Mobil
Travel Guide®

Great Plains
2002

ExxonMobil Travel Publications

ACKNOWLEDGMENTS

We gratefully acknowledge the help of our representatives for their efficient and perceptive inspection of the lodging and dining establishments listed; the establishments' proprietors for their cooperation in showing their facilities and providing information about them; the many users of previous editions of the Mobil Travel Guides who have taken the time to share their experiences; and for their time and information, the thousands of chambers of commerce, convention and visitors bureaus, city, state, and provincial tourism offices, and government agencies who assisted in our research.

PHOTO CREDITS

Abilene Convention and Visitors Bureau Civic Center: 84; **Ellen Barone/Houserstock:** 446; **Tom Bean Photography:** 97, 213, 354, 399, 410; **Bismarck-Mandan Convention and Visitors Bureau:** 419; **Corbis:** 388; Jan Butchofsky-Houser: 273; David G. Houser: 329; Peter Turnley: 472; **Dick Dietrich Photography:** 322; **John Elk III Photography:** 490; **FPG:** Dennie Cody: 89; Richard H. Smith: 241; Travelpix: 510; **Greater St. Charles Convention and Visitors Bureau:** 314; **Jeff Greenberg/Photri, Inc.:** 198; **kellymooney.com:** 204, 209; **Fred J. Maroon/Folio, Inc.:** 263; **G. Alan Nelson Photography:** 95, 167, 179, 430; **Jack Olson Photography:** 350; **James P. Rowan Photography:** 278, 279; **Greg Ryan-Sally Beyer Photography:** 57, 152, 235, 245, 432; **Michael C. Snell/Shade of the Cottonwood:** 130, 132; **SuperStock:** 201, 324, 364, 428, 496, 518, 521; **Tom Till Photography:** 1, 37, 75; **Unicorn Stock Photos:** Jim Argo: 466; Terry Barner: 63; Eric R. Berndt: 313; Andre Jenny: 393; Martha McBride: 9; Chuck Schmeiser: 186, 505; Jim Shippee: 289; **Steve Warble Photography:** 456.

Maps © MapQuest 2001, www.mapquest.com

Published by Publications International, Ltd.
7373 North Cicero Avenue
Lincolnwood, Illinois 60712

info@exxonmobiltravel.com

ISBN 0-7853-5811-0

Manufactured in China.

10 9 8 7 6 5 4 3 2 1

CONTENTS

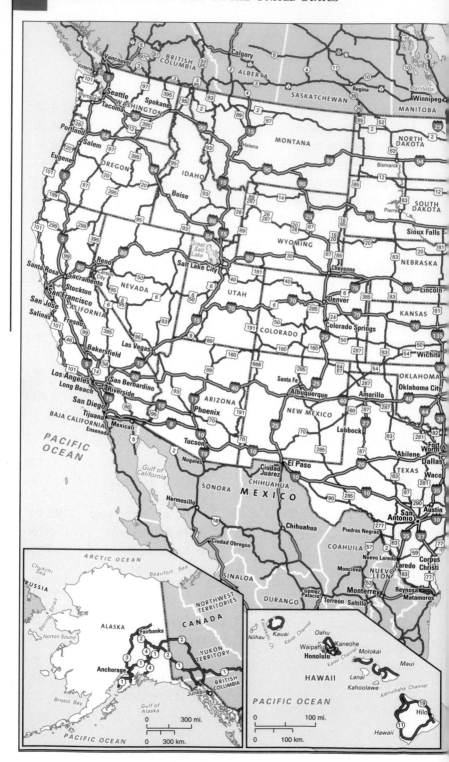

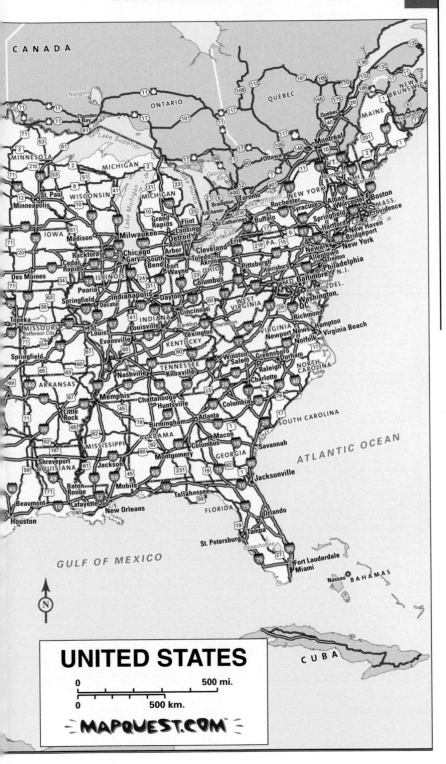

UNITED STATES

0 — 500 mi.

0 — 500 km.

MAPQUEST.COM

Mileage Chart

Distances in chart are in miles. To convert miles to kilometers, multiply the distance in miles by 1.609

Example:
New York, NY to Boston, MA = 215 miles or 346 kilometers (215 x 1.609)

	ALBUQUERQUE, NM	ATLANTA, GA	BALTIMORE, MD	BILLINGS, MT	BIRMINGHAM, AL	BISMARCK, ND	BOISE, ID	BOSTON, MA	BUFFALO, NY	BURLINGTON, VT	CHARLESTON, SC	CHARLESTON, WV	CHARLOTTE, NC	CHEYENNE, WY	CHICAGO, IL	CINCINNATI, OH	CLEVELAND, OH	DALLAS, TX	DENVER, CO	DES MOINES, IA	DETROIT, MI	EL PASO, TX	HOUSTON, TX	INDIANAPOLIS, IN	JACKSON, MS	KANSAS CITY, MO	LAS VEGAS, NV
ALBUQUERQUE, NM		1490	1902	991	1274	1333	966	2240	1808	2178	1793	1568	1649	538	1352	1409	1619	754	438	1091	1608	263	994	1298	1157	894	578
ATLANTA, GA	1490		679	1889	150	1559	2218	1100	910	1158	317	503	238	1482	717	476	726	792	1403	967	735	1437	800	531	386	801	2067
BALTIMORE, MD	1902	679		1959	795	1551	2401	422	370	481	583	352	441	1665	708	521	377	1399	1690	1031	532	2045	1470	600	1032	1087	2445
BILLINGS, MT	991	1889	1959		1839	413	626	2254	1796	2181	2157	1755	2012	455	1246	1552	1597	1433	554	1007	1534	1255	1673	1432	1836	1088	965
BIRMINGHAM, AL	1274	150	795	1839		1509	2170	1215	909	1241	466	578	389	1434	667	475	725	647	1356	919	734	1292	678	481	241	753	1852
BISMARCK, ND	1333	1559	1551	413	1509		1039	1846	1388	1773	1749	1347	1604	594	838	1144	1189	1342	693	675	1126	1597	1582	1024	1548	801	1378
BOISE, ID	966	2218	2401	626	2170	1039		2697	2239	2624	2520	2182	2375	737	1708	1969	2040	1711	833	1369	1977	1206	1952	1852	2115	1376	760
BOSTON, MA	2240	1100	422	2254	1215	1846	2697		462	214	1003	741	861	1961	1003	862	654	1819	2004	1326	741	2465	1890	940	1453	1427	2757
BUFFALO, NY	1808	910	370	1796	909	1388	2239	462		375	899	431	695	1502	545	442	197	1393	1546	868	277	2039	1513	508	1134	995	2299
BURLINGTON, VT	2178	1158	481	2181	1241	1773	2624	214	375		1061	782	919	1887	930	817	567	1763	1931	1253	652	2409	1916	878	1479	1366	2684
CHARLESTON, SC	1793	317	583	2157	466	1749	2520	1003	899	1061		468	204	1783	907	622	724	1109	1705	1204	879	1754	1110	721	703	1102	2371
CHARLESTON, WV	1568	503	352	1755	578	1347	2182	741	431	782	468		265	1445	506	209	255	1072	1367	802	410	1718	1192	320	816	764	2122
CHARLOTTE, NC	1649	238	441	2012	389	1604	2375	861	695	919	204	265		1637	761	476	520	1031	1559	1057	675	1677	1041	575	625	956	2225
CHEYENNE, WY	538	1482	1665	455	1434	594	737	1961	1502	1887	1783	1445	1637		972	1233	1304	979	100	633	1241	801	1220	1115	1382	640	843
CHICAGO, IL	1352	717	708	1246	667	838	1708	1003	545	930	907	506	761	972		302	346	936	1015	337	283	1543	1108	184	750	532	1768
CINCINNATI, OH	1409	476	521	1552	475	1144	1969	862	442	817	622	209	476	1233	302		253	958	1200	599	261	1605	1079	116	700	597	1955
CLEVELAND, OH	1619	726	377	1597	725	1189	2040	654	197	567	724	255	520	1304	346	253		1208	1347	669	171	1854	1328	319	950	806	2100
DALLAS, TX	754	792	1399	1433	647	1342	1711	1819	1393	1763	1109	1072	1031	979	936	958	1208		887	752	1218	647	241	913	406	554	1331
DENVER, CO	438	1403	1690	554	1356	693	833	2004	1546	1931	1705	1367	1559	100	1015	1200	1347	887		676	1284	701	1127	1088	1290	603	756
DES MOINES, IA	1091	967	1031	1007	919	675	1369	1326	868	1253	1204	802	1057	633	337	599	669	752	676		606	1283	992	481	931	194	1429
DETROIT, MI	1608	735	532	1534	734	1126	1977	741	277	652	879	410	675	1241	283	261	171	1218	1284	606		1799	1338	318	960	795	2037
EL PASO, TX	263	1437	2045	1255	1292	1597	1206	2465	2039	2409	1754	1718	1677	801	1543	1605	1854	647	701	1283	1799		758	1489	1051	1085	717
HOUSTON, TX	994	800	1470	1673	678	1582	1952	1890	1513	1916	1110	1192	1041	1220	1108	1079	1328	241	1127	992	1338	758		1033	445	795	1474
INDIANAPOLIS, IN	1298	531	600	1432	481	1024	1852	940	508	878	721	320	575	1115	184	116	319	913	1088	481	318	1489	1033		675	485	1843
JACKSON, MS	1157	386	1032	1836	241	1548	2115	1453	1134	1479	703	816	625	1382	750	700	950	406	1290	931	960	1051	445	675		747	1735
KANSAS CITY, MO	894	801	1087	1088	753	801	1376	1427	995	1366	1102	764	956	640	532	597	806	554	603	194	795	1085	795	485	747		1358
LAS VEGAS, NV	578	2067	2445	965	1852	1378	760	2757	2299	2684	2371	2122	2225	843	1768	1955	2100	1331	756	1429	2037	717	1474	1843	1735	1358	
LITTLE ROCK, AR	900	528	1072	1530	381	1183	1808	1493	1066	1437	900	745	754	1076	662	632	882	327	984	567	891	974	447	587	269	382	1478
LOS ANGELES, CA	806	2237	2705	1239	2092	1702	1033	3046	2572	2957	2554	2374	2453	1116	2042	2215	2374	1446	1029	1703	2310	801	1558	2104	1851	1632	274
LOUISVILLE, KY	1320	419	602	1547	369	1139	1933	964	545	915	610	251	464	1197	299	106	356	852	1118	595	366	1499	972	112	594	516	1874
MEMPHIS, TN	1033	389	933	1625	241	1337	1954	1353	927	1297	760	606	614	1217	539	493	742	466	1116	720	752	1112	586	464	211	536	1611
MIAMI, FL	2155	661	1109	2554	812	2224	2883	1529	1425	1587	583	994	730	2147	1382	1141	1250	1367	2069	1632	1401	1959	1201	1196	915	1466	2733
MILWAUKEE, WI	1426	813	805	1175	763	767	1748	1100	642	1027	1003	601	857	1012	89	398	443	1010	1055	378	380	1617	1193	279	835	573	1808
MINNEAPOLIS, MN	1339	1129	1121	839	1079	431	1465	1417	958	1343	1319	918	1173	881	409	714	760	999	924	246	697	1530	1240	596	1151	441	1677
MONTRÉAL, QC	2172	1241	564	2093	1289	1685	2535	313	397	92	1145	822	1003	1799	841	815	588	1772	1843	1165	564	2363	1892	872	1514	1359	2596
NASHVILLE, TN	1248	242	716	1648	194	1315	1976	1136	716	1086	543	395	397	1240	474	281	531	681	1162	725	541	1328	801	287	423	559	1826
NEW ORLEANS, LA	1276	473	1142	1955	351	1734	2234	1563	1254	1588	783	926	713	1502	935	820	1070	525	1409	1117	1079	1118	360	826	185	932	1854
NEW YORK, NY	2015	869	192	2049	985	1641	2491	215	400	299	773	515	631	1755	797	636	466	1589	1799	1121	622	2235	1660	715	1223	1202	2552
OKLAHOMA CITY, OK	546	944	1354	1227	729	1136	1506	1694	1262	1632	1248	1022	1102	773	807	863	1073	209	681	546	1062	737	449	752	612	348	1124
OMAHA, NE	973	989	1168	904	941	616	1234	1463	1005	1390	1290	952	1144	497	474	736	806	669	541	136	743	1236	910	618	935	188	1294
ORLANDO, FL	1934	440	904	2333	591	2003	2662	1324	1221	1383	379	790	525	1926	1161	920	1045	1146	1847	1411	1180	1738	980	975	694	1245	2512
PHILADELPHIA, PA	1954	782	104	2019	897	1611	2462	321	414	371	685	454	543	1725	768	576	437	1501	1744	1091	592	2147	1572	655	1135	1141	2500
PHOENIX, AZ	466	1868	2366	1199	1723	1662	993	2706	2274	2644	2184	2035	2107	1004	1819	1876	2085	1077	904	1558	2074	432	1188	1764	1482	1360	285
PITTSBURGH, PA	1670	676	246	1719	763	1311	2161	592	217	587	642	217	438	1425	467	292	136	1246	1460	791	292	1893	1366	370	988	857	2215
PORTLAND, ME	2338	1197	520	2352	1313	1944	2795	107	560	233	1101	839	959	2059	1101	960	751	1917	2102	1424	838	2563	1988	1038	1550	1525	2855
PORTLAND, OR	1395	2647	2830	889	2599	1301	432	3126	2667	3052	2948	2610	2802	1166	2137	2398	2469	2140	1261	1798	2405	1767	2381	2280	2544	1805	1188
RAPID CITY, SD	841	1511	1626	379	1463	320	930	1921	1463	1848	1824	1422	1678	305	913	1219	1264	1077	404	629	1201	1105	1318	1101	1458	710	1035
RENO, NV	1020	2440	2623	960	2392	1372	430	2919	2460	2845	2741	2403	2595	959	1930	2191	2262	1933	1054	1591	2198	1315	2072	2073	2337	1598	442
RICHMOND, VA	1876	527	152	2053	678	1645	2496	572	485	630	428	322	289	1760	802	530	471	1309	1688	1126	627	1955	1330	641	914	1085	2444
ST. LOUIS, MO	1051	549	841	1341	501	1053	1628	1181	749	1119	850	512	704	892	294	350	560	635	855	436	549	1242	863	239	505	252	1610
SALT LAKE CITY, UT	624	1916	2100	548	1868	960	342	2395	1936	2322	2218	1880	2072	436	1406	1667	1738	1410	531	1067	1675	864	1650	1549	1813	1074	417
SAN ANTONIO, TX	818	1000	1671	1500	878	1599	1761	2092	1665	2036	1310	1344	1241	1046	1270	1231	1481	271	946	1009	1490	556	200	1186	644	812	1272
SAN DIEGO, CA	825	2166	2724	1302	2021	1765	1096	3065	2632	3020	2483	2393	2405	1179	2105	2234	2437	1375	1092	1766	2373	730	1487	2122	1780	1695	337
SAN FRANCISCO, CA	1111	2618	2840	1176	2472	1749	646	3135	2677	3062	2934	2620	2759	1176	2146	2407	2478	1827	1271	1807	2415	1181	1938	2290	2232	1814	575
SEATTLE, WA	1463	2705	2775	816	2657	1229	500	3070	2612	2997	2973	2571	2827	1234	2062	2368	2413	2208	1329	1822	2350	1944	2449	2249	2612	1872	1256
TAMPA, FL	1949	455	960	2348	606	2018	2677	1380	1276	1438	434	845	581	1941	1176	935	1101	1161	1862	1426	1194	1753	995	990	709	1259	2526
TORONTO, ON	1841	958	565	1762	958	1354	2204	570	106	419	1006	537	802	1468	510	484	303	1441	1512	834	233	2032	1561	541	1183	1028	2265
VANCOUVER, BC	1597	2838	2908	949	2791	1362	633	3204	2745	3130	3106	2705	2960	1368	2196	2501	2547	2342	1463	1956	2483	2087	2583	2383	2746	2007	1390
WASHINGTON, DC	1896	636	38	1953	758	1545	2395	458	384	517	539	346	397	1659	701	517	370	1362	1686	1025	526	2008	1433	596	996	1083	2441
WICHITA, KS	707	989	1276	1067	838	934	1346	1616	1184	1554	1291	953	1145	613	728	785	995	367	521	390	984	898	608	674	771	192	1276

LITTLE ROCK, AR	LOS ANGELES, CA	LOUISVILLE, KY	MEMPHIS, TN	MIAMI, FL	MILWAUKEE, WI	MINNEAPOLIS, MN	MONTRÉAL, QC	NASHVILLE, TN	NEW ORLEANS, LA	NEW YORK, NY	OKLAHOMA CITY, OK	OMAHA, NE	ORLANDO, FL	PHILADELPHIA, PA	PHOENIX, AZ	PITTSBURGH, PA	PORTLAND, ME	PORTLAND, OR	RAPID CITY, SD	RENO, NV	RICHMOND, VA	ST. LOUIS, MO	SALT LAKE CITY, UT	SAN ANTONIO, TX	SAN DIEGO, CA	SAN FRANCISCO, CA	SEATTLE, WA	TAMPA, FL	TORONTO, ON	VANCOUVER, BC	WASHINGTON,DC	WICHITA, KS
900	806	1320	1033	2155	1426	1339	2172	1248	1276	2015	546	973	1934	1954	466	1670	2338	1395	841	1020	1876	1051	624	818	825	1111	1463	1949	1841	1597	1896	707
528	2237	419	389	661	813	1129	1241	242	473	869	944	989	440	782	1868	676	1197	2647	1511	2440	527	549	1916	1000	2166	2618	2705	455	958	2838	636	989
1072	2705	602	933	1109	805	1121	564	716	1142	192	1354	1168	904	104	2366	246	520	2830	1626	2623	152	841	2100	1671	2724	2840	2775	960	565	2908	38	1276
1530	1239	1547	1625	2554	1175	839	2093	1648	1955	2049	1227	904	2333	2019	1199	1719	2352	889	379	960	2053	1341	548	1500	1302	1176	816	2348	1762	949	1953	1067
381	2092	369	241	812	763	1079	1289	194	351	985	729	941	591	897	1723	763	1313	2599	1463	2392	678	501	1868	878	2021	2472	2657	606	958	2791	758	838
1183	1702	1139	1337	2224	767	431	1685	1315	1734	1641	1136	616	2003	1611	1662	1311	1944	1301	320	1372	1645	1053	960	1599	1765	1749	1229	2018	1354	1362	1545	934
1808	1033	1933	1954	2883	1748	1465	2535	1976	2234	2491	1506	1234	2662	2462	993	2161	2795	432	930	430	2496	1628	342	1761	1096	646	500	2677	2204	633	2395	1346
1493	3046	964	1353	1529	1100	1417	313	1136	1563	215	1694	1463	1324	321	2706	592	107	3126	1921	2919	572	1181	2395	2092	3065	3135	3070	1380	570	3204	458	1616
1066	2572	545	927	1425	642	958	397	716	1254	400	1262	1005	1221	414	2274	217	560	2667	1463	2460	485	749	1936	1665	2632	2677	2612	1276	106	2745	384	1184
1437	2957	915	1297	1587	1027	1343	92	1086	1588	299	1632	1390	1383	371	2644	587	233	3052	1848	2845	630	1119	2322	2036	3020	3062	2997	1438	419	3130	517	1554
900	2554	610	760	583	1003	1319	1145	543	783	773	1248	1290	379	685	2184	642	1101	2948	1824	2741	428	850	2218	1310	2483	2934	2973	434	1006	3106	539	1291
745	2374	251	606	994	601	918	822	395	926	515	1022	952	790	454	2035	217	839	2610	1422	2403	322	512	1880	1344	2393	2620	2571	845	537	2705	346	953
754	2453	464	614	730	857	1173	1003	397	713	631	1102	1144	525	543	2107	438	959	2802	1678	2595	289	704	2072	1241	2405	2759	2827	581	802	2960	397	1145
1076	1116	1197	1217	2147	1012	881	1799	1240	1502	1755	773	497	1926	1725	1004	1425	2059	1166	305	959	1760	892	436	1046	1179	1176	1234	1941	1468	1368	1659	613
662	2042	299	539	1382	89	409	841	474	935	797	807	474	1161	768	1819	467	1101	2137	913	1930	802	294	1406	1270	2105	2146	2062	1176	510	2196	701	728
632	2215	106	493	1141	398	714	815	281	820	636	863	736	920	576	1876	292	960	2398	1219	2191	530	350	1667	1231	2234	2407	2368	935	484	2501	517	785
882	2374	356	742	1250	443	760	588	531	1070	466	1073	806	1045	437	2085	136	751	2469	1264	2262	471	560	1738	1481	2437	2478	2413	1101	303	2547	370	995
327	1446	852	466	1367	1010	999	1772	681	525	1589	209	669	1146	1501	1077	1246	1917	2140	1077	1933	1309	635	1410	271	1375	1827	2208	1161	1441	2342	1362	367
984	1029	1118	1116	2069	1055	924	1843	1162	1409	1799	681	541	1847	1744	904	1460	2102	1261	404	1054	1688	855	531	946	1092	1271	1329	1862	1512	1463	1686	521
567	1703	595	720	1632	378	246	1165	725	1117	1121	546	136	1411	1091	1558	791	1424	1798	629	1591	1126	436	1067	1009	1766	1807	1822	1426	834	1956	1025	390
891	2310	366	752	1401	380	697	564	541	1079	622	1062	743	1180	592	2074	292	838	2405	1201	2198	627	549	1675	1490	2373	2415	2350	1194	233	2483	526	984
974	801	1499	1112	1959	1617	1530	2363	1328	1118	2235	737	1236	1738	2147	432	1893	2563	1767	1105	1315	1955	1242	864	556	730	1181	1944	1753	2032	2087	2008	898
447	1558	972	586	1201	1193	1240	1892	801	360	1660	449	910	980	1572	1188	1366	1988	2381	1318	2072	1330	863	1650	200	1487	1938	2449	995	1561	2583	1433	608
587	2104	112	464	1196	279	596	872	287	826	715	752	618	975	655	1764	370	1038	2280	1101	2073	641	239	1549	1186	2122	2290	2249	990	541	2383	596	674
269	1851	594	211	915	835	1151	1514	423	185	1223	612	935	694	1135	1482	988	1550	2544	1458	2337	914	505	1813	644	1780	2232	2612	709	1183	2746	996	771
382	1632	516	536	1466	573	441	1359	559	932	1202	348	188	1245	1141	1360	857	1525	1805	710	1598	1085	252	1074	812	1695	1814	1872	1259	1028	2007	1083	192
1478	274	1874	1611	2733	1808	1677	2596	1826	1854	2552	1124	1294	2512	2500	285	2215	2855	1188	1035	442	2444	1610	417	1272	337	575	1256	2526	2265	1390	2441	1276
	1706	526	140	1190	747	814	1446	355	455	1262	355	570	969	1175	1367	920	1590	2237	1093	2030	983	416	1507	600	1703	2012	2305	984	1115	2439	1036	464
1706		2126	1839	2759	2082	1951	2869	2054	1917	2820	1352	1567	2538	2760	369	2476	3144	971	1309	519	2682	1856	691	1356	124	385	1148	2553	2538	1291	2702	1513
526	2126		386	1084	394	711	920	175	714	739	774	704	863	678	1786	394	1062	2362	1215	2155	572	264	1631	1125	2144	2372	2364	878	589	2497	596	705
140	1839	386		1051	624	940	1306	215	396	1123	487	724	830	1035	1500	780	1451	2382	1247	2175	843	294	1652	739	1841	2144	2440	845	975	2574	896	597
1190	2759	1084	1051		1478	1794	1671	907	874	1299	1609	1654	232	1211	2390	1167	1627	3312	2176	3105	954	1214	2581	1401	2688	3140	3370	274	1532	3504	1065	1655
747	2082	394	624	1478		337	939	569	1020	894	880	514	1257	865	1892	564	1198	2063	842	1970	899	367	1446	1343	2145	2186	1991	1272	607	2124	799	769
814	1951	711	940	1794	337		1255	886	1337	1211	793	383	1573	1181	1805	881	1515	1727	606	1839	1216	621	1315	1257	2014	2055	1654	1588	924	1788	1115	637
1446	2869	920	1306	1671	939	1255		1094	1632	383	1625	1300	1466	454	2637	607	282	2963	1758	2756	714	1112	2232	2043	2931	2972	2907	1522	330	3041	600	1547
355	2054	175	215	907	569	886	1094		539	906	703	747	686	818	1715	569	1234	2405	1269	2198	626	307	1675	954	2056	2360	2463	701	764	2597	679	748
455	1917	714	396	874	1020	1337	1632	539		1332	731	1121	653	1245	1548	1108	1660	2663	1643	2431	1002	690	1932	560	1846	2298	2731	668	1302	2865	1106	890
1262	2820	739	1123	1299	894	1211	383	906	1332		1469	1258	1094	91	2481	367	313	2920	1716	2713	342	956	2189	1861	2839	2929	2864	1150	507	2998	228	1391
355	1352	774	487	1609	880	793	1625	703	731	1469		463	1388	1408	1012	1124	1792	1934	871	1727	1331	505	1204	466	1370	1657	2002	1403	1295	2136	1350	161
570	1567	704	724	1654	514	383	1300	747	1121	1258	463		1433	1228	1440	928	1561	1662	525	1455	1263	440	932	927	1630	1672	1719	1448	971	1853	1162	307
969	2538	863	830	232	1257	1573	1466	686	653	1094	1388	1433		1006	2169	963	1422	3091	1955	2884	750	993	2360	1180	2467	2918	3149	82	1327	3283	860	1434
1175	2760	678	1035	1211	865	1181	454	818	1245	91	1408	1228	1006		2420	306	419	2890	1686	2683	254	895	2160	1774	2779	2900	2835	1062	522	2968	140	1330
1367	369	1786	1500	2390	1892	1805	2637	1715	1548	2481	1012	1440	2169	2420		2136	2804	1335	1308	883	2343	1517	651	987	358	750	1513	2184	2307	1655	2362	1173
920	2476	394	780	1167	564	881	607	569	1108	367	1124	928	963	306	2136		690	2590	1386	2383	341	611	1859	1519	2494	2599	2534	1019	321	2668	240	1046
1590	3144	1062	1451	1627	1198	1515	282	1234	1660	313	1792	1561	1422	419	2804	690		3223	2019	3016	670	1279	2493	2189	3162	3233	3168	1478	668	3301	556	1714
2237	971	2362	2382	3312	2063	1727	2963	2405	2663	2920	1934	1662	3091	2890	1335	2590	3223		1268	578	2925	2057	771	2322	1093	638	170	3106	2633	313	2824	1775
1093	1309	1215	1247	2176	842	606	1758	1269	1643	1716	871	525	1955	1686	1308	1386	2019	1268		1151	1720	963	628	1335	1372	1368	1195	1970	1429	1328	1620	712
2030	519	2155	2175	3105	1970	1839	2756	2198	2431	2713	1727	1455	2884	2683	883	2383	3016	578	1151		2718	1850	524	1870	642	217	755	2899	2426	898	2617	1568
983	2682	572	843	954	899	1216	714	626	1002	342	1331	1263	750	254	2343	341	670	2925	1720	2718		834	2194	1530	2684	2934	2869	805	660	3003	108	1274
416	1856	264	294	1214	367	621	1112	307	690	956	505	440	993	895	1517	611	1279	2057	963	1850	834		1326	968	1875	2066	2125	1008	782	2259	837	441
1507	691	1631	1652	2581	1446	1315	2232	1675	1932	2189	1204	932	2360	2160	651	1859	2493	771	628	524	2194	1326		1419	754	740	839	2375	1902	973	2094	1044
600	1356	1125	739	1401	1343	1257	2043	954	560	1861	466	927	1180	1774	987	1519	2189	2322	1335	1870	1530	968	1419		1285	1737	2275	1195	1714	2410	1635	624
1703	124	2144	1841	2688	2145	2014	2931	2056	1846	2839	1370	1630	2467	2779	358	2494	3162	1093	1372	642	2684	1875	754	1285		508	1271	2481	2601	1414	2720	1531
2012	385	2372	2144	3140	2186	2055	2972	2360	2298	2929	1657	1672	2918	2900	750	2599	3233	638	1368	217	2934	2066	740	1737	508		816	2933	2643	958	2834	1784
2305	1148	2364	2440	3370	1991	1654	2907	2463	2731	2864	2002	1719	3149	2835	1513	2534	3168	170	1195	755	2869	2125	839	2275	1271	816		3164	2577	140	2769	1843
984	2553	878	845	274	1272	1588	1522	701	668	1150	1403	1448	82	1062	2184	1019	1478	3106	1970	2899	805	1008	2375	1195	2481	2933	3164		1383	3297	916	1448
1115	2538	589	975	1532	607	924	330	764	1302	507	1295	971	1327	522	2307	321	668	2633	1429	2426	660	782	1902	1714	2601	2643	2577	1383		2711	563	1217
2439	1291	2497	2574	3504	2124	1788	3041	2597	2865	2998	2136	1853	3283	2968	1655	2668	3301	313	1328	898	3003	2259	973	2410	1414	958	140	3297	2711		2902	1977
1036	2702	596	896	1065	799	1115	600	679	1106	228	1350	1162	860	140	2362	240	556	2824	1620	2617	108	837	2094	1635	2720	2834	2769	916	563	2902		1272
464	1513	705	597	1655	769	637	1547	748	890	1391	161	307	1434	1330	1173	1046	1714	1775	712	1568	1274	441	1044	624	1531	1784	1843	1448	1217	1977	1272	

MAPQUEST.COM™

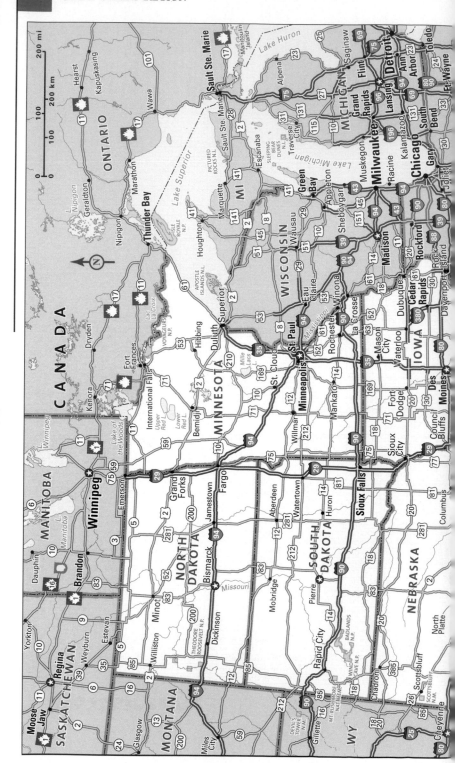

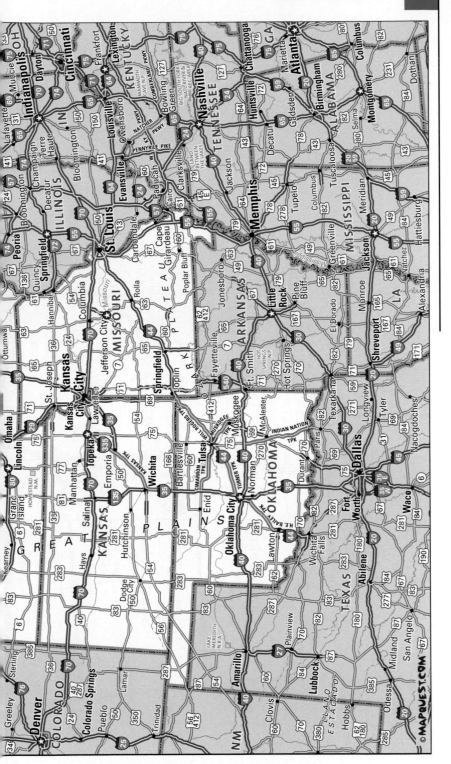

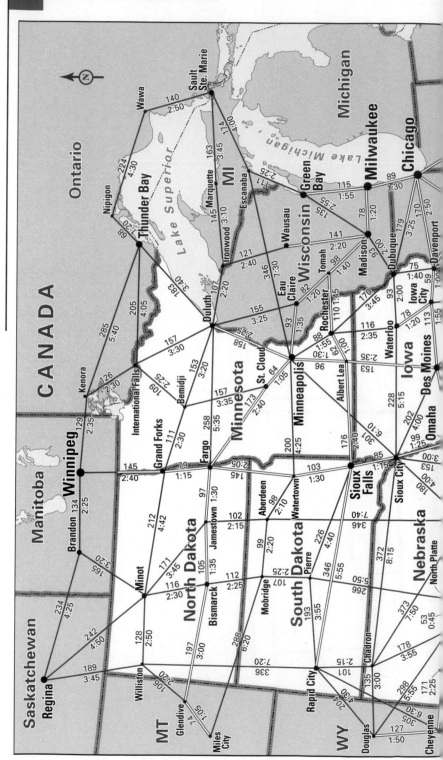

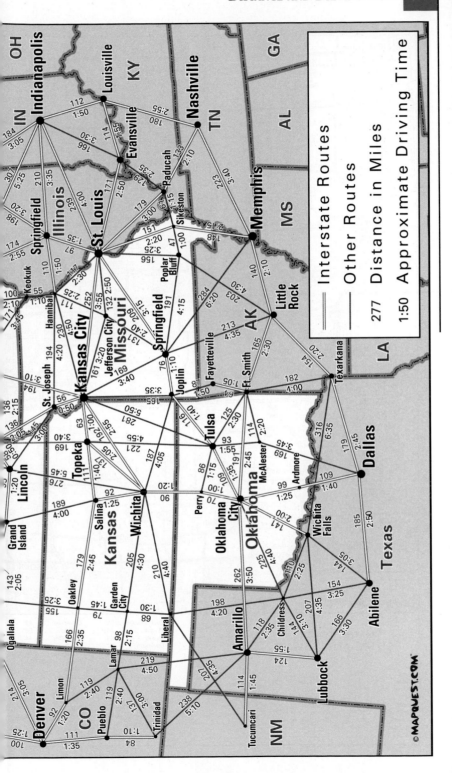

© MAPQUEST.COM

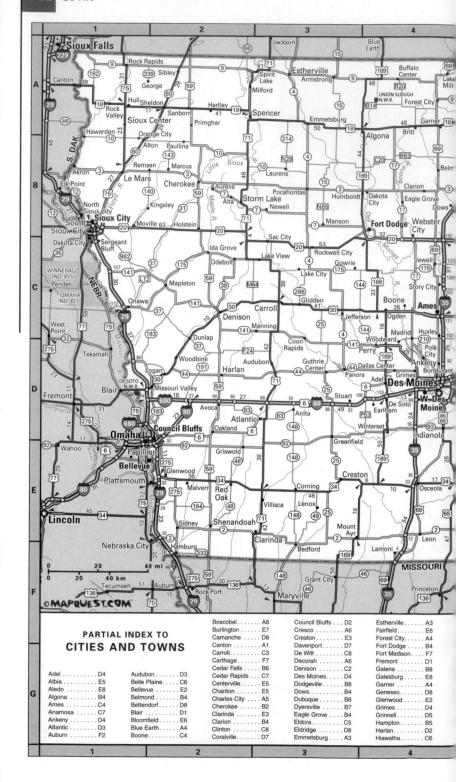

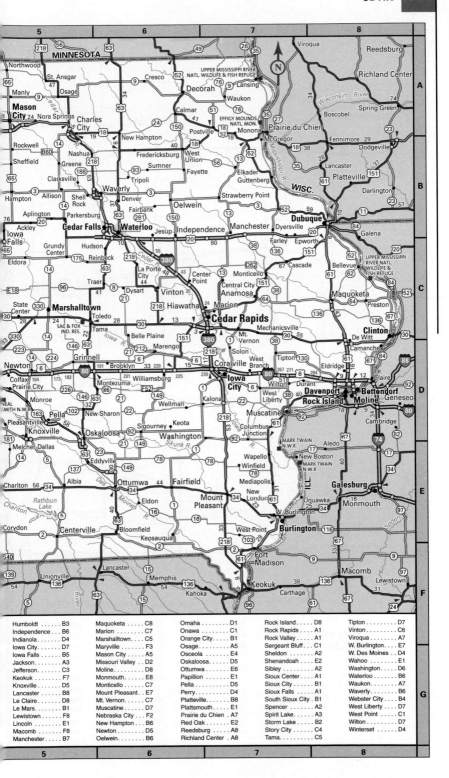

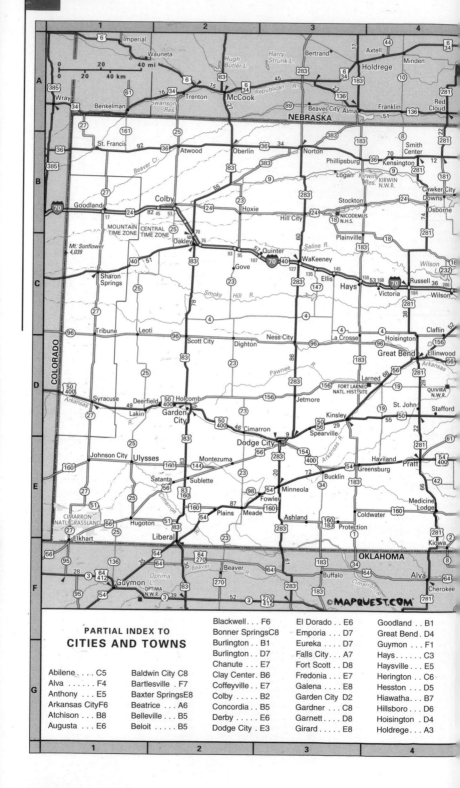

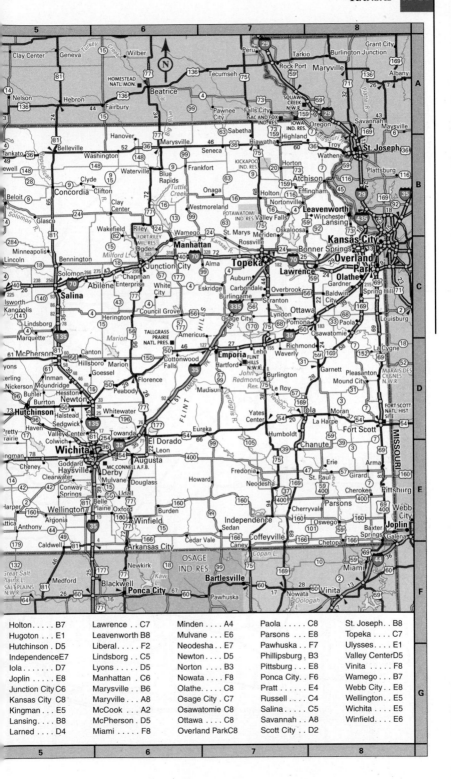

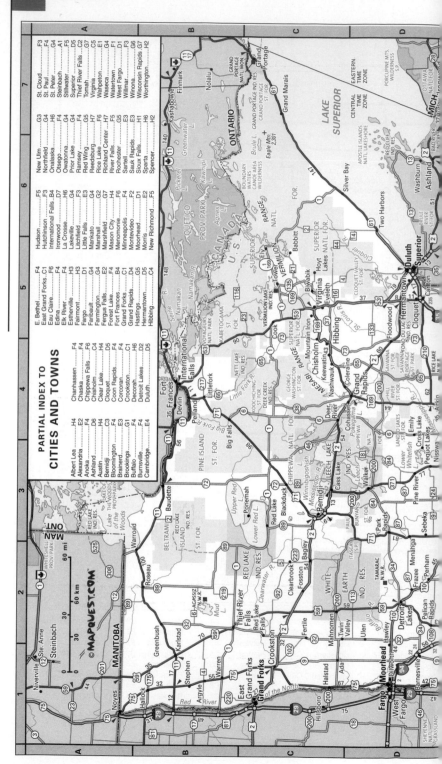

PARTIAL INDEX TO CITIES AND TOWNS

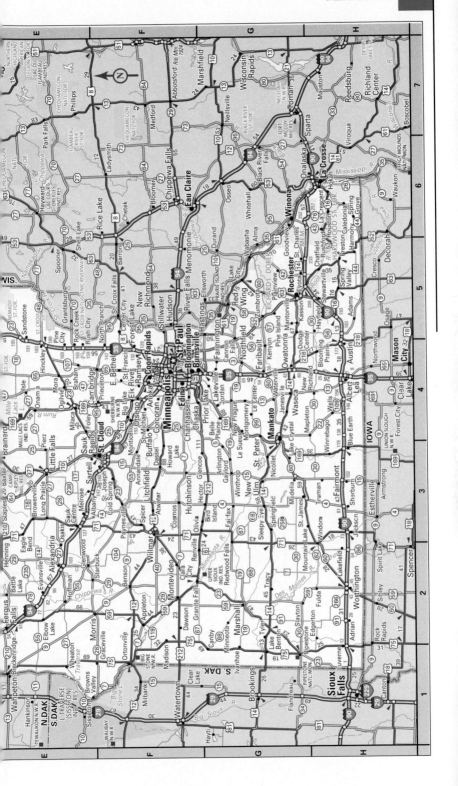

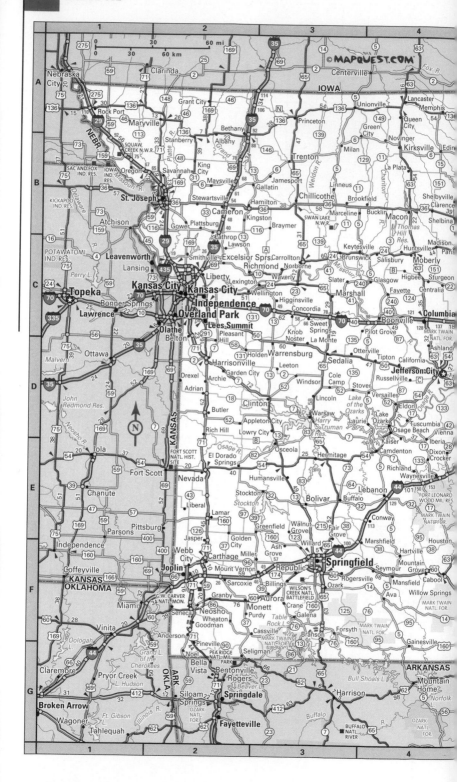

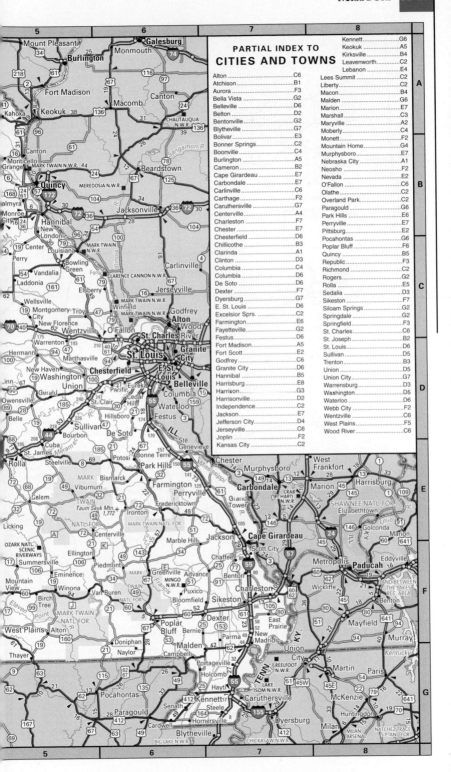

PARTIAL INDEX TO
CITIES AND TOWNS

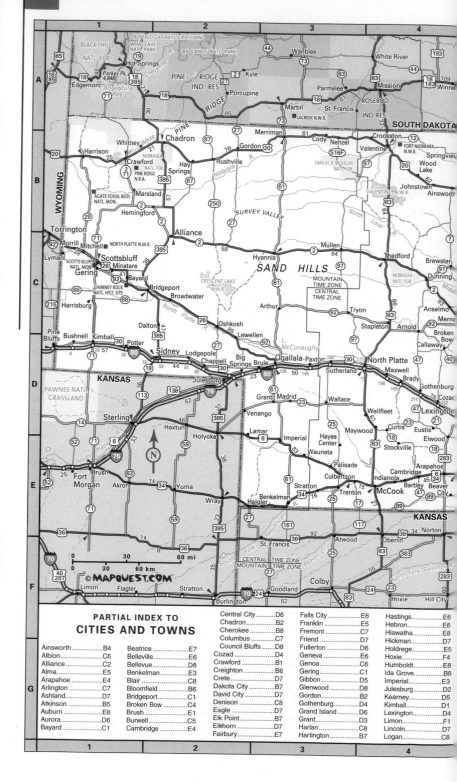

PARTIAL INDEX TO
CITIES AND TOWNS

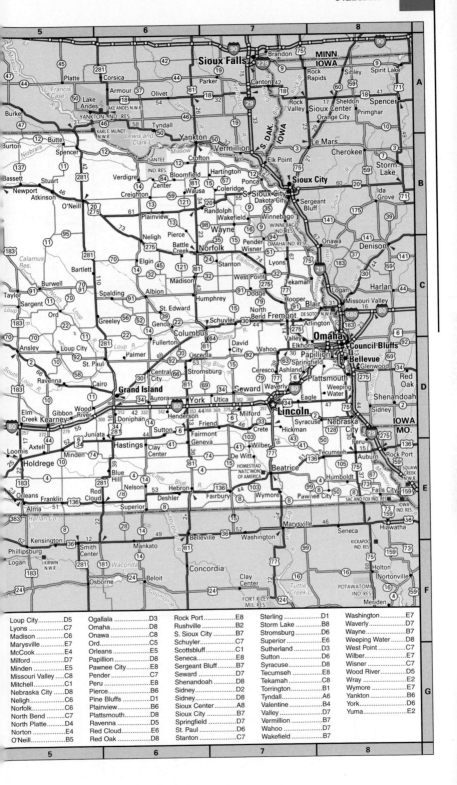

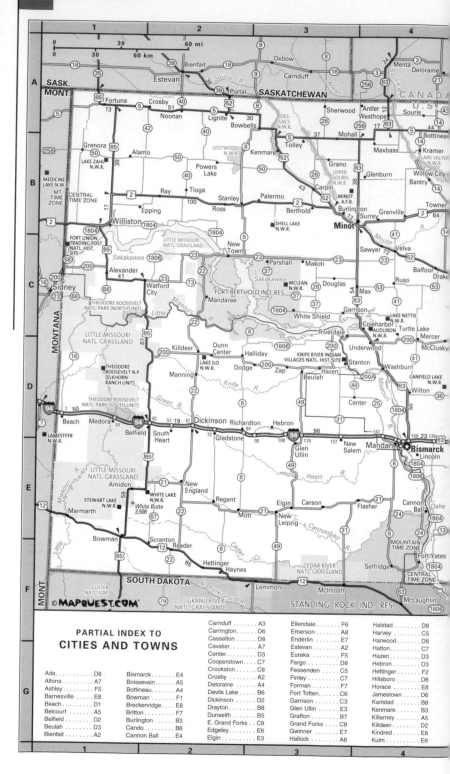

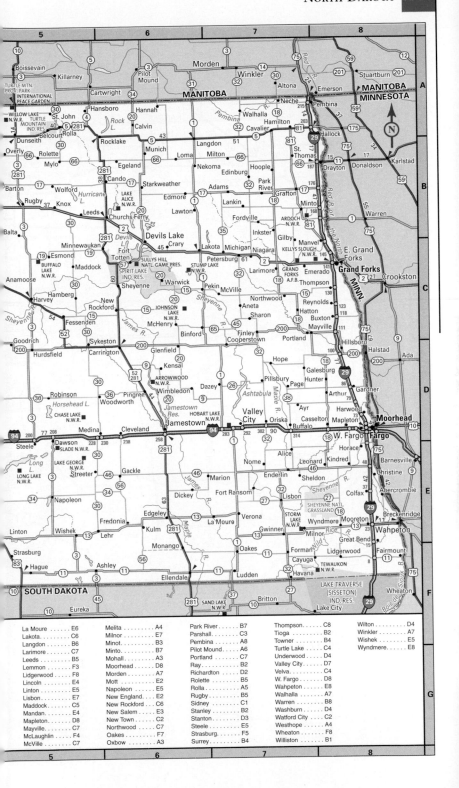

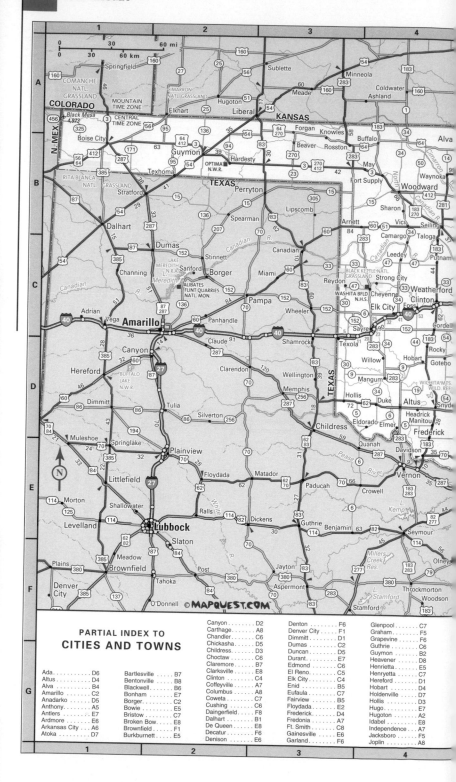

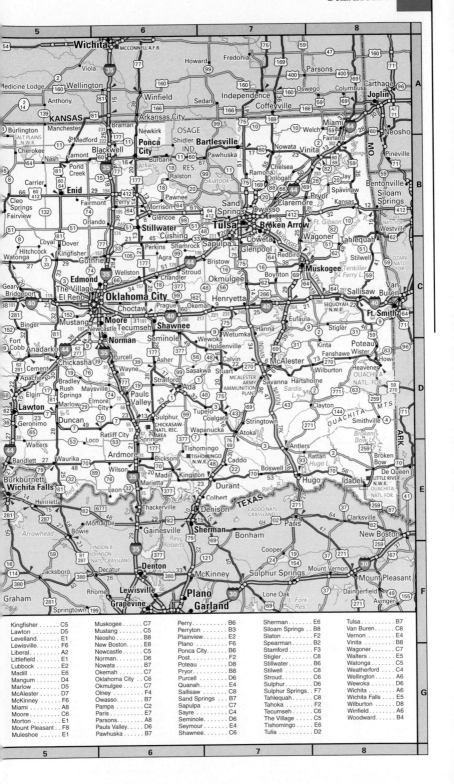

Kingfisher C5	Muskogee C7	Perry B6	Sherman E6	Tulsa B7
Lawton D5	Mustang C5	Perryton B3	Siloam Springs . . B8	Van Buren C8
Leverland. E1	Neosho B8	Plainview E2	Slaton F2	Vernon E4
Lewisville. F6	New Boston E8	Plano F6	Spearman B2	Vinita B8
Liberal A2	Newcastle C5	Ponca City B6	Spearman B2	Wagoner C7
Littlefield E1	Norman D6	Post. F2	Stamford F3	Walters E5
Lubbock E2	Nowata B7	Poteau D8	Stigler C8	Watonga C5
Madill E6	Okemah C7	Pryor B8	Stillwater B6	Weatherford C4
Mangum D4	Oklahoma City . . C6	Purcell D6	Stilwell C8	Wellington A6
Marlow D5	Okmulgee C7	Quanah E4	Stroud C6	Wewoka D6
McAlester D7	Olney F4	Sallisaw C8	Sulphur D6	Wichita A6
McKinney F6	Owasso B7	Sand Springs B7	Sulphur Springs. . F7	Wichita Falls E5
Miami A8	Pampa C2	Sapulpa C7	Tahlequah C8	Wilburton D8
Moore C6	Paris E7	Sayre C4	Tahoka F2	Winfield A6
Morton E1	Parsons A8	Seminole D6	Tecumseh C6	Woodward B4
Mount Pleasant . . F8	Pauls Valley D6	Seymour E4	The Village C5	
Muleshoe E1	Pawhuska B7	Shawnee. C6	Tishomingo E6	
			Tulia D2	

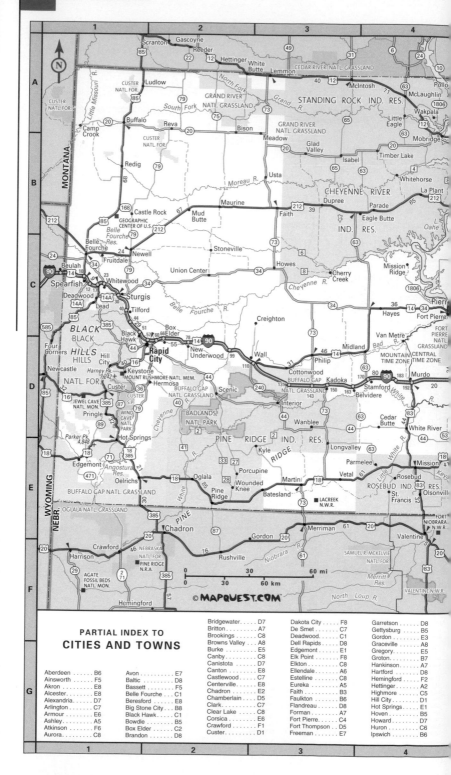

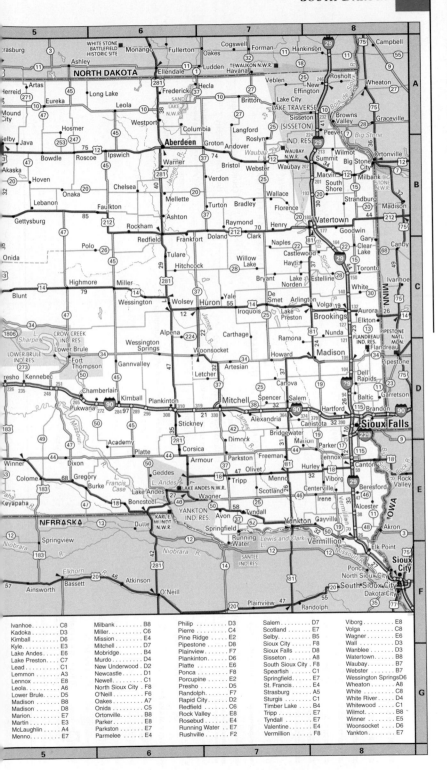

MAP LEGEND

TRANSPORTATION

CONTROLLED-ACCESS HIGHWAYS

Free

Toll; Toll Booth

Under Construction

Interchange and Exit Number

Ramp
Downtown maps only

OTHER HIGHWAYS

Primary Highway

Secondary Highway

Multilane Divided Highway
Primary and secondary highways only

Other Paved Road

Unpaved Road
Check conditions locally

HIGHWAY MARKERS

Interstate Route

US Route

State or Provincial Route

County or Other Route

Business Route

Trans-Canada Highway

Canadian Provincial Autoroute

Mexican Federal Route

OTHER SYMBOLS

Distances Along Major Highways
Miles in US; kilometers in Canada and Mexico

Tunnel; Pass

One-Way Street

Airport

Railroad
Downtown maps only

Auto Ferry; Passenger Ferry

RECREATION AND FEATURES OF INTEREST

National Park

National Forest; National Grassland

Other Large Park or Recreation Area

Military Lands

Indian Reservation

Small State Park with and without Camping

Public Campsite

Trail

Point of Interest

Golf Course
Professional tournament location

Hospital
City maps only

Ski Area

CITIES AND TOWNS

National Capital; State or Provincial Capital

County Seat
State maps only

Cities, Towns, and Populated Places
Type size indicates relative importance

Urban Area
State and province maps only

Large Incorporated Cities

OTHER MAP FEATURES

JEFFERSON   County Boundary and Name

Time Zone Boundary

+ Mt. Olympus   Mountain Peak; Elevation
  7,965   Feet in US; meters in Canada and Mexico

Perennial; Intermittent River

Perennial; Intermittent or Dry Water Body

Dam

Swamp

Whoever said the world's getting smaller never had to fuel it.

Each year millions of people become drivers. Meeting this growing demand for energy is complicated, but as ExxonMobil we try to make it look simple. So not only are the familiar faces of Exxon and

Mobil still there to help you, they now accept each other's credit cards. We figure you have enough stuff in your wallet already, so now one card works like two.

Ex*x***onMobil**

WHETHER YOU'RE IN A...

...TRACK RACE

...TRUCK RACE

...DRAG RACE

...OR THE RAT RACE,

...SUPERFLO® GIVES PROTECTION THAT'S FAST, PROTECTION THAT LASTS.

High-speed straightaways of the Busch Series. Treacherous mud pits of CORR (Championship Off Road Racing). Earth-shaking quarter miles of NHRA. They're all brutal on a car and its engine. Yet the drivers of these Exxon Superflo® racing vehicles can tell you firsthand, Exxon Superflo motor oil goes the distance. And if it can protect their engines, imagine what it can do for yours.

Superflo races its protection to your engine's vital parts at the start and keeps protecting mile after mile after mile. So protect your car's engine with Exxon Superflo motor oil. Protection That's Fast, Protection That Lasts!™

Would you like to spend less time buying gas?

With *Speedpass,* getting gas just got a little more exciting. All you have to do is wave it at the pump, gas up and go. Fast and easy. You can link it to a major credit card or check card that you *already* have. So call our toll-free number, **1-877-MY MOBIL**, or visit www.speedpass.com to enroll. Join the millions of people who already use *Speedpass.* It's safe, secure and best of all...it's *free.*

Speedpass
Today's way to pay. Mobil

Only your garage
could protect it better.

But if you actually use your car, then protect it with Mobil 1® oil and a Mobil 1 filter. They're like a tag team in your engine. Each one is engineered for a specific job, but together they're unbeatable. It's the perfect give-and-take relationship. So, on your next oil change play matchmaker and be sure to ask for Mobil 1 oil as well as the Mobil 1 filter.

www.mobil1.com/estore
1-800-ASK-MOBIL

Nothing outperforms
Mobil 1

WELCOME

Dear Traveler,

Since 1958, *Mobil Travel Guides,* an ExxonMobil Travel Publication, has provided North American travelers with reliable advice on finding good value, special getaways, and entertaining attractions. Today, our Mobil, Exxon, and Esso brands provide a full array of products and services to accommodate your travel needs.

We appreciate the opportunity to assist you with your leisure and business travels. Our nationwide network of independent, professional evaluators offers their expertise on thousands of lodging, dining, and attraction options, allowing you to plan an economical family vacation, a scenic business retreat, or a memorable 5-Star experience.

Your feedback is important to us as we strive to improve our product offerings and better meet the needs of the modern traveler. Whether you dine out only occasionally or travel extensively, please take the time to complete the customer feedback form at the back of this book. Or, contact us at www.exxonmobiltravel.com. We hope to hear from you soon.

Best wishes for safe and enjoyable travels.

Lee R Raymond

Lee R. Raymond
Chairman
Exxon Mobil Corporation

A WORD TO OUR READERS

The exciting and complex development of the US interstate highway system was formally—and finally—established in 1956, allowing Americans to take to the roads in enormous numbers. They have been going on day trips, long weekends, extended family vacations, and business trips ever since. Traveling across the country—stopping at National Parks, major cities, small towns, monuments, and landmarks—remains a fantasy trip for many.

Airline travel, too, is on the increase. Whether for business or pleasure, we can take flights between relatively close cities and from coast to coast.

You, the traveler, deserve the best food and accommodations available in every city, town, or village you visit. But finding suitable accommodations can be problematic. You could try to meet and ask local residents about appropriate places to stay and eat, but that time-consuming option comes with no guarantee of getting the best advice.

That's where the *Mobil Travel Guides* come in. This trusted, well-established tool can direct you to satisfying places to eat and stay, as well as to interesting events and attractions in thousands of locations across North America. Prior to the merger with Exxon Corporation, Mobil Corporation had sponsored the *Mobil Travel Guides* since 1958. Now ExxonMobil presents the latest edition of our annual Travel Guide series in partnership with Consumer Guide publications.

In 2001, we introduced driving tours and walking tours to the *Mobil Travel Guides*. This year we've taken that idea a bit further by adding additional walking and driving tours that are more detailed and more colorful. With more specific directions, the driving tours will help you navigate off the beaten path, so you can spend the day (or two if you choose) getting a taste of local history and culture by exploring the sites around your destination city. Walking tours let you stretch your legs and explore your destination more thoroughly, pointing you in the direction of historic points of interest, must-see attractions, and even a great place to grab a bite.

Last year's inclusion of full-color photos was a great success. This year we've filled the guides with even more new pictures to help you envision your trip and perhaps encourage you to stop and take your own pictures. The photos aren't the only color in the guides, though. MapQuest's maps are also in full-color.

The hi-tech information database that is the foundation of every title in the *Mobil Travel Guide* series is an astonishing resource: It is enormous, detailed, and continually updated, making it as accurate and useful as it can be. Highly trained field representatives, spread out across the country, generate exhaustive, computerized inspection reports. Senior staff members then evaluate these reports, along with the comments of more than 100,000 readers. All of this information is used to arrive at fair, accurate, and useful assessments of hotels, motels, and restaurants. Mobil's respected and world-famous one- to five-star rating system highlights valuable capsulized descriptions of each site. All of this dependable information, plus details about thousands of attractions and things to do, is in the dynamic Mobil database!

Although the ten-book set allows us to include many more hotels, restaurants, and attractions than in past years, space limitations still make it impossible for us to include every hotel, motel, and restaurant in America. Instead, our database consists of a generous, representative sampling, with information about places that are above-average in their type. In essence, you can confidently patronize any of the restaurants, places of lodging, and attractions contained in the *Mobil Travel Guide* series.

What do we mean by "representative sampling"? You'll find that the *Mobil Travel Guide* books include information about a great variety of establishments. Perhaps you favor rustic lodgings and restaurants, or perhaps you're most comfortable with elegance and high style. Money may be no object or, like most of us, you may be on a budget. Some travelers place a high premium on 24-hour room service or special menu items. Others look for quiet seclusion. Whatever your travel needs and desires, they will be reflected in the *Mobil Travel Guide* listings.

Allow us to emphasize that we have charged no establishment for inclusion in our guides. We have no relationship with any of the businesses and attractions we list and act only as a consumer advocate. In essence, we do the investigative legwork so you won't have to.

Look over the "How to Use This Book" section that follows. You'll discover just how simple it is to quickly and easily gather all the information you need—before your trip or while on the road. For terrific tips on saving money, travel safety, and other ways to get the most out of your travels, be sure to read our special section, "Making the Most of Your Trip."

Keep in mind that the hospitality business is ever-changing. Restaurants and places of lodging—particularly small chains or stand-alone establishments—can change management or even go out of business with surprising quickness. Although we have made every effort to double-check information during our annual updates, we nevertheless recommend that you call ahead to be sure a place you have selected is open and still offers all the features you want. Phone numbers are provided, and, when available, we also list fax and Web site information.

We hope that all your travel experiences are easy and relaxing. If any aspects of your accommodations or dining motivate you to comment, please drop us a line. We depend a great deal on our readers' remarks, so you can be assured that we will read and assimilate your comments into our research. General comments about our books are also welcome. You can write us at Mobil Travel Guides,

7373 N Cicero Ave, Lincolnwood, IL 60712, or send email to info@exxonmobiltravel.com.

Take your *Mobil Travel Guide* books along on every trip. You'll be pleased by their convenience, ease of use, and breadth of dependable coverage.

Happy travels in the new millennium!

EDITORIAL CONTRIBUTOR AND CONSULTANT FOR DRIVING TOURS, WALKING TOURS, ATTRACTIONS, EVENTS, AND PHOTOGRAPHY:

Bill McRae is a native of eastern Montana and now resides in Oregon. He is the author of eight guidebooks to the western US and Canada including *Pacific Northwest USA: A Travel Survival Kit, Montana Handbook,* and *Frommer's Canada.* His other travel writing accomplishments and credits include *National Geographic's The American Road Atlas and Travel Planner* and assignments for GORP.com and Expedia.com.

HOW TO USE THIS BOOK

The *Mobil Travel Guides* are designed for ease of use. Each state has its own chapter. The chapter begins with a general introduction, which provides both a general geographical and historical orientation to the state; it also covers basic statewide tourist information, from state recreation areas to seatbelt laws. The remainder of each chapter is devoted to the travel destinations within the state—cities and towns, state and national parks, and tourist areas—which, like the states, are arranged alphabetically.

The following is an explanation of the wealth of information you'll find regarding those travel destinations—information on the area, on things to see and do there, and on where to stay and eat.

Maps and Map Coordinates

Next to each destination is a set of map coordinates. These are referenced to the appropriate state map in the front of this book. In addition, we have provided maps of selected larger cities and of key neighborhoods within the city sections.

Destination Information

Because many travel destinations are close to other cities and towns where visitors might find additional attractions, accommodations, and restaurants, cross-references to those places are included whenever possible. Also listed are addresses and phone numbers for travel information resources—usually the local chamber of commerce or office of tourism—as well as pertinent vital statistics and a brief introduction to the area.

What to See and Do

Almost 20,000 museums, art galleries, amusement parks, universities, historic sites and houses, plantations, churches, state parks, ski areas, and other attractions are described in the *Mobil Travel Guides*. A white star on a black background ◼ signals that the attraction is one of the best in the state. Because municipal parks, public tennis courts, swimming pools, and small educational institutions are common to most towns, they are generally not represented with the white star on the black background.

Following the attraction's description, you'll find the months and days it's open, address/location and phone number, and admission costs (see the inside front cover for an explanation of the cost symbols). Note that directions are given from the center of the town under which the attraction is listed, which may not necessarily be the town in which the attraction is located. Zip codes are listed only if they differ from those given for the town.

Driving and Walking Tours

The driving tours are usually day trips—though they can be longer—that make for interesting side trips. This is a way to get off the beaten track and visit an area often overlooked. These trips frequently cover areas of natural beauty or historical significance. The walking tours focus on a particularly interesting area of a city or town. Again, these can be a break from more everyday tourist attractions. The tours often include places to stop for a meal or snack.

Special Events

Special events can either be annual events that last only a short time, such as festivals and fairs, or longer, seasonal events such as horse racing, summer theater and concerts, and professional sports. Special event listings might also include an infrequently occurring occasion that marks a certain date or event, such as a centennial or other commemorative celebration.

Major Cities

Additional information on airports and ground transportation, suburbs, and neighborhoods may be included for large cities.

Lodging and Restaurant Listings

ORGANIZATION

For both lodgings and restaurants, when a property is in a town that does not have its own heading, the listing appears under the town nearest its location with the address and town immediately after the establishment name. In large cities, lodgings located within five miles of major commercial airports are listed under a separate "Airport" heading, following the city listings.

LODGING CLASSIFICATIONS

Each property is classified by type according to the characteristics below. Because the following features and services are found at most motels and hotels, they are not shown in those listings:

- Year-round operation with a single rate structure unless otherwise quoted
- European plan (meals not included in room rate)
- Bathroom with tub and/or shower in each room
- Air-conditioned/heated, often with individual room control
- Cots
- Daily maid service
- In-room phones
- Elevators

Motels/Motor Lodges. Accommodations are in low-rise structures with rooms easily accessible to parking (which is usually free). Properties have outdoor room entry and small, functional lobbies. Service is often limited, and dining may not be offered in lower-rated motels and lodges. Shops and businesses are found only in higher-rated properties, as are bellhops, room service, and restaurants serving three meals daily.

Hotels. To be categorized as a hotel, an establishment must have most of the following facilities and services: multiple floors, a restaurant and/or coffee shop, elevators, room service, bellhops, a spacious

lobby, and recreational facilities. In addition, the following features and services not shown in listings are also found:
- Valet service (one-day laundry/cleaning service)
- Room service during hours restaurant is open
- Bellhops
- Some oversize beds

Resorts. These specialize in stays of three days or more and usually offer American plan and/or housekeeping accommodations. Their emphasis is on recreational facilities, and a social director is often available. Food services are of primary importance, and guests must be able to eat three meals a day on the premises, either in restaurants or by having access to an on-site grocery store and preparing their own meals.

All Suites. All Suites' guest rooms consist of two rooms, one bedroom and one living room. Higher rated properties offer facilities and services comparable to regular hotels.

B&Bs/Small Inns. Frequently thought of as a small hotel, a bed-and-breakfast or an inn is a place of homelike comfort and warm hospitality. It is often a structure of historic significance, with an equally interesting setting. Meals are a special occasion, and refreshments are frequently served in late afternoon. Rooms are usually individually decorated, often with antiques or furnishings representative of the locale. Phones, bathrooms, or TVs may not be available in every room.

Guest Ranches. Like resorts, guest ranches specialize in stays of three days or more. Guest ranches also offer meal plans and extensive outdoor activities. Horseback riding is usually a feature; there are stables and trails on the ranch property, and trail rides and daily instruction are part of the program. Many guest ranches are working ranches, ranging from casual to rustic, and guests are encouraged to participate in ranch life. Eating is often family style and may also include cookouts. Western saddles are assumed; phone ahead to inquire about English saddle availability.

Extended Stay. These hotels specialize in stays of three days or more and usually offer weekly room rates. Service is often limited and dining might not be offered at lower-rated extended-stay hotels.

Villas/Condos. Similar to Cottage Colonies, these establishments are usually found in recreational areas. They are often separate houses, often luxuriously furnished, and rarely offer restaurants and only a small variety of services on the premises.

Conference Centers. Conference Centers are hotels with extended meeting space facilities designed to house multiday conferences and seminars. Amenities are often geared toward groups staying for longer than one night and often include restaurants and fitness facilities. Larger Conference Center Hotels are often referred to as Convention Center Hotels.

Casinos. Casino Hotels incorporate areas that offer games of chance like Blackjack, Poker, Slot machines, etc. and are only found in states that legalize gambling. Casino Hotels offer a wide range of services and amenities, comparable to regular hotels.

Cottage Colonies. These are housekeeping cottages and cabins that are usually found in recreational areas. Any dining or recreational facilities are noted in our listing.

DINING CLASSIFICATIONS

Restaurants. Most dining establishments fall into this category. All have a full kitchen and offer table service and a complete menu. Parking on or near the premises, in a lot or garage, is assumed. When a property offers valet or other special parking features, or when only street parking is available, it is noted in the listing.

Unrated Dining Spots. These places, listed after Restaurants in many cities, are chosen for their unique atmosphere, specialized menu, or local flavor. They include delis, ice-cream parlors, cafeterias, tearooms, and pizzerias. Because they may not have a full kitchen or table service, they are not given a *Mobil Travel Guides* rating. Often they offer extraordinary value and quick service.

QUALITY RATINGS

The *Mobil Travel Guides* have been rating lodgings and restaurants on a national basis since the first edition was published in 1958. For years the guide was the only source of such ratings, and it remains among the few guidebooks to rate restaurants across the country.

All listed establishments were inspected by experienced field representatives or evaluated by a senior staff member. Ratings are based upon their detailed inspection reports of the individual properties, on written evaluations of staff members who stay and dine anonymously, and on an extensive review of comments from our readers.

You'll find a key to the rating categories, ★ through ★★★★★, on the inside front cover. All establishments in the book are recommended. Even a ★ place is above average, usually providing a basic, informal experience. Rating categories reflect both the features the property offers and its quality in relation to similar establishments.

For example, lodging ratings take into account the number and quality of facilities and services, the luxury of appointments, and the attitude and professionalism of staff and management. A ★ establishment provides a comfortable night's lodging. A ★★ property offers more than a facility that rates one star, and the decor is well planned and integrated. Establishments that rate ★★★ are professionally managed and staffed and often beautifully appointed; the lodging experience is truly excellent, and the range of facilities is extensive. Properties that have been given ★★★★ not only offer many services but also have their own style and personality; they are luxurious, creatively decorated, and superbly maintained. The ★★★★★ properties are among the best in North America, superb in every respect and entirely memorable, year in and year out.

Restaurant evaluations reflect the quality of the food and the ingredients, preparation, presentation, service levels, as well as the property's decor and ambience. A restaurant that has fairly simple goals for menu and decor but that achieves those goals superbly might receive the same number of stars as a restaurant with somewhat loftier ambitions, but the execution of which falls short of the mark. In general, ★ indicates a restaurant that's a good choice in its area, usually fairly simple and perhaps catering to a clientele of locals and families; ★★ denotes restaurants that are more highly recommended in their area; ★★★ restaurants are of national caliber, with professional and attentive service and a skilled chef in the kitchen; ★★★★ reflect superb dining choices, where remarkable food is served in equally remarkable surroundings; and ★★★★★ represent that rare group of the best restaurants in the country, where in addition to near perfection in every detail, there's that special something extra that makes for an unforgettable dining experience.

A list of the four-star and five-star establishments in each region is located just before the state listings.

Each rating is reviewed annually and each establishment must work to maintain its rating (or improve it). Every effort is made to assure that ratings are fair and accurate; the designated ratings are published purely as an aid to travelers. In general, properties that are very new or have recently undergone major management changes are considered difficult to assess fairly and are often listed without ratings.

LODGINGS

Each listing gives the name, address, directions (when there is no street address), neighborhood and/or directions from downtown (in major cities), phone number (local and 800), fax number, number and type of rooms available, room rates, and seasons open (if not year-round). Also included are details on recreational and dining facilities on the property or nearby, the presence of a luxury level, and credit card information. A key to the symbols at the end of each listing is on the inside front cover. (Note that Exxon or Mobil Corporation credit cards cannot be used for payment of meals and room charges.)

All prices quoted in the *Mobil Travel Guide* publications are expected to be in effect at the time of publication and during the entire year; however, prices cannot be guaranteed. In some localities there may be short-term price variations because of special events or holidays. Whenever possible, these price charges are noted. Certain resorts have complicated rate structures that vary with the time of year; always confirm listed rates when you make your plans.

RESTAURANTS

Each listing gives the name, address, directions (when there is no street address), neighborhood and/or directions from downtown (in major cities), phone number, hours and days of operation (if not open daily year-round), reservation policy, cuisine (if other than American), price range for each meal served, children's menu (if offered), specialties, and credit card information. In addition, special features such as chef ownership, ambience, and entertainment are noted. By carefully reading the detailed restaurant information and comparing prices, you can easily determine whether the restaurant is formal and elegant or informal and comfortable for families.

TERMS AND ABBREVIATIONS IN LISTINGS

The following terms and abbreviations are used throughout the listings:

A la carte entrees With a price, refers to the cost of entrees/main dishes that are not accompanied by side dishes.

AP American plan (lodging plus all meals).

Bar Liquor, wine, and beer are served in a bar or cocktail lounge and usually with meals unless otherwise indicated (e.g., "wine, beer").

Business center The property has a designated area accessible to all guests with business services.

Business servs avail The property can perform/arrange at least two of the following services for a guest: audiovisual equipment rental, binding, computer rental, faxing, messenger services, modem availability, notary service, obtaining office supplies, photocopying, shipping, and typing.

Cable Standard cable service; "premium" indicates that HBO, Disney, Showtime, or similar cable services are available.

Ck-in, ck-out Check-in time, check-out time.

Coin lndry Self-service laundry.

Complete meal Soup and/or salad, entree, and dessert, plus nonalcoholic beverage.

Continental bkfst Usually coffee and a roll or doughnut.

Cr cds: A, American Express; C, Carte Blanche; D, Diners Club; DS, Discover; ER, enRoute; JCB, Japanese Credit Bureau; MC, MasterCard; V, Visa.

D Followed by a price, indicates room rate for a "double"—two people in one room in one or two beds (the charge may be higher for two double beds).

Downhill/X-country ski Downhill and/or cross-country skiing within 20 miles of property.

Each addl Extra charge for each additional person beyond the stated number of persons at a reduced price.

Early-bird dinner A meal served at specified hours, typically around 4:30-6:30 pm.

Exc Except.

Exercise equipt Two or more pieces of exercise equipment on the premises.

Exercise rm Both exercise equipment and room, with an instructor on the premises.

Fax Facsimile machines available to all guests.

Golf privileges Privileges at a course within ten miles.

Hols Holidays.

In-rm modem link Every guest room has a connection for a modem that's separate from the phone line.

Kit. or **Kits.** A kitchen or kitchenette that contains stove or microwave, sink, and refrigerator and that is either part of the room or a separate room. If the kitchen is not fully equipped, the listing will indicate "no equipt" or "some equipt."

Luxury level A special section of a lodging, covering at least an entire floor, that offers increased luxury accommodations. Management must provide no less than three of these four services: separate check-in and check-out, concierge, private lounge, and private elevator service (key access). Complimentary breakfast and snacks are commonly offered.

MAP Modified American plan (lodging plus two meals).

Movies Prerecorded videos are available for rental.

No cr cds accepted No credit cards are accepted.

No elvtr In hotels with more than two stories, it's assumed there are elevators; only their absence is noted.

No phones Phones, too, are assumed; only their absence is noted.

Parking There is a parking lot on the premises.

Private club A cocktail lounge or bar available to members and their guests. In motels and hotels where these clubs exist, registered guests can usually use the club as guests of the management; the same is frequently true of restaurants.

Prix fixe A full meal for a stated price; usually one price is quoted.

Res Reservations.

S Followed by a price, indicates room rate for a "single," i.e., one person.

Serv bar A service bar, where drinks are prepared for dining patrons only.

Serv charge Service charge is the amount added to the restaurant check in lieu of a tip.

Table d'hôte A full meal for a stated price, dependent upon entree selection; no a la carte options are available.

Tennis privileges Privileges at tennis courts within five miles.

TV Indicates color television.

Under certain age free Children under that age are not charged if staying in room with a parent.

Valet parking An attendant is available to park and retrieve a car.

VCR VCRs in all guest rooms.

VCR avail VCRs are available for hookup in guest rooms.

Special Information for Travelers with Disabilities

The *Mobil Travel Guides* D symbol shown in accommodation and restaurant listings indicates establishments that are at least partially accessible to people with mobility problems.

The *Mobil Travel Guides* criteria for accessibility are unique to our publication. Please do not confuse them with the universal symbol for wheelchair accessibility. When the D symbol appears following a listing, the establishment is equipped with facilities to accommodate people using wheelchairs or crutches or otherwise needing easy access to doorways and rest rooms. Travelers with severe mobility problems or with hearing or visual impairments may or may not find facilities they need. Always phone ahead to make sure that an establishment can meet your needs.

All lodgings bearing our D symbol have the following facilities:

- ISA-designated parking near access ramps
- Level or ramped entryways to building
- Swinging building entryway doors minimum 39"
- Public rest rooms on main level with space to operate a wheelchair; handrails at commode areas
- Elevators equipped with grab bars and lowered control buttons
- Restaurants with accessible doorways; rest rooms with space to operate wheelchair; handrails at commode areas
- Minimum 39" width entryway to guest rooms
- Low-pile carpet in rooms
- Telephone at bedside and in bathroom
- Bed placed at wheelchair height
- Minimum 39" width doorway to bathroom
- Bath with open sink—no cabinet; room to operate wheelchair
- Handrails at commode areas; tub handrails
- Wheelchair-accessible peephole in room entry door
- Wheelchair-accessible closet rods and shelves

All restaurants bearing our Ⓓ symbol offer the following facilities:
- ISA-designated parking beside access ramps
- Level or ramped front entryways to building
- Tables to accommodate wheelchairs
- Main-floor rest rooms; minimum 39" width entryway
- Rest rooms with space to operate wheelchair; handrails at commode areas

In general, the newest properties are apt to impose the fewest barriers.

To get the kind of service you need and have a right to expect, do not hesitate when making a reservation to question the management in detail about the availability of accessible rooms, parking, entrances, restaurants, lounges, or any other facilities that are important to you, and confirm what is meant by "accessible." Some guests with mobility impairments report that lodging establishments' housekeeping and maintenance departments are most helpful in describing barriers. Also inquire about any special equipment, transportation, or services you may need.

MAKING THE MOST OF YOUR TRIP

A few hardy souls might look with fondness upon the trip where the car broke down and they were stranded for a week. Or maybe even the vacation that cost twice what it was supposed to. For most travelers, though, the best trips are those that are safe, smooth, and within their budget. To help you make your trip the best it can be, we've assembled a few tips and resources.

Saving Money

ON LODGING

After you've seen the published rates, it's time to look for discounts. Many hotels and motels offer them—for senior citizens, business travelers, families, you name it. It never hurts to ask—politely, that is. Sometimes, especially in late afternoon, desk clerks are instructed to fill beds, and you might be offered a lower rate, or a nicer room, to entice you to stay. Look for bargains on stays over multiple nights, in the off-season, and on weekdays or weekends (depending on location). Many hotels in major metropolitan areas, for example, have special weekend package plans that offer considerable savings on rooms; they may include breakfast, cocktails, and meal discounts. Prices can change frequently throughout the year, so phone ahead.

Another way to save money is to choose accommodations that give you more than just a standard room. Rooms with kitchen facilities enable you to cook some meals for yourself, reducing restaurant costs. A suite might save money for two couples traveling together. Even hotel luxury levels can provide good value, as many include breakfast or cocktails in the price of the room.

State and city sales taxes, as well as special room taxes, can increase your room rates as much as 25 percent per day. We are unable to include this specific information in the listings, but we strongly urge that you ask about these taxes when placing reservations to understand the total cost of your lodgings.

Watch out for telephone-usage charges that hotels frequently impose on long-distance calls, credit-card calls, and other phone calls—even those that go unanswered. Before phoning from your room, read the information given to you at check-in, and then be sure to read your bill carefully before checking out. You won't be expected to pay for charges that they did not spell out. (On the other hand, it's not unusual for a hotel to bill you for your calls after you return home.) Consider using your cell phone; or, if public telephones are available in the hotel lobby, your cost savings may outweigh the inconvenience.

ON DINING

There are several ways to get a less expensive meal at a more expensive restaurant. Early-bird dinners are popular in many parts of the country and offer considerable savings. If you're interested in sampling a 4- or 5-star establishment, consider going at lunchtime. While the prices then are probably relatively high, they may be half of those at dinner and come with the same ambience, service, and cuisine.

ON PARK PASSES

Although many national parks, monuments, seashores, historic sites, and recreation areas may be used free of charge, others charge an entrance fee (ranging from $1 to $6 per person to $5 to $15 per carload) and/or a "use fee" for special services and facilities. If you plan to make several visits to federal recreation areas, consider one of the following National Park Service money-saving programs:

Park Pass. This is an annual entrance permit to a specific unit in the National Park Service system that normally charges an entrance fee. The pass admits the permit holder and any accompanying passengers in a private noncommercial vehicle or, in the case of walk-in facilities, the holder's spouse, children, and parents. It is valid for entrance fees only. A Park Pass may be purchased in person or by mail from the National Park Service unit at which the pass will be honored. The cost is $15 to $20, depending upon the area.

Golden Eagle Passport. This pass, available to people who are between 17 and 61, entitles the purchaser and accompanying passengers in a private noncommercial vehicle to enter any outdoor National Park Service unit that charges an entrance fee and admits the purchaser and family to most walk-in fee-charging areas. Like the Park Pass, it is good for one year and does not cover use fees. It may be purchased from the National Park Service, Office of Public Inquiries, Room 1013, US Department of the Interior, 18th and C sts NW, Washington, D.C. 20240, phone 202/208-4747; at any of the ten regional offices throughout the country; and at any National Park Service area that charges a fee. The cost is $50.

Golden Age Passport. Available to citizens and permanent residents of the United States 62 years or older, this is a lifetime entrance permit to fee-charging recreation areas. The fee exemption extends to those accompanying the permit holder in a private noncommercial vehicle or, in the case of walk-in facilities, to the holder's spouse and children. The passport also entitles the holder to a 50 percent discount on use fees charged in park areas but not to fees charged by concessionaires. Golden Age Passports must be obtained in person. The applicant must show proof of age, i.e., a driver's license, birth certificate, or signed affidavit attesting to age (Medicare cards are not acceptable proof). These passports are available at most park service units where they're used, at National Park Service headquarters (see above), at park system regional offices, at National Forest Supervisors' offices, and at most Ranger Station offices. The cost is $10.

Golden Access Passport. Issued to citizens and permanent residents of the United States who are physically disabled or visually impaired, this passport is a free lifetime entrance permit to fee-charging recreation areas. The fee exemption extends to those accompanying the permit holder in a private noncommercial vehicle or, in the case of walk-in facilities, to the holder's spouse and children. The passport also entitles the holder to a 50 percent discount on use fees charged in park areas but not to fees charged by concessionaires. Golden Access Passports must be obtained in person. Proof of eligibility to receive federal benefits is required (under programs such as Disability Retirement, Compensation for Military Service-Connected Disability, Coal Mine

Safety and Health Act, etc.), or an affidavit must be signed attesting to eligibility. These passports are available at the same outlets as Golden Age Passports.

FOR SENIOR CITIZENS

Look for the senior-citizen discount symbol in the lodging and restaurant listings. Always call ahead to confirm that the discount is being offered, and be sure to carry proof of age. At places not listed in the book, it never hurts to ask if a senior-citizen discount is offered. Additional information for mature travelers is available from the American Association of Retired Persons (AARP), 601 E St NW, Washington, D.C. 20049, phone 202/434-2277.

Tipping

Tipping is an expression of appreciation for good service, and often service workers rely on tips as a significant part of their income. However, you never need to tip if service is poor.

IN HOTELS

Door attendants in major city hotels are usually given $1 for getting you a cab. Bellhops expect $1 per bag, usually $2 if you have only one bag. Concierges are tipped according to the service they perform. It's not mandatory to tip when you've asked for suggestions on sightseeing or restaurants or help in making reservations for dining. However, when a concierge books you a table at a restaurant known to be difficult to get into, a gratuity of $5 is appropriate. For obtaining theater or sporting event tickets, $5-$10 is expected. Maids, often overlooked by guests, may be tipped $1-$2 per days of stay.

AT RESTAURANTS

Coffee shop and counter service waitstaff are usually given 8 percent–10 percent of the bill. In full-service restaurants, tip 15 percent of the bill, before sales tax. In fine restaurants, where the staff is large and shares the gratuity, 18 percent–20 percent for the waiter is appropriate. In most cases, tip the maitre d' only if service has been extraordinary and only on the way out; $20 is the minimum in upscale properties in major metropolitan areas. If there is a wine steward, tip him or her at least $6 a bottle, more if the wine was decanted or if the bottle was very expensive. If your bus person has been unusually attentive, $2 pressed into his hand on departure is a nice gesture. An increasing number of restaurants automatically add a service charge to the bill instead of a gratuity. Before tipping, carefully review your check. If you are in doubt, ask your server.

AT AIRPORTS

Curbside luggage handlers expect $1 per bag. Car-rental shuttle drivers who help with your luggage appreciate a $1 or $2 tip.

Staying Safe

The best way to deal with emergencies is to be prepared enough to avoid them. However, unforeseen situations do happen, and you can prepare for them.

IN YOUR CAR

Before your trip, make sure your car has been serviced and is in good working order. Change the oil, check the battery and belts, and make sure tires are inflated properly (this can also improve gas mileage). Other inspections recommended by the car's manufacturer should be made, too.

Next, be sure you have the tools and equipment to deal with a routine breakdown: jack, spare tire, lug wrench, repair kit, emergency tools, jumper cables, spare fan belt, auto fuses, flares and/or reflectors, flashlights, first-aid kit, and, in winter, windshield wiper fluid, a windshield scraper, and snow shovel.

Bring all appropriate and up-to-date documentation—licenses, registration, and insurance cards—and know what's covered by your insurance. Also bring an extra set of keys, just in case.

En route, always buckle up! In most states it is required by law.

If your car does break down, get out of traffic as soon as possible—pull well off the road. Raise the hood and turn on your emergency flashers or tie a white cloth to the roadside door handle or antenna. Stay near your car. Use flares or reflectors to keep your car from being hit.

IN YOUR LODGING

Chances are slim that you will encounter a hotel or motel fire. The ▣ in a listing indicates that there were smoke detectors and/or sprinkler systems in the rooms we inspected. Once you've checked in, make sure that any smoke detector in your room is working properly. Ascertain the locations of fire extinguishers and at least two fire exits. Never use an elevator in a fire.

For personal security, use the peephole in your room's door.

PROTECTING AGAINST THEFT

To guard against theft wherever you go, don't bring anything of more value than you need. If you do bring valuables, leave them at your hotel rather than in your car, and if you have something very expensive, lock it in a safe. Many hotels have one in each room; others will store your valuables in the hotel's safe. And of course, don't carry more money than you need; use traveler's checks and credit cards, or visit cash machines.

For Travelers with Disabilities

A number of publications can provide assistance. The most complete listing of published material for travelers with disabilities is available from The Disability Bookshop, Twin Peaks Press, Box 129, Vancouver, WA 98666, phone 360/694-2462.

The Reference Section of the National Library Service for the Blind and Physically Handicapped (Library of Congress, Washington, D.C. 20542, phone 202/707-9276 or 202/707-5100) provides information and resources for persons with mobility problems and hearing and vision impairments, as well as information about the NILS talking program (or visit your local library).

IMPORTANT TOLL-FREE NUMBERS AND ONLINE INFORMATION

Hotels and Motels

Adams Mark   800 444-2326
   www.adamsmark.com
Amerisuites   800 833-1516
   www.amerisuites.com
AMFA Parks & Resorts   800 236-7916
   www.amfac.com
Baymont Inns   800 229-6668
   www.baymontinns.com
Best Western   800 780-7234
   www.bestwestern.com
Budget Host Inn   800 283-4678
   www.budgethost.com
Canadian Pacific   800 441-1414
   www.fairmont.com
Candlewood Suites   888 226-3539
   www.candlewoodsuites.com
Clarion Hotels   800 252-7466
   www.choicehotels.com
Clubhouse Inns   800 258-2466
   www.clubhouseinn.com
Coast Hotels & Resorts   800 663-1144
   www.coasthotels.com
Comfort Inns   800 252-7466
   www.choicehotels.com
Concorde Hotels   800 888-4747
   www.concorde-hotel.com
Country Hearth Inns   800 848-5767
   www.countryhearth.com
County Inns   800 456-4000
   www.countryinns.com
Courtyard by Marriott   888 236-2437
   www.courtyard.com
Crown Plaza Hotels   800 227-6963
   www.crowneplaza.com
Days Inn   800 544-8313
   www.daysinn.com
Delta Hotels   800 268-1133
   www.deltahotels.com
Destination Hotels & Resorts
   800 434-7347
   www.destinationhotels.com
Doubletree   800 222-8733
   www.doubletree.com
Drury Inns   800 378-7946
   www.druryinn.com
Econolodge   800 553-2666
   www.econolodge.com
Embassy Suites   800 362-2779
   www.embassysuites.com
Fairfield Inns   800 228-2800
   www.fairfieldinn.com

Fairmont Hotels   800 441-1414
   www.fairmont.com
Family Inns of America   800 251-9752
   www.familyinnsofamerica.com
Forte Hotels   800 300-9147
   www.fortehotels.com
Four Points by Sheraton
   888 625-5144   www.starwood.com
Four Seasons   800 545-4000
   www.fourseasons.com
Hampton Inns   800 426-7866
   www.hamptoninn.com
Hilton   800 774-1500
   www.hilton.com
Holiday Inn   800 465-4329
   www.holiday-inn.com
Homestead Village   888 782-9473
   www.stayhsd.com
Homewood Suites   800 225-5466
   www.homewoodsuites.com
Howard Johnson   800 406-1411
   www.hojo.com
Hyatt   800 633-7313
   www.hyatt.com
Inn Suites Hotels & Suites
   800 842-4242   www.innsuites.com
Inter-Continental   888 567-8725
   www.interconti.com
Jameson Inns   800 526-3766
   www.jamesoninns.com
Kempinski Hotels   800-426-3135
   www.kempinski.com
Kimpton Hotels   888-546-7866
   www.kimptongroup.com
La Quinta   800-531-5900
   www.laquinta.com
Leading Hotels of the World
   800-223-6800   www.lhw.com
Loews Hotels   800-235-6397
   www.loewshotels.com
Mainstay Suites   800-660-6246
   www.choicehotels.com
Mandarin Oriental   800-526-6566
   www.mandarin-oriental.com
Marriott   888-236-2427
   www.marriott.com
Nikko Hotels   800-645-5687
   www.nikkohotels.com
Omni Hotels   800-843-6664
   www.omnihotels.com
Preferred Hotels & Resorts Worldwide
   www.preferredhotels.com
   800-323-7500

Quality Inn   800-228-5151
www.qualityinn.com
Radisson Hotels   800-333-3333
www.radisson.com
Ramada   888-298-2054
www.ramada.com
Red Lion Inns   800-733-5466
www.redlion.com
Red Roof Inns   800-733-7663
www.redroof.com
Regal Hotels   800-222-8888
www.regal-hotels.com
Regent International   800-545-4000
www.regenthotels.com
Renaissance Hotels   888-236-2427
www.renaissancehotels.com
Residence Inns   888-236-2427
www.residenceinn.com
Ritz Carlton   800-241-3333
www.ritzcarlton.com
Rodeway Inns   800-228-2000
www.rodeway.com
Rosewood Hotels & Resorts
888-767-3966
www.rosewood-hotels.com
Sheraton   888-625-5144
www.sheraton.com
Shilo Inns   800-222-2244
www.shiloinns.com
Shoney's Inns   800-552-4667
www.shoneysinn.com
Sierra Suites   800-474-3772
www.sierrasuites.com
Sleep Inns   800-453-3746
www.sleepinn.com
Small Luxury Hotels   800-525-4800
www.slh.com
Sofitel   800-763-4835
www.sofitel.com
Sonesta Hotels & Resorts
800-766-3782   www.sonesta.com
SRS Worldhotels   800-223-5652
www.srs-worldhotels.com
Summerfield Suites   800-833-4353
www.summerfieldsuites.com
Summit International   800-457-4000
www.summithotels.com
Swissotel   800-637-9477
www.swissotel.com
The Peninsula Group
www.peninsula.com
Travelodge   800-578-7878
www.travelodge.com
Westin Hotels & Resorts
800-937-8461   www.westin.com
Wingate Inns   800-228-1000
www.wingateinns.com
Woodfin Suite Hotels
www.woodfinsuitehotels.com
800-966-3346
Wyndham Hotels & Resorts
800-996-3426   www.wyndham

Airlines

Air Canada   888-247-2262
www.aircanada.ca
Alaska   800-252-7522
www.alaska-air.com
American   800-433-7300
www.aa.com
America West   800-235-9292
www.americawest.com
British Airways   800-247-9297
www.british-airways.com
Continental   800-523-3273
www.flycontinental.com
Delta   800-221-1212
www.delta-air.com
Island Air   800-323-3345
www.islandair.com
Mesa   800-637-2247
www.mesa-air.com
Northwest   800-225-2525
www.nwa.com
SkyWest   800-453-9417
www.skywest.com
Southwest   800-435-9792
www.southwest.com
TWA   800-221-2000
www.twa.com
United   800-241-6522
www.ual.com
US Air   800-428-4322
www.usair.com

Car Rentals

Advantage   800-777-5500
www.arac.com
Alamo   800-327-9633
www.goalamo.com
Allstate   800-634-6186
www.bnm.com/as.htm
Avis   800-831-2847
www.avis.com
Budget   800-527-0700
www.budgetrentacar.com
Dollar   800-800-3665
www.dollarcar.com
Enterprise   800-325-8007
www.pickenterprise.com
Hertz   800-654-3131
www.hertz.com
National   800-227-7368
www.nationalcar.com
Payless   800-729-5377
www.800-payless.com
Rent-A-Wreck.com   800-535-1391
www.rent-a-wreck.com
Sears   800-527-0770
www.budget.com
Thrifty   800-847-4389
www.thrifty.com

FOUR-STAR AND FIVE-STAR ESTABLISHMENTS IN THE GREAT PLAINS

Minnesota

★★★★ Lodging
The Saint Paul Hotel, *St. Paul*

★★★★ Restaurant
Goodfellow's, *Minneapolis*

Missouri

★★★★ Lodgings
The Fairmont Kansas City at The Plaza, *Kansas City*
Hyatt Regency Crown Center, *Kansas City*
The Ritz-Carlton, St. Louis, *Clayton*

★★★★ Restaurants
American, *Kansas City*
Cafe de France, *St. Louis*
Tony's, *St. Louis*

Oklahoma

★★★★ Lodging
The Inn At Jarrett Farm, *Tulsa*

IOWA

Iowa, the heartland of American agriculture, is also a growing center of industry. Iowa is a leader in corn and soybean production, but Iowa industry generates about 3½ times the revenue of agriculture. The 3,600 manufacturing firms in the state produce more than 3,000 different products, ranging from motor homes to microwave ovens. Major appliances, farm implements, and plastics are exported all over the world. Iowa is the only state bordered by two navigable rivers, with the Mississippi River forming its eastern boundary and the Missouri River most of its western boundary. The Sioux called Iowa the "beautiful land."

Iowa's countryside offers tourists a wide range of recreational activities, from boating and fishing on lakes, rivers, and reservoirs to hiking and picnicking at the many state parks and forests. Iowa also offers medium-sized cities with cultural activities, including performing arts, historic sites, and art museums. This is the land of Native American warrior Black Hawk and the birthplace of Buffalo Bill Cody, John Wayne, Herbert Hoover, Meredith Willson, and Dr. James Van Allen.

Population: 2,869,413
Area: 55,965 square miles
Elevation: 480-1,670 feet
Peak: Near Ocheyedan (Osceola County)
Entered Union: December 28, 1846 (29th state)
Capital: Des Moines
Motto: Our liberties we prize and our rights we will maintain
Nickname: The Hawkeye State
Flower: Wild Rose
Bird: Eastern Goldfinch
Tree: Oak
Fair: August 8-18, 2002, in Des Moines
Time Zone: Central
Website: www.state.ia.us

Iowa cornfield

Four glacial epochs and centuries of untouched wilderness fertilized the soil of Iowa before Marquette and Jolliet came in 1673. A favorite Native American hunting ground, Iowa was part of the Louisiana Purchase. Lewis and Clark passed through in 1804 on their arduous trip to find out what the United States had bought. Treaties with the Native Americans in 1832, 1837, and 1842 opened the area to European settlers. Pioneer settlements were made in Lee County in 1820, at Burlington in 1832, and at Dubuque in 1833. The Territory of Iowa was created from the Territory of Wisconsin in 1838.

In its 300-mile east-west sweep and 210-mile north-south stretch, Iowa has nearly 56,000 acres of natural and man-made lakes; 19,000 miles of interior fishing streams; and 72 state parks and recreation areas.

When to Go/Climate

Typical midwestern weather is the norm in Iowa. Summers are hot and humid, winters are cold and harsh. Long Indian summers can stretch into November, while spring is usually very short and rainy.

AVERAGE HIGH/LOW TEMPERATURES (°F)

DES MOINES

Jan 28/11	**May** 73/52	**Sept** 76/55
Feb 34/16	**June** 82/67	**Oct** 64/43
Mar 47/28	**July** 87/67	**Nov** 48/30
Apr 62/40	**Aug** 84/64	**Dec** 33/16

DUBUQUE

Jan 24/8	**May** 69/48	**Sept** 72/52
Feb 30/13	**June** 78/62	**Oct** 61/40
Mar 43/25	**July** 82/62	**Nov** 45/28
Apr 58/37	**Aug** 80/60	**Dec** 29/14

Parks and Recreation Finder

Directions to and information about the parks and recreation areas below are given under their respective town/city sections. Please refer to those sections for details.

NATIONAL PARK AND RECREATION AREAS

Key to abbreviations. I.H.S. = International Historic Site; I.P.M. = International Peace Memorial; N.B. = National Battlefield; N.B.P. = National Battlefield Park; N.B.C. = National Battlefield and Cemetery; N.C.A. = National Conservation Area; N.E.M. = National Expansion Memorial; N.F. = National Forest; N.G. = National Grassland; N.H.P. = National Historical Park; N.H.C. = National Heritage Corridor; N.H.S. = National Historic Site; N.L. = National Lakeshore; N.M. = National Monument; N.M.P. = National Military Park; N.Mem. = National Memorial; N.P. = National Park; N.Pres. = National Preserve; N.R.A. = National Recreational Area; N.R.R. = National Recreational River; N.Riv. = National River; N.S. = National Seashore; N.S.R. = National Scenic Riverway; N.S.T. = National Scenic Trail; N.Sc. = National Scientific Reserve; N.V.M. = National Volcanic Monument.

Place Name	Listed Under
Effigy Mounds N.M.	MARQUETTE
Herbert Hoover N.H.S.	IOWA CITY

STATE PARK AND RECREATION AREAS

Key to abbreviations. I.P. = Interstate Park; S.A.P. = State Archaeological Park; S.B. = State Beach; S.C.A. = State Conservation Area; S.C.P. = State Conservation Park; S.Cp. = State Campground; S.F. = State Forest; S.G. = State Garden; S.H.A. = State Historic Area; S.H.P. = State Historic Park; S.H.S. = State Historic Site; S.M.P. = State Marine Park; S.N.A. = State Natural Area; S.P. = State Park; S.P.C. = State Public Campground; S.R. = State Reserve; S.R.A. = State Recreation Area; S.Res. = State Reservoir; S.Res.P. = State Resort Park; S.R.P. = State Rustic Park.

Place Name	Listed Under
Ambrose A. Call S.P.	ALGONA
Backbone S.P.	STRAWBERRY POINT

CALENDAR HIGHLIGHTS

MARCH

St. Patrick's Day Celebration (Emmetsburg). Parade, pageant, cultural exhibits. Irish stew dinner, dances, and a guest member of Irish Parliament. Phone 712/852-4326.

APRIL

Veishea Spring Festival (Ames). Iowa State campus. Parade, sports, theatrical events, academic open houses. Phone 515/294-1026.

MAY

Snake Alley Criterium Bicycle Races (Burlington). Olympic-style racing. Phone 319/752-0015. Memorial Day weekend.

JUNE

All-Iowa Fair (Cedar Rapids). Hawkeye Downs. Stock car races, fine arts, exhibits, entertainment. Phone Cedar Rapids Area Convention and Visitors Bureau, 319/365-8656.

Glenn Miller Festival (Clarinda). Musical event in honor of Glenn Miller and his birthplace. Phone 712/542-2461.

My Waterloo Days Festival (Waterloo). Citywide festival features air show, balloon rallies, parade, laser and fireworks show, music, renaissance fair, food. Phone 319/233-8431.

Burlington Steamboat Days & the American Music Festival (Burlington). Downtown riverfront. Athletic competitions, fireworks, midway, parade, entertainment. Phone 319/754-4334.

JULY

Freedom Festival (Cedar Rapids). Eighty events for all ages held citywide, topped off by large fireworks display. Phone 319/365-8313.

AUGUST

Iowa State Fair (Des Moines). Fairgrounds. One of the oldest and largest in the country; includes 20 acres of farm machinery, fine arts, grandstand stage and track events, free entertainment, exhibits, demonstrations, contests; camping. Phone 515/262-3111.

SEPTEMBER

Midwest Old Threshers Reunion (Mount Pleasant). Iowa's largest working craft show, antique car show; steam and gas engines, vintage tractors; Midwest Village, log village, narrow-gauge steam railroad, and electric trolley cars; entertainment. Phone 319/385-8937.

OCTOBER

Covered Bridge Festival (Winterset). Late 19th-century crafts, entertainment; parade, bus tour of covered bridges. Phone 515/462-1185.

Beed's Lake S.P.	HAMPTON
Bellevue S.P.	DUBUQUE
Black Hawk S.P.	CARROLL
Brush Creek Canyon S.P.	STRAWBERRY POINT
Clear Lake S.P.	CLEAR LAKE
Dolliver Memorial S.P.	FORT DODGE
Fort Atkinson State Preserve	DECORAH
Fort Defiance S.P.	ESTHERVILLE

Geode S.P.	BURLINGTON
George Wyth Memorial S.P.	CEDAR FALLS
Green Valley S.P.	CRESTON
Gull Point S.P.	SPENCER
Honey Creek S.P.	CENTERVILLE
Lacey-Keosauqua S.P.	FAIRFIELD
Lake Ahquabi S.P.	INDIANOLA
Lake Darling S.P.	WASHINGTON
Lake Keomah S.P.	OSKALOOSA
Lake Macbride S.P.	IOWA CITY
Lake Manawa S.P.	COUNCIL BLUFFS
Lake of Three Fires S.P.	CLARINDA
Lake Wapello S.P.	OTTUMWA
Ledges S.P.	BOONE
Lewis and Clark S.P.	ONAWA
Maquoketa Caves S.P.	MAQUOKETA
McIntosh Woods S.P.	CLEAR LAKE
Mini-Wakan S.P.	SPIRIT LAKE
Nine Eagles S.P.	OSCEOLA
Palisades-Kepler S.P.	CEDAR RAPIDS
Pikes Peak S.P.	MARQUETTE
Pikes Point S.P.	OKOBOJI
Pilot Knob S.P.	GARNER
Prairie Rose S.P.	AVOCA
Red Haw S.P.	CHARITON
Rice Lake S.P.	GARNER
Rock Creek S.P.	GRINNELL
Shimek S.F.	FORT MADISON
Stephens S.F.	CHARITON
Stone S.P.	SIOUX CITY
Twin Lakes S.P.	FORT DODGE
Viking Lake S.P.	RED OAK
Volga River S.R.A.	WEST UNION
Wapsipinicon S.P.	CEDAR RAPIDS
Wildcat Den S.P.	MUSCATINE
Wilson Island S.R.A.	MISSOURI VALLEY

Water-related activities, hiking, riding, various other sports, picnicking and visitor centers, as well as camping, are available in many of these areas. Swimming fees at supervised beaches (bathhouse included) vary. Camping (limited to two weeks; no reservations accepted): $6-$8/night/site (electricity $5 additional; sewer and water $3 additional). Cabins (no bedding, linens): $18-$100/day or $110-$600/week; cot, where available, 50¢/cot/day; deposit $25. Modern (bath facilities) $9/night. Nonmodern $7/night. Pets on leash only. State properties open daily. At most parks, water facilities are not available mid-October-mid-April. Contact the Department of Natural Resources, Wallace State Office Building, Des Moines 50319; 515/281-5145 (automated system).

SKI AREA

Place Name	Listed Under
Sundown Mountain Ski Area	DUBUQUE

FISHING AND HUNTING

Fishing for walleye, muskellunge, northern pike, perch, bluegill, smallmouth bass, catfish, and bullhead is good in the natural lakes of northern Iowa. The man-made lakes in the southern half of the state are abundant with large-mouth bass, catfish, crappie, and bluegill. There are 87,000 farm ponds in the state, 50 spring-fed trout streams in the northeastern section, and more than 56,000 acres of natural and man-made lakes. Public access to fishing water is furnished at more than 200 state-owned areas, 19,000 miles of meandering inland streams, and 600 miles of boundary streams.

Ring-necked pheasant is a popular target, with all counties open for a 50-plus day season. Quail hunting, primarily in the southern half of the state, lasts for approximately 90 days. Ruffed grouse provide a challenge to hunters in north-eastern hills while gray partridge offer good hunting opportunities in the north and north central counties. Raccoons, rabbits, fox, and gray squirrels are numerous.

Nonresident season hunting license, $60.50; duck stamp, $5.50 more. Non-resident season fishing license, $22.50; seven-day license, $8.50; trout stamp, $10.50 more. Required for all hunters and fur harvesters: state habitat stamp, $5. Nonresident fur harvester license $180.50. Nonresident deer tag $150.50; nonresident turkey tag $75.50; both require habitat stamp. For full information contact the Department of Natural Resources, Wallace State Office Building, Des Moines 50319-0034; 515/281-5918.

Driving Information

Safety belts are mandatory for all persons in front seat of vehicle. Children under age six must be in an approved passenger restraint anywhere in vehicle; children ages three to six may use a regulation safety belt; children under age three must use an approved safety seat. For further information phone 515/281-3907.

INTERSTATE HIGHWAY SYSTEM

The following alphabetical listing of Iowa towns in *Mobil Travel Guide* shows that these cities are within ten miles of the indicated Interstate highways. A highway map, however, should be checked for the nearest exit.

Highway Number	Cities/Towns within ten miles
Interstate 29	Council Bluffs, Missouri Valley, Onawa, Sioux City.
Interstate 35	Ames, Clear Lake, Des Moines, Mason City, Osceola.
Interstate 80	Atlantic, Avoca, Council Bluffs, Davenport, Des Moines, Grinnell, Iowa City, Newton.

Additional Visitor Information

The Department of Economic Development, Iowa Division of Tourism, 200 E Grand Ave, Des Moines 50309, has further information, including an Iowa Travel Guide, Camping & Outdoor Guide, and Calendar of Events; phone 515/242-4705 or 800/345-IOWA.

Two periodicals worth looking at are *Annals of Iowa,* quarterly, State Historical Society of Iowa, 402 Iowa Ave, Iowa City 52240; and *The Iowan,* quarterly, Mid-America Publishing Corp, Box 130, Shenandoah 51601.

There are 22 welcome centers in Iowa; visitors will find information and brochures most helpful in planning stops at points of interest. They are located near the following cities: Amana, Bloomfield, Burlington, Clear Lake, Davis City, Des Moines, Dows, Dubuque, Elk Horn, Elkader, Emmetsburg, Lamoni, LeClaire, Missouri Valley, Sergeant Bluff, Sioux City, Underwood, Victor, and Wilton.

FROM THE BRIDGES OF MADISON COUNTY TO LOESS HILLS

This route begins at I-80, exit 110 at De Soto, west of Des Moines. Follow Highway 169 south to Winterset. Surrounded by wooded hills, Winterset—originally a Quaker settlement—is the hub of several short side trips to the six covered bridges made famous by Robert Waller's *Bridges of Madison County*. If you want to make the full circuit, pick up a free brochure and map to all the bridges from local businesses (most are on remote county roads). If you don't have time for the full tour, one of the bridges is now preserved in Winterset's city park. The Madison County Historical Complex is an 18-acre park with a number of historic buildings, including a limestone barn and the old Winterset train depot.

Quaker-founded Winterset was also a station along the Underground Railroad, along which slaves traveled north to freedom from the Confederate states (such as neighboring Missouri). A painted brick house, now in the Winterset Art Center, served as a temporary home for hundreds of displaced slaves during the 1850s and 1860s, including scholar George Washington Carver, who lived here after experiencing discrimination elsewhere in the Midwest. Winterset is also the birthplace of actor John Wayne—born Marion Robert Morrison. His family home is open to visitors.

Continue south on Highway 169, and turn west on Highway 34 to Creston, an old railroading center with an impressive core of late Victorian homes and storefronts. The town's McKinley Park houses the Union County Historical Museum, with remnants of Creston's heyday in the 1880s. Continue on Highway 34 to the village of Corning, once home to the Icarian Colony, the longest operating nonreligious utopian community in the United States. Founded in 1850, the 80-member community disbanded in 1900 after establishing vineyards, lilac hedges, and stands of rhubarb in the area (rhubarb pie is still a favorite in local cafes). The town's original jail is now the Adams County House of History, which preserves relics from the disbanded agrarian commune.

Follow Highway 34 across the prairies to Red Oak, then south on Highway 59 to Shenandoah, originally a Mormon settlement during that group's westward migration. Today, the fertile soil that surrounds the town supports three national seed nurseries. From Shenandoah, turn west on Highway 2 toward Sidney, a village in Iowa's famous Loess Hills. These green, heavily eroded hills were formed at the end of the last Ice Age. The Missouri River brought silt-rich waters from the north, where massive glaciers were busy grinding rock into till. As the silt deposits dried, winds blew the fine sand into dunes hundreds of feet high. Now covered with virgin prairie grasslands and upland forests, the Loess Hills are home to wildlife such as coyotes, deer, bald eagles, and prairie dogs and were considered for national park status during the Clinton administration.

While in Sidney, be sure to stop at the Penn Drug Store. Built in 1865, the store is still operated by the Penn family—it's the oldest family-owned business in the state—and features an old-fashioned soda fountain. From Sidney, two scenic backroads, the Pleasant Overview Loop and the Spring Valley Loop, wind into the Loess Hills. South along Highway 2 is Waubonsie State Park, which features hiking and biking trails into the hills. To see more of this curious landscape, continue north on Highway 275 toward Glenwood and Council Bluffs. **(APPROX 205 MI)**

THE DES MOINES RIVER VALLEY

This route travels through picture-perfect farming communities founded by European settlers, then along the lower Des Moines River, where historic towns have changed little since the great riverboat era. From Des Moines, drive east on Highway 163 toward Pella. Founded in 1847 by Dutch settlers who came to this valley to escape religious persecution in Holland, Pella retains a sense of Dutch orderliness and is filled with trim historic homes and tulip-filled public parks. The Pella Historical Village Museum features a number of the town's original structures clustered around a central flower-filled courtyard. The downtown area is filled with Dutch-style bakeries, gift shops, and restaurants featuring Dutch fare.

East on Highway 163 through rolling hills is Oskaloosa, a farming town settled by Quakers. The town's past is retold at Nelson Pioneer Farm and Craft Museum, which preserves a farm community from the 1850s. The 21-building site includes farm structures, a one-room schoolhouse, a Friends Meeting Room, and a country store. From Oskaloosa, follow Highway 163 to Ottumwa, a busy industrial center. The John Deere Factory here is open for tours.

Continuing on, turn east on Highway 34, then turn south on Highway 16, which closely follows the Des Moines River. One of the earliest settled regions of Iowa, this section of the Des Moines valley is lined with tiny towns founded in the 1830s when the river was the only avenue for travel. Bypassed by the rail lines and the freeway system, these towns were forgotten by the forward rush of time. Today, they are beautifully preserved testaments to a long-past era, with handsome period architecture, newly refurbished small hotels and inns, historical museums, and antique stores.

The town of Eldon contains one of the most archetypical structures in the Midwest: At the corner of Gothic and Burton streets is the house painted by Grant Wood as the backdrop to his famous portrait *American Gothic*. The rustic couple in the painting were the painter's sister and his dentist. Fronting onto the Des Moines River, Keosauqua is home to the oldest courthouse in the state, as well as the imposing Manning Hotel, 150 years old and still in operation. Farther downstream, the entire village of Bentonsport—once a sizable river port—is a National Historic District. The Mason House Hotel, built by Mormon craftsmen in the 1840s, is open both for tours and for paying guests. At the town of Bonaparte, the original grist and woolen mills are preserved. A number of artisans work out of historic storefronts.

From Bonaparte, follow Highway 81 south to Farmington, with the oldest Congregational church west of the Mississippi (1848) and a stone carriage factory. Continue east to Highway 218 and turn south to Keokuk, at the confluence of the Des Moines and Mississippi rivers. Keokuk was head of steamboat navigation on the Mississippi before Lock Number 19—the largest on the river system—was built in 1913. The lock is part of Keokuk Dam, which was the world's largest hydroelectric dam until the 1930s. Fittingly, the sternwheeler George M. Verity houses the Keokuk River Museum. Also here is the Keokuk National Cemetery, established after the Civil War as a place of interment for soldiers killed on both sides of the conflict. **(APPROX 185 MI)**

Algona

(B-4) *See also Emmetsburg*

Settled 1854 **Pop** 6,015 **Elev** 1,200 ft
Area code 515 **Zip** 50511
Information Chamber of Commerce,
123 E State St; 515/295-7201
Web www.algona.org

Originally known as Call's Grove, the
town later chose its present name, a
shortened form of "Algonquin." In
1857 a fort enclosed the town hall;
after the frontier hostilities abated,
this was torn down and the wood
used for a plank road. On the wide
bend of the east fork of the Des
Moines River, Algona is the seat and
crossroads city of Kossuth County.

What to See and Do

Ambrose A. Call State Park. These
130 acres of rolling timbered hills
incl hiking trails. Frisbee golf course.
Picnicking; playground. Camping
(no hookups); lodge. Standard hrs,
fees. 1½ mi S on US 169, then W on
paved road. Phone 515/295-3669.

Smith Lake Park. The 124 acres incl
53-acre Smith Lake. Swimming, fishing, boating (electric motors only);
picnicking, playground, hiking trail,
tree garden. Camping (fee; dump station addl). Standard hrs, fees. 3 mi N
on US 169. Phone 515/295-2138.

Motel/Motor Lodge

★ **BURR OAK.** *IA 169 S (50511).*
515/295-7213; fax 515/295-2979.
www.burroakmotel.com. 42 rms. S $34-
$44; D $42-$47. Crib $5. Pet accepted,
some restrictions. TV; cable (premium). Complimentary continental
bkfst. Restaurant adj 5-11 pm. Ck-out
10 am. Meeting rm. Cr cds: A, C, D,
DS, MC, V.

Restaurant

★★ **SISTER SARAH'S.** *US 18
(50511). 515/295-7757.* Hrs: 11 am-2
pm, 5-9:30 pm; Fri, Sat to 10:30 pm.
Closed Mon. Res accepted. Bar.
Lunch $3.75-$6.25, dinner $5.95-
$28.50. Children's menu. Specializes
in chicken kiev, prime rib, seafood.
Salad bar. Outdoor dining. Rms vary
from 1920s and 1950s to contemporary decor. Cr cds: DS, MC, V.

Amana Colonies

See also Cedar Rapids, Iowa City

Settled 1855 **Pop** 71,640 **Elev** 715 ft
Area code 319 **Zip** 52203
Information Amana Colonies Con-
vention & Visitors Bureau, 39 38th
Ave, Suite 100, Amana; 319/622-7622
or 800/245-5465
Web www.jeonet.com/amanas

A religiously motivated community,
the Amana Colonies produce smoked
meats, woolen goods, bakery products, furniture, ovens and radar
ranges, refrigerators, food freezers,
and air conditioners. The history of
the community goes back to the
founding in Germany of the "Inspi-
rationists" (1714), a Lutheran sepa-
ratist group. Members migrated to
America and settled near Buffalo,
New York. Later they bought 25,000
acres of prairie land in Iowa and
moved west. Their first Iowa village
was called Amana, a Biblical name
meaning "remain faithful." Five
more villages were built (West, High,
Middle, East, and South Amana). The
village of Homestead was purchased
outright to acquire use of its railroad
terminal.

At first the members of the Amana
Colonies lived a simple communal
life. Families were assigned living
quarters where there were common
kitchen and dining facilities. Goods
and gains were shared equally. Farming was and still is a mainstay of the
group.

The community finally yielded to
the pressures of the 20th century. In
1932 common property was dis-
solved and redistributed on a stock
corporation basis. The new corporation, encouraging individual skills
and vigor, prospered mostly because
of the quality work of its artisans.
Today nearly every family owns its
own house.

What to See and Do

⭐ **Amana.** This community has a furniture factory that offers tours of the production area; a woolen mill with salesrm (daily); woodworking shops, meat shop, general store, brewery, wineries, restaurants, and shops. The residence of the late Christian Metz, former leader of Amana Colonies, is in Amana. At jct US 151 and IA 220. Also here is

Museum of Amana History. Exhibits incl schoolhouse, crafts and trades, lithographs, documents; audiovisual presentation of history of the Amanas. (Apr-Nov, Mon-Sat, also Sun afternoons) Phone 319/622-3567. ¢¢

Old Creamery Theatre Company. Professional theatre company performs variety of productions. (May-mid-Dec, Thurs-Sun; closed Thanksgiving) 39 38th Ave, Price Creek Stage. Phone 800/352-6262. ¢¢¢¢

East Amana. 1 mi NE of Amana on IA 220.

High Amana. Amana Arts Guild Center; old-fashioned general store. 2 mi W of Middle Amana on IA 220. Phone 319/622-3797.

Homestead. Meat shop; winery. 5 mi E of South Amana on US 6. Phone 319/622-3931.

Middle Amana. Restored original Amana communal kitchen, hearth-oven bakery; coopers shop; Amana Refrigeration, incl Amana Lily Lake. 2 mi W of Amana on IA 220.

South Amana. Winery, miniature-barn museum, furniture factory and refinishing shops; agricultural museum with displays of early farm equipt. 2 mi S of West Amana on IA 220.

West Amana. General store, basket and antique shops. 1 mi W of High Amana on IA 220. Phone 319/622-3945.

Broommaker, Amana Colonies

Motels/Motor Lodges

★★ **BEST WESTERN QUIET HOUSE SUITES.** *1708 N Highland St, Williamsburg (52361). 319/668-9777; fax 319/668-9770; toll-free 800/528-1234. www.bestwestern.com.* 33 rms, 2 story, 7 suites. S $98; D $120; suites $89-$99; under 12 free; higher rates: wkends, hols. Crib free. Pet accepted; $15. TV; cable (premium). Complimentary continental bkfst, coffee in rms. Meeting rms. Business servs avail. Exercise equipt. Indoor/outdoor pool; whirlpool. Cr cds: A, D, DS, MC, V.
🄳 🐾 🏊 🏃 🎿 🔥

★ **GUEST HOUSE MOTOR INN.** *4712 220th Tr (52203). 319/622-3599; toll-free 877/331-0828.* 38 rms, 2 story. Apr-Dec: S $36-$45; D $42-$47; each addl $3; under 12 free; lower rates rest of yr. Crib free. TV; cable (premium). Restaurant nearby. Ck-out 11 am. Cr cds: A, DS, MC, V.
🐾 **SC**

★★ **HOLIDAY INN AMANA COLONIES.** *I-80, exit 225 (52203). 319/668-1175; fax 319/668-2853; toll-free 800/633-9244. www.amanaholiday inn.com.* 155 rms, 2 story. S, D $84; under 19 free. Crib free. Pet accepted. TV; cable (premium). Indoor pool; wading pool, whirlpool, poolside serv. Playground. Complimentary coffee in rms. Restaurant 6 am-10 pm. Bar noon-11 pm. Ck-out 11 am. Coin lndry. Meeting rms. Business servs avail. Exercise equipt; sauna. Game rm. Little Amana complex adj; old-time general store and winery. Cr cds: A, MC, V.
🐾 ≈ 🏃 🔥

★ **RAMADA LTD.** *220 Hawkeye Dr, Williamsburg (52361). 319/668-1000. www.ramada.com.* 40 rms, 2 story. S $42-$65; D $49-$75; each addl $7. Crib free. TV. Complimentary continental bkfst. Restaurant opp 5 am-midnight. Ck-out 11 am. Exercise equipt. Opp Tanger Factory Outlet Center. Cr cds: A, MC, V.
🏃 🔥

★ **SUPER 8 MOTEL.** *2228 U Ave, Williamsburg (52361). 319/668-2800; toll-free 800/800-8000. www.super8. com.* 63 rms, 2 story. May-Oct: S, D $49.88; each addl $6; under 12 free; lower rates rest of yr. Crib $3. Pet accepted, some restrictions; $6. TV; cable (premium). Complimentary continental bkfst. Restaurant adj 6 am-10 pm. Ck-out 11 am. Business servs avail. Cr cds: A, C, D, DS, ER, JCB, MC, V.
🄳 🐾 🏃 ≈ 🔥 SC

B&Bs/Small Inns

★ **DIE HEIMAT COUNTRY INN.** *4430 V St, Homestead (52236). 319/622-3937.* 19 rms, 2 story. S, D $49-$76; each addl $5; under 6, $3. Crib $3. Pet accepted, some restrictions; $10. TV, some B/W. Complimentary full bkfst. Ck-out 10:30 am. Some refrigerators. Restored inn (1858). Cr cds: DS, MC, V.
🐾 ≈ 🔥

★ **DUSK TO DAWN BED & BREAKFAST.** *2616 K St, Middle Amana (52307). 319/622-3029; res 800/669-5773.* 7 rms, 4 with shower only, 2 story. No rm phones. S $58; D $63. Crib free. TV; cable (premium). Complimentary continental bkfst. Restau-rant nearby. Ck-out 10:30 am, ck-in 2-6 pm. Whirlpool. Microwaves avail. Picnic tables, grills. Built in 1868; original communal settlement house. Totally nonsmoking. Cr cds: A, DS, MC, V.
🄳 ≈ 🔥

Restaurants

★★ **THE AMANA BARN RESTAURANT.** *4709 220th Tr (52203). 319/ 622-3214. www.amanabarn.com.* Hrs: 11 am-8:30 pm; Fri, Sat to 9 pm; Sun 10 am-8 pm; hrs vary Jan-Mar. Closed hols. German, American menu. Res accepted. Bar. Lunch $5.25-$8.25, dinner $6.50-$15.95. Children's menu. Specialties: sauer-braten, schnitzel. Family-style serv. Parking. Country decor. Cr cds: A, C, D, DS, MC, V.
🄳 🕞

★★ **BRICK HAUS.** *728 47th Ave, Amana (52203). 319/622-3278.* Hrs: 7 am-8 pm. Closed Jan 1, Dec 25. German, American menu. Res accepted. Wine, beer. Complete meals: bkfst $6.35, lunch $5.95-6.95, dinner $9.95-$14.95. Children's menu. Specialties: Wiener schnitzel, Amana ham and bratwurst, smoked pork chops. Parking. Photos on wall detail history of village. Totally nonsmoking. Cr cds: A, C, D, MC, V.
🄳

★★ **COLONY VILLAGE.** *2224 U Ave, Williamsburg (52361). 319/668-1223. www.colonyvillage.com.* Hrs: 7 am-10 pm. German, American menu. Res accepted. Bar. Bkfst $2.89-$6.85, lunch $2.25-$7, dinner $8.95-$14.25. Children's menu. Specializes in home-made pie, cinnamon and pecan rolls. Entertainment Fri, Sat. Parking. Bavarian decor, beer garden. Family-owned. Cr cds: A, D, DS, MC, V.
🄳 🕞

★★ **OX YOKE INN.** *4420 220th Tr, Amana (52203). 319/622-3441. www. oxyokeinn.com.* Hrs: 11 am-9 pm; Sun 9 am-7 pm; Sept-mid-May 11 am-2 pm, 5-8 pm; Sun 9 am-7 pm; Sun brunch to noon. Closed Mon Nov-Feb; hols. German, American menu. Res accepted. Bar. Lunch, dinner $3.95-$17.95. Sun brunch $9.95. Children's menu. Specialties: Wiener schnitzel, sauerbraten, rhubarb custard pie. Family-style serv. Parking.

Old German decor; display of antiques. Family-owned. Cr cds: A, D, DS, MC, V.

★★ **RONNEBURG.** *4408 220 Tr, Amana (52203). 319/622-3641.* Hrs: 11 am-8 pm. Closed hols. Res accepted. German, American menu. Bar 9 am-10 pm. Lunch $3.50-$9.95, dinner $10.95-$15.95. Specialties: sauerbraten, Wiener schnitzel. Family-style serv. Parking. Antiques. Family-owned. Cr cds: DS, MC, V.

★★ **ZUBER'S.** *4406 V St (52203). 319/622-3911.* Hrs: 11 am-2 pm, 4:30-8 pm; Sun 11 am-7:30 pm. Closed Dec 24, 25. German, American menu. Res accepted. Serv bar. Lunch $5-$6.50, dinner $8-$13. Children's menu. Specializes in oven-baked steak, chicken. Own pies. Family-style serv. Parking. Baseball memorabilia. Restored century-old inn. Cr cds: A, C, D, DS, MC, V.

Ames

(C-4) *See also Boone*

Settled 1864 **Pop** 47,198 **Elev** 921 ft
Area code 515 **Zip** 50010
Information Convention & Visitors Bureau, 213 N Duff Ave; 515/232-4032 or 800/288-7470
Web www.ames.ia.us

Located near the geographical center of the state, Ames's economy beats to the pulse of Iowa State University. There are 38 small factories and a regional medical center complex but no major industrial activity. Ames has 500 clubs and organizations. A municipal band performs weekly during the summer. The town is named in honor of a Massachusetts congressman, Oakes Ames, who was financially interested in a local railroad project.

What to See and Do

Iowa Arboretum. Arboretum incl 340 acres of trees, shrubs, and gardens. Trails, horticultural plantings, scenic overlooks, ravines, streams. Guided and self-guided tours; educational programs (fee). (Daily) 18 mi SW via US 30, IA 17, and County E-57. Phone 515/795-3216. ¢

Iowa State University. (1858) 25,250 students. One of the oldest land grant universities in the US, ISU is known for its spacious, green central campus with sculptures and fountains by artist Christian Petersen and for its many historic buildings. The school is also the birthplace of the electronic digital computer, built by John V. Atanasoff in the basement of the Physics Building in the late 1930s. N of US 30. Phone 515/294-4777. Major places of interest are

Campanile. (1899) The 50-bell carillon is played during the academic year (Mon-Fri) and also on special occasions. On central campus.

Christian Petersen Sculptures. Works, executed in 1930s and 1940s when Petersen was artist-in-residence at ISU, are on display at Memorial Union fountain, State Gym, Dairy Industry Building, MacKay Hall, and several other locations.

Farm House. (1860) Restored original residence on the Iowa State Agricultural College farm; period furnishings. (Early Apr-Dec, Sun, Tues, and Thurs; rest of yr, by appt; closed some hols) Near Dairy Industry Building, off Union Dr. Phone 515/294-3342. **FREE**

Grant Wood Murals. Considered among the best works of this Iowa artist, the nine murals were begun as a WPA project during the Great Depression. They depict various academic divisions of the school as well as the breaking of the sod by pioneer farmers. In the Parks Library, on Morrill Rd.

Iowa State Center. Complex of four buildings incl auditorium, coliseum, two theaters; Brunnier Museum and Art Gallery (Tues-Sun; closed most hols). For information on theatrical and musical performances, phone 515/294-3347.

Reiman Gardens. Peonies, irises, geraniums, many varieties of roses. Teaching garden on NE edge of campus. Phone 515/294-2710.

Special Event

Veishea Spring Festival. Iowa State campus. Parade, sports, theatrical events, academic open houses. Mid-late Apr.

Motels/Motor Lodges

★★ BAYMONT INN & SUITES. *2500 Elwood Dr (50010). 515/296-2500; fax 515/296-2874. www. baymontinns.com.* 89 rms, 2 story. S $50; D $56; under 18 free. Crib free. Pet accepted. TV; cable (premium). Indoor pool; whirlpool. Complimentary continental bkfst. Restaurant nearby. Ck-out noon. Meeting rms. Some refrigerators. Cr cds: A, MC, V.

★★ BEST WESTERN. *2601 E 13th St (50010). 515/232-9260; toll-free 800/528-1234. www.bestwestern.com.* 131 rms, 3 story. S $50-$55; D $60-$65; each addl $6; higher rates special events. Crib $6. Pet accepted. TV; cable (premium), VCR avail. Indoor pool; whirlpool. Sauna. Restaurant 6 am-10 pm. Rm serv to 9 pm. Bar noon-2 am. Ck-out noon. Meeting rms. Valet serv. Game rm. Cr cds: A, C, D, DS, MC, V.

★ COMFORT INN. *1605 S Dayton Ave (50010). 515/232-0689; res 800/228-5150. www.comfortinn.com.* 52 rms, 2 story, 6 suites. May-Aug: S $54; D $59; each addl $5; suites $69; under 18 free; higher rates: football season; lower rates rest of yr. Crib free. Pet accepted; fee. TV; cable. Indoor pool; whirlpool. Complimentary continental bkfst. Restaurant adj open 24 hrs. Ck-out 11 am. Business servs avail. Some refrigerators. Cr cds: A, MC, V.

★ HEARTLAND INN. *I-35 and IA 30 (50010). 515/233-6060; fax 515/233-1911; toll-free 800/334-3277. www. heartlandinns.com.* 91 rms, 2 story. S $65; D $70; each addl $7; under 16 free. Crib free. Pet accepted. TV; cable. Complimentary continental bkfst. Restaurant nearby. Ck-out noon. Indoor pool; whirlpool. Sauna. Cr cds: A, C, D, DS, MC, V.

★★ HOLIDAY INN GATEWAY CENTER. *US 30 and Elwood Dr (50014). 515/292-8600; fax 515/268-2224; res 800/465-4329. www.thegate wayames.com.* 188 rms, 8 story. S $95; D $105; each addl $10; suites $180-$270; studio rms $89; under 18 free. Crib free. Pet accepted, some restrictions. TV; cable (premium), VCR avail. Indoor pool; whirlpool. Restaurant 6:30 am-2 pm, 5-10 pm; Sun from 7 am. Bar 4 pm-midnight; Sun 4-10 pm. Ck-out noon. Meeting rms. Business center. In-rm modem link. Valet serv. Sundries. Free airport transportation. Exercise equipt; sauna. Cr cds: A, C, D, DS, JCB, MC, V.

★ RAMADA INN. *1206 S Duff Ave (50010). 515/232-3410; fax 515/232-6036; toll-free 800/272-6232. www. ramada.com.* 103 rms, 2 story. S $56; D $66; each addl $10; suites $80-$150; under 18 free. Crib free. TV; cable (premium), VCR avail. Pool. Restaurant 6:30 am-10 pm. Bar 4 pm-2 am. Ck-out noon. Meeting rms. Fireplace in lobby. Cr cds: A, C, D, DS, JCB, MC, V.

★ UNIVERSITY INN. *229 S Duff Ave (50010). 515/232-0280; fax 515/232-4578; toll-free 800/422-5250. www. ameshotels.com.* 120 rms, 2 story. S $45-$90; D $49-$99; each addl $6-$10; under 12 free. Crib free. TV; cable (premium). Restaurant 5-10 pm. Bar 4 pm-2 am; entertainment. Ck-out noon. Meeting rms. Valet serv. Cr cds: A, C, D, DS, MC, V.

Restaurants

★★ BROILER STEAKHOUSE. *6008 Lincoln Way (50014). 515/292-2516. www.broilersteakhouse.com.* Hrs: 5:30-9:30 pm; Sun 11:30 am-2 pm, 5-9 pm. Closed hols. Res accepted. Bar. Lunch, dinner $7.95-$28.95. Children's menu. Specializes in seafood, steak. Family-owned. Cr cds: A, C, D, DS, MC, V.

★★ ELWELL'S CHEF'S INN. *6400 W Lincoln Way (50014). 515/292-*

4454. www.chefsinn.com. Hrs: 5-10 pm; Fri, Sat to 11 pm; Sun brunch 10 am-2 pm. Closed Dec 25. Res accepted. Bar. Dinner $7.95-$15.95. Sun brunch $10.95. Children's menu. Specializes in prime rib, seafood, steak. Multilevel dining areas. Cr cds: A, D, DS, MC, V.

★ **HICKORY PARK.** 1404 S Duss (50010). 515/232-8940. Hrs: 11 am-9 pm; Fri, Sat to 10 pm. Closed Thanksgiving, Dec 25. Lunch $1.95-$4.95, dinner $1.95-$12. Children's menu. Specializes in barbecue. 1890s atmosphere. Family-owned. Cr cds: A, D, DS, MC, V.

★ **LUCULLANS.** 400 Main St (50010). 515/232-8484. Hrs: 11 am-10 pm; Fri, Sat to 11 pm; Sun to 9 pm. Closed hols. Res accepted. Italian menu. Bar. Lunch $5.95-$8.50, dinner $10.50-$15.95. Children's menu. Own bread. Contemporary decor; informal atmosphere. Cr cds: A, D, DS, MC, V.

Atlantic

(D-3) See also Avoca

Pop 7,432 **Elev** 1,215 ft
Area code 712 **Zip** 50022
Information Chamber of Commerce, 614 Chestnut; 712/243-3017

What to See and Do

Danish Windmill. Built in Denmark (1848), this 60-ft-high working windmill was dismantled and shipped to Elk Horn where it was reassembled by community volunteers. Tours. (Daily; closed Jan 1, Dec 25) 15 mi N via IA 173; 7 mi N of I-80 exit 54 in Elk Horn. Phone 712/764-7472. ¢

Motels/Motor Lodges

★ **ECONO LODGE.** I-80, exit 60 (50022). 712/243-4067; fax 712/243-1713. www.econolodge.com. 51 rms, 1-2 story. S $35-$37; D $39-$45; each addl $2. Crib $2. Pet accepted. TV; cable. Pool. Coffee in rms. Restaurant

nearby. Ck-out 11 am. Meeting rm. Sundries. Cr cds: A, MC, V.

★ **SUPER 8 MOTEL.** 1902 E 7th St (50022). 712/243-4723; fax 712/243-2864; toll-free 888/243-2378. www.super8.com. 44 rms. S $39-$45; D $50-$59; each addl $2. Crib $2. TV; cable (premium). Complimentary continental bkfst. Coffee in rms. Restaurant 5-10 pm. Ck-out 11 am. Meeting rm. Business servs avail. In-rm modem link. Sundries. Whirlpool. Cr cds: A, MC, V.

B&B/Small Inn

★★★ **CHESTNUT CHARM BED & BREAKFAST.** 1409 Chestnut St (50022). 712/243-5652. 9 rms, 1 with shower only. Many rm phones. S $60-$200; D $70-$225; guest house $60-$250; each addl $10. Adults only. TV in many rms; cable (premium). Complimentary full bkfst. Ck-out 11 am, ck-in 4 pm. Concierge serv. Gift shop. Many in-rm whirlpools, refrigerators, microwaves, fireplaces. Victorian mansion built in 1898; antiques, gazebo. Totally non-smoking. Cr cds: MC, V.

Avoca

(D-2) See also Atlantic

Pop 1,497 **Elev** 1,138 ft
Area code 712 **Zip** 51521

What to See and Do

Prairie Rose State Park. More than 650 acres of wind-formed hills surround a 204-acre lake. Swimming, fishing, boating (ramp); snowmobiling, picnicking, camping (electricity, dump station). Standard hrs, fees. 2 mi N via US 59, then 6 mi E on I-80, exit 46, then 9 mi N on paved road. Phone 712/773-2701.

Motel/Motor Lodge

★ **CAPRI MOTEL.** 110 E Pearshing St (51521). 712/343-6301; fax 712/343-2652. 27 rms. S $35; D $41; each addl $5. Crib $5. Pet accepted, some restrictions. TV; cable (premium). Complimentary coffee in lobby. Restaurants nearby. Ck-out 10:30 am. Cr cds: A, DS, MC, V.

Bettendorf

(D-8) *See also Clinton, Davenport*

Pop 28,132 **Elev** 565 ft **Area code** 319 **Zip** 52722

Information Quad Cities Convention & Visitors Bureau, 102 S Harrison St, Davenport 52801; 309/788-7800 or 800/747-7800

Web www.quadcities.com

Bettendorf began as a quiet rural village called Gilbert. In 1903 the town's future changed with the arrival of the Bettendorf Axle and Wagon Company, which became the largest manufacturer of railroad cars west of the Mississippi. The growing city changed its name in honor of the company. Today Bettendorf, on the Mississippi River, is part of the Quad Cities metropolitan area that incl Davenport, Iowa, and Moline and Rock Island, Illinois.

What to See and Do

Buffalo Bill Cody Homestead.
Restored boyhood home of Buffalo Bill Cody, built by his father in 1847. On grounds are buffalo, deer, and farm animals. (Apr-Oct, daily; rest of yr, by appt) 3 mi N on US 67, then W on 280th/Bluff Rd near McCausland. Phone 319/225-2981. **Donation**

Family Museum of Arts & Science.
Hands-on exhibits; Rhythm Alley, Heartland, The Homestead, Kinder Garten; also traveling exhibit gallery, children's program area. (Tues-Sun; closed hols) 2900 18th St. Phone 319/344-4106. ¢

Lady Luck Casino. Casino gambling; restaurant, gift shop, lodging. Valet parking. Riverfront, just E of I-74. Phone 319/359-7280.

Motels/Motor Lodges

★★ **COURTYARD BY MARRIOTT.**
895 Golden Valley Dr (52722). 319/ *355-3999; fax 319/355-0308. www.* *marriott.com.* 108 rms, 3 story. S, D $86; suites $109. Crib free. TV; cable (premium). Indoor pool; whirlpool. Complimentary coffee in rms. Restaurant 6-9:30 am; Sat, Sun 7-11 am. Bar 5-10 pm. Ck-out noon. Coin lndry. Meeting rm. Business servs avail. In-rm modem link. Valet serv. Sundries. Exercise equipt. Health club privileges. Some refrigerators; microwaves avail. Balconies. Cr cds: A, C, D, DS, ER, JCB, MC, V.

★ **ECONO LODGE.** *2205 Kimberly Rd (52722). 319/355-6471; fax 319/* *359-0559; toll-free 800/638-7949. www.* *econolodge.com.* 67 rms. S, D $40-$70; each addl $4; under 18 free. Crib free. Pet accepted, some restrictions. TV; cable (premium). Pool. Playground. Complimentary continental bkfst. Restaurant 10 am-10 pm. Bar from 11 am. Ck-out noon. Meeting rm. Business servs avail. Cr cds: A, C, D, DS, MC, V.

★ **HEARTLAND INN.** *815 Golden Valley Dr (52722). 319/355-6336; fax 319/355-0039; toll-free 800/334-3277. www.heartlandinns.com.* 85 rms, 3 story. May-Aug: S $70; D $75; each addl $7; suites $110-$140; under 16 free; lower rates rest of yr. Crib free. TV; cable, VCR avail. Pool. Complimentary continental bkfst. Ck-out 11 am. Meeting rms. Business servs avail. In-rm modem link. Sundries. Valet serv. Sauna. Health club privileges. Microwaves avail. Cr cds: A, C, D, DS, MC, V.

★★ **HOLIDAY INN.** *909 Middle Rd (57277). 319/355-4761; fax 319/355-5572; toll-free 800/465-4329. www.* *holiday-inn.com.* 157 rms, 2 story. S, D $65-$86; each addl $7; under 18 free. Crib free. TV; cable (premium), VCR avail. Heated pool. Restaurant 6 am-1:30 pm, 5-10 pm. Bar 4 pm-2 am. Ck-out noon. Coin lndry. Meeting rms. Business servs avail. In-rm modem link. Valet serv. Complimentary airport transportation. Exercise equipt. Cr cds: A, C, D, DS, JCB, MC, V.

★★ **SIGNATURE INN.** *3020 Utica Ridge Rd (52722). 319/355-7575. www.*

signatureinn.com. 124 rms, 3 story. S, D $52-$67; each addl $7; suite $109; under 17 free. Crib free. TV; cable (premium), VCR avail (movies). Pool. Complimentary full bkfst. Ck-out noon. Business center. In-rm modem link. Free airport transportation. Exercise equipt. Health club privileges. Cr cds: A, D, DS, MC, V.

Hotel

★★★ JUMER'S CASTLE LODGE. *900 Spruce Hills Dr (52722). 319/359-7141; toll-free 800/285-8637. www. jumers.com.* 210 rms. S $80; D $89; each addl $9; suites $90-$144; under 18 free. Crib free. Pet accepted, some restrictions; $35 refundable. TV; cable (premium). 2 pools, 1 indoor; whirlpool. Restaurant (see also JUMER'S). Bars 11-1 am; entertainment. Ck-out noon. Convention facilities. Business servs avail. Free airport, bus depot transportation. Putting green. Exercise equipt; sauna. Health club privileges. Rec rm. Lawn games. Bavarian architecture and decor; antiques, tapestries. Cr cds: A, D, DS, MC, V.

B&B/Small Inn

★★★ ABBEY HOTEL. *1401 Central Ave (52722). 319/355-0291; fax 319/ 355-7647; res 800/438-7535. www. theabbeyhotel.com.* 19 rms, 3 story. S $75; D $85; each addl $10; suite $125; under 12 free. Crib free. TV; cable (premium), VCR avail. Complimentary full bkfst. Rm serv 3-11 pm. Bar 5 pm-midnight. Ck-out noon, ck-in 2 pm. Meeting rms. Business servs avail. In-rm modem link. Free airport transportation. Exercise equipt. Heated pool. Romanesque structure was once a Carmelite monastery. Totally nonsmoking. Cr cds: A, DS, MC, V.

Restaurants

★★★ JUMER'S. *900 Spruce Hills Dr (52722). 319/359-1607. www.jumers. com.* Hrs: 6 am-10 pm; Fri, Sat to 11 pm; Sun from 7 am; Sun brunch 10 am-2 pm; hols to 8 pm. Res accepted.

German, American menu. Bar. Bkfst $2.25-$6.50, lunch $4.45-$8.45, dinner $7.95-$19.95. Children's menu. Specialties: Wiener schnitzel, sauerbraten, Kirschtorte. Own baking. Pianist. Bavarian decor; antiques. Cr cds: A, D, DS, MC, V.

★★ STUBBS EDDY RESTAURANT/PUB. *1716 State St (52722). 319/355-0073.* Hrs: 2-10 pm. Closed Sun; hols. Res accepted. Bar. Dinner $4.95-$38.95. Children's menu. Specializes in pasta, fresh seafood. Entertainment Tues, Thurs eves. Cr cds: A, MC, V.

Boone

(C-4) *See also Ames*

Founded 1865 **Pop** 12,392 **Elev** 960 ft
Area code 515 **Zip** 50036
Information Chamber of Commerce, 806 7th St; 515/432-3342 or 800/266-6312

In the fertile Des Moines River valley, Boone is a farming center with several factories. There are a number of summer camps for children in the surrounding area.

What to See and Do

Boone and Scenic Valley Railroad. The ride on this shortline railroad incl a scenic 12-mi (round-trip) tour (1¾ hr) in vintage 1920s cars pulled by a steam engine (wkends, hols; three trips daily) or diesel (wkdays; one trip daily); steam locomotive, made in China, is the only engine of its class in the US; train crosses the highest "single-track, interurban bridge" in US. Depot has snack bar and **Iowa Railroad Museum** with railroad history exhibits. (Memorial Day wkend-Oct, daily) 225 10th St. Phone 515/432-4249. ¢¢

Ledges State Park. More than 1,200 acres with foot trails, streams, and twenty-five 150-ft-high sandstone ledges. Fishing; hiking, snowmobiling, picnicking, camping (electric hookups, dump station). Standard

fees. 6 mi S on IA 164. Phone
515/432-1852.

Mamie Doud Eisenhower Birthplace.
One-story frame house restored to
original Victorian style incl such
period furnishings as the bed in
which Mamie Eisenhower was born.
Summer kitchen, library, museum.
(June-Oct, daily; Apr-May, Tues-Sun
afternoons; also by appt) 709 Carroll
St. Phone 515/432-1896. ¢¢

Special Event

Pufferbilly Days. Features train rides,
model railroad display, handcar
races, spike driving contest; antique
car show; parade, entertainment,
food, bike races. Wkend after Labor
Day.

Hotel

★★★ **HOTEL PATTEE.** *1112 Willis
Ave, Perry (50220). 515/465-3511; fax
515/465-3909. www.hotelpattee.com.*
40 rms, 3 story. S, D $150-$225; each
addl $20; under 17 free. Crib avail.
TV; cable (premium), VCR avail.
Complimentary coffee, newspaper in
rms. Restaurant 6 am-10 pm. Ck-out
noon. Meeting rms. Business servs
avail. Exercise rm. Cr cds: A, D, DS,
MC, V.
🐾 🛉

Burlington

(E-7) *See also Fort Madison*

Settled 1832 **Pop** 27,208 **Elev** 540 ft
Area code 319 **Zip** 52601
Information Convention & Tourism
Bureau, 807 Jefferson St; 319/752-
6365 or 800/827-4837
Web www.visit.burlington.ia.us

Burlington, a river port, shopping,
industrial, and farm center, traces its
history back to the days when it was
called Flint Hills by Native Americans and served as neutral ground
where tribes hunted flint for implements. Zebulon Pike raised the Stars
and Stripes here in 1805, and a trading post was built in 1808. The city
became capital of the Wisconsin Territory in 1837, then capital of the
Iowa Territory from 1838-1840. Its
retail trade draws shoppers from

three states; factories turn out tractors, chemicals, electronic instruments, furniture, and other products.

What to See and Do

The Apple Trees Historical Museum.
The museum, a remaining wing of
railroad magnate Charles E. Perkins's
mansion, contains Victorian furnishings; antique tools, costumes, dolls,
toys, buttons, glass, china; Native
American artifacts; changing exhibits.
Maintained by Des Moines County
Historical Society. Guided tours (by
appt; fee). (May-Oct, Wed and Sun
afternoons) 1616 Dill St, in Perkins
Park. Phone 319/753-2449. **FREE** The
society also maintains

> **Hawkeye Log Cabin.** Replica (1910)
> of pioneer cabin; antique furnish-
> ings and tools. Guided tours (by
> appt; fee). (May-Sept, Wed and Sun
> afternoons) On bluff in Crapo
> Park. Phone 319/753-2449. **FREE**
>
> **Phelps House.** (ca 1850) Mansard-
> roofed, Italianate Victorian man-
> sion with original furnishings used
> by three generations of the Phelps
> family; extensive collection of rare
> china; family portraits. Guided
> tours (by appt; fee). (May-Oct, Wed
> and Sun afternoons) 521 Columbia
> St. Phone 319/753-2449. ¢

Crapo and Dankwardt Parks. The
parks (approx 175 acres) are situated
along the Mississippi on the site
where the American flag first flew
over Iowa soil (1805); incl illuminated fountain, arboretum, formal
flower garden. Swimming. Black
Hawk Spring Indian trail; tennis,
archery range, ice-skating. Picnicking; playground. (Daily) On Great
River Rd at SE corner of city. Phone
319/753-8110. **FREE**

Geode State Park. More than 1,600
heavily wooded acres along limestone bluffs rising out of 187-acre
lake. Swimming, supervised beach,
fishing, boating (ramps, rentals); hiking trails, snowmobiling, picnicking,
camping (electricity, dump station).
Standard hrs, fees. 6 mi W on US 34,
then 6 mi W on IA 79 and County
J20. Phone 319/392-4601.

Grandpa Bill's Farm. This 100-acre
"country fun park" was created from
an actual Iowa farm. Original buildings have been converted to house
attractions: country barn theater features live musical shows and dances;

play barn has play area, hay loft, educational exhibits; mini-farm contains examples of conventional farm buildings and animals. Hayrides, crafts fair. Restaurant. (June-late Aug, daily; May and late Aug-Oct, wkends only) 13 mi N on US 61 in Sperry. Phone 319/985-2262. ¢

Heritage Hill National Historic District. This 29-sq-blk area contains churches, mansions, and houses in a wide variety of architectural styles, incl a full range of Victorian buildings from the 1870s to the turn of the century. Walking tours, auto cassette tours, and brochures avail. Contact the Convention & Tourism Bureau. N of downtown, between Washington and High sts. Also here is

Snake Alley. According to Ripley's Believe It or Not, this zigzagging brick-paved street, built in 1894, is the "crookedest street in the world." Between Washington and Columbia sts.

Mosquito Park. Located on a bluff overlooking the city and the Mississippi River just N of downtown. 3rd and Franklin sts.

Special Events

Snake Alley Criterium Bicycle Races. Olympic-style racing. Memorial Day wkend.

Burlington Steamboat Days & the American Music Festival. Downtown riverfront. Athletic competitions, fireworks, midway, parade, name entertainment. Phone 319/754-4334. Six days ending Father's Day, mid-June.

The Sight of Music. In Bracewell Stadium. Drum and bugle corps competition. Mid-July.

Jazz Fest on the River. Live jazz on the Mississippi River. Nationally known jazz ensembles. Late Sept.

Motels/Motor Lodges

★★ **BEST WESTERN PZAZZ MOTOR INN.** *3001 Winegarden Dr. (52601). 319/753-2223; fax 319/753-2224; toll-free 800/373-1223. www. bestwestern.com.* 151 rms, 3 story. S $77; D $67; each addl $4; suites $115; studio rms $60-$90; under 18 free. Crib free. Pet accepted. TV; cable (premium), VCR (movies).

Indoor pool; whirlpool. Restaurant 6:30 am-10 pm. Bar 11:30-2 am; entertainment. Ck-out noon. Balconies. Coin lndry. Meeting rms. Business servs avail. In-rm modem link. Gift shop. Barber, beauty shop. Airport transportation. Game rm. Exercise equipt; sauna. Cr cds: A, C, D, DS, MC, V.

★ **COMFORT INN.** *3051 Kirkwood (52601). 319/753-0000; toll-free 800/ 228-5150. www.comfortinn.com.* 52 rms, 2 story. S $35-$50; D $45-$60; each addl $5; suites $99; under 18 free; higher rates: hol wkends, special events. Crib avail. Pet accepted. TV; cable (premium). Pool. Complimentary continental bkfst. Restaurant nearby. Ck-out 11 am. Business servs avail. In-rm modem link. Cr cds: A, C, D, DS, ER, JCB, MC, V.

★★ **HOLIDAY INN EXPRESS.** *1601 N Roosevelt (52601). 319/752-0000; toll-free 800/465-4329. www. holiday-inn.com.* 43 rms. S $35-$45; D $45-$55; each addl $5; under 12 free. Crib free. Pet accepted. TV; cable (premium). Restaurant nearby. Ck-out 11 am. Meeting rm. Microwaves avail. Cr cds: A, DS, MC, V.

★ **SUPER 8 MOTEL.** *3001 Kirkwood (52601). 319/752-9806; toll-free 800/ 800-8000. www.super8.com.* 63 rms, 3 story. No elvtr. S $32.98-$60.98; D $39.73-$68.98; under 12 free. Crib $2.24. TV; cable (premium). Complimentary continental bkfst. Restaurant nearby. Ck-out 11 am. Sundries. Microwaves avail. Cr cds: A, C, D, DS, MC, V.

Carroll (C-3)

Pop 9,579 **Elev** 1,261 ft
Area code 712 **Zip** 51401

Information Chamber of Commerce, 223 W 5th St, PO Box 307; 712/792-4383

Web www.carrolliowa.com

This town is named for Charles Carroll, a signer of the Declaration of Independence.

What to See and Do

Black Hawk State Park. Park consists of 86 acres along 925-acre Black Hawk Lake. Swimming, fishing, boating (ramps); snowmobiling, picnicking, camping (electricity, dump station). Standard hrs, fees. 23 mi NW on US 71 in Lake View. Phone 712/657-8712.

Swan Lake Park. The 510 acres incl 115-acre Swan Lake. Swimming, fishing. Nature trails, wildlife exhibit. Access to Sauk Rail Trail. Winter activities. Picnicking. Camping (fee). (Daily) 2 mi S, then ½ mi E. Phone 712/792-4614.

War Memorial Monuments. Monument for each war beginning with the Civil War and the latest monument for Desert Storm. E 1st St, S of Grant Rd.

Special Events

Great Raccoon River Fun Float. Float down the Raccoon River; rest stops on several beaches. Second Sat July.

Holiday Animated Lighting Extravaganza. In Swan Lake Park. Campground full of lighted scenes. Thanksgiving-Jan 1.

Motel/Motor Lodge

★★★ **CARROLLTON INN.** *1730 US 71 N (51401). 712/792-5600; toll-free 877/798-3535. www.carrolltoninn.com.* 87 rms, 2 story. S $49; D $59; each addl $5; suites $89-$93. Crib free. Pet accepted; $6/day. TV; cable (premium), VCR avail (movies). Indoor pool; whirlpool. Sauna. Restaurant 6:30 am-10 pm. Bar 4 pm-2 am. Ckout noon. Coin lndry. Meeting rms. Sundries. Beauty shop. Cr cds: A, C, D, DS, MC, V.

Restaurant

★★ **TONY'S.** *1012 US 71 N (51401). 712/792-3792.* Hrs: 7 am-10:30 pm. Closed Jan 1, Dec 25. Res accepted. Continental menu. Bkfst $3.45-$5.95, lunch $4.45-$7.95, dinner $5-$13. Sun brunch $6.95. Children's menu. Specializes in chicken,

lasagna. Salad bar. Family-owned. Cr cds: A, C, D, DS, MC, V.

Cedar Falls

(B-6) *See also Waterloo, Waverly*

Settled 1845 **Pop** 34,298 **Elev** 900 ft
Area code 319 **Zip** 50613
Information Chamber of Commerce, Tourism & Visitors Bureau, PO Box 367; 319/266-3593 or 800/845-1955
Web www.ci.cedar-falls.ia.us

Once one of the most important milling centers in the state, today Cedar Falls is a university town and home to a diverse industrial base.

What to See and Do

Black Hawk Park. Fishing, boating; hiking, shooting and archery ranges, x-country skiing, ice-skating, snowshoeing, ice fishing. Picnicking. Camping (fee). (Daily) 3 mi N on US 218, then 1 mi W on Lone Tree Rd. Phone 319/266-6813.

Cedar Falls Historical Society Victorian Home Museum. Civil War-era Victorian house furnished in 1890s period style. **Carriage House Museum** contains library, archives, fashions, Lenoir train exhibit, memorabilia of the first permanent settlement in Black Hawk County (1845). (Wed-Sun afternoons) 308 W 3rd. Phone 319/266-5149. **FREE**

George Wyth House. The residence of George Wyth, founder of the Viking Pump Company, was built in 1907; now furnished in Art Deco style of 1920s; incl pieces by Gilbert Rhode. Viking Pump Company museum on third floor. Tours (Sun afternoons, also by appt; closed Jan-Mar). 303 Franklin St. Phone 319/266-5149. **FREE**

George Wyth Memorial State Park. The 494-acre park incl several lakes. Swimming, fishing, boating (ramp); nature, hiking, bicycle trails; snowmobiling, picnicking, camping (electricity, dump station). Standard hrs, fees. Between Cedar River and US 20. Phone 319/232-5505.

Icehouse Museum. This round structure, 100 ft in diameter, was once used for storing up to 8,000 tons of ice from the Cedar River. The icehouse now displays antique tools for the harvesting, storing, selling, and use of natural ice; also antique farm equipt; early American kitchen; military memorabilia. (May-Oct, Wed, Sat and Sun afternoons; closed hols) 1st and Franklin sts, enter off Clay St. Phone 319/266-5149. **FREE**

The Little Red School. Country school (1909) has been authentically furnished to reflect turn-of-the-century education. (May-Oct, Wed, Sat and Sun afternoons; closed hols) 1st and Clay sts. Phone 319/266-5149.

University of Northern Iowa. (1876) 13,150 students. Campanile in Italian Renaissance style, 100-ft high; chimes played daily. UNI-Dome, Iowa's first and only multipurpose domed coliseum. Also on campus is a museum (Mon-Fri; closed hols) with exhibits on geology and natural history. College St between 23rd St and University Ave. Phone 319/273-6864. Campus incl

> **Gallery of Art.** Permanent collection and changing exhibits. (Daily; closed school hols and between exhibits) 27th St and Hudson Rd in Kamerick Art Building-South. Phone 319/273-2077. **FREE**

Special Events

Band concerts. In Overman Park. Tues eves, June-July.

Sturgis Falls Days Celebration. Overman and Island parks. Incl Dixieland jazz festival, parade, street fair, arts and crafts. Last full wkend June.

College Hill Arts Festival. Juried arts festival showcasing over 75 Midwest artists. Third wkend July.

Motels/Motor Lodges

★★ **HOLIDAY INN UNIVERSITY PLAZA.** *5826 University Ave (50613). 319/277-2230; fax 319/277-0364; toll-free 800/465-4329. www.holiday-inn.com.* 182 rms, 2 story. S $69; D $79; each addl $10; suites $125-$150. Crib free. Pet accepted. TV; cable (premium). Heated pool; poolside serv. Complimentary coffee in rms. Restaurant 6 am-10 pm. Bar 4 pm-

midnight. Ck-out noon. Coin lndry. Meeting rms. Business servs avail. In-rm modem link. Bellhops. Valet serv. Free airport transportation. Exercise equipt. Game rm. Cr cds: A, C, D, DS, MC, V.

★★ **VILLAGER LODGE.** *4410 University Ave (50613). 319/277-1550; fax 319/277-8947. www.villager.com.* 96 rms, 2 story. S $43-$55; D $54-$59; each addl $5; under 12 free. Crib free. TV; cable (premium), VCR avail (movies). Indoor pool; whirlpool. Complimentary continental bkfst, coffee in rms. Restaurant nearby. Ck-out noon. Business servs avail. In-rm modem link. Sundries. Valet serv. Sauna. Balconies. Cr cds: A, C, D, DS, MC, V.

Restaurant

★★ **OLDE BROOM FACTORY.** *125 W First St (50613). 319/268-0877.* Hrs: 11 am-2:30 pm, 5-10 pm; Sat 11 am-2 pm, 4:30-11 pm; Sun 10 am-10 pm, brunch to 2 pm. Closed hols. Res accepted. Continental menu. Bar 4 pm-midnight. A la carte entrees: lunch, dinner $6-$17. Sun brunch $8.95. Children's menu. Specializes in prime rib, desserts. Parking. Structure built 1862. Cr cds: A, D, DS, MC, V.

Cedar Rapids

(C-7) See also Amana Colonies

Settled 1838 **Pop** 108,751 **Elev** 730 ft
Area code 319

Information Cedar Rapids Area Convention & Visitors Bureau, 119 1st Ave SE, PO Box 5339, 52406-5339; 319/398-5009 or 800/735-5557

Web www.cedar-rapids.com

Cedar Rapids, located at the rapids of the Cedar River, is the industrial leader of the state. More than $475 million worth of cereals, corn products, milk processing machinery, farm hardware, stock feeds, and electronic material are exported to worldwide markets.

What to See and Do

Brucemore. (1886) Queen Anne-style 21-rm mansion with visitor center, gift and flower shops, formal gardens, lawns, orchard, and pond; sunrm decorated by native artist Grant Wood. The estate serves as community cultural center. (Feb-Dec, Tues-Sat; closed hols) 2160 Linden Dr SE. Phone 319/362-7375. ¢¢

Cedar Rapids Museum of Art. Extensive collection of work by Grant Wood, Marvin Cone, and Mauricio Lasansky; changing exhibits; children's gallery. Gift shop. (Tues-Sun; closed hols) 410 3rd Ave SE. Phone 319/366-7503. ¢¢

⭐ **Czech Village.** Bakery, gift shops, restaurants, historic structures preserving Czech heritage. (See SPECIAL EVENTS) On 16th Ave SW near Downtown. Phone 319/362-2846. In village is

National Czech and Slovak Museum & Library. Houses large collection of folk costumes. Permanent and changing exhibits; museum grounds incl restored immigrant home. Tours. (Tues-Sat, also Sun afternoons mid-May-Dec; closed hols) 30 16th Ave SW. Phone 319/362-8500. ¢¢

Indian Creek Nature Center. On this 210-acre nature preserve is an observatory/museum in a remodeled dairy barn which offers changing exhibits. Hiking trails. (Daily; closed hols) 6665 Otis Rd SE. Phone 319/362-0664. ¢

Masonic Library. (1955) Houses most complete Masonic collection in the US; also three museum rms in this late-*moderne*, Vermont-marble structure with bas-relief decoration and stained-glass windows. Tours. (Mon-Fri, afternoons; closed hols) Grand Lodge Office Building, 813 1st Ave SE. Phone 319/365-1438. **FREE**

Palisades-Kepler State Park. This 970-acre park incl limestone palisades that rise 75 ft above the Cedar River; timbered valleys, wildflowers. Fishing, boating (ramps), nature and hiking trails, snowmobiling, picnicking. Lodge. Camping (electricity, dump station); cabins. Standard hrs, fees. 12 mi E via US 30. Phone 319/895-6039.

Paramount Theatre. Restored theater (ca 1925). Stage productions, films; home of Cedar Rapids Symphony. 123 Third Ave SE. Phone 319/398-5211.

Science Station. Science and technology museum features unusual hands-on exhibits incl a working hot-air balloon and giant kaleidoscope. In historic fire station. (Tues-Sun; closed hols) 427 1st St SE. Phone 319/366-0968. ¢¢

US Cellular Center. This 10,000-seat entertainment center features sports events, concerts, exhibits, rodeos, ice shows, other events. 370 1st Ave NE. Phone 319/398-5211.

Wapsipinicon State Park. This 251-acre park is along the west bank of the Wapsipinicon River and incl high rock cliffs, open meadows, wooded hills, caves, wildflowers. Fishing, boating (ramp); nine-hole golf course, hiking trails, snowmobiling, picnicking. Lodge. Camping (electric hookups). Standard hrs, fees. 27 mi NE, off US 151 in Anamosa. Phone 319/462-2761.

Special Events

Houby Days. Czech Village. Features Czech fine arts, folk arts and customs, music, dancing, food; mushroom hunt contests, races. Wkend after Mother's Day.

All-Iowa Fair. Hawkeye Downs. Stock car races, fine arts, exhibits, name entertainment. June.

Celebration of the Arts. Brucemore. Open-air festival celebrating all performing and visual arts. Father's Day.

Freedom Festival. Eighty events for all ages held citywide, topped off by large fireworks display. Wk preceding and incl July 4.

Motels/Motor Lodges

★★ **BEST WESTERN COOPERS MILL.** *100 F Ave NW (52405). 319/366-5323; toll-free 800/858-5511. www.bestwestern.com.* 86 rms, 4 story. S $49-$59; D $59-$69; under 18 free. Crib $5. Pet accepted; $5/day. TV; cable (premium). Restaurant 6-3 am; Sun to midnight. Bar 11-2 am; closed Sun. Ck-out noon. Meeting rms.

Business servs avail. In-rm modem link. Valet serv. Cr cds: A, MC, V.

⊟ 👍 SC

★★ BEST WESTERN LONG-BRANCH. *90 Twixt Town Rd NE (52402). 319/377-6386; toll-free 800/ 443-7660. www.bestwestern.com.* 106 rms, 4 story. S $59-$89; D $69-$99; suites $85.95-$199.95; under 18 free; wkend rates. Crib $5. TV; cable (premium), VCR avail. Heated pool. Restaurant 6 am-10 pm. Bars 11 am-midnight; entertainment. Ck-out noon. Meeting rms. Business servs avail. In-rm modem link. Bellhops. Valet serv. Free airport transportation. Health club privileges. Cr cds: A, C, D, DS, ER, JCB, MC, V.

D ⊟ ✈ ⊠ 👍 SC

★ CEDAR RAPIDS INN AND CONFERENCE CENTER. *2501 Williams Blvd SW (52404). 319/365-9441; fax 319/365-0255.* 184 rms, 2 story. S, D $68-$78; under 19 free. Crib free. Pet accepted. TV; cable. Indoor pool; whirlpool. Restaurant 6 am-2 pm, 5-10 pm. Bar 4 pm-midnight; Sun to noon. Ck-out noon. Coin lndry. Meeting rms. Business servs avail. In-rm modem link. Free airport transportation. Sauna. Cr cds: A, C, D, DS, JCB, MC, V.

D ⊟ ⊠ ⊠ 👍 SC

★ COMFORT INN. *5055 Rockwell Dr (52402). 319/393-8247. www.comfort inn.com.* 59 rms, 2 story. May-Aug: S, D $50-$65; under 18 free; lower rates rest of yr. Crib free. Pet accepted, some restrictions. TV; cable (premium), VCR avail. Complimentary continental bkfst. Ck-out 11 am. Business servs avail. In-rm modem link. Whirlpool. Some refrigerators. Cr cds: A, D, DS, MC, V.

D ⊟ ⊠ ⊠

★ COMFORT INN SOUTH. *390 33rd Ave SW (52404). 319/363-7934; toll-free 800/228-5150. www.comfort inn.com.* 60 rms, 3 story. S $43-$60; D $45-$65; each addl $5; suites $53-$65; under 18 free. Crib free. Pet accepted. TV; cable (premium). Complimentary continental bkfst. Restaurant nearby. Ck-out 11 am. Meeting rms. Cr cds: A, C, D, DS, ER, JCB, MC, V.

D ⊟ ⊠ 👍 SC

★ DAYS INN. *3245 Southgate Pl SW (52404). 319/365-4339. www.daysinn. com.* 40 rms, 2 story, 4 suites. S $42-$50; D $44-$52; each addl $5; suites $55-$65; under 18 free. Crib free. Pet accepted. TV; cable. Indoor pool; whirlpool. Complimentary continental bkfst. Restaurant nearby. Ck-out 11 am. Business servs avail. In-rm modem link. Some refrigerators. Cr cds: A, MC, V.

D ⊟ ⊠ ⊠ 👍 SC

★ ECONO LODGE. *622 33rd Ave SW (52404). 319/363-8888; fax 319/ 363-7504; toll-free 800/228-5050. www. econolodge.com.* 50 rms, 2 story. S $38.95-$58.95; D $42.95-$58.95; each addl $5; suites $70-$125; under 18 free; higher rates: farm show, conventions. Crib free. Pet accepted. TV; cable. Indoor pool; whirlpool. Complimentary continental bkfst. Restaurant nearby. Ck-out 11 am. Coin lndry. Cr cds: A, C, D, DS, MC, V.

D ⊟ ⊠ ⊠ 👍 SC

★ EXEL INN. *616 33rd Ave SW (52404). 319/366-2475; fax 319/366-5712. www.exelinns.com.* 102 rms, 2 story. S $32.99-$41.99; D $37.99-$47.99; each addl $4; under 18 free. Crib free. Pet accepted. TV; cable. Complimentary continental bkfst. Restaurant nearby. Ck-out noon. Guest lndry. Business servs avail. In-rm modem link. Cr cds: A, C, D, DS, ER, JCB, MC, V.

D ⊟ 🦮 ⊠ 👍

★★ FAIRFIELD INN. *3243 Southridge Dr SW (52404). 319/364-2000; toll-free 800/228-2800. www.fair fieldinn.com.* 105 rms, 3 story. S $40-$65; D $45-$72; each addl $7; under 18 free. Crib free. TV; cable (premium). Heated pool. Continental bkfst. Ck-out noon. Coin lndry. Meeting rm. Business servs avail. In-rm modem link. Cr cds: A, D, DS, MC, V.

D ⊠ ⊠ 👍 SC

★★ FOUR POINTS BY SHERATON. *525 33rd Ave SW (52404). 319/ 366-8671; fax 319/362-1420; toll-free 800/325-3535. www.sheratoncr.com.* 157 rms, 6 story. S $99-$103; D $109-$113; each addl $10; suites $185; under 18 free; wkend rates. Crib free. Pet accepted. TV; cable (premium). Indoor pool; whirlpool, poolside serv. Restaurant 6:30 am-10 pm; Sat 7 am-11 pm. Bar 11-2 am; Sun noon-10 pm; entertainment. Ck-out noon. Meeting rms. Business servs avail. In-rm modem link. Bellhops. Valet serv. Sundries. Free airport transportation. Exercise equipt; sauna. Game rm. Rec rm. Cr cds: A, C, D, DS, MC, V.

D ◆ ≈ ⚡ ✕ ⚓ 🔥 SC

★★ **HAMPTON INN.** *3265 SW 6th St (52404). 319/364-8144; fax 319/399-1877. www.hamptoninn.com.* 106 rms, 3 story. S, D $79-$99; suite $89-$99; under 18 free. Crib free. TV; cable (premium), VCR avail (movies). Indoor pool; whirlpool. Complimentary continental bkfst. Restaurant adj open 24 hrs. Bar 6-2 am. Ck-out noon. Meeting rms. Business servs avail. Valet serv. Coin lndry. Exercise equipt. Cr cds: A, D, DS, MC, V.

D ≈ ⚡ ⚓ 🔥

★ **HEARTLAND INN.** *3315 Southgate Ct SW (52404). 319/362-9012; fax 319/362-9694; toll-free 800/334-3277. www.heartlandinns.com.* 117 units, 2 story, 30 suites. S $49-$60; D $58-$71; each addl $8; suites $68-$150; under 16 free. Crib free. TV. Complimentary bkfst. Restaurant adj open 24 hrs. Ck-out noon. Meeting rm. Sauna. Cr cds: A, MC, V.

D ✕ 🔥

★ **RED ROOF INN.** *3325 Southgate Ct SW (52404). 319/366-7523; fax 319/366-7639. www.redroof.com.* 108 rms, 2 story. S $29.99-$41.99; D $35.99-$53.99; each addl $8; under 18 free. Crib free. TV; cable (premium). Complimentary coffee. Restaurant opp open 24 hrs. Ck-out noon. Cr cds: A, D, DS, MC, V.

D ⚡ ⚓ 🔥

Hotels

★★★ **COLLINS PLAZA.** *1200 Collins Rd NE (52402). 319/393-6600; fax 319/393-2308. www.jghotels.com.* 221 units, 7 story, 85 suites. S, D $90-$98; each addl $8; suites $107-$125; under 18 free. Crib free. TV; cable. Indoor pool; whirlpool. Restaurants 6 am-11 pm. Bars 11-1 am; entertainment. Ck-out noon. Coin lndry. Meeting rms. Business center. In-rm modem link. Gift shop. Free airport, bus depot transportation. Exercise equipt; sauna, steam

rm. Refrigerator, wet bar in suites. Cr cds: A, D, DS, MC, V.

D ⚡ ≈ ⚓ ⚡ ✕

★★★ **CROWNE PLAZA FIVE SEA-SONS.** *350 First Ave NE (52401). 319/363-8161; fax 319/363-3804. www.crowneplaza.com.* 275 rms, 16 story. S $79-$105; D $89-$115; each addl $10; suites $175-$325; under 18 free; wkend rates. Crib free. Parking $3. TV; cable. Indoor pool; whirlpool. Complimentary coffee in rms. Restaurant 6:30 am-11 pm. Rm serv 24 hrs. Bar. Ck-out noon. Convention facilities. Business center. In-rm modem link. Concierge. Free airport transportation. Exercise equipt; sauna. Game rm. Cr cds: A, MC, V.

D ≈ ⚡ ⚓ 🔥 SC ✕

Centerville (E-5)

Founded 1846 **Pop** 5,936 **Elev** 1,010 ft **Area code** 641 **Zip** 52544
Information Chamber of Commerce, 128 N 12th St; 641/437-4102 or 800/611-3800
Web www.centervillecofc.org

Once an important ferry point for Chariton River traffic, Centerville today is an agricultural, industrial, and retail center.

What to See and Do

Rathbun Lake. Offers swimming, bathhouse, fishing, boating (ramps, two marinas); picnicking, camping (electricity, dump station May-Sept; fee). 7 mi NW. Phone 641/647-2464. On N shore is

Honey Creek State Park. On 828 acres. Swimming, fishing, boating; hiking trails, snowmobiling, picnicking, camping (electric hookups, dump station). Scenic overlook. Standard hrs, fees. 12 mi N on IA 5, then 9½ mi W on IA 142, 3 mi SE on unnumbered road. Phone 641/724-3739.

Sharon Bluffs Park. More than 140 acres on the Chariton River; scenic view from high bluffs of clay and shale. Boating (ramp). Hiking trails. Picnicking, shelter. Camping (hookups, fee). (Daily) 3 mi E on

IA 2, then 1 mi S. Phone 641/856-8528.

Special Events

Croatian Fest. Courthouse lawn on city square. Ethnic festival featuring entertainment, dancing, and food. Last Sat July.

Pancake Day. Entertainment, parade, craft show, free pancakes. Last Sat Sept.

Motel/Motor Lodge

★ **SUPER 8 MOTEL.** *1021 18th Hwy 5 N (52544). 641/856-8888; toll-free 800/800-8000. www.super8.com.* 41 rms, 2 story. S $43-$48; D $58-$62; each addl $4; suites $55-$85; under 12 free. Crib $5. TV; cable (premium). Complimentary continental bkfst. Ck-out 11 am. Meeting rm. Business servs avail. Cr cds: A, C, D, DS, MC, V.
⊡ ⊠ ⊠ SC

Restaurant

★ **GREEN CIRCLE INN.** *22984 Hwy 55 (52544). 641/437-4472.* Hrs: 11 am-2 pm, 4:30-9 pm; Mon, Sat from 4:30 pm; Sun brunch 10:30 am-2 pm. Closed Dec 25. Res accepted. Bar. Lunch, dinner $4.75-$16.95. Specializes in steak, seafood, pasta. Family-owned. Cr cds: A, DS, MC, V.
⊡ ⊟

Chariton

(E-5) *See also Osceola*

Pop 4,616 **Elev** 1,041 ft
Area code 515 **Zip** 50049
Information Chariton Chamber and Development Corp, 104 N Grand, PO Box 488; 515/774-4059

The site of this town was recorded as Chariton by Lewis and Clark after the French corrupted the Native American word "thier-aton," meaning "two rivers."

What to See and Do

John L. Lewis Museum of Mining and Labor. Exhibits; library; theater; mining tools collection. (Mid-Apr-mid-Oct, Tues-Sat; also by appt) 102 Division St, Lucas. Approx 10 mi W on US 34, jct US 65. Phone 515/766-6831. ¢

Lucas County Historical Museum. Restored and furnished 1907 home; rural Puckerbrush school and Otterbein church; John L. Lewis building with library, replica of mine, antique farm machinery. (Memorial Day-Oct, Sun and Wed) 123 17th St at Braden Ave. Phone 515/774-4464. **FREE**

Red Haw State Park. Approx 420 acres with 72-acre lake. Swimming beach, fishing, boating (electric motors only; ramps, rentals); snowmobiling, picnicking, camping (electricity, dump station). Standard hrs, fees. 1 mi E on US 34. Phone 515/774-5632.

Stephens State Forest. Five units totaling 8,466 acres of evergreens and hardwoods; pond. Fishing, boating (electric motors only); hiking, bridle trails, hunting, snowmobiling, picnicking. Primitive camping. Standard hrs, fees. 10 mi W on US 34 to Lucas, then 2 mi S on US 65, then W on county road. Phone 515/774-4559.

Wayne County Historical Museum. More than 80,000 artifacts from county's history; replicas of 17 buildings incl doctor's office, bank, jail, toy shop and music rm; Jesse James exhibit incl the safe he robbed in Corydon; bird and animal exhibits; old machinery and vehicles; genealogy section; Mormon exhibit; collection of 150 creche figures from Italy and Germany. (Mid-Apr-mid-Oct, daily) Approx 18 mi S via IA 14 to IA 2 in Corydon. Phone 515/872-2211. ¢¢

Charles City

(A-5) *See also Mason City, Waverly*

Settled 1852 **Pop** 7,878 **Elev** 1,000 ft
Area code 641 **Zip** 50616
Information Charles City Area Chamber of Commerce, 610 S Grand Ave; 641/228-4234
Web www.charles-city.com

One of the first gasoline tractor engines for agricultural and industrial use was produced here.

What to See and Do

Floyd County Historical Society Museum. Incl authentic 1873 drug-store, barber shop, model railroad display, military exhibits, Native American artifacts, doctor and dentist offices, farm equipt, blacksmith shop, country store, newspaper printshop. (May-Sept, Tues-Sun; rest of yr, Tues-Fri; also by appt) 500 Gilbert St on US 218 and 18. Phone 641/228-1099. ¢

Special Event

Art-a-Fest. Central Park, Main St. Fine arts festival with arts and craft displays, ethnic foods, music, drama, dance performances. Third wkend Aug.

Motel/Motor Lodge

★ **HARTWOOD INN.** *1312 Gilbert St (50616). 641/228-4352; fax 515/257-2488; toll-free 800/972-2335.* 35 rms, 1 and 2 story. S $36-$45; D $49-$65; each addl $5; under 16 free. Crib free. TV; cable (premium). Complimentary continental bkfst. Coffee in rms. Restaurant nearby. Ck-out 11 am. Coin lndry. Cr cds: A, MC, V.
[D] [≈] [🐾] [SC]

Restaurant

★ **BROOKS.** *102 Cedar Mall (50616). 515/228-7162.* Hrs: 6:30 am-10 pm. Closed Jan 1, Memorial Day, Dec 25. Res accepted. Bar from 4 pm. Bkfst $1-$5, lunch $1.50-$6, dinner $3.99-$16.99. Specializes in steak. Diner atmosphere. Cr cds: A, DS, MC, V.
[D] [SC] [⊸]

Cherokee

(B-2) *See also Storm Lake*

Pop 6,026 **Area code** 712 **Zip** 51012
Information Chamber of Commerce, 228 W Main St; 712/225-6414

Center of one of the heaviest cattle feeding and hog raising areas of Iowa, Cherokee is home to many processing and manufacturing plants. The Cherokee Community Center houses a symphony orchestra and an active community theater.

What to See and Do

City Parks. Wescott. Canoeing, picnicking, playgrounds, sand volleyball courts. S 2nd St on Little Sioux River. **Spring Lake.** Fishing, x-country skiing, ice-skating, picnicking, camping (hookups, dump station; fee). S 2nd St. **Gillette.** Swimming pool (Memorial Day-Aug, daily; fee). Tennis. W Bluff St. S 2nd St on Little Sioux River. Phone 712/225-2715.

Sanford Museum and Planetarium. Natural history, science, historical and changing art exhibits. Classes by appt; planetarium programs (last Sun of month; also by appt). (Daily; closed hols) 117 E Willow St. Phone 712/225-3922. **FREE**

Special Events

Cherokee Rodeo. PRCA sanctioned. Wkend after Memorial Day wkend.
Cherokee County Fair. July.

Motels/Motor Lodges

★★ **BEST WESTERN LA GRANDE HACIENDA.** *1401 N 2nd St (51012). 712/225-5701; fax 712/225-3926; toll-free 800/924-3765. www.bestwestern. com.* 55 rms, 2 story. S $59-$65; D $65-$71; each addl $8. TV; cable (premium), VCR avail (movies). Indoor pool; whirlpool. Complimentary bkfst. Restaurant 4-10 pm. Ck-out 11 am. Meeting rm. Business servs avail. In-rm modem link. Sundries. Cr cds: A, C, D, DS, JCB, MC, V.
[D] [≈] [≋] [🐾] [SC]

★ **SUPER 8 MOTEL.** *1400 N 2nd St (51012). 712/225-4278; fax 712/225-4678; toll-free 800/800-8000. www. super8.com.* 34 rms, 2 story. S $38; D $48; suites $41-$47; under 12 free. Crib $5. TV. Complimentary coffee in lobby. Restaurant adj open 24 hrs. Ck-out 11 am. Exercise equipt. Cr cds: A, C, D, DS, MC, V.
[D] [🕅] [≈] [🐾] [SC]

Clarinda

(E-3) *See also Shenandoah*

Settled 1853 **Pop** 5,104
Area code 712 **Zip** 51632
Information Association of Business
& Industry, 200 S 15th St; 712/542-
2166

Clarinda is the birthplace of Big
Band-era legend Glenn Miller. It's
also where, at the turn of the century, rural school teacher Jessie Field
Shambaugh started the Boys' Corn
Clubs and Girls' Home Clubs, which
later became the 4-H movement.

What to See and Do

Lake of Three Fires State Park. Park
has 691 acres with 97-acre lake.
Swimming, fishing, electric boating
(ramps, rentals); hiking, bridle trails;
snowmobiling, picnicking, camping
(electricity, dump station), cabins.
Standard hrs, fees. 18 mi E on IA 2 to
Bedford, then 3 mi NE on IA 49.
Phone 712/523-2700.

Nodaway Valley Historical Museum.
Exhibits on history of Nodaway River
area incl agricultural displays, artifacts from early days of 4-H movement, and Glenn Miller
memorabilia. Visits to the nearby
Glenn Miller Birthplace Home (by
appt only; addl fee) can be arranged
through the museum. (Tues-Sun
afternoons) 1600 S 16th St. Phone
712/542-3073. ¢

Special Events

Glenn Miller Festival. Honoring his
music and birthplace. Second wkend
June.

Page County Fair. Last wk July.

Southwest Iowa Band Jamboree.
High school bands from three states
participate. First Sat Oct.

Motel/Motor Lodge

★ **CELEBRITY INN MOTEL.** *1323 S
16th St (51632). 712/542-5178; fax
712/542-5085; toll-free 877/542-5178.
www.celebrityinnmotel.com.* 36 rms. S
$32-$38; D $40-$48; under 16 free.
Crib $4. TV; cable. Complimentary
coffee. Restaurant opp 7 am-11 pm.

Ck-out 11 am. Meeting rms. Cr cds:
A, DS, MC, V.
Ⓓ ⌂

Restaurant

★ ★ **J. BRUNER'S.** *1100 E Washington (51632). 712/542-3364.* Hrs: 5-
10:30 pm; Sun 11:30 am-2 pm.
Closed Mon; hols. Bar 4:30-11:30
pm. Lunch, dinner $9-$35. Children's menu. Specializes in steak,
seafood, onion rings. Country French
decor. Cr cds: A, D, DS, MC, V.
Ⓓ ⊟

Clear Lake

See also Garner, Mason City

Settled 1851 **Pop** 8,183 **Elev** 1,236 ft
Area code 641 **Zip** 50428
Information Chamber of Commerce,
205 Main Ave, PO Box 188; 641/357-
2159 or 800/285-5338
Web www.clearlakeiowa.com

Scene of a Native American uprising
in 1854, Clear Lake rivaled Mason
City (see) for honors as the county
seat but lost out because it was not
in the geographic center of the area.
Taking its name from the nearby
lake, Clear Lake is an ancient Native
American fishing and hunting
ground. Today it is a popular, modern resort town.

What to See and Do

State parks. Swimming, fishing,
boating (ramps); snowmobiling, picnicking, camping (electric hookups).
Standard hrs, fees.

Clear Lake. Park has 102 acres
with 3,684-acre lake. Picnicking.
Also dump station. 2 mi S on IA
107. Phone 641/357-4212.

McIntosh Woods. Also nature trails
in this 62-acre park. On N shore of
lake, off US 18. Phone 641/829-
3847.

◪ **Surf Ballroom.** Site of Buddy
Holly's last concert before Holly,
Ritchie Valens, and J. P. Richardson
(the Big Bopper) died in local plane
crash on Feb 2, 1959. Ballrm features
varied entertainment wkends; plaque

and monument outside commemo-rate the musicians; museum of musical history. Tours avail. 460 North Shore Dr. Phone 641/357-6151.

Tours. Main Street Trolley. Vintage-style trolley avail for regular narrated tours, charters, and special events. (Thurs-Sun, Memorial Day-Sept) Phone 800/285-5338. ¢¢¢

Motels/Motor Lodges

★★ **BEST WESTERN HOLIDAY LODGE.** *I-35 S (50428). 641/357-5253; fax 641/357-8153; toll-free 800/528-1234. www.bestwestern.com.* 144 rms, 5 story. S $49-$59; D $59-$69; each addl $8; suites $70-$150; under 12 free. Crib free. Pet accepted. TV; cable. Indoor pool; whirlpool. Sauna. Complimentary bkfst. Restaurant 11 am-midnight. Ck-out 11 am. Valet serv. Sundries. Free airport transportation. Cr cds: A, C, D, DS, JCB, MC, V.

★ **BUDGET INN.** *1306 N 25th St (50428). 641/357-8700; fax 641/357-8811; res 888/357-8700.* 60 rms, 2 story. S $35-$49; D $40-$59; each addl $5; under 16 free. Crib free. Pet accepted. TV; cable (premium). Heated pool. Playground. Restaurant adj open 24 hrs. Ck-out 11 am. Meeting rms. Sundries. Cr cds: A, DS, MC, V.

★ **HEARTLAND INN.** *1603 S Shore Dr (50428). 641/357-5123; fax 641/357-2228; toll-free 800/334-3277. www.heartlandinns.com.* 18 rms, 2 story. June-Aug: S, D $109; children free; lower rates rest of yr. Crib free. TV; cable. Restaurant nearby. Ck-out 11 am. In-rm modem link. Some refrigerators. Some balconies. On lake; dock. Cr cds: A, C, D, DS, MC, V.

★ **SUPER 8 MOTEL.** *I-35 (50428). 641/357-7521; fax 641/357-5999; toll-free 800/800-8000. www.super8.com.* 60 rms, 3 story. No elvtr. S $38.88; D $42.88-$47.88; each addl $2. Crib $2. TV; cable. Complimentary continental bkfst. Restaurant adj open 24 hrs. Ck-out 11 am. Sundries. Cr cds: A, C, D, DS, MC, V.

Clinton (C-8)

Founded 1855 **Pop** 29,201 **Elev** 600 ft
Area code 563 **Zip** 52732
Information Convention & Visitors Bureau, 333 4th Ave S, PO Box 1024; 563/242-5702 or 800/828-5702

Agriculture, industry, and business are blended in this city of wide streets and modern buildings on the Mississippi River. First called New York, it was later renamed after DeWitt Clinton, former governor of New York. Once the largest lumber-producing city in the world, Clinton today is the home of a diverse group of industries. It is also the seat of a county famous for its prime beef production.

What to See and Do

Eagle Point Park. Flower gardens; picnicking (shelters), lodge; playground, observation tower; children's nature center; petting zoo. (Apr-mid-Nov, daily) On US 67 at N city limits, overlooking the Mississippi. Phone 563/243-1260. **FREE**

Riverview Park. Swimming pool (Memorial Day-Labor Day, daily; fee); marina, boat ramp; lighted tennis courts, fountain; playground, recreational trail, baseball stadium, horseshoes, picnicking; RV parking (fee). (Daily) 6th Ave N, on the Mississippi. Phone 563/243-1260. **FREE** Also here are

Lillian Russell Theatre. Aboard the paddlewheel showboat *The City of Clinton.* Musicals and comedies. (June-Aug) Phone 563/242-6760.

Mississippi Belle II. Offers yr-round casino gambling along the Mississippi River. Entertainment. Concession. Showboat Landing. Phone 563/243-9000.

Special Events

Civil War Reenactment. Eagle Point Park. Battle for Burnside Bridge; Military Ball with period music and costumes. Mother's Day wkend.

Riverboat Days. Pageant, events, tractor pulls, entertainment, shows, carnival. July 4th wkend.

Symphony of Lights. Eagle Point Park. Over 800,000 individual lights;

Babes in Toyland, medieval castles, illuminated arches, animated snowball throwers (fee per vehicle). Phone 888/725-4689. Dec.

Motels/Motor Lodges

★★ **BEST WESTERN FRONTIER MOTOR INN.** *2300 Lincolnway St (52732). 563/242-7112; fax 563/242-7117; toll-free 800/728-7112. www. bestwestern.com.* 117 rms, 1-2 story. S, D $46-$79; each addl $6; suites $99-$149; under 12 free. Crib $6. Pet accepted, some restrictions. TV; cable (premium). Indoor pool; whirlpool. Restaurant 6 am-9 pm. Bar 11:30-2 am; closed Sun. Ck-out noon. Meeting rms. Business servs avail. Valet serv. Sundries. Exercise equipt. X-country ski 5 mi. Some refrigerators. Cr cds: A, MC, V.

★ **RAMADA INN.** *1522 Lincolnway St (52734). 563/243-8841; fax 563/242-6202. www.ramada.com.* 103 rms, 2 story, 10 suites. S $56-$58; D $62-$64; each addl $6; suites $80-$90; under 18 free; package plans. Crib free. Pet accepted, some restrictions. TV; cable (premium), VCR avail. Complimentary coffee in lobby. Indoor pool. Bar 11-2 am. Ck-out noon. Meeting rms. Business servs avail. Game rm. Some refrigerators, microwaves. Cr cds: A, D, DS, MC, V.

★ **SUPER 8 MOTEL.** *1711 Lincolnway St (52732). 563/242-8870; toll-free 800/800-8000. www.super8.com.* 63 rms, 3 story. No elvtr. S $43.98; D $52.98; under 12 free. Crib $2. TV; cable (premium). Complimentary coffee in lobby. Restaurant nearby. Ck-out 11 am. Business servs avail. Sundries. Cr cds: A, C, D, DS, MC, V.

★ **TRAVEL INN.** *302 6th Ave S (52732). 563/243-4730; fax 563/243-4732; res 877/237-5261.* 51 rms, 2 story. S $38; D $48; each addl $5; under 17 free. Crib $5. Pet accepted. TV; cable (premium). Pool. Complimentary coffee. Restaurant adj 11 am-8 pm. Ck-out 11 am. Some refrigerators. Some private patios. Cr cds: A, DS, MC, V.

Council Bluffs
(D-2) *Also see Omaha, NE*

Settled 1824 **Pop** 54,315 **Elev** 986 ft **Area code** 712
Information Convention & Visitors Bureau, 7 N 6th St, PO Box 1565, 51502; 712/325-1000 or 800/228-6878
Web www.councilbluffsiowa.com

The Lewis and Clark expedition stopped in Council Bluffs in 1804 to rest and hold their first "council bluff" with local Native American tribes. Council Bluffs was settled in 1846 by Mormons who were fleeing religious persecution. They called the town "Kanesville"; but the city officially took the name Council Bluffs in 1853. The town subsequently became a booming hub of commerce as the nation's fifth-largest rail center. Today the Loess Hills Scenic Byway (see MISSOURI VALLEY) passes through the area. A mix of insurance, gaming, telecommunications, agriculture, and manufacturing industries have created a diverse employment base.

What to See and Do

Golden Spike. Erected in 1939, this 56-ft golden concrete spike commemorates the junction of the Union Pacific and Central Pacific railroads in Council Bluffs. 21st St and 9th Ave.

Historic General Dodge House. (1869) Restored Victorian home built by Grenville M. Dodge, chief construction engineer for Union Pacific Railroad and general in Civil War. Guided tours (Tues-Sun; closed hols; also Jan). 605 3rd St. Phone 712/322-2406. ¢¢

Historic Pottawattamie County Jail. (1885) This unique three-story rotary jail is sometimes referred to as the "human squirrel cage" or "lazy Susan jail." (Apr-Sept, or by appt; closed hols) 226 Pearl St. Phone 712/323-2509. ¢¢

Lake Manawa State Park. More than 1,500-acre park with 660-acre lake. "Dream Playground" designed by and for children. Swimming, supervised beach, fishing, boating (ramps, rentals); hiking trails, bicycle trails, snowmobiling, picnicking, camping (electricity). Standard hrs, fees. 1 mi S on IA 92/275. Phone 712/366-0220.

Lewis and Clark Monument. Shaft of native stone on bluffs depicts Lewis and Clark holding council with Oto and Missouri. Rainbow Point, N on 8th St.

Lincoln Monument. Granite shaft marks spot from which Lincoln designated the town as the eastern terminus of the Union Pacific Railroad. 323 Lafayette Ave.

Mississippi Belle II. Offers yr-round casino gambling along the Mississippi River. Entertainment. Concession. Phone 319/243-9000 or 800/457-9975.

Mormon Trail Memorial. Huge boulder marks passage of Mormons out of city on trek to Utah. Bayliss Park, Pearl St and 1st Ave.

RailsWest Railroad Museum. Historic Rock Island depot (1899); railroad memorabilia, HO gauge model trains on display. (Memorial Day-Labor Day, Tues-Sun and hols; rest of yr, by appt) 16th Ave and South Main St. Phone 712/323-5182 or 712/322-0612. ¢¢

Ruth Anne Dodge Memorial. Commissioned by the daughters of G.M. Dodge in memory of their mother, this bronze statue of an angel is the work of Daniel Chester French. N 2nd and Lafayette aves.

Western Historic Trails Center. Explore preserved and restored sites along Lewis and Clark, Mormon Pioneer, California, and Oregon trails. Discover history of Native American tribes and trails heritage in the region. Guided group tours. (Daily; closed hols) Jct I-80 and S 24th St. Phone 712/366-4900. **FREE**

Special Event

Renaissance Faire of the Midlands. Renaissance period crafts, entertainment, concessions; jousting contests, street performers. Phone 402/330-8446 or 712/328-4992. June.

Motels/Motor Lodges

★ **ECONO LODGE.** *3208 S 7th St (51501). 712/366-9699; fax 712/366-* 6129; toll-free 800/228-5150. www. conolodge.com. 60 rms, 3 story. No elvtr. May-Oct: S, D $42-$49; each addl $5; suites $90-$99; under 16 free; lower rates rest of yr. Crib $5. TV; cable (premium). Complimentary continental bkfst. Restaurant adj open 24 hrs. Ck-out noon. Coin lndry. Meeting rms. Business servs avail. Valet serv. Exercise equipt. Refrigerator in suites. Cr cds: A, MC, V.

D 🖈 🖎 🔥 SC

★★ **FAIRFIELD INN.** *520 30th Ave (51501). 712/366-1330; toll-free 800/ 228-2800. www.fairfieldinn.com.* 62 rms, 3 story. May-Sept: S, D $59.95-$79.95; under 18 free; higher rates special events; lower rates rest of yr. Crib free. TV; cable (premium), VCR avail. Complimentary continental bkfst. Restaurant opp 6 am-10 pm. Ck-out noon. Meeting rms. Business servs avail. Indoor pool; whirlpool. Cr cds: A, D, DS, MC, V.

D 🖎 🖎 🔥 SC

★ **HEARTLAND INN.** *1000 Woodbury Ave (51503). 712/322-8400; fax 712/322-4022; toll-free 800/334-3277. www.heartlandinns.com.* 89 rms, 2 story. S $51-$61; D $59-$66; under 16 free. Crib avail. TV; cable (premium). Complimentary continental bkfst. Restaurant opp 6-3 am. Ck-out 11 am. Meeting rm. Business servs avail. Sauna. Whirlpool. Microwaves avail. Cr cds: A, MC, V.

D 🔥

★★ **QUALITY INN.** *3537 W Broadway (51501). 712/328-3171; fax 712/ 328-2205. www.qualityinn.com.* 89 rms, 2 story, 43 suites. May-Oct: S, D $49-$69; each addl $6; under 18 free; higher rates rest of yr. Crib avail. Pet accepted. TV; cable (premium). Complimentary continental bkfst, coffee in rms. Restaurant 6 am-10 pm. Ck-out noon. Meeting rms. Business servs avail. In-rm modem link. Free airport transportation. Indoor pool. Refrigerators; microwave in suites. Cr cds: A, C, D, DS, JCB, MC, V.

D 🐾 🖎 ✈ 🖎 🔥 🖎

★★ **WESTERN INN MOTOR LODGE.** *1842 Madison Ave, Council Bluff (51503). 712/322-4499; toll-free 712/322-1842.* 51 rms, 2 story. S $48; D $56; each addl $7; suites $69.95-$88; under 12 free. Crib free. TV;

cable (premium). Indoor pool; whirl-pool. Restaurant adj 6 am-midnight. Ck-out 11 am. Business servs avail. Cr cds: A, MC, V.

Hotel

★★★ **AMERISTAR CASINO.** *2200 River Rd (51501). 712/328-8888; fax 712/328-8882; res 877/462-7827. www.ameristarcasinos.com.* 160 rms, 5 story. S, D, suites $65-$295; wkend rates; higher rates special events. Crib free. TV; cable, VCR avail. Restaurants open 24 hrs. Rm serv to 11 pm. Bar 11-2 am. Ck-out 11 am. Meeting rms. Business servs avail. Gift shop. Exercise equipt; sauna. Indoor pool; whirlpool. Game rm. Bathrm phones; some in-rm whirlpools. Cr cds: A, D, DS, MC, V.

Creston (E-3)

Founded 1869 **Pop** 7,911 **Elev** 1,314 ft **Area code** 641 **Zip** 50801

Information Chamber of Commerce, 208 W Taylor, PO Box 471; 641/782-7021

Web www.creston.heartland.net

In the heart of Iowa's High Lakes country, Creston has long been a railroad town and shopping, medical, and educational hub for southwest Iowa.

What to See and Do

Green Valley State Park. The 991-acre park amid rolling hills has a 428-acre lake. Swimming, fishing, boating (ramps, rentals); snowmobiling, picnicking, camping (electricity, dump station). Standard hrs, fees. 2½ mi N off IA 25. Phone 515/782-5131.

Special Event

Creston Hot Air Balloon Days. Municipal Airport on S Cherry St Rd. Three balloon races; parade, marching band contest, art and book fairs. Mid-Sept. Phone 515/782-2383.

Motels/Motor Lodges

★ **BERNING MOTOR INN.** *301 W Adams St (50801). 641/782-7001; fax 641/782-9941.* 48 rms, 2 story. S $28-$35; D $35-$40; each addl $5; under 10 free. Crib $1. TV; cable (premium). Restaurant 5:30 am-10:30 pm; Sun to 2 pm. Bar 11 am-midnight; Sun to 2 pm. Ck-out 11 am. Meeting rms. Cr cds: A, MC, V.

★ **SUPER 8.** *804 W Taylor St (50801). 641/782-6541. www.super8.com.* 83 rms, 2 story. S $38-$43; D $45-$50; each addl $2. Crib $2. TV; cable (premium). Complimentary coffee in lobby. Restaurant adj open 24 hrs. Ck-out 11 am. Business servs avail. In-rm modem link. Cr cds: A, D, DS, MC, V.

Davenport

(D-7) *See also Muscatine*

Founded 1808 **Pop** 95,333 **Elev** 589 ft **Area code** 563

Information Quad Cities Convention & Visitors Bureau, 102 S Harrison St, 52801; 563/788-7800 or 800/747-7800

Web www.quadcities.com

Stretching five miles along the Mississippi River, Davenport is part of the Quad Cities metropolitan area, which also includes Bettendorf, Iowa, and Moline and Rock Island, Illinois. Principally a regional retail center, Davenport also produces machinery, agricultural goods, and food products. Davenport's Palmer College of Chiropractic is the fountainhead of that practice in the United States. The city is named for its founder, a former US Army officer who explored this bank of the river while stationed on Rock Island. The state's first railroad came here when tracks were put across the Mississippi at this point in 1854. In pre-Civil War days, Dred Scott claimed the town as his home, and John Brown provisioned here before his attack on Harpers Ferry.

What to See and Do

Dan Nagle Walnut Grove Pioneer Village. Three-acre walk-through site contains ten historic buildings moved from various locations in the county. Visitors can explore a blacksmith shop, schoolhouse, pioneer family home; also St. Anne's Church. (Apr-Oct, daily) 8 mi N on US 61, Long Grove. Phone 319/285-9903. **Donation**

Davenport Museum of Art. Rotating displays from permanent collection of 19th- and 20th-century paintings, Mexican Colonial, Oriental, native Haitian art collections; works by regional artists Grant Wood and Thomas Hart Benton. (Tues-Sun; closed hols) 1737 W 12th St. Phone 319/326-7804. **Donation**

Parks.

Fejevary Park. Swimming pool, picnic areas, playground (Apr-Oct). A zoo in the park features North American animals (late May-early Sept, Tues-Sun). 1800 W 12th St. Phone 319/326-7812.

Scott County Park. More than 1,000 acres with pioneer village, nature center. Swimming (fee), fishing. Ball fields. 18-hole golf. Skiing, tobogganing, ice-skating. Picnicking. Camping, trailer sites (fee; electricity addl). (Daily) 8 mi N on US 61, follow signs. Phone 319/285-9656.

President Casino. Departs from River Drive, between Centennial and Government bridges.

Putnam Museum of History & Natural Science. Permanent and changing exhibits of regional history, natural science, and world cultures. (Tues-Sat, also Sun afternoons; closed Mondays and hols) 1717 W 12th St. Phone 319/324-1933. ¢¢

Special Event

Bix Beiderbecke Memorial Jazz Festival. Riverfront at LeClaire Park. Honors Davenport-born musician. Incl three indoor venues: Davenport Holiday Inn, Col Ballroom, Danceland Ballroom. Phone 319/324-7170. July 20-23.

Motels/Motor Lodges

★★ **BEST WESTERN STEEPLE-GATE INN.** *100 W 76th St (52806). 563/386-6900; fax 563/388-9955; toll-free 800/373-6900. www.bestwestern. com.* 121 rms, 2 story. S, D $79-$99; each addl $6; suites $145-$155; under 16 free. Crib $5. Pet accepted; $5. TV; cable (premium). Indoor pool; whirlpool. Restaurant 6 am-9 pm; Fri, Sat to 10 pm. Bar 11-2 am; entertainment. Ck-out noon. Business servs avail. Valet serv. Free airport, bus depot, transportation. Exercise equipt. Game rm. Some refrigerators, microwaves. Cr cds: A, C, D, DS, JCB, MC, V.

🄳 ✈🖼🏃✈🛏🔥🆂🅲

★ **CLARION HOTEL.** *227 LeClaire St (52801). 563/324-1921; fax 563/324-9621; toll-free 800/553-1879. www. clarioninns.com.* 150 rms, 6 story. S $55; D $59; each addl $6; studio rms $55-$80. Crib $5. TV; cable (premium). 2 pools, 1 indoor; whirlpool. Complimentary continental bkfst. Coffee in rms. Restaurant 6 am-2 pm, 5-10 pm. Bar 3 pm-1 am. Ck-out 11 am. Coin lndry. Meeting rms. Business center. In-rm modem link. Valet serv. Sauna. Game rm. Rec rm. Refrigerators. Some rms with view of the Mississippi. Cr cds: A, C, D, DS, ER, JCB, MC, V.

🄳 ☕🖼🏃🛏🔥🏃

★ **COMFORT INN.** *7222 Northwest Blvd (52806). 563/391-8222; fax 563/391-1595. www.comfortinn.com.* 89 rms, 2 story. S $45.50; D $54.50; each addl $4. Pet accepted, some restrictions; $20 refundable and $2/day. TV; cable (premium), VCR avail. Complimentary continental bkfst. Restaurant adj 6 am-10 pm. Ck-out 11 am. Business servs avail. Exercise equipt. Microwaves avail. Cr cds: A, C, D, DS, ER, MC, V.

🄳 ✈☕🛏🔥

★ **DAYS INN.** *3202 E Kimberly Rd (52807). 563/355-1190; toll-free 800/329-7466. www.daysinn.com.* 65 rms, 2 story. Apr-Sept: S $40-$85; D $44-$85; under 13 free; lower rates rest of yr. Crib free. Pet accepted, some restrictions. TV; cable (premium). Indoor pool; whirlpool. Complimentary continental bkfst. Restaurant nearby. Ck-out 11 am. Meeting rms. Business servs avail.

DAVENPORT AND MISSISSIPPI RIVER ISLANDS

Davenport is one of the Quad Cities, a four-city metropolitan area that straddles the Mississippi and that includes Moline and Rock City in Illinois, plus Bettendorf, just upriver from Davenport. This hike explores the old waterfront of Davenport, as well as two park islands in the Mississippi between Illinois and Iowa. Begin on Credit Island Park, the site of a turn-of-the-century amusement park. Scenic trails loop around the island, which is now a community park with a playground area and a municipal golf course. A number of public art pieces are also found here, part of the Quad Cities' Art in the Park project.

Cross over to the Iowa mainland from the east end of Credit Island Park, and walk along the Mississippi through two more riverside parks. Centennial Park features riverside walkways past sports fields and stadiums. Atop the bluff on Division Street is Museum Hill, home of the Putnam Museum of Science and Natural History (1717 West 12th Street) and the Davenport Museum of Art (1737 West 12th Street). The Putnam houses two permanent exhibits about the Mississippi River; the art museum's permanent collection includes works by Midwestern painters, such as Thomas Hart Benton and Grant Wood, an Iowa native famous for his painting *American Gothic*. Just to the east is LeClaire Park, home to summer outdoor events and concerts.

The Davenport Downtown Levee includes a riverboat casino, restaurants, nightclubs, and the renovated Union Station railroad depot, which houses the Quad Cities Convention and Visitors Center. A local Farmers Market is also held here on Wednesday and Saturday mornings from May through October.

Just downstream from the historic Government Bridge, Dam 15 provides a navigational pool for commercial shipping on the Mississippi. Lock 15 allows boats to transfer between the river's pools. Cross Government Bridge to Arsenal Island, which was acquired by the US Government in 1804 under a treaty with the Sauk and Fox Indians. Fort Armstrong was established in 1816 on the tip of the island, where a replica now stands. Manufacturing began on the island in 1840, and in 1869 it became home to the Rock Island Arsenal, a major military manufacturing facility. The island contains a number of historic homes and structures, including the Rock Island Arsenal Museum; the restored Colonel George Davenport Mansion, filled with furnishings from the mid-1800s; and the Mississippi River Visitors Center, with exhibits about the history of navigation on the river. A Confederate Soldiers' Cemetery and National Military Cemetery date back to the 1800s. Hikers and bikers can enjoy a five-mile trail around the island.

Valet serv. Game rm. Cr cds: A, D, DS, MC, V.

★ **DAYS INN.** *101 W 65th St (52806). 563/388-9999; fax 563/391-9072; toll-free 800/329-7466. www.daysinn.com.* 64 rms, 2 story, 7 suites. Apr-Sept: S $40-$60; D $45-$70; each addl $5; suites $60-$109; under 13 free; lower rates rest of yr. Crib free. TV; cable (premium), VCR avail. Indoor pool; whirlpool. Complimentary continental bkfst. Restaurant nearby. Ck-out 11 am. Meeting rm. Business servs avail. In-rm modem link. Exercise equipt; sauna. Game

rm. Some refrigerators. Cr cds: A, C, D, DS, MC, V.

★ **EXEL INN.** *6310 N Brady St (52806). 563/386-6350; fax 563/388-1548; toll-free 800/356-8013. www.exelinns.com.* 103 rms, 2 story. S $37; D $44; each addl $5; under 18 free. Crib free. Pet accepted. TV; cable. Complimentary continental bkfst. Ck-out noon. In-rm modem link. Valet serv. Cr cds: A, C, D, DS, MC, V.

★★ **FAIRFIELD INN.** *3206 E Kimberly Rd (52807). 563/355-2264. www.*

fairfieldinn.com. 62 rms, 3 story. S, D $55.95-$63.95; each addl $6; under 18 free; higher rates Bix Jazz Festival; lower rates rest of yr. Crib free. TV; cable (premium). Indoor pool; whirlpool. Complimentary continental bkfst. Restaurant nearby. Ck-out 11 am. Meeting rms. Business servs avail. Sundries. Valet serv. Game rm. Refrigerator in suites. Cr cds: A, D, DS, MC, V.

⬛ 🛏 〰 🏔 🔥

★★ **HAMPTON INN.** *3330 E Kimberly Rd (52807). 563/359-3921; fax 563/359-1912; toll-free 800/426-7866. www.hamptoninn.com.* 132 rms, 2 story. S $52-$59; D $54-$64; under 18 free. Crib free. Pet accepted, some restrictions. TV; cable (premium). Indoor pool. Complimentary continental bkfst. Ck-out noon. Business servs avail. In-rm modem link. Bellhops. Free airport transportation. Exercise equipt. Cr cds: A, C, D, DS, MC, V.

⬛ 🐾 〰 🏋 🏔 🔥 SC

★ **HEARTLAND INN.** *6605 Brady St (52806). 563/386-8336; fax 563/386-6005; toll-free 800/334-3277. www.heartlandinns.com.* 86 rms, 3 story. S, D $70-$77; each addl $9; suites $110-$140. Crib free. Pet accepted. TV; cable (premium). Indoor pool. Complimentary continental bkfst. Restaurant adj 6 am-11 pm. Ck-out 11 am. Meeting rm. Business servs avail. Sundries. Rec rm. Cr cds: A, C, D, DS, MC, V.

⬛ 〰 🏋 🏔 🔥

★★ **HOLIDAY INN.** *5202 N Brady St (52806). 563/391-1230; fax 563/391-6715; toll-free 800/465-4329. www.holiday-inn.com.* 295 rms, 2-3 story. S $58-$75; D $65-$85; under 19 free. Crib free. TV; cable (premium). Indoor pool. Restaurant 6 am-1 pm, 5-9:30 pm. Rm serv from 7 am. Bar 4 pm-midnight. Ck-out noon. Coin lndry. Meeting rms. Business servs avail. Bellhops. Sundries. Gift shop. Free airport transportation. Exercise equipt. Miniature golf. Game rm. Cr cds: A, C, D, DS, JCB, MC, V.

⬛ 〰 🏋 🏔 🔥 SC

★ **SUPER 8 MOTEL.** *410 E 65th St (52807). 563/388-9810. www.super8.com.* 61 rms, 2 story. Apr-Sept: S $45-$56; D $50-$60; each addl $5; suites $50.88-$52.88; under 12 free; higher

rates: jazz festival, special events; lower rates rest of yr. Crib free. Pet accepted. TV; cable (premium). Complimentary continental bkfst. Restaurant adj 11 am-10 pm; Sat, Sun from 8 am. Ck-out 11 am. Business servs avail. Microwaves avail. Cr cds: A, D, DS, MC, V.

⬛ 🐾 🏔 SC

Hotel

★★ **PRESIDENT CASINO'S BLACKHAWK HOTEL.** *200 E 3rd St (52801). 563/328-6000; fax 563/328-6047; toll-free 800/553-1173. www.rhythmcitycasino.com.* 189 rms, 11 story. S $75; D $85; each addl $10; suites $79-$95; under 12 free. Crib free. TV; cable (premium). Restaurant 6 am-2 pm, 5-10 pm. Bar 11-2 am. Ck-out noon. Meeting rms. Business servs avail. Gift shops. Barber, beauty shop. Free airport transportation. Exercise equipt. Microwaves avail. Cr cds: A, C, D, DS, MC, V.

⬛ 🏋 🏔 🔥

B&B/Small Inn

★★ **FULTON'S LANDING GUEST HOUSE.** *1206 E River Dr (52803). 563/322-4069; fax 563/322-8186. www.fultonslanding.com.* 5 rms, 2 story. S, D $60-$125. Crib $10. TV; VCR avail. Complimentary full bkfst, coffee in rms. Ck-out noon. Antique furnishings; overlooks Mississippi. Cr cds: A, MC, V.

🏔 🔥

Restaurants

★ **GRAMMA'S KITCHEN.** *I-80 exit 284, Walcott (52773). 563/284-5055.* Hrs: 6 am-10 pm; Nov-Apr to 9 pm; Sun 7 am-10 pm. Closed hols. Bkfst $2.60-$6.25, lunch $4.95-$6.95, dinner $5.99-$9.95. Specialties: homemade pot pies, chicken-fried steak, apple dumplings. Salad bar. Country decor; crafts, collectibles displayed. Gift shop. Cr cds: A, D, DS, MC, V.

⬛ 🍴

★ **IOWA MACHINE SHED.** *7250 Northwest Blvd (52806). 563/391-2427.* Hrs: 6 am-10 pm; Sun 7 am-9 pm. Closed hols. Bar. Bkfst $2-$7, lunch $3.50-$10, dinner $5-$20. Children's menu. Specializes in stuffed pork loin, beef. Salad bar.

Own desserts. "Down-on-the-farm" atmosphere; country artifacts. Cr cds: A, D, DS, MC, V.

D ⊟

★★ **THUNDER BAY GRILLE.** *6511 Brady St (52806). 563/386-2722.* Hrs: 11 am-10 pm; Fri to 11 pm; Sat 8 am-11 pm; Sun 8 am-9 pm; Sat, Sun brunch to 1:30 pm. Closed hols. Res accepted. Bar. Lunch $4.99-$6.99, dinner $4.99-$19.95. Sat, Sun brunch $6.99. Children's menu. Specializes in fish, steak, seafood. Bilevel dining. Cr cds: A, C, D, DS, ER, MC, V.

D ⊟

Decorah

Pop 8,063 **Elev** 904 ft **Area code** 563 **Zip** 52101

Information Decorah Area Chamber of Commerce, 111 Winnebago St; 563/382-3990 or 800/463-4692

Web www.decorah-iowa.com

A center of Norwegian culture in the United States, Decorah is the seat of Winneshiek County, one of the state's most picturesque areas. Within a short distance are Siewers and Twin Springs and towering spires of limestone along the Upper Iowa River. The town is named for a Native American chief who aided settlers during the Black Hawk War.

What to See and Do

Antonin Dvorak Memorial. Tablet on huge boulder is monument to famed Czech composer who lived here one summer. Titles of some of his outstanding works are inscribed on base of monument. In Spillville.

Bily Clocks. Collection of elaborately carved musical clocks with moving figures, some nine ft tall. (May-Oct, daily) Phone 319/562-3569. ¢¢

Fort Atkinson State Preserve. Fort built in 1840 as federal protection for the Winnebago from the Sac, Fox, and Sioux. Restored buildings incl barracks, blockhouse, magazine. Museum exhibits Native American and pioneer relics. (Mid-May-mid-Oct, daily) 16 mi SW via US 52, IA 24. Phone 319/425-4161. **FREE**

Seed Savers Heritage Farm. 173-acre farm features displays of endangered vegetables, apples, grapes, and ancient White Park cattle. Preservation Gardens house 15,000 rare vegetable varieties; Cultural History Garden displays old-time flowers and vegetables. Historic Orchard has 650 19th-century apples and 160 hardy grapes. Meeting center; gift shop. (Daily) 3076 N Winn Rd, 6 mi N of town off US 52. Phone 319/382-5990. ¢

Upper Iowa River. Popular for canoeing and tubing. Phone 800/463-4692.

★ **Vesterheim, the Norwegian-American Museum.** Extensive exhibits relate history of Norwegians in America and Norway. Pioneer objects, handicrafts, ship gallery, arts displayed in complex of 13 historic buildings; restored mill. (Daily; closed hols) 502 W Water St. Phone 319/382-9681. ¢¢

Special Event

Nordic Fest. Parades, dancing, pioneer tool display; demonstrations of cooking, needlework, and rosemaling. Phone 800/382-FEST. Last full wkend July.

Motels/Motor Lodges

★ **HEARTLAND INN.** *705 Commerce Dr (52101). 563/382-2269; fax 563/382-4767; toll-free 800/334-3277. www.heartlandinns.com.* 59 rms, 2 story. S $65; D $71; each addl $7; suites $65-$115; under 16 free. Crib free. TV; cable. Complimentary continental bkfst. Restaurant nearby. Ck-out 11 am. Meeting rms. Sundries. Exercise equipt. Cr cds: A, C, D, DS, MC, V.

D ⚹ ⊠ ⧆

★ **SUPER 8 MOTEL.** *IA 9 E (52101). 563/382-8771; toll-free 800/800-8000. www.super8.com.* 60 rms, 2 story. S $38.88-$43; D $49.88-$54.88; each addl $4; suites $53.88-$70.88. Crib $2. Pet accepted. TV; cable (premium), VCR avail. Complimentary continental bkfst. Restaurant nearby. Ck-out 11 am. Coin lndry. Meeting rm. Business servs avail. In-rm modem link. Cr cds: A, C, D, DS, MC, V.

D ⧉ ⊠ ⧆ SC

Restaurant

★ **STONE HEARTH INN.** *811 Commerce Dr (52101). 563/382-4614.* Hrs: 11 am-9:30 pm; Fri, Sat to 11 pm; Sun brunch 10:30 am-2 pm. Closed hols. Res accepted. Bar. Lunch $3.50-$5.50, dinner $5.95-$16.95. Sun brunch $6.95. Children's menu. Specializes in prime rib. Casual decor. Cr cds: A, DS, MC, V.
D ⟶

Denison (C-2)

Founded 1855 **Pop** 6,604
Area code 712 **Zip** 51442
Information Chamber of Commerce, 109 N 14th St; 712/263-5621

J. W. Denison, an agent for the Providence Western Land Company and a Baptist minister, came to this area in 1855 and gave the new town his name. The following year the town survived raids by Native Americans. In 1933 Denison survived martial law brought about when farmers nearly rioted during land foreclosures triggered by the Great Depression. Denison is the seat of Crawford County.

What to See and Do

Yellow Smoke Park. A 320-acre recreation area with swimming beach, fishing, boating (no power boats); hiking, winter sports, picknicking, camping (fee). (Daily) 1 mi E on US 30, then ½ mi N on county road. Phone 712/263-2070. **FREE**

Special Event

Donna Reed Festival for the Performing Arts. Special workshops in the performing arts conducted by professionals from around the nation. Parade. Golf tourney. 10K run. Sat night gala. Street fair. Phone 712/263-3334. Late June.

Motel/Motor Lodge

★ **SUPER 8.** *502 Boyer Valley Rd (51442). 712/263-5081; fax 712/263-2898. www.super8.com.* 40 rms, 2 story. S $30-$34; D $38-$46. Crib $4. TV; cable. Continental bkfst. Restau-

rant nearby. Ck-out 11 am. Cr cds: A, D, DS, MC, V.
D 🐾 ⟶ 🔥

Restaurant

★ **CRONK'S.** *812 4th Ave S (51442). 712/263-4191.* Hrs: 6 am-10 pm; Fri, Sat to 11 pm. Closed Dec 25. Res accepted. Bar to midnight. Bkfst $1.95-$4.95, lunch $1.95-$5.95, dinner $1.95-$9.95. Specializes in steak. Salad bar. Casual decor. Cr cds: A, C, D, MC, V.
D SC ⟶

Des Moines

(D-4) *See also Indianola*

Founded 1843 **Pop** 193,187 **Elev** 803 ft **Area code** 515
Information Greater Des Moines Convention & Visitors Bureau, 40 S Sixth Ave, Suite 201, 50309; 515/286-4960 or 800/451-2625
Web www.desmoinesia.com

Des Moines (De-MOYN) is the capital and largest city in the state. This metropolis is the industrial, retail, financial, and political hub of Iowa. A military garrison established Fort Des Moines at a point on the Raccoon and Des Moines rivers in 1843. Two years later the territory was opened to settlers, and the town of Fort Des Moines was chosen as the county seat. The word "fort" was abandoned when the community became a city in 1857; the next year it became the state capital. Today more than 60 insurance companies have their home offices here.

Additional Visitor Information

The Greater Des Moines Convention & Visitors Bureau, Two Ruan Center, Suite 222, 601 Locust St, 50309, has tourist guidebooks, maps, and brochures, as well as a guide to events; phone 515/286-4960 or 800/451-2625. There is a visitor information center located at the Des Moines International Airport, Fleur

Dr, phone 515/287-4396 (Mon-Fri, Sun).

Transportation

Car Rental Agencies. See IMPORTANT TOLL-FREE NUMBERS.

Public Transportation. Buses (Metropolitan Transit Authority), phone 515/283-8100.

Airport Information

Des Moines International Airport. Information 515/256-5100; lost and found 515/256-5000; weather 515/270-2614; cash machines, Terminal Building.

What to See and Do

Adventureland Park. Amusement park with more than 100 rides, shows, and attractions. Features the Dragon, Spaceshot double-looping, Tornado, and Outlaw roller coasters; Raging River, whitewater rapids; live musical entertainment. (June-Aug,

daily; May and Sept, wkends) 5091 NE 56th St. Phone 515/266-2121. ¢¢¢¢

Blank Park Zoo. Animal and bird areas designed for close viewing; Australian and African walk-through displays; farm animal contact area; camel rides and Old West train ride; concession. (May-mid-Oct, daily) 7401 SW 9th St. Phone 515/285-4722. ¢¢

Civic Center. Varied musical and theatrical entertainment, symphony concerts, and ballet performances all yr. Free tours by appt. 221 Walnut St. Phone 515/243-1120.

Des Moines Art Center. Exhibits of 19th- and 20th-century paintings and sculptures in striking contemporary building; original buildings by Eliel Saarinen, additions by Meier and Pei; changing exhibits; library, museum shop, restaurant. (Tues-Sun; closed Jan 1, Dec 25, Dec 31) 4700 Grand Ave, in Greenwood Park. Phone 515/277-4405. **FREE**

Des Moines Botanical Center. Displays of nearly 1,500 species from all over the world; seasonal floral displays. (Daily; closed hols) 909 E River Dr. Phone 515/323-8900. ¢

Drake University. (1881) 6,500 students. Six colleges and schools. Many buildings designed by distinguished architects, incl Eliel and Eero Saarinen; Harry Weese & Associates; Brooks, Borg & Skiles; Ludwig Mies van der Rohe. Campus tours. (See SPECIAL EVENTS) 2507 University Ave. Phone 515/271-2011.

Francesca's House. (1870) Victorian farmhouse used in the film *The Bridges of Madison County*. (May-Oct, daily) I-35 S to exit 65, 3 mi W. Phone 515/981-5268. ¢¢

Heritage Village. Century-old barn, exposition hall (1886) with display of early farm machinery; authentically furnished country school; replicas of 1834 church, Fort Madison blockhouse, turn-of-the-century pharmacy, general store, telephone building, totem pole; state fair museum, barber shop, and railroad station. Tours (mid-Apr to mid-Oct, by appt), State Fairgrounds, 12 blks E of I-235 on E University. Phone 515/262-3111. ¢

Hoyt Sherman Place. (1877) Once home of General Sherman's brother. Now features the city's oldest art gallery, incl artifacts, antique furniture, and art collection. Tours (by appt; fee). Theater (1,400 seats) added in 1922. (Mon-Fri) 1501 Woodland Ave. Phone 515/244-0507.

Iowa Historical Building. Modern cultural center houses state historical museum; displays portray Iowa history and heritage. Library contains county, state, and family history materials, rare books and manuscripts about Iowa, census records and newspapers. Museum (Tues-Sun). 600 E Locust, Capitol Complex. Phone 515/281-5111. **FREE**

★ **Living History Farms.** Complex has four farms and town on 600 acres: Native American settlement of 1700 incl gardens, shelters, crafts of Ioway tribe; pioneer farm of 1850 features log cabin and outbuildings, demonstrations of early farming methods; horse-powered farm of 1900 depicts farm and household chores typical of period; crop center emphasizes modern agriculture and crops. The 1875 town of Walnut Hill incl Victorian mansion; schoolhouse; pottery, blacksmith, and carpentry shops; veterinary infirmary; church, law, bank, newspaper, and doctor's offices; general store. (May-late Oct, daily) 2600 NW 111th St, Urbandale, W via I-35, I-80 exit 125, to Hickman Rd (US 6). Phone 515/278-5286. ¢¢¢

Polk County Heritage Gallery. Formerly the city's main post office (1908), the building's lobby was restored to its original Beaux Arts classical architecture. The gallery houses changing art exhibits and historical material, incl brass writing desks and gas lamps. (Mon-Fri; closed between exhibits) 2nd Ave and Walnut. Phone 515/286-3215. **FREE**

Prairie Meadows Racetrack & Casino. Live thoroughbred, quarter horse, and harness racing (May-Aug); simulcasts of thoroughbred and greyhound racing (daily); 24-hr casino with over 1,000 slots (daily). 10 mi E on I-80, exit 142. Phone 800/325-9015. **FREE**

Salisbury House. A 42-rm replica of King's House in Salisbury, England, on 11 acres of woodland. Houses authentic furnishings of Tudor age; classic paintings and sculpture; tapestries; 80 Oriental rugs; stained-glass windows; huge fireplaces; collector's library contains a leaf from the Gutenberg Bible. Guided tours only. 4025 Tonawanda. Phone 515/274-1777. ¢¢

Science Center of Iowa. Natural and physical science exhibits, live demonstrations; Digistar planetarium shows; laser shows (addl fee). (Daily; closed Thanksgiving, Dec 25) 4500 Grand Ave, in Greenwood Park. Phone 515/274-4138. ¢¢¢

State Capitol. (1871) Towering central dome covered with 23-carat gold leaf; four smaller domes have golden seam marks. State offices and Supreme Court on first floor. House and Senate chamber, law library on second floor. Paintings, mosaics, collection of war flags. Building (daily). Call for tour times Mon-Sat. E 9th St and Grand Ave. Phone 515/281-5591. **FREE**

★ **Terrace Hill.** (1869) Extravagant Italianate/Second Empire mansion, now residence of Iowa governors, is situated on commanding knoll above downtown. Restored house is out-

Living History Farms

standing example of Victorian residential architecture. Tours incl first and second floors, carriage house, and gardens. (Open Tues-Sat 10-1:30; closed hols, also Jan) 2300 Grand Ave. Phone 515/281-3604. ¢¢

White Water University. Water park featuring wave pool, slides, tubing, hot tub; children's pool; picnicking, refreshments. (Memorial Day-Labor Day, daily) Miniature golf, go-karts (also open wkends spring and fall; addl fee). 5401 E University, E on I-235, then 3½ mi E on E University. Phone 515/265-4904. ¢¢¢¢

Special Events

Drake Relays. Drake University. One of the most prestigious intercollegiate track and field events in the country; more than 5,000 athletes compete. Phone 515/271-3647. Apr 28-29.

Iowa State Fair. Fairgrounds, E 30th and University Ave. One of the oldest and largest in country; incl 20 acres of farm machinery, fine arts, giant midway, grandstand stage and track events, free entertainment, exhibits, demonstrations, contests; camping. Phone 515/262-3111. Aug 8-18.

Doors to the Past. Walking tour of six-ten historic houses in Sherman Hill area. Phone 515/284-5717. Last two wkends Sept.

Motels/Motor Lodges

★★★ **ADVENTURE-LAND INN.** *I-80 and Hwy 65, Altoona (50316). 515/265-7321; fax 515/265-3506; res 800/910-5382. www.adventureland-usa. com.* 130 rms, 2 story. June-Aug: S $70-$90; D $80-$100; each addl $5; suites $140-$155; under 12 free; lower rates rest of yr. Crib free. TV; cable (premium). Indoor pool; poolside serv. Playground. Restaurant 6:30 am-9 pm. Bar 4 pm-midnight; entertainment. Ck-out 11 am. Meeting rms. Business servs avail. Sundries. Gift shop. Game rm. Some private patios, balconies. Amusement park adj. Cr cds: A, C, D, DS, MC, V.
D ⊠ ⊠ 🔥 🎿

★★ **BEST INN.** *5050 Merle Hay Rd, Johnston (50131). 515/270-1111; res 800/237-8466. www.bestinn.com.* 92 rms, 2 story, 14 suites. S $49.88; D $52.88-$62.88; each addl $10; suites $67-$77; under 18 free. Crib free. Pet accepted. TV; cable (premium), VCR avail (movies $3). Indoor pool; whirlpool. Complimentary continental bkfst. Ck-out 1 pm. Meeting rms. Business servs avail. Health club privileges. Microwaves avail. Cr cds: A, C, D, DS, MC, V.
D 🐾 ⊠ ⊠ 🎿 SC

★★ **BEST WESTERN INN.** *133 SE Delaware Ave, Ankeny (50021). 515/964-1717; fax 515/964-8781; toll-free 800/528-1234. www.bestwestern.com.* 116 rms, 2 story. June-Aug: S $48-$53; D $53-$62; each addl $5; kits. $120; under 12 free; wkly rates; lower rates rest of yr. Crib $3. Pet accepted, some restrictions. TV; cable. Indoor pool; whirlpool. Restaurant 6 am-10 pm. Bar 1 pm-2 am; Sun to 10 pm. Meeting rms. Business servs avail. Sundries. Microwaves avail. Cr cds: A, D, DS, MC, V.

★ **COMFORT INN SOUTH.** *5231 Fleur Dr (50321). 515/287-3434. www. comfortinn.com.* 55 rms, 3 story, 16 suites. No elvtr. May-Aug: S $49-$64; D $59-$79; each addl $5; suites $59-$95; under 18 free; higher rates special events; lower rates rest of yr. Pet accepted, some restrictions. TV; cable (premium). Indoor pool; whirlpool. Complimentary continental bkfst. Restaurant nearby. Ck-out 11 am. Meeting rm. Business servs avail. In-rm modem link. Sundries. Free airport transportation. Refrigerator in suites. Cr cds: A, D, DS, MC, V.

★★ **COMFORT SUITES LIVING.** *11167 Hickman Rd, Urbandale (50322). 515/276-1126; fax 515/276-8969; toll-free 800/395-7675. www. hoari.com.* 101 rms, 2 story. S $79-$169; D $89-$179; each addl $10; under 18 free; higher rates special events. Crib free. TV; cable (premium). Heated pool; whirlpool. Complimentary continental bkfst, coffee in rms. Restaurant adj 6 am-10 pm. Bar. Ck-out noon. Meeting rms. Business servs avail. Bellhops. Sundries. Exercise equipt. Game rm. Refrigerators. Living History Farms adj. Cr cds: A, MC, V.

★★ **FAIRFIELD INN.** *1600 114th St, Clive (50325). 515/226-1600. www. fairfieldinn.com.* 135 rms, 3 story. S, D $39-$75; each addl $7; under 18 free. Crib free. TV; cable (premium). Pool. Complimentary continental bkfst. Restaurant nearby. Ck-out noon. Business servs avail. Health club privileges. Cr cds: A, D, DS, MC, V.

★★ **FOUR POINTS BY SHERA-TON.** *1810 Army Post Rd (50321). 515/287-6464; fax 515/287-5818. www.fourpoints.com.* 145 rms. S $62; D $72; each addl $5; suites $99; under 17 free. Crib free. Pet accepted. TV; cable, VCR avail (movies). Indoor pool; poolside serv. Complimentary continental bkfst. Restaurant 11 am-2 pm, 5-9 pm. Bar 4 pm-1 am. Ck-out noon. Coin lndry. Meeting rms. Business servs avail. Bellhops. Valet serv. Free airport transportation. Cr cds: A, D, DS, MC, V.

★★ **FOUR POINTS BY SHERA-TON.** *11040 Hickman Rd and I-80 (50325). 515/278-5575; fax 515/278-4078. www.fourpoints.com.* 157 rms, 6 story. S $99; D $109; each addl $5; under 17 free. Crib free. TV; cable (premium). Indoor pool; wading pool, whirlpool. Coffee in rms. Restaurant 6:30 am-2 pm, 5-10 pm. Bar 4 pm-midnight. Ck-out noon. Coin lndry. Meeting rms. Business servs avail. In-rm modem link. Valet serv. Exercise equipt; sauna. Health club privileges. Cr cds: A, C, D, DS, MC, V.

★★ **HAMPTON INN.** *5001 Fleur Dr (50321). 515/287-7300; fax 515/287-6343. www.hamptoninn.com.* 122 rms, 4 story. S $64; D $74; under 18 free. Crib free. TV; cable. Pool. Complimentary continental bkfst. Restaurant nearby. Ck-out 11 am. Meeting rm. Business servs avail. In-rm modem link. Bellhops. Valet serv. Sundries. Free airport transportation. Exercise equipt. Cr cds: A, C, D, DS, JCB, MC, V.

★ **HEARTLAND INN.** *11414 Forest Ave (50325). 515/226-0414; fax 515/226-9769; toll-free 800/334-3277. www.heartlandinns.com.* 87 rms, 2 story. S $70; D $77; each addl $5; under 16 free. Crib free. Pet accepted, some restrictions; $10. TV; cable (premium). Complimentary continental bkfst. Restaurant nearby. Ck-out 11 am. Business servs avail. Sauna. Health club privileges. Whirlpool. Microwaves avail. Cr cds: A, C, D, DS, MC, V.

★★ **HOLIDAY INN AIRPORT & CONFERENCE CENTER.** *6111 Fleur Dr (50321). 515/287-2400; fax 515/287-4811; toll-free 800/248-4013. www. holiday-inn.com.* 227 rms, 3 story. S, D $99. TV; cable (premium), VCR avail. Indoor pool; whirlpool. Restaurant 6 am-10 pm. Bar 11-1 am. Ck-out noon. Meeting rms. Business center. In-rm modem link. Bellhops. Valet serv. Sundries. Free airport transportation. Indoor putting green. Exercise equipt; sauna. Microwaves avail. Cr cds: A, C, D, DS, MC, V.

★★ **HOLIDAY INN EXPRESS AT DRAKE.** *1140 24th St (50311). 515/ 255-4000; fax 515/255-1192. www. hiexpress.com.* 52 rms, 2 story. S, D $59-$79; each addl $5; under 19 free. Crib free. TV; cable (premium). Complimentary continental bkfst. Restaurant adj 7 am-11 pm; Sun to 10 pm. Ck-out noon. Meeting rms. Business servs avail. Sundries. Health club privileges. Microwaves avail. Cr cds: A, D, DS, MC, V.

★ **MOTEL 6.** *3225 Adventureland Dr, Altoona (50009). 515/967-5252; fax 515/957-8637. www.motel6.com.* 110 rms, 2 story. S $45.50-$57.50; D $62.50-$66.50; suites $80.50; under 14 free. Crib $3. Pet accepted; $6. TV; cable (premium). Indoor pool; whirlpool. Complimentary coffee in lobby. Restaurant adj open 24 hrs. Ck-out 11 am. Meeting rm. Business servs avail. Cr cds: A, D, DS, MC, V.

★ **QUALITY INN & SUITES.** *4995 Merle Hay Rd (50322). 515/278-2381; fax 515/278-9760. www.qualityinn. com.* 120 rms, 2 story. S, D $59-$159; each addl $6; suites $90-$225; under 18 free. Crib free. TV; cable (premium). Indoor/outdoor pool; whirlpool. Complimentary continental bkfst. Bar. Ck-out noon. Coin lndry. Meeting rms. Business servs avail. Sauna. Microwave in suites. Cr cds: A, C, D, DS, ER, JCB, MC, V.

★★ **RAMADA INN AT MERLE HAY.** *5055 Merle Hay Rd, Johnston (50131). 515/276-5411; fax 515/276-0696. www.ramada.com.* 146 rms. S $50-$80; D $59-$90; suites $129-$159; under 16 free. Crib $5. Pet accepted; $40 ($30 refundable). TV; cable (premium). Indoor pool; whirlpool. Complimentary coffee in rms. Restaurant 6:30 am-11 pm. Bar. Ck-out noon. Meeting rms. Business servs avail. Bellhops. Free airport, bus depot transportation. Microwaves avail. Cr cds: A, D, DS, ER, MC, V.

★★ **RAMADA INN WEST DES MOINES.** *3530 Westown Pkwy, West Des Moines (50266). 515/225-1144; fax 515/225-6463; toll-free 800/272-6232. www.ramada.com.* 100 rms, 2 story. S $50; D $55; each addl $5; suites $75-$150; under 12 free. Crib $6. TV; cable (premium). Indoor/outdoor pool; whirlpool. Complimentary continental bkfst. Coffee in rms. Restaurant 11 am-11 pm; Fri 11 am-midnight; Sat 9 pm-midnight. Bar 4 pm-midnight. Ck-out 11 am. Meeting rms. Business servs avail. Sundries. Exercise equipt; sauna. Health club privileges. Refrigerators; microwaves avail. Balconies. Cr cds: A, C, D, DS, JCB, MC, V.

★ **TRAVELODGE.** *5626 Douglas Ave (50310). 515/278-1601; fax 515/278-9816; toll-free 800/578-7878. www. travelodge.com.* 48 rms, 2 story. S $31.95-$52; D $35.95-$60; each addl $5; under 18 free. Crib free. TV; cable (premium). Complimentary continental bkfst. Restaurant nearby. Ck-out 11 am. Business servs avail. Microwaves avail. Cr cds: A, C, D, DS, ER, JCB, MC, V.

Hotels

★★ **HOLIDAY INN DOWNTOWN.** *1050 6th Ave (50314). 515/283-0151; toll-free 800/465-4329. www. holiday-inn.com.* 253 rms, 12 story. S, D $89; each addl $10; suites $225; under 19 free. Crib free. TV; cable (premium), VCR avail. Indoor pool. Restaurant 6 am-2 pm, 5-10 pm. Bar noon-2 am. Meeting rms. Business servs avail. Gift shop. Airport transportation. Cr cds: A, D, DS, MC, V.

★★★ **HOTEL FORT DES MOINES.** *1000 Walnut St (50309). 515/243-1161; fax 515/243-4317; toll-free 800/532-1466. www.hotelfortdes moines.com.* 242 rms, 11 story, 56 suites. S, D $109-$119; suites $75-$250; under 18 free; wkend rates. Pet accepted. TV; cable. Pool; whirlpool. Restaurant 6:30 am-10:30 pm. Bar 11-2 am. Ck-out noon. Meeting rms.

In-rm modem link. Gift shop. Free airport transportation. Exercise equipt. Refrigerator in some suites. Cr cds: A, C, D, DS, MC, V.

★ **KIRKWOOD CIVIC CENTER HOTEL.** *400 Walnut St (50309). 515/244-9191; fax 515/282-7004; toll-free 800/798-9191.* 150 rms, 12 story. S, D $54-$79; suites $99-$200; under 14 free. Crib free. TV; cable. Restaurant 6 am-2 pm. Ck-out noon. Health club privileges. Some in-rm whirlpools. Cr cds: A, D, DS, MC, V.

★★★ **MARRIOTT DES MOINES.** *700 Grand Ave (50309). 515/245-5500; fax 515/245-5567. www.marriott.com.* 415 rms, 33 story. S, D $70-$140; suites $125-$600; under 18 free; wkend rates. Crib free. Pet accepted, some restrictions. Covered parking $10/day, valet $10/day. TV; cable (premium), VCR avail. Indoor pool; whirlpool, poolside serv. Restaurants 6:30 am-11 pm. Bar. Ck-out noon. Convention facilities. Business servs avail. Free airport transportation. Barber, beauty shop. Exercise equipt; sauna. Some bathrm phones. Luxury level. Cr cds: A, C, D, DS, MC, V.

★★★ **MARRIOTT WEST DES MOINES.** *1250 74th Ave, West Des Moines (50266). 515/267-1500. www.marriott.com.* 219 rms, 9 story. S, D $150-$225; each addl $20; under 17 free. Crib avail. Pet accepted. Indoor pool. TV; cable (premium), VCR avail. Complimentary coffee, newspaper in rms. Restaurant 6 am-10 pm. Ck-out noon. Meeting rms. Business center. Gift shop. Exercise rm. Some refrigerators, minibars. Cr cds: A, C, D, DS, ER, JCB, MC, V.

★★ **SAVERY HOTEL AND SPA.** *401 Locust St (50309). 515/244-2151; fax 515/244-1408; toll-free 800/798-2151. www.shanerhotel.com.* 221 units, 12 story, 20 kits. S, D $95-$125; each addl $10; suites $225-$500. Crib $10. Pet accepted, some restrictions. TV; cable. Indoor pool; whirlpool. Restaurants 6:30 am-2 pm, 5-10 pm. Rm serv 6:30 am-10 pm. Bar 2 pm-12 am; entertainment. Ck-out noon. Meeting rms. Beauty shop. Free air-

port, bus depot transportation. Valet parking. Exercise equipt; sauna. Built 1919. Cr cds: A, C, D, DS, ER, MC, V.

★★ **WILDWOOD LODGE.** *11431 Forest Ave, Clive (50325). 515/222-9876; res 800/728-1223.* 104 rms, 3 story. S $80-$100; D $90-$110. Crib free. TV; cable (premium), VCR avail. Indoor pool; whirlpool. Complimentary continental bkfst. Restaurant nearby. Bar 10 am-11 pm. Ck-out noon. Meeting rms. Business servs avail. In-rm modem link. Gift shop. Exercise equipt. Microwaves avail. Cr cds: A, D, DS, ER, JCB, MC, V.

All Suite

★★ **EMBASSY SUITES.** *101 E Locust St (50309). 515/244-1700; fax 515/244-2537; toll-free 800/362-2779. www.embassysuites.com.* 234 suites, 8 story. S, D $159; each addl $15; under 18 free; special wkend plans. Crib free. Parking $3; garage $7. TV; cable (premium), VCR avail. Indoor pool; whirlpool. Complimentary full bkfst, coffee in rms. Restaurant 11 am-2 pm, 5-10 pm. Rm serv to midnight. Bar to 2 am; entertainment. Ck-out noon. Coin lndry. Meeting rms. Business servs avail. Gift shop. Free airport, bus depot transportation. Exercise equipt; sauna. Refrigerators, microwaves, wet bars. Cr cds: A, C, D, DS, MC, V.

Extended Stay

★★ **CHASE SUITES HOTEL.** *11428 Forest Ave, Clive (50325). 515/223-7700; fax 515/223-7222; toll-free 888/433-6140. www.woodfinsuitehotels.com/chase.* 112 kit. suites, 2 story. S $74-$99; D $84-$110; wkly, monthly rates. Crib free. Pet accepted; $50. TV; cable (premium). Pool; whirlpool. Complimentary continental bkfst, coffee in rms. Restaurant nearby. Ck-out noon. Coin lndry. Meeting rms. Business servs avail. In-rm modem link. Valet serv. Sundries. Exercise equipt. Health club privileges. Microwaves. Balconies. Picnic tables, grills. Cr cds: A, C, D, DS, JCB, MC, V.

Restaurants

★★★ **BRIX.** *2249 NW 86th St, Clive (50325). 515/251-6867. www.brix restaurant.com.* Specializes in brix filet, honey herb pork, seafood manicotti. Hrs: 5-10 pm. Closed Sun. Res accepted. Wine, beer. Dinner $13-$25. Children's menu. Entertainment. Cr cds: A, D, DS, MC, V.
D ⊟

★★ **CHINA PALACE.** *2800 University Ave, West Des Moines (50266). 515/225-2800.* Hrs: 11:30 am-10 pm; Fri, Sat to 11 pm; Sun brunch to 2:30 pm. Res accepted. Chinese menu. Bar. A la carte entrees: lunch $4.25-$6, dinner $5.95-$12.95. Sun brunch $10.95. Specializes in Szechwan, Mandarin, Hunan dishes. Parking. Formal atmosphere. Cr cds: A, C, D, DS, MC, V.
D ⊟

★★ **CHINA WOK.** *1960 Grand Ave, Suite 23, West Des Moines (50265). 515/223-8408.* Hrs: 11:30 am-10 pm; Fri, Sat to 11 pm; Sun brunch 11 am-2:30 pm. Closed Thanksgiving. Res accepted. Chinese menu. Bar. Lunch $3.85-$5.95, dinner $6.95-$13.95. Sun brunch $8.95. Specialties: China Wok delicacy, Neptune catch in a bird's nest, General Tso's chicken. Parking. Dining rm features Asian art, figurines, fans, porcelain. Cr cds: A, D, DS, MC, V.
D ⊟

★★★ **CHRISTOPHER'S.** *2816 Beaver Ave (50310). 515/274-3694.* Hrs: 5-10:30 pm; Fri, Sat to 11:30 pm. Closed Sun; hols. Res accepted. Italian, American menu. Bar 3 pm-2 am; Sat from 2 pm. Dinner $7-$18.95. Children's menu. Specializes in prime rib, steak, seafood. Own pasta. Parking. Family-owned. Cr cds: A, D, DS, MC, V.
D ⊟

★★★ **GREENBRIER.** *5810 Merle Hay Rd, Johnston (50131). 515/253-0124.* Hrs: 11:30 am-2 pm, 5-9:30 pm; Fri to 10:30 pm; Sat 5-10:30 pm; early-bird dinner Mon-Thurs 5-6:30 pm. Closed Sun; hols. Lunch $4.95-$7.95, dinner $8.95-$19.95. Children's menu. Specializes in prime rib, rack of lamb, fresh seafood. Patio dining. Cr cds: A, DS, MC, V.
D ⊟

★ **HOUSE OF HUNAN.** *6810 Douglas Ave (50322). 515/276-5556.* Hrs: 11:30 am-10 pm; Fri, Sat to 11 pm. Res accepted wkends. Chinese menu. Bar. A la carte entrees: lunch $3.95-$5.95, dinner $5.50-$11.95. Buffet: lunch (Sun) $8.95. Parking. Asian decor. Cr cds: A, C, D, DS, MC, V.
D SC ⊟

★ **JESSE'S EMBERS.** *3301 Ingersoll (50312). 515/255-6011. www.jesses embers.com.* Hrs: 11:30 am-2 pm, 5-10:30 pm; Sat 5-11 pm. Closed Sun; hols. Bar. Lunch $4.50-$11.95, dinner $6.95-$34. Specializes in steak, seafood, ribs. Parking. Family-owned. Cr cds: A, MC, V.
⊟

★ **THE MACHINE SHED.** *11151 Hickman Rd, Urbandale (50322). 515/270-6818. www.hoari.com.* Hrs: 6 am-10 pm; Sun 7 am-9 pm. Closed hols. Bar. Complete meals: bkfst $3.25-$7.50, lunch $4.95-$11.95, dinner $6.99-$20. Children's menu. Specialties: roast pork loin, stuffed pork chops, barbecued ribs. Parking. Family atmosphere. Farm implements on display. Cr cds: A, DS, MC, V.
D ⊟

★ **MAXIE'S.** *1311 Grand Ave, West Des Moines (50265). 515/223-1463.* Hrs: 11 am-2 pm, 5-10 pm; Mon-Fri, Sat 5-11 pm. Closed Sun; hols. Res accepted. Bar. Lunch $5-$8, dinner $7-$25. Children's menu. Specializes in chicken, ribs, steak. Parking. Cr cds: A, C, D, DS, ER, MC, V.
D ⊟

★ **NACHO MAMMAS.** *216 Court Ave (50309). 515/280-6262.* Hrs: 11 am-10 pm; Fri, Sat to 11 pm; Sun noon-9 pm. Closed hols. Res accepted. Mexican, Southwestern menu. Bar. Lunch $3.95-$6.50, dinner $6.99-$10.99. Children's menu. Specializes in tortillas. Sidewalk patio dining. Cr cds: A, D, DS, MC, V.
D ⊟

★ **OHANA STEAKHOUSE.** *2900 University Ave, West Des Moines (50266). 515/225-3325.* Hrs: 5-9 pm; Fri, Sat to 10:30 pm. Closed Mon;

some hols. Res accepted. Japanese menu. Bar. Complete meals: dinner $10-$16.50. Children's menu. Specializes in chicken, steak, seafood. Tableside preparation. Japanese rock garden. Cr cds: A, DS, MC, V.
D ⌐

★ **SPAGHETTI WORKS.** *310 Court Ave (50309). 515/243-2195.* Hrs: 11:15 am-10:15 pm; Fri to 11 pm; Sat, Sun from noon. Closed Thanksgiving, Christmas. Italian, American menu. Bar. Lunch $3.29-$6.99, dinner $3.99-$9.95. Children's menu. Specializes in spaghetti. Salad bar. Own sauces. Big band music Mon (fall and winter); comedy Fri, Sat. Outdoor dining. Cr cds: A, MC, V.
D ⌐

★ **A TASTE OF THAILAND.** *215 E Walnut St (50309). 515/243-9521.* Hrs: 11 am-2 pm, 5-9 pm; Fri, Sat to 10 pm. Closed Sun; hols. Res accepted. Thai menu. Wine, beer. Lunch $4.50, dinner $5.50-$11.50. Parking. Specializes in vegetarian dishes. Cr cds: A, C, D, DS, MC, V.
D SC ⌐

★ **WATERFRONT SEAFOOD MARKET.** *2900 University Ave, West Des Moines (50266). 515/223-5106.* Hrs: 11 am-2:30 pm, 5-10 pm; Fri, Sat 11 am-11 pm. Closed Sun; hols. Bar. Lunch $5-$9, dinner $9-$25. Children's menu. Specializes in clam chowder, fresh seafood. Oyster bar. Cr cds: A, DS, MC, V.
D SC ⌐

Dubuque (B-8)

Settled 1833 **Pop** 57,546 **Elev** 650 ft
Area code 319 **Zip** 52001
Information Convention and Visitors Bureau, 770 Town Clock Plaza, PO Box 705, 52004-0705; 319/557-9200 or 800/798-8844
Web www.dubuque.org

Facing both Wisconsin and Illinois across the broad Mississippi River, Dubuque became the first known European settlement in Iowa when Julien Dubuque, a French Canadian, came from Quebec in 1788 and leased land from the Native Americans to mine lead. After his death, Native Americans barred settlement until 1833 when the territory was opened under a treaty with Chief Black Hawk. Once a boisterous river and mining town, Dubuque had the first bank and the first newspaper in what is now Iowa. Dubuque now prospers as a center of more than 300 industries, including publishing, software development, and manufacturing.

What to See and Do

Bellevue State Park. Approx 540 acres on a high bluff; river view. Native American mounds, rugged woodlands. Hiking trails, snowmobiling, picnicking, camping (electricity, dump station). Nature center. Standard hrs, fees. 26 mi S on US 52, 67, near Bellevue. Phone 319/872-3243.

Cathedral Square. Surrounding square are stylized figures of a lead miner, farmer, farmer's wife, priest, and river hand; opposite square is architecturally and historically significant St. Raphael's Cathedral. 2nd and Bluff St.

Clarke College. (1843) 1,000 students. Music performance hall, art gallery, library, and chapel open from 56-ft-high glass atrium plaza. Tours (by appt). 1550 Clarke Dr at W Locust St. Phone 319/588-6318.

Crystal Lake Cave. Network of passageways carved by underground streams; surrounding lake with glittering stalactites and stalagmites. Guided tours (Memorial Day-late Oct, daily; May, Sat and Sun). 3 mi S off US 52. Phone 319/556-6451. ¢¢¢

Diamond Jo Casino. Casino gambling on river. 400 E 3rd St, Ice Harbor. Phone 319/583-7005.

Dubuque Arboretum and Botanical Gardens. Features annual and perennial gardens, rose, water, formal gardens; ornamental trees, woodland and prairie wildflower walk. (Daily) 3800 Arboretum Dr. Phone 319/556-2100. **FREE**

Dubuque County Courthouse. This gold-domed courthouse is on the National Historic Register of Places. Guided tours. (Daily; closed hols) 720 Central Ave. Phone 319/589-4445. **FREE** Adj is

Dubuque Museum of Art/Old County Jail. Museum is housed in a brand-new facility; gallery is an example of Egyptian Revival architechture. (Tues-Fri, also wkend afternoons) 701 Locust St. Phone 319/557-1851.

Eagle Point Park. On a high bluff above the Mississippi, the 164-acre park overlooks three states. A WPA project, the park's Prairie School pavillions and naturalistic landscaping were designed by Alfred Caldwell, who studied under Frank Lloyd Wright. Floral displays. Tennis. Picnicking (shelters), playgrounds. (Mid-May-mid-Oct, daily) Off Shiras Ave, NE corner of city. Phone 319/589-4263. ¢

Fenelon Place Elevator. One of world's shortest, steepest incline railways; connects Fenelon Place with 4th St, providing three-state view. In operation since 1882. (Apr-Nov, daily) 512 Fenelon Place. Phone 319/582-6496. ¢

★ *Field of Dreams* **Movie Site.** Background set of movie *Field of Dreams,* incl baseball diamond. (Daily) Gift shop (Early Apr-early Nov, daily). 25 mi W on US 20, on Lansing Rd in Dyersville. Phone 319/875-2311. **FREE**

Five Flags Theater. (1910) Designed by Rapp and Rapp, premier theater architects of their day, the Five Flags was modeled after Parisian music halls. Tours (by appt). (Daily) Fourth and Main sts. Phone 319/589-4254.

General Zebulon Pike Lock and Dam. Steady stream of barges and other river traffic moves through lock. Can be seen from Eagle Point Park.

Grand Opera House. Century-old opera house offers a variety of entertainment throughout the yr. 135 8th St. Phone 319/588-1305.

Heritage Trail. Trail provides 26 mi of scenic hiking, biking, and x-country skiing on old railroad along rugged Little Maquoketa River valley. Level, surfaced trail crosses from wooded, hilly, "driftless" area to rolling prairie near Dyersville. Self-guided tour identifies railroad landmarks, incl water-powered mill sites. (Daily). 2 mi N on US 52. Phone 319/556-6745. ¢

Iowa Welcome Center. 3rd St, Ice Harbor. Phone 319/556-4372.

Julien Dubuque Monument. Tower built in 1897 at site of Dubuque's mine and the spot where Native Americans buried him in 1810. Provides excellent view of Mississippi River. On 18 acres. ½ mi from end of Julien Dubuque Dr. Phone 319/556-0620.

Loras College. (1839) 1,900 students. Liberal arts. On campus is Heitkamp Planetarium (academic yr, Fri eves; also by appt; free). Wahlert Memorial Library has collection of 2,200 rare books, many printed before 1500. 1450 Alta Vista St. Phone 319/588-7100.

Mathias Ham House Historic Site. (1857) Italianate villa/Victorian mansion (32 rms) with cupola, offering spectacular views of Mississippi River. Built by lead miner Mathias Ham. Also Iowa's oldest log cabin and one-room schoolhouse. (June-Oct, daily) 2241 Shirs Ave, below Eagle Point Park. Phone 319/583-2812. ¢¢

Mines of Spain Recreation Area. This 1,380-acre park features nature trails, limestone quarry, wetlands, prairie. (Daily) 8999 Bellevue Heights. Phone 319/556-0620.

★ **Mississippi River Museum.** Complex of six Dubuque County Historical Society museums, all emphasizing the city's river history. (Daily) Ice Harbor, downtown. Phone 319/557-9545. ¢¢ Two-day pass incl

Boatyard. Exhibits and replicas of small craft that plied the Mississippi; boat building and restoration demonstrations.

Dubuque Heritage Center. Changing exhibits on riverboating and other local history.

National Rivers Hall Of Fame. Museum celebrating nation's river heroes—Samuel Clemens, Lewis and Clark, Robert Fulton, and others.

Paddlewheel Towboat Logsdon. One of the last wooden-hulled paddlewheel towboats on inland waterways; first operated in 1940.

River of Dreams. Interactive film (15 min) on history of Mississippi River. (Daily) Shown in Iowa Welcome Center. Phone 319/556-4372.

Sidewheeler William M. Black. One of the last steam-powered sidewheelers. Tour main deck, boiler and hurricane decks, pilothouse with speaking tubes and brass gauges, and engine rm. (May-Oct only)

Woodward Riverboat Museum. Dramatizes 300 yrs of Mississippi River history: Native Americans, explorers, lead miners, boat builders, and steamboat captains; lead mines; pilothouse and log raft displays. Phone 319/557-9545.

National Farm Toy Museum. A wide array of farm toys are displayed amid agricultural scenes. Theater has ten-min film on "Toys to Treasure." Annual toy show held in early June. (Daily; closed hols) Children five and under admitted free. 1110 16th Ave SE, Dyersville. Phone 319/875-2727. ¢¢

Old Shot Tower. (1856) Tower, 140 ft high, produced three tons of shot daily during Civil War; lead melted on ninth floor was dropped through screens into water at bottom as finished shot. River and Tower sts.

Redstone Inn. (1894) Red sandstone Queen Anne/Victorian mansion built by a prominent Dubuque industrialist as a wedding present for his daughter. Overnight stays avail (see THE REDSTONE INN), restaurant; open all yr. 504 Bluff St. Phone 319/582-1894.

Rustic Hills Carriage Tours. Thirty-min narrated tours; horse-drawn carriage. Sleigh and hay rides. (Daily) 4th and Bluff sts. Phone 319/556-6341. ¢¢

Skiing. Sundown Mountain Ski Area. Five chairlifts, rope tow; patrol, school, rentals; snowmaking; cafeteria, concession, bar. Twenty-one runs; longest run ½ mi; vertical drop 475 ft. (Late Nov-mid-Mar, daily; closed Dec 25) 17017 Asbury Rd. Phone 319/556-6676. ¢¢¢¢

Spirit of Dubuque. Sightseeing and dinner cruises (1½-hr) on Mississippi River aboard paddlewheeler (May-Oct). 3rd St, Ice Harbor, in the Port of Dubuque. Phone 319/583-8093. ¢¢¢¢

Storybook Hill Children's Zoo. Recreation area and petting zoo; playground; concession; train ride. (Memorial Day-Labor Day, daily) N Cascade Rd (Fremont Rd extension). Phone 319/588-2195.

Trolleys of Dubuque, Inc. One-hr narrated tours explore history of town, offer panoramic views of Dubuque, Mississippi River, Wisconsin, and Illinois. (Apr-Oct, daily) Depart from Iowa Welcome Center, 3rd St, Ice Harbor. Phone 319/582-0077. ¢¢¢

University of Dubuque. (1852) 1,200 students. Liberal arts; theological seminary. Historic Alumni Hall (1907), a replica of a 15th-century English structure, features changing art exhibits; Blades Hall has impressive stained-glass windows; Steffens Arcade serves as doorway to the campus. Carillon on campus plays concerts. Tours (Mon-Fri, by appt). 2000 University Ave. Phone 319/589-3000.

Special Events

Mighty Summer Farm Toy Show. Antique tractors and farm machinery; city-wide garage sales; indoor/outdoor farm toy show. Phone 319/875-2311. Early June.

Dubuque Catfish Festival. Catfish tournament; carnival; music; craft show; food and entertainment. Phone 319/583-8535. Late June.

Music on the March. Midwest drum and bugle corps competition. Ten corps; youth competition. Phone 319/582-4872. July.

Dubuque County Fair. Dubuque County Fairgrounds. Phone 319/588-1406. Late July.

Motels/Motor Lodges

★★ **BEST WESTERN INN.** *3434 Dodge St (US 20 W) (52003). 319/556-7760; fax 319/556-4003; toll-free 800/747-7760. www.bestwestern.com.* 153 rms, 3 story. S, D $79-$99; each addl $5; suites $125-$199; under 18 free; package plans. Crib free. TV; cable (premium). Indoor pool; whirlpool. Complimentary coffee in rms. Restaurant 6 am-2 pm, 4:30-10 pm. Bar. Ck-out 11 am. Meeting rms. Business servs avail. In-rm modem link. Valet serv. Free airport transportation. Downhill/x-country ski 5 mi. Game rm. Sauna. Some refrigerators, microwaves. Cr cds: A, C, D, DS, JCB, MC, V.

★★ **BEST WESTERN MIDWAY HOTEL.** *3100 Dodge St (52003). 319/556-7760; fax 319/557-7692; res 800/336-4392. www.midwayhotels. com.* 149 rms, 4 story. June-Oct: S $79; D $95; each addl $5; suites $125-$150; under 18 free; wkend rates; lower rates rest of yr. Crib $3. Pet accepted, some restrictions. TV; cable, VCR (movies). Complimentary bkfst buffet Mon-Fri, coffee in rms. Restaurant 6:30 am-10 pm; Sat from 7 am; Sun 7 am-1 pm, 5-9 pm. Bar 11 am-midnight; wkends to 1 am. Ck-out 1 pm. Meeting rms. Business servs avail. In-rm modem link. Bellhops. Free airport transportation. Exercise equipt; sauna. Indoor pool; whirlpool. Game rm. Refrigerator, wet bar in suites. Picnic tables. Cr cds: A, C, D, DS, JCB, MC, V.

★ **COMFORT INN.** *4055 McDonald Dr (52003). 319/556-3006. www. comfortinn.com.* 52 rms, 3 story, 14 suites. May-Oct: S, D $59-$79; each addl $5; suites $69-$89; under 18 free; lower rates rest of yr. Crib free. Pet accepted. TV; cable (premium). Indoor pool; whirlpool. Complimentary continental bkfst. Ck-out 11 am. Meeting rms. Business servs avail. In-rm modem link. Sundries. Downhill ski 6 mi; x-country ski 5 mi. Refrigerator, microwave in suites. Cr cds: A, D, DS, MC, V.

★ **DAYS INN.** *1111 Dodge St (52003). 319/583-3297; fax 319/583-5900; toll-free 800/772-3297. www.daysinn.com.* 154 rms, 2 story. S $49-$69; D $59-$69; under 18 free. Crib free. Pet accepted. TV; cable (premium), VCR avail. Pool. Complimentary continental bkfst. Restaurant 11 am-10 pm. Bar to midnight. Ck-out 11 am. Meeting rms. Business servs avail. Bellhops. Valet serv. Sundries. Free airport transportation. Exercise equipt. Refrigerators, microwaves in suites. Picnic tables. Cr cds: A, C, D, DS, JCB, MC, V.

★★ **HEARTLAND INN.** *2090 Southpark Ct (52003). 319/556-6555; fax 319/556-0542; toll-free 800/334-3277. www.heartlandinns.com.* 59 rms, 2 story, 6 suites. S $70; D $75; each addl $5; suites $75-$115; under 16 free. Crib free. Pet accepted, some restrictions. TV; cable (premium). Indoor pool. Complimentary continental bkfst. Restaurant nearby. Ck-out 11 am. Business servs avail. In-rm modem link. Downhill ski/x-country ski 12 mi. Exercise equipt. Some microwaves. Cr cds: A, C, D, DS, MC, V.

★★ **HEARTLAND INN.** *4025 McDonald Dr (52003). 319/582-3752; fax 319/582-0113; toll-free 800/334-3277. www.heartlandinns.com.* 88 rms, 2 story. S $70; D $75; each addl $6; under 16 free; ski plans. Crib free. Pet accepted, some restrictions. TV; cable (premium). Whirlpool. Complimentary continental bkfst. Ck-out 11 am. Meeting rm. Business servs avail. Downhill/x-country ski 5 mi. Sauna. Cr cds: A, C, D, DS, MC, V.

★★ **HOLIDAY INN.** *450 Main St (52001). 319/556-2000; fax 319/556-2303; toll-free 800/465-4329. www. khconline.com.* 193 rms, 5 story. May-Oct: S $89-$109; D $99-$119; suites $120-$148; under 18 free; lower rates rest of yr. Crib free. Pet accepted, some restrictions; $75. TV; cable (premium), VCR avail. Indoor pool. Restaurant 6:30 am-10 pm. Bar. Ck-out noon. Meeting rms. Business center. Free airport transportation. Exercise equipt. Some refrigerators, microwaves. Cr cds: A, C, D, DS, MC, V.

★★ **JULIEN INN.** *200 Main St (52004). 319/556-4200; fax 319/582-5023; toll-free 800/798-7098.* 145 rms, 8 story. Apr-Oct: S $24-$59; D $39-$59; each addl $6; suites $75-$125; under 12 free; lower rates rest of yr. Crib free. TV; cable. Complimentary coffee in lobby. Restaurant 7 am-9 pm. Bar 3 pm-2 am. Ck-out 11 am. Meeting rms. Business servs avail. Bellhops. Free airport transportation. Exercise equipt. Cr cds: A, MC, V.

★ **SUPER 8 MOTEL.** *2730 Dodge St; Hwy 20 (52003). 319/582-8898; toll-free 800/800-8000. www.super8.com.* 61 rms, 3 story. No elvtr. S $42-$48; D $50-$57; each addl $4; under 12 free. Crib $3. Pet accepted, some restrictions. TV; cable (premium).

Complimentary continental bkfst. Restaurant nearby. Ck-out 11 am. Business servs avail. Downhill ski 7 mi. Cr cds: A, C, D, DS, MC, V.

⊡ ⬛ ⬛ ⬛ ⬛ SC

★★ **TIMMERMAN'S HOTEL & RESORT.** *7777 Timmerman Dr, East Dubuque (61025). 815/747-3181; fax 815/747-6556; toll-free 800/336-3181.* 74 rms, 3 story. S $49-$85; D $64-$85; each addl $5; suites $149; under 18 free. Crib $4. Pet accepted. TV; cable, VCR (movies). Indoor pool; whirlpool. Restaurant 7 am-2 pm. Bar. Ck-out noon. Coin lndry. Meeting rm. Business servs avail. In-rm modem link. Sundries. Downhill ski 10 mi; x-country ski ¼ mi. Sauna. Game rm. Rec rm. Private patios, balconies. Cr cds: A, DS, MC, V.

⊡ ⬛ ⬛ ⬛ ⬛ ⬛ SC

B&B/Small Inn

★★ **THE REDSTONE INN.** *504 Bluff St (52001). 319/582-1894; fax 319/582-1893. www.theredstoneinn. com.* 14 units, 3 story. S, D $70-$195; each addl $10; suites $115-$195. TV; cable. Complimentary continental bkfst. Ck-out noon, ck-in 3 pm. Business servs avail. In-rm modem link. Whirlpool in some rms. Victorian mansion (1894) built by prominent Dubuque industrialist; fireplaces, antiques. Totally nonsmoking. Cr cds: A, DS, MC, V.

⬛ ⬛

Restaurants

★ **MARIO'S.** *1298 Main St (52001). 319/556-9424.* Hrs: 11 am-11 pm; Sun 4-10:30 pm. Closed hols. Res accepted. Italian, American menu. Bar. Lunch $3.25-$7, dinner $3.25-$25.25. Specializes in pasta, pizza, steak. Casual atmosphere, contemporary decor. Cr cds: A, D, MC, V.

⊡ ⬛

★ **YEN CHING.** *926 Main St (52001). 319/556-2574.* Hrs: 11 am-2 pm, 5-9:30 pm. Closed Sun; hols. Res accepted. Mandarin, Hunan menu. Lunch $4.50-$6, dinner $7-$10. Specialties: twice-cooked pork, cashew chicken, Szechuan spicy shrimp. Traditional Chinese decor. Cr cds: A, C, D, DS, MC, V.

⊡ SC ⬛

Emmetsburg

(A-3) *See also Spencer, West Bend*

Settled 1858 **Pop** 3,940 **Elev** 1,234 ft **Area code** 712 **Zip** 50536
Information Chamber of Commerce & Iowa Welcome Center, 1013 Broadway; 712/852-2283

In the Des Moines River valley, flanked by Kearney Park, Emmetsburg is the seat of Palo Alto County. A colony of Irish families built the first settlement here and named the community in honor of Irish patriot Robert Emmet. A statue of Emmet stands in the courthouse square. The town is Dublin, Ireland's official "Sister City."

What to See and Do

Kearney Park. 45 acres on Five Island Lake, which covers 945 acres. Boating, fishing; golf, picknicking. Camping (fee). NW edge of town. Phone 712/852-4030.

Special Event

St. Patrick's Day Celebration. Features a guest member of Irish Parliament. Parade, pageant, cultural exhibits, Irish stew dinner, dances. Phone 712/852-4326. Three days around Mar 17.

Motel/Motor Lodge

★ **BEST VALUE SUBURBAN MOTEL.** *3635 450th Ave (50536). 712/852-2626; fax 712/852-2821; res 800/341-8000. www.bestvalueinn.com.* 41 rms. S $39-$45; D $49-$55; each addl $5. Crib $3. TV; cable. Coffee in lobby. Restaurant nearby. Ck-out 11 am. Sundries. Guest lndry. Cr cds: A, MC, V.

⬛ ⬛

B&B/Small Inn

★ **QUEEN MARIE VICTORIAN BED & BREAKFAST.** *707 Harrison St (50536). 712/852-4700; fax 712/852-3090; toll-free 800/238-9485.* 5 rms, 2 share bath. No rm phones. S, D $55. TV; cable (premium). Complimentary full bkfst. Restaurant nearby. Ck-out 11 am, ck-in 3-7 pm. Built 1890 by local lumber baron. Totally non-smoking. Cr cds: DS, MC, V.

Estherville

(A-3) *See also Okoboji, Spirit Lake*

Settled 1857 **Pop** 6,720
Area code 712 **Zip** 51334
Information Chamber of Commerce, PO Box 435; 712/362-3541

What to See and Do

Fort Defiance State Park. Memorial to fort erected during Civil War to protect settlers from attacks by Native Americans. 181 acres; picnic area surrounded by wooded hills, wildflowers. Bridle, hiking trails. Snowmobiling. Picnicking, lodge. Primitive camping. Standard hrs, fees. 1 mi W on IA 9, then 1½ mi S on County N 26. Phone 712/362-2078.

Special Events

Winter Sports Festival. Ice and snow sculptures, skiing, skating; art, quilt shows; dance, concert. Phone 712/362-3541. First wkend Feb.

Sweet Corn Days. Parade, craft show, carnival, street dance. Phone 712/362-3541. Late July-early Aug.

Fairfield

(E-6) *See also Mount Pleasant, Ottumwa*

Settled 1839 **Pop** 9,768 **Elev** 778 ft
Area code 641 **Zip** 52556

What to See and Do

⭐ **Bentonsport-National Historic District.** Preserved 1840s village with 13 original buildings; Mason House Inn (1846) with original furnishings offers lodging and tours (fee); churches, stately brick houses; antique and craftshops; lodging. Canoeing. Special events. Village (Apr-Nov, daily). 20 mi S on IA 1, then 5 mi E on County J40, in Keosauqua. Phone 319/592-3133.

Jefferson County Park. This 175-acre area is mostly oak and hickory timberland, which provides an excellent wildlife habitat; three ponds stocked with bass, bluegill, and catfish. Hiking, bicycle trails. X-country skiing. Picnicking, playground. Camping (fee; electricity addl). ½ mi SW on County H33 (Libertyville Rd). Phone 515/472-4421. **FREE**

Lacey-Keosauqua State Park. Approx 1,500 acres incl Ely's Ford, famous Mormon crossing. Heavily wooded; scenic views; 22-acre lake. Swimming, supervised beach, fishing, boating (ramp, rentals); hiking trails, snowmobiling, picnicking, lodge. Camping (electricity, dump station), cabins. Standard hrs, fees. 23 mi S on IA 1, near Keosauqua. Phone 319/293-3502.

Old Settlers Park. An 11-acre park; Bonnifield Cabin (1838); grave of first settler. B St, N edge of town.

Motels/Motor Lodges

⭐⭐ **BEST WESTERN FAIRFIELD INN.** 2200 W Burlington Ave (52556). 641/472-2200; fax 641/472-7642; toll-free 800/528-1234. www.bestwestern.com. 52 rms, 2 story. S $55-$64; D $63-$72; each addl $8; under 18 free. Crib free. Pet accepted, some restrictions. TV. Indoor pool; whirlpool. Complimentary continental bkfst. Restaurant 11 am-9 pm. Ck-out noon. Meeting rms. Cr cds: A, C, D, DS, ER, JCB, MC, V.

⭐ **ECONOMY INN.** 2701 W Paulington, US 34 W (52556). 641/472-4161. 42 rms, 1-2 story. S $35; D $36-$45; each addl $5; Crib $3. Pet accepted, some restrictions. TV; cable. Restaurant opp 6 am-11 pm. Ck-out 11 am. Meeting rm. Cr cds: A, MC, V.

Fort Dodge

(B-4) *See also Humboldt, Webster City*

Founded 1853 **Pop** 25,894 **Elev** 1,030 ft **Area code** 515 **Zip** 50501

Information Chamber of Commerce, 1406 Central Ave, PO Box T; 515/955-5500 or 800/765-1438

Astride the Des Moines River, atop a gypsum bed that covers nearly 30 square miles and nestled amid fertile farms, Fort Dodge has every ingredient for prosperity. Major industries are veterinary pharmaceuticals, gypsum products, pet food, and aluminum cans.

Fort Dodge was established to protect settlers. Its commander, Major William Williams, was given a large tract of land as part of his compensation, and here the town was laid out. Fort Dodge was an innocent party to a scientific hoax when a huge slab of gypsum cut here was freighted to Chicago and carved into the celebrated Cardiff Giant, falsely claimed to be a petrified prehistoric man (now at the Farmer's Museum, Cooperstown, NY).

What to See and Do

Blanden Memorial Art Museum. American and European paintings and sculpture; Asian paintings and decorative arts; African, Pre-Columbian art, graphic art; photography; changing exhibits. (Tues-Sun) 920 3rd Ave S. Phone 515/573-2316. **FREE**

🔲 **Fort Dodge Historical Museum, Fort Museum and Frontier Village.** Replica of 1862 fort houses museum, trading post, blacksmith shop, general store, log home, drugstore, cabinet shop, newspaper office, church, jail, and one-rm school. A replica of the "Cardiff Giant" is on display at the Fort Museum. (May-Oct, daily; rest of yr, by appt) At jct US 20 Business, Museum Rd. Phone 515/573-4231.

John F. Kennedy Memorial Park. Swimming, fishing, boating (ramp; no motors); picnicking, shelter; "children's forest," playground; golfing. Tent and trailer sites (mid-Apr-Oct; fee). (Daily) 5 mi N on County P56. Phone 515/576-4258. **FREE**

Kalsow Prairie. Approx 160 acres preserving untouched Iowa prairie. 15 mi W on IA 7 to Manson, then 2 mi N on county road.

Site of Old Fort Dodge. Boulder with bronze tablet marks spot where fort stood. 1st Ave N and N 4th St.

State parks.

Dolliver Memorial. This 572-acre park features deep ravines, 75-ft limestone walls, Native American mounds, and scenic overlook. Fishing, boating (ramp); hiking trails, picnicking, camping (electricity, dump station). Cabins, lodges. Standard hrs, fees. 8 mi S on US 169, then 5 mi E on IA 50, then 1 mi N. Phone 515/359-2539.

Twin Lakes. Approx 15 acres adj to N Twin Lake. Swimming, fishing, boating (ramps); picnicking. Standard hrs, fees. 26 mi W on IA 7, then 3 mi S on IA 4, then E on IA 124. Phone 712/657-8712.

Motels/Motor Lodges

★★ **BEST WESTERN STARLITE VILLAGE MOTELS.** *1518 3rd Ave NW (50501). 515/573-7177; fax 515/573-3999; toll-free 800/903-0009. www.bestwestern.com.* 120 rms, 1-2 story. S $40-$46; D $54-$60; each addl $5. TV; cable. Indoor pool; whirlpool, poolside serv. Coffee in rms. Restaurant 6 am-2 pm, 5-10 pm. Ck-out noon. Exercise equipt. Meeting rms. Game rm. Cr cds: A, C, D, DS, MC, V.
🄳 ⇔ 🕱 🖾 🖎 **SC**

★ **COMFORT INN.** *2938 5th Ave S (50501). 515/573-3731; fax 515/573-2820; toll-free 800/228-5150. www.comfortinn.com.* 48 rms, 2 story. S $45-$110; D $47-$110; each addl $6; under 18 free. Crib free. TV; cable. Indoor pool; whirlpool. Complimentary continental bkfst. Restaurant adj open 24 hrs. Ck-out 11 am. Some refrigerators. Cr cds: A, D, DS, JCB, MC, V.
🄳 ⇔ 🖾 🖎 **SC**

★★ **HOLIDAY INN.** *2001 US 169 S (50501). 515/955-3621; fax 515/955-3643. www.holiday-inn.com.* 102 rms, 2 story. S, D $65; under 19 free. Crib free. TV. Heated pool; wading pool. Playground. Restaurant 6 am-10 pm, Sun 7 am-3 pm. Bar 11-1 am; Sun 3-8 pm. Ck-out 1 pm. Meeting rms. Cr cds: A, C, D, DS, JCB, MC, V.
🄳 ⬧ ⇔ 🕱 🖾 🖎

Fort Madison

(F-7) *See also Burlington, Keokuk*

Settled 1808 **Pop** 11,618 **Elev** 536 ft
Area code 319 **Zip** 52627
Information Riverbend Regional Convention & Visitors Bureau, 933 Ave H, PO Box 425; 319/372-5472 or 800/210-8687
Web www.tourriverbend.org

Fort Madison began as the first military outpost (1808-1813) on the upper Mississippi River. Settlers established the town in the early 1830s; steamboats and logging were important early industries. Fort Madison entered an era of prosperity when the Sante Fe Railroad arrived in the 1880s. Today the manufacture of pens and paints is important to the economy. Fort Madison is also home to the state's only maximum-security prison.

What to See and Do

Lee County Courthouse. (1841) Oldest courthouse in continuous use in the state. (Mon-Fri; closed hols) 701 Ave F. Phone 319/372-3523. **FREE**

Riverview Park. Approx 35 landscaped acres. Marina; flower garden; picnicking. Reflecting pool and fountain. (May-Sept, daily) Between river and business section at E end of town. Phone 319/372-7700. ¢¢ Also here is

Old Fort Madison. Full-scale replica of fort that existed from 1808-1813. Complete living history experience incl uniformed soldiers loading and firing muskets. (Memorial Day-Aug, daily; May, Sept, Oct, wkends) Phone 319/372-6318. ¢¢

Rodeo Park. 234 acres. Picnicking, camping (Apr-Oct, fee), nature trails. (Daily) 1 mi N on IA 88. Phone 319/372-7700. **FREE**

Santa Fe Railway Bridge. The largest double-track, double-decked railroad swing-span bridge in the world. E edge of town.

Sante Fe Depot Historic Museum and Complex. Local historical displays, farm machinery, old fire engine; replica of old icehouse;

prison and railroad displays. (Apr-Sept, daily) 9th and Ave H. Phone 319/372-7661.

Shimek State Forest. Park has 7,940 acres with 20-acre lake. Fishing, boating (electric motors only); hunting, hiking, bridle trails. Snowmobiling. Picnicking. Primitive camping. Standard hrs, fees. 25 mi W on IA 2, E of Farmington. Phone 319/878-3811.

Special Event

Tri-State Rodeo. Rodeo Arena, N on County X32, at Old Denmark Rd. Rated one of top ten PRCA rodeos in US. Preceded by wk of festivities. Phone 319/372-2550 or 800/369-3211. Thurs-Sat following Labor Day.

Motel/Motor Lodge

★ **MADISON INN.** 3440 Ave L (52627). 319/372-7740; fax 319/372-1315; toll-free 800/728-7316. www.madisoninnmotel.com. 20 rms. S $44-$47; D $48-$52; each addl $5; higher rates Tri-State Rodeo. Pet accepted, some restrictions; $5. TV; cable (premium). Complimentary coffee in rms. Restaurant adj 6 pm-11 pm. Ck-out 11 am. Business servs avail. In-rm modem link. Cr cds: A, C, D, DS, MC, V.
◻ ⬚ ⬚ ⬚

B&B/Small Inn

★★★ **KINGSLEY INN.** 707 Ave H (52627). 319/372-7074; fax 319/372-7096; toll-free 800/441-2327. www.kingsleyinn.com. 14 rms, 3 story. Apr-Oct: S, D $80-$85; package plans; lower rates rest of yr. Children over 12 yrs. TV; cable (premium). Complimentary full bkfst. Restaurant adj 11 am-11 pm; Fri, Sat to midnight. Ck-out 11 am, ck-in 3 pm. Gift shop. Health club privileges. Microwaves avail. Some balconies. Restored historic building (1860s); antiques. Opp Mississippi River. Cr cds: A, C, D, DS, MC, V.
⬚ ⬚

Garner

(A-4) *See also Clear Lake, Mason City*

Pop 2,916 **Elev** 1,216 ft
Area code 515 **Zip** 50438

What to See and Do

Pilot Knob State Park. Glacial formation rising to one of the highest points in state. More than 700 heavily wooded acres with 15-acre lake. Fishing, boating (electric motors only); bridle and hiking trails, snowmobiling, picnicking. Observation tower. Camping (electricity, dump station). Standard hrs, fees. 3 mi W via US 18, then 10 mi N on US 69, then 6 mi E on IA 9, then 1 mi S on IA 332 near Forest City. Phone 515/581-4835.

Rice Lake State Park. Park has 47 acres on 612-acre lake. Fishing; picnicking. 3 mi W via US 18, then 24 mi NE on US 69, then S on unnumbered road. Phone 515/581-4835.

Grinnell

(D-5) *See also Marshalltown, Newton*

Founded 1854 **Pop** 8,902 **Elev** 1,016 ft **Area code** 515 **Zip** 50112
Information Chamber of Commerce, 1010 Main St, PO Box 538; 515/236-6555

When Horace Greeley said, "Go west, young man, go west and grow up with the country!" he was talking to Josiah Bushnell Grinnell, who took the advice, went west to a bit of prairie between the Iowa and Skunk rivers, and established the town of Grinnell. Today, Grinnell is a thriving college town prospering on the fruits of the surrounding farmland and its more than 20 factories and processing plants.

What to See and Do

Brenton National Bank—Poweshiek County. (1914) The second in the series of "jewel box" banks that architect Louis Henri Sullivan designed late in his career. This unique structure, one of the more important designs in the series, has been restored within the confines of a working bank environment. (Mon-Fri) Downtown, on corner opposite town square.

Grinnell College. (1846) 1,243 students. Considered one of top coeducational, liberal arts colleges in US. Tours (by appt). On US 6, NE of business district. Phone 515/269-3400.

Grinnell Historical Museum. Historical furnishings; relics, documents of J. B. Grinnell and aviator Billy Robinson in late Victorian house. (June-Aug, Tues-Sun afternoons; rest of yr, Sat afternoons) 1125 Broad St. Phone 515/236-3252. **Donation**

Rock Creek State Park. More than 1,260 acres on 602-acre lake. Swimming, fishing, boating (ramp, rentals); hiking trails, snowmobiling, picnicking, camping (electricity, dump station). Standard hrs, fees. 7 mi W on US 6, then 3 mi N on IA 224. Phone 515/236-3722.

Motels/Motor Lodges

★ **DAYS INN MOTEL.** *1902 West St S (50112). 515/236-6710; fax 515/236-5783; toll-free 800/325-2525. www.daysinn.com.* 41 rms, 2 story. S $49; D $65; under 12 free. Pet accepted; $5. TV; cable. Indoor pool. Complimentary continental bkfst. Ck-out 11 am. Cr cds: A, MC, V.

★ **SUPER 8 MOTEL.** *2111 West St S (50112). 515/236-7888; toll-free 800/800-8000. www.super8.com.* 53 rms, 2 story. S $42.88; D $52.88; each addl $3; under 12 free; higher rates: special events, wknds. Crib $4. Pet accepted, some restrictions. TV; cable (premium). Complimentary continental bkfst. Restaurant opp 6:30 am-9 pm. Ck-out 11 am. Cr cds: A, C, D, DS, MC, V.

Restaurant

★★ **KELCY'S FINE FOODS.** *812 6th Ave (50112). 515/236-3132. www.grinnelliowa.com.* Hrs: 11 am-1:30 pm, 5:30-10 pm. Closed Sun; hols. Res accepted. Bar. Lunch $3.20-$5.75, dinner $6.95-$15.95. Children's menu. Specializes in steak, prime rib. Cr cds: DS, MC, V.

D ⊒

Hampton (B-5)

Founded 1856 **Pop** 4,133 **Elev** 1,145 ft **Area code** 641 **Zip** 50441
Information Chamber of Commerce, 5 First St SW; 515/456-5668
Web www.hamptoniowa.org

What to See and Do

Beed's Lake State Park. Park of 319 acres; dam creates 100-acre lake. Swimming, beach, fishing, boating (ramps); hiking, snowmobiling, picnicking. Camping (electricity, dump station). Standard hrs, fees. 3 mi NW near jct US 65, IA 3. Phone 515/456-2047.

Motel/Motor Lodge

★ **GOLD KEY.** *1570 B US 65 N (50441). 641/456-2566; fax 641/456-3622.* 20 rms. S $30-$35; D $39-$44; each addl $4-$7. Crib free. Pet accepted. TV; cable. Sundries. Ck-out 11 am. Cr cds: A, C, DS, MC, V.

D ◗ ⬤ ⚡ ⊠ ▥

Humboldt

(B-3) *See also Fort Dodge*

Pop 4,438 **Elev** 1,089 ft
Area code 515 **Zip** 50548
Information Humboldt/Dakota City Chamber of Commerce, 29 S 5th St, PO Box 247; 515/332-1481

A small religious sect led by the Reverend S. H. Taft came to this site on the West Fork of the Des Moines River and founded the community of Springvale, later renamed Humboldt in honor of the German scientist.

What to See and Do

Frank A. Gotch Park. A 67-acre park at the confluence of the east and west forks of the Des Moines River. Fishing, boating; picnicking, camp-

ing (fee). 3 mi SE off US 169. Phone 515/332-4087.

Humboldt County Historical Museum. Housed in eight buildings; Mill Farm House (1879), a handmade two-story brick house with summer kitchen, enclosed summer porch, Victorian furnishings, doll and toy collections; Red Barn exhibits incl Native American artifacts, farm equipt, tools, carpenter and blacksmith shops, and old-time post office; Willow School (1883), restored as a one-room 1890s schoolhouse. Also an authentically furnished log cabin, kettle shed, jail (ca 1907), and chicken house (ca 1875). (May-Sept, Mon, Tues, Thurs-Sun) E edge of Dakota City, S of IA 3 and County P 56. Phone 515/332-5280. ¢

Joe Sheldon Park. An 81-acre park with camping (fee); fishing, boating (ramp); picnicking. 2 mi W of US 169, S of IA 3. Phone 515/332-4087.

Motel/Motor Lodge

★ **BROADWAY INN MOTEL.** *812 13th St N (50548). 515/332-3545.* 38 rms, 13 with shower only, 2 story. S $36.95; D $28-$40; each addl $2; under 16 free. TV; cable. Complimentary continental bkfst. Restaurant nearby. Ck-out 11 am. Cr cds: A, DS, MC, V.

D ⊠ ▥

Indianola

(D-4) *See also Des Moines, Winterset*

Pop 11,340 **Elev** 970 ft **Area code** 515 **Zip** 50125
Information Chamber of Commerce, 515 N Jefferson, Suite D; 515/961-6269
Web www.cityofindianola.com

What to See and Do

Lake Ahquabi State Park. More than 770 acres with 114-acre lake. Swimming, supervised beach, fishing, boating (ramps, rentals); hiking trail, snowmobiling, picnicking. Lodge. Camping (electricity, dump station). Standard hrs, fees. 5 mi S off US 69. Phone 515/961-7101.

National Balloon Museum. Balloon-ing artifacts and history spanning more than 200 yrs. (Daily; closed hols) N edge of town on US 65/69. Phone 515/961-3714. **FREE**

Simpson College. (1860) 1,700 students. On campus are George Washington Carver Science Building, Dunn Library with historic exhibit, Blank Performing Arts Center, and Amy Robertson Music Center. Tours. N Buxton St and W Clinton Ave. Phone 515/961-6251.

Special Events

Des Moines Metro Opera Summer Festival. Blank Performing Arts Center, Simpson College. Three operas performed in repertory by the Des Moines Metro Opera Company. For schedule, res phone 515/961-6221. Mid-June-mid-July.

National Balloon Classic. 2 mi E on IA 92. Phone 515/961-8415. Late July or early Aug.

Motel/Motor Lodge

★★ **APPLE TREE INN.** *1215 N Jefferson (50125). 515/961-0551; fax 515/961-0555; toll-free 800/961-0551.* 60 rms, 2 story. S $46; D $52; each addl $3; suites $60; under 10 free. Crib $3. TV; cable (premium). Complimentary coffee in lobby. Restaurant adj 6 am-11 pm. Ck-out noon. Meeting rm. Business servs avail. Refrigerator, microwave in suites. Cr cds: A, MC, V.

Iowa City

(D-7) *See also Amana Colonies, Cedar Rapids*

Founded 1839 **Pop** 59,738 **Elev** 698 ft **Area code** 319
Information Iowa City/Coralville Convention & Visitors Bureau, 408 First Ave, Riverview Square, Coralville 52241; 319/337-6592 or 800/283-6592
Web www.icccvb.org

Fondly referred to as "the river city," Iowa City is the home of the University of Iowa and the state's first capi-tal. Founded to become Iowa's terri-torial capital, Iowa City boomed as a backwoods metropolis, with the Ter-ritorial Legislative Assembly meeting here for the first time in 1841. A Doric stone capitol was erected, but with the shift of population the leg-islators moved to Des Moines in 1857. As a conciliatory gesture to Iowa City they selected it as the site of the new university. The "Old Capitol" and ten acres of land were given for use by the university.

The university is the major enter-prise, but the community is also important as one of the top medical centers in the country, the key city of hog, cattle, and grain-raising in Johnson County, and an industrial center.

What to See and Do

Coralville Lake. A 4,900-acre lake; swimming, boating (marinas, ramps), fishing; off-road biking, hunting. Pic-nicking. Improved camping (eight areas, seven with fees). Flooding that occurred during the summer of 1993 eroded a 15-ft-deep channel expos-ing the underlying bedrock. Now called Devonian Fossil Gorge, it offers a rare opportunity to view Iowa's geological past. An Army Corps of Engineers project. (Daily) 3½ mi N of I-80. Phone 319/338-3543.

Herbert Hoover National Historic Site. The 187-acre park incl restored house in which President Hoover was born; Quaker meetinghouse where he worshiped as a boy; school; blacksmith shop; graves of President and Lou Henry Hoover. (Daily; build-ings closed Jan 1, Thanksgiving, Dec 25) 10 mi E on I-80 exit 254 to West Branch. Phone 319/643-2541. ¢ Also in park is

> **Herbert Hoover Presidential Library-Museum.** (1962) Adminis-tered by the National Archives and Records Administration. Features a museum with re-created historic settings in China, Belgium, Wash-ington, and other places promi-nent in Hoover's 50 yrs of public service. Changing exhibits, film. Research library (by appt). (Daily; closed Jan 1, Thanksgiving, Dec 25) Phone 319/643-5301. ¢

Iowa Children's Museum. Interactive exhibits for the young and young at heart. (Daily) I-80 exit 240, Coralville, 52241. Phone 319/625-5500. ¢¢

✪ Kalona Historical Village. Amish traditions and lifestyle are preserved in village containing the Wahl Museum, the Mennonite Museum and Archives, and an implement building; restored 110-yr-old depot, log house (1842), one-room school, country store, outdoor bake oven, Victorian house, working windmill, post office (1880), and church (1869). (Mon-Sat) Approx 18 mi SW via IA 1 in Kalona. Phone 319/656-3232. ¢¢

Lake Macbride State Park. More than 2,150 acres with 812-acre lake. Swimming, bathhouse, supervised beach, fishing, boating (ramps, rentals); hiking, snowmobile trails. Picnicking, concession. Improved and primitive camping (electricity, dump station; fee). Standard hrs, fees. 11 mi N on IA 1, then 4 mi W on IA 382 in Solon. Phone 319/644-2200.

Plum Grove. (1844) Residence of territory's first governor, Robert Lucas; restored and furnished. (Mid-Apr-mid-Oct, Wed-Sun) 1030 Carroll St. Phone 319/337-6846. ¢

University of Iowa. (1847) 28,000 students. More than 90 major buildings on 1,900 acres; 10 colleges, 6 schools, 82 departments. In the central section of city on both sides of Iowa River. Phone 319/335-3055. On campus are

Carver-Hawkeye Arena. Seats 15,500. Big Ten basketball games, wrestling meets, gymnastics, volleyball; also concerts and special events. On Elliott Dr, between Hawkins Dr and Newton Rd.

Iowa Hall. An exhibit gallery showing the state's geological, cultural, and environmental history. **FREE**

Medical Museum. Photographs, artifacts, and hands-on displays focusing on history of medicine and patient care in Iowa. Changing exhibits. (Mon-Fri; also Sat and Sun afternoons; closed hols) On W campus at The University of Iowa Hospitals and Clinics, Patient and Visitor Activities Center, eighth floor. Phone 319/356-7106. **FREE**

Museum of Art. Paintings, prints, lithographs; sculpture; silver; African art. (Tues-Sun; closed hols) W bank of Iowa River, near jct of Riverside Dr and River St. **FREE**

Museum of Natural History. Habitat dioramas; mounted mammals, fish, reptiles, birds. (Daily; closed hols) In Macbride Hall, Jefferson and Capitol sts, on east campus. **FREE**

Old Capitol. First capital of state; restored to original appearance of 1840s-1850s. (Daily; closed hols) Clinton St and Iowa Ave, on E campus. **FREE**

Special Events

Iowa Arts Festival. Celebration of the arts. Phone 319/337-7944. Mid-June.

Kalona Fall Festival. At Kalona Historical Village. Amish food, crafts, and displays. Last wkend Sept. Phone 319/656-3232.

Motels/Motor Lodges

★ **CLARION HOTEL AND CONFERENCE CENTER.** *1220 1st Ave, Coralville (52241). 319/351-5049; fax 319/354-4214; toll-free 800/252-7466. www.ncghotels.com.* 96 rms, 4 story. No elvtr. S $54-$59; D $64-$69; under 18 free. Crib free. Indoor pool. TV; cable (premium). Complimentary continental bkfst. Restaurant 11 am-2 pm, 5-10 pm; Fri, Sat to 11 pm. Ck-out noon. Meeting rms. Business servs avail. Exercise equipt. Cr cds: A, C, D, DS, ER, JCB, MC, V.

★★ **HAMPTON INN.** *1200 1st Ave, Coralville (52241). 319/351-6600; fax 319/351-3928. www.hamptoninn.com.* 115 rms, 4 story. S, D $59-$69; under 10 free. TV; cable (premium). Complimentary continental bkfst. Restaurant 5-10 pm. Ck-out noon. Meeting rms. Business center. In-rm modem link. Free airport transportation. Exercise equipt. Indoor pool; whirlpool. Some refrigerators, microwaves. Cr cds: A, C, D, DS, MC, V.

★ **HEARTLAND INN.** *87 2nd St, Coralville (52241). 319/351-8132; fax 319/351-2916; res 800/334-3277. www.heartlandinns.com.* 171 rms, 3 story. S $75; D $80; each addl $8; suites $80-$225; under 16 free; hospital rates. Crib free. TV; cable (premium), VCR avail. Complimentary continental bkfst. Restaurant adj 10 am-10 pm. Ck-out 11 am. Business servs avail. In-rm modem link. Cr cds: A, C, D, DS, MC, V.

⌨ ✕ ⊠ 🔥

★ **PRESIDENTIAL MOTOR INN.**
711 S Downey Rd, West Branch (52358). 319/643-2526; fax 319/643-5166. 38 rms, 2 story. S $39-$55; D $47-$67; each addl $12; wkly rates. Crib $3. Pet accepted, some restrictions. TV; cable (premium). Complimentary coffee in lobby. Ck-out 11 am. Coin lndry. Refrigerators; microwaves avail. Cr cds: A, C, D, DS, ER, JCB, MC, V.

⌨ 🐾 ⌁ ⊠ 🔥

★ **RAMADA INN.** *2530 Holiday Rd, Coralville (52241). 319/354-7770; toll-free 800/528-1234. www.ramada.com.* 155 rms, 2 story. S $57-$65; D $65-$73; each addl $8; under 17 free; package plans. Pet accepted. TV; cable (premium). Indoor pool; whirlpool. Complimentary continental bkfst. Restaurant 6:30 am-2 pm, 5-10 pm. Bar 4 pm-midnight. Ck-out 11 am. Meeting rms. Business servs avail. Airport transportation. Exercise equipt; sauna. Putting green. Game rm. Rec rm. Microwaves avail. Cr cds: A, C, D, DS, MC, V.

⌨ 🐾 ⌁ 🎣 ⊠ 🔥 SC

★ **SUPER 8 OF IOWA CITY.** *611 1st Ave, Coralville (52241). 319/337-8388; fax 319/337-4327. www.super8.com.* 87 rms, 2 story. S $47.98; D $56.98; each addl $3. Crib $2. TV; cable (premium). Complimentary continental bkfst. Restaurant nearby. Ck-out 11 am. Business servs avail. Sundries. Microwaves avail. Cr cds: A, MC, V.

⌨ ⊠ 🔥 SC

Hotel

★★★ **SHERATON IOWA CITY HOTEL.** *210 S Dubuque St (52240). 319/337-4058; fax 319/337-9045; toll-free 800/848-1335. www.sheraton.com.* 236 rms, 9 story. S, D $169; each addl $10; suites $145-$160; under 19 free. Pet accepted, some restrictions. TV; cable (premium). Indoor pool; whirlpool. Restaurant 6 am-2 pm, 5-10 pm. Bar 4 pm-1 am. Ck-out noon.

Meeting rms. Business servs avail. Bellhops. Beauty shop. Airport transportation. Exercise equipt; sauna. Game rm. Refrigerators. Cr cds: A, C, D, DS, JCB, MC, V.

⌨ 🐾 ⌁ 🎣 ✕ ⊠ 🔥

Restaurants

★★ **IOWA RIVER POWER COMPANY.** *501 First Ave, Coralville (52241). 319/351-1904.* Hrs: 5-9:30 pm; Fri to 10 pm; Sat 4-10:30 pm; Sun 4-9:30 pm; Sun brunch 10 am-2 pm. Closed Dec 25. Res accepted. Bar. Dinner $10.95-$28.95. Sun brunch $10.95. Children's menu. Specializes in prime rib, fowl, seafood. Salad bar. Multitiered dining in former power generating building. Overlooks river. Cr cds: A, C, D, DS, MC, V.

⌨ ⊰

★ **L B STEAKHOUSE.** *102 W Main St, West Branch (52358). 319/643-5420.* Hrs: 5-9 pm; Fri, Sat to 10 pm. Closed Mon; hols. Res accepted. Bar. Dinner $8.45-$18.50. Children's menu. Salad bar. Brick charcoal grill where customers grill own steak. Cr cds: A, C, DS, MC, V.

⊰

Keokuk

(F-7) *See also Fort Madison*

Settled 1820 **Pop** 12,451 **Elev** 550 ft **Area code** 319 **Zip** 52632

Information Keokuk Area Convention & Tourism Bureau, Pierce Building, 401 Main St; 319/524-5599 or 800/383-1219

Web www.keokuk.com

At the foot of the Des Moines rapids on the Mississippi, Keokuk served as a gateway to the west and north and a manufacturing center for the pioneer frontier. The town was named for a Native American chief and developed as a fur trading center. Manufacturing and agricultural industries are its mainstays now.

What to See and Do

Keokuk Dam. (1910-1913) Union Electric Company Hydroelectric

Power Plant with a mi-long dam across the Mississippi River to Hamilton, IL. Offers half-hr tours (Memorial Day-Labor Day, daily; rest of yr, by appt; lobby open Mon-Fri; closed hols). Lock 19, operated by Army Corps of Engineers, has observation platform. End of N Water St at riverfront. Phone 319/524-4091. **FREE**

Keokuk River Museum. In Sternwheel towboat *George M. Verity,* houses historical items of upper Mississippi River valley. (Apr-Oct, Mon, Thurs-Sun) Victory Park, foot of Johnson St. Phone 319/524-4765. ¢

National Cemetery. Unknown Soldier monument, Civil War graves. S 18th and Ridge sts. **FREE**

Rand Park. Statue and grave of Chief Keokuk. Flower gardens, picnic area. (Daily) Orleans Ave between N 14th and N 17th sts. **FREE**

Samuel F. Miller House and Museum. Restored home of US Supreme Court Justice appointed by Abraham Lincoln. (Fri-Sun afternoons) 318 N 5th St. Phone 319/524-5599. ¢

Special Events

Bald Eagle Appreciation Days. Mid-Jan.

Civil War Reenactment. Late Apr.

Motels/Motor Lodges

★★ **HOLIDAY INN EXPRESS.** *4th and Main sts (52632). 319/524-8000; fax 319/524-4114. www.holiday-inn.com.* 80 rms, 5 story. S $59; D $67; each addl $8. Crib free. TV; cable (premium). Indoor pool; whirlpool. Complimentary continental bkfst. Ck-out noon. Meeting rms. Business servs avail. In-rm modem link. Exercise equipt; sauna. Game rm. Cr cds: A, DS, MC, V.

D ≈ 🏋 🔄 🐾 SC

★ **SUPER 8.** *3511 Main St (52632). 319/524-3888. www.super8.com.* 62 rms, 2 story. S $43.98; D $52.98; suites $56.98. Crib $2. TV; cable. Restaurant adj 11 am-9 pm. Ck-out 11 am. Business servs avail. Microwaves avail. Cr cds: A, D, DS, MC, V.

D 🔄 🔄 🐾

Le Mars

(B-1) *See also Sioux City*

Settled 1869 **Pop** 8,454 **Elev** 1,231 ft
Area code 712 **Zip** 51031
Information Chamber of Commerce, 50 Central Ave SE; 712/546-8821
Web www.lemarsiowa.com

A young English gentleman learned of the opportunities in this part of Iowa, formed a land company, and induced a colony of Englishmen to settle here. A training farm, cricket and polo fields, and a tavern called "The House of Lords" soon blossomed. Le Mars was well known in Great Britain and was advertised there as a training ground for second sons in the areas of farming and stock raising. However, as the young Englishmen preferred horse racing, pubs, and sports to working the soil, the Germans, Irish, Luxembourgers, and Scandinavians took over the serious business of farming.

Today, Le Mars is the financial, educational, and recreational center for the area. As home to Wells Dairy, Inc, it has earned the name "Ice Cream Capital of the World."

What to See and Do

Plymouth County Historical Museum. More than 100 antique musical instruments; antique farm machinery, tools and furnishings; Native American artifacts; restored log cabin; four 1900 period rms. (Tues-Sun; closed hols) 355 1st Ave SW. Phone 712/546-7002. **FREE**

Special Events

Ice Cream Days. Citywide event incl Art in the Park, children's learning fair, parade, street dance, fireworks. July 4th wkend.

Plymouth County Fair. Pioneer village and historic round barn; exhibits, arts and crafts; entertainment. Last wk July.

Motels/Motor Lodges

★ **AMBER INN.** *635 8th Ave SW (51031). 712/546-7066; fax 712/548-4058.* 70 rms. S $34-$40; D $45-$50;

each addl $5. Crib $5. Pet accepted. TV; cable. Continental breakfast. Restaurant nearby. Ck-out 11 am. Meeting rm. Business servs avail. Cr cds: A, DS, MC, V.

★ **LEMARS SUPER 8 MOTEL.** *1201 Hawkeye Ave (51031). 712/546-8800. www.super8.com.* 61 rms, 3 story. S $36.88; D $41.88; suites $49.88-$63.88. Crib $3. TV. Complimentary bkfst. Restaurant nearby. Ck-out 11 am. Meeting rms. Business servs avail. Whirlpool. Cr cds: A, MC, V.

Maquoketa (C-8)

Founded 1838 **Pop** 6,111 **Elev** 700 ft
Information Chamber of Commerce, 1175 Main St; 319/652-4602

From 1840-1870 this town was a stopping point for wagon trains before they ferried across the Maquoketa River heading west. Today Maquoketa is a beef and dairy production center and the home of several diversified industries.

What to See and Do

Costello's Old Mill Gallery. Restored stone mill with waterwheel, built in 1867; inside constructed entirely of oak. Art gallery. (Apr-Dec, daily; rest of yr, Wed-Sun) 1 mi E on IA 64. Phone 319/652-3351. **FREE**

Jackson County Historical Museum. Replicas of general store and one-rm country school; 19th-century bedrm, living rm, and kitchen; old fire equipt, log cabin, buggies; barn with antique machinery, blacksmith shop; church; medical center; entertainment center, tent show; toy shop; wildlife display. Changing exhibits; exhibits by local artists. (Mar-Dec, Tues-Sun; closed hols) E Quarry St at Fairgrounds. Phone 319/652-5020. **FREE**

Maquoketa Caves State Park. Park of 272 acres. Large limestone caves; natural bridge rises 50 ft above valley floor; 17-ton rock balanced on cliff. Hiking trail, picnicking, camping.

Standard hrs, fees. 7 mi NW on IA 428. Phone 319/652-5833.

Special Event

Octoberfest of Bands. Forty marching bands; parade, field marching competitions. Phone 319/652-4602 or contact Chamber of Commerce. First Sat Oct.

B&B/Small Inn

★★ **SQUIERS MANOR BED & BREAKFAST.** *418 W Pleasant St (52060). 319/652-6961; fax 319/652-5995. www.squiresmanor.com.* 8 rms, 2 with shower only, 3 story, 3 suites. S, D $80-$110; each addl $15-$25; suites $160-$195. Crib free. TV. Complimentary full bkfst; eve refreshments. Restaurant nearby. Ck-out 11 am, ck-in 4 pm. X-country ski 12 mi. Many in-rm whirlpools; fireplace in suites. First Maquoketa residence with utilities. Built in 1882; antiques. Cr cds: A, DS, MC, V.

Marquette

Settled 1779 **Pop** 479 **Elev** 627 ft
Area code 319 **Zip** 52158
Information McGregor/Marquette Chamber of Commerce, PO Box 105, 52157; 319/873-2186 or 800/895-0910

First known as North McGregor, this town was later renamed for Father Jacques Marquette; he and Louis Jolliet were the first to see Iowa territory from the mouth of the Wisconsin River in 1673. Within a 15-mile radius of the town are hundreds of effigy mounds, fortifications, and earthworks.

What to See and Do

☒ Effigy Mounds National Monument. Preserves traces of indigenous civilization from 2,500 yrs ago. Mounds built in shapes of animals, birds, other forms. Area divided by Yellow River; Great Bear Mound is the largest known bear effigy in state, 70 ft across shoulders, 137 ft long, 5 ft high. Footpath leads from headquarters to Fire Point Mound

Pikes Peak State Park, Marquette

Group, to scenic viewpoints over-looking Mississippi and Yellow rivers. Guided walks (Memorial Day-Labor Day, daily). Visitor center has museum, 15-min film. (Daily; closed Dec 25) 3 mi N on IA 76. Phone 319/873-3491. ¢

Pikes Peak State Park. Park of 970 acres on bluffs overlooking Missis-sippi River. Native American mounds, colored sandstone outcroppings, woods, and wild flowers. Trail leads across rugged terrain to Bridal Veil Falls. Hiking. Picnicking. Camping (electricity, dump station). Observa-tion point. Boardwalks. Views of river. Standard hrs, fees. 5 mi SE on IA 340. Phone 319/873-2341.

Spook Cave and Campground. Guided 35-min tour of underground cavern via power boat. Campground has swimming beach, lake fishing; hiking trails, picnic areas. (May-Oct, daily) 5 mi SW on US 18, then 2 mi N on unnumbered road, near McGre-gor. Phone 319/873-2144. ¢¢¢

Motels/Motor Lodges

★ **HOLIDAY SHORES.** *101 Front St; US 18 Business, McGregor (52157). 319/873-3449; fax 319/873-3328.* 33

rms, 2-3 story. No elvtr. S, D $55-$90. Crib $4. TV; cable. Indoor pool; whirlpool. Restaurant nearby. Ck-out 10:30 am. Game rm. Balconies. Over-looks Mississippi River. Cr cds: DS, MC, V.

★ **ISLE OF CAPRI MARQUETTE.** *100 Anti Monopoly (52158). 319/873-3531; toll-free 800/496-8238. www.isleofcapricasino.com.* 24 rms, 3 story. No elvtr. S, D $79. TV; cable. Ck-out noon, ck-in 3 pm. Balconies. On bluff overlooking Mississippi River. Cr cds: A, DS, MC, V.

Marshalltown

(C-5) *See also Grinnell*

Founded 1853 **Pop** 25,178 **Elev** 938 ft
Area code 641 **Zip** 50158

Information Convention & Visitors Bureau, 709 S Center St, PO Box 1000; 515/753-6645 or 800/697-3155

Web www.marshalltown.org

The business center of Marshall County prides itself on its symbols of the "good life" in the Midwest—the historic courthouse, pleasant parks, and numerous churches. Perhaps its most famous son is "Cap" Anson, son of the founder, who is enshrined in the Baseball Hall of Fame in Cooperstown, New York.

What to See and Do

Fisher Community Center Art Gallery. Art collection incl paintings by Sisley, Utrillo, and Cassatt. (Daily; closed hols) Contact Convention and Visitors Bureau. 709 S Center St. **FREE**

Glick-Sower Historical Homestead. Contains original furnishings of post-Civil War era; also furnished one-rm country school with world maps of 1880. (Apr-Oct, Sat; groups by appt yr-round) 2nd Ave and State St. Phone 515/752-6664. **FREE**

Riverview Park. Swimming pool (June-Aug, daily). Camping. Picnicking, playground, ballfields. Park (Apr-Oct, daily). Some fees. N 3rd Ave and Woodland. Phone 515/754-5715.

Motels/Motor Lodges

★★ **BEST WESTERN REGENCY INN.** *3303 S Center St (50158). 641/ 752-6321; fax 641/752-4412; res 800/ 241-2974. www.bestwestern.com.* 105 rms, 2 story. S $59-$89; D $66-$96; each addl $7; under 18 free. Crib free. TV; cable. Indoor pool; whirlpool. Coffee in rms. Restaurant 6:30 am-2 pm, 5-9 pm; Sat, Sun from 7 am. Bar 4 pm-2 am. Ck-out noon. Meeting rms. Bellhops. Cr cds: A, C, D, DS, ER, JCB, MC, V.
D ⬧ ⬧ ⬧ ⬧

★ **COMFORT INN.** *2613 S Center St (50158). 641/752-6000; fax 641/752-8762. www.comfortinn.com.* 62 rms, 2 story. May-Aug: S $60, D $65; suites $139.95; under 18 free; lower rates rest of yr. Crib free. Pet accepted; $10. TV; cable (premium). Indoor pool; whirlpool. Complimentary full bkfst. Restaurant nearby. Ck-out noon. Business servs avail. Cr cds: A, C, D, DS, MC, V.
D ⬧ ⬧ ⬧ ⬧

★ **SUPER 8 MOTEL.** *3014 S Center St (50158). 641/753-8181; toll-free 800/ 800-8000. www.super8.com.* 61 rms, 2

story. S $39.88-$44.88; D $48.88; under 12 free. Crib $2. TV; cable. Complimentary coffee in lobby. Restaurant adj open 24 hrs. Ck-out 11 am. Cr cds: A, C, D, DS, MC, V.
D ⬧ ⬧ ⬧

Mason City

(A-5) *See also Clear Lake*

Settled 1853 **Pop** 29,040 **Elev** 1,138 ft **Area code** 641 **Zip** 50401

Information Convention & Visitors Bureau, 15 W State St, PO Box 1128, 50402-1128; 641/423-5724 or 800/423-5724

Web www.masoncityia.com

A trading, manufacturing, farming, and transportation hub, Mason City is a major producer of cement; it also processes meat and dairy products. A Native American uprising slowed growth of the city after the first settlement, but pioneers, many of whom were Masons, gradually returned. The town was first known as Shibboleth, later as Masonic Grove. This is the seat of Cerro Gordo County and was the inspiration for the classic musical *The Music Man*.

What to See and Do

Charles H. MacNider Museum. Art Center features changing and permanent exhibits with emphasis on American art; gallery featuring "Bil Baird: World of Puppets," films, music, lectures, classes. (Tues-Sun; closed legal hols) 303 2nd St SE. Phone 515/421-3666. **FREE** Just E of the museum is

   Meredith Wilson Footbridge. Formerly called the Willow Creek Bridge, featured in the movie *The Music Man*.

Kinney Pioneer Museum. Local history, pioneer, military exhibits; antique cars; original log cabin (ca 1854); one-rm schoolhouse; old farm machinery, railroad caboose; artifacts, fossils. (May, Sept, Wed-Fri, Sun; June-Aug, Wed-Sun) 7 mi W on US 18, at entrance to Municipal Airport. Phone 515/423-1258. ¢¢

Lime Creek Nature Center. On limestone bluffs in the Lime Creek Conservation Area, center incl plant, bird, mammal, insect, and fish displays. Five trails wind throughout 400 acres of forest, field, prairie, pond, and river. (Daily; closed hols) 3501 Lime Creek Rd. Phone 515/423-5309. **FREE**

Margaret M. MacNider/East Park. Winnebago River divides this park into two areas. Swimming pool, fishing; hiking trails, picnicking facilities, playground. Improved camping (fees). (Apr-Oct, daily) 841 Birch Dr at Kentucky Ave NE. Phone 515/421-3673.

Meredith Wilson Boyhood Home. Birthplace of author of *The Music Man.* (May-Oct, Fri-Sun afternoons) 314 S Pennsylvania Ave. Phone 515/423-3534. ¢¢

Stockman House. (1908) Only Prairie School house in Iowa designed by Frank Lloyd Wright; one of few houses built by Wright during this period to address middle-class housing needs. Tours. (June-Aug, Thurs-Sat, also Sun afternoons; Sept-Oct, wkends) 530 First St NE. Phone 515/421-3666. ¢¢

Van Horn's Antique Truck Museum. Features large collection of some of the oldest and most unusual trucks in the nation. Also on display is a scale model circus. (Late May-mid-Sept, daily) 2 mi N on US 65. Phone 515/423-0550. ¢¢

Special Events

Buddy Holly Tribute. Surf Ballroom, 460 North Shore Dr, in Clear Lake. Event commemorates Holly's last concert with local and national entertainers. Phone 515/357-6151. First wkend Feb.

North Iowa Band Festival. East Park, 841 Birch Dr. Music, entertainment. Phone 515/423-5724. Early June.

North Iowa Fair. Fairgrounds, US 18 W. Nine-county area fair; carnival; food, wine, and livestock exhibits; crafts; concessions, entertainment. Mid-Aug.

Motels/Motor Lodges

★ **COMFORT INN.** *410 5th St SW (50401). 641/423-4444; fax 515/424-*5358; toll-free 800/228-5150. www.comfortinn.com.* 60 rms, 3 story. S $54-$60; D $60-$66; each addl $6; suites $90-$115; under 16 free. Crib free. TV; cable (premium). Indoor pool; whirlpool. Complimentary continental bkfst. Restaurant nearby. Ck-out 11 am. Refrigerator in suites. Cr cds: A, C, D, DS, ER, JCB, MC, V.
D ⊠ 🐾 SC

★ **DAYS INN.** *2301 4th St SW (50401). 641/424-0210; fax 641/424-5284; toll-free 800/329-7466. www.daysinn.com.* 58 rms, 2 story. S $32-$44; D $42-$59; each addl $6; under 18 free. Crib free. Pet accepted. TV; cable. Complimentary continental bkfst. Ck-out noon. Business servs avail. Cr cds: A, C, D, DS, MC, V.
D 🐾 ⊠ 🐾 SC

Missouri Valley

(D-2) *See also Council Bluffs; also see Blair, NE*

Settled 1858 **Pop** 2,888 **Elev** 1,019 ft
Area code 712 **Zip** 51555
Information Chamber of Commerce, 400 E Erie, PO Box 130; 712/642-2553
Web www.missourivalley.com

A town rich in Native American history, this was the site of the first settler's cabin in the Missouri Valley along the Willow River.

What to See and Do

DeSoto National Wildlife Refuge. Partly in Nebraska and partly in Iowa, this approx 7,800-acre refuge surrounds DeSoto Lake, once a bend in the Missouri River. In spring and fall thousands of geese and ducks may be found here. Self-guided auto tours (Mid-Oct-mid-Nov). Excavation site of the *Bertrand,* a steamboat sunk in 1865. Visitor center (Daily; closed hols) houses steamboat's artifacts and wildlife exhibits. Fishing, boating; hunting, nature trails, picnicking. 6 mi W on US 30. Phone 712/642-4121. ¢¢

Harrison County Historical Village/Welcome Center. Incl a two-story log display building. The village consists of a school (1868), log cabin (1853), harness shop, print shop, and chapel. Contains relics of pioneer period. Museum (Mid-Apr-mid-Nov, daily). Welcome center (Daily; closed hols) 3 mi NE on US 30. Phone 712/642-2114. ¢

Loess Hills Scenic Byway. This 220-mi paved byway takes travelers through the Loess Hills region of Western Iowa, traversing seven counties and revealing beautiful geologic formations along the way. For map and information contact Chamber of Commerce. Phone 712/642-2553. **FREE**

Missouri Valley Antique and Craft Mall. 60 antique dealers in mall; over 40 booths in craft mall; vintage soda fountain. (Daily; closed hols). 1931 US 30. Phone 712/642-2125.

Wilson Island State Recreation Area. More than 550 acres. Fishing, boating (ramps); hunting, hiking, x-country skiing, snowmobiling. Picnicking, playground. Camping (electricity addl; dump station). Standard hrs, fees. US 30 to I-29 S, exit Loveland, then 7 mi W on IA 362. Phone 712/642-2069.

Mount Pleasant

(E-7) *See also Fairfield*

Settled 1834 **Pop** 8,027 **Elev** 725 ft **Area code** 319 **Zip** 52641
Information Henry County Tourism Assn, 502 W Washington; 319/385-2460 or 800/421-4282

The first courthouse in Iowa was constructed here. One of the first roads in the state was a plank road between Burlington and Mount Pleasant.

What to See and Do

Iowa Wesleyan College. (1842) 550 students. Harlan-Lincoln Home is on campus (open by appt at IWC Chadwick Library). 601 N Main St. Phone 319/385-6215. **FREE**

✪ **Midwest Old Threshers Heritage Museum.** Houses one of nation's largest collections of steam engines, steam-powered farm machines; agri-

cultural artifacts; turn-of-the-century farmhouse and barn; women's exhibit. **The Theatre Museum** has memorabilia of early tent, folk and repertory theater (Sept-May, Mon-Fri; rest of yr, Tues-Sun; fee). Camping (fee). (Memorial Day-Labor Day, daily; mid-Apr-Memorial Day and after Labor Day-Oct, Mon-Fri) S of town. Phone 319/385-8937. ¢¢

Oakland Mills Park. Approx 104 wooded acres with picnic area overlooking Skunk River. Fishing, boating. Hiking trails. Camping (electrical hookups; fee). 4 mi S, off US 34. Phone 319/986-5067. **FREE**

Special Event

Midwest Old Threshers Reunion. Iowa's largest working craft show, antique car show; steam and gas engines, vintage tractors; Midwest Village, log village, narrow-gauge steam railroad and electric trolley cars; entertainment. Phone 319/385-8937. Five days ending Labor Day.

Motels/Motor Lodges

★ **HEARTLAND INN.** *810 N Grand Ave, Mt Pleasant (52641).* 319/385-2102; fax 319/385-3223; toll-free 800/334-3277. www.heartlandinns.com. 59 rms, 2 story. S $42-$56; D $50-$64; each addl $8; under 16 free. Crib free. Pet accepted. TV; cable (premium). Indoor pool. Complimentary continental bkfst. Restaurant adj 11 am-9 pm. Ck-out 11 am. Business servs avail. Sauna. Whirlpool. Cr cds: A, MC, V.
D ⊠ ⌧ ⊠ 🐾 SC

★ **SUPER 8 MOTEL.** *1000 N Grand Ave (52641).* 319/385-8888; fax 319/385-8888; res 800/800-8000. www.super8.com. 55 rms, 2 story. S $46.98; D $55.98; each addl $3; under 12 free. Crib $2. TV; cable (premium). Complimentary continental bkfst. Restaurant opp 11 am-9:30 pm. Ck-out 11 am. Meeting rms. Business servs avail. Microwaves avail. Cr cds: A, C, D, DS, MC, V.
D ⊠ 🐾 SC

Muscatine

(D-7) *See also Davenport*

Founded 1836 **Pop** 22,881 **Elev** 550 ft
Area code 319 **Zip** 52761
Information Convention & Visitors
Bureau, 319 E 2nd St, PO Box 297;
319/263-8895 or 800/25-PEARL
Web www.muscatine.com

Famous Muscatine cantaloupes and
watermelons, as well as plastics,
grain handling, food processing, and
manufacturing, are the major industries of this city. Samuel Clemens,
who once lived here, declared Muscatine's summer sunsets unsurpassed.

What to See and Do

Mark Twain Overlook. Three acres
with panoramic view of Mississippi
River valley, boat harbor and downtown Muscatine; picnicking. Lom-
bard and 2nd sts.

Muscatine Art Center. Consists of
the Laura Musser Museum and the
Stanley Gallery. Museum is housed
in an Edwardian mansion; changing
art exhibits, special events, Estey
player pipe organ with 731 pipes,
antiques and historical displays;
Asian carpets, furniture, paintings,
drawings, prints, sculpture, graphics
in permanent collection. (Tues-Sun;
closed hols) 1314 Mulberry Ave.
Phone 319/263-8282. **FREE**

Pearl Button Museum. Dedicated to
pearl button industry. Exhibits on
making buttons from Mississippi
River mussel shells. (Sat) Iowa Ave
and 2nd St. **FREE**

Saulsbury Bridge Recreation Area.
Approx 675 acres. Fishing, canoeing;
picnicking, playground, nature trails
and center, x-country skiing. Camping (Hookups mid-Apr-mid-Oct only;
fee). Park (Daily). W on IA 22. Phone
319/649-3379. **FREE**

Shady Creek Recreation Area. 15
acres. Boat ramp. Picnicking, playground, shelter. Improved camping
(May-Oct; fee). Park (daily). 7 mi E
on IA 22, on Mississippi River. Phone
319/263-7913. ¢¢¢

Wildcat Den State Park. A 321-acre
park with historic mid-19th-century
gristmill, one-rm schoolhouse, Pine

Creek Bridge; scenic overlook. Hiking
trails. Picnicking. Primitive camping.
Standard hrs, fees. 12 mi E on IA 22.
Phone 319/263-4337.

Motels/Motor Lodges

★ **ECONO LODGE.** *2402 Park Ave
(52761). 319/264-3337; fax 319/263-
0413; toll-free 800/234-7829. www.
econolodge.com.* 91 rms, 2 story. S
$39.95-$59; D $49.95-$69; each addl
$6; suites $99-$179; under 18 free;
wkend rates. Crib free. TV; cable (premium). Indoor pool. Restaurant 5-9
pm. Bar 4:30-11 pm; Fri, Sat to midnight. Ck-out noon. Coin lndry.
Meeting rm. Business servs avail. Cr
cds: A, C, D, DS, MC, V.
⊠ ⊠ ⊠ **SC**

★★ **HOLIDAY INN.** *2915 N Hwy 61
(52761). 319/264-5550; fax 319/264-
0451. www.holiday-inn.com.* 112 rms,
3 story. S, D $89; each addl $10.
Crib free. Pet accepted, some restrictions; $10. TV; cable (premium).
Indoor pool; wading pool, whirlpool.
Restaurant 6 am-2 pm, 5-10 pm. Bar
5 pm-midnight. Coin lndry. Ck-out
noon. Meeting rms. Business center.
In-rm modem link. Exercise equipt;
sauna. Health club privileges. Rec rm.
Some refrigerators. Cr cds: A, C, D,
DS, ER, JCB, MC, V.
D ⊠ ⊠ ⊠ ⊠ ⊠ **SC** ⊠

Newton

(D-5) *See also Grinnell*

Pop 14,789 **Elev** 950 ft **Area code** 641
Zip 50208
Information Visitor & Conference
Bureau, 113 1st Ave W; 641/792-
0299
Web www.newtongov.org

The washing machine industry was
born here in 1898, and the Maytag
Company continues to make Newton
the "home laundry appliance center
of the world."

What to See and Do

Fred Maytag Park. Donated by
founder of Maytag Company. Tennis,
picnicking, playground; amphithe-

ater, log cabin, concession. Pool and water slide (June-Aug, daily; fee). Park (Daily). W 3rd St S. Phone 515/792-1470. **FREE**

Jasper County Historical Museum. Local historical displays incl bas-relief sculpture of natural history of the county, Victorian home, school-room, chapel, tool and farm equipt collections, sound film of early county scenes. Also the Maytag historical display of washing machines. (May-Sept, afternoons) 1700 S 15th Ave W. Phone 515/792-9118. ¢

Trainland, USA. Toy train museum exhibits depict development of the railroad across the US in three eras: frontier, steam, and diesel; original railroad memorabilia and toy trains dating from 1916 to the present. (Memorial Day-Labor Day, daily; rest of Sept, wkends) 12 mi W via I-80, then 2½ mi N on IA 117, in Colfax. Phone 515/674-3813. ¢¢

Motels/Motor Lodges

★★ **BEST WESTERN NEWTON INN.** *I-80 at IA 14 (50208). 641/792-4200; fax 641/792-0108; res 800/528-1234. www.bestwestern.com.* 118 rms, 2 story. S $49-$59; D $59-$69; each addl $6; under 18 free; higher rates Knoxville racing season. Crib $3. Pet accepted. TV; cable (premium), VCR avail. Indoor pool; whirlpool. Complimentary full bkfst. Restaurant 6 am-1 pm, 5:30-10 pm. Bar 5:30 pm-1 am. Ck-out noon. Meeting rms. Business servs avail. Putting green. Exercise equipt; sauna. Game rm. Cr cds: A, C, D, DS, ER, JCB, MC, V.
⊗ ⋈ ✕ ⊠ ⊛ SC

★ **DAYS INN.** *1605 W 19th St S (50208). 641/792-2330; fax 641/792-1045. www.daysinn.com.* 59 rms, 2 story. S $43-$48; D $49-$54; each addl $5. Crib free. Pet accepted. TV; cable (premium), VCR avail. Complimentary continental bkfst. Restaurant adj open 24 hrs. Ck-out 11 am. Business servs avail. Cr cds: A, C, D, DS, ER, JCB, MC, V.
D ⊗ ✦ ⊠ ⊛

★ **SUPER 8.** *1635 S 12th Ave W (50208). 641/792-8868. www.super8. com.* 43 rms, 2 story. S $37-$54; D $47-$60; under 12 free; higher rates: Knoxville National Race, wkends.

Crib $4. TV; cable (premium). Complimentary continental bkfst. Restaurant adj 6-10 am. Ck-out 11 am. Meeting rms. Business servs avail. Cr cds: A, D, DS, MC, V.
D ✦ ⊠ ⊛

B&B/Small Inn

★★★ **LA CORSETTE MAISON INN.** *629 1st Ave E (50208). 641/792-6833. www.innbook.com.* 7 units, 2 story, 2 suites. S, D $75-$85; suites $80-$175; kit. unit $80; higher rates special events. TV in some rms. Complimentary full bkfst. Restaurant (see also LA CORSETTE MAISON INN). Ck-out 11:30 am, ck-in 4-6 pm. Business servs avail. 1909 Mission-style mansion with all original woodwork; art nouveau stained-glass windows; some original brass light fixtures and furnishings. Unique decor in each rm. Totally nonsmoking. Cr cds: A, MC, V.
⊠ ⊛

Restaurant

★★★ **LA CORSETTE MAISON INN.** *629 1st Ave E (US 6) (50208). 641/792-6833. www.innbook.com.* Hrs: one sitting per day, usually at 7 pm; phone for schedule. Closed Mon, Tues, Sun. Res required 24-48 hrs in advance. French, Continental menu. Complete meals: dinner $35.50-$38.50. Specialties: roasted beef tenderloin, medallions of Iowa pork, La Corsette French bread. Gourmet dining in 1909 Mission-style mansion; original dining rm furnishings; 3 sets of floral patterned leaded glass French doors lead to enclosed, mosiac-tiled atrium. Totally nonsmoking. Cr cds: A, MC, V.
D

Okoboji

See also Spencer, Spirit Lake

Founded 1855 **Pop** 775 **Elev** 1,450 ft **Area code** 712 **Zip** 51355
Information Tourism, US 71, PO Box 215; 712/332-2209 or 800/270-2574
Web www.vacationokoboji.com

Lewis and Clark keelboat replica, Lewis and Clark State Park

Lake Okoboji and the surrounding area are among the most popular resort areas in Iowa.

What to See and Do

Arnolds Park Amusement Park. Century-old amusement park with classic old rides and newer favorites, plus entertainment and games. (May-mid-June, late Aug, wkends; mid-June-mid-Aug, daily; hrs vary) Phone 712/332-2183.

Boji Bay. Family water park features water slides, wave pool, tube rides, sand volleyball courts, arcades, and games. Concessions. Gift shop. (Memorial Day-Labor Day) Jct US 71 and IA 86, N of town. Phone 712/338-2473.

Gardner Cabin. (1856) Restored; period furnishings; displays on pioneer life and history of the region. (Memorial Day-Labor Day, afternoons) 3 mi SW on US 71 in Arnolds Park, one blk W of Arnolds Park Amusement Park. Phone 712/332-7248. **FREE**

Higgins Museum. Displays notes and artifacts of the National Banks. (Memorial-Labor Day, Tues-Sun; May and Sept, wkends) 1507 Sanborn Ave. Phone 712/332-5859. **FREE**

Okoboji Queen II. One-hr steamship cruises on West Okoboji Lake. Schedule varies; call ahead. (Several cruises daily in summertime) Docks at Arnolds Park Amusement Park (see). Phone 712/332-5159. ¢¢¢

State parks. Swimming, fishing, boating; snowmobiling, picnicking. Standard fees. On 3,847-acre West Okoboji Lake. Phone 712/337-3211.

Gull Point. On 165 acres. Also boating. Hiking trails. Picnicking, lodge. Camping (electricity, dump station). Approx 6 mi SW off US 71.

Pikes Point. On 15 acres. Picnicking. Approx 3 mi W.

Special Event

Okoboji Summer Theater. 1 mi N on US 71. New play each wk; operated by Stephens College of Columbia, MO. Tues-Sun. Also children's theater. For res, schedule phone 712/332-7773. Mid-June-mid-Aug.

Motels/Motor Lodges

★ **COUNTRY CLUB MOTEL.** *1107 Sanborn Ave (51355). 712/332-5617; fax 712/332-7705; toll-free 800/831-5615.* 53 rms. Memorial Day-late Sept: S, D $80-$150; lower rates rest of yr. Crib $5. Pet accepted. TV; cable (premium). Heated pool. Restaurant nearby. Ck-out 10 am. Business servs avail. Picnic tables, grills. Cr cds: A, D, DS, MC, V.

★★ **FILLENWARTH BEACH.** *87 Lakeshore Dr, Arnolds Park (51331). 712/332-5646. www.fillenwarthbeach. com.* 93 kit. units in motel, cottages, 1-3 story. No elvtr. Late June-late Aug: apts for 2-8, $500-$1,380/wk; daily rates; lower rates Apr-mid-June, Sept. Closed rest of yr. Crib free. Pet accepted. TV; cable, VCR. Indoor/ outdoor pool. Playground. Supervised children's activities (late May-early Sept). Restaurant opp 6 am-midnight. Ck-out noon. Business servs avail. Free airport, bus depot transportation. Sports dir in season. Tennis. Rec rm. Private beach. Waterskiing, instruction. Boat dock, canoes, boats. Free sail and cruiser boat rides. Balconies. Picnic tables, grills. On West Okoboji Lake. Cr cds: A, DS, MC, V.

★ **FOUR SEASONS RESORT.** *US 71, Arnolds Park (51331). 712/332-2103; toll-free 800/876-2103.* 32 units, 1-2 story. S, D, suites $45-$125. Pet accepted. Restaurant 9 am-11 pm. Bar to 2 am. Ck-out 11 am. Lakefront motel. Cr cds: A, DS, MC, V.

★★★ **INN AT OKOBOJI.** *3301 Lakeshore Dr (51355). 712/332-2113; fax 712/332-2714.* 152 1-2 rm studio units, 1-2 story. June-Aug: S, D $120-$150; lower rates May and Sept. Closed rest of yr. Crib $10. TV; cable. 2 pools, 1 indoor; poolside serv. Playground. Free supervised children's activities (Memorial Day-Labor Day); ages 4 and up. Restaurant 7 am-10 pm. Bar 11-2 am; entertainment Tues-Sat. Ck-out noon. Meeting rms. Business servs avail. Concierge. Sundries. Gift shop. Tennis. 9-hole golf, putting green, driving range. Soc dir. Lawn games. Boating; rentals, docks. Refrigerators. Spacious grounds on West Okoboji Lake. Cr cds: A, D, DS, MC, V.

★★★ **VILLAGE EAST.** *1405 US 71 N (51355). 712/332-2161; fax 712/ 332-7727. www.villageeast.com.* 99 rms, 2 story. Late May-Sept: S $139; each addl $10; lower rates rest of yr. Pet accepted. TV; cable. 2 pools; whirlpool. Restaurant 6 am-10 pm. Bar. Ck-out 11 am. Meeting rms. Business servs avail. Beauty shop. Indoor and outdoor tennis. 18-hole golf, greens fee $49. X-country ski on site. Exercise rm; sauna. Rec rm. Private patios. Lake opp. Cr cds: A, D, DS, MC, V.

Onawa (C-1)

Pop 2,936 **Elev** 1,052 ft
Area code 712 **Zip** 51040

What to See and Do

Lewis and Clark State Park. Park of 176 acres on 250-acre lake. Swimming, fishing, boating (ramp); hiking trails, snowmobiling, picnicking. Replica of Lewis and Clark keelboat *Discovery.* Camping (electricity, dump station). Standard hrs, fees. 3 mi NW via IA 175, 324. Phone 712/423-2829.

Motel/Motor Lodge

★ **SUPER 8.** *22868 Filbert Ave (51040). 712/423-2101; fax 712/423-3480. www.super8.com.* 80 rms. S $40-$65; D $45-$65; each addl $3. Pet accepted. TV; cable. Restaurant nearby. Ck-out 11 am. Picnic table. Cr cds: A, D, DS, MC, V.

Osceola

(E-4) *See also Chariton*

Settled 1850 **Pop** 4,164 **Elev** 1,139 ft
Area code 641 **Zip** 50213
Information Chamber of Commerce, 100 S Fillmore St, PO Box 1; 641/342-4200

The seat of Clarke County is named for a Seminole warrior; a 30-foot figure of Osceola, carved from a cedar tree trunk, stands on the west side of the city. The town was settled by pioneers from Indiana and Ohio.

What to See and Do

Nine Eagles State Park. Timbered 1,119-acre park with 67-acre lake. Swimming, supervised beach, fishing, electric boating (ramps, rentals); hiking, snowmobiling, picnicking. Camping (electricity, dump station). Standard hrs, fees. 29 mi S on US 69 to Davis City, then 6 mi SE on county road. Phone 515/442-2855.

Motel/Motor Lodge

★ **BLUE HAVEN MOTEL.** *325 S Main St (50213). 641/342-2115; toll-free 800/333-3180.* 24 rms, 1-2 story. S $33-$43; D $41-$49; each addl $4; higher rates hunting seasons. Crib free. Pet accepted. TV; cable (premium). Restaurant nearby. Ck-out 11 am. Cr cds: A, DS, MC, V.
⊠ ⊠ ⊠ **SC**

Oskaloosa

(D-5) *See also Ottumwa, Pella*

Settled 1843 **Pop** 10,632 **Elev** 845 ft
Area code 641 **Zip** 52577
Information Chamber & Development Group, 124 N Market St; 641/672-2591
Web www.oskaloosa.ia.us

Native American tribes lived here when the site was picked for the county seat, and the name of a Native American maiden ("last of the beautiful") was chosen as the name of the new community. Oskaloosa has a thriving retail trade and is the home of several manufacturers. It is also a center of production of corn, hay, hogs, cattle, and soybeans.

What to See and Do

Lake Keomah State Park. More than 370 acres with 84-acre lake. Swimming, supervised beach, fishing, electric boating (ramps, rentals); hiking trails, snowmobiling, picnicking, lodge. Camping (electricity, dump station). Standard hrs, fees. 5 mi E off IA 92. Phone 641/673-6975.

Nelson Pioneer Farm & Craft Museum. Family farm of 1800s incl house, barn, one-room schoolhouse, log cabin, quilt collection, Friends Meeting House; post office and country store (1900); museum with historical exhibits; mule cemetery. (Mid-May-mid-Oct, Tues-Sun) 2 mi NE of Penn College on Glendale Rd. Phone 515/672-2989. ¢¢

Special Events

Art On The Square. Arts and crafts demonstrations and workshops; children's activities. Second Sat June.

Southern Iowa Fair. Classic county fair. Late July.

Lighted Christmas Parade. Thurs-Fri night after Thanksgiving.

Motels/Motor Lodges

★ **OSKALOOSA SUPER 8.** *306 S 17th St (52577). 641/673-8481; res 800/800-8000. www.super8.com.* 51 rms, 2 story, 4 suites. S $47.98; D $56.98; each addl $3; under 12 free. Crib $2. TV; cable (premium). Complimentary coffee in lobby. Restaurant nearby. Ck-out 11 am. Business servs avail. Cr cds: A, MC, V.
D ⊠ ⊠ **SC**

★ **RED CARPET INN.** *2278 US 63 N (52577). 641/673-8641; fax 641/673-4111; toll-free 800/255-2110.* 41 rms, 2 story. S $37-$47; D $44-$54; each addl $5. Pet accepted. TV; cable (premium). Complimentary continental bkfst. Cr cds: A, DS, MC, V.
⊠ ⊠ ⊠

★ **RODEWAY INN.** *1315 A Ave E (52577). 641/673-8351; toll-free 800/ 228-5050. www.rodewayinn.com.* 42 rms, 1-2 story. S $35-$50; D $45-$60; each addl $3. Crib $2. TV; cable (premium). Playground. Coffee in rms. Restaurant nearby. Ck-out 11 am. Meeting rm. Business servs avail. Picnic table. Cr cds: A, C, D, DS, MC, V.
D ⊠ ⊠ **SC**

Ottumwa

(E-6) *See also Oskaloosa*

Settled 1843 **Pop** 24,488 **Elev** 650 ft
Area code 641 **Zip** 52501

Information Ottumwa Area Convention & Visitors Bureau, 217 E Main St, PO Box 308; 641/682-3465
Web www.ottumwachamber.com

A major Iowa trade center, Ottumwa is an industrial and agricultural city. The city was born in a land rush as settlers staked out this site on both sides of the Des Moines River. The name Ottumwa comes from a Native American word meaning "swift rapids" and later "perseverance." Historical marker east of town marks the site of the 1842 Indian Council, which resulted in the purchase of much of Iowa from the Sac and Fox.

What to See and Do

The Beach—Ottumwa. Water recreation park featuring 22,000-sq-ft wave pool, 340-ft body slide, 200-ft speed slide, and four-acre lagoon with kayak and paddleboats. Children's activity pool. Sand volleyball courts. Concessions. Some indoor recreational facilities operate yr-round. Phone 641/682-7873. ¢¢¢

John Deere Ottumwa Works. Hay, forage implements; 90-min guided tour (Mon-Fri; no tours last wk July, Aug, Dec 25-Jan 2). Over 12 yrs only; no sandals or tennis shoes. 928 E Vine St. Phone 641/683-2394. **FREE**

Lake Wapello State Park. A 1,168-acre park with 289-acre lake. Swimming beach, fishing, boating (ramp); hiking trails, snowmobiling, picnicking. Camping (electricity, dump station), cabins. Standard hrs, fees. 16 mi S on US 63, then 10 mi W on IA 273 near Drakesville. Phone 641/722-3371.

Ottumwa Park. A 365-acre recreation area in center of city incl camping (fee), fishing, tennis, horseshoes, bocce. (Apr-mid-Oct, daily) At jct US 34, 63.

Special Events

Ottumwa Pro Balloon Races. Ottumwa Park. Balloon flights, races; concessions, fireworks. Phone 515/684-8838. Last wkend June.

Octoberfest. Downtown. Parade. Beer tent. Nightly entertainment. First full wkend Oct.

Motels/Motor Lodges

★★ **FAIRFIELD INN.** 2813 N Court St (52501). 641/682-0000; toll-free 800/228-2800. www.fairfieldinn.com. 63 rms, 3 story. Mar-Oct: S $39-$48; D $47-$54; under 18 free; higher rates special events. Crib free. TV; cable. Indoor pool; whirlpool. Complimentary continental bkfst. Restaurant nearby. Ck-out noon. Coin lndry. Meeting rms. Health club privileges. Some refrigerators; microwaves avail. Cr cds: A, D, DS, MC, V.
D ⊠ ⊠ 🔥 SC

★ **HEARTLAND INN.** 125 W Joseph Ave (52501). 641/682-8526; fax 641/682-7124; toll-free 800/334-3277. www.heartlandinns.com. 89 units. S $47; D $55-$65; each addl $8; under 17 free. Crib free. Pet accepted. TV; cable (premium). Pool; whirlpool. Complimentary continental bkfst. Restaurant nearby. Ck-out noon. Coin lndry. Meeting rm. Business servs avail. Sauna. Cr cds: A, DS, MC, V.
D 🐾 ⊠ 🐕

★ **SUPER 8 MOTEL.** 2823 N Court St (52501). 641/684-5055; fax 641/682-6622; toll-free 800/800-8000. www.super8.com. 62 rms, 2 story. S $45.88; D $54.88; suites $68.88-$78.88; under 13 free. Crib $3. TV; cable (premium). Indoor pool; whirlpool. Complimentary continental bkfst. Restaurant nearby. Ck-out 11 am. Coin lndry. Meeting rm. Sauna. Cr cds: A, D, DS, MC, V.
D ⊠ ⊠ 🔥 SC

Restaurant

★ **FISHERMAN'S BAY.** 221 N Wapello St (52501). 641/682-6325. Hrs: 11 am-9 pm; Fri, Sat to 10 pm. Closed Dec 25. Res accepted. Bar. Lunch $2.95-$7, dinner $7.95-$18. Children's menu. Specializes in seafood, french fries. Salad bar. Casual dining; nautical decor. Cr cds: A, DS, MC, V.
D SC ⊠

Pella

(D-5) *See also Oskaloosa*

Settled 1847 **Pop** 9,270 **Elev** 878 ft
Area code 641 **Zip** 50219
Information Chamber of Commerce,
518 Franklin St; 641/628-2626
Web www.pella.org

Dutch refugees from religious intolerance first settled Pella, and the town retains many Dutch customs. Dutch influence can be seen in the architectural design of the business district and in the many tulip gardens in the area. Pella was the boyhood home of Wyatt Earp. It is the headquarters of the Pella Corporation, a major manufacturer of prefabricated windows.

What to See and Do

Central College. (1853) 1,700 students. Liberal arts. Mills Gallery with changing exhibits. Tours. 812 University St. Phone 641/628-9000.

Klokkenspel at Franklin Place. A 147-bell carillon in the Franklin Place Arch with figurines representing Pella's early history, town founders, Wyatt Earp, and others; Sinterklaas and his faithful companion, Black Piet, during the Christmas season. Courtyard on S side of arch has scenes of Holland in Dutch tiles. Concerts (five times daily). ½ blk E of town square. **FREE**

⊠ Pella Historical Village Museum. Restoration project of 21 buildings housing exhibits and antiques; pottery and blacksmith shops, pioneer log cabin, Wyatt Earp Boyhood Home, Heritage Hall, Dutch museum and bakery; gristmill in garden. (Apr-Dec, Mon-Sat; rest of yr, Mon-Fri; closed hols exc during summer) 507 Franklin St. Phone 641/628-4311. ¢¢

Red Rock Lake. A 19,000-acre lake formed by Army Corps of Engineers dam impounding Des Moines River. Swimming, boating, fishing; picnicking. Approx 400 developed campsites (mid-Apr-mid-Oct; fee). 4½ mi SW. Phone 641/828-7522.

Scholte House. Oldest permanent dwelling in Pella built by town founder H. P. Scholte; many original furnishings and possessions, collection of old world French and Italian furniture; gardens with more than 25,000 tulips. (Mon-Sat afternoons; also by appt; closed Easter and Dec 25) 728 Washington. Phone 641/628-3684. ¢¢

Special Event

Tulip Time Festival. Citizens dress in Dutch costumes; scrubbing the streets is a colorful and traditional feature; Dutch dancers; stage performances, parades. Phone 515/628-4311. Mid-May.

Pocahontas

(B-3) *See also Humboldt, Storm Lake*

Pop 2,085 **Elev** 1,227 ft
Area code 712 **Zip** 50574

Named in honor of the famous daughter of Powhatan, this town, in pheasant-hunting country, is also the seat of Pocahontas County.

Motel/Motor Lodge

★ **CHIEF MOTEL.** *801 W Elm Ave (50574).* 712/335-3395. 34 rms, 1-2 story, 4 kits. S $37.15-$45; D $46.67-$57; each addl $7. Crib free. TV; cable. Restaurant nearby. Ck-out 11 am. Sundries. Cr cds: A, C, DS, MC, V. ⊠⊠

Red Oak (E-2)

Pop 6,264 **Elev** 1,077 ft
Area code 712 **Zip** 51566

What to See and Do

Viking Lake State Park. More than 950 acres on 137-acre lake. Swimming, fishing, boating (ramp, rentals); hiking trail, snowmobiling. Picnicking. Camping (electricity, dump station). Standard hrs, fees. 12 mi E off US 34. Phone 712/829-2235.

Motel/Motor Lodge

★ **RED COACH INN.** *1200 Senate Ave (51566).* 712/623-4864; fax 712/

623-2389; toll-free 800/544-6002. 74 rms, 2 story. S $40; D $44; each addl $5; studio rm $38-$48. Crib free. TV; cable (premium), VCR avail. Heated pool. Bar 4 pm-10:30 pm. Ck-out noon. Meeting rms. Business servs avail. Valet serv. Cr cds: A, C, DS, MC, V.

D ⌇ ⊠ 🐾 SC

Sheldon (A-2)

Pop 4,937 **Elev** 1,420 ft
Area code 712 **Zip** 51201

Motel/Motor Lodge

★ **IRON HORSE INN.** *1111 S Hwy 60 (51201).* 712/324-5353. 33 rms, 2 story. S $39; D $50; under 10 free. TV; cable. Complimentary continental bkfst. Restaurant 11 am-midnight. Bar. Ck-out 11 am. Cr cds: A, D, DS, MC, V.

D 🐾

Shenandoah

(E-2) *See also Clarinda, Red Oak*

Founded 1870 **Pop** 5,572 **Elev** 981 ft
Area code 712 **Zip** 51601
Information Chamber and Industry Association, 301 S Maple, PO Box 38; 712/246-3455

Mormons settled here, moving in from Manti (Fisher's Grove). Other early settlers fought with General Sheridan in the Shenandoah Valley of Virginia and brought the name back with them. The town is now the home of three large seed and nursery companies, a truck transmissions plant, and a windows and doors plant.

Motel/Motor Lodge

★★ **COUNTRY INN.** *US 59 and 48; 1503 Sheridan Ave (51601).* 712/246-1550; fax 712/246-4773. 65 rms, 1-2 story. S $34; D $54; each addl $5; family rates. Crib $5. Pet accepted. TV; cable (premium). Restaurant 6 am-9 pm. Bar 5 pm-1 am. Ck-out 11 am. Meeting rms. Business servs

avail. Airport transportation. Cr cds: A, C, D, DS, MC, V.

🔌 ⊠ 🐾

Sioux City (B-1)

Settled 1854 **Pop** 80,505 **Elev** 1,117 ft
Area code 712
Information Sioux City Convention Center/Tourism Bureau, 801 4th St, PO Box 3183, 51102; 712/279-4800 or 800/593-2228
Web www.siouxland.com

At the heart of a tristate region bordered by the Sioux and Missouri rivers, Sioux City has historically been a hub for shipping, transportation, and agriculture. The Lewis and Clark expedition followed the Missouri River; the only fatality of that historic march is commemorated here with the Sergeant Floyd Monument, the first registered historic landmark in the United States.

Today, the Missouri River is important to the city from a recreational standpoint. A developed riverfront with parks, a dance pavilion, and a riverboat casino greets visitors. Sioux City has also grown to be a cultural and historical destination with many theaters, parks, an art center, nature center, historical attractions, and festivals and events throughout the year.

What to See and Do

Belle of Sioux City. Trilevel riverboat casino. (May-Oct, daily) 100 Larsen Park Rd. Phone 712/255-0080.

Morningside College. (1894) 1,400 students. Liberal arts. Fine Arts Building contains lobby art gallery. Tours. 1501 Morningside Ave. Phone 712/274-5000.

Sergeant Floyd Monument. First registered national historic landmark in the US. The 100-ft obelisk marks burial place of Sergeant Charles Floyd, the only casualty of the Lewis and Clark expedition. Glenn Ave and US 75, on E bank of Missouri River.

Sergeant Floyd Welcome Center and Museum. Former Missouri River inspection ship now houses museum, information center, and gift shop. (Daily) Exit 149 off I-29, Hamilton Blvd to S Larsen Park Rd. Phone 712/279-0198. **FREE**

Sioux City Art Center. Contemporary traveling exhibits and permanent collection. Three-story glass atrium. Special programs. (Tues-Sat, also Sun afternoon; closed hols) 225 Nebraska St. Phone 712/279-6272. **FREE**

Sioux City Public Museum. Exhibits show Sioux City history and life in pioneer days; geological, archaeological, and Native American materials. Located in Romanesque 23-rm mansion. Museum store. (Tues-Sat; hols) 2901 Jackson St. Phone 712/279-6174. **FREE**

Stone State Park. 1,069 acres. Park overlooks the Missouri and Big Sioux river valleys; view of three states from Dakota Point Lookout near Big Sioux River. Fishing. Bridle, hiking trails. Snowmobiling. Picnicking. Camping. Standard hrs, fees. Ten-acre **Dorothy Pecant Nature Center** (Tues-Sun; closed hols). 4800 Sioux River Rd, I-29 exit 151. Phone 712/255-4698.

Trinity Heights. A 30-ft stainless steel statue of the Immaculate Heart of Mary, Queen of Peace. Life-size carving of the Last Supper. Outdoor cathedral with 33-ft statue of Christ. (Daily) 33rd and Floyd Blvd. Phone 712/239-8670. ¢¢

Woodbury County Courthouse. (1916-1918) Courthouse was the largest structure ever completed in the architectural style of Chicago's Prairie School. Designed by Purcell and Elmslie, long-time associates of Louis Sullivan, the city-blk-long building is constructed of Roman brick, ornamented with massive pieces of Sullivanesque terra-cotta, stained glass, and relief sculpture by Alfonso Ianelli, who also worked with Frank Lloyd Wright. Both exterior and highly detailed interior are in near-pristine condition; courtrms still contain original architect-designed furniture, lighting fixtures. (Mon-Fri) Between 7th and Douglas sts. Phone 712/279-6624.

Special Events

Saturday in the Park. Day-long music festival. Late June.

River-Cade Festival. Features fireworks, antique show, entertainment, midway, baseball, bowling, "fun run." Phone 712/277-4226. Last wk July.

Motels/Motor Lodges

★★ **BEST WESTERN CITY CENTRE.** *130 Nebraska St (51101). 712/277-1550; fax 712/277-1120; toll-free 800/528-1234. www.bestwestern.com.* 114 rms, 2 story. S $50-$63; D $58-$69; each addl $10; suites $113-$173; under 18 free. Crib $6. Pet accepted, some restrictions. TV; cable. Heated pool. Bar 5-8 pm. Ck-out noon. Coin lndry. Meeting rms. Business servs avail. Free airport transportation. Cr cds: A, C, D, DS, JCB, MC, V.

★ **COMFORT INN.** *4202 S Lakeport St (51106). 712/274-1300; fax 712/274-7592. www.comfortinn.com.* 70 rms, 2 story. S $60; D $65; suites $90-$100; under 18 free. Crib free. TV. Indoor pool; whirlpool. Complimentary continental bkfst. Restaurant nearby. Ck-out 11 am. Meeting rms. Business servs avail. In-rm modem link. Cr cds: A, D, DS, MC, V.

★★ **HOLIDAY INN EXPRESS.** *4230 S Lakeport St (51106). 712/274-1400; fax 712/276-2136; toll-free 800/465-4329. www.holiday-inn.com.* 58 rms, 2 story. S $55-$70; D $60-$80; under 18 free. Crib free. TV; cable, VCR avail (free movies). Complimentary continental bkfst. Restaurant nearby. Ck-out 11 am. Meeting rms. Business servs avail. In-rm modem link. Exercise equipt. Whirlpool. Cr cds: A, C, D, DS, ER, JCB, MC, V.

★ **PALMER HOUSE MOTEL.** *3440 Gordon Dr (51105). 712/276-4221; fax 712/276-9535; toll-free 800/833-4221.* 59 rms, 1-2 story. S $40; D $45; Pet accepted. TV; cable. Complimentary continental bkfst. Restaurant adj. Ck-out 11 am. Business servs avail. Cr cds: A, MC, V.

★ **SUPER 8 MOTEL.** *4307 Stone Ave (51106). 712/274-1520; toll-free 800/800-8000. www.super8.com.* 60 rms, 2 story. Mid-May-mid-Oct: S $37; D

$46; each addl $5. Crib. Pet accepted. TV; cable. Continental bkfst. Restaurant 5-10 pm. Ck-out 11 am. Cr cds: A, C, D, DS, MC, V.

🄳 🌊 🈁 🐾 🆂🄲

Hotel

★ ★ ★ **HILTON SIOUX CITY.** *707 Fourth St (51101). 712/277-4101; fax 712/277-3168; toll-free 800/593-0555. www.hilton.com.* 193 units, 12 story. S, D $89; each addl $10; suites $125-$500; family rates; wkend rates. Crib free. Pet accepted, some restrictions; $10/day. TV; cable (premium). Indoor pool. Restaurant 6 am-10 pm; Sat, Sun from 6:30 am. Bar 4 pm-2 am. Ck-out noon. Meeting rms. Business servs avail. In-rm modem link. Free airport transportation. Exercise equipt; sauna. Cr cds: A, C, D, DS, JCB, MC, V.

🄳 🌊 🈁 🏃 🈁 🐾

Restaurants

★ **GREEN GABLES.** *1800 Pierce St (51105). 712/258-4246.* Hrs: 11 am-10 pm; Fri, Sat to 11 pm. Closed Dec 25. Res accepted. Beer, wine. Lunch $3-$7.95, dinner $5.25-$11.50. Children's menu. Specializes in chicken, barbecued ribs, steak. Parking. Family-owned. Cr cds: A, DS, MC, V.

🄳 🍴

★ **HUNAN PALACE.** *4280 Sergeant Rd (51106). 712/274-2336.* Hrs: 11:30 am-2:30 pm; 4:30-9:30 pm; Fri, Sat to 10:30 pm. Closed Thanksgiving, Dec 25. Res accepted. Chinese menu. Bar. A la carte entrees: lunch $3.25-$4.95, dinner $5.75-$9.75. Specializes in seafood, duck, Szechwan dishes. Several dining areas. Cr cds: A, C, DS, MC, V.

🄳 🍴

Spencer

(A-2) *See also Okoboji, Spirit Lake*

Founded 1859 **Pop** 11,066 **Elev** 1,321 ft **Area code** 712 **Zip** 51301

Information Spencer Area Association of Business & Industry, 122 W 5th St, PO Box 7937; 712/262-5680

In 1859 George E. Spencer gave his name to this city. In 1878 the first railroad was built through the black, fertile prairie, and in less than a year the settlement known as Spencer grew from 300 to a bustling town of 1,000. Its growth has continued, and due to its location in the middle of a large agricultural area, the town is now a prosperous business center serving surrounding farm communities.

What to See and Do

East Leach Park Campground. Campground with tent and trailer sites (dump station); fishing; playground. Campground (Mid-Apr-mid-Oct, daily). 305 4th St SE. Phone 712/264-7265. ¢¢¢

Gull Point State Park. Park has 160 wooded acres overlooking scenic Little Sioux River valley. Hiking, picnicking. 16 mi S on US 71, then 10 mi W on IA 10 in Peterson. Phone 712/337-3211.

Special Events

Flagfest Summer Festival. Art festival, craft fair, parade, air show, dance, talent contest, entertainment. Phone 712/262-5680. June 5-7.

Clay County Fair. Nine days early Sept.

Motels/Motor Lodges

★ **THE HOTEL.** *605 Grand (51301). 712/262-2010; fax 712/262-5610.* 41 rms, 39 shower only, 4 story. S, D $38-$68; each addl $4; under 12 free; wkly rates; higher rates county fair. TV; cable. Restaurant 6 am-2 pm. Bar 11-2 am. Ck-out 11 am. Meeting rms. Business servs avail. Valet serv. Free airport transportation. Some refrigerators, wet bars. Cr cds: A, MC, V.

🐾

★ **IRON HORSE MOTEL.** *1411 St SE (51301). 712/262-3720; fax 712/262-4538.* 94 rms, 2 story. S $35; D $60; under 12 free. TV; cable. Complimentary coffee. Restaurant nearby. Ck-out 11 am. Cr cds: A, D, DS, MC, V.

🄳 🐾 🈁 🐾

★ **PLAZA ONE MOTEL.** *102 11th St SW Plaza; jct US 18 and 71 S (51301). 712/262-6100; fax 712/262-5742.* 58 rms, 2 story. S $45.95; D $67.79; each addl $4; suites $70.95-$75;

under 12 free. Crib free. TV; cable. Complimentary continental bkfst. Restaurant adj 6 am-11 pm. Ck-out 11 am. Meeting rm. Business servs avail. Cr cds: A, D, DS, MC, V.
🅳 ⌨ 🔄 🔥

★ **SUPER 8 MOTEL.** *209 11th St SW (51301). 712/262-8500. www.super8. com.* 31 rms, 2 story. S $33.20-$39.88; D $41.30. Crib $3. TV; cable. Complimentary coffee in lobby. Restaurant adj 6 am-10 pm. Ck-out 11 am. Cr cds: A, DS, MC, V.
🅳 ⌨ 🔄 🔥

Spirit Lake

(A-3) *See also Estherville, Okoboji, Spencer*

Settled 1856 **Pop** 3,871 **Elev** 1,450 ft
Area code 712 **Zip** 51360
Information Okoboji Tourism, US 71, PO Box 215; 712/332-2209 or 800/270-2574
Web www.vacationokoboji.com

Spirit Lake serves tourists in the resort region and farming community flanking it. This area was a popular Native American meeting ground, visited by French explorers about 1700. The so-called Indian Massacre of Spirit Lake actually took place on the shores of three lakes—Spirit, East Okoboji, and West Okoboji. This is the scene of McKinlay Kantor's book *Spirit Lake.*

What to See and Do

Mini-Wakan State Park. 20 acres. Swimming, fishing, boating (ramp); snowmobiling, picnicking. Off IA 276, on N shore of Spirit Lake. Phone 712/337-3211.

Spirit Lake. 4,169 acres; largest glacier-carved lake in state. Swimming, fishing, boating (ramp). Camping (fee). Access area at Marble Beach, 3 mi NW on IA 276.

Storm Lake

(B-2) *See also Cherokee*

Pop 8,769 **Elev** 1,435 ft
Area code 712 **Zip** 50588
Information Chamber of Commerce, 119 W 6th, PO Box 584; 712/732-3780
Web www.stormlake.org

A college town—Buena Vista University is located here—and county seat on the north shore of Storm Lake, this community is also a meat and poultry center for the surrounding farms.

What to See and Do

Buena Vista County Historical Museum. Exhibits on early county history; changing displays; genealogy library. Changing exhibits and video presentations. (Mon-Fri mornings) 200 E 5th St, annex at 214 W 5th St. Phone 712/732-4955. **Donation**

Living Heritage Tree Museum. Seedlings and cuttings of more than 30 noteworthy trees, incl the Charter Oak Tree and the NASA seedling sent into space with Apollo 14. Descriptive plaques; pamphlets avail at City Hall. Illuminated at night. (Daily) In Sunset Park, W Lakeshore Dr. **FREE**

Storm Lake. Fourth-largest natural lake in Iowa with water surface of over 3,000 acres. Storm Lake offers swimming on the north, east, and south shores; fishing for bullhead, walleye, crappie, catfish, northern, and bass. Along shore are 135 acres of state and municipal parks with boating (docks, ramps). Golf. Camping at Sunrise Campground (Apr-Oct, daily; hookups; fee). Phone 712/732-8023.

Special Events

Star-Spangled Spectacular. North side of lake. July 4.

Balloon Days. Airport. Hot-air balloon races, fireworks, parade, amusement rides, food. Three days Labor Day wkend.

Santa's Castle. More than 70 detailed animated characters, some dating to the early 1900s. Daily. Thanksgiving-Dec 25.

Motel/Motor Lodge

★ **BUDGET INN.** *1504 N Lake Ave (50588). 712/732-2505; fax 712/732-7056; toll-free 800/383-7666.* 50 rms, 2 story. S $33; D $43; each addl $3. TV; cable (premium). Pool. Complimentary coffee in lobby. Restaurant adj. Ck-out 11 am. Meeting rm. In-rm modem link. Cr cds: A, C, D, DS, MC, V.
⊠ ⊠ ⊠ SC

Strawberry Point

(B-7) *See also Dubuque*

Pop 1,357 **Elev** 1,200 ft
Area code 319 **Zip** 52076

This town took its name from the wild strawberries that once grew nearby.

What to See and Do

State parks.

Backbone. Approx 1,780 acres with limestone bluffs rising 140 ft from Maquoketa River, scenic overlook and 100-acre lake. Swimming, supervised beach, fishing on stocked trout stream, boating (ramps, rentals); hiking trails, snowmobiling, picnicking. Improved and primitive camping (electricity, dump station), cabins. Civilian Conservation Corps museum. Standard hrs, fees. 4 mi SW on IA 410. Phone 319/924-2527.

Brush Creek Canyon. More than 210 acres featuring gorge with steep limestone walls that cut through 100 ft of bedrock; diversity of wildlife; state preserve. Hiking trails. Picnicking. 6 mi W on IA 3, then 5 mi N on IA 187 to Arlington, then 2 mi N. Phone 319/425-4161.

Wilder Memorial Museum. More than 850 dolls and three dollhouses; many rms furnished in style of late 1800s; art glassware, porcelain; oil paintings; rare Queen Anne doll; model of Iowa farm; display of Norwegian rosemaling; spinning wheels; Victorian lamps. (Schedule varies, call for appt) 123 W Mission St. Phone 319/933-4615. ¢¢

Washington

(D-6) *See also Iowa City*

Pop 7,074 **Elev** 762 ft **Area code** 319 **Zip** 52353

What to See and Do

Lake Darling State Park. A 1,387-acre park with 299-acre lake. Swimming, fishing, boating (ramps, rentals). Hiking trail. Snowmobiling. Picnicking. Camping (electricity, dump station). Standard hrs, fees. 12 mi SW on IA 1, then 3 mi W on IA 78, near Brighton. Phone 319/694-2323.

Waterloo

(B-6) *See also Cedar Falls*

Settled 1845 **Pop** 66,467 **Elev** 867 ft **Area code** 319
Information Convention & Visitors Bureau, 215 E 4th St, PO Box 1587, 50704; 319/233-8350 or 800/728-8431
Web www.waterloocvb.org

One of the largest tractor production facilities in the world is located here and contributes to the area's production of more than $1 billion worth of goods per year. On both banks of the wide Cedar River, Waterloo has established park and picnic areas, docks, and boating facilities along the shoreline.

What to See and Do

Grout Museum of History and Science. Permanent and changing exhibits on regional history and science; Discovery Zone offers many hands-on activities. Pioneer Hall, photo history area, industrial hall; genealogy library. Planetarium shows. (Tues-Sat; closed hols). W Park Ave and South St, on US 218. Phone 319/234-6357. ¢¢

John Deere Waterloo Works. Guided
2½-hr tours of farm tractor facility
(Mon-Fri; closed hols; also two wks
late July-early Aug). Over 12 yrs only;
low-heeled shoes advised; no open-
toed sandals. Also tours of John
Deere Component Works and John
Deere Engine Works. Res advised.
3500 E Donald St. Phone 319/292-
7801. **FREE**

Rensselaer Russell House Museum.
(1861) Guided tours of restored Victorian mansion; period furnishings.
(June-Aug, Tues-Fri, also Sat afternoons; Apr-May and Sept-Oct, Tues-
Sat afternoons) 520 W 3rd St. Phone
319/233-0262. ¢

Waterloo Community Playhouse.
Since 1916; offers seven productions
yrly incl comedies, dramas, myster-
ies, and classics. 225 Commercial St.
Phone 319/235-0367. ¢¢¢

Waterloo Museum of Art. Permanent
collections incl Haitian, American,
and regional art; Grant Wood drawings. Changing exhibits. Gift shop
offers works by Midwest artists.
(Daily; closed Jan 1, Thanksgiving,
Dec 25) 225 Commercial St. Phone
319/291-4491. **FREE**

Special Event

My Waterloo Days Festival. Citywide
festival features air show, balloon rallies, parade, laser and fireworks show,
music, renaissance fair, food. Phone
319/233-8431. Ten days beginning
Fri after Memorial Day.

Motels/Motor Lodges

★★ **BEST WESTERN STARLITE
VILLAGE.** *214 Washington St (50701).
319/235-0321; fax 319/235-6343; toll-
free 800/903-0009. www.bestwestern.
com.* 219 rms, 11 story. S, D $52-$59;
each addl $7; suites $95-$150; under
12 free. Crib free. Pet accepted. TV;
cable. Indoor pool. Restaurant 6:30
am-2 pm, 5-9 pm; Sun 7 am-2 pm.
Bar 4 pm-2 am. Ck-out noon. Meeting rms. Business servs avail. In-rm
modem link. Airport, railroad station, bus depot transportation. Cr
cds: A, MC, V.

★★ **FAIRFIELD INN.** *2011 Laporte
Rd (71202). 319/234-5452; toll-free
800/228-2800. www.fairfieldinn.com.*

57 rms, 3 story. S $48; D $48-$53;
under 18 free. Crib free. Pet accepted,
some restrictions. TV; cable. Indoor
pool; whirlpool. Complimentary
continental bkfst. Restaurant opp
open 24 hrs. Ck-out 11 am. Cr cds:
A, D, DS, MC, V.

★★ **HEARTLAND INN.** *1809
LaPorte Rd (50702). 319/235-4461; fax
319/235-0907; toll-free 800/334-3277.
www.heartlandinns.com.* 118 rms, 2
story. S $65; D $71; each addl $5;
suites $120-$150; under 17 free. Crib
free. Pet accepted; $10. TV; cable.
Complimentary bkfst. Restaurant
nearby. Ck-out noon. Meeting rm.
Business servs avail. In-rm modem
link. Exercise equipt; sauna. Cr cds:
A, C, D, DS, MC, V.

★ **HEARTLAND INN.** *3052 Marnie
Ave (50701). 319/232-7467; fax 319/
232-0403; toll-free 800/334-3277. www.
heartlandinns.com.* 56 rms, 2 story. S
$42-$51; D $49-$58; suites $115-
$130; under 17 free. Crib free. Pet
accepted; $10. TV; cable. Compli-
mentary bkfst. Restaurant adj 6 am-
10 pm. Ck-out noon. Meeting rms.
Business servs avail. Cr cds: A, C, D,
DS, MC, V.

★★ **HOLIDAY INN.** *205 W 4th St
(50701). 319/233-7560; fax 319/236-
9590. www.holiday-inn.com.* 229 rms,
10 story. S $58-$66; D $60-$67; suites
$85-$190; under 18 free. Crib free.
Pet accepted. TV; cable. Indoor pool;
whirlpool, poolside serv. Restaurant 6
am-2 pm; dining rm 5-10 pm. Bar
11-2 am; entertainment. Ck-out
noon. Meeting rms. In-rm modem
link. Airport transportation. Some
refrigerators. Atrium lobby. Cr cds: A,
D, DS, MC, V.

★ **SUPER 8.** *1825 LaPorte Rd
(50702). 319/233-1800. www.super8.
com.* 62 rms, 3 story. S $42; D $47;
under 16 free. Crib free. Pet accepted,
some restrictions. TV; cable. Complimentary continental bkfst. Restaurant opp open 24 hrs. Ck-out 11 am.
Sundries. Cr cds: A, C, D, DS, MC, V.

★ **TRAVEL INN.** *3350 University Ave (50701). 319/235-2165; fax 319/235-7175.* 98 rms, 2 story. S $35; D $45; each addl $5; under 17 free. Pet accepted. TV; cable. Complimentary continental bkfst. Restaurant nearby. Ck-out noon. Coin lndry. In-rm modem link. Game rm. Cr cds: A, DS, MC, V.
🔲 🔲 🔲 SC

Waverly

(B-6) *See also Cedar Falls, Waterloo*

Pop 8,539 **Elev** 919 ft **Area code** 319 **Zip** 50677

Information Chamber of Commerce, 118 W Bremer Ave; 319/352-4526

Astride the Cedar River, Waverly serves a rich farm area as a major retail and industrial center.

What to See and Do

Iowa Star Clipper Dinner Train. Scenic round-trip, four-course dining excursions (three hrs) through Cedar River Valley in 1950s-era dining cars. (All yr, days vary) Departs from Waverly depot for afternoon or eve trips. Phone 319/352-5467. ¢¢¢¢
Wartburg College. (1852) 1,450 students. Liberal arts. The Becker Hall of Science has collection of New Guinea artifacts (Daily; closed Sun June-Aug, hols). Also Schield International Museum (fee), a planetarium and art gallery. The Wartburg College Lageschulte Prairie is 3 mi NE. (Sept-May, Mon-Fri; closed hols) 9th St NW and Bremer Ave. Phone 319/352-8200.

Webster City

(B-4) *See also Fort Dodge*

Settled 1850 **Pop** 7,894
Area code 515 **Zip** 50595
Information Area Association of Business & Industry, 628 2nd St, PO Box 310; 515/832-2564

What to See and Do

Country Relics Little Village and Homestead. Reproduction of turn-of-the-century Midwestern town features 1/2- to 2/3-scale model buildings; incl church, one-rm schoolhouse, general store, and railway depot. Also on display are tractors and memorabilia relating early history of International Harvester. Gift shop. (May-Oct, daily) Approx 10 mi S on IA 17; just N of Stanhope. Phone 515/826-3491. ¢¢

Depot Museum Complex. Log cabin, original courthouse, other historic buildings. (May-Sept, daily) Ohio and Superior sts. Phone 515/832-2847. **FREE**

Motels/Motor Lodges

★★ **BEST WESTERN NORSEMAN INN.** *3086 220th St, Williams (50271). 515/854-2281; fax 515/855-2621. www.bestwestern.com.* 33 rms. S $39; D $51; each addl $6. Crib $6. Pet accepted. TV; cable. Complimentary continental bkfst. Restaurant nearby. Bar. Ck-out noon. Cr cds: A, C, D, DS, ER, JCB, MC, V.
🔲 🔲 🔲 🔲 🔲

★ **EXECUTIVE INN.** *1700 Superior St (50595). 515/832-3631; fax 515/832-6830; toll-free 800/322-3631.* 39 rms, 2 story. S, D $38-$53. Crib $3. TV; cable. Indoor pool. Complimentary continental bkfst. Ck-out 11 am. Meeting rm. Business servs avail. Sauna. Cr cds: A, DS, MC, V.
🔲 🔲 🔲 🔲 SC

West Bend

See also Algona, Emmetsburg

Founded 1880 **Pop** 862 **Elev** 1,203 ft
Area code 515 **Zip** 50597
Information Chamber of Commerce, PO Box 366; 515/887-4721

The large bend in the West Fork of the Des Moines River gives this town its name.

What to See and Do

Grotto of the Redemption. Begun in 1912 by Reverend P. M. Dobberstein,

One of the "Bridges of Madison County," near Winterset

the grotto, which covers entire city blk, tells the story of the fall and redemption of man. Constructed of ornamental stones from many states and countries, the shrine is reputed to be the largest collection of shells, minerals, fossils, and other petrified material in the world. Illuminated at night. Camping (hookups, dump station). (Daily; guided tours June-mid-Oct; also by appt) 2 blks off IA 15 at N end of town. Phone 515/887-2371. **Donation**

West Union (B-6)

Pop 2,490 **Elev** 1,107 ft
Area code 319 **Zip** 52175
Information Chamber of Commerce, 101 N Vine St, PO Box 71; 319/422-3070

What to See and Do

Montauk. (1874) Former home of William Larrabee, Iowa's 12th governor. Original furnishings; art objects; personal memorabilia; 40-acre grounds. Tours (Late May-Oct, daily; mid-Mar-Apr, by appt). 9 mi NE on US 18, near Clermont. Phone 319/423-7173. ¢¢

Volga River State Recreation Area. A 5,500-acre wooded area with lake; boating, fishing; hunting, hiking, horseback riding. X-country skiing, snowmobiling. Camping. Standard hrs, fees. 6 mi S via IA 150. Phone 319/425-4161.

Motel/Motor Lodge

★ **LILAC MOTEL.** *310 US 150 N (52175). 319/422-3861.* 27 rms. S $35; D $45; under 12 free. TV; cable. Restaurant nearby. Ck-out 11 am. In-rm modem link. Cr cds: A, C, D, DS, MC, V.
⬛ ⬛ ⬛

Winterset

(D-4) *See also Indianola*

Settled 1846 **Pop** 4,196 **Elev** 1,100 ft
Area code 515 **Zip** 50273
Information Chamber of Commerce, 73 Jefferson; 515/462-1185
Web www.madisoncounty.com

What to See and Do

⬛ **Covered bridges.** Six remain in Madison County; for leaflet, map and information on guided tours contact Chamber of Commerce.

John Wayne Birthplace. House where the actor was born May 26, 1907; front parlor and kitchen restored to era when he lived here; other rms contain memorabilia. Visitor center. (Daily; closed Jan 1, Thanksgiving, Dec 25) 216 S 2nd St. Phone 515/462-1044. ¢

Madison County Museum and Complex. Twelve buildings and restored Bevington Mansion (1856). Fossils, Native American artifacts, memorabilia; old barn with live poultry display, log cabin school, log post office, 1881 church, general store, train depot. (May-Oct, daily; also by appt) 815 S 2nd Ave. Phone 515/462-2134. ¢¢

Special Events

National Skillet-Throwing Contest. 15 mi SW via US 169 and County G61 in Macksburg. Contestants throw skillets at stuffed dummies. Second full wkend June.

Madison County Fair. Fairgrounds. Aug.

South River Festival. S via county P71 and County G68 to Truro. Features National Dry-land Canoe Race, in which canoes race down Main St using brooms for paddles. Phone 515/765-4586. Aug.

Covered Bridge Festival. Late 19th-century crafts, entertainment; parade, bus tour of two covered bridges. Second full wkend Oct.

Motel/Motor Lodge

★ **VILLAGE VIEW MOTEL.** *711 E US 92 (50273). 515/462-1218; fax 515/462-1231; toll-free 800/862-1218.* 16 rms, 1 story. S $54.88; D $64.88; under 12 free. Crib free. Pet accepted. TV; cable (premium), VCR avail. Complimentary coffee in lobby. Restaurant nearby. Ck-out 11 am. Rec rm. Cr cds: A, D, DS, MC, V.
🐾 ⊠ 🐾 **SC**

KANSAS

Native Americans inhabited Kansas thousands of years before Spanish conquistador Francisco Vasquez de Coronado explored the territory in 1541. Though looking for gold and the fabled Land of Quivira, Coronado instead found what he called "the best country I have ever seen for producing all the products of Spain." Other early explorers of Kansas were partners Meriwether Lewis and William Clark. Army Captain Zebulon Pike also explored the area, continuing westward to discover what is now Pikes Peak in Colorado.

By the 1840s traders and immigrants had established the Santa Fe and Chisholm Trails across the region. Kansas pre-Civil War activity included the exploits of John Brown, who operated the Underground Railway for runaway slaves escaping through Kansas. Many clashes occurred between antislavery and proslavery forces as Kansas was being admitted to the Union. As railroads expanded westward, the era of cattle drives made such towns as Abilene, Hays, Wichita, and Dodge City centers of the legendary Old West, as did such men as Bat Masterson, Wyatt Earp, "Wild Bill" Hickock, and the Dalton Gang.

Population: 2,654,052
Area: 82,280 square miles
Elevation: 680-4,039 feet
Peak: Mount Sunflower (Wallace County)
Entered Union: January 29, 1861 (34th state)
Capital: Topeka
Motto: To the stars through difficulties
Nickname: The Sunflower State
Flower: Native Sunflower
Bird: Western Meadowlark
Tree: Cottonwood
Fair: September 6-15, 2002, in Hutchinson
Time Zone: Central and Mountain
Website: www.kansascommerce.com

Eastern Kansas is green, fertile, and hilly, with woods, streams, and lakes. Western Kansas is a part of the Great Plains, once the grass-covered haunt of the buffalo. In 1874 Mennonite immigrants from Russia introduced their Turkey Red wheat seed to Kansas soil, helping to establish Kansas as the "breadbasket of the nation." Today agriculture has expanded to include a wide range of crops, cattle, and other livestock. Other leading industries include the manufacturing of airplanes and farm equipment, salt mining, and oil refining.

Crappie, walleye, bass, and channel catfish abound in many lakes and streams to lure the fishing enthusiast. Deer, quail, pheasant, ducks, geese, and many other species of game attract the hunter.

When to Go/Climate

Expect to encounter typical midwestern temperatures in Kansas—hot summers, with more humidity in the eastern part of the state; cold, sometimes harsh, winters; and a propensity for tornadoes, thunderstorms, and blizzards. Tornadoes are most likely from May-June; half the annual precipitation falls between May-August. Summer, despite the heat, is the most popular time to visit.

AVERAGE HIGH/LOW TEMPERATURES (°F)

TOPEKA

Jan 37/16	May 76/53	Sept 80/56
Feb 43/22	June 84/63	Oct 69/44
Mar 55/32	July 89/68	Nov 54/32
Apr 67/43	Aug 88/65	Dec 41/21

WICHITA

Jan 40/19	May 77/54	Sept 81/59
Feb 46/24	June 87/65	Oct 71/47
Mar 57/34	July 93/70	Nov 55/34
Apr 68/45	Aug 91/68	Dec 43/23

Parks and Recreation Finder

Directions to and information about the parks and recreation areas below are given under their respective town/city sections. Please refer to those sections for details.

NATIONAL PARK AND RECREATION AREAS

Key to abbreviations. I.H.S. = International Historic Site; I.P.M. = International Peace Memorial; N.B. = National Battlefield; N.B.P. = National Battlefield Park; N.B.C. = National Battlefield and Cemetery; N.C.A. = National Conservation Area; N.E.M. = National Expansion Memorial; N.F. = National Forest; N.G. = National Grassland; N.H.P. = National Historical Park; N.H.C. = National Heritage Corridor; N.H.S. = National Historic Site; N.L. = National Lakeshore; N.M. = National Monument; N.M.P. = National Military Park; N.Mem. = National Memorial; N.P. = National Park; N.Pres. = National Preserve; N.R.A. = National Recreational Area; N.R.R. = National Recreational River; N.Riv. = National River; N.S. = National Seashore; N.S.R. = National Scenic Riverway; N.S.T. = National Scenic Trail; N.Sc. = National Scientific Reserve; N.V.M. = National Volcanic Monument.

Place Name	Listed Under
Fort Larned N.H.S.	LARNED
Fort Scott N.H.S.	FORT SCOTT

STATE PARK AND RECREATION AREAS

Key to abbreviations. I.P. = Interstate Park; S.A.P. = State Archaeological Park; S.B. = State Beach; S.C.A. = State Conservation Area; S.C.P. = State Conservation Park; S.Cp. = State Campground; S.F. = State Forest; S.G. = State Garden; S.H.A. = State Historic Area; S.H.P. = State Historic Park; S.H.S. = State Historic Site; S.M.P. = State Marine Park; S.N.A. = State Natural Area; S.P. = State Park; S.P.C. = State Public Campground; S.R. = State Reserve; S.R.A. = State Recreation Area; S.Res. = State Reservoir; S.Res.P. = State Resort Park; S.R.P. = State Rustic Park.

Place Name	Listed Under
Cedar Bluff S.P.	WAKEENEY
Cheney S.P.	WICHITA
Clinton S.P.	LAWRENCE
Crawford S.P.	PITTSBURG
Eisenhower S.P.	EMPORIA
El Dorado S.P.	EL DORADO
Elk City S.P.	INDEPENDENCE

CALENDAR HIGHLIGHTS

FEBRUARY
International Pancake Race (Liberal). Women compete simultaneously with women in Olney, England, running a 415-yd S-shaped course with a pancake in a skillet, flipping it en route.

MARCH
National Junior College Basketball Tournament (Hutchinson). Sports Arena.

MAY
Wichita River Festival (Wichita). Includes twilight pop concert and fireworks; antique bathtub races; hot-air balloon launch; athletic events; entertainment. Phone 316/267-2817.

JUNE
Washburn Sunflower Music Festival (Topeka). International symphonic musicians perform nightly. Phone 785/231-1010.

JULY
Indian Powwow (Wichita). Tribes gather from all over the country and Canada. Traditional dances; crafts; ethnic food. Phone 316/262-5221.

AUGUST
Central Kansas Free Fair & PRCA Wild Bill Hickock Rodeo (Abilene). Phone 785/263-4570.
National Baseball Congress World Series (Wichita). Lawrence Stadium. Amateur Series. Phone 316/267-3372.

SEPTEMBER
Historic Fort Hays Days (Hays). Two full days of living history including demonstrations of butter churning, tatting, ropemaking, rug weaving, whittling, stonepost cutting. Phone 785/625-6812, 785/628-8202 or 800/569-4505.
Kansas State Fair (Hutchinson). Fairgrounds. Exhibits, carnival, entertainment, car racing, etc. Phone 316/669-3600.
Renaissance Festival (Kansas City)(Bonner Springs). Seven wkends of festivities. Phone 800/373-0357. Begins Labor Day wkend.

Fall River S.P.	EUREKA
Glen Elder S.P.	BELOIT
Kanopolis S.P.	LINDSBORG
Kaw Mission S.H.S.	COUNCIL GROVE
Lake Scott S.P.	SCOTT CITY
Lovewell S.P.	MANKATO
Meade S.P.	MEADE
Milford S.P.	JUNCTION CITY
Perry S.P.	TOPEKA
Pomona S.P.	OTTAWA
Prairie Dog S.P.	NORTON
Shawnee Indian Mission S.H.S.	OVERLAND PARK
Toronto S.P.	YATES CENTER
Tuttle Creek S.P.	MANHATTAN
Webster S.P.	STOCKTON
Wilson S.P.	RUSSELL

Water-related activities, hiking, riding, various other sports, picnicking and visitor centers, as well as camping, are available in many of these areas. Annual vehicle permit $30; daily vehicle permit $5. There is camping at most areas (two week maximum). Daily camping permit $5.50; electricity, water, trailer utility hookup $5-$8. Pets on hand-held leash or in cage only; no pets on bathing beaches. A camping guide is published by the Kansas Department of Wildlife and Parks, Public Information, 512 SE 25th Ave, Pratt 67124-8174; 316/672-5911.

FISHING AND HUNTING

The state maintains more than 35 state fishing lakes and 48 wildlife management and public hunting areas.

Nonresident fishing license: annual $35.50; 5-day $15.50; 24-hour $3.50. Nonresident hunting license: annual $65.50; 48-hr nonresident waterfowl license $20; Kansas migratory habitat stamp $3.50; handling fee on all licenses $1. Hunters born on or after July 1, 1957, must have a hunter's education course certificate card in order to purchase a license.

For digests of hunting and fishing regulations, contact Kansas Department of Wildlife and Parks, Public Information, 512 SE 25th Ave, Pratt 67124; 316/672-5911. The department also publishes hunting and fishing guides.

Driving Information

Safety belts are mandatory for all persons in front seat of vehicle. Children under the age of four must be in an approved safety seat anywhere in vehicle. Children ages 4-13 must wear a safety belt anywhere in vehicle. For further information phone 800/416-2522.

INTERSTATE HIGHWAY SYSTEM

The following alphabetical listing of Kansas towns in *Mobil Travel Guide* shows that these cities are within ten miles of the indicated Interstate highways. A highway map should, however, be checked for the nearest exit.

Highway Number	Cities/Towns within ten miles
Interstate 35	El Dorado, Emporia, Kansas City, Ottawa, Wichita.
Interstate 70	Abilene, Colby, Goodland, Hays, Junction City, Kansas City, Lawrence, Manhattan, Oakley, Russell, Salina, Topeka, WaKeeney.
Interstate 135	Lindsborg, McPherson, Newton, Salina, Wichita.

Additional Visitor Information

The Kansas Department of Commerce and Housing, Travel and Tourism Development Division, 700 SW Harrison St, Suite 1300, Topeka 66603-3712, phone 785/296-2009 or 800/2-KANSAS, distributes the *Kansas Attractions Guide, Kansas Transportation Map* and *Calendar of Events.*

Visitors to Kansas will find welcome centers on I-70 W, just W of Goodland; at the Kansas City exit on I-70 E (milepost 415); at the southern entrance into Kansas on the turnpike in Belle Plaine; at 229 E Pancake Blvd in Liberal; at 231 E Wall St in Fort Scott; at the Civic Center Depot in Abilene; at the Santa Fe Depot/Chamber in Atchison; at the Brown Mansion on US 169 in Coffeeville; on US 81 near North Belleville; and at the State Capitol in Topeka. Visitors will find information and brochures helpful in planning stops at points of interest.

WILDLIFE ON THE PRAIRIE

East Central Kansas boasts beautiful tallgrass prairies, some of the few remaining in the United States. Take this drive in early spring, when the old grass is burned to make way for spring growth, or in early summer, when wildflowers are abundant. Head west from Topeka on I-70 to Manhattan. Nearby, the Konza Prairie is a major site for prairie research, with hiking and wildlife watching. Continue south on Highway 177 to the Tallgrass Prairie National Preserve near Strong Falls. Covered-wagon train trips are offered at El Dorado, northeast of Wichita on Highway 177. From Wichita, take I-135 north to McPherson and visit the McPherson-Maxwell Game Preserve, with one of the state's largest bison herds, as well as elk, deer, and buffalo. Return to I-70 at Salina, then head back east to your starting point. If possible, stop en route in Abilene to visit the Eisenhower Center, featuring the president's boyhood home, museum, and gravesite. **(APPROX 380 MI)**

ACROSS THE PRAIRIE LANDSCAPE

This loop trail passes through prairie landscapes and across the Kansas of past, present, and future. Begin in Witchita, the state's largest city and a prosperous oil and agricultural center. Three of the city's best attractions are found in the Arthur Sim Memorial Park, along a bend of the Arkansas River. The city's historic role as a "cow capital" along the Chisholm Trail is preserved at the Old Cowtown Museum, a historic village with 40 buildings from the city's early boom years in the 1870s. Nearby is the Witchita Art Museum, with a fine collection of American Impressionists and a grand outdoor sculpture garden. Gardeners will enjoy Botanica, The Witchita Garden, with a number of theme gardens.

Drive northeast on I-35 to Cassoday, home to several good antique stores, and join Highway 177 northbound. Known as the Flint Hills Scenic Byway, this route passes through a rugged landscape of rolling hills, mesas, and virgin prairie. At the town of Cottonwood Falls, stop to visit the Chase County Courthouse, the oldest in Kansas. The building was constructed from local limestone in a striking French Renaissance style.

Just north is the Tallgrass Prairie National Preserve, which protects 11,000 acres of native prairie grassland that is home to 40 species of grasses, 200 species of birds, 30 species of mammals, and up to 10 million insects per acre. A number of trails lead across the plains, which in spring are carpeted with wildflowers. The preserve's headquarters are located at the Z Bar Ranch, an imposing stone ranch house cum mansion from the 1880s.

Council Grove is one of Kansas's most historic towns; in fact, the entire settlement has been designated a National Historic Landmark. Council Grove was the last provisioning stop on the old Sante Fe Trail between the Missouri River and Sante Fe, and the town is filled with landmarks of the frontier West. The Council Oak marks the site of the signing of an 1825 peace treaty between the Osage and the United States. The nearby Post Office Oak served as a drop box for letters written by travelers along the Sante Fe Trail. The Last Chance Store and the Hays House Restaurant have both been in business since 1857—the latter is the oldest continuously operating restaurant west of the Mississippi.

Continue north on Highway 57 to Junction City, located at the confluence of the Republican and Smoky Hill rivers. The town owes its existence to Fort Riley, founded in 1853 to protect pioneers traveling along the Sante Fe and Oregon trails. The fort, just north of town along Highway 57, contains a number of historic sites, including the state's first territorial capital, an early home of General George Custer, and the US Cavalry Museum, which chronicles the history of the mounted horse soldier from the Revolutionary War to 1950.

Continue east on I-70 to Abilene, famous as an Old West cowtown and as the boyhood home of President Dwight Eisenhower. In addition to the frontier and presidential museums you'd expect, Abilene offers a couple of unusual attractions, including dinner excursions in an antique train and the American Indian Art Center, which represents 90 artists from 30 Native American nations.

From Abilene, travel north on Highway 15 and north on Highway 106 to visit Rock City, where hiking trails wind through a curious wonderland of house-sized sandstone concretions scattered across a prairie meadow. It's easy to imagine these formations as a prehistoric town turned to stone!

Return to Highway 18, and head east to join I-135 southbound. At McPherson, turn southwest on Highway 61 at exit 58. Hutchinson offers travelers two unusual attractions. The Dillon Nature Center comprises 100 acres of trail-linked prairie and ponds containing 150 plains animal species. The Kansas Cosmosphere and Space Center is one of the nation's foremost museums dedicated to the exploration of space. Displays include rockets and capsules from both the US and Soviet space programs, plus spy planes, space equipment, and an IMAX Theater. Return to Wichita on I-96. **(APPROX 350 MI)**

Abilene

(C-5) *See also Junction City, Salina*

Founded 1858 **Pop** 6,242 **Elev** 1,153 ft **Area code** 785 **Zip** 67410
Information Convention & Visitors Bureau, 201 NW 2nd, PO Box 146; 785/263-2231 or 800/569-5915
Web www.jc.net/~cityhall

Once famous as a Kansas "cow town," Abilene in 1867 was the terminal point of the Kansas Pacific (later Union Pacific) Railroad and the nearest railhead for the shipment of cattle brought north over the Chisholm Trail. The number shipped east from here between 1867-1871 has been estimated at more than a million, and often 500 cowboys were paid off at a time. City marshals Tom Smith and Wild Bill Hickock brought in law and order in the 1870s. Today Abilene is a wheat center, perhaps best known as the boyhood home of Dwight D. Eisenhower.

What to See and Do

Abilene Smoky Valley Excursion Train. Hundred-yr-old wooden coach/diner makes trips through historic countryside. (Memorial Day-Labor-Day, daily) I-70, S on Buckeye St. Phone 785/263-1077. ¢¢

Dickinson County Historical Museum. Exhibits depict life of early pioneer days, the Native Americans, and the buffalo; antique toys and household items used at the turn of the century; cowboys and cattle trails; Heritage Center, carousel, log cabin. Teaching tours for children by appt. (Early Apr-late Oct, daily; rest of yr, by appt) 412 S Campbell St. Phone 785/263-2681. Admission incl

> **Museum of Independent Telephony.** More than a century of telephones from 1876 to present; insulators, cables, pay stations. Exhibits incl old switchboard and crank-type phones. (Same days as Dickinson County Historical Museum) Guided tours by appt. Phone 785/263-2681.

🗙 **Eisenhower Center.** This house (1887), where Dwight Eisenhower and his five brothers were raised, was

purchased by the family in 1898. Interior and most furnishings are original. Museum houses changing exhibits of mementos, souvenirs, and gifts received during Dwight D. Eisenhower's career; murals in lobby depict his life. Thirty-min orientation film shown in Visitor Center. Library contains presidential papers. President and Mrs. Eisenhower buried in the Meditation Chapel. (Daily; closed Jan 1, Thanksgiving, Dec 25) 200 SE 4th St, E of KS 15. Phone 785/263-4751. ¢¢

Greyhound Hall of Fame. Exhibits, ten-min film on breeding and racing of greyhounds. (Daily; closed Jan 1, Thanksgiving, Dec 25) 407 S Buckeye St. Phone 785/263-3000. **FREE**

Lebold-Vahsholtz Mansion. Restored Victorian mansion with period furnishings. (All yr, by appt; closed Thanksgiving, Dec 25) 106 N Vine. Phone 785/263-4356. ¢¢

Seelye Mansion and Museum. Twenty-five-rm Georgian mansion listed on the National Register of Historic Places. Built in 1905 by A. B. Seelye, patent medicine entrepreneur. Museum depicts turn-of-the-century medicine business. Tours. (Daily) 1105 N Buckeye. Phone 785/263-1084. ¢¢¢

Special Events

National Greyhound Meet. 1½ mi W on US 40 at the Greyhound Association. Greyhound racing in the hometown of the National Greyhound Assn. Last wk Apr and second wk Oct.

Central Kansas Free Fair and PRCA Wild Bill Hickock Rodeo. Third wk Aug.

Garden Tour. Phone 800/569-5915. Third wk Aug.

Chisholm Trail Festival. First Sat Oct.

Motels/Motor Lodges

★★ **BEST WESTERN ABILENE'S PRIDE.** *1709 N Buckeye Ave (67410). 785/263-2800; fax 785/263-3285; toll-free 800/701-1000. www.bestwestern. com.* 80 rms, 1-2 story. S $39-$55; D $44-$75; each addl $4. Crib free. TV; cable. Heated pool; whirlpool. Complimentary continental bkfst. Restaurant 11 am-8 pm; Fri, Sat to 9 pm, Sun to 8 pm. Bar. Ck-out 11 am.

Eisenhower Center, Abilene

Meeting rm. In-rm modem link. Exercise equipt. Cr cds: A, C, D, DS, MC, V.

★ **DIAMOND MOTEL.** *1407 NW 3rd St (67410). 785/263-2360; fax 785/ 263-2186.* 30 rms. S $28; D $32-$38; each addl $4. Pet accepted, some restrictions. TV; cable (premium). Complimentary coffee in lobby. Ck-out 11 am. Refrigerators. Cr cds: A, DS, MC, V

★ **SUPER 8 MOTEL.** *2207 N Buckeye Ave (67410). 785/263-4545; fax 785/ 263-7448; res 800/800-8000. www. super8.com.* 62 rms, 3 story. No elvtr. S $34-$39; D $42-$50; each addl $4; suites $47-$59; under 12 free. Crib free. Pet accepted, some restrictions; $10. TV; cable (premium). Complimentary coffee in lobby. Restaurant adj 6:30 am-midnight. Ck-out 11 am. Meeting rms. Business servs avail. Cr cds: A, C, D, DS, ER, MC, V.

Restaurants

★★ **BROOKVILLE HOTEL DINING ROOM.** *105 E Lafayette (67410). 785/263-2244. www.brookvillehotel.com.* Hrs: 5-8:30 pm; Sun 11 am-7:30 pm. Closed Mon; Dec 25, Thanksgiving. Res accepted. Serv bar. Complete meals: family-style chicken dinner $10.75. Own biscuits. In historic frontier hostelry; period decor. Cr cds: DS, MC, V.
D

★★★ **KIRBY HOUSE.** *205 NE 3rd St (67410). 785/263-7336. www. kirby-house.com.* Hrs: 11 am-2 pm, 5-9 pm; Sun to 3 pm. Closed Jan 1, Dec 25. Res accepted. Bar. Lunch $2.95-$5.95, dinner $4.95-$15.95. Children's menu. Specialties: chicken Marco Polo, country-fried steak, peppercorn steak. Ten dining rms in Victorian house (1885). Totally non-smoking. Cr cds: DS, MC, V.
D

Arkansas City

(F-6) *See also Winfield; also see Ponca City, OK*

Founded 1870 **Pop** 12,762 **Elev** 1,120 ft **Area code** 620 **Zip** 67005
Information Chamber of Commerce, 126 E Washington; 316/442-0230
Web www.arkcity.org

Situated near the Oklahoma border, Arkansas City is home to meat packing, oil refining, and aircraft-related industries. Approximately 100,000 homesteaders started the run for the Cherokee Strip on September 16, 1893, from here. The run was a race held by the US government as a means to give away land for settlement in what was then the Oklahoma Territory.

What to See and Do

Chaplin Nature Center. More than 200 acres of woodland, prairie, and streams along the Arkansas River; visitor center, nature center, self-guided trails. (Daily; guided tours by appt) 3 mi W on US 166, then 2 mi N on gravel road (follow signs). Phone 316/442-4133. **FREE**

Cherokee Strip Land Rush Museum. Articles related to the Cherokee Strip Run; reference library on Run, Native Americans, genealogy. (Tues-Sun; closed hols) 1 mi S on US 77. Phone 316/442-6750. ¢¢

Special Events

River Valley Art Festival. Wilson Park. More than 80 juried artists display and sell their works. Entertainment, international foods. Phone 316/442-5895. First wkend June.

Last Run Car Show. Fourth wkend Sept. Agri-Business Building, 712 W Washington.

Arkalalah Celebration. Phone 316/442-6077. Last wkend Oct.

Motels/Motor Lodges

★ **HALLMARK INN.** *1617 N Summit St (67005). 620/442-1400; fax 620/442-4729.* 47 rms. S $44; D $49; each addl $6; under 12 free. Crib free. Pet accepted. TV; cable (premium). Pool. Complimentary continental bkfst, coffee in rms. Ck-out 11 am. Business servs avail. Microwaves avail. Cr cds: A, DS, MC, V.
🔧 🐾 🖥 🖨 🔥

★★ **REGENCY COURT INN.** *3232 N Summit St (67005). 620/442-7700; fax 620/442-1218; toll-free 800/325-9151.* 86 rms. S $53; D $65; each addl $6; under 12 free. Crib free. TV; cable. Indoor pool; whirlpool. Restaurant 7 am-1:30 pm, 5-8:30 pm; Fri, Sat to 9 pm; Sun 7 am-1:30 pm. Bar 5 pm-midnight, closed Sun. Ck-out 11 am. Meeting rms. Business servs avail. Game rm. Cr cds: A, C, D, DS, JCB, MC, V.
D 🖨 🖥 SC

Atchison

(B-8) *See also Hiawatha, Leavenworth; also see St. Joseph, MO*

Founded 1854 **Pop** 10,656 **Elev** 810 ft
Area code 913 **Zip** 66002
Information Atchison Area Chamber of Commerce, 200 S 10th St, Box 126; 913/367-2427 or 800/234-1854
Web www.atchison.org

Atchison grew up around a desirable landing site on the Missouri River—an important factor in its crowded history. Lewis and Clark camped here in 1804; so did Major Stephen Longstreet's Yellowstone Expedition in 1819; French explorers from the colony of Louisiana preceded both. In the 1850s and 1860s steamboat and wagon traffic to the west was bustling; mail coaches left daily on the 17-day round trip to Denver. A railroad from St. Joseph, Missouri, established in 1859 by means of an Atchison city bond issue, was the first direct rail connection eastward from a point this far west. Another Atchison bond issue the same year made the Atchison, Topeka, and Santa Fe Railroad possible, although the first lines were not opened until 1872. The town's position in the Missouri-Kansas border struggles of the 1850s caused it to be named for US Senator David Rice Atchison of Missouri (who, it is claimed, was president of the United States from noon, March 4 to noon, March 5, 1849). Today Atchison is a manufacturing and wholesale center, producing flour, feeds, alcohol, and steel castings. It is also the birthplace of aviatrix Amelia Earhart. A one-acre "earthwork" portrait by crop artist Stan Herd pays tribute to this accomplished pilot.

What to See and Do

Amelia Earhart Birthplace. House built in 1861 by Judge Alfred Otis, Amelia Earhart's grandfather. Earhart was born here July 24, 1897, and lived her early yrs here. Incl exhibits of her life and flying accomplishments. (May-Oct, Mon-Sat, also Sun afternoons; rest of yr, by appt) 223 N Terrace. Phone 913/367-4217. ¢

Atchison County Historical Society Museum. Amelia Earhart exhibit; WWI collection; gun collection; pictures, local historical items. (Daily) 200 S 10th St. Phone 913/367-6238. ¢

Atchison Trolley. One-hr tours of city history and visitor highlights. (May, Aug-Oct, Fri-Sun; June-July, Wed-Sun) Santa Fe Depot, 200 S 10th St. Phone 913/367-2427. ¢¢

City parks.

Independence Park. Five-acre park with boat landing on Missouri River; Lewis and Clark Trail landmark. Near Downtown. **FREE**

Jackson Park. Covers 115 acres with iris-bordered drives; scenic view of the Missouri River valley from Guerrier Hill. Pavilion (fee), picnicking (May-Oct, daily) 1500 S 6th St. **FREE**

Warnock Lake Recreation Area. Fishing, swimming, beach; picnicking, camping (fee). (Daily) 2 mi SW. Phone 913/367-4179. **FREE**

Evah C. Cray Historical Home Museum. Nineteenth-century period rms and country store, children's display. (Mar-Oct, daily; Jan-Feb, Sat and Sun; rest of yr, by appt) Children only with adult. 805 N 5th St. Phone 913/367-3046. ¢

International Forest of Friendship. A bicentennial gift to the United States from the city and the Ninety Nines Inc, an international organization of women pilots. The forest incl trees from all 50 states and from 33 countries. A concrete walkway (wheelchair accessible) winds through the forest; embedded in the walkway are granite plaques honoring those people who have contributed to the advancement of aviation and the exploration of space; statue of Amelia Earhart; NASA astronaut memorial. (Daily) 2 mi SW, just S of Warnock Lake. Phone 913/367-2427. **FREE**

Special Events

Antique Airplane Fly-In. Phone 913/367-2427. Memorial Day wkend.

Historic Homes Tour. Mid-June.

Amelia Earhart Festival. Mid-July.

Atchison County Fair. Mid-Aug.

Oktoberfest. First wkend Oct.

Haunted Home Tours. Phone 913/367-2427. Halloween wk.

Motel/Motor Lodge

★ **COMFORT INN.** 509 S 9th St (66002). 913/367-7666; fax 913/367-7566; res 800/228-5150. www.comfort inn.com. 45 rms, 3 story, 10 suites. No elvtr. S $42; D $46; each addl $4; suites $54; under 18 free. Crib $4. Pet accepted. TV; cable. Complimentary continental bkfst. Restaurant nearby. Bar 5 pm-2 am, closed Sun. Ck-out 11 am. Meeting rms. Picnic tables. Cr cds: A, D, DS, MC, V.
D ⊠ ⚓ ⛧ ⊠ ⚑

Restaurant

★ **TIME OUT FAMILY RESTAURANT.** 337 S 10th St (66002). 913/367-3372. Hrs: 6 am-9 pm; Fri, Sat to 2:30 am; Sun 7 am-9 pm. Closed hols. Bkfst $1.95-$5.95, lunch, dinner $1.95-$7.95. Children's menu. Salad bar. Cr cds: DS, MC, V.
D SC ⊐

Belleville

(B-5) *See also Concordia, Mankato*

Pop 2,517 **Elev** 1,550 ft

Information Chamber of Commerce, 1819 L St; 785/527-2310

Belleville's Rocky Pond was used in early railroad days to provide water for steam engines and supply ice for refrigerated cars. Fishing, picnicking, and camping are allowed in Rocky Pond Park.

A Sandzen mural from WPA days hangs in the post office at 18th and L streets.

What to See and Do

Crossroads of Yesteryear Museum. Log cabin (1870), rural school, church (1900), and museum on five acres. Exhibits feature artifacts of the county, the history of agriculture, and the Bertil Olson Tool Collection. (Daily; closed Thanksgiving, Dec 25) 2726 US 36. Phone 785/527-5971. **FREE**

Pawnee Indian Village Museum. Built on site of a Pawnee village (ca 1820); excavated earth lodge floor; displays depicting Pawnee culture. (Tues-Sun;

closed hols) 13 mi W on US 36, then 8 mi N on KS 266. Phone 785/361-2255. **FREE**

Special Events

North Central Kansas Free Fair. Features Midget Nationals car races. Phone 785/527-2488. First wkend Aug.

Pawnee Indian Village Rendezvous. Phone 785/361-2255. Sept.

Motel/Motor Lodge

★★ **BEST WESTERN BEL VILLA.** *215 W US 36 (66935). 785/527-2231; fax 785/527-2572; toll-free 800/528-1234. www.bestwestern.com.* 40 rms. S $49; D $64; each addl $4; higher rates: Memorial Day wkend, racing events, hunting season. Crib free. Pet accepted, some restrictions. TV; cable (premium). Pool. Playground. Restaurant 6 am-10 pm. Bar. Ck-out 11 am. Meeting rms. In-rm modem link. Sundries. Cr cds: A, D, DS, MC, V.

Beloit

(B-5) *See also Concordia, Mankato*

Pop 4,066 **Elev** 1,386 ft
Area code 785 **Zip** 67420

What to See and Do

Glen Elder State Park. A 1,250-acre park on 12,600-acre lake. An early Native American historical site. It was here that Margaret Hill McCarter wrote some of her well-loved tales of Kansas. Swimming beach, fishing, boating (ramp, marina); picnicking, more than 300 primitive and improved campsites (dump station). Amphitheater. Standard fees. (Daily) 12 mi W on US 24. Phone 785/545-3345. ¢¢

Chanute

(E-7) *See also Iola, Parsons, Yates Center*

Founded 1873 **Pop** 9,488 **Elev** 943 ft
Area code 316 **Zip** 66720

Information Chamber of Commerce, 21 N Lincoln Ave, PO Box 747; 316/431-3350

What to See and Do

Chanute Art Gallery. Houses permanent collection of more than 500 works. Changing exhibits. (Mon-Sat) 17 N Lincoln Ave. Phone 316/431-7807. **FREE**

Martin and Osa Johnson Safari Museum. Contains artifacts and photographs of the South Seas, Borneo, and African trips of photo-explorers Martin and Osa Johnson (she was born in Chanute); exhibits illustrating West African village life incl ceremonial artifacts and musical instruments; ten-min film shown upon request. Wildlife paintings and sketches, other art objects displayed in the Selsor Gallery. Stott Explorers Library houses expedition journals, monographs, books on exploration. (Daily; closed hols) 111 N Lincoln Ave, located in a renovated Santa Fe train depot. Phone 316/431-2730. ¢¢

Special Events

Mexican Fiesta. Celebration of Mexican independence from Spain. Phone 316/431-3350. Second wkend Sept.

Artist Alley and Fall Festival. Incl parade, art booths. Fourth wkend Sept.

Coffeyville

(E-7) *See also Independence, Parsons*

Founded 1869 **Pop** 12,917 **Elev** 736 ft
Area code 316 **Zip** 67337
Information Convention & Visitors Bureau, 811 Walnut PO Box 457; 316/251-1194 or 800/626-3357

Named for Colonel James A. Coffey, who in 1869 built a house and trading post near the Verdigris River. With the coming of the railroad shortly after its settlement, Coffeyville followed the usual pattern of cow towns. The famous Dalton raid occurred here October 5, 1892, when the three Dalton brothers and two confederates attempted to rob two banks at once and fought a running battle with armed citizens. Several of the defenders were killed or wounded; of the gang, only Emmett Dalton survived.

The town prospered with the development of natural gas and oil fields in 1903. Today its chief industries are oil refineries, smelters, oil field equipment, lawn mowers, power transmissions, and foundries. Wendell Willkie, the Republican presidential candidate in 1940, lived and taught school here.

What to See and Do

Brown Mansion. (1904) Designed by proteges of Stanford White; original furniture, hand-painted canvas wall coverings; Tiffany chandelier in dining rm. (June-Aug, daily; hrs vary rest of yr; closed hols) 2019 Walnut St. Phone 316/251-0431. ¢¢

Dalton Defenders Museum. Dalton raid souvenirs; mementos of Wendell Willkie and Walter Johnson. (Daily) 113 E 8th St. Phone 316/251-5944. ¢¢

Special Events

New Beginning Festival. Phone 316/251-1194. Last wkend Apr.

Inter-State Fair and Rodeo. Phone 316/251-1194. Second full wk Aug.

Dalton Defenders Day. Commemorates the Dalton raid on Coffeyville. First wkend Oct.

Intertribal Pow Wow. Phone 316/252-6819. First wkend Nov.

Motel/Motor Lodge

★★ **APPLE TREE INN.** *820 E 11th St (67337). 316/251-0002; fax 316/251-1615.* 64 rms, 2 story. S $46; D $54; charge for each addl. Crib $2. Pet accepted; $3. TV; cable (premium). Indoor pool; whirlpool. Complimentary continental bkfst. Restaurant nearby. Ck-out noon. Business servs avail. In-rm modem link. Some refrigerators; microwaves avail. Cr cds: A, C, D, DS, MC, V.

Colby

(B-2) *See also Goodland, Oakley*

Founded 1885 **Pop** 5,396 **Elev** 3,160 ft **Area code** 785 **Zip** 67701
Information Convention & Visitors Bureau, 350 S Range, PO Box 572; 785/462-7643 or 800/611-8835
Web www.colbychamber.com

This town is the hub of northwest Kansas due to its cultural, shopping, and hospitality facilities. Agribusiness drives the economy.

What to See and Do

Northwest Research Extension Center. Branch of Kansas State University. Crop, soil, irrigation, and horticulture research. (Mon-Fri) W of city, ¼ mi S of US 24. 105 Experiment Farm Rd. Phone 785/462-7575. **FREE**

Prairie Museum of Art & History. Museum complex is located on a 24-acre site. On exhibit are rare bisque and china dolls; Meissen, Tiffany, Sèvres, Capo de Monte, Royal Vienna, Satsuma, Ridgway, Wedgwood, and Limoges; glass and crystal, such as Redford, Stiegel, Steuben, Gallé; Chinese and Japanese artifacts; textiles; furniture. On the museum site are a sod house, restored 1930s farmstead, one-rm schoolhouse, a country church, and one of the largest barns in Kansas. (Tues-Sun; closed hols) 1905 S Franklin St, adj to I-70 between exits 53 and 54. Phone 785/462-4590. ¢¢

Special Events

Prairie Heritage Day. Third Sat June.

Thomas County Free Fair. Phone 785/426-4511. July.

Bluegrass Festival. Phone 785/462-7643. Third wkend July.

Motels/Motor Lodges

★★ **BEST WESTERN CROWN HOTEL.** *2320 S Range Ave (67701). 785/462-3943; res 800/528-1234. www.bestwestern.com.* 29 rms. June-Sept: S, D $69-$79; each addl $6; lower rates rest of yr. Crib free. Pet accepted. TV; cable (premium). Heated pool. Complimentary coffee in rms. Restaurant

Monument Rocks, near Colby

nearby. Ck-out 11 am. Business servs avail. In-rm modem link. Airport transportation. Cr cds: A, C, D, DS, MC, V.

★ **RAMADA INN.** *1950 S Range Ave (67701). 785/462-3933; fax 785/462-7255; toll-free 800/750-7160. www. ramada.com.* 117 rms, 2 story. S $45-$60; D $55-$75; each addl $5; under 18 free. Crib free. TV; cable (premium). Heated pool. Restaurant 6:30 am-9 pm. Bar 5 pm-midnight. Ck-out noon. Meeting rms. Business servs avail. In-rm modem link. Valet serv. Sundries. Cr cds: A, C, D, DS, JCB, MC, V.

Concordia

(B-5) *See also Belleville, Beloit*

Pop 6,167 **Elev** 1,369 ft
Area code 785 **Zip** 66901
Information Chamber of Commerce, 606 Washington St; 785/243-4290 or 800/343-4290

Web www.dustdevil.com/towns/ concordia

What to See and Do

★ **The Brown Grand Theatre.** Built in 1907 by Colonel Napoleon Bonaparte Brown at a cost of $40,000, the restored 650-seat theater has two balconies and features a grand drape which is a reproduction of a Horace Vernet painting entitled "Napoleon at Austerlitz." Theater currently hosts plays, concerts, and shows. Guided tours (daily, limited hrs; fee). 310 W 6th St. Phone 785/243-2553.

Special Events

Cloud County Fair. Phone 785/243-4290. Mid-July.

North Central Kansas Rodeo. Phone 785/243-1313. Mid-Aug.

Fall Fest. Phone 785/243-4290. Last Sat Sept.

Motel/Motor Lodge

★★ **ECONO LODGE.** *89 Lincoln St (66901). 785/243-4545; fax 785/243-4545. www.econolodge.com.* 50 rms. S $39; D $46; each addl $5; under 12 free. Crib free. Pet accepted, some restrictions. TV; cable (premium). Pool. Restaurant 6 am-9 pm; wkend hrs vary. Private club 5 pm-midnight; closed Sun. Ck-out 11 am. Coin lndry. Meeting rms. Business servs avail. Sundries. Cr cds: A, C, D, DS, MC, V.

🔲 ▭ ▭ ▭ SC

Council Grove

(C-6) *See also Emporia, Junction City*

Founded 1858 **Pop** 2,228 **Elev** 1,233 ft **Area code** 620 **Zip** 66846
Information Convention & Visitor's Bureau, 200 W Main St; 620/767-5882 or 800/732-9211
Web www.councilgrove.com

As the last outfitting place on the Santa Fe Trail between the Missouri River and Santa Fe, Council Grove, now a National Historic Landmark, holds historic significance in the development of the West. The town grew up around a Native American campground in a grove of oaks near the Neosho River. It is an agricultural and merchandising center. The town also has many lovely turn-of-the-century buildings, several parks, and two lakes.

What to See and Do

Council Grove Federal Lake. Covers 3,200 acres. Fishing, boating, marina

A WALK THROUGH THE OLD WEST

Forget Dodge City. If you're looking for an authentic Old West town, journey to Council Grove, a bustling trading center on the Sante Fe Trail during the 1840s and 1850s—and largely unchanged since. Council Grove contains some of the best-preserved frontier-era architecture in Kansas, and many of the buildings are still used for their original commercial purpose.

Begin your tour at the Kaw Mission State Historic Site, at 500 North Mission Street. Methodist missionaries built this school for native Kaw children in 1851. Today the structure contains a museum dedicated to the Kaw, the Santa Fe Trail, and early Council Grove. From here, walk south on Mission Street to Main Street, which follows the route of the Santa Fe Trail through town. The Cottage House Hotel (25 North Neosho) is a beautifully maintained Victorian hotel with wraparound porches and striking Queen Anne turrets and gazebos. Still in operation, this is a marvelous place to spend the night in period splendor. Across Main Street, the Farmers and Drovers Bank (201 West Main), is a handsome landmark of redbrick and limestone, with eclectic architectural features like Romanesque arches, stained-glass windows, and a Byzantine dome.

One block east on Main Street is another still-in-operation historic structure. The Hays House Restaurant (112 West Main) is the oldest continuously operating restaurant west of the Mississippi. Since it was constructed in 1857, the restaurant has served the likes of General George Custer and Jesse James. Although the ambiance is frontier-era, the food is up-to-date and delicious—stop by for a piece of peach pie. Also on this block of Main Street is the stone Last Chance Store—in operation since 1857 as well—and the Council Grove National Bank Building.

Before crossing the Neosho River Bridge, turn south two blocks to the Seth Hays Home. Built in 1867, this home has been preserved in period condition and is open to visitors on Sundays and by appointment. Cross the Neosho River on Main Street. In a shelter along the riverbank is the remains of the Council Oak, a once-vast oak tree under which representatives of the United States and the Osage tribe signed a treaty in 1825 that guaranteed settlers safe passage across Indian territory. On the north corner of Main and Union streets is a small park containing the *Madonna of the Trail*, a statue of a pioneer mother and children erected in 1925 by the Daughters of the American Revolution. Along with a museum of frontier history, the park is home to the Post Office Oak, a 300-year-old bur oak that served as an unofficial post depository for travelers along the Santa Fe Trail. Continue east on Main to Durland Park (at 5th Street) where Council Grove's first jail, constructed in 1849, still stands. Also in Durland Park are two 19th-century train depots.

(seasonal); hunting, camping (some fees/night). (Daily) 1 mi N on KS 177. Phone 620/767-5195.¢

Council Oak Shrine. Here the treaty of 1825 was signed between US government commissioners and the Osage. 313 W Main St.

Custer's Elm Shrine. Elm trunk stands as a shrine to the tree that was 100 ft tall, 16 ft in circumference, and reputedly sheltered the camp of General George Custer in 1867 when he was leading an expedition in western Kansas. Neosho St, six blks S of Main St.

Hays House. (1857) This National Registered Historic Landmark houses a restaurant (see). 112 W Main St. Phone 620/797-5911.

Kaw Mission State Historic Site. Stone building (1851) where members of the Methodist Church once taught Native Americans; also one of the first Kansas schools for children of settlers. (Tues-Sun; closed hols) 500 N Mission St. Phone 620/767-5410. **FREE**

The Madonna of the Trail Monument. One of 12 statues erected in each of the states through which the National Old Trails Roads passed. The Madonna pays tribute to pioneer mothers and commemorates the trails that opened the West. Union and Main sts.

Old Calaboose. (1849) Only pioneer jail on Santa Fe Trail in early days. 502 E Main St, on US 56.

Post Office Oak. Mammoth oak tree with a cache at its base served as an unofficial post office for pack trains and caravans on the Santa Fe Trail 1825-1847. E Main St between Union and Liberty sts.

Special Event

Wah-Shun-Gah Days. Kaw Intertribal Powwow, Santa Fe trail ride and supper, antique tractor pull, street dance. Third wkend June.

Motel/Motor Lodge

★★ **THE COTTAGE HOUSE HOTEL & MOTEL.** *25 N Neosho (66846). 620/767-6828; fax 620/767-6414; toll-free 800/717-7903.* 36 rms, 1-2 story. S $30-$52; D $38-$68; each addl $8; suites $85-$90; under 12

free. Crib $8. Pet accepted, some restrictions; $8. TV; cable, VCR avail. Continental bkfst. Restaurant nearby. Ck-out 11 am. Meeting rm. Business servs avail. In-rm modem link. Gift shop. Whirlpool, sauna. Some refrigerators, in-rm whirlpools. Built in 1867 as a cottage and blacksmith shop; some antiques; gazebo. Cr cds: A, MC, V.

Restaurant

★★ **HAYS HOUSE 1857.** *112 W Main St (US 56) (66846). 620/767-5911. www.hayshouse.com.* Hrs: 7 am-9 pm; Sun buffet 11 am-2 pm. Closed Mon; Jan 1, Dec 25. Res accepted. Bar from 5 pm. Bkfst, lunch $2.95-$8.50, dinner $5.50-$13.75. Sun brunch $9.50. Children's menu. Specializes in aged beef, skillet-fried chicken. Own desserts, breads. Building erected 1857; Old West atmosphere. National Register of Historic Landmarks on Santa Fe Trail. Cr cds: DS, MC, V.

Dodge City (E-3)

Settled 1872 **Pop** 21,129 **Elev** 2,530 ft
Area code 620 **Zip** 67801
Information Convention & Visitors Bureau, 400 W Wyatt Earp Blvd, PO Box 1474; 316/225-8186 or 800/OLD-WEST
Web www.dodgecity.org

Memorable for buffalo hunts, longhorn cattle, and frontier marshals, Dodge City was laid out by construction crews of the Santa Fe Railroad and named for nearby Fort Dodge. Vast herds of buffalo—estimated at 24 million or more—which then covered the surrounding plains, had been hunted for years. But the railroad provided transportation to make the hides commercially profitable. A skilled hunter could earn $100 in a day at the industry's height; by 1875 the herds were nearly exterminated. Cattle drives, also stimulated by the railroad, took the buffalo's place in the town's economy. In the 1870s Dodge City became the cowboy capital of the region. Among its notable peace officers were Bat Masterson and Wyatt Earp. The prevalence of sudden and violent death resulted in the establishment of Boot Hill cemetery. In the mid-1880s the era of the cattle drives ended; by 1890 much of the grazing land had been plowed for crops. Dodge City is now the hub of one of the nation's greatest wheat-producing areas and a growing production and marketing center for cattle.

What to See and Do

Dodge City Trolley. Narrated tour of city's history and folklore. (Memorial Day-Labor Day, daily; rest of yr, by appt) 4th and W Wyatt Earp Blvd. Phone 620/225-8186. ¢¢

☒ Historic Front Street. Reconstruction of two blks of main street of 1870s: Long Branch Saloon, Saratoga Saloon, general store, blacksmith, saddle shop, drugstore, many other businesses. Beeson Gallery contains exhibits, many objects of historical significance from the Southwest and Dodge City; Hardesty House, home of an early cattle baron, has been restored and furnished with original pieces; exhibits of early banking.

  Boot Hill Museum. Museum and cemetery are on site of original Boot Hill Cemetery; depot, locomotive, "Boot Hill Special." Old Fort Dodge Jail; gun collection. Stagecoach rides in summer. (Daily; closed Jan 1, Thanksgiving, Dec 25) Front St. Phone 620/227-8188. ¢¢¢

Home of Stone & Ford County Museum. (1881) Preserved Victorian home with many original furnishings; occupied until 1964. Guided tours (June-Aug, daily; rest of yr, by appt). 112 E Vine St. Phone 316/227-6791.

Special Events

Dodge City Days. Parades; PRCA rodeo features cowboy competition in several events. Phone 620/227-9501. Last wk July-first wkend Aug.

Long Branch Saloon. Front St. Variety show, nightly (fee). Stagecoach rides; reenacted gunfights, daily.

Phone 620/227-8188. Late May-late Aug.

Motels/Motor Lodges

★★ **BEST WESTERN SILVER SPUR LODGE.** 1510 W Wyatt Earp Blvd (67801). 620/227-2125; fax 620/227-2030; toll-free 800/817-2125. www.bestwestern.com. 121 rms, 1-2 story. S $44-$54; D $52-$62; each addl $5; suites $60-$70. Crib $2. Pet accepted, some restrictions; $5. TV; cable (premium), VCR avail. Heated pool. Restaurant 6 am-9 pm. Bar 4 pm-midnight; entertainment, dancing. Ck-out noon. Meeting rms. Business servs avail. Valet serv Mon-Sat. Free airport transportation. Cr cds: A, DS, MC, V.

★★ **DODGE HOUSE HOTEL AND CONVENTION CENTER.** 2408 W Wyatt Earp Blvd (67801). 620/225-9900; fax 620/227-5012. www.dodgehousehotel.com. 111 rms, 2 story. S, D $46; each addl $6; suites $75-$120; under 12 free. Crib free. Pet accepted, some restrictions. TV; cable (premium), VCR avail (movies). 2 pools, 1 indoor. Sauna. Restaurant 6 am-4 pm; Fri, Sat to 10 pm; Sun from 6:30 am. Bar 11 am-midnight; closed Sun. Ck-out 11 am. Meeting rms. Business servs avail. Free airport transportation. Game rm. Cr cds: A, C, D, DS, ER, JCB, MC, V.

★ **SUPER 8.** 1708 W Wyatt Earp Blvd (67801). 620/225-3924; fax 620/225-5793; res 800/800-8000. www.super8.com. 64 rms, 3 story. S $34.88-$40.88; D $42.88-$54.88; under 12 free; higher rates special events. Crib free. Pet accepted. TV; cable (premium), VCR avail. Pool. Complimentary continental bkfst, coffee in rms. Restaurant adj 6 am-10 pm. Ck-out noon. Cr cds: A, D, DS, MC, V.

El Dorado

(E-6) *See also Eureka, Newton, Wichita*

Pop 11,504 **Elev** 1,291 ft
Area code 316 **Zip** 67042

Information Chamber of Commerce, 383 E Central, PO Box 509; 316/321-3150

El Dorado, the seat of Butler County, is located on the western edge of the Flint Hills. The city's growth can be attributed to oil; two refineries are here. Stapleton No. 1, the area's first gusher (1915), is commemorated by a marker at the northwestern edge of the town.

What to See and Do

El Dorado State Park. The largest of Kansas's state parks, El Dorado is made up of four areas totaling 4,000 acres. Rolling hills, wooded valleys, and open prairie make up the natural environment of the park. El Dorado Lake, 8,000 acres, is also within the park. Swimming beaches, fishing (with license), boating (ramps, marina); hiking trails. Picnicking, concession. More than 1,100 primitive and improved campsites (hookups, dump stations). Standard fees. (Daily) 5 mi NE on KS 177. Phone 316/321-7180. ¢¢

Kansas Oil Museum and Butler County Historical Museum. Interpretive displays depicting oil, ranching, and agricultural history, incl a model rotary drilling rig; outdoor historic oil field exhibits incl restored cable-tool drilling rig, shotgun lease house, antique engines. Library, archives. Gift shop. Walking tour, nature trail. (Daily, afternoons; closed hols) 383 E Central Ave. Phone 316/321-9333. **FREE**

Motel/Motor Lodge

★★ **BEST WESTERN RED COACH INN.** *2525 W Central St (67042). 316/321-6900; res 800/528-1234. www.bestwestern.com.* 73 rms, 2 story, 1 kit. unit. S $38-$58; D $42-$62; each addl $5. Crib $4. Pet accepted, some restrictions. TV; cable (premium). Indoor pool; whirlpool. Restaurant 6 am-11 pm. Ck-out 11 am. Business servs avail. Exercise equipt; sauna. Game rm. Some in-rm whirlpools. Cr cds: A, C, D, DS, MC, V.

Emporia

(D-7) *See also Council Grove*

Founded 1857 **Pop** 25,512 **Elev** 1,150 ft **Area code** 620 **Zip** 66801

Information Convention & Visitors Bureau, 719 Commercial St, PO Box 703; 316/342-1803 or 800/279-3730.

Web www.emporia.com

This was the home of one of America's most famous newspaper editors, William Allen White. His Emporia *Gazette* editorials attracted nationwide attention. The seat of Lyon County and "front porch" to the Flint Hills, Emporia is a center of education, industry, agriculture, and outdoor recreation.

What to See and Do

Eisenhower State Park. A 1,785-acre park on 6,900-acre lake. Crappie, walleye, catfish, and bass. Beach, bathhouse, fishing, boating (ramp); picnicking, walking trail. Camping (electricity, dump station). Standard fees. (Daily) 20 mi E on I-35, 7 mi N on US 75. Phone 316/528-4102.

Emporia Gazette Building. Houses White's widely quoted newspaper; small one-rm museum displays newspaper machinery used in White's time. (Mon-Fri; wkends by appt; closed hols) 517 Merchant St. Phone 316/342-4800. **FREE**

Flint Hills National Wildlife Refuge. Hiking, camping. Wild food gathering permitted. Bald eagles present in fall and winter. Fishing and hunting in legal seasons. (Daily; some portions closed during fall migration of waterfowl) 10 mi E on I-35, then 8 mi S on KS 130. Phone 316/392-5553. **FREE**

Lyon County Historical Museum. In Carnegie Library Building (1904). Rotating exhibits, gift gallery with locally made items. (Tues-Sat; closed hols) 118 E 6th Ave. Phone 316/342-0933. **FREE** Opp is

Research Center and Archives. Valuable collection of city directories, newspapers dating from 1857 on microfilm; a complete file of the Gazette; genealogy collection for Lyon County, incl marriage and cemetery records. (Tues-Sat; closed hols) 225 E 6th Ave. Phone 316/342-8120. **FREE**

National Teachers Hall of Fame. Galleries and tributes to some of the best teachers in America. (Mon-Fri, also Sat mornings; closed hols). 1320 C of E Dr. Phone 316/341-5660. **Donation**

Peter Pan Park. Approx 50 acres given to the city by the White family; bust of William Allen White by Jo Davidson. Swimming pool, wading pool (June-Aug, daily), lake (children under age 14 and senior citizens may fish here). Softball fields. Picnic grounds. (Daily) Kansas Ave and Neosho St. Phone 316/342-5105. **FREE**

Prairie Passage. Eight massive limestone sculptures reflecting Emporia's heritage, each weighing from five-nine tons and standing 10-15 ft high. (Daily) W US 50 and Industrial Rd. **FREE**

Soden's Grove Park. Thirty acres bordered by Cottonwood River; baseball field, picnic area; miniature train (seasonal, eves). S Commercial and Soden Rd. Located in park is

> **Emporia Zoo.** More than 80 species of native and exotic wildlife in natural habitat exhibits. Drive or walk through. (Daily; closed Jan 1, Thanksgiving, Dec 25) Phone 316/342-6558. **FREE**

Special Events

Twin Rivers Festival. Emporia State University campus. Celebration of the arts featuring arts and crafts; children's section; concerts; street dance; recreational activities; concessions. Phone 316/343-6473. Third wkend June.

Lyon County Free Fair. Fairgrounds, W US 50. Exhibits, entertainment, carnival, rodeos. Phone 316/342-5014. Late July-early Aug.

Mexican-American Fiesta. Fairgrounds. Celebration of Emporia's Hispanic heritage. Entertainment, food, dance. Phone 316/342-1803 or 800/279-3730. Wkend after Labor Day.

Motels/Motor Lodges

★ ★ **BEST WESTERN.** *3021 US 50 W (66801). 620/342-3770; fax 620/* 342-9271; toll-free 800/362-2036. www. bestwestern.com. 56 rms. S $36-$50; D $44-$60; each addl $7; suites $75; under 18 free. Crib free. Pet accepted. TV; cable (premium). Indoor pool; whirlpool. Restaurant 6 am-9 pm. Ck-out 11 am. Meeting rm. Business servs avail. In-rm modem link. Exercise equipt. Game rm. Cr cds: A, C, D, DS, MC, V.

★ **DAYS INN.** *3032 US 50 W (66801). 620/342-1787; fax 620/342-2292; res 800/329-7466. www.daysinn.com.* 39 rms, 1-2 story. S $36-$48; D $48-$58; each addl $6. Crib free. Pet accepted, some restrictions. TV; cable (premium). Indoor pool; whirlpool. Complimentary continental bkfst. Coffee in rms. Restaurant opp 6 am-9 pm. Ck-out 11 am. Business servs avail. In-rm modem link. Game rm. Some refrigerators. Cr cds: A, C, D, DS, MC, V.

★ **RAMADA INN AND CONFERENCE CENTER.** *2700 W 18th Ave (66801). 620/343-2200; fax 620/343-1609. www.ramada.com.* 133 rms, 2 story. S, D $53-$65; suites $80-$140; under 19 free. Crib free. TV; cable (premium). Indoor/outdoor pool; whirlpool. Sauna. Restaurant 6 am-10 pm. Ck-out noon. Coin lndry. Meeting rms. Business servs avail. Bellhops. Game rm. Cr cds: A, C, D, DS, ER, JCB, MC, V.

Eureka

(D-7) *See also El Dorado, Yates Center*

Pop 2,974 **Elev** 1,084 ft
Area code 316 **Zip** 67045
Information Eureka Area Chamber of Commerce, 112 N Main; 316/583-5452

What to See and Do

Fall River State Park. Park encompasses 917 acres that overlook a 2,500-acre reservoir. Rolling uplands forested by native oak adjoining native tallgrass prairies. Beach, bathhouse, fishing, boating (ramps, docks). Trails. Picnicking. Tent and

Kansas tallgrass prairie

trailer camping (electricity, dump station). Standard fees. (Daily) 17 mi SE, just off KS 96. Phone 316/637-2213. ¢¢

Greenwood County Historical Society and Museum. Collection of historical artifacts; 19th-century kitchen and farm display; county newspapers from 1868-1986; genealogy section. (Mon-Sat; closed hols) 120 W 4th St. Phone 316/583-6682. **FREE**

Hawthorne Ranch Trail Rides. View the beautiful Flint Hills from horseback. Trail rides twice daily (res required; must be age ten or over). 960-acre ranch also has wilderness campsite, fishing, hiking. (Apr-Nov, daily) 8 mi N on gravel road. Phone 316/583-5887. ¢¢¢¢

Special Event

Quarter horse racing. Eureka Downs, 210 N Jefferson. Phone 316/583-5201. May-July 4.

Motel/Motor Lodge

★ **BLUE STEM LODGE.** *1314 E River St (67045).* 316/583-5521. 27 rms. S $28-$32; D $32-$38; each addl $4. Pet accepted, some restrictions. Crib $2. Pool. Complimentary coffee in lobby. Restaurant nearby. Ck-out 11 am. Business servs avail. In-rm modem link. Golf privileges. Cr cds: A, MC, V.

🄳 🛱 🍽 🏊 🏃 🐾

Fort Scott

(D-8) *See also Pittsburg; also see Nevada, MO*

Founded 1842 **Pop** 8,362 **Elev** 846 ft
Area code 620 **Zip** 66701
Information Visitor Information Center, 231 E Wall St, PO Box 205; 316/223-3566 or 800/245-FORT
Web www.fortscott.com

Named for General Winfield Scott and established as a military post between Fort Leavenworth and lands designated for the displaced Cherokee, Fort Scott was manned by troops in 1842. Although the fort was abandoned in 1853 and its buildings sold at auction in 1855, the town survived. Located only five miles from the Missouri border, it became a center for pre-Civil War agitation by those for, as well as those against, slavery. Rival groups had headquarters on the Plaza—the former parade ground—in the Free State Hotel and Western Hotel. John Brown and James Montgomery were among the antislavery leaders who met here.

During the Civil War, the fort was again active as a supply center for Union troops. Today the town is a livestock center, with an economy based on service and manufacturing.

What to See and Do

Fort Scott National Cemetery. Designated by President Abraham Lincoln in 1862. (Daily) E National St.

Fort Scott National Historic Site. Established in 1842, the fort was the base for infantry and dragoons protecting the frontier. The buildings have been restored and reconstructed to represent the fort (ca 1845-55). Visitor center located in restored post hospital; officers' quarters, powder magazine, dragoon stable, guardhouse, bakery, quartermaster's storehouse, post headquarters, and barracks; museum exhibits, audiovisual programs (Daily). Some special events. Living history and interpretive programs (June-Aug, wkends). (Daily; closed Jan 1, Thanksgiving, Dec 25) Old Fort Blvd, at business jct US 69 and 54. Phone 316/223-0310. ¢

Gunn Park. Along the Marmaton River. Covers 135 acres, two lakes. Fishing (fee). Picnicking, playground. Camping (fee). (Daily) W edge of town. Phone 316/223-0550. **FREE**

Historic Trolley Tour. Narrated trolley tours pass the historic 1840s fort, one of the country's oldest national cemeteries, and several miles of Victorian architecture. (Mid-Mar-early Dec, daily) Contact Visitor Information Center for schedule. 231 E Wall. ¢¢

Special Events

Good Ol' Days Celebration. Phone 800/245-3678. First wkend June.

Bourbon County Fair. Fairgrounds. Phone 800/245-3678. Late July.

Pioneer Harvest Fiesta. Fairgrounds. Steam, gas engine, and tractor show; demonstrations of farm activities. Phone 800/245-3678. Early Oct.

Motel/Motor Lodge

★★ **BEST WESTERN INN.** *101 State St (66701). 620/223-0100; fax 620/ 223-1746; toll-free 888/800-3175. www.bestwestern.com.* 78 rms, 1-2 story. S $55; D $61; under 12 free. Crib free. Pet accepted; $5. TV; cable (premium), VCR avail. Pool; whirl-

pool. Complimentary continental bkfst. Ck-out 11 am. Coin lndry. Meeting rms. Business servs avail. Exercise equipt; sauna. Picnic tables. Cr cds: A, C, D, DS, MC, V.

🔊 🏊 🎿 🛄 🐾 SC

Garden City (D-2)

Founded 1878 **Pop** 24,097 **Elev** 2,839 ft **Area code** 620 **Zip** 67846

Information Chamber of Commerce, Finney County Convention & Tourism Bureau, 1511 E Fulton Terrace; 316/276-3264 or 800/879-9803

Web www.gcnet.com

This is the center for raising and processing much of the state's beef for shipment throughout the world. The city is also the heart of the state's irrigation operations, which are important to wheat, alfalfa, and corn crops in the area. It is home to one of the oldest known state-owned bison herds.

What to See and Do

Finney Game Refuge. Some 3,670 acres of sandsage prairie biome which is home to more than 100 head of bison, lesser prairie chickens, jackrabbits, quail, deer, and other wildlife. Wildflowers are abundant, and the lake is stocked with trout in the spring and fall. US 83. Phone 316/276-3264.

Finnup Park and Lee Richardson Zoo. More than 300 mammals and birds can be found in the zoo incl the Wild Asia Exhibit. Picnic area, playgrounds; food and gift shop (fee for vehicles; closed Jan 1, Thanksgiving, Dec 25). Swimming pool (Mar-Nov, daily). Museum with memorabilia of early settlers (Daily) S city limits, on US 83. Phone 316/276-1250. **FREE**

Special Events

Beef Empire Days. Phone 316/275-6807. Early June.

Finney County Fair. Mid-Aug.

Tumbleweed Festival. Phone 316/276-3264. Late Aug.

Mexican Fiesta. Phone 316/276-3264. Second wkend Sept.

Motels/Motor Lodges

★★ **BEST WESTERN WHEAT LANDS HOTEL AND CONFERENCE CENTER.** *1311 E Fulton St (67846). 620/276-2387; fax 620/276-4252; toll-free 800/333-2387. www. wheatlands.com.* 112 units, 1-2 story. S $51; D $63; each addl $4; suites $59-$69; under 12 free; wkly rates. Crib $3. Pet accepted. TV; cable (premium), VCR avail. Heated pool. Complimentary coffee in lobby. Restaurant adj 6 am-9 pm. Bar 4 pm-2 am, closed Sun; entertainment. Ck-out 1 pm. Coin lndry. Meeting rms. Business servs avail. In-rm modem link. Valet serv. Gift shop. Barber, beauty shop. Airport, railroad station, bus depot transportation. Golf privileges. Some bathrm phones, refrigerators. Cr cds: C, D, DS, MC, V.

★★ **GARDEN CITY PLAZA INN.** *1911 E Kansas (67846). 620/275-7471; fax 620/275-4028; toll-free 800/875-5201.* 109 rms, 2 story. S $52-$58; D $62-$68; each addl $10; suites $84-$94. Crib free. Pet accepted. TV; cable (premium), VCR avail (movies). Indoor pool; whirlpool. Sauna. Restaurant 6 am-10 pm; Sun 7 am-8 pm. Bar 4 pm-1 am; entertainment. Ck-out noon. Meeting rms. Business servs avail. Bellhops. Free airport transportation. Golf privileges. Game rm. Cr cds: A, C, D, DS, MC, V.

Goodland

(B-1) *See also Colby*

Pop 4,983 **Elev** 3,683 ft
Area code 785 **Zip** 67735
Information Convention and Visitors Bureau, 104 W 11th, PO Box 628; 785/899-3515 or 888/824-4222

What to See and Do

High Plains Museum. Houses replica of the first patented American helicopter (built 1910). Also display of Native American artifacts; farm implements, 19th-century clothing and household goods; miniature local history dioramas. (Mon-Sat, also Sun afternoons; closed hols) 17th and Cherry sts. Phone 785/899-4595. **FREE**

Special Events

Northwest Kansas District Free Fair. Phone 888/824-4222. Early Aug.
Sunflower Festival. Phone 785/899-7130. Second wkend Aug.

Buffalo herd on Kansas prairie

Flatlander Fall Classic. Phone 222/824-4222. IMCA race. Last Sat Sept.

Motels/Motor Lodges

★★ **BEST WESTERN.** *830 W US 24 (67735). 785/899-3621; fax 785/899-5072; toll-free 800/433-3621. www. bestwestern.com.* 93 rms, 2 story. June-Sept: S $40; D $55-$65; each addl $5-$8; lower rates rest of yr. Crib $5. Pet accepted, some restrictions. TV; cable (premium), VCR avail. Indoor pool; wading pool, whirlpool. Playground. Restaurant 6 am-9 pm; summer to 10 pm. Bar 5-10 pm. Ck-out 11 am. Guest lndry. Meeting rm. Business servs avail. Airport transportation. Cr cds: A, C, D, DS, MC, V.
D ⊷ ⌘ ✕ ⊠ 🔥 SC

★ **HOWARD JOHNSON.** *2218 Commerce Rd (67735). 785/899-3644; fax 785/899-3646. www.hojo.com.* 79 rms, 2 story. S $49-$70; D $54-$75. Crib free. Pet accepted. TV; cable (premium), VCR avail. Indoor pool; whirlpool. Playground. Coffee in rms. Restaurant 6 am-2 pm, 5-10 pm. Bar 5 pm-midnight. Ck-out noon. Guest lndry. Meeting rms. Business servs avail. In-rm modem link. Airport, bus depot transportation. Miniature golf. Sauna. Game rm. Cr cds: A, D, DS, MC, V.
D ⊷ ⌘ ⊠ 🔥

Great Bend

(D-4) *See also Larned*

Founded 1871 **Pop** 15,427 **Elev** 1,849 ft **Area code** 620 **Zip** 67530
Information Convention & Visitors Bureau, 1307 Williams, PO Box 400; 316/792-2401
Web www.greatbend.com

Great Bend, named for its location on the Arkansas River, was an early railhead on the Santa Fe Trail.

What to See and Do

Barton County Historical Society Museum and Village. Village contains church (ca 1895), schoolhouse (ca 1915), agricultural buildings, native stone blacksmith shop, Dodge home-stead, depot, and post office. Museum exhibits incl local Native American history, furniture, clothing, antique doll collection, farm machinery, fire truck. (Apr-mid-Nov, Tues-Sun; rest of yr, by appt). S Main St. Phone 316/793-5125. **Donation**

Brit Spaugh Park and Zoo. Swimming pool (fee). Zoo. Picnicking, playground. (Daily) N Main St. Phone 316/793-4160. **FREE**

Cheyenne Bottoms. Migratory waterfowl refuge, public hunting area, and bird-watching area. Water area about 13,000 acres. Fishing from shoreline in all pools (catfish, bullheads, carp). (Daily) 5 mi N on US 281, then 2 mi E. Phone 316/793-7730. **FREE**

Quivira National Wildlife Refuge. This 21,820-acre refuge incl 5,000 acres of managed wetlands and 15,000 acres of tall grass prairie. It was established in 1955 to provide a feeding and resting area for migratory waterfowl during spring and fall migrations. Auto tour route and wildlife drive (daily). Hunting and fishing permitted some seasons. 34 mi SE via US 281 and County Rd 636. Phone 316/486-2393. **FREE**

Special Event

Barton County Fair. Phone 316/797-3247. Mid-July.

Motels/Motor Lodges

★★ **BEST WESTERN ANGUS INN.** *2920 10th St (67530). 620/792-3541; fax 620/792-8621; toll-free 800/862-6487. www.bestwestern.com.* 90 units, 2 story. S $55; D $65; studio rm $49-$59; each addl $4; under 18 free. Crib $3. Pet accepted, some restrictions. TV; cable (premium), VCR avail (movies $4). Indoor pool; whirlpool. Restaurant 6 am-11 pm. Rm serv from 5 pm. Ck-out 11 am. Meeting rms. Business servs avail. Airport transportation. Exercise equipt; sauna. Game rm. Rec rm Cr cds: A, C, D, DS, JCB, MC, V.
D ⊷ ⌘ 🏋 ✕ ⊠ 🔥

★★ **GREAT BEND HOLIDAY INN.** *3017 W 10th St (67530). 620/792-2431; fax 620/792-5561; res 800/465-4329. www.holiday-inn.com.* 173 rms, 2 story. S, D $50-$55; under 18 free. Crib free. Pet accepted. TV; cable (premium). Indoor pool; whirlpool.

Sauna. Restaurant 6 am-10:30 pm. Bar 5 pm-1 am. Ck-out noon. Coin lndry. Meeting rms. Business servs avail. Airport transportation. Cr cds: A, MC, V.

D ◆ ◪ ◪ ◪ SC

Greensburg

(E-3) *See also Pratt*

Pop 1,792 **Elev** 2,230 ft
Area code 620 **Zip** 67054
Information Chamber of Commerce, 315 S Sycamore; 620/723-2261 or 800/207-7369

Incorporated in 1886, Greensburg is named for pioneer stagecoach driver "Cannonball" Green. This community came to life in 1884 when two railroads extended their lines here and brought settlers. In 1885 the railroads began construction of what has been called the world's largest hand-dug well; it is still in good condition today.

What to See and Do

Big Well. The well is 32 ft wide and 109 ft deep; steps lead downward to water level (fee). Gift shop contains 1,000-lb pallasite meteorite found on a nearby farm and said to be largest of its type ever discovered. (Daily; closed Thanksgiving, Dec 25) 315 S Sycamore St, 3 blks S of US 54. Phone 620/723-2261. ¢

Motel/Motor Lodge

★★ **BEST WESTERN J-HAWK.** *515 W Kansas Ave (67054). 620/723-2121; fax 620/723-2650; res 800/528-1234. www.bestwestern.com.* 30 rms. S $38-$41; D $48-$58; each addl $5; under 12 free. Crib $5. TV; cable (premium). Indoor pool; whirlpool. Complimentary continental bkfst. Ck-out 11 am. Meeting rms. In-rm modem link. Free airport transportation. Cr cds: A, C, D, DS, MC, V.

D ◪ ◪ ◪ ◪

Hays

(C-3) *See also Russell, WaKeeney*

Founded 1867 **Pop** 17,767 **Elev** 1,997 ft **Area code** 785 **Zip** 67601
Information Convention & Visitors Bureau, 1301 Pine, Suite B; 785/628-8202 or 800/569-4505
Web www.visithaysks.net

Fort Hays, military post on the old frontier, gave this railroad town its name. Oil, grain, cattle, educational and medical facilities, tourism, and light industry are important to the area.

What to See and Do

Ellis County Historical Society and Museum. More than 26,000 items on display in museum; incl antique toys and games, musical instruments; rotating exhibits incl quilts from the 1800s-present (selected days Apr-June). Also here are one-rm schoolhouse and oldest stone church in Ellis County. (June-Aug, Tues-Fri; also Sat and Sun afternoons; rest of yr, Tues-Fri; closed hols). 100 W 7th St. Phone 785/628-2624. **Donation**

Historic Fort Hays. Parade grounds, small buffalo herd. Museums in original guardhouse, officers' quarters, and blockhouse; visitor center. (Daily; closed hols). Frontier Historical Park, 1472 Hwy 183 Alt. Phone 785/625-6812. **Donation**

Sternberg Museum of Natural History. Natural history, paleontological, and geological collections. (Call for schedule; closed Jan 1, Thanksgiving, Dec 25) 2911 Canterbury Dr. Phone 785/628-4286. ¢¢

Special Events

Wild West Festival. Family oriented activities; concerts, food booths, fireworks display. Early July.

Ellis County Fair. Ellis County Fairground. Entertainment, activities, tractor pull, arts and crafts. Phone 785/628-8202. Last full wkend July.

Historic Fort Hays Days. Two full days of living history incl demonstrations of butter churning, tatting, ropemaking, rug weaving, whittling, stonepost cutting. Phone 785/625-6812 or 785/628-8202. Sept.

Oktoberfest. Arts and crafts, entertainment. Phone 785/628-8202. Early Oct.

Motels/Motor Lodges

★★ **BEST WESTERN VAGABOND.** *2524 Vine St (67601). 785/625-2511; fax 785/625-8879; res 800/528-1234. www.bestwestern.com.* 92 rms, 1-2 story. S $48-$58; D $58-$68; each addl $4; suites $80-$140; under 12 free. Crib $4. Pet accepted. TV; cable (premium). Pool; whirlpool. Complimentary coffee in rms. Restaurant 7 am-9 pm. Bar 5-10 pm. Ck-out noon. Meeting rms. Business servs avail. In-rm modem link. Valet serv. Cr cds: A, C, D, DS, MC, V.

🐾 ➤ 🛏 🎿 🔥

★ **BUDGET HOST VILLA INN.** *810 E 8th St (67601). 785/625-2563; fax 785/625-3967; toll-free 800/283-4678. www.budgethost.com.* 49 rms, 1-2 story. S $25-$40; D $30-$50; each addl $3; suites $49-$65. Crib $5. Pet accepted, some restrictions. TV; cable. Pool. Coffee in rms. Restaurant nearby. Ck-out noon. Business servs avail. Free airport transportation. Picnic tables. Cr cds: A, C, D, DS, MC, V.

🅓 🐾 ➤ 🛏 🔥 SC

★ **DAYS INN.** *3205 N Vine St (67601). 785/628-8261; res 800/329-7466. www.daysinn.com.* 104 rms, 2 story. S $40-$52; D $52-$62; each addl $5; suites $85-$90; under 17 free. Crib free. Pet accepted; $5. TV; cable (premium), VCR avail. Heated pool. Playground. Complimentary coffee in rms. Restaurant day 6 am-11 pm. Ck-out noon. Meeting rms. Business servs avail. In-rm modem link. Bathrm phones. Cr cds: A, C, D, DS, MC, V.

🅓 🐾 ➤ 🛏 🔥

★★ **HAMPTON INN.** *3801 Vine St (67601). 785/625-8103; fax 785/625-3006. www.hamptoninn.com.* 116 rms, 2 story. S, D $47-$60; suites $90. Crib free. Pet accepted. TV; cable (premium). Pool privileges adj. Complimentary continental bkfst. Restaurant adj. Ck-out noon. Business servs avail. In-rm modem link.

Free airport transportation. Cr cds: A, D, DS, MC, V.

🅓 🐾 🐸 🛏 🔥

★★ **HOLIDAY INN.** *3603 Vine St (67601). 785/625-7371; fax 785/625-7250; res 800/465-4329. www. holiday-inn.com.* 190 rms, 2 story. S, D $60-$75; suites $75-$100; under 19 free. Crib free. Pet accepted. TV; cable (premium). Indoor pool; whirlpool. Sauna, steam rm. Restaurant 6:30 am-2 pm, 5-10 pm. Ck-out noon. Business servs avail. In-rm modem link. Valet serv. Gift shop. Airport transportation. Rec rm. Cr cds: A, D, DS, MC, V.

🅓 🐾 🛏 🔥 🐸

Restaurant

★ **GUTIERREZ.** *1106 E 27th (67601). 785/625-4402. www.gutierrez restaurant.com.* Hrs: 11 am-10 pm; Sun to 9 pm. Closed hols. Res accepted. Mexican, American menu. Bar. Lunch $2.75-$8, dinner $5-$9. Children's menu. Specializes in fajitas, quesadillas, chimichangas. Own chips. Cr cds: A, DS, MC, V.

🅓 🍽

Hiawatha

(B-7) *See also Atchison, Seneca; also see St. Joseph, MO*

Pop 3,603 **Elev** 1,136 ft
Area code 785 **Zip** 66434
Information Chamber of Commerce, 602 Oregon St; 785/742-7136

What to See and Do

Brown County AG Museum. Features display of windmills, the Old Barn, Ernie's cabinet shop, blacksmith shop, horsedrawn implement building, antique tractor and car display. (Display Mon-Sat) E Iowa St. Phone 785/742-3702. ¢¢

🟥 **Davis Memorial.** Eccentric $500,000 tomb features 11 life-size Italian marble statues depicting John Davis and his wife in various periods of their lives. Completed in 1937. ½ mi E on Iowa St in Mt Hope Cemetery.

Special Event

Halloween Parade. Afternoon and evening parade held every yr since 1914. Phone 785/742-7136. Oct 31.

Motel/Motor Lodge

★★ **HIAWATHA INN.** *1100 S 1st St (66434). 785/742-7401; fax 785/742-3334.* 40 rms, 2 story. S $38; D $42; each addl $4; under 12 free. TV; cable, VCR avail. Heated pool. Restaurant (see HEARTLAND). Ck-out 11 am. Meeting rms. Business servs avail. Free airport transportation. Private patios, balconies. Cr cds: A, C, D, DS, ER, JCB, MC, V.

🄳 ⛵ ⌁ ⊠ 🐾

Restaurant

★ **HEARTLAND.** *1100 S 1st St (66434). 785/742-7401.* Hrs: 6 am-9 pm. Res accepted. Bar 5 pm-midnight. Bkfst $1.50-$5.25, lunch $3.75-$5.75, dinner $4.99-$14.99. Buffet $6.95. Children's menu. Specializes in chicken, ribs, steak. Salad bar. Cr cds: A, C, D, DS, MC, V.

🄳 ⊸

Hutchinson

(D-5) See also McPherson, Newton, Wichita

Founded 1872 **Pop** 39,308 **Elev** 1,538 ft **Area code** 620

Information Greater Hutchinson Convention & Visitors Bureau, 117 N Walnut, PO Box 519, 67504; 316/662-3391 or 800/691-4282

Web www.hutchchamber.com

In 1887, drillers for natural gas discovered some of the world's richest rock salt deposits under the town of Hutchinson. The industry was promptly established; today the town is a major salt-producing center, with a mine and processing plants. Hutchinson, the principal city and county seat of Reno County, also is a wholesale and retail trade center for central and western Kansas.

What to See and Do

Dillon Nature Center. More than 150 species of birds, along with deer, coyote, and other animals, can be spotted at the 100-acre center, which incl special gardens, nature trails, a discovery building, and two ponds for fishing and canoeing. Guided nature tours (by appt), discovery building (Mon-Fri). Grounds (daily; days vary for canoe rentals and fishing). 3002 E 30th St. Phone 316/663-7411. **FREE**

Historic Fox Theatre. Restored 1931 theater exemplifies Art Deco architecture. Named the "state movie palace of Kansas," the theater is on the National Register of Historic Places. Professional entertainment for all ages; classic and independent film; arts education programs. Guided tours (daily, by appt). 18 E First. Phone 316/663-5861.

Kansas Cosmosphere and Space Center. Major Space Science Center for Midwest, featuring Hall of Space Museum exhibits from the US and Soviet space programs. Displays incl a full-scale space shuttle replica, the actual Apollo 13 command module "Odyssey," a Northrup T-38 jet used for pilot training, and an SR-71 Blackbird spy plane—one of only 29 in the world. Cosmosphere with planetarium (fee) and Omnimax (70 mm) projectors. Cosmosphere shows (Daily). (Daily; closed Dec 25) 1100 N Plum. Phone 316/662-2305. ¢¢

Reno County Museum. Features four rotating exhibit galleries; two interactive areas for children (101 and 102 Children's Place), along with several temporary exhibits. Educational program offers lectures, classes, and workshops. (Tues-Sun; closed hols) 100 S Walnut St. Phone 316/662-1184. **FREE**

Special Events

National Junior College Basketball Tournament. Sports Arena. Mid-Mar.

Kansas State Fair. Fairgrounds, 2000 N Poplar. Phone 316/669-3600. Sept.

Motels/Motor Lodges

★ **COMFORT INN.** *1621 Super Plaza (67501). 620/663-7822; fax 620/663-1055; res 800/424-6423. www.comfort inn.com.* 63 rms, 3 story. S, D $59-

$69; under 18 free; wkend rates; higher rates special events. Crib free. Pet accepted. TV; cable (premium). Pool; whirlpool. Complimentary continental bkfst. Restaurant nearby. Ck-out noon. Business servs avail. In-rm modem link. Valet serv. Cr cds: A, D, DS, MC, V.

🅳 🏊 🖭 ✈ 🔏 🛥

★ **QUALITY INN.** *15 W 4th Ave (67501). 620/663-1211; toll-free 800/ 228-5151. www.qualityinn.com.* 98 rms, 2 story. S $40.95-$48.95; D $48.95-$58.95; suites $48.95-$130; under 18 free; wkly rates; higher rates: state fair, college basketball tournament. Crib free. Pet accepted, some restrictions. TV; cable (premium), VCR avail. Pool. Restaurant 6:30 am-9 pm; Sun 7 am-2 pm. Bar 4 pm-midnight. Ck-out noon. Meeting rms. Business servs avail. In-rm modem link. Sundries. Golf privileges. Balconies. Cr cds: A, C, D, DS, ER, JCB, MC, V.

🅳 🏊 🖭 🍴 🔏 🛥 SC

★ **RAMADA CONFERENCE CENTER.** *1400 N Lorraine St (67501). 620/ 669-9311; fax 620/669-9830; toll-free 800/362-5018. www.ramada.com.* 220 rms, 2 story. S, D $66-$72; each addl $6; suites $175-$250; under 18 free; higher rates state fair, special events. Crib free. TV; cable (premium), VCR avail. Heated pool; whirlpool. Sauna. Restaurants 6 am-2 pm, 5-10 pm. Bar. Ck-out noon. Coin lndry. Meeting rms. Business servs avail. In-rm modem link. Lighted tennis. Rec rm. Picnic tables. Cr cds: A, C, D, DS, ER, JCB, MC, V.

🅳 🎾 🖭 🍴 🔏 🛥

Independence

(E-7) *See also Coffeyville, Parsons*

Founded 1870 **Pop** 9,942 **Elev** 826 ft **Area code** 620 **Zip** 67301

Information Convention & Visitors Bureau, 322 N Penn, PO Box 386; 316/331-1890 or 800/882-3606

Montgomery County, of which Independence is the seat, was part of the Osage Indian Reservation. In 1869 the Independent Town Company from Oswego, Kansas, obtained 640 acres from the tribe. When the Osage moved to Oklahoma following a treaty in 1870 the entire reservation was opened to settlement. The discovery of natural gas in 1881 and of oil in 1903 caused temporary booms. Today leading industrial products are cement, electrical and electronic parts and equipment, wood products, small aircraft, truck bodies, and gas heaters. Farming in the area produces beef cattle, dairy products, hogs, wheat, beans, alfalfa, corn, and grain sorghums.

Alfred M. Landon, presidential candidate in 1936, playwright William Inge, author Laura Ingalls Wilder, oilman Harry F. Sinclair, and actress Vivian Vance lived here.

What to See and Do

Independence Museum. Miscellaneous collections on display; period rms and monthly exhibits. (Thurs-Sat) 8th and Myrtle sts. Phone 316/331-3515. ¢

Independence Science & Technology Center. Hands-on museum; anti-gravity simulator; Van de Graaff generator. (Daily; closed hols) 125 S Main St. Phone 316/331-1999. ¢

"Little House on the Prairie." Reproduction of log cabin occupied by Laura Ingalls Wilder's family from 1869-1870. Also one-rm schoolhouse (ca 1870) and old post office. (Mid-May-Aug, daily). 13 mi SW on US 75. Phone 800/882-3606. **Donation**

Recreation areas. Elk City State Park. An 857-acre park on 4,500-acre lake. Nearby is Table Mound, overlooking Elk River valley, site of one of the last Osage villages. Arrowheads and other artifacts are still found. Beach; fishing, boating (ramp, dock); hiking, nature trails, picnicking, camping (electricity, dump station). Standard fees. (Daily) 7 mi NW off US 160.

Montgomery State Fishing Lake. Fishing, boating; picnicking. Primitive camping. 4 mi S via 10th St Rd, then 1 mi E. Phone 316/331-6295. ¢¢

Riverside Park. Covers 124 acres. Ralph Mitchell Zoo, Kiddy Land, miniature train (fee), merry-go-round (fee), and miniature golf (fee) (May-Labor Day, daily; rest of yr, hrs vary). Swimming pool (Memorial Day-Labor Day, daily; fee). Tennis courts; playground; picnic grounds, shelter houses. Park (daily). Oak St and Park Blvd. Phone 316/332-2513. **FREE**

Special Event

"Neewollah." Wk-long Halloween festival. Musical entertainment. Last full wk Oct.

Motels/Motor Lodges

★★ **APPLETREE INN.** *201 N 8th St (67301). 620/331-5500; fax 620/331-0641.* 64 rms, 2 story. S $47-$49; D $53-$56; each addl $4; suites $58-$100; higher rates Neewollah. Crib avail. Pet accepted. TV, cable (premium). Indoor pool; whirlpool. Complimentary continental bkfst. Restaurant opp 11 am-10 pm. Ck-out noon. Business servs avail. In-rm modem link. Health club privileges. Some refrigerators. Cr cds: A, C, D, DS, MC, V.

D 🐾 ≈ 🏋 🔥

★★ **BEST WESTERN PRAIRIE INN.** *3222 W Main St (67301). 620/331-7300; fax 620/331-8740; res 800/528-1234. www.bestwestern.com.* 40 rms. S $46-$50; D $50-$56; each addl $4. Crib $3. Pet accepted, some restrictions; $3/day. TV; cable (premium). Pool. Complimentary continental bkfst. Ck-out 11 am. Business servs avail. Cr cds: A, C, DS, MC, V.

D 🐾 🛄 ≈ 🏋 🔥

Iola

(D-7) *See also Chanute, Yates Center*

Pop 6,351 **Elev** 960 ft **Area code** 620 **Zip** 66749

Information Chamber of Commerce, 208 W Madison, PO Box 722; 316/365-5252

Web www.ci.iola.ks.us

What to See and Do

Allen County Historical Museum Gallery. Display of historical artifacts and memorabilia. (May-Sept, Tues-Sat or by appt) 207 N Jefferson. Phone 316/365-3051. **FREE** Adj is

Old Jail Museum. Historic building; downstairs is solitary confinement cell (1869) and cell cage (1891);

upper floor is re-creation of sheriff's living quarters (1869-1904). (Schedule same as Museum Gallery) 207 N Jefferson. **FREE**

Bowlus Fine Arts Center. Hosts a number of cultural attractions in the 750-seat capacity auditorium. 205 E Madison. Phone 316/365-4765. **FREE**

Boyhood Home of Major General Frederick Funston. Built in 1860; originally located on homestead about five mi north of Iola. Restored according to the Victorian decor of the 1880s and 1890s. Many original family items on display. (May-Sept, Wed-Sat). 207 N Jefferson **FREE**

Museum Room. Collection and display of historical artifacts. (Mon-Fri; closed hols) Allen County Courthouse, on Courthouse Square. Phone 316/365-1407. **FREE**

Special Events

Allen County Fair. Fairgrounds and Riverside Park. Phone 316/365-5252. First wk Aug.

Buster Keaton Festival. Bowlus Fine Arts Center. Phone 316/365-4765. Last wkend Sept.

Farm City Days. Town Square. Phone 316/365-5252. Third wkend Oct.

Motels/Motor Lodges

★★ **BEST WESTERN INN.** *1315 N State St (66749). 620/365-5161; fax 620/365-6808; res 800/769-0007. www.bestwestern.com.* 59 rms. S $42-$46; D $46-$52; each addl $4; suites $51-$59. Crib $2. TV; cable (premium). Pool. Complimentary coffee in rms. Restaurant 6 am-9 pm; Sun 7 am-2 pm. Private club 5-11 pm. Ck-out noon. Meeting rm. Business servs avail. Refrigerators; some microwaves, bathrm phones. Cr cds: A, MC, V.

D ≈ 🏋 🔥 SC

★ **CROSSROADS MOTEL.** *14 N State St (66749). 620/365-2183.* 54 rms, 1-2 story. S $29; D $36; each addl $3; suites $35-$38. Crib $3. TV; cable (premium). Pool. Complimentary coffee in rms. Restaurant nearby. Ck-out 11 am. Cr cds: A, C, D, DS, MC, V.

≈ 🏋 🔥 SC

Junction City

(C-6) *See also Abilene, Council Grove, Manhattan*

Settled 1855 **Pop** 20,604 **Elev** 1,107 ft **Area code** 785 **Zip** 66441

Information Geary County Convention & Visitors Bureau, 425 N Washington, PO Box 1846; 785/238-2885 or 800/JCT-CITY

Web www.junctioncity.org

Its situation at the junction of the Republican and Smoky Hill rivers gave the town its name. The seat of Geary County, it has long been a trading point for soldiers from Fort Riley.

What to See and Do

Fort Riley. (1853) A 101,000-acre military reservation; once a frontier outpost and former home of the US Cavalry School. Marked tour. (Daily) N on KS 57, NE on KS 18; located along I-70. Phone 785/239-6727. Here are

1st Infantry Division Museum. Division history and memorabilia. (Tues-Sat; closed Jan 1, Thanksgiving, Dec 25) **FREE**

Custer House. The George Armstrong Custers lived in quarters similar to this house. (Memorial Day-Labor Day, daily; hrs vary rest of yr) **FREE**

First Territorial Capitol. "Permanent" capitol July 2-6, 1855, before Free Staters won legislative majority. (Thurs-Sun; closed hols) **FREE**

St. Mary's Chapel. (1855) Kansas's first native limestone church; still in use.

US Cavalry Museum. Army memorabilia and local history. (Daily; closed hols) **FREE**

Geary County Historical Museum. Three-story native limestone building is example of the stonecutter's art and houses the first Junction City High School. Galleries feature changing and rotating exhibits portraying the Native American Indian period to present day. (Tues-Sun; closed hols) 6th and Adams sts. **FREE**

Milford Lake. A 15,700-acre reservoir with a 163-mi shoreline; arboretum, fish hatchery, nature center. Swimming, fishing, boating (marinas); picnicking, camping (fee). (Daily) 4 mi NW via US 77, KS 57. Phone 785/238-5714. ¢¢

Milford State Park. A 1,084-acre park on 16,200-acre lake. Largest manmade lake in Kansas. Native red cedars border shoreline. Nearby is Fort Riley, a major military reservation. Beach, bathhouse, fishing, boating (rentals, ramps, docks, marina). Concession. Tent and trailer camping (electricity, dump station). Standard fees. (Daily) 5 mi NW on KS 57. Phone 785/238-3014.

Motels/Motor Lodges

★ **DAYS INN.** *1024 S Washington St (66441). 785/762-2727; fax 785/762-2751; toll-free 800/860-1020. www.daysinn.com.* 108 rms, 2 story. S $40-$58; D $47-$60; each addl $5; under 17 free. Crib free. Pet accepted, some restrictions. TV; cable (premium). 2 pools, 1 indoor; whirlpool. Sauna. Complimentary continental bkfst. Coffee in rms. Restaurant adj open 24 hrs. Bar 4 pm-midnight, closed Sun. Ck-out noon. Coin lndry. Meeting rms. Business servs avail. Valet serv. Game rm. Rec rm. Cr cds: A, D, DS, MC, V.
🄳 🐾 🕭 🏊 🖨 🔥

★ **GOLDEN WHEAT BUDGET INN.** *820 S Washington St (66441). 785/238-5106; fax 785/233-6137.* 20 rms, 6 with shower only. Mar-Oct: S $30; D $35-$40; each addl $5; under 14 free; lower rates rest of yr. Crib $3. TV; cable (premium). Complimentary coffee in lobby. Restaurant nearby. Ck-out 11 am. Cr cds: A, DS, MC, V.
🕭 🔥

★★ **RED CARPET INN.** *110 E Flinthills Blvd (66441). 785/238-5188; fax 785/238-7585.* 48 rms, 1-2 story, 20 kits. S $35-$45; D $45-$55; each addl $4; kit. units $38-$56; under 12 free. Crib $4. Pet accepted. TV; cable (premium), VCR avail. Pool. Complimentary coffee in rms. Restaurant nearby. Ck-out noon. Some refrigerators. Picnic tables. Cr cds: A, DS, MC, V.
🄳 🐾 🕭 🏊 🖨 🔥

★ **SUPER 8 MOTEL.** *1001 E 6th St (66441). 785/238-8101; fax 785/238-7470; toll-free 800/800-8000. www.super8.com.* 99 rms, 2 story. May-

Sept: S $40; D $47; suites $65; under 12 free; wkly rates; lower rates rest of yr. Crib free. Pet accepted, some restrictions. TV; cable (premium). Pool. Restaurant 7 am-2 pm, 5-9 pm. Bar 5-10 pm. Ck-out noon. Coin lndry. Meeting rm. Business servs avail. In-rm modem link. Some refrigerators. Picnic tables. Cr cds: A, C, D, DS, MC, V.

D ↩ ⊵ ⊠ ♨ SC

Kansas City

(C-8) *See also Independence, Kansas City, Lawrence, Leavenworth, Overland Park*

Settled 1843 **Pop** 149,767 **Elev** 744 ft
Area code 913
Information Kansas City, Kansas Area Convention & Visitors Bureau, 727 Minnesota Ave, PO Box 171517, 66117; 913/371-3070 or 800/264-1563
Web www.kckcvb.org

Kansas City as it is today was formed by the consolidation of eight individual towns. The earliest of these, Wyandot City, was settled in 1843 by the Wyandot, an emigrant tribe from Ohio, who bought part of the Delaware tribe's land. This cultured group brought government, schools, churches, business, and agricultural methods to the area. In 1849, alarmed at the influx of settlers on their way to seek California gold, the Wyandot took measures to dispose of their property at a good price. Their successors created a boomtown and changed the spelling to "Wyandotte." Other towns arose nearby, especially as the meat packing industry developed. Eventually they all merged into the present city, which took the name of one of the earliest towns.

Kansas City has several grain elevators, in addition to fabricating steel mills, automobile manufacturers, soap factories, railway yards, and various other industries.

What to See and Do

The Children's Museum of Kansas City. Learning museum for children ages 4-12 has more than 40 hands-on exhibits dealing with science, history, art, and technology. Exhibits incl a shadow retention wall, grocery store, a slice of city streets, a crawl-around salt water aquarium, chain reaction demonstrations, and simple machines. (Tues-Sun) 4601 State Ave, in the Indian Springs Shopping Center. Phone 913/287-8888. ¢¢

Grinter House. (1857) Home of Moses Grinter, first European settler in Wyandotte County; period furnishings. (Wed-Sat, also Sun afternoons; closed hols) Maintained by the Kansas State Historical Society. 1420 S 78th St. Phone 913/299-0373. **FREE**

Huron Indian Cemetery. The tribal burial ground of the Wyandots; an estimated 400 burials (1844-1855). In Huron Park, Center City Plaza, between 6th and 7th sts, in the heart of the business district.

National Agricultural Center and Hall of Fame. National Farmer's Memorial; history and development of agriculture; library/archives, gallery of rural art; Museum of Farming; "Farm-town USA" exhibit; 1-mi nature trail. (Mid-Mar-Nov, daily; closed Memorial Day, Labor Day, Thanksgiving) 18 mi W on I-70, at 630 Hall of Fame Dr (N 126th St) in Bonner Springs. Phone 913/721-1075. ¢¢

The Woodlands. Thoroughbred, quarter horse, and greyhound racing; two grandstands. (Horse racing Oct-Nov, Wed-Sun; greyhound racing all yr) 99th and Leavenworth Rd. Phone 913/299-9797. ¢

Wyandotte County Historical Society and Museum. Native American artifacts, horse-drawn fire engine, pioneer furniture, costumes, county history; research library, archives. (Fri-Sat; closed mid-Dec-Jan 2) 15 mi W on I-70, Bonner Springs exit, at 631 N 126th St in Bonner Springs. Phone 913/721-1078. **FREE**

Special Event

Renaissance Festival. Adj to Agricultural Hall of Fame in Bonner Springs.

Phone 800/373-0357. Seven wkends beginning Labor Day wkend.

Restaurant

★★ **PAULO & BILL.** *16501 Midland Dr, Shawnee (66217). 913/962-9900.* Hrs: 11 am-10 pm; Fri, Sat to midnight; Sun brunch 10:30 am-2:30 pm. Closed July 4, Thanksgiving, Dec 25. Res accepted. Italian, American menu. Bar. Lunch $5.95-$9.95, dinner $8.95-$15.95. Sun brunch $13.95. Children's menu. Specialties: osso buco, lasagna al forno, wood-fired pizza. Outdoor dining. Contemporary decor. Cr cds: A, D, DS, MC, V.

[D] [⊒]

Larned

(D-4) *See also Great Bend*

Founded 1872 **Pop** 4,490 **Elev** 2,004 ft **Area code** 620 **Zip** 67550

Information Chamber of Commerce, 502 Broadway, PO Box 240; 316/285-6916 or 800/747-6919

Web www.larned.net/~chamber

What to See and Do

Fort Larned National Historic Site. (1859-1878). Considered one of the best-preserved frontier military posts along the Santa Fe Trail; quadrangle of nine original stone buildings plus reconstructed blockhouse. Incl officers' quarters, enlisted men's barracks, blacksmith and carpenter shops, post bakery, hospital, quartermaster and commissary storehouses. Visitor center contains museum, orientation program, and bookstore. Conducted tours (Mon-Fri in summer). Living history programs, demonstrations, and special events (most summer wkends). One-mi history/nature trail. Picnic area. (Daily; closed Jan 1, Thanksgiving, Dec 25) 6 mi W on KS 156. Phone 316/285-6911. ¢

Santa Fe Trail Center. Museum and library with exhibits explaining exploration, transportation, settlement, and cultural development along the Santa Fe Trail. On the grounds are a sod house, frontier schoolhouse, limestone cooling

house, dugout, and depot. (Memorial Day-Labor Day, daily; rest of yr, Tues-Sun; closed Jan 1, Thanksgiving, Dec 25) 2 mi W on KS 156. Phone 316/285-2054. ¢¢

Motel/Motor Lodge

★★ **BEST WESTERN TOWNSEND.** *123 E 14th St (67550). 620/285-3114; fax 620/285-7139; res 800/399-3114. www.bestwestern.com.* 44 rms. S $40-$50; D $50-$55; each addl $3; under 12 free. Crib $2. Pet accepted. TV; cable (premium), VCR avail. Pool. Coffee in rms. Restaurant opp 6 am-10 pm. Ck-out noon. Business servs avail. In-rm modem link. Sundries. Tennis privileges. Golf privileges. Cr cds: A, MC, V.

[D] [≈] [†] [⊱] [≈] [⊠] [♨] [SC]

Lawrence

(C-7) *See also Kansas City, Leavenworth, Ottawa, Topeka*

Founded 1854 **Pop** 65,608 **Elev** 850 ft **Area code** 785

Information Convention & Visitors Bureau, 734 Vermont, PO Box 586, 66044; 785/865-4411 or 800/LAWKANS

Web www.visitlawrence.com

Lawrence had a stormy history in the territorial years. It was founded by the New England Emigrant Aid Company and named for one of its prominent members. The center of Free State activities, the town was close to a state of war from 1855 until the Free Staters triumphed in 1859. The Confederate guerrilla leader William Quantrill made one of his most spectacular raids on Lawrence in 1863, burning the town and killing 150 citizens. After the Civil War the town experienced a gradual and peaceful growth as an educational, cultural, trading, and shipping point, and developed a variety of industries.

What to See and Do

Baker University. (1858) 850 students. Oldest university in state. Original building is now Old Castle Museum and Complex, housing pioneer relics and Native American artifacts (Tues-Sun; closed hols); Quayle Bible collection (Daily), res required at Collins Library. Campus tours. 13 mi S on US 59, then 5 mi E on US 56 in Baldwin City. Phone 785/594-6451.

Clinton State Park. A 1,485-acre park on 7,000-acre lake. High, heavily wooded hills and grassland on the north shore. Beach, bathhouse, fishing, boating (ramps, docks); nature trails, picnicking, concession. Camping (electricity, dump station). Standard fees. (Daily) 4 mi W off US 40. Phone 785/842-8562. ¢¢

Haskell Indian Nations University. (1884) 1,000 students. A 320-acre campus. More than 120 tribes are represented among the students. Campus is a registered historic landmark; cultural activities; American Indian Athletic Hall of Fame. (Mon-Fri) 155 Indian Ave. Phone 785/749-8450.

Lawrence Arts Center. Galleries featuring work of local artists and craftspeople; performance hall for theater, dance, and music; art classes and workshops for all ages. (Mon-Sat) 200 W 9th St. **FREE**

Old West Lawrence Historic District. Self-guided tour through area of notable 19th-century homes. (Daily) 2 blks W of downtown on Tennessee and Missouri sts. Phone 785/865-4499. **FREE**

University of Kansas. (1866) 26,000 students. Λ 1,000-acre campus. Some of the campus attractions are the Campanile Bell Tower; Museum of Natural History (daily; phone 785/864-4450); Museum of Anthropology (daily; phone 785/864-4245); and Spencer Museum of Art (Tues-Sun; phone 785/864-4710). (All buildings closed hols) Tours of campus. Phone 785/864-3131.

Watkins Community Museum. Museum housed in 1888 bank building; Victorian era children's playhouse; 1920 Milburn Light Electric car; Quantrill Raid artifacts; permanent and changing exhibits pertaining to the history of Lawrence and Douglas County. (Tues-Sun; closed hols) 1047 Massachusetts St. Phone 785/841-4109. **FREE**

Special Events

Douglas County Free Fair. Early Aug.

Indian Arts Show. University of Kansas Museum of Anthropology. Juried exhibit featuring work by contemporary American Indian artists from across the US. Phone 785/864-4245. Sept-Oct.

Motels/Motor Lodges

★★ **BEST WESTERN INN.** *730 Iowa St (66044). 785/841-6500; fax 785/841-6612; res 800/528-1234. www. bestwestern.com.* 59 rms, 2 story. S $42-$55; D $46-$55; each addl $4; under 12 free; higher rates university events. Crib free. Pet accepted, some restrictions. TV; cable (premium). Pool. Complimentary continental bkfst, coffee in rms. Restaurant nearby. Ck-out noon. Coin lndry. Business servs avail. In-rm modem link. Cr cds: A, D, DS, MC, V.

★ **BISMARCK INN.** *1130 N 3rd St (66044). 785/749-4040; fax 785/749-3016.* 53 rms, 3 story. S, D $37.90-$51.90; each addl $6; under 16 free; higher rates university football season. Crib free. TV; cable (premium). Complimentary continental bkfst. Restaurant nearby. Ck-out 11 am. Coin lndry. Game rm. Refrigerators avail. Cr cds: A, D, DS, MC, V.

★ **DAYS INN.** *2309 Iowa St (66047). 785/843-9100; fax 785/843-1572; res 800/329-7466. www.daysinn.com.* 101 rms, 3 story. S, D $42-$75; each addl $4; suite $95; under 18 free; monthly rates. Crib free. Pet accepted, some restrictions. TV; cable (premium). Pool. Complimentary continental bkfst. Coffee in rms. Ck-out noon. Restaurant adj 11:30 am-10:30 pm. Coin lndry. Business servs avail. In-rm modem link. Sundries. 18-hole golf privileges, greens fee $35-$45. Some refrigerators. Cr cds: A, DS, MC, V.

★★ **HOLIDAY INN.** *200 McDonald Dr (66044). 785/841-7077; fax 785/841-2799; res 800/465-4329. www. holiday-inn.com.* 192 rms, 4 story. S, D $69-$129; suites $125-$225; under 17 free; higher rates major college activities. Crib free. Pet accepted. TV; cable, VCR avail. Indoor pool; whirlpool, poolside serv. Coffee in rms. Restaurant 6 am-2 pm, 5-10 pm. Bar 2 pm-1 am. Ck-out noon. Business servs avail. Coin lndry. Exercise equipt; sauna. Game rm. Rec rm. Cr cds: A, D, DS, MC, V.

★ **WESTMINSTER INN.** *2525 W 6th St (66049). 785/841-8410; fax 785/ 841-1901; toll-free 888/937-8646.* 60 rms, 2 story. S $40; D $50-$58; each addl $4. Crib free. Pet accepted. TV; cable (premium). Pool. Complimentary coffee in lobby. Restaurant nearby. Ck-out noon. Meeting rm. Cr cds: A, C, D, DS, ER, MC, V.

Hotel

★ ★ ★ **ELDRIDGE HOTEL.** *701 Massachusetts St (66044). 785/749-5011; fax 785/749-4512; toll-free 800/ 527-0909. www.eldridgehotel.com.* 48 suites, 5 story. S $78-$92; D $86-$235; under 12 free; higher rates major college events. Crib free. Valet parking. TV; cable, VCR avail. Complimentary coffee in rms. Restaurant 7 am-2 pm, 5-9 pm; Fri, Sat to 10 pm. Bar 11-10 pm. Ck-out noon. Meeting rms. Business servs avail. Barber, beauty shop. Exercise equipt; sauna. Whirlpool. Refrigerators, wet bars. Built in 1855 as a Free State hostelry for abolitionists; many fights during the Civil War took place here. Cr cds: A, D, DS, MC, V.

B&B/Small Inn

★ ★ **HALCYON HOUSE BED & BREAKFAST.** *1000 Ohio St (66044). 785/841-0314; fax 785/843-7273; toll-free 888/441-0314. www.thehalcyon house.com.* 9 rms, 4 share bath, 3 story. D $45-$85. Children over 12 yrs only. TV in some rms; VCR avail (movies). Complimentary full bkfst. Ck-out 11 am, ck-in 1 pm. Tennis privileges. 27-hole golf privileges. Health club privileges. Balconies. Victorian inn built 1885. Cr cds: A, MC, V.

Restaurant

★ ★ ★ **FIFI'S.** *925 Iowa St (US 59) (66044). 785/841-7226.* Hrs: 11 am-2 pm, 5-10 pm; Sun, Mon 5-9 pm. Closed hols. Res accepted. Continental menu. Wine list. Lunch $2.95-$6.25, dinner $3.95-$13.95. Bar. Specialties: steak Diane, lobster fettucine, fresh seafood. Cr cds: A, MC, V.

Leavenworth

(B-8) *See also Atchison, Kansas City, Lawrence; also see Kansas City and St. Joseph, MO*

Founded 1854 **Pop** 38,495 **Elev** 800 ft **Area code** 913 **Zip** 66048

Information Leavenworth Convention & Visitors Bureau, 518 Shawnee St, PO Box 44; 913/682-4113 or 800/844-4114

Web www.lvarea.com

Leavenworth was the first incorporated town in Kansas Territory. At first strongly pro-slavery, Leavenworth had many border conflicts, but during the Civil War it was loyal to the Union. In the years just before the war, the town was the headquarters for a huge overland transportation and supply operation sending wagons and stagecoaches northwest on the Oregon Trail and southwest on the Santa Fe Trail. Fort Leavenworth, adjoining the city, is the oldest military post in continuous operation (since 1827) west of the Mississippi River. A federal penitentiary is on the grounds adjacent to the fort. Industries in the city of Leavenworth include the Hallmark Card Company and the production of flour, milling machinery, and agricultural chemicals.

What to See and Do

Fort Leavenworth. Features of interest are US Army Command and General Staff College, US Disciplinary Barracks, National Cemetery, Buffalo Soldier Monument, branches of the Oregon and Santa Fe trails. Frontier Army Museum features artifacts of pioneer history and the Army of the

West. (Daily; closed hols) Fort (daily). Obtain self-guided Historical Wayside Tour brochure at information center inside fort entrance on Grant Ave. 3 mi N on US 73. Phone 913/684-5604. **FREE**

Leavenworth's Victorian Carroll Museum. 1867 Victorian home and furnishings; school rm; local mementos. Gift shop. (Daily; closed hols, also Jan) 1128 5th Ave. Phone 913/682-7759. ¢¢

Parker Carousel. Restored 1913 carousel features hand-carved, one-of-a-kind horses, ponies, and rabbits. (Daily) Downtown historic riverfront area. Phone 913/682-4113. ¢

Special Events

Fort Homes Tour and Frontier Army Encampment. Mid-Apr.

Lansing Daze. Community-wide festival. Phone 913/727-3233. First wkend May.

Leavenworth River Fest. Historic riverfront downtown. Mid-Sept.

Motels/Motor Lodges

★★ **HALLMARK INN LEAVEN-WORTH.** 3211 S 4th St (66048). 913/651-6000; fax 913/651-7722; toll-free 888/540-4020. 52 rms, 2 story. S $52; D $60-$67; each addl $6; under 12 free. Crib free. TV; cable (premium). Pool. Complimentary continental bkfst. Coffee in rms. Restaurant nearby. Ck-out noon. Business servs avail. In-rm modem link. Coin lndry. Valet serv. Sundries. Cr cds: A, MC, V.
D ➣ ⊠ ⚹ SC

★ **RAMADA INN.** 101 S 3rd St (66048). 913/651-5500; fax 913/651-6981; res 888/298-2054. www.ramada. com. 97 rms, 2 story. S $40-$70; D $46-$70; each addl $6; suites $60-$70; under 18 free. Crib free. Pet accepted, some restrictions. TV; cable (premium). Pool. Restaurant 6 am-2 pm, 5-9pm. Bar 5-11 pm. Ck-out 1 pm. Meeting rms. Business servs avail. Valet serv. Sundries. Cr cds: A, D, DS, MC, V.
D ➤ ➣ ✕ ⊠ ⚹

Restaurant

★★ **SKYVIEW.** 504 Grand (66048). 913/682-2653. www.skyview

restaurant.net. Hrs: 5:30-8:30 pm. Closed Mon, Sun; Dec 24-30; also 1st 2 wks July. Res accepted. Bar. Dinner $10-$30. Specializes in steak, chicken, seafood. Victorian house (1892); antique tile fireplaces, hand-woven portieres (ca 1850). Gazebo and herb garden. Cr cds: DS, MC, V.

Liberal (F-2)

Founded 1888 **Pop** 16,573 **Elev** 2,836 ft **Area code** 620 **Zip** 67901
Information Tourist Information Center, 1 Yellow Brick Rd; 316/626-0170
Web www.liberal.net

Liberal's name comes from the generosity of one of its first settlers, Mr. S. S. Rogers. Although water was scarce in southwestern Kansas, Mr. Rogers never charged parched and weary travelers for the use of his well—a "liberal" fee.

Liberal, on the eastern edge of the Hugoton-Oklahoma-Texas Panhandle natural gas field, has many gas and oil company offices. Its agricultural products have become more diversified through irrigation. Beef processing and health care are also important.

What to See and Do

Coronado Museum. Displays depict early life of town; some exhibits trace Francisco Coronado's route through Kansas. Also incl are Dorothy's House from *The Wizard of Oz* and animated display of the story. (Memorial Day-Labor Day, daily; rest of yr, Tues-Sat; closed hols) 567 E Cedar St. Phone 316/624-7624. ¢¢

Liberal Air Museum. Aviation collection of more than 100 aircraft incl civilian aircraft, military aircraft from WWII, and planes of the Korean and Vietnam era. Also here are NASA traveling exhibits and Liberal Army Airfield exhibit. Theater, library, special events, and guest speakers. (Daily; closed Jan 1, Thanksgiving, Dec 25) 2000 W Second St. Phone 316/624-5263.

Special Events

International Pancake Race. Downtown. Women compete simultaneously with women in Olney, England, running a 415-yd S-shaped course with a pancake in a skillet, flipping it en route. Shrove Tues in Feb. Phone 316/626-0171.

Five-State Free Fair. Fairgrounds. Aug. Phone 316/624-3743.

Oztoberfest. Munchkin parade, carnival. Oct. Phone 316/624-7624.

Motels/Motor Lodges

★★ **GATEWAY INN.** 720 E Pancake Blvd (67901). 620/624-0242; fax 620/624-1952; toll-free 800/833-3391. 101 rms, 2 story. S $36-$39; D $44-$47; each addl $3; under 12 free. Crib free. Pet accepted, some restrictions. TV; cable (premium). Pool. Restaurant 6 am-2 pm, 5-9 pm. Bar 4 pm-2 am. Ck-out noon. Coin lndry. Meeting rms. Business servs avail. In-rm modem link. Valet serv (wkdays only). Gift shop. Free airport transportation. Tennis. Picnic tables, grill. Cr cds: A, C, D, DS, MC, V.

★★ **LIBERAL INN.** 603 E Pancake Blvd (67901). 620/624-7254; toll-free 800/458-4667. 123 rms, 2 story. S $55; D $64; each addl $5; suites $65-$100; under 12 free; higher rates: pheasant season, Compressor Institute. Crib free. Pet accepted. TV; cable (premium). Indoor pool; whirlpool. Restaurant 6 am-10:30 pm; Sun from 7 am. Private club 5 pm-1 am. Ck-out noon. Coin lndry. Meeting rms. In-rm modem link. Bellhops. Valet serv Mon-Fri. Sundries. Free airport transportation. Picnic tables. Cr cds: A, C, D, DS, MC, V.

Restaurant

★ **KING'S PIT BAR-B-Q.** 355 E Pancake Blvd (US 54) (67901). 620/624-2451. Hrs: 11 am-9 pm. Closed Sun; hols. Res accepted. Lunch, dinner $3.95-$11.95. Children's menu. Specializes in family-style barbecue, steak, seafood. Cr cds: A, D, DS, MC, V.

Lindsborg

(C-5) *See also McPherson, Salina*

Founded 1869 **Pop** 3,076 **Elev** 1,333 ft **Area code** 785 **Zip** 67456
Information Chamber of Commerce, 104 E Lincoln; 785/227-3706 or 888/227-2227
Web www.lindsborg.org

Lindsborg was founded by Swedish immigrants who pioneered cooperative farming in Kansas. The Swedish heritage of Lindsborg is evident in the Old World motifs of its business district, Bethany College, and in its cultural life, which includes many ethnic festivals.

What to See and Do

Birger Sandzen Memorial Art Gallery. Paintings and prints by Birger Sandzen and other artists; fountain by Carl Milles. (Wed-Sun afternoons; closed hols) 401 N 1st St, on Bethany College campus. Phone 785/227-2220. ¢

Kanopolis State Park. A 1,585-acre park on 3,550-acre lake. Excellent fishing for white bass, crappie, walleye, catfish, and largemouth bass. Hiking and bridle trails in rugged Horsethief Canyon, site of 150-ft-high Inscription Rock, with petroglyphs representing three Native American cultures covering the face of the cliff. N of reservoir is Mushroom Rock area, containing unique sandstone formations shaped like giant toadstools. Beach, bathhouse, fishing, boating (ramp, dock, marina); picnicking, concession. Tent and trailer camping (electricity, dump station). Standard fees. (Daily) 19 mi W on KS 4, then N on KS 141. Phone 785/546-2565. ¢¢

McPherson County Old Mill Museum and Park. Museum features Native American history, natural history, collections on pioneer and Swedish culture. Smoky Valley Roller Mill and Swedish Pavilion (1904) have been restored. (Daily; closed hols) 120 Mill St, on the Smoky Hill River. Phone 785/227-3595. ¢

REO Auto Museum. Collection of antique autos (1906-36) displayed in annex to 1930 service station complete with antique hand-operated gas pumps. (Mon-Sat; also Sun afternoons; closed hols) US 81 Business (KS 4), at Lincoln. Phone 785/227-3252. ¢

Special Events

Messiah Festival. Presser Hall, Bethany College campus. Special art shows, concerts, and recitals, incl oratorios of Handel and Bach; presented annually since 1882. For ticket info phone 785/227-3311. Eight days, Palm Sunday-Easter.

Midsummer's Day Festival. Swedish ethnic celebration. Folk dancing, arts and crafts. Phone 785/227-3706. Third Sat June.

Lucia Fest. Christmas season ushered in according to 18th-century Swedish tradition. Phone 785/227-3706. Second Sat Dec.

Motel/Motor Lodge

★ **VIKING MOTEL.** *446 Harrison (67456). 785/227-3336; res 800/326-8390.* 24 rms, 2 story. S $43; D $49; each addl $4; higher rates special events. Crib $4. TV; cable. Pool. Complimentary coffee. Ck-out 11 am. Cr cds: A, C, D, DS, ER, JCB, MC, V.
🌊 🏊 🔥

B&B/Small Inn

★★ **SWEDISH COUNTRY INN.** *112 W Lincoln St (67456). 785/227-2985; fax 785/227-2795; toll-free 800/231-0266. www.swedishcountryinn.com.* 19 rms, 2 story. S $49.50-$70; D $61-$77; under 6 free. Crib free. TV. Complimentary buffet bkfst. Dining rm 7-10 am; Sat, Sun to 11 am. Ck-out 11 am, ck-in 1 pm. Street parking. Bicycles avail. Sauna. Built 1901; handmade Swedish pine furnishings. Totally nonsmoking. Cr cds: A, DS, MC, V.
🦽 🏊 🔥

Restaurant

★★ **SWEDISH CROWN.** *121 N Main St (67456). 785/227-2076.* Hrs: 11 am-9 pm; Sun 10:30 am-8 pm; winter hrs vary. Closed Jan 1, July 4, Dec 25. Res accepted. Swedish, American menu. Lunch $3.50-$5.95, dinner $6.95-$12.95. Children's menu. Specialties: Swedish meatballs, seafood, beef, Swedish ham loaf. Entertainment Fri, Sat. Cr cds: A, DS, MC, V.
D SC 🔄

Manhattan

(C-6) *See also Junction City*

Founded 1857 **Pop** 37,712 **Elev** 1,056 ft **Area code** 785 **Zip** 66502

Information Convention & Visitors Bureau, 501 Poyntz Ave; 785/776-8829 or 800/759-0134

Web www.manhattan.org

Several early settlements were combined to form Manhattan. Lying in a limestone bowl-shaped depression resulting from glacial action, the town developed as a trading center for farm products. Later, when the Rock Island Railroad extended a branch here, it became a shipping point. Kansas State University is in Manhattan; its forerunner, Bluemont Central College, opened in 1863.

What to See and Do

City Park. Picnicking, tennis, playground, games; swimming (Memorial Day-Labor Day); rose garden with 400 varieties of roses (spring-summer). Also here is a pioneer log cabin with farm and shop tools on display (Apr-Oct, Sun; also by appt; phone 785/565-6490). Historic cast-iron fountain, monument to Quivera. (Daily) Poyntz Ave between 11th and 14th sts. Phone 785/587-2757. **FREE**

Goodnow House Museum. (ca 1860) Original limestone home of Isaac T. Goodnow, pioneer educator; period furnishings. (Tues-Sun; closed hols) 2301 Claflin Rd, in Pioneer Park. Phone 785/565-6490. **FREE**

Hartford House. (1855) Period furnishings in restored prefabricated house. One of ten buildings brought to Manhattan in 1855 on a riverboat by a group of Free Staters (those who wished to establish Kansas as anti-slavery territory). (Tues-Sun; closed hols) 2309 Claflin Rd, in Pioneer Park. Phone 785/565-6490. **FREE**

Kansas State University. (1863) 21,500 students. Buildings constructed of native limestone on 664-acre campus. Geological displays in Thompson Hall (Mon-Fri). Tours, Anderson Hall (Mon-Fri). 17th and Anderson sts, center of town. Phone 785/532-6250.

Riley County Historical Museum. Changing exhibits depict history of Riley County; lifestyle of early Kansas settlers; farm, household, and Native American tools; clothing, musical instruments, furniture; archives and library. (Tues-Sun; closed hols) 2309 Claflin Rd, in Pioneer Park. Phone 785/565-6490. **FREE**

Sunset Zoo. Houses more than 300 animals, incl snow leopards and red pandas. Incl the Australian Outback, with wallabies and kangaroos, Primate Building, Asian Forest Preserve, and a children's petting zoo. (Daily; closed Jan 1, Thanksgiving, Dec 25) 2333 Oak St at Summit Ave, SW edge of city off US 24, KS 18. ¢¢

Tuttle Creek State Park. A 1,156-acre park on 13,350-acre lake. Special observation area with distant views of the Blue River valley and Randolph Bridge, largest in Kansas. Beach, bathhouse, fishing, boating (marina); picnicking, concession. Tent and trailer camping (electricity, dump station). Standard fees. 5 mi N on US 24. Phone 785/539-7941. ¢¢

Motels/Motor Lodges

★ **DAYS INN.** 1501 Tuttle Creek Blvd (66502). 785/539-5391; fax 785/539-0847; res 800/329-7466. www.daysinn. com. 119 rms, 2 story. S $45-$65; D $50-$65; each addl $4; under 18 free. Crib free. Pet accepted. TV; cable (premium), VCR avail. Heated pool. Playground. Complimentary coffee in rms, continental bkfst. Ck-out noon. Coin lndry. Meeting rms. Business servs avail. In-rm modem link. Valet serv. Sundries. Lawn games. Some refrigerators. Picnic tables, grills. Cr cds: A, DS, MC, V.

D 🐾 **t** ⇌ ⊠ 🐾

★★ **HOLIDAY INN.** 530 Richards Dr (66502). 785/539-5311; fax 785/539-8368; res 800/465-4329. www. holiday-inn.com. 197 rms, 3 story. S, D $76-$89; each addl $5; suites $165-$260; under 19 free; higher rates special events. Crib free. Pet accepted. TV; cable (premium). Indoor pool; wading pool, whirlpool. Sauna. Coffee in rms. Restaurant 6 am-10 pm. Bar 4 pm-midnight. Ck-out noon. Coin lndry. Meeting rms. Business servs avail. In-rm modem link. Gift shop. Local airport transportation. Health club privileges. Game rm. Balconies. Cr cds: A, D, DS, MC, V.

D 🐾 ⇌ ⊠ 🐾

★ **RAMADA PLAZA.** 1641 Anderson Ave (66502). 785/539-7531; fax 785/539-3909; toll-free 800/962-0014. www. ramada.com. 116 rms, 6 story. S, D $67-$88; each addl $6; under 18 free. Crib free. Pet accepted. TV; cable (premium), VCR avail. Heated pool. Restaurant 6:30 am-2 pm, 5-10 pm; Sun 6 am-2 pm, 5-10 pm. Bar 2-10 pm; Fri, Sat to 11 pm. Ck-out noon. Meeting rms. Business servs avail. In-rm modem link. Valet serv. Sundries. Free airport transportation. Health club privileges. Some refrigerators. Cr cds: A, D, DS, MC, V.

D 🐾 ⇌ ⊠ 🐾

★ **SUPER 8.** 200 Tuttle Creek Blvd (66502). 785/537-8468; toll-free 800/800-8000. www.super8.com. 87 rms, 3 story. No elvtr. S $49.98; D $58.98; under 12 free. Crib $2. TV; cable (premium), VCR avail. Complimentary continental bkfst. Restaurant opp open 24 hrs. Ck-out 11 am. Business servs avail. In-rm modem link. Cr cds: A, MC, V.

✈ 🐾

Restaurant

★★ **HARRY'S UPTOWN SUPPER CLUB.** 418 Poyntz (66502). 785/537-1300. Hrs: 11 am-9 pm; Fri, Sat to 10 pm; Sun to 2 pm. Closed hols. Bar to midnight. Lunch $3.95-$6.95, dinner $11.50-$23.95. Specializes in beef, chicken, fresh seafood. Cr cds: A, DS, MC, V.

D ⊣

Mankato

(B-5) See also Belleville, Beloit, Smith Center

Pop 1,037 **Elev** 1,776 ft
Area code 785 **Zip** 66956

Information Chamber of Commerce, 703 N West; 785/378-3652

What to See and Do

Lovewell State Park. A 1,100-acre park on 3,000-acre lake shaded by dense growth of cedar and burr oak. The State Historical Society's Pawnee Indian Village and Archaeological Museum is nearby, E of Lovewell Dam. Beach, bathhouse; boating (ramps, dock, marina); picnicking, playground, concession, camping (electricity, dump station). Interpretive center. Standard fees. (Daily) 20 mi NE via US 36, KS 14, unnumbered road. Phone 785/753-4971. ¢¢

Motel/Motor Lodge

★ **CREST-VUE MOTEL.** *E US 36 (66956). 785/378-3515.* 12 rms. S $30; D $38; each addl $2; under 5 free; higher rates hunting season. Crib free. Pet accepted. TV; cable. Complimentary coffee in lobby. Restaurant adj 11 am-1:30 pm, 5-9 pm. Ck-out 11 am. Picnic tables. Cr cds: A, DS, MC, V.

Marysville

(B-6) *See also Seneca*

Founded 1854 **Pop** 3,359 **Elev** 1,202 ft **Area code** 785 **Zip** 66508

Information Chamber of Commerce, 101 N 10th St, Box 16; 785/562-3101

This was the first home station out of St. Joseph, Missouri, on the Pony Express route. Many emigrant parties camped near here in the 1840s-1850s, including the ill-fated Donner Party, for which Donner Pass in California is named.

What to See and Do

Hollenberg Pony Express Station. Built in 1857; believed to be first house in Washington County. Six-rm frame structure served as a family house, neighborhood store, and tavern, as well as a station on the Pony Express. (Wed-Sat, also Sun afternoons; closed hols) N on KS 148, E on KS 243, near Hanover. Phone 785/337-2635. **FREE**

Koester House Museum. Restored Victorian home of 1872; original furnishings, costumes. (May-Oct, Tues-Sun; rest of yr, by appt; closed hols) 919 Broadway. Phone 785/562-2417. ¢¢

Pony Express Barn Museum. Original Pony Express barn (1859), home station #1; houses Native American artifacts, Pony Express memorabilia; doll collection, displays of old tools, and harness equipt. (May-Oct, daily) 106 S 8th St. Phone 785/562-3825. ¢

Motels/Motor Lodges

★★ **BEST WESTERN SURF MOTEL.** *2105 Center St (66508). 785/562-2354; res 800/528-1234. www.bestwestern.com.* 52 rms. S $30-$40; D $38-$48; each addl $4-$6. Crib free. Pet accepted, some restrictions. TV; cable (premium), VCR avail. Playground. Complimentary coffee in lobby. Restaurant nearby. Ck-out 11 am. Coin lndry. Business servs avail. Exercise equipt; sauna. Refrigerators. Cr cds: A, D, DS, MC, V.

★ **THUNDERBIRD INN.** *819 Pony Express Hwy (66508). 785/562-2373; fax 785/562-2531; toll-free 800/662-2373.* 21 rms. S $28-$34; D $37-$42; each addl $4. Crib $4. Pet accepted, some restrictions. TV; cable (premium). Continental bkfst, coffee in rms. Ck-out 11 am. In-rm modem link. Golf privileges. Refrigerators. Cr cds: A, C, D, DS, MC, V.

McPherson

(D-5) *See also Hutchinson, Lindsborg, Newton, Salina*

Pop 12,422 **Elev** 1,495 ft
Area code 620 **Zip** 67460

Information Convention & Visitors Bureau, 306 N Main, PO Box 616; 620/241-3340 or 800/324-8022

Web www.mcphersonks.org

Both the city and the county it is in bear the name of Civil War hero General James Birdseye McPherson, who was killed in the Battle of

Atlanta in 1864. Today the center of a diversified agricultural region, McPherson also has a large oil refinery and manufactures plastic pipe, RVs, pharmaceutical products, fiberglass insulation, and other products.

What to See and Do

Maxwell Wildlife Refuge. A 2,650-acre prairie provides natural environment for elk, deer, buffalo. Observation tower; 46-acre fishing lake, boat ramp; nature trail. Primitive campsites. Tram tours (Memorial Day-Oct, wkends). (Daily) 14 mi NE via US 56, Canton exit. Phone 620/628-4455. ¢¢¢

McPherson Museum. 1920s mansion houses America's first synthetic diamond, a collection of meteorites, wood carvings, bell collection, art, dolls, Asian items, Native American artifacts, pioneer relics, mounted birds and eggs, saber-tooth tiger, giant ground sloth, fossils, rocks, and minerals. (Tues-Sun afternoons; closed hols) 1130 E Euclid. Phone 620/245-2574. **Donation**

Special Events

Prairie Day Celebration. At Maxwell Wildlife Refuge. Phone 620/241-3340. June.

Scottish Festival and Highland Games. Phone 620/241-3340. Fourth wkend Sept.

Motels/Motor Lodges

★★ **BEST WESTERN HOLIDAY MANOR.** *2211 E Kansas Ave (67460). 620/241-5343; fax 620/241-8086; res 888/841-0038. www.bestwestern.com.* 110 rms, 2 story. S $52; D $58; suites $85-$100; each addl $2; under 12 free. Crib $2. Pet accepted, some restrictions. TV; cable (premium). 2 pools, 1 indoor; whirlpool. Restaurant 6 am-10 pm. Private club 5 pm-midnight. Ck-out noon. Meeting rms. Business servs avail. Valet serv. Cr cds: A, C, D, DS, MC, V.
🅳 🐾 ⇌ ⊠ 🐾

★★ **RED COACH INN.** *2111 E Kansas Ave (67460). 620/241-6960; fax 620/241-4340.* 88 rms, 1-2 story. S $38-$48; D $43-$55; each addl $5; suites $60-$85. Crib $5. Pet accepted, some restrictions. TV; cable (premium), VCR avail (movies $3). Indoor

pool; whirlpool. Sauna. Playground. Restaurant 6 am-11 pm. Ck-out noon. Meeting rms. Business servs avail. In-rm modem link. Sundries. Rec rm. Cr cds: A, D, DS, MC, V.
🅳 🐾 ⇌ ⊠ 🐾

Meade (E-2)

Pop 1,526 **Elev** 2,497 ft
Area code 316 **Zip** 67864

What to See and Do

Meade County Historical Society. History of Meade County through exhibits of furnished rooms. (Daily; closed Dec 25). 200 E Carthage. Phone 316/873-2359. **Donation**

Meade State Park. Originally carved out of the Turkey Track Ranch, this 443-acre park has varied terrain of prairie, rolling hills, bogs, and a small lake. Beach, bathhouse, fishing, boating (ramps, dock); picnicking, camping (electricity, dump station; fee). Standard fees. (Daily) 13 mi SW on KS 23. Phone 316/873-2572. ¢¢

Medicine Lodge

(E-4)

Founded 1873 **Pop** 2,453 **Elev** 1,510 ft **Area code** 316 **Zip** 67104
Information Chamber of Commerce, 209 W Fowler, PO Box 274; 316/886-3417

Long before settlers came to Kansas, Native Americans of all the Plains tribes peacefully shared the use of a "medicine lodge" on the Medicine River in a spot they regarded as sacred. In 1867, when the US Government planned a peace council to end the Indian wars, the site of the present town was chosen by the tribes for the meeting. Two weeks of negotiations with 15,000 Native Americans and 600 government commissioners present resulted in a treaty that fixed the Kansas southern boundary and opened the area to settlement. The town was officially chartered in 1879. Today the town of

Medicine Lodge is a shipping point for cattle and wheat and has a large gypsum plant. It was the home of the hatchet-wielding temperance crusader Carry Nation.

What to See and Do

Carry A. Nation Home Memorial. WCTU shrine and museum; original furnishings. (Daily) 211 W Fowler Ave, at Oak St. Phone 316/886-3553. Admission incl

Medicine Lodge Stockade. Replica of 1874 stockade. Log house with authentic 1800s furnishings; house built of gypsum; museum with pioneer relics. (Daily) 209 W Fowler. Phone 316/886-3417.

Gypsum Hills. Deep canyons in hills carved by erosion. "Gyp Hills Scenic Drive" is well marked. 4 mi W on US 160. Phone 316/886-9815.

Motel/Motor Lodge

★ **COPA.** *401 W Fowler Ave (67104). 316/886-5673; fax 316/886-5241; toll-free 800/316-2673.* 54 rms, 2 story. S $31-$37; D $35-$40; each addl $3. Crib $3. Pet accepted. TV; cable (premium). Pool. Complimentary continental bkfst. Restaurant adj 6 am-10 pm. Ck-out 11 am. Picnic tables. Lake 1 mi. Cr cds: A, D, DS, MC, V.
🐾 🏋 ⚓ 🖼 🔥

Newton

(D-5) *See also El Dorado, Hutchinson, McPherson, Wichita*

Founded 1871 **Pop** 16,700 **Elev** 1,448 ft **Area code** 316 **Zip** 67114

Information Convention & Visitors Bureau, 500 N Main, PO Box 353; 316/283-7555 or 800/899-0455

Web www.newtonkansas.com

When the Santa Fe Railroad extended its line to Newton in 1871 the town succeeded Abilene as the terminus of the Chisholm Cattle Trail and the meeting place of cowboys, gamblers, and gunmen.

Mennonites migrating from Russia settled in this area in the 1870s, bringing the Turkey Red hard winter wheat they had developed on the steppes. This revolutionized Kansas agriculture and made it one of the world's greatest wheat areas. Newton still has a large Mennonite population, with the oldest educational institution of the sect, Bethel College. Active in historic preservation, Newton has adapted such buildings as the Old Mill, 500 Main Place, and Newton Station into interesting shopping, eating, and business sites.

What to See and Do

Kansas Learning Center for Health. Exhibits on human body; transparent "talking" model. (Mon-Fri, Sun; closed hols) 10 mi W on US 50, then 2 mi S on KS 89, at 505 Main St in Halstead. Phone 316/835-2662. ¢

Kauffman Museum. A Mennonite museum devoted to the environment and people of the plains. Exhibits incl prairie animals and birds, and the cultural history of the Cheyenne and the central Kansas Mennonites. Log cabin, 1880s farmhouse, barn, and windmill. (Tues-Sun) 1 mi N via KS 15, in North Newton opp entrance to Bethel College. Phone 316/283-1612. ¢

Warkentin House. (1887) Victorian mansion with original furnishings; also carriage house and gazebo (June-Aug, Tues-Sun afternoons; Apr-May and Sept-Dec, Sat and Sun only). For tours contact the Convention and Visitors Bureau. 211 E 1st St. Phone 316/283-7555. ¢¢

Special Events

Chisholm Trail Festival. Athletic Park. Phone 316/283-7555. July 4 holiday.

Newton Fiesta. Athletic Park. Phone 316/283-7555. Second wkend Sept.

Bethel College Fall Festival. Early Oct. Phone 316/283-2500.

Motel/Motor Lodge

★ ★ **BEST WESTERN RED COACH INN.** *1301 E 1st St (67114). 316/283-9120; fax 316/283-4105; toll-free 800/777-9120. www.bestwestern.com.* 81 rms, 1-2 story. S $49; D $55; each addl $6; suites $89; under 18 free. Crib $4. Pet accepted, some restrictions. TV; cable (premium), VCR avail. Indoor pool; whirlpool. Restaurant 6 am-11 pm; closed Dec 25. Ck-out 11 am. Meeting rm. Valet serv. Free airport transportation. Exercise equipt; sauna. Game rm. Rec rm. Cr cds: A, C, D, DS, ER, JCB, MC, V.

D ⤵ ≈ 🛉 ⊠ 🔥

Restaurant

★★ **SPEARS.** *301 N Main St (67114). 316/283-3510.* Hrs: 11 am-9 pm; Fri to 10 pm; Sat 5-10 pm; Sun brunch 11 am-2 pm. Closed hols. Res accepted. Bar. Lunch $3.95-$6, dinner $4.50-$14.95. Sun brunch $9.95. Children's menu. Specializes in steak, seafood. Own baking. Located in old historic flour mill. Cr cds: A, C, D, DS, MC, V.

D

Norton

(B-3) *See also Oberlin, Phillipsburg*

Founded 1871 **Pop** 3,017 **Elev** 2,339 ft
Information Chamber of Commerce, 108 W Main, PO Box 97; 785/877-2501

What to See and Do

✪ **Gallery of Also-Rans.** Photographs and biographies of unsuccessful presidential candidates. (Mon-Fri; closed hols) First State Bank mezzanine, 105 W Main. **FREE**

Prairie Dog State Park. A 1,000-acre park on 600-acre lake. Site of a restored sod house furnished with articles of the homestead era and an original old schoolhouse (ca 1880). Wildlife observation. Beach, bathhouse, fishing, boating (ramps, dock); picnicking, camping (electricity, dump station). Standard fees. (Daily) 4 mi W via US 36 to KS 261, S 1 mi. Phone 785/877-2953. ¢¢

Station 15. "Look in" building; 1859 stagecoach depot replica; costumed figures. (Daily) US 36, Wayside Park. **FREE**

Motels/Motor Lodges

★ **THE BROOKS.** *900 N State St, US 283 and 36 (67654). 785/877-3381; fax 785/877-2188; toll-free 800/494-9244.* 35 rms, 1-2 story. S $35-$39; D $42-$48; each addl $3. TV; cable. Pool. Coffee in rms. Restaurant nearby. Ck-out 11 am. Business servs avail. In-rm modem link. Free airport transportation. Cr cds: A, DS, MC, V.

D ⤵ ⚓ ♿ ≈ 🛫 ⊠ 🔥

★★ **HILLCREST MOTEL.** *US 36 W (67654). 785/877-3343; fax 785/877-3377; res 800/444-8773.* 25 rms. S $31-$36; D $41-$46; each addl $3; higher rates special events, hols. Crib $3. TV; cable (premium). Pool. Playground. Complimentary coffee in rms. Restaurant nearby. Ck-out 11 am. Free airport transportation. City park adj. Cr cds: A, C, D, DS, MC, V.

≈ 🛫 ⊠ 🔥 SC

Oakley

(C-2) *See also Colby*

Pop 2,045 **Elev** 3,029 ft
Area code 785 **Zip** 67748

What to See and Do

Fick Fossil and History Museum. Fossils, rocks, minerals; shark tooth collection (11,000 teeth); unique fossil paintings, photographs; general store, sod house, depot replica. Changing exhibits. Tours. (Mon-Sat; May-Labor Day, also Sun afternoons; closed hols) 700 W 3rd St. Phone 785/672-4839. **Donation**

Motels/Motor Lodges

★ **1ST INTERSTATE INN.** *I-70 and US 40 (67748). 785/672-3203; fax 785/672-3330; res 800/462-4667.* 29 rms, 1-2 story. S $34-$49; D $39-$54; each addl $5; under 12 free. Pet accepted. Crib free. TV; cable (premium). Restaurant opp open 24 hrs. Ck-out 11 am. Business servs avail. Cr cds: A, C, D, DS, MC, V.

⚓ 🛫 ⊠ 🔥 SC

★★ **BEST WESTERN GOLDEN PLAINS.** *3506 US 40 (67748). 785/672-3254; fax 785/672-3200; res 800/528-1234. www.bestwestern.com.* 26 rms, 2 story. S $45-$55; D $53-$63; each addl $4; suites $65-$85; higher rates pheasant season. TV; cable. Heated pool. Complimentary continental bkfst. Ck-out 11 am. Golf

privileges. Some patios. Picnic table.
Cr cds: A, C, D, DS, MC, V.
⊠ 👬 ✕ ⤢ 👌

Restaurant

★★ **COLONIAL STEAK HOUSE.**
464 US 83 (67748). 785/672-4720.
Hrs: 6 am-11 pm. Closed Thanksgiving, Dec 25. Res accepted. Bkfst
$2.45-$4.65, lunch $3-$12.95, dinner
$4.50-$12.95. Buffet: lunch, dinner
$5.95. Children's menu. Specializes
in steak, fried chicken. Own desserts.
Salad bar. Many antiques. Cr cds: A,
DS, MC, V.
SC ⟶

Oberlin

(B-2) *See also Norton*

Founded 1873 **Pop** 2,197 **Elev** 2,562 ft
Information Convention & Visitors
Bureau, 132 S Penn; 785/475-3441

What to See and Do

Decatur County Museum. Native
American artifacts, tools, sod house,
church, school, doctor's office, 19th-
century depot, jail. (Apr-Nov, Tues-
Sat; closed hols) 258 S Penn Ave.
Phone 785/475-2712. ¢¢

Special Events

Decatur County Fair. 4-H exhibits,
parade, carnival, theater production.
Phone 785/475-3441. Early Aug.

Mini-Sapa Days. Decatur County
Museum (see). Two-day fall festival
honors those killed in Northern
Cheyenne Native American Raid of
1878. Phone 785/475-3441. First
wkend Oct.

Osawatomie

(C-8) *See also Ottawa*

Founded 1855 **Pop** 4,590 **Elev** 865 ft
Area code 913 **Zip** 66064
Information Chamber of Commerce,
526 Main St, PO Box 338; 913/755-
4114

Osawatomie is chiefly associated
with John Brown (1800-1859), most
famous of the militant abolitionists.
In the 1856 Battle of Osawatomie
five of his men were killed. He was
later executed in Charles Town, West
Virginia, and buried at his home in
North Elba, New York.

What to See and Do

Driving tour. One-hr driving tour incl
six sites on the National Register of
Historic Places. Contact Chamber of
Commerce for details.

Fishing. Marais des Cygnes Wildlife
Refuge and Pottawatomie River. City
Lake, 4 mi NW.

John Brown Memorial Park. Site of
one of the first battles of the Civil
War. Contains a life-size statue of
Brown; also a log cabin he used (now
a state museum) with period furnishings. (Wed-Sun; closed Jan 1, Thanksgiving, Dec 25) Picnic facilities.
Campsites (hookups; fee). Park (all
yr, daily). 10th and Main sts, W side
of town. Phone 913/755-4384. **FREE**

Special Event

John Brown Jamboree. Parade, carnival, and entertainment. Phone
913/755-4114. Late June.

Ottawa

(C-8) *See also Lawrence, Osawatomie*

Founded 1837 **Pop** 10,667
Area code 785 **Zip** 66067
Information Franklin County
Tourism Bureau, 109 E 2nd St, PO
Box 580; 785/242-1411

In 1832 the Ottawa were given land
in this area in exchange for their
Ohio lands. In 1837 the Reverend
Jotham Meeker established the
Ottawa Indian Baptist Mission. During the border warfare it was headquarters for Free State men,
including John Brown. Today the
town is a trading and manufacturing
center.

What to See and Do

Dietrich Cabin Museum. In Pioneer log cabin (1859); restored, period furnishings. (May-Sept, Sat and Sun afternoons; rest of yr, by appt) City Park, Main and 5th sts. Phone 785/242-4097. **FREE**

Old Depot Museum. Historical museum housing relics of area; model railroad rm; general store; period rms. 135 Tecumseh St, ½ blk S of KS 68. Phone 785/242-4097. ¢

Ottawa Indian Burial Grounds. Jotham Meeker is buried here. NE of city.

Pomona Reservoir. A 4,000-acre reservoir; eight developed public use areas, one access area. Swimming, fishing, boating; hunting (rentals). Nature trails. Picnicking. Primitive camping (free); improved camping, group camping (fee). (Daily) 20 mi W on KS 68, 268. Phone 785/453-2201. **FREE** Also on reservoir is

> **Pomona State Park.** A 490-acre park on 4,000-acre lake. Beach, bathhouse, fishing, boating (rentals, ramps, docks, marina); picnicking, shelters; cafe. Nature trail. Tent and trailer camping (hookups, dump station). Interpretive programs. Standard fees. (Daily) 15 mi W on KS 68, 5 mi W on KS 268, then N on KS 368. Phone 785/828-4933. ¢¢

Special Events

Franklin County Fair. Fairgrounds. Rodeo. Third wk July.

Yule Feast Weekend. Ottawa University. Parade, Christmas homes tours, craft fair. Res required for madrigal dinner. Phone 785/242-5200 or 800/755-5200. First wkend Dec.

Motel/Motor Lodge

★ **HALLMARK INN.** 2209 S Princeton St (66067). 785/242-7000; fax 785/242-8572; res 888/540-4024. 60 rms, 2 story. S $49-$54; D $59-$64; each addl $5; under 12 free. Crib $5. Pet accepted, some restrictions. TV; cable (premium). Pool. Complimentary continental bkfst, coffee in rms. Restaurant adj 6 am-11 pm; wkends open 24 hrs. Ck-out noon. Coin lndry. Meeting rm. Business servs avail. Cr cds: A, C, D, DS, MC, V.

D 🐾 🏊 🖎 🐾

Overland Park

(C-8) *See also Kansas City*

Pop 111,790 **Elev** 950 ft
Area code 913
Information Convention & Visitors Bureau, 10975 Benson, Suite 360, 66210; 913/491-0123 or 800/262-PARK
Web www.opcvb.org

The suburb Overland Park is located directly south of Kansas City.

What to See and Do

Old Shawnee Town. Re-creation of a typical Midwestern pioneer town of the 1800s-early 1900s. Collection of buildings and structures incl both originals and replicas; all are authentically furnished. (Tues-Sun; closed hols) N on I-35 to Johnson Dr, then W to 57th and Cody, in Shawnee. Phone 913/268-8772. ¢

Overland Park Arboretum and Botanical Gardens. Six hundred acres incl three mi of hiking trails (½-mi wheelchair accessible) through gardens; picnic facilities. Naturalized areas feature a Meadow Garden, Butterfly Garden, and Woodland Garden. Continuous development occurring. Guided tours (by appt). (Daily, weather permitting) 179th and Antioch. Phone 913/685-3604. **FREE**

Shawnee Indian Mission State History Site. Established in 1839 as mission and school; three original buildings. (Tues-Sun; closed hols) 3403 W 53rd St, at Mission Rd, 1 blk N of Shawnee Mission Pkwy in Fairway. Phone 913/262-0867. **FREE**

Motels/Motor Lodges

★★ **AMERISUITES.** 6801 W 112th St (66211). 913/451-2553; fax 913/451-3098; toll-free 800/833-1516. www.amerisuites.com. 126 suites, 6 story. May-Nov: suites $89-$129; under 18 free; wkend rates; lower rates rest of yr. Crib free. Pet accepted, some restrictions. TV; cable (premium), VCR (movies). Complimentary continental bkfst, coffee in rms. Restaurant nearby. Ck-out 11 am. Meeting rms. Business center. In-rm modem link. Sundries. Coin lndry. Exercise equipt. Health club privileges. Pool. Refrigerators, microwaves. Cr cds: A, D, DS, MC, V.

★ **CLUBHOUSE INN.** *10610 Marty St (66212). 913/648-5555; fax 913/648-7130; res 800/258-2466. www.clubhouseinn.com.* 143 rms, 3 story, 22 suites. S $75-$99; D $85-$99; each addl $10; suites $89-$109; under 16 free; wkly rates. Crib free. TV; cable (premium). Heated pool; whirlpool. Complimentary full bkfst. Restaurant nearby. Ck-out noon. Coin lndry. Meeting rms. Business servs avail. Valet serv. Exercise equipt. Microwaves avail. Refrigerator, wet bar in suites. Balconies. Grills. Cr cds: A, C, D, DS, MC, V.

★★ **COURTYARD BY MARRIOTT.** *11301 Metcalf Ave (66210). 913/339-9900; fax 913/339-6091. www.courtyard.com.* 149 rms, 3 story. S $119; D $129; each addl $10; suites $134-$154; under 16 free; wkly, wkend rates. Crib free. TV; cable (premium). Indoor pool; whirlpool. Complimentary coffee in rms. Bar 4:30-11 pm. Ck-out 1 pm. Coin lndry. Meeting rms. Business servs avail. In-rm modem link. Valet serv. Sundries. Exercise equipt. Microwaves avail. Refrigerator in suites. Balconies. Cr cds: A, C, D, DS, ER, JCB, MC, V.

★★ **DRURY INN.** *10951 Metcalf Ave (66210). 913/451-0200; res 800/378-7946. www.druryinn.com.* 155 rms, 4 story. S $75-$81; D $85-$91; each addl $10; under 18 free. Crib free. Pet accepted, some restrictions. TV; cable (premium). Pool. Complimentary continental bkfst. Restaurant nearby. Ck-out noon. Meeting rms. Business servs avail. In-rm modem link. Valet serv. Health club privileges. Microwaves avail. Cr cds: A, C, D, DS, MC, V.

★★ **FAIRFIELD INN.** *4401 W 107th St (66207). 913/381-5700; toll-free 800/228-2800. www.fairfieldinn.com.* 134 rms, 3 story. S, D $64-$73; under 18 free. Crib free. TV; cable (premium). Pool. Complimentary continental bkfst. Restaurant nearby. Ck-out noon. Business servs avail. In-rm modem link. Valet serv. Sundries.

Health club privileges. Cr cds: A, C, D, DS, MC, V.

★★ **HAMPTON INN.** *10591 Metcalf Frontage Rd (66212). 913/341-1551; fax 913/341-8668; toll-free 900/426-7866. www.hamptoninn.com.* 134 rms, 5 story. S, D $84-$99; under 18 free. Crib free. TV; cable (premium). Pool; whirlpool. Complimentary continental bkfst, coffee in rms. Restaurant nearby. Ck-out noon. Meeting rms. Business servs avail. In-rm modem link. Health club privileges. Cr cds: A, MC, V.

★★ **HOLIDAY INN EXPRESS.** *7200 W 107th Terr (66212). 913/648-7858; fax 913/648-1867; res 800/465-4329. www.holiday-inn.com.* 82 rms, 4 story. S, D $85-$95; each addl $8; suites $105; under 18 free; family rates; package plans; higher rates football games. Crib free. TV; cable (premium), VCR avail. Complimentary continental bkfst, coffee in rms. Restaurant nearby. Ck-out noon. Meeting rms. Business servs avail. In-rm modem link. Valet serv. Pool. Cr cds: A, MC, V.

★★ **HOLIDAY INN KANSAS CITY/LENEXA.** *12601 W 95th St, Lenexa (66215). 913/888-6670; fax 913/888-9528; res 800/527-0582. www.holidayinnlenexa.com.* 296 rms, 4 story. S, D $90-$100; suites $125-$175; under 12 free; family rates. Crib free. TV; cable (premium), VCR avail. Restaurant 6:30 am-2 pm, 6-10 pm. Bar 5 pm-1 am. Ck-out noon. Convention facilities. Business servs avail. In-rm modem link. Bellhops. Valet serv. Sundries. Gift shop. Coin lndry. Exercise equipt; sauna. Indoor pool; whirlpool, poolside serv. Playground. Game rm. Refrigerators avail; bathrm phone, wet bar in suites. Some balconies. Picnic tables. Cr cds: A, C, D, DS, JCB, MC, V.

★★ **LA QUINTA INN.** *9461 Lenexa Dr, Lenexa (66215). 913/492-5500; fax 913/492-2935; res 800/687-6667. www.laquinta.com.* 106 rms, 3 story. S $69; D $77; each addl $8; suites $89; under 18 free. Crib free. Pet accepted, some restrictions. TV; cable (premium). Complimentary continental bkfst, coffee in rms. Restaurant adj open 24 hrs. Ck-out noon. Business servs avail. In-rm modem link. Sundries. Pool. Microwaves avail; refrigerator, microwave in suites. Cr cds: A, D, DS, MC, V.

★★ **WHITE HAVEN MOTOR LODGE.** *8039 Metcalf Ave (66204). 913/649-8200; fax 913/901-8199; toll-free 800/752-2892. www.white-haven. com.* 100 rms, 1-2 story, 10 kit. units. S $45; D $52; suites, kit. units $82. Crib $2. Pet accepted, some restrictions. TV; cable (premium). Pool. Complimentary coffee. Restaurant nearby. Ck-out noon. Business servs avail. Refrigerators; microwaves avail. Cr cds: A, C, D, DS, MC, V.

★★ **WYNDHAM GARDEN HOTEL.** *7000 W 108th St (66211). 913/383-2550; fax 913/383-2099; res 800/996-3426. www.wyndham.com.* 180 rms, 2 story. S $85-$105; D $95-$115; each addl $10; under 12 free. Crib free. TV; cable (premium). Complimentary coffee in rms. Restaurant 6:30 am-10 pm. Rm serv from 5 pm. Bar 4 pm-midnight. Ck-out noon. Meeting rms. Business center. In-rm modem link. Bellhops. Concierge. Sundries. Coin lndry. Exercise equipt. Pool. Refrigerators, microwaves avail. Cr cds: A, C, D, DS, JCB, MC, V.

Hotels

★★ **DOUBLETREE.** *10100 College Blvd (66210). 913/451-6100; fax 913/451-3873; toll-free 800/528-0444. www.doubletree.com.* 357 rms, 18 story. S, D $142; suites $175-$450; under 18 free; wkend rates. Crib free. Pet accepted, some restrictions. TV; cable (premium). Indoor pool; whirlpool, poolside serv. Coffee in rms. Restaurants 6 am-11 pm (see also ROTIS-SERIE). Bar 4-1 am, Sun 4 pm-midnight. Ck-out noon. Convention facilities. Business center. In-rm modem link. Gift shop. Airport transportation. Exercise equipt; sauna. Some refrigerators. Cr cds: A, C, D, DS, JCB, MC, V.

★★ **HOLIDAY INN HOTEL & SUITES.** *8787 Reeder Rd (66214).* 913/888-8440; fax 913/888-3438; res 800/465-4329. www.holiday-inn.com. 192 rms, 8 story. S, D $79; suites $109-$149; under 18 free. Crib free. TV; cable (premium). Heated indoor/outdoor pool; whirlpool. Complimentary coffee in rms. Restaurant 6 am-1 pm, 5-9 pm. Bar; entertainment. Ck-out noon. Meeting rms. In-rm modem link. Valet serv. Exercise equipt; sauna. Airport transportation. Cr cds: A, C, D, DS, ER, JCB, MC, V.

★★★ **MARRIOTT OVERLAND PARK.** *10800 Metcalf Ave (66210). 913/451-8000; fax 913/451-5914; res 800/468-3571. www.marriott.com.* 397 rms, 11 story. S, D $109-$139; suites $225-$400; under 18 free; wkly, wkend rates. Crib free. TV; cable (premium), VCR avail. Indoor/outdoor pool; whirlpool, poolside serv. Complimentary coffee. Restaurant (see NIKKO). Bar 3 pm-1 am. Ck-out noon. Meeting rms. Business servs avail. In-rm modem link. Concierge. Gift shop. Guest lndry. Airport transportation. Exercise equipt. Game rm. Luxury level. Cr cds: A, D, DS, MC, V.

All Suites

★★ **CHASE SUITE HOTEL.** *6300 W 110th S (66211). 913/491-3333; fax 913/491-1377; toll-free 800/433-9765. www.woodfinsuitehotels.com.* 112 suites, 2 story. S, D $99-$135; under 12 free; wkly, monthly rates. Crib free. Pet accepted, some restrictions. TV; cable (premium). Pool; whirlpool. Complimentary continental bkfst. Ck-out noon. Coin lndry. Meeting rm. Business servs avail. In-rm modem link. Valet serv. Exercise equipt. Sports court. Microwaves; some fireplaces. Private patios, balconies. Picnic tables, grills. Cr cds: A, C, D, DS, ER, JCB, MC, V.

★★ **EMBASSY SUITES.** *10601 Metcalf Ave (66212). 913/649-7060; fax 913/649-9382; res 800/362-2779. www.embassy-suites.com.* 199 suites, 7 story. Aug: suites $139-$169; under 12 free; lower rates rest of yr. Crib free. TV; cable (premium). Indoor pool; whirlpool. Complimentary full bkfst, coffee in rms. Restaurant 6:30 am-11 pm. Rm serv from 11 am. Bar

3 pm-midnight. Ck-out noon. Meeting rms. Business servs avail. In-rm modem link. Gift shop. Exercise equipt; sauna. Health club privileges. Game rm. Refrigerators; microwaves avail. Cr cds: A, C, D, DS, JCB, MC, V.

🅳 ⛵ 🏋 ⬇ 🔥

Restaurants

★★ CAFE ITALIA. *6522 Martway, Mission (66202). 913/262-7564.* Hrs: 11 am-2 pm, 5-9 pm; Fri, Sat to 10 pm. Closed Sun; hols. Res accepted. Italian menu. Bar. Lunch $6.75-$12, dinner $8-$25. Specializes in veal, lamb, seafood, pasta. Parking. Italian decor.

🅳 ➖

★★ COYOTE GRILL. *4843 Johnson Dr, Mission (66205). 913/362-3333. www.coyotegrill.com.* Hrs: 11 am-10 pm; wkends to 11 pm; Sun brunch to 3 pm. Southwestern menu. Bar. Lunch $5.99-$12.99, dinner $5.99-$20. Sun brunch $4.50-$10.99. Southwestern art. Cr cds: A, D, DS, MC, V.

🅳 ➖

★ DON CHILITO'S. *7017 Johnson Dr, Mission (66202). 913/432-4615. www.donchilitos.com.* Hrs: 11 am-9 pm; Fri, Sat to 10 pm; Sun from noon. Closed Thanksgiving, Dec 25. Mexican menu. Beer. Lunch, dinner $3-$9.99. Specializes in burritos. Parking. Family-owned. Cr cds: DS, MC, V.

🅳 ➖

★★ EL CARIBE. *12112 W 87th St, Lenexa (66215). 913/599-2270.* Hrs: 11 am-2 pm, 5-9:30 pm; Fri to 10:30 pm; Sat noon-midnight. Closed Mon, Sun; also hols. Res accepted. Caribbean menu. Bar. Lunch $5.95-$6.95, dinner $9.95-$19.95. Children's menu. Specialties: conch fritters, Spanish paella, jerk chicken. Entertainment Sat. Parking. Caribbean atmosphere and decor. Cr cds: A, D, DS, ER, MC, V.

🅳 ➖

★★★ HEREFORD HOUSE. *5001 Town Center Dr, Leawood (66211). 913/327-0800. www.herefordhouse. com.* Hrs: 11 am-10 pm; Fri to 11 pm; Sat 4-11 pm; Sun 4-9 pm. Closed

Thanksgiving, Dec 25. Res accepted. Bar. Wine list. Lunch $5.95-$12.50, dinner $14.95-$29.95. Children's menu. Specialties: whiskey steak, baseball-cut sirloin, prime rib. Own desserts. Outdoor dining. Western decor; artwork, branding irons, tack, cowboy hats; stone fireplace. Cr cds: A, C, D, DS, ER, MC, V.

🅳 ➖

★★ HOUSTON'S. *7111 W 95th St (66212). 913/642-0630.* Hrs: 11 am-11 pm; Fri, Sat to midnight. Closed Thanksgiving, Dec 25. Bar. Lunch, dinner $6-$22. Children's menu. Specializes in steak, fresh fish. Parking. Casual elegance. Cr cds: A, C, D, MC, V.

🅳 ➖

★★ IL TRULLO. *9056 Metcalf Ave (66212). 913/341-3773.* Hrs: 11 am-2 pm, 5-9 pm; Fri to 10 pm; Sat 5-10 pm; Sun from 5 pm. Closed hols. Res accepted. Italian menu. Bar. Lunch $4.95-$7.95, dinner $5.95-$17.95. Specialties: zuppa di mare, orecchiette con cime di rapa. Parking. Cr cds: A, D, DS, MC, V.

🅳 ➖

★★ INDIA PALACE. *9918 W 87th St (66212). 913/381-1680.* Hrs: 11:30 am-2:15 pm, 5-10 pm. Closed Thanksgiving, Dec 25. Res accepted. Indian menu. Lunch, dinner $5.95-$12.95. Lunch buffet $5.95; wkends $6.95. Specializes in Indian-style barbecue. Parking. Indian atmosphere. Elegant dining. Totally nonsmoking. Cr cds: A, C, D, DS, MC, V.

★★ JACK STACK BARBECUE. *9520 Metcalf Ave (66212). 913/385-7427. www.jackstackbbq.com.* Hrs: 11 am-10 pm; Fri, Sat to 11 pm. Closed Thanksgiving, Dec 25. Barbecue menu. Lunch $5.75-$13.95, dinner $6.25-$22.95. Children's menu. Specialties: crown prime short ribs, rack of lamb, salmon. Parking. Casual dining. Cr cds: A, D, DS, MC, V.

🅳 ➖

★★ J GILBERT'S WOOD FIRED STEAKS. *8901 Metcalf Ave (66212). 913/642-8070.* Hrs: 5-10 pm; Fri, Sat to 10:30 pm; Sun to 9:30 pm. Closed hols. Res accepted. Bar from 4:30 pm; Fri, Sat 4-11:30 pm. Dinner $12.95-$25.95. Children's menu. Specialties: Louisiana skillet-seared pep-

per fillet, grilled barbecue salmon. Cr cds: A, D, DS, MC, V.
D ⌐

★★ **JOHNNY CASCONE'S.** *6863 W 91st St (66212).* 913/381-6837. Hrs: 11 am-10 pm; Sun 4-9 pm. Closed hols. Res accepted Mon-Thurs, Sun. American menu. Bar. Lunch $6-$8, dinner $9-$17.95. Children's menu. Specializes in lasagne, seafood, steak. Parking. Cr cds: A, D, DS, MC, V.
D ⌐

★ **JUN'S JAPANESE RESTAURANT.** *7660 State Line Rd, Prairie Village (66208).* 913/341-4924. Hrs: 11:30 am-2 pm, 5-10 pm. Closed Sun; hols. Res accepted. Japanese menu. Bar. Lunch $4.95-$9.95, dinner $9.95-$19.50. Specializes in sushi, teriyaki tempura. Parking. Japanese atmosphere. Cr cds: D.
D

★★ **K.C. MASTERPIECE.** *10985 Metcalf (66210).* 913/345-1199. *www.kcmrestaurants.com.* Hrs: 11 am-10 pm; Fri, Sat to 11 pm; Sun to 9:30 pm. Closed Thanksgiving, Dec 25. Bar. Lunch $6.59-$16.49, dinner $6.59-$17.99. Children's menu. Specialties: baby-back ribs, filet of pork, turkey. Parking. Authentic 1930s decor; ornamental tile floor. Display of barbecue memorabilia. Cr cds: A, C, D, DS, MC, V.
D ⌐

★★ **LEONA YARBROUGH'S.** *10310 W 63rd St, Fairway (66203).* 913/248-0500. Hrs: 11 am-8 pm; Sun to 7 pm. Closed Mon; also Dec 25. Lunch $3.25-$10.25, dinner $7.95-$11.25. Children's menu. Specialties: fried chicken, liver and onions, roast pork. Parking. Full bakery on premises. Family-owned. Cr cds: MC, V.
D ⌐

★★★ **NIKKO.** *10800 Metcalf Rd (66210).* 913/451-8000. Hrs: 5-10 pm; Fri, Sat to 11 pm. Closed hols. Res accepted. Japanese menu. Bar. Dinner $11.95-$24.95. Children's menu. Specialties: swordfish, filet mignon. Parking. Japanese decor; teppanyaki table service. Cr cds: A, C, D, DS, MC, V.
D SC ⌐

★★ **RAOUL'S VELVET ROOM.** *7222 W 119th St (66213).* 913/469-0466. *www.raoulsvelvetroom.com.* Hrs: 5-

10:30 pm. Closed Mon, Tues, Sun; also hols. Res accepted. Contemporary American menu. Bar 4:30 pm-1 am. A la carte entrees: dinner $14-$22. Specialties: cured grilled pork chop, grilled stuffed quail, pan-seared halibut. Parking. Cr cds: A, D, DS, MC, V.
D ⌐

★★★ **ROTISSERIE.** *10100 College Blvd (66210).* 913/451-6100. Hrs: 6:30 am-10 pm; wkends from 7 am; Sun brunch 10 am-2 pm. Res accepted. Bar 4 pm-1 am. Wine list. Bkfst $3.95-$8.95, lunch $5.50-$10, dinner $14.95-$21.95. Buffet: bkfst $8.95, lunch $7.95. Sun brunch $16.95. Children's menu. Specializes in prime rib, steak, seafood. Parking. Skylight, waterfall and many plants give the 3 dining areas a relaxing atmosphere. Cr cds: A, C, D, DS, MC, V.
D SC ⌐

★ **SUSHI GIN.** *9559 Nall Ave (66207).* 913/649-8488. Hrs: 11:30 am-2 pm, 5:30-9:30 pm; Fri to 10 pm; Sat 5-10 pm. Closed Sun; hols. Res accepted. Japanese menu. Serv bar. Lunch $5.45-$12.95, dinner $9.95-$20.95. Children's menu. Specializes in boat combinations, chicken or beef sukiyaki, tempura. Japanese tapestries. Cr cds: D, DS, MC, V.
D ⌐

★★★ **TATSU'S.** *4603 W 90th St, Prairie Village (66207).* 913/383-9801. Hrs: 11:30 am-2 pm, 5:30-9:30 pm; Fri to 10 pm; Sat 5:30-10 pm. Closed Sun; hols. Res accepted. French menu. Bar. Lunch $6.95-$15.95, dinner $16.95-$24.95. Specialties: Saumon poche au champagne, boeuf a la bourguignonne. Small, elegant dining area. Cr cds: A, D, DS, MC, V.
D ⌐

★★ **THE WOKS.** *8615 Hauser Dr, Lenexa (66215).* 913/541-1777. Hrs: 11 am-9:30 pm; Fri, Sat to 10:30 pm; Sun buffet to 2:30 pm. Closed hols. Res accepted. Chinese menu. Bar. Lunch $4.75-$5.50, dinner $7.25-$10.95. Sun buffet $6.95. Children's menu. Specializes in beef, chicken. Chinese decor. Cr cds: A, C, DS, MC, V.
D ⌐

★★ **YAHOOZ.** *4701 Town Center Dr, Leawood (66211). 913/451-8888. www. yahooz.com.* Hrs: 11 am-10 pm; Fri, Sat to midnight; Sun from 10:30 am. Closed July 4, Dec 25. Res accepted. Bar. Lunch $6.95-$12.95, dinner $14.95-$25.95. Children's menu. Specializes in steaks, daily specials. Parking. Outdoor dining. Rustic western interior; wall murals, fireplaces. Cowboy atmosphere and cuisine. Cr cds: A, C, D, DS, ER, MC, V.

D ⬅

★★ **YIAYIAS EUROBISTRO.** *4701 W 119th St (66209). 913/345-1111.* Hrs: 11 am-10 pm; Fri, Sat to midnight; Sun 10:30 am-10 pm, Sun brunch to 2:30 pm. Closed Thanksgiving, Dec 25. Res accepted. Bar to 11 pm; Fri, Sat to 1 am. Lunch $5.95-$10.95, dinner $7.95-$24.95. Sun brunch $5.95-$12.95. Specializes in steak, fresh seafood, pasta. Parking. Outdoor dining. European bistro decor. Cr cds: A, C, D, DS, ER, MC, V.

D ⬅

Unrated Dining Spots

DICK CLARK'S AMERICAN BANDSTAND GRILL. *10975 Metcalf Ave (66210). 913/451-1600. www.kcdick clarksgrille.com.* Hrs: 11 am-11 pm; Fri, Sat, Sun to midnight. Closed Thanksgiving, Dec 25. Bar to 2 am. Lunch $4-$7, dinner $6-$15. Children's menu. Specialties: voodoo chicken, Memphis meatloaf, Philadelphia cheese steak. Band wkends. Parking. Pictures and memorabilia on walls depicting eras of rock and roll. Cr cds: A, C, D, DS, ER, MC, V.

D ⬅

GATES BAR-B-QUE. *2001 W 103 Rd, Leawood (66211). 913/383-1752.* Hrs: 10 am-11 pm; Fri, Sat to midnight. Closed Thanksgiving, Dec 25. Beer. A la carte entrees: lunch, dinner $4.50-$14. Specializes in barbecue ribs, beef. Parking. Cr cds: A, DS, V.

Parsons

(E-8) *See also Chanute, Coffeyville, Independence, Pittsburg*

Founded 1871 **Pop** 11,924 **Elev** 907 ft **Area code** 316 **Zip** 67357

Information Chamber of Commerce, 1715 Corning, PO Box 737; 316/421-6500 or 800/280-6401

Parsons's economy is based on industry and agriculture. The Union Pacific Railroad is here as well as assorted industries. Dairying, beef cattle, and cereal grains are important.

What to See and Do

Fishing, picnicking, boating. Neosho County State Fishing Lake. Campgrounds. 5 mi N on US 59, then 3 mi E on unnumbered road. Lake Parsons. Beach, bathhouses; camping, electrical hookups (fee). 4 mi N on US 59, then 3½ mi W. Marvel Park. Camping, electrical hookups. E Main St. (Daily) Phone 316/421-7077. **FREE**

Pearson-Skubitz Big Hill Lake. Swimming, fishing, boating (ramps); hiking, picnic area, camping (fee). (Mar-Oct, daily) 9 mi W on US 160, then 5 mi S on unnumbered road, then 3 mi W on unnumbered road. Phone 316/336-2741. **FREE**

Oakwood Cemetery. Contains Civil War graves and monuments. S Leawood.

Parsons Historical Museum. Display of items dating from 1871; memorabilia related to Missouri-Kansas-Texas Railroad. (May-Oct, Fri-Sun or by appt) 401 S 18th St. **FREE**

Motels/Motor Lodges

★ **CANTERBURY INN.** *400 Main St (67357). 316/421-5000; fax 316/421-9123; toll-free 800/835-0369.* 81 rms, 2 story. S $30.45-$33.20; D $36.90-$47.98; each addl $5; suites $52-$63. Crib free. TV; cable (premium). Pool.

Restaurant 6:30 am-9 pm; Sun to 2 pm. Private club 5-11 pm. Ck-out 11 am. Coin lndry. Meeting rms. Business servs avail. In-rm modem link. Bathrm phones. Cr cds: A, D, DS, MC, V.

≈ 🖳 🔥

★ **TOWNSMAN MOTEL.** *US 59 S (67357). 316/421-6990; fax 316/421-4767.* 38 rms. S $28-$30; D $35-$37; each addl $2; under 4 free. Crib free. Pet accepted, some restrictions. TV; cable (premium). Pool. Restaurant 6 am-9 pm. Ck-out 11 am. Business servs avail. Refrigerators avail. Cr cds: A, DS, MC, V.

🐾 🛉 ≈ 🖳 🔥 🖾

Hotel

★ **PARSONIAN HOTEL.** *1725 Broadway (67357). 316/421-4400.* 55 rms, 8 story. S $34; D $38; each addl $3. Crib free. TV; cable (premium), VCR avail. Restaurant 6 am-7:30 pm. Private club 4-11 pm. Ck-out 11 am. Meeting rms. No bellhops. Cr cds: A, D, MC, V.

D 🐾

Phillipsburg

(B-3) *See also Norton, Smith Center, Stockton*

Pop 2,828 **Elev** 1,951 ft
Area code 785 **Zip** 67661
Information Phillipsburg Area Chamber of Commerce, 270 State St; 785/543-2321 or 800/543-2321

What to See and Do

Kirwin National Wildlife Refuge. An overlay project on a flood control reservoir. Auto tour route, nature trail, bird watching, fishing, hunting. (Daily) 5 mi S on US 183, then 6 mi E on KS 9 near Kirwin. Phone 785/543-6673. **FREE**

Old Fort Bissell. Replicas of fort and sod house; authentic log cabin; one-rm schoolhouse (ca 1870); depot; store; old gun collection. (Mid-Apr-Sept, Tues-Sun). City Park, W edge of town, on US 36. Phone 785/543-6212. **Donation**

Special Events

Phillips County Fair. Phillips County Fairgrounds. Phone 785/543-6845. Late July.

Rodeo. One of the largest in the state. Phone 785/543-2321. Early Aug.

Motel/Motor Lodge

★ **MARK V MOTEL.** *320 W State St (67661). 785/543-5223; fax 785/543-2323; toll-free 800/219-3149.* 33 rms, 2 story. S $29; D $37. Crib free. TV; cable (premium). Outdoor pool. Complimentary coffee in lobby. Restaurant nearby. Ck-out 10 am. In-rm modem link. Park adj. Cr cds: A, DS, MC, V.

≈ 🖳 🔥 SC

Pittsburg

(E-8) *See also Fort Scott, Parsons*

Founded 1876 **Pop** 17,775 **Elev** 944 ft
Area code 620 **Zip** 66762
Information Convention & Visitors Bureau, 117 W 4th, PO Box 1115; 316/231-1212 or 800/879-1112
Web www.chamber.pitton.com

Rich in natural resources, this coal center of Kansas began as a mining camp and was named for Pittsburgh, Pennsylvania. Surviving depressions and strikes, today it is a prosperous consumer, industrial, and educational center.

What to See and Do

Crawford County Historical Museum. Artifacts related to coal industry of area; also old schoolhouse and store. (Wed-Sun afternoons; closed hols) N of 20th St on US 69 Bypass . Phone 316/231-1440. **FREE**

Crawford State Park. In the heart of the strip coal mining area, here is a tiny piece of the Ozarks with redbuds and flowering trees in the spring and brilliant autumn colors in the fall. Located on small lake. Beach, bathhouse, fishing, boating (rentals, ramps, dock, marina); picnicking, concession. Camping (electricity, dump station). Standard fees. (Daily) 7 mi N on US 69, then 7 mi W on KS

57, then 9 mi N on KS 7. Phone 316/362-3671. ¢¢

Lincoln Park. Pittsburg Family Aquatic Center (Late May-Aug, daily); wading pool, picnic and campgrounds, tennis courts, batting cage, playground, kiddie rides. Park (Mid-Apr-mid-Oct). Eighteen-hole golf, driving range, miniature golf (all yr). Fee for activities. (Daily) Memorial Dr and US 69 Bypass. Phone 316/231-8310.

Motel/Motor Lodge

★★ **HOLIDAY INN EXPRESS.** *4020 Parkview Dr (66762). 620/231-8700; fax 620/230-0154; res 800/465-4329. www.holiday-inn.com.* 100 rms, 2 story. S, D $51-$90; each addl $6; under 20 free; higher rates special events. TV; cable (premium), VCR avail. Pool; whirlpool. Complimentary bkfst buffet. Ck-out noon. Coin lndry. Meeting rms. Business servs avail. In-rm modem link. Valet serv. Exercise equipt. Picnic tables. Game rm. Cr cds: A, C, D, DS, JCB, MC, V.

⧈ ⚓ ⌇ ✦ ✈ ⊠ ♨ ⟨SC⟩

Pratt

(E-4) See also Greensburg, Medicine Lodge

Founded 1884 **Pop** 6,687 **Elev** 1,891 ft **Area code** 620 **Zip** 67124

Information Chamber of Commerce, 114 N Main, PO Box 469; 316/672-5501

Web www.pratt.net

What to See and Do

Kansas State Fish Hatchery/Nature Center. Covers 187 acres and has more than 90 brood ponds, a nature center, aquarium; picnicking. One of the first channel catfish hatcheries. (Spring, daily; rest of yr, Mon-Fri) Operations headquarters of the Department of Wildlife and Parks are located on the grounds. 2 mi E on US 54, then 1 mi S on KS 64. Phone 316/672-5911. **FREE**

Pratt County Historical Society Museum. Pioneer Room settings incl complete dentist's office, 1890

kitchen, blacksmith shop, gun collection and artifacts, old-time Main St. (Tues-Sun afternoons; also by appt) 208 S Ninnescah. Phone 316/672-7874. **FREE**

Special Events

Miss Kansas Pageant. Pratt Community College. Phone 316/672-5501. First full wkend June.

Pratt County Fair. Fairgrounds, S of town. Phone 316/672-6121. Late July.

Motel/Motor Lodge

★★ **BEST WESTERN.** *1336 E 1st (67124). 620/672-6407; fax 620/672-6707; toll-free 800/336-2279. www. bestwestern.com.* 42 rms. S $32-$38; D $38-$43; each addl $4; under 12 free. Crib $4. Pet accepted. TV; cable (premium), VCR avail. Pool. Complimentary continental bkfst. Restaurant nearby. Ck-out noon. Meeting rm. Business servs avail. In-rm modem link. Refrigerators. Cr cds: A, D, DS, MC, V.

⧈ ⥁ ⚓ ⌇ ⊠ ♨

Russell

(C-4) See also Hays

Pop 4,781 **Elev** 1,826 ft **Area code** 785 **Zip** 67665

Information Russell County Convention & Visitors Bureau, 610 Main; 785/483-6960 or 800/658-4686

Web www.russellks.org

Russell is located in the heart of an oil district.

What to See and Do

Deines Cultural Center. Houses permanent and traveling art exhibits; collection of wood engravings by E. Hubert Deines. (Tues-Sun afternoons) 820 N Main St. Phone 785/483-3742. **FREE**

Fossil Station Museum. History of Russell County. Also houses furniture and artifacts of settlers in building made of hand-hewn post rock. (May-Sept, Tues-Sun; winter, by appt) 331

Kansas St. Phone 785/483-3637. **FREE**

Oil Patch Museum. History of the oil industry in Russell County. Outdoor displays of oil equipt are also incl. (May-Labor Day, daily) Guided tours. Jct I-70 and US 281. Phone 785/483-6640. **FREE**

Wilson Dam and Reservoir. Swimming, fishing, boating; camping (fee) (Daily). 21 mi E on I-70 to Wilson, then 8 mi N on KS 232. On southern shore is

> **Wilson State Park.** A 927-acre park on 9,000-acre lake. An area of unique beauty with deep canyons and steep hills devoid of trees and brush. Rugged chimney rocks and arches rim the lake on Hell Creek Canyon. Home to thousands of migratory water fowl. Beach, bathhouse, fishing, boating (rentals, ramps, dock, marina); hiking trails, picnicking, concession. Camping (electricity, dump station). Standard fees. (Daily) 21 mi E on I-70, then 5 mi N on KS 232. Phone 785/658-2465. ¢¢

Salina

(C-5) *See also Abilene, Lindsborg, McPherson*

Founded 1858 **Pop** 42,303 **Elev** 1,220 ft **Area code** 785 **Zip** 67401
Information Chamber of Commerce, 120 W Ash, PO Box 586; 785/827-9301
Web www.salinakansas.org

The Salina site was chosen by a New York newspaper correspondent who established a store to trade with Native American hunting parties. Business improved in 1860 when gold hunters stocked up on their way to Pikes Peak. The arrival of the Union Pacific Railroad in 1867 brought new growth and the wheat crops in the 1870s established a permanent economy. Alfalfa, now one of the state's major crops, was first introduced in Kansas by a Salina resident in 1874. The city was rebuilt in 1903 after the Smoky Hill flood destroyed most of the community. Today it is a leading agricultural, regional trade, and medical center.

Manufacturing also contributes to its economic base.

What to See and Do

Bicentennial Center. Concerts; trade shows and expositions; athletic events; special events. 800 The Midway. Phone 785/826-7200.

Central Kansas Flywheels Historical Museum. Museum features antique farm machinery and other artifacts from central Kansas. Craft show (Apr or May). (Apr-Sept, Tues-Sun; closed hols) 1100 W Diamond Rd. Phone 785/825-8473. ¢

Salina Art Center. Features art exhibits; also hands-on art laboratory for children. (Tues-Sun afternoons; closed hols) 242 S Santa Fe. Phone 785/827-1431. **FREE**

Smoky Hill Museum. Area history represented by photos and artifacts; changing exhibits; general store period rm. (Tues-Sun; closed hols) 211 W Iron Ave. Phone 785/826-7460. **FREE**

Special Events

Smoky Hill River Festival. Phone 785/826-7410. Mid-June.

Steam Engine and Antique Farm Engine Show. At Central Kansas Flywheels Historical Museum. Antique tractor pull. Wheat threshing, log sawing, and other early farming skills. Phone 785/825-8473. Mid-Aug.

Tri-Rivers Fair and Rodeo. Phone 785/826-6532. Mid-Aug.

Motels/Motor Lodges

★★ **BEST WESTERN MID-AMERICA INN.** *1846 N 9th St (67401). 785/827-0356; fax 785/827-7688; res 800/528-1234. www.bestwestern.com.* 108 rms, 2 story. Mid-May-mid-Oct: S $45-$47; D $52-$60; each addl $3; suites $70-$75; under 18 free; lower rates rest of yr. Crib $1. Pet accepted, some restrictions. TV; cable (premium), VCR avail. Indoor/outdoor pool; whirlpool, poolside serv. Sauna. Restaurant 6 am-10 pm. Bar 5 pm-1 am. Ck-out noon. Meeting rms. Business servs avail. In-rm modem link. Sundries. Cr cds: A, C, D, DS, ER, JCB, MC, V.

D ⊁ ⊠ ⊠ ☀ SC

★ **COMFORT INN.** *1820 W Crawford St (67401). 785/826-1711; fax 785/827-6530; res 800/228-5150. www.comfortinn.com.* 60 rms. S $50-$57; D $52-$73; each addl $7; under 18 free. Crib free. Pet accepted, some restrictions. TV; cable (premium), VCR avail. Indoor pool; whirlpool. Complimentary continental bkfst. Restaurant nearby. Ck-out 11 am. Business servs avail. In-rm modem link. Some refrigerators. Cr cds: A, D, DS, MC, V.

★★ **HOLIDAY INN.** *1616 W Crawford St (67401). 785/823-1739; fax 785/823-1791; res 800/465-4329. www.holiday-inn.com.* 192 rms, 3 story. S, D $50-$65; suites $75-$115; under 12 free. Crib free. TV; cable (premium). Indoor/outdoor pool; whirlpool, poolside serv. Playground. Restaurant 6 am-10 pm; Sun to 9 pm. Bar 4 pm-midnight. Ck-out noon. Coin lndry. Meeting rms. Business servs avail. In-rm modem link. Bellhops. Valet serv. Sundries. Airport, bus depot transportation. Miniature golf. Exercise equipt; sauna. Game rm. Cr cds: A, D, DS, MC, V.

★ **RAMADA INN.** *1949 N 9th St (67401). 785/825-8211; fax 785/823-1048. www.ramada.com.* 103 rms, 2 story. May-Nov: S $50; D $58; each addl $6; under 18 free. Crib free. Pet accepted; $10 deposit. TV; cable (premium). Heated pool. Restaurant 7 am-9 pm. Bar 5 pm-midnight. Ck-out noon. Meeting rms. Business servs avail. Cr cds: A, C, D, DS, MC, V.

★★ **SALINA RED COACH INN.** *2110 W Crawford (67401). 785/825-2111; fax 785/825-6973; toll-free 800/332-0047.* 112 rms, 2 story. S $32-$56; D $56-$61; each addl $5; suites $89-$125; under 12 free. Crib $3. Pet accepted, some restrictions. TV; cable (premium), VCR (movies). Indoor pool; whirlpool, sauna. Playground. Complimentary continental bkfst. Restaurant 6 am-9 pm; wkends to 11 pm. Ck-out noon. Meeting rms. Business servs avail. In-rm modem link. Sundries. Coin lndry. Lighted tennis. Miniature golf. Game

rm. Refrigerator in suites. Cr cds: A, C, D, DS, MC, V.

★ **VAGABOND INN.** *217 S Broadway Blvd (67401). 785/825-7265; fax 785/825-7003; res 888/203-1413.* 45 rms, 2 story. S $32-$40; D $34-$45; each addl $4; kit. $4/day addl. Crib $1. Pet accepted. TV; cable (premium). Pool. Complimentary coffee in rms. Restaurant adj 6 am-10 pm; Sun to 2 pm. Ck-out 11 am. Business servs avail. Cr cds: A, DS, MC, V.

Restaurant

★ **GUTIERREZ.** *1935 S Ohio (67401). 785/825-1649.* Hrs: 11 am-10 pm. Closed Easter, Dec 25. Res accepted. Mexican, American menu. Lunch $5-$7, dinner $8-$12. Children's menu. Specializes in chimichangas. Cr cds: A, DS, MC, V.

Scott City (D-2)

Pop 3,785 **Elev** 2,978 ft
Area code 316 **Zip** 67871

What to See and Do

Lake Scott State Park. A memorial marker notes the 17th-century pueblo ruins of El Cuartelejo; the old Steele home is open for viewing. Spring-fed lake is bordered by willow, cedar, elm, pine, and cottonwood trees. Beach, bathhouse, boats (rentals, ramp, dock); picnicking, concession, camping (electricity, dump station). Standard fees. (Daily) 10 mi N on US 83, N on KS 95. Phone 316/872-2061. ¢¢

Seneca

(B-7) *See also Hiawatha, Marysville*

Pop 2,027 **Elev** 1,131 ft
Area code 785 **Zip** 66538
Information Chamber of Commerce, PO Box 135; 785/336-2294

What to See and Do

Fort Markley and Indian Village. Old Western town with Victorian home (fee), museum, gift shop, antique shop; boating, fishing; tent and trailer sites (fee); restaurant. (Daily) ½ mi W on US 36. Phone 785/336-2285. ¢

Nemaha County Historical Museum. Old county jail with a resident sheriff; memorabilia from a local farmer; variety of items used over a century ago. (May-Sept, Mon-Fri, also Sun afternoons; hols and rest of yr by appt). 6th and Nemaha sts. Phone 785/336-6366.

Motels/Motor Lodges

★ **SENECA MOTEL.** *1106 North St (66538). 785/336-6127.* 12 rms. S $24; D $30; each addl $2. Crib avail. Pet accepted, some restrictions. TV; cable. Complimentary coffee in lobby. Restaurant nearby. Ck-out 11 am. Many refrigerators. Cr cds: A, D, DS, MC, V.
🐾 🖼 🎿

★ **STAR LITE MOTEL.** *US 36 (66538). 785/336-2191.* 16 rms. S $27; D $30-$34; each addl $3; under 12 free. Crib $3. Pet accepted, some restrictions. TV; cable (premium). Complimentary coffee in lobby. Restaurant opp 11 am-9 pm. Ck-out 11 am. Cr cds: A, C, D, DS, MC, V.
🐾 🖼 🎿

Smith Center

(B-4) *See also Mankato, Phillipsburg*

Pop 2,016 **Elev** 1,804 ft
Information Smith Center Area Chamber of Commerce, 219 S Main; 785/282-3895

What to See and Do

Home on the Range Cabin. Restored cabin where homesteader Dr. Brewster M. Higley wrote the words to the song "Home on the Range" in 1872. (Daily) 8 mi W on US 36, then 8 mi N on KS 8, then ¾ mi W. Phone 785/282-6258. **FREE**

Old Dutch Mill. In Wagner Park. (May-Sept, daily) Phone 785/456-7344. **FREE**

Motels/Motor Lodges

★ **MODERN AIRE MOTEL.** *117 W US 36 (66967). 785/282-6644; fax 758/282-6817; toll-free 800/727-7332.* 16 rms. S $26-$36; D $38-$46; each addl $4; higher rates pheasant hunting season. Crib $4. Pet accepted, some restrictions. TV; cable (premium). Pool. Complimentary coffee in lobby. Restaurant nearby. Ck-out 11 am. Airport transportation. Cr cds: A, DS, MC, V.
🐾 🖼 🎿 🎿

★ **US CENTER MOTEL.** *116 E US 36 (66967). 785/282-6611; toll-free 800/875-6613.* 21 rms. S $34; D $46; each addl $4; family units. Crib $2. TV; cable (premium). Indoor pool. Playground. Restaurant adj 6 am-9 pm. Ck-out 11 am. Free airport transportation. Picnic tables. Cr cds: A, DS, MC, V.
🖼 ✈ 🎿 🎿

Stockton

(B-3) *See also Phillipsburg*

Pop 1,507 **Elev** 1,792 ft
Area code 785 **Zip** 67669

Information City of Stockton, 115 S Walnut, PO Box 512; 785/425-6162

What to See and Do

Log Hotel. Replica of first log hotel. Main St.

Rooks County Museum. Houses artifacts related to Rooks County history; records, old newspapers, photographs, family heirlooms; horse-drawn buggy; displays incl old-time general store, schoolrm, and doctor's office. (Mon-Wed; other times by appt) 921 S Cedar. Phone 785/425-7217. **FREE**

Webster State Park. An 880-acre park located on Webster Reservoir on South Fork of Solomon River, with 1,400 acres of water. Walleye, catfish, bass, crappie, and bullheads. Beach, bathhouse, fishing, boating (ramps, dock); trails, picnicking, camping (electricity, dump station). Standard fees. (Daily) 9 mi W on US 24. Phone 785/425-6775. ¢¢

Topeka

(C-7) *See also Lawrence; also see Kansas City, MO*

Founded 1854 **Pop** 119,883 **Elev** 951 ft **Area code** 785

Information Convention & Visitors Bureau, 1275 SW Topeka Blvd, 66612; 785/234-1030 or 800/235-1030

Web www.topekacvb.com

The capital city of Kansas was born because a young Pennsylvanian, Colonel Cyrus K. Holliday, wanted to build a railroad. The present Topeka site on the Kansas River (familiarly the Kaw) was chosen as a suitable terminus, and a town company was formed in 1854. It flourished, becoming the Shawnee county seat in 1857; in 1861 when Kansas became a state, Topeka was designated state capital. Colonel Holliday's railroad, the Atchison, Topeka, and Santa Fe, began to build westward from Topeka in 1869; its general offices and machine shops were established there in 1878 and are still important to the city. Other industries today include tires, steel products, cellophane, printing, insurance, grain milling, and meat packing. World-famous psychiatric clinic and research center the Menninger Foundation is in Topeka. Herbert Hoover's vice president, Charles Curtis, who was part Kaw and a descendant of one of Topeka's earliest settlers, was born here.

What to See and Do

Combat Air Museum. Jets, cargo transports, bombers, fighters, and trainers from 1917-1980 are displayed here, as well as military artifacts. Guided tours (by appt). (Daily; closed Jan 1, Thanksgiving, Dec 25) Forbes Field, Hanger 602, 5 mi S on US 75. Phone 785/862-3303. ¢¢

Governor's Mansion (Cedar Crest). Period architecture with Loire Valley

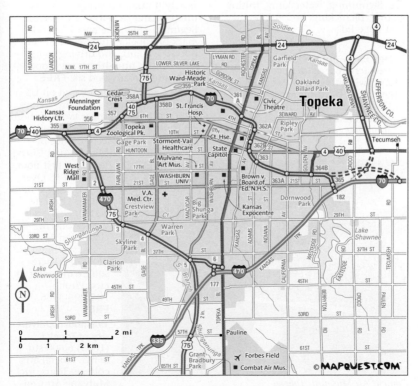

overtones on 244 acres. Built in 1928, bequeathed to state in 1955. Became governor's residence in 1962. Guided tours (Mon afternoons). Fairlawn Rd at I-70, 1 mi N. Phone 785/296-3966. **FREE**

Heartland Park Topeka. Motorsports complex featuring professional and amateur race events. (Daily) 7530 SW US 75. Phone 785/862-4781.

Kansas Museum of History. Contains displays relating to the history of Kansas and the plains. Museum, changing exhibits, hands-on Discovery Place. (Daily; closed hols) 6425 SW 6th St. Phone 785/272-8681. **Donation**

Kansas State Historical Society. Library of Kansas, Native American, and Western history and genealogy; one of largest newspaper collections in the nation; manuscript, photograph, and map collections. State Historic Preservation Office; State Archaeology Office. (Mon-Sat; closed hols) Center for Historical Research, 6425 SW 6th S. Phone 785/272-8681. **FREE**

Lake Shawnee. A 411-acre man-made lake. Swimming, waterskiing, fishing, boating; picnicking. SE 29th St and West Edge Rd.

Parks.

Gage Park. Approx 160 acres; incl three-acre rose garden, conservatory; swimming pool (Memorial Day-Labor Day); tennis courts, picnic facilities; miniature train ride and restored 1908 carousel (May-Labor Day, fee). (Daily) Gage Blvd

between W 6th and W 10th sts. ¢ Also in park is

Topeka Zoo. Discovering Apes Building with orangutans and gorillas; Black Bear exhibit; Lions Pride exhibit; tropical rain forest under geodesic dome with plants and free-roaming animals. (Daily; closed Dec 25) 6th and 10th St entrances. Inside Gage Park on Gage Blvd. Phone 785/272-5821. ¢¢

Ward-Meade Historical Home. Historical Ward-Meade house, restored rock livery stable, log cabin, depot, general store, caboose, and one-rm schoolhouse (Tues-Fri; two tours daily). Botanical gardens (free). Gift shop. 124 NW Fillmore. Phone 785/295-3888. ¢¢

Perry State Park. A 1,600-acre park on 12,200-acre lake. Beach, bathhouse, fishing, boating (ramps, docks); trails, picnicking, camping (electricity, dump station). Standard fees. (Daily) 16 mi E via US 24, 4 miles N on KS 237, near Ozawkie. Phone 785/246-3449. ¢¢

⭐ **Potwin Place.** Community of stately homes, towering trees, distinctive circular parks on 70 acres. Begun in 1869, the area is a landmark of Topeka's heritage. Self-conducted walking and driving tours. Between 1st and 4th sts on Woodlawn and Greenwood sts. **FREE**

State Capitol. Design based on US Capitol. On the grounds are statues of Lincoln and Pioneer Woman, both by Topeka-born sculptor Merrell Gage; murals on second floor by John Steuart Curry; those on first floor by David H. Overmeyer; second floor statuary by Pete Felten. Guide service (Mon-Fri; closed Jan 1, Thanksgiving, Dec 25). On 20-acre square in center of city. Phone 785/296-3966. **FREE**

Washburn University of Topeka. (1865) 6,600 students. Liberal arts college. Tours, incl Mulvane Art Cen-

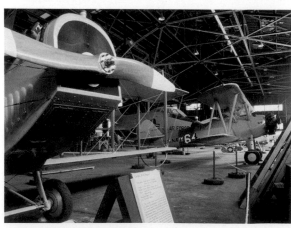

Combat Air Museum, Topeka

ter, Petro Allied Health Center, observatory, and planetarium. 17th St and College Ave. Phone 785/231-1010.

Special Events

Washburn Sunflower Music Festival. International symphonic musicians perform nightly. Phone 785/231-1010. First two wks June.

Huff 'n Puff Balloon Rally. Phillip Billard Airport. Hot-air balloons. Phone 785/234-1030. Sept.

Motels/Motor Lodges

★★ **BEST WESTERN MEADOW ACRES.** *2950 S Topeka Blvd (66611). 785/267-1681; toll-free 800/528-1234. www.bestwestern.com.* 83 rms. S $36-$42; D $54-$62; each addl $6; under 12 free. Crib $4. TV; cable (premium). Indoor pool. Complimentary continental bkfst, coffee in rms. Restaurant nearby. Ck-out noon. Business servs avail. Some refrigerators. Cr cds: A, C, D, DS, MC, V.
D 🏊 🚫 🐾 SC

★ **CAPITAL CENTER INN.** *914 SE Madison (66607). 785/232-7721; fax 785/290-0465.* 196 rms, 9 story. S, D $65; each addl $6; under 18 free. Crib free. Pet accepted, some restrictions. TV; cable (premium). Pool. Restaurant 6 am-2 pm, 5-10 pm. Bar 11 am-midnight; closed Sun. Ck-out noon. Coin lndry. Meeting rms. Business servs avail. In-rm modem link. Bellhops. Valet serv. Airport transportation. Health club privileges. Luxury level. Cr cds: A, D, DS, MC, V.
D 🐾 🏊 🚫 🐾

★★ **CLUBHOUSE INN.** *924 SW Henderson Rd (66615). 785/273-8888; fax 785/273-5809. www.clubhouse inn.com.* 121 rms, 2 story, 17 suites. S $65; D $75; each addl $10; suites $81; under 10 free; wkly, wkend rates. Crib free. TV; cable (premium). Heated pool; whirlpool. Complimentary full bkfst. Ck-out noon. Coin lndry. Meeting rms. Business servs avail. In-rm modem link. Valet serv. Health club privileges. Refrigerator, wet bar in suites. Balconies. Grills. Cr cds: A, D, DS, MC, V.
D 🐾 🏊 🚫 🐾

★ **DAYS INN.** *1510 SW Wanamaker Rd (66604). 785/272-8538; toll-free*

800/329-7466. 62 rms, 2 story, 6 suites. S $42-$59; D $47-$69; each addl $5; suites $49-$69; under 12 free; higher rates Heartland auto races. Crib $5. Pet accepted. TV; cable (premium). Indoor pool; whirlpool. Complimentary continental bkfst. Restaurant nearby. Ck-out 11 am. Business servs avail. Game rm. Refrigerator in suites. Cr cds: A, D, DS, MC, V.
D 🐾 🏊 🚫 🐾 SC

★ **LIBERTY INN.** *3839 SW Topeka Blvd (66609). 785/266-4700.* 132 rms, 2 story. S $37-$48; D $41-$55; each addl $6; suites $95. Crib free. Pet accepted, some restrictions. TV; cable. Pool. Playground. Restaurant 6:30 am-2 pm. Bar 5 pm-2 am, closed Sun. Ck-out noon. Meeting rms. Business servs avail. Valet serv. Airport transportation. Many refrigerators. Private patios, balconies. Cr cds: A, C, D, DS, ER, JCB, MC, V.
D 🐾 🏊 🚫 🐾 SC

★ **RAMADA INN DOWNTOWN.** *420 E 6th St (66607). 785/234-5400; fax 785/233-0460; res 888/298-2054. www.ramada.com.* 422 rms, 3-11 story. S, D $48-$76; each addl $7; suites $80-$250; under 18 free; wkend rates. Crib free. Pet accepted, some restrictions; $20. TV; cable (premium), VCR avail. Pool; whirlpool. Restaurants 6 am-9 pm. Bar 4 pm-midnight; entertainment. Ck-out noon. Coin lndry. Convention facilities. Business servs avail. Bellhops. Valet serv. Sundries. Gift shop. Barber, beauty shop. Free airport transportation. Exercise equipt; sauna. Some bathrm phones, refrigerators. Cr cds: A, D, DS, MC, V.
D 🐾 🛗 🏊 🚶 🚫 🐾

★★ **SENATE LUXURY SUITES.** *900 SW Tyler St (66612). 785/233-5050; fax 785/233-1614; toll-free 800/488-3188. www.senatesuites.com.* 52 suites, 3 story. S $59-$69; D $69-$79; under 13 free; higher rates Heartland races. TV; cable (premium). Complimentary continental bkfst. Ck-out noon. Coin lndry. Meeting rms. Business center. Valet serv. Exercise equipt. Whirlpool. Health club privileges. Many refrigerators. Balconies. Cr cds: A, C, D, DS, MC, V.
D 🚶 🚫 🐾 🚶

Potwin Place, Topeka

Restaurants

★ **CARLOS O'KELLY'S.** *3425 S Kansas Ave (66611). www.carlos.kellys. com 785/266-3457.* Hrs: 11 am-10 pm; Fri and Sat to 11 pm. Closed Thanksgiving, Dec 25. Res accepted. Mexican, American menu. Bar. Lunch $1.95-$5.95, dinner $1.95-$10.95. Lunch buffet $4.99. Children's menu. Specialties: fajitas, enchilada de Monterey. Hacienda atmosphere. Cr cds: A, C, D, DS, MC, V.
D ⊸

★★ **KOBE STEAK HOUSE OF JAPAN.** *5331 SW 22nd Pl (66614). 785/272-6633.* Hrs: 5:30-9 pm; Fri, Sat 5-10 pm; Sun 4-8 pm. Res accepted. Japanese menu. Bar. Dinner $7.95-$22. Children's menu. Specializes in chicken, seafood, hibachi steak. Japanese artwork. Cr cds: MC, V.
⊸

★★ **MCFARLAND'S.** *4133 W Gage Center Dr (66604). 785/272-6909.* Hrs: 11 am-8 pm; Fri, Sat to 8:30 pm; Sun 11 am-2:30 pm. Closed hols. Bar. Lunch $2.50-$8, dinner $6-$12.50. Children's menu. Specializes in beef, chicken. Family-owned. Cr cds: MC, V.
D

WaKeeney

(C-3) *See also Hays*

Founded 1877 **Pop** 2,161 **Elev** 2,465 ft **Area code** 785 **Zip** 67672
Information Chamber of Commerce, 216 Main St; 785/743-2077

This county seat halfway between Denver and Kansas City produces extra-high-protein wheat. It is known as "Christmas City of the High Plains."

What to See and Do

Cedar Bluff State Park. A 1,700-acre park on 1,600-acre lake. Channel catfish, bass, crappie, and walleye. Dam is 12,500 ft long and rises 134 ft above the stream bed. Sweeping view of the Smoky Hill River valley as it winds through prehistoric, fossil-rich chalk beds. Beach, bathhouse, fishing, boating (ramps, docks); trails, picnicking. Tent and trailer camping (electricity, dump station). Standard fees. (Daily) 8 mi SE on I-70, then 13 mi S on KS 147, exit 135. Phone 785/726-3212. ¢¢

Chalk beds. Rich in fossils. In Smoky Hill River valley. W of town.

Special Events

The Gathering. Eisenhower Park. Phone 785/743-2077. First Sat May.

Trego County Free Fair. County fairgrounds. Phone 785/743-5806. First wk Aug.

Motel/Motor Lodge

★ **TRAVEL INN BUDGET HOST.** *668 S 13th St, Wakeeney (67672).* 785/743-2121; fax 785/743-2458; tollfree 800/283-4678. www.budgethost. com. 27 rms. S $28-$35; D $35-$55; each addl $3; under 18 free. Crib free. Pet accepted. TV; cable (premium). Pool. Restaurant adj 6 am-10 pm. Ck-out 11 am. Cr cds: A, MC, V.
🔧 ≈ ✕ 🐾

B&B/Small Inn

★★ **THISTLE HILL BED & BREAKFAST.** *Rural Rte 1, Wakeeney (67672).* 785/743-2644. www.thistlehillonline. com. 3 rms, 2 with shower only, 2 story. Rm phone avail. S $45; D $85; each addl $10. Complimentary full bkfst. Ck-out 11 am, ck-in 4 pm. Luggage handling. Gift shop. Whirlpool. Picnic tables. Covered patio overlooking gardens. On 320-acre farm with 60-acre wildflower preserve. Cr cds: MC, V.
🛇 ✕ 🔄 🐾

Wichita

(E-5) *See also El Dorado, Hutchinson, Newton*

Settled 1864 **Pop** 304,011 **Elev** 1,305 ft **Area code** 316

Information Convention & Visitors Bureau, 100 S Main, Suite 100, 67202; 316/265-2800 or 800/288-9424

Web www.wichita-cvb.org

The largest city in Kansas has a definite metropolitan flavor, with its tall buildings, wide streets, and bustling tempo. Still a major marketing point for agricultural products, it is now best known as an aircraft production center. McConnell Air Force Base is here. Wichita is the petroleum capital of Kansas, with many independent oil companies represented. Some of the nation's largest grain elevators for wheat storage are here.

The town's first settlers were the Wichita, who built a village of grass lodges on the site. The following year James R. Mead set up a trading post and in 1865 sent his assistant, Jesse Chisholm, on a trading expedition to the Southwest. His route became famous as the Chisholm Trail, over which longhorn cattle were driven through Wichita to the Union Pacific at Abilene. As the railroad advanced to the southwest, Wichita had its turn as the "cow capital" in the early 1870s. By 1880 farmers drawn by the land boom had run fences across the trail and the cattle drives were shifted west to Dodge City. The interrupted prosperity was restored by wheat crops of the next two decades and the discovery of oil after World War I.

What to See and Do

Allen-Lambe House Museum and Study Center. Designed in 1915 by Frank Lloyd Wright as a private residence, it is considered the last of Wright's prairie houses. Living and dining rm surround a sunken garden; furniture designed by Wright in collaboration with interior designer George M. Niedecken. Visitor center, bookstore. Guided tours (by appt only). 255 N Roosevelt St. Phone 316/687-1027. ¢¢

Botanica, The Wichita Gardens. Display of exotic flowers as well as plants native to Kansas. Among the gardens are the Butterfly Garden, Shakespearean Garden, Aquatic Collection, and Xeriscape Demonstration Garden. (Apr-Dec, Mon-Sat, also Sun afternoons; rest of yr, Mon-Fri) 701 Amidon. Phone 316/264-9799. ¢¢

Century II Convention Center. Circular structure houses convention and exhibition halls, meeting rms, theater, concert hall. 225 W Douglas. Phone 316/264-9121.

Cheney State Park. A 1,913-acre park at 9,537-acre lake. Popular with sailboat and windsurfing enthusiasts. Large-scale regattas are a featured part of the many lake activities. Beach, bathhouse, fishing, boating (ramps, docks, marina); picnicking, concession, camping (electricity,

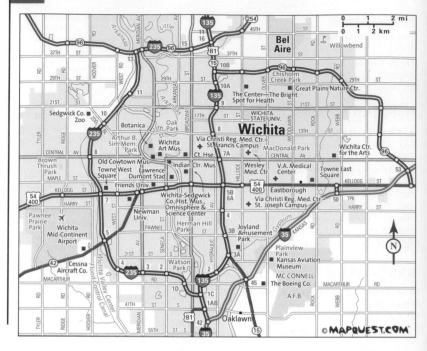

dump station). Standard fees. (Daily) 20 mi W on US 54, then 4 mi N on KS 251. Phone 316/542-3664. ¢¢

Clifton Square Shopping Village. 19th-century houses converted into shops; brick walkways and old-fashioned lampposts. (Daily) 3700 E Douglas at Clifton, in historic College Hill neighborhood. Phone 316/686-2177.

Edwin A. Ulrich Museum of Art. Exhibitions of contemporary art; also outdoor mosaic mural by Joan Miró. (Daily) Tours by appt. On Wichita State University campus, in the McKnight Art Center. Phone 316/978-3664. Also on campus are

  Corbin Education Center. Designed by Frank Lloyd Wright. (Mon-Fri) 1845 Fairmount, near Yale and 21st sts.

  Martin H. Bush Outdoor Sculpture Collection. Boasts a 56-piece collection of 20th-century sculpture by internationally known artists.

Indian Center Museum. Changing exhibits of past and present Native American art. (Apr-Dec, daily; rest of yr, Tues-Sun; closed hols) 650 N Seneca. Phone 316/262-5221. ¢

Lake Afton Public Observatory. Public programs (two hrs) offer opportunity to view a variety of celestial objects through a 16-inch reflecting telescope; astronomy computer games; exhibits and displays. Programs begin ½ hr after sunset. (Sept-May, Fri and Sat; June-Aug, Fri-Sun; closed Dec 23-Jan 1) 25000 W 39th St S; 15 mi SW via US 54, Viola Rd exit. Phone 316/978-7827. ¢¢

O. J. Watson Park. Covers 119 acres; fishing, boats; miniature golf; pony, train, and hayrack rides (fees). Picnic area, concession. (Mar-Nov) S Lawrence Rd at Carp St, just S of Arkansas River. Phone 316/529-9940. **FREE**

Old Cowtown Museum. A 40-building historic village museum depicting Wichita life in the 1870s; restaurant, shops. (Mar-Oct, Mon-Sat, also Sun afternoons; rest of yr, wkends only) (See SPECIAL EVENTS) 1871 Sim Park Dr. Phone 316/264-0671. ¢¢

Omnisphere and Science Center. Planetarium and hands-on science center. (Tues-Sat; closed hols) 220 S Main St. Phone 316/337-9178. ¢¢

Sedgwick County Zoo and Botanical Garden. Animals in their natural habitat; African veldt; herpetarium; jungle; pampas; prairie; outback; boat and train rides (summer).

(Daily) 5555 Zoo Blvd. Phone 316/942-2212. ¢¢¢

Wichita Art Museum. Traveling exhibits; collection of American art; paintings and sculpture by Charles M. Russell; pre-Columbian art; works by contempory and historic Kansas artists. (Tues-Sun; closed hols) 619 Stackman Dr. Phone 316/268-4921. **FREE**

Wichita Center for the Arts. Changing and permanent exhibits. (Tues-Sun; closed hols) Also School of Art for adults and children, theatre with concerts, plays, and recitals. 9112 E Central. Phone 316/634-2787. **FREE**

Wichita-Sedgwick County Historical Museum. Local history, Native American artifacts, period rms, costume collection, 1917 Jones Auto display. (Tues-Sun; closed hols) 204 S Main St. Phone 316/265-9314. ¢¢

Special Events

Jazz Festival. Jazz clinic; entertainment. Phone 316/262-2351. Apr.

Wichita River Festival. Incl twilight pop concert and fireworks; antique bathtub races; hot-air balloon launch; athletic events; entertainment. Phone 316/267-2817. Mid-May.

Indian Powwow. Tribes gather from all over the country and Canada. Traditional dances; crafts; ethnic food. Phone 316/262-5221. July.

National Baseball Congress World Series. (amateur) Lawrence Stadium, Maple and Sycamore sts. Phone 316/267-3372. Aug.

Old Sedgwick County Fair. Old Cowtown Museum. Re-creation of 1870s fair; crafts, livestock, demonstrations, music, food, games. Phone 316/264-0671. First full wkend Oct.

Motels/Motor Lodges

★★ **AIRPORT PLAZA CONVENTION CENTER.** *5805 W Kellogg Dr (67209). 316/942-7911; fax 316/942-0854.* 206 rms, 2 story. S $75; D $85; each addl $5; suites $125-$195; under 18 free; wkend rates. Crib free. TV; cable (premium), VCR avail. Pool; wading pool. Restaurant 6 am-2 pm, 5-10 pm; Sat, Sun from 7 am. Bar noon-2 am, Sun to 1 am; entertainment. Ck-out noon. Meeting

rms. Business servs avail. In-rm modem link. Bellhops. Valet serv. Free airport transportation. Some private patios, balconies, refrigerators. Cr cds: A, C, D, DS, ER, JCB, MC, V.

[D] [≈] [✕] [⊿] [⚑] [SC]

★★ **BEST WESTERN RED COACH INN.** *915 E 53rd St N (67219). 316/832-9387; fax 316/832-9443; toll-free 800/362-0095. www.bestwestern.com.* 152 rms, 2 story. S $60; D $68; each addl $5; suites $89-$119; under 12 free. Crib $3. TV; cable (premium), VCR avail (movies $3). Indoor pool; whirlpool. Sauna. Playground. Restaurant 6 am-11 pm. Ck-out noon. Meeting rms. Business servs avail. Sundries. Game rm. Rec rm. Golf course opp. Cr cds: A, C, D, DS, MC, V.

[D] [≈] [⊿] [⚑]

★★ **CAMBRIDGE SUITES.** *120 W Orme St (67213). 316/263-1061; fax 316/263-3817; res 800/946-6200. www.candlewoodsuites.com.* 64 kit. suites, 2 story. S, D $95-$125; wkend, wkly, monthly rates. Crib avail. Pet accepted. TV; cable (premium), VCR avail. Pool. Complimentary continental bkfst. Ck-out noon. Business servs avail. In-rm modem link. Health club privileges. Many fireplaces. Private patios, balconies. Grill. Cr cds: A, C, D, DS, ER, JCB, MC, V.

[D] [🐾] [≈] [⊿] [⚑]

★★ **COMFORT SUITES WICHITA AIRPORT.** *658 Westdale Dr (67209). 316/945-2600; fax 316/945-5033; toll-free 800/318-2607. www.comfort suites.com.* 50 suites, 3 story. S, D $79-$86. TV; cable (premium). Heated pool. Complimentary bkfst. Coffee in rms. Bar. Ck-out noon. Meeting rms. Business servs avail. Airport transportation. Refrigerators. Cr cds: A, C, D, DS, ER, JCB, MC, V.

[D] [≈] [✕] [⊿] [⚑]

★ **DAYS INN.** *550 S Florence St (67209). 316/942-1717; toll-free 800/329-7466. www.daysinn.com.* 43 rms, 2 story. S $44.95; D $49.95; each addl $5; family rates. Crib free. TV; cable (premium). Complimentary continental bkfst. Restaurant adj 11 am-11 pm. Ck-out 11 am. Business servs avail. In-rm modem link. Many refrigerators. Near airport. Cr cds: A, C, D, DS, MC, V.

D ⊠ ⊠ SC

★ **DAYS INN EAST.** *9100 E Kellogg (67207). 316/685-0371; fax 316/685-4668; res 800/329-7466. www.daysinn. com.* 116 rms, 2 story. May-Aug: S, D $40.99-$42.99; each addl $2; suites $75; under 14 free; lower rates rest of yr. Crib $6. TV; cable (premium). Pool. Complimentary continental bkfst. Ck-out 11 am. Meeting rms. Business servs avail. Valet serv. Refrigerator, whirlpool in suites. Cr cds: A, C, D, DS, MC, V.

D ⊠ ⊠ ⊠ SC

★★ **HOLIDAY INN.** *5500 W Kellogg (67209). 316/943-2181; fax 316/943-6587; toll-free 800/255-6484. www. holiday-inn.com.* 152 rms, 5 story. S, D $89; each addl $8; under 12 free; wkend rates. Crib free. Pet accepted. TV; cable, VCR avail. Indoor pool; whirlpool, poolside serv. Sauna. Complimentary coffee in rms. Restaurant 6 am-10 pm. Bar 5 pm-1 am. Ck-out noon. Coin lndry. Meeting rms. Business servs avail. Bellhops. Valet serv. Free airport transportation. Cr cds: A, C, D, DS, ER, JCB, MC, V.

D ⊠ ⊠ ⊠ ⊠ ⊠ SC

★★★ **HOLIDAY INN SELECT.** *549 S Rock Rd (67207). 316/686-7131; fax 316/686-0018; res 800/465-4329. www.holiday-inn.com.* 260 rms, 9 story. S, D $89-$159; suites $175-$350; wkend, family rates. Crib free. Pet accepted; $125 ($100 refundable). TV; cable (premium), VCR avail. Pool. Coffee in rms. Restaurant 6:30 am-10 pm; Sun from 7 am. Bar 2 pm-midnight. Ck-out noon. Meeting rms. Business servs avail. In-rm modem link. Free airport transportation. Cr cds: A, D, DS, JCB, MC, V.

D ⊠ ⊠ ⊠ ⊠

★★ **LA QUINTA INN.** *7700 E Kellogg (67207). 316/681-2881; fax 316/681-0568. www.laquinta.com.* 122 rms, 2 story. S $55-$65; D $63-$73; each addl $7; under 18 free. Crib free. Pet accepted, some restrictions. TV; cable (premium). Pool. Complimentary continental bkfst. Restaurant adj 11:30 am-11 pm; Fri, Sat to midnight; Sun to 10 pm. Ck-out noon. Meeting rms. Business servs

avail. In-rm modem link. Cr cds: A, C, D, DS, MC, V.

D ⊠ ⊠ ⊠ ⊠

★ **RAMADA INN.** *7335 E Kellogg (67207). 316/685-1281; fax 316/685-8621.* 192 rms, 6 story. S, D $69-$82; suites $82-$150; under 18 free. Crib free. Pet accepted. TV; cable (premium), VCR avail. Indoor pool; whirlpool. Coffee in rms. Restaurant 6-10 am, 6-10 pm; wkends 7-11 am, 6-10 pm. Bar 5 pm-midnight. Ck-out noon. Coin lndry. Meeting rms. Business servs avail. In-rm modem link. Bellhops. Valet serv. Free airport transportation. Exercise equipt. Game rm. Cr cds: A, D, DS, MC, V.

D ⊠ ⊠ ⊠ ⊠ ⊠

★ **SCOTMAN INN WEST.** *5922 W Kellogg (67209). 316/943-3800; toll-free 800/950-7268. www.scotsmaninn. com.* 72 rms, 3 story. S $34; D $38; each addl $2; suites $49-$64; under 17 free. Crib $3. TV; cable (premium). Complimentary coffee in lobby. Restaurant nearby. Ck-out noon. Coin lndry. Business servs avail. Refrigerators. Cr cds: A, C, D, DS, MC, V.

D ⊠ ⊠ ⊠

★ **STRATFORD HOUSE INNS.** *5505 W Kellogg (67209). 316/942-0900.* 40 rms, 2 story. S $35.95; D $39.95-$43.95; under 12 free. Crib free. Pet accepted. TV; cable (premium). Complimentary continental bkfst. Restaurant nearby. Ck-out 11 am. Business servs avail. Cr cds: A, DS, MC, V.

D ⊠ ⊠ ⊠

★ **WICHITA INN EAST.** *8220 E Kellogg (67207). 316/685-8291; fax 316/685-0835; toll-free 888/685-8291.* 96 rms, 3 story. S $35; D $39; each addl $4; under 10 free. Crib free. TV; cable (premium). Complimentary continental bkfst. Restaurant nearby. Ck-out 11 am. Coin lndry. Business servs avail. In-rm modem link. Valet serv. Cr cds: A, MC, V.

D ⊠ ⊠

★★ **WICHITA SUITES HOTEL.** *5211 E Kellogg (67218). 316/685-2233; fax 316/685-4152; toll-free 800/243-5953.* 90 suites, 4 story. S $69-$76; D $79-$86; each addl $7; under 6 free. Crib free. TV; cable (premium). Heated pool; whirlpool. Complimentary full bkfst; afternoon refreshments. Restaurant nearby. Ck-out noon. Coin lndry. Meeting rms. In-rm modem link. Valet serv. Sundries. Exercise equipt; sauna. Refrigerators. Cr cds: A, MC, V.

[D] [≈] [ⅉ] [⤓] [♨]

★★ WYNDHAM GARDEN HOTEL.
515 S Webb Rd (67207). 316/684-1111; fax 316/684-0538; res 800/996-3426. www.wyndham.com. 120 rms, 2 story. S, D $94; each addl $5; suites $89-$110; under 16 free; wkend, wkly rates. Crib free. TV; cable (premium). Heated pool; whirlpool. Complimentary full bkfst. Restaurant nearby. Ck-out noon. Business servs avail. Refrigerator in suites. Many balconies. Cr cds: A, C, D, DS, ER, JCB, MC, V.

[D] [≈] [⤓] [♨] [SC]

Hotels

★★★ HILTON AIRPORT.
2098 Airport Rd (67206). 316/945-5272; fax 316/945-7620. www.hilton.com. 175 rms, 6 story. S, D $150-$225; each addl $20; under 17 free. Crib avail. TV; cable (premium), VCR avail. Complimentary coffee, newspaper in rms. Restaurant 6 am-10 pm. Ck-out noon. Meeting rms. Business center. Gift shop. Exercise rm. Some refrigerators, minibars. Cr cds: A, C, D, DS, ER, JCB, MC, V.

[ⅉ] [♨] [♀]

★★★ HYATT REGENCY WICHITA.
400 W Waterman (67202). 316/293-1234. www.hyatt.com. 303 rms, 17 story. S, D $150-$225; each addl $20; under 17 free. Crib avail. Pet accepted. 2 heated pools. TV; cable (premium), VCR avail. Complimentary coffee, newspaper in rms. Restaurant 6 am-10 pm. Ck-out noon. Meeting rms. Business center. Gift shop. Exercise rm. Some refrigerators, minibars. Cr cds: A, C, D, DS, ER, JCB, MC, V.

[➘] [≈] [ⅉ] [♨] [♀]

★★★ MARRIOTT WICHITA.
9100 E Corporate Hills Dr (67207). 316/651-0333; fax 316/651-0990; toll-free 800/610-0673. www.marriott.com. 294 units, 11 story. S $139; D $149; suites $175-$275; under 18 free; wkly, wkend rates. Crib free. Pet accepted. TV; cable (premium), VCR avail. Indoor/outdoor pool; whirlpool,

poolside serv. Coffee in rms. Restaurant 6:30 am-11 pm. Bar noon-2 am. Ck-out noon. Business center. Concierge. Gift shop. Free airport transportation. Exercise equipt; sauna. Luxury level. Cr cds: A, C, D, DS, JCB, MC, V.

[D] [➘] [≈] [ⅉ] [✕] [⤓] [♨] [♀]

B&B/Small Inn

★★★ INN AT THE PARK.
3751 E Douglas (67218). 316/652-0500; fax 316/652-0525; toll-free 800/258-1951. www.innathepark.com. 12 suites, 3 story. S, D $89. TV; cable. Complimentary continental bkfst, coffee in rms. Restaurant nearby. Ck-out 11 am, ck-in 4 pm. Business servs avail. Whirlpool. Picnic tables. Built 1909; suites designed individually by local designers. Cr cds: A, DS, MC, V.

[⤓] [♨]

Extended Stay

★★ RESIDENCE INN BY MARRIOTT.
411 S Webb Rd (67207). 316/686-7331; fax 316/686-2345; res 800/331-3131. www.residenceinn.com. 64 kit. suites, 2 story. S $99; D $124; wkend rates. Crib free. Pet accepted; $50 refundable and $7/day. TV; cable (premium), VCR avail. Pool; whirlpool. Complimentary continental bkfst. Ck-out noon. Coin lndry. Business servs avail. In-rm modem link. Health club privileges. Lawn games. Refrigerators. Many fireplaces. Grills. Cr cds: A, MC, V.

[D] [➘] [≈] [⤓] [♨] [SC]

Restaurants

★★ GRAPE.
550 N Rock Rd (67206). 316/634-0113. www.the-grape.com. Hrs: 4 pm-2 am. Closed Jan 1, Thanksgiving, Dec 25. Bar. A la carte entrees: $7.95-$16.50. Specializes in cheese boards, fish, charbroiled steaks. Entertainment Fri, Sat. Outdoor dining. Cr cds: A, DS, MC, V.

[D] [SC] [⊟]

★★★ OLIVE TREE.
2949 N Rock Rd (67226). 316/636-1100. Hrs: 11 am-10 pm; Fri, Sat to 11 pm; Sun 5-10 pm. Closed Dec 25. Res accepted. Continental menu. A la carte entrees: lunch $6-$9, dinner $12.95-$21.95. Specializes in fresh salmon, lamb,

duck. Outdoor dining. Cr cds: A, C, D, DS, MC, V.

D ⟶

Winfield

(E-6) *See also Arkansas City*

Founded 1870 **Pop** 11,931 **Elev** 1,127 ft **Area code** 316 **Zip** 67156
Information Chamber of Commerce, 205 E 9th, PO Box 640; 316/221-2420

Settled on land leased from Osage Chief Chetopah for $6, Winfield manufactures crayons, water coolers, and ice chests and has oil and gas wells.

What to See and Do

Cowley County Historical Museum. Glass collection, period rms, early artifacts, library, archives. (Sat and Sun afternoons) 1011 Mansfield. Phone 316/221-4811. **FREE**

Recreation.

City Lake. A 2,400-acre recreation area incl reservoir with 21-mi shoreline. Swimming, fishing, boating (launching ramp). Tent and trailer camping. (Daily) 10 mi NE. Phone 316/221-5635. ¢¢

Fairgrounds and Pecan Grove. Surrounded by Walnut River. Fishing. Picnicking, playground. (Daily) W end of North Ave. **FREE**

Motel/Motor Lodge

★ **BEST VALUE INN CAMELOT MOTOR INN.** *1710 Main St (67156). 316/221-9050; fax 316/221-7062; res 888/315-2378. www.bestvalueinn.com.* 30 rms, 2 story. S $42-$55; D $49-$65; each addl $4; higher rates special events. Crib $5. TV; cable (premium). Coffee in rms. Restaurant nearby. Ck-out 11 am. Cr cds: A, C, D, DS, MC, V.

⚓ ⟶ 🔥

Yates Center

(D-7) *See also Chanute, Eureka, Iola*

Pop 1,815 **Elev** 1,136 ft
Area code 316 **Zip** 66783

What to See and Do

Toronto State Park. A 1,075-acre park at 2,800-acre lake. Located in the Chautauqua Hills region, the forested uplands of Black Jack and Post Oak overlook the 2,800-acre reservoir nestled in the Verdigris Valley. Beach, bathhouse, fishing, boating (ramps, docks); trails, picnicking, concession. Tent and trailer camping (fee; reservations accepted; hookups, dump station). (Daily) 12 mi W on US 54, then S on KS 105. Phone 316/637-2213. ¢¢

MINNESOTA

Mother of the Mississippi and dotted by more than 4,000 square miles of water surface, Minnesota is not the "land of 10,000 lakes" as it so widely advertises—a recount indicates that the figure is closer to 12,000. Natives of the state may tell you that the lakes were stamped out by the hooves of Paul Bunyan's giant blue ox, "Babe"; geologists say they were created by retreating glaciers during the Ice Age. They are certainly the Minnesota vacationland's prize attraction.

Although Minnesota borders on Canada and is 1,000 miles from either ocean, it is nevertheless a seaboard state thanks to the St. Lawrence Seaway, which makes Duluth, on Lake Superior, an international port and the world's largest inland freshwater port.

Dense forests, vast grain fields, rich pastures, a large open pit iron mine, wilderness parks, outstanding hospitals and universities, high technology corporations, and a thriving arts community—these are facets of this richly endowed state.

Population: 4,375,099
Area: 79,548 square miles
Elevation: 602-2,301 feet
Peak: Eagle Mountain (Cook County)
Entered Union: May 11, 1858 (32nd state)
Capital: St. Paul
Motto: Star of the North
Nickname: Gopher State, North Star State
Flower: Pink and White Ladyslipper
Bird: Common Loon
Tree: Norway Pine
Fair: August 22-September 2, 2002, in St. Paul
Time Zone: Central
Website: www.exploreminnesota.com

This is the get-away-from-it-all state: you can fish in a lake, canoe along the Canadian border, or search out the Northwest Angle, which is so isolated that until recently it could be reached only by boat or plane. In winter you can ice fish, snowmobile, or ski the hundreds of miles of downhill and cross-country areas. If you are not the outdoor type, there are spectator sports, nightlife, shopping, music, theater, and sightseeing in the Twin Cities (Minneapolis/St. Paul).

Explored by Native Americans, fur traders, and missionaries since the dawn of its known history, Minnesota surged ahead on the economic tides of lumber, grain, and ore. The state has 92,000 farms covering 30 million acres; its agricultural production ranks high in sugar beets, butter, turkeys, sweet corn, soybeans, sunflowers, spring wheat, hogs, and peas. Manufacturing is important to Minnesota's economy. It also is a wholesale transportation hub and financial and retailing center of the Upper Midwest.

The flags of four nations have flown over Minnesota as it passed through Spanish, French, and British rule, finally becoming part of the United States in segments in 1784, 1803, and 1818. A territory in 1849, Minnesota was admitted as a state less than a decade later. The Dakota (Sioux) War was a turning point in the state's history, claiming the lives of 400 settlers and an unknown number of Native Americans in 1862. It marked the end of Sioux control in the domain they called "the land of the sky-tinted waters." The vast forests poured out seemingly unending streams of lumber and the people spun legends of Paul Bunyan, an enduring part of American folklore. With the first shipment of iron ore in 1884, Minnesota was on its way to a mine-farm-factory future.

When to Go/Climate

This state of lakes and prairieland offers warm summers, cool falls, wet springs, and cold winters.

AVERAGE HIGH/LOW TEMPERATURES (°F)

INTERNATIONAL FALLS

Jan 12/-10	May 65/40	Sept 64/43
Feb 19/-4	June 73/55	Oct 52/33
Mar 33/11	July 79/55	Nov 33/17
Apr 50/28	Aug 76/52	Dec 17/-2

MINNEAPOLIS/ST. PAUL

Jan 21/3	May 69/48	Sept 71/50
Feb 27/9	June 79/63	Oct 59/39
Mar 39/23	July 84/63	Nov 41/25
Apr 57/36	Aug 81/60	Dec 26/10

Parks and Recreation Finder

Directions to and information about the parks and recreation areas below are given under their respective town/city sections. Please refer to those sections for details.

NATIONAL PARK AND RECREATION AREAS

Key to abbreviations. I.H.S. = International Historic Site; I.P.M. = International Peace Memorial; N.B. = National Battlefield; N.B.P. = National Battlefield Park; N.B.C. = National Battlefield and Cemetery; N.C.A. = National Conservation Area; N.E.M. = National Expansion Memorial; N.F. = National Forest; N.G. = National Grassland; N.H.P. = National Historical Park; N.H.C. = National Heritage Corridor; N.H.S. = National Historic Site; N.L. = National Lakeshore; N.M. = National Monument; N.M.P. = National Military Park; N.Mem. = National Memorial; N.P. = National Park; N.Pres. = National Preserve; N.R.A. = National Recreational Area; N.R.R. = National Recreational River; N.Riv. = National River; N.S. = National Seashore; N.S.R. = National Scenic Riverway; N.S.T. = National Scenic Trail; N.Sc. = National Scientific Reserve; N.V.M. = National Volcanic Monument.

Place Name	Listed Under
Chippewa N.F.	GRAND RAPIDS
Grand Portage N.M.	GRAND PORTAGE
Pipestone N.M.	same
St. Croix and the Lower St. Croix N.S.R.	TAYLORS FALLS
Superior N.F.	same
Voyageurs N.P.	INTERNATIONAL FALLS

STATE PARK AND RECREATION AREAS

Key to abbreviations. I.P. = Interstate Park; S.A.P. = State Archaeological Park; S.B. = State Beach; S.C.A. = State Conservation Area; S.C.P. = State Conservation Park; S.Cp. = State Campground; S.F. = State Forest; S.G. = State Garden; S.H.A. = State Historic Area; S.H.P. = State Historic Park; S.H.S. = State Historic Site; S.M.P. = State Marine Park; S.N.A. = State Natural Area; S.P. = State Park; S.P.C. = State Public Campground; S.R. = State Reserve; S.R.A. = State Recreation Area; S.Res. = State Reservoir; S.Res.P. = State Resort Park; S.R.P. = State Rustic Park.

Place Name	Listed Under
Blue Mounds S.P.	LUVERNE
Camden S.P.	MARSHALL
Charles A. Lindbergh S.P.	LITTLE FALLS

CALENDAR HIGHLIGHTS

FEBRUARY

John Beargrease Sled Dog Marathon (Duluth). Approximately 500-mile, five-day marathon from Duluth to Grand Portage and back. About 20 to 25 mushers compete. Phone 218/722-7631.

Winter Carnival (St. Paul). Citywide happening, with ice and snow carving; parades, sports events, parties, pageants. Phone 651/223-4700.

JUNE

Judy Garland Festival (Grand Rapids). Museum. Discussions and presentations on Judy Garland's life and accomplishments. Viewing of *The Wizard of Oz*, children's activities, gala dinner. Phone 218/327-9276 or 800/664-JUDY.

Vikingland Drum Corps Classic (Alexandria). National drum and bugle corps perform in the state's only field show competition. Phone Chamber of Commerce, 320/763-3161 or 800/235-9441.

JULY

Laura Ingalls Wilder Pageant (Tracy). Celebration of the life of Laura Ingalls Wilder, author of the *Little House* books. Phone 507/859-2174.

Paul Bunyan Water Carnival (Bemidji). Water show, parade, fireworks. Phone Chamber of Commerce, 218/751-3541 or 800/458-2223.

Minneapolis Aquatennial (Minneapolis). Parades, aquatic events, sports events, entertainment.

Heritagefest (New Ulm). Old World-style celebration highlighting German traditions and culture; music, food, arts and crafts. Features entertainers from around the area and from Europe. Phone 507/354-8850.

AUGUST

WE Country Music Fest (Detroit Lakes). Soo Pass Ranch. Three-day event featuring many top country musicians and groups. Phone 218/847-1340 or 800/493-3378.

Bayfront Blues Festival (Duluth). Three days of nonstop blues performances. Phone 218/722-4011.

Minnesota State Fair (St. Paul). Fairgrounds. Horse show, kids' days, allstar revue; agricultural exhibitions and contests; more than one million visitors each year; 300 acres of attractions. Phone 651/642-2200.

Flandrau S.P.	NEW ULM
Forestville S.P.	SPRING VALLEY
Fort Ridgely S.P.	NEW ULM
Fort Snelling S.P.	ST. PAUL
Gooseberry Falls S.P.	TWO HARBORS
Hayes Lake S.P.	ROSEAU
Interstate S.P.	TAYLORS FALLS
Itasca S.P.	same
Jay Cooke S.P.	DULUTH
Kilen Woods S.P.	JACKSON
Lac qui Parle S.P.	GRANITE FALLS
Lake Bemidji S.P.	BEMIDJI

Lake Carlos S.P.	ALEXANDRIA
Lake Shetek S.P.	TRACY
McCarthy Beach S.P.	HIBBING
Mille Lacs Kathio S.P.	ONAMIA
Minneopa S.P.	MANKATO
Myre-Big Island S.P.	ALBERT LEA
Nerstrand Woods S.P.	NORTHFIELD
St. Croix S.P.	HINCKLEY
Savanna Portage S.P.	AITKIN
Scenic S.P.	GRAND RAPIDS
Sibley S.P.	WILLMAR
Soudan Underground Mine S.P.	TOWER
Split Rock Creek S.P.	PIPESTONE
Split Rock Lighthouse S.P.	TWO HARBORS
Upper Sioux Agency S.P.	GRANITE FALLS
Whitewater S.P.	ROCHESTER
Wild River S.P.	TAYLORS FALLS
William O'Brien S.P.	STILLWATER
Zippel Bay S.P.	BAUDETTE

Water-related activities, hiking, riding, various other sports, picnicking and visitor centers as well as camping are available in many of these areas. A $20 annual permit is required for vehicles entering a state park: good for a calendar year. A $4 daily permit is also available. Permits may be purchased at parks. Camping: $8-$12/night, limited to two weeks in any one park, and reservations are accepted in all parks. In state forests, camping, backpack, or canoe-in sites are $7/night. There are small fees for other services. Fees subject to change. Parks are open year-round; however, summer facilities vary in their opening and closing dates. All state parks are game refuges; hunting is prohibited. Pets are allowed on leash only. For further information contact Information Center, Minnesota Department of Natural Resources, 500 Lafayette Rd, St. Paul 55155; 651/296-6157.

SKI AREAS

Place Name	Listed Under
Afton Alps Ski Area	HASTINGS
Buck Hill Ski Area	MINNEAPOLIS
Detroit Mountain Ski Area	DETROIT LAKES
Hyland Hills Ski Area	MINNEAPOLIS
Lutsen Mountains Ski Area	LUTSEN
Mountain Frontenac Ski Area	RED WING
Mountain Kato Ski Area	MANKATO
Powder Ridge Ski Area	ST. CLOUD
Quadna Mountain Resort Ski Area	GRAND RAPIDS
Spirit Mountain Ski Area	DULUTH
Welch Village Ski Area	RED WING
Wild Mountain Ski Area	TAYLORS FALLS

FISHING AND HUNTING

There's every kind of freshwater fishing here. Many of the lakes have more than 50 pounds of game fish per acre; the total catch in the state is as high as 20 million pounds a year. Dip a line for walleye, large or smallmouth bass, crappie, northern pike, muskellunge, brook, brown, rainbow or lake trout, or panfish.

Nonresident fishing license, $35; nonresident family license, $47; nonresident 24-hr license, $9.50; nonresident three-day license, $21; nonresident seven-day license, $25; trout stamp, $8.50. Nonresident small game license, $78. Fees subject to change. For a more complete summary of hunting, fishing, and trapping regulations contact Department of Natural Resources, 500 Lafayette Rd, St. Paul 55155-4040; 651/296-6157.

Driving Information

Safety belts are mandatory for all persons in front seat of a vehicle. Children under 12 yrs must be restrained anywhere in vehicle: ages 4-11 must use a regulation safety belt; under age 4 must be in a federally approved safety seat. For further information phone 651/282-6558.

INTERSTATE HIGHWAY SYSTEM

The following alphabetical listing of Minnesota towns in *Mobil Travel Guide* shows that these cities are within ten miles of the indicated Interstate highways. A highway map, however, should be checked for the nearest exit.

Highway Number	Cities/Towns within ten miles
Interstate 35	Albert Lea, Bloomington, Cloquet, Duluth, Faribault, Hinckley, Lakeville, Minneapolis, Northfield, Owatonna, St. Paul.
Interstate 90	Albert Lea, Austin, Blue Earth, Fairmont, Jackson, Luverne, Rochester, Winona.
Interstate 94	Alexandria, Anoka, Bloomington, Elk River, Fergus Falls, Minneapolis, Moorhead, St. Cloud, St. Paul, Sauk Centre.

Additional Visitor Information

Minnesota travel information is available free from the Minnesota Travel Information Center, 500 Metro Square, 121 7th Pl East, St. Paul 55101. Phone 651/296-5029 or 800/657-3700, for information on special events, recreational activities, and places of interest. Also available are: *Minnesota Guide; Minnesota Explorer,* a free seasonal newspaper with events and attraction information, including a calendar of events for each season; canoeing, hiking, backpacking, biking, and fishing brochures; a state map and directories to restaurants, accommodations, and campgrounds, as well as regional and community tourism publications.

There are 12 travel information centers at entry points and along several traffic corridors of Minnesota; visitors will find the information provided at these stops very helpful in planning their trip through the area. Their locations are as follows: northbound I-35 at Iowa border; US 53, 10 mi S of Eveleth; I-90 at South Dakota border near Beaver Creek; I-90 at Wisconsin border near La Crescent; US 2, 10 mi E of North Dakota border near Fisher; US 61, 5 mi S of Canadian border near Grand Portage (May-Oct); US 53 in International Falls; I-94 at North Dakota border in Moorhead; I-94 at Wisconsin border near Lakeland; I-35 and US 2W in Duluth; US 59 and MN 60, 5 mi N of Iowa border near Worthington; US 10 S of St. Cloud.

MINNESOTA'S RIVER TOWNS

Though the Mississippi River starts far to the northwest of Minneapolis and St. Paul, its most scenic and oft-visited section is found along Highway 61. Drive southeast out of the Twin Cities, tracing the Mississippi River along Minnesota's border with Wisconsin to the southern end of Highway 16. The sights begin in earnest in Hastings, a town started in 1819 and home to some very well-preserved Hudson River Gothic Revival-style residences. The road passes the Cannon River, where travelers can make a pit stop for some fine biking along a multiuse path. Red Wing is a still-thriving old wheat town with excellent bed-and-breakfast inns, hotels, and a theater. Water lovers enjoy little Frontenac State Park, which rests along the shoreline of Lake Pepin, the widest spot on the Mississippi River. Wabasha is one of the state's oldest towns; many of its ornate Victorian buildings have been renovated. South of Wabasha, numerous antebellum structures have been lovingly restored and are open for tours. (**APPROX 125 MI**)

EXPLORING THE LAKES AND FORESTS OF THE GREAT NORTH WOODS

Departing from Grand Rapids, this loop route winds through the Chippewa National Forest, along the shores of innumerable lakes (there are over 1,000 in the national forest alone) and through massive stands of sugar maple, pine, oak, and birch. Historically, the vast forests of northern Minnesota have been home to logging camps and lumbermen; more mythically, these are the woods where the legends of Paul Bunyan took root.

From Grand Rapids, drive west on Highway 2 toward Deer River, a logging and agricultural center. Immediately west of town, take Highway 46 northward. The route, designated the Avenue of Pines Scenic Byway, enters the Chippewa National Forest. Wildlife is plentiful throughout the Chippewa National Forest; the highest concentration of breeding eagles in the lower 48 states can be found here. Also watch for black bears, beavers, timber wolves, and white-tailed deer. The lakes are filled with walleye.

Turn at signs for Lake Winnibigoshish and Winnie Dam. The lake—affectionately called Big Winnie—pools the waters of the Mississippi River, and canoeing and rafting the fast-flowing stream are popular activities below Winnie Dam. Campgrounds, swimming beaches, and picnic areas line the lake.

North of Winnie Dam, the route enters the corridor of red pines for which the byway is named. Many of the pines along the highway were planted in the 1930s by the Civilian Conservation Corps (CCC). Cut Foot Sioux Lake is named for a warrior slain in a 1748 battle between the Chippewa and the Sioux. On the shores of the lake are a fish hatchery and a national forest visitor center, with evening naturalist events and exhibits about the flora and fauna of the forest. Adjacent to the center is a historic log ranger station, built in 1908.

Just east of Highway 46, on the shores of Little Cut Foot Sioux Lake, is Turtle Mound, a sacred ritual site for the Native Americans of the area. This turtle-effigy is actually an intaglio, a rare form of "mound" building where the image is sunk in the ground rather than raised above it. The Dakota Sioux constructed the effigy in the 18th century, before the arrival of Europeans to the area. After the Ojibwe people drove the Sioux westward, they adopted the site into their religious observances. A short 1/2-mile trail leads to this curious site, which continues to be used as a place of worship for practitioners of traditional native religion.

North of Squaw Lake, pastures and farms break up the dense forest; at Northome, the byway terminates at Highway 71. Turn west, drive 16 miles to Blackduck, then turn south on Highway 39. In fall this route, locally called the Scenic Highway, is especially beautiful as it cuts through forests of oak, maple, aspen, and birch turned a brilliant mosaic of color by the first frost. Creeks and rivers provide openings in the forest, and you can glimpse black spruce bogs and expansive wetlands occupied by waterfowl, beavers, and songbirds.

Across from Rabideau Lake is Camp Rabideau, a restored CCC camp open to visitors in summer. The camp was built in 1935, and until 1940 it housed hundreds of workers who spent summers planting trees and building roads, ranger stations, fire towers, and other infrastructure projects in Chippewa National Forest. A one-mile interpretive trail winds through the camp.

The largest lake along this route is Cass Lake. On the lake's south shore is Norway Beach, with a long white-sand swimming beach, four campgrounds, and hiking trails. The interpretive center here offers ranger-led activities in summer and also rents boats. A popular boat excursion is Star Island, unusual because the island has another lake at its center. At Highway 2, turn east and return to Grand Rapids. (APPROX 150 MI)

Aitkin

(D-4) *See also Brainerd, Deerwood, Onamia*

Pop 1,698 **Elev** 1,201 ft
Area code 218 **Zip** 56431
Information Aitkin Area Chamber of Commerce, PO Box 127; 218/927-2316

Once the bed of Lake Aitkin and since drained by the deep channel of the Mississippi, the city now produces wild rice and other crops. Fishing enthusiasts, bound for one of the hundreds of lakes in Aitkin County, often stop here.

What to See and Do

Mille Lacs Lake. 14 mi S on US 169. (See ONAMIA)

Rice Lake National Wildlife Refuge. An 18,127-acre refuge that incl 4,500-acre Rice Lake; migration and nesting area for ducks and Canada geese along Mississippi Flyway. Walking and auto trails; fishing. Headquarters (Mon-Fri; closed hols). Area (daily). 23 mi E on MN 210, then 5 mi S, off MN 65 near McGregor. Phone 218/768-2402. **FREE**

Savanna Portage State Park. A 15,818-acre wilderness area built around historic portage linking Mississippi River and Lake Superior. Swimming, fishing, boating (electric motors only; rentals), canoeing; hiking, x-country skiing, snowmobiling, picnicking, camping. Standard fees. 8 mi NE on US 169, then 14 mi E on US 210 to McGregor, then 7 mi N on MN 65, 10 mi NE on County 14. Phone 218/426-3271.

Special Events

Riverboat Heritage Days. Third wkend July. Phone 218/927-2316.
Fish House Parade. Fri after Thanksgiving. Phone 218/927-2316.

Motel/Motor Lodge

★ **RIPPLE RIVER MOTEL & RV PARK.** *701 Minnesota Ave S (56431). 218/927-3734; fax 218/927-3734; toll-free 800/258-3734. www.ripplerivermotel.com.* 29 rms, 1 suite. S $38-$49; D $45-$55; each addl $6. Pet

accepted. TV; cable. Complimentary coffee in lobby. Restaurant nearby. Ck-out 11 am. Business servs avail. X-country ski ¼ mi. Some refrigerators, microwaves. On 7 acres. Cr cds: A, DS, MC, V.

Albert Lea

(H-4) *See also Austin, Blue Earth*

Settled 1855 **Pop** 18,310 **Elev** 1,299 ft
Area code 507 **Zip** 56007
Information Convention & Visitors Bureau, 202 N Broadway; 507/373-3938 or 800/345-8414
Web www.albertlea.org/cvb

An important agriculture, manufacturing, and distribution center, Albert Lea bears the name of the officer who surveyed the area. Albert Lea is the seat of Freeborn County.

What to See and Do

Fountain Lake. Numerous parks offer fishing, swimming, boating; picnicking, hiking. NW part of city. Phone 507/377-4370.

Freeborn County Historical Museum, Library, and Village. Restored buildings incl schoolhouse, general store, sheriff's office and jail, blacksmith and wagon shops, post office, train depot, church, and log cabin. Museum has displays of tools, household items, firefighting equipment, toys, musical instruments. Library specializes in Freeborn County history and genealogy. (Apr-mid-Dec, Tues-Sun) 1031 N Bridge Ave. Phone 507/373-8003.

Myre-Big Island State Park. On 1,600 acres. Prairie pothole landscape incl rare white pelicans; hundreds of wildflowers; Native American displays; hiking, x-country skiing, camping. Interpretive center. Standard fees. 3 mi E at jct I-35 and I-90. Phone 507/373-3403. ¢

Story Lady Doll and Toy Museum. Collection of 400 storybook dolls on display. Every other month museum exhibits uinque dolls from area collectors. Gift shop has antique, designer, and ethnic dolls. (Apr-Dec, Tues-Sun; closed hols). 131 N Broadway Ave. Phone 507/377-1820.

Special Events

Freeborn County Fair. Fairgrounds. Just N of city limits on Bridge St. Entertainment; livestock exhibits; midway. Phone 507/373-6965. Five days late July or early Aug.

Big Island Rendezvous and Festival. Bancroft Bay Park. Reenactment of the fur trade period; bluegrass music; ethnic food. Phone 507/373-3938 or 800/658-2526. First wkend Oct.

Motels/Motor Lodges

★ **BEL-AIRE MOTOR INN.** *700 US 69 S (56007). 507/373-3983; fax 507/373-5161; toll-free 800/373-4073. www.belairemotel.com.* 46 rms, 1 story. S $35-$42; D $38-$55; each addl $4; under 14 free. Crib free. Pet accepted. TV; cable. Pool. Playground. Complimentary continental bkfst. Restaurant nearby. Ck-out 11 am. Cr cds: A, DS, MC, V.

★★ **BUDGET HOST.** *2301 E Main St (56007). 507/373-8291; fax 507/373-4043; toll-free 800/218-2989. www.budgethost.com.* 124 rms, 3 story. S $46-$56; D $59-$69; each addl $5; under 18 free. Crib free. Pet accepted. TV. Indoor pool; wading pool; whirlpool. Restaurant 6:30 am-9:30 pm. Bar 5 pm-midnight, closed Sun; entertainment wkends. Ck-out 11 am. Coin lndry. Meeting rms. Business servs avail. Sundries. X-country ski 1 mi. Exercise equipt; sauna. Game rm. Cr cds: A, C, D, DS, MC, V.

★ **DAYS INN.** *2306 E Main St (56007). 507/373-6471; fax 507/373-7517; res 800/329-7466. www.daysinn.com.* 128 rms, 2 story. S, D $59-$75; each addl $5; under 18 free. Crib free. Pet accepted. TV. Indoor pool. Restaurant 6:30 am-9 pm. Bar 4 pm-12:30 am. Ck-out 11 am. Coin lndry. Meeting rms. Business servs avail. In-rm modem link. Sundries. X-country ski 1 mi. Cr cds: D, DS, MC, V.

★ **SUPER 8 MOTEL.** *2019 E Main St (56007). 507/377-0591; res 800/800-8000. www.super8.com.* 60 rms, 3 story. No elvtr. S $38; D $52; each addl $4. Crib $2. Pet accepted. TV; cable, VCR avail (movies $5). Complimentary coffee in lobby Mon-Fri. Restaurants adj. Ck-out 11 am. Business servs avail. Sundries. X-country ski 1 mi. Snowmobile trail adj. Cr cds: A, MC, V.

Alexandria

(E-2) *See also Glenwood, Sauk Centre*

Settled 1866 **Pop** 7,838 **Elev** 1,400 ft **Area code** 320 **Zip** 56308
Information Chamber of Commerce, 206 Broadway; 320/763-3161 or 800/245-ALEX
Web www.alexandriamn.org

Easy access to hundreds of fish-filled lakes attracts a steady stream of tourists. The city has a manufacturing and trade industry base. Red River fur traders first explored this area, followed by settlers, one of whom gave the city his name.

What to See and Do

Lake Carlos State Park. A 1,261-acre park. Swimming, fishing, boat ramp; hiking, bridle trails, ski trails, snowmobiling, picnicking, camping. Sandy shoreline. Standard fees. 8 mi N on MN 29, then 2 mi W on County 38. Phone 320/852-7200.

Runestone Museum. Runic inscriptions on graywacke stone carry a 1362 date, supporting belief of exploration of North America long before Columbus discovered the New World. Found at the roots of a tree in 1898, authenticity of the stone has been the subject of great controversy. Also restored log cabins, farm artifacts, horse-drawn machinery, schoolhouse. (Mon-Sat, also Sun afternoons) Children with adult only. 206 Broadway. Phone 320/763-3160. ¢¢

Special Events

Ole Oppe Fest. Dunk tanks, face painting, museum tours, street dance. Late May.

Vikingland Drum Corps Classic. National drum and bugle corps perform in state's only field show competition. Last Sat June.

Vikingland Band Festival. Twenty select high school marching bands compete in state's largest summer marching band competition. Last Sun June.

Motels/Motor Lodges

★★ **AMERICINN MOTEL.** *4520 S Hwy 29 (56308). 320/763-6808; fax 320/763-6808; toll-free 800/634-3444. www.americinn.com.* 53 rms, 2 story. Memorial Day-Labor Day: S $64.90-$120.90; D $64.90-$140.90; each addl $6; under 12 free; lower rates rest of yr. Crib free. Pet accepted. TV; cable (premium). Indoor pool; whirlpool. Complimentary continental bkfst. Restaurant adj 6 am-11 pm. Ck-out 11 am. Business servs avail. Health club privileges. Cr cds: A, C, D, DS, MC, V.

[icons]

★★ **BEST INN.** *507 W 50th Ave (56308). 320/762-5161; fax 320/762-5337; res 800/237-1234. www.bestinn.com.* 46 rms, 2 story. May-Aug: S $45.90-$66.90; D $56.90-$66.90; each addl $5; under 18 free; lower rates rest of yr. Crib avail. TV; cable (premium). Indoor pool; whirlpool. Complimentary continental bkfst. Restaurant nearby. Ck-out 11 am. Meeting rms. Business servs avail. In-rm modem link. Downhill ski 10 mi; x-country ski 1 mi. Cr cds: A, C, D, DS, ER, MC, V.

[icons]

★ **DAYS INN.** *4810 MN 29 S (56308). 320/762-1171; fax 320/762-1171; res 800/329-7466. www.daysinn.com.* 59 rms, 2 story. S $44-$54; D $54-$64; each addl $6; under 18 free. Crib free. TV; cable (premium). Complimentary continental bkfst. Restaurant adj open 24 hrs. Ck-out 11 am. Business servs avail. Sundries. Cr cds: A, C, D, DS, MC, V.

[icons]

★★ **HOLIDAY INN.** *5637 MN 29 S (56308). 320/763-6577; fax 320/762-*2092; toll-free 800/465-4329. www.holiday-inn.com.* 149 rms, 2 story. S, D $59-$109; under 18 free. Crib free. Pet accepted. TV; cable (premium), VCR (movies). Indoor pool; wading pool, whirlpool. Restaurant 6 am-10 pm; from 7 am Mon, Sat, Sun. Bar 4 pm-1 am; entertainment Mon-Sat. Ck-out noon. Free lndry. Meeting rms. Business servs avail. In-rm modem link. Valet serv. Sundries. Exercise equipt; sauna. Rec rm. Cr cds: A, C, D, DS, MC, V.

[icons]

★ **SUPER 8.** *4620 MN 29 S (56308). 320/763-6552; fax 320/762-6591; res 800/800-8000. www.super8.com.* 57 rms, 2 story. May-Sept: S $40-$45; D $47-$56; under 12 free; lower rates rest of yr. Crib $2. Pet accepted. TV; cable (premium). Complimentary continental bkfst. Restaurant nearby. Ck-out 11 am. Business servs avail. Game rm. Cr cds: A, C, D, DS, MC, V.

[icons]

Resort

★★★ **ARROWWOOD, A RADISSON RESORT.** *2100 Arrowwood Ln (56308). 320/762-1124; fax 320/762-0133; res 800/333-3333. www.radisson.com.* 200 rms, 5 story, 18 suites. June-Sept: S, D $119-$179; each addl $15; suites $209-$269; family, wkly rates; golf plans; lower rates rest of yr. Pet accepted, some restrictions; $50 deposit. TV; cable (premium), VCR avail (movies). 2 pools, 1 indoor; whirlpool, poolside serv. Playground. Supervised children's activities (June-Sept). Dining rm 6:30 am-10 pm. Box lunches. Snack bar. Bars 11-1 am. Ck-out noon, ck-in after 4 pm. Convention facilities. Business servs avail. In-rm modem link. Free airport, bus depot transportation. Indoor/outdoor tennis. 18-hole golf, greens fee $25. Exercise equipt; sauna. Private beach. Waterskiing. Jet skis. Boats, launching ramp, dockage, motors, rowboats, canoes, pontoon boats, sailboats, paddleboats. Downhill ski 20 mi; x-country ski adj. Tobogganing, snowmobiles, sleighrides. Ice-skating. Bicycles. Hayrides. Nature trails. Soc dir. Rec rm. Game rm. Some refrigerators; microwaves avail.

Balconies. Picnic tables. Cr cds: A, MC, V.

Anoka

(F-4) *See also Minneapolis, St. Paul*

Settled 1844 **Pop** 17,192 **Elev** 870 ft **Area code** 763
Information Anoka Area Chamber of Commerce, 222 E Main St, Suite 108, 55303; 763/421-7130
Web www.anokaareachamber.com

Once rivaling Minneapolis as the metropolitan center of the state, Anoka continues as a thriving industrial city at the confluence of the Mississippi and Rum rivers. A city of parks and playgrounds, Anoka is minutes away from ten well-stocked lakes.

What to See and Do

Colonial Hall Museum. Built in 1904 as a home and medical office for two doctors. Now it preserves the history of the county. Photographs, artifacts. Tours (fee). (Tues-Fri, afternoons; first Sat of each month, mornings) 1900 3rd Ave S. Phone 763/421-0600. ¢¢

Father Hennepin Stone. Inscription reads "Father Louis Hennepin—1680"; possibly carved by the Franciscan explorer. Near mouth of Rum River.

Jonathan Emerson Monument. Old settler inscribed 2,500 words from the Bible and personal philosophy on monument, erected it, and died a yr later. City Cemetery.

Special Event

Anoka County Suburban Fair. NTPA Tractor/truck pull, PRCA rodeo, demolition derbies, free entertainment, beer garden. Exhibits and an "old farm place." Phone 763/427-4070. Early Aug.

Restaurants

★★ **SEASONS.** *MN 242 and Foley Blvd, Coon Rapids (55448). 763/755-4444.* Hrs: 11:30 am-2 pm, 5-9 pm; Sun brunch 10 am-1 pm. Res accepted. Continental menu. Bar. Lunch $4.25-$7.25, dinner $8.25-$19.95. Sun brunch $9.95. Children's menu. Specializes in steak, seafood, pasta. Overlooks golf course. Cr cds: A, DS, MC, V.

★★ **THE VINEYARD.** *1125 W Main St (55303). 763/427-0959.* Hrs: 11 am-10 pm; Sat from 4 pm; Sun from noon. Closed Thanksgiving, Dec 25. Bar. Lunch $4.95-$10.90, dinner $9.95-$16.95. Children's menu. Specializes in homemade soup, seafood, steak. Cr cds: A, DS, MC, V.

Austin

(H-4) *See also Albert Lea, Owatonna*

Founded 1856 **Pop** 21,907 **Elev** 1,198 ft **Area code** 507 **Zip** 55912
Information Convention & Visitors Bureau, 329 Main St, Suite 106L, PO Box 613; 507/437-4563 or 800/444-5713

Named for a pioneer settler, Austin became the county seat after two citizens stole the county records from another contender. The act aroused the voters, who cast their ballots for Austin. The Hormel Institute here, a unit of the Graduate School of the University of Minnesota, does research on fats and oils and their effect on heart disease. Austin's meat and food processing plants are an important industry; livestock, grain, and vegetables from a 100-mile radius are delivered here.

What to See and Do

Austin Fine Arts Center. Features local artists. (Fri-Sun) Oak Park Mall. Phone 507/433-8451. **FREE**

J. C. Hormel Nature Center. Located on the former estate of Jay Hormel, the center incl interpretive building (Mon-Sat, also Sun afternoons; closed hols); footpaths; woods, pond, streams, meadows; also x-country skiing in winter, canoeing in summer. (Daily) ¼ mi N off I-90, at 1304 NE 21st St. Phone 507/437-7519. **FREE**

Mower County Historical Center. Restored buildings incl original Hormel building, log cabin, church, depot, country school; also steam locomotive, firefighting equipt, and horse-drawn carriages; Native American artifacts; telephone museum; guide service (summer only). (June-Aug, daily; rest of yr, by appt) 12th St and 6th Ave SW, at County Fairgrounds. Phone 507/437-6082. **Donation**

Special Events

SpamTown USA Festival/Spam Jam. Phone 507/437-4561. First wkend July.

Mower County Fair. Fairgrounds, 12th St and 4th Ave SW. Mid-Aug.

National Barrow Show. Fairgrounds. Phone 507/437-5306. Second wk Sept.

Motel/Motor Lodge

★ ★ **HOLIDAY INN.** *1701 4th St NW (55912). 507/433-1000; fax 507/433-8749; toll-free 800/985-8850. www. holiday-inn.com.* 121 rms, 12 suites, 2 story. S $59-$79; D $69-$89; each addl $10; suites $88-$150; under 19 free. Crib avail. Pet accepted. TV; cable (premium). Indoor pool; wading pool, whirlpool, poolside serv. Complimentary coffee in lobby. Restaurant 6 am-10 pm. Bar 11-1 am; entertainment Mon-Sat. Ck-out 11 am. Coin lndry. Meeting rms. Business servs avail. In-rm modem link. Airport, railroad station transportation. Exercise equipt; sauna. Game rm. Refrigerator in suites. Cr cds: A, MC, V.

D 🐾 ≈ 🏋 🖎 🐾 SC

Baudette (B-3)

Pop 1,146 **Elev** 1,086 ft
Area code 218 **Zip** 56623
Information Lake of the Woods Area Tourism Bureau, PO Box 518; 218/634-1174 or 800/382-3474

Web www.lakeofthewoodsmn.com

On the Rainy River, Baudette is the gateway to the waters and thousands of islands of the Lake of the Woods area. Across the border from Ontario, it is an important trade and commerce center for a farm area producing seed potatoes, flax, alfalfa, clover, and small grain crops. It is also a 24-hour port of entry, with a toll-free bridge to Canada. (For Border Crossing Regulations, see MAKING THE MOST OF YOUR TRIP.)

What to See and Do

Lake of the Woods. This lake is partly in the US, partly in Canada. Noted for fishing, sandy beaches, and scenic beauty; more than 2,000 sq mi in area, with 14,000 charted islands and 65,000 mi of shoreline. Famous for walleyed pike. Maps of driving tours through lush forests and wildlife areas are avail from the Tourism Bureau. 12 mi N on MN 172. Also here is

> **Zippel Bay State Park.** A 2,946-acre park. Swimming, fishing, boating (ramps); hiking, snowmobiling, picnicking, camping. Beach area. Standard fees. 1 mi W on MN 11 to MN 172, 12 mi N to County 8, then 9 mi W. Phone 218/783-6252.

Lake of the Woods County Museum. Museum of local history. (May-Sept, Tues-Sat) 8th Ave SE. Phone 218/634-1200. **FREE**

Northwest Angle/Islands. A Minnesota peninsula connected to Canada and separated by Lake of the Woods. Fishing. Lodging.

Rainy River. Fishing, boating. Begins 70 mi E, flows NW into Lake of the Woods.

Red Lake Wildlife Management Area and Norris Camp. On 285,000 acres. Songbirds, bald eagles, moose, wolf, bear, grouse, deer, and waterfowl; hunting permitted in season; blueberry picking; camping (permit required). Norris Camp is a historic CCC camp from the 1930s. Phone 218/783-6861. **FREE**

Motel/Motor Lodge

★ **WALLEYE INN MOTEL.** *MN 11 W (56623). 218/634-1550; fax 218/634-1596; toll-free 888/634-5944.* 39 rms, 2 story. S $35; D $45.50-$52.90;

each addl $5; suites $59-$90; under 12 free. Crib $4. TV; cable (premium). Complimentary continental bkfst. Restaurant nearby. Ck-out 11 am. Business servs avail. Health club privileges. Microwaves avail. Cr cds: A, DS, MC, V.

D ⬛ 🐾

Cottage Colony

★ **SPORTSMAN'S LODGE.** *3244 Bur Oak Rd NW (56623). 218/634-1342; fax 218/634-9497; toll-free 800/862-8602.* 29 rms in 3-story lodge, 21 kit. cabins (1-3 bedrm). S $45-$49; D $65-$69; suites $75-$100; cabins for 2-10, $66-$199. TV; cable. Indoor pool; whirlpool. Dining rm 6-10 pm. Box lunches, snacks. Bar 8-1 am. Ck-out 11 am, ck-in 2 pm. Grocery 1 mi. Coin lndry 1 mi. Meeting rms. Business servs avail. Gift shop. Waterskiing. Boats; motors; boat dockage, charter fishing trips. X-country ski 4 mi. Snowmobile trails. Entertainment. Rec rm. Hunting in season. Freezers. Microwaves avail in cabins. Picnic tables, grill. Cr cds: A, DS, MC, V.

⛵ 🎣 🚤 🐾

Bemidji (C-3)

Settled 1894 **Pop** 11,245 **Elev** 1,350 ft
Area code 218
Information Chamber of Commerce, PO Box 850, 56619; 218/751-3541 or 800/458-2223, ext 100
Web www.visitbemidji.com

Northland vacations support this city in a lake and forest area at the foot of Lake Bemidji (beh-MID-jee). Logging and Native American trails, wooded shorelines, and scenic rivers are just a few minutes away. Bemidji started as a trading post, became a lumber boomtown, a dairy and farming center, and is now enjoying the bounty of a new cycle of forest harvests. Once strictly a summer vacation area, Bemidji is host to winter sports enthusiasts, spring anglers, fall hunters, and nature lovers.

What to See and Do

Bemidji State University. (1919) 5,400 students. Renowned for peat research, music programs, environmental studies, accounting, industrial technology. Guided tours. Overlooking Diamond Point and Lake Bemidji. Phone 218/755-2040.

Bemidji Tourist Information Center. Houses collection of Paul Bunyan tools and artifacts with amusing descriptions. Fireplace of the States has stones from every state (exc Alaska and Hawaii) and most Canadian provinces. (Memorial Day-Labor Day, daily; rest of yr, Mon-Fri) MN 197 (Paul Bunyan Dr). **FREE** Adj is

> **Paul Bunyan and "Babe."** Giant replicas of Paul Bunyan and "Babe," the Blue Ox; one of the most photographed statues in America.

Lake Bemidji State Park. A 1,688-acre park. Swimming, fishing; picnicking, hiking in a virgin pine forest. Boating (ramp, rentals); x-country skiing, camping, biking. Naturalist programs. Visitor center. Standard fees. 6 mi NE off US 71. Phone 218/755-3843.

Special Events

Paul Bunyan Playhouse. Downtown. Plays and musicals; professional casts. Wed-Sun. Res advised. Phone 218/751-7270. Mid-June-mid-Aug.

Beltrami County Fair. Agricultural exhibits, carnival rides, nightly entertainment. July or Aug.

Paul Bunyan Water Carnival. Water show, parade, fireworks. July 4 wkend.

Motels/Motor Lodges

★★ **AMERICINN.** *1200 Paul Bunyan Dr NW (56601). 218/751-3000; fax 218/751-3000; toll-free 800/634-3444. www.americinn.com.* 59 rms, 2 story. June-Sept: S $65-$111, D $71-$125; each addl $6; under 12 free; ski plan; lower rates rest of yr. Crib free. TV; cable (premium). Indoor pool; whirlpool. Complimentary continental bkfst. Restaurant adj open 24 hrs. Ck-out 11 am. Coin lndry. In-rm modem link. Downhill/x-country ski 18 mi. Sauna. Some in-rm whirl-

Paul Bunyan and "Babe" statues, Bemidji

pools, refrigerators. Cr cds: A, D, DS, MC, V.

★★ **BEST WESTERN.** *2420 Paul Bunyan Dr NW (56601). 218/751-0390; fax 218/751-2887; res 800/780-7234. www.bestwestern.com.* 60 rms, 2 story. July-Labor Day: S $39-$55; D $40-$75; each addl $6; under 18 free; lower rates rest of year. Crib free. TV; cable, VCR avail (movies). Indoor pool; whirlpool. Complimentary continental bkfst. Restaurant adj open 24 hrs. Ck-out 11 am. Business servs avail. Health club privileges. Downhill ski 12 mi; x-country ski 4 mi. Cr cds: A, C, D, DS, MC, V.

★ **COMFORT INN.** *3500 Comfort Dr (56619). 218/751-7700; fax 218/751-8742; res 800/228-5150. www.comfort inn.com.* 61 rms, 2 story, 18 suites. Mid-June-early Sept: S $49; D $59; each addl $5; suites $59-$89; under 19 free; lower rates rest of yr. Crib free. TV; cable, VCR avail (movies). Indoor pool; whirlpool. Sauna. Complimentary continental bkfst. Restaurant adj 6 am-10 pm. Ck-out noon. Business servs avail. In-rm modem link. Valet serv. Sundries. Airport transportation. Refrigerator in suites; whirlpool in some suites. Cr cds: A, C, D, DS, MC, V.

★★★ **NORTHERN INN.** *3600 Moberg Dr NW (56601). 218/751-9500; fax 218/751-8122; toll-free 800/667-8485.* 123 rms, 2 story. Mid-May-Oct: S $59-$69; D $69-$79; each addl $10; suites $130; family rates; lower rates rest of yr. Crib free. Pet accepted. TV; cable, VCR avail (movies). Indoor pool; whirlpool, poolside serv. Restaurant 6 am-10 pm; Fri, Sat to 11 pm. Bar 3 pm-1 am; Sat, Sun from noon. Ck-out noon. Coin lndry. Meeting rms. Business servs avail. In-rm modem link. Valet serv. Sundries. Beauty shop. Free airport, bus depot transportation. Indoor putting green. Downhill ski 10 mi; x-country ski 4 mi. Exercise equipt; sauna. Game rm. Rec rm. Cr cds: A, D, DS, MC, V.

★ **SUPER 8 MOTEL.** *1815 Paul Bunyan Dr NW (56601). 218/751-8481; fax 218/751-8870; toll-free 800/800-8000. www.super8.com.* 101 rms, 2 story. S $38-$65; D $40-$59; suites $45-$70; each addl $5; under 12 free. Crib free. TV; cable (premium). Complimentary continental bkfst. Restaurant nearby. Ck-out 11 am. Business servs avail. Downhill ski 15 mi; x-country ski 3 blks. Whirlpool. Sauna. Cr cds: A, C, D, DS, MC, V.

Resort

★★★ RUTTGER'S BIRCHMONT

LODGE. *530 Birchmont Beach Rd NE (56601). 218/751-1630; fax 218/751-9519; toll-free 888/788-8437. www. ruttger.com.* 28 rms in 3-story lodge, 29 cottages (1-4 bedrm), 11 kits. Some A/C. No elvtr. Late June-mid-Aug: S $66-$69; D $78-$148; MAP avail; family rates; package plans; lower rates rest of yr. Fewer units late Sept-early May. Crib $4. TV; cable. 2 pools, 1 indoor; whirlpool, poolside serv. Free supervised children's activities (June-Labor Day). Dining rm (seasonal) 7:30-10:30 am, 11:30-2 pm, 5:30-8:30 pm. Bar (seasonal) noon-1 am. Ck-out 11:30 am, ck-in after 4:30 pm. Coin lndry. Grocery, package store 4 mi. Meeting rms. Business servs avail. In-rm modem link. Airport, bus depot transportation. Sports dir. Tennis. 18-hole golf privileges, greens fee $28. Private beach. Waterskiing instruction. Boats, motors, sailboats, boat launch, dockage. Downhill ski 15 mi; x-country ski on site. Indoor, outdoor games. Soc dir. Movies. Exercise rm; sauna. Some refrigerators; fireplace in most cabins. Screened porches. Cr cds: A, DS, MC, V.

Cottage Colony

★★★ FINN AND FEATHER

RESORT. *Rural Rte 3, Box 870 (56601). 218/335-6598; fax 218/335-6151; toll-free 800/776-3466. www. finn-n-feather.com.* 20 kit. cottages (1-4 bedrm). No A/C. Mid-June-Labor Day, wkly: $600-$1,400 for 2-6 persons; lower rates mid-May-mid-June, Labor Day-mid-Oct. Closed rest of yr. Crib avail. Heated pool; whirlpool. Box lunches, snacks. Ck-out 9 am, ck-in 4 pm. Coin lndry. Grocery, package store 1 mi. Tennis. 18-hole golf privileges. Private beach. Boats, motors, canoes, pontoon boat. Lawn games. Movies. Game rm. Rec rm. Some fireplaces. Many screened porches. Picnic tables, grills. Sand beach on Lake Andrusia. Cr cds: MC, V.

Bloomington

(F-4) *See also Minneapolis*

Pop 86,335 **Elev** 830 ft **Area code** 952
Information Bloomington Convention and Visitors Bureau, 7900 International Dr, Suite 990, 55425; 952/858-8500 or 800/346-4289
Web www.bloomingtonmn.org

Bloomington, located south of Minneapolis, is one of the state's largest cities.

What to See and Do

⭐ **Mall of America.** A retail/family entertainment complex with more than 500 stores and restaurants. Features Knott's Camp Snoopy, a seven-acre indoor theme park with rides and entertainment; LEGO Imagination Center with giant LEGO models and play areas; Golf Mountain miniature golf course; 14-screen movie complex; Under Water World, a walk-through aquarium. (Daily) Separate fees for activities. I-494 exit 24th Ave S, bounded by 81st St, Killebrew Dr, MN 77, and 24th Ave S. Phone 952/883-8800.

Minnesota Valley National Wildlife Refuge. One of the only urban wildlife refuges in the nation. A 34-mi corridor of marsh and forest that is home to coyotes, badgers, and bald eagles; the refuge offers mi of trails for hiking, biking, horseback riding, and skiing. (Daily) 3815 E 80th St. Phone 952/854-5900.

Minnesota Zoo. Simulated natural habitats house 450 species of animals and 2,000 varieties of plants. Incl Discovery Bay, IMAX theater, Minnesota tropics, Ocean and Discovery Trails sections; 1¼-mi monorail. (Daily; closed Dec 25) E on I-494, then S on MN 77 in Apple Valley. Phone 952/432-9000. ¢¢¢

Valleyfair. A 68-acre family amusement park bordering the Minnesota River. More than 50 rides and attractions, incl four roller coasters, three water rides, antique carousel, and special rides for children. Entertainment: IMAX Theater plus musical shows. (Memorial Day-Labor Day, daily; May and Sept, some wkends) 7 mi S on I-35 W, then 9 mi W on MN 101 in Shakopee. Phone 952/445-6500. ¢¢¢¢

Special Event

Renaissance Festival. Re-creation of 16th-century Renaissance village celebrating a harvest holiday. Entertainment, ethnic foods, 250 arts and crafts shops, games, equestrian events. Phone 952/445-7361. 7 wkends beginning mid-Aug. Phone 800/966-8215.

Motels/Motor Lodges

★★ **BAYMONT INN.** *7815 Nicollet Ave (55420). 612/881-7311; fax 612/881-0604; res 800-301-0200. www.baymontinn.com.* 190 rms, 2 story. S $55; D $63; under 18 free. No elvtr. Crib free. Pet accepted, some restrictions. TV; cable (premium). Complimentary continental bkfst. Restaurant nearby. Ck-out noon. Meeting rms. Business servs avail. In-rm modem link. Downhill ski 10 mi; x-country ski ½ mi. Cr cds: A, C, D, DS, MC, V.

⊡ ⚐ ⌦ ⊠ ⏁

★★ **BEST WESTERN THUNDER-BIRD HOTEL.** *2201 E 78th St (55425). 952/854-3411; fax 952/854-1183; toll-free 800/328-1931. www.thunderbirdhotel.com.* 263 rms, 2 story. S, D $97-$140; each addl $6; suites $135-$370; under 13 free. Crib free. Pet accepted. TV; cable. 2 pools, 1 indoor; whirlpool. Restaurant 6:30 am-10:30 pm. Rm serv to 11 am. Bar 5 pm-midnight; entertainment. Ck-out 11 am. Convention facilities. Business center. Valet serv. Sundries. Gift shop. Free airport transportation. Downhill ski 10 mi; x-country ski 1 mi. Exercise equipt; sauna. Game rm. Refrigerators, microwaves avail. Cr cds: A, C, D, DS, ER, JCB, MC, V.

⊡ ⚐ ⌦ ⌧ ⏁ ⏁ ⊠ ⏁ SC ⏁

★ **COMFORT INN.** *1321 E 78th St (55425). 952/854-3400; fax 952/854-2234; res 800/228-5150. www.comfort innmsp.com.* 272 rms, 4 suites, 5 story. S, D $79-129; each addl $7; suites $145; under 17 free. Crib free. TV; cable (premium). Indoor pool. Coffee in rms. Restaurant 6-11 am, 5-

10 pm; Sat 7 am-midnight; Sun 8 am-10 pm. Bar 11-1 am. Ck-out 11 am. Meeting rms. Business servs avail. Valet serv. Sundries. Free airport transportation. Downhill ski 10 mi; x-country ski 1 mi. Exercise equipt. Health club privileges. Cr cds: A, C, D, DS, ER, JCB, MC, V.

⊡ ⌦ ⌧ ⏁ ⌧ ⊠ ⏁ SC

★★ **COUNTRY INN & SUITES - BLOOMINGTON.** *2221 Killebrew Dr (55425). 612/854-5555; fax 952/854-5564; res 800/456-4000. www.country inns.com.* 234 rms, 6 story. S, D, suites $119-$169; each addl $10; under 19 free. Crib free. TV; cable (premium). Indoor pool; whirlpool. Complimentary continental bkfst. Restaurant adj 11 am-midnight. Ck-out noon. Meeting rms. Business servs avail. Free airport transportation. Downhill ski 14 mi; x-country 1 mi. Exercise equipt. Refrigerators; microwaves avail. Cr cds: A, C, D, DS, MC, V.

⊡ ⌦ ⌧ ⏁ ⊠ ⏁

★ **DAYS INN.** *1901 Killebrew Dr (55425). 952/854-8400; fax 952/854-3331; toll-free 800/329-7466. www. daysinn.com.* 207 rms, 2 story. May-Oct: S $110; D $120-$130; under 17 free; lower rates rest of yr. Crib avail. TV; cable (premium). Heated pool; whirlpool. Complimentary coffee in lobby. Restaurant nearby. Ck-out 11 am. Meeting rms. Free airport transportation. Downhill ski 10 mi; x-country 1 mi. Sauna. Game rm. Some balconies. Cr cds: A, C, D, DS, MC, V.

⊡ ⌦ ⌧ ⌧ ⊠ ⏁

★ **EXEL INN.** *2701 E 78th St (55425). 952/854-7200; fax 952/854-8652; res 800/367-3935. www.exelinns. com.* 204 rms, 2 story. S $50-$70; D $60-$75; whirlpool rms $85.99-$125.99; under 18 free. Crib free. TV; cable (premium), VCR avail. Complimentary continental bkfst. Restaurant nearby. Ck-out noon. Business servs avail. In-rm modem link. Sundries. Free airport transportation. Downhill ski 10 mi; x-country ski 2 mi. Exercise equipt. Microwaves avail. Cr cds: A, D, DS, MC, V.

⊡ ⌦ ⌧ ⊠ ⏁

★★ **FAIRFIELD INN.** *2401 E 80th St S (55425). 952/858-8475; res 800/228-2800. www.fairfieldinn.com.* 134 rms,

14 suites, 4 story. May-Oct: S, D $79-$140; under 18 free; lower rates rest of yr. Crib avail. Pet accepted. TV; cable (premium). Indoor pool; whirlpools. Complimentary continental bkfst. Restaurant adj 6 am-11 pm. Ck-out noon. Business servs avail. Downhill ski 15 mi; x-country ski 1 mi. Rec rm. Some refrigerators. Cr cds: A, MC, V.

★★ **HAMPTON INN.** 7740 Flying Cloud Dr, Eden Prairie (55344). 952/942-9000; fax 952/942-0725; res 800/426-7866. www.hamptoninn.com. 122 rms, 3 story. S $69-$79; D $75-$79; under 18 free. Crib free. TV; cable (premium). Complimentary continental bkfst. Coffee in rms. Restaurant nearby. Ck-out noon. Meeting rms. Business servs avail. In-rm modem link. Downhill ski 6 mi; x-country ski 1 mi. Cr cds: A, C, D, DS, MC, V.

★★ **HAMPTON INN.** 4201 W 80th St (55437). 952/835-6643; fax 952/835-7217; res 800/426-7866. www.hampton-inn.com. 135 rms, 4 story. S $84-$99; D $94-$109; each addl $10; suites $89-$119; under 18 free. Crib free. TV; cable (premium). Complimentary continental bkfst. Coffee in rms. Restaurant adj open 24 hrs. Ck-out noon. Meeting rms. Business servs avail. In-rm modem link. Valet serv. Free airport transportation. Downhill/x-country ski 2 mi. Health club privileges. Private balconies. Cr cds: A, C, D, DS, ER, JCB, MC, V.

★★ **HAWTHORN SUITES.** 3400 Edinborough Way, Edina (55435). 952/893-9300; fax 952/893-9885; res 800/983-9300. 140 kit. suites, 7 story. S, D $135-$145; under 18 free; wkend rates. Crib free. Pet accepted. TV; cable (premium), VCR (movies $6). Indoor pool. Playground. Complimentary full bkfst, coffee in rms. Restaurant nearby. No rm serv. Ck-out noon. Coin lndry. Meeting rms. Business servs avail. In-rm modem link. Sundries. Airport transportation. Downhill ski 7 mi; x-country ski 1 mi. Health club privileges. Microwaves. Cr cds: A, C, D, DS, MC, V.

★★ **HOLIDAY INN.** 814 E 79th St (55420). 952/854-5558; fax 952/854-4623; res 800/465-4329. www.holiday-inn.com. 142 rms, 6 suites, 4 story. S $74-$90; D $79-$95; each addl $10; suites $90; under 18 free. Crib free. TV; cable (premium). Complimentary continental bkfst. Restaurant open 24 hrs. Ck-out noon. Business servs avail. In-rm modem link. Free airport transportation. Downhill ski 15 mi; x-country ski 2 mi. Refrigerator in suites. Cr cds: A, C, D, DS, JCB, MC, V.

★★ **HOLIDAY INN.** 1201 W 94th St (55431). 952/884-8211; fax 952/881-5574; res 800/465-4329. www.holiday-inn.com. 168 rms, 2 suites, 4 story. S, D $89-$109; under 19 free. Crib avail. TV; cable. Indoor pool; whirlpool. Coffee in rms. Restaurant 6:30 am-10 pm. Bar. Ck-out 11 am. Coin lndry. Meeting rms. Business center. In-rm modem link. Sundries. Free airport transportation. Downhill ski 6 mi. Exercise equipt; sauna. Game rm. Refrigerators avail. Cr cds: A, D, DS, MC, V.

★★ **HOLIDAY INN SELECT.** 3 Appletree Sq (55425). 952/854-9000; fax 952/876-8700; res 800/465-4329. www.holiday-inn.com. 430 rms, 130 suites, 13 story. S, D $119-$129; each addl $10; suites $103-$250; under 19 free; wkend rates. Crib free. TV; cable (premium), VCR avail. Indoor pool; whirlpool, poolside serv. Restaurant 6 am-11 pm. Bar 11-1 am. Ck-out noon. Convention facilities. Business center. In-rm modem link. Free covered parking. Free airport transportation. Downhill/x-country ski 10 mi. Exercise rm; sauna. Massage. Some refrigerators. Cr cds: A, C, D, DS, JCB, MC, V.

★★ **RAMADA INN MINNEAPOLIS AIRPORT.** 2500 E 79th St (55425). 952/854-1771; fax 952/854-5898; res 800/228-2828. www.ramada.com. 250 rms, 2-4 story. S, D $110-$120; suites $140-$160; each addl $10; under 18 free. Crib free. TV; cable (premium), VCR avail. Indoor pool; whirlpool. Restaurant 6 am-10:30 pm; Sat, Sun from 7 am. Bar 11:30-1 am. Ck-out noon. Meeting rms. Business servs avail. Valet serv. Sundries. Free airport transportation. Downhill ski 10 mi; x-country ski 2 mi. Exercise equipt. Microwaves avail. Near Mall of America. Cr cds: A, D, DS, JCB, MC, V.

D ⬛⬛⬛⬛⬛⬛⬛

★★ **RAMADA LIMITED.** *250 N River Ridge Cir, Burnsville (55337).* 952/890-9550; fax 952/890-5161; res 800/228-2828. www.ramada.com. 94 rms, 2 story, 30 suites. May-Oct: S $69; D $79; each addl $8; suites $99-$280; under 18 free; lower rates rest of yr. TV; cable (premium), VCR avail (movies). Indoor/outdoor pool; whirlpool. Bar. Ck-out noon. Meeting rms. Business servs avail. Balconies. Suites decorated in different themes. Cr cds: A, D, DS, MC, V.

D ⬛⬛⬛⬛

★ **SELECT INN.** *7851 Normandale Blvd (55435).* 952/835-7400; fax 952/835-4124; toll-free 800/641-1000. www.selectinn.com. 148 rms, 2 story. S $65-$70; D $73-$80; each addl $10; under 13 free. Crib $3. Pet accepted; $25. TV; cable. Indoor pool. Complimentary continental bkfst. Restaurant nearby. Ck-out 11 am. Coin lndry. Meeting rms. Business servs avail. Free airport transportation. Downhill ski 5 mi. Exercise equipt; weights, treadmill. Cr cds: A, D, DS, MC.

D ⬛⬛⬛⬛⬛⬛⬛⬛

★ **SUPER 8.** *11500 W 78th St, Eden Prairie (55344).* 952/829-0888; fax 952/829-0854; res 800/800-8000. www.super8.com. 61 rms, 3 story. No elvtr. S $50.88; D $60.88; each addl $6; under 12 free. Crib free. TV; cable (premium). Complimentary continental bkfst. Ck-out 11 am. Coin lndry. Business servs avail. X-country ski. Cr cds: A, D, DS, MC, V.

D ⬛⬛⬛⬛⬛⬛⬛

★★ **WYNDHAM GARDEN HOTEL.** *4460 W 78th St Cir (55435).* 952/831-3131; fax 952/831-6372; res 800/822-4200. www.wyndham.com. 209 rms, 13 suites, 8 story. S $119-$129; D $129-$139; each addl $10; suites $99-$145; under 19 free; wkend rates. Crib free. TV; cable (premium). Indoor pool; whirlpool. Coffee in rms. Restaurant 7 am-10 pm. Rm serv from 5 pm. Bar. Ck-out noon. Meeting rms. Business servs avail. In-rm modem link. Valet serv. Sundries.

Free airport transportation. Exercise equipt. Downhill/x-country ski 2 mi. Wet bar in suites. Cr cds: A, C, D, DS, ER, JCB, MC, V.

D ⬛⬛⬛⬛⬛⬛⬛⬛ SC

Hotels

★★ **DOUBLETREE MINNEAPOLIS AIRPORT AT THE MALL.** *7901 24th Ave S (55425).* 952/854-2244; fax 952/854-4737; res 800/222-8733. www.doubletree.com. 321 rms, 15 story. S $89-$169; D $99-$179; each addl $20; suites $225-$400; wkend rates. TV; cable (premium), VCR. Indoor pool; whirlpool, poolside serv. Restaurant 6 am-10 pm. Rm serv 24 hrs. Bar from 11 am. Ck-out noon. Business center. In-rm modem link. Gift shop. Free airport transportation. Exercise equipt; sauna. Some private patios, balconies. Luxury level. Cr cds: A, C, D, DS, JCB, MC, V.

D ⬛⬛⬛⬛⬛⬛⬛⬛⬛

★★★ **HILTON MINNEAPOLIS/ST. PAUL AIRPORT.** *3800 E 80th St (55425).* 952/854-2100; fax 952/854-8002. www.hilton.com. 300 rms, 15 story. S, D $150-$225; each addl $20; under 17 free. Crib avail. Indoor pool. TV; cable (premium), VCR avail. Complimentary coffee, newspaper in rms. Restaurant 6 am-10 pm. Ck-out noon. Meeting rms. Business center. Gift shop. Exercise rm. Some refrigerators, minibars. Cr cds: A, C, D, DS, MC, V.

⬛⬛⬛⬛⬛

★★★ **MARRIOTT MINNEAPOLIS AIRPORT.** *2020 E 79th St (55425).* 952/854-7441; fax 952/854-7671; res 800/228-9290. www.marriott.com. 473 rms, 12 suites, 2-5 story. S $69-$175; D $69-$195; under 18 free; wkend rates. Crib free. TV; cable (premium), VCR. Indoor pool; whirlpool. Restaurant 6 am-10 pm; Sat, Sun 7 am-11 pm. Bar 11-1 am. Ck-out noon. Meeting rms. Business center. In-rm modem link. Gift shop. Free airport transportation. Exercise equipt. Game rm. Luxury level. Cr cds: A, DS, MC, V.

D ⬛⬛⬛⬛⬛⬛

★★ **PARK INN SUITES INTERNATIONAL.** *7770 Johnson Ave S (55435).* 952/893-9999; toll-free 800/670-7275. www.parkinnbloomington.com. 163 rms, 6 story. S, D $74-$99; each addl

$10; under 16 free. Crib free. TV; cable. Pool. Complimentary bkfst buffet. Restaurant adj. Ck-out noon. Meeting rms. Business servs avail. In-rm modem link. Airport transportation. Downhill/x-country ski 1 mi. Health club privileges. Refrigerators. Cr cds: A, D, DS, MC, V.

🄳 ⊱ ⊷ ⊠ ⋀

★★★ **RADISSON HOTEL SOUTH & PLAZA TOWER.** *7800 Normandale Blvd (55439). 952/835-7800; fax 952/893-8419; toll-free 800/333-3333. www.radisson.com/minneapolismn_south.* 565 rms, 22 story. S $149; D $159; each addl $15; suites $250-$450; under 18 free; wkend rates. Crib free. TV; VCR avail. Indoor pool; whirlpool. Coffee in rms. Restaurant 6:30 am-10 pm. Bar 11-1 am. Ck-out noon. Convention facilities. Business servs avail. In-rm modem link. Airport transportation avail. Downhill/x-country ski 2 mi. Exercise equipt; sauna. Cr cds: A, C, D, DS, ER, JCB, MC, V.

🄳 ⊷ 𐦂 ⊠ ⋀ SC

★★★ **SOFITEL.** *5601 W 78th St (55439). 952/835-1900; fax 952/835-2696; res 800/763-4835. www.sofitel.com.* 282 rms, 6 story. S $149-$167; D $164-$181; each addl $15; suites $185-$275; wkend rates. Crib free. TV; cable (premium), VCR avail. Indoor pool. Restaurants 6:30-1 am (see also LA FOUGASSE, Unrated Dining). Bars 11-1 am; Sun 10 am-midnight. Ck-out noon. Convention facilties. Business center. In-rm modem link. Concierge. Valet parking. Airport transportation. Downhill/x-country ski 1 mi. Exercise equipt. Massage. Cr cds: A, C, D, MC, V.

🄳 ⊷ ⚓ 𐦂 𐦂 ⊠ ⋀ 𐦂

All Suites

★ **CLARION HOTEL.** *8151 Bridge Rd (55437). 952/830-1300; fax 952/830-1535; toll-free 800/328-7947. www.thebloomingtonhotel.com.* 252 rms, 18 story. S $59-$119; D $69-$129; under 16 free; wkend rates. Crib free. Pet accepted. TV. Indoor pool; whirlpool. Restaurant 6 am-1:30 pm, 5:30-9:30 pm; wkend hrs vary. Bar. Ck-out 11 am. Convention facilities. Business servs avail. In-rm modem link. Free

airport transportation. Downhill ski 5 mi; x-country ski 1 mi. Sauna. Health club privileges. Game rm. Balconies. Cr cds: A, C, D, DS, JCB, MC, V.

🄳 ⚓ ⊱ ⊠ ✈ ⋀ 𐦂 SC

★★ **EMBASSY SUITES.** *7901 34th Ave S (55425). 952/854-1000; fax 952/854-6557; res 800/362-2779. www.embassysuites.com.* 310 rms, 10 story. S, D $149-$159; each addl $10; under 18 free. Crib free. TV; cable (premium). Indoor pool; whirlpool. Complimentary full bkfst. Restaurant 11 am-10 pm. Bar to 1 am. Ck-out noon. Meeting rms. Business center. In-rm modem link. Gift shop. Free airport transportation. Downhill ski 15 mi; x-country ski 2 mi. Exercise equipt; sauna. Microwaves. Private balconies. All rms open to courtyard atrium. Cr cds: A, C, MC, V.

🄳 ⚓ 𐦂 ⊱ ⊠ 𐦂 ✈ ⋀ 𐦂 𐦂

★★ **EMBASSY SUITES BLOOM-INGTON.** *2800 W 80th St (55431). 952/884-4811; fax 952/884-8137; toll-free 800/362-2779. www.embassybloomington.com.* 219 rms, 8 story. S $139-$189; D $149-$199; each addl $10; under 12 free. Crib free. TV; cable (premium). Indoor pool; whirlpool. Restaurant 11:30 am-10 pm. Bar to 1 am. Ck-out noon. Coin lndry. Meeting rms. Business servs avail. In-rm modem link. Free airport transportation. Downhill ski 8 mi; x-country ski 1 mi. Exercise equipt; sauna, steam rm. Game rm. Refrigerators, microwaves. Private patios, balconies. Cr cds: A, C, D, DS, JCB, MC, V.

🄳 ⊱ ⊠ 𐦂 ✈ ⋀ 𐦂

Extended Stay

★★ **RESIDENCE INN BY MAR-RIOTT.** *7780 Flying Cloud Dr, Eden Prairie (55344). 952/829-0033; fax 952/829-1935; res 800/331-3131. www.residenceinn.com.* 126 kit. suites, 1-2 story. S, D $129-$195; under 18 free. Pet accepted, some restrictions; $50. TV; cable (premium), VCR (movies $3.50). Heated pool; whirlpool. Complimentary bkfst buffet. Ck-out noon. Coin lndry. Meeting rms. Business servs avail. In-rm modem link. Valet serv. Airport transportation. Downhill ski 10 mi; x-country ski 1 mi. Exercise equipt. Health club privileges. Refrigerators. Private patios, balconies. Cr cds: A, D, DS, MC, V.

D ⛵ 🐕 ➳ 🏋 🔻 🔥

Restaurants

★★ **ASIA GRILLE.** *549 Prairie Center Dr, Eden Prairie (55344). 952/944-4095.* Hrs: 11 am-10 pm; Fri, Sat to 11 pm. Closed hols. Asian menu. Bar. Lunch $6.95-$9.95, dinner $6.95-$14.95. Specialties: spit-roasted garlic chicken, Asian pork with mushrooms. Contemporary decor. Cr cds: A, MC, V.

D

★★★ **CIAO BELLA.** *3501 Minnesota Dr (55435). 952/841-1000.* Italian menu. Menu changes seasonally. Hrs: 11 am-10 pm; Fri to 11 pm; Sun 4-9 pm. Closed hols. Res accepted. Wine, beer. Lunch $ Cr cds: A, DS, MC, V.

D ⊒

★ **DAVID FONG'S.** *9329 Lyndale Ave S (55420). 952/888-9294. www.david fongs.com.* Hrs: 11 am-9 pm; Thurs-Sat to 10 pm. Closed Sun; hols. Res accepted. Chinese menu. Bar to 1 am. Lunch, dinner $10.75-$21.95. Children's menu. Asian decor. Cr cds: A, D, MC, V.

D ⊒

★★★ **KINCAID'S.** *8400 Normandale Lake Blvd (55437). 952/921-2255.* Classic steakhouse menu. Specialties: Copper River king salmon, handmade small batch Maytag bleu cheese, fresh tropical Pacific game fish, rosemary-crusted lamb sirloin. Own bread. Hrs: 11 am-2:30 pm, 5-10 pm, Fri to 11 pm; Sat 4:30-11 pm; Sun 10 am-2 pm (brunch), 5-9 pm. Bar. Extensive wine list. Res accepted. Live band New Year's Eve. Patio dining. Cr cds: A, D, DS, MC, V.

D

★★ **LEEANN CHIN.** *14023 Aladrich Ave S, Burnsville (55337). 952/898-3303.* Hrs: 11:30 am-10 pm; Fri, Sat to 11 pm; Sun, Mon to 9 pm. Closed Memorial Day, Thanksgiving, Dec 25. Res accepted. Chinese menu. Bar. Lunch $5-$7, dinner $7-$12. Specialties: Asian tacos, soy-garlic rotisserie chicken. Own noodles. Outdoor dining. Casual, Asian decor. Cr cds: A, DS, MC, V.

D

★ **TEJAS.** *3910 W 50th St (55424). 952/926-0800. www.tejasrestaurant. com.* Hrs: 11:30 am-10 pm; Fri, Sat to 10:30 pm; Sun from 11 am. Res accepted. Southwestern menu. Wine, beer. A la carte entrees: lunch $5.25-$8.50, dinner $7-$17. Specialties: smoked chicken nachos, braised lamb shank. Patio dining in summer. Totally nonsmoking. Cr cds: A, D, MC, V.

D ⊒

Unrated Dining Spots

DA AFGHAN. *929 W 80th St (55420). 952/888-5824.* Hrs: 4:30-9:30 pm; Thurs, Fri 11 am-1:30 pm, 4:30-9:30 pm; Sat 4-9:30 pm; Sun 4-9 pm. Closed July 4. Res accepted. Middle Eastern, Greek menu. Wine, beer. Lunch $4.95-$9.95, dinner $8.95-$16. Children's menu. Specializes in lamb, chicken, vegetarian dishes. Parking. Cr cds: A, MC, V.

D

LA FOUGASSE. *5601 W 78th St (55439). 952/835-1900. www.sofitel. com.* Hrs: 11 am-midnight; Fri-Sat to 1 am; Sun 10:30 am-midnight; Sun brunch to 2:30 pm. French menu. Bar to 1 am. Lunch, dinner $5.75-$11.50. Sun brunch $8.50. Specializes in soup, seasonal French dishes. Valet parking. Outdoor dining. Cr cds: A, D, DS, MC, V.

D ⊒

PLANET HOLLYWOOD. *402 South Ave (55425). 952/854-7827. www. planethollywood.com.* Hrs: 11-1 am; Sun to midnight. Closed Dec 25. Bar. Lunch, dinner $6.50-$17.95. Specialties: chicken crunch, fajitas. Children's menu. Authentic Hollywood memorabilia displayed. Gift shop. Cr cds: A, D, DS, MC, V.

D ⊒

RAINFOREST CAFE. *102 South Ave (Mall of America) (55425). 952/854-7500. www.rainforestcafe.com.* Hrs: 11 am-10 pm; Sat 11 am-11 pm; Sun to 9 pm. Closed Thanksgiving, Dec 25. Bar. Lunch, dinner $8.95-$15.95. Children's menu. Specialties: rasta pasta, pita quesadillas. Rainforest atmosphere with flashing "lightning", roaring thunder. Cr cds: A, DS, MC, V.

D

Blue Earth

(H-3) *See also Albert Lea, Fairmont*

Pop 3,745 **Elev** 1,093 ft
Area code 507 **Zip** 56013
Information Chamber of Commerce, 119 N Main, Suites 1 and 2; 507/526-2916
Web www.chamber.blue-earth.mn.us

The city gets its name from the Blue Earth River, which circles the town. The river was given the Native American name "Mahkota" (meaning blue earth) for a blue-black clay found in the high river banks. The town is the birthplace of the ice cream sandwich, and a 55½ foot statue of the Jolly Green Giant stands in Green Giant Park.

What to See and Do

Faribault County Historical Society. (Wakefield House) Maintained as a pioneer home with furnishings depicting life between 1875-1900 (Tues-Sat afternoons; also by appt). Also 1870 rural school, an original log house, an Episcopal Church (1872), and the Etta C. Ross Museum (limited hrs). 405 E 6th St. Phone 507/526-5421. **FREE**

The Woodland School and Krosch Log House. The Woodland School (ca 1870) is furnished as were one-rm schools in the early 20th century. The Krosch Log House (ca 1860) was once home to a family of 11 children. Inquire for tours. Located at Faribault County Fairgrounds, N Main St, jct I-90 and US 169. Phone 507/526-5421.

Special Events

Citywide Garage Sales. Phone 507/526-2916. First Sat May and last Sat Sept.

Faribault County Fair. Fairgrounds. Carnival, 4-H exhibits, entertainment. Phone 507/854-3374. Fourth wk July.

Upper Midwest Woodcarvers and Quilters Expo. Phone 507/526-2916. Last full wkend Aug.

Motel/Motor Lodge

★ **SUPER 8 MOTEL.** *1420 Giant Dr (56013). 507/526-7376; fax 507/526-2246; toll-free 800/800-8000. www. super8.com.* 42 rms. S $59.98; D $60.98; each addl $6; under 12 free. Crib. TV; cable (premium), VCR avail. Restaurant adj 6 am-10 pm. Ck-out 11 am. Meeting rms. Continental breakfast. Business servs avail. Gift shop. Whirlpool. Cr cds: A, C, D, DS, MC, V.

Ⓓ ⊠ 🐾 SC

Brainerd

(E-3) *See also Aitkin, Deerwood, Little Falls, Onamia*

Founded 1870 **Pop** 12,353 **Elev** 1,231 ft **Area code** 218 **Zip** 56401
Information Brainerd Lakes Area Chamber of Commerce, 124 N 6th St, PO Box 356; 218/829-2838 or 800/450-2838
Web www.brainerd.com

Brainerd calls itself the "hometown of Paul Bunyan" and is the center of lore and legend about the giant lumberjack and his blue ox, Babe. On the Mississippi River at the geographical center of the state, the city was once part of a dense forest used by the Chippewa as a hunting ground and blueberry field. Created by the Northern Pacific Railroad, Brainerd was named for the wife of a railroad official. There are 465 pine-studded, sandy-bottomed lakes within a 25-mile radius and over 180 lodging choices. Golfing, fishing, canoeing, swimming, and water sports are available in the summer; skiing and snowmobiling in the winter.

What to See and Do

Crow Wing County Historical Society Museum. Restored sheriff's residence and remodeled jail features exhibits on domestic life, logging, mining, and the railroad. Research library. (Mon-Sat; closed hols) 320 Laurel St, adj to Courthouse. Phone 218/829-3268. ¢¢

Paul Bunyan Amusement Center. A 26-ft animated Paul Bunyan, 15-ft Babe, the blue ox; 27 rides in amusement park, lumbering exhibits, trained animals, picnic grounds. 21-hole miniature golf. (Memorial Day-Labor Day, daily) 1 mi W at jct MN 210, 371. Phone 218/829-6342. ¢¢¢

Paul Bunyan State Trail. Hundred-mi recreational trail for joggers, walkers, bikers, hikers, and snowmobilers (rentals avail). Trail passes by six communities, nine rivers, and 21 lakes.

Potlatch Paper Mill. Free one-hr tours (June-Labor Day, Mon-Fri), No open-toed shoes or children under eight. 1 mi N of East Brainerd Mall on Hwy 25. Phone 218/828-3200.

Recreational Areas. Swimming at hundreds of lakes in the area. Also boating, canoe routes, fishing, water-skiing; playground, golf courses, picnicking, hiking, biking, camping, snowmobile and ski trails. Phone Chamber of Commerce.

Special Events

Icefest. Ice sculptures, carving. Bands, races, dance, golf. Usually wkends Jan.

Crow Wing County Fair. Amusement rides; livestock; entertainment. Phone 218/824-1065 Five days early Aug.

Brainerd International Raceway. 7 mi N on MN 371. Motor racing events. Phone 810/249-5530. Mid-Apr-early Oct.

Motels/Motor Lodges

★★ **AMERICINN OF BAXTER.** 600 Dellwood Dr N, Baxter (56425). 218/829-3080; fax 218/829-9715; toll-free 800/634-3444. www.americinn.com. 59 rms, 2 story. Memorial Day-Oct: S $69-$72; D $79-$82; each addl $6; suites $78-$108; under 13 free; higher rates racing events; lower rates rest of yr. Crib free. TV; cable (premium). Indoor pool; whirlpool. Complimentary continental bkfst. Restaurant adj 10 am-10 pm. Ck-out noon. Coin lndry. Business servs avail. Sundries. Valet serv. Downhill ski 11 mi; x-country ski 1 mi. Health club privileges. Some refrigerators, in-rm whirlpools. Microwaves in suites. Cr cds: A, D, DS, MC, V.

D ⬛ ⬛ ⬛ ⬛

★★ **COUNTRY INN & SUITES - BAXTER.** 1220 Dellwood Dr N, Baxter (56401). 218/828-2161; fax 218/825-8419; res 8000/456-4000. www.country inns.com. 68 rms, 2 story. Mid-May-Sept: S, D $73-$83; suites $99-$119; under 18 free; higher rates auto races; lower rates rest of yr. Crib free. Pet accepted. TV; cable (premium), VCR avail (movies). Complimentary continental bkfst, coffee in rms. Ck-out noon. Meeting rms. Business servs avail. In-rm modem link. Valet serv. Coin lndry. X-country ski 1½ mi. Health club privileges. Indoor pool; whirlpool. Sauna. Refrigerators, microwaves; many wet bars; some in-rm whirlpools. Cr cds: A, C, D, DS, MC, V.

D ⬛ ⬛ ⬛ ⬛ ⬛ ⬛ ⬛

★ **DAYS INN.** 1630 Fairview Rd, Baxter (56425). 218/829-0391; fax 218/828-0749; res 800/329-7460. www.daysinn.com. 60 rms, 2 story. May-Sept: S $48-$57; D $54-$66; each addl $6; higher rates special events; lower rates rest of yr. Crib free. Pet accepted, some restrictions. TV; cable (premium). Complimentary continental bkfst. Restaurant adj open 24 hrs. Ck-out 11 am. Business servs avail. Downhill ski 15 mi; x-country ski 1 mi. Cr cds: A, MC, V.

D ⬛ ⬛ ⬛ ⬛ SC

★ **DAYS INN.** 45 N Smiley Rd, Nisswa (56468). 218/963-3500; fax 218/963-4936; toll-free 800/329-7466. www.daysinn.com. 43 rms, 2 story. Mid-May-Sept: S $51-$65; D $54-$73; each addl $5; suites $84-$95; under 12 free; higher rates special events; lower rates rest of yr. Crib free. Pet accepted; $25 deposit. TV; cable, VCR avail (movies). Indoor pool; whirlpool. Complimentary continental bkfst. Restaurant nearby. Ck-out 11 am. Coin lndry. Downhill ski 15 mi; x-country ski 3 blks. Cr cds: A, C, D, DS, MC, V.

D ⬛ ⬛ ⬛ ⬛ ⬛ SC

★★ **HOLIDAY INN.** 2115 S 6th St (56401). 218/829-1441; fax 218/829-1444; toll-free 888/562-2944. www.holiday-inn.com. 150 rms, 2 story. Mid-May-early Sept: S, D $65-$89; under 18 free; lower rates rest of yr.

Crib free. Pet accepted. TV; cable. Indoor pool; whirlpool, poolside serv. Restaurant 6 am-2 pm, 5-10 pm. Bar 3 pm-1 am. Ck-out noon. Coin lndry. Meeting rms. Business servs avail. In-rm modem link. Bellhops. Valet serv. Free airport, bus depot transportation. Tennis. Downhill ski 7 mi; x-country ski 3 mi. Sauna. Rec rm. Cr cds: A, C, D, DS, JCB, MC, V.

★★ **PAUL BUNYAN INN.** *1800 Fairview Rd N, Baxter (56425). 218/ 829-3571; fax 218/829-0506; toll-free 877/728-6926. www.paulbunyan center.com.* 34 rms, 8 suites. Memorial Day wkend-Labor Day: S $38-$60; D $60-$70; suites $85-$110; lower rates rest of yr. Crib $2. TV; cable (premium). Indoor pool; whirlpool. Complimentary continental bkfst. Coffee in rms. Restaurant adj open 24 hrs. Ck-out noon. Business servs avail. Sundries. Downhill ski 15 mi; x-country ski 1 mi. Sauna. Microwaves in suites. Picnic tables. Paul Bunyan Amusement Center adj. Cr cds: A, D, DS, MC, V.

★ **SUPER 8 MOTEL.** *501 Edgewood Dr, Baxter (56425). 218/828-4288; toll-free 800/800-8000. www.super8. com.* 63 rms, 2 story. S $48; D $56. Crib avail. TV; cable (premium). Continental bkfst. Restaurant nearby. Ck-out 11 am. Guest lndry. Business servs avail. Sundries. Downhill ski 13 mi; x-country ski 1 mi. Game rm. Cr cds: A, D, DS, MC, V.

Resorts

★★★ **BREEZY POINT RESORT TIME SHARES.** *9252 Breezy Point Dr, Breezy Point (56472). 218/562-7811; fax 218/562-4930; toll-free 800/432-3777. www.breezypointresort.com.* 37 units in lodge, 1-2 story; 149 motel rms, 2 story; 15 condominium buildings; 10 units in Fawcett House, 2 story; 7 homes. Memorial Day-Labor Day, MAP: $78.95-$145/person; EP: D $61.50-$725; family rates; package plans; lower rates rest of yr. Crib avail. TV; cable (premium), VCR avail. 5 pools, 2 indoor; whirlpools. Playground. Supervised children's activities (Memorial Day-Labor Day).

Dining rm 7 am-10:30 pm. Box lunches, snack bar. Bars 11:30-1 am. Ck-out noon, ck-in 5 pm. Package store. Meeting rms. Business servs avail. Tennis, pro. 36-hole golf, greens fee $28-$39. Private beach; water sports. Marina; boats, motors; guided tours. Downhill ski 20 mi; x-country ski on site. Exercise equipt; sauna. Ice-skating. Lawn games. Entertainment. Rec rm. Game rm. Refrigerator in motel rms. 2,600-ft airstrip. Cr cds: A, C, D, DS, MC, V.

★★★ **CRAGUN'S PINE BEACH LODGE AND CONFERENCE CENTER.** *11000 Cragun's Rd (56401). 218/829-3591; fax 218/829-9188; toll-free 800/272-4867.* 285 rms, 1-2 story. 50 kits., 105 lake view units. July-Aug and wkends: S, D $139-$187; family, wkly rates; package plans; MAP avail; lower rates rest of yr. Serv charge 15 percent. Crib avail. TV. 2 pools, 1 indoor; whirlpools. Free supervised children's activities (mid-June-mid-Sept); ages 4-12. Dining rm 6:30-8 pm. Restaurant 5:30-9 pm (summer). Snack bar. Barbecues. Bar 5 pm-1 am; entertainment. Ck-out noon, ck-in 5 pm. Coin lndry. Grocery 1 mi. Deli. Meeting rms. Business servs avail. Airport, bus depot transportation. 8 tennis courts, 2 indoor, 6 lighted. Golf privileges. Downhill ski 9 mi; x-country ski on site. Private beaches. Boats, motors, canoes, sailboats, pontoon boats. Lake excursions. Exercise equipt; saunas. Snowmobile trails. Many refrigerators, microwaves, fireplaces. Balconies. Cr cds: A, DS, MC, V.

★★★ **GRAND VIEW LODGE.** *23521 Nokomis Ave, Nisswa (56468). 218/963-2234; fax 218/963-0261; toll-free 800/432-3788. www.grandview lodge.com.* 12 rms in 1-2 story lodge, 65 cottages. Mid-June-mid-Aug, MAP: S, D $205-$290; AP, EP avail; family, wkly rates; lower rates rest of yr. Serv charge 15 percent, no tipping. Crib avail. TV; cable, VCR avail. Heated pool; whirlpool, poolside serv. Free supervised children's activities (Memorial Day-Labor Day, Mon-Sat); ages 3-12. Dining rm 7-10 am, noon-1 pm, 6-9 pm. Box lunches. Bar 11:30-1 am. Ck-out 12:30 pm, ck-in 4:30 pm. Meeting rms. Business servs avail. Airport, bus depot transportation. Sports dir. Tennis, pro. 54-hole golf course, driving range, putting green. X-country ski on site. Private beach. Waterskiing. Boats, motors, canoes, paddle boats, kayaks, pontoon boat. Water sports. Bicycles. Lawn games. Soc dir; entertainment Mon-Sat. Rec rm. Game rm. Refrigerators; some fireplaces. Some private patios, decks (all cottages). Overlooks Gull Lake. Garden walk. Cr cds: A, DS, MC, V.

⊡ ⚓ ✶ 🏊 ⛷ 🏃 ≈ ✈ ⊠ 🔥

★★★ **MADDEN'S ON GULL LAKE.**
11266 Pine Beach Peninsula (56401). 218/829-2811; fax 218/829-6583; toll-free 800/642-5363. www.maddens.com. 41 rms in 3-story lodge; 24 units in three 2-story villas; 16 units in three 2-story bay view buildings; 86 units in 74 cottages. July-late Aug, MAP: $102-$155/person; EP: S, D $81-$284; each addl $30; family, wkly rates; wkly and package plans off-season; lower rates mid-Apr-June, late Aug-mid-Oct. Closed rest of yr. Crib avail. TV; cable, VCR avail. 5 pools, 3 indoor; whirlpools, poolside serv. Playground. Supervised children's activities (July-mid-Aug); ages 4-12. Dining rm (July-Aug) 8 am-6 pm. Pizzeria 5:30 pm-1 am. Bar 11-1 am; entertainment. Ck-out 1 pm, ck-in 4:30 pm. Coin lndry. Convention facilities. Business servs avail. In-rm modem link. Grocery, package store. Shopping arcade. Airport, bus depot transportation. Tennis. 63-hole golf, greens fee $23, putting green, driving range. Exercise equipt; saunas. Private beaches. Boats; motors, sailboats, kayaks, water bikes, pontoon boats, rowboats, speedboats. Marina, dockage, launching facilities. Bicycles. Lawn games. Movies. Rec rm. Game rm. Sun deck. Refrigerators; many fireplaces. Private patios. On Gull Lake. 2,600-ft airstrip ½ mi. Cr cds: A, MC, V.

⊡ ⚓ ✶ 🏃 ⛷ ≈ 🏃 ✈ ⊠ 🔥

Restaurants

★ **BAR HARBOR SUPPER CLUB.**
8164 Interlaken Rd (56468). 218/963-2568. Hrs: noon-1 am; Sun from 10 am. Closed Dec 24-25. Bar. Lunch, dinner $8.95-$24.95. Children's menu. Specializes in charcoal-broiled steak, lobster, barbecued ribs. Enter-

tainment Wed-Sun. Outdoor dining. Overlooks Gull Lake; dockage. Family-owned. Cr cds: A, C, D, DS, MC, V.
⊡

★ **IVEN'S ON THE BAY.** *5195 MN 371 N (56401). 218/829-9872.* Hrs: 5-9 pm; Fri, Sat to 10 pm; Sun brunch 9:30 am-1:30 pm. Early bird dinner to 5:30 pm. Closed hols. Res accepted. Bar. Dinner $10.95-$19.75. Sun brunch $6.95-$10.95. Children's menu. Specializes in fresh seafood, pasta. Contemporary nautical decor; lakeside dining. Cr cds: A, MC, V.
⊡ ⊡

Cloquet

(D-5) *See also Duluth*

Pop 10,885 **Elev** 1,204 ft
Area code 218 **Zip** 55720

Motel/Motor Lodge

★★ **AMERICINN.** *111 Big Lake Rd (55720). 218/879-1231; fax 218/879-2237; toll-free 800/634-3444. www.americinn.com.* 51 rms, 2 story. S $55; D $64; each addl $4. Crib free. Pet accepted. TV; cable (premium). Indoor pool; whirlpool. Complimentary continental bkfst. Restaurant adj open 24 hrs. Ck-out 11 am. Meeting rm. Business servs avail. Sauna. Many refrigerators. Cr cds: A, D, DS, MC, V.
⊡ 🐾 ≈ ⊠ 🔥

Cook (C-5)

Pop 680 **Elev** 1,306 ft **Area code** 218
Zip 55723

Almost at the center of the "arrow-head country," Cook provides access to outdoor vacations, serves the logging industry, and is the western gateway to Superior National Forest (see). A Ranger District office of the forest is located here.

What to See and Do

Lakes. Fishing in this area is excellent for northern pike, panfish, crappie, and walleye.

Elbow Lake. Two thousand acres, 12 islands. 10 mi N on County 24. Phone 218/685-4711.

Lake Vermilion. 5½ mi NE via County 24 or County 78. (See TOWER) Phone 218/666-2627.

Pelican Lake. Fifty-four mi of shoreline, 50 islands, sandy beaches; fishing for northern pike and panfish. 21 mi N on US 53.

Motel/Motor Lodge

★ **NORTH COUNTRY INN.** *4483 US 53, Orr (55771). 218/757-3778. www.northcountryinn.com.* 12 rms. May-Sept: S,$44.90, D $52.90; each addl $6; under 12 free; lower rates rest of yr. Crib free. Pet accepted. TV; cable (premium), VCR avail. Complimentary coffee in lobby. Restaurant nearby. Ck-out 11 am. Picnic tables. Cr cds: A, DS, MC, V.

Cottage Colony

★★★ **LUDLOW ISLAND LODGE.** *8166 Ludlow Rd (55723). 218/666-5407; fax 218/666-2488; toll-free 877/583-5697. www.ludlowsresort.com.* 20 kit. cabins (1-5 bedrm), some 2 story. No A/C. Mid-June-Aug wkly: D $1,400-$2,000; each addl $30-$150; lower rates mid-May-mid-June, Sept-early Oct. Closed rest of yr. Crib avail. TV in some cabins; VCR avail (movies). Playground. Free supervised children's activities (June-Aug). Ck-out Sat 9 am, ck-in Sat 5 pm. Grocery. Coin lndry. Meeting rm. Business center. Airport transportation. Tennis. Golf privileges. Exercise equipt; sauna. Private beach; waterskiing (equipt). Boats, motors; rowboats; sailboats; kayaks, pontoon boats; paddleboats. Covered dockage; launching facilities. Fishing guides, fish clean and store. Racquetball. Rec rm. Lawn games. Exercise, nature trails. Fireplaces, microwaves; some whirlpools. Private decks; some screened porches. Grills. Secluded cabins on 11 acres. Cr cds: A, DS, MC, V.

Crane Lake

See also Cook

Pop 350 **Elev** 1160 ft **Area code** 218 **Zip** 55725

A natural entry to the Voyageur Country, Crane Lake, in Superior National Forest (see), is bounded on the north by the Canadian Quetico Provincial Park. (For Border Crossing Regulations, see MAKING THE MOST OF YOUR TRIP.)

Cottage Colony

★★★ **NELSON'S RESORT.** *7632 Nelson Rd (55725). 218/993-2295; fax 218/993-2242; toll-free 800/433-0743. www.nelsonsresort.com.* 28 cabins, 16 kits. No A/C. Early-June-early Sept, AP: D $124/person; MAP: D $109/person; family rates. Closed rest of yr. Crib avail. TV in lodge. Playground. Dining rm 6:30 am-9:30 pm. Box lunches. Bar 5 pm-1 am. Ck-out 11 am, ck-in 3 pm. Grocery. Coin lndry. Gift shop. Meeting rm. Business servs avail. Airport, bus depot transportation. Waterskiing. Boats, motors, canoes; launching ramp, docks, canoe trips. Nature trails; naturalist program. Guide serv. Bicycle rentals. Lawn games. Rec rm. Sauna. Fish clean and store facilities. Some microwaves, fireplaces. Spacious grounds; private sand beach. Cr cds: DS, MC, V.

Crookston

(C-1) *See also Thief River Falls*

Settled 1872 **Pop** 8,119 **Elev** 890 ft **Area code** 218 **Zip** 56716

Information Crookston Area Chamber of Commerce, PO Box 115, Suite 2; 218/281-4320 or 800/809-5997

Crookston is the major city of the broad and level Red River valley, carved by glacial Lake Agassiz. A branch of the University of Minnesota is located here.

What to See and Do

Central Park. Playground, picnicking, boat ramp, fishing, canoeing; tent, trailer and RV camping (Mid-May-Oct 1, fee), showers. Indoor swimming pool adj. Civic arena, roller skating (May-Oct), ice-skating (Nov-Mar), indoor tennis (Apr-Oct). N Ash St, on Red Lake River. Phone 218/281-1232. ¢¢¢

Polk County Historical Museum. Houses several rms depicting early days of America incl an original log cabin, one-rm schoolhouse, and a building with antique machinery. Also on the premises are a chapel and miniature train exhibit. (Mid-May-mid-Sept, daily; rest of yr, by appt) US 2 E. Phone 218/281-1038. **Donation**

Special Event

Ox Cart Days. Phone 800/809-5997. Third wkend Aug.

Motel/Motor Lodge

★★ **NORTHLAND INN.** *2200 University Ave (56716). 218/281-5210; fax 218/281-1019; toll-free 800/423-4541.* 74 rms, 2 story. S $49-$56; D $55-$62; each addl $6. Crib free. TV; cable (premium). Indoor pool; whirlpool. Restaurant 6:30 am-2 pm, 5-9:30 pm; Fri, Sat to 10 pm. Bar 4 pm-1 am. Ck-out noon. Meeting rms. Business servs avail. In-rm modem link. Sundries. Game rm. Cr cds: A, D, DS, MC, V.
D ⊠ ⊠ 🐾 SC

Crosslake

(D-3) *See also Aitkin, Brainerd, Pine River*

Pop 1,132 **Elev** 1,240 ft
Area code 218 **Zip** 56442

Cottage Colony

★★★ **BOYD LODGE.** *36653 Silver Peak Rd (56442). 218/543-4125; fax 218/543-6108; toll-free 800/450-2693. www.boydlodge.com.* 35 kit. cottages (1-5 bedrm), 1-3 story. Jan-Mar, May-Labor Day, wkly for 2-6: $700-$1,600; family rates; package plans; lower rates rest of yr. No maid serv. Crib free. TV; cable. 2 pools; wading pool, 2 whirlpools. 2 saunas. Playground. Free supervised children's activities (June-Aug). Snack bar. Ck-out 9:30 am, ck-in 3 pm. Coin lndry. Business servs avail. Grocery, package store 4 mi. Meeting rm. Free airport transportation. Tennis. 9-hole golf privileges, greens fee $29. Private beach; launching ramp. Boats, motors, canoes, pontoon boat, water bikes avail. X-country ski on site. Snowmobile trails. Lawn games. Soc dir. Rec rm. Fireplaces. Deck on cottages. Marina with lifts. Picnic tables, grills. On 200 acres. Cr cds: MC, V.
🐾 ⊠ ⊠ 🎿 🐾 ⊠ 🐾

Deer River

(C-4) *See also Grand Rapids, Hibbing*

Pop 838 **Elev** 1,291 ft **Area code** 218
Zip 56636

A harvesting point for lumber products of Chippewa National Forest, Deer River also serves nearby farms as well as hunting and fishing camps. A Ranger District office of the Chippewa National Forest (see GRAND RAPIDS) is located here.

What to See and Do

Chippewa National Forest. At W edge of city, access on MN 46. (See GRAND RAPIDS) Phone 218/335-8600.

Cut Foot Sioux Lakes. Fishing; hunting, camping. Turtle and snake Indian mounds along shore. 15 mi NW on both sides of MN 46.

Deerwood

See also Aitkin, Brainerd, Crosslake

Pop 524 **Elev** 1,079 ft **Area code** 218 **Zip** 56444

Motel/Motor Lodge

★★ **COUNTRY INN.** *23884 Front St (56444). 218/534-3101; fax 218/534-3685. www.countryinns.com.* 38 rms, 2 story. Late May-Aug: S, D $65-$85; each addl $6; under 18 free; lower rates rest of yr. Crib free. Pet accepted, some restrictions. TV; cable (premium), VCR avail (movies). Indoor pool; whirlpool. Complimentary continental bkfst, coffee in rms. Restaurant nearby. Ck-out 11 am. Coin lndry. X-country ski 1 mi. Sauna. Game rm. Some refrigerators, wet bars. Cr cds: A, D, DS, ER, JCB, MC, V.

⬛🔧🛉🛗🏊🖼️🐾

Resort

★★★ **RUTTGER'S BAY LAKE LODGE.** *25039 Tame Fish Lake Rd (56444). 218/678-2885; fax 218/678-2864; toll-free 800/450-4545. www.ruttgers.com.* 30 rms in lodges, 37 cottages (1-3 bedrm), 1-2 story, 88 town houses, 2 story. MAP, July-Aug: for 2-6, $122-$155/person; EP: $125-$335/day; family rates; package plans; lower rates rest of yr. Crib free. TV; cable, VCR avail (movies). 3 pools, 1 indoor; whirlpools. Free supervised children's activities (MAP guests mid-June-Labor Day); ages 4-12. Dining rm (public by res) 7-10 am, noon-2 pm, 6-8 pm. Bar noon-midnight. Ck-out noon, ck-in 5 pm. Coin lndry. Meeting rms. Business servs avail. Gift shop. 27-hole golf, pro, putting green, pro shop. Exercise equipt; saunas. Private beach. Water-skiing instruction. Boats, launching ramp, motors; canoes, sailboat, kayaks, paddleboat. Lawn games. Soc dir (July-Aug); naturalist, trails, entertainment; movies. Rec rm. Game rm. Some fireplaces in kit. units. Lodge overlooks lake. Cr cds: A, DS, MC, V.

⬛🛉🛗🏌️🖼️🚶🎿🐾

Detroit Lakes

(D-2) *See also Moorhead, Park Rapids*

Pop 6,635 **Elev** 1,365 ft
Area code 218 **Zip** 56501

Information Detroit Lakes Regional Chamber of Commerce, PO Box 348, 56502; 218/847-9202 or 800/542-3992

Web www.detroitlakes.com

A French missionary visiting this spot more than 200 years ago commented on the beautiful *détroit* (strait), and this came to be the name of the town. "Lakes" was added to promote the 412 lakes found within 25 miles. Tourism and agriculture are major sources of income.

What to See and Do

Becker County Historical Society Museum. Exhibits pertaining to history of county. (Memorial Day-Labor Day, daily; rest of yr, Mon-Fri; closed hols) Corner of Summit and W Front, two blks off US 10. Phone 218/847-2938. **FREE**

Detroit Lakes City Park. Picnic tables, grills, shelters; tennis courts, lifeguard (Mid-June-Aug), shuffleboard, ball diamonds; playground, boat rentals, fishing. One-mi-long beach, bathhouse. Motorboat sightseeing services nearby. Shops. (June-Labor Day, daily) Washington Ave and W Lake Dr. **FREE**

Skiing. Detroit Mountain Ski Area. Double and triple chairlifts, two T-bars, four rope tows; patrol, school, rentals, snowmaking; cafeteria. Vertical drop 235 ft. (Mid-Nov-Mar, Fri-Sun) 2 mi E, off MN 34. Phone 218/847-1661. ¢¢¢

Tamarac National Wildlife Refuge. On 43,000 acres. Twenty-one lakes, abundant wild rice; trumpeter swans, grouse, beaver, deer; flyway sanctuary for thousands of songbirds, ducks, geese; picnicking, fishing. (Daily) Visitor center (Memorial Day-Labor Day, daily; rest of yr, Mon-Fri; closed hols). 8 mi E on MN 34, then 9 mi N on County 29. Phone 218/847-2641. **FREE**

Special Events

Polar Fest. Wkend filled with sports, entertainment, polar plunge. Mid-Feb.

Festival of Birds. Three-day migration celebration. Workshop, speakers, displays, and guided field trips. Mid-May.

White Earth Powwow. Celebrates the treaty between the Sioux and Chippewa. Phone 800/542-3992. Mid-June.

Northwest Water Carnival. Detroit Lake, throughout city. Incl water show, races, fishing derby, parade, flea markets. Mid-July.

WE Country Music Fest. Soo Pass Ranch, 3 mi S on MN 59. 3-day event featuring many top country musicians and groups. Phone 218/847-1681. First wkend Aug.

Becker County Fair. Late Aug.

Motels/Motor Lodges

★★ **BEST WESTERN HOLLAND HOUSE.** *615 US 10 E (56501). 218/847-4483; fax 218/847-1770; toll-free 800/338-8547. www.bestwestern.com.* 56 rms, 1-2 story. D $59-$99; each addl $6; suites $79-$139. Crib free. Pet accepted, some restrictions. TV; cable (premium), VCR avail. Indoor pool; whirlpool, wading pool, waterslide. Sauna. Complimentary continental bkfst. Coffee in rms. Restaurant adj. Ck-out 11 am. Coin lndry. Meeting rms. Business servs avail. In-rm modem link. Golf privileges. Downhill ski 2 mi. Refrigerators; some bathrm phones, in-rm whirlpools. Cr cds: A, MC, V.

D ◆ ❄ ⚔ ≈ ⬄ 🐾 SC

★★ **HOLIDAY INN.** *1155 US 10 E (56501). 218/847-2121; fax 218/847-2121; res 800/465-4329. www.holiday-inn.com.* 98 rms, 4 suites, 4 story. Late May-Labor Day: S, D $89-$119; under 18 free; family rates; lower rates rest of yr. Crib free. Pet accepted. TV; cable. Indoor pool; whirlpool. Sauna. Restaurant 6:30 am-10 pm. Bar 11-1 am; entertainment. Ck-out noon. Coin lndry. Meeting rms. Business servs avail. In-rm modem link. Valet serv. Sundries. Downhill ski 2 mi; x-country ski on site. Rec rm. Paddleboat rentals. Some minibars. Some poolside rms. Lakeside rms with private balconies.

On lake; 500-ft private beach, dockage. Cr cds: A, C, D, DS, JCB, MC, V.

D ◆ ⚡ ❄ ≈ 🏋 ✈ ⬄ 🐾 SC

★ **SUPER 8 MOTEL.** *400 Morrow Ave (56501). 218/847-1651; fax 218/847-1651; toll-free 800/800-8000. www.super8.com.* 39 rms, 2 story. S $37.88-$43.88; D $42.88-$52.88; each addl $4; under 13 free. Crib free. TV; cable. Complimentary coffee in lobby. Restaurant adj open 24 hrs. Ck-out 11 am. Business servs avail. Downhill/x-country ski 5 mi. Cr cds: A, C, D, DS, MC, V.

D ❄ ⬄ 🐾 SC

Resort

★★★ **FAIR HILLS.** *24270 County Hwy 20 (56501). 218/532-2222; fax 218/532-2068; toll-free 800/323-2849. www.fairhillsresort.com.* 100 units. Late June-mid-Aug, AP: wkly, S, D $634 each; kit. cabins; EP: wkly $542-$1,554; family rates; varied lower rates mid-May-late June, mid-Aug-late Sept. Closed rest of yr. Serv charge 15 percent. Crib avail. Heated pool; wading pool, whirlpool. Free supervised children's activities (mid-June-mid Aug); ages 4-14. Dining rm (public by res) 8-9 am, noon-1 pm, 5:30-7 pm. Box lunches, snacks. Ck-out noon, ck-in 4 pm. Coin lndry. Business servs avail. Airport, bus depot transportation. Rec dirs. Tennis. 27-hole golf. Private beach. Waterskiing, instruction; boats, motors, canoes, sailboats, water bikes, windsurfing; launching ramp, dockage. Indoor, outdoor games. Soc dir; entertainment, bingo. Some fireplaces. Picnic tables, grills. On Pelican Lake. Cr cds: A, D, DS, MC, V.

D ⚡ 🏋 ⛷ ≈ ✈ ⬄ 🐾

Restaurants

★★ **FIRESIDE.** *1462 E Shore Dr (56501). 218/847-8192.* Hrs: 5:30-10:30 pm; days vary off-season. Closed late Nov-Mar. Dinner $7.95-$16.75. Children's menu. Specializes in charcoal-grilled steak, barbecued ribs, seafood. Open charcoal grill. Fireplace. Overlooks Big Detroit Lake. Family-owned. Cr cds: A, D, DS, MC, V.

D ⬄

★ **LAKESIDE.** *200 W Lake Dr (56501).* 218/847-7887. Hrs: 5-10 pm; Fri, Sat to 11 pm; Sun brunch 10 am-1 pm. Closed hols. Res accepted. Bar. Dinner $9.50-$16.25. Sun brunch $7.95. Children's menu. Specializes in tableside cooking. Outdoor dining. Rustic decor. Former hotel built in 1891. Cr cds: DS, MC, V.

D

Duluth (D-5)

Founded 1856 **Pop** 85,493 **Elev** 620 ft
Area code 218

Information Convention & Visitors Bureau, 100 Lake Place Dr, 55802; 218/722-4011 or 800/4-DULUTH

Web www.visitduluth.com

At the western tip of Lake Superior, Duluth is a world port thanks to the St. Lawrence Seaway. Ships of many countries fly their flags at its 49 miles of docks. This gives the products of Minnesota and the Northwestern states better access to markets of the world and stimulates development of new industries converting raw materials to finished goods. One of the foremost grain exporting ports in the nation, Duluth-Superior Harbor also handles iron ore, coal, limestone, petroleum products, cement, molasses, salt, grain, soybean oil, soybeans, wood pulp, paper, and chemicals. The twin ports are the westernmost water terminus for goods consigned to the Northwest.

High bluffs rise from the lakeshore, protecting the harbor from the elements. Minnesota Point, a sandbar extending seven miles from Minnesota to the Wisconsin shore, protects the inner harbor.

There are two ways for ships to enter the Duluth-Superior Harbor: one by way of the Superior side, called the Superior Entry; and the other, the Duluth Ship Canal, with an aerial lift bridge located a few blocks south of downtown Duluth. The distance between the two is about eight miles.

As the state's gateway to the sea, Duluth is a business, industrial, cultural, recreational, and vacation center. The great Minnesota northwoods begin almost at the city's boundaries. From here the North Shore Drive (see GRAND MARAIS) follows Lake Superior into Canada; other highways fan out to the lake country, the great

Aerial Lift Bridge, Duluth

forests, and south to the Twin Cities. The headquarters of the Superior National Forest (see) is located here.

Long a fur trading post, Duluth is the city of early voyageurs, Chippewa, and French and British explorers. The first major shipment from the twin ports of Duluth and Superior was 60 canoe loads of furs in 1660. Modern commerce started in 1855 following construction of the lock at Sault Ste. Marie, Michigan, the eastern entrance to Lake Superior. The French explorer Daniel Greysolon, Sieur du Lhut, landed here in 1679. The city takes its name from him.

What to See and Do

Aerial Lift Bridge. (138 ft high, 336 ft long, 900 tons in weight) Connects mainland with Minnesota Point, lifting 138 ft in less than a minute to let ships through. Foot of Lake Ave. Phone 218/722-3119.

★ **The Depot, St. Louis County Heritage and Arts Center.** Building was originally Union Depot (1890); houses three museums, a visual arts institute, and four performing arts organizations. (Daily; closed hols) 506 W Michigan St. Phone 218/727-8025. ¢¢¢ Admission incl

  Depot Square. (lower level) Reproduction of 1910 Duluth street scene with ice cream parlor, storefronts, gift shops, trolley rides.

  Duluth Children's Museum. Natural, world, and cultural history; featuring giant walk-through tree in habitat exhibit. Phone 218/733-7543.

  Lake Superior Railroad Museum. Extensive displays of historic railroad equipment and memorabilia. Trolley car rides and periodical excursions, some using steam locomotives.

  St. Louis County Historical Society. Settlement of northern Minnesota; logging, mining, railroading, and pioneer life exhibits. Phone 218/733-7580.

Duluth-Superior Excursions. Two-hr tour of Duluth-Superior Harbor and Lake Superior on the *Vista King* and *Star.* (Mid-May-mid-Oct, daily) Also dinner and dance cruises. Foot of 5th Ave W and waterfront. Phone 218/722-6218. ¢¢¢

Enger Tower. Tower providing best view of Duluth-Superior; dedicated in 1939 by Norway's King Olav V, then Crown Prince; dwarf conifer and Japanese gardens, picnic tables on grounds. On Skyline Dr at 18th Ave W. **FREE**

Fitger's Brewery Complex. Historic renovated brewery transformed into more than 25 specialty shops and restaurants on the shore of Lake Superior. Summer courtyard activities. (Daily; closed Jan 1, Easter, Thanksgiving, Dec 25) 600 E Superior St. Phone 218/722-8826. **FREE** From here take the

  Duluth Lakewalk. Walk along Lake Superior to the Aerial Lift Bridge; statues, kiosks; horse and buggy rides.

Glensheen. (ca 1905-1908) Historic 22-acre Great Lake estate on W shore of Lake Superior; owned by University of Minnesota. Tours. Grounds (Daily). Mansion (May-Oct, daily; rest of yr, wkends; closed hols) 3300 London Rd. Phone 218/726-8910. ¢¢

Jay Cooke State Park. Located on 8,813 acres of rugged country; fishing; x-country skiing, snowmobiling, picnicking, camping (electric hookups, dump station), visitor center. Standard fees. SW via MN 23, 210, adjoining gorge of St. Louis River. Phone 218/384-4610.

Karpeles Manuscript Library Museum. Holds original drafts of *US Bill of Rights, Emancipation Proclamation,* Handel's *Messiah,* and others. (June-Aug, daily; rest of yr, Tues-Sun) 902 E 1st St. Phone 218/728-0630. **FREE**

Lake Superior Maritime Visitors Center. Ship models, relics of shipwrecks, reconstructed ship cabins; exhibits related to maritime history of Lake Superior and Duluth Harbor and the Corps of Engineers. Vessel schedules and close-up views of passing ship traffic. (Apr-mid-Dec, daily; rest of yr, Fri-Sun; closed Jan 1, Thanksgiving, Dec 25) Canal Park Dr next to Aerial Bridge. Phone 218/727-2497. **FREE**

Lake Superior Zoological Gardens. Twelve-acre zoo with more than 80 exhibits; picnicking. (Daily) 72nd and Grand aves W, on MN 23. Phone 218/733-3770. ¢¢

Leif Erikson Park. Statue of Norwegian explorer and half-size replica of boat he sailed to America in A.D. 997. Rose Garden. (May-mid-Sept, daily) 11th Ave E and London Rd. **FREE**

North Shore Scenic Railroad. Narrated sightseeing trips along 28 mi of Lake Superior's scenic North Shore, from Duluth to Two Harbors. Other excursions avail: Duluth to Lester River, Two Harbors to Tom's Logging Camp, Pizza Train. Trips range from 90 min to six hrs. (Apr-Oct, daily) Departs from the Depot, 506 W Michigan St. Phone 218/722-1273. ¢¢¢

Park Point Recreation Center. Two hunded-acre playground; picnicking; boat ramp; swimming facilities, lifeguard. (June-Labor Day, daily) At tip of Minnesota Point. **FREE**

Scenic North Shore Drive. MN 61 from Duluth to Canada along Lake Superior.

Site of Fond du Lac. Originally a Native American village, later a trading post; school, mission established here in 1834. On St. Louis River.

Skyline Parkway Drive. A 27-mi scenic road along bluffs of city constructed during 1930s; view from 600 ft overlooks harbor, lake, bay, and river.

S/S *William A. Irvin.* Guided tours of former flagship of United States Steel's Great Lakes fleet that journeyed inland waters from 1938-1978. Explore decks and compartments of restored 610-ft ore carrier, incl the engine rm, elaborate guest staterms, galley, pilothouse, observation lounge, elegant dining rm. Free parking. (May-mid-Oct) 350 Harbor Dr; on the waterfront, adj to Duluth Convention Center. Phone 218/722-5573. ¢¢

Skiing. Spirit Mountain Ski Area. Two quad, two triple, double chairlifts; patrol, school, rentals, snowmaking; bar, cafeteria; children's center. Twenty-four runs, longest run 5,400 ft; vertical drop 700 ft. (Nov-Mar, daily) Half-day rates. Snowboarding; tubing. X-country trails (Dec-Apr, daily). 9500 Spirit Mtn Pl, 10 mi S on I-35, exit 249. Phone 218/628-2891 or 800/642-6377. ¢¢¢¢

University of Minnesota, Duluth. (1902) 7,800 students. 10 University Dr. Phone 218/726-8000. On campus are

Marshall W. Alworth Planetarium. Shows (Wed; closed hols). Phone 218/726-7129. **FREE**

Tweed Museum of Art. Exhibits of 19th- and 20th-century paintings; contemporary works. (Tues-Sun; closed hols) Phone 218/726-8222. **Donation**

Special Events

John Beargrease Sled Dog Marathon. Phone 218/722-7631. Mid-Jan.

International Folk Festival. Leif Erikson Park. Folk music, dancing, crafts, foods. Phone 218/722-7425. First Sat Aug.

Bayfront Blues Festival. Phone 218/722-4011. Second wkend Aug.

Motels/Motor Lodges

★ **ALLYNDALE MOTEL.** *510 N 66th Ave W (55807).* 218/628-1061; toll-free 800/341-8000. 21 rms. Mid-Apr-mid-Oct: S $38; D $43-$48; each addl $5; lower rates rest of yr. Crib $5. Pet accepted, some restrictions; $5. TV; cable. Playground. Complimentary coffee. Restaurant nearby. Ck-out 11 am. Downhill/x-country ski 1½ mi. Refrigerators, microwaves. Picnic tables. Cr cds: A, C, D, DS, MC, V.

🔲 🔲 🔲 🔲

★★ **BEST WESTERN EDGEWATER.** *2400 London Rd (55812).* 218/728-3601; fax 218/728-3727; toll-free 800/777-7925. www.bestwestern.com. 282 rms, 5 story. June-mid-Oct: S $59-$99, D $69-$139; each addl $6; suites $98-$169; under 18 free; ski plans; lower rates rest of yr. Crib $2. Pet accepted, some restrictions. TV; cable (premium). Indoor pool; whirlpool. Playground. Complimentary continental bkfst. Coffee in rms. Restaurant adj. Ck-out noon. Meeting rm. Business center. Valet serv. Miniature golf. Downhill ski 7 mi; x-country ski 1 mi. Exercise equipt; sauna. Game rm. Lawn games. Refrigerators. Many rms with balcony, view of Lake Superior. Cr cds: A, C, D, DS, ER, JCB, MC, V.

🔲 🔲 🔲 🔲 🔲 🔲 🔲 🔲

★ **COMFORT INN.** *3900 W Superior St (55807).* 218/628-1464; fax 218/

624-7263; toll-free 800/228-5151.
www.comfortinn.com. 81 rms, 2 story,
10 kit. units. May-Oct: S $61; D $72;
each addl $5; suites $108; kit. units
(no equipt) $82; under 18 free; lower
rates rest of yr (exc wkends). Crib
free. TV; cable (premium). Indoor
pool; whirlpool. Complimentary
continental bkfst. Restaurant adj
open 24 hrs. Ck-out 11 am. Coin
lndry. Meeting rm. Business servs
avail. Sauna. Microwaves avail. Cr
cds: A, C, D, DS, MC, V.

D ≋ ⊠ 🐾 SC

★★ **COMFORT SUITES.** *408 Canal
Park Dr (55802). 218/727-1378; fax
218/727-1947; toll-free 800/228-5151.
www.comfortinn.com.* 82 rms, 3 story.
Early June-Sept: S, D $105-$115;
suites $155; under 18 free; higher
rates special events; lower rates rest
of yr. Crib free. TV; cable (premium).
Indoor pool; whirlpools. Complimentary continental bkfst. Restaurant adj 8 am-11 pm. Ck-out 11 am.
Coin lndry. Meeting rm. Business
servs avail. In-rm modem link. Bellhops (in season). Downhill/x-country
ski 5 mi. Refrigerators; some in-rm
whirlpools. Cr cds: A, MC, V.

D ≋ ⊠ 🐾 SC

★ **DAYS INN.** *909 Cottonwood Ave
(55811). 218/727-3110; fax 218/727-
3110; res 800/329-7466. www.daysinn.
com.* 86 rms, 2-3 story. No elvtr. June-
mid-Oct: S $59-$82; D $68-$82; each
addl $6; higher rates special events;
lower rates rest of yr. Crib free. Pet
accepted. TV; cable (premium), VCR
avail. Complimentary continental
bkfst. Restaurant opp open 24 hrs.
Ck-out noon. Business servs avail. Cr
cds: A, C, D, DS, ER, JCB, MC, V.

D 🐾 ✗ ⊠ 🐾

★ **SUPER 8.** *4100 W Superior St
(55807). 218/628-2241; fax 218/628-
2241; res 800/800-8000. www.duluth.
com/super8.* 59 rms, 2 story. Late
May-early Sept: S $56-$69; D $66-
$69; each addl $3; under 12 free;
higher rates special events; lower
rates rest of yr. Crib free. TV; cable
(premium). Complimentary continental bkfst. Restaurant opp open 24
hrs. Ck-out 11 am. Coin lndry. Business servs avail. Downhill/x-country
ski 5 mi. Sauna. Whirlpool. Cr cds:
A, C, D, DS, MC, V.

D 🐾 ⊠ 🐾

Hotels

★★★ **FITGERS INN.** *600 E Superior
St (55802). 218/722-8826; fax 218/
722-8826; toll-free 888/348-4377.
www.fitgers.com.* 62 rms, 5 story, 20
suites. May-Oct: S $80-$95, D $80-
$135; suites $150-$250; under 17
free; lower rates rest of yr. Pet
accepted, some restrictions. TV; cable
(premium), VCR avail. Bar 11 am-11
pm; entertainment wkends. Ck-out
noon. Meeting rms. Business servs
avail. In-rm modem link. Shopping
arcade. Exercise equipt. Health club
privileges. Some in-rm whirlpools,
fireplaces. Most rms overlook Lake
Superior. Part of renovated 1858
brewery; shops, theater adj. Cr cds:
A, C, D, DS, MC, V.

D 🐾 🛏 ✗ ⊠ 🐾

★★ **HOLIDAY INN HOTEL &
SUITES - DOWNTOWN WATER-
FRONT.** *200 W First St (55802).
218/722-1202; fax 218/722-0233; toll-
free 800/477-7089. www.holidayinn
duluth.com.* 353 rms, 16 story. S, D
$89-$119; each addl $10; suites $89-
$235; ski, package plans. Crib free.
TV; cable. Indoor pools; whirlpools.
Coffee in rms. Restaurant 6:30 am-11
pm. Bar 11-1 am. Ck-out noon.
Meeting rms. In-rm modem link.
Free garage parking. Downhill/x-
country ski 7 mi. Exercise equipt;
saunas. Health club privileges. Refrigerators; microwave, wet bar in suites.
Adj large shopping complex. Cr cds:
A, C, D, DS, ER, JCB, MC, V.

D 🐾 ⊠ ✗ ⊠ 🐾 SC

★★ **RADISSON HOTEL DULUTH-
HARBORVIEW.** *505 W Superior St
(55802). 218/727-8981; fax 218/
727-0162; res 800/333-3333. www.
radisson.com.* 268 rms, 16 story. June-
mid-Oct: S, D $80-$110; each addl
$10; suites $135-$250; under 18 free;
package plans; lower rates rest of yr.
Crib free. Pet accepted. TV; cable,
VCR avail. Indoor pool; whirlpool,
poolside serv. Restaurant (see also
TOP OF THE HARBOR). Bar 11:30-1
am; closed Sun. Ck-out noon. Meeting rms. Business servs avail. Down-
hill/x-country ski 10 mi. Sauna.
Health club privileges. Cr cds: A, C,
D, DS, ER, JCB, MC, V.

D 🐾 🛏 🐾 ⊠ ✗ ⊠ 🐾

Restaurants

★ ★ ★ **BELLISIO'S.** *405 Lake Ave S (55802). 218/727-4921. www.grand masrestaurants.com.* Hrs: 11:30 am-2 pm, 5-9 pm; Fri to 10 pm; Sat 11:30 am-3 pm, 5-10 pm; Sun 11:30 am-3 pm, 5-9 pm. A la caret entrees: $7.99-$24.99. Bar. Wine cellar. Specialties: rigatoni Bolognese, chicken a la Milanese. Cr cds: A, C, D, DS, MC, V.
[D]

★ **GRANDMA'S CANAL PARK.** *522 Lake Ave S (55802). 218/727-4192.* Hrs: 11 am-10:30 pm; Sun to 10 pm. Closed hols. Res accepted. Bar to 1 am. Lunch $4.50-$8.99, dinner $6.99-$18.99. Children's menu. Specializes in sandwiches, pasta. Under Aerial Lift Bridge at entrance to harbor. Early 1900s building; antiques. Cr cds: A, D, DS, MC, V.
[D] [SC] [→]

★ ★ **PICKWICK.** *508 E Superior St (55802). 218/727-8901.* Hrs: 11 am-11 pm. Closed Sun; hols. Bar 8-1 am. Lunch $6.25-$8.50, dinner $9.95-$20.95. Children's menu. Specializes in charcoal-broiled steak, seafood. Open-hearth grill. View of Lake Superior; pub atmosphere. Family-owned. Cr cds: A, C, D, DS, MC, V.
[D]

★ **TOP OF THE HARBOR.** *505 W Superior St (55802). 218/727-8981. www.radisson.com.* Hrs: 6:30 am-2 pm, 4:30-10 pm; Fri, Sat 5-11 pm; early-bird dinner Thurs-Sun 4:30-6 pm. Res accepted. Serv bar. Bkfst $4.25-$9.95, lunch $4.95-$8.95, dinner $9.95-$19.95. Children's menu. Specializes in steak, salmon, trout. Panoramic view of city, Duluth Harbor, Lake Superior from 16th-floor revolving restaurant. Cr cds: A, C, D, DS, ER, MC, V.
[SC] [→]

Elk River

(F-4) *See also Anoka, Minneapolis, St. Cloud, St. Paul*

Pop 11,143 **Elev** 924 ft **Area code** 763 **Zip** 55330

Information Elk River Area Chamber of Commerce, 509 US 10; 763/441-3110
Web www.elkriver-mn.com

What to See and Do

Oliver H. Kelley Farm. Birthplace of National Grange and organized agriculture. Now a living history farm of the mid-19th century (May-Oct, daily). Visitor center only (Nov-mid-Apr, Sat-Sun; closed hols; free). 2 mi SE on US 10, 52. Phone 763/441-6896. ¢¢

Sherburne National Wildlife Refuge. Canoeing, fishing; wildlife observation, interpretive hiking and x-country skiing trails in season, hunting. Incl a self-guided auto tour route (wkends and hols). 13 mi N on MN 169, then 5 mi W on County 9. Phone 763/389-3323. **FREE**

Motel/Motor Lodge

★ ★ **AMERICINN.** *17432 US 10 (55330). 763/441-8554; toll-free 800/634-3444.* 41 rms, 2 story. S $54-$69; D $95-$110; under 12 free. Crib free. Pet accepted, some restrictions; $5. TV; cable, VCR (movies). Indoor pool; whirlpool. Complimentary continental bkfst. Restaurant opp 6 am-11 pm. Ck-out 11 am. Meeting rms. X-country ski 3 blks. Sauna. Mississippi River 1 blk. Cr cds: A, D, DS, MC, V.
[D] [icons]

Ely

(C-5) *See also Tower*

Settled 1883 **Pop** 3,968 **Elev** 1,473 ft **Area code** 218 **Zip** 55731
Information Chamber of Commerce, 1600 E Sheridan St; 218/365-6123 or 800/777-7281
Web www.ely.org

A vacation and resort community, Ely is also gateway to one of the finest canoeing areas, Boundary Waters Canoe Area Wilderness, and is in the heart of the Superior National Forest (see). A Ranger District office of this forest is located here. From the Laurentian Divide, south of here, all waters flow north to the Arctic.

What to See and Do

Canoe trips. Canoes, equipt, supplies. Guides avail. Phone Chamber of Commerce for info.

Canoe Country Outfitters. Offers complete and partial ultra-light outfitting for trips to BWCAW and Quetico Park. Boat fishing trips and fly-in canoe trips; also camping, cabins on Moose Lake. (May-Oct, daily) 629 E Sheridan St. Phone 218/365-4046.

Tom and Woods' Moose Lake Wilderness Canoe Trips. Family, wkly rates. Specializes in ultra-lightweight canoe trips. (May-Sept) 20 mi NE on Moose Lake. Phone 800/322-5837.

Dorothy Molter Museum. Last living resident of the Boundary Waters Canoe Area Wilderness who passed away Dec 1986. Museum has two of her furnished cabins as they were in the wilderness. (Memorial Day-Sept, daily) 2002 E Sheridan. Phone 218/365-4451. ¢¢

Greenstone outcropping. Only surface ellipsoidal greenstone in US, judged to be more than two billion yrs old. 13th Ave E and Main St.

International Wolf Center. Houses wolf pack; exhibits. (May-mid-Oct, daily; rest of yr, Fri-Sun) E on MN 169.

Native American Pictographs. Cliff paintings can be seen on Hegman Lake. These are simple exhibits of art painted by tribes who inhabited the region long ago. 7 mi N via MN 88 and 116 (Echo Tr).

Superior-Quetico Wilderness. Superior in the US, Quetico in Canada. (See SUPERIOR NATIONAL FOREST)

Vermilion Interpretive Center. Presentation of local history through photos, tapes, film, artifacts, and displays; focuses on heritage of local people and land. (Apr-Oct, daily) 1900 E Camp St. Phone 218/365-3226. ¢

Special Events

Voyageur Winter Festival. Ten days beginning first Sat Feb.

Blueberry/Art Festival. Last full wkend July.

Full Harvest Moon Festival. Wkend after Labor Day.

Motels/Motor Lodges

★ **BUDGET HOST ELY.** *1047 E Sheridan St (55731). 218/365-3237; fax 218/365-3099; toll-free 800/283-4678. www.budgethost.com.* 17 rms. S $44; D $54-$74; each addl $5-$10; family rates. Crib free. Pet accepted; $10/day. TV; cable (premium). Complimentary coffee in rms. Restaurant nearby. Ck-out 10 am. Business servs avail. Free airport transportation. X-country ski ½ mi. Sauna. Cr cds: DS, MC, V.

★ **SUPER 8 MOTEL.** *1605 E Sheridan St (55731). 218/365-2873; fax 218/365-5632; res 800/800-8000. www.super8.com.* 30 rms, 2 story. S $55; D $65; each addl $5; under 12 free. Crib free. TV; cable. Complimentary coffee in lobby. Ck-out 11 am. Business servs avail. X-country ski 1 mi. Whirlpool. Sauna. Cr cds: A, C, D, DS, MC, V.

★ **WESTGATE MOTEL.** *110 N 2nd Ave W (55731). 218/365-4513; fax 218/365-5364; toll-free 800/806-4979.* 17 units, 2 story. S $40-$50; D $55-$65; each addl $5; under 5 free. Crib free. Pet accepted, some restrictions; $5/day. TV; cable. Complimentary continental bkfst. Restaurant nearby. Ck-out 10:30 am. Business servs avail. Free airport transportation. Downhill ski 20 mi; x-country ski 1 mi. Cr cds: A, MC, V.

Cottage Colony

★★ **TIMBER BAY LODGE AND HOUSEBOATS.** *8347 Timber Bay Rd, Babbitt (55706). 218/827-3682; toll-free 800/846-6821. www.timberbay.com.* 12 kit. cabins (1-3-bedrm), 11 houseboats. No A/C. Mid-June-mid-Aug: houseboats for 2-10, $150-$300/day (3-day min); cabins: $650-$1,075/wk; daily rates; lower rates mid-May-mid-June, mid-Aug-Sept. Closed rest of yr. Pet accepted; $6/day, $30/wk. No maid serv. TV in cabins. Free supervised children's activities (mid-June-mid-Aug). Ck-out 10 am, ck-in 3 pm. Grocery, coin lndry, package store 2 mi. Golf privileges. Private beach. Boats, motors, canoes, kayaks, marina. Naturalist program. Lawn games. Rec rm. Game rm. Microwaves in cabins. Cabins with fireplaces and decks. On Birch Lake, among tall pines. Cr cds: DS, MC, V.

Eveleth

(C-5) *See also Cook, Hibbing, Tower, Virginia*

Founded 1893 **Pop** 4,064 **Elev** 1,610 ft **Area code** 218 **Zip** 55734
Information Eveleth Area Chamber of Commerce, PO Box 556; 218/744-1940
Web www.evelethchamber.com

Site of a large taconite operation, mines within a 50-mile radius produce a large amount of the nation's requirements of iron ore. Located about one mile west of town on County Highway 101, Leonidas Overlook provides a panoramic view of the taconite operations and Minntac Mine.

What to See and Do

US Hockey Hall of Fame. Museum honoring American players and the sport; theater. (Mid-May-Dec, daily; rest of yr, Mon-Tues; closed hols) 801 Hat Trick Ave (US 53). Phone 218/744-5167. ¢¢

Motels/Motor Lodges

★ ★ ★ **EVELETH INN.** *US 53 (55734). 218/744-2703; fax 218/744-5865; res 888/354-6230.* 145 rms, 2 story. S, D $59-$92; under 19 free. Crib free. Pet accepted. TV; cable (premium). Indoor pool. Restaurant 6 am-10 pm. Bar 4 pm-1 am. Ck-out noon. Coin lndry. Meeting rms. Business servs avail. Sundries. Gift shop. Sauna. Rec rm. Some refrigerators, microwaves. Cr cds: A, C, D, DS, JCB, MC, V.

★ **SUPER 8 MOTEL - EVELETH.** *1080 Industrial Park Dr, US 53 (55734). 218/744-1661; fax 218/744-4343; res 800/800-8000. www.super8.com.* 54 rms, 2 story. Mid-May-late Oct: S $55.88; D $59.88-$64.88; each addl $5; under 12 free; ski, golf plans; lower rates rest of yr. Crib $1. TV; cable (premium). Complimentary continental bkfst, coffee in rms. Restaurant opp 6 am-10 pm. Ck-out 11 am. Meeting rms. Business servs avail. Coin lndry. Downhill ski 20 mi; x-country ski 10 mi. Indoor pool; whirlpool. Sauna. Game rm. Cr cds: A, MC, V.

Fairmont

(H-3) *See also Blue Earth, Jackson*

Pop 11,265 **Elev** 1,185 ft
Area code 507 **Zip** 56031
Information Fairmont Area Chamber of Commerce, PO Box 826; 507/235-5547
Web www.fairmont.org

Fairmont, the seat of Martin County, is 10 miles north of the Iowa line at the junction of I-90 and MN 15. Situated on a north-south chain of lakes, fishing and water sports are popular pastimes. A group of English farmers who arrived in the 1870s and were known as the "Fairmont sportsmen" introduced fox hunting into southern Minnesota.

What to See and Do

Fairmont Opera House. Built in 1901, historic theater has been completely restored. Guided tours. Fees for productions vary. (Mon-Fri, also by appt; closed hols) 45 Downtown Plaza. Phone 507/238-4900. **FREE**

Pioneer Museum. Operated by Martin County Historical Society; pioneer memorabilia, Native American artifacts. (May-Sept, Mon-Sat; rest of yr, by appt) Under 12 yrs with adult only. 304 E Blue Earth Ave. Phone 507/235-5178. **FREE**

Motels/Motor Lodges

★ **BUDGET INN.** *1122 N State St (56031). 507/235-3373; fax 507/235-3286.* 43 rms. S $26-$42; D $35-$49. Crib free. TV; cable. Indoor pool; whirlpool. Sauna. Complimentary coffee in lobby. Restaurant nearby. Ck-out 11 am. Meeting rm. X-country ski 2 mi. Cr cds: A, C, D, DS, MC, V.
⊠ ⊠ ⊠ ⊠ SC

★★ **HOLIDAY INN.** *I-90 and Hwy 15 (56031). 507/238-4771; fax 507/238-9371; res 800/465-4329. www.holiday innfairmont.com.* 105 rms, 2 story. S $62-$79; D $72-$89; under 18 free. TV; cable. Indoor pool; wading pool, whirlpool, poolside serv. Sauna. Restaurant 6 am-10 pm. Bar 11-1 am. Ck-out noon. Coin lndry. Meeting rms. Business servs avail. In-rm modem link. Sundries. Free airport transportation. X-country ski 2 mi. Balconies. Cr cds: A, C, D, DS, JCB, MC, V.
D ⊠ ⊠ ⊠ ⊠ ⊠

★ **SUPER 8 MOTEL.** *1200 Torgerson Dr (56031). 507/238-9444; fax 507/238-9371; toll-free 800/800-8000. www.super8.com.* 47 rms, 2 story. S, D $47-$57; each addl $5; under 12 free. Crib $5. Pet accepted. TV; cable. Continental bkfst. Restaurant opp 6 am-10 pm. Ck-out noon. Business servs avail. Free airport transportation. Cr cds: A, C, D, DS, MC, V.
D ⊠ ⊠ ⊠ SC

Restaurant

★ **THE RANCH FAMILY RESTAURANT.** *1330 N State St (56031). 507/235-3044.* Hrs: 6 am-10 pm; Fri, Sat to 11 pm. Closed Dec 25. Res accepted. Bar. Bkfst $2.50-$4, lunch $3.50-$6, dinner $6.75-$10.95. Children's menu. Specializes in steak, seafood, salad. Salad bar. Casual, family-style dining. Cr cds: DS, MC, V.
D SC ⊟

Faribault

(G-4) See also Lakeville, Le Sueur, Mankato, Northfield, Owatonna, St. Peter

Settled 1826 **Pop** 17,085 **Elev** 971 ft
Area code 507 **Zip** 55021
Information Faribault Area Chamber of Commerce, 530 Wilson Ave, PO Box 434; 507/334-4381 or 800/658-2354
Web www.faribaultmn.org

In 1826 Alexander Faribault, a French-Canadian fur trader, built the largest of his six trading posts here. Faribault now is known for Faribo wool blankets and Tilt-A-Whirl amusement rides. The town, seat of Rice County, is surrounded by 20 area lakes and 3,000 acres of parkland. Faribault is also home to several historic landmarks, incl the Cathedral of Our Merciful Saviour, built in 1869, and the limestone buildings of Shattuck-St. Mary's Schools, founded in 1858.

What to See and Do

Alexander Faribault House. (1853) House of the fur trader for whom the town was named. Period furnishings; museum of Native American artifacts and historical items. (May-Sept, Mon-Fri (daily); rest of yr, by appt) 12 NE 1st Ave. Phone 507/334-7913. ¢

Faribault Woolen Mill Company. Wool blankets, items made in century-old mill on the Cannon River. Factory store, mill seconds. Check in at store for 45-min guided tour (Mon-Fri; closed first two wks July). Store (daily; closed hols). 1500 NW 2nd Ave. Phone 507/334-1644. **FREE**

Rice County Historical Society Museum. Slide show; video presentation; Native American and pioneer artifacts; turn-of-the-century Main St; works of local artists. Nearby are log cabin, church, one-rm schoolhouse, and two steel annexes. (June-Aug, wkends; rest of yr, Tues-Fri, daily) 1814 NW 2nd Ave, adj to county fairgrounds. Phone 507/332-2121. ¢

River Bend Nature Center. These 646 acres of mixed habitat incl wood-

lands, prairie, ponds, and rivers. Ten
mi of trails (x-country in winter)
meander through the area. (Daily) SE
via MN 60, on Rustad Rd. Phone
507/332-7151. **FREE**

Special Event

Tree Frog Music Festival. 122 1st Ave
NE. Two-day event featuring head-
liner concert each day. Arts and
crafts. Mid-Sept.

Motels/Motor Lodges

★★ **GALAXIE INN & SUITES.** *1401
MN 60 W (55021).* 507/334-5508; fax
507/334-2165; toll-free 888/334-9294.
59 rms, 2 story. S $39-$43; D $56-
$68; each addl $3. Crib $2. TV; cable
(premium). Indoor pool; whirlpool.
Sauna. Complimentary continental
bkfst. Restaurant adj 6 am-11 pm.
Ck-out 11 am. Meeting rms. Business
servs avail. In-rm modem link. Cr
cds: A, D, DS, MC, V.
🛍 🖾 🐾

★★ **SELECT INN.** *4040 MN 60 W
(55021).* 507/334-2051; fax 507/334-
2051; toll-free 800/641-1000. www.
selectinn.com. 67 rms, 2 story. S $37;
D $43-$58; each addl $5; under 13
free. Crib $3. Pet accepted. TV; cable
(premium). Indoor pool. Complimentary continental bkfst. Restaurant adj open 24 hrs. Ck-out 11 am.
Meeting rms. Business servs avail.
Game rm. Cr cds: A, D, DS, MC, V.
D 🐾 🖾 🏝 🐾 SC

Restaurant

★ **LAVENDER INN.** *2424 N Lyndale
Ave (55021).* 507/334-3500. www.
lavenderinn.com. Hrs: 11 am-10 pm.
Closed Jan 1, Thanksgiving, Dec 24
eve, Dec 25. Res accepted. Bar. Lunch
$6-$10, dinner $9-$25. Children's
menu. Specializes in steak, broasted
chicken, seafood. Art display. Family-
owned. Cr cds: A, D, DS, MC, V.
D

Fergus Falls (E-2)

Settled 1857 **Pop** 12,362 **Elev** 1,196 ft
Area code 218 **Zip** 56537

Information Chamber of Commerce,
202 S Court St; 218/736-6951
Web www.fergusfalls.com

Fergus Falls was named in honor of
James Fergus, who financed Joseph
Whitford, a frontiersman who led an
expedition here in 1857. The town is
the seat of Otter Tail County, which
has 1,029 lakes. The city has a remarkable park and recreation system.

What to See and Do

**Otter Tail County Historical Society
Museum.** Modern facility featuring
dioramas and changing exhibits
interpreting regional history; also
library, archives, and genealogical
materials. (Daily; closed hols) 1110
W Lincoln Ave. Phone 218/736-
6038. ¢

**Recreation areas. Pebble Lake City
Park.** Swimming, beach; picnicking.
Eighteen-hole golf (Apr-Sept, daily;
fee). Park (Early June-late Aug, daily).
DeLagoon Park. Swimming, beach,
fishing, boating (ramp); picnicking,
camping (fee). Park (Mid-May-Oct,
daily). SE on US 59. Phone 218/739-
3205.

Motels/Motor Lodges

★ **COMFORT INN.** *425 Western Ave
(56537).* 218/736-5787; fax 218/736-
2640; res 800/228-5150. www.
comfortinn.com. 35 rms, 2 story. May-
Oct: S $61; D $71; each addl $5;
suites $99; under 19 free; lower rates
rest of yr. Crib free. TV; cable (premium), VCR avail (movies). Complimentary continental bkfst.
Restaurant nearby. Ck-out 11 am.
Business servs avail. Valet serv. Coin
lndry. X-country ski 15 mi. Some
refrigerators. Cr cds: A, C, D, DS, ER,
JCB, MC, V.
🖾 🗷 🏝 🐾 SC

★ **DAYS INN.** *610 Western Ave
(56537).* 218/739-3311; fax 218/736-
6576; toll-free 800/329-7466. www.
daysinn.com. 57 rms, 2 story. S $38-
$42.90; D $48.90-$52.90; each addl
$3; under 12 free. Crib free. Pet
accepted; $5. TV; cable. Indoor pool;
whirlpool. Complimentary continental bkfst. Restaurant adj 6 am-midnight. Ck-out 11 am. Business servs
avail. Sundries. Health club privi-

leges. Downhill/x-country ski 2 mi.
Cr cds: A, C, D, DS, MC, V.

[icons]

★ **SUPER 8 MOTEL.** *2454 College Way (56537). 218/739-3261; res 800/800-8000. www.super8.com.* 32 rms, 2 story. S, D $35-$55; each addl $5. Crib $2. TV; cable (premium). Complimentary coffee. Restaurant adj open 6 am-midnight. Ck-out 11 am. Business servs avail. Cr cds: A, MC, V.

[icons]

Restaurant

★★ **MABEL MURPHY'S EATING LTD.** *MN 210 W (56537). 218/739-4406.* Hrs: 11 am-2 pm, 5-10 pm; Sun 5-9 pm. Bar 11-1 am. Lunch $4.25-$6.95, dinner $8.95-$24.95. Children's menu. Specializes in seafood, prime rib, pastas. Salad bar. Own desserts. Country inn decor; fireplaces, antiques. Cr cds: A, D, DS, MC, V.

[icons]

Glenwood

(E-2) *See also Alexandria, Morris, Sauk Centre*

Pop 2,573 **Elev** 1,350 ft
Area code 320 **Zip** 56334
Information Glenwood Area Chamber of Commerce, 200 N Franklin St; 320/634-3636 or 800/304-5666

What to See and Do

Chalet Campsite. Boating (launch), swimming beach; bicycling, picnicking, playground, tennis court, camping (fee), rest rms, showers. (Mid-May-Sept, daily) ½ mi S on MN 104. Phone 320/634-5433.

Department of Natural Resources, Area Fisheries Headquarters. Trout in display ponds (Mon-Fri; closed hols). Grounds (Daily). 1½ mi W on N Lakeshore Dr, MN 28, 29. **FREE**

Pope County Historical Museum. Helbing Gallery of Native American arts and crafts; country store, school and church; exhibits of local history, farm machinery, and artifacts; furnished log cabin (1880). (Memorial Day-Labor Day, daily; rest of yr,

Mon-Fri) ½ mi S on MN 104. Phone 320/634-3293. ¢¢

Special Events

Scout Fishing Derby. First wkend Feb.
Terrace Mill Heritage Festival. Phone 320/278-3289. Last wkend June.
Waterama. Water carnival; contests, parade. Last full wkend July.
Pope County Fair. First wk Aug.
Terrence Mill Fiddlers' Contest. Phone 320/278-3289. First Sun Oct.

Motel/Motor Lodge

★ **SCOTWOOD MOTEL.** *MN 55 and MN 28 (56334). 320/634-5105.* 46 rms, 2 story. S $35-$42; D $42-$45; each addl $5. Crib $5. TV; cable (premium). Indoor pool; whirlpool. Complimentary continental bkfst. Restaurant nearby. Ck-out 11 am. Game rm. Cr cds: A, D, DS, MC, V.

[icons]

Resort

★★★ **PETERS' SUNSET BEACH RESORT.** *20000 S Lakeshore Dr (56334). 320/634-4501; toll-free 800/356-8654. www.petersresort.com.* 24 lodge rms, 27 kit. cottages. Some rm phones. Mid-June-mid-Aug: cottages for 1-9, $114-$267; MAP, family rates; golf plans; 2-4 day min stay: hols, some wkends; lower rates May-mid-June, mid-Aug-Oct. Closed rest of yr. Crib $8. TV; VCR avail (movies). Dining rm (public by res) 7:30-9:30 am, 7-8:30 pm. Snack bar. Ck-out 12:30 pm, ck-in 4:30 pm. Business servs avail. Package store 3 mi. Tennis. 18-hole golf, greens fee $28, putting green. Private beach. Boats, motors, rowboats; launching ramp. Bicycles. Saunas. Cr cds: A, MC, V.

[icons]

Restaurant

★★ **MINNEWASKA HOUSE SUPPER CLUB.** *24895 MN 28 (56334). 320/634-4566.* Hrs: 11 am-2 pm, 5-10 pm; Sun 5-9 pm. Closed hols. Res accepted. Bar to 1 am. Lunch $4.95-$12.50, dinner $8.50-$29.50. Specializes in steak. Entertainment. Open charcoal grill. Cr cds: A, MC, V.

[icons]

Grand Marais

(C-7) *See also Grand Portage, Lutsen*

Pop 1,171 **Elev** 688 ft **Area code** 218
Zip 55604
Information Grand Marais Information Center, PO Box 1048; 218/387-2524 or 800/622-4014
Web www.grandmarais.com

This municipality on the rocky north shore of Lake Superior is the major community in the northeast point of Minnesota. The area resembles the tip of an arrow and is known as the "arrowhead country." The cool climate and pollen-free air, as well as lake and stream fishing, abundant wildlife, water sports, camping, and stretches of wilderness, make this a leading resort area. A Ranger District office of the Superior National Forest (see) is located here.

What to See and Do

Canoe trips. Canoes, equipt, guides. For map, folder, names of outfitters contact Grand Marais Information Center.

Grand Portage National Monument. 38 mi NE on MN 61. (See GRAND PORTAGE)

Gunflint Trail. Penetrates into area of hundreds of lakes where camping, picnicking, fishing, canoeing are avail. Starting at NW edge of town, the road goes N and W 58 mi to Saganaga Lake on the Canadian border.

North Shore Drive. Considered one of the most scenic shore drives in the US. MN 61 along Lake Superior from Duluth to Pigeon River (150 mi).

Special Events

Fisherman's Picnic. Parade, rides, dancing, queen's coronation; food. First wk Aug.

Cook County Fair. Five blks N on MN 61. Late Aug.

Motels/Motor Lodges

★★ **ASPEN LODGE.** *US 61 E (55604). 218/387-2500; fax 218/387-2647; res 800/247-6020.* 52 rms. Mid-June-mid-Oct, mid-Dec-mid-Mar: S $39-$88; D $42-$129; suites $65-$145; package plans; lower rates rest of yr. Pet accepted, some restrictions. TV; cable (premium). Indoor pool; whirlpool. Sauna. Complimentary continental bkfst. Restaurant nearby. Ck-out 11 am. Guest lndry. Meeting rm. Business servs avail. In-rm modem link. Downhill ski 18 mi; x-country ski 1 mi. Snowmobiling. Refrigerators; some in-rm whirlpools. Cr cds: A, D, DS, MC, V.

★★ **BEST WESTERN.** *US 61 E (55604). 218/387-2240; fax 218/387-2244; res 800/842-8439. www.bestwestern.com.* 66 rms, 2-3 story. June-Oct: D $79-$129; suites $109-$179; lower rates rest of yr. Crib free. Pet accepted. TV; cable (premium), VCR avail (movies). Complimentary continental bkfst. Coffee in rms. Restaurant nearby. Ck-out 11 am. Coin lndry. Meeting rm. Business servs avail. Downhill ski 18 mi; x-country ski ½ mi. Snowmobiling. Whirlpool. Refrigerators; some bathrm phones, whirlpools, fireplaces. Balconies. Private beach on lake. Views of Lake Superior. Cr cds: A, C, D, DS, ER, JCB, MC, V.

★★ **EAST BAY HOTEL AND DINING ROOM.** *Wisconsin St (55604). 218/387-2800; fax 218/387-2801; res 800/414-2807. www.eastbayhotel.com.* 36 rms, 2-3 story, 4 suites. No A/C. Mid-May-Oct: S, D $51-$124.50; suites $125-$150; under 12 free; lower rates rest of yr. Crib free. Pet accepted. TV; cable. Restaurant 7 am-2 pm, 5-9 pm. Bar 11 am-9 pm; entertainment. Ck-out 11 am. Downhill ski 18 mi; x-country ski 5 mi. Massage. Whirlpool. Many refrigerators. Some in-rm whirlpools, refrigerators. Microwave, wet bar, fireplace in suites. On lake. Cr cds: A, DS, MC, V.

★★ **NANIBOUJOU LODGE.** *20 Naniboujou Tr (55604). 218/387-2688. www.naniboujou.com.* 24 rms, 2 story. No A/C. No rm phones. Mid-May-late Oct: S $65; D $80; each addl $10; under 3 free; lower rates rest of yr. Winter hrs wkends only. Crib $10. Restaurant 8 am-10:30 am, 11:30 am-2:30 pm, 5:30-8:30 pm. Ck-out 10:30

am. Business servs avail. X-country ski on site. Some fireplaces. On lake/river. Totally nonsmoking. Cr cds: DS, MC, V.

⊡ 📭 🐟 🛒

★ **SHORELINE.** *20 S Broadway (55604). 218/387-2633; fax 218/387-2499; toll-free 800/247-6020. www. grandmaraismn.com.* 30 rms, 2 story. No A/C. Mid-June-mid-Oct, mid-Dec-mid-Mar: S, D $49-$99; each addl $8; package plans; lower rates rest of yr. Crib free. TV; cable (premium). Complimentary continental bkfst. Restaurant nearby. Ck-out 11 am. Business servs avail. In-rm modem link. Gift shop. Downhill ski 18 mi; x-country ski 1 mi. Snowmobiling. Refrigerators. Beach on Lake Superior. Cr cds: A, C, D, DS, MC, V.

🐟 ✈ 🛒 🔥 SC

★ **SUPER 8.** *1711 US 61 W (55604). 218/387-2448; fax 218/387-9859; toll-free 800/247-6020. www.super8.com.* 35 rms. Mid-June-mid-Oct and mid-Dec-mid-Mar: S, D $40-$108; each addl $8; package plans; lower rates rest of yr. Crib free. Pet accepted, some restrictions. TV; cable (premium). Complimentary continental bkfst. Restaurant nearby. Ck-out 11 am. Guest lndry. Business servs avail. In-rm modem link. Downhill ski 18 mi; x-country ski 2 mi. Snowmobiling. Sauna. Whirlpool. Refrigerators. Cr cds: A, D, DS, MC, V.

⊡ 🐟 🐾 📭 💈 🛒 🔥

Resorts

★★ **BEARSKIN LODGE.** *124 E Bearskin Rd (55604). 218/388-2292; fax 218/388-4410; toll-free 800/338-4170. www.bearskin.com.* 4 kit. units (1-3 bedrm) in 2-story lodge, 11 kit. cottages (2-3 bedrm). No A/C. Lodge: S, D $125-$208; each addl $46; kit. cottages: D $90-$306; each addl $46; package plans. Crib avail. Playground. Free supervised children's activities (June-Aug); ages 3-13 yrs. Dining rm (res required) 6 pm. Box lunches. Wine, beer. Ck-out 10 am, ck-in 4 pm. Coin lndry. Business servs avail. Grocery. Package store 5 mi. Private swimming beach. Boats, motors, canoes. X-country ski on site. Hiking trails. Mountain bikes. Nature program. Sauna. Whirlpool. Fishing guides. Microwaves, fireplaces. Some balconies, screened porches. Picnic tables, grills. Private docks. Cr cds: A, DS, MC, V.

⊡ 📭 🐟 💈 🐟 🔥 🛒

★ **CLEARWATER CANOE OUTFITTERS AND LODGE.** *774 Clearwater Rd (55604). 218/388-2254; toll-free 800/527-0554. www.canoe-bwca.com.* 6 kit. log cabins (2-3 bedrm); 5 rms in lodge, 2 story. No A/C. Mid-May-mid-Oct, cabins: D $730-$770/wk; each addl $60-$100; lodge rms: S $60; D $75; family rates; lower rates. Closed rest of yr. Pet accepted. Playground. Box lunches avail. Ck-out 10 am, ck-in 2 pm. Grocery 6 mi. Coin lndry 8 mi. Sand beach. Private docks; boats, motors, kayaks, canoe outfitting (with bunkhouses). Hiking trails. Nature program. Mountain bikes. Sauna. Microwaves, fireplaces. Some porches. Picnic tables, grills. Cr cds: A, DS, MC, V.

📭 🐾 🛒 🔥

★ **MOOSEHORN LODGE BED & BREAKFAST.** *196 N Gunflint Lake Rd (55604). 218/388-2233; fax 218/388-2019; toll-free 888/238-5975. www. moosehorn.com.* 4 kit. units, 2 story, 3 kit. cottages, 1 villa. May-Sept, mid-Dec-mid-Mar: S, D, kit. cottages $490-$900/wk; daily rates avail; ski plans; lower rates Oct-mid-Dec. Closed rest of yr. Crib free. Playground. Dining rm 7-9 am, 6:30-8 pm. Box lunches. Ck-out 10 am, ck-in 2 pm. Coin lndry 3 mi. Package store 16 mi. Gift shop. Swimming beach. Boats. X-country ski on site. Hiking. Mountain bikes (rentals). Sauna. Fishing guides. Microwaves; some fireplaces. Picnic tables, grills. On peninsula; overlooks Gunflint Lake. Cr cds: MC, V.

📭 💈 🐟 🐟 🛒 🔥

★ **NORWESTER LODGE.** *7778 Gunflint Tr (55604). 218/388-2252; res 800/992-4386.* 10 kit. cottages (1-4 bedrm), 1-2 levels. No A/C. EP, wkly: D $774-$1,134; each addl $120-$180; under 3 free; spring, fall rates. Crib avail. Pet accepted; $40/wk. TV; cable in lodge, VCR avail (movies). Playground. Ck-out 10 am, ck-in 3 pm. Grocery. Coin lndry. Package store 1 mi. Gift shop. Private sand beach. Waterskiing. Pontoon boat, motors, canoes and outfitting serv; boat launch. X-country ski 4 mi. Snowmobile trails. Hunting. Lawn games. Sauna. Fishing guide. Trophy display in lodge. Fireplaces, microwaves. Picnic tables, grills. Private docks. Cr cds: A, DS, MC, V.

★★ **ROCKWOOD LODGE & OUT-FITTERS.** *50 Rockwood Rd (55604). 218/388-2242; toll-free 800/942-2922. www.rockwood-bwca.com.* 9 kit. cottages (1-3 bedrm). No A/C. 2-8 persons, EP, wkly: $700-$1,800; AP, dinner plan avail; family rates. Crib avail. Playground. Dining rm (guests only). Box lunches. Bar. Ck-out 10:30 am, ck-in 2 pm. Business servs avail. Grocery 2 mi. Coin lndry 2 mi. Private and children's beaches. Boats, motors, canoes. Canoe outfitting (with bunkhouses). Hiking trail. Lawn games. Saunas. Fishing/hunting guides. Microwaves; many fireplaces. Cr cds: A, DS, MC, V.

Restaurants

★ **ANGRY TROUT CAFE.** *408 W US 61 (55604). 218/387-1265.* Hrs: 11 am-9 pm. Closed late Oct-Apr. No A/C. Wine, beer. Lunch $3.95-$7.95, dinner $13.50-$16.95. Specialty: grilled lake trout. Outdoor dining. Solarium overlooking Lake Superior;

building and its furnishings all hand-crafted. Totally nonsmoking. Cr cds: DS, MC, V.

★ **BIRCH TERRACE.** *W 6th Ave (55604). 218/387-2215.* Hrs: 5-11 pm. Res accepted. No A/C. Bar 4 pm-1 am. Dinner $8.95-$16.95. Children's menu. Specializes in seafood, ribs, steak. Northwoods mansion built 1898; fireplaces. Native American burial grounds in front yard. Overlooks Lake Superior. Family-owned. Cr cds: DS, MC, V.

Grand Portage

(C-7) *See also Grand Marais*

Pop 250 **Elev** 610 ft **Area code** 218 **Zip** 55605

What to See and Do

Ferry Service to Isle Royale National Park. From Grand Portage there is passenger ferry service to Isle Royale National Park within Michigan state

Pigeon River High Falls, Grand Portage State Park

waters (Mid-May-late Oct). Phone 715/392-2100.

Grand Portage. The Grand Portage begins at the stockade and runs 8½ mi NW from Lake Superior to Pigeon River. Primitive camping at Ft Charlotte (accessible only by hiking the Grand Portage or by canoe). Trail (all-yr). **FREE**

Grand Portage National Monument. Once this area was a rendezvous point and central supply depot for fur traders operating between Montreal and Lake Athabasca. Partially reconstructed summer headquarters of the North West Company incl stockade, great hall, kitchen, and warehouse. Buildings and grounds (mid-May-mid-Oct, daily). S of MN 61, 5 mi from Canadian border. Phone 218/387-2788. ¢

Grand Rapids

(D-4) *See also Deer River, Hibbing*

Settled 1877 **Pop** 7,976 **Elev** 1,290 ft
Area code 218 **Zip** 55744
Information Grand Rapids Area Chamber of Commerce, The Depot, 1 NW 3rd St; 218/326-6619 or 800/472-6366
Web www.grandmn.com

At the head of navigation on the Mississippi River, Grand Rapids was named for nearby waters. For years it served as a center for logging. Paper production and tourism are the principal industries today. Seat of Itasca County, Grand Rapids serves as a diverse regional center at the western end of the Mesabi Iron Range. A number of open pit mines nearby have observation stands for the public. The forested area surrounding the town incl more than a thousand lakes. Four of them—Crystal, Hale, Forest, and McKinney—are within the city limits.

What to See and Do

Canoeing. On Mississippi River, N on Bigfork waters to Rainy Lake, Lake of the Woods; also to Lake Itasca and on many nearby rivers.

Central School. Heritage center housing historical museum, Judy Garland display, antiques, shops, and a restaurant. (Daily) 10 NW 5th St. Phone 218/327-1843.

Chippewa National Forest. Has 661,400 acres of timbered land; 1,321 lakes, with 699 larger than ten acres; swimming, boating, canoeing, fishing; hiking, hunting, picnicking, camping (fee), winter sports. Bald eagle viewing; several historic sites. Between Grand Rapids and Bemidji on US 2. Phone 218/335-8600.

Forest History Center. Center incl a museum building, re-created 1900 logging camp and log drive wanigan maintained by Minnesota Historical Society as part of an interpretive program. Early Forest Service cabin and fire tower, modern pine plantation, living history exhibits; nature trails. (Mid-May-mid-Oct, daily). 3 mi SW via S US 169. Phone 218/327-4482. ¢¢

Judy Garland Birthplace and Children's Museum. Childhood home of actress. (Tues-Sat, also Sun afternoon) 2727 US 169 S. Phone 218/327-9276. ¢

Pokegama Dam. Camping on 16 trailer sites (hookups, dump station; 14-day max); picnicking, fishing. 2 mi W on US 2. Phone 218/326-6128. ¢¢¢

Scenic State Park. Primitive area of 3,000 acres with seven lakes. Swimming, fishing, boating (ramp, rentals); hiking, x-country skiing, snowmobiling, picnicking, camping (electrical hookups), lodging, interpretive programs. Standard fees. 12 mi N on US 169, then 32 mi N on County 7. Phone 218/743-3362.

Skiing. Quadna Mountain Resort Ski Area. Quad chairlift, two T-bars, rope tow; patrol, school, rentals, snowmaking; motel, lodge and restaurant. X-country trails. Sixteen runs, longest run more than 2,000 ft, vertical drop 350 ft. (Thanksgiving-mid-Mar; Mon, Tues, Fri-Sun) Also golf, outdoor tennis, horseback riding, lake activities in summer. 18 mi S on US 169, 1 mi S of Hill City. Phone 218/697-8444. ¢¢¢¢

Special Events

Judy Garland Festival. Museum. Phone 218/327-9276. Late June.

Mississippi Melodie **Showboat.** 16th Ave W, on Mississippi River. Amateur musical variety show. Phone 800/722-7814. Three wkends July.

Northern Minnesota Car Show and Swap Meet. Itasca County Fairgrounds. Phone 218/326-5640. Late July.

North Star Stampede. Three-day rodeo. Phone 218/743-3893. Late July.

Tall Timber Days and US Chainsaw Carving Championships. Downtown. Phone 800/472-6366. Early Aug.

Itasca County Fair. Fairgrounds, on Crystal Lake. Mid-Aug.

Motels/Motor Lodges

★★ **AMERICINN OF GRAND RAPIDS.** *1812 S Pokegama Ave (55744). 218/326-8999; fax 218/326-9190; toll-free 800/634-3444. www.americinn.com.* 43 rms, 2 story. Mid-June-Labor Day: S $52-$66, D $71-$86; each addl $6; under 17 free; lower rates rest of yr. Crib free. TV; cable (premium). Indoor pool; whirlpool. Sauna. Complimentary continental bkfst. Coffee in rms. Restaurant nearby. Ck-out 11 am. Business servs avail. Downhill/x-country ski 18 mi. Cr cds: A, D, DS, MC, V.

🅳 ⛷ ≋ ✈ ⛷ 🔥

★ **BUDGET HOST INN.** *311 US 2 E (55744). 218/326-3457; fax 218/326-3795; res 800/283-4678. www.budgethost.com.* 34 rms, 2 story. Mid-Apr-late Sept: S, D $45-$85; each addl $4; under 12 free; lower rates rest of yr. Crib free. Pet accepted. TV; cable. Playground. Complimentary coffee in lobby. Restaurant adj open 24 hrs. Ck-out 11 am. Business servs avail. Free airport, bus depot transportation. Health club privileges. Cr cds: A, DS, MC, V.

⛷ ✈ 🔥 🔥

★★ **COUNTRY INN.** *2601 US 169 S (55744). 218/327-4960; fax 218/327-4964; res 800/456-4000.* 59 rms, 2 story. June-Aug: S, D $74; each addl $5; under 18 free; lower rates rest of yr. Crib free. Pet accepted, some restrictions. TV; cable (premium). Indoor pool; whirlpool. Complimentary continental bkfst. Restaurant adj 6:30 am-10 pm. Ck-out noon. Down-

hill ski 10 mi; x-country 2 mi. Some refrigerators. Cr cds: A, D, DS, MC, V.

🅳 ⛷ 🔥 ⛷ ≋ ✈ 🔥 🔥

★★ **THE RAINBOW INN.** *1300 US 169 E (55744). 218/326-9655; fax 218/326-9651; toll-free 888/248-8050.* 80 rms, 2 story. S $45-$60; D $52-$75; each addl $8; suites $75-$90; under 12 free. Crib free. Pet accepted; $50 deposit. TV; cable. Indoor pool; whirlpool. Sauna. Restaurant 7 am-9 pm. Bar noon-1 am; entertainment Fri, Sat. Ck-out noon. Meeting rms. Business center. Airport transportation. Downhill/x-country ski 10 mi. Cr cds: A, C, D, DS, MC, V.

🅳 ⛷ ≋ ✈ 🔥 🔥 SC 🔥

★★★ **SAWMILL INN.** *2301 S Pokegama Ave (55744). 218/326-8501; fax 218/326-1039; toll-free 800/235-6455. www.sawmillinn.com.* 124 rms, 2 story. S $57-$85; D $67-$85; each addl $4; suites $88-$110; under 12 free. Crib free. Pet accepted. TV; cable. Indoor pool; whirlpool, poolside serv. Restaurant 6:30 am-10 pm; Sun to 9 pm. Bar 11-1 am. Ck-out noon. Coin lndry. Meeting rms. Business servs avail. Sundries. Free airport, bus depot transportation. Downhill/x-country ski 18 mi. Sauna. Game rm. Cr cds: A, C, D, DS, MC, V.

🅳 ⛷ 🔥 ⛷ ≋ ✈ 🔥

★ **SUPER 8 MOTEL.** *1702 S Pokegama Ave (55744). 218/327-1108; res 800/800-8000. www.super8.com.* 58 rms, 2 story. S, D $59-$62. Crib $2. TV; cable (premium). Complimentary continental bkfst. Restaurants nearby. Ck-out 11 am. Guest lndry. Business servs avail. In-rm modem link. Downhill ski 18 mi; x-country ski 1 mi. Shopping nearby. Cr cds: A, MC, V.

⛷ ✈ 🔥

Granite Falls

(F-2) *See also Marshall, Redwood Falls*

Pop 3,083 **Elev** 920 ft **Area code** 320 **Zip** 56241

Information Chamber of Commerce, 155 7th Ave, PO Box 220; 320/564-4039

What to See and Do

Lac qui Parle State Park. Approx 529 acres. On Lac qui Parle and Minnesota rivers. Dense timber. Swimming, fishing, boating (ramps); hiking, riding, x-country skiing, picnicking, camping. Standard fees. (Daily) 14 mi NW on US 212, 8 mi NW on US 59, then 4½ mi W on County 13. Phone 320/752-4736.

Olof Swensson Farm Museum. A 22-rm brick family-built farmhouse, barn, and family burial plot on a 17-acre plot. Olof Swensson ran unsuccessfully for governor of Minnesota, but the title was given to him by the community out of respect and admiration. (Memorial Day-Labor Day, Sun) 4 mi N on County 5, then 2½ mi W on County 15. Phone 320/269-7636. ¢¢

Upper Sioux Agency State Park. On 1,280 acres. Boating (ramps, canoe campsites); bridle trails, snowmobiling, picnicking, primitive camping. Visitor center. Standard fees. 8 mi SE on MN 67. Phone 320/564-4777.

Yellow Medicine County Museum. Depicts life in the county and state dating from the 1800s. Two authentic log cabins and bandstand on site. Also here is an exposed rock outcropping estimated to be 3.8 billion yrs old. (Mid-May-mid-Oct, Tues-Sun; mid-Apr-mid-May, Tues-Fri) ½ mi from center of town via MN 67. Phone 320/564-4479. **FREE**

Special Event

Western Fest Stampede Rodeo. 155 7th Ave. Rodeo, street dances, parade. Phone 320/564-4039. Wkend after Father's Day.

Motel/Motor Lodge

★ **VIKING JR MOTEL.** *1250 US 212 W (56241). 320/564-2411.* 20 rms. S $28; D $31-$42; each addl $3. Crib $3. Pet accepted. TV; cable, VCR avail (movies). Ck-out 11 am. Cr cds: A, DS, MC, V.
🔾 🖼 🐾 SC

Hastings

(G-5) *See also Minneapolis, Northfield, Red Wing, St. Paul*

Settled 1850 **Pop** 15,445 **Elev** 726 ft
Area code 651 **Zip** 55033
Information Hastings Area Chamber of Commerce & Tourism Bureau, 111 E 3rd St; 651/437-6775 or 888/612-6122
Web www.hastingsmn.org

Diversified farming and industry are the mainstays of this community, founded by a trader who felt the area was a good town site.

What to See and Do

Alexis Bailly Vineyard. First vineyard to make wine with 100 percent Minnesota-grown grapes. Wine tastings (June-Oct, Fri-Sun). Group tours (by appt). 18200 Kirby Ave. Phone 651/437-1413.

Carpenter St. Croix Valley Nature Center. Environmental education center with more than 15 mi of hiking trails and one mi of shoreline on the St. Croix River. Various seasonal programs and activities (some fees). (Daily; closed hols) 12805 St. Croix Tr, 2 mi N via US 61, then 3 mi E via US 10. Phone 651/437-4359.

Historic Walking Tour. A self-guided tour featuring the historic buildings of Hastings, incl the LeDuc-Simmons Mansion and Norrish "Octagon House." Tour booklets with background detail and map are avail at the Chamber of Commerce. Guided tours by appt.

Ramsey Mill. Remains of first flour mill in state, built by Governor Alexander Ramsey in 1857. On MN 291 on the Vermillion River. Phone 800/222-7077.

Skiing. Afton Alps. Three triple, 15 double chairlifts, two rope tows; patrol, school, rentals; snowmaking; store, cafeteria, snack bar; bar. Longest run 3,000 ft; vertical drop 330 ft. (Nov-Mar, daily) 10 mi N via US 61, MN 95. Phone 651/436-5245 or 800/328-1328. ¢¢¢¢

Treasure Island Casino and Bingo. This 24-hr casino offers blackjack, slots, bingo, and pull-tabs. Buffet, sports bar. Marina. Comedy shows

(Tues night). (Daily) 5734 Sturgeon Lake Rd. S on US 61, 316 to Welch, follow signs. Phone 800/222-7077.

Special Event

Rivertown Days. Gala community-wide festival. Riverfront activities; exhibits and tours; sporting events; fireworks. July 17-19.

Motels/Motor Lodges

★ ★ **AMERICINN MOTEL.** *2400 Vermillion St (55033). 651/437-8877; fax 651/437-8184; toll-free 800/634-3444. www.americinn.com.* 44 rms, 2 story. S $52.90-$95.90; D $58.90-$95.90; each addl $6; under 12 free. Crib free. TV; cable (premium), VCR avail. Complimentary continental bkfst. Restaurant nearby. Ck-out 11 am. Meeting rms. Business servs avail. Downhill ski 11 mi; x-country ski 1 mi. Cr cds: A, C, D, DS, MC, V.
🄳 ⬛ ⬛ ⬛ SC

★ **HASTINGS INN.** *1520 Vermillion St (55033). 651/437-3155.* 43 rms. S $28-$44; D $35-$59.95; each addl $5; family units to 8, $75-$79. TV; cable. Indoor pool. Sauna. Complimentary coffee. Restaurant nearby. Ck-out 11 am. In-rm modem link. Sundries. Downhill ski 11 mi; x-country ski 1 mi. Game rm. Sun deck. Cr cds: A, C, D, DS, MC, V.
⬛ ⬛ ⬛ ⬛ SC

★ **SUPER 8 MOTEL.** *2250 Vermillion St (55033). 651/438-8888; res 800/800-8000. www.super8.com.* 49 rms, 2 story. Apr-Sept: S $43-$46; D $49-$56; each addl $6; lower rates rest of yr. Crib $3. TV; cable. Complimentary continental bkfst. Restaurant nearby. Ck-out 11 am. Cr cds: A, MC, V.
🄳 ⬛ ⬛ SC

B&B/Small Inn

★ ★ ★ **THORWOOD BED AND BREAKFAST INN.** *315 Pine St (55033). 651/437-3297; fax 651/437-4129; toll-free 888/746-7966. www.thorwoodinn.com.* 6 rms, 2 suites, 3 story. S, D $137-$177; suites $247; each addl $15; under 12 free. TV avail; VCR. Complimentary full bkfst. Ck-out noon, ck-in 4 pm. Business servs avail. In-rm modem link. Downhill ski 6 mi; x-country ski 3 mi. Some in-rm whirlpools. Historic houses built 1880; antiques, feather comforters, marble fireplaces. Dinner avail with notice. Cr cds: A, DS, MC, V.
⬛ ⬛ ⬛

Restaurant

★ **MISSISSIPPI BELLE.** *101 E 2nd St (55033). 651/437-4814.* Hrs: 11 am-2 pm, 4:30-9 pm; Fri to 10 pm; Sat 4:30-10 pm; Sun noon-7 pm. Closed Mon. Res accepted. Lunch $6.35-$7.50, dinner $10.95-$41. Children's menu. Specializes in fresh seafood, steak. Dining in the tradition of the riverboat era (1855-1875); riverboat steel engravings. Cr cds: A, MC, V.
🄳 ⬛

Hibbing

(C-4) *See also Cook, Deer River, Eveleth, Grand Rapids, Virginia*

Founded 1893 **Pop** 18,046 **Elev** 1,489 ft **Area code** 218 **Zip** 55746
Information Chamber of Commerce, 211 E Howard St, PO Box 727; 218/262-3895 or 800/4-HIBBING
Web www.hibbing.org

Here is the world's largest open-pit iron mine, which produced one-quarter of the ore mined in the country during World War II. Hibbing calls itself the "iron ore capital of the world." On the Mesabi (Native American for "sleeping giant") Iron Range, Hibbing mines and processes taconite, yielding a rich iron concentrate. Frank Hibbing, the town's founder, built the first hotel, sawmill, and bank building. In 1918, when the Hull-Rust pit encroached on the heart of town, the community was moved on wheels two miles south. The move was not completed until 1957. A local bus line, begun here in 1914 with an open touring car, is now the nationwide Greyhound Bus system. Hibbing was the boyhood home of singer-guitarist Bob Dylan.

What to See and Do

Bus tour. Four-hr bus tour of town and nearby taconite plant. Incl stops at Hull-Rust Mine, Paulucci Space Theatre, high school. (Mid-June-mid-Aug, Mon-Fri) Phone 218/262-3895. ¢¢

Hull-Rust Mahoning Mine. Observation building provides view of "Grand Canyon of Minnesota," mining area extending three mi. Individual mines have merged through the yrs into single pit producing hundreds of millions of tons. Deepest part of pit, on east side, dips 535 ft into earth. Observation building; self-guided walking tours. (Mid-May-Sept, daily) Contact the Chamber of Commerce for further information. N of town. Phone 218/262-3895. **FREE**

⭐ **Ironworld USA.** Displays and audiovisual presentations interpret culture and history of the iron mining industry and its people. Ethnic craft demonstrations and food specialties; entertainment; scenic train rides; outdoor amphitheater. (Apr-Oct, daily) (See SPECIAL EVENTS) 5 mi NE on US 169 in Chisholm. Phone 218/254-3321. ¢¢¢

McCarthy Beach State Park. Approx 2,566 acres. Virgin pine, two lakes. Swimming, fishing, boating (ramp, rentals); x-country skiing, hiking, snowmobiling, camping. naturalist (summer). Standard fees. 20 mi NW on County 5. Phone 218/254-2411. ¢¢

Minnesota Museum of Mining. Records the past 70 yrs of iron mining; equipt, exhibits, models; jet and rotary drills, steam engine, ore cars, and railroad caboose, 120-ton Euclid, and fire trucks; first Greyhound bus. (Mid-May-mid-Sept, daily) Self-guided tours. Picnicking. Memorial Park Complex. 6 mi NE via MN 73, on W Lake St in Chisholm. Phone 218/254-5543. ¢¢

Paulucci Space Theatre. General interest programs from astronomy to dinosaurs, using stars, slides, special effects, and hemispheric film projection; multimedia theater with tilted-dome screen; display area; gift shop. Shows (June-Aug, daily; hrs vary). Phone 218/262-6720. ¢¢

Special Events

Winter Frolic. Wk-long festival incl giant treasure hunt, ice fishing contest. Mid-Feb.

Last Chance Curling Bonspiel. Memorial Building. International curling competition on 14 sheets of ice. Early Apr.

Minnesota Ethnic Days. Ironworld USA. A series of celebrations of ethnic heritage. Entertainment, history, crafts, and food. Each day devoted to different nationality. July.

St. Louis County Fair. Fairgrounds, 12th Ave. Cattle and rock exhibits, auto races, carnival midway. Early Aug.

Hibbing World Classic Rodeo. Memorial Building. First wkend Oct.

Motel/Motor Lodge

★ **SUPER 8.** *1411 E 40th St (55746). 218/263-8982; fax 218/263-8982; res 800/800-8000. www.super8.com.* 49 rms, 2 story. Apr-Sept: S, D $37-$50; suites $42-$64; each addl $3; under 13 free; wkly rates; higher rates special events; lower rates rest of yr. Crib free. Pet accepted, some restrictions; $25 deposit. TV; cable (premium), VCR avail. Complimentary coffee in lobby. Restaurant opp 6 am-11 pm. Ck-out 11 am. Meeting rms. Business servs avail. X-country ski 2 mi. Cr cds: A, D, DS, MC, V.

Hinckley

(E-4) *See also Mora*

Pop 946 **Elev** 1,030 ft **Area code** 320 **Zip** 55037

What to See and Do

Hinckley Fire Museum. Old Northern Pacific Railroad Depot houses museum that depicts the disastrous forest fire that swept across Hinckley in 1894. Mural, video tape, diorama, reconstructed living quarters. (May-Oct, daily) 106 US 61. Phone 320/384-7338. ¢¢

North West Company Fur Post. A reconstruction of an 1800 fur trade outpost, based on archaeological findings and other research; picnic area. (May-Labor Day, Tues-Sat and

Sun afternoons) 2 mi W of I-35 Pine City exit. Phone 320/629-6356. **FREE**

St. Croix State Park. A 34,037-acre park. Swimming (lake), fishing, canoeing (Memorial Day-Labor Day, rentals); hiking, riding trails, x-country skiing, snowmobiling, picnicking, six-mi blacktop wooded bike trail, camping (electric, dump station). Standard fees. 15 mi E on MN 48, then S. Phone 320/384-6591.

Motels/Motor Lodges

★ **DAYS INN OF HINCKLEY.** *104 Grindstone Ct (55037). 320/384-7751; fax 320/384-6403; toll-free 800/559-8951. www.daysinn.com.* 69 rms, 2 story. S $55-$85; D $60-$90; each addl $5; suites $90-$135; under 18 free. Crib free. Pet accepted; $5. TV; cable, VCR avail. Indoor pool; whirlpool. Complimentary continental bkfst, coffee in rms. Restaurant adj open 24 hrs. Ck-out 11 am. Coin lndry. Business servs avail. X-country ski 10 mi. Sauna. Some refrigerators; microwaves avail. Cr cds: A, C, D, DS, JCB, MC, V.

★ **GOLD PINE INN.** *MN 48 and I-35 (55037). 320/384-6112; fax 320/384-6194; toll-free 888/384-6112. www.goldpinebw.com.* 50 rms, 2 story. May-Nov: S $49; D $59, suites $63; each addl $6; under 18 free; lower rates rest of yr. Crib $2. Pet accepted. TV; cable (premium), VCR avail. Complimentary coffee in rms. Restaurant adj. Ck-out 11 am. Business servs avail. X-country ski 15 mi. Some refrigerators; microwaves avail. Cr cds: A, C, D, DS, MC, V.

★★ **GRAND NORTHERN INN.** *604 Weber Ave (55037). 320/384-7171; fax 320/745-4659; toll-free 800/558-0612.* 101 rms, 2 story. May-Sept: D $69-$89; each addl $10; whirlpool rms $85-$129; under 19 free; lower rates rest of yr. Crib free. Pet accepted. TV; cable. Indoor pool; whirlpool. Complimentary continental bkfst. Coffee in rms. Ck-out noon. X-country ski 10 mi. Sauna. Microwaves avail. Cr cds: A, MC, V.

★ **SUPER 8.** *2811 MN 23, Finlayson (55735). 320/245-5284; fax 320/245-*
2233; res 800/800-8000. www.super8. com.* 31 rms, 2 story. S $45-$98; D $61-$148; each addl $4; under 12 free. Crib free. Pet accepted. TV; cable (premium). Complimentary continental bkfst. Restaurant opp 6 am-10 pm. Ck-out 11 am. Coin lndry. Business servs avail. X-country ski opp. Whirlpool. Game rm. Cr cds: A, C, D, DS, MC, V.

Restaurants

★ **CASSSIDY'S.** *I-35 and MN 48 (55037). 320/384-6129.* Hrs: 6 am-10 pm; Sat bkfst buffet 7-10:45 am. Res accepted. Wine, beer. Bkfst $.99-$7.95, lunch $4-$8.95, dinner $5.50-$11.95. Buffet (Sat): bkfst $5.95. Children's menu. Specialties: barbecued ribs, pressure-fried chicken. Salad bar. Own baking, soups. Cr cds: DS, MC, V.

★ **TOBIE'S.** *I-35 and MN 48 (55037). 320/384-6174. www.tobies.com.* Hrs: Coffee shop open 24 hrs. Closed Dec 25. Res accepted. Bar 11-1 am. Bkfst $2-$6, lunch $3-$6, dinner $5-$12. Specializes in prime rib, salads, pastries. Entertainment Thurs-Sun. Bistro atmosphere. Bakery on premises. Family-owned. Cr cds: A, D, DS, MC, V.

International Falls (B-4)

Pop 8,325 **Elev** 1,124 ft
Area code 218 **Zip** 56649
Information International Falls Area Chamber of Commerce, 301 2nd Ave; 218/283-9400 or 800/325-5766
Web www.ci.international-falls.mn.us

In addition to tourism, converting trees and wood chips into paper is big business here. The town takes its name from a 35-foot drop of the Rainy River, now concealed by a reservoir above a dam that harnesses

Smokey the Bear Statue, International Falls

the water power. International Falls is a port of entry to Canada by way of Fort Frances, ON. (For border crossing regulations, see MAKING THE MOST OF YOUR TRIP.)

What to See and Do

Boise Cascade Paper Mill. No cameras allowed. No children under ten yrs. Proper footwear required. Tours (June-Aug, Mon-Fri; closed hols). Res advised. 2nd St. Phone 218/285-5511. **FREE**

Fishing. Rainy Lake. E along international boundary. Walleye, sand pike, muskie, crappie, perch, bass. **Rainy River.** W along international boundary. Walleye, sand pike, sturgeon, northern pike.

Grand Mound History Center. Several ancient Native American burial mounds exist in this area, the largest being the Grand Mound, which has never been excavated. Interpretive center offers audiovisual program, sound system exhibit, and ¼-mi trail to mound site. (May-Aug, daily; rest of yr, wkends; also by appt) 17 mi W

via MN 11. Phone 218/285-3332. **FREE**

International Falls City Beach. Sandy beach for swimming; picnic grounds, play equipt. 3½ mi E on MN 11.

Smokey the Bear Statue. Giant symbol of the campaign against forest fires. In park is a giant thermometer, standing 22 ft tall; it electronically records the temperature. Municipal Park. NW edge of business district. Also in the park is

Bronko Nagurski Museum. Highlighting the life and career of football hero Bronko Nagurski; features exhibits, diorama, audiovisual program, photographs, and archives. Located in the same building and incl in admission is

Koochiching County Historical Museum. Exhibits, manuscripts, pictures, articles used by early settlers in area. (Mid-May-mid-Sept, daily; research center Mon and Tues rest of yr) Phone 218/283-4316. ¢¢

⭐ **Voyageurs National Park.** Approx 219,000 acres of forested lake country along the northern Minnesota border. Fishing, boating; camping, naturalist-guided activities, hiking trails. Off US 53 on country rds 122 and 123 or E on MN 11. Phone 800/325-5766. **FREE**

Motels/Motor Lodges

★ **DAYS INN.** *2331 MN 53 S (56649). 218/283-9441; toll-free 800/329-7466. www.daysinn.com.* 60 rms, 2 story. S $46-$58; D $60-$70; under 18 free. Crib free. Pet accepted, some restrictions. TV; cable (premium). Complimentary continental bkfst. Restaurant adj open 24 hrs. Ck-out noon. Business servs avail. Exercise equipt; sauna. Whirlpool. Cr cds: A, C, D, DS, JCB, MC, V.
🐾 🏋 🏊 🐾 SC

★★ **HOLIDAY INN.** *1500 MN 71 (56649). 218/283-8000; fax 218/283-3774; toll-free 800/331-4443. www.*

holidayinnifalls.com. 127 rms, 2 story. S, D $79.95-$89; suites $85-$149; family rates. Crib free. Pet accepted. TV; cable (premium). Indoor pool; wading pool, whirlpool. Restaurant 6:30 am-10 pm. Bar. Ck-out noon. Coin lndry. Meeting rms. Business servs avail. In-rm modem link. Bellhops. Sundries. Free airport transportation. Sauna. Health club privileges. Some refrigerators; microwaves avail. View of Rainy River. Cr cds: A, D, DS, JCB, MC, V.

★ **SUPER 8 MOTEL.** *2326 MN 53 Frontage Rd (56649). 218/283-8811; fax 218/283-8880; res 800/800-8000. www.super8.com.* 53 rms, 2 story. Mid-May-Sept: S $33-$37; D $45-$62, suites $62-$76; each addl $6; under 12 free; lower rates rest of yr. Crib free. TV; cable (premium). Complimentary coffee in lobby. Restaurant nearby. Ck-out 11 am. Coin lndry. Business servs avail. In-rm modem link. Refrigerator, whirlpool, minibar in suites; some microwaves. Cr cds: A, C, D, DS, MC, V.

Cottage Colonies

★ **ISLAND VIEW LODGE.** *1817 MN 11 E (56649). 218/286-3511; fax 218/286-5036; toll-free 800/777-7856. www.rainy-lake.com.* 9 A/C rms in 2-story lodge, 12 kit. cottages (1-6 bedrm), 5 A/C. S, D $65-$70; each addl $11; cottages (3-day min) 1-6 bedrm, $115-$250/day. Pet accepted, some restrictions. TV in lodge rms, some cabins. Dining rm 6:30 am-2 pm, 5-10 pm. Box lunches, snack bar. Bar noon-1 am. Ck-out 10 am, ck-in 3 pm. Grocery, coin lndry 12 mi. Package store. Free airport transportation. Private beach; dockage, boats, motors, guides. Whirlpool. Sauna. Snowmobiling. National park tours. Jukebox dancing. Rec rm. Picnic table, grills. Cr cds: A, MC, V.

★ **NORTHERNAIRE HOUSEBOATS OF RAINY LAKE.** *2690 County Rd 94 (56649). 218/286-5221.* 15 power-driven floating kit. lodges on pontoon boats. No A/C. Mid-May-mid-Oct (3-day min): for 2-10, $795-$2,100/wk; package plans; daily rates. Res, deposit required. Closed rest of yr. Pet accepted, some restrictions. Ck-out noon. Grocery. Water-skiing, motors. Hunting; guides, cooks. Unique houseboat living. Cr cds: MC, V.

Restaurant

★★ **SPOT FIREHOUSE.** *1801 Second Ave W (56649). 218/283-2440.* Hrs: 5-11 pm. Closed Sun; hols. Res accepted. Bar. Dinner $6.50-$19.95. Children's menu. Specializes in barbecued ribs, charbroiled steak, prime rib. Salad bar. Parking. Firefighter theme and memorabilia. Family-owned. Cr cds: A, D, DS, MC, V.

Itasca State Park

See also Bemidji, Park Rapids

28 mi N on US 71.

In the deep forests that cover most of the 32,000 acres of this park, there is a small stream just 15 steps across; this is the headwaters of the Mississippi River at its source, Lake Itasca. The name of the park and the lake itself is a contraction of the Latin *veritas caput,* meaning "true head." The lake is the largest of more than 100 that sparkle amid the virgin woodlands. The park offers swimming, fishing, boating (ramp, rentals); snowmobiling, cross-country skiing, biking (rentals), and hiking. There are cabins, camping and picnic grounds, and a lodge that offers food service (see RESORT). In the summer there are daily boat cruises aboard the *Chester Charles,* from Douglas Lodge Pier to the headwaters of the Mississippi River (fee). A lookout tower, Aiton Heights, in the southeastern part of the park just off the ten-mile wilderness drive, provides a bird's eye view of the park. American Indian burial mounds and a pioneer cabin are some of the many historical sites preserved at Itasca. The University of Minnesota's forestry school and biological station operate here during the summer.

Naturalist program provides self-guided and guided hikes, auto tours, boat launch tours, campfire programs, and evening movies on history and features of the area. Exhibits show many animals and plants native to the state, as well as park history. Inquire at the entrance gates for details. Standard entrance fees. (For further information contact Itasca State Park, HC05, Box 4, Lake Itasca, 56470-9702; phone 218/266-2114.)

Resort

★ **DOUGLAS LODGE.** *36750 Main Park Dr, Lake Itasca (56470). 218/266-2122; fax 218/266-3942.* 25 rms, annexes, 3 suites, 4 guestrooms, 18 rooms in courtyard area, 9 A/C, 12 cabins (1-3 bedrm), 1 clubhouse, central shower area. Memorial Day-mid-Oct, lodge, annexes: S, D $45-$47; each addl $10; cabins $73-$130; kit. cabins $75. Closed rest of yr. Crib avail. Playground. Dining rm 8 am-8 pm. Picnic lunches. Ck-out 11 am, ck-in 4 pm. Grocery 2 mi. Coin lndry 8 mi. Meeting rms. Business servs avail. Sand beach 3 mi; boats, canoes; launch tours. Hiking trails and naturalist program. Bicycles. Some cabins with fireplace, screened porch. State park sticker required for entry to park and lodge. Cr cds: A, DS, MC, V.
D 🛆 🖼 🔥

Jackson

(H-3) *See also Fairmont*

Founded 1856 **Pop** 3,559 **Elev** 1,312 ft **Area code** 507 **Zip** 56143
Information Chamber of Commerce, 1000 US 71 N; 507/847-3867
Web www.jacksonmn.com

A peaceful community on the banks of the Des Moines River, Jackson processes the farm produce of the fertile river valley and also manufactures industrial farm equipment. Thirteen blocks of Jackson's business district are on the National Register of Historic Places.

What to See and Do

Fort Belmont. Museum with antique automobiles; log chapel, sodhouse, waterwheel-operated flour mill, and other buildings; Native American artifacts. Museum (Memorial Day-Labor Day, daily). 2 mi S of jct US 71 and I-90. Phone 507/847-5840. ¢¢

Kilen Woods State Park. 219 acres of forested hills in Des Moines Valley. Fishing; hiking, snowmobiling, picnicking, camping (hookups, dump station); visitor center. Standard fees. 4 mi N on US 71, then 5 mi W. Phone 507/662-6258.

Monument to Slain Settlers. Marks scene of attack by the Sioux in 1857. Ashley Park, State St and Riverside Dr.

Special Events

Town and Country Day Celebration. Main St. Third Sat July.

County Fair. Late July, early Aug.

Motels/Motor Lodges

★★ **BEST WESTERN COUNTRY MANOR INN.** *2007 US 71 N (56143). 507/847-3110; toll-free 800/528-1234. www.bestwestern.com.* 41 rms. S $40-$48; D $50-$62; each addl $4. Crib free. TV; cable. Indoor pool; wading pool, whirlpool. Sauna. Restaurant 6 am-10 pm. Bar 11-12:30 am. Ck-out noon. Meeting rms. Business servs avail. In-rm modem link. Sundries. Cr cds: A, C, D, DS, MC, V.
D 🛌 🖼 🔥 SC

★ **BUDGET HOST.** *950 US 71 N (56143). 507/847-2020; fax 507/847-2022; toll-free 800/283-4678. www.budgethost.com.* 24 rms. S, D $36-$55; each addl $4. Crib $4. TV; cable. Coffee in rms. Restaurant nearby. Ck-out 10 am. In-rm modem link. Sundries. X-country ski 2 mi. Golf opp. Cr cds: A, C, D, DS, MC, V.
🏊 🏋 🖼 🔥

Lake Kabetogama

See also International Falls

Pop 60 **Elev** 1,155 ft **Area code** 218
Zip 56669
Information Kabetogama Lake Association, Inc, 9707 Gamma Rd;
218/875-2621 or 800/524-9085

Kabetogama Lake is the central entrance to Voyageurs National Park (see INTERNATIONAL FALLS).

What to See and Do

Kabetogama Lake. Twenty-two mi long, six mi wide, with hundreds of mi of rugged shoreline, numerous islands, secluded bays for fishing, sand beaches; woodland trails, snowmobiling, x-country skiing, hunting for partridge, deer, bear; many resorts. 7 mi NE off US 53.

Voyageurs National Park. Off US 53 on county rds 122 and 123. (See INTERNATIONAL FALLS) Phone 218/283-9821.

Lakeville

(G-4) *See also Faribault, Hastings, Minneapolis, Northfield, Red Wing, St. Paul*

Pop 24,854 **Elev** 974 ft **Area code** 952
Zip 55044

Motels/Motor Lodges

★ **IMA FRIENDLY HOST INN.**
*17296 I-35 W (55044). 952/435-7191;
fax 952/435-6220; res 800/341-8000.*
48 rms. S $35-$55; D $45-$70; each addl $5; kit. units $5 addl. Crib $4. Pet accepted. TV; cable, VCR avail (movies). Indoor pool; whirlpool. Complimentary coffee in lobby. Restaurant nearby. Ck-out 11 am. Sundries. Downhill/x-country ski 1 mi. Game rm. Cr cds: A, D, DS, MC, V.

★ **MOTEL 6.** *11274 210th St (55044).
952/469-1900; fax 952/469-5359; toll-*

free 800/466-8356. www.motel6.com.
85 rms, 2 story. S $30-$34; D $36-$42; under 17 free. Crib free. Pet accepted. Complimentary coffee in lobby. Restaurant opp 7 am-11 pm. Ck-out noon. Downhill ski 5 mi; x-country ski 2 mi. Cr cds: A, C, D, DS, MC, V.

B&B/Small Inn

★★★ **SCHUMACHER'S HOTEL.**
*212 W Main St, New Prague (56071).
952/758-2133; fax 952/758-2400; toll-free 800/283-2049. www.schumachers
hotel.com.* 16 rms, 2 story. S, D $140-$250. Restaurant (see also SCHUMACHER'S). Bar to 11 pm; Fri, Sat to midnight. Ck-out 11:30 am, ck-in 3 pm. Business servs avail. Valet serv. Gift shop. X-country ski 1 mi. Built in 1898. Decor resembles country inns, hotels in Bavaria, southern Bohemia, and Austria. Cr cds: A, C, D, DS, MC, V.

Restaurant

★★ **SCHUMACHER'S.** *212 W Main
St (56071). 952/758-2133. www.
schumachershotel.com.* Hrs: 7 am-9 pm; Fri, Sat to 10 pm. Res accepted. Continental menu. Bar. Wine list. Bkfst $3-$10, lunch $5-$19, dinner $19-$27. Specializes in veal, game dishes. Own baking. Decor resembles country inns in Bavaria, Austria, and southern Bohemia. Cr cds: A, C, D, DS, MC, V.

Le Sueur

(G-4) *See also Faribault, Mankato, St. Peter*

Pop 3,714 **Elev** 800 ft **Area code** 507
Zip 56058
Information Chamber of Commerce, 500 N Main St, Suite 106; 507/665-2501

This town on the Minnesota River was named for Pierre Charles le Sueur, who explored the river valley at the end of the 17th century. The

Green Giant Company, one of the world's largest packers of peas and corn, was founded here and merged with Pillsbury in 1980. Home office of Le Sueur Inc. and plant sites for ADC Telcommunications, UNIMIN, and Le Sueur Cheese are located here.

What to See and Do

W. W. Mayo House. (1859) Home of Mayo Clinic founder; restored to 1859-1864 period when Dr. Mayo carried on a typical frontier medical practice from his office on the second floor. Adj park is location of Paul Granland's bronze sculpture *The Mothers Louise*. (June-Aug, Tues-Sun; May and Sept-Oct, wkends and hols only) 118 N Main St. Phone 507/665-3250. ¢

Litchfield

(F-3) *See also Minneapolis, Willmar*

Pop 6,041 **Elev** 1,132 ft
Area code 320 **Zip** 55355

What to See and Do

Meeker County Historical Society Museum. The museum stands behind the Grand Army of the Republic Hall (see). Incl a log cabin, old barn display, blacksmith shop, general store, and Native American display. Original newspapers, furniture, and uniforms are also exhibited. (Tues-Sun afternoons, also by appt; closed hols exc Memorial Day) 308 N Marshall Ave. Phone 320/693-8911. **Donation**

   Grand Army of the Republic Hall. Built in 1885, the hall has two rms in original condition. Commemorates the members of the GAR (Grand Army of the Republic).

Motels/Motor Lodges

★ **LAKE RIPLEY RESORT.** *1205 S Sibley Ave (55355). 320/693-3227.* 17 rms. S $31; D $40; each addl $4; under 8 free. Crib free. TV; cable (premium). Complimentary coffee in rms. Restaurant nearby. Ck-out 11 am. Cr cds: A, DS, MC, V.
🐾 ✈ 🐾

★ **SCOTWOOD.** *1017 MN 12 E (55355). 320/693-2496; fax 320/693-2496; toll-free 800/225-5489.* 35 rms, 2 story. S $44.95-$59.50; D $58.95-$99.75; each addl $5. Crib free. Pet accepted, some restrictions. TV; cable (premium). Pool and hot tub. Complimentary continental bkfst. Restaurant nearby. Ck-out 11 am. Sundries. Cr cds: A, DS, MC, V.
🄳 🐾 🐾 🌊 ✈ 🐾 🐾

Little Falls

(E-3) *See also Brainerd, Onamia, St. Cloud*

Pop 7,232 **Elev** 1,120 ft
Area code 320 **Zip** 56345
Information Chamber of Commerce, 200 First St NW; 320/632-5155 or 800/325-5916.
Web www.littlefallsmn.com

This town gets its name from the rapids of the Mississippi River. The seat of Morrison County, it is a paper milling town and a center of the small boat industry.

What to See and Do

Charles A. Lindbergh House and History Center. Home of Charles A. Lindbergh, Sr., former US congressman, and Charles A. Lindbergh, Jr., famous aviator. Homestead restored to its 1906-1920 appearance with much original furniture; history center has exhibits, audiovisual program. (May-Labor Day, daily) 1200 Lindbergh Dr S, S edge of town, on W bank of Mississippi River. Phone 320/632-3154. ¢¢ Adj is

   Charles A. Lindbergh State Park. On 294 acres. Hiking, x-country skiing, picnicking, camping (hookups, dump station). Standard fees. Phone 320/616-2525.

Charles A. Weyerhaeuser Memorial Museum. Museum and resource center for Morrison County and regional history. (May-Sept, Tues-Sun; rest of yr, Tues-Sun; closed hols) 2 mi SW of town via Lindbergh Dr S. Phone 320/632-4007. **FREE**

Minnesota Military Museum. Located in a former regimental headquarters, the museum documents US military history as experienced by Minnesotans, from frontier garrisons to the Persian Gulf. Exhibits; military decorations; tanks and aircraft. (Sept-May, Thurs-Fri; late May-late Aug, Wed-Sun) Camp Ripley, 7 mi N on MN 371, W on MN 115. Phone 320/632-7374. **FREE**

Primeval Pine Grove Municipal Park. Picnicking, playground, zoo with native animals (all yr); stand of virgin pine. (May-Sept, daily) W on MN 27. Phone 320/632-2341. **FREE**

Motel/Motor Lodge

★ **SUPER 8 MOTEL.** *300 12th St NE (56345). 320/632-2351; fax 320/632-2351; res 800/800-8000. www.super8. com.* 51 rms, 2 story. S $48; D $55-$60. Crib free. TV; cable. Coffee in rms. Restaurant nearby. Ck-out 11 am. Sundries. Cr cds: A, C, D, DS, MC, V.

Lutsen

See also Grand Marais

Pop 290 **Elev** 671 ft **Area code** 218 **Zip** 55612

What to See and Do

Skiing. Lutsen Mountains Ski Area. Six double chairlifts, surface lift; school; rentals; snowmaking; lodge (see RESORTS); cafeteria, bar. Longest run two mi; vertical drop 1,088 ft. Gondola. (Mid-Nov-mid-Apr, daily) X-country trails. 1½ mi SW on MN 61, then 1½ mi N. Phone 218/663-7281. ¢¢¢¢ Also here are

Alpine Slide. Chairlift takes riders up mountain to slide; riders control sled on ½-mi track down mountain. (May-mid-Oct) Concession and picnic area. Phone 218/663-7281. ¢¢¢¢

Gondola Skyride. Two-mi round trip sightseeing ride to the highest point on the North Shore. Particularly scenic view in fall. (May-mid-Oct) Phone 218/663-7281. ¢¢¢

Motels/Motor Lodges

★★ **BEST WESTERN CLIFF DWELLER.** *6452 US 61 (55604). 218/663-7273; res 800/528-1234.* 22 rms, 2 story. April-Oct: S $69-$99; Dec-May $69-$99; each addl $8; package plans; lower rates rest of yr. Crib free. Pet accepted, some restrictions. TV; cable (premium). Restaurant (late June-Sept) 7 am-9 pm. Ck-out 11 am. Business servs avail. In-rm modem link. Downhill ski 3 mi; x-country ski adj. 18-hole golf privileges. Balconies. On lake; scenic view. Cr cds: A, C, D, DS, ER, JCB, MC, V.

★★★ **BLUEFIN BAY ON LAKE SUPERIOR.** *US 61, Tofte (55615). 218/663-7296; fax 218/663-8025; toll-free 800/258-3346. www.bluefinbay. com.* 72 units, 2 story, 56 kits. No A/C. Late Dec-Mar, June-Oct: S, D, kit. units $69-$345; each addl $10; under 12 free; ski plans; higher rates; ski wkends, hols; lower rates rest of yr. Crib free. Pet accepted. TV; cable, VCR avail (movies). 2 pools, 1 indoor; whirlpool. Supervised children's activities. Playground. Complimentary coffee in rms. Restaurant 7:30 am-10 pm. Bar 3 pm-1 am. Ck-out noon. Coin lndry. Meeting rms. Business servs avail. Gift shop. Tennis. 18-hole golf privileges. Downhill ski 9 mi; x-country ski opp. Exercise equipt; sauna. Massage. Game rm. Lawn games. Many in-rm whirlpools, fireplaces; microwaves avail. Balconies. Grills. On Lake Superior. Cr cds: DS, MC, V.

★ **MOUNTAIN INN.** *County Rd 5 (55612). 218/663-7244; fax 218/663-7248; res 800/663-7248. www.mtn-inn. com.* 30 rms, 2 story. Jan-Mar, July-mid-Oct: S, D $55-$99; each addl $8; under 18 free; wkend rates; ski, golf plans; hols (2-day min); lower rates rest of yr. Crib free. Pet accepted, some restrictions. TV; cable (premium). Complimentary continental bkfst. Restaurant opp 7 am-11 pm. Ck-out noon. Business servs avail. 18-hole golf privileges, greens fee $41, pro, putting green, driving range. Downhill ski 1 blk; x-country ski on site. Sauna. Whirlpool. Many refrigerators, microwaves, wet bars.

Picnic tables. Opp lake. Cr cds: DS, MC, V.

Resorts

★★★ **CARIBOU HIGHLANDS LODGE.** *371 Ski Hill Rd (55612). 218/663-7241; fax 218/663-7920; res 800/642-6036. www.caribouhighlands. com.* 110 units, 1-3 story. Feb-Mar: S, D $100-$600; kit. units $180-$600; wkly, wkend, hol rates; ski, golf plans; wkends Feb-Mar (3-day min), also wkends mid-July-Labor Day (2-day min); lower rates rest of yr. Crib free. TV; cable, VCR avail (movies). Complimentary coffee in lobby. Restaurant 7-1 am. Box lunches, snack bar, picnics. Bar 11-1 am. Ck-out 11 am, ck-in 4:30 pm. Grocery 2½ mi. Coin lndry 18 mi. Package store 2½ mi. Meeting rms. Business servs avail. Sports dir. Tennis. 18-hole golf privileges, greens fee $39, pro, putting green, driving range. Down-hill/x-country ski on site. Rental equipt avail. Sleighing. Hiking. Horse stables. Bicycle rentals. Social dir. Game rm. Exercise equipt; sauna. Spa. Fishing/hunting guides. 2 pools, 1 indoor. Playground. Supervised children's activities; ages 4-12. Many refrigerators; microwaves, fireplaces. Many balconies. Picnic tables, grills. Cr cds: MC, V.

★★ **CASCADE LODGE.** *3719 US 61 W (55612). 218/387-1112; toll-free 800/322-9543. www.cascadelodge mn.com.* 12 rms in 2-story lodge, 11 cabins, 4 motel units (1-2 bedrm), 8 kits. No A/C. Late June-mid-Oct and late Dec-late Mar: Lodge D $66-$110; each addl $11-$13; cabins, kit. units $106-$185; motel units D $66-$106; family rates; package plans. Crib $5. TV; VCR avail (movies). Playground. Dining rm 7:30 am-8 pm. Box lunches. Ck-out 11 am, ck-in after 1 pm. Grocery, coin lndry, package store 10 mi. Meeting rms. Business servs avail. Downhill ski 11 mi; x-country ski adj. Bicycles. Canoes. Hiking trails. Indoor, outdoor games. Rec rm. Sauna. Many refrigerators; some in-rm whirlpools, fireplaces. Picnic tables, grill. Overlooks Lake Superior. Lodge rms totally non-smoking. Cr cds: A, DS, MC, V.

Luverne

(H-1) *See also Pipestone*

Pop 4,382 **Elev** 1,450 ft
Area code 507 **Zip** 56156

What to See and Do

Blue Mounds State Park. A 2,028-acre park. Main feature is Blue Mound, 1½-mi-long quartzite bluff. Buffalo can be observed in park. Swimming, fishing, boating; snow-mobiling; picnicking; camping; visitor center. Standard fees. 5 mi N of I-90 on US 75, 1 mi E on County 20. Phone 507/283-1307. ¢¢

Motel/Motor Lodge

★ **SUPER 8 MOTEL.** *I-90 and US 75 (56156). 507/283-9541; res 800/800-8000. www.super8.com.* 36 rms, 2 story. S, D $42-$65; suites $56-$67; each addl $5. Crib free. Pet accepted. TV; cable (premium). Ck-out 11 am. Cr cds: A, D, DS, MC, V.

Mankato

(G-4) *See also Faribault, Le Sueur, New Ulm, St. Peter*

Founded 1852 **Pop** 31,477 **Elev** 785 ft
Area code 507
Information Chamber & Convention Bureau, PO Box 999, 56002; 507/345-4519
Web www.ci.mankato.mn.us

In a wooded valley where the Minnesota and Blue Earth rivers join, Mankato (Native American for "blue earth") takes its name from the blue clay that lines the riverbanks. Settled by Eastern professional men, farmers, and Scandinavian and German immigrants, Mankato today enjoys an economy based on farming, retailing, manufacturing, and distributing.

What to See and Do

Hubbard House. (1871) Historic Victorian home with cherry woodwork, three marble fireplaces, silk wall coverings, signed Tiffany lampshade; carriage house; Victorian gardens. 606 S Broad St. Phone 507/345-4154. ¢¢

Land of Memories. Fishing, boating (launch); picnicking, camping (hookups, dump station, rest rms), nature trails. S via US 169, then E at municipal campground sign. Camping ¢¢¢

Minneopa State Park. A 1,145-acre park. Scenic falls and gorge; historic mill site; fishing; hiking, picnicking, camping. Standard fees. 3 mi W off US 60. Phone 507/389-5464. Adj is

Minneopa-Williams Outdoor Learning Center. Wide variety of native animals and vegetation; information stations; outdoor classrm. (Daily) Phone 507/625-3281. **FREE**

Sibley Park. Fishing; picnicking; river walk, playground, zoo (daily); rest rms; beautiful gardens, scenic view of rivers. End of Park Ln. **FREE**

Skiing. Mount Kato Ski Area. Five quad, three double chairlifts; patrol, school, rental; snowmaking; cafeteria; bar. (Nov-Apr, daily) 1 mi S on MN 66. Phone 507/625-3363. ¢¢¢¢¢

Tourtelotte Park. Picnicking, playground. Swimming pool (early June-Labor Day, daily; fee), wading pool. N end of Broad St, on Mabel St. ¢

Motels/Motor Lodges

★★ **BEST WESTERN.** *1111 Range St (56003). 507/625-9333; fax 507/386-4592; toll-free 800/780-7234. www.bestwestern.com.* 147 rms, 2 story. S $53-$84; D $69-$99; each addl $6; under 18 free. Crib free. TV; cable, VCR avail (movies). Indoor pool; whirlpool. Sauna. Coffee in rms. Restaurant 6 am-9 pm. Bar. Ck-out noon. Coin lndry. Meeting rms. Business servs avail. Sundries. Free airport transportation. Downhill ski 6 mi; x-country ski 1 mi. Rec rm. Cr cds: A, C, D, DS, JCB, MC, V.

★ **DAYS INN.** *1285 Range St (56001). 507/387-3332; res 800/329-7466. www.daysinn.com.* 50 rms, 2 story. S $39-$64; D $49-$69; suites $65-$135; under 18 free. Crib free. Pet accepted. TV; cable. Indoor pool; whirlpool.

Complimentary continental bkfst. Restaurant nearby. Ck-out 11 am. Business servs avail. In-rm modem link. Downhill/x-country ski 5 mi. Cr cds: A, C, D, DS, MC, V.

★ **ECONO LODGE.** *111 W Lind Ct (56001). 507/345-8800; fax 507/345-8921; res 800/533-2666. www.econolodge.com.* 66 rms, 2 story. S $35-$39; D $44-$49; under 18 free. Crib free. Pet accepted, some restrictions. TV; cable. Continental bkfst. Coffee in rms. Restaurant adj 7 am-11 pm. Ck-out noon. Business servs avail. Valet serv. Sundries. Downhill ski 6 mi; x-country ski 2 mi. Whirlpool. Sauna. Cr cds: A, C, D, DS, MC, V.

★★ **HOLIDAY INN.** *101 E Main St (56001). 507/345-1234; fax 507/345-1248; res 800/465-4329. www.holiday-inn.com.* 151 rms, 4 suites, 4 story. S $59-$69; D $69-$79; each addl $6; suites $89; under 19 free. Crib free. TV; cable. Indoor pool; whirlpool, poolside serv. Restaurant 7 am-10 pm. Bar 3 pm-1 am. Ck-out noon. Coin lndry. Meeting rms. Business servs avail. In-rm modem link. Valet serv. Sundries. Putting green. Downhill ski 4 mi; x-country ski 1 mi. Exercise equipt. Rec rm. Civic Center nearby. Cr cds: A, C, D, DS, JCB, MC, V.

★ **RIVERFRONT INN.** *1727 N Riverfront Dr (56001). 507/388-1638; fax 507/388-6111.* 19 rms. S $30-$59; D $39-$79; each addl $7. Crib free. Pet accepted, some restrictions. TV; cable, VCR avail (movies). Complimentary coffee in rms. Restaurant nearby. Ck-out 11 am. Business servs avail. In-rm modem link. Downhill ski 5 mi; x-country ski 1 mi. Refrigerators. Cr cds: A, DS, MC, V.

★ **SUPER 8 MOTEL.** *US 169 N and 14 (56001). 507/387-4041; fax 507/387-4107; toll-free 800/800-8000. www.super8.com.* 61 rms, 3 story. S, D $45-$85; Crib $1. TV; cable. Complimentary coffee in lobby. Restaurant adj open 24 hrs. Ck-out 11 am. Business servs avail. In-rm modem link. Downhill ski 5 mi; x-country ski 2 mi. Whirlpool. Cr cds: A, C, D, DS, MC, V.

☑ ⛄ ⚓ 🔥 SC

Marshall

(G-2) *See also Granite Falls, Redwood Falls, Tracy*

Pop 12,023 **Elev** 1,170 ft
Area code 507 **Zip** 56258
Information Marshall Area Chamber of Commerce, 1210 E College Dr, PO Box 352B; 507/532-4484
Web www.marshall-mn.org

Crossroads of five highways, Marshall is a major industrial and retail center for the southwest part of Minnesota.

What to See and Do

Camden State Park. Approx 1,500 acres in forested Redwood River Valley. Swimming, fishing; hiking, riding, x-country skiing, snowmobiling, picnicking, camping; visitor center. Standard fees. 10 mi S, off MN 23. Phone 507/865-4530.

Southwest State University. (1963) 3,000 students. Liberal arts and technical programs. Planetarium (fee), museum and greenhouse (daily; closed hols; free). 1501 State St. Phone 507/537-6255. **FREE**

Special Events

Shades of the Past 50's Revival Weekend. More than 500 classic and collector cars. Flea market, swap meet, street dance. First wkend June.

International Rolle Bolle Tournament. More than 100 teams compete for prize money. Mid-Aug.

Motels/Motor Lodges

★★ **BEST WESTERN.** *1500 E College Dr (56258). 507/532-3221; fax 507/532-4089; res 800/800-8000. www.bestwestern.com.* 100 rms, 2 story. S $43-$60; D $53-$60; suites $79-$84; under 17 free. Crib free. Pet accepted. TV; cable. Indoor pool; whirlpool, poolside serv. Sauna. Restaurant 6:30 am-2 pm, 5-9:30 pm; wkend hrs vary. Bar noon-11:30 pm. Ck-out noon. Meeting rms. Business

servs avail. In-rm modem link. Sundries. Free airport, bus depot transportation. X-country ski 1 mi. Cr cds: A, C, D, DS, MC, V.

☑ 🐾 🖐 ⛄ ≋ ⚓ 🔥

★ **COMFORT INN.** *1511 E College Dr (56258). 507/532-3070; fax 507/532-9641; res 800/228-5150. www.comfortinn.com.* 49 rms, 2 story. S $48-$100; D $54-$100; each addl $6; under 18 free. Crib free. Pet accepted. TV; cable (premium). Complimentary continental bkfst. Coffee in rms. Restaurant nearby. Ck-out 11 am. Meeting rm. Business servs avail. In-rm modem link. Whirlpool. Cr cds: A, C, D, DS, ER, JCB, MC, V.

☑ 🐾 ⚓ 🔥 SC

★ **SUPER 8.** *1106 E Main St (56258). 507/537-1461; res 800/800-8000. www.super8.com.* 50 rms, 2 story. S $42-$52; D $42-$75; suites $78-$130; each addl $5. Crib free. Pet accepted. TV; cable (premium). Restaurant adj 6 am-10 pm. Ck-out 11 am. Coin lndry. Meeting rm. Business servs avail. X-country ski 1 mi. Cr cds: A, C, D, DS, MC, V.

☑ 🐾 🖐 🚲 ⛄ ≋ ⚓ 🔥

★★ **TRAVELER'S LODGE.** *1425 E College Dr (56258). 507/532-5721; fax 507/532-4911; toll-free 800/532-5721.* 90 rms, 1-2 story. S $36; D $44; each addl $4; under 12 free. Crib free. Pet accepted. TV; cable (premium), VCR avail (movies $3.50). Complimentary continental bkfst. Restaurant adj open 24 hrs. Ck-out noon. Meeting rm. Business servs avail. Sundries. Free airport transportation. X-country ski 1 mi. Cr cds: A, C, D, DS, MC, V.

🐾 ⛄ ✈ ⚓ 🔥

Minneapolis

(F-4) *See also Bloomington, St. Paul*

Settled 1847 **Pop** 368,383 **Elev** 687-980 ft **Area code** 612
Information Greater Minneapolis Convention & Visitors Association, 4000 Multifoods Tower, 33 S 6th St, 55402; 612/661-4700 or 888/676-6757
Web www.minneapolis.org

Across the Mississippi from Minnesota's capital, St. Paul, is this handsome city with skyscrapers, lovely parks, and teeming industries. Minneapolis still has a frontier vigor; it is growing and brimming with confidence in itself and its future. Clean and modern, a north country fountainhead of culture, Minneapolis is also a university town, a river town, and a lake town.

A surprising array of nightlife, a revitalized downtown with many fine stores, a rich, year-round sports program, a symphony orchestra, and theaters provide an excellent opportunity to enjoy the niceties of city life. Minneapolis has one of the largest one-campus universities in the country and more than 400 churches and synagogues. Hunting and fishing, which are among the state's major tourist attractions, are easily accessible. The Minneapolis park system, with more than a hundred parks, has been judged one of the best in the country. The city has also been a consistent winner of traffic safety awards.

Capital of Upper Midwest agriculture, with one of the largest cash grain markets in the world, Minneapolis is the processing and distribution center for a large sector of America's cattle lands and grainfields. Several of the largest milling companies in the world have their headquarters here. Graphic arts, electronics, medical technology, machinery, lumber, paper, and chemicals are also major industries.

Minneapolis was born when two mills were built to cut lumber and grind flour for the men of a nearby fort. Despite the fact that these were reservation lands and that cabins were torn down by army troops almost as soon as settlers raised them, the community of St. Anthony developed at St. Anthony Falls around the twin mills. In 1885, the boundaries of the reservation were changed, and the squatters' claims became valid. The swiftly-growing community took the new name of Minneapolis (*Minne,* a Sioux word for water, and *polis,* Greek for city).

Additional Visitor Information

For further information contact the Greater Minneapolis Convention & Visitors Association, 4000 Multifoods Tower, 33 S 6th St, 55402; phone 612/661-4700 or 800/445-7412. The Minneapolis Park and Recreation Board, 400 4th Ave S, 55415, phone 612/661-4800, provides city park information.

Transportation

Car Rental Agencies. See IMPORTANT TOLL-FREE NUMBERS.

Public Transportation. Buses (Metropolitan Transit Commission), phone 612/349-7000.

Rail Passenger Service. Amtrak 800/872-7245.

Airport Information

Minneapolis/St. Paul International Airport. Information 612/726-5555; 612/726-5141 (lost and found); 952/361-6680 (weather); cash machines, Main Terminal, between entrances to Blue and Green Concourses.

What to See and Do

American Swedish Institute. Museum housed in turn-of-the-century 33-rm mansion; features hand-carved woodwork, porcelainized tile stoves, sculpted ceilings, plus Swedish fine art and artifacts. (Tues-Sun; closed hols) 2600 Park Ave S. Phone 612/871-4907. ¢¢

Basilica of St. Mary. Renaissance architecture patterned after Basilica of St. John Lateran in Rome. (Daily) Hennepin Ave and 16th St. Phone 612/333-1381.

Eloise Butler Wildflower Garden and Bird Sanctuary. Horseshoe-shaped glen contains natural bog, swamp; habitat for prairie and woodland flowers and birds. Guided tours. Phone 612/370-4903. **FREE**

Fort Snelling State Park. (See ST. PAUL) Phone 612/725-2389.

Guthrie Theater. Produces classic plays in repertory. (June-Feb, nightly Tues-Sun; matinees Wed, Sat, Sun) Vineland Pl, 1 blk S of jct I-94 and I-394. Phone 612/377-2224.

Hennepin History Museum. Permanent and temporary exhibits on the history of Minneapolis and Hennepin County. Incl collection of textiles, costumes, toys, and material

© MAPQUEST.COM.

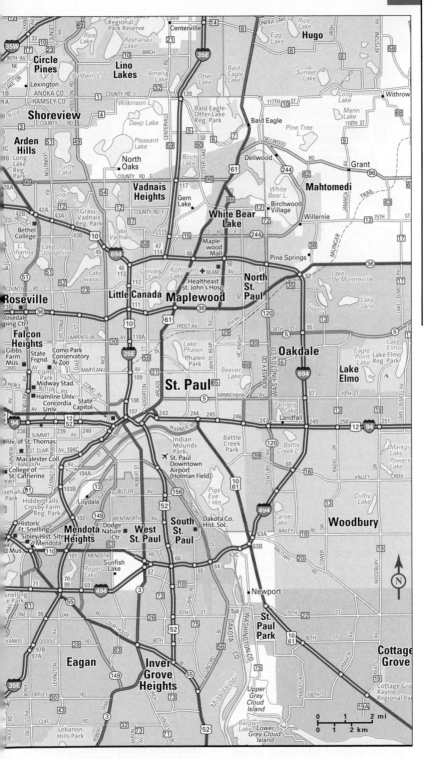

Spoon Bridge Sculpture, Minneapolis Sculpture Garden

unique to central Minnesota. Research library and archive. (Tues-Sun; closed hols) 2303 3rd Ave S. Phone 612/870-1329. ¢

Hubert H. Humphrey Metrodome. Sports stadium. Home of Minnesota Twins (baseball), Vikings (football), and University of Minnesota football. (Mon-Fri and special events) 500 11th Ave S. Phone 612/332-0386. ¢¢

Lyndale Park. Garden displays of roses, bulbs, other annuals and perennials; exotic and native trees; rock garden; two decorative fountains; bird sanctuary. Apr-Sept is best time to visit. (Daily) Off E Lake Harriet Pkwy and Roseway Rd, on NE shore of Lake Harriet. **FREE**

Minneapolis City Hall. (1891) Father of Waters statue in rotunda, carved of largest single block of marble produced from quarries of Carrara, Italy. Self-guided tours. (Mon-Fri; closed hols) 5th St and 3rd Ave S. Phone 612/673-2491. **FREE**

Minneapolis College of Art and Design. (1886) 650 students. Four-yr college of fine arts, media arts, and design. MCAD Gallery (daily; closed hols). 2501 Stevens Ave S. Gallery **FREE**

Minneapolis Grain Exchange. Visit cash grain market and futures market. Tours (Tues-Thurs). Visitors' balcony; res required (mornings; closed

hols). 400 S 4th St. Phone 612/321-7101. **FREE**

Minneapolis Institute of Arts. Masterpieces from every age and culture. Collection of more than 80,000 objects covering American and European painting, sculpture, decorative arts; period rms, prints and drawings, textiles, photography; American, African, Oceanic, ancient, and Asian objects. Lectures, classes, films (fee), special events (fee), monthly expertise clinic; restaurants. (Tues-Sat, also Sun afternoons; closed July 4, Thanksgiving, Dec 25) 2400 3rd Ave S. Phone 612/870-3131. **FREE**

Minneapolis Planetarium. More than 2,000 stars, the visible planets, the sun, moon, and a multitude of other celestial phenomena are projected onto 40-ft dome; astronomically oriented multimedia presentations. Laser light show (eves). (Closed hols) 300 Nicollet Mall, at Public Library. Phone 612/630-6150. ¢¢

Minnehaha Park. Minnehaha Falls, immortalized as the "laughing water" of Longfellow's epic poem *Song of Hiawatha;* statue of Hiawatha and Minnehaha; picnicking; Stevens House, first frame house built west of the Mississippi. Park (May-mid-Oct, daily). Minnehaha Pkwy and Hiawatha Ave S, along the Mississippi. Phone 612/370-4939. **FREE**

Minnesota Transportation Museum. Display museum and restoration shop; two-mi rides in early 1900s electric streetcars along reconstructed Como-Harriet line (Memorial Day wkend-Labor Day, daily; after Labor Day-Oct, wkends). W 42nd St and Queen Ave S. Phone 651/228-0263. ¢

✖ **Nicollet Mall.** The world-famous shopping promenade with a variety of shops, restaurants, museums, art galleries; also entertainment ranging from an art show to symphony orchestra performances (see SPECIAL EVENTS). No traffic is allowed on this avenue except for buses and cabs. Beautifully designed with spacious walkways, fountains, shade trees, flowers, and a skyway system, it is certainly worth a visit. Downtown. Phone 612/332-3101. Also here is

   IDS Tower. Stands 775 ft, 57 stories; one of the tallest buildings between Chicago and the West Coast. 80 S 8th St.

Professional sports.

   Minnesota Lynx (WNBA). Target Center, 600 First Ave N. Phone 612/637-8400.

   Minnesota Timberwolves (NBA). Target Center, 600 First Ave N. Phone 612/337-DUNK.

   Minnesota Twins (MLB). Metrodome, 34 Kirby Puckett Pl. Phone 612/375-1366.

   Minnesota Vikings (NFL). Metrodome, 500 11th Ave S. Phone 612/338-4537.

St. Anthony Falls. Head of the navigable Mississippi, site of village of St. Anthony. A public vantage point at the upper locks and dam provides a view of the falls and of the operation of the locks. Also incl a renovated warehouse with shops and restaurants. Main St SE and Central Ave.

Ski Areas.

   Buck Hill. Quad, three double chairlifts, J-bar, three rope tows; snowmaking; patrol, school, rentals; restaurant, bar, cafeteria. (Thanksgiving-Mar, daily) 15400 Buck Hill Rd, 14 mi S on I-35 W or E, in Burnsville. Phone 952/435-7174. ¢¢¢¢

   Hyland Hills. Three triple chairlifts, rope tow; patrol, school, rentals; snowmaking; cafeteria, snack bar; nursery. Longest run 2,000 ft; vertical drop 175 ft. (Thanksgiving-

mid-Mar, daily; closed Dec 25) X-country trails. Chalet Rd, 2 mi SW off I-494. Phone 952/835-4250. ¢¢¢¢

Tours.

   Gray Line bus tours. Tours of the Twin Cities area (summer). Phone 952/469-5020.

   MetroConnections. Stops incl Minnehaha Falls, Mall of America, and Minnesota History Center. (June-Aug, daily; Sept-Oct, Fri-Sun) Phone 612/333-8687. ¢¢¢¢

   River City Trolley. A 40-min loop traverses the core of downtown, passing through the Mississippi Mile, St. Anthony Falls, and the Warehouse District. On-board narration; runs approx every 20 mins. (May-Oct, daily, also Fri and Sat eves) Phone 612/204-0000. ¢

University of Minnesota, Twin Cities. (1851) 39,315 students. One of the largest single campuses in United States. Several art galleries and museums on campus. Tours. On E and W banks of Mississippi, University Ave SE. Phone 612/626-8687. On campus are

   Bell Museum of Natural History. Dioramas show Minnesota birds and mammals in natural settings; special traveling exhibits; exhibits on art, photography, and natural history research change frequently. Touch and See Room encourages hands-on exploration and comparison of natural objects. (Tues-Sun; closed Thanksgiving, Dec 25) Free admission Sun. 17th and University Ave SE. Phone 612/624-7083. ¢¢

   Frederick R. Weisman Art Museum. Striking exterior is oddly shaped stainless steel designed by Frank Gehry. Inside are collections of early 20th-century and contemporary American art, Asian ceramics, and Native American Mimbres pottery. Special exhibits. Group tours (by appt, phone 612/625-9656 three wks in advance). Museum store. (Tues-Sun; closed hols) 333 East River Rd. Phone 612/625-9494. **FREE**

Walker Art Center. Permanent collection of 20th-century painting, sculpture, prints and photographs; also changing exhibits, performances, concerts, films, lectures.

(Tues-Sun) Vineland Pl. Phone
612/375-7577. ¢¢ Opp is

Minneapolis Sculpture Garden.
Ten-acre urban garden featuring
more than 40 sculptures by leading
American and international artists;
glass conservatory. (Daily) Phone
612/375-7577. **FREE**

Special Events

Showboat. On University of Minnesota campus, on Mississippi River.
During the 1800s, melodramas,
comedies, and light opera were presented on riverboats; University Theater productions preserve this
tradition aboard an authentic, air-
conditioned sternwheeler moored on
the river. Tues-Sun. Phone 612/625-
4001 for schedule and ticket information. July-Aug.

Sommerfest. Orchestra Hall, 1111
Nicollet Mall. Summer concert series
of Minnesota Orchestra (see) with
Viennese flavor; food booths. Phone
612/371-5656. July-Aug.

Minneapolis Aquatennial. Parades,
aquatic events, sports events, entertainment. Mid-July.

Minnesota Orchestra. Orchestra Hall,
1111 Nicollet Mall. Box office phone
612/371-5656. Mid-Sept-June.

University Theatre. 120 Rarig Center,
330 21st Ave S, on University of
Minnesota campus. Student-profes-
sional productions of musicals,
comedies, and dramas in four-theatre
complex. Phone 612/625-4001. Early
Oct-late May.

Motels/Motor Lodges

★ **AMERICINN.** 21800 Industrial
Blvd, Rogers (55374). 763/428-4346;
fax 763/428-2117; res 800/634-3444.
www.americinn.com. 35 rms, 2 story. S
$39-$48; D $46-$57; each addl $5;
whirlpool rms $89-$109; under 12
free. Crib free. Pet accepted. TV; cable
(premium), VCR. Complimentary
continental bkfst. Restaurant adj open
24 hrs. Ck-out 11 am. Business servs
avail. Cr cds: A, C, D, DS, MC, V.
D 🔧 🐾 🖭 🎿

★ **AQUA CITY MOTEL.** 5739 S Lyndale Ave (55419). 612/861-6061; fax
612/861-5737; toll-free 800/861-6061.
37 rms, 1-2 story, 8 kit. units. S $35-
$42; D $45-$50; each addl $5; under
5 free. Crib $5. TV; cable (premium).

Complimentary coffee. Restaurant
nearby. Ck-out 11 am. X-country ski
½ mi. Game rm. Cr cds: A, MC, V.
🎿 🐾 SC

★★ **BAYMONT INN AND SUITES.**
6415 James Cir N, Brooklyn Center
(55430). 763/561-8400; fax 763/560-
3189; res 800/301-0200. 99 rms, 3
story. S $43-$66; D $51-$74. Crib
free. TV; cable (premium). Complimentary continental bkfst, coffee in
rms. Restaurant nearby. Ck-out noon.
Meeting rm. Business servs avail. In-
rm modem link. Valet serv. X-country
ski ½ mi. Cr cds: A, D, DS, MC, V.
D 🎿 🖭 🐾

★★ **BEST WESTERN DOWN-
TOWN.** 405 S 8th St (55404). 612/
370-1400; fax 612/370-0351; toll-free
800/372-3131. www.bestwestern.
com. 159 rms, 4 story. S $74.50-
$104.50; D $82-$108.50; each addl
$7.50; under 18 free. Crib free. TV;
cable (premium). Indoor pool; whirlpool, poolside serv. Complimentary
continental bkfst. Bar 4:30-11 pm.
Ck-out noon. Meeting rms. Business
servs avail. In-rm modem link. Valet
serv. Sundries. Exercise equipt; sauna.
Cr cds: A, C, D, DS, ER, MC, V.
D 🖭 🏋 🐾

★★ **BEST WESTERN KELLY INN.**
2705 N Annapolis Ln, Plymouth
(55441). 763/553-1600; fax 763/553-
9108; res 800/780-7234. www.best
western.com. 150 rms, 4 story. S $89-
$99; D $99; each addl $8; suites $91-
$185; under 18 free. Crib free. TV;
cable. Indoor pool; whirlpool. Complimentary coffee in rms. Restaurant
7 am-midnight. Bar 11-1 am. Ck-out
11 am. Meeting rms. Business servs
avail. Downhill ski 20 mi; x-country
ski 1 mi. Exercise equipt; sauna.
Some refrigerators. Some balconies.
Cr cds: A, C, D, DS, ER, JCB, MC, V.
D 🎿 🖭 🏋 🖭 🐾

★★ **BEST WESTERN KELLY INN.**
5201 NE Central Ave, Fridley (55441).
763/571-9440; fax 763/571-1720; toll-
free 800/780-7234. www.bestwestern.
com. 95 rms, 2 story. S, D $64-$72;
each addl $8; suites $105-$185;
under 18 free. Crib free. Pet accepted.
TV; cable (premium). Indoor pool;
whirlpool. Restaurant 6 am-9 pm.
Ck-out 11 am. Meeting rms. Business
servs avail. Exercise equipt; sauna.

St. Anthony Falls, Minneapolis

Game rm. Some refrigerators. Cr cds: A, D, DS, MC, V.

★★ **CHANHASSEN INN.** *531 W 79th St, Chanhassen (55317). 952/ 934-7373; fax 952/934-7373; res 800/ 242-6466.* 7 rms, 2 story. S $56-$61; D $61-$66; each addl $5; under 16 free. Crib free. TV; cable. Complimentary continental bkfst. Ck-out 2 pm. Business servs avail. Refrigerators, microwaves. In-rm modem link. Guest lndry. Cr cds: A, C, D, DS, MC, V.

★ **COMFORT INN.** *1600 James Cir N, Brooklyn Center (55430). 612/560-7464; fax 612/560-7464; toll-free 800/228-5150. www.comfortinn.com.* 60 rms, 3 story. June-Sept: S $74.95-$79.95; D $79.95-$84.95; each addl $5; under 19 free; lower rates rest of yr. TV; cable (premium). Complimentary continental bkfst. Restaurant adj 6 am-11 pm. Ck-out 11 am. Meeting rms. Business servs avail. Game rm. Some refrigerators, microwaves. Cr cds: A, C, D, DS, MC, V.
SC

★ **DAYS INN.** *2407 University Ave SE (55414). 612/623-3999; fax 612/331-2152; res 800/329-7466. www.daysinn. com.* 131 rms, 6 story. S $73-$99; D $79-$99; each addl $10; under 18 free. Crib free. TV; cable. Compli-

mentary continental bkfst. Restaurant nearby. Ck-out 11 am. Coin lndry. Meeting rms. Business servs avail. In-rm modem link. Downhill ski 10 mi; x-country ski 1 mi. Some refrigerators. Cr cds: A, C, D, DS, JCB, MC, V.

★★ **DAYS INN MOUNDS VIEW.** *2149 Program Ave, Mounds View (55112). 763/786-9151; fax 612/786-2845; res 800/329-7466. www.days inn.com.* 70 rms, 2 story. S $37-$51; D $46-$71; each addl $5; under 15 free; higher rates special events. Crib $3. TV; cable (premium). Complimentary continental bkfst. Restaurant adj open 24 hrs. Bar. Ck-out 11 am. Coin lndry. Meeting rms. Business servs avail. Sundries. X-country ski 3 mi. Cr cds: A, C, D, DS, MC, V.

★ **ECONO LODGE.** *2500 University Ave SE (55414). 612/331-6000; fax 612/331-6821; res 800/533-2666. www. econolodge.com.* 80 rms, 2 story. May-Sept: S $55-$65; D $61-$71; each addl $6; under 18 free; lower rates rest of yr. Crib free. TV; cable (premium). Complimentary coffee in rms. Restaurant nearby. Ck-out 11 am. Business servs avail. In-rm modem link. Pool. Cr cds: A, C, D, DS, MC, V.

[D] [⚡] [🏊] [🎿] [🏄] [🔥]

★★ **FOUR POINTS BY SHERATON MINNEAPOLIS.** *1330 Industrial Blvd (55413). 612/331-1900; fax 612/331-6827; res 800/777-3277. www.four points.com.* 252 rms, 8 story. S $99; D, studio rms $115-$195; each addl $10; suites $150-$280; wkend rates. Crib free. TV; cable (premium). Indoor pool; whirlpool, poolside serv. Coffee in rms. Restaurant 6:30 am-10:30 pm; Sat, Sun 7:30-11 pm. Bar 11-1 am; entertainment Mon-Sat. Ck-out 11 am. Meeting rms. Business servs avail. In-rm modem link. Airport transportation. X-country ski 1 mi. Exercise equipt; sauna. Luxury level. Cr cds: A, C, D, DS, MC, V.

[D] [🏄] [🏊] [🎿] [🏋] [🏄] [🔥]

★★ **HAMPTON INN.** *10420 Wayzata Blvd, Minnetonka (55305). 952/541-1094; fax 612/541-1905; toll-free 800/426-7866. www.hamptoninn. com.* 127 rms, 4 story. S $74-$89; D $89-$94; under 18 free. Crib free. TV; cable (premium). Complimentary continental bkfst. Restaurant nearby. Ck-out noon. Meeting rms. Business servs avail. In-rm modem link. Downhill ski 25 mi; x-country ski 1 mi. Cr cds: A, D, DS, MC, V.

[D] [🏄] [🏄] [🔥]

★ **METRO INN.** *5637 Lyndale Ave S (55419). 612/861-6011; fax 612/869-1041.* 35 rms. Apr-Oct: S $35-$44; D $42-$52; each addl $6; lower rates rest of yr. Crib $4-$5. Pet accepted, some restrictions; $3. TV; cable (premium). Ck-out 11 am. X-country ski ½ mi. Cr cds: A, C, DS, MC, V.

[🐾] [🏄] [🏄] [🔥]

★ **QUALITY INN & SUITES.** *41 N 10th St (55403). 612/339-9311; fax 612/339-4765; toll-free 800/423-4100. www.qualityinnminneapolis.com.* 192 rms, 3 story. S, D $59-$109; each addl $6; suites $85-$110; under 18 free; wkend rates. Crib free. TV; cable, VCR avail. Indoor pool; whirlpool, poolside serv. Restaurant 6:30 am-2 pm, 4-11 pm; Sat, Sun from 7:30 am. Bar 4 pm-1 am; entertainment Mon-Sat. Ck-out noon. Coin lndry. Meeting rms. Business servs avail. In-rm modem link. Bellhops.

Sundries. X-country ski 1 mi. Cr cds: A, D, DS, MC, V.

[D] [🏄] [🏊] [🏋] [🏄] [🔥]

★★ **RAMADA INN.** *2540 N Cleveland Ave, Roseville (55113). 651/636-4567; fax 651/636-7110; res 800/298-2054. www.ramada.com.* 256 rms, 4 story. June-Labor Day: S, D $69-$119; each addl $10; under 19 free; lower rates rest of yr. Crib free. TV; cable. Indoor pool; wading pool, whirlpool. Complimentary coffee in rms. Restaurant 6:30 am-10 pm. Bar 3 pm-1 am. Ck-out noon. Meeting rms. Business servs avail. Valet serv. Coin lndry. Exercise equipt; sauna. Game rm. Some refrigerators. Cr cds: A, C, D, DS, JCB, MC, V.

[D] [🏊] [🏋] [🏄] [🏄] [SC]

★ **RAMADA PLAZA.** *12201 Ridgedale Dr, Minnetonka (55305). 952/593-0000; toll-free 800/588-0443. www.ramada.com.* 222 rms, 4 story. S $119; D $129; each addl $10; suites $150; under 18 free; wkend rates. Crib free. TV; cable (premium). Indoor pool; poolside serv. Coffee in rms. Restaurant 6:30 am-10 pm. Rm serv 6:30-10 pm. Bar 4 pm-1 am. Ck-out noon. Meeting rms. Business servs avail. In-rm modem link. Gift shop. X-country ski 2 mi. Exercise equipt. Some private patios, balconies. Cr cds: A, C, D, DS, MC, V.

[D] [🏄] [🏊] [🏋] [🏄] [🔥]

★ **SUPER 8.** *6445 James Cir N, Brooklyn Center (55430). 763/566-9810; fax 763/566-8680; res 800/800-8000. www. super8.com.* 102 rms, 2 story. S, D $63-$73; suites $89-$119; each addl $5; under 12 free. Crib free. TV; cable (premium). Complimentary continental bkfst. Restaurant adj. Ck-out 11 am. Business servs avail. Cr cds: A, C, D, DS, MC, V.

[D] [♿] [🏄] [🔥]

Hotels

★★★ **CROWNE PLAZA NORTHSTAR HOTEL.** *618 Second Ave S (55402). 612/338-2288; fax 612/338-6194; toll-free 800/556-7827. www. crowneplaza.com.* 226 rms, 11 story. June-Sept: S, D $169-$279; each addl $15; suites $250-$500; under 17 free; wkend rates; lower rates rest of yr. Crib free. Garage parking $12.95. TV; cable, VCR avail (movies). Restaurants 6:30 am-11:30 pm. Bar 11-1 am. Ck-out 1 pm. Meeting rms. Business servs avail. In-rm modem link. Barber, beauty shop. X-country ski 1 mi. Exercise equipt. Luxury level. Cr cds: A, C, D, DS, ER, JCB, MC, V.

[icons]

★★ DOUBLETREE GUEST SUITES.
1101 LaSalle Ave (55403). 612/332-6800; fax 612/332-8246; toll-free 800/662-3232. www.doubletree. com. 230 suites, 12 story. S, D $149-$189; each addl $10; under 17 free; wkend rates. Covered parking $9.75. Crib free. TV; cable (premium). Restaurant 6:30 am-midnight. Bar 11-1 am. Ck-out noon. Meeting rms. Business servs avail. In-rm modem link. Exercise equipt; sauna. X-country ski 1 mi. Refrigerators, microwaves. Cr cds: A, D, DS, MC, V.

[icons]

★★ DOUBLETREE PARK PLACE.
1500 Park Pl Blvd (55416). 612/542-8600; fax 612/542-8063; res 800/222-8733. www.doubletree.com. 297 rms, 15 story. S, D $89-$109; each addl $10; suites $109-$139; under 18 free; wkend rates. Crib free. TV; cable (premium). Indoor pool; whirlpool. Restaurant 6:30 am-midnight. Rm serv 24 hrs. Bar 11-1 am. Ck-out noon. Convention facilities. Business servs avail. In-rm modem link. X-country ski 2 mi. Exercise equipt; sauna. Game rm. Cr cds: A, D, DS, MC, V.

[icons]

★★★ THE GRAND HOTEL MINNEAPOLIS.
615 Second Ave S (55402). 612/288-8888. www. minneapolisgrandhotel.com. 140 rms, 12 story. S, D $195-$275; each addl $20; under 17 free. Crib avail. TV; cable (premium), VCR avail. Complimentary coffee, newspaper in rms. Restaurant 6 am-10 pm. Ck-out noon. Meeting rms. Business center. Gift shop. Exercise rm. Some refrigerators, minibars. Cr cds: A, C, D, DS, ER, JCB, MC, V.

[icons]

★★★ HILTON.
1001 Marquette Ave S (55403). 612/376-1000; fax 612/397-4875; res 800/445-8667. www.hilton. com. 821 rms, 25 story. S $150-$225; D $170-$245; each addl $20; suites $700-$1,000; under 18 free. Crib avail. Valet parking $17.50; garage $10.50. TV; cable (premium), VCR avail. Heated pool; whirlpool, poolside serv. Restaurant 6:30 am-11 pm. Bar 11-1 am. Ck-out noon. Convention facilities. Business servs avail. In-rm modem link. Concierge. Sundries. Shopping arcade. X-country ski 1 mi. Exercise equipt; sauna. Some refrigerators. Cr cds: A, D, DS, MC, V.

[icons]

★★★ HILTON MINNEAPOLIS NORTH.
2200 Freeway Blvd (55430). 763/566-8000. www.hilton.com. 176 rms, 10 story. S, D $150-$225; each addl $20; under 17 free. Pool. TV; cable (premium), VCR avail. Complimentary coffee, newspaper in rms. Restaurant 6 am-10 pm. Ck-out noon. Meeting rms. Business center. Gift shop. Exercise rm. Some refrigerators, minibars. Cr cds: A, C, D, DS, MC, V.

[icons]

★★ HOLIDAY INN.
1500 Washington Ave S (55454). 612/333-4646; fax 612/333-7910; toll-free 800/448-3663. www.metrodome.com. 265 rms, 14 story. S, D $119-$159; each addl $10; suites $149.50; under 18 free. Crib free. Garage $8. TV; cable (premium), VCR avail. Indoor pool. Coffee in rms. Restaurant 6:30 am-11 pm. Bar 11-1 am; pianist. Ck-out noon. Meeting rms. Business servs avail. In-rm modem link. Gift shop. Airport transportation. Exercise equipt. Cr cds: A, C, D, DS, ER, MC, V.

[icons]

★★★ HYATT REGENCY.
1300 Nicollet Mall (55403). 612/370-1234; fax 612/370-1463; res 800/233-1234. www.hyatt.com. 533 rms, 23 suites, 24 story. S $199; D $224; each addl $25; suites $290-$800; under 18 free. Crib free. Parking $9.75. TV; VCR avail (movies). Indoor pool. Restaurants 6:30-1 am; Sun 7 am-11 pm (see also MANNY'S). Bar 11-1 am. Ck-out noon. Convention facilities. Business servs avail. In-rm modem link. Concierge. Shopping arcade. Barber, beauty shop. Airport transportation. Indoor tennis privileges. X-country ski 1 mi. Health club privileges. Luxury level. Cr cds: A, C, D, DS, MC, V.

[icons]

★★★ HYATT WHITNEY.
150 Portland Ave (55401). 612/375-1234; fax

Riding high at the Minnesota State Fair, Minneapolis

612/376-7512. www.hyatt.com. 96 rms, 8 story, 40 suites. S, D $160-$170; suites 195-$1,600; under 10 free. Crib free. Parking $6. TV; cable (premium), VCR avail. Restaurant (see also WHITNEY GRILLE). Rm serv 24 hrs. Bar 11:30-1 am; pianist. Ck-out noon. Meeting rms. Business servs avail. In-rm modem link. Concierge. Airport transportation. Bathrm phones, refrigerators. Elegantly renovated hotel located on the banks of the Mississippi River; outdoor plaza with fountain. Cr cds: A, C, D, DS, MC, V.

★★★ THE MARQUETTE HOTEL.
710 Marquette Ave (55402). 612/333-4545; fax 612/288-2188; res 800/328-4782. www.marquettehotel.com. 278 rms, 19 story. S, D $229; each addl $15; suites $379-$810; family rates; wkend rates. Crib free. Pet accepted; $200 deposit. Garage parking $16; wkends $7. TV; cable (premium), VCR avail. Restaurant 6:30 am-10:30 pm. Bar 11:30-1 am. Ck-out noon. Convention facilities. Business center. In-rm modem link. X-country ski 1 mi. Exercise equipt. Steam bath in suites. Luxury level. Cr cds: C, D, DS, JCB, MC, V.

★★★ MARRIOTT CITY CENTER
MINNEAPOLIS. 30 S 7th St (55402).

612/349-4000; fax 612/332-7165; toll-free 800/228-9290. www.marriott.com. 583 rms, 83 suites, 31 story. S $189; D $209; each addl $10; suites $250-$650; under 18 free; wkend rates. Crib free. Valet parking $17. TV; cable (premium), VCR avail (movies). Restaurants 6:30 am-11 pm. Bar 11-1 am. Ck-out noon. Convention facilities. Business center. In-rm modem link. Shopping arcade. X-country ski 1 mi. Exercise rm; sauna. Massage. Health club privileges. Whirlpool. Some bathrm phones. Luxury level. Cr cds: A, C, D, DS, MC, V.

★★★ MARRIOTT SOUTHWEST
MINNEAPOLIS. 5801 Opus Pkwy, Minnetonka (55343). 952/935-5500; fax 952/935-0753. www.marriott.com. 321 rms, 17 story. S, D $150-$225; each addl $20; under 17 free. Crib avail. Pet accepted. Indoor pool. TV; cable (premium), VCR avail. Complimentary coffee, newspaper in rms. Restaurant 6 am-10 pm. Ck-out noon. Meeting rms. Business center. Gift shop. Exercise rm. Some refrigerators, minibars. Cr cds: A, C, D, DS, ER, JCB, MC, V.

★★★ MILLENNIUM HOTEL MIN-
NEAPOLIS. 1313 Nicollet Mall (55403). 612/332-6000; fax 612/359-2160. www.millennium-hotels.com. 325

rms, 14 story. S $175; D $195; suites $190-$350. Crib free. Pet accepted. TV; cable (premium). Indoor pool. Restaurant (see also 1313 NICOLLET). Bars 11-1 am. Ck-out noon. Coin lndry. Convention facilities. Business servs avail. In-rm modem link. Gift shop. Airport transportation avail. X-country ski 1 mi. Exercise equipt; sauna. Health club privileges. Cr cds: A, D, DS, MC, V.

D ❄ ➤ ➤ ⅞ ➷ ♨

★★★ **NORTHLAND INN AND EXECUTIVE CONFERENCE CENTER.** *7025 Northland Dr, Brooklyn Park (55428). 763/536-8300; fax 763/536-8790; toll-free 800/441-6422. www.northlandinn.com.* 231 rms, 8 story. S, D $125-$195; under 12 free. Crib free. TV; cable (premium), VCR avail. Indoor pool; whirlpool, poolside serv. Restaurant 6:30 am-10 pm. Bar to 1 am. Ck-out noon. Meeting rms. Business servs avail. In-rm modem link. Concierge. Sundries. Gift shop. Valet serv. Downhill ski 20 mi; x-country 1 mi. Exercise equipt. Game rm. Refrigerators avail. Cr cds: A, C, D, DS, MC, V.

D ➤ ➤ ⅞ ➷ ♨

★★ **RADISSON.** *3131 Campus Dr, Plymouth (55441). 763/559-6600; fax 763/559-1053; res 800/333-3333.* 243 rms, 6 story. S, D $124; each addl $10; suites $159-$249; under 18 free. Crib free. TV; cable (premium), VCR avail. Indoor pool; whirlpool, poolside serv. Restaurant 6:30 am-10 pm. Bar 11-1 am. Ck-out noon. Meeting rms. Business servs avail. In-rm modem link. Gift shop. Lighted tennis. Downhill ski 20 mi; x-country ski 2 mi. Exercise rm; sauna. Racquetball. Rec rm. Refrigerators. On wooded site. Cr cds: A, D, DS, MC, V.

D ➤ ⛳ ➤ ⅞ ➷ ♨

★★ **RADISSON HOTEL METRODOME.** *615 Washington Ave SE (55414). 612/379-8888; fax 612/379-8436; toll-free 800/822-6757. www.radisson.com.* 304 rms, 8 story. S $139-$149; D $149-$159; each addl $10; suites $135-$325; under 18 free. Crib free. Pet accepted. Valet parking $9.50; garage $6.50. TV; cable, VCR avail. Pool privileges. Complimentary coffee in rms. Restaurants 6:30 am-10:30 pm (see also MEADOWS). Bar to 1 am. Ck-out noon.

Meeting rms. Business servs avail. In-rm modem link. Gift shop. Downhill ski 20 mi; x-country ski 1 mi. Exercise equipt. Health club privileges. Some refrigerators. Cr cds: A, D, DS, JCB, MC, V.

❄ ➤ ➤ ⅞ ➷ ♨ SC

★★ **RADISSON PLAZA.** *35 S 7th St (55402). 612/339-4900; fax 612/337-9766; toll-free 800/333-3333. www.radisson.com.* 357 rms, 17 story. S, D $178-$258; each addl $10; suites $310-$410; under 18 free. Crib free. Parking $10. TV; cable (premium), VCR avail. Restaurant 6 am-11 pm. Rm serv 24 hrs. Bar 11-1 am; entertainment. Ck-out noon. Meeting rms. Business servs avail. In-rm modem link. Concierge. Shopping arcade. X-country ski 1 mi. Exercise rm; sauna. Whirlpool. Atrium lobby; fountain, marble columns. Luxury level. Cr cds: A, C, D, DS, ER, JCB, MC, V.

D ➤ ⅞ ➷ ♨

B&Bs/Small Inns

★★★ **INN ON THE FARM.** *6150 Summit Dr N, Brooklyn Center (55430). 612/569-6330; fax 612/569-6321; toll-free 800/428-8382. www.innonthefarm.com.* 10 rms, 2 story. S, D $100-$130. TV. Complimentary full bkfst; afternoon refreshments. Restaurant nearby. Ck-out 11 am, ck-in 4 pm. Business servs avail. X-country ski 1/2 mi. Built in the 1880s; antiques. Cr cds: DS, MC, V.

D ⅞ ➤ ➷ ♨

★★ **NICOLLET ISLAND INN.** *95 Merriam St (55401). 612/331-1800; fax 612/331-6528; toll-free 800/331-6528. www.nicolletislandinn.com.* 24 rms, 2 story. S, D $140; TV; cable (premium). Restaurant 7 am-9:30 pm. Ck-out noon, ck-in 3 pm. Business servs avail. In-rm modem link. Cr cds: A, C, D, DS, ER, JCB, MC, V.

D ⅞ ➷ ♨

All Suite

★★★ **EMBASSY SUITES DOWNTOWN MINNEAPOLIS.** *425 S 7th St (55415). 612/333-3111; fax 612/333-7984. www.embassysuites.com.* 217 suites, 6 story. S $155-$189; D $165-$185; each addl $10; under 13 free;

wkend rates. Crib free. TV; cable (premium). Indoor pool; whirlpool. Complimentary full bkfst. Restaurant 11 am-2:30 pm, 5-10 pm; Fri, Sat 5-11 pm. Bar 11-1 am. Ck-out noon. Meeting rms. Business servs avail. In-rm modem link. X-country ski 1 mi. Exercise equipt; sauna, steam rm. Refrigerators, microwaves. Cr cds: A, MC, V.

D ⏏ 🏊 🕵 🛏 🔥 SC

Restaurants

★ **AUGUST MOON.** *5340 Wayzata Blvd, St. Louis Park (55416). 612/544-7017. www.augustmoon.com.* Hrs: 11 am-9 pm; Fri to 10 pm; Sat 4-10 pm; Sun 4-9 pm. Closed Dec 25. New Asian menu. Wine, beer. Lunch $5-$11.95, dinner $8-$15. Specialties: Cal-Asian crab cakes, tandoori chicken. Parking. Asian artwork. Cr cds: A, D, MC, V.

D 🛏

★ **BACKSTAGE AT BRAVO.** *900 Hennepin Ave (55403). 612/338-0062.* Hrs: 5-11 pm; Fri to 12:30 am; Sat to midnight. Closed Thanksgiving, Dec 24, 25. Res accepted. Continental menu. Bar 5 pm-1 am. Lunch $5.95-$18.50, dinner $12.50-$25. Specializes in fresh seafood, steak, pasta. Valet parking (dinner). Outdoor dining. Broadway theatre decor with rooftop dining. Cr cds: A, D, DS, V.

D 🛏

★ **BLACK FOREST INN.** *1 E 26th St (55404). 612/872-0812. www.black forestinnmpls.com.* Hrs: 11-1 am; Sun noon-midnight. German menu. Lunch $3.50-$8, dinner $5.50-$15. Specialties: sauerbraten, Wiener schnitzel, bratwurst. Outdoor dining. German decor. Family-owned. Cr cds: A, C, D, DS, MC, V.

D 🛏

★ **BUCA DI BEPPO.** *11 S 12th St (55403). 612/288-0138. www.bucadi beppo.com.* Hrs: 5-10 pm; Fri, Sat to 11 pm. Closed Thanksgiving, Dec 24, 25. Italian menu. Bar to midnight. Dinner $8.95-$22.95. Specialties: chicken marsala, ravioli with meat sauce. Pictures of Italian celebrities along walls. Cr cds: A, D, DS, MC, V.

D 🛏

★★ **CAFE BRENDA.** *300 1st Ave N (55401). 612/342-9230. www.cafe brenda.com.* Hrs: Mon-Fri 11:30 am-2 pm, 5:30-9 pm; Fri and Sat 5:30-10 pm. Closed Sun; hols. Res accepted. Vegetarian, seafood menu. Bar. Lunch $6-$10, dinner $9-$16. Specializes in fresh broiled rainbow trout, organic chicken enchiladas. Parking (dinner). Totally nonsmoking. Cr cds: A, D, DS, MC, V.

D

★★★ **CAFE UN DEUX TROIS.** *114 S 9th St (55402). 612/673-0686.* Hrs: 11:30 am-10 pm; Fri, Sat to 11 pm. Closed Sun; hols. Res accepted. French bistro menu. Bar. Lunch $7.95-$17.50, dinner $12.95-$19.50. Specialties: poulet rôti, roast Long Island duck. Own pasta. Free valet parking (dinner). Eclectic, bistro atmosphere with murals, mirrors on walls. Cr cds: A, C, D, MC, V.

D 🛏

★★ **CAMPIELLO.** *1320 W Lake St (55408). 612/825-2222. www. campiello.damico.com.* Hrs: 5-10 pm; Fri, Sat to 11 pm; Sun 10:30 am-2:30 pm (brunch), 5-10:30 pm. Closed Dec 25. Res accepted. Italian menu. Bar to midnight. Dinner $8.95-$17.95. Sun brunch $8.95-$13.95. Specialties: Balsamic-glazed shortribs, wood-oven pizzas. Own pasta. Valet parking. Outdoor dining. Upscale atmosphere with high ceilings, chandeliers. Cr cds: A, D, DS, MC, V.

D 🛏

★ **CARAVELLE.** *2529 Nicollet Ave S (55404). 612/871-3226.* Hrs: 11 am-9 pm; Sat from noon; Sun noon-7 pm. Closed July 4, Thanksgiving, Dec 25. Res accepted. Chinese menu. Lunch, dinner $5.95-$8.95. Buffet: lunch $5.50, dinner $5.95. Specializes in shrimp, scallops. Parking. Asian decor. Cr cds: MC, V.

D 🛏

★ **CHEZ BANANAS.** *129 N 4th St (55401). 612/340-0032. www.chez bananas.net.* Hrs: 11:30 am-10 pm; Sat, Sun 5-10 pm. Closed Mon; hols. Caribbean menu. Bar. Lunch $5-$10, dinner $7-$19. Specialties: mustard-pepper chicken, Caribbean barbecue. Informal, fun atmosphere; inflatable animals hanging from ceiling, toys at tables. Cr cds: A, D, DS, MC, V.

D

★★ **CHRISTOS.** *2632 Nicollet Ave S (55408). 612/871-2111. www.christos. com.* Hrs: 11 am-10 pm; Fri to 10:30 pm; Sat noon-10:30 pm; Sun noon-9 pm. Closed hols. Res accepted. Greek menu. Wine, beer. Lunch $4.50-$7.50, dinner $7.95-$12.95. Specialties: spanakopita, moussaka, shish kebab. Cr cds: A, C, D, DS, MC, V.
D ⊟

★★★ **D'AMICO CUCINA.** *100 N 6th St (55403). 612/338-2401. www. damico.com.* Hrs: 5:30-10 pm; Fri, Sat to 11 pm; Sun 5-9 pm. Closed hols. Res accepted. Italian menu. Bar. Dinner $21-$29.50. Specializes in modern Italian cuisine. Piano Fri, Sat. Restored warehouse. Cr cds: A, D, DS, MC, V.
D

★★ **FIGLIO.** *3001 Hennepin Ave S (55408). 612/822-1688.* Hrs: 11:30-1 am; Fri, Sat to 2 am. Res accepted. Italian menu. Bar. Lunch, dinner $7.50-$18.95. Specializes in pasta, pizza, sandwiches. Outdoor dining. Art Deco decor. Cr cds: A, D, DS, MC, V.
D ⊟

★★ **510 RESTAURANT.** *510 Groveland Ave (55403). 612/874-6440.* Hrs: 5:30-10 pm. Closed Sun. Res accepted. French, American menu. Wine cellar. Dinner $12-$22. Complete meals: 3-course dinner $19.95. Specializes in rack of lamb, seafood. Own baking. Family-owned. Cr cds: A, C, D, DS, MC, V.
D

★ **GARDENS - SALONICA.** *19 5th St NE (55413). 612/378-0611.* Hrs: 11 am-9 pm; Fri, Sat to 10 pm. Closed Sun; Thanksgiving, Dec 25. Greek menu. Bar. Lunch, dinner $5-$10. Specializes in lamb dishes. Own pasta. Casual dining; Greek decor. Cr cds: A, C, D, DS, MC, V.
D ⊟

★★ **GIORGIO.** *2451 Hennepin Ave (55408). 612/374-5131.* Hrs: 11:30 am-2:30 pm, 5-11 pm; Sun 5-11 pm. Closed Thanksgiving, Dec 24, 25. Res accepted wkdays. Italian menu. Wine, beer. Lunch $2.95-$10.95, dinner $2.95-$16.50. Specialties: marinated leg of lamb, calamari steak.

Outdoor dining. Italian decor. Cr cds: D, MC, V.
D

★★★★ **GOODFELLOW'S.** *40 S 7th St (55402). 612/332-4800. www.good fellowsrestaurant.com.* This former Forum-Cafeteria space feels like a trip back to the 1930s, albeit a luxurious trip, with a decor of polished wood, Art Deco fixtures, and jade accents. Executive chef Kevin Cullen's regional American offerings highlight local, seasonal ingredients and may incl a lamb trio of grilled chop, sweet-onion strudel, and seared leg with marjoram sauce. The Forum space offers four private dining/meeting rooms. Specialties: grilled salmon, hickory-grilled Wisconsin veal chop. Hrs: 11:30 am-2 pm, 5:30-9 pm; Fri to 10 pm; Sat 5:30-10 pm. Closed Sun; hols. Res accepted. Bar. Wine list. Lunch $6-$13, dinner $20-$31. Beamed ceiling. Cr cds: A, C, D, DS, MC, V.
D ⊟

★ **ICHIBAN JAPANESE STEAK HOUSE.** *1333 Nicollet Mall Ave (55403). 612/339-0540.* Hrs: 4:30-9:30 pm; Fri, Sat to 10 pm. Closed Thanksgiving, Dec 24. Res accepted. Japanese menu. Bar. Dinner $13.95-$29.50. Specializes in sushi, tempura. Tableside cooking. Japanese decor. Cr cds: A, C, D, DS, MC, V.
D SC

★ **IT'S GREEK TO ME.** *626 W Lake St (55408). 612/825-9922.* Hrs: 4 pm-midnight; Sat, Sun from 11 am. Closed Mon; hols. Greek menu. Bar. Outdoor Patio. Lunch, dinner $7.75-$13.95. Specialties: lamb kebab, pastitsio. Parking. Cr cds: A, MC, V.
D ⊟

★★★ **JAX CAFE.** *1928 University Ave NE (55418). 612/789-7297.* Hrs: 11 am-10:30 pm; Sun to 9 pm; Sun brunch 10 am-1:30 pm. Closed hols. Res accepted. Wine list. Lunch $7.95-$13.95, dinner $15-$35. Sun brunch $14.50. Specialties: prime rib, rainbow trout (in season). Pianist Thurs-Sun. Parking. Overlooks trout pond; waterwheel. Fireplace. Family-owned. Cr cds: A, D, DS, MC, V.
D ⊟

★ **J. D. HOYT'S.** *301 Washington Ave N (55401). 612/338-1560. www.jdhoyts. com.* Hrs: 7-1 am; Sat from 7:30 am; Sun 10 am-midnight; Sun brunch 10 am-2 pm. Closed hols. Res accepted. Bar. Bkfst $1.99-$7, lunch $7.50-$9.95, dinner $8-$27.95. Sun brunch $9.95. Specializes in pork chops, charcoal-grilled steak. Valet parking. Casual dining; roadhouse atmosphere. Cr cds: A, D, DS, MC, V.
D ⊐

★ **JERUSALEM'S.** *1518 Nicollet Ave S (55403). 612/871-8883.* Hrs: 11 am-10 pm; Fri to 11 pm; Sat, Sun noon-10 pm. Closed Thanksgiving, Dec 25. Res accepted. Middle Eastern menu. Bar. Lunch $4.25-$8.25, dinner $9.95-$15.95. Specializes in vegetarian combinations. Middle Eastern tapestries on walls. Cr cds: C, D, DS, MC, V.
D ⊐

★ **KIKUGAWA.** *43 SE Main St (55414). 612/378-3006. www.kiku gawa-sushi.com.* Hrs: 11:30 am-2 pm, 5-10 pm; Sat noon-2 pm, 5-11 pm; Sun noon-2:30 pm, 4:30-9:30 pm. Closed Jan 1, Thanksgiving, Dec 25. Res accepted. Japanese menu. Bar. Lunch $4.95-$10, dinner $9.50-$26.50. Specialties: sukiyaki, sushi bar. Parking. Modern Japanese decor. Overlooks Mississippi River. Cr cds: A, D, DS, MC, V.
D

★ **THE KING AND I.** *1346 LaSalle Ave (55403). 612/332-6928. www. kingandithai.com.* Hrs: 11 am-1 am; Sat from 5 pm. Closed Sun. Res accepted. Thai menu. Wine, beer. Lunch, dinner $7.25-$17.95. Specialties: pad Thai, king's spring roll, tom yum goong. Informal dining. Cr cds: A, C, D, DS, MC, V.
D ⊐

★★ **LINGUINI AND BOB.** *100 N 6th St (55403). 612/332-1600. www. damico.com.* Hrs: 5-9:30 pm; Fri, Sat to 11 pm. Closed Sun; hols. Res accepted. Italian menu. Bar. Dinner $8.95-$17.95. Specializes in shrimp, pasta. 2nd floor overlooks Butler Sq. Cr cds: A, D, DS, MC, V.
D ⊐

★★★ **LORD FLETCHER'S OF THE LAKE.** *3746 Sunset Dr, Spring Park (55384). 952/471-8513. www.*

lordfletchers.com. Hrs: 11:30 am-2:30 pm, 5-10 pm; Sun 4:30-9:30 pm; Sun brunch 11 am-2 pm. Closed Jan 1, Dec 24 eve, Dec 25. Res accepted. English, American menu. Bar. Wine list. Lunch $6.25-$11.50, dinner $12.95-$22.95. Sun brunch $10.95. Specializes in beef, fish, prime rib. Outdoor dining. Mesquite charcoal grill. Old English decor; fireplaces, wine kegs, antiques. Boat dockage. Cr cds: A, D, DS, MC, V.
D

★★ **LORING CAFE.** *1624 Harmon Pl (55403). 612/332-1617. www.loring cafe.com.* Hrs: 11:30 am-3:30 pm, 5:30-11 pm; Fri, Sat 11:30 am-3 pm, 4 pm-midnight; Sun 11:30 am-3 pm, 5:30-11 pm. Closed Dec 24, 25. Res accepted. Bar. Lunch $9-$15, dinner $18-$35. Specialty: artichoke ramekin. Entertainment. Outdoor dining. Restored 1918 building. Eclectic decor. Cr cds: A, C, D, MC, V.
D ⊐

★★★ **LUCIA'S.** *1432 W 31st St (55408). 612/825-1572. www. lucias.com.* Hrs: 11:30 am-2:30 pm, 5:30-9:30 pm; Fri, Sat to 10 pm; Sun 10 am-2 pm, 5:30-9 pm; Sat, Sun brunch 10 am-2 pm. Closed Mon; hols. Res accepted. Contemporary American menu. Bar. Lunch $5.50-$8.95, dinner $8.95-$16.95. Sat, Sun brunch $5.95-$8.95. Specialties: polenta, crostini. Parking. Outdoor dining. Menu changes wkly. Cr cds: MC, V.
D

★★★ **MANNY'S.** *1300 Nicollet Mall (55403). 612/339-9900.* Hrs: 5:30-10 pm; Sun to 9 pm. Closed hols. Res accepted. Bar. A la carte entrees: $28-$50. Specializes in steak, lobster. Contemporary decor. Cr cds: A, D, DS, MC, V.
D ⊐

★★ **MARSH.** *15000 Minnetonka Blvd, Minnetonka (55345). 952/935-2202.* Hrs: 7 am-9 pm; Sat 8 am-8:30 pm; Sun 8 am-5 pm; Sun brunch 11 am-2 pm. Closed Thanksgiving, Dec 25. Res accepted. Bar. Lunch $3.50-$8.50, dinner $8-$15. Sun brunch $8.50. Children's menu. Specialties: portobello mushroom melt, fish of the day. Own baking, pasta. Outdoor dining. Adj large fitness facility;

Statue in Minnehaha Park

menu changes daily, features healthy choices. Cr cds: A, MC, V.
[D]

★★ **MEADOWS.** *615 Washington Ave SE (55414). 612/379-8888. www. radisson.com.* Hrs: 5:30-10 pm. Closed Sun; hols. Res accepted. Continental menu. Bar 4 pm-1 am. Dinner $18.95-$30.95. Specializes in wild game, walleye. Own pasta. Pianist Fri, Sat. Valet parking. Elegant, semi-formal atmosphere; brass ceiling fans, high-backed chairs. Cr cds: A, DS, MC, V.
[D]

★★★ **MORTON'S OF CHICAGO.** *555 Nicollet Mall (55402). 612/673-9700. www.mortons.com.* Hrs: 11:30 am-2:30 pm, 5:30-11 pm; Sun 5-10 pm. Closed hols. Res accepted. Continental menu. Bar. Lunch $9.95-$29.95, dinner $29.95-$59.95.

Specializes in steak, lobster. Contemporary decor. Cr cds: A, D, MC, V.
[D]

★★ **NEW FRENCH CAFE.** *128 N 4th St (55401). 612/338-3790.* Hrs: 7 am-2 pm, 5:30-10 pm; Fri to 11 pm; Sat 5:30-11 pm; Sun 5-9 pm; Sat, Sun brunch 8 am-2 pm. Res accepted. Country and contemporary French menu. Bar 11-1 am, Sun from 6 pm. Bkfst $3.95-$7.95, lunch $6.95-$11, dinner $16.95-$23. Prix fixe dinner: $18. Sat, Sun brunch $3.50-$10.75. Specializes in duck, seafood. Outdoor dining (bar). Remodeled building (1900); French bistro theme. Cr cds: A, D, MC, V.
[D]

★ **NYE'S POLONAISE.** *112 E Hennepin Ave (55414). 612/379-2021.* Hrs: 11 am-11 pm; Sun 5-10 pm. Closed Dec 25. Res accepted. Polish, American menu. Bar to 1 am. Lunch $4.95-$7.95, dinner $11.95-$17.95. Specialties: prime rib, pierogi. Polka Thurs-Sat. Casual decor. Cr cds: A, D, DS, MC, V.
[D]

★★★ **OCEANAIRE SEAFOOD INN.** *1300 Nicollet Mall (55403). 612/333-2277.* Fresh seafood menu changes daily. Specialties: fresh seafood. Hrs: 5-10 pm, Fri, Sat to 11 pm. Dinner: $10.95-$59.95. Res recommended. Parking. Cr cds: A, C, D, DS, MC, V.
[D]

★★ **ORIGAMI.** *30 N 1st St (55401). 612/333-8430. www.origami restaurant.com.* Hrs: 11 am-2 pm, 5-9:30 pm; Fri, Sat to 11 pm, Sun 5-9 pm. Closed hols. Japanese menu. Bar. Lunch $5-$12, dinner $7-$25. Specialties: sushi bar, sashimi. Parking. Outdoor dining. Cr cds: A, D, DS, MC, V.
[D]

★★★ **PALOMINO.** *825 Hennepin Ave (55402). 612/339-3800.* Hrs: 11:15 am-2:30 pm, 5-10 pm; Fri, Sat to 11 pm; Sun 5-10 pm. Closed hols. Res accepted. Mediterranean menu. Bar to 1 am. Lunch $4.50-$16.95, dinner $6.95-$25.95. Specialties: spit-roasted garlic chicken, hardwood-grilled salmon. Contemporary decor. Cr cds: A, D, DS, MC, V.
D

★ **PICKLED PARROT.** *26 N 5th St (55403). 612/332-0673.* Hrs: 11-1 am; Sun 10 am-10 pm; Sun brunch 10 am-2 pm. Closed Jan 1, Dec 24, 25. Res accepted. Bar. Lunch $7.95-$13, dinner $12.95-$22.50. Sun brunch $12.95. Specialties: barbecued ribs, pork sandwich, Southern dishes. Colorful decor. Cr cds: A, C, D, DS, MC, V.
D

★★ **PING'S SZECHUAN BAR AND GRILL.** *1401 Nicollet Ave S (55403). 612/874-9404.* Hrs: 11 am-10 pm; Fri to midnight; Sat noon-midnight; Sun noon-9 pm. Closed Easter, Thanksgiving, Dec 24, 25. Res accepted. Chinese menu. Bar. Lunch buffet $6.95. Dinner $9-$14. Specialties: Peking duck, Ping's wings, Szechwan trio. Valet parking. Cr cds: A, C, D, DS, MC, V.
D

★ **PRACNA ON MAIN.** *117 Main St (55414). 612/379-3200.* Hrs: 11:30 am-10 pm. Bar to 1 am. Lunch $6-$10, dinner $12-$17.95. Outdoor dining. Warehouse (1890); turn-of-the-century decor. Overlooks Mississippi River. Cr cds: A, D, DS, MC, V.
D

★★★ **RUTH'S CHRIS STEAK HOUSE.** *920 2nd Ave S (55402). 612/672-9000. www.ruthschris.com.* Hrs: 5-10:30 pm. Closed Thanksgiving, Dec 25. Res accepted. Bar. Dinner $35-$45. Specializes in steak. Elegant decor. Cr cds: A, D, DS, MC, V.
D

★ **SAWATDEE.** *607 Washington Ave S (55415). 612/338-6451. www.sawatdee.com.* Hrs: 11 am-10 pm; Fri, Sat to 11 pm. Res accepted. Thai menu. Bar. A la carte entrees: lunch, dinner $8.25-$14.95. Buffet: lunch $8.95. Specialties: pad Thai, Bangkok

seafood special. Parking. Cr cds: A, C, D, DS, MC, V.
D

★ **SHUANG CHENG.** *1320 SE 4th St (55414). 612/378-0208.* Hrs: 10 am-10 pm; Fri, Sat 11 am-11 pm; Sun 4-10 pm. Chinese menu. Lunch $3.55-$4.75, dinner $4.50-$10.95. Specializes in seafood, pork, chicken. Casual decor. Cr cds: A, D, DS, MC, V.
D

★ **SIDNEY'S PIZZA CAFE.** *2120 Hennepin Ave (55405). 612/870-7000.* Hrs: 7 am-11 pm; Fri to midnight; Sat 10 am-midnight; Sun 10 am-11 pm. Closed Dec 24, 25. Italian, American menu. Wine, beer. Bkfst $4.95-$9.95, lunch, dinner $4.95-$9.95. Specializes in pizza, pasta. Outdoor dining. Casual decor. Cr cds: D, DS, V.
D

★★ **SOPHIA.** *65 SE Main St (55414). 612/379-1111. www.sophia-mpls.com.* Hrs: 11 am-3 pm, 5-9:45 pm; Fri, Sat to 11:45 pm; Sun 11 am-3 pm. Closed Jan 1, Dec 25. Res accepted. French, Continental menu. Bar. Lunch $5.95-$10.95, dinner $11.95-$19.95. Specializes in Norwegian salmon, steaks. Pianist Tues-Sat. Outdoor dining. Many ingredients are provided through restaurant's own ranch. Overlooks river. Cr cds: A, D, DS, MC, V.
D

★★ **TABLE OF CONTENTS.** *1310 Hennepin Ave (55403). 612/339-1133. www.tableofcontents.net.* Hrs: 11:30 am-2 pm, 5-10 pm; Fri, Sat to 11 pm; Sun 10 am-3 pm, 5-9 pm. Closed hols. Res accepted. Contemporary American menu. Bar. Lunch $7.50-$12.50, dinner $12.50-$22.95. Sun brunch $4.95-$11.95. Specializes in grilled fish, grilled beef. Contemporary decor. Cr cds: A, D, DS, MC, V.
D

★★ **1313 NICOLLET.** *1313 Nicollet Mall (55403). 612/332-6000. www.millennium-hotels.com.* Hrs: 6:30 am-2 pm, 5-10 pm. Res accepted. Bar to 1 am. Bkfst $6.25-$7.50, lunch $6.25-$8.50, dinner $7.50-$16.95. Children's menu. Specializes in pasta, steak. Contemporary decor. Cr cds: A, C, D, DS, MC, V.

D

★★★ **WHITNEY GRILLE.** *150 Portland Ave (55401). 612/372-6405. www. hyatt.com.* Hrs: 6:30 am-10 pm; Sat 7 am-10 pm; Sun 7 am-2 pm. Closed Dec 25. Res accepted. Bar to midnight. Bkfst, lunch, dinner $19-$29. Sun brunch $19.95. Specialty: tournedos Rossini. Entertainment Fri, Sat. Outdoor dining. Formal decor. Totally nonsmoking. Cr cds: A, D, DS, MC, V.

D

Unrated Dining Spots

EMILY'S LEBANESE DELI. *641 University Ave NE (55413). 612/379-4069.* Hrs: 9 am-9 pm; Fri, Sat to 10 pm. Closed Tues; Easter, Thanksgiving, Dec 25. Lebanese menu. Lunch, dinner $4.50-$7.50. Specialties: spinach pie, tabooleh salad. Parking. No cr cds accepted.

MARKET BAR-B-QUE. *1414 Nicollet Ave S (55403). 612/872-1111. www. marketbbq.com.* Hrs: 11:30-2:30 am; Sun noon-midnight. Bar. Lunch $5-$9, dinner $9-$15.95. Specializes in barbecued chicken, ribs, pork. Free parking. 1930s cafe atmosphere. Cr cds: A, C, D, DS, MC, V.

D

MUD PIE. *2549 Lyndale Ave S (55405). 612/872-9435.* Hrs: 11 am-10 pm; Sat, Sun from 8 am. Closed hols. Vegetarian menu. Wine, beer. Bkfst $2-$4.50, lunch $4-$12, dinner $7-$15. Outdoor dining. Cr cds: A, D, DS, MC, V.

D

Moorhead

(D-1) *See also Detroit Lakes; also see Fargo, ND*

Founded 1871 **Pop** 32,295 **Elev** 903 ft
Area code 218 **Zip** 56560
Information Chamber of Commerce of Fargo Moorhead, 321 N 4th St, PO Box 2443, Fargo, ND, 58108-2443; 701/237-5678
Web www.fmchamber.com

Along with the neighboring city to the west, Fargo, North Dakota, Moorhead is considered an agricultural capital. A shipping and processing center for agricultural products, the town is also a retailing and distribution point. The biggest industries are sugar refining and grain malting. Millions of pounds of sugar are produced annually from beets raised in and near Clay County. Moorhead is the home of Moorhead State University, Concordia College, and Northwest Technical College-Moorhead.

What to See and Do

Comstock Historic House. (1882) Eleven-rm home of Solomon Comstock, the founder of Moorhead State University, and his daughter Ada Louise Comstock, who was the first full-time president of Radcliffe College (1923-1943). House has period furniture, historical artifacts. Guided tours. (June-Sept, Sat and Sun) 506 8th St S. Phone 218/233-0848. ¢

Heritage-Hjemkomst Interpretive Center. Home of the *Hjemkomst,* a replica Viking ship that sailed to Norway in 1982; also home of Clay County Museum. (Mon-Sat, also Sun afternoons; closed hols) 202 1st Ave N. Phone 218/233-5604. ¢¢

Regional Science Center-Planetarium. Offers variety of astronomy programs. (Sept-May, Mon, Sun; summer, Thurs) Moorhead State University campus, 11th St and 8th Ave S. Phone 218/236-3982. ¢¢

Viking Mooring Stones. These stones are believed to be evidence of the presence of Viking explorers in the area (1362). Stones are approx 6 x 4 x 5 ft, embedded above the highest water line level and at the foot of nearby hills. Anglers now use them as piers to moor their boats. 21 mi E of town in Hawley.

Special Event

Scandinavian Hjemkomst Festival. Phone 218/233-8484. Late June.

Motel/Motor Lodge

★ **SUPER 8 MOTEL.** *3621 S 8th St (56560). 218/233-8880; res 800/800-8000. www.super8.com.* 61 rms, 2 story. S $35; D $40-$49; each addl

$4; under 12 free. Crib $2. TV; cable. Complimentary continental bkfst. Restaurant nearby. Ck-out 11 am. Coin lndry. Business servs avail. Game rm. Cr cds: A, MC, V.

D ⊠ ⚒ SC

Mora

(E-4) *See also Hinckley*

Pop 2,905 **Elev** 1,010 ft
Area code 320 **Zip** 55051
Information Mora Area Chamber of Commerce, Tourist Information Center, 114 Union St S; 800/291-5729

Rich in Swedish heritage, Mora's name led to its sister city affiliation with Mora, Sweden.

What to See and Do

Fishing. Snake River. Runs along N, S, and W perimeters of city. Canoeing. **Fish Lake.** 5 mi S off MN 65. **Ann Lake.** 8 mi NW, off MN 47. **Knife Lake.** 8 mi N on MN 65.
Kanabec History Center. Exhibits, gift shop, picnic area, hiking and ski trails; research information. (Daily; closed Jan 1, Thanksgiving, Dec 24-25) W Forest Ave. Phone 320/679-1665. ¢

Special Events

Vasaloppet Cross-Country Ski Race. Second Sun Feb.
Canoe Race. First Sat May.
Half-Marathon. Third Sat Aug.
Bike Tour. Third Sat Sept.

Morris

(E-2) *See also Glenwood*

Pop 5,613 **Area code** 320 **Zip** 56267
Information Morris Area Chamber of Commerce & Agriculture, 507 Atlantic Ave; 320/589-1242

Morris is the county seat of Stevens County and provides a regional shopping center for west central Minnesota. The surrounding area offers good fishing and hunting and is known for wildfowl, especially pheasants. The Wetland Management office is located here and manages seven counties along with 43,000 acres of waterfowl protection areas.

What to See and Do

Pomme de Terre City Park. A 363-acre public recreational area along Pomme de Terre River. Picnicking; canoeing, fishing; camping (hook-ups; fee), nature and bicycle trail; swimming beach; sand volleyball court; concession. (Apr-Oct, daily) 2¾ mi E on County 10. **FREE**
University of Minnesota, Morris. (1960) 2,000 students. Humanities Fine Arts Center Gallery presents changing contemporary exhibits (Oct-mid-June, Mon-Fri) and performing arts series (Oct-Apr). Tours. 4th and College sts. Phone 320/589-6050.

Special Event

Prairie Pioneer Days. Arts and crafts, parade, games and activities. Second wkend July.

Motels/Motor Lodges

★★ **BEST WESTERN PRAIRIE INN.** *200 MN 28 E (56267).* 320/589-3030; toll-free 800/565-3035. *www.best western.com.* 78 rms, 2 story. S, D $34-$84; under 17 free. Crib free. Pet accepted, some restrictions. TV; cable (premium). Indoor pool; wading pool, whirlpool, poolside serv. Complimentary continental bkfst. Restaurant 6:30 am-10 pm. Bar 4 pm-1 am. Ck-out 11 am, Sun noon. Meeting rms. Business servs avail. Sauna. Game rm. Cr cds: A, D, DS, MC, V.

D ⚐ ⛱ ⇌ ⊠ ⚒

★ **MORRIS MOTEL.** *207 S MN 9 (56267).* 320/589-1212. 14 rms. S $30; D $38; each addl $2.50. TV; cable (premium). Complimentary coffee in rms. Ck-out 11 am. Cr cds: DS, MC, V.

✈ ⊠ ⚒

New Ulm

(G-3) See also Mankato, Redwood Falls, St. Peter

Founded 1854 **Pop** 13,132 **Elev** 896 ft
Area code 507 **Zip** 56073
Information New Ulm Convention & Visitors Bureau, 1 N Minnesota, Box 862; 507/354-4217 or 888/4-NEWULM
Web www.ic.new-ulm.mn.us

Settled by German immigrants who borrowed the name of their home city, New Ulm is one of the few planned communities in the state. After more than a century, it still retains the order and cleanliness of the original settlement. The city today is in the center of a prosperous agricultural and dairy area and has developed a substantial business community. There is a visitor center at 1 North Minnesota Street (May-October, daily; November-April, Monday-Saturday).

What to See and Do

Brown County Historical Museum. Former post office. Historical exhibits on Native Americans and pioneers; artwork; research library with 4,000 family files. (Mon-Fri, also Sat and Sun afternoons; closed hols) Center St and Broadway. Phone 507/354-2016. ¢

The Glockenspiel. A 45-ft-high musical clock tower with performing animated figures; carillon with 37 bells. Performances (three times daily; noon, 3 pm and 5 pm). 4th N and Minnesota sts. Phone 507/354-4217.

Harkin Store. General store built by Alexander Harkin in 1870 in the small town of West Newton. The town died when it was bypassed by the railroad, but the store stayed open as a convenience until 1901, when rural free delivery closed the post office. The store has been restored to its original appearance and still has many original items on the shelves. Special programs in summer months. (Summer, Tues-Sun; May-Sept, wkends) 8 mi NW of town via County 21. Phone 507/354-2016. ¢

Hermann's Monument. Erected by a fraternal order, monument recalls Hermann the Cheruscan, a German hero of A.D. 9. Towering 102 ft, monument has winding stairway to platform with view of city and Minnesota Valley. (June-Labor Day, daily) Picnic area. On the bluff W of city in Hermann Heights Park. Phone 507/354-4217. ¢

Schell Garden and Deer Park. Garden with deer and peacocks (all yr). Brewery tours, museum, gift shop. (Memorial Day-Labor Day, daily) S on MN 15, then W on 18th St; on Schell Brewery grounds. Phone 507/354-5528. ¢

State parks.

 Flandrau. Comprised of 801 acres on Cottonwood River. Swimming; x-country skiing (rentals), camp-

Glockenspiel clock tower, New Ulm

ing, hiking. Standard fees. Located at the city limits, on S Summit Ave; 1 mi S on MN 15, then W. Phone 507/354-3519.

Fort Ridgely. A 584-acre park. Fort partly restored; interpretive center (May-Labor Day, daily). Nine-hole golf course (fee); x-country skiing; camping; hiking; annual historical festival. Standard fees. 14 mi W on US 14, then 12 mi N on MN 4. Phone 507/426-7840.

Special Events

Fasching. Traditional German winter festival. Incl German food, music; costume ball. Phone 507/354-8850. Late Feb.

Heritagefest. Old World-style celebration highlighting German traditions and culture through music, foods, arts and crafts. Features entertainers from around the area and from Europe. Phone 507/354-8850. Mid-July.

Brown County Fair. Fairgrounds. Aug.

Motels/Motor Lodges

★ **BUDGET HOLIDAY.** *1316 N Broadway St (56073). 507/354-4145; fax 507/354-4146.* 45 rms. S $26.95-$32.95; D $29.95-$34.95; each addl $5. Crib $5. Pet accepted. TV; cable (premium). Restaurant nearby. Ck-out 11 am. Business servs avail. X-country ski 2 mi. Cr cds: A, DS, MC, V.
🐕 🛝 ♿ 🏊 🔌 🔥

★ **COLONIAL INN.** *1315 N Broadway St (97060). 507/354-3128; toll-free 888/215-2143.* 24 rms, 10 with shower only. S $26-$50; D $34-$65. Crib free. TV; cable (premium). Complimentary coffee in lobby. Restaurant nearby. Ck-out 11 am. X-country ski 1 mi. Cr cds: A, DS, MC, V.
✈ 🔌 🏊 🔥

★★ **HOLIDAY INN.** *2101 S Broadway St (56073). 507/359-2941; fax 507/354-7147; toll-free 877/359-2941. www.holiday-inn.com.* 120 rms, 6 suites, 2 story. S, D $69-$89; each addl $10; suites $89-$129; under 19 free. Crib free. TV; cable (premium). Indoor pool; whirlpool. Sauna. Restaurant 6:30 am-2 pm, 5-10 pm. Bar 11-1 am; entertainment. Ck-out

noon. Meeting rms. Business center. In-rm modem link. Valet serv. X-country ski 2 mi. Game rm. Cr cds: A, D, DS, JCB, MC, V.
🅳 🍴 🏊 🏊 🔌 🔥 🏃

Restaurants

★ **D. J.'S.** *1201 N Broadway St (56073). 507/354-3843.* Hrs: 6 am-9 pm; Sat, Sun from 7 am. Closed Dec 24, 25. German, American menu. Bkfst $1.59-$4.99, lunch $3.15-$4.99, dinner $5.25-$11.95. Specialties: broasted chicken, bratwurst with sauerkraut. Informal atmosphere.
🅳 🆂🅲 ➖

★ **VEIGEL'S KAISERHOF.** *221 N Minnesota St (56073). 507/359-2071.* Hrs: 11 am-10:30 pm; Sun 11 am-10 pm. Closed Dec 24, 25. Res accepted. Bar to 1 am. Lunch $4-$8, dinner $9-$18. Children's menu. Specialty: barbecued ribs. Bavarian decor. Family-owned. Cr cds: A, C, D, DS, MC, V.
🅳 ➖

Northfield

(G-4) *See also Faribault, Hastings, Lakeville, Minneapolis, Owatonna, Red Wing, St. Paul*

Founded 1855 **Pop** 14,684 **Elev** 919 ft **Area code** 507 **Zip** 55057

Information Northfield Area Chamber of Commerce, 500 Water St S, PO Box 198; 507/645-5604 or 800/658-2508

Web www.northfieldchamber.com

This bustling, historic river town, located 30 miles south of the Twin Cities, offers a captivating blend of the old and new. Its history is one of the most dramatic of any Midwestern community. Each year on the weekend after Labor Day, thousands flock here to share in the retelling of the defeat of Jesse James and his gang who, on September 7, 1876, were foiled in their attempt to raid the Northfield Bank in what proved to be one of the last chapters in the brutal saga of the Old West.

This history has been preserved in the Northfield Bank Museum at 408 Division Street, keystone of the city's unique historical downtown district. The well-preserved storefronts house boutiques, antique stores, and other interesting shops.

What to See and Do

Carleton College. (1866) 1,800 students. Liberal arts. Arboretum (455 acres) has hiking and jogging trails along Cannon River. Also here is a 35-acre prairie maintained by college. Tours of arboretum and prairie with advance notice. Summer theater programs. NE edge of town on MN 19. Phone 507/646-4000.

Nerstrand Woods State Park. More than 1,280 acres, heavily wooded; hiking, x-country skiing, snowmobiling, picnicking, camping (dump station). Standard fees. 12 mi SE, off MN 246. Phone 507/334-8848.

Northfield Arts Guild. Exhibits of local and regional fine arts housed in historic YMCA Building (1885); juried handcrafted items. (Mon-Sat; closed hols) Downtown. Phone 507/645-8877. **FREE**

St. Olaf College. (1874) 3,000 students. Famous for its choir, band, and orchestra, which tour nationally and abroad. Steensland Art Gallery (Daily). Home of national offices and archives of Norwegian-American Historical Association. 1 mi W of business district. Phone 507/646-2222.

Special Event

Defeat of Jesse James Days. Raid reenactment, parade, outdoor arts fair, rodeo. Four days beginning wkend after Labor Day.

Motels/Motor Lodges

★ **COLLEGE CITY MOTEL.** *875 MN 3 N (55057). 507/645-4426; fax 507/645-7756.* 24 rms. S $24-$27; D $29-$39; Crib free. TV, cable. Complimentary coffee 7 am-noon. Ck-out 11 am. Sundries. X-country ski 1 mi. Cr cds: A, DS, MC, V.

★★ **COUNTRY INN BY CARLSON, NORTHFIELD.** *300 S MN 3 (55057). 507/645-2286; fax 507/645-2958; toll-free 800/456-4000.* 54 rms, 2 story. S $47-$82; D $53-$88; each addl $6; suites $82-$88; under 18 free. Crib

free. TV; cable (premium). Indoor pool; whirlpool. Complimentary continental bkfst. Restaurant nearby. Ck-out noon. Coin lndry. Downhill ski 20 mi; x-country ski 1 mi. Some refrigerators. Cr cds: A, C, D, DS, MC, V.

★ **SUPER 8 MOTEL.** *1420 Riverview Dr (55057). 507/663-0371; toll-free 800/800-8000. www.super8.com.* 40 rms, 2 story. S $40-$49; D $51-67; suite $76-$81. Crib free. TV. Restaurant adj. Ck-out 11 am. Business servs avail. X-country ski 1 mi. Cr cds: A, C, D, DS, MC, V.

B&B/Small Inn

★★ **ARCHER HOUSE HOTEL.** *212 Division St (55057). 507/645-5661; fax 507/645-4295; toll-free 800/247-2235. www.archerhouse.com.* 34 rms, 3 story. D $40. Crib avail. Pet accepted. TV; cable (premium), VCR avail. Dining rm 6:30 am-10 pm. Ck-out noon, ck-in 3 pm. Downhill ski 20 mi; x-country ski 1 mi. On river. Built 1877; antiques, country decor. Cr cds: A, DS, MC, V.

Onamia

(E-4) *See also Aitkin, Brainerd, Little Falls*

Pop 676 **Elev** 1,264 ft **Area code** 320 **Zip** 56359

What to See and Do

Fort Mille Lacs Village. Recreational complex incl tame animal park; paddleboats (addl fee); Native American museum; art gallery; picnic area. Three gift shops; amusement park (fee). (May-Oct, daily) 6 mi N via US 169, then 1 mi S on County Rd, on SW shore of Mille Lacs Lake. Phone 320/532-3651. **FREE**

Mille Lacs Kathio State Park. Comprises 10,577 acres surrounding main outlet of Mille Lacs Lake. Evidence of Native American habitation and culture dating back over 4,000 yrs. Here in 1679, Daniel Greysolon, Sieur du

Lhut, claimed the upper Mississippi region for France. Swimming, fishing, boating (rentals); hiking, riding trails; x-country skiing (rentals), snowmobiling; picnicking; camping (dump station). Interpretive center. Standard fees. 8 mi NW on US 169, then 1 mi S on County Rd 26. Phone 320/532-3523. ¢¢

Mille Lacs Lake. Has 150 mi of shoreline; one of the largest and loveliest in the state. Near lakeshore are nearly 1,000 Native American mounds. Fishing, boating, camping. 4 mi N on US 169. Phone 218/829-2838.

Resort

★ ★ ★ **IZATY'S GOLF AND YACHT CLUB.** *40005 85th Ave (56359). 320/ 532-3101; fax 320/532-3208; toll-free 800/533-1728. www.izatys.com.* 87 units, 28 rms in lodge, 2 story, 59 townhouses. D $65-$125; townhouses $115-$389 (2-day min wkends); family rates; golf plan. Crib avail. TV; cable; VCR avail (movies). 2 pools, 1 indoor; whirlpool. Free supervised children's activities (Memorial Day-Labor Day); ages 4-10 yrs. Coffee in rms. Dining rm 7 am-10 pm. Box lunches, snacks, barbecues. Bar 11-1 am. Ck-out noon, ck-in 4 pm. Meeting rms. Business servs avail. Tennis. 18-hole golf, greens fee $25-$55, pro. Sauna. Motors, pontoons, launch serv, boat marina. Jet ski rentals. X-country ski on site. Snowmobiling. Lawn games. Game rm. Fishing guides. Fireplaces; microwaves in townhouses. Private patios. Balconies. Cr cds: A, D, DS, MC, V.
🅳 ⬧ 🐟 ⛷ 🏊 🏴 🐾 🎿

Owatonna

(G-4) *See also Austin, Faribault, Northfield, Rochester*

Settled 1854 **Pop** 19,386 **Elev** 1,154 ft
Area code 507 **Zip** 55060
Information Convention & Visitors Bureau, 320 Hoffman Dr; 507/451-7970 or 800/423-6466
Web www.owatonna.org

Legend has it that the city was named after a beautiful but frail Native American princess named Owatonna. It is said that her father, Chief Wabena, had heard about the healing water called "minnewaucan." When the waters' curing powers restored his daughter's health, he moved his entire village to the site now known as Mineral Springs Park. A statue of Princess Owatonna stands in the park and watches over the springs that are still providing cold, fresh mineral water.

What to See and Do

Heritage Halls Museum. Transportation museum featuring one-of-a-kind trains, planes, and automobiles. Interactive discovery zone. Gift shop. (Daily; closed hols) 2300 Heritage Place. Phone 507/451-2060. ¢¢¢

Minnesota State Public School Orphanage Museum. Museum on site of former orphanage that housed nearly 13,000 children from 1866 to 1943. Main building is on the National Registry of Historic Places. (Daily) 540 W Hills Cir. Phone 507/451-2149. **FREE**

Norwest Bank Owatonna, NA Building. Completed in 1908 as the National Farmers Bank, this nationally acclaimed architectural treasure was designed by one of America's outstanding architects, Louis H. Sullivan. The cubelike exterior with huge, arched stained-glass windows by Louis Millet quickly earned the building widespread recognition as, according to one historian, "a jewel box set down in a prairie town." 101 N Cedar Ave, at Broadway. Phone 507/451-7970.

Owatonna Arts Center. Housed in a historic Romanesque structure. Permanent collection incl 100-piece collection of garments from around the world and 14-ft stained-glass panels featured in the Performing Arts Hall. Outdoor sculpture garden has works by Minnesota artists John Rood, Richard and Donald Hammel, Paul Grandlund, and Charles Gagnon. Changing gallery shows every month. (Tues-Sun; closed hols) 435 Garden View Ln, West Hills Complex. Phone 507/451-0533. **Donation**

Village of Yesteryear. Eleven restored pioneer buildings from mid-1800s incl church, two log cabins, schoolhouse, large family home, old fire department and country store; depot, farm machinery building, blacksmith shop; museum; period furnishings, memorabilia and a C-52 locomotive caboose (1905). (May-Oct, afternoons Tues-Sun) 1448 Austin Rd. Phone 507/451-1420. ¢¢

Motels/Motor Lodges

★ **BUDGET HOST INN.** *745 State Ave (55060). 507/451-8712; fax 507/451-4456.* 27 rms, 2 story. S $29-$38; D $32-$48; each addl $5. Crib $5. TV; cable. Coffee in lobby. Restaurant adj. Ck-out 11 am. Meeting rm. X-country ski 1 mi. Cr cds: A, MC, V.
🎿 ▶ 🐾

★ **RAMADA INN.** *1212 N I-35 (55060). 507/455-0606; fax 507/455-3731; res 800/228-2828. www.ramada.com.* 117 rms, 2 story. S $54-$64; each addl $5. Crib free. TV; cable. Indoor pool; whirlpool. Sauna. Restaurant 6 am-2 pm, 5-9 pm. Bar 4 pm-1 am. Ck-out noon. Coin lndry. Business servs avail. Sundries. Free airport transportation. X-country ski 1 mi. Cr cds: A, C, D, DS, MC, V.
🅳 🐾 ▶ ➳ 🏋 ➳ 🐾

★ **SUPER 8 MOTEL.** *1818 US 14 W; I-35 and US 14 W (55060). 507/451-0380; res 800/800-8000.* 60 rms, 2 story. S $44-$48; D $53-$60; each addl $3-$5. Crib $3. TV; VCR (movies). Complimentary continental bkfst. Restaurant adj open 24 hrs. Ck-out 11 am. Business servs avail. Sundries. X-country ski 1 mi. Cr cds: A, C, D, DS, MC, V.
🅳 ▶ ➳ 🐾 SC

Park Rapids

(D-3) *See also Detroit Lakes, Walker*

Founded 1880 **Pop** 2,863 **Elev** 1,440 ft **Area code** 218 **Zip** 56470
Information Chamber of Commerce, PO Box 249; 218/732-4111 or 800/247-0054
Web www.parkrapids.com

This resort center is surrounded by 400 lakes, nearly as many streams, and beautiful woods. There are more than 200 resorts within 20 miles. Fishing is excellent for bass, walleye, northern pike, muskie, and trout.

What to See and Do

Hubbard County Historical Museum/North Country Museum of Arts. Historical museum has displays on pioneer life, incl a pioneer farm house and one-rm schoolhouse, and foreign wars. Museum of arts has five galleries of contemporary art, but also features a section on 15th-through 18th-century European art. (May-Sept, Tues-Sun) Court Ave at Third St. Phone 218/732-5237.

Rapid River Logging Camp. Authentic logging camp with nature trail; antiques; serves lumberjack meals; logging demonstrations (Tues and Fri). See sluiceway in the river. (Memorial Day wkend-Labor Day wkend, daily) 3 mi N via US 71, 2½ mi E on County 18 and follow signs. Phone 218/732-3444. **FREE**

Smoky Hills Artisan Community. North country's artists and crafters produce and sell their wares in a miniature village. Nature trails. Live music; scenic lookout tower. Restaurant. (Memorial Day wkend-Labor Day, daily) 10 mi W on MN 34. Phone 218/573-3300. ¢¢

Motel/Motor Lodge

★ **SUPER 8 MOTEL.** *1020 E 1st St (56470). 218/732-9704; toll-free 800/800-8000. www.super8.com.* 62 rms, 2 story. S $45-$75; D $60-$80; suites $95-$125; each addl $5; under 13 free. Crib $2. TV; cable. Complimentary bkfst. Restaurant nearby. Ck-out 11 am. Guest lndry. Business servs avail. In-rm modem link. Whirlpool. Sauna. Rec rm. Cr cds: A, C, D, DS, JCB, MC, V.
🅳 ➳ 🐾 SC

Cottage Colonies

★★ **BROOKSIDE RESORT.** *31671 County 50 (56470). 218/732-4093; toll-free 800/247-1615. www.brookside-resort.com.* 28 kit. cottages (2-4 bedrm). Mid-July-mid-Aug, wkly (with boat): kit. cottages for 4-8, $1,000-$1,400; each addl $100; lower rates late May-mid-July, mid-Aug-Sept. Closed rest of yr. No maid serv.

Crib avail. TV in lodge. Indoor/outdoor pool. Sauna. Supervised children's activities (May-Aug); ages 2-16. Snack bar. Ck-out Sat, 9:30 am, ck-in Sat, 4:30 pm. Coin lndry. Business servs avail. Grocery 2½ mi. Package store 16 mi. Airport, bus depot transportation. Tennis. Golf, greens fee $8, putting green. Miniature golf. Private beach; waterskiing. Boats, motors, canoes, pontoon boats, sailboats; dock, launching ramps. Hayrides. Lawn games. Movies. Library. Some fireplaces. Picnic tables, grills. Cr cds: MC, V.

★★ **EVERGREEN LODGE FAMILY RESORT AND GOLF.** *17838 Goldeneye Ln (56470). 218/732-4766; fax 218/732-0762.* 18 kit. cabins (2-4 bedrm) (no towels, maid serv). July-early Aug: wkly (with boat) for 1-4, $600-$770; 1-6, $755-$915; 1-8, $725-$1,000; each addl $40; under 2 free; lower rates mid-May-June, early Aug-Labor Day. Closed rest of yr. Playground. Free supervised children's activities (June-Aug). Ck-out 9:30 am, ck-in 3 pm. Grocery, coin lndry, package store 7 mi. Free airport transportation. Tennis. Par-3 golf, greens fee $7. Private beach. Motorboats, canoes, pontoon boat; launching ramp. Lawn games. Rec rm. Sauna. Picnic tables, grills.

★★ **SUNSET LODGE.** *28017 Green Pine Rd (56470). 218/732-4671.* 11 kit. cottages (2-4 bedrm). Late June-mid-Aug: wkly (with boat) for 1-4, $570; 1-6, $770; 1-8, $995; each addl $10/day; varied lower rates mid-May-late June and mid-Aug-mid Nov (2-day min). Closed rest of yr. Crib avail. TV. Playground. Ck-out Sat, 10 am, ck-in 4 pm. Grocery 4 mi. Coin lndry. Package store 8 mi. Airport transportation. Tennis. 18-hole golf privileges, greens fee. Private beach. Boats, canoes, sailboats, water bikes; launching ramp. Lawn games. Rec rm. Picnic tables, grills. Cr cds: A, MC, V.

Pine River

(D-3) *See also Brainerd, Crosslake, Walker*

Pop 871 **Elev** 1,290 ft **Area code** 218 **Zip** 56474

Resorts

★★★ **DRIFTWOOD RESORT AND GOLF COURSE.** *Rural Rte 1, Box 404 (56474). 218/568-4221; fax 218/568-4222. www.driftwoodresort.com.* 27 cottages (1-4 bedrm), 8 kits. AP, July-mid-Aug, wkly: $546 each; MAP avail; family rates; daily rates avail; lower rates mid-May-June, mid-Aug-late Sept. Closed rest of yr. Crib avail. Heated pool; wading pool. Free supervised children's activities (mid-May-Sept); ages 2-13. Dining rm 8-9:30 am, noon-1 pm, 6-7:30 pm. Box lunches, snacks. Barbecues, outdoor buffet Mon. Ck-out noon, ck-in 4 pm. Business servs avail. Grocery, package store 4½ mi. Coin lndry. Rec dir. Tennis, pro. 9-hole golf, putting greens. Private sand beach. Canoes, rowboats, sailboats, motors; launching facilities. Pony rides. Bicycles. Indoor, outdoor games. Rec hall. Nature trails. Entertainment; movies, dancing. Refrigerators. Minnesota resort museum. 55 acres. Sternwheel paddleboat cruises avail. Cr cds: A, MC, V.

★★ **PINEY RIDGE LODGE.** *6023 Wildamere Dr (56474). 218/587-2296; fax 218/587-4323; toll-free 800/450-3333. www.pineyridge.com.* 12 cottages (1-4 bedrm), 8 with kit. 14 deluxe condo kit. units. Mid-June-late Aug, wkly: $700-$1,575 (2-6 persons); MAP, wkend rates; lower rates May-mid-June, late Aug-late Sept. Closed rest of yr. Crib avail. Pool. Sauna. Free supervised children's activities (mid-June-Labor Day). Dining rm 8-10 am, 11:30-3 pm, 5-10 pm. Box lunches, snack bar. Private club 8-11 pm. Ck-out 10 am, ck-in 4 pm. Grocery, package store 6½ mi. Coin lndry. Business servs avail. Airport, bus depot transportation. Tennis. 18-hole golf, pro shop. Miniature golf. Private beach. Dockage, boats, motors, canoes. Lawn games. Soc dir. Movies. Rec rm. Refrigerators; fireplaces. Picnic tables, grills. Cr cds: MC, V.

D ♿ 🚷 🧖 🏊 ➰ 🔥

Pipestone

(G-1) *See also Luverne; also see Sioux Falls, SD*

Settled 1874 **Pop** 4,554 **Elev** 1,738 ft
Area code 507 **Zip** 56164
Information Chamber of Commerce, 117 8th Ave SE, PO Box 8; 507/825-3316 or 800/336-6125
Web www.pipestone.mn.us

County seat and center of a fertile farming area, Pipestone is host to visitors en route to Pipestone National Monument (see). Some of the red Sioux quartzite from the quarries shows up in Pipestone's public buildings. George Catlin, famous painter of Native Americans, was the first white man to report on the area.

What to See and Do

Pipestone County Museum. Prehistory, early settlement, pioneer exhibits; research library. Tours. (Daily, closed hols) Phone 507/825-2563. ¢

Split Rock Creek State Park. On 238 acres. Swimming, fishing (accessible to the disabled), boating (rentals); hiking, x-country skiing, picnicking, camping (dump station). Standard fees. 6 mi SW on MN 23, then 1 mi S on County 20. Phone 507/348-7908.

Special Events

Watertower Festival. Courthouse lawn. Large arts and crafts show; parade. Last Fri and Sat June.

Song of Hiawatha Pageant. Just S of Pipestone National Monument entrance. Outdoor performance. All seats reserved; ticket office opens 1 pm on show dates, phone 507/825-3316 or contact the Chamber of Commerce. Last two wkends July and first wkend Aug.

Motels/Motor Lodges

★ **ARROW MOTEL.** *600 8th Ave NE (56164).* 507/825-3331; fax 507/825-5638. 17 rms. S $27; D $39; each addl $4. Crib. Pet accepted. TV; cable (premium). Pool. Complimentary continental bkfst. Restaurant opp 6 am-9 pm. Ck-out 11 am. Gift shop. Shaded lawn. Cr cds: A, DS, MC, V.

D ➴ ✕ ➰ 🔥

★ **SUPER 8.** *605 8th Ave SE (56164).* 507/825-4217; fax 507/825-4219; res 800/800-8000. www.super8.com. 39 rms, 2 story. S $38-$50; D $72-$80; each addl $4; under 12 free. Crib $1. TV; cable (premium). Restaurant adj 6 am-10 pm. Ck-out 11 am. Business servs avail. Some in-rm whirlpools. Cr cds: A, C, D, DS, MC, V.

D 🧖 ➰ 🔥

Hotel

★ ★ ★ **HISTORIC CALUMET INN.** *104 W Main St (56164).* 507/825-5871; fax 507/825-4578; res 800/535-7610. 40 rms, 4 story. S, D $50-$65; each addl $4; under 12 free. Crib free. TV; cable (premium), VCR avail (movies). Complimentary continental bkfst. Restaurant 9 am-9 pm. Bar 4 pm-1 am. Ck-out 11 am. Meeting rms. Business servs avail. In-rm modem link. Gift shop. Cr cds: A, MC, V.

D ➰ 🔥 SC

Restaurant

★ **LANGE'S CAFE.** *110 8th Ave SE (56164).* 507/825-4488. Open 24 hrs. Res accepted. Bkfst $1.29-$6.95, lunch $3.25-$6.95, dinner $4.25-$13.95. Specializes in roast beef, homemade pastries. Casual, family-style dining. Family-owned. Cr cds: MC, V.

Pipestone National Monument

See also Pipestone; also see Sioux Falls, SD

(On US 75, MN 23, 30, adj to north boundary of Pipestone)

The ancient pipestone in the quarries of this 283-acre area is found in few other places. The Native Americans quarried this reddish stone and carved it into ceremonial pipes. Pipestone deposits, named catlinite for George Catlin, who first described the stone, run about a foot thick, though most usable sections are about two inches thick. Principal features of the monument are **Winnewissa Falls**, flowing over quartzite outcroppings; **Three Maidens**, group of glacial boulders near quarries; **Leaping Rock**, used by Native Americans as a test of strength of young men who attemped to leap from the top of quartzite ridge to its crest, 11 feet away; **Nicollet Marker**, inscription on boulder recalls visit here in 1838 of Joseph Nicollet's exploring party. He carved his name and initials of members of his party, incl Lieutenant John C. Frémont.

Established as a national monument in 1937, Pipestone protects the remaining red stone and preserves it for use by Native Americans of all tribes. The visitor center has exhibits, slides, pipe-making demonstrations, and a self-guided tour booklet for the circle trail and other information; also here is Upper Midwest Indian Cultural Center with craft displays. (Daily; visitor center closed January 1, December 25) Phone 507/825-5464.

Red Wing

(G-5) *See also Hastings, Lakeville, Northfield, St. Paul*

Founded 1836 **Pop** 15,134 **Elev** 720 ft
Area code 651 **Zip** 55066

Information Visitors and Convention Bureau, 418 Levee St; 651/385-5934 or 800/498-3444
Web www.redwing.org

Established as a missionary society outpost, this community bears the name of one of the great Dakota chiefs, Koo-Poo-Hoo-Sha ("wing of the wild swan dyed scarlet"). Red Wing industries produce leather, shoes, precision instruments, malt, flour, linseed oil, diplomas, rubber, and wood products.

What to See and Do

Biking. Wheel passes needed for biking. For further information, contact the Cannon Valley Trail office. Phone 507/263-3954.

Goodhue County Historical Museum. One of state's most comprehensive museums. Permanent exhibits relate local and regional history from glacial age to present. Extensive collection of Red Wing pottery; artifacts from Prairie Island Native American community. (Tues-Sun; closed hols) 1166 Oak St. Phone 651/388-6024. **FREE**

Hiking. A 1½ mi hiking trail to top of Mt LaGrange (Barn Bluff) with scenic overlook of Mississippi River. Cannon Valley Trail provides 25 mi of improved trail following Cannon Bottom River to Cannon Falls. **FREE**

Red Wing Stoneware. Popular stoneware facility; visitors can watch artisans create various types of pottery. Call for hrs. Phone 651/388-4610.

Sheldon Theatre. The first municipal theater in the US, opened 1904. Performances avail regularly. Free tours (June-Oct, Thurs-Sat; Nov-May, Sat). Phone 651/385-3667.

Ski Areas.

Cannon Valley Trail. Twenty-mi x-country skiing trail connects Cannon Falls, Welch, and Red Wing. Phone 651/296-6157. ¢¢

Mount Frontenac. Three double chairlifts, three rope tows; patrol, school, rentals; snowmaking; cafeteria. Vertical drop 420 ft. (Nov-mid-Mar, Wed-Sun; closed Dec 25) Also 18-hole golf course (Mid-Apr-Oct; fee). 9 mi S on US 61. Phone 651/388-5826 or 800/488-5826. ¢¢¢¢

Welch Village. Three quad, five double, triple chairlifts, Mitey-mite; patrol, rentals; snowmaking; cafeteria. Longest run 4,000 ft; vertical drop 350 ft. (Nov-Mar, daily; closed Dec 25) 12 mi NW on US 61, then 3 mi S on County 7 to Welch. Phone 651/258-4567. ¢¢¢¢

Soldiers' Memorial Park/East End Recreation Area. Skyline Dr. On plateau overlooking city and river; 476 acres; five mi of hiking trails. **Colvill Park.** On Mississippi. Also pool (June-Aug, fee), playground; boat launching, marina. **Bay Point Park.** On Mississippi. Showers, boat launching, marina, picnicking, playground, walking trail. (May-Oct, daily)

Special Events

River City Days. First wkend Aug.
Fall Festival of the Arts. Second wkend Oct.

Motels/Motor Lodges

★★ **BEST WESTERN.** 752 Withers Harbor Dr (55066). 651/388-1577; fax 612/388-1150; res 800/780/7234. www.quiethouse.com. 51 rms, 2 story. S $74-$157; D $84-$167; under 12 free. Pet accepted. TV; cable. Indoor/outdoor pool; whirlpool. Complimentary coffee. Restaurant nearby. Ck-out 11 am. In-rm modem link. Exercise equipt. Some refrigerators. Balconies. Cr cds: A, D, DS, MC, V.
🄳 🔌 🕓 🛏 🎿 🏊 🐾

★ **DAYS INN.** 955 E 7th St (55066). 651/388-3568; fax 651/385-1901; toll-free 800/329-7466. www.daysinn.com. 48 rms. S, D $40.50-$80.50; each addl $5; under 13 free. Pet accepted. TV; cable. Indoor pool; whirlpool. Complimentary continental bkfst, coffee in rms. Restaurant nearby. Ck-out 11 am. Business servs avail. Downhill ski 7 mi; x-country ski 1 mi. Municipal park, marinas opp. Cr cds: A, C, D, DS, JCB, MC, V.
🄳 🔌 🏊 🛏 🎿 🏊 🐾 SC

★ **RODEWAY INN.** 235 Withers Harbor Dr (55066). 651/388-1502; fax 651/388-1501; toll-free 800/228-2000. 39 rms, 2 story. S $39-$57; D $49-$67; each addl $5; suites $59-$130. Crib $5. TV; cable (premium), VCR avail (movies). Indoor pool; whirl-pool. Restaurant adj 6 am-midnight. Ck-out 11 am. Business servs avail. Downhill ski 12 mi; x-country ski 1 mi. Cr cds: A, C, D, DS, MC, V.
🄳 🏊 🛏 🎿 🏊 SC

★ **SUPER 8.** 232 Withers Harbor Dr (55066). 651/388-0491; fax 651/388-1066; res 800/800-8000. www.super8.com. 60 rms, 2 story. June-Dec: S $48-$57; D $57-$67; suites $70-$100; higher rates Sat; lower rates rest of yr. Crib $3. TV; cable (premium), VCR avail, (movies). Indoor pool. Complimentary continental bkfst in lobby. Restaurant adj 6 am-11 pm. Ck-out 11 am. Business servs avail. Downhill ski 12 mi. Cr cds: A, C, D, DS, MC, V.
🄳 🕓 🎿 🏊 🛏 🎿 🐾

Hotel

★★★ **ST. JAMES.** 406 Main St (55066). 651/388-2846; fax 651/388-5226; toll-free 800/252-1875. www.st-james-hotel.com. 60 rms, 2-5 story. S, D $96-$225; under 18 free. TV; cable (premium), VCR avail. Restaurant 6:30 am-9:30 pm. Bars 11-12:30 am; entertainment Fri, Sat. Meeting rms. Business servs avail. In-rm modem link. Shopping arcade. Beauty shop. Free covered parking. Airport transportation. Downhill/x-country ski 10 mi. Health club privileges. Some whirlpools. Built in 1875; each rm completely different; antiques. Overlooks Mississippi. Cr cds: A, C, D, DS, MC, V.
🄳 🕓 🎿 🛏 🐾

B&Bs/Small Inns

★★ **GOLDEN LANTERN INN.** 721 East Ave (55066). 651/388-3315; fax 651/385-9178; toll-free 888/288-3315. www.goldenlantern.com. 5 rms, 2 story. No rm phones. S, D $89-$125. Children over 12 yrs only. Complimentary full bkfst. Restaurant nearby. Ck-out 11 am, ck-in 4-5:30 pm. Downhill ski 8 mi; x-country ski 1 mi. Tudor brick house built 1932. Totally nonsmoking. Cr cds: DS, MC, V.
🕓 🎿 🎿 🛏 🐾

Restaurant

★ **LIBERTY'S.** 303 W 3rd (55066). 651/388-8877. Hrs: 8 am-11 pm; Fri, Sat to 1 am. Sun brunch 9:30 am-2

pm. Closed hols. Res accepted. Continental menu. Bar to 1 am. Bkfst $1.95-$6.50, lunch $3-$7, dinner $3-$14.95. Sun brunch $8.25. Specializes in ribs, burgers. Entertainment Fri, Sat. Casual decor. Cr cds: A, D, DS, MC, V.
D SC

Redwood Falls

(G-3) *See also Granite Falls, Marshall, New Ulm*

Pop 4,859 **Elev** 1,044 ft
Area code 507 **Zip** 56283
Information Redwood Area Chamber and Tourism, 610 E Bridge St; 507/637-2828

What to See and Do

Lower Sioux Agency and History Center. Exhibits trace history of the Dakota in Minnesota from the mid-17th century through the present. (May-Oct, daily; rest of yr, by appt) Redwood City Hwy 2, 7 mi E of Redwood Falls. Phone 507/697-6321.

Ramsey Park. A 200-acre park of rugged woodland carved by Redwood River and Ramsey Creek. Incl picnicking, trail riding, x-country ski trail, hiking; golf; camping. Small zoo, playground shelters, 30-ft waterfall. W edge of town, off MN 19.

Special Event

Minnesota Inventors Congress. Redwood Valley School. Exhibit of inventions by adult and student inventors; seminars. Food; arts and crafts; parade; also resource center. Phone 507/637-2344. Three days second full wkend June.

Rochester

(G-5) *See also Owatonna, Spring Valley*

Settled 1854 **Pop** 70,745 **Elev** 1,297 ft
Area code 507
Information Convention & Visitors Bureau, 150 S Broadway, Suite A, 55904; 507/288-4331 or 800/634-8277

Web www.rochestercvb.org

The world-famous Mayo Clinic has made what was once a crossroads campground for immigrant wagon trains a city of doctors, hospitals, and lodging places. Each year thousands of people come here in search of medical aid. One of the first dairy farms in the state began here, and Rochester still remains a central point for this industry. Canned goods, fabricated metals, and electronic data processing equipment are among its industrial products.

What to See and Do

Mayo Clinic. Over 30 buildings now accommodate the famous group practice of medicine that grew from the work of Dr. William Worrall Mayo and his sons, Dr. William James Mayo and Dr. Charles Horace Mayo. There are now 1,041 doctors at the clinic as well as 935 residents in training in virtually every medical and surgical specialty. The 14-story Plummer Building (1928) incl medical library and historical exhibit. The Conrad N. Hilton and Guggenheim buildings (1974) house clinical and research laboratories. The 19-story Mayo Building (1955, 1967) covers an entire block. It houses facilities for diagnosis and treatment. Clinic tours (Mon-Fri; closed hols). 200 1st St SW. Phone 507/284-9258. **FREE** Also here is

The Rochester Carillon. In the tower of the Plummer Building. Concerts (schedule varies). **FREE**

Mayowood. Home of Drs C. H. and C. W. Mayo, historic 55-rm country mansion on 15 acres; period antiques, works of art. Phone 507/282-9447. ¢¢¢

Olmsted County History Center and Museum. Changing historical exhibits (Daily; closed hols); research library (Mon-Fri; closed hols). Corner of County Rds 22 and 25. Phone 507/282-9447. ¢

Plummer House of the Arts. Former estate of Dr. Henry S. Plummer, a 35-yr member of the Mayo Clinic. Eleven acres remain, with formal gardens, quarry, water tower. Five-story house is English Tudor mansion (ca 1920) with original furnishings and slate roof. Tours (June-Aug, Wed afternoons, also first and third Sun afternoons). Entrance is at corner of 12th Ave and 9th St. Phone 507/281-6160. ¢

Whitewater State Park. A 1,822-acre park. Limestone formations in a hardwood forest. Swimming, fishing; hiking, x-country skiing; picnicking; primitive camping. Interpretive center. Standard fees. 20 mi E on US 14, then 7 mi N on MN 74. Phone 507/932-3007.

Motels/Motor Lodges

★ **AMERICINN STEWARTVILLE.** *1700 Second Ave NW, Stewartville (55976). 507/533-4747; fax 507/533-4747; toll-free 800/634-3444.* 29 rms. S $40-$45; D $45-$50; each addl $6; under 12 free. Crib free. TV; cable. Complimentary continental bkfst. Restaurant nearby. Ck-out 11 am. Business servs avail. Cr cds: A, MC, V.
🄳 ⅏ 🐾 🅂🄲

★★ **BEST WESTERN FIFTH AVENUE.** *20 NW 5th Ave (55901). 507/289-3987; res 800/780-7234. www. bestwestern.com.* 63 rms, 3 story. S, D $56; each addl $5; under 18 free. Crib free. Pet accepted. TV; cable (premium). Indoor pool. Complimentary coffee in lobby. Restaurant nearby. Ck-out noon. X-country ski 1 mi. Cr cds: A, C, D, DS, ER, JCB, MC, V.
🄳 🐾 ⅏ ⅏ 🅂🅂

★★ **BEST WESTERN INN.** *1517 16th St SW (55902). 507/289-8866; fax 507/292-0000; res 800/780-7234. www.bestwestern.com.* 151 rms, 3 story. S $60-$199; D $64-$219; each addl $5; suites $85-$159; under 18 free; wkend rates. Pet accepted. TV; cable (premium), VCR avail. Indoor pool; whirlpool. Complimentary bkfst. Restaurant 6:30 am-10 pm. Bar 5 pm-1 am. Ck-out noon. Meeting rms. Business servs avail. In-rm modem link. Valet serv. Sundries. Free airport transportation. X-country ski 2 mi. Game rm. Tropical atrium. Cr cds: A, C, D, DS, JCB, MC, V.
🄳 🐾 🅇 ⅏ 🅂 ⅏ 🅂🅂

★★ **BEST WESTERN SOLDIERS' FIELD.** *401 6th St SW (55902). 507/288-2677; fax 507/282-2042; res 800/780-7234. www.bestwestern.com.* 218 rms, 8 story, 90 kit. suites. S, D, kit. suites $69-$84; each addl $5; under 12 free. Crib free. TV; cable. Indoor pool; wading pool, whirlpool. Complimentary bkfst Mon-Fri. Restaurant 6 am-10 pm. Bar 4 pm-closing; entertainment. Ck-out noon. Coin lndry. Meeting rms. Business servs avail. Gift shop. Free airport, bus depot transportation. X-country ski 1 blk. Exercise equipt. Game rm. Rec rm. Cr cds: A, C, D, DS, JCB, MC, V.
🄳 🐾 ⅏ 🅇 🅇 ⅏ ⅏ 🅂🅂

★ **BLONDELL.** *1406 2nd St SW (55902). 507/282-9444; fax 507/282-8683; toll-free 800/441-5209. www. blondell.com.* 60 rms, 3 story, 7 suites. S, D $53-$68; each addl $5; suites $90-$130; kit. units $52-$57; under 12 free. Crib free. Pet accepted. TV; cable (premium). Restaurant 6 am-10 pm. Bar 11-1:30 am. Ck-out 1 pm. Meeting rms. Business servs avail. Gift shop. X-country ski 1 mi. Cr cds: A, DS, MC, V.
🄳 🐾 🐾 ⅏ ⅏

★ **COMFORT INN & CONFERENCE CENTER.** *1625 S Broadway (55904). 507/281-2211; fax 507/288-8979; toll-free 800/305-8470. www. comfortinn.com.* 162 rms, 5 story. S, D $79; each addl $10; under 17 free. Crib free. Pet accepted, some restrictions. TV; cable (premium). Indoor pool; whirlpool. Complimentary continental bkfst. Coffee in rms. Restaurant 11 am-2 pm, 5-10 pm. Bar 4 pm-midnight. Ck-out noon. Coin lndry. Meeting rms. Business servs avail. In-rm modem link. Valet serv. Sauna. Refrigerators, microwaves. Some private patios. Cr cds: A, MC, V.
🄳 🐾 ⅏ ⅏ ⅏ 🅂🅂

★ **DAYS INN.** *111 28th SE St (55904). 507/286-1001; toll-free 800/329-7466. www.daysinn.com.* 128 rms. S $46-$62; D $52-$62; each addl $5; under 18 free. Crib free. Pet accepted. TV; cable (premium). Complimentary continental bkfst. Restaurant nearby. Ck-out noon. Business servs avail. Free airport transportation. X-country ski 2 mi. Cr cds: A, C, D, DS, ER, JCB, MC, V.
🄳 🐾 🐾 ⅏ ⅏ 🅂🅂

★ **DAYS INN.** *6 1st Ave NW (55901). 507/282-3801; toll-free 800/329-7466. www.daysinn.com.* 71 rms, 5 story. S $43-$75; D $49-$75; each addl $6; under 17 free. Crib free. Pet accepted. TV; cable. Restaurant 6 am-8 pm. Ck-out noon. Coin lndry. Some refrigerators. Cr cds: A, C, D, DS, MC, V.

★ **ECONO LODGE.** *519 3rd Ave SW (55902). 507/288-1855; toll-free 800/553-2666. www.econolodge.com.* 62 rms, 2 story, 6 kits. S, D $43-$46; each addl $5; kit. units $45; under 18 free. Crib free. TV; cable. Restaurant nearby. Ck-out noon. Coin lndry. X-country ski 1 mi. City park opp. Cr cds: A, C, D, DS, MC, V.

★ **EXECUTIVE INN.** *116 5th St SW (55902). 507/289-1628; toll-free 888/233-9470.* 59 rms, 2 story. S, D $29-$39; under 18 free. Crib free. TV; cable. Indoor pool. Sauna. Complimentary continental bkfst. Ck-out noon. Coin lndry. Sundries. X-country ski 2 mi. Some refrigerators. Cr cds: A, DS, MC, V.

★★ **EXECUTIVE SUITES AND INN.** *9 3rd Ave NW (55901). 507/289-8646; fax 507/282-4478; toll-free 800/533-1655. www.kahler.com.* 266 rms, 9 story. S $71-$102; D $81-$112; each addl $10; under 18 free. Crib free. Pet accepted. TV; cable (premium). Indoor pool; whirlpool. Complimentary continental bkfst. Restaurant 6 am-9 pm. Bar 3-9 pm. Ck-out 2 pm. Meeting rm. Business servs avail. In-rm modem link. Sundries. Grocery store. Valet serv. Coin lndry. X-country ski 1 mi. Exercise equipt; sauna. Rec rm. Some refrigerators. Cr cds: A, MC, V.

★ **FIKSDAL HOTEL AND SUITES.** *1215 2nd St SW (55902). 507/288-2671; fax 507/285-9325; toll-free 800/366-3451.* 55 rms, 6 story. S $46-$55; D $71; each addl $6. Crib free. TV; cable. Complimentary continental bkfst. Restaurant adj 6 am-10 pm. Ck-out 11 am. Business servs avail. Airport transportation. X-country ski 1 mi. Refrigerators, microwaves. Sun deck. Cr cds: A, D, DS, MC, V.

★ **GASLIGHT INN.** *1601 2nd St SW (55902). 507/289-1824; fax 507/289-3611; toll-free 800/658-7016.* 25 rms, 2 story. S $43; D $50; each addl $5; under 12 free. Crib free. TV; cable. Complimentary coffee in rms.

Restaurant adj open 24 hrs. Ck-out noon. Coin lndry. Business servs avail. In-rm modem link. Sundries. Refrigerators, microwaves. Balconies. Cr cds: A, DS, MC, V.

★★ **HAMPTON INN.** *1755 S Broadway (55904). 507/287-9050; fax 507/287-9139; toll-free 800/426-7866. www.hamptoninn.com.* 105 rms, 3 story. S $74-$79; D $84-$89; under 18 free. Crib free. TV; cable (premium). Indoor pool; whirlpool. Complimentary continental bkfst. Restaurant nearby. Ck-out noon. Meeting rm. Business servs avail. Valet serv. Coin lndry. X-country ski 1 mi. Exercise equipt. Refrigerator avail. Cr cds: A, D, DS, MC, V.

★★ **HOLIDAY INN SOUTH.** *1630 S Broadway (55904). 507/288-1844; res 800/465-4329. www.holiday-inn.com.* 195 rms, 5 suites, 2 story, 7 kits. S, D $59-$69; each addl $7; kit. units $79-$119. Crib free. Pet accepted. TV; cable. Indoor pool. Restaurant 6 am-10 pm; Fri, Sat to 11 pm. Bar 11:30-1 am. Ck-out 2 pm, Sat noon. Coin lndry. Meeting rms. Business servs avail. Valet serv. Sundries. Free airport, bus depot transportation. Rec rm. Cr cds: A, MC, V.

★ **LANGDON'S UPTOWN MOTEL.** *526 3rd Ave SW (55902). 507/282-7425.* 38 rms, 2 story. S $26-$29; D $28-$33; each addl $3. TV; cable. Complimentary coffee in rms. Restaurant nearby. Ck-out 11 am. Refrigerators. City pool, park opp. Cr cds: A.

★ **QUALITY INN AND SUITES.** *1620 1st Ave SE (55904). 507/282-8091; toll-free 800/228-5151. www.qualityinn.com.* 41 suites, 2 story. S, D $69-$165; each addl $7; under 18 free. Crib free. Pet accepted. TV; cable (premium). Complimentary continental bkfst, coffee in rms. Restaurant nearby. Ck-out noon. Coin lndry. In-rm modem link. Airport transportation. Cr cds: A, D, DS, MC, V.

★ **RAMADA LIMITED.** *435 16th Ave NW (55901). 507/288-9090; fax 507/*

292-9442; res 888/298-2054. www. ramada.com. 120 rms, 3 story, 20 kit. units. S $52-$72; D $57-$77; each addl $10; under 18 free. Crib free. Pet accepted. TV; cable (premium). Indoor pool. Coffee in rms. Restaurant 11 am-10 pm. Ck-out noon. Coin lndry. Valet serv. Sundries. Refrigerators, microwaves. Cr cds: A, MC, V.

🄳 ⌨ ➳ ➳ 🔥 SC

★ **RED CARPET INN.** *2214 S Broadway (55904).* 507/282-7448; toll-free 800/658-7048. 47 rms, 2 story, 6 kits. S $36; D $40-$42; each addl $5; kit. units $28.95-$31.95; under 12 free; wkend rates. Crib free. Pet accepted. TV; cable. Indoor pool. Complimentary coffee in lobby. Restaurant nearby. Ck-out noon. Coin lndry. Meeting rm. Business servs avail. Sundries. X-country ski 1 mi. Cr cds: A, DS, MC, V.

🔥 ⌨ ➳ ➳ ➳ 🔥

★ **ROCHESTER INN.** *1837 S Broadway (55904).* 507/282-2031; toll-free 800/800-3871. 27 rms. S, D $33-$50; each addl $5. Crib free. Pet accepted. TV; cable. Complimentary coffee in lobby. Restaurant nearby. Ck-out noon. X-country ski 1 mi. Cr cds: A, C, D, DS, MC, V.

⌨ ➳ ➳ 🔥 SC

★ **SUPER 8.** *106 21st St SE (55904).* 507/282-1756; res 800/800-8000. *www. super8.com.* 80 rms, 2 story. S, D $45-$60; under 18 free. Crib free. TV; cable (premium). Complimentary continental bkfst. Restaurant nearby. Ck-out noon. Business servs avail. X-country ski 2 mi. Some refrigerators, wet bars. Cr cds: A, C, D, DS, MC, V.

🄳 ➳ ➳ 🔥

★ **SUPER 8.** *1230 S Broadway (55904).* 507/288-8288; res 800/800-8000. *www.super8.com.* 88 rms. S $52-$60; D $57-$65; each addl $5; under 18 free. Crib free. Pet accepted. TV; cable. Restaurant adj open 24 hrs. Ck-out noon. In-rm modem link. X-country ski adj. Cr cds: A, DS, MC, V.

🄳 ⌨ 🏊 ➳ ➳ 🔥

Hotels

★★ **HOLIDAY INN CITY CENTRE.** *220 S Broadway (55904).* 507/252-8200; fax 507/288-6602; toll-free

800/241-1597. www.kahler.com. 170 rms, 8 story. S, D $89-$99; each addl $10; suites $89-$252; under 18 free. Crib free. TV; cable (premium). Restaurant 6:30 am-2 pm, 5:30-10 pm; Sat, Sun from 7 am. Bars 5 pm-midnight. Meeting rms. Business servs avail. In-rm modem link. X-country ski 2 mi. Cr cds: A, C, D, DS, JCB, MC, V.

🄳 ➳ ➳ 🔥 SC

★★★ **KAHLER HOTEL.** *20 2nd Ave SW (55902).* 507/282-2581; fax 507/285-2775; toll-free 800/533-1655. *www.kahler.com.* 700 rms, 11 story. S $59-$140; D $69-$150; each addl $10; suites $350-$1,500; under 18 free. Crib free. Pet accepted. TV; cable. Indoor pool; whirlpool, poolside serv. Restaurant 6:30 am-11 pm, 5:30-9 pm. Bars 11-12:45 am; entertainment Mon-Sat. Ck-out 2 pm. Meeting rms. Business servs avail. In-rm modem link. Drugstore. Barber, beauty shop. Airport transportation. X-country ski 2 mi. Exercise equipt; sauna. Health club privileges. Game rm. Refrigerators. Original section English Tudor; vaulted ceilings, paneling. Walkway to Mayo Clinic. Cr cds: A, C, D, JCB, MC.

🄳 ➳ ⌨ ➳ 🏋 ➳ 🔥

★★★ **MARRIOTT AT MAYO CLINIC ROCHESTER.** *101 1st Ave SW (55902).* 507/280-6000; fax 507/280-8531. *www.kahler.com.* 194 rms, 9 story. S, D $179-$219; suites $295-$1,800; under 18 free. Crib free. Pet accepted, some restrictions. TV; cable. Indoor pool; whirlpool. Restaurant 6:30 am-10 pm. Bar 11 am-11 pm; entertainment. Ck-out 2 pm. Meeting rms. Business servs avail. In-rm modem link. Concierge. Gift shop. Drugstore. Barber, beauty shop. Exercise equipt; sauna. Game rm. Refrigerators; some bathrm phones, minibars. Mayo Medical Complex adj. Luxury level. Cr cds: A, MC, V.

🄳 ⌨ 🏊 ➳ 🏋 ➳ 🔥

★★ **RADISSON PLAZA.** *150 S Broadway (55904).* 507/281-8000; fax 507/281-4280; toll-free 800/333-3333. *www.radisson.com.* 212 rms, 11 story. S, D $89-$119; suites $139-$295. Crib free. TV; cable (premium). Indoor pool; whirlpool. Restaurant 6:30 am-midnight. Bar 11-1 am. Ck-out noon.

Coin lndry. Meeting rms. Business servs avail. In-rm modem link. Concierge. Gift shop. X-country ski 1 mi. Exercise equipt; sauna. Refrigerator in suites. Cr cds: A, C, D, DS, ER, JCB, MC, V.

D ▨ ▨ ▨ ⚐ ▨ ▨ SC

Restaurants

★ **AVIARY.** *4320 US 52 N (55901).* *507/281-5141.* Hrs: 11-1 am. Closed hols. Res accepted. Bar. Lunch $5-$7, dinner $8-$12. Specialties: blackened steak sandwich, garlic shrimp fettucine. Parking. Many trees, plants. Cr cds: A, D, DS, MC, V.

D ▨

★★ **BROADSTREET CAFE AND BAR.** *300 1st Ave NW (55901). 507/281-2451.* Hrs: 11 am-9:30 pm; Sat, Sun 5-9:30 pm. Closed Easter, Thanksgiving, Dec 25. Res accepted. Mediterranean menu. Bar. Lunch $7-$10, dinner $19-$23. Specialties: boursin chicken breast, Canadian walleye. Former warehouse. Casual decor. Cr cds: A, D, MC, V.

D

★★ **CHARDONNAY.** *723 2nd St SW (55902). 507/252-1310.* Hrs: 11 am-2 pm, 5:30-9:30 pm; Sat from 5:30 pm. Closed Sun; hols. Res accepted. French, American menu. Wine, beer. Lunch $6.50-$10, dinner $16-$24. Specialties: breast of duck with foie gras Hollandaise. Parking. 4 dining rms in remodeled house. Cr cds: A, C, D, DS, MC, V.

D

★ **HENRY WELLINGTON.** *216 1st Ave SW (55902). 507/289-1949.* Hrs: 11 am-midnight; Sat 4 pm-midnight; Sun 4-11 pm. Closed July 4, Thanksgiving, Dec 24, 25. Bar. Lunch $5-$7, dinner $9-$18. Specialties: filet Wellington, clam chowder. Outdoor dining. Antique decor. Cr cds: A, D, MC, V.

D

★★ **HUBBELL HOUSE.** *MN 57, Mantorville (55955). 507/635-2331. www.hubbell-house.com.* Hrs: 11:30 am-2 pm, 5-10 pm; Sun 11:30 am-9:30 pm; early-bird dinner Tues-Fri 5-6 pm. Closed Mon; Jan 1, Thanksgiving, Dec 24-25. Res accepted; required wkends. Bar to 1 am. Lunch $5-$7.95, dinner $9.95-$19.95. Chil-

dren's menu. Specializes in steak, barbecued ribs, seafood. Parking. Country inn built in 1854; antiques. Family-owned. Cr cds: A, D, DS, MC, V.

D

★ **JOHN BARLEYCORN.** *2780 S Broadway (55904). 507/285-0178.* Hrs: 11 am-2 pm, 5-10 pm; Sat, Sun from 5 pm. Closed Dec 24, 25. Res accepted. Bar. Lunch $4.25-$7.25, dinner $5.95-$23.95. Specialties: prime rib, barbecued ribs. Salad bar. Parking. Atmosphere of 1890s dining halls; Western decor. Cr cds: A, C, D, DS, MC, V.

D ▨

★ **MICHAEL'S FINE DINING.** *15 S Broadway (55904). 507/288-2020. www.michaelsfinedining.com.* Hrs: 11 am-11 pm; early-bird dinner Mon-Thurs 3-5 pm, Fri, Sat to 5:30 pm. Closed Sun; hols. Res accepted. Bar to midnight. Greek, American menu. Lunch $6-$8, dinner $8-$21.95. Children's menu. Specializes in steak, chops, seafood. Own baking. Parking. Art display. Family-owned. Cr cds: A, D, DS, MC, V.

D ▨

★ **SANDY POINT.** *18 Sandy Point Ct NE (55906). 507/367-4983.* Hrs: 4:30-10 pm; Fri to 11 pm; Sat noon-11 pm; Sun 11:30 am-10 pm. Closed Dec 25. Bar. Lunch, dinner $9.95-$19.95. Children's menu. Specializes in seafood, steak. Parking. Overlooks river. Cr cds: A, C, D, DS, MC, V.

D SC

Roseau

(B-2) *See also Baudette*

Pop 2,396 **Elev** 1,048 ft
Area code 218 **Zip** 56751

What to See and Do

Hayes Lake State Park. A 2,950-acre park. Swimming, fishing, hiking, x-country skiing, snowmobiling, picnicking, camping (dump station). Standard hrs, fees. 15 mi S on MN 89, then 9 mi E on County 4. Phone 218/425-7504.

Pioneer Farm and Village. Restored buldings incl log barn, museum, church, parish hall, equipped printery, log house, school, store, blacksmith shop, and post office. Picnicking. (Mid-May-mid-Sept; schedule varies) 2½ mi W via MN 11. Phone 218/463-2187. **FREE**

Roseau City Park. Forty-acre park with canoeing, hiking, and picnicking. Camping (electric and water hook-ups, dump station). 11th Ave SE.

Roseau County Historical Museum and Interpretive Center. Natural history, collection of mounted birds and eggs; Native American artifacts and pioneer history. (Tues-Sat; closed hols) 110 2nd Ave NE. Phone 218/463-1918. ¢

Roseau River Wildlife Management Area. More than 2,000 ducks raised here annually on 65,000 acres. Birdwatching area, canoeing on river, hunting during season, with license. 20 mi W and N via MN 11, 89 and County Rd 3. Phone 218/463-1557. **FREE**

St. Cloud

(F-3) *See also Elk River, Little Falls*

Founded 1856 **Pop** 48,812 **Elev** 1,041 ft **Area code** 320

Information St Cloud Area Covention & Visitors Bureau, 30 S 6th Ave, PO Box 487, 56302; 320/251-2940 or 800/264-2940

Web www.stcloudcvb.com

Its central location makes St. Cloud a convention hub and retail center for the area. The granite quarried here is prized throughout the United States. This Mississippi River community's architecture reflects the German and New England roots of its early settlers.

What to See and Do

City recreation areas. Riverside Park. Monument to Zebulon Pike, who discovered and named the nearby Beaver Islands in 1805 during exploration of the Mississippi. Shelter; flower gardens; wading pool, tennis, picnicking, lighted x-country skiing.

1725 Kilian Blvd. **Wilson Park,** picnicking, boat landing; tennis. 625 Riverside Dr NE. **Lake George Eastman Park,** swimming (Early June-mid-Aug, daily; fee); skating (Late Dec-early Feb, daily; free); paddleboats (fee), fishing, picnicking. 9th Ave and Division. **Municipal Athletic Center,** indoor ice-skating (Mid-June-mid-May, phone 320/255-7223 for fee and schedule information). 5001 8th St N. **Whitney Memorial Park,** walking trails, softball, and soccer. Northway Dr. **Heritage Park,** nature trails, skating, x-country skiing, earth-covered shelter; nearby is an interpretive heritage museum (Memorial Day-Labor Day, daily; rest of yr, Tues-Sun; closed hols; fee) with replica of working granite quarry and historical scenes of central Minnesota. 33rd Ave S. Phone 320/255-7256.

Clemens Gardens & Munsinger Gardens. Clemens Gardens features, among other gardens, the White Garden, based upon Kent, England's White Garden at Sissinghurst Garden. Munsinger Gardens is surrounded by pine and hemlock trees. (Memorial Day-Labor Day) 13th St S, along the Mississippi River. Phone 800/264-2940. **FREE**

College of St. Benedict. (1887) 1,742 women. On campus is the $6-million Ardolf Science Center. Guided tours. Art exhibits, concerts, plays, lectures, and films in Benedicta Arts Center. 7 mi W on I-94 in St. Joseph. Phone 320/363-5777. Also here is

St. Benedict's Convent. (1857) Community of more than 400 Benedictine women. Tours of historic Sacred Heart Chapel (1913), and archives. Gift and crafts shop; Monastic Gardens. NW via I-94, in St. Joseph at 104 Chapel Lane. Phone 320/363-7100.

Minnesota Baseball Hall of Fame. Features great moments from amateur and professional baseball. (Mon-Fri) St. Cloud Civic Center. Second floor. Phone 320/255-7272. **FREE**

St. Cloud State University. (1869) 16,500 students. Marked historical sites; anthropology museum, planetarium, art gallery (Mon-Fri; closed hols and school breaks). 4th Ave S, overlooking Mississippi River. Phone 320/255-3151.

St. John's University and Abbey, Preparatory School. (1857) 1,771 university students. Impressive modern abbey, university, church, and nine Hill Monastic manuscript library, other buildings designed by the late Marcel Breuer; 2,450 acres of woodlands and lakes. 13 mi W on I-94 in Collegeville. Phone 320/363-2573.

Skiing. Powder Ridge Ski Area. Quad, two double chairlifts, J-bar, rope tow; patrol, school, rentals; snowmaking; bar, cafeteria. (Nov-Apr, daily) Fifteen runs. 16 mi S on MN 15. Phone 800/348-7734. ¢¢¢¢

Stearns County Heritage Center. Located in a 100-acre park, the center showcases cultural and historical aspects of past and present life in central Minnesota; contains replica of working granite quarry; agricultural and automobile displays; research center and archives. (Tues-Sun; June-Aug, daily; closed hols) 235 S 33rd Ave. Phone 320/253-8424. ¢¢

Special Events

Mississippi Music Fest. Riverside Park. May.

Big Sing USA. College of St. Benedict. Phone 320/363-5011. June.

Wheels, Wings & Water Festival. June.

America Fest. Court House Plaza, downtown. July.

Motels/Motor Lodges

★★ **BEST WESTERN AMERICANNA INN AND CONFERENCE CENTER.** *520 US 10 E (56304). 320/252-8700; fax 320/252-8700; toll-free 800/950-8701. www.best western.com.* 63 rms, 2 story. S $57-$73; D $67-$80; each addl $5; suites for 2-6, $74.95-$99.95; under 19 free. Crib $2. Pet accepted, some restrictions. TV; cable (premium). Indoor pool; whirlpool. Complimentary coffee in rms. Restaurant 11 am-10 pm; Sun to 9 pm. Bar 10:30-1 am; entertainment. Ck-out 11 am. Meeting rms. Business servs avail. In-rm modem link. Valet serv. Sundries. Sauna. Game rm. Cr cds: A, MC, V.

🐾 ➰ 🐾

★★ **BEST WESTERN KELLY INN.** *MN 23 and 4th Ave S (56301).*

320/253-0606; fax 320/202-0505; toll-free 800/635-3559. www.bestwestern. com.* 229 rms, 6 story. S $58-$81; D $65-$79; each addl $6; suites $95-$175; under 18 free. Crib free. Pet accepted, some restrictions. TV; cable (premium), VCR avail (movies). Indoor pool; wading pool, whirlpool. Restaurant 6:30 am-10 pm. Bar 11-1 am; Sun to midnight. Ck-out 11 am. Coin lndry. Meeting rms. Business servs avail. In-rm modem link. Valet serv. Sundries. Gift shop. Sauna. Game rm. Poolside rms. Cr cds: A, D, DS, MC, V.

D 🐾 ➰ ➰ 🐾

★ **COMFORT INN.** *4040 2nd St S (56301). 320/251-1500; fax 320/251-1111; toll-free 800/228-5150. www. comfortinn.com.* 63 rms, 2 story. S, D $45.95-$66.95; each addl $6; under 18 free. Crib $7. TV; cable (premium). Complimentary continental bkfst. Restaurant nearby. Ck-out 11 am. Coin lndry. Meeting rms. Business servs avail. Sundries. Exercise equipt; sauna. Cr cds: A, C, D, DS, ER, JCB, MC, V.

D 🖈 ➰ 🐾 SC

★ **DAYS INN.** *420 US 10 SE (56304). 320/253-0500; fax 320/253-0500; toll-free 800/329-7466. www.daysinn.com.* 78 rms, 2 story. S $38.95-$56.95; D $45.95-$59.95; each addl $7; under 18 free. Crib free. Pet accepted. TV; cable (premium). Indoor pool; whirlpool. Complimentary continental bkfst. Ck-out 11 am. Business servs avail. Sundries. Downhill ski 10 mi; x-country ski 1 mi. Cr cds: A, C, D, DS, MC, V.

D 🐾 ➰ ➰ 🐾 SC

★★ **FAIRFIELD INN.** *4120 2nd St S (56301). 320/654-1881; res 800/238-2800. www.fairfieldinn.com.* 57 rms, 10 suites, 3 story. S $46.95-$64.95; D $49.95-$69.95; each addl $6; under 19 free. Crib free. TV; cable (premium). Indoor pool; whirlpool. Complimentary continental bkfst. Restaurant adj open 24 hrs. Ck-out 11 am. Meeting rms. Business servs avail. In-rm modem link. Downhill ski 18 mi; x-country ski 1 mi. Game rm. Some refrigerators. Cr cds: A, MC, V.

D ➰ ➰ 🐾 🐾 SC

★★ **HOLIDAY INN ST. CLOUD.** *75 37th Ave S (56301). 320/253-9000; fax*

320/253-5998; toll-free 800/465-4329.
www.holiday-inn.com. 257 rms, 43
suites, 3 story. S, D $74-$99; suites
$89-$179; under 19 free. Crib free.
TV; cable (premium). 5 indoor pools;
wading pool, whirlpool, poolside
serv. Coffee in rms. Restaurant 6 am-
2 pm, 5-10 pm; Sun from 7 am. Bar
11-1 am. Ck-out 11 am. Meeting
rms. Business servs avail. Exercise
equipt; sauna. Cr cds: A, C, D, DS,
MC, V.

★ **MOTEL 6.** *815 S 1st St, Waite Park
(56387).* 320/253-7070; fax 320/253-
0436; toll-free 800/466-8356. *www.
motel6.com.* 93 rms, 2 story. S $29-
$39; D $35-$45; under 18 free. Crib
free. TV; cable (premium). Restaurant
nearby. Ck-out noon. Business servs
avail. In-rm modem link. Downhill
ski 10 mi. Cr cds: A, C, D, DS, MC, V.

★ **QUALITY INN.** *70 S 37th Ave
(56301).* 320/253-4444; fax 320/259-
7809; res 800/228-5151. *www.
qualityinn.com.* 89 units, 2 story. Mid-
June-early Sept: S $39-$42; D $44-
$49; each addl $7; under 18 free;
lower rates rest of yr. Crib free. Pet
accepted, some restrictions. TV; cable
(premium). Restaurant nearby. Ck-
out noon. Sauna. Whirlpool. Cr cds:
A, C, D, DS, MC, V.

★ **SUPER 8 MOTEL.** *50 Park Ave S
(56302).* 320/253-5530; fax 320/253-
5292; toll-free 800/843-1991. *www.
super8.com.* 68 rms, 2 story. S $36-
$43; D $42.88-$58.88; each addl $5;
under 13 free. Crib free. Pet accepted.
TV; cable (premium). Complimentary
continental bkfst. Restaurant adj
open 24 hrs. Ck-out 11 am. Meeting
rms. Business servs avail. Downhill
ski 8 mi; x-country ski 1 mi. Cr cds:
A, C, D, DS, MC, V.

★ **TRAVELODGE.** *3820 Roosevelt Rd
(56301).* 320/253-3338; fax 320/253-
3627; res 800/515-6375. *www.
travelodge.com.* 28 rms, 2 story. S, D
$26-$51; each addl $3. TV. Continen-
tal bkfst. Bar noon-1 am. Ck-out 11
am. Refrigerators. Cr cds: A, D, DS,
MC, V.

Restaurant

★ **D. B. SEARLE'S.** *18 5th Ave S
(56301).* 320/253-0655. Hrs: 11 am-
10 pm; Fri, Sat to 11 pm; Sun 3-10
pm. Closed hols. Res accepted. Bar to
1 am; Sun 3 pm-midnight. Lunch
$6.49-$7.39, dinner $9.39-$19.69.
Specialties: French onion soup,
stuffed popovers. Built 1886. Cr cds:
A, MC, V.

St. Paul

(F-4) *See also Hastings, Minneapolis,
Stillwater*

Settled 1840 **Pop** 272,235 **Elev** 874 ft
Area code 651

Information Convention and Visitors
Bureau, 175 W Kellogg Blvd, Suite
502, 55102; 651/265-4900 or
800/627-6101

Web www.stpaulcvb.org

Distribution center for the great
Northwest and dignified capital of
Minnesota, stately St. Paul had its
humble beginnings in a settlement
known as "Pig's Eye." At the great
bend of the Mississippi and tangent
to the point where the waters of the
Mississippi and Minnesota rivers
meet, St. Paul and its twin city, Minneapolis, form a mighty northern
metropolis. Together they are a center for computers, electronics, medical technology, printing, and
publishing. In many ways they com-
plement each other, yet they are also
friendly rivals. Fiercely proud of their
professional athletes (the baseball
Minnesota Twins, the football Minnesota Vikings, and the basketball
Minnesota Timberwolves), the parti-
sans of both cities troop to the
Hubert H. Humphrey Metrodome
Stadium in Minneapolis (see), as well
as other arenas in the area, to watch
their heroes in action.

A terraced city of diversified industry and lovely homes, St. Paul boasts
30 lakes within a 30-minute drive, as
well as more than 90 parks. St. Paul

is home to 3M Companies and other major corporations.

The junction of the Mississippi and Minnesota rivers was chosen in 1807 as the site for a fort that later became known as Fort Snelling. Squatters soon settled on the reservation lands nearby, only to be expelled in 1840 with one group moving a few miles east and a French-Canadian trader, Pierre Parrant, settling at the landing near Fort Snelling. Parrant was nicknamed "Pig's Eye," and the settlement that developed at the landing took this name.

When Father Lucien Galtier built a log cabin chapel there in 1841, he prevailed on the settlers to rename their community for Saint Paul. A Mississippi steamboat terminus since 1823, St. Paul prospered on river trade, furs, pioneer traffic, and agricultural commerce. Incorporated as a town in 1849, it was host to the first legislature of the Minnesota Territory and has been the capital ever since.

A number of institutions of higher education are located in St. Paul, incl University of Minnesota—Twin Cities Campus, University of St. Thomas, College of St. Catherine, Macalester College, Hamline University, Concordia University, Bethel College, and William Mitchell College of Law.

Transportation

Car Rental Agencies. See IMPORTANT TOLL-FREE NUMBERS.

Public Transportation. Buses (Metropolitan Council Transit Operations)

Rail Passenger Service. Amtrak 800/872-7245.

Airport Information

Minneapolis/St. Paul International Airport. Information 605/726-5555; 605/726-5141 (lost and found); 952/361-6680 (weather); cash machines, Main terminal between Blue and Green Concourses.

What to See and Do

Alexander Ramsey House. (1872) Home of Minnesota's first territorial governor; original furnishings. Guided tours; res suggested. (Apr-Dec, limited hrs; closed Thanksgiving, Dec 25) 265 S Exchange St. Phone 651/296-0100. ¢¢

Capitol City Trolley. Downtown. (Mon-Fri) Phone 651/223-5600. ¢¢¢

Cathedral of St. Paul. (1915) Roman Catholic. Dome 175 ft high; central rose window. (Daily) 239 Selby Ave. Phone 651/228-1766.

City Hall and Court House. (1932) Prominent example of Art Deco, with Carl Milles's 60-ton, 36-ft-tall onyx *Vision of Peace* statue in the lobby. 15 W Kellogg Blvd. Phone 651/266-8023.

Fort Snelling State Park. A 4,000-acre park at confluence of the Minnesota and Mississippi rivers. Swimming, fishing, boating; hiking, biking, x-country skiing, picnicking; visitor center. Standard fees. At jct MN 5 and Post Rd, just S of Main Terminal exit. Phone 612/725-2390. Incl

> **Historic Fort Snelling.** Stone frontier fortress restored to its appearance of the 1820s; daily drills and cannon firings; craft demonstrations (June-Aug, daily; May and Sept-Oct, wkends only). Visitor center with films, exhibits. (May-Oct, daily) Phone 612/725-2724. ¢¢

Gray Line bus tours. Greyhound Bus Depot. (See MINNEAPOLIS)

James J. Hill House. (1891) Showplace of city when built for famous railroad magnate. Res suggested. (Wed-Sat; closed hols) 240 Summit Ave. Phone 651/297-2555. ¢¢

Landmark Center. Restored Federal Courts Building constructed in 1902; currently center for cultural programs and gangster history tours. Houses four courtrms and four-story indoor courtyard (the Cortile). Incl restaurant, archive gallery, auditorium, Schubert Club Keyboard Instrument Collection (Mon-Fri), and the Minnesota Museum of American Art. (Daily; closed hols) 45-min tours (Thurs and Sun; also by appt); self-guided tours (Daily). 75 W 5th St. Phone 651/292-3228. **FREE**

Luther Northwestern Theological Seminary. (1869) 780 students. On campus is the Old Muskego Church (1844), first church built by Norse immigrants in America; moved to present site in 1904. Tours. 2481 Como Ave. Phone 651/641-3456.

HISTORIC ST. PAUL

The center of St. Paul contains a number of historic structures and cultural institutions, as well as the Minnesota state capitol. A morning or afternoon stroll easily links all of the following sites.

Begin at Rice Park, located at 5th and Market streets. Established 150 years ago, this park—with its vast old trees, manicured lawns, flowers, and fountains, is an oasis of nature in the midst of urban St. Paul. Surrounding the park are some of the city's most noted landmarks. Facing the park to the east is the St. Paul Hotel (350 Market Street), built in 1910 as the city's finest. After a loving refurbishment, it is once again one of the city's premier luxury hotels. Step inside to wander the lobby, which is filled with chandeliers, oriental carpets, and fine furniture.

Facing Rice Park from the south is the handsome turn-of-the-20th-century St. Paul Public Library. To the west, the Ordway Music Theatre (345 Washington Street) is an elegant concert hall where the St. Paul Chamber Orchestra and the Minnesota Orchestra frequently perform. The Landmark Center, facing Rice Park to the north (75 West 5th Street), is a castlelike federal courthouse built in 1902. A number of galleries and arts organizations are now housed in the structure, including the Minnesota Museum of American Art.

Cross St. Peter Street and continue east on East 6th Street. At Cedar Street is Town Center Park, the world's largest indoor park, complete with trees, fountains, flowers, and a carousel. From the north side of the park there are good views of the state capitol. Exit the north end of the park onto 7th Street, walk one block east to Wabasha Street, and turn north. At the corner of Wabasha and Exchange streets is the World Theater (10 Exchange Street), from where Garrison Keillor frequently broadcasts *The Prairie Home Companion*, the acclaimed public radio show.

One block north is the Science Museum of Minnesota (30 East 10th Street) with exhibits on geology, paleontology, and the sciences, and the William L. McKnight-3M Omnitheater, with a 76-foot-wide domed screen. From the main entrance of the Science Museum, walk up Cedar Street toward the capitol building, passing through the parklike Capitol Mall. The magnificent Minnesota Capitol sits on a hill overlooking the city and is crowned by the world's largest unsupported dome. Wander the marble-clad hallways, or join a free tour of the legislative chambers.

From the capitol, follow John Ireland Boulevard south to the Cathedral of St. Paul. Modeled after St. Peter's Basilica in Rome, this 3,000-seat church occupies the highest point in St. Paul. Just south of the cathedral is the James J. Hill House at 240 Summit Avenue. This late 19th-century, five-story mansion was built by James Hill, founder of the Great Northern Railroad. When built, this mansion was the largest and most expensive private home in the upper Midwest. Tours are offered. Return to downtown St. Paul along Kellogg Boulevard.

Minnesota Children's Museum. Hands-on learning exhibits for children up to 12 yrs old; museum store stocked with unique puzzles, maps, toys, games, books. Self-guiding. (June-Aug and school hols, daily; rest of yr, Tues-Sun) 10 W 7th St. Phone 651/225-6000. ¢¢

Minnesota History Center. Home to the Historical Society, the center houses a museum with interactive exhibits, extensive genealogical collection; special events, gift shop, restaurant. (Daily; hrs may vary) Phone 651/296-6126. **FREE**

Minnesota Museum of American Art—Landmark Center. Changing exhibits and gallery of contemporary Midwest artists and new art forms. Also Museum School and store. (Tues-Sun; closed hols) Fifth at Market St. Phone 651/292-4355. **Dona-tion**

Norwest Center Skyway. Created out of the second level of Norwest Center's five-story parking garage. The center incl shops and restaurants. (Daily; closed hols) 56 E 6th St, located in the center of downtown.

Parks.

Como Park. A 448-acre park with 70-acre lake. Conservatory features authentic Japanese garden and tea house; "Gates Ajar" floral display, zoo. (Daily) Amusement area (Memorial Day-Labor Day, daily) with children's rides (fee). 18-hole golf course (fee). Midway and Lexington pkwys. Phone 651/266-6400.

Mounds Park. More than 25 acres of park containing prehistoric Native American burial mounds. 18 mounds existed on this site in 1856, six remain. Picnic facilities, ball field, view of Mississippi River. Mounds Blvd and Burns Ave, in Dayton's Bluff section. Phone 651/266-6400.

Town Square Park. Glass-enclosed indoor park incl waterfalls, streams, pools, and greenery, giving it a tropical atmosphere. (Daily; closed hols) 7th and Cedar sts, downtown. Phone 651/266-6400.

Professional Sports Team. Minnesota Wild (NHL). Xcel Energy Center, 317 Washington St, St. Paul, MN. Phone 651/222-WILD.

Science Museum of Minnesota. Technology, anthropology, paleontology, geography, and biology exhibits; William L. McKnight 3M Omnitheater. (Daily; Labor Day-Dec 25, Tues-Sun) 120 W Kellogg Phone 651/221-9444. ¢¢¢ Also here is

Great American History Theatre. Original works with American and Midwestern themes. (Sept-May, Thurs-Sun) Phone 651/292-4323.

Sibley Historic Site. (1835) Home of General Henry Sibley, first governor, now preserved as museum. On same grounds is Faribault House Museum (1837), home of pioneer fur trader Jean Baptiste Faribault, a museum of the Native American and fur trade era. (May-Oct, Tues-Sun) 1357 Sibley Memorial Hwy (MN 13). Phone 651/452-1596. ¢¢

⚄ **Sightseeing cruises.** Authentic Mississippi River sternwheelers *Harriet Bishop, Josiah Snelling,* and *Jonathan Padelford* make 1¾-hr narrated trips to historic Fort Snelling. Side-wheeler *Anson Northrup* makes trip through lock at St. Anthony Falls. Dinner, brunch cruises also avail. (Memorial Day-Labor Day, daily; May and Sept, wkends) Harriet Island Park, W of Wabasha bridge. Phone 651/227-1100.

State Capitol. (1896-1905) Designed in the Italian Renaissance style by Cass Gilbert and decorated with murals, sculpture, stencils, and marble, the Capitol opened in 1905. 45-min guided tours leave on the hr; last tour leaves one hr before closing (group res required). (Daily; closed hols) 75 Constitution Ave. Phone 651/296-2881. **FREE**

University of Minnesota, Twin Cities Campus. (1851) 39,315 students. Campus tours; animal barn tours (for small children). Phone 612/625-5000. Near campus is

Gibbs Farm Museum. (1854) Restored furnished farmhouse depicting life on an urban fringe farm at the turn of the century. Incl two barns and a one-rm schoolhouse. Interpretations, demonstrations, summer schoolhouse program. (May-Oct, Tues-Fri, also Sat and Sun afternoons) 2097 W Larpenteur Ave, Falcon Heights. Phone 651/646-8629. ¢¢

Special Events

Winter Carnival. Throughout city. One of the leading winter festivals in America; ice and snow carving; parades, sports events, parties, pageants. Phone 651/223-4700. Last wkend Jan-first wkend Feb.

Minnesota State Fair. Fairgrounds, N 1265 Snelling Ave. Midway, thrill show, horse show, kids' days, all-star revue; more than one million visitors each year; 300 acres of attractions. Phone 651/642-2200. Late Aug-early Sept.

Motels/Motor Lodges

★★ **BEST WESTERN.** *1780 E County Rd D, Maplewood (55109). 651/770-2811; toll-free 800/528-1234. www.bestwesternmaplewood.com.* 118 rms, 2 story. S, D $89-$129; each addl $4; under 18 free. Crib free. Pet accepted; $5 deposit. TV; cable (premium). Indoor pool; whirlpool. Coffee in rms. Restaurant 6:30 am-2 pm, 5-10 pm. Bar 4 pm-1 am; entertainment Fri, Sat. Ck-out noon. Coin lndry. Meeting rms. Business servs avail. In-rm modem link. Valet serv. Sundries. Sauna. Health club privileges. Game rm. Microwaves avail. Cr cds: A, C, D, DS, MC, V.

🐾 ➥ 🛏 🎿 SC

★★ **BEST WESTERN DROVER'S INN AND CONFERENCE CENTER.** *701 S Concord St, South St. Paul (55075). 651/455-3600; fax 651/455-0282; toll-free 800/780-7234. www.bestwestern.com.* 85 rms, 4 story. S, D $70-$90; each addl $10; under 19 free. Crib free. TV; cable (premium). VCR avail. Indoor pool; whirlpool. Coffee in rms. Restaurant 6:30 am-2 pm, 5-9 pm; Sun 8 am-1 pm. Bar 2 pm-1 am; closed Sun. Ck-out noon. Meeting rms. Business servs avail. Valet serv. Sundries. Free airport transportation. Microwaves avail. Cr cds: A, C, D, DS, MC, V.

D ➥ 🛏 🎿

★★ **BEST WESTERN KELLY INN.** *161 St. Anthony Ave (55103). 651/227-8711; fax 651/227-1698; res 800/780-7234. www.bestwestern.com.* 126 rms, 7 story. S, D $89-$99; each addl $8; suites $125-$195; under 15 free; higher rates special events. Crib free. Pet accepted. TV; cable. Indoor pool; wading pool, whirlpool. Restaurant 6:30 am-9 pm. Bar 11-1 am; Sat 4 pm-midnight; Sun 4-10 pm. Meeting rms. Business servs avail. In-rm modem link. Sundries. Game rm. Valet serv. Downhill ski 20 mi; x-country ski 4 mi. Sauna. Game rm. Microwaves in suites. Cr cds: A, C, D, DS, ER, JCB, MC, V.

D 🐾 ➥ 🛏 🎿 SC

★★ **COUNTRY INN.** *6003 Hudson Rd, Woodbury (55125). 651/739-7300; fax 651/731-4007; toll-free 800/456-4000. www.countryinnwoodbury.com.* 158 rms, 2 story. S, D $69-$119; each addl $8; under 19 free. Crib free. TV; cable (premium). Indoor pool; whirlpool. Complimentary continental bkfst, coffee in rms. Restaurant 11 am-10 pm; Fri, Sat to midnight. Bar from 11 am. Ck-out noon. Coin lndry. Meeting rms. Business servs

avail. In-rm modem link. Concierge. Valet serv. Downhill ski 12 mi, x-country ski 11 mi. Exercise equipt; sauna. Game rm. Many refrigerators. Cr cds: A, C, D, DS, MC, V.

D 🎿 ➥ 🛏 🎿 SC

★ **EXEL INN OF ST. PAUL.** *1739 Old Hudson Rd (55106). 651/771-5566; fax 651/771-1262; res 800/367-3935. www.exelinns.com.* 100 rms, 3 story. S $43.99-$59.99; D $48.99-$63.99; each addl $5; under 18 free; ski, wkly plans; higher rates special events. Crib free. Pet accepted. TV; cable (premium). Complimentary continental bkfst. Restaurant adj open 24 hrs. Ck-out noon. Coin lndry. Business servs avail. In-rm modem link. Downhill ski 15 mi; x-country ski 2 mi. Game rm. Refrigerators; microwaves avail. Cr cds: A, MC, V.

D 🐾 🎿 🛏 🎿 SC

★★ **HAMPTON INN.** *1000 Gramsie Rd, Shoreview (55126). 651/482-0402; fax 651/482-8917; toll-free 800/426-7866. www.hamptoninn.com.* 120 rms, 2 story. S, D $69-$89; under 16 free. Crib free. TV; cable (premium). Indoor pool; whirlpool. Complimentary continental bkfst. Restaurant 11 am-11 pm. Bar to 1 am. Ck-out 11 am. Meeting rms. Business servs avail. In-rm modem link. Coin lndry. Exercise equipt. Cr cds: A, C, D, DS, MC, V.

➥ 🛏 🎿 SC

★★ **HOLIDAY INN.** *2201 Burns Ave (55119). 651/731-2220; fax 651/731-0243; toll-free 800/465-4329. www.holiday-inn.com.* 192 rms, 8 story. S, D $125; under 19 free; wkend rates. Crib free. TV; cable (premium). Indoor pool; whirlpool. Restaurant 6 am-2 pm, 5-10 pm; Sat, Sun from 7 am. Bar 4 pm-1 am. Ck-out noon. Coin lndry. Meeting rms. Business servs avail. In-rm modem link. Bellhops. Valet serv. Sundries. Gift shop. Downhill ski 10 mi; x-country ski ½ mi. Exercise equipt; sauna. Game rm. Some bathrm phones. Luxury level. Cr cds: A, C, D, DS, JCB, MC, V.

D 🎿 ➥ 🛏 🎿

★★ **HOLIDAY INN.** *1010 W Bandana Blvd (55108). 651/647-1637; fax 651/647-0244; toll-free 800/465-4329. www.holiday-inn.com.* 109 rms, 6 suites, 2 story. S, D $81-$101; suites

$101-$131. Crib free. TV; cable (premium). Indoor pool; wading pool, whirlpool. Complimentary continental bkfst. Ck-out noon. Meeting rms. Business servs avail. In-rm modem link. Valet serv. Downhill ski 15 mi; x-country ski 1 mi. Sauna. Some refrigerators. Motel built within exterior structure of old railroad repair building; old track runs through lobby. Shopping center adj; connected by skywalk. Cr cds: A, C, D, DS, ER, MC, V.

🅳 ⛷ ➴ 🆂🅲

★★ **HOLIDAY INN ST. PAUL NORTH.** *1201 County Rd E (55112). 651/636-4123; fax 651/636-2526; toll-free 800/777-2232. www.holiday-inn. com.* 156 rms, 15 suites, 4 story. S, D $89-$130; each addl $10; suites $99-$149; under 19 free. Crib free. TV; cable (premium). Indoor pool; whirlpool. Complimentary full bkfst. Coffee in rms. Restaurant 6:30 am-10 pm. Bar to 1 am. Ck-out noon. Meeting rms. Business servs avail. Valet serv. Coin lndry. Exercise equipt. Some refrigerators. Cr cds: A, MC, V.

🅳 ➴ 🕴 🔆🆂🅲

★ **RED ROOF INN ST. PAUL.** *1806 Wooddale Dr, Woodbury (55125). 651/738-7160; fax 651/738-1869; res 800/843-7663. www.redroof.com.* 108 rms, 2 story. S $33.99-$58.99; D $46.99-$68.99; each addl $8; under 18 free. Crib free. Pet accepted. TV; cable (premium). Complimentary coffee. Restaurant nearby. Ck-out noon. Business servs avail. In-rm modem link. Downhill ski 15 mi; x-country ski 3 mi. Cr cds: A, C, D, DS, MC, V.

🅳 🍴 ⛷ ➴ 🕴 🔆

★ **SUPER 8 MOTEL.** *285 Century Ave N, Maplewood (55119). 651/738-1600; fax 651/738-9405; toll-free 800/800-8000. www.super8.com.* 110 rms, 4 story. Late May-early Sept: S $48.88-$61.88; D $55.88-$66.88; each addl $5; under 12 free; lower rates rest of yr. Crib free. Pet accepted; $50 refundable. TV; cable (premium). Complimentary bkfst buffet. Restaurant adj. Ck-out 11 am. Coin lndry. Business servs avail. In-rm modem link. Game rm. Sundries. Airport transportation. Downhill ski 15 mi; x-country ski 2 mi. Refrigerators, microwaves avail. Whirlpool in some

suites. Picnic tables. On lake. Cr cds: A, D, DS, MC, V.

🅳 🍴 ⛷ ➴ 🔆🆂🅲

Hotels

★★★ **CROWNE PLAZA.** *2700 Pilot Knob Rd, Eagan (55121). 651/454-3434; fax 651/454-4904; toll-free 800/465-4329. www.crowneplaza.com.* 187 rms, 6 story. S, D $119-$129; suites $129-$149; under 20 free. Crib free. TV; cable (premium). Indoor pool; whirlpool. Coffee in rms. Restaurant 7 am-11 pm. Bar. Ck-out noon. Coin lndry. Meeting rms. Business servs avail. In-rm modem link. Free airport transportation. Exercise equipt; sauna. Health club privileges. Cr cds: A, C, D, DS, JCB, MC, V.

🅳 ➴ 🕴 ✈ 🔆🆂🅲

★★ **EMBASSY SUITES.** *175 E 10th St (55101). 651/224-5400; fax 651/224-0957; toll-free 800/362-2779. www. embassystpaul.com.* 210 suites, 8 story. S $159-$179; D $169-$189; each addl $10; under 12 free; wkend, hol rates. Crib free. TV; cable (premium). Indoor pool; whirlpool. Complimentary full bkfst. Coffee in rms. Restaurant 11 am-10 pm. Bar to 1 am. Ck-out noon. Coin lndry. Meeting rms. Business servs avail. In-rm modem link. Gift shop. Free airport transportation. Exercise equipt; sauna, steam rm. Refrigerators, microwaves, wet bars. Atrium with pond, waterfalls, fountains, ducks; many plants and trees. Cr cds: A, C, D, DS, ER, JCB, MC, V.

🅳 ➴ 🕴 ✈ 🔆🆂🅲

★★ **RADISSON RIVERFRONT HOTEL.** *11 E Kellogg Blvd (55101). 651/292-1900; fax 651/224-8999; res 800/333-3333. www.radisson.com.* 475 rms, 22 story. S $110; D $140; each addl $10; under 18 free; package plans. Crib free. Garage parking $12.50. TV; cable (premium), VCR avail. Indoor pool. Restaurant 6:30 am-10:30 pm; Fri, Sat to 11:30 pm. Bars 11:30-1 am. Ck-out noon. Convention facilities. Business servs avail. In-rm modem link. Concierge. Downhill ski 15 mi; x-country ski 4 mi. Exercise equipt. Health club privileges. Some refrigerators. Indoor skyway to major stores, businesses. Luxury level. Cr cds: A, MC, V.

🅳 ⛷ ➴ 🕴 🔆🆂🅲

★★★★ **THE SAINT PAUL HOTEL.**
350 Market St (55102). 651/292-9292; fax 612/228-9506; toll-free 800/292-9292. A Historic Hotel of America, this beautifully restored property was founded in 1910 by wealthy businessman Lucius Ordway and still maintains an old-style, European charm. The 254-room hotel has hosted many famous individuals while still maintaining a commitment to business and leisure visitors to this capital city. Most rooms have splendid downtown, Rice Park, or St. Paul Cathedral views. 254 rms, 12 story. S $180; each addl $15; suites $250-$650; under 19 free; wkend rates; package plans. Crib free. Garage $15. TV; cable. Restaurant (see also THE ST. PAUL GRILL). Bar 11-1 am. Ck-out noon. Convention facilities. Business center. In-rm modem link. Concierge. Rooftop exercise rm. Health club privileges. Connected to downtown skyway system. Cr cds: A, MC, V.

★★ **SHERATON INN.** *400 Hamline Ave N (55104). 651/642-1234; fax 651/642-1126; toll-free 800/535-2339. www.sheraton.com.* 198 rms, 4 story. S $95-$125; D $102-$125; each addl $10; under 18 free; wkend rates. Crib free. TV; cable (premium). Indoor pool; whirlpool. Complimentary coffee in rms. Restaurant 6:30 am-10:30 pm. Bar 11 am-midnight, Sun from noon. Ck-out noon. Meeting rms. Business servs avail. In-rm modem link. Bellhops. Downhill ski 15 mi; x-country ski 7 mi. Exercise equipt. Health club privileges. Cr cds: A, D, DS.

Restaurants

★ **BUCA DI BEPPO.**
2728 Gannon Rd (55116). 651/772-4388. www.

bucadibeppo.com. Hrs: 5-10 pm; Fri to 11 pm; Sat 4-11 pm; Sun 4-10 pm. Closed Thanksgiving, Dec 24, 25. Italian menu. Bar. A la carte entrees: dinner $13-$17. Specializes in pasta, seafood. Outdoor dining. Italian decor. Cr cds: A, D, DS, MC, V.

★★ **CARAVAN SERAI.** *2175 Ford Pkwy (55116). 651/690-1935.* Hrs: 5-10 pm; Fri, Sat to 11 pm; Sun to 9 pm; closed hols. Res accepted. Afghani, Northern Indian menu. Wine, beer. Lunch $3.25-$6.25, dinner $8.95-$16.95. Children's menu. Specialties: tandoori chicken, vegetarian combination platter. Guitarist, Egyptian dancers Tues, Thurs-Sat. Hand-crafted tapestries, floor seating. Cr cds: A, MC, V.

★ **CIATTI'S.** *850 Grand Ave (55105). 651/292-9942.* Hrs: 11 am-10 pm; Fri, Sat to 11 pm; Sun from 2:30 pm; Sun brunch 10 am-2 pm. Closed Thanksgiving, Dec 24, 25. Italian menu. Res accepted. Bar to 1 am. Lunch $6.95-$9.95, dinner $7.95-$14.95. Sun brunch $6.95-$11.95. Children's

Victorian home on Summit Hill, St. Paul

menu. Specializes in northern Italian dishes. Own sauces. Cr cds: A, DS, MC, V.

D 🍽

★★★ **DAKOTA BAR AND GRILL.** *1021 E Bandana (55108). 651/642-1442. www.dakotacooks.com.* Hrs: 5-10 pm; Sun brunch 11 am-2:30 pm. Closed hols. Res accepted. Bar 4 pm-midnight; Fri, Sat to 1 am. Dinner $13-$26.95. Sun brunch $9.95-$18.95. Specializes in regional and seasonal dishes. Jazz eves. Parking. Outdoor dining. Located in restored railroad building in historic Bandana Sq. Modern decor. Cr cds: A, D, DS, MC, V.

D

★ **DIXIE'S.** *695 Grand Ave (55105). 651/222-7345.* Hrs: 11 am-midnight; Sun 2:30-11 pm; Sun brunch 10 am-2 pm. Closed Thanksgiving. Res accepted. Southern, Cajun menu. Bar to 1 am; Sun to midnight. Lunch $4.50-$9.95, dinner $4.95-$15.95. Sun brunch $10.95. Specialties; hickory-smoked ribs, Key lime pie. Parking. Informal dining. Cr cds: A, C, D, DS, MC, V.

D 🍽

★★★ **FOREPAUGH'S.** *276 S Exchange St (55102). 651/224-5606. www.forepaughs.com.* Hrs: 11:30 am-2 pm, 5:30-9:30 pm; Sat from 5:30 pm; Sun 5-8:30 pm; Sun brunch 10:30 am-1:30 pm. Closed hols. Res accepted. French menu. Bar to 1 am; Sun to midnight. Lunch $7.50-$9.95, dinner $12.25-$19.25. Sun brunch $13.75. Children's menu. Specialties: shrimp scampi, twin tournedos, veal Calvados. Valet parking. Outdoor dining. Restored mansion (1870); 9 dining rms. Cr cds: A, D, MC, V.

D

★ **GALLIVAN'S.** *354 Wabasha St (55102). 651/227-6688.* Hrs: 11 am-10 pm; Fri, Sat to 11 pm; Sun 4-8 pm. Closed hols. Res accepted. Bar to 1 am. Lunch $3.95-$8.45, dinner $9.95-$21.95. Specializes in steak, prime rib, seafood. Entertainment Fri, Sat. Cr cds: A, C, D, DS, MC, V.

D 🍽

★★★ **KOZLAKS ROYAL OAK.** *4785 Hodgson Rd, Shoreview (55126). 651/484-8484.* Hrs: 11 am-2:30 pm, 4-9:30 pm; Fri to 10:30 pm; Sat 4-10:30 pm; Sun 10 am-1:30 pm (brunch), 4-8:30 pm; early-bird dinner Sun-Fri to 5:45 pm. Closed hols. Res accepted. Bar to midnight; Fri, Sat to 1 am. Lunch $5.50-$12, dinner $15.50-$27. Sun brunch $9.95-$16.95. Children's menu. Specialties: steer tenderloin filet, duckling, salmon. Salad bar. Own baking. Strolling jazz musicians Sun brunch. Outdoor dining. Elegant decor with arched windows, etched glass. Family-owned. Cr cds: A, DS, MC, V.

D

★★★ **LAKE ELMO INN.** *3442 Lake Elmo Ave, Lake Elmo (55042). 651/777-8495.* Hrs:11 am-2 pm, 5-10 pm; Sun 10 am-2 pm, 4:30-8:30 pm. Closed hols. Res accepted. Continental menu. Bar to midnight. Wine list. Lunch $6-$8.95, dinner $14-$22. Sun brunch $14.95. Children's menu. Specialties: rack of lamb, roast duckling. Outdoor dining. Casual elegance in restored inn (1881). Cr cds: A, C, D, DS, MC, V.

D

★ **LEEANN CHIN.** *214 E 4th St (55101). 651/224-8814. www.leeannchin.com.* Hrs: 11 am-2:30 pm, 5-9 pm; Fri, Sat to 10 pm. Closed hols. Res accepted. Chinese menu. Serv bar. Buffet: lunch $7.95, dinner $13.95. Children's menu. Specializes in Cantonese, mandarin, and Szechwan dishes. Contemporary decor. Totally nonsmoking. Cr cds: A, D, DS, MC, V.

D

★★ **LEXINGTON.** *1096 Grand Ave (55105). 651/222-5878.* Hrs: 11 am-10 pm; Fri, Sat to 11 pm; Sun 4-9 pm; Sun brunch 10 am-3 pm. Closed July 4, Dec 24 eve, 25. Res accepted. Bar. Lunch $6.95-$11.95, dinner $9.95-$27. Sun brunch $4.95-$11.95. Children's menu. Specializes in prime rib, fresh walleye. Parking. French Provincial decor. Cr cds: A, D, DS, MC, V.

D 🍽

★ **LINDEY'S PRIME STEAKHOUSE.** *3600 Snelling Ave N, Arden Hills (55112). 651/633-9813.* Hrs: 5-10:30 pm; Fri, Sat to 11:30 pm. Closed Sun; hols. Bar. Dinner $13.65-$19.85. Children's menu. Specializes in steak.

Rustic, Northwoods lodge atmosphere. Cr cds: A, DS, MC, V.

★ **MANCINI'S CHAR HOUSE.** *531 W 7th St (55102). 651/224-7345.* Hrs: 5-11 pm; Fri, Sat to 12:30 am. Closed hols. Bar to 1 am. Dinner $10-$29. Specializes in steak, lobster. Entertainment Wed-Sat. Parking. Open charcoal hearths; 2 fireplaces. Family-owned. Cr cds: DS, MC, V.

★★ **MUFFULETTA IN THE PARK.** *2260 Como Ave (55108). 651/644-9116.* Hrs: 11:30 am-2:30 pm, 5-9:30 pm; Fri, Sat to 10 pm; Sun 10 am-2 pm, 5-8 pm; winter hrs vary. Closed hols. Res accepted. Continental menu. Wine, beer. Lunch $6.95-$11.95, dinner $7.95-$15.95. Sun brunch $7.95-$11.95. Specializes in pasta, fresh fish. Own soup, dressings. Parking. Outdoor dining. Cafe decor. Totally nonsmoking. Cr cds: A, D, DS, MC, V.

★★★ **RISTORANTE LUCI.** *470 Cleveland Ave S (55105). 651/699-8258.* Hrs: 5-9:30 pm; Fri, Sat to 10:30 pm; Sun 4:30-9 pm. Closed hols. Res accepted. Italian menu. Wine, beer. Dinner $7.75-$18.95. Children's menu. Specializes in pasta, seafood. Italian decor. Totally nonsmoking. Cr cds: A, MC, V.

★★★ **THE ST. PAUL GRILL.** *350 Market St (55102). 651/224-7455. www.stpaulhotel.com.* Hrs: 11 am-2 pm, 5:30-11 pm; Mon to 10 pm; Sun 5-10 pm; Sun brunch to 2 pm. Res accepted. Wine list. Lunch $6-$12, dinner $9-$26. Sun brunch $9-$15. Specializes in fresh fish, regional cuisine. Valet parking. Cr cds: A, DS, MC, V.

★★ **SAKURA.** *350 St. Peter St, #338 (55102). 651/224-0185.* Hrs: 11:30 am-2:30 pm, 5-10:30 pm; Fri, Sat to 11 pm; Sun to 9:30 pm. Closed Jan 1, Thanksgiving, Dec 25. Res accepted. Japanese menu. Bar. Lunch $6-$10, dinner $10-$15. Specializes in sushi, sashimi, teriyaki. Validated parking.

Contemporary Japanese decor; sushi bar. Cr cds: A, D, DS, MC, V.

★ **SAWATDEE.** *289 E 5th St (55101). 651/222-5859. www.sawatdee.com.* Hrs: 11 am-10 pm; Fri, Sat to 11 pm. Closed hols. Res accepted. Thai menu. Bar. Lunch, dinner $6-$8. Buffet: lunch $5.95. Specializes in noodle dishes, curry dishes. Thai decor. Cr cds: A, DS, MC, V.

★★ **TABLE OF CONTENTS.** *1648 Grand Ave (55105). 651/699-6595. www.tableofcontents.net.* Hrs: 11:30 am-2 pm, 5:30-9:30 pm; Fri, Sat to 10:30 pm; Sun 10 am-2 pm, 5-9 pm. Closed hols. Res accepted. Contemporary American menu. Wine, beer. Lunch $5.95-$11.95, dinner $10.95-$19.95. Sun brunch $5.25-$9.75. Specializes in pasta, seafood. Contemporary decor. Adj bookstore. Cr cds: A, D, DS, MC, V.

★★ **TOBY'S ON THE LAKE.** *249 Geneva Ave N (55128). 651/739-1600. www.tobysonthelake.com.* Hrs: 11 am-2:30 pm, 5-10 pm; Sat 11 am-11 pm; Sun 11 am-9 pm; Sun brunch to 2 pm. Closed Dec 25. Res accepted. Bar. Lunch $5.95-$11.95, dinner $10.95-$23.95. Sun brunch $5.95-$8.95. Children's menu. Specializes in prime rib, steak, fresh seafood. Parking. Outdoor dining. Olde English atmosphere. Overlooks Tanners Lake. Cr cds: A, D, DS, MC, V.

★ **TULIPS.** *452 Selby Ave (55102). 651/221-1061.* Hrs: 11:30 am-3 pm, 5-10 pm; Fri, Sat to 11 pm; Sun brunch to 2:30 pm. Closed hols. Res accepted. French menu. Wine, beer. Lunch $6-$12, dinner $10-$20. Sun brunch $6-$15. Specialties: sea scallops, herbed walnut walleye, filet mignon with bearnaise sauce. Outdoor dining. Country French decor; intimate dining. Cr cds: A, D, MC, V.

★★ **VENETIAN INN.** *2814 Rice St, Little Canada (55113). 651/484-7215.* Hrs: 11 am-10 pm; Fri, Sat to 11 pm. Closed Sun; hols. Res accepted. Italian, American menu. Bar to 1 am. Lunch $6.50-$8.50, dinner $7.95-

$17.95. Complete meals: Sicilian dinner (for 2 or more) $22.50. Children's menu. Specializes in steak, barbecued ribs, lasagne. Theatre entertainment Fri, Sat. Parking. Family-owned. Cr cds: A, D, DS, MC, V.
D

★★★ **W. A. FROST AND COMPANY.** *374 Selby Ave (55102). 651/224-5715.* Hrs: 11-1 am; Sun 10:30 am-midnight; Sun brunch to 2 pm. Closed hols. Res accepted. Bar. Lunch $7-$11, dinner $6.95-$22. Sun brunch $5-$10. Children's menu. Specialties: dry-aged ribeye, Nantucket chicken, chocolate silk pie. Valet parking Fri, Sat. Outdoor dining in garden area. Three dining rms; Victorian-style decor. Renovated pharmacy (1887). Totally nonsmoking. Cr cds: A, C, D, DS, MC, V.
D

Unrated Dining Spots

CECIL'S. *651 S Cleveland (55116). 651/698-0334. www.visi.com~zodiac/cecils.* Hrs: 9 am-8 pm. Bkfst $1.75-$4.50, lunch, dinner $3-$6.50. Specialties: corned beef, pastrami sandwiches. Own baking, soups. Parking. Family-owned since 1949. Cr cds: MC, V.

GREEN MILL INN. *57 S Hamline Ave (55105). 651/698-0353. www.greenmill.com.* Hrs: 11 am-2 pm, 4-10 pm; Fri to 11 pm; Sat 4-11 pm; Sun 4-10 pm. Closed Dec 24 eve-Dec 25. Italian, American menu. Wine, beer. Lunch, dinner $2.95-$10.75. Specializes in deep-dish pizza, sandwiches. Own soups, chili. Cr cds: A, D, DS, MC, V.
D

NO WAKE CAFE. *100 Yacht Club Rd, Pier One (55107). 651/292-1411. www.covingtoninn.com.* Hrs: 8 am-2 pm; Thur also 5-9 pm; Fri, Sat also 5-10 pm; Sun 8 am-noon. Closed Mon; hols; also Jan-Feb. Wine, beer. Bkfst $4-$6, lunch $3.50-$7, dinner $9-$15. Specialties: Tuscan tenderloin, almond-crusted walleye. Vintage towboat on Mississippi River. Cr cds: MC, V.
D

St. Peter

(G-4) *See also Faribault, Le Sueur, Mankato, New Ulm*

Founded 1853 **Pop** 9,421 **Elev** 770 ft **Area code** 507 **Zip** 56082

Information St. Peter Area Chamber of Commerce, 101 S Front St; 507/931-3400 or 800/473-3404

Web www.tourism.st-peter.mn.us

What to See and Do

Eugene Saint Julien Cox House. (1871) Fully restored home is best example of Gothic Italianate architecture in the state. Built by town's first mayor; late Victorian furnishings. Guided tours. (June-Aug, Wed-Sun; May and Sept, Sat and Sun afternoons) 500 N Washington Ave. Phone 507/931-2160. ¢¢

Gustavus Adolphus College. (1862) 2,300 students. On campus are Old Main (dedicated 1876); Alfred Nobel Hall of Science and Gallery; Lund Center for Physical Education; Folke Bernadotte Memorial Library; Linnaeus Arboretum; Schaefer Fine Arts Gallery; Christ Chapel, featuring door and narthex art by noted sculptor Paul Granlund. At various other locations on campus are sculptures by Granlund, sculptor-in-residence, incl one depicting Joseph Nicollét, mid-19th-century French explorer and cartographer of the Minnesota River valley. Campus tours. In Oct, the college hosts the nationally known Nobel Conference, which has been held annually since 1965. 800 W College Ave. Phone 507/933-8000.

Treaty Site History Center. County historical items relating to Dakota people, explorers, settlers, traders, and cartographers and their impact on the 1851 Treaty of Traverse des Sioux. Archives. Museum shop. (Daily; closed hols) 1851 N Minnesota Ave. Phone 507/931-2160. ¢¢

Sauk Centre

(E-3) *See also Alexandria, Glenwood*

Pop 3,581 **Elev** 1,246 ft
Area code 320 **Zip** 56378
Information Sauk Centre Area Chamber of Commerce, PO Box 222; 320/352-5201
Web www.saukcentre.com

This is "Gopher Prairie," the boyhood home of Sinclair Lewis and the setting for *Main Street,* as well as many of his other novels. The town is at the southern tip of Big Sauk Lake.

What to See and Do

Sinclair Lewis Boyhood Home.
Restored home of America's first Nobel Prize-winning novelist. Original furnishings; family memorabilia. (Memorial Day-Labor Day, daily; rest of yr, by appt) 812 Sinclair Lewis Ave. Phone 320/352-5201. ¢¢

Sinclair Lewis Interpretive Center.
Exhibits incl original manuscripts, photographs, letters; 15-min video on the author's life; research library. (Labor Day-Memorial Day, Mon-Fri; Memorial Day-Labor Day, daily) At jct I-94, US 71. Phone 320/352-5201.
FREE

Special Event

Sinclair Lewis Days. Third wkend July.

Motels/Motor Lodges

★ **HILLCREST MOTEL.** *965 S Main St (56378).* 320/352-2215; fax 320/352-6881; toll-free 800/858-6333. 21 rms. S $24; D $32; each addl $4. Pet accepted, some restrictions; $5. TV; cable (premium). Restaurant nearby. Ck-out 11 am. Cr cds: A, DS, MC, V.

★ **SUPER 8.** *322 12th St S (56378).* 320/352-6581; fax 320/352-6584; res 800/800-8000. www.super8.com. 38 rms, 2 story. S, D $43-$62; each addl $5; under 12 free. Crib $2.50. Pet accepted, some restrictions. TV; cable (premium). Indoor pool. Ck-out 11

am. Business servs avail. Cr cds: A, DS, MC, V.

Spring Valley

(H-5) *See also Austin, Rochester*

Pop 2,461 **Elev** 1,279 ft
Area code 507 **Zip** 55975

As the name suggests, there are many large springs in this area. Geologists find the underground rivers, caves, and limestone outcroppings here of particular interest.

What to See and Do

Forestville/Mystery Cave State Park.
A 3,075-acre park in Root River valley with historic townsite. Fishing; hiking; bridle trails. X-country skiing, snowmobiling; picnicking; camping. Standard fees. 6 mi E on MN 16, 4 mi S on County 5, then 2 mi E on County 12. Phone 507/352-5111. ¢ Also in park is

Mystery Cave. Sixty-min guided tours; 48°F in cave. (Memorial Day-Labor Day, daily; mid-Apr-Memorial Day, wkends) Picnicking. Vehicle permit required (addl fee). Phone 507/352-5111. ¢¢¢

Historic buildings.

Methodist Church. (1878) Victorian Gothic architecture; 23 stained-glass windows. Laura Ingalls Wilder site. Lower-level displays incl country store, history rm; military and business displays. (June-Aug, daily; Sept-Oct, wkends; also by appt) 221 W Courtland St. Phone 507/346-7659. ¢

Washburn-Zittleman House.
(1866) Two-story frame house with period furnishings, quilts; farm equipt, one-rm school, toys. (Memorial Day-Labor Day, daily; Sept-Oct, wkends; also by appt) 220 W Courtland St. Phone 507/346-7659. ¢¢

Stillwater

(F-5) *See also St. Paul, Taylors Falls*

Settled 1839 **Pop** 13,882 **Elev** 700 ft
Area code 651 **Zip** 55082
Information Chamber of Commerce, 423 S Main St, Brick Alley Building; 651/439-7700

Center of the logging industry in pioneer days, Stillwater became a busy river town, host to the men who rode the logs downriver and the lumbermen who cleared the forests.

What to See and Do

⬛ **St. Croix Scenic Highway.** MN 95 runs 50 mi from Afton to Taylors Falls (see) along the "Rhine of America," the St. Croix River.

Washington County Historical Museum. Former warden's house at old prison site; mementos of lumbering days (1846-1910); pioneer kitchen, furniture. (May-Oct, Tues, Thurs, Sat and Sun; also by appt) 602 N Main St. Phone 651/439-5956. ¢

William O'Brien State Park. A 1,273-acre park. Swimming, fishing, boating (ramp); hiking, x-country skiing, picnicking, camping (hookups, dump station). Standard fees. 16 mi N on MN 95. Phone 651/433-0500.

Special Events

Rivertown Art Fair. Lowell Park. Third wkend May.
Lumberjack Days. Last wkend July.

Motels/Motor Lodges

★★ **BEST WESTERN.** *1750 W Frontage Rd (55082). 651/430-1300; fax 651/430-0596; toll-free 800/647-4039. www.bestwestern.com/still waterinn.* 60 rms, 2 story. Mid-May-mid-Oct: S $72-$75; D $79-$82; each addl $4; under 18 free; lower rates rest of yr. Crib free. Pet accepted. TV; cable (premium). Complimentary continental bkfst. Restaurant nearby. Ck-out 11 am. Business servs avail. In-rm modem link. Downhill ski 20 mi; x-country ski 2 mi. Exercise equipt. Whirlpool. Picnic table. Cr cds: A, C, D, DS, ER, JCB, MC, V.
🄳 🍴 ⚡ ⛵ 🎿 ⚓ 🔥

★★ **COUNTRY INN AND SUITES BY CARLSON.** *2200 W Frontage Rd (55082). 651/430-2699; fax 651/430-1233; toll-free 800/456-4000.* 52 rms, 2 story, 20 suites. S, D $69-$79; each addl $6; suites $78-$129; under 18 free. Crib free. TV; cable (premium). Complimentary continental bkfst, coffee in rms. Restaurant nearby. Ck-out noon. Meeting rms. Business servs avail. In-rm modem link. Valet serv. Coin lndry. Downhill ski 15 mi; x-country ski 2 mi. Exercise equipt. Indoor pool; whirlpool. Game rm. Some in-rm whirlpools; refrigerator, microwave in suites. Cr cds: A, D, DS, MC, V.
🄳 ⚡ ⛵ 🎿 ⚓ 🔥 SC

★ **SUPER 8 MOTEL.** *2190 W Frontage Rd (55082). 651/430-3990; toll-free 800/800-8000. www.super8. com.* 49 rms, 2 story. S, D $43-$70; each addl $7; under 12 free. Crib free. TV; cable (premium). Complimentary continental bkfst. Restaurant adj open 24 hrs. Ck-out 11 am. Coin lndry. Business servs avail. Downhill ski 15 mi; x-country ski 2 mi. Near St. Croix River. Cr cds: A, C, D, DS, MC, V.
🄳 ⚡ ⚓ 🔥 SC

Hotel

★★★ **LUMBER BARON'S HOTEL.** *101 S Water St (55082). 651/439-6000; fax 651/430-9393. www. lumberbarons.com.* 42 rms, 3 story. S, D $139-$199; each addl $15; under 5 free. Crib free. TV. Complimentary full bkfst. Restaurant 7 am-3 pm, 5-11 pm. Bar 11-1 am. Ck-out 11 am. Business servs avail. Fireplaces, in-rm whirlpools. Cr cds: A, D, DS, MC, V.
🄳 🏊 ⚡ ⚓ 🔥

B&Bs/Small Inns

★★★ **AFTON HOUSE INN.** *3291 S St. Croix Tr, Afton (55001). 651/436-8883; fax 651/436-6859; toll-free 877/436-8883. www.aftonhouse inn.com.* 15 rms, 2 story. S, D $49; AP avail; mid-wk rates. Crib free. TV; VCR avail. Restaurant (see also AFTON HOUSE). Ck-out 11 am, ck-in 2 pm. Business servs avail. Airport transportation. Downhill/x-country ski 2 mi. Some in-rm whirlpools, fireplaces. Some balconies. Historic inn

Boundary Waters Canoe Area Wilderness

(1867); antiques. River cruises avail.
Cr cds: A, DS, MC, V.

⬛ 🖼 🖼 🖼 🖼 🖼

★★ **COVER PARK MANOR BED AND BREAKFAST.** *15330 58th St N (55082). 651/430-9292; fax 651/430-0034; toll-free 877/430-9292. www. coverpark.com.* 4 rms, 2 suites, 2 story. No elvtr. No rm phones. S $95-$149, D $109-$149; hols (2-day min). Complimentary full bkfst; afternoon refreshments. Restaurant nearby. Ck-out 11:30 am, ck-in 4 pm. Some fireplaces, in-rm whirlpools Victorian house built in 1882; antiques. Totally nonsmoking. Cr cds: A, DS, MC, V.

⬛ 🖼 🖼

★★ **JAMES A. MULVEY INN.** *622 W Churchill St (55082). 651/430-8008; fax 651/430-2801; toll-free 800/820-8008. www.jamesmulveyinn.com.* 7 rms, 2 story. No rm phones. June-Oct: S, D $149-$219; lower rates rest of yr. Children over 12 yrs only. Complimentary full bkfst; afternoon refreshments. Restaurant nearby. Ck-out noon, ck-in 4 pm. Downhill ski 15 mi; x-country ski 3 mi. Lawn games. Fireplaces, in-rm whirlpools. Victorian house built in 1878 furnished with antiques. Totally nonsmoking. Cr cds: DS, MC, V.

🖼 🖼 🖼 🖼

★★★ **LOWELL INN.** *102 2nd St N (55082). 651/439-1100; fax 651/439-4686; toll-free 888/569-3554. www. lowellinn.com.* 21 rms, 3 story. S $89; D $129; higher rates Fri, Sat (MAP). TV. Bkfst 8-10:30 am. Restaurant (see also LOWELL INN). Bar 11:30 am-2:30 pm, 5:30 pm-1 am; Sun, hols noon-11 pm. Ck-out noon. Business servs avail. Downhill ski 15 mi; x-country ski 9 mi. Antique furnishings. Cr cds: A, C, D, DS, MC, V.

🖼 🖼 🖼

Restaurants

★★ **AFTON HOUSE.** *3291 S St. Croix Tr (55001). 651/436-8883. www. aftonhouseinn.com.* Hrs: 11:30 am-10 pm; Sat to 11 pm; Sun 10 am-9 pm; Sun brunch to 2 pm. Closed Dec 24; also Mon, Jan-Apr. Res accepted. Bar to 1 am. Lunch $5.95-$9.95, dinner $13.95-$20.95. Sun brunch $12.95. Children's menu. Specializes in seafood. Entertainment Fri-Sat. Parking. Renovated inn (1867); nautical decor. Dockage on St. Croix River. Tableside preparation. Cr cds: A, DS, MC, V.

⬛

★★★ **BAYPORT AMERICAN COOKERY.** *328 5th Ave N, Bayport (55003). 651/430-1066. www.bayport cookery.com.* Sitting: 6:30 pm; Fri, Sat

7:30 pm. Closed Mon, Sun; hols. Res required. Contemporary American menu. Wine, beer. Prix fixe: dinner $29.95. Children's menu. Specializes in regional ingredients. Contemporary decor with local artwork displayed. Totally nonsmoking. Cr cds: A, C, D, DS, MC, V.

D

★ **ESTEBAN'S.** *423 S Main St (55082). 651/430-1543.* Hrs: 11 am-10 pm; Fri, Sat to 11 pm. Closed Dec 24, 25. Mexican, American menu. Bar. Lunch, dinner $5-$15. Children's menu. Specializes in fajitas, fried ice cream. Parking. Mexican/Southwest decor. Cr cds: A, C, D, DS, MC, V.

D ⊟

★ **GASTHAUS BAVARIAN HUNTER.** *8390 Lofton Ave N (55082). 651/439-7128. www.gasthaus bavarianhunter.com.* Hrs: 11 am-9 pm; Fri to 10 pm; Sat noon-10 pm; Sun noon-8 pm. Closed hols. Res accepted. German menu. Bar. Lunch $4-$7, dinner $9-$17. Sun dinner buffet: $11.95. Children's menu. Specialties: schnitzel, pork hock. Accordianist Fri eve, Sun afternoon. Parking. Outdoor dining in beer garden. Authentic Bavarian decor. Family-owned since 1966. Cr cds: A, MC, V.

D ⊟

★★ **HARVEST INN.** *114 Chestnut St (55082). 651/430-8111.* Hrs: 11:30 am-2 pm, 5:30-9:30 pm; Sat from 5:30 pm; early-bird dinner Mon-Fri to 6:15 pm. Closed Sun; hols. Res accepted. Continental menu. Wine, beer. A la carte entrees: lunch $7.95-$9.95, dinner $15.95-$17.95. Children's menu. Specialties: frutti di mare, steak au poivre, chicken Marsala. Own baking. Street parking. Outdoor dining. Restored Victorian home (1848) is oldest surviving wood frame structure in city; antique interior; intimate dining. Totally nonsmoking. Cr cds: A, DS, MC, V.

D

★★ **LOWELL INN.** *102 N 2nd St (55082). 651/439-1100. www.lowell inn.com.* Hrs: 8 am-10 pm. Closed Thanksgiving, Dec 24, 25. Res accepted. Swiss, American menu. Bar to 1 am; Sun, hols to 11 pm. Bkfst $4.35-$8.95, lunch $11.75-$20.75, dinner $20.95-$35.95. Serv charge 20 percent. Children's menu. Specializes in fresh brook trout in season (select your own from pool). Prix fixe: dinner $60 (Swiss fondue Bourguigonne). Own baking. Parking. Elegant furnishings; wood carvings, paintings. Antique silverware, china. Formal dining. Family-owned. Cr cds: A, D, DS, MC, V.

D SC

★ **VITTORIO'S.** *402 S Main St (55082). 651/439-3588.* Hrs: 11 am-10 pm; Fri, Sat to 11 pm. Closed Thanksgiving, Dec 24 eve, 25. Res accepted. Italian menu. Bar. Lunch $4.50-$8.75, dinner $5.95-$19.95. Children's menu. Specialties: canelloni, antipasto salad. Parking. Outdoor dining. Unique dining experience in caves used as "brewery" from 1870s through prohibition. Family-owned. Cr cds: A, D, DS, MC, V.

D ⊟

Superior National Forest

See also Crane Lake, Ely, Grand Marais, Tower, Virginia

(On N side of Lake Superior, W to Virginia, N to Canadian border, E to Grand Marais)

With more than 2,000 beautiful clear lakes, rugged shorelines, picturesque islands, and deep woods, this is a magnificent portion of Minnesota's famous northern area.

The Boundary Waters Canoe Area Wilderness, part of the forest, is perhaps the finest canoe country in the United States (travel permits required for each party, $9 for advance reservations, phone 800/745-3399). Scenic water routes through wilderness near the international border offer opportunities for adventure. Adjacent Quetico Provincial Park is similar, but guns are prohibited. Entry through Canadian Customs. and Park Rangers' Ports of Entry.

Boating, swimming, water sports; fishing and hunting under Minnesota game and fish regulations; winter sports; camping (fee), picnicking, and scenic drives along Honeymoon, Gunflint, Echo, and Sawbill trails.

For further information contact Forest Supervisor, 8901 Grand Avenue Pl, Duluth 55808; 218/626-4300.

Taylors Falls

See also St. Paul, Stillwater

Settled 1838 **Pop** 694 **Elev** 900 ft
Area code 612 **Zip** 55084
Information Taylors Falls Chamber of Commerce, PO Box 235; 612/465-6315, 612/257-3550 (Twin Cities) or 800/447-4958 (outside 612 area)
Web www.wildmountain.com

What to See and Do

Boat Excursions. Taylors Falls Scenic Boat Tour. Base of bridge, downtown. (Early May-mid-Oct, daily); 30-min, three-mi trip through St. Croix Dalles; also 1⅓-hr, seven-mi trip on *Taylors Falls Queen* or *Princess*. Scenic, brunch, luncheon, and dinner cruises; fall color cruises. Also Taylors Falls one-way canoe rentals, trips (with shuttle) (May-mid-Oct, daily). Phone 612/465-6315.

⚔ St. Croix and Lower St. Croix National Scenic Riverway. From its origins in northern Wisconsin the St. Croix flows southward to form part of the Minnesota-Wisconsin border before joining the Mississippi near Point Douglas. Two segments of the river totaling more than 250 mi have been designated National Scenic Riverways and are administered by the National Park Service. Information headquarters (mid-May-Oct, daily; rest of yr, Mon-Fri); three information stations (Memorial Day-Labor Day, daily). For information contact PO Box 708. Phone 612/483-3284.

Skiing. Wild Mountain Ski Area. Four quad chairlifts, two rope tows; patrol, school, rentals; snowmaking; cafeteria. Twenty-three runs, longest run 5,000 ft; vertical drop 300 ft. (Nov-Mar, daily) 7 mi N on County 16. Phone 651/257-3550 or 800/447-4958. ¢¢¢¢ Also here is

Water Park. Alpine slides and go-karts. (Memorial Day-Labor Day, daily). Phone 651/257-3550. ¢¢¢¢
State parks.
Interstate. A 295-acre park. Geologic formations. Boating (ramp), canoe rentals, fishing, hiking, picnicking, camping (electric hookups, dump station). Excursion boat (fee). Standard fees. 1 mi S on MN 8. Phone 612/465-5711.
Wild River. On 6,706 acres in the St. Croix River valley. Fishing, canoeing (rentals); 35 mi of trails for hiking, x-country skiing and 20 mi of horseback riding trails; picnicking; primitive and modern camping (electric hookups, dump station). Interpretive center and Trail Center (Daily). Standard hrs, fees. 10 mi NW via MN 95, then 3 mi N on County 12. Phone 612/583-2125.
W.H.C. Folsom House. (1855) Federal/Greek Revival mansion reflects New England heritage of early settlers; many original furnishings. (Memorial Day wkend-mid-Oct, daily) 120 Government Rd. Phone 612/465-3125. ¢¢

Thief River Falls

(C-2) *See also Crookston*

Pop 8,010 **Elev** 1,133 ft
Area code 218 **Zip** 56701

What to See and Do

Agassiz National Wildlife Refuge. Approx 61,500 acres of forest, water, and marshland. A haven for 280 species of migratory and upland game birds; 41 species of resident mammals. Observation tower; refuge headquarters (Mon-Fri; closed hols); auto tour route (daily, exc winter). No camping. 23 mi NE via MN 32 to County 7 E. Phone 218/449-4115. **FREE**

Motels/Motor Lodges

★ ★ **BEST WESTERN INN.** *1060 MN 32 S (56701). 218/681-7555; fax*

218/681-7721; toll-free 800/780-7234. www.bestwestern.com. 78 rms. S, studio rms $49-$57; D $59-$67; each addl $4; under 18 free. Crib free. TV; cable (premium). Indoor pool; whirlpool. Complimentary coffee in rms. Restaurant 6 am-10 pm. Bar 3 pm-1 am; entertainment. Ck-out noon. Meeting rms. Business servs avail. In-rm modem link. Sundries. Free airport transportation. X-country ski 3 mi. Exercise equipt. Game rm. Refrigerators. Cr cds: A, C, D, DS, MC, V.

D ⌧ ⌫ 🕎 ⌦ 🐾 SC

★ **C'MON INN.** 1586 Hwy 59 S (56701). 218/681-3000; fax 218/681-3060; toll-free 800/950-8111. 44 rms, 2 story. S $44-$57; D $51-$65; each addl $7; suites $74-$94; under 12 free. Crib free. Pet accepted, some restrictions. TV; cable (premium). Indoor pool; whirlpool. Complimentary continental bkfst. Restaurant nearby. Ck-out noon. Meeting rm. Business servs avail. In-rm modem link. Game rm. Balconies. Cr cds: A, DS, MC, V.

D 🐾 ⌫ ⌦ 🐾 SC

★ **SUPER 8 MOTEL.** 1915 Hwy 59 S (56701). 218/681-6205; fax 218/681-7519; toll-free 888/890-9568. www.super8.com. 46 rms. S, D $40-$60; each addl $4; under 16 free. Crib free. TV; cable (premium). Complimentary continental bkfst. Restaurant adj 6:30 am-11 pm. Ck-out 11 am. Business servs avail. Cr cds: A, D, DS, MC, V.

D ⌦ 🐾 SC

Tower

(C-5) See also Cook, Crane Lake, Ely, Virginia

Founded 1882 **Pop** 502 **Elev** 1,400 ft
Area code 218 **Zip** 55790

Oldest mining town in northern Minnesota, Tower today serves as a shopping center for Lake Vermilion, Superior National Forest (see), and the "arrowhead country."

What to See and Do

Lake Vermilion. 40 mi long, 1,250 mi of wooded shoreline, 365 islands varying in size from specklike rocks

to Pine Island, which is nine mi long and has its own lake in its interior. Fishing for walleye, northern pike, bass, panfish. Swimming, boating, water sports; hunting for duck, deer, and small game in fall; snowmobiling and x-country skiing; camping and lodging. Primarily located in Superior National Forest (see). Phone 218/753-2301.

Soudan Underground Mine State Park. Has 1,300 acres incl site of the Soudan Mine, the state's first underground iron mine (52°F; 2,400 ft) in operation 1882-1962. Self-guided tour of open pits, engine house, crusher building, drill shop, interpretive center; one-hr guided underground mine tour incl train ride (fees). Hiking trails. Picnic area. (Memorial Day-Labor Day, daily) Standard fees. 2 mi E on MN 169, in Soudan. Phone 218/753-2245. ¢¢

Steam locomotive and coach. Locomotive (1910) served Duluth & Iron Range Railroad. Coach is now a museum housing early logging, mining, and Native American displays. (Memorial Day-Labor Day, daily; early spring and late fall, by appt) On grounds is a tourist information center. W end Main St, near jct MN 135, 169. Phone 218/753-2301. **Donation**

Tracy

(G-2) See also Marshall, Pipestone, Redwood Falls

Pop 2,059 **Elev** 1,395 ft
Area code 507 **Zip** 56175
Information Chamber of Commerce, Prairie Pavilion, 372 Morgan St; 507/629-4021

What to See and Do

Lake Shetek State Park. Comprises 1,011 acres on one of largest lakes in SW Minnesota. Monument to settlers who were victims of the Dakota Conflict in 1862; restored pioneer cabin. Swimming, fishing, boating (ramp, rentals); hiking, snowmobiling, picnicking, camping. Standard fees. Naturalist (Late May-early Sept). 14 mi S on County 11 and 38. Phone 507/763-3256.

⭐ **Laura Ingalls Wilder Museum and Tourist Center.** This tribute to Laura Ingalls Wilder is located in an old railroad depot. The depression in the ground where the dugout used to be, and the rock and spring mentioned in *On the Banks of Plum Creek* are all 1½ mi N of Walnut Grove; fee per vehicle at farm site. (May-Oct, daily; rest of yr, by appt) 7 mi E on US 14, in Walnut Grove at 330 8th St. Phone 507/859-2358. **FREE**

Special Event

Laura Ingalls Wilder Pageant. 7 mi E on US 14, 1 mi W of Walnut Grove. Story of the Ingalls family of Walnut Grove in the 1870s. Daughter was Laura Ingalls Wilder, author of the *Little House* books. Phone 507/859-2174. July.

Two Harbors

(D-6) *See also Duluth*

Founded 1884 **Pop** 3,651 **Elev** 699 ft
Area code 218 **Zip** 55616

Information Two Harbors Area Chamber of Commerce, 603 7th Ave; 800/777-7384
Web www.twoharbors.com/chamber

Two Harbors was given its start when the Duluth & Iron Range Railroad reached Lake Superior at Agate Bay. Ore docks were constructed immediately, and the city became an important ore shipping terminal. Today it is a bustling harbor community nestled between the twin harbors of Agate Bay and Burlington Bay.

What to See and Do

Depot Museum. Historic depot (1907) highlights the geological history and the discovery and mining of iron ore. Mallet locomotive (1941), world's most powerful steam engine, on display. (Mid-May-Oct, daily; winter, wkends) In depot of Duluth & Iron Range Railroad, foot of Waterfront Dr. Phone 218/834-4898. ¢

Gooseberry Falls State Park. A 1,662-acre park. Fishing, hiking, x-country skiing, snowmobiling, picnicking, camping (dump station). State park vehicle permit required.

Gooseberry Falls State Park, near Two Harbors

Standard fees. 14 mi NE on MN 61. Phone 218/834-3855.

Lighthouse Point and Harbor Museum. Displays tell the story of iron ore shipping and the development of the first iron ore port in the state. A renovated pilot house from an ore boat is located on the site. Tours of operating lighthouse. (May-Nov 1, daily) Off MN 61, on Waterfront Dr at Lighthouse Point. Phone 218/834-4898. ¢

Split Rock Lighthouse State Park. 1,987 acres. Lighthouse served as guiding sentinel for north shore of Lake Superior from 1910-1969. Also in the park is a historic complex (fee) which incl fog-signal building, keeper's dwellings, several outbuildings, and the ruins of a tramway (mid-May-mid-Oct, daily). Waterfalls. Picnicking. Cart-in camping (fee) on Lake Superior, access to Superior Hiking Trail. State park vehicle permit required. Standard hrs, fees. 20 mi NE on MN 61. Phone 218/226-6377. ¢¢

Motel/Motor Lodge

★★ **COUNTRY INN BY CARLSON.** *1204 7th Ave (55616). 218/834-5557; fax 218/834-3777; toll-free 800/456-4000.* 46 rms, 2 story. Mid-May-mid-Oct: S, D $59-$109; each addl $5; under 18 free; higher rates special events; lower rates rest of yr. Crib free. Pet accepted, some restrictions; $5/day. TV; cable (premium), VCR avail (movies). Indoor pool; whirlpool. Complimentary continental bkfst, coffee in rms. Restaurant adj 6 am-11 pm. Ck-out 11 am. Coin lndry. Business servs avail. X-country ski 1 mi. Sauna. Some refrigerators, microwaves, wet bars. Near Lake Superior. Cr cds: A, C, D, DS, MC, V.

D ★ ★ ★ ★ ★ ★ SC

Resort

★★★ **SUPERIOR SHORES RESORT.** *1521 Superior Shores Dr (55616). 218/834-5671; fax 218/834-5677; toll-free 800/242-1988. www.superiorshores.com.* 104 rms in 3-story lodge, 42 kit. units in 3-story townhouses. Mid-June-mid Oct: S, D $49-$69; under 18 free; wkly rates; wkends (2-day min); wkends (3-day min); lower rates rest of yr. Pet accepted. TV; cable, VCR (movies). 3 pools, 1 indoor; whirlpool. Restaurant 7 am-9 pm. Bar 11-1 am. Ck-out 11 am, ck-in by arrangement. Gift shop. Meeting rms. Business servs avail. Tennis. X-country ski opp. Sauna. Snowmobiles. Hiking trails. Game rm. Many refrigerators, microwaves. Balconies. Picnic tables, grills. On Lake Superior. Cr cds: A, DS, MC, V.

D ★ ★ ★ ★ ★ ★ ★

Virginia

(C-5) See also Cook, Eveleth, Hibbing, Tower

Founded 1892 **Pop** 9,410 **Elev** 1,437 ft **Area code** 218 **Zip** 55792

Information Virginia Area Chamber of Commerce, 403 1st St N, PO Box 1072; 218/741-2717

Born of lumbering, Virginia is nurtured by mining and vacationing. Great open iron ore pits mark the surrounding green countryside—man-made canyons are right at the city limits. Vacationers come to Virginia en route to the Boundary Waters Canoe Area Wilderness, Superior National Forest, and Voyagers National Park. A Ranger District office of the Superior National Forest (see) is located nearby.

What to See and Do

Mine View in the Sky. Observation building (and visitor information center) gives view of a Mesabi Range open-pit mine 650 ft below. (May-Sept daily) S edge of town on US 53. Phone 218/741-2717. **FREE**

World's Largest Floating Loon. Listed in the *Guinness Book of World Records*, this 20-ft long, 10-ft high, 7½-ft wide, fiberglass loon swims on Silver Lake (located in the heart of the city) during the summer months. Phone 507/289-6412.

Motels/Motor Lodges

★ **LAKESHORE MOTOR INN.** *404 N 6th Ave (55792). 218/741-3360; fax 218/741-3363; toll-free 800/569-8131.* 11 rms, 3 suites, 2 story. Mid-May-Aug: S $36; D $44-$48; each addl $4; family rates; lower rates rest of yr.

Crib avail. Pet accepted. TV; cable. Complimentary coffee in rms. Whirlpool. Restaurant nearby. Ck-out 11 am. Gift shop. Downhill ski 18 mi; x-country ski 4 mi. Cr cds: A, MC, V.

★ **SKI VIEW.** *903 17th St N (55792). 218/741-8918; fax 218/749-3279; toll-free 800/255-7106.* 59 rms, 2 story. S $32; D $44; each addl $4. Crib $5. Pet accepted. TV; cable (premium). Complimentary continental bkfst, coffee in rms. Restaurant nearby. Ck-out 11 am. Downhill/x-country ski 20 mi. Snowmobile trails adj. Sauna. Microwaves avail. Cr cds: A, C, D, DS, MC, V.

Walker

(D-3) *See also Bemidji, Park Rapids, Pine River*

Pop 950 **Elev** 1,336 ft **Area code** 218 **Zip** 56484

Information Chamber of Commerce, PO Box 1089; 218/547-1313 or 800/833-1118

Web www.leech-lake.com

At the foot of Chippewa National Forest and Leech Lake, Walker serves tourists heading for adventures among woods and waters. Snowmobiling and cross-country skiing are popular sports here. The town is named for a pioneer lumberman and landowner. A Ranger District office of the Chippewa National Forest (see GRAND RAPIDS) is located here.

What to See and Do

Leech Lake. Third-largest in state; fishing and swimming. MN 200/371.

Motel/Motor Lodge

★★ **AMERICINN.** *MN 371, Box 843 (56484). 218/547-2200; toll-free 800/757-9135.* 37 rms, 2 story. S $43.90-$56.90; D $59.90-$65.90; each addl $6; suites $64.90-$96.90; under 12 free. Crib free. TV; cable, VCR avail (movies). Indoor pool; whirlpool. Sauna. Complimentary continental bkfst. Restaurant adj 7 am-9 pm. Ck-out 11 am. X-country ski 10 mi. Some refrigerators, wet bars. Cr cds: A, D, DS, MC, V.

Cottage Colony

★ **BIG ROCK RESORT.** *7860 Hawthorn Tr NW (56484). 218/547-1066; fax 218/547-1402; toll-free 800/827-7106. www.bigrockresort.com.* 20 kit. cottages (1-3 bedrm). June-Aug, wkly: D $425; each addl $75; 4-6 persons $605-$830; lower rates rest of yr. No maid serv. Crib avail. Pet accepted; $10/day. TV; cable. Heated pool; whirlpool. Playground. Snack bar 7 am-11 pm. Ck-out 9 am, ck-in 4 pm Sat. Grocery. Coin lndry, package store 5 mi. Free airport, bus depot transportation. Tennis. Private sand beach. Boat harbors. Boats, motors, canoes, paddleboat, boat ramp, dockage. X-country ski 10 mi. Snowmobile trails. Indoor, outdoor games. Rec rm. Picnic tables, grills. Screened porches, patios. Cr cds: MC, V.

Willmar

(F-3) *See also Granite Falls, Litchfield*

Founded 1869 **Pop** 17,531 **Elev** 1,130 ft **Area code** 320 **Zip** 56201

Information Willmar Area Chamber of Commerce, 2104 E US 12; 320/235-0300 or 800/845-8747

What to See and Do

Kandiyohi County Historical Society Museum. Steam locomotive, country schoolhouse, restored house (1893); historical exhibits, agriculture building, research library. (Memorial Day-Labor Day, daily; rest of yr, Mon-Fri, Sun; also by appt; closed hols) 1 mi N on US 71 Business. Phone 320/235-1881. **FREE**

Sibley State Park. A 2,300-acre park; was a favorite hunting ground of first governor of state, for whom park is named. Swimming, fishing, boating (ramps, rentals); horseback riding, hiking; x-country skiing, snowmobiling; camping (dump station); nature center. Standard fees. 15 mi N on US 71. Phone 320/354-2055.

Motels/Motor Lodges

★★ **AMERICINN MOTEL AND SUITES.** 2404 E US 12 (56201). 320/231-1962; toll-free 800/634-3444. www.americinn.com. 30 rms, 2 story. S $59.99; D $69.99; each addl $6; under 13 free. Crib free. TV; cable (premium). Indoor pool; whirlpool. Complimentary continental bkfst. Restaurant adj open 24 hrs. Ck-out 11 am. Meeting rms. Business servs avail. X-country ski 1 mi. Cr cds: A, DS, MC, V.

⬛ 🏊 ≋ ✈ ⛷ 🔥

★ **DAYS INN WILLMAR.** 225 28th St SE (56201). 320/231-1275; fax 320/231-1275; toll-free 877/241-5235. www.torgersonproperties.com. 59 rms, 2 story. S, D $59; each addl $6; under 18 free. Crib free. Pet accepted. TV; cable (premium). Complimentary continental bkfst. Restaurant nearby. Ck-out 11 am. Exercise equipt; sauna. Whirlpool. Cr cds: A, C, D, DS, JCB, MC, V.

⬛ 🐾 ⛷ ⛷ 🔥

★★ **HOLIDAY INN.** 2100 E US 12 (56201). 320/235-6060; fax 320/235-4231; toll-free 877/405-4466. www.holiday-inn.com. 98 rms, 2 story. S $63-$69; D $73-$79; each addl $10; under 18 free. Crib free. Pet accepted. TV; cable (premium). Complimentary coffee in lobby. Restaurant 6 am-10 pm. Bar 4 pm-1 am. Ck-out noon. Business servs avail. In-rm modem link. Indoor pool; wading pool, whirlpool, poolside serv. Some balconies. Cr cds: A, D, DS, MC, V.

⬛ 🐾 🏋 🔥 ≋ ⛷ 🔥

★ **SUPER 8 MOTEL.** 2655 S 1st St (56201). 320/235-7260; fax 320/235-5580; toll-free 800/800-8000. www.super8.com. 60 rms, 3 story. No elvtr. S, D $37-$55; each addl $5; under 12 free. Crib free. Pet accepted. TV; cable (premium). Complimentary coffee in lobby. Restaurant nearby. Ck-out 11 am. Business servs avail. Cr cds: A, DS, MC, V.

⬛ 🐾 ⛷ 🔥 SC

Winona

(G-6) *See also Rochester*

Settled 1851 **Pop** 25,399 **Elev** 666 ft
Area code 507 **Zip** 55987
Information Convention & Visitors Bureau, 67 Main St, PO Box 870; 507/452-2272 or 800/657-4972; or the Visitors Center, Huff St and US 61; 507/452-2278
Web www.visitwinona.com

New Englanders and Germans came to this site on the west bank of the Mississippi and built an industrial city graced with three colleges. An early lumbering town, Winona today is one of the state's leading business and industrial centers and home of Winona State University.

What to See and Do

Fishing. Whitman Dam and Locks #5. 12 mi N on US 61. **Dresbach Dam and Locks #7.** 15 mi S on US 61. **Lake Winona.** S side of town. Float and boat fishing.

Garvin Heights. Park with 600-ft bluff, offering majestic views of the Mississippi River valley. Picnic area. (Dawn-dusk) Accessible via Huff St.

Julius C. Wilkie Steamboat Center. Replica and exhibits. (June-Oct, Tues-Sun) Levee Park. Phone 507/454-1254. ¢

Prairie Island Park. Camping (Apr-Oct), picnicking, water, rest rms, fireplaces. Fishing (all-yr). Some fees. Prairie Island Rd, 3 mi N off US 61.

Upper Mississippi River National Wildlife and Fish Refuge. From Wabasha, MN, extending 261 mi to Rock Island, IL, the refuge encompasses 200,000 acres of wooded islands, marshes, sloughs, and backwaters. Abounds in fish, wildlife, and plants. (Daily) Twenty percent of the refuge is closed for hunting and trapping until after duck hunting season. Boat required for access to most parts of refuge. 51 E 4th St. Phone 507/452-4232.

Winona County Historical Society Museum. Country store, kitchen; blacksmith, barber shops; Native American artifacts; logging and lumbering exhibits; early vehicles and fire fighting equipt. (Daily; closed

hols) 160 Johnson St. Phone
507/454-2723. ¢¢ The society also
maintains

Bunnell House. (ca 1850) Unusual
mid-19th-century Steamboat
Gothic architecture; period furnishings. (Memorial Day-Labor
Day, Wed-Sun; Labor Day-second
wkend Oct, wkends only; rest of
yr, by appt) Also here is Carriage
House Museum Shop (same schedule). 5 mi S on US 14, 61 in
Homer. Phone 507/452-7575. ¢¢

Special Events

Winona Steamboat Days. Wk of
July 4.

Victorian Fair. Living history; costumed guides; boat rides. Late Sept.

Motels/Motor Lodges

★★ **BEST WESTERN RIVERPORT
INN.** *900 Bruski Dr (55987). 507/452-
0606; fax 507/452-6489; toll-free 800/
595-0606. www.bestwestern.com.* 106
rms, 3 story. May-Oct: S $59-$89; D
$69-$99; each addl $10; suites $69-
$89; under 13 free; lower rates rest of
yr. Crib free. Pet accepted; $10. TV;
cable (premium), VCR avail. Indoor
pool; whirlpool. Complimentary
continental bkfst. Restaurant 11 am-
10 pm. Bar 11-1 am. Ck-out 11 am.
Meeting rms. Gift shop. Downhill ski
8 mi; x-country ski 1 mi. Game rm.
Some refrigerators. Cr cds: A, C, D,
DS, MC, V.
[icons]

★ **DAYS INN.** *420 Cottonwood Dr
(55987). 507/454-6930; fax 507/454-
7917; toll-free 800/329-7466. www.
daysinn.com.* 58 rms, 2 story. S $42-
$56; D $43-$62; each addl $6; under
18 free. Crib free. TV; cable. Complimentary continental bkfst. Restaurant nearby. Ck-out 11 am.
X-country ski 1 mi. Cr cds: A, C, D,
DS, MC, V.
[icons]

★ **QUALITY INN.** *956 Mankato Ave
(55987). 507/454-4390; fax 507/452-
2187; toll-free 800/228-5151. www.
qualityinn.com.* 112 rms, 2 story. S
$50-$75; D $55-$85; each addl $10;
family rates. Crib free. TV; cable.
Indoor pool; whirlpool. Complimentary coffee in rms. Restaurant open
24 hrs. Bar 4 pm-1 am, Sun from 11

am. Ck-out 11 am. Meeting rms.
Valet serv. Sundries. X-country ski 1
mi. Cr cds: A, C, D, DS, JCB, MC, V.
[icons]

★ **STERLING MOTEL.** *1450 Gilmore
Ave (55987). 507/454-1120; toll-free
800/452-1235.* 32 rms. S $29-$38; D
$45-$59; each addl $4; family rates.
Crib free. TV; cable (premium).
Restaurant adj open 24 hrs. Ck-out
11 am. X-country ski 1 mi. Cr cds: A,
D, DS, MC, V.
[icons]

★ **SUPER 8 MOTEL.** *1025 Sugar Loaf
Rd (55987). 507/454-6066; toll-free
800/800-8000. www.super8.com.* 61
rms, 3 story. No elvtr. S, D $41-$59;
each addl $5; family rates. Crib $2.
TV; cable. Complimentary continental bkfst. Restaurant nearby. Ck-out
11 am. X-country ski 1 mi. Cr cds: A,
C, D, DS, MC, V.
[icons]

MISSOURI

Since the migration and settlement of Missouri followed the Mississippi and Missouri rivers, the eastern border and the northern and central areas have many points of historic interest. When the first French explorers came down the Mississippi in the late 17th century Missouri was included in the vast territory claimed for the French king and named Louisiana in his honor. The transfer to Spanish dominion in 1770 made little lasting impression; French names and traditions have remained throughout the state, especially south of St. Louis along the Mississippi. When the United States purchased all of Louisiana in 1803, Missouri, with its strategic waterways and the already-thriving town of St. Louis, became a gateway to the West and remained one throughout the entire westward expansion period. The Pony Express began in St. Joseph in the northwestern corner of the state. The extreme northeast, along the Mississippi, is the land of Mark Twain. The central area north of the Missouri River was the stomping ground of Daniel Boone, and to the west the Santa Fe, Oregon, and California trails crossed the land. Missouri's southeastern section contains some of the oldest settlements in the state. Settlers came here from the South and New England; later Germans and other Europeans arrived. Consequently, traditions are as varied as the state's topography. Missouri's admission to the Union in 1821 resulted from a famous compromise between free and slave-holding states; in the Civil War its people were sharply divided.

Population: 5,117,073
Area: 68,945 square miles
Elevation: 230-1,772 feet
Peak: Taum Sauk Mountain (Iron County)
Entered Union: August 10, 1821 (24th state)
Capital: Jefferson City
Motto: Let the welfare of the people be the supreme law
Nickname: The Show Me State
Flower: Hawthorn
Bird: Bluebird
Tree: Dogwood
Fair: August 8-18, 2002, in Sedalia
Time Zone: Central
Website: www.missouritourism.org

Topographically, Missouri is divided into four regions: the northeastern glacial terrain, the central and northwestern prairie, the Ozark highlands in most of the southern portion, and the southeastern alluvial plain. Indicative of the northeastern section are picturesque river scenery, souvenirs of steamboat days, prosperous farmlands, and fine saddle horses. Westward along the Iowa border is rich, prairie farm country. Long-staple cotton is an important crop in the fertile alluvial plain of the Mississippi River. Southwest of St. Louis is Meramec Valley, a forested rural area. It stretches to the northern edge of the Ozarks, which extend south and west to the state borders and afford varied and beautiful mountain scenery. Lakes of all sizes, including Lake of the Ozarks, one of the largest man-made lakes in the United States, and swift-flowing streams where fish are plentiful abound in this area. The southeastern section of the state has large springs and caves.

Missouri's diverse farm economy includes the production of corn, soybeans, wheat, fruit, cotton, and livestock. Missouri's lead mines provide more than three-quarters of the nation's supply. Other mineral products include zinc, coal, limestone, iron ores, and clays. The variety of manufactured products is almost endless: shoes, clothing, beer, transportation equipment, and foundry and machine shop products are among the most important. St. Louis on Missouri's eastern border and Kansas City on the western side provide the state's metropolitan areas.

When to Go/Climate

Missouri enjoys four distinct seasons. Summers can be oppressively hot, although it remains the most popular time to visit; winters are cold; and April-June is the wettest period. The state lies in Tornado Alley and experiences an average of 27 twisters a year, peak season running from May through early June. Snowfall is generally light—four to six inches in January is the norm.

AVERAGE HIGH/LOW TEMPERATURES (°F)

ST. LOUIS

Jan 38/21	May 76/56	Sept 80/61
Feb 43/25	June 85/66	Oct 69/48
Mar 55/36	July 89/70	Nov 55/38
Apr 67/46	Aug 87/68	Dec 42/26

SPRINGFIELD

Jan 42/20	May 76/53	Sept 80/58
Feb 46/25	June 84/62	Oct 70/46
Mar 57/34	July 90/67	Nov 57/36
Apr 68/44	Aug 89/65	Dec 45/25

Parks and Recreation Finder

Directions to and information about the parks and recreation areas below are given under their respective town/city sections. Please refer to those sections for details.

NATIONAL PARK AND RECREATION AREAS

Key to abbreviations. I.H.S. = International Historic Site; I.P.M. = International Peace Memorial; N.B. = National Battlefield; N.B.P. = National Battlefield Park; N.B.C. = National Battlefield and Cemetery; N.C.A. = National Conservation Area; N.E.M. = National Expansion Memorial; N.F. = National Forest; N.G. = National Grassland; N.H.P. = National Historical Park; N.H.C. = National Heritage Corridor; N.H.S. = National Historic Site; N.L. = National Lakeshore; N.M. = National Monument; N.M.P. = National Military Park; N.Mem. = National Memorial; N.P. = National Park; N.Pres. = National Preserve; N.R.A. = National Recreational Area; N.R.R. = National Recreational River; N.Riv. = National River; N.S. = National Seashore; N.S.R. = National Scenic Riverway; N.S.T. = National Scenic Trail; N.Sc. = National Scientific Reserve; N.V.M. = National Volcanic Monument.

Place Name	Listed Under
George Washington Carver N.M.	same
Harry S Truman N.H.S.	INDEPENDENCE
Jefferson N.E.M.	ST. LOUIS
Mark Twain N.F.	BONNE TERRE, CASSVILLE, POPLAR BLUFF, ROLLA
Ozark N.S.R.	VAN BUREN
Ulysses S. Grant N.H.S.	ST. LOUIS
Wilson's Creek N.B.	SPRINGFIELD

Mark Twain National Forests offer swimming, float trips, fishing, hunting, hiking, horseback riding, and picnicking. Camping (regular season, April-September; some areas open year-round; $6-$14/site/night). Trailer sites at many campgrounds (no hookups). For further information contact the Forest Supervisor, 401 Fairgrounds Rd, Rolla 65401; 573/364-4621.

CALENDAR HIGHLIGHTS

APRIL

World Fest (Branson). In Silver Dollar City. Contact Chamber of Commerce, 417/334-4136 or 800/952-6626.

MAY

Apple Blossom Parade & Festival (St. Joseph). Originally a celebration of area apple growers. Parade with more than 200 entries; food, music, crafts. Contact Convention & Visitors Bureau, 816/233-6688 or 800/785-0360.

Gypsy Caravan (St. Louis). One of the largest flea markets in the Midwest, with more than 600 vendors; arts and crafts, entertainment, concessions.

JULY

National Tom Sawyer Days (Hannibal). National fence painting championship, Tom and Becky contest, entertainment. Contact Chamber of Commerce, 573/221-2477.

Kansas City Blues & Jazz Festival (Kansas City). Penn Valley Park, Liberty Memorial Area. Phone 816/753-3378.

Boone County Fair (Columbia). First held in 1835, earliest fair west of the Mississippi; includes exhibits, horse show. Contact Convention & Visitors Bureau, 573/875-1231.

AUGUST

Missouri State Fair (Sedalia). Fairgrounds, 16th St & Limit Ave. One of the country's leading state fairs; held here since 1901. Stage shows, rodeo, competitive exhibits, livestock, auto races. Phone 660/530-5600.

SEPTEMBER

National Festival of Craftsmen (Branson). In Silver Dollar City. Fiddle making, mule-powered sorghum molasses making, wood carving, barrel making, and dozens of other crafts. Contact Chamber of Commerce, 417/334-4136.

OCTOBER

Octoberfest (Hermann). Area wineries. Wine cellar tours, wine samples; craft demonstrations; German music, food. Contact Historic Hermann Information Center, 573/486-2017.

American Royal Livestock, Horse Show, and Rodeo (Kansas City). At the American Royal Center. Phone 816/221-9800.

STATE PARK AND RECREATION AREAS

Key to abbreviations. I.P. = Interstate Park; S.A.P. = State Archaeological Park; S.B. = State Beach; S.C.A. = State Conservation Area; S.C.P. = State Conservation Park; S.Cp. = State Campground; S.F. = State Forest; S.G. = State Garden; S.H.A. = State Historic Area; S.H.P. = State Historic Park; S.H.S. = State Historic Site; S.M.P. = State Marine Park; S.N.A. = State Natural Area; S.P. = State Park; S.P.C. = State Public Campground; S.R. = State Reserve; S.R.A. = State Recreation Area; S.Res. = State Reservoir; S.Res.P. = State Resort Park; S.R.P. = State Rustic Park.

Place Name	Listed Under
Arrow Rock S.H.S.	ARROW ROCK
Battle of Lexington S.H.S.	LEXINGTON
Bennett Spring S.P.	LEBANON
Big Lake S.P.	MOUND CITY
Bollinger Mill S.H.S.	CAPE GIRARDEAU
Bothwell Lodge S.H.S.	SEDALIA
Cuivre River S.P.	WENTZVILLE
Deutschheim S.H.S.	HERMANN
Dr. Edmund A. Babler Memorial S.P.	ST. LOUIS
First Missouri State Capitol S.H.S.	ST. CHARLES
Felix Valle Home S.H.S.	STE. GENEVIEVE
General John J. Pershing Boyhood Home S.H.S.	CHILLICOTHE
Graham Cave S.P.	HERMANN
Ha Ha Tonka S.P.	CAMDENTON
Harry S Truman Birthplace S.H.S.	LAMAR
Harry S Truman S.P.	CLINTON
Jefferson Landing S.H.S.	JEFFERSON CITY
Johnson's Shut-Ins S.P.	PILOT KNOB
Katy Trail S.P.	ST. CHARLES
Knob Noster S.P.	SEDALIA
Lake of the Ozarks S.P.	LAKE OF THE OZARKS
Lake Wappapello S.P.	POPLAR BLUFF
Lewis & Clark S.P.	WESTON
Long Branch S.P.	MACON
Mark Twain S.P.	MONROE CITY
Mastodon S.H.S.	ST. LOUIS
Meramec S.P.	SULLIVAN
Montauk S.P.	ROLLA
Onondaga Cave S.P.	SULLIVAN
Pershing S.P.	CHILLICOTHE
Pomme de Terre S.P.	CAMDENTON
Prairie S.P.	LAMAR
Roaring River S.P.	CASSVILLE
St. Francois S.P.	BONNE TERRE
Sam A. Baker S.P.	PILOT KNOB
Stockton S.P.	STOCKTON
Sugar Creek S.F.	KIRKSVILLE
Table Rock S.P.	BRANSON/TABLE ROCK LAKE AREA
Thousand Hills S.P.	KIRKSVILLE
Trail of Tears S.P.	CAPE GIRARDEAU
Van Meter S.P.	ARROW ROCK
Wallace S.P.	CAMERON
Washington S.P.	BONNE TERRE
Watkins Woolen Mill S.H.S.	EXCELSIOR SPRINGS

Water-related activities, hiking, riding, various other sports, picnicking and visitor centers, as well as camping, are available in many of these areas. Tent, trailer sites: April-October, $7/day/basic, $12-$15/day/improved; November-March, $6/day/basic, $10-$11/day/improved; limit 15 consecutive days; water and sanitary facilities April-October only in most parks; reservations accepted at some parks. Lodging reservations: one-day deposit (two-day minimum Memorial Day-Labor Day), contact concessionaire in park. Most cabins, dining lodges are open mid-April-October. Parks are open daily, year-round. Senior citizen discounts. Pets on leash only. For further information contact the Missouri Department of Natural Resources, Division of State Parks; PO Box 176, Jefferson City 65102; 573/751-2479,800/334-6946 or 800/379-2419 (TDD).

SKI AREAS

Place Name	Listed Under
Hidden Valley Ski Area	ST. LOUIS
Snow Bluff Ski Area	SPRINGFIELD
Snow Creek Ski Area	WESTON

FISHING AND HUNTING

Float trips combine scenic river floating with fishing. Trips vary from half-day to one week. Anglers can bring their own canoes, rent canoes, or hire professional guides to manipulate johnboats (flat-bottomed boats suited to shallow waters). Some outfitters provide equipment and food. About 35 Ozark rivers have black bass, goggle-eye, walleye, sunfish, or trout. *Missouri Ozark Waterways* provides information on float fishing and may be purchased from the Missouri Dept of Conservation.

Squirrel, rabbit, and quail hunting are fair to good in most areas. Deer, doves, and wild turkeys are relatively plentiful. The larger lakes and rivers are used by migrating ducks, geese, and other waterfowl. Contact the Department of Conservation for outdoor maps.

Nonresident fishing permit: $35; one-day $5; trout permit $7. Nonresident hunting permit: deer $125; turkey $125; small game $65; nonresident archer's hunting permit $100. Nonresident furbearer hunting and trapping permit: $80. To purchase permits and obtain regulations contact Missouri Dept of Conservation, PO Box 180, Jefferson City, 65102.

Driving Information

Safety belts are mandatory for all persons in front seat of passenger vehicle. Children under four yrs must be in an approved child passenger restraint system. For further information phone 573/526-6115.

INTERSTATE HIGHWAY SYSTEM

The following alphabetical listing of Missouri towns in *Mobil Travel Guide* shows that these cities are within ten miles of the indicated interstate highways. A highway map should be checked, however, for the nearest exit.

Highway Number	Cities/Towns within ten miles
Interstate 29	Kansas City, Mound City, St. Joseph, Weston.
Interstate 35	Bethany, Cameron, Excelsior Springs, Kansas City.
Interstate 44	Carthage, Clayton, Joplin, Lebanon, Mount Vernon, Rolla, St Louis, Springfield, Sullivan, Waynesville.
Interstate 55	Cape Girardeau, Ste. Genevieve, St. Louis, Sikeston.
Interstate 70	Blue Springs, Columbia, Fulton, Independence, Kansas City, St. Charles, St. Louis, Wentzville.

Additional Visitor Information

For general information contact the Missouri Division of Tourism, 301 W High St, Box 1055, Jefferson City 65102; 573/751-4133. For a Missouri travel information packet, phone 800/877-1234. An official state highway map may be obtained from Highway Maps, Department of Transportation, Box 270, Jefferson City 65102. Another good source of information on Missouri is *The Ozarks Mountaineer*, bimonthly, PO Box 20, Kirbyville 65679.

Visitor centers are located in St. Louis, I-270 at Riverview Dr; Joplin, I-44 at state line; Kansas City, I-70 at the Truman Sports Complex; Hannibal, US 61, 2 mi S of jct with US 36; Rock Port, I-29, just S of jct with US 136; and New Madrid, I-55, at Marston rest area. They are open all year; the hrs vary.

COUNTRY MUSIC AND THE DUCKS

The beautiful Ozark hills drew people to southwest Missouri long before Branson became famous for its country music theaters. From Springfield, drive 41 miles south on US 65 to Branson. Touring options here include a railroad that travels through the Ozarks to Arkansas, and "the Ducks," amphibious vehicles that roll around town and onto Table Rock Lake. Other area attractions—beyond the music theaters packing MO 76 (Country Boulevard)—include the Shepherd of the Hills homestead and outdoor theater and Silver Dollar City theme park. Once you've had your fill of Branson, head east out of town on MO 76, a scenic stretch through part of the Mark Twain National Forest, then take MO 5 north. Stop at Mansfield to see the Laura Ingalls Wilder farm, where the author wrote the Little House books. Return to Springfield via US 60 west. **(APPROX 150 MI)**

EL CAMINO REAL

This driving tour follows a transportation route with its beginnings in prehistory. Originally an Indian trail, this route became the El Camino Real, laid out during the late 18th century when Spain ruled the North American territory west of the Mississippi.

Leave St. Louis on I-55 south to exit 186, then drive east to Highway 61. Head south on Highway 61 to Kimmswick, a little town on the Mississippi that thrived from the 1860s to the end of the 19th century, when it was a busy center for riverboat traffic. Shortly thereafter, time and traffic bypassed the village and it fell into a deep slumber for almost 70 years. Lucianna Gladney Ross, daughter of the founder of the 7-Up soft-drink company, discovered the handsome but dilapidated town and spearheaded a movement to restore the town to its original condition. Today, Kimmswick is part open-air museum, part shopping boutique. Many of the older buildings contain restaurants, antique stores, and other specialty retail shops. The Old House Restaurant, at 2nd and Elm, was once a stagecoach stop and tavern frequented by Ulysses S. Grant. Today it features old-fashioned home-cooked meals and desserts.

Just west of Kimmswick, the 425-acre Mastodon Historic Site preserves an important archaeological site that contains the bones of American mastodons. The fossil remains of mastodons and other now-extinct animals were first found in the early 1800s in what is now known as the Kimmswick Bone Bed. The area became known as one of the most extensive Pleistocene bone beds in the country, attracting archaeological and paleontological interest from around the world. A museum tells the natural and cultural story of the area, while picnicking and hiking along the Tom Stockwell Wildflower Trail offer chances to explore the land where mastodons once lived.

Follow Highway 61 south along the Mississippi to Ste. Genevieve, founded in the 1750s as a French village. Ste. Genevieve is one of the oldest European settlements west of the Mississippi and contains an important collection of French Colonial architecture. Now a National Historic District, the entire town gives testament to the lasting quality of French craftsmanship. Nine original structures are open to the public; the Guibourd-Valle House and the Bolduc House are especially noteworthy. Located at 66 South Main, the Interpretive Center has historical displays and shows a movie about the town's past.

Drive south on Highway 66 to Perryville. St. Mary's of the Barrens, a Catholic seminary established in 1818, contains a number of museums and the Tuscan-style Church of the Assumption, begun in 1827. The seminary is the oldest institution of higher learning west of the Mississippi. The French were not the only Europeans to settle this area. South of Perryville to the east of Highway 66 is a cluster of villages settled by Germans: Altenburg, Frohna, and Wittenberg. Altenburg has a collection of original structures from the 1830s and a museum that commemorates the early Lutheran farming history of the area. Continue south on Highway 66, and follow Highway 177 east to Trail of Tears State Park. This 3,415-acre park is a memorial to the Cherokee Indians who lost their lives during a forced relocation to Oklahoma. The park is located on the site where 9 of 13 groups of Cherokee Indians crossed the Mississippi River during the harsh winter of 1838-1839. Thousands lost their lives on the trail, including dozens on or near the park's grounds. The visitor center features exhibits that interpret the forced march, and numerous picnic areas and campsites are scattered throughout the park. Trails offer opportunities for hiking, and the bluffs and cliffs along the river are noted as roosting sites for bald eagles.

From there, follow Highway 177 to Cape Girardeau, which began its history as a fur-trading fort. The town sweeps up from the Mississippi to a high promontory, and besides a number of 19th-century buildings along the waterfront, has the distinction of being the birthplace of Rush Limbaugh.

From Cape Girardeau, follow Highway 61 south to New Madrid. In 1789, this site was selected to be the capital of the colony that Spain hoped to establish in the Louisiana Territory. Not much became of Spain's plans for this colony, and now New Madrid is most famous for the devastating 1811 earthquake that centered on the New Madrid Fault. With an estimated magnitude over eight on the Richter Scale, this earthquake was one of the largest in recent geologic history. **(APPROX 190 MI)**

Arrow Rock

See also Columbia

Pop 70 **Elev** 700 ft **Area code** 660
Zip 65320
Information Historic Site Administrator, PO Box 1; 660/837-3330

What to See and Do

Arrow Rock State Historic Site. A 200-acre plot with many restored buildings and historical landmarks of the Old Santa Fe Trail. Picnicking, concession, camping (dump station; standard fees). Visitor center. (Daily; closed Jan 1, Thanksgiving, Dec 25) In town. Phone 660/837-3330. Park incl

  George Caleb Bingham House. (1837) Restored house built by the artist; period furnishings. (June-Aug, daily) On guided walking tour.

  Old Tavern. (ca 1834) Restored; period furnishings, historical exhibits, and general store; restaurant. (May-Sept, Tues-Sun) Phone 660/837-3200. On guided walking tour.

Van Meter State Park. More than 900 acres. Remains found at this archaeological site date from 10,000 B.C.; Old Fort, only known earthworks of its kind west of the Mississippi. Visitor Center explains history of area. Fishing; picnicking, playground, camping. Standard fees. (Daily) 22 mi NW on MO 41, then W and N on MO 122. Phone 660/886-7537.

Walking tour. Guided tour incl restored log courthouse (1839), gunshop and house (ca 1844), printshop (1868), stone jail (1870), medical museums, and Arrow Rock State Historic Site. Tour begins at Main St boardwalk. (Memorial Day-Labor Day, daily; spring and fall, wkends; also by appt) Phone 660/837-3231. ¢¢

Special Events

Antique Show/Sale. Stolberg-Jackson Center and Main St. Phone 660/846-3031. Mid-May.

Arrow Rock Lyceum Theater. In town on MO 41. Missouri's oldest professional regional theater. Wed, Fri-Sun. Phone 660/837-3311. June-Aug.

Bethany

See also Cameron

Settled 1840 **Pop** 3,005 **Elev** 904 ft
Area code 660 **Zip** 64424
Information Chamber of Commerce, 116 N 16th St, PO Box 202; 660/425-6358
Web www.netins.net/showcase/bethany

Motel/Motor Lodge

★★ **FAMILY BUDGET INN.** *4014 Miller St (64424). 660/425-7915; fax 660/425-3697; toll-free 877/283-4388.* 78 rms. S $45-$51; D $51-$61; each addl $5. Crib free. Pet accepted. TV; cable. Complimentary continental bkfst. Restaurant adj 6 am-11 pm. Ck-out 11 am. Coin lndry. Business servs avail. Whirlpool. Picnic tables. Cr cds: A, D, DS, MC, V.

Blue Springs

See also Independence, Kansas City

Pop 40,153 **Elev** 950 ft **Area code** 816
Information Chamber of Commerce, 1000 Main St, 64015; 816/229-8558

What to See and Do

Civil War Museum of Jackson County. Exhibits, historic battlefield, and soldiers' cemetery. (Apr-Oct, Mon-Sat and Sun afternoons; rest of yr, Sat and Sun; closed Jan 1, Thanksgiving, Dec 25) S on MO 7 to US 50, then 7 mi E, in Lone Jack. Phone 816/566-2272. **Donation**

Fleming Park. This more than 4,400-acre park incl 970-acre Lake Jacomo and 960-acre Blue Springs Lake. Fishing, boating (rentals, marina); camping. Wildlife exhibit, special activities (fee). Park (Daily). S on MO 7, then 2 mi W on US 40 to Woods Chapel Rd S. **FREE** In park is

  Missouri Town 1855. More than 20 original western Missouri buildings from 1820-1860 brought to the site and restored. Mercantile store, blacksmith and cabinetmaker's shop. Furnishings, gardens, live-stock, and site interpreters in period attire. Special events; candlelight tours (fee). (Mid-Apr-mid-Nov, Wed-Sun; rest of yr, Sat and Sun; closed Jan 1, Thanksgiving, Dec 25) 8010 E Park Rd. E side of Lake Jacomo. Phone 816/524-8770. ¢¢

Restaurant

★★★ **MARINA GROG & GALLEY.**
22A N Lake Shore Dr, Lake Lotowana (64806). 816/578-5511. Specializes in seafood, steak. Hrs: 5-9:30 pm; Fri, Sat to 10 pm. Closed Jan 1, Dec 25. Bar. Wine list. Res accepted. Dinner $16.95-$42.95. Children's menu. Outdoor dining overlooking lake. Nautical theme incl 1,500-gallon aquarium that separates dining area from bar. Cr cds: A, D, MC, V.
D ➘

Bonne Terre

(E-6) *See also Ste. Genevieve*

Pop 3,871 **Elev** 830 ft **Area code** 573
Zip 63628

What to See and Do

Bonne Terre Mine Tours. One-hr walking tours through lead and silver mines that operated from 1864-1962; historic mining tools, ore cars, ore samples, underground lake (boat tour), flower garden; museum exhibits. (May-Sept, daily; rest of yr, Fri-Mon) On MO 47, at Park and Allen sts. Phone 573/358-2148.

Mark Twain National Forest. (Potosi Ranger District) Swimming beach, boat launching at Council Bluff Recreation Area; nature trails, camping. Standard fees. (Daily) W via MO 47, S via MO 21, E via MO 8. Phone 573/438-5427. **FREE**

St. Francois State Park. A 2,700-acre park with fishing, canoeing; hiking, picnicking, improved camping. Naturalists. Standard fees. (Daily) 4 mi N on US 67. Phone 573/358-2173.

Washington State Park. More than 1,400-acre park containing petroglyphs (interpretations avail). Swimming pool, fishing, canoeing in Big River; hiking trails, playground, cab-ins, improved camping. Standard fees. (Daily) 15 mi NW via MO 47, 21. Phone 636/586-2995. **FREE**

Branson/Table Rock Lake Area

(F-3) *See also Cassville, Rockaway Beach, Springfield*

Pop 3,706 **Elev** 722 ft **Area code** 417
Zip 65616
Information Branson/Lakes Area Chamber of Commerce, US 65 and MO 248, PO Box 1897; 417/334-4084 or 800/214-3661
Web www.bransonchamber.com

The resort town of Branson, situated in the Ozarks, is in the region that provided the setting for Harold Bell Wright's novel *The Shepherd of the Hills.* Both Lake Taneycomo and Table Rock Lake have excellent fishing for trout, bass, and crappie. In recent years Branson has become a mecca for fans of country music.

What to See and Do

Branson Scenic Railway. Forty-mi round-trip through Ozark Foothills. (Mid-Mar-mid-Dec, schedule varies; closed Easter, Thanksgiving) 206 E Main St. Phone 417/334-6110.

College of the Ozarks. (1906) 1,500 students. Liberal arts college where students work, rather than pay, for their education. 100 Opportunity Ave. Phone 417/334-6411. On campus are

Edwards Mill. Working reproduction of an 1880s water-powered gristmill. Weaving studio on second floor; store. (Mon-Sat; closed mid-Dec-Jan) **FREE**

Ralph Foster Museum. Ozark-area Native American artifacts, relics; apothecary, cameo, gun, coin collections; mounted game animals; Ozarks Hall of Fame. (Mon-Sat; closed Thanksgiving, also mid-Dec-Jan) Phone 417/334-6411. ¢¢

Entertainment shows.

Al Brumley's Memory Valley Show. Mar-Dec. 1945 W MO 76. Phone 417/335-2484.

Andy Williams Moon River Theatre. Apr-Dec. 2500 W MO 76. Phone 417/334-4500.

Baldknobbers Jamboree. Mar-mid-Apr, Fri and Sat; mid-Apr-mid-Dec, Mon-Sat. 2043 W MO 76. Phone 417/334-4528.

Blackwood Family Music Show. Mar-Dec. MO 248 (Shepherd of the Hills Expy). Phone 417/336-5863.

Blackwood Quartet. W MO 76. Phone 417/336-5863.

Branson's Magical Mansion. Featuring Van Burch and Wellford. Apr-Dec. MO 248 (Shepherd of the Hills Expy). Phone 417/336-3986.

Charley Pride Theatre. Phone 417/337-7433.

Dutton Family Theatre. Apr-Dec. 3454 W MO 76. Phone 417/332-2772.

Elvis and the Superstars Show. Yr-round. 205 S Commercial. Phone 417/336-2112.

The Grand Palace. Late Apr-Dec. 2700 W MO 76.

Jim Stafford Theatre. 3440 W MO 76. Phone 417/335-8080.

Lawrence Welk Show. Lawrence Welk Champagne Theatre. 1984 MO 165. Phone 417/336-3575.

Mel Tillis Theater. Mar-Dec. 2527 N MO 248 (Shepherd of the Hills Expy). Phone 417/335-6635.

Osmond Family Theater. Apr-Dec. 3216 W MO 76. Phone 417/336-6100.

Presleys' Jubilee. Mar-mid-Dec. 2920 W MO 76. Phone 417/334-4874.

Roy Clark Celebrity Theatre. Phone 417/334-0076.

★ 76 Music Hall. 1945 W MO 76. Phone 417/335-2484.

Shoji Tabuchi Theatre. Mar-Dec. 3260 MO 248 (Shepherd of the Hills Expy). Phone 417/334-7469.

Sons of the Pioneers. Early May-Oct. 3446 MO 76. Phone 888/322-6394.

Will Rogers Theatre. MO 65 and MO 248 (Shepherd of the Hills Expy). Phone 417/336-1333.

Mutton Hollow Craft and Entertainment Village. Ozark crafters at work. Musical entertainment; carnival rides. Restaurants. (Late Apr-Oct, daily) 5 mi W on MO 76. Phone 417/334-4947. ¢¢¢

Ripley's Believe It Or Not! Museum. Hundreds of exhibits in eight galleries. 3326 W Hwy 76. Phone 417/337-5300. ¢¢¢¢

★ Shepherd of the Hills. Jeep-drawn conveyance tours (70 min) incl authentically furnished Old Matt's Cabin, home of the prominent characters in Harold Bell Wright's Ozark novel *The Shepherd of the Hills;* Old Matt's Mill, an operating steam-powered saw and gristmill; 230-ft Inspiration Tower; craft demonstrations, horseback riding, and music shows. (Late Apr-late Oct, daily) 5586 W MO 76. Phone 417/334-4191. On grounds is

Outdoor Theater. Outdoor historical pageant adapted from Harold Bell Wright's best-selling novel. (May-late Oct, nightly) 5586 W MO 76. Phone 417/334-4191.

Shepherd of the Hills Trout Hatchery. Largest trout hatchery in state. Visitor Center has aquariums, exhibits, slide presentation. Guided tours (Memorial Day-Labor Day, Mon-Fri). Hiking trails, picnicking. (Daily; closed Jan 1, Thanksgiving, Dec 25) 483 Hatchery Rd. Phone 417/334-4865. **FREE**

Sightseeing.

Lake Queen Cruises. A 1 ¼-hr narrated cruise of scenic Lake Taneycomo aboard 149-passenger *Lake Queen;* also dinner and bkfst cruises. (Early Apr-Dec, daily) 280 N Lake Dr. Phone 417/334-3015. ¢¢

Polynesian Princess. Sightseeing, bkfst, and dinner cruises. Departs from Gages Long Creek Marina, on MO 86. Phone 417/337-8366. ¢¢¢¢

Ride the Ducks. Scenic 70-min land and water tour on amphibious vehicles. (Mar-Now, daily) 2½ mi W on MO 76. 2½ mi W on MO 76. Phone 417/334-3825.

Sammy Lane Pirate Cruise. Narrated folklore cruise (70 min) on Lake Taneycomo leaves several times a day. (Apr-Oct, daily) 280 N Lake Dr. Phone 417/334-3015. ¢¢

Showboat Branson Belle. Bkfst, lunch, and dinner cruises. (Mid-Apr-mid-Dec, daily) Departs from

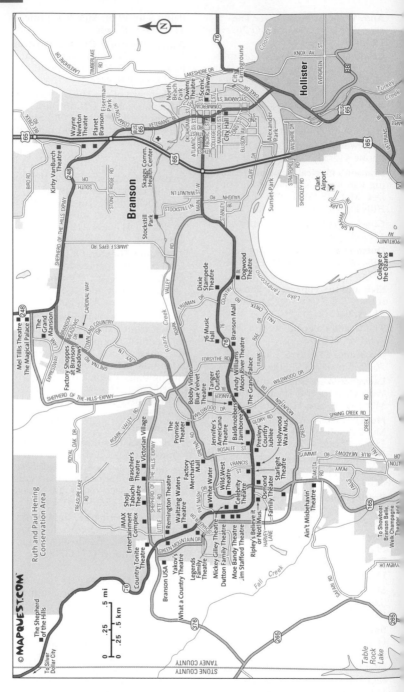

MO 165 near Table Rock Dam. Phone 417/336-7171. ¢¢¢¢¢

Table Rock Helicopters. Scenic tours of lakes area. (Mar-Nov,

daily) 3309 W MO 76. Phone 417/334-6102. ¢¢¢¢¢

Stone Hill Winery. Guided tours and bottling demonstrations. Gift shop. (Mon-Sat, also Sun afternoons; closed

Jan 1, Thanksgiving, Dec 25) 601 State Hwy 165. Phone 417/334-1897. **FREE**

Table Rock Dam and Lake. This 43,100-acre reservoir, formed by impounding waters of White River, offers swimming, waterskiing, scuba diving, fishing for bass, crappie, and walleye, boating (rentals; commercial docks; marine dump station); hunting for deer, turkey, rabbit, and waterfowl, picnicking, playgrounds, camping (15 parks, fee charged in most areas; showers, trailer dump stations). (Daily) 4600 State Hwy 165, Suite A. Phone 417/334-4101. ¢¢

Table Rock State Park. More than 350 acres. Fishing, sailing (docks, ramp), boating (marina, launch, rentals), scuba service; picnicking; improved camping (dump station). Standard fees. (Daily) 5272 State Hwy 165. Phone 417/334-4704. **FREE**

Waltzing Waters. Colored fountains set to music create a display more than 20 ft high and 60 ft wide. Indoor performances hrly. Also stage shows. (Tues-Sun) 3617 W MO 76. Phone 417/334-4144.

White Water. Family water park; streams, slides, flumes, wave pool. (May-early Sept, Wed-Sun) 399 Indian Point Rd. Phone 417/334-7487. ¢¢¢¢

Special Events

Great American Music Festival. In Silver Dollar City. More than 200 musicians play rhythm and blues, jazz, gospel, swing, Cajun, and more. Mid-May-early June.

Festival of America. In Silver Dollar City. Celebrating arts, crafts, and cooking from across America, with demonstrations, exhibits, and entertainment. Early Sept-late Oct.

National Festival of Craftsmen. In Silver Dollar City. Fiddle making, mule-powered sorghum molasses making, wood carving, barrel making, and dozens of other crafts. Mid-Sept-late Oct.

Motels/Motor Lodges

★★ **BEST WESTERN MOUNTAIN OAK LODGE.** *8514 MO 76, Branson (65737). 417/338-2141; fax 417/338-8320; toll-free 800/868-6625.* 150 rms,

3 story. Mar-Dec: S, D $49-$79; each addl $5; suites $99; under 18 free; lower rates rest of yr. Crib free. TV; cable (premium). Indoor pool. Complimentary continental bkfst. Restaurant 6:30 am-noon, 4:30-8 pm. Bar 5-10 pm. Ck-out noon. Coin lndry. In-rm modem link. Meeting rms. Tennis. Game rm. Balconies. Cr cds: A, C, D, DS, MC, V.

[icons]

★★★ **BIG CEDAR LODGE.** *612 Devils Pool Rd, Ridgedale (65739). 417/335-2777; fax 417/339-5060. www.bigcedarlodge.com.* 224 rms in 3 buildings, 11 suites, 81 cottages. May-Oct: S, D $115-$125; suites $189-$240; cottages $155-$272; log cabins $249-$549; lower rates rest of yr. Crib free. TV; cable (premium). Heated pool; poolside serv. Playground. Supervised children's activities (Memorial Day-Labor Day); ages 4-12. Dining rm 6 am-10 pm. Bar noon-1 am; entertainment. Ck-out 11 am. Coin lndry. Meeting rms. Business servs avail. Sundries. Gift shop. Lighted tennis. Miniature golf. Exercise equipt; sauna. Lawn games. Water sports. Many balconies. Elegant, rustic atmosphere, wooded grounds, stone pathways. On lake; marina. Cr cds: A, DS, MC, V.

[icons]

★★ **BRANSON INN.** *448 MO 248, Branson (25401). 417/334-5121; fax 417/334-6039; res 800/334-5121.* 272 rms, 2-4 story. Sept-Dec: S $45-$68; D $49-$72; each addl $5; suites $125-$135; under 17 free; lower rates rest of yr. Crib $5. Pet accepted. TV; cable. Pool; wading pool, whirlpool. Complimentary coffee in rms. Restaurant nearby. Ck-out 11 am. Game rm. Picnic tables. Cr cds: A, C, D, DS, MC, V.

[icons]

★ **DAYS INN.** *3524 Keeter St, Branson (65616). 417/334-5544; fax 417/334-2935; toll-free 800/325-2525. www.bransonusa.com.* 425 rms, 4 story. Mid-Apr-Oct: S, D $40-$95; each addl $6; under 12 free; lower rates rest of yr. Pet accepted; $10/day. TV. Pool; wading pool, whirlpool. Playground. Complimentary continental bkfst. Restaurant 7 am-8 pm.

Ck-out 11 am. Business servs avail. Sundries. Cr cds: A, C, D, DS, MC, V.

★ **DOGWOOD INN.** *1420 W MO 76, Branson (65615). 417/334-5101; fax 417/334-0789; toll-free 888/334-3649. www.dogwoodinn.com.* 220 rms, 1-3 story. No elvtr. Apr-Dec: S, D $55-$70; each addl $10; suites $100-$125; under 19 free; lower rates rest of yr. TV; cable (premium). Pool; wading pool, whirlpool. Complimentary coffee in rms. Restaurant 7 am-1 pm, 5-7 pm. Ck-out 11 am. Coin lndry. Meeting rms. Business servs avail. Cr cds: A, C, D, DS, JCB, MC, V.

★★ **FOXBOROUGH INN.** *235 Expy Ln, Branson (65616). 417/335-4369; fax 417/335-5043; toll-free 800/335-4369.* 171 rms, 3-4 story. May-Sept: S, D $52.95-$62.95; each addl $5; under 18 free; lower rates rest of yr. Crib free. TV; cable; VCR avail. Pool. Complimentary continental bkfst, coffee in lobby. Snack bar. Restaurant nearby. Ck-out 11 am. Coin lndry. Meeting rms. Business servs avail. Gift shop. Cr cds: A, C, D, DS, MC, V.

★ **GAZEBO INN.** *2424 W MO 76, Branson (65616). 417/335-3826; fax 417/335-3889; toll-free 800/873-7990.* 73 rms, 3 story, 14 suites. S, D $49-$69; suites $79.95-$130. Crib free. TV; cable. Pool. Complimentary continental bkfst. Restaurant adj 7 am-9 pm. Ck-out 11 am. Totally nonsmoking. Cr cds: A, DS, MC, V.

★★ **HAMPTON INN BRANSON WEST.** *3695 W MO 76, Country Music Blvd, Branson (65616). 417/337-5762; fax 417/337-8733. www.hamptoninn.com.* 110 rms, 5 story. S, D $65-$85; under 17 free. Closed mid-Dec-mid-Apr. Crib free. TV; cable (premium); VCR avail (movies). Indoor pool; whirlpool. Complimentary continental bkfst. Restaurant nearby. Ck-out noon. Business servs avail. Cr cds: A, MC, V.

★★ **HOLIDAY INN EXPRESS.** *1000 W Main St, Branson (65616). 417/334-1985; fax 417/334-1984; toll-free 800/465-4329. www.holiday-inn.com.* 90 rms, 5 story. May-Dec: S, D $65-$69.50; lower rates rest of yr. TV; cable (premium). Indoor pool; whirlpool. Complimentary continental bkfst. Ck-out 11 am. Business servs avail. Valet serv. Some in-rm whirlpools. Totally nonsmoking. Cr cds: A, C, D, DS, JCB, MC, V.

★★ **HOLIDAY INN EXPRESS.** *2801 Green Mountain Dr, Branson (65616). 417/336-2100; fax 417/336-6319. www.holiday-inn.com.* 120 rms, 5 story. May, Sept-Oct: S, D $59.95; suites $105-$145; under 16 free; lower rates rest of yr. Closed Jan-Feb. Crib free. TV; cable. Pool; whirlpool. Restaurant nearby. Ck-out 11 am. Business servs avail. Valet serv. 18-hole golf privileges. Some refrigerators. Cr cds: A, DS, MC, V.

★★★ **LODGE OF THE OZARKS ENTERTAINMENT COMPLEX.** *3431 W MO 76, Branson (65616). 417/334-7535; fax 417/334-6861; toll-free 887/840-3946. www.lodgeoftheozarks. com.* 190 rms, 4 story. Apr-Dec: S, D $59-$99; lower rates rest of yr. Crib $5. TV; cable. Indoor pool; whirlpool. Complimentary continental bkfst. Restaurants 6:30 am-7 pm. Bar 4 pm-1 am; entertainment. Ck-out 11 am. Meeting rms. Business servs avail. In-rm modem link. Gift shop. Bellhops. Concierge. Barber, beauty shop. Massage. Game rm. Some refrigerators, wet bars. Cr cds: A, DS, MC, V.

★ **MAGNOLIA INN.** *3311 Shepherd of the Hills Expy, Branson (65616). 417/334-2300; fax 417/336-4165.* 152 rms, 2 story. May-Dec: S, D $54-$77; each addl $4; under 12 free; lower rates rest of yr. Crib free. TV; cable. Pool; whirlpool. Complimentary coffee in lobby. Restaurant opp 6-2 am. Ck-out 11 am. Coin lndry. Business servs avail. Gift shop. Barber, beauty shop. Game rm. Cr cds: A, MC, V.

★ **MELODY LANE INN.** *2821 W MO 76, Branson (65615). 417/334-8598; fax 417/334-3799; toll-free 800/338-8598. www.melodylaneinn.com.* 140 rms, 2-3 story. No elvtr. Mar-Dec: S, D $45.25-$65.25; each addl $5. Closed rest of yr. Crib $5. TV; VCR avail. Pool; whirlpool. Complimentary continental bkfst. Ck-out 11 am. Business servs avail. Coin lndry. Cr cds: A, MC, V.

D ⇔ ⊠ ⊠ SC

★★ **PALACE INN.** *2820 W MO 76, Branson (65615). 417/334-7666; fax 417/334-7720; toll-free 800/725-2236. www.palaceinn.com.* 166 rms, 7 story. Late May-Oct: S, D $77-$88; each addl $5; suites $95-$140; lower rates rest of yr. Crib $5. TV; cable. Heated pool; whirlpool. Complimentary continental bkfst. Restaurant 7-11 am, 4:30-9 pm. Bar noon-5 pm; closed Sun. Ck-out 11 am. Coin lndry. Business servs avail. Concierge. Barber, beauty shop. Free airport transportation. Sauna. Massage. Some refrigerators. Many balconies. Cr cds: A, D, DS, MC, V.

D ⇔ ✗ ⊠ ⊠ SC

★ **RAMADA INN.** *1700 W MO 76, Branson (65616). 417/334-1000; fax 417/339-3013. www.ramada.com.* 296 rms, 2-6 story. S, D $29.99-$69.99; each addl $10. Crib $10. TV. Pool. Complimentary coffee in lobby. Restaurant adj 6:30 am-8 pm. Ck-out 11 am. Coin lndry. Meeting rms. Business servs avail. Picnic tables, grills. Cr cds: A, DS, MC, V.

D ⇔ ⊠ ⊠ SC

★★ **SETTLE INN.** *3050 Green Mountain Dr, Branson (65616). 417/335-4700; fax 417/335-3906; toll-free 800/677-6906. www.bransonsettleinn. com.* 300 rms, 3-4 story. S, D $50-$80; suites $99-$129; under 5 free. Crib free. Pet accepted; $5. TV; cable (premium). 2 indoor pools; whirlpool. Sauna. Complimentary continental bkfst. Restaurant 11 am-midnight. Bar; entertainment. Ck-out 11 am. Coin lndry. Meeting rms. Business center. Concierge. Gift

Silver Dollar City, Branson

shop. Exercise equipt. Game rm. Balconies. Cr cds: A, D, DS, MC, V.

D ⌨ ⇔ ✗ ✗ ⊠ ⊠

★ **SOUTHERN OAKS INN.** *3295 Shepherd of the Hills Expy, Branson (65616). 417/335-8108; fax 417/335-8861; toll-free 800/324-8752. www. southernoaksinn.com.* 150 rms, 2 story. May-Oct: S, D $57.95; suites $95; under 17 free; lower rates rest of yr. Crib free. TV; cable (premium), VCR avail. 2 pools, 1 indoor; whirlpool. Complimentary bkfst. Restaurant opp 6 am-10 pm. Ck-out 11 am. Coin lndry. Meeting rms. Business servs avail. Refrigerator in suites. Some balconies. Cr cds: A, DS, MC, V.

D ⇔ ⊠ ⊠ SC

★ **SUNTERRA RESORT AT FALL CREEK.** *1 Fall Creek Dr, Branson (65616). 417/334-6404; fax 417/336-1158.* 250 kit. units, (1, 2, and 3 bedrms), 10 studio rms. 1-bedrm condos $89; 2-bedrm condos $119-$139; 3-bedrm condos $189; studio rms $72. TV; cable, VCR avail (movies). 5 pools, 1 indoor. Playground. Restaurant 8 am-7 pm. Ck-out 10:30 am. Coin lndry. Business servs avail. Tennis. Miniature golf. Exercise equipt. Marina, boat rentals. Patio tables, grills. Cr cds: A, C, D, DS, JCB, MC, V.

★ **TRAVELODGE FORGET-ME-NOT INN.** *3102 Falls Pkwy, Branson (65616). 417/334-7523; fax 417/336-2495; res 800/899-1097. www. travelodge.com.* 81 rms, 2 story. May-Dec: S, D $45-$73; each addl $5; under 17 free. TV; cable (premium). Pool. Complimentary continental bkfst. Ck-out 11 am. Meeting rm. Business servs avail. Gift shop. Cr cds: A, C, D, DS, MC, V.

Hotel

★★ **RADISSON HOTEL BRANSON.** *120 S Wildwood Dr, Branson (65616). 417/335-5767; fax 417/335-7979; toll-free 888/566-5290. www. radisson.com.* 500 rms, 10 story. Mid-Apr-Sept: S, D $89-99; suites $150; under 19 free; lower rates rest of yr. Crib free. TV; cable (premium). Indoor/outdoor pool; whirlpool, poolside serv. Complimentary coffee in rms. Restaurant 6 am-10 pm. Bar 4 pm-1 am. Ck-out 11 am. Meeting rms. Business servs avail. In-rm modem link. Concierge. Gift shop. Barber, beauty shop. Exercise equipt; sauna. Cr cds: A, C, D, DS, JCB, MC, V.

Resorts

★★★ **CHATEAU ON THE LAKE.** *415 N MO 265 (65616). 417/334-1161; fax 417/339-5566.* 300 rms, 10 story. S, D $150-$225; each addl $20; under 17 free. Crib avail. Pet accepted. Pool. TV; cable (premium), VCR avail. Complimentary coffee, newspaper in rms. Restaurant 6 am-10 pm. Ck-out noon. Meeting rms. Business center. Gift shop. Exercise rm. Some refrigerators, minibars. Cr cds: A, C, D, DS, ER, JCB, MC, V.

★★ **POINTE ROYALE.** *158-A Pointe Royale Dr, Branson (65616). 417/334-5614; fax 417/334-5620; toll-free*

800/962-4710. pointeroyale.com. 275 kit. condos, 3 story. May-Oct: S, D $69-$97; lower rates rest of yr. Crib $3. TV; cable, VCR avail (movies). Pool. Sauna. Restaurants 8 am-midnight. Bar. Ck-out 10 am. Meeting rms. Business servs avail. Lndry facilities. Maid serv wkly. Lighted tennis. 18-hole golf, greens fee $40, putting green. Picnic tables, grills. On Lake Taneycomo. Cr cds: A, MC, V.

B&Bs/Small Inns

★★ **BRANSON HOTEL BED & BREAKFAST.** *214 W Main St, Branson (65616). 417/335-6104; fax 417/339-3224. www.bransonhotelbb.com.* 9 rms, 2 story. S, D $95. Closed Jan-Feb. Children over 9 yrs only. TV; cable. Complimentary full bkfst. Restaurant opp 5 am-11 pm. Ck-out 11 am, ck-in 4-8 pm. Built 1903. Victorian decor, antiques. Author Harold Bell Wright stayed here while writing "Shepherd of the Hills." Totally non-smoking. Cr cds: MC, V.

★★ **BRANSON HOUSE BED & BREAKFAST.** *120 N 4th St, Branson (78208). 417/334-0959. www.branson houseinn.com.* 6 rms, 4 with shower only, 2 story. No rm phones. S $55-$85; D $65-$90; each addl $10. Children over 9 only. TV in parlor. Complimentary full bkfst. Restaurant adj 7 am-10 pm. Ck-out 11 am, ck-in 3-6 pm. Individually decorated rms; antiques. Cr cds: A, MC, V.

Cottage Colony

★ **BRIARWOOD RESORT.** *1685 Lakeshore Dr, Branson (65615). 417/334-3929; fax 417/334-1324. www. briarwoodresort.com.* 16 kit. cottages. Mid-May-Nov: 1-bedrm $45-$55; 2-bedrm $61-$80; 3-bedrm $112-$122; each addl $5; wkly rates; lower rates Mar-mid-May. Closed rest of yr. Crib free. TV; cable. Pool. Playground. Ck-out 10 am. Sundries. Game rm. Lawn games. Grills. On Lake Taneycomo; boats, motors, dock, fish storage.

Restaurants

★★ **CANDLESTICK INN.** *127 Taney St, Marvel Cave Park (65616). 417/ 334-3633. www.candlestickinn.com.* Specializes in steak and seafood. Hrs: 5-9 pm; Fri and Sat to 10 pm. Closed Thanksgiving, Dec 25. Bar 4-10 pm. Res accepted. Dinner $10.95-$31.50. Children's menu. Overlooks Lake Taneycomo. Cr cds: A, DS, V.
D

★★ **DIMITRIS.** *500 E Main, Branson (61656). 417/334-0888. www.dimitris gourmet.com.* Continental menu. Specializes in salads, seafood, beef. Hrs: 5-10 pm. Closed Jan. Res accepted. Wine, beer. Dinner $14.99-$29.99. Children's menu. Contemporary decor. Cr cds: A, D, DS, MC, V.
D

★ **FRIENDSHIP HOUSE.** *College of the Ozarks, Point Lookout (65726). 417/334-6411.* Specializes in Ozark country-style cooking. Hrs: 7 am-7:30 pm; Sun to 3 pm. Res accepted. Bkfst $1-$4.65, lunch, dinner $3.25-$6.95. Sun buffet $6.50. Overlooks Ozarks college campus. Student operated. Totally nonsmoking. Cr cds: A, DS, MC, V.
D

★ **MR G'S CHICAGO STYLE PIZZA.** *202½ N Commercial, Marvel Cave Park (65616). 417/335-8156.* Italian menu. Specializes in Chicago-style pizza, pasta. Hrs: 11 am-11 pm. Closed hols. Res accepted. Bar. Lunch, dinner $3.95-$9.95. Cr cds: MC, V.
D ⮥

★ **UNCLE JOE'S BAR-B-Q.** *2819 MO 76 W, Branson (65616). 417/334-4548.* Specializes in hickory-smoked ribs, ham. Salad bar. Hrs: 11 am-10 pm; Apr to 8 pm. Closed mid-Dec-late Jan. Lunch $4.95-$6.40, dinner $7.20-$14.60. Children's menu. Totally nonsmoking. Cr cds: A, D, MC, V.
D SC

Camdenton

(E-4) *See also Lake Ozark, Osage Beach*

Pop 2,561 **Elev** 1,043 ft
Area code 573 **Zip** 65020
Information Chamber of Commerce, PO Box 1375; 573/346-2227 or 800/769-1004
Web www.odd.net/ozarks/cchamber

Camdenton is near the Niangua Arm of the Lake of the Ozarks (see).

What to See and Do

Bridal Cave. Tour (one hr) incl colorful onyx formations, underground lake; temperature constant 60°F; lighted concrete walks. Nature trails, visitor center, picnic area, gift shop. (Daily; closed Thanksgiving, Dec 25) 2 mi N on MO 5, then 1½ mi on Lake Rd 5-88. Phone 573/346-2676. ¢¢

Ha Ha Tonka State Park. More than 2,500 acres on the Niangua Arm of the Lake of the Ozarks; classic example of "karst" topography characterized by sinks, caves, underground streams, large springs, and natural bridges, all remnants of an immense ancient cavern system. Features incl the Colosseum, a natural theaterlike pit; Whispering Dell, 150-ft sink basin that transmits sound along its entire length; Natural Bridge, 70 ft wide, 100 ft high, and spanning 60 ft; remains of burned castle (ca 1910). Fishing; hiking, picnicking. Standard fees. (Daily) 5 mi SW via US 54. Phone 573/346-2986. **FREE**

Pomme de Terre State Park. On the shore of 7,800-acre Pomme de Terre Reservoir; a favorite for water activities, incl muskie fishing. Swimming, beaches, fishing, boating (rentals, marina); hiking trails, picnicking, camping (hookups, dump station). Standard fees. (Daily) 30 mi W via US 54, then S on County D, near Nemo. Phone 417/852-4291. **FREE**

Special Event

Dogwood Festival. Entertainment, crafts, food, carnival, parade. Mid-Apr.

Cameron

(B-2) *See also Excelsior Springs, St. Joseph*

Established 1855 **Pop** 4,831
Elev 1,036 ft **Area code** 816
Zip 64429
Information Chamber of Commerce, PO Box 252; 816/632-2005

Cameron was laid out by Samuel McCorkle, who named the town after his wife, Malinda Cameron. The completion of the railroad in 1858 spurred population and economic growth, making Cameron an agricultural trade center.

What to See and Do

Wallace State Park. More than 500 acres. Swimming, fishing, canoeing; hiking trails, picnicking, playground, improved camping (dump station). Standard fees. (Daily) 7 mi S on US 69, I-35, then E on MO 121. Phone 816/632-3745. **FREE**

Motel/Motor Lodge

★ **ECONO LODGE INN.** *220 E Grand Ave (64429). 816/632-6571; res 800/350-8763.* 36 rms, 1-2 story. S $33-$41; D $36-$47; each addl $5. Pet accepted. TV; cable. Pool. Complimentary continental bkfst. Restaurants nearby. Ck-out 11 am. Cr cds: A, D, DS, MC, V.
🔧 ≈ 🕌 ≈ 🎨

Restaurant

★ **CACTUS GRILL.** *923 N Walnut (64429). 816/632-6110.* Specializes in fried chicken, steak, seafood. Salad bar. Hrs: 11 am-10 pm. Bar. Lunch $4.95-$6.95, dinner $4.95-$15. Children's menu. Early American decor, antiques. Family-owned. Cr cds: A, D, DS, MC, V.
D ≈

Cape Girardeau

(E-7) *See also Ste. Genevieve, Sikeston*

Settled 1793 **Pop** 34,438 **Elev** 400 ft
Area code 573 **Zip** 63701
Information Convention & Visitors Bureau, 100 Broadway, PO Box 617; 573/335-1631 or 800/777-0068
Web www.capegirardeaucvb.org

On early maps, a rocky promontory on the Mississippi River 125 miles below St. Louis was labeled "Cape Girardot" (or "Girardeau"), named for a French ensign believed to have settled there about 1720. In 1792 an agent for the Spanish government, Louis Lorimier, set up a trading post at the site of the present city and encouraged settlement through the Spanish policy of offering tax-exempt land at nominal cost.

Cape Girardeau's location assured flourishing river traffic before the Civil War; sawmills, flour mills, and packing houses contributed to the prosperity. The war, however, ended river trade, and the earliest railroads bypassed the town, triggering further decline. In the late 1880s, the arrival of new railroads and the 1928 completion of a bridge across the Mississippi contributed to industrial growth and the widening of Cape Girardeau's economic base. Southeast Missouri State University (1873), which has a mural in its library depicting the history of the area, is located in the town.

What to See and Do

Bollinger Mill State Historic Site. Day-use park features historic 19th-century gristmill. Also oldest covered bridge in the state (1868). (Daily; closed hols) 113 Bollinger Rd. Phone 573/243-4591. ¢

Cape River Heritage Museum. Exhibits on Cape Girardeau's early heritage, 19th-century industry, education, and culture. Gift shop. (Mar-Dec, Wed, Fri, and Sat; also by appt; closed Thanksgiving, Dec 25) 538 Independence. Phone 573/334-0405. ¢

Cape Rock Park. Site of original trading post. Scenic river views. Reached by Cape Rock Dr. Phone 800/777-0068.

Court of Common Pleas Building.
Central portion built about 1854 to
replace previous log structure. During the Civil War, cells in the basement housed prisoners. Outstanding
view of Mississippi River from park.
Spanish and Themis sts.

Glenn House. (ca 1885) Victorian
house with period furnishings, memorabilia of Mississippi River and
steamboat era; tours. (Apr-Dec, Fri-
Sun; closed Thanksgiving, Dec 25)
325 S Spanish St. Phone 573/334-
1177. ¢¢

Old St. Vincent's Church. English
Gothic Revival church showing
Roman influences. More than 100
medieval-design plaster masks. Hand-
carved doors. Tours by appt (fee).
Spanish and Main sts.

Rose Display Garden. Test garden
(approx 300 plants) for new roses;
blooming season May-Sept. Garden
(Daily). Perry Ave and Parkview Dr in
Capaha Park. **FREE**

**St. Louis Iron Mountain and Southern
Railway.** A 1946 steam locomotive
pulls vintage 1920s cars through
scenic woodlands; trips range from
80 min-5 hrs. (Apr-Oct, Sat and Sun;
also by charter) NW via I-55 exit 99,
then 4 mi W on US 61 (MO 72) at jct
MO 25 in Jackson. Phone 573/243-
1688. ¢¢¢

Trail of Tears State Park. More than
3,000-acre park on limestone bluffs
overlooking Mississippi River. Commemorates forced migration of the
Cherokee Nation over Trail of Tears
from their homeland to Oklahoma.
Fishing, boating; hiking and equestrian trails, picnicking, primitive and
improved camping (showers, trailer
hookups, standard fees). Interpretive
center (seasonal). (Daily) 429 Moccasin Spring. Phone 573/334-1711.
FREE

Special Events

Riverfest. Water and Main sts, downtown. Festival along the Mississippi
River incl arts and crafts, food, entertainment. First full wkend June.

Semo District Fair. Arena Park. Agricultural products, crops, animals;
entertainment, carnival, food. One
wk mid-Sept.

Motels/Motor Lodges

★★ **DRURY LODGE.** *104 S Vantage
Dr (63701). 573/334-7151; toll-free
800/378-7946. www.druryinn.com.* 139
rms, 2 story. S $63; D $73; each addl
$8; under 18 free. Crib free. Pet
accepted, some restrictions. TV; cable
(premium), VCR avail. Pool; wading
pool. Playground. Complimentary
bkfst buffet. Restaurant 6 am-10 pm.
Bars 4 pm-1:30 am. Ck-out noon.
Meeting rms. Business servs avail.
Valet serv. Exercise equipt. Health
club privileges. Sundries. Game rm.
Microwaves avail. Cr cds: A, D, DS,
MC, V.

★★ **DRURY SUITES.** *3303 Campster
Dr (63701). 573/339-9500; toll-free
800/325-8300.* 87 suites, 5 story. S
$78.95; D $88.95; each addl $10;
under 18 free; golf plans. Crib free.
Pet accepted, some restrictions. TV;
cable (premium). Complimentary
continental bkfst, coffee in rms.
Restaurant adj 4-10 pm. Bar. Ck-out
noon. Meeting rms. Business servs
avail. Health club privileges. Indoor
pool; whirlpool. Refrigerators, microwaves. Cr cds: A, C, D, DS, MC, V.

★★ **HAMPTON INN.** *103 Cape W
Pkwy (65065). 573/651-3000; fax
573/651-0882.* 80 rms, 3 story. S
$64.95-$69.95; D $74.95-$79.95;
under 18 free. Crib free. Pet accepted,
some restrictions. TV; cable (premium). Complimentary continental
bkfst. Restaurant nearby. Ck-out
noon. Meeting rms. Business servs
avail. Valet serv. Cr cds: A, C, D, DS,
MC, V.

★★ **HOLIDAY INN WEST PARK.**
*3257 William St (63703). 573/334-
4491; fax 573/334-7459; toll-free
800/645-3379. www.holiday-inn.com.*
186 rms, 2 story. S, D $79-$89; each
addl after 1, $10; under 18 free. Crib
free. Pet accepted. TV; cable (premium). Indoor/outdoor pool; wading
pool. Restaurant 6 am-2 pm, 5-9 pm.
Bar 4 pm-midnight. Ck-out 11 am.
Coin lndry. Meeting rms. Business
servs avail. In-rm modem link. Valet
serv. Free airport transportation.
Exercise equipt. Health club privi-

leges. Rec rm. Bathrm phones. Cr
cds: A, MC, V.

[D] [☎] [≈] [术] [≣] [🔥] [SC]

★ **PEAR TREE INN.** *3248 William St,
I-55 and Rte K (63703). 573/334-3000;
toll-free 800/378-7946.* 78 rms, 3
story. No elvtr. S $48-$54; D $58-$64;
each addl $8; under 18 free. Crib
free. Pet accepted, some restrictions.
TV; cable (premium). Complimentary
continental bkfst. Restaurant adj 6
am-10 pm. Ck-out noon. Business
servs avail. Pool; wading pool. Cr
cds: A, C, D, DS, MC, V.

[D] [☎] [≈] [≣] [🔥] [SC]

Restaurants

★ **BG'S OLDE TYME DELI &
SALOON.** *205 S Plaza Way (63703).
573/335-8860.* Specialties: deli sandwiches, fried chicken, Cajun catfish.
Salad bar. Hrs: 11 am-10 pm; Fri, Sat
to 11 pm. Closed hols. Bar. Lunch,
dinner $3.99-$6.49. Children's
menu. Continuous showings of contemporary movies. Cr cds: A, D, DS,
MC, V.

[⊣]

★ **BROUSSARD'S CAJUN CUISINE.**
120 N Main St (63701). 573/334-7235.
Cajun menu. Specializes in crawfish
étouffée, seafood. Hrs: 10 am-10 pm;
Fri, Sat to 11 pm; Sun from 11 am.
Closed Thanksgiving, Dec 25. Bar. Res
accepted. Bar. Lunch, dinner $2.95-
$16.95. Blues band Thurs-Sat. Cr cds:
A, D, MC, V.

[D] [⊣]

Carthage

See also Joplin, Lamar, Mount Vernon

Founded 1842 **Pop** 10,747 **Elev** 1,002
ft **Area code** 417 **Zip** 64836
Information Chamber of Commerce,
107 E 3rd St; 417/358-2373
Web www.carthagenow.com

Carthage was founded as the seat of
Jasper County in 1842. The first
major Civil War battle west of the
Mississippi River was fought here
July 5, 1861. Among early residents
were Belle Starr, Confederate spy and
outlaw, who lived here as a girl;
Annie Baxter, the first woman in the

United States to hold elective office,
who was elected County Clerk here
in 1890; and James Scott, ragtime
musician and composer who began
his career here in 1906. Many interesting Victorian houses can still be
found in Carthage.

What to See and Do

**Battle of Carthage Civil War
Museum.** Features artifacts, wall-sized
mural, and diorama depicting
progress of battle. (Daily) 205 E
Grant. Phone 417/358-6643. **FREE**

**George Washington Carver National
Memorial.** (see) Approx 14 mi S on
US 71A.

Jasper County Courthouse. (1894)
Built of Carthage marble, with mural
by Lowell Davis depicting local history. (Mon-Fri; closed hols) Courthouse Sq, downtown. Phone
417/358-0421.

Powers Museum. Museum devoted to
local history and arts. Rotating
exhibits on late 19th- to early 20th-
century clothing, furniture, holiday
celebrations. Research library; gift
shop. (Feb-Dec, Tues-Sun; closed
hols) 1617 Oak St. Phone 417/358-
2667. **FREE**

Precious Moments Chapel. Structure
houses murals by Samuel J. Butcher.
Also museum; gardens; gift shops;
cafes. (Mar-Dec, daily; Jan and Feb,
limited hrs) 480 Chapel Rd. S on US
71A to Hwy HH, then W to Chapel
Rd. Phone 417/358-7599. ¢

Special Event

Maple Leaf Festival. Parade, marching band competition, arts and
crafts, house tours. Mid-Oct.

Motels/Motor Lodges

★ **DAYS INN.** *2244 Grand Ave
(64836). 417/358-2499; toll-free 888/
454-2499. www.daysinn.com.* 40 rms.
S $34; D $40-$44; each addl $5; under
12 free. Crib free. TV; cable (premium). Complimentary continental
bkfst. Restaurant nearby. Ck-out 11
am. Business servs avail. In-rm
modem link. Cr cds: A, D, DS, MC, V.

[D] [≣] [🔥] [SC]

★ **ECONO LODGE.** *1441 W Central
(64886). 417/358-3900; fax 417/358-
6839; toll-free 800/553-2666. www.*

econolodge.com. 82 rms, 2 story. S $47.95-$54.95; D $52.95-$59.95; each addl $5; under 18 free. Crib $3. TV; cable (premium). Indoor pool; whirlpool. Complimentary continental bkfst. Ck-out 11 am. Meeting rm. Cr cds: A, MC, V.

D ⊠ ⊠ ⊠ SC

B&B/Small Inn

★★ GRAND AVENUE BED AND BREAKFAST. 1615 Grand Ave (64836). 417/358-7265; toll-free 888/380-6786. www.grand-avenue.com. 4 rms, 2 story. Rm phones avail. Apr-Dec: D $69-$89; suite $119; wkly rates; lower rates rest of yr. TV in library. Pool. Complimentary full bkfst. Ck-out 11 am, ck-in 4-6 pm. Queen Anne-style, Victorian house (1890); antiques. Cr cds: DS, MC, V.

⊠ ⊠ ⊠ SC

Restaurant

★ BAMBOO GARDEN. 102 N Garrison Ave (64836). 417/358-1611. Chinese menu. Specialties: cashew chicken, sweet and sour chicken. Hrs: 11 am-9 pm; Fri to 10 pm. Closed Sun; Jan 1, Thanksgiving, Dec 25; also 1st wk Aug. Res accepted Mon-Thurs. Buffet: lunch $5.49, dinner $6.49. Cr cds: MC, V.

D ⊠

Cassville

(F-3) See also Branson/Table Rock Lake Area

Pop 2,371 Elev 1,324 ft
Area code 417 Zip 65625
Information Chamber of Commerce, 504 Main St; 417/847-2814

What to See and Do

Mark Twain National Forest. (Cassville Ranger District) Approx 70,300 acres. Fishing, boat launching; camping at Big Bay Campground (standard fees), picnicking at Piney Creek Wilderness Area. (Daily) E via MO 76 or MO 86; S via MO 112. Phone 417/847-2144.

Ozark Wonder Cave. Seven rms with multicolored onyx, stalactites, and stalagmites; 45-min tour. (Daily) 45 mi W via MO 76, then 5 mi S on MO 59, near Noel. Phone 417/475-3579. ¢¢

Roaring River State Park. Approx 3,300 acres of spectacular hill country. Trout fishing; hiking, picnicking; dining lodge, general store. Improved camping (dump station), cabins, motel. Naturalist program and nature center; fish hatchery. Standard fees (Mar-Oct, daily). 7 mi S on MO 112. Phone 417/847-2539. FREE

Chillicothe (B-3)

Settled 1837 Pop 8,804 Elev 798 ft
Area code 660 Zip 64601
Information Chamber of Commerce, 715 Washington St, 2nd Floor, PO Box 407; 660/646-4050
Web www.chillicothemo.com

Chillicothe, seat of Livingston County, is a Shawnee word meaning "our big town." Named for Chillicothe, Ohio, the city is located in a rich farming, livestock, and dairy region. Sloan's Liniment was developed here about 1870 by Earl Sloan. An Amish community located approximately 25 miles northwest of town, near Jamesport, has many interesting shops.

What to See and Do

General John J. Pershing Boyhood Home State Historic Site. This 11-rm house built in 1858 has been restored to and furnished in the 1860s-1880s period; museum; guided tours. Also here is statue of "Black Jack" Pershing, Wall of Honor, and relocated Prairie Mound School, one-rm schoolhouse where Pershing taught before entering West Point. (Daily; closed hols) 20 mi E on US 36, the 1 mi N on MO 5 in Laclede. Phone 660/963-2525.

Pershing State Park. This 3,000-acre memorial to General John J. Pershing offers fishing, canoeing; hiking trails, picnicking, improved camping (dump station). N of the park is the Locust Creek covered bridge, the longest of four remaining covered bridges in the state. Standard fees. (Daily) 18 mi E on US 36, then S on MO 130. Phone 660/963-2299. **FREE**

Swan Lake National Wildlife Refuge. This 10,795-acre resting and feeding area attracts one of the largest concentrations of Canada geese in North America. Fishing; hunting. Observation tower (Daily), visitor center with exhibits, specimens, and wildlife movies (Mon-Fri). Refuge and fishing (Mar-mid-Oct, Mon-Fri). Self-guided interpretive trail. 19 mi E on US 36 to Laclede jct, then 13 mi S on MO 139 to Sumner; main entrance 1 mi S. Phone 660/856-3323. **FREE**

Motels/Motor Lodges

★★ **BEST WESTERN.** *1020 S Washington St (64601).* 660/646-0572; fax 660/646-1274; res 800/990-9150. *www.bestwestern.com.* 60 rms, 1-2 story. S $39-$49; D $42-$52; each addl $5. Crib $5. Pet accepted; $5. TV; cable. Pool. Continental bkfst. Restaurants nearby. Ck-out noon. Meeting rm. Business servs avail. In-rm modem link. Coin lndry. Refrigerators. Cr cds: A, D, DS, MC, V.
[icons]

★★ **GRAND RIVER INN.** *606 W Business 36 (64601).* 660/646-6590. 60 rms, 2 story, 5 suites. S $54-$58; D $63-$67; each addl $9; suites $63-$83; family rates; wkend, wkly rates; golf plans. Crib free. Pet accepted, some restrictions. TV; cable (premium), VCR avail (movies). Heated pool; whirlpool. Sauna. Complimentary continental bkfst. Restaurant 6:30 am-9 pm; Fri to 10 pm; Sat 7 am-10 pm; Sun 7 am-2 pm. Bar 5 pm-1:30 am; closed Sun. Ck-out noon. Meeting rms. Business servs avail. In-rm modem link. Valet serv. Health club privileges. Some refrigerators. Cr cds: A, C, D, DS, MC, V.
[icons]

Clayton

See also St. Louis

Settled 1820 **Pop** 13,874 **Elev** 550 ft
Area code 314 **Zip** 63105
Information Chamber of Commerce, 225 S Meramec, Suite 300; 314/726-3033

Clayton, a central suburb of St. Louis, was first settled by Virginia-born Ralph Clayton, for whom the city is named. In 1877 the budding town became the seat of St. Louis County when Clayton and another early settler, Martin Hanley, donated part of their land for a new courthouse. Today Clayton is a major suburban St. Louis residential and business center.

What to See and Do

Craft Alliance Gallery. Contemporary ceramic, fiber, metal, glass, and wood exhibits. (Tues-Sat; closed hols) N on Hanley Rd to Delmar Blvd, E to 6640 Delmar Blvd in University City. Phone 314/725-1177. **FREE**

Forest Park. (See ST. LOUIS) Approx 2 mi E via Clayton Rd or Forsyth Blvd.

Washington University. (1853) 11,000 students. On campus are Graham Chapel, Edison Theatre, and Francis Field, site of first Olympic Games in US (1904). E on Forsyth Blvd, hilltop campus entrance at Hoyt Dr. Phone 314/935-5000. Also here is

> **Washington University Gallery of Art.** Established in 1888, this was the first art museum west of the Mississippi River; a branch of the museum later became the St. Louis Art Museum. Collections of 19th- and 20th-century American and European paintings; sculpture and old and modern prints. (Mon-Fri, also Sat and Sun afternoons; closed hols) Steinberg Hall. Phone 314/935-5490. **FREE**

Special Event

St. Louis Art Fair. Central Business District. One of top three juried art fairs in nation. Phone 314/863-0278. First full wkend Sept.

Hotels

★★★ **DANIELE HOTEL.** *216 N Meramac, St. Louis (13105).* 314/721-0101; fax 314/721-0609; res 800/325-8302. 82 rms, 4 story. S, D $139; suites $200-$700; under 18 free; wkend rates. Pet accepted. TV; cable (premium), VCR avail. Pool. Restaurant (see DANIELE). Bar. Ck-out noon. Meeting rms. Business servs avail. In-rm modem link. Free covered parking. Free airport transportation. Health club privileges. Some refrigerators, wet bars. Cr cds: A, MC, V.

[D] [≈] [✕]

★★ **RADISSON HOTEL CLAYTON.** *7750 Carondelet Ave (63105). 314/726-5400; fax 314/719-1126; toll-free 800/333-3333. www.radisson.com.* 194 rms, 2-8 story. S $159; D $169; each addl $10; suites $129-$200; under 18 free; wkly rates, wkend package plan. Crib free. TV; cable. Indoor/outdoor pool; whirlpool. Complimentary continental bkfst. Coffee in rms. Restaurant 6 am-11 pm. Bar 11-1 am. Ck-out noon. Meeting rms. Business center. In-rm modem link. Barber. Free garage parking; valet. Airport transportation. Exercise rm. Game rm. Refrigerators. Cr cds: A, C, D, DS, ER, JCB, MC, V.

[D] [≈] [🏃] [✕] [⊠] [🐾] [🏃]

★★★★ **THE RITZ-CARLTON, ST. LOUIS.** *100 Carondelet Plaza (63105). 314/863-6300; fax 314/863-3525; toll-free 800/241-3333. www.ritzcarlton. com.* The fashionable suburban location of this luxury property is near both downtown St. Louis and Lambert Airport. All 301 rooms and suites have French doors opening to beautiful, private balconies, many overlooking the skyline and Mississippi River. In this brand's signature style, there are many first-rate dining options including the Lobby Lounge's afternoon tea and evening sushi bar. 301 rms, 18 story, 34 suites. S, D $175-$350; suites $295-$2,000; under 12 free; wkend rates, package plans. Crib free. Garage, valet parking $15/day. TV; cable (premium), VCR avail. Indoor pool; whirlpool, poolside serv. Restaurant. (see also THE GRILL) Rm serv 24 hrs. Bar 11-1 am; entertainment. Ck-out noon. Convention facilities. Business center. In-rm modem link. Concierge. Gift shop. Exercise rm; sauna, steam rm. Massage. Bathrm phones, refrigerators, minibars; microwaves avail. Cr cds: A, C, D, DS, MC, V.

[D] [≈] [🏃] [✕] [⊠] [🐾] [🏃]

B&Bs/Small Inns

★ **DAS GAST HAUS NADLER.** *125 Defiance Rd, Defiance (63341). 636/987-2200.* 4 rms, all share bath. No rm phones. S, D $70-$90; under 12 free. Complimentary full bkfst. Restaurant 9 am-9 pm. Ck-out 11 am, ck-in 4 pm. Whirlpool. Game rm. Built in 1907. Cr cds: MC, V.

[⊠] [🐾] [SC]

★★★ **SEVEN GABLES.** *26 N Meramec Ave (63105). 314/863-8400; fax 314/863-8846; res 800/433-6590. sevengablesinn.com.* 32 rms, 3 story. No elvtr. S, D $155; suites $159-$260; wkend rates. Valet parking $8.50. TV; cable (premium). Restaurant 6:30 am-11 pm. Bar 11-12:30 am. Ck-out 1 pm, ck-in 2 pm. Meeting rm. Bellhops. Valet serv. Health club privileges. Designed in early 1900s; inspired by sketches in Hawthorne's novel *House of Seven Gables.* Renovated inn; European country-style furnishings. Cr cds: A, C, D, DS, MC, V.

[⊠] [🐾]

Restaurants

★★ **ANNIE GUNN'S.** *16806 Chesterfield Airport Rd, Chesterfield (63005). 636/532-7684.* Specializes in steak, seafood. Hrs: 11 am-10:30 pm; Fri, Sat to 11:30 pm; Sun to 8 pm. Closed Mon; hols. Res accepted. Bar. Lunch $5.95-$11.95, dinner $5.95-$29.95. Outdoor dining; view of gardens. Originally built in 1935 as a meat market and smokehouse. Cr cds: A, DS, MC, V.

[D] [⊟]

★★★ **BENEDETTO'S.** *10411 Clayton Rd, Frontenac (63131). 314/432-8585.* Italian menu. Specializes in veal, fresh fish, beef. Hrs: 11:30 am-2 pm, 5-11 pm. Closed hols. Res accepted. Bar. Wine cellars. A la carte entrees: lunch $8-$11, dinner $13.95-$18.95. Pianist, vocalist Fri, Sat. Tableside preparation. Cr cds: A, D, DS, MC, V.

[D] [⊟]

★ **CAFE MIRA.** *12 N Meramec Ave (63105). 314/721-7801.* Contemporary menu. Specialties: risotto, beef, fisa with seafood. Own baking. Hrs: 5-10 pm; Fri, Sat to 10:30 pm. Closed Sun. Res accepted. Bar. Dinner $16.95-$23.95. Outdoor dining. Cr cds: A, D, DS, MC, V.

[D]

★ **CAFE NAPOLI.** *7754 Forsyth (63105).* *314/863-5731.* Italian menu. Specializes in veal, salmon, pasta. Hrs: 11 am-2 pm, 5:30-10 pm; Fri to 11 pm; Sat 5:30-11 pm. Closed Sun; hols. Bar. Res accepted. Lunch $4.95-$25, dinner $10.95-$29.95. Italian atmosphere. Cr cds: A, MC, V.
D

★★ **CAFE PROVENCAL.** *40 N Central (63105).* *314/725-2755.* *www.cafeprovencal.com.* Specializes in southern French cuisine. Hrs: 6-10 pm. Closed Mon, Sun; also Easter, Thanksgiving, Dec 25. Bar. Res accepted. Dinner $13-$24. Entertainment Wed, Thurs. French country decor. Cr cds: A, DS, MC, V.
D

★★★ **CARDWELL'S.** *8100 Maryland (63105).* *314/726-5055.* *www.cardwellsrestaurant.com.* Specializes in fresh seafood, prime aged beef, poultry. Hrs: 11:30 am-3 pm, 5:30-10 pm; Fri, Sat to 11 pm. Closed Sun; hols. Bar to 1:30 am. Res accepted. Lunch $5.95-$12.95, dinner $14.95-$23.95. Children's menu. Outdoor dining. Contemporary decor. Cr cds: A, DS, MC, V.
D ☒

★ **CRAZY FISH FRESH GRILL.** *15 N Meramec Ave (63105).* *314/726-2111.* Continental menu. Specialties: bison meatloaf, shrimp voodoo pasta, potato crusted grouper. Hrs: 11:30 am-11 pm; Fri, Sat to midnight; Sun 10 am-10 pm. Closed Thanksgiving, Dec 25. Bar. Res accepted. Lunch $6.95-$11.95, dinner $12.95-$22.95. Children's menu. Outdoor dining. Modern decor. Cr cds: A, D, DS, MC, V.
D

★★ **DANIELE.** *216 N Meramac (63105).* *314/721-0101.* *www.thedanielehotel.com.* Continental menu. Specializes in steak, veal, prime rib. Hrs: 6 am-10 pm; Sun to 2 pm. Closed hols. Bar. Res accepted. Bkfst $4.95-$7.95, lunch $6.95-$10.95, dinner $10.95-$18.95. Complete meals: dinner $16.95. Sun brunch $14.95. Valet parking. Elegant dining. Cr cds: A, D, DS, MC, V.
D ☒

★★★ **FIO'S LA FOURCHETTE.** *7515 Forsyth Ave (63105).* *314/863-6866.* *www.saucecafe.com/fiosla fourchette.* French menu. Specializes in souffles, mussels, wild game. Own baking. Hrs: 6-9 pm. Closed Mon, Sun; hols; also 2 wks in summer. Bar. Extensive wine list. Res accepted. Dinner $19-$24. Complete meal: dinner $58.75. Valet parking. Intimate dining. Cr cds: A, DS, MC, V.
D

★★★ **THE GRILL.** *100 Carondelet Plaza (63105).* *314/863-6300.* *www.ritzcarlton.com.* Hrs: 5:30-11 pm. Res accepted. Bar. Wine cellar. Dinner $22-$48. Children's menu. Specialties: Dover sole, Aquanor salmon, lobster Tempura. Own baking. Valet parking. Marble fireplace in main rm; English pub atmosphere. Cr cds: A, D, DS, MC, V.
D

★★ **PORTABELLA.** *15 N Cental Ave (63105).* *314/725-6588.* *www.portabellarestaurant.com.* Continental menu. Specialty: porcini-encrusted sea bass. Own baking. Hrs: 11 am-3 pm, 5:30-10:30 pm; Fri to 11 pm; Sat 5:30-11 pm. Closed Sun; hols. Res accepted. Bar to 1:30 am. Lunch $6.50-$10.95, dinner $11.50-$18.95. Valet parking. Modern art. Cr cds: A, D, DS, MC, V.
D ☒

★★ **REMY'S.** *222 S Bemiston (63105).* *314/726-5757.* Hrs: 11:30 am-2:30 pm, 5:30-10 pm; Fri, Sat 5:30 pm-midnight. Closed Sun; also hols. Res accepted. Mediterranean menu. Bar. Lunch $5.95-$7.95, dinner $12-$16. Specialties: bronzed snapper filet, braised lamb shank and stuffed grape vine leaves. Outdoor dining. Modern decor. Totally nonsmoking. Cr cds: A, D, DS, MC, V.
D

Clinton

(D-3) *See also Harrisonville, Sedalia*

Pop 8,703 **Elev** 803 ft **Area code** 660 **Zip** 64735

Information Tourism Association, 200 S Main St; 660/885-8167 or 800/222-5251

Selected as the county seat in 1837, Clinton was called "the model town of the prairies." It has a large and attractive downtown square and is the northern gateway to Harry S. Truman Lake.

What to See and Do

Harry S. Truman State Park. Swimming, beach, fishing, boating (ramp, rentals, marina); hiking, picnicking, camping (hookups, dump station). Standard fees. (Mar-Nov, daily) Approx 20 mi E on MO 7, then 2 mi N on County UU, on Truman Lake. Phone 660/438-7711. ¢¢

Henry County Historical Society Museum and Cultural Arts Center. Built in 1886 by Anheuser-Busch as a distributing point, restored structure now houses historical documents, cemetery records, war relics, Native American artifacts, antique dolls, glass, china; Victorian parlor and old-fashioned kitchen; stable. Turn of the Century Village has 1890s store, bank, saddle shop; art gallery. (Apr-Dec, Tues-Sat, limited hrs; also by appt) 203 W Franklin St. Phone 660/885-8414. ¢¢

Kumberland Gap Pioneer Settlement. Re-creation of a typical 1870s village featuring general store, trading post, blacksmith shop, schoolhouse, and a reconstructed log cabin. (Mid-May-Oct, wkends only) 9 mi E

on MO 7 to County C, continue E to County T, then S to County TT, then W, near Truman Lake. Phone 660/547-3899. ¢¢

Restaurant

★ **UCHIE'S FINE FOODS.** *127 W Franklin (64735). 660/885-3262.* Hrs: 5 am-8 pm. Closed Sun; hols; also 1st 2 wks Jan. Bkfst $1.30-$6.45, lunch, dinner $3.25-$9.95. Specialties: biscuits and gravy, Missouri-cured country ham. Salad bar. Located in pre-1865 building. Cr cds: D, MC, V.

Columbia

(D-6) *See also Fulton, Hermann, Jefferson City*

Settled 1819 **Pop** 69,101 **Elev** 758 ft
Area code 573

Information Convention & Visitors Bureau, 300 S Providence Rd, PO Box N, 65205; 573/875-1231 or 800/652-0987

Web www.visitcolumbia.mo

An educational center from its earliest years, Columbia is the home of Columbia College, Stephens College, and the University of Missouri, the

Hot-air balloons fly high at Balbon Classic

oldest state university west of the Mississippi. Established as Smithton, the town was moved a short distance to ensure a better water supply and renamed Columbia. In 1822 the Boone's Lick Trail was rerouted to pass through the town. The University of Missouri was established in 1839, and the citizens of Boone County raised $117,900—in hard times and often with personal hardship—to secure the designation of a state university. Classes began in 1841, and the town has revolved around the institution ever since. The School of Journalism, founded in 1908, was the first journalism school in the world to grant degrees.

What to See and Do

Nifong Park. Park incl visitor center, restored 1877 Maplewood house (Apr-Oct, Sun, limited hrs), Maplewood Barn Theater (summer; fee), Boone County Historical Society Museum; petting zoo, lake, picnicking. Park (Daily). Nifong Blvd at Ponderosa Dr, off US 63. Phone 573/443-8936. **FREE**

Shelter Gardens. Miniature mid-American environment with a pool and stream, domestic and wild flowers, more than 300 varieties of trees and shrubs, rose garden, garden for visually impaired; replica of one-rm schoolhouse, gazebo. Concerts in summer, weather permitting; closed Dec 25) On grounds of Shelter Insurance Co, 1817 W Broadway; S at I-70 Stadium Blvd exit. Phone 573/445-8441. **FREE**

Stephens College. (1833) 800 women. On 240-acre campus is the Firestone Baars Chapel on Walnut St (Mon-Fri), designed in 1956 by Eero Saarinen; art gallery (Sept-May, daily), solar-heated visitor center. E Broadway and College Ave. Phone 573/442-2211.

University of Missouri-Columbia. (1839) 22,140 students. This 1,334-acre campus contains numerous collections, exhibits, galleries, and attractions. Campus tours (Mon-Fri). Campus map/guide at the Visitor Relations office, Reynolds Alumni and Visitor Center, Conley Ave. 311 Jesse Hall. Phone 573/882-6333. Of special interest are

> **Botany Greenhouses and Herbarium.** Greenhouse has tropical and desert rms displaying cacti, yucca, orchids, palms, and climbing bougainvillea. (Mon-Fri, by appt) Tucker Hall, off Hitt St, E of McKee Gymnasium. Phone 573/882-6888. **FREE**

Edison Electric Dynamo. The recently restored dynamo, given to the university in 1882 by its inventor, Thomas Alva Edison, was used on campus in 1883 for the first demonstration of incandescent lighting west of the Mississippi. (Mon-Fri) Lobby of Engineering Building, E 6th St between Stewart Rd and Elm St.

Ellis Library. One of the largest libraries in the Midwest. Exhibits; rare book rm contains page from a Gutenberg Bible. **State Historical Society of Missouri,** east ground wing, has early newspapers and works by Missouri artists (phone 573/882-7083); Western Historical Manuscripts, incl holdings from Great Plains region (phone 573/882-6028 for schedule). Main library (Daily; closed hols; schedule varies). Lowry Mall between Memorial Union and Jesse Hall. Phone 573/882-4391.

Museum of Anthropology. Artifacts from 9000 B.C. to present. Gift shop. (Mon-Fri; closed hols) Swallow Hall on Francis Quadrangle. Phone 573/882-3764. **FREE**

Museum of Art and Archaeology. Comprehensive collection incl more than 13,000 objects from around the world, from paleolithic period to the present. Cast gallery has casts made from original Greek and Roman sculptures. Gift shop. (Tues-Sun; closed hols) Pickard Hall on Francis Quadrangle. Phone 573/882-3591. **FREE**

Research Reactor Facility. Guided tours incl displays and a view of the reactor core. (Tues-Fri; appt req) S of Memorial Stadium on Providence Rd in University Research Park. Phone 573/882-4211. **FREE**

Special Events

Boone County Fair. First held in 1835, earliest fair west of the Mississippi; incl exhibits, horse show. Phone 573/474-9435. Late July-early Aug.

Show-Me State Games. Missouri's largest amateur athletic event with approx 20,000 participants in 30 different events. Late July.

United States Cellular Balloon Classic. Hot-air balloon events incl mass ascensions, ballumination (after dark glow). Last wkend Aug.

Boone County Heritage Festival. Mid-Sept.

Motels/Motor Lodges

★ **CAMPUS INN.** *1112 E Stadium Blvd (65201). 573/449-2731; fax 573/449-6691.* 97 rms, 2 story. S $40; D $48; suites $89; wkly rates; higher rates wkends. Crib free. TV; cable (premium). Pool. Restaurant 7 am-1 pm, 5-10 pm. Bar. Ck-out noon. Meeting rms. Business servs avail. Cr cds: A, C, D, DS, MC, V.
D ≈ ⊠ ⌂

★★ **HOLIDAY INN.** *2200 Interstate 70 Dr SW (65203). 573/445-8531; fax 573/445-7607; toll-free 800/465-4329. www.holiday-inn.com.* 311 rms, 6 story. S, D $85; mini-suites $135-$250, suites $175-$250. Crib free. Pet accepted. TV; cable, VCR avail. 2 pools, 1 indoor; whirlpool, poolside serv. Restaurant open 24 hrs. Bar 11-1:30 am, Sun noon-midnight. Ck-out 11 am. Meeting rms. Business servs avail. In-rm modem link. Bellhops. Concierge. Gift shop. Beauty shop. Exercise equipt; sauna. Microwave avail. Adj Exposition Center. Luxury level. Cr cds: A, C, D, DS, MC, V.
D ⊷ ≈ ⊼ ⊠ ⌂

★★ **HOLIDAY INN EAST.** *1612 N Providence Rd (65202). 573/449-2491; fax 573/874-6720; toll-free 800/465-4329. www.holiday-inn.com.* 142 rms, 2 story. S $59-$79; D $60-$79; suites $175; under 18 free. Crib free. Pet accepted, some restrictions. TV; cable. Heated pool; whirlpool. Restaurant 6 am-2 pm, 5-10 pm. Bar 5 pm-midnight. Ck-out noon. Meeting rms. Sundries. Exercise equipt; sauna. Cr cds: A, C, D, DS, JCB, MC, V.
D ⊷ ≈ ⊼ ⊠ ⌂ SC

★ **SUPER 8 MOTEL.** *3216 Clark Ln (65202). 573/474-8488; fax 573/474-4180; res 800/800-8000. www.super8.com.* 75 rms, 3 story. S $51-$73; D $63-$73; each addl $5; suites $70.88-$118.88; under 12 free; higher rates special events. Crib avail. TV; cable (premium), VCR avail. Complimentary continental bkfst. Restaurant adj 6 am-10 pm. Ck-out 11 am. Business servs avail. Cr cds: A, C, D, DS, MC, V.
⊠ ⌂

★ **TRAVELODGE.** *900 Vandiver Dr (65202). 573/449-1065; fax 573/442-6266; toll-free 800/456-1065. www.travelodge.com.* 156 rms, 2 story. S $40-$50; D $50-$60; each addl $5; under 12 $1; wkly rates; higher rates special events. Crib $5. Pet accepted, some restrictions; $3. TV; cable. Heated pool. Complimentary continental bkfst. Restaurant nearby. Ck-out 11 am. Coin lndry. Business servs avail. Sundries. Some refrigerators. Picnic tables. Cr cds: A, C, D, DS, JCB, MC, V.
D ⊷ ⌂ ⊹ ≈ ⊠ ⌂

Restaurants

★★ **BOONE TAVERN.** *811 E Walnut St (65201). 573/442-5123. www.boonetavern.com.* Hrs: 11 am-midnight; Sun from 10 am. Closed Thanksgiving, Dec 25. Bar. Lunch $4.95-$8.95, dinner $9.95-$18.95. Sun brunch $8.95. Children's menu. Specializes in prime rib, seafood. Outdoor dining. Turn-of-the-century memorabilia. Cr cds: A, D, MC, V.
D ⊟

★ **FLAT BRANCH PUB & BREWING.** *115 S 5th St (65201). 573/499-0400. www.flatbranch.com.* Hrs: 11-1 am; Sun to 11:30 pm. Closed Thanksgiving, Dec 25. Res accepted (exc wkends). Bar. Lunch, dinner $5.95-$12.95. Children's menu. Specialties: chokes and cheese, chicken fuente, hobgobbler. Own baking. Outdoor dining. Casual atmosphere; brewery visible through windows in dining area. Cr cds: A, D, DS, MC, V.
D ⊟

Excelsior Springs

(C-2) *See also Independence, Kansas City*

Pop 10,354 **Elev** 900 ft **Area code** 816 **Zip** 64024

Information Chamber of Commerce, 101 E Broadway; 816/630-6161

Excelsior Springs was established in 1880 when two settlers, Anthony W. Wyman and J.V.D. Flack, discovered various natural springs on Wyman's property. Today the city is a health resort offering the visitor bottled water from the springs and medicinal baths in the city-operated bathhouse.

What to See and Do

Excelsior Springs Historical Museum. Incl murals, bank, antiques, antique bedrm, doctor's office, dental equipt. (Daily) 101 E Broadway. Phone 816/630-3712. **FREE**

Hall of Waters. Samples of mineral water may be purchased. Mineral baths for both men and women (by appt). 201 E Broadway. Phone 816/630-0753. ¢¢¢¢

☒ **Jesse James' Farm.** House where outlaw James was born and raised with brother Frank; original furnishings; guided tours. Theater production of *The Life and Times of Jesse James* (Aug, Fri-Sun; fee). Visitor center; slide program, historical museum. (Mon-Sat, also Sun afternoons) Approx 12 mi W on MO 92 to Kearney, then follow signs 3 mi on Jesse James Farm Rd. Phone 816/628-6065. ¢¢ Opp is

Historic Claybrook Plantation. Restored pre-Civil War house, which later was residence of James' daughter. Guided tours (fee). (Mid-May-Aug, daily) Phone 816/628-6065.

Watkins Woolen Mill State Historic Site. Woolen factory and gristmill built and equipped in 1860; contains original machinery. Original owner's house, summer kitchen, ice house, smokehouse, fruit dryhouse, family cemetery, church, and school. Guided tours. (Daily; closed hols) Recreation area adjoining site has swimming, fishing; bicycle and hiking trail, camping (dump station). Standard fees. (Daily) 6½ mi N on US 69, then 1½ mi W on County MM. Phone 816/296-3357. ¢

B&B/Small Inn

★★★ **THE INN ON CRESCENT LAKE.** *1261 St. Louis Ave (64024). 816/630-6745; fax 816/630-9326.*

www.crescentlake.com. 8 rms, 1 with shower only, 2 suites. No elvtr. S $95-$135; D $150; suites $95-$155. Children over 16 yrs only. TV; cable. Complimentary full bkfst. Restaurant 7-9 pm. Ck-out 11 am, ck-in 3-6 pm. Business servs avail. Exercise equipt. Massage. Pool. Some in-rm whirlpools. Picnic tables. On lake. Built in 1915; antiques. Totally nonsmoking. Cr cds: MC, V.
D ⚓ ≈ 🛪 ⊠ 🔥

Fulton

See also Columbia, Jefferson City

Pop 10,033 **Elev** 770 ft **Area code** 573 **Zip** 65251
Information Kingdom of Callaway Chamber of Commerce, 409 Court St; 573/642-3055 or 800/257-3554
Web www.vax2.rainis.net/~cocomerce

Named in honor of Robert Fulton, inventor of the steamboat, this town was home to both architect General M. F. Bell, who designed many of Fulton's historic buildings, and Henry Bellaman, author of the best-selling novel *King's Row,* which depicted life in Fulton at the turn of the century. The town is home to Westminster College (1851), William Woods University (1870), and the Missouri School for the Deaf. A Ranger District office of the Mark Twain National Forest is located here.

What to See and Do

Kingdom Expo and Car Museum. Collection of 75 rare automobiles, classic fire trucks, model trains, and restored tractors. Rotating exhibits incl arrowheads, over 300 china doll heads, Kennedy family memorabilia, and ladies' hats. Exhibition hall. Gift shop. (Daily; closed Jan 1, Thanksgiving, Dec 25) 1920 N Bluff St (Business 54 N). Phone 573/642-2080. ¢¢

Little Dixie Lake Conservation Area. More than 600 acres with 205-acre lake; fishing (permit required), boating (ramp, 10 hp limit), rowboat rentals (Apr-Oct); hiking, picnicking. (Daily) 10 mi NW via County F or I-

70, in Millersburg. Phone 573/592-4080. **FREE**

Westminster College. (1851) 750 students. Winston Churchill delivered his "Iron Curtain" address here on Mar 5, 1946. 7th St and Westminster Ave. Phone 573/642-3361. On campus is

Winston Churchill Memorial and Library. To memorialize Churchill's "Iron Curtain" speech, the bombed ruins of Sir Christopher Wren's 17th-century Church of St. Mary, Aldermanbury, were dismantled, shipped from London to Westminster College, reassembled, and finally restored. The church was rehallowed in 1969 with Lord Mountbatten of Burma and Churchill's daughter, Lady Mary Soames, in attendance. The undercroft of the church houses a museum, gallery, and research library with letters, manuscripts, published works, photos, memorabilia; five original Churchill oil paintings; philatelic collections; antique maps; clerical vestments; slide show. (Daily; closed Jan 1, Thanksgiving, Dec 25) Phone 573/592-1369. ¢¢ Adj to the memorial is

Breakthrough. This 32-ft sculpture by Churchill's granddaughter was created to memorialize the Berlin Wall. The piece uses eight concrete sections of the actual wall; two human silhouettes cut through the concrete represent "freedom passing through."

Special Event

Kingdom Days. Three-day festival celebrating the Civil War incident that residents claim made the county a sovereign entity; entertainment, concessions, events. Last full wkend June.

George Washington Carver National Monument

See also Joplin

(2 mi W of Diamond on County V, then ½ mi S)

Born a slave on the farm of Moses Carver, George Washington Carver (1864?-1943) rose to become an eminent teacher, humanitarian, botanist, agronomist, and pioneer conservationist. Carver was the first African American to graduate from Iowa State University. He received both a bachelor's and a master's degree in science. He then headed the Department of Agriculture at Booker T. Washington's Tuskegee Institute in Alabama.

Authorized as a national monument in 1943, this memorial to Carver perpetuates a vital part of the American historical heritage. The visitor center contains a museum and audiovisual presentation depicting Carver's life and work. A ¾-mile, self-guided trail passes the birthplace site, the statue of Carver by Robert Amendola, the restored 1881 Moses Carver house, the family cemetery, and the woods and streams where Carver spent his boyhood. Children's Discovery Center. (Daily; closed January 1, Thanksgiving, December 25). Contact Superintendent, 5646 Carver Rd, Diamond 64840-8314; 417/325-4151.

Hannibal

(B-5) *See also Monroe City*

Settled 1818 **Pop** 18,004 **Elev** 491 ft **Area code** 573 **Zip** 63401

Information Visitors & Convention Bureau, 505 N 3rd; 573/221-2477

Web www.hanmo.com/twainweb/

Hannibal is world-famous as the home town of the great novelist Samuel Clemens (Mark Twain) as well as the setting of *The Adventures of Tom Sawyer,* which records many actual events of Clemens's boyhood. Here he served his printer's apprenticeship and gained a fascination for "steamboating" in the days when the river was the source of the town's prosperity.

What to See and Do

Adventures of Tom Sawyer Diorama Museum. *The Adventures of Tom Sawyer* in 3-D miniature scenes carved by Art Sieving. (Daily; closed hols) 323 N Main St. Phone 573/221-3525. ¢

Becky Thatcher House. House where Laura Hawkins (Becky Thatcher) lived during Samuel Clemens's boyhood; upstairs rms have authentic furnishings. (Daily; closed Jan 1, Thanksgiving, Dec 25) 209-211 Hill St. Phone 573/221-0822. **FREE**

Hannibal Trolley. Narrated tour aboard trolley. Open-air summer months, enclosed rest of season. (Mid-Apr-Oct, daily; rest of yr, by appt) 301 N Main St. Phone 573/221-1161. ¢¢

Haunted House on Hill Street. Life-size wax figures of Mark Twain, his family, and his famous characters; gift shop. (Mar-Nov, daily) 215 Hill St. Phone 573/221-2220. ¢¢

Mark Twain Cave. This is the cave in *The Adventures of Tom Sawyer* in which Tom and Becky Thatcher were lost and where Injun Joe died; 52°F temperature. One-hr guided tours (Daily; closed Thanksgiving, Dec 25). Lantern tours to nearby Cameron Cave (Memorial Day-Labor Day, daily. Campground adj. 1 mi S, off MO 79. Phone 573/221-1656. ¢¢

⭐ **Mark Twain Museum and Boyhood Home.** Museum houses Mark Twain memorabilia, incl books, letters, photographs, and family items. Two-story white frame house in which the Clemens family lived in the 1840s and 1850s, restored and furnished with period pieces and relics. Gift shop. (Daily; closed Jan 1, Thanksgiving, Dec 25) 208 Hill St. Phone 573/221-9010. Admission incl

John M. Clemens Law Office. Restored courtrm and law office where Twain's father presided as justice of the peace. Hill St.

Museum Annex. Audiovisual presentations on Mark Twain and Hannibal; displays. 415 N Main. Phone 573/221-9603.

Pilaster House and Grant's Drugstore. (1846-1847) The Clemens family lived in this Greek Revival house, which contains a restored old-time drugstore, pioneer kitchen, doctor's office, and living quarters where John Clemens, Twain's father, died. Hill and Main sts.

Mark Twain Museum and Boyhood Home, Hannibal

Mark Twain Riverboat Excursions. One-hr cruises on the Mississippi River; also two-hr dinner cruises. (Early May-Oct, daily) Departs from foot of Center St. Phone 573/221-3222.

Molly Brown Birthplace and Museum. Antique-filled home has memorabilia of the "unsinkable" Molly Brown, who survived the Titanic disaster. (Apr-May, Sept-Oct, wkends; Jun-Aug, daily) 600 Butler St. Phone 573/221-2100. ¢¢

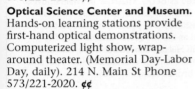

Tom and Huck Statue, Hannibal

Optical Science Center and Museum. Hands-on learning stations provide first-hand optical demonstrations. Computerized light show, wrap-around theater. (Memorial Day-Labor Day, daily). 214 N. Main St Phone 573/221-2020. ¢¢

Riverview Park. This 400-acre park on bluffs overlooking the Mississippi River contains a statue of Samuel Clemens at Inspiration Point. Nature trails. Picnicking; playground. (Mon-Fri) Phone 573/221-0154. **FREE**

Rockcliffe Mansion. Restored Beaux Arts mansion overlooking river; 30 rms, many original furnishings. Samuel Clemens addressed a gathering here in 1902. Guided tours. (Daily; closed Jan 1, Thanksgiving, Dec 25) 1000 Bird St. Phone 573/221-4140. ¢¢

Tom and Huck Statue. Life-size bronze figures of Huck Finn and Tom Sawyer by F.C. Hibbard. Main and North Sts, at the foot of the hill that was their playground.

Twainland Express. Narrated tours past points of interest in historic Hannibal, some aboard open-air, train-style trams. (Apr-Oct, daily) 400 N 3rd St. Phone 573/221-5593. ¢¢¢

Special Events

Molly Brown Dinner Theater. 200 N Main St. Professional musicals, including *Twain and Company* and Christmas hol show. Res required for dinner show. Phone 573/221-8940. Apr-Dec.

Mississippi River Art Fair. Phone 573/221-6545. Memorial Day wkend.

Mark Twain Outdoor Theater. 4 mi S on US 61 at Clemens Landing. Performances based on the books of Mark Twain. Stage setting is a reconstruction of mid-1800s Hill St, where Twain lived. Phone 573/985-3581. June-Aug.

Tom Sawyer Days. National fence-painting contest, frog jumping, entertainment. Phone 573/221-2477. Four days early July.

Autumn Historic Folklife Festival. Mid-1800s crafts, food, entertainment. Phone 573/221-6545. Third wkend Oct.

Motels/Motor Lodges

★★ **BEST WESTERN HOTEL CLEMENS.** *401 N 3rd St (63401). 573/248-1150; fax 573/248-1155; toll-free 800/528-1234. www.bestwestern. com.* 78 rms, 3 story. Mid-May-mid-Sept: S $55-$75; D $68-$95; each addl $6; higher rates: Memorial Day, July 4, Labor Day; lower rates rest of yr. Crib $5. Pet accepted. TV; cable (premium), VCR avail. Indoor pool; whirlpool. Complimentary continental bkfst. Restaurant opp 6 am-10 pm. Ck-out 11 am. Coin lndry. Meeting rms. Business servs avail. Free airport, bus depot transportation. Game rm. In historic district near the Mississippi River. Cr cds: A, C, D, DS, ER, JCB, MC, V.

D 🐾 ≈ ≥ 🐾 SC

★★★ **HANNIBAL INN AND CONFERENCE CENTER.** *4141 Market St (63401). 573/221-6610; fax 573/221-*

MARK TWAIN'S HANNIBAL

Start a tour of Hannibal, an old Mississippi riverboat town and hometown to Samuel Longhorn Clemens—better known as Mark Twain—at the Hannibal Convention and Visitors Bureau (505 North 3rd). Towering above the visitor center is the Mark Twain Lighthouse, located at the crest of Cardiff Hill. It's a hefty climb up to the lighthouse, the largest inland lighthouse in the United States, but the views of Hannibal and the Mississippi are worth it.

A block south of the Visitors Bureau is the Mark Twain Boyhood Home and Museum (208 Hill Street), which features the original 1843 Clemens home, restored to look as it did when Twain lived here in the 1840s. Directly across the street at 215 Hill Street is the Haunted House on Hill Street Wax Museum, which contains 27 lifelike, hand-carved wax figures of Twain, his family, and many characters from his books, plus several "haunted" rooms with ghostly inhabitants. Next door at 211 Hill Street is the period home of Laura Hawkins, Mark Twain's youthful sweetheart, who is represented as Becky Thatcher in Twain's novels. On the corner of Hill and Main streets is the Clemens Law office, where Twain's father, J. M. Clemens, presided as Hannibal's justice of the peace. Attached to the building is a historic courtroom, which served as the model for scenes from *The Adventures of Tom Sawyer*. At the base of Cardiff Hill at Main Street is the Tom and Huck Statue, which commemorates Twain's most famous characters, Huck Finn and Tom Sawyer. Frederick Hibbard sculpted this bronze statue in 1926.

Stretching along Main Street are a number of historic buildings and interesting shops. Follow Main Street south, passing shops and boutiques in historic storefronts. A worthy stop is Mrs. Clemens Antique Mall (305 North Main), which features two floors of antiques and an ice-cream parlor. At Bird and Main streets stands the handsome Pilaster House/Grant's Drug Store, dating from the 1830s. The Clemens family lived here briefly in the 1940s, and Judge Clemens died here in 1847. Today, the building is preserved as an 1890s apothecary. An interesting anomaly amidst all this Twain-ania is the Optical Center and Museum (214 North Main), a science center that details how contact lenses and eyeglasses, as well as other optical equipment, are made.

At Main and Center streets is the New Mark Twain Museum and Gift Shop, a newly restored structure that contains a collection of original Norman Rockwell paintings that were used for illustrated editions of *The Adventures of Huckleberry Finn*. The museum also serves as a memento of Hannibal's riverboat past. Speaking of riverboats, conclude your visit to Hannibal with a riverboat cruise. At the base of Center Street is Mississippi Riverboat Cruises, which features a one-hour excursion tour on the river, with great views of this historic river town.

3840; res 800/325-0777. 241 rms, 2 story. Memorial Day-Labor Day: S $65-$85; D $75-$85; each addl $8; under 19 free; lower rates rest of yr. Crib free. Pet accepted. TV; cable (premium). Indoor pool; whirlpool, poolside serv. Sauna. Complimentary continental bkfst. Restaurant 6 am-10 pm. Rm serv 7 am-2 pm, 5-9 pm. Bar 4 pm-1 am. Ck-out 11 am. Coin lndry. Meeting rms. Business servs avail. In-rm modem link. Bellhops. Gift shop. Beauty shop. Cr cds: A, C, D, DS, JCB, MC, V.

★ **SUPER 8 MOTEL.** *120 Huckleberry Heights Dr (63401). 572/221-5863; fax 573/221-5478; toll-free 800/800-8000. www.super8.com.* 59 rms, 3 story. No elvtr. Late May-early Sept: S $50.88-$55.88; D $58.88-$72.88; each addl $5; suites $98.88-$110.88; higher rates special events; lower rates rest of yr. Crib $5. TV; cable. Pool. Complimentary continental bkfst. Ck-out 11 am. Meeting rm. Business servs avail. City park adj. Cr cds: A, MC, V.

B&Bs/Small Inns

★★ **5TH STREET MANSION BED AND BREAKFAST.** *213 S 5th St (63401). 573/221-0445; fax 573/221-3335; toll-free 800/874-5661.* 7 rms, 3 story. Rm phones avail. S, D $65-$99; each addl $15. Complimentary full bkfst. Restaurant nearby. Ck-out 11 am, ck-in 4 pm. Italianate house (1858) where Samuel Clemens dined in 1902. Original Tiffany stained-glass windows, light fixtures, fireplaces; walnut-paneled library; antiques. In historic district near river. Cr cds: A, DS, MC, V.

★★★ **GARTH WOODSIDE MANSION B&B.** *11069 New London Rd (63401). 573/221-2789; toll-free 888/427-4809. garthmansion.com.* 8 rms, 3 story. No rm phones. S, D $83-$150; each addl $20. Complimentary full bkfst. Restaurant nearby. Ck-out 11 am, ck-in 4 pm. Some balconies. Second-empire/Victorian mansion (1871) where Mark Twain was often a guest. On 39 acres with pond, woods. Many antiques original to house; 3-story "flying" staircase. Totally nonsmoking. Cr cds: MC, V.

Restaurant

★ **LOGUE'S.** *121 Huckleberry Heights Dr (63401). 573/248-1854.* Hrs: 6 am-9 pm. Closed Jan 1, Thanksgiving, Dec 25. Bkfst $1.50-$4.95, lunch $2-$5, dinner $3.50-$6.50. Children's menu. Specializes in fried chicken, homemade tenderloin.

Harrisonville

(D-2) *See also Independence, Kansas City*

Pop 7,683 **Elev** 904 ft **Area code** 816 **Zip** 64701
Information Chamber of Commerce, 400 E Mechanic; 816/380-5271
Web www.harrisonville.com

Harrisonville, the retail and government center of Cass County, was named for Albert Harrison, a Missouri congressman.

Special Event

Log Cabin Festival. Phone 816/887-2393. First wkend Oct.

Motel/Motor Lodge

★★ **BEST WESTERN INN.** *2201 N Rockhaven Rd (64701). 816/884-3200; fax 816/884-3200; toll-free 800/528-1234. www.bestwestern.com.* 45 rms. S $40-$70; D $47-$75; each addl $5; under 12 free. Crib $4. TV; cable (premium). Pool. Playground. Complimentary coffee in lobby. Ck-out 11 am. In-rm modem link. Some refrigerators. Cr cds: A, C, D, DS, ER, JCB, MC, V.

Hermann

(D-5) *See also Columbia*

Founded 1836 **Pop** 2,754 **Elev** 519 ft **Area code** 573 **Zip** 65041
Information Visitor Information Center, German School Building, PO Box 104; 573/486-2744 or 800/932-8687
Web www.hermanmo.com

German immigrants unhappy with the English atmosphere of Philadelphia bought this land and founded the town with the purpose of maintaining their German culture. Grape cultivation and winemaking started early and was a thriving business until Prohibition. Today winemaking has been revived in the area, and German culture is still in evidence.

What to See and Do

Deutsche Schule Arts and Crafts. Exhibits from more than 100 craftspeople, incl handmade quilting, china painting, basketmaking, toll painting, woodcutting. Demonstrations by crafters during festival wkends. (Daily; closed Easter, Thanksgiving; also Dec 25-mid-Jan) German School Building, 4th and Schiller sts. Phone 573/486-3313. **FREE**

Deutschheim State Historic Site.
Dedicated to Missouri's German immigrants and German-American folk art and material culture, 1830-1920. Incl authentically furnished Pommer-Gentner House (1840) on Market St and Strehly House and Winery (ca 1840-67) on W 2nd St. Kitchen, herb, and flower gardens; special events. Tours. (Daily; closed hols) 109 W 2nd St. Phone 573/486-2200. ¢

Graham Cave State Park. Native Americans occupied this cave approx 10,000 yrs ago. About 350 acres with fishing; nature trails, playground, improved camping (dump station). Visitor center. (Daily) Standard fees. 13 mi N on MO 19, then 5 mi W, off I-70. Phone 573/564-3476. **FREE**

Historic Hermann Museum. Heritage Museum in 1871 building, with artifacts of early settlers; River Room depicts history of early river men; children's museum has toys, furniture of 1890s; handmade German bedrm set; 1886 pump organ. Mechanism of town clock may be seen. (Apr-Oct, daily) German School Building, 4th and Schiller sts. Phone 573/486-2017. ¢

White House. (Late 1860s) Restored hotel; tours; doll collection, mineral collection. (Apr-mid-Nov, schedule varies) 232 Wharf St. Phone 573/486-3200. ¢

Wineries.

Hermannhof Winery. This 150-yr-old winery incl ten wine cellars. Sausage making; cheeses. Sampling. (Daily) 330 E 1st St. Phone 573/486-5959. ¢

Stone Hill Winery. Guided tour of wine cellars; wine tasting. Restaurant. Gift shop. (See SPECIAL EVENTS) (Daily) 1110 Stone Hill Hwy. Phone 573/486-2120. ¢

Special Events

Maifest. Dancing, parades; crafts; house tour. Third full wkend May.

Great Stone Hill Grape Stomp. Stone Hill Winery. Phone 800/909-9463. Second Sat Aug.

Octoberfest. Area wineries. Wine cellar tours; wine samples; craft demonstrations; German music, food. First four wkends Oct.

KristKindl Markt. Stone Hill Winery. Traditional German Christmas market; music, food. Phone 800/909-9463. First wkend Dec.

Motels/Motor Lodges

★ **HERMANN.** *112 E 10th St (65041). 573/486-3131; fax 573/486-5244.* 24 rms. S $39.58-$43.86; D $54.56-$64.18; each addl $2. Crib $5. TV; cable (premium). Coffee in rms. Restaurant opp 6 am-8 pm. Ck-out 11 am. Cr cds: A, DS, MC, V.
🐾 ⬛ 🦽

★ **LEWIS AND CLARK INN.** *6054 MO 100, Washington (63090). 314/239-0111; fax 314/239-3657. www.justabouttown.com.* 50 rms, 2 story. S $46; D $50.50; each addl $4.50; under 12 free; higher rates special events. Crib $2.50. TV; cable. Complimentary continental bkfst. Restaurant nearby. Ck-out 11 am. Business servs avail. Cr cds: A, C, D, DS, MC, V.
D ⬛ 🦽 SC

B&Bs/Small Inns

★ **AUGUSTA LINDENHOF BED & BREAKFAST.** *5596 Walnut St, Augusta (63332). 636/228-4617. www.lindenhof-augusta.com.* 4 rms, 2 story. S $85-$175; D $120. TV. Complimentary full bkfst. Restaurant nearby. Ck-out 11 am, ck-in 4-6 pm. Street parking. Free railroad station transportation. Whirlpool. Built in 1857; Colonial Victorian style. Totally nonsmoking. Cr cds: A, DS, MC, V.
⬛ 🦽

★ **ESTHER'S AUSBLICK BED & BREAKFAST.** *236 W 2nd St (65041). 573/486-2170.* 4 rms, 2 story. No rm phones. S $65-$70; D $80-$85; each addl $15. Complimentary full bkfst. Restaurant nearby. Ck-out noon, ck-in 2 pm. Business servs avail. Free railroad station transportation. Whirlpool. Built in 1939; view of Missouri River. Totally nonsmoking. Cr cds: A, MC, V.
🐾 ⬛ 🦽

★ **SCHWEGMANN HOUSE BED & BREAKFAST.** *438 W Front St, Washington (63090). 636/239-5025; fax 636/239-3920; res 800/949-2262. schwegmannhouse.com.* 9 rms, 3 story. S $85; D $95; each addl $15; suites $120-$150; higher rates: Feb 14, Dec 31. Adults only Fri, Sat. Complimentary full bkfst. Restaurant adj 11 am-11 pm. Ck-out noon, ck-in 4-6 pm. Business servs avail. Built in 1861; antiques. Overlooks Missouri River. Totally nonsmoking. Cr cds: A, MC, V.

★ **WINDHOMME HILL.** *301 Schomberg Rd, Marthasville (63357). 636/932-4234; fax 314/932-4809; res 800/633-0582.* 4 rms, 2 share bath, some with shower only. Mid-May-mid-Sept, MAP: S, D $135-$275; EP avail; lower rates rest of yr. Adults only. TV. Complimentary full bkfst. Restaurant nearby. Ck-out 11:30 am, ck-in 4 pm. Business servs avail. In-rm modem link. Free railroad station transportation. Bicycles. Whirlpool. Lawn games. Built in 1915; country decor. Guests can help harvest crops for dinner. Totally nonsmoking. Cr cds: A, MC, V.

Restaurants

★ **CHAR-TONY'S.** *116 W Front St, Washington (63090). 636/239-2111.* Hrs: 11 am-9 pm; Fri to 10 pm; Sat 4-10 pm; Sun noon-8 pm. Closed Mon; hols. Res accepted. Italian menu. Bar. Lunch $4.95-$6.95, dinner $5.95-$15.95. Children's menu. Specializes in pasta, steak, veal. Outdoor dining. On riverfront; European decor. Cr cds: A, DS, MC, V.

★★ **VINTAGE.** *1110 Stone Hill Hwy (65041). 573/486-3479. www.stonehill winery.com.* Hrs: 11 am-8:30 pm; Fri to 9 pm; Sat to 10 pm. Closed 1st wk of Jan, Thanksgiving, Dec 25. Res accepted; required Sat. Continental menu. Wine. Lunch $4.95-$9.95, dinner $9.95-$17.95. Children's menu. Specializes in European cuisine, fresh seafood, steak. In former stable and carriage house of working winery. Cr cds: A, D, DS, MC, V.

Independence

(C-2) *See also Blue Springs, Kansas City*

Founded 1827 **Pop** 112,301 **Elev** 900 ft **Area code** 816

Information Tourism Division, 111 E Maple, 64050; 816/325-7111 or 800/748-7323
Web www.ci.independence.mo.us

Independence was an outfitting point for westbound wagon trains from 1830-1850. The scene of much of the "Mormon Wars" of the early 1830s, it was ravaged by raiders and occupied by Union and Confederate troops during the Civil War. Today it is best known as the home town of President Harry S. Truman.

What to See and Do

Bingham-Waggoner Estate. Famous Missouri artist George Caleb Bingham lived here from 1864-1870; also the homestead of the Waggoner family, millers of "Queen of the Pantry" flour. (Apr-Oct, daily) 313 W Pacific. Phone 816/461-3491. ¢¢

1859 Marshall's Home and Jail Museum. Restored building contains dungeonlike cells, marshall's living quarters, regional history museum. One-rm schoolhouse (1870). (Apr-Oct, daily; Nov, Dec, Mar, Tues-Sun; closed Jan-Feb) 217 N Main St. Phone 816/252-1892. ¢¢

Fort Osage. Restoration of one of the first US outposts in the Louisiana Territory following the purchase from France. Built in 1808 by William Clark of the Lewis and Clark expedition, fort incl officers' quarters, soldiers' barracks, trading post, factor's house, museum; costumed guides. Visitor center contains dioramas, exhibits, gift shop. Special events; candlelight tours (fee). (Mid-Apr-mid-Nov, Wed-Sun; rest of yr, Sat and Sun; closed Jan 1, Thanksgiving, Dec 25) 10 mi E of MO 291 on US 24 to Buckner, then 3 mi N to Sibley, then 1 mi N following signs. Phone 816/795-8200. ¢¢

Harry S. Truman Courtroom and Office Museum. Restored office and courtrm where Truman began his political career as presiding county judge; 30-min audiovisual show on Truman's boyhood and early career. Tours. (Mon-Thurs, Sun by appt) Jackson County Courthouse, 112 W Lexington. Phone 816/795-8200. ¢¢

Harry S. Truman Library and Museum. Incl presidential papers; mementos of public life; reproduction of President Truman's White House office; Thomas Hart Benton mural. Graves of President and Mrs. Truman in courtyard. Museum (Daily; closed Jan 1, Thanksgiving, Dec 25). Library (Mon-Fri). US 24 and Delaware St. Phone 816/833-1225. ¢¢

⭐ **Harry S. Truman National Historic Site (Truman House).** Truman's residence from the time of his marriage to Bess Wallace in 1919 until his death in 1972; an excellent example of late 19th-century Victorian architecture, the house, built by Bess Truman's grandfather, was the birthplace of Margaret Truman and served as the summer White House from 1945-1953. Guided tours. Ticket Center at Truman Rd and Main St. (Memorial Day- Labor Day, daily; rest of yr, Tues-Sun; closed Jan 1, Thanksgiving, Dec 25) 219 N Delaware St. Phone 816/254-9929. 219 N Delaware St.

National Frontier Trails Center. Partially restored flour mill at site of Santa Fe, California, and Oregon trails serves as museum, interpretive center, library, and archive of westward pioneer expansion; film (17 min), exhibits. (Daily; closed Jan 1, Thanksgiving, Dec 25). 318 W Pacific, at Osage St. Phone 816/325-7575. ¢¢

Pioneer Spring Cabin. Cabin furnished with items typical of those brought westward by the pioneers; spring was meeting place of Native Americans and settlers. (Apr-Oct, Mon-Fri) Truman and Noland rds. Phone 816/325-7111. **FREE**

Truman Farm Home. Truman lived in this two-story, white frame house in the decade preceding WWI; during these yrs—"the best years," according to Truman—he farmed the surrounding 600 acres, worked as a mason and postmaster, served as a soldier, and courted Bess Wallace. Interior features period furnishings, incl original family pieces; outbuildings incl garage, outhouse, chicken coop, and smokehouse. (Mid-May-late Aug; Fri-Sun) 19 mi S via I-435 to US 71, S on US 71 to 12301 Blue Ridge Blvd in Grandview. Phone 816/254-2720. **FREE**

Vaile Mansion. (1881) House designed for local entrepreneur Colonel Harvey Vaile has 30 rms and is an example of Second Empire architecture; ceiling murals. (Apr-Oct, daily) 1500 N Liberty. Phone 816/325-7111. ¢¢

World Headquarters Complex, Reorganized Church of Jesus Christ of Latter Day Saints. Auditorium, museum, and art gallery; 6,300-pipe organ; recitals (June-Aug, daily; rest of yr, Sun only). Japanese meditation garden. Guided tours (Daily; closed Jan 1, Thanksgiving, Dec 25). River and Walnut sts. Phone 816/833-1000.

Special Events

Truman Celebration. Tribute to President Truman. Early May.

Santa-Cali-Gon. Celebration commemorating the Santa Fe, California, and Oregon trails; melodrama, contests, arts and crafts, square dancing. Phone 816/252-4745. Labor Day wkend.

Motels/Motor Lodges

★ **COMFORT INN.** *4200 S Noland Rd (64055). 816/373-8856; fax 816/373-3312; toll-free 800/228-5150. www.comfortinn.com.* 171 rms, 2 story. S $59-$89; D $69-$89; suites $89; under 18 free. Crib free. Pet accepted. TV; cable (premium). 2 pools, 1 indoor; whirlpool. Coffee in rms. Restaurant adj open 24 hrs. Ck-out noon. Meeting rms. Business servs avail. In-rm modem link. Valet serv. Saunas. Refrigerators. Private patios, balconies. Cr cds: A, MC, V.

🄳 ⭐ ➰ ⊠ 🐾 SC

★ **RED ROOF INN.** *13712 E 42nd Terr (64055). 816/373-2800; fax 816/373-0067; toll-free 800/843-7663. www.redroof.com.* 108 rms, 2 story. S, D $40-$65; each addl $8; under 18 free. Crib free. Pet accepted. TV; cable. Complimentary coffee. Restaurant nearby. Ck-out noon. Business servs avail. Health club privileges. Cr cds: A, C, D, DS, MC, V.

🄳 🐾 ⊠ 🔥

B&B/Small Inn

★ ★ **WOODSTOCK INN BED & BREAKFAST.** *1212 W Lexington Ave (64050). 816/833-2233; fax 816/461-7226; res 800/276-5202. www.independence-missouri.com.* 11 rms, 2 story. S $85; D $100; each addl $8; suites $85. Crib $3. TV in some rms, lobby; cable. Complimentary full bkfst. Restaurant nearby. Ck-out 11 am, ck-in 4 pm. Airport, bus depot transportation. In historic area of town near Truman house and library. Totally nonsmoking. Cr cds: A, DS, MC, V.

D ⤢ ⬚

Restaurants

★ **GAROZZO'S DUE.** *12801 US 40 E (64055). 816/737-2400. www.garozzos. com.* Hrs: 11 am-10 pm; Fri to 11 pm; Sat noon-11 pm; Sun 3-9 pm. Closed hols. Italian menu. Bar. Lunch $6.95-$14, dinner $7.95-$22. Children's menu. Specialties: vitello Marion, bistecca Modiga, chicken spiedini. Outdoor dining. Cr cds: A, D, DS, MC, V.

D ⤢

★★ **RHEINLAND.** *208 N Main St (64050). 816/461-5383.* Hrs: 11 am-9 pm; Sun noon-8 pm. Closed Mon; hols. Res accepted. German menu. Wine, beer. Lunch $4.25-$7.95, dinner $9.95-$14.95. Children's menu. Specialties: strammer max, jaegerschnitzel. Entertainment wkends. Bavarian decor. Cr cds: A, D, MC, V.

D ⤢

★ **TIPPINS.** *2931 S Noland Rd (64055). 816/252-8890.* Hrs: 7 am-10 pm; Fri to 11 pm; Sat 8 am-11 pm; Sun 8 am-10 pm. Closed Dec 25. Bkfst $2.25-$6.25, lunch $4-$7, dinner $6-$10.95. Children's menu. Specializes in soups, salads, homemade pies. Cr cds: A, D, DS, MC, V.

D

★★ **V'S ITALIANO.** *10819 US 40 E (64055). 816/353-1241. www.vs restaurant.com.* Hrs: 11:30 am-10 pm; Fri, Sat to 11 pm; Sun 10 am-8 pm; Sun brunch 10 am-2 pm. Closed hols. Res accepted. Italian, American menu. Bar. Lunch $5-$9.50, dinner $8-$16.50. Children's menu. Specialties: lasagne, veal parmesan, rum cake. Family-owned. Cr cds: A, D, DS, MC, V.

D SC ⤢

Jefferson City

(D-4) *See also Columbia, Fulton*

Settled ca 1825 **Pop** 35,481 **Elev** 702 ft **Area code** 573

Information Jefferson City Convention & Visitors Bureau, 213 Adams St, PO Box 776, 65102; 573/634-3616 or 800/769-4183
Web www.jcchamber.org

Jefferson City was chosen for the state capital in 1826. Near a river landing, it consisted of a foundry, a shop, and a mission. Its growth was not steady, and as late as 1895 efforts were being made to move the seat of government. Since 1900, however, the city has prospered. The present capitol, completed in 1917, confirmed its status. Named for Thomas Jefferson, it is known locally as "Jeff City."

What to See and Do

Cole County Historical Society Museum. (ca 1870) One of three 4-story row houses built in the Federal style, the museum features Victorian furnishings and household items; inaugural gowns from Missouri's first ladies dating from 1877; research library. Guided tours (Tues-Sat). 109 Madison St. Phone 573/635-1850. ¢

Governor's Mansion. (1871) Renaissance Revival architecture by George Ingham Barnett; period furnishings, stenciled ceilings, period wall coverings, and late 19th-century chandeliers. Tours (Tues and Thurs; closed Aug and Dec). 100 Madison St. Phone 573/751-4141. **FREE**

Runge Conservation Nature Center. Hiking trails, aquarium, nature exhibits. (Daily; closed hols) 2901 W Truman Blvd. Phone 573/526-5544. **FREE**

State Capitol. (1918) On a bluff overlooking the Missouri River, this building of Carthage stone is the third state capitol in Jefferson City; both predecessors burned. A Thomas Hart Benton mural is in the House Lounge, third floor, west wing; also paintings by N. C. Wyeth and Frank Brangwyn. Tours (30 min). (Daily; closed hols) High St and Broadway. Phone 573/751-4127. **FREE** Also here is

> **Missouri State Museum.** Offers two permanent exhibits; History Hall, with several themes of Missouri history, and Resources Hall. (Daily; closed hols) Phone 573/751-4127. **FREE** Near here is

Jefferson Landing State Historic Site. Restored mid-1800s riverboat landing. Lohman Building (1839) features exhibits and audiovisual presentation on history of Jefferson City and Missouri Capitol. Union Hotel (1855) contains gallery of exhibits by local artists. (Daily; closed hols) 100 blk of Jefferson St. Phone 573/751-3475. **FREE**

Special Events

Cole County Fair. Fairgrounds. Rides, shows, arts and crafts. Last wk July.

Festival Weekend. Craft fair, jazzfest, parade, Shakespeare Festival. Second wkend Sept.

Motels/Motor Lodges

★★ **BEST WESTERN INN.** *1937 Christy Dr (65101). 573/635-4175; fax 573/635-6769; 800/528-1234. www. bestwestern.com.* 79 rms, 1-2 story. S $59; D $69; suites $89; under 18 free. Crib $2. TV; cable (premium). Indoor pool. Complimentary continental bkfst. Coffee in rms. Restaurant 6 am-2 pm, 4:30-9 pm; Sun 7 am-3 pm. Bar 3 pm-1 am; entertainment. Ck-out noon. Guest lndry. Meeting rms. Business servs avail. In-rm modem link. Valet serv. Exercise equipt. Sundries. Cr cds: A, MC, V.
D ⇌ 🏋 ⅀ 🖘 SC

★★ **HOTEL DEVILLE.** *319 W Miller St (65101). 573/636-5231; fax 573/636-5260; toll-free 800/392-3366. devillehotel.com.* 98 rms, 3 story. S $75; D $85; each addl $10; suites $81.90; under 17 free. Crib free. Pet accepted. TV; cable (premium), VCR avail (movies). Pool. Restaurant 6 am-10 pm. Bar 11-1 am, closed Sun. Ck-out noon. Meeting rms. Business servs avail. Valet serv. Health club privileges. Cr cds: A, C, D, DS, MC, V.
D 🕐 🛠 ✈ 🖘 🖘 ⇌

★ **RAMADA INN.** *1510 Jefferson St (65109). 573/635-7171; fax 573/635-8006; toll-free 800/392-0202. www. ramadajeffcity.com.* 234 rms, 2 story. S $64; D $69; each addl $5; suites $140; under 18 free. Crib free. Pet accepted. TV; cable (premium). Pool. Coffee in rms. Restaurant 6:30 am-2 pm, 5-10 pm; Sat, Sun from 7 am. Bar 5 pm-1:30 am, Sun noon-8 pm; entertainment Tues-Sat. Ck-out 11 am. Meeting rms. Business center. Sundries. Free railroad station, bus depot transportation. Airport transportation. Exercise equipt. Game rm. Refrigerator, microwave in suites. Cr cds: A, MC, V.
D 🕐 ⇌ 🏋 ⅀ 🖘 SC 🏋

Hotel

★★★ **CAPITOL PLAZA HOTEL.** *451 W McCarty St (65101). 573/635-1234; fax 573/635-4565; toll-free 800/338-8088.* 255 rms, 9 story, 40 suites. S $85-$95; D $105-$110; each addl $10; suites $105-$250; under 18 free; wkend rates. Crib free. TV; cable (premium). Indoor pool; poolside serv. Restaurant 6 am-10 pm. Bar 11-2 am, Sun to 10 pm; entertainment. Ck-out noon. Convention facilities. Business servs avail. In-rm modem link. Exercise equipt. Gift shop. Covered parking. Refrigerator, wet bar. Cr cds: A, MC, V.
D ⇌ 🏋 ⅀ 🖘 SC

Restaurants

★★ **MADISON'S CAFE.** *216 Madison St (65101). 573/634-2988.* Hrs: 11 am-10 pm; Fri to 11 pm; Sat noon-11 pm. Closed Sun; hols. Italian menu. Serv bar. Lunch $5-$15, dinner $10-$20. Children's menu. Specializes in salads, pasta, steak. Casual dining; Italian decor. Cr cds: A, D, DS, MC, V.
D ⅀

★ **VEIT'S DIAMOND.** *2001 Missouri Blvd (65109). 573/635-1213.* Hrs: 11 am-2:30 pm, 5-10 pm; Sat from 5 pm. Closed Sun; hols; 10 days early July. Bar. Lunch $3.95-$5.95, dinner $9.50-$20.50. Children's menu. Specializes in seafood, steak, barbecue ribs. Family-style dining. Family-owned since 1934. Cr cds: A, D, DS, MC, V.
D ⅀

Joplin

(F-2) *See also Carthage, Mount Vernon*

Settled 1838 **Pop** 40,961 **Elev** 972 ft
Area code 417

Information Convention & Visitors Bureau, 222 W 3rd St, 64802; 417/625-4789 or 800/657-2534
Web www.joplincvb.com

The discovery of lead here convinced an early settler to establish a town and name it after another settler, Reverend Harris G. Joplin. As the mining boom continued another community, Murphysburg, grew up on the west side of Joplin Creek. The two towns were rivals until 1873 when both agreed to incorporate into one city. Today Joplin, one of Missouri's larger cities, is home to many manufacturing industries.

What to See and Do

Missouri Southern State College. (1937) 6,000 students. This 332-acre campus incl Taylor Performing Arts Center, Mission Hills estate, and Spiva Art Center (phone 417/623-0183) with changing exhibits (Tues-Sun; closed hols; also early Aug). Tours. Newman and Duquesne rds. Phone 417/625-9300. **FREE**

Museum Complex. Schifferdecker Park. W edge of city on US 66. Here are

Dorothea B. Hoover Historical Museum. Period rms with late 19th-century furnishing; miniatures, incl a circus, photographs, musical instruments, Victorian doll house and playhouse; antique toys; dolls; Native American artifacts; cut glass. (Wed-Sun afternoons; closed hols, late Dec-early Jan) Under 12 only with adult. Phone 417/623-1180. **FREE**

Tri-State Mineral Museum. Models of lead- and zinc-mining equipt, mineral and history displays. (May-Sept, daily; rest of yr, Wed-Sun afternoons; closed hols) Phone 417/623-2341. **FREE**

Post Memorial Art Reference Library. Art research facility resembling 16th-century English hall. Furniture and artwork date to 13th century. (Mon-Sat; closed hols) 300 Main St. Phone 417/782-7678. **FREE**

Thomas Hart Benton Exhibit. Incl mural "Joplin at the Turn of the Century, 1896-1906," as well as photographs, clay models, personal letters, and other paintings by Benton. (Mon-Fri; closed hols) In Municipal Building, 303 E 3rd St. **FREE**

Motels/Motor Lodges

★★ **DRURY INN.** *3601 S Range Line Rd (64804). 417/781-8000.* 109 rms, 4 story. Memorial Day-Labor Day: S $58; D $64-$80; each addl $5; under 18 free; lower rates rest of yr. Crib free. Pet accepted, some restrictions. Coffee in rms. TV; cable (premium), VCR avail. Indoor pool; whirlpool. Complimentary continental bkfst. Restaurant adj 6 am-10 pm. Ck-out noon. Meeting rms. Business servs avail. In-rm modem link. Exercise equipt. Health club privileges. Some refrigerators. Cr cds: A, D, DS, MC, V.
🄳 🔧 ➦ 🛅 📓

★ **HALLMARK INN.** *3600 S Rangeline Rd (64804). 417/624-8400; fax 417/781-5625; toll-free 800/825-2378.* 96 rms, 2 story. S $43-$50; D $48-$54; each addl $6; suites $85; under 12 free. Pet accepted. TV; cable (premium). Pool. Complimentary continental bkfst. Restaurant nearby. Ck-out noon. Business servs avail. In-rm modem link. Coin lndry. Refrigerators avail. Cr cds: A, D, DS, MC, V.
🄳 🔧 ➦ 📓

★★ **HOLIDAY INN & CONVENTION CENTER.** *3615 S Range Line Rd (64804). 417/782-1000; fax 417/623-4093; toll-free 800/465-4329. www.holiday-inn.com.* 264 rms, 2-5 story. S, D $88; each addl $10; suites $89.50-$145; under 18 free. Crib free. Pet accepted, some restrictions. TV; cable (premium), VCR avail. 2 pools, 1 indoor; whirlpool. Restaurant 6 am-10 pm. Bar; entertainment. Ck-out noon. Meeting rms. Business servs avail. In-rm modem link. Bellhops. Valet serv. Free airport, bus depot transportation. Exercise equipt; sauna, steam rm. Game rm. Atrium. Cr cds: A, C, D, DS, JCB, MC, V.
🄳 🔧 ➦ 🛅 ✈ 📓

★ **RAMADA INN.** *3320 Range Line Rd (64804). 417/781-0500; fax 417/781-9388; toll-free 800/228-2828. www.ramada.com.* 171 rms, 2-3 story. S $58-$64; D $60-$80; each addl $8; suites $95-$130; under 18 free. Crib free. Pet accepted. TV; cable (premium). 2 pools, 1 indoor; whirlpool. Sauna. Playground. Restaurant 6:30

am-10 pm. Bar. Ck-out noon. Meeting rms. Business servs avail. In-rm modem link. Bellhops. Valet serv. Free airport transportation. Lighted tennis. Cr cds: A, C, D, DS, MC, V.

★ **WESTWOOD.** *1700 W 30th St (64804). 417/782-7212; fax 417/624-0265. www.westwoodmotel.com.* 33 rms, 2 story. S $36; D $40; each addl $4; kits. $44; under 12 free; wkly rates. Crib $5. Pet accepted; $25. TV; cable (premium). Pool. Complimentary coffee in lobby. Ck-out 11 am. Coin lndry. Health club privileges. Cr cds: A, DS, MC, V.

Restaurants

★ **KITCHEN PASS.** *1212 S Main St (64801). 417/624-9095.* Hrs: 11 am-10 pm; wkends to 11 pm. Closed Sun; hols. Res accepted. Bar to 1:30 am; entertainment Fri and Sat. Lunch $3.25-$5.75, dinner $7.75-$12.95. Children's menu. Specializes in seafood, steak, chicken. Cr cds: A, MC, V.

★ **WILDER'S.** *1216 Main St (64801). 417/623-7230.* Hrs: 11 am-2 pm, 4:30-10 pm. Closed Sun; hols. Res accepted. Bar. Lunch, dinner $5.75-$15.95. Specializes in steaks, seafood, pasta. Operating since 1929; nostalgic decor. Cr cds: A, DS, MC, V.

Kansas City (C-2)

Settled 1838 **Pop** 435,146 **Elev** 800 ft
Area code 816

Information Kansas City Convention & Visitors Bureau, 1100 Main St, Suite 2550, 64105; 816/221-5242 or 800/767-7700

Web www.visitkc.com

Suburbs In Missouri: Blue Springs, Excelsior Springs, Independence. In Kansas: Kansas City, Overland Park. (See individual alphabetical listings.)

Kansas City is the distributing point for a huge agricultural region. It is one of the country's leading grain and livestock markets and is famous for its steak and barbecue. The city is also a great industrial center, with food processing, milling, petroleum refining, and vehicle assembly high in importance. Kansas City, Kansas, across the Missouri River, is politically separate, but the two cities form an economic unit constituting the Greater Kansas City area.

Kansas City, Missouri, developed as a steamboat landing for the town of Westport, four miles south on the Santa Fe Trail, and a competitor with Independence as the trail's eastern terminus and outfitting point. The buildings that sprang up along this landing soon eclipsed Westport, which was eventually incorporated into the new city. Kansas City's roaring overland trade was disturbed by the border warfare of the 1850s and the Civil War, but peace and the railroads brought new growth and prosperity. A network of railway lines following the natural water-level routes that converge at the mouth of the Kansas River made Kansas City a great terminus.

Famous for their "booster" spirit, its citizens were aroused to the need for civic improvement in the 1890s by the crusade of William Rockhill Nelson, *Kansas City Star* publisher. As a result, today's Kansas City boasts 52 boulevards totaling 155 miles, and more fountains than any city except Rome.

Transportation

Car Rental Agencies. See IMPORTANT TOLL-FREE NUMBERS.

Public Transportation. Area Transit Authority, phone 816/221-0660.

Rail Passenger Service. Amtrak 800/872-7245.

Airport Information

Kansas City International Airport. Information 816/243-5237; lost and found 816/243-5215; cash machines, Terminals A, B, C.

What to See and Do

✪ *Arabia* **Steamboat Museum.** Excavated pioneer artifacts from steamboat *Arabia*, which went down in 1856. The boat, discovered in 1988,

Arabia Steamboat Museum

carried 200 tons of cargo. Replica of main deck; hands-on displays. (Mon-Sat and Sun afternoons; closed hols) 400 Grand Blvd. Phone 816/471-4030.

Art and Antique Center. More than 20 shops and galleries located in old historic area. 45th and State Line. Phone 913/362-2002.

Benjamin Ranch. Re-creation of early Western town; horseback and pony rides, sleigh rides, hayrides; chuck-wagon food, western equipt and live-stock. Picnic facilities. (Apr-Nov, daily) Fees vary by activity. (See SPECIAL EVENTS) On the Old Santa Fe Trail, I-435 and E 87th. Phone 816/761-5055.

Board of Trade. Stock index trading and world's largest hard winter wheat market. Visitors may observe trading from third floor. (Mon-Fri) 4800 Main St. Phone 816/753-7500. **FREE**

City Market. Outdoor market since early 1800s (daily). Indoor farmers market (Apr-Sept, Mon-Sat, also Sun afternoons). Main to Grand sts, 3rd to 5th sts. Phone 816/842-1271.

Country Club Plaza. The nation's first planned shopping center (1922) consists of 55 acres encompassing more than 180 shops and 25 restaurants in and around Spanish/Moorish-style arcaded buildings. The plaza features tree-lined walks, statues, fountains, and murals; re-creations of

Spain's Seville light and Giralda tower; horse-drawn carriage rides; free entertainment. Shops (Daily). 47th between Nichols Pkwy and Madison Ave, S of downtown. Phone 816/753-0100.

☆ **Crown Center.** This entertainment complex offers shopping, theaters, restaurants, and hotels around a landscaped central square; exhibits and ice-skating (mid-Nov-Mar). Shops (daily). 2501 McGee Phone 816/274-8444. In Crown Center are

    Coterie—Kansas City's Family Theatre. Nonprofit professional theater. (Early Feb-late Dec, Tues-Sun) 2450 Grand Ave. Phone 816/474-6552. ¢¢

    Hallmark Visitors Center. Exhibit areas focus on history of the greeting card industry. Incl are audiovisual and interactive displays; die-making and manufacturing demonstrations; film presentation. (Mon-Sat; closed hols) Phone 816/274-5672. **FREE**

    Kaleidoscope. Participatory creative art exhibit for children ages 5-12 only; Discovery Room features hands-on creative area; studio with specially designed art projects. (Mid-June-Aug, Mon-Sat; rest of yr, Sat or Mon-Fri with advance res) Adults may view activity through one-way mirrors. Three 90-min sessions per day; tickets avail half-hour before each session. 25th and McGee sts. Phone 816/274-8300. **FREE**

Government Buildings. Incl City Hall with observation roof on 30th floor (Mon-Fri; closed hols); federal, state and county buildings. 11th to 13th Sts, Holmes to McGee sts. **FREE**

Jesse James Bank Museum. (1858) Restored site of first daylight bank robbery by James gang (1866). Jesse James memorabilia; hand-scribed bank ledger books and other relics of early banking. (Mon-Sat; closed Jan 1, Thanksgiving, Dec 25) 15 mi N via I-35, in Liberty, on Old Town Sq. Phone 816/781-4458. ¢¢

John Wornall House Museum. (1858) Restored farmhouse interprets lives of prosperous Missouri farm families from 1830-1865; herb garden; gift shop. (Tues-Sat, also Sun afternoons; closed hols and Jan). 61st Terrace and Wornall. Phone 816/444-1858. ¢¢

Kansas City Art Institute. (ca 1885) 4415 Warwick Blvd. Phone 816/472-4852.

Kansas City Museum. Science, history, and technology exhibits housed in former estate of lumber millionaire Robert A. Long; Challenger Learning Center space flight simulator (fee); re-creation of 1821 trading post, 1860 storefront, and functioning 1910 drugstore; planetarium; gift shop. (Tues-Sat; closed hols) 3218 Gladstone Blvd. Phone 816/483-8300. ¢¢

Kansas City Zoological Gardens. Zoo incl 95-acre African exhibit, Deramus education pavilion, Australian walkabout, IMAX theatre; miniature train, pony and camel rides; interpretive programs. (Daily; closed Jan 1, Dec 25) Swope Park, Meyer Blvd and Swope Pkwy, just off I-435. Phone 816/871-5700. ¢¢¢

Kemper Museum of Contemporary Art and Design. (Tues-Sun; closed hols) 4420 Warwick Blvd. Phone 816/561-3737. **FREE**

Nelson-Atkins Museum of Art. Collections range from Sumerian art of 3000 B.C. to contemporary paintings and sculpture; period rms; decorative arts; Kansas City Sculpture Park featuring Henry Moore sculpture garden. Guided tours (free). (Tues-Sun; closed hols) Free admission Sat. 4525 Oak St, at 47th St. ¢¢

Oceans of Fun. This 60-acre family water park features wave pool, twisting water slides, boats, children's pools, and playgrounds. (Late May-Labor Day, daily) One- and two-day passports; also combination Worlds of Fun/Oceans of Fun passports. 10 mi NE via I-435 exit 54, between Parvin Rd and NE 48th St. Phone 816/454-4545. ¢¢¢¢

Professional sports.

    Kansas City Blades (IHL). Kemper Memorial Arena, 1800 Gennessee. Phone 816/842-1063.

    Kansas City Chiefs (NFL). Arrowhead Stadium, One Arrowhead Dr. Phone 816/920-9300.

    Kansas City Royals (MLB). Kauffman Stadium, One Royal Way.

    Kansas City Wizards (MLS). Arrowhead Stadium, One Arrowhead Dr. Phone 816/920-9300.

Sightseeing.

Kansas City Trolley. Trolley makes continuous circuit from downtown through Crown Center to Westport Square, Country Club Plaza and the River Market; 16 stops incl museums, hotels, restaurants. (Early Mar-late Dec, daily; closed Thanksgiving) Phone 816/221-3399. ¢¢

Thomas Hart Benton Home and Studio State Historic Site. (1903-1904) Eclectic-style residence of the artist from 1939 until his death in 1975; studio contains many of Benton's tools and equipt; changing exhibits. (Daily; closed hols) 3616 Belleview. Phone 816/931-5722. ¢

Toy and Miniature Museum of Kansas City. Miniatures, antique doll houses and furnishings from 1840s to mid-20th century. (Wed-Sat, also Sun afternoons; closed hols; also first two wks Sept) 5235 Oak St at 52nd St, on University of Missouri-Kansas City campus. Phone 816/333-2055. ¢¢

Union Cemetery. (1857) Some notables buried here incl artist George Caleb Bingham and Alexander Majors, founder of the Pony Express; graves of more than 1,000 Civil War soldiers. Self-guided walking tours. 227 E 28th St Terr. Phone 816/221-4373.

University of Missouri-Kansas City. (1933) 11,500 students. On campus is Toy and Miniature Museum of Kansas City, library with Americana and local historical exhibits, Marr Sound Archives, Jazz Film Archives, Geosciences Museum and Gallery of Art. Performances by Conservatory of Music and Academic Theater. 5100 Rockhill Rd. Phone 816/235-1000.

Westport. Renovated 1830s historic district incl specialty shops, galleries and restaurants; Pioneer Park traces Westport's role in founding of Kansas City. Shops (Daily). Broadway at Westport Rd. Phone 816/756-2789.

Worlds of Fun. A 170-acre entertainment complex with amusement rides, live entertainment, children's area, special events, restaurants; incl looping steel and wooden roller coasters and whitewater raft, spill water, log flume, and hydroflume rides. (Late May-late Aug, daily; Apr-late May and Sept-Oct, Sat and Sun) 10 mi NE via I-435 exit 54. Phone 816/454-4545. ¢¢¢¢

Special Events

St Patrick's Parade. Downtown. Mar 17.

Lyric Opera. 11th St and Central. Opera productions in English. Mon, Wed, Fri, and Sat. Phone 816/471-7344. Apr-May and mid-Sept-mid-Oct; holiday production in Dec.

Starlight Theater. Near 63rd and Swope Pkwy in Swope Park. Outdoor amphitheater featuring Broadway musicals and contemporary concerts. Performances nightly. Phone 816/363-STAR. Early June-Aug.

Kansas City Pro Rodeo. Benjamin Ranch. Phone 816/761-1234. Wk of July 4.

Kansas City Blues and Jazz Festival. Phone 816/753-3378. Third wkend July.

Ethnic Enrichment Festival. Many nationalities celebrate with music, dance, cuisine, and crafts. Phone 816/842-7530. Three days Aug.

Kansas City Symphony. 1020 Central. Concert series of symphonic and pop music. Fri-Sun, some Wed. Phone 816/471-0400. Sept-May.

Missouri Repertory Theatre. Center for the Performing Arts, 50th and Cherry sts. Professional equity theater company; classic and contemporary productions. Annual performance of *A Christmas Carol.* Tues-Sun. Phone 816/235-2700. Sept-May.

American Royal Barbecue. Kemper Arena Phone 816/221-9800. First wkend Oct.

American Royal Livestock, Horse Show and Rodeo. American Royal Center, 1701 American Royal Court. Phone 816/221-9800. 18 days early-mid-Nov.

Motels/Motor Lodges

★★ **BAYMONT INN & SUITES.** *2214 Taney St, North Kansas City (64116). 816/221-1200; fax 816/471-6207; toll-free 800/301-0200. www. baymontinns.com.* 94 rms, 3 story. S $47.95-$65.95; D $54.95-$74.95; each addl $7; under 18 free. Pet accepted, some restrictions. TV; cable (premium). Complimentary continental bkfst. Restaurant adj 7 am-midnight. Ck-out noon. Business servs avail. In-rm modem link. Sun-

dries. Microwaves avail. Cr cds: A, C, D, DS, MC, V.

[D] [🐾] [≍] [🔥] [SC]

★★ **BEST WESTERN COUNTRY INN.** *7100 NE Parvin Rd (64117). 816/453-3355. www.bestwestern.com.* 86 rms, 2 story. May-Sept: S $79.95-$109.95; D $89.95-$129.95; each addl $5; under 12 free; lower rates rest of yr. Crib free. TV; cable (premium). Pool. Complimentary continental bkfst. Restaurant nearby. Ck-out 11 am. Business servs avail. In-rm modem link. Cr cds: A, C, D, DS, MC, V.

[D] [🐾] [≍] [≍] [🔥]

★★ **DAYS INN.** *6101 E 87th St (64138). 816/765-4331; fax 816/765-7395. www.daysinn.com.* 250 rms, 3-4 story. S $64-$75; D $75-$88; each addl $6; suites $100-$175; studio rms $75; under 18 free; wkend rates. Crib free. TV; cable (premium), VCR avail. Heated pool. Restaurant 6:30 am-2 pm, 5-10 pm; Fri, Sat to 11 pm; Sun 7 am-2 pm, 5-10 pm. Rm serv 7 am-10 pm. Bar 1 pm-1 am, Sun to midnight. Ck-out noon. Convention facilities. Business servs avail. In-rm modem link. Bellhops. Health club privileges. Microwaves. Private patios, balconies. Cr cds: A, C, D, DS, MC, V.

[D] [≍] [≍] [🔥]

★★ **HOLIDAY INN.** *7333 NE Parvin Rd (64117). 816/455-1060; fax 816/455-0250; toll-free 800/465-4329. www. holiday-inn.com.* 167 rms, 3 story. June-Aug: S, D $105-$143; under 18 free; lower rates rest of yr. Crib free. TV; cable (premium). Indoor pool; whirlpool. Sauna. Restaurant 6:30-10 am, 6-10 pm. Bar 4 pm-midnight. Ck-out noon. Coin lndry. Meeting rms. Business servs avail. In-rm modem link. Bellhops. Valet serv. Sundries. Free airport transportation. Game rm. Near Worlds of Fun. Cr cds: A, C, D, DS, JCB, MC, V.

[D] [≍] [≍] [🔥] [SC]

★★ **HOLIDAY INN AIRPORT.** *11832 NW Plaza Cir (65615). 816/464-2345; fax 816/464-2543; toll-free 800/465-4329. www.holiday-inn.com.* 196 rms, 5 story. S, D $99; family, wkend and hol rates. Crib free. TV; cable (premium), VCR avail. Pool. Coffee in rms. Restaurant 6 am-11 pm. Bar 1:30 pm-1 am. Ck-out noon.

Coin lndry. Meeting rms. Business servs avail. In-rm modem link. Bellhops. Gift shop. Valet serv. Free airport transportation. Exercise equipt; sauna. Game rm. Lawn games. Some refrigerators. Cr cds: A, C, D, DS, ER, JCB, MC, V.

★★ HOLIDAY INN EXPRESS AIRPORT. 11130 NW Ambassador Dr (64153). 816/891-9111; fax 816/891-8811; res 800/465-4329. www.holiday-inn.com. 80 rms, 3 story. S, D $79-$150; each addl $10; suites $135-$165; family rates; package plans. Crib free. TV; cable (premium). Complimentary continental bkfst, coffee in rms. Restaurant nearby. Ck-out noon. Meeting rms. Business servs avail. In-rm modem link. Sundries. Free airport transportation. Exercise equipt. Indoor pool; whirlpool. Many refrigerators, microwaves; in-rm whirlpool in suites. Cr cds: A, D, DS, MC, V.

★★ HOLIDAY INN SPORTS COMPLEX. 4011 Blue Ridge Cutoff (64133). 816/353-5300; fax 816/353-1199; toll-free 800/465-4329. www.holiday-inn.com. 163 rms, 6 story. S, D $59-$149; each addl $8; under 18 free. Crib free. TV; cable (premium), VCR avail. Indoor pool; whirlpool. Restaurant 6 am-10 pm. Bar 4 pm-midnight. Ck-out noon. Coin lndry. Meeting rms. Business center. In-rm modem link. Bellhops. Valet serv. Gift shop. Sundries. Underground parking. Exercise equipt; sauna. Game rm. Microwaves avail. Overlooks Harry S. Truman Sports Complex. Cr cds: A, C, D, DS, MC, V.

★★ PLAZA HOTEL WESTPORT. 4309 Main St (64111). 816/561-9600; fax 816/561-4677. www.countryclub plazahotels.com. 77 rms, 4 story. S $79-$89; D $89-$99; each addl $5; under 18 free; higher rates: hols, Plaza Lights Festival. Crib free. TV; cable (premium), VCR avail. Complimentary continental bkfst. Coffee in rms. Restaurant nearby. Ck-out noon. Meeting rms. Business servs avail. In-rm modem link. Bellhops. Valet serv. Whirlpool. Health club privileges. Refrigerators. Cr cds: A, C, D, DS, MC, V.

★★ QUARTERAGE HOTEL. 560 Westport Rd (64111). 816/931-0001; fax 816/931-8891; toll-free 800/942-4233. www.quarteragehotel.com. 123 rms, 4 story. S, D $99; each addl $10; under 17 free; higher rates special events; wkend rates. Crib free. TV; cable (premium). Complimentary bkfst buffet. Coffee in rms. Restaurant adj 7 am-10 pm. Ck-out noon. Meeting rms. Business servs avail. Sauna. Whirlpool. Health club privileges. Some bathrm phones, in-rm whirlpools, refrigerators, wet bars; microwaves avail. Some balconies. Cr cds: A, MC, V.

★ SUPER 8. 6900 NW 83rd Terr (64152). 816/587-0808; toll-free 800/800-8000. www.super8.com. 50 rms, 3 story. Apr-Sept: S $43-$53; D $43-$69; each addl $6; suites $64-$72; under 12 free; package plans; higher rates special events; lower rates rest of yr. Crib free. Pet accepted; $25 deposit. TV; cable (premium). Complimentary coffee in lobby. Restaurant nearby. Ck-out 11 am. Business servs avail. In-rm modem link. Sundries. Cr cds: A, C, D, DS, ER, JCB, MC, V.

Hotels

★★ ADAM'S MARK. 9103 E 39th St (64133). 816/737-0200; fax 816/737-4713. www.adamsmark.com. 374 rms, 15 story. S $89-$129; D $89-$139; each addl $10; suites $225-$485; studio rms $175; under 18 free; wkend rates. Crib free. TV; cable. 2 heated pools, 1 indoor; whirlpool, poolside serv. Restaurant 6 am-11 pm. Bars 11-3 am; Sun noon-midnight; entertainment. Ck-out noon. Coin lndry. Convention facilities. Business servs avail. In-rm modem link. Gift shop. Exercise rm; sauna. Rec rm. Some bathrm phones. Adj to Truman Sports Complex. Cr cds: A, D, DS, MC, V.

★★ DOUBLETREE HOTEL. 1301 Wyandotte St (63801). 816/474-6664; fax 816/474-0424; toll-free 800/843-6664. www.doubletree.com. 388 rms, 28 story, 99 suites. S, D $169-$199; each addl $10; suites $189-$219; family, wkend, hol rates. Crib free. Valet parking $9, garage $6. Pet accepted. TV; cable (premium), VCR avail. Complimentary coffee in rms. Restaurant 6:30 am-10 pm. Bar 5 pm-1 am. Ck-out noon. Convention facilities. Business center. In-rm modem link. Concierge. Gift shop. Exercise equipt. Pool; poolside serv. Health club privileges. Refrigerator, microwave, wet bar in suites. Luxury level. Cr cds: A, C, D, DS, MC, V.

⊡ ⩲ 🛉 ⩓ 🐾 SC 🛉

★★★★ **FAIRMONT KANSAS CITY AT THE PLAZA.** *401 Ward Pkwy (64112). 816/756-1500; fax 816/756-1635; toll-free 800/866-5577. www. fairmont.com.* Located ten minutes from downtown in historic Country Club Plaza, guests will find immediate luxury at this former Ritz-Carlton property with an elegant, mahogany-walled lobby accented with marble and crystal. Creative, Midwestern-inspired cuisine is served at Cafe 401 in a bright, sun-yellow room overlooking the Plaza. 366 rms, 12 story. S, D $139-$279; suites $235-$1,400; under 12 free; wkend rates; higher rates Thanksgiving. Crib free. Valet parking $12. TV; cable (premium), VCR avail. Heated pool; wading pool; poolside serv. Restaurant 6:30 am-11 pm; Fri, Sat to 1 am. Rm serv 24 hrs. Bar 5 pm-midnight; entertainment. Ck-out noon. Convention facilities. Business center. In-rm modem link. Concierge. Airport transportation avail. Exercise equipt; sauna, steam rm. Massage. Bathrm phones, refrigerators, mini-bars. Private patios, balconies. Luxury level. Cr cds: A, C, D, DS, JCB, MC, V.

⊡ ⩲ 🛉 ⩓ 🐾 🛉

★★★ **HILTON KANSAS CITY AIRPORT.** *8801 NW 112th St (64153). 816/891-8900; fax 816/891-8030. www.hilton.com.* 347 rms, 11 story. S $109-$139; D $119-$149; each addl $10; suites $249-$369; under 18 free; wkend rates. Crib free. TV; cable (premium). Complimentary coffee in lobby. Restaurant 6 am-10 pm. Bar 11:30-1 am. Ck-out noon. Convention facilities. Business center. In-rm modem link. Bellhops. Sundries. Coin lndry. Free airport transportation. Lighted tennis. Exercise equipt. Indoor/outdoor pool; whirlpool; poolside serv. Some bathrm phones; wet bar in some suites. Cr cds: A, MC, V.

⊡ ⩲ 🛉 ✈ ⩓ 🐾 SC 🛉 ⛷

★★ **HISTORIC SUITES OF AMERICA.** *612 Central (64105). 816/842-6544; fax 816/842-0656; toll-free 800/733-0612. www.historicsuites.com.* 100 suites, 5 story. S, D $150-$225; under 18 free; wkly rates; lower rates hol wkends. Crib free. Pet accepted, some restrictions. TV; cable (premium). Pool; whirlpool. Complimentary continental bkfst, coffee in rms. Restaurant nearby. No Coin lndry. Meeting rms. Business servs avail. In-rm modem link. No bellhops. Garage parking. Exercise equipt; sauna. Health club privileges. Microwaves. Turn-of-the-century design. Cr cds: A, MC, V.

⊡ 🐾 ⩲ 🛉 ⩓ 🐾 SC

★★ **HOLIDAY INN.** *1215 Wyandotte (64105). 816/471-1333; fax 816/283-0541; toll-free 800/465-4329. www. holiday-inn.com.* 190 rms, 16 story. S, D $79-$109; each addl $10; suites $99-$125; under 13 free; wkend rates. Crib free. TV; cable (premium). Ck-out noon. Meeting rms. Business servs avail. Covered parking. Exercise equipt. Health club privileges. Some refrigerators, microwaves. Cr cds: A, C, D, DS, JCB, MC, V.

⊡ 🛉 ⩓ 🐾

★★★ **HOTEL PHILLIPS.** *106 W 12th St (64105). 816/221-7000; fax 816/221-8902; toll-free 800/333-3333.* 240 suites, 20 story, 43 kit. units. S, D $89-$179; each addl $10; kit. units $99-$199; under 18 free; wkend rates. Crib free. TV; cable (premium). Complimentary continental bkfst. Restaurants 6:30 am-11 pm. Bar 10:30 am-midnight; Sat, Sun 11-3 am. Ck-out noon. Guest lndry. Meeting rms. In-rm modem link. Valet parking. Exercise equipt. Health club privileges. Cr cds: A, C, D, DS, ER, MC, V.

⊡ 🛉 ⩓ 🐾 SC

★★ **HOTEL SAVOY.** *219 W 9th St (64105). 816/842-3575; toll-free 800/728-6922.* 100 suites, 6 story. S, D $79-$150; each addl $10-$20; under 8 free. TV; cable (premium). Complimentary full bkfst. Complimentary coffee in rms. Restaurant (see SAVOY GRILL). Bar. Ck-out 1 pm. Coin lndry. Business servs avail. Concierge. Wet bars. Restored 1888 landmark building with original architectural detail; stained and leaded glass, tile floors, tin ceilings. Cr cds: A, C, D, DS, MC, V.

★★★★ **HYATT REGENCY CROWN CENTER.** *2345 McGee St (64108). 816/421-1234; fax 816/435-4190; toll-free 800/233-1234. www. hyatt.com.* 731 rms, 42 story. S $189; D $214; each addl $25; suites $250-$850; under 18 free; wkend rates. Crib free. Valet parking $12.50, garage $10. TV; cable (premium). Heated pool; whirlpool, poolside serv. Restaurants 6:30 am-midnight. Bars 11-1 am; entertainment. Ck-out noon. Convention facilities. Business center. In-rm modem link. Concierge. Gift shop. Lighted tennis. Exercise equipt; sauna, steam rm. Minibars. Luxury level. Cr cds: A, C, D, DS, ER, JCB, MC, V.

★★★ **MARRIOTT COUNTRY CLUB PLAZA KANSAS CITY.** *4445 Main St (64111). 816/531-3000; fax 816/531-3007; toll-free 800/810-3708. www.marriotthotels.com/mcipl.* 296 rms, 19 story. S, D $169; each addl $10; suites $350-$550; under 18 free. Crib free. Garage free; valet parking $5. TV; cable. Indoor pool; whirlpool. Restaurant 6:30 am-10 pm. Bar 3 pm-1 am. Ck-out noon. Convention facilities. Business servs avail. In-rm modem link. Gift shop. Concierge. Exercise rm. Some refrigerators. Luxury level. Cr cds: A, C, D, DS, JCB, MC, V.

★★★ **MARRIOTT DOWNTOWN KANSAS CITY.** *200 W 12th St (64105). 816/421-6800; fax 816/855-4418; toll-free 800/228-9290. www. marriott.com.* 986 rms, 18 and 22 story. S $150; D $170; each addl $20; suites $325-$600; wkend rates. Crib free. TV; cable (premium), VCR avail. Indoor pool. Restaurant 6 am-midnight. Bar 11:30-1:30 am; entertainment Wed-Sat. Ck-out noon. Convention facilities. Business center. In-rm modem link. Concierge. Gift shop. Exercise rm. Some refrigerators. Luxury level. Cr cds: A, C, D, DS, MC, V.

★★★ **MARRIOTT KANSAS CITY AIRPORT.** *775 Brasilia Ave (64153). 816/464-2200; fax 816/464-5915; toll-free 800/228-9290. www.marriott.com.* 382 rms, 9 story. S, D, studio rms $69-$150; suites $250-$450; under 18 free; wkend plan. Crib free. Pet accepted. TV; cable (premium). Indoor pool; whirlpool. Restaurant 6 am-11 pm. Bar 11:30-1 am, Sun 12:30 pm-midnight. Ck-out noon. Coin lndry. Meeting rms. Business center. In-rm modem link. Bellhops. Valet serv. Gift shop. Free airport transportation. Downhill ski 15 mi. Exercise equipt; sauna. Rec rm. Lawn games. Private patios, picnic tables. On lake. Luxury level. Cr cds: A, C, D, DS, JCB, MC, V.

★ **PARK PLACE HOTEL.** *1601 N Universal Ave (64210). 816/483-9900; fax 816/231-1418; toll-free 800/821-8532.* 330 rms, 9 story. S, D $79-$89; under 18 free; wkend rates; package plans. Crib free. Pet accepted, some restrictions; $25 deposit. TV; cable (premium). Indoor/outdoor pool. Complimentary full bkfst, coffee in rms. Restaurant 6:30 am-10 pm; Fri, Sat to 11 pm. Bar 11-1:30 am; entertainment Mon-Sat. Ck-out noon. Meeting rms. Business servs avail. Gift shop. Exercise equipt; sauna. Some bathrm phones, refrigerators. Private patios; some balconies. Cr cds: A, C, D, DS, MC, V.

★★★ **RAPHAEL.** *325 Ward Pkwy (64112). 816/756-3800; fax 816/802-2131; toll-free 800/821-5343. www. raphaelkc.com.* 123 rms, 9 story. S $125-$145; D $144-$175; each addl $20; under 18 free; hol, wkend plans. Crib free. TV; cable (premium), VCR avail. Restaurant (see RAPHAEL DINING ROOM). Rm serv 24 hrs. Bar to 1 am; closed Sun. Ck-out 1 pm. Business servs avail. In-rm modem link. Free garage, valet parking. Health club privileges. Refrigerators, minibars. Cr cds: A, D, DS, MC, V.

★★★ **SHERATON SUITES COUNTRY CLUB PLAZA.** *770 W 47th St (64112). 816/931-4400; fax 816/561-7330. www.starwood.com.* 258 suites, 18 story. S $150; D $160; each addl $20; under 16 free; wkend rates. Crib free. Valet parking $7.50. TV; cable (premium), VCR avail. Indoor/outdoor pool; whirlpool, poolside serv. Complimentary coffee in rms. Restaurant 6 am-10:30 pm. Bar 11:30

am-midnight. Ck-out noon. Coin lndry. Meeting rms. Business servs avail. In-rm modem link. Exercise equipt. Health club privileges. Refrigerators; some wet bars; microwaves avail. Some balconies. Cr cds: A, C, D, DS, MC, V.

D ~ ~ ~

★★★ WESTIN CROWN CENTER.

One Pershing Rd (64108). 816/474-4400; fax 816/391-4438; toll-free 800/228-3000. www.westin.com. 725 rms, 18 story. S $99-$205; D $99-$230; each addl $25; suites $300-$1,000; under 18 free; wkend package. Crib free. Pet accepted. TV; cable, VCR avail. Heated pool; whirlpool, poolside serv. Supervised children's activities; ages 6-12. Restaurants 6 am-midnight. Bars 11:30-1 am; entertainment. Ck-out noon. Convention facilities. Business center. In-rm modem link. Barber. Airport transportation. Lighted tennis. Exercise rm; sauna, steam rm. Rec rm. Lawn games. Refrigerators, wet bars. Private patios, balconies. Indoor tropical waterfall and garden. Luxury level. Cr cds: A, C, D, DS, ER, JCB, MC, V.

D ~ ~ ~ ~ ~ ~ ~ SC ~

★★ WYNDHAM GARDEN HOTEL.

11828 NW Plaza Cir (64153). 816/464-2423; fax 816/464-2560; toll-free 800/996-3426. wyndham.com. 138 rms, 7 story. S $59-$95; D $59-$105; each addl $10; suites $125-$135; under 10 free. Crib free. TV; cable (premium). Indoor pool; whirlpool. Restaurant 6:30-10 am, 11 am-2 pm, 5-10 pm; Sat 7 am-noon, 5-10 pm; Sun 7 am-2 pm, 5-10 pm. Bar 4 pm-midnight. Ck-out noon. Coin lndry. Meeting rms. Business servs avail. In-rm modem link. Free airport transportation. Downhill ski 15 mi. Exercise equipt. Some refrigerators; microwaves avail. Wet bar in suites. Balconies. Cr cds: A, D, DS, JCB, MC, V.

D ~ ~ ~ ~ ~ ~

B&Bs/Small Inns

★★★ SOUTHMORELAND ON THE PLAZA.

116 E 46th St (64112). 816/531-7979; fax 816/531-2407. www.southmoreland.com. 13 rms, 3 story. S, D $105-$170. Children over 13 only. TV in sitting rm; cable (premium), VCR in general rm. Complimentary full bkfst; afternoon refreshments. Restaurants nearby. Ck-out 11 am, ck-in 4:30 pm. Business servs avail. In-rm modem link. Health club privileges. Solarium. Totally nonsmoking. Cr cds: A, MC, V.

D ~ ~

All Suite

★★ EMBASSY SUITES.

7640 NW Tiffany Springs Pkwy (64153). 816/891-7788; fax 816/891-7513; toll-free 800/362-2779. www.embassy suites.com. 236 suites, 8 story. Suites $145; under 18 free. Crib free. TV; cable (premium), VCR avail. Indoor pool; whirlpool. Complimentary full bkfst, coffee in rms. Restaurant 11 am-2 pm, 5-10 pm; wkends from 7 am. Bar 11-1 am, wkends to 3 am; entertainment. Ck-out noon. Coin lndry. Convention facilites. Business center. In-rm modem link. Gift shop. Free airport transportation. Exercise equipt; sauna. Refrigerators, microwaves, wet bars. Cr cds: A, D, DS, MC, V.

D ~ ~ ~ ~ ~ ~ ~

Extended Stay

★★ CHASE HOTEL.

9900 NW Prairie View Rd (64153). 816/891-9009; fax 816/891-8623. www.wood finsuitehotels.com. 110 kit. suites, 2 story. S, D $69-$159; wkly, monthly rates. Crib free. Pet accepted, some restrictions; $50 and $5/day. TV; cable (premium), VCR avail (movies). Heated pool; wading pool, whirlpool. Complimentary continental bkfst. Ck-out noon. Coin lndry. Meeting rms. Business servs avail. In-rm modem link. Valet serv. Sundries. Free airport transportation. Lawn games. Exercise equipt. Microwaves. Private patios, balconies. Gazebo area with grills. Cr cds: A, C, D, DS, JCB, MC, V.

D ~ ~ ~ ~ ~ ~ SC

Restaurants

★★★★ AMERICAN.

2450 Grand Blvd, Suite #321 (64108). 816/426-1133. www.theamericanrestaurant kc.com. For over 25 years, this con-

temporary American restaurant in Hall's Crown Center has been a favorite destination for romantic dinners and special occasions. The multilevel dining room has a magnificent view of downtown and a sparkling ceiling of scalloped lighting. Tuxedo-clad waiters serve cochefs Debbie Gold and Michael Smith's Asian and Latin-accented menu of seasonally changing cuisine using many local ingredients. Specializes in contemporary American cuisine with ethnic influences and traditional American cuisine. Own baking, ice cream. Hrs: 11:15 am-2 pm, 6-10 pm, Fri to 11 pm; Sat 6-11 pm. Closed Sun; hols. Res accepted. Bar. Wine cellar. A la carte entrees: dinner $18-$38. Pianist. Free valet parking. Jacket. Cr cds: A, D, DS, MC, V.
D

★ **ARTHUR BRYANT'S BARBEQUE.** *1727 Brooklyn (64127). 816/231-1123.* Specializes in ribs, ham, pork, turkey. Hrs: 10 am-9:30 pm; Fri, Sat to 10 pm; Sun 11 am-8:30 pm. Res accepted. Beer. Lunch, dinner $7.36-$16.27. Entertainment. Cr cds: A, MC, V.
D

★ **BERLINER BEAR.** *7815 Wornall (64114). 816/444-2828.* Hrs: 11 am-9 pm; Fri, Sat to 10 pm. Closed Mon, Sun; hols. Res accepted. German menu. Bar. Lunch, dinner $8.50-$11.95. Specialties: German goulash, cordon bleu, fresh seafood. German decor. Cr cds: D, MC, V.
D

★★ **BUGATTI'S LITTLE ITALY.** *3200 N Ameristar Dr (64161). 816/414-7000. www.ameristars.com.* Hrs: 5-10 pm; Fri, Sat to midnight. Closed Mon. Res accepted. Italian menu. Bar. Dinner $9.95-$19.95. Specialties: veal parmesan, scampi linguini, aged KC strip steak. Parking. Italian cafe atmosphere. Cr cds: A, D, DS, MC, V.
D

★★★ **CAFE ALLEGRO.** *1815 W 39th St (64111). 816/561-3663. www.cafe-allegro.com.* Hrs: 11:30 am-2 pm, 6-10 pm; Sat 6-10 pm. Closed Sun; hols; also 1 wk Jan; wk of July 4. Res accepted. Continental menu. Bar. Wine list. Lunch $6-$12, dinner $18-$25. Specialties: grilled salmon, rack of lamb with Tuscan cranberry beans. Intimate dining rm with original art.

Totally nonsmoking except at the bar. Cr cds: A, DS, MC, V.
D

★★★ **CAFE BARCELONA.** *520 Southwest Blvd (64108). 816/471-4944.* Hrs: 11 am-10 pm; Fri to 11 pm; Sat 4-11 pm. Closed Sun; hols. Spanish/Italian menu. Bar to 1:30 am. Lunch $6.95-$8.95, dinner $9.95-$18.95. Children's menu. Specialties: paella Valencia, salmon with bernaise sauce. Entertainment Sat. Outdoor dining. Mediterranean decor. Cr cds: A, C, D, DS, MC, V.
D

★★ **CALIFORNOS.** *4124 Pennsylvania (64111). 816/531-7878. www.californos.com.* Hrs: 11 am-3 pm, 5-10 pm; Fri, Sat to 11 pm; Sun noon-9 pm. Closed hols. Res accepted. Bar to midnight. Lunch, dinner $5.50-$19.95. Specializes in bistro and steakhouse cuisine. Pianist Sat eves. Valet parking wkends. Outdoor dining. Casual atmosphere. Cr cds: A, MC, V.

★ **CANYON CAFE.** *4626 Broadway (64112). 816/561-6111. www.canyon-cafe.com.* Hrs: 11 am-11 pm; Fri, Sat to midnight; Sun to 10 pm; Sun brunch to 2 pm. Closed Dec 25. Res accepted. Southwestern menu. Bar. Lunch $6.59-$12.99, dinner $7.99-$18.99. Children's menu. Specialties: Southwest chicken piccata, desert fire pasta, Tahoe tenderloin. Own baking. Southwestern decor. Cr cds: A, D, DS, MC, V.
D

★★ **CASCONE'S.** *3733 N Oak (64116). 816/454-7977. www.cascones.con.* Hrs: 11 am-10 pm; Fri, Sat to 11 pm; Sun 4-9 pm. Closed July 4, Dec 25. Res accepted. Italian, American menu. Bar. Lunch $6.50-$9, dinner $12-$24. Children's menu. Specializes in chicken, steak, seafood. Outdoor dining. Cr cds: A, D, DS, MC, V.
D SC

★★ **CHAPELL'S.** *323 Armour Rd, North Kansas City (64116). 816/421-0002. www.chapellsrestaurant.com.* Hrs: 11 am-10 pm; Fri, Sat to 11 pm. Closed Sun; hols. Bar. Lunch $4.95-$7.95, dinner $4.99-$16.99. Children's menu. Specializes in steak, prime rib, hamburgers. Extensive collection of sports memorabilia. Cr cds: A, C, D, DS, MC, V.

D ⚏

★★ **CLASSIC CUP.** *4130 Pennsylvania (64111). 816/756-0771.* Hrs: 11 am-10 pm; Mon to 3 pm; Fri, Sat to 11 pm; Sun to 3 pm. Closed Jan 1, Thanksgiving, Dec 25. Res accepted. Continental menu. Bar to 1 am. Lunch $6-$10, dinner $4.95-$20. Specialties: crabby portabello, mustard shrimp, grilled duck salad. Parking. Cr cds: A, D, MC, V.

D ⚏

★★★ **CLASSIC CUP SIDEWALK CAFE.** *301 W 47th St (64112). 816/ 753-1840. www.missourirestaurant association.com.* Hrs: 7 am-midnight; Fri, Sat 8-1 am; Sun brunch 10 am-3:30 pm. Closed hols. Res accepted. Bar. Lunch $6.99-$12.98, dinner $8.99-$26.75. Sun brunch $8.95. Children's menu. Specialties: Thai chicken pizza, steak medallions. Outdoor dining. Casual dining. Cr cds: A, D, MC, V.

D

★★★ **EBT.** *1310 Carondelet Dr (64114). 816/942-8870.* Hrs: 11 am-2 pm, 5-9:30 pm; Fri to 10 pm; Sat 5-10 pm. Closed Sun; hols. Res accepted. Bar. Wine cellar. Lunch $6.50-$11.95, dinner $12.95-$25.95. Children's menu. Specializes in seafood, steak, chicken. Pianist Wed-Sat. Decorated with palm trees, fountain; antiques, gilded iron elevator. Cr cds: A, D, DS, MC, V.

D ⚏

★★ **FEDORA CAFE.** *210 W 47th St (64112). 816/561-6565. www.kcfedora. com.* Hrs: 11:30 am-11 pm; Fri, Sat to midnight; Sun 9 am-10 pm. Res accepted. Bar. A la carte entrees: lunch $4.25-$11.95, dinner $7.95-$24.95. Specializes in seafood, pasta, steak. Jazz Thurs-Sat. European bistro-style cafe; art deco. Cr cds: A, D, DS, MC, V.

D SC

★★ **FIGLIO.** *209 W 46th Terr (64112). 816/561-0505. www.kcfiglio. com.* Hrs: 11 am-10 pm; Fri, Sat to 11 pm; Sun 10:30 am-10 pm; Sun brunch to 2:30 pm. Closed Dec 25. Res accepted. Italian, American

menu. Bar. Lunch $7.25-$8.95, dinner $7.75-$16.95. Sun brunch $11.95. Children's menu. Specializes in pasta, gourmet pizza. Accordionist Wed-Sun. Valet parking wkends. Outdoor porch dining. Cr cds: A, C, D, DS, MC, V.

D ⚏

★★★ **FIORELLA'S JACK STACK BAR-B-Q.** *13441 Holmes Rd (64145). 816/942-9141. www.jackstackbbq.com.* Hrs: 11 am-10 pm; Fri, Sat to 10:30 pm. Closed Thanksgiving, Dec 25. Lunch $5.25-$10, dinner $7.25-$23. Specializes in barbecue, fresh seafood, steak. Museumlike atmosphere; antiques. Cr cds: A, C, D, DS, MC, V.

D ⚏

★ **GAROZZO'S.** *526 Harrison (64106). 816/221-2455.* Hrs: 11 am-10 pm; Fri to 11 pm; Sat 4-11 pm. Closed Sun; also hols. Italian menu. Bar. Lunch $4.95-$10.50, dinner $8.50-$24.95. Specialties: chicken spidini, stuffed artichoke. Casual decor. Cr cds: A, D, DS, MC, V.

D SC ⚏

★★ **GOLDEN OX.** *1600 Genessee (64102). 816/842-2866.* Hrs: 11 am-10 pm; Sat 4-10:30 pm; Sun 4-9 pm. Closed Dec 25. Bar. Lunch $4.50-$7.95, dinner $14.95-$24.95. Children's menu. Specializes in steak, prime rib. Western decor with stockyard influence. Family-owned. Cr cds: A, D, DS, MC, V.

D ⚏

★★ **GRAND STREET CAFE.** *4740 Grand Ave (64112). 816/561-8000.* Hrs: 11 am-10 pm; Fri, Sat to midnight; Sun from 10:30 am; Sun brunch to 3 pm. Closed Dec 25. Res accepted. Bar. Lunch $4.95-$10.95, dinner $5.95-$24.95. Sun brunch $4.95-$10.95. Children's menu. Specializes in lamb chops, pork chops, grilled tenderloin. Outdoor dining. Eclectic, contemporary decor. Cr cds: A, D, DS, MC, V.

D ⚏

★★ **HARDWARE CAFE.** *5 E Kansas Ave, Liberty (64068). 816/792-3500. www.thehardwarecafe.com.* Hrs: 11 am-9 pm; Mon to 2 pm; Fri, Sat to 10 pm. Closed Sun; hols. Serv bar. Lunch $4.25-$7.50, dinner $4.25-$18.95. Children's menu. Specialties:

fried chicken, chicken puff pastries. Own baking. Converted hardware store; old-fashioned soda fountain, historical building. Gift shop upstairs. Cr cds: D, MC, V.
D -⬛

★ **HARRY'S BAR & TABLES.** *501 Westport Rd (64111). 816/561-3950.* Hrs: 11:30 am-midnight; Fri to 2 am; Sat 5 pm-2 am; Sun 5 pm-midnight. Res accepted. Continental menu. Bar. Complete meal: lunch $12-$18. Dinner $4-$14.50. Specialties: steak sandwich with garlic mashed potatoes, filet of salmon. Outdoor dining. Two dining areas. Casual decor. Cr cds: A, DS, MC, V.
D SC -⬛

★★ **HEREFORD HOUSE.** *2 E 20th St (64108). 816/842-1080. www.herefordhouse.com.* Hrs: 11 am-10 pm; Fri to 10:30 pm; Sat 4-10:30 pm; Sun 4-9 pm. Closed hols. Res accepted. Bar. Lunch $6-$15, dinner $15-$30. Children's menu. Specializes in steak, Maine lobster tails. Casual atmosphere. Cr cds: A, D, DS, MC, V.
D -⬛

★ **ILIKI CAFE.** *6427 N Cosby Ave (64151). 816/587-0009. www.iliki.com.* Hrs: 11 am-2:30 pm, 5-10 pm; Fri to 11 pm; Sat noon-3 pm, 5-11 pm. Closed Sun; also hols. Mediterranean menu. Wine, beer. Lunch $4.95-$14.95, dinner $7.95-$14.95. Specializes in kabobs, dips. Parking. Cr cds: A, D, DS, MC, V.
D -⬛

★★ **ITALIAN GARDENS.** *1110 Baltimore (64105). 816/221-9311.* Hrs: 11 am-9 pm; Fri to 10 pm; Sat 11:30 am-10 pm. Closed Sun; hols. Res accepted. Italian, American menu. Bar. Lunch $4.50-$6, dinner $7-$15. Children's menu. Specializes in pasta, veal, seafood. Valet parking. Cr cds: A, D, DS, MC, V.
D -⬛

★★ **JAPENGO.** *600 Ward Pkwy (64112). 816/931-6600. www.japengo-kc.com.* Hrs: 11 am-10 pm; Fri, Sat to 11 pm; Sun from noon. Closed Jan 1, Dec 24, 25. Res accepted. Pacific Rim menu. Bar. Wine list. Lunch $6.95-$9.95, dinner $14.95-$29.95. Children's menu. Specialties: sizzling whole fish, Thai curry Mahi Mahi, burnt spice filet. Valet parking.

Murals; large dome ceiling with skylight. Totally nonsmoking. Cr cds: A, D, DS, MC, V.
D SC

★★ **JESS & JIM'S STEAK HOUSE.** *517 E 135th St (64145). 816/941-9499. www.jessandjims.com.* Hrs: 11 am-10 pm; Fri, Sat to 11 pm; Sun noon-9 pm. Closed July 4, Thanksgiving, Dec 25. Bar. Lunch $4.95-$6.95, dinner $9.95-$25.95. Children's menu. Specializes in steak, seafood. Casual atmosphere, Western decor. Family-owned since 1938. Cr cds: A, D, DS, MC, V.
D SC -⬛

★★★ **JJ'S.** *910 W 48th St (64112). 816/561-7136.* Hrs: 11 am-10 pm; Fri to 11 pm; Sat 5-11 pm; Sun 5-10 pm. Closed hols. Res accepted. Continental menu. Bar to 3 am. Wine list. Lunch $6.95-$10.95, dinner $13.95-$24.95. Specialties: lamb chops, chicken marsala. Valet parking. Cr cds: A, D, DS, MC, V.
D -⬛

★★ **K. C. MASTERPIECE.** *4747 Wyandotte St (64112). 816/531-3332.* Hrs: 11 am-10 pm; Fri, Sat to 11 pm; Sun to 9:30 pm. Closed Thanksgiving, Dec 25. Bar. Lunch $6.49-$14.99, dinner $6.99-$18.99. Children's menu. Specializes in pork, turkey, brisket. Kansas City memorabilia. Casual atmosphere. Cr cds: A, D, DS, MC, V.
D

★ **L. C.'S BAR-B-Q.** *5800 Blue Park Way (64129). 816/923-4484.* Specializes in BBQ ribs, sandwiches. Hrs: 11:30 am-9:30 pm; Fri, Sat to 11 pm. Lunch, dinner $3.99-$12.99. Entertainment. Cr cds: A, C, D, DS, MC, V.
D -⬛

★★★ **LE FOU FROG.** *400 E 5th St (64106). 816/474-6060.* Hrs: 11 am-2 pm, 6-11 pm; Sat from 6 pm; Sun 5-9 pm. Closed Mon, Tues; hols. Res accepted. French menu. Bar to 1 am. Wine cellar. Lunch $6.25-$9.25, dinner $16.75-$28. Specialties: pork loin with orange, steak au poivre, grilled marinated venison chop. Own desserts. Outdoor dining. French bistro atmosphere; globe lights, antique French posters. Cr cds: A, D, DS, MC, V.
D

★★★ **LIDIA'S.** *101 W 22nd St (64108). 816/221-3722. www.lidias italy.com.* Northern Italian cuisine. Lunch Mon-Sun 11 am-2 pm. Dinner Mon-Thurs 5:30-9:30 pm, Fri 5-10:30 pm, Sat 4-10:30 pm, Sun 5-9 pm. Lunch $7-$12, dinner $11-$25. Bar. Cr cds: A, D, MC, V.
D

★★ **MACALUSO'S.** *1403 W 39th St (64111). 816/561-0100.* Hrs: 5:30-10 pm; Fri, Sat to 11 pm. Closed Sun; also hols. Res accepted. Italian, Continental menu. Bar. Dinner $12.95-$24.95. Specialties: crab cakes, manicotti, rack of lamb. Casual decor. Cr cds: A, D, DS, MC, V.
D

★★★ **MAJESTIC STEAKHOUSE.** *931 Broadway (64105). 816/471-8484. www.majesticgroup.com.* Hrs: 11:30 am-10 pm; Fri to 10:30 pm; Sat 5-11 pm; Sun 4-9 pm. Closed hols. Res accepted. Bar. Wine cellar. Lunch $3.95-$15, dinner $12.50-$35. Specialties: Kansas City strip steak, prime rib, grilled fresh salmon. Jazz. Valet parking. In former Garment District building; turn-of-the-century decor with stained-glass windows, ceiling fans, ornate tin ceiling. Cr cds: A, D, DS, MC, V.

★★ **METROPOLIS AMERICAN GRILL.** *303 Westport Rd (64111). 816/753-1550.* Hrs: 5:30-10 pm; wkends to 11 pm. Closed Sun; hols. Res accepted. Bar. A la carte entrees: dinner $11.95-$22.95. Specialties: tandoori sea bass, rosemary scented rack of lamb, wild mushroom strudel. Contemporary decor. Cr cds: A, C, D, DS, MC, V.

★★ **MILANO.** *2450 Grand Ave (64108). 816/426-1130.* Hrs: 11:30 am-9 pm; Fri, Sat to 10 pm; Sun from noon. Closed hols. Res accepted. Italian menu. Bar. Lunch $5-$10.50, dinner $8.95-$19.95. Children's menu. Patio dining. Casual Italian decor. Cr cds: A, D, DS, MC, V.
D

★★★ **O'DOWD'S LITTLE DUBLIN.** *4742 Pennsylvania (64112). 816/561-2700. www.odowds.com.* Hrs: 11-1:30 am; Fri, Sat to 3 am. Closed Dec 25.

Irish menu. Bar. Lunch $5.95-$8.50, dinner $8.75-$16.95. Specialties: Guiness beef crostini, Dublin fish and chips, corned beef boxty. Own baking. Irish vocalists Wed and Sun eves. Rooftop dining. Authentic Irish pub decor; entire interior shipped from Ireland. Cr cds: A, DS, MC, V.
D

★★ **PAPAGALLO.** *3535 Broadway (64111). 816/756-3227.* Hrs: 11 am-11 pm; Sat 5-11 pm; Sun 5-9 pm. Closed Mon; hols. Res accepted. Continental menu. Bar. Lunch $4.95-$11.95, dinner $11.95-$22. Specializes in kabobs, fresh seafood, pasta. Entertainment Fri, Sat. Valet parking. Original artwork. Contemporary decor. Cr cds: A, D, DS, MC, V.
D

★ **PARADISE GRILL.** *5225 NW 64th St (64151). 816/587-9888.* Hrs: 11 am-10 pm; Fri, Sat to 11 pm; Sun 10:30 am-9 pm. Closed Thanksgiving, Dec 25. Res accepted. Bar. Lunch, dinner $3.99-$18.99. Children's menu. Specializes in chicken, fish. Modern decor. Cr cds: A, D, DS, MC, V.
D

★ **PHOENIX PIANO BAR & GRILL.** *302 W 8th St (64105). 816/472-0001.* Hrs: 11-1 am. Closed Sun; hols. Res accepted. Bar. Lunch, dinner $5.60-$7.50. Specializes in sandwiches. Jazz nightly. Parking. Outdoor dining. Piano bar; pictures of famous jazz musicians. Cr cds: A, DS, MC, V.

★★★ **PLAZA III THE STEAK-HOUSE.** *4749 Pennsylvania Ave (64112). 816/753-0000.* Hrs: 11:30 am-2:30 pm, 5:30-10 pm; Fri, Sat to 11 pm; Sun 5-10 pm. Res accepted. Bar 11-1 am; Sun to midnight. Wine list. A la carte entrees: lunch $5.95-$9.95, dinner $15.95-$28.95. Children's menu. Specializes in prime midwestern beef, veal chops, fresh seafood. Entertainment. Valet parking. Cr cds: A, D, DS, MC, V.
D

★★★ **RAPHAEL DINING ROOM.** *325 Ward Pkwy (64112). 816/756-3800. www.raphaelkc.com.* Hrs: 6:30-10 am, 11 am-3 pm, 5-11 pm; Sat 7 am-3 pm, 5-11 pm; Sun 7-11 am. Closed hols. Res accepted. Continen-

tal menu. Bar to 1 am. Lunch $7-$10.95, dinner $11.95-$22.95. Specializes in fresh fish, veal, New Zealand rack of lamb. Entertainment Fri, Sat. Valet parking. Romantic elegance in European-style setting. Cr cds: A, D, DS, MC, V.
D ⊿

★★ RUTH'S CHRIS STEAK HOUSE. *700 W 47th St (64112). 816/531-4800. www.ruthschris.com.* Hrs: 5-10:30 pm; Fri, Sat to 11 pm. Closed Thanksgiving, Dec 25. Res accepted. Bar. Wine list. A la carte entrees: $16.25-$36.95. Specializes in porterhouse steak, shrimp, lobster. Valet parking. Outdoor dining. Upscale atmosphere; large wine display cabinet; ornate artwork. Cr cds: A, D, DS, MC, V.
D ⊿

★★★ SAVOY GRILL. *219 W 9th St (64105). 816/842-3890.* Hrs: 11 am-11 pm; Fri, Sat to midnight; Sun 4-10 pm. Closed Dec 25. Res accepted. Bar. Lunch $4.50-$12, dinner $14-$27. Specializes in fresh seafood, Maine lobster, prime dry-aged beef. Parking. 19th-century hotel dining rm; oak paneling, stained-glass windows, murals of Santa Fe Trail. Ornate back bar. Cr cds: A, D, DS, MC, V.
D ⊿

★★ SHIRAZ. *320 Southwest Blvd (64108). 816/472-0015.* Hrs: 11 am-2 pm, 5-10 pm; Fri and Sat to 11 pm. Closed Sun; also hols. Res accepted. Continental menu. Bar. Lunch $5-$8, dinner $8.95-$20. Specialties: curry chicken, grilled scallops with black bean salsa. Contemporary decor. Cr cds: A, D, DS, MC, V.
D

★ SMUGGLER'S INN. *1650 Universal Plaza Dr (64120). 816/483-0400.* Hrs: 11 am-10 pm; Sat 5-11 pm; Sun 10 am-9 pm. Res accepted. Bar to 1 am. Complete meals: lunch $6.95-$12.95, dinner $10.95-$21.95. Specializes in prime rib, fresh fish. Salad bar. Entertainment Wed-Sat. Casual atmosphere; wood-burning fireplaces. Cr cds: A, D, DS, MC, V.
D ⊿

★★★ STEPHENSON'S APPLE FARM. *16401 E US 40 (64136). 816/373-5400.* Hrs: 11:30 am-10 pm; Sun 10 am-9 pm; Sun brunch 10 am-2 pm exc hols. Closed Dec 24 and 25. Res accepted. Bar. Lunch $7-$14, dinner $12.95-$18.95. Sun brunch $13.95. Children's menu. Specialties: hickory-smoked meats, apple fritters and dumplings. Own baking. Outdoor dining. Started as a fruit stand (1900). Early American decor; farm implements, cider keg in lobby. Country store. Family-owned. Cr cds: A, D, MC, V.
D ⊿

★★ STOLEN GRILL. *904 Westport Rd (64111). 816/960-1450.* Hrs: 5:30-10:30 pm; Fri, Sat to 11 pm. Closed Sun; hols. Res accepted. Contemporary American menu. Dinner $6-$26. Specialties: crispy celery root roesti, artichoke salad, beef filet. Parking. Bistro decor and atmosphere. Totally nonsmoking. Cr cds: A, D, MC, V.
D

★★ STROUD'S. *1015 E 85th St (64131). 816/333-2132. www.strouds restaurant.com.* Hrs: 4-10 pm; Fri 11 am-11 pm; Sat 2-11 pm; Sun 11 am-10 pm. Closed Thanksgiving, Dec 25. Bar. Lunch $5.95-$10.95, dinner $8.95-$19.95. Specialties: pan-fried chicken. Pianist. Cr cds: A, DS, MC, V.
D ⊿

★ THE VELVET DOG. *400 E 31st St (64108). 816/753-9990. www.velvet dog.com.* Hrs: 4 pm-1:30 am; Fri, Sat to 3 am; Sun 6 pm-1:30 am. Closed hols. Res accepted. Italian menu. Bar. Dinner $9.95-$14.95. Specialties: artichoke heart fritters, lemon butter bowtie pasta. Outdoor dining. Old storefront brick building with wood floors, brick walls, ceiling fans. Cr cds: A, D, MC, V.
D ⊿

Unrated Dining Spot

ANDRE'S CONFISERIE SUISSE. *5018 Main St (64112). 816/561-3440. www.andreschocolates.com.* Hrs: 11 am-2:30 pm. Closed Mon, Sun; hols. Swiss menu. Complete meal: lunch $9.25. Specializes in quiche, chocolate candy, pastries. Swiss chalet atmosphere. Family-owned since 1955. Totally nonsmoking. Cr cds: A, DS, MC, V.
D

LAMAR'S DONUTS. *14131 E Hwy 40 (64136). 816/220-8900.* Specializes in donuts. Hrs: 6 am-2 pm. Lunch $ .11-$.97. Entertainment. Cr cds: DS, MC, V.

D ⬛

Kirksville

(B-4) *See also Macon*

Founded 1841 **Pop** 17,152 **Elev** 981 ft
Area code 660 **Zip** 63501
Information Kirksville Area Chamber of Commerce, 304 S Franklin, Box 251; 660/665-3766
Web www.truman.edu/kirksville/kirk.html

Kirksville is a trade center for surrounding communities and the home of Kirksville College of Osteopathic Medicine (1892), the world's first such college. An early pioneer, Jesse Kirk, traded a turkey dinner for the right to name the town after himself.

What to See and Do

Sugar Creek State Forest. A 2,609 acre forest. Hunting, primitive camping, horseback riding trails. (Daily) 8 mi SW on MO 11. Phone 660/785-2420.

Thousand Hills State Park. More than 3,000 acres. Swimming, bathhouse, fishing, boating (ramp, marina, rentals), canoeing; hiking trails, picnicking, dining lodge, store, improved camping (dump station), cabins. Standard fees. (Daily) 4 mi W on MO 6, then 2 mi S on MO 157. Phone 660/665-6995. **FREE**

Truman State University. (1867) 6,000 students. E. M. Violette Museum on campus has gun collection, Native American artifacts, historical items (by appt only). Pickler Memorial Library has Schwengel-Lincoln Collection of memorabilia on Abraham Lincoln (Mon-Fri); also historical textiles and related arts (by appt). Campus tours. Phone 660/785-4016.

Motels/Motor Lodges

★ **BUDGET HOST VILLAGE INN.** *1304 S Baltimore (63501). 660/665-3722; fax 816/665-6334; toll-free 888/333-5475.* 30 rms, 1-2 story. S $40-$42; D $44-$49; each addl $5; under 10 free. Crib free. Pet accepted, some restrictions. TV; cable (premium). Complimentary coffee in office. Restaurant nearby. Ck-out noon. Business servs avail. In-rm modem link. In-rm steam baths. Cr cds: A, C, D, DS, ER, MC, V.

🔲 ⬛ ⬛ SC

★★ **SHAMROCK INN.** *2501 S Business 63 (63501). 660/665-8352; fax 660/665-0072; res 800/301-2772.* 45 rms. S $48; D $56; each addl $10; under 12 free. Crib free. Pet accepted, some restrictions. TV; cable (premium), VCR avail (movies). Pool. Playground. Restaurant 6 am-10 pm. Ck-out 11 am. Meeting rms. Sundries. Cr cds: A, C, D, DS, MC, V.

🔲 ⬛ ⬛ ⬛ SC

★ **SUPER 8 MOTEL.** *1101 Country Club Dr (63501). 660/665-8826; toll-free 800/800-8000. www.super8.com.* 61 rms, 2-3 story. No elvtr. S $55; D $55; under 12 free. Crib $2. TV; cable. Complimentary coffee. Restaurants nearby. Ck-out 11 am. Health club privileges. Cr cds: A, C, D, DS, MC, V.

D ⬛ ⬛ SC

B&B/Small Inn

★ **TRAVELER'S INN.** *301 W Washington St (63501). 660/665-5191; fax 660/665-0825; toll-free 800/320-5191. www.travelers-inn-bnb.com.* 22 rms, 4 story. S $23-$32.95; D $39.95; each addl $5; suites $60; wkly, monthly rates. Crib free. TV; cable (premium), VCR avail. Bar 3 pm-1:30 am, Sun noon-midnight. Ck-out noon. Meeting rms. Business center. In-rm modem link. Barber, beauty shop. Built in 1923. Cr cds: A, D, DS, MC, V.

D ⬛ ⬛ ⬛

Lake of the Ozarks

See also Camdenton, Lake Ozark, Osage Beach

(Approx 42 mi SW of Jefferson City on US 54)

Completed in 1931, 2,543 ft-long Bagnell Dam impounds the Osage River to form this 54,000 acre recreational lake, which has a very irregular 1,150-mile shoreline. Fishing, boating, and swimming are excellent. Boats may be rented.

What to See and Do

Jacob's Cave. Famous for its depth illusion, reflective pools, prehistoric bones, and the world's largest geode. One-mile tours on concrete, wheelchair-accessible walkways. (Daily; closed Dec 25) N on AR 5, exit at State Rd TT. Phone 573/378-4374. ¢¢¢

Lake cruises.

Casino Pier. One- and two-hr cruises aboard the Commander depart hrly (Apr-Oct, daily); also bkfst, brunch, and dinner and dance cruises. ½ blk S of Bagnell Dam, on US 54 Business. Phone 573/365-2020. ¢¢¢¢

Paddlewheeler *Tom Sawyer* Excursion Boat. One- and 2-hr narrated sightseeing excursions on sternwheeler (Apr-Oct, daily); charters avail. Scenic helicopter rides (fee). W end of Bagnell Dam. Phone 573/365-3300.

Lake of the Ozarks State Park. This more than 17,000-acre park, the largest in the state, has 89 mi of shoreline with two public swimming and boat launching areas. Public Beach #1 is at end of MO 134, and Grand Glaize Beach is ½ mi from US 54, 2 mi south of Grand Glaize Bridge. On the grounds is a large cave with streams of water that continuously pour from stalactites. Fishing, canoeing; hiking, horseback riding, picnicking, improved camping (dump station). Naturalist. (Daily) Standard fees. SE of Osage Beach on MO 42. Phone 573/348-2694. **FREE**

Cottage Colony

★ **BASS POINT RESORT.** *Rural Rte 1 Box 127, Sunrise Beach (65079). 573/374-5205; fax 573/374-0545. www.basspoint.com.* 37 kit. cottages. No rm phones. June-Aug: S $48-$82; D $48-$99; each addl $9; wkly rates; lower rates Apr-May and Sept-Oct. Closed rest of yr. TV; cable. 2 pools, 1 indoor; wading pool. Playground. Ck-out 11 am, ck-in 4 pm. Grocery 3 mi. Coin lndry. Pkg store 3 mi. Lighted tennis. Boats. Water skiing. Game rm. Microwaves. Picnic tables. Cr cds: DS, MC, V.

🛈 🏊 ✈ 🔥

Lake Ozark

(D-4) *See also Camdenton, Lake of the Ozarks, Osage Beach*

Pop 681 **Elev** 703 ft **Area code** 573 **Zip** 65049

Motel/Motor Lodge

★★ **HOLIDAY INN SUNSPREE RESORT.** *120 Holiday Ln (65049). 573/365-2334; fax 573/365-6887; toll-free 800/532-3575. www.holiday-inn.com.* 211 rms, 2 story. Late May-early Sept: S, D $99-$149; suites $169-$299; under 20 free; lower rates rest of yr. Crib free. Pet accepted. TV; cable (premium). 3 pools, 1 indoor; whirlpool. Playground. Complimentary continental bkfst. Restaurant 6:30 am-10 pm. Bar noon-midnight. Ck-out 11 am. Coin lndry. Meeting rms. Business servs avail. In-rm modem link. Bellhops. Gift shop. Exercise equipt; sauna. Miniature golf. Game rm. Rec rm. Lawn games. Microwaves avail. On lake. Cr cds: A, MC, V.

🄳 🐾 🏊 🖈 🔚 🔥 **SC**

Resort

★★★ **LODGE OF FOUR SEASONS.** *State Rd HH (65049). 573/365-3000; fax 573/365-8525; toll-free 800/843-5253. www.4seasonsresort.com.* 304 lodge rms, 18 rms over marina, 1-4 story. May-Sept: S, D $134-$214; suites $300-$450; 2-3 bedrm condos $229-$339; under 18 free; package plans; varied lower rates rest of yr. Crib free. TV; cable (premium), VCR avail. 4 pools, 1 indoor/outdoor; wading pool, whirlpool, poolside serv. Playground. Supervised children's activities; ages 2-14. Restaurants 7 am-10 pm (see also TOLEDO'S). Rm serv 6 am-10 pm. Box lunches, snacks; barbecues, outdoor buffets. Bars 11-1 am; Sun noon-midnight. Ck-out 11 am, ck-in 4 pm. Meeting rms. Business servs avail. Valet serv. Airport transportation. Package store 2 mi. Tennis. Two 18-hole golf courses, one 9-hole course, greens fee $35-$79, pro, putting greens, driving range. Private beach; waterskiing; boats, fishing guides; marina. Trap shooting. Lawn games. Soc dir; movies, entertainment. Rec rm. Game rm. Bowling alley. Exercise equipt; sauna, steam rm. Health club privileges. Private patios, balconies. More than 200 acres of natural wooded Ozark countryside. Japanese garden and tropical fish. Panoramic views of lake. Cr cds: A, D, DS, MC, V.

Restaurants

★★ **BENTLEY'S.** *US 54 (Business) (65049).* 573/365-5301. Hrs: 5-10 pm; Fri, Sat to 11 pm. Closed Sun off-season; also Jan-Feb. Res accepted. Bar. Dinner $12.95-$24.95. Children's menu. Specializes in prime rib, seafood. English decor. Cr cds: A, D, DS, MC, V.

★★ **J B HOOK'S GREAT OCEAN FISH.** *2260 Bagnell Dam Blvd (65049). 573/365-3255. www.jbhooks. com.* Hrs: 11 am-10 pm. Closed Thanksgiving, Dec 25. Bar. Lunch $5.95-$8.95, dinner $13.95-$26.95. Specialties: 16-oz porterhouse steak, orange roughy supreme. Oyster, shrimp bar. Piano bar. Outdoor dining (lunch only). View of lake. Cr cds: A, D, DS, MC, V.

★★★ **TOLEDO'S.** *State Rd HH (65049). 573/365-8507. www.4seasons resort.com.* Hrs: 5:30-10 pm; Sun brunch 10 am-2 pm. Res accepted. Bar. A la carte entrees: dinner $8-$20. Children's menu. Own baking. Specializes in beef, chicken. Entertain-

ment Tues-Sun. Valet parking. Mediterranean decor; scenic view of Japanese garden and lake. Cr cds: A, D, DS, V.

Lamar

(E-2) *See also Carthage, Nevada*

Pop 4,168 **Elev** 985 ft **Area code** 417 **Zip** 64759
Information Barton County Chamber of Commerce, 824B W 12th St; 417/682-3595

What to See and Do

★ **Harry S. Truman Birthplace State Historic Site.** Restored 1½ story house where Truman was born May 8, 1884, and lived until he was 11 months old; six rms with period furnishings, outdoor smokehouse, and hand-dug well. Guided tours. (Mon-Sat, also Sun afternoons; closed hols) 1009 Truman Ave. Phone 417/682-2279. **FREE**

Prairie State Park. This nearly 3,500-acre park preserves an example of Missouri's original prairie; on site are a flock of prairie chickens and small herd of buffalo. Hiking. Picnicking. Visitor center; wildlife observation. Standard fees. (Daily) 16 mi W on US 160. Phone 417/843-6711. **FREE**

Special Events

Truman Days. Celebrates Truman's birthday. Parade, contests, entertainment, Truman drama, and impersonator. Second Sat May.

Lamar Free Fair. Lamar Square. Livestock exhibits; contests, displays; parade, carnival, entertainment. Phone 417/682-3911. Third full wk Aug.

Motel/Motor Lodge

★ **BLUE TOP INN.** *65 S E 1st Ln (64759). 417/682-3333; fax 417/682-3336; toll-free 800/407-3030.* 25 rms. S $28-$35; D $35-$45; each addl $3. Crib $3. TV; cable (premium). Pool.

Restaurant adj 6 am-9 pm; winter hrs vary. Ck-out 11 am. Cr cds: A, MC, V.
D ⬛ ⬛ ⬛

Lebanon

(E-4) *See also Camdenton, Waynesville*

Founded 1849 **Pop** 9,983 **Elev** 1,266 ft **Area code** 417 **Zip** 65536
Information Lebanon Area Chamber of Commerce, 321 S Jefferson; 417/588-3256

Lebanon was founded in the mid-1800s beside an Indian trail that today is Interstate 44. As the seat of the newly created Laclede County, the town was originally called Wyota; however, the name was changed when a respected minister asked that it be renamed after his home town of Lebanon, Tennessee.

What to See and Do

Bennett Spring State Park. Nearly 3,100 acres. Swimming pool, trout fishing (Mar-Oct); picnicking, store, dining lodge, improved camping (dump station), cabins. Nature center, naturalist. Standard fees. (Daily) (See SPECIAL EVENTS). 12 mi W on MO 64. Phone 417/532-4338. **FREE**

Laclede County Museum. (ca 1872) County jail until 1955; exhibits. (May-Sept, Mon-Fri; closed Memorial Day, July 4, Labor Day) 262 Adams St. Phone 417/588-2441. ¢

Special Events

Bennett Spring Hillbilly Days. Bennett Spring State Park. Arts and crafts, contests, country music, antique cars. Father's Day wkend. Phone 417/532-4338.

Laclede County Fair. Fairgrounds. One wk mid-July.

Motels/Motor Lodges

★ ★ **BEST WESTERN WYOTA INN.** *I-44 at exit 130 (65536). 417/532-6171; fax 417/532-6174. www.best western.com.* 52 rms, 1-2 story. May-Oct: S $36-$50; D $42-$52; each addl $5; under 12 free; lower rates rest of yr. Crib $5. Pet accepted, some restrictions. TV; cable (premium).

Pool. Complimentary continental bkfst. Coffee in rms. Restaurant 6 am-9 pm. Ck-out 11 am. Coin lndry. Cr cds: A, C, D, DS, MC, V.
⬛ ⬛ ⬛ ⬛ ⬛ ⬛

★ **DAYS INN.** *2071 W Elm (65536). 417/532-7111; fax 417/532-7005; toll-free 800/228-5151. www.daysinn.com.* 82 rms, 2 story. S, D $48-$65.88; each addl $5; under 19 free. Crib free. Pet accepted. TV; cable, VCR avail. Pool; poolside serv. Complimentary continental bkfst. Coffee in rms. Restaurant 6:30 am-2 pm, 5-10 pm. Bar 3 pm-midnight. Ck-out noon. Coin lndry. Meeting rm. Business servs avail. Cr cds: A, C, D, DS, ER, JCB, MC, V.
⬛ ⬛ ⬛ ⬛ ⬛

Restaurant

★ **STONEGATE STATION.** *1475 S Jefferson (65536). 417/588-1387.* Hrs: 11 am-9 pm; Fri, Sat to 10 pm; Sun to 2:30 pm. Closed hols. Serv bar. Lunch $3.95-$7.65, dinner $5.95-$15.95. Children's menu. Specializes in steak, seafood, Mexican dishes. Salad bar. Rustic atmosphere; antique farm implements. Totally nonsmoking. Cr cds: A, D, DS, MC, V.

Lexington

(C-3) *See also Independence, Kansas City*

Settled 1822 **Pop** 4,860 **Elev** 849 ft **Area code** 660 **Zip** 64067
Information Tourism Bureau, 817 Main St, PO Box 132; 660/259-4711

This historic city with more than 110 antebellum houses was founded by settlers from Lexington, Kentucky. The site of a three-day battle during the Civil War, many of the Union Army's entrenchments are still visible today. Situated on bluffs overlooking the Missouri River, Lexington was an important river port during the 19th century. Today the area is one of the state's largest producers of apples.

What to See and Do

Battle of Lexington State Historic Site. Site of one of the Civil War's largest western campaign battles

(Sept 18-20, 1861). Anderson House, which stood in the center of the battle and changed hands from North to South three times, has been restored. Visitor Center with exhibits and video. Guided tours. (Daily; closed hols) N 13th St. Phone 660/259-4654. ¢

Lafayette County Courthouse. (1847) Oldest courthouse in constant use west of Mississippi. Has Civil War cannonball embedded in E column. (Mon-Fri; closed hols) 10th and Main sts. Phone 660/259-4315.

Lexington Historical Museum. Built as a Presbyterian church in 1846; contains Pony Express and Battle of Lexington relics, photographs, and other historical Lexington items. (Mid-Apr-mid-Oct, daily) 112 S 13th St. Phone 660/259-6313. ¢

Log House Museum. Exhibits incl candle making, quilting, hearth cooking. (Wed-Sat and Sun afternoons; also by appt) Main St at Broadway. Phone 660/259-4711. ¢

Motel/Motor Lodge

★ **LEXINGTON INN PROPERTIES INC.** *1078 N Outer Rd W (64067). 660/259-4641; fax 660/259-6604; toll-free 800/289-4641.* 60 rms, 2 story. S $39; D $45; each addl $5; under 5 free. Crib $3. Pet accepted; $100 deposit. TV; cable. Pool. Restaurant 6 am-10 am; closed Sun. Bar 4 pm-1:30 am; entertainment. Ck-out 11 am. Coin lndry. Meeting rms. Business servs avail. Cr cds: A, C, D, DS, MC, V.
D ◀ 🛏 🏊 🎇

Macon

(B-4) *See also Kirksville*

Pop 5,571 **Elev** 859 ft **Area code** 660 **Zip** 63552

Information Macon Area Chamber of Commerce, 218 N Rollins, Suite 102A; 660/385-5484

What to See and Do

Long Branch State Park. Approx 1,800-acre park on western shore of Long Branch Lake offers swimming, beach, fishing, boating (ramps,

marina); picnicking (shelters), camping (hookups, dump station). Standard fees. (Daily) 2 mi W on US 36. Phone 660/773-5229. **FREE**

Motel/Motor Lodge

★★ **BEST WESTERN INN.** *28933 Sunset Dr (63552). 660/385-2125; fax 660/385-4900; toll-free 800/901-2125. www.bestwestern.com.* 46 rms, 2 story. S $39-$43; D $47; each addl $4. Crib $4. Pet accepted, some restrictions. TV; cable. Pool. Coffee in rms. Restaurant adj 6 am-9 pm; Sun 7 am-8 pm. Ck-out 11 am. Meeting rm. Business servs avail. In-rm modem link. Cr cds: A, MC, V.
◀ 🛏 🛏 🎇 **SC**

Restaurants

★★ **GASLIGHT ROOM.** *205 N Rollins St (63552). 660/385-4013. www.gaslightroom.com.* Hrs: 10 am-9:30 pm; Sun 11 am-1:30 pm. Closed Jan 1, Thanksgiving, Dec 25. Res accepted. Bar. Lunch $2.50-$6, dinner $6.50-$30. Specializes in seafood, steak, pork chops. Salad bar. Entertainment Fri, Sat. In historic hotel. Cr cds: A, D, MC, V.
D ⬛

★ **LONG BRANCH.** *28855 Sunset Dr (63552). 660/385-4600.* Hrs: 6 am-9 pm; Sun 7 am-8 pm; Sun brunch to 3 pm. Closed Jan 1, Dec 25. Res accepted. Bar 3:30 pm-1 am. Bkfst $1.49-$6.50, lunch $1.59-$5.25, dinner $4.39-$12.99. Sun brunch $6.49. Children's menu. Specializes in beef, chicken. Salad bar. Western decor. Cr cds: A, D, DS, MC, V.
D ⬛

Mexico

See also Columbia

Founded 1836 **Pop** 11,290 **Elev** 802 ft **Area code** 573 **Zip** 65265

Information Mexico Area Chamber of Commerce, 100 W Jackson, PO Box 56; 573/581-2765 or 800/581-2765

According to local lore, Mexico got its name from a sign on a local tavern reading "Mexico that-a-way." Known as an agricultural trade center, its heritage includes world-famous saddlehorse breeding and training stables. The Missouri Military Academy, founded in 1889, is located on a beautiful 70-acre campus at the eastern end of Jackson Street.

What to See and Do

Graceland: Audrain County Historical Society Museum. Restored 1857 mansion; Victorian parlor, dining rm, library, period bedrm, children's rm with doll collection; Audrain County School, original rural schoolhouse and furnishings. Also here is American Saddle Horse Museum. (Mar-Dec, Tues-Sun afternoons; closed hols) 501 S Muldrow St. Phone 573/581-3910. ¢

Motel/Motor Lodge

★★ **BEST WESTERN INN.** *1010 E Liberty St (65265). 573/581-1440; fax 573/581-1487; toll-free 800/528-1234.* 63 rms, 2 story. S $36-$40; D $43-$48; each addl $4; under 12 free. Crib $4. Pet accepted; $5/day. TV; cable (premium). Pool. Complimentary continental bkfst. Restaurant 11 am-2 pm, 5-9 pm; closed Sun. Bar 11-1:30 am; closed Sun. Ck-out noon. Coin lndry. Meeting rm. Business servs avail. Sundries. Refrigerators. Cr cds: A, C, D, DS, ER, MC, V.
D ⬛ ⬛ ⬛ ⬛ SC

Unrated Dining Spot

G & D STEAK HOUSE. *US 54 S (65265). 573/581-0171.* Specializes in steak, Greek dishes, spaghetti. Salad bar. Hrs: 11 am-9 pm. Closed Dec 25. Lunch, dinner $5. Cafeteria-style line serv. Cr cds: A, DS, MC, V.
D SC

Monroe City

(B-5) *See also Hannibal*

Founded 1857 **Pop** 2,701 **Elev** 749 ft **Area code** 573 **Zip** 63456

Information Chamber of Commerce, 314 S Main St, in Nutrition Center, Box 22; 800/735-4391

What to See and Do

⭐ **Mark Twain Birthplace and State Park.** Almost 2,000 acres of wooded park; museum has frame house where Samuel Clemens (Mark Twain) was born Nov 30, 1835, exhibits on the author's life and some personal artifacts; slide show (daily); movies (summer wkends). Swimming, fishing, boating; picnicking, camping (dump station; standard fees). (Daily; museum closed hols) 9 mi SW on US 24 to MO 107, then 7 mi S. Phone 573/565-2228.

Motels/Motor Lodges

★ **MONROE CITY INN.** *3 Gateway Sq (63456). 573/735-4200; toll-free 800/446-6676.* 47 rms, 2 story. Mar-Oct: S $40-$50; D $45-$55; under 12 free; lower rates rest of yr. Crib free. Pet accepted, some restrictions; $5. TV; cable. Indoor pool; whirlpool. Ck-out 11 am. Cr cds: A, D, DS, MC, V.
D ⬛ ⬛ ⬛ ⬛ SC

★ **RAINBOW.** *308 5th St (63456). 573/735-4526.* 20 rms. S $24-$30; D $36-$40; each addl $5; under 6 free. Crib $5. TV; cable (premium). Pool. Complimentary coffee. Ck-out 11 am. Cr cds: A, DS, MC, V.
⬛ ⬛ ⬛ ⬛ ⬛

Mound City

See also St. Joseph

Pop 1,273 **Elev** 900 ft **Area code** 816 **Zip** 64470

What to See and Do

Big Lake State Park. Located at 625-acre natural oxbow lake. Swimming pool, fishing, boating, canoeing; picnicking, dining lodge, improved camping (dump station), cabins. Standard fees. (Daily) 7 mi SW on MO 118, then S on MO 111. Phone 816/442-3770. **FREE**

Squaw Creek National Wildlife Refuge. View bald eagles, geese, ducks, pelicans (during migrations), deer, and pheasant along ten-mi auto tour route; hiking trail; display in office (Mon-Fri). Refuge (Daily). For information contact Refuge Manager, PO Box 158. 5 mi S via I-29, exit 79, then 3 mi W on US 159. Phone 816/442-3187. **FREE**

Mount Vernon

(F-3) *See also Joplin, Springfield*

Pop 3,726 **Elev** 1,176 ft
Area code 417 **Zip** 65712

Motels/Motor Lodges

★ **BUDGET HOST.** *1015 E Mount Vernon Blvd (65712).* 417/466-2125; *fax 417/466-4440; toll-free 800/283-4678. www.budgethost.com.* 21 rms. S $40-$44; D $48-$55; each addl $3; wkly rates winter. Crib $3. Pet accepted, some restrictions. TV; cable (premium), VCR avail. Pool. Restaurant nearby. Ck-out 11 am. Picnic tables. Cr cds: A, DS, MC, V.

★★ **VILLAGER INN.** *900 E Mount Vernon Blvd (65712).* 417/466-2111; *fax 417/466-4776.* 43 rms. S $38-$55; D $43-$60; each addl $3; under 12 free. Crib free. TV; cable. Pool. Restaurant adj open 24 hrs. Ck-out 11 am. Meeting rm. Cr cds: A, DS, MC, V.

Nevada

(E-2) *See also Lamar; also see Fort Scott, KS*

Founded 1855 **Pop** 8,597 **Elev** 880 ft
Area code 417 **Zip** 64772
Information Chamber of Commerce, 110 S Adams; 417/667-5300

Settled by families from Kentucky and Tennessee, Nevada became known as the "bushwhackers capital" due to the Confederate guerrillas headquartered here during the Civil War. The town was burned to the ground in 1863 by Union troops and was not rebuilt until after the war. Today Nevada is a shopping and trading center for the surrounding area.

What to See and Do

Bushwhacker Museum. Museum operated by Vernon County Historical Society incl restored 19th-century jail; exhibits incl original cell rm; Civil War relics; period clothing, tools, medical items; Osage artifacts. (May-Sept, daily; Oct, Sat and Sun) 231 N Main St at Hunter St, 3 blks N of US 54. Phone 417/667-5841. ¢

Schell Osage Wildlife Area. Winter home to bald eagles and thousands of wild ducks and geese. (Daily; some areas closed during duck hunting season) 12 mi E on US 54 then 12 mi N on County AA, near Schell City. Phone 417/432-3414. **FREE**

Special Event

Bushwhacker Days. Parade; arts and crafts, antique machine and car shows; street square dance, midway. Mid-June.

Motels/Motor Lodges

★★ **RAMBLER MOTEL.** *1401 E Austin (64772).* 417/667-3351; *fax 417/667-3390.* 53 rms. S $38-$44; D $44-$48; each addl $4. Crib $4. TV; cable (premium). Pool. Ck-out 11 am. Cr cds: A, D, DS, MC, V.

★★ **RAMSEY'S.** *1514 E Austin Blvd (64772).* 417/667-5273. 26 rms. S $32; D $42; each addl $2. Crib $5. TV; cable (premium). Pool. Ck-out 11 am. Meeting rm. Airport transportation. Some refrigerators. Microwaves avail. Cr cds: A, C, D, DS, MC, V.

★ **SUPER 8 MOTEL.** *2301 E Austin St (64772).* 417/667-8888; *fax 417/667-8883; toll-free 800/800-8000. www.super8.com.* 60 rms, 2 story. S $40.88-$47.88; D $48.88-$60.88; each addl $2. Crib avail. Pet accepted. TV; cable (premium), VCR avail. Indoor pool; whirlpool. Complimentary continental bkfst. Restaurant nearby. Ck-out 11 am. Business servs avail. Coin lndry. Cr cds: A, C, D, DS, MC, V.

★ **WELCOME INN.** *2345 Marvel Dr (64772).* 417/667-6777; *fax 417/667-6135.* 46 rms, 2 story. S $44.95; D

$49.95; suites $51.95-$71.95; under 12 free; higher rates special events. Pet accepted, some restrictions; $25. TV; cable (premium). Pool; whirlpool. Complimentary continental bkfst. Restaurant nearby. Ck-out 11 am. Coin lndry. Meeting rms. Cr cds: A, C, D, DS, MC, V.
🅳 ⬛ ⬛ ⬛ ⬛ SC

Restaurants

★ **EL SAMBRE.** *1402 W Austin (64772).* 417/667-8242. Hrs: 11 am-9 pm; Fri, Sat to 10 pm. Closed Easter, Thanksgiving, Dec 25. Mexican menu. Lunch, dinner $1.20-$13.35. Children's menu. Specializes in Mexican cuisine. Mexican decor. Cr cds: A, DS, MC, V.
🅳 SC ⬛

★ **J.T. MALONEY'S.** *2117 E Austin (64772).* 417/667-7719. Hrs: 11 am-2 pm, 4-10 pm; Sat from 4 pm; Sun brunch 11 am-2 pm. Closed hols. Mexican, American menu. Bar to midnight. Lunch $3-$5.25, dinner $4-$19. Sun brunch $2.75-$5. Children's menu. Specializes in prime rib, chicken, seafood. Cr cds: A, DS, MC, V.
🅳 ⬛

Osage Beach

(D-4) *See also Camdenton, Lake Ozark*

Pop 2,599 **Elev** 895 ft **Area code** 573 **Zip** 65065
Information Lake Area Chamber of Commerce, US 54, PO Box 1570, Lake Ozark 65049; 573/365-3002 or 800/451-4117
Web www.odd.net/ozarks/chamber

A major resort community on the Lake of the Ozarks (see), the town came into existence with the 1931 completion of the lake. Today Osage Beach features some of the lake area's most popular attractions.

What to See and Do

Big Surf Water Park. This 22-acre park features river and tube rides, wave pool, body flumes; volleyball, changing facilities, concession. (Memorial Day-Labor Day, daily) 3 mi SW on US 54 to County Y. Phone 573/346-6111. ¢¢¢¢ Adj is

Big Shot Family Action Park. Miniature golf, bumper boats, go-carts, and other rides. Gift shop; concession. (Mar-Nov, daily, weather permitting) Admission to park is free; fees charged at each attraction. Phone 573/346-6111. ¢¢¢¢

Special Events

Lee Mace's Ozark Opry. On US 54. Mon-Sat eves. Phone 573/348-2270. Late Apr-Nov.

Main Street Opry. On US 54. Mon-Sat eves. Phone 573/348-4848. Mid-Apr-Oct.

Motels/Motor Lodges

★★ **BEST WESTERN DOGWOOD HILLS RESORT INN.** *1252 State Hwy KK (65065).* 573/348-1735; fax 573/348-0014; toll-free 800/528-1234. www.dogwoodhillsresort.com. 47 rms, 4 fairway villas, 2-3 story. S, D $72-$97; each addl $8; villas $250-$372; under 19 free; wkend rates. Crib $5. TV; cable. Pool; whirlpool. Dining rm 7 am-2 pm; closed Nov-Feb. Bar. Ck-out 11 am, ck-in 4 pm. Package store 1 mi. Meeting rm. Business servs avail. 18-hole golf, pro, putting green, driving range. Some refrigerators. Some private patios, balconies. Extensive grounds. Cr cds: A, D, DS, MC, V.
🅳 ⬛ ⬛ ⬛ ⬛ ⬛

★★ **INN AT GRAND GLAIZE.** *5142 US 54 (65065).* 573/348-4731; fax 573/348-4694; toll-free 800/348-4731. www.innatgrandglaize.com. 151 rms, 5 story. May-Oct: S, D $59-$139; under 18 free; lower rates rest of yr. Crib free. TV; cable. Heated pool; wading pool, whirlpool, poolside serv. Restaurant 6:30 am-10 pm. Bar 5 pm-1 am. Ck-out noon. Meeting rms. Business servs avail. Bellhops. Exercise equipt; sauna. Massage. Tennis. Game rm. Marina. Boat rentals. Fishing guides. Some bathrm phones, refrigerators. Private patios, balconies. Cr cds: A, C, D, DS, MC, V.
🅳 ⬛ ⬛ ⬛ ⬛ ⬛ ⬛ ⬛

★ **LAKE CHATEAU RESORT INN.** *5066 US 54 W (65065).* 573/348-2791; fax 573/348-1340; res 888/333-6927. www.lakeozark.com/lakechateau/.

49 rms, 2 story. Mid-May-mid-Sept: S, D $44-$89; each addl $5; under 18 free; lower rates rest of yr. Crib free. TV; cable. 2 pools; whirlpool. Playground. Restaurant 7 am-2 pm. Ck-out noon. Coin lndry. Business servs avail. Private patios, balconies. On lake; private sand beach, dock. Cr cds: A, D, DS, MC, V.

🅳 🐾 ➰ 📶 🔥 🆂🅲

★ **OSAGE VILLAGE MOTEL.** *4616 US 54 (65065). 573/348-5207; fax 573/348-9499.* 53 rms, 2 story. May-Oct: S $40-$65; D $45-$75; each addl $5; lower rates rest of yr. Crib $5. TV; cable (premium). Complimentary continental bkfst. Restaurant nearby. Ck-out 11 am. Pool; whirlpool. Some in rm whirlpools, refrigerators. Some balconies. Cr cds: A, DS, MC, V.

🅳 ➰ 📶 🔥 🆂🅲

★ **POINT BREEZE RESORT.** *1166 Jeffries Rd (65065). 573/348-2929. www.funlake.com.* 34 kits., 2 story. No rm phones. Memorial Day-Labor Day: S $48-$63; D $58-$76; each addl $6; suites $88; lower rates Apr-late May, early Sept-Oct. Closed rest of yr. Crib $6. TV; cable. Pool; wading pool. Playground. Restaurant nearby. Ck-out 11 am. Tennis. Rec rm. Lawn games. Private patio, balconies. Boats, motors. Picnic tables, grills.

🐾 🏌 ➰ 🔥

★★ **SUMMERSET INN RESORT.** *1165 Jeffries Rd (65065). 573/348-5073; fax 573/348-4676.* 35 units, 33 kits, 1-3 story. No rm phones. June-Aug: S, D $63-$260; wkly rates; golf plans; lower rates Mar-May and Sept-Oct. Closed rest of yr. Crib free. TV; cable (premium). Pool; wading pool, whirlpool. Playgrounds. Restaurant nearby. Ck-out 10:30 am, ck-in 4 pm. Business servs avail. Grocery store 1½ mi. Coin lndry. Dockage. Lawn games. Game rm. Fishing guide. Microwaves avail. Picnic tables, grills. Cr cds: A, MC, V.

➰ 🔥

Resorts

★ **KALFRAN LODGE.** *Lake Rd 54-39 (65065). 573/348-2266; fax 573/348-2747; toll-free 800/417-2266. www.funlake.com.* 56 rms, 1-2 story, 44 kits. June-Aug: S, D $68-$78; each addl $5; kit. units $62-$95; cottages with

kit. $52-$92; lower rates Apr-May, Sept-Oct. Closed rest of yr. Crib $5. TV; cable. 2 heated pools; wading pool. Playground. Restaurant nearby. Ck-out 10 am, ck-in 3 pm. Grocery ¼ mi. Coin lndry. Package store ¼ mi. Meeting rms. Tennis. Boats. Lawn games. Rec rm. Refrigerators. Some private patios, balconies. Picnic tables, grills. Cr cds: A, MC, V.

🐾 🏌 ➰ 🔥

★★ **THE KNOLLS.** *Baydy Peak Rd and KK (65065). 573/348-2236; fax 573/348-7198; toll-free 800/648-0339. www.funlake.com.* 50 kit condo units. Mid-May-mid-Sept: 1-bedrm $199-$244; 2-bedrm $244-$259; 3-bedrm $269-$324; 4-bedrm $414; lower rates rest of yr. Crib $5. TV; cable. 2 pools, 1 indoor; poolside serv. Playground. Coffee in rms. Box lunches. Snack bar in season. Picnic area. Bar in season. Ck-out noon, ck-in 4 pm. Grocery 1 mi. Meeting rms. Business servs avail. Airport transportation. Indoor tennis. Lawn games. Dock; waterskiing; boats, pontoons. Fishing guides. Game rm. Fireplaces; some in-rm whirlpools; microwaves avail. Balconies, grills. Cr cds: A, DS, MC, V.

🐾 🏌 🏌 ➰ 🔥

★★★ **TAN-TAR-A RESORT GOLF CLUB AND SPA.** *State Rd KK (65065). 573/348-3131; fax 573/348-3206; toll-free 800/826-8272. www.tan-tar-a.com.* 365 lodge rms, 1-8 story; 195 kit. units, 1-3 story. Apr-Oct: S, D $89-$185; suites, kit. units $175-$380; family rates; wkend, package plans; seasonal rates. Crib free. TV; cable (premium), VCR avail. 5 pools, 1 indoor, 1 heated; 2 wading pools, whirlpool, poolside serv. Playground. Supervised children's activities (Memorial Day-Labor Day, daily; rest of yr, Fri-Sun; also hols). Coffee in rms. Restaurant 6 am-midnight. Box lunches. Snack bar. Picnics. Rm serv 6 am-midnight. Bars to 1 am, Sun to midnight. Ck-out noon, ck-in 4 pm. Grocery on site. Coin lndry. Meeting rms. Business servs avail. Valet serv. Shopping arcade. Barber, beauty shop. Rec dir. Indoor, outdoor tennis. 27-hole golf, greens fee $55-$79, putting green, driving range. Waterskiing; parasailing; marina, excursion boat, pontoon boat. Go-carts, touring carts. Soc dir; entertainment, rainy day program. Indoor ice

rink (Oct-Apr). Racquetball courts.
Indoor basketball. Bowling. Miniature
golf. Rec rm. Exercise equipt; sauna.
Fishing guides, children's fishing
area. Refrigerators, fireplaces; microwaves avail. Many private patios; balconies overlook lake. On 550-acre
peninsula. Cr cds: A, MC, V.

⬜🎿🛶🏈🎣🏊🏃🎿🚴SC

Restaurants

★★ **BRASS DOOR.** *US 54 (65065).*
573/348-9229. www.brassdoor.com.
Hrs: 5-10 pm. Dinner $13.99-$23.99.
Children's menu. Specializes in sea-
food, prime rib, steak. Entertainment
Fri-Sat eves. Cr cds: A, MC, V.
🎿

★★ **DOMENICO'S CARRY-OUT
PIZZA.** *4737 US 54 (65065). 573/348-
2844.* Hrs: 5-10:30 pm; to 10 pm off
season. Closed hols; also Super Bowl
Sun. Italian, American menu. Bar.
Dinner $6.95-$25.95. Children's
menu. Specializes in charbroiled
prime rib, pasta, chicken. Cr cds: A,
DS, MC, V.
⬜🎿

★★ **HAPPY FISHERMAN.** *US 54
(65065). 573/348-3311.* Hrs: 11:30
am-10 pm. Closed mid-Dec-mid-Jan.
Bar. Lunch, dinner $3.95-$17.50.
Children's menu. Specializes in
seafood. Salad bar. Nautical decor. Cr
cds: A, DS, MC, V.
⬜SC🎿

★★ **POTTED STEER.** *US 54
(65065). 573/348-5053.* Hrs: 5-10 pm.
Closed Mon, Sun; hols; also Dec-Feb.
Bar. Wine list. $18.65-$34.75. Specialties: batter-fried lobster tail, strip
steaks. View of lake. Family-owned.
Cr cds: A, DS, MC, V.
⬜

★★ **VISTA GRANDE.** *US 54 (65065).*
573/348-1231. Hrs: 11:30 am-10 pm.
Closed Thanksgiving, Dec 24-25.
Mexican, American menu. Bar.
Lunch $4.25-$6.95, dinner $6.75-
$13.95. Children's menu. Specializes
in Mexican cuisine. Mexican decor.
Cr cds: A, DS, MC, V.
⬜🎿

Pilot Knob
See also Bonne Terre

Pop 783 **Elev** 1,000 ft **Area code** 573
Zip 63663

What to See and Do

Johnson's Shut-Ins State Park. This
nearly 8,500-acre area, left in its
wilderness state, has a spectacular
canyonlike defile along river. The
park is at the southern end of 20-mi-
long Ozark backpacking trail which
traverses Missouri's highest mountain, Taum Sauk. Swimming, fishing;
hiking, picnicking, playground,
improved camping (dump station).
Standard fees. (Daily) 4 mi N on MO
21 to Graniteville, then 13 mi SW on
County N. Phone 573/546-2450.
FREE

Sam A. Baker State Park. The St.
François and Big Creek rivers flow
through this more than 5,000-acre
park. Canoe rentals; hiking trails;
picnicking, playground, store, cabins,
dining lodge (Apr-Oct), improved
camping (dump station). Nature center. Standard fees. (Daily) 30 mi S on
MO 21 and MO 49 to Des Arc, then
12 mi SE on MO 143. Phone
573/856-4411.

Resort

★★ **WILDERNESS LODGE.** *Peola
Rd, Lesterville (63654). 573/637-2295;
fax 573/637-2504; toll-free 888/969-
9129. www.wildernesslodgeresort.com.*
27 cottages (1-3 bedrm). MAP, Apr-
Nov: S $69-$109; D $109-$138; each
addl $69; suites $79/person; family
rates; lower rates rest of yr. Crib free.
TV; cable (premium), VCR avail
(movies). Pool. Playground. Complimentary coffee in rms. Dining rm
(public by res) 8-9 am, 11:30 am-1
pm, 7-8 pm. Box lunches. Bar 6-9
pm. Ck-out 1 pm, ck-in 4:30 pm.
Meeting rms. Business center. Tennis.
Private beach, canoes, inner tube
rentals. Lawn games. Hiking trails
with maps. Hay rides (fee). Refrigerators; some screened porches, fireplaces. Some private patios, balconies.
On Black River. Cr cds: A, D, MC, V.
⬜🎿🛶🎣🏊🏃🎿

Poplar Bluff

(F-6) *See also Sikeston, Van Buren*

Settled 1819 **Pop** 16,996 **Elev** 344 ft
Area code 573 **Zip** 63901
Information Chamber of Commerce,
1111 W Pine, PO Box 3986, 63902-
3986; 573/785-7761
Web www.ims-l.com/~pbchamber/

Solomon Kittrell, the first settler
here, immediately set up two vital
industries—a tannery and a distillery.
Poplar Bluff is now an industrial and
farm marketing center.

What to See and Do

Lake Wappapello State Park. Approx
1,800 acres. Swimming, fishing; hiking, playground, improved camping
(dump station), cabins. Standard
fees. (Daily) 15 mi N on US 67, then
9 mi E on MO 172. Phone 573/297-
3232. **FREE**

Mark Twain National Forests. (Poplar
Bluff Ranger District). More than
150,000 acres on rolling hills of
Ozark Plateau, with 49 acres of lakes,
33 mi of horseback riding trails. Fishing, float trips (Black River); hunting,
hiking, camping (standard fees). 7 mi
N on US 67. Phone 573/785-1475.

Motels/Motor Lodges

★★ **DRURY INN.** *Business 60 and US
67 N (63901).* 573/686-2451; *toll-free
800/325-8300. www.druryinn.com.* 78
rms, 3 story. S $55-$59; D $63-$68;
each addl $8; under 18 free. Crib
free. Pet accepted, some restrictions.
TV; cable. Pool. Complimentary
bkfst. Restaurant adj 6 am-11 pm.
Ck-out noon. Business servs avail. In-
rm modem link. Valet serv. Cr cds: A,
C, D, DS, MC, V.
D 🍴 🏋 ⊠ 🗑 SC

★ **RAMADA INN.** *2115 N Westwood
Blvd (63901).* 573/785-7711; *fax
573/785-5215; toll-free 888/298-2054.
www.ramada.com.* 143 rms, 1-2 story.
S $55; D $63; each addl $8; suites
$150; under 18 free. Crib free. Pet
accepted. TV; cable (premium). Pool.
Restaurant 6 am-10 pm. Bar 11-1:30
am, Sun 1-10 pm; entertainment

Mon-Sat. Ck-out noon. Meeting rms.
Cr cds: A, C, D, DS, MC, V.
D 🍴 🏋 ⊠ 🗑 🔥

★ **SUPER 8 MOTEL.** *2831 N Westwood Blvd (63901).* 573/785-0176; *fax
573/785-2865; toll-free 800/800-8000.
www.super8.com.* 63 rms, 2 story. S
$44; D $50-$62; each addl $4; under
12 free. Crib free. TV; cable. Complimentary continental bkfst. Restaurant 6 am-10 pm. Ck-out 11 am. Cr
cds: A, C, D, DS, MC, V.
D ⊠ 🗑 SC

Rockaway Beach

See also Branson/Table Rock Lake Area

Pop 275 **Elev** 800 ft **Area code** 417
Zip 65740
Information Bureau of Tourism; PO
Box 1004; 417/561-4280 or 800/798-
0178

This popular resort area is on the
shores of Lake Taneycomo, which
was created by the impounding of
the White River by a 1,700-foot dam
near Ozark Beach. Attractions
include fishing, boating (rentals),
tennis, golf, flea markets, and
arcades.

Motel/Motor Lodge

★ **TANEYCOMO MOTOR LODGE.**
2518 MO 176 (65740). 417/561-4141.
27 rms. S $35; D $39-$43. Crib free.
TV; cable (premium). Pool. Playground. Complimentary coffee.
Restaurant nearby. Ck-out 11 am. On
lake; marina. Cr cds: A, DS, MC, V.
🏋 ⊠ 🗑 🔥

Restaurant

★ **HILLSIDE INN.** *Main St (65740).*
417/561-8252. Hrs: 7 am-9 pm; May-
Sept 7 am-10 pm. Closed Dec 24-25.
Res accepted. Mexican, American
menu. Bkfst $2.50-$5.50, lunch
$2.95-$7, dinner $4-$11.95. Children's menu. Specializes in chicken,
Mexican dishes.
🗑

Rolla

(E-5) *See also Sullivan, Waynesville*

Settled 1855 **Pop** 14,090 **Elev** 1,119 ft
Area code 573 **Zip** 65401
Information Rolla Area Chamber of
Commerce, 1301 Kings Hwy;
573/364-3577
Web www.rollanet.org/atcommerce

According to legend, the town was
named by a homesick settler from
Raleigh, North Carolina, who spelled
the name as he pronounced it.
Called "the child of the railroad"
because it began with the building of
the St. Louis-San Francisco Railroad,
the town is located in a scenic area
with several fishing streams nearby.
Mark Twain National Forest maintains its headquarters in Rolla.

What to See and Do

**Ed Clark Museum of Missouri Geol-
ogy.** Displays of mineral resources,
geological history, and land survey-
ing. (Mon-Fri; closed hols) In Buehler
Park, on City I-44, 111 Fairgrounds
Rd. Phone 573/368-2100. **FREE**

**Maramec Spring Park and Remains
of Old Ironworks.** The spring dis-
charges an average of 96.3 million
gallons per day. The ironworks was
first established in 1826; the present
furnace was built in 1857. Trout fishing (Mar-Oct); trails, scenic road, picnicking, playground, campground
(fee). Nature center; observation
tower; two museums. (Daily) 8 mi E
on I-44 to St. James, then 7 mi SE on
MO 8. Phone 573/265-7387. ¢

Mark Twain National Forests. (Rolla-
Houston Ranger Districts) More than
192,000 acres; cradles headwaters of
Gasconade, Little Piney, and Big
Piney rivers. Swimming, fishing;
hunting; boating. Picnicking. Camping (standard fees). Paddy Creek
Wilderness Area covers about 6,800
acres with 30 mi of hiking and riding
trails. SW via I-44, US 63. Phone
573/364-4621.

Memoryville, USA. More than 30
antique cars; art gallery, restoration
shop; antique, gift shop; lounge,
restaurant. (Daily; closed Jan 1,
Thanksgiving, Dec 25). On US 63 N
at jct I-44. Phone 573/364-1810. ¢¢

Montauk State Park. Approx 1,300
acres. Trout fishing; hiking trail, picnicking, store, motel, dining lodge,
improved camping (dump station),
cabins. Standard fees. (Daily) 35 mi S
on US 63 to Licking, then 2 mi S on
MO 137, then 10 mi E on County
VV. Phone 573/548-2201. **FREE**

St. James Winery. Dry and semi-dry
wines, champagne, sparkling wines,
Concord, Catawba, and berry wines
all produced here. Hrly tours; tasting
rm; gift shop. (Daily; closed Dec 25)
10 mi E via I-44, St. James exit, then
3 blks E on County B (north access
road). Phone 573/265-7912.

University of Missouri-Rolla. (1870)
5,000 students. N Pine St. Phone
573/341-4328. On campus are

Minerals Museum. Begun in 1904
as part of the Missouri mining
exhibit for the St. Louis World's
Fair, today the exhibit contains
4,000 specimens from around the
world. (Mon-Fri; closed hols) First
floor, McNutt Hall. Geology
Department. Phone 573/341-4616.
FREE

UMR Nuclear Reactor. Swimming
pool-type reactor, contains 32,000
gallons of water. Tours. (Mon-Fri;
closed hols and Aug) Phone
573/341-4236. **FREE**

UM-Rolla Stonehenge. Partial
reproduction of Stonehenge, the
ancient circle of megaliths on Salisbury Plain in England. Features
five trilithons standing 13 ft high.
Interpretive guides avail. Phone
573/341-4328. **FREE**

Special Events

St. Pat's Celebration. University of
Missouri celebration of St. Patrick,
patron saint of engineers; parade,
painting Main St green, beard judging contests, shillelagh judging,
entertainment. Mar.

Rte 66 Summerfest. Downtown. Second wkend July.

Central Missouri Regional Fair. Fairgrounds, ½ mi S on US 63. Early Aug.

Motels/Motor Lodges

★★ **BEST WESTERN COACH-
LIGHT.** *1403 Martin Springs Dr
(65401). 573/341-2511; fax 573/308-*

3055; toll-free 800/937-8376. www. bestwestern.com. 88 rms, 2 story. May-Oct: S, D $55; each addl $4; under 17 free; higher rates special events; lower rates rest of yr. Crib $8. Pet accepted. TV; cable (premium). Pool. Playground. Complimentary continental bkfst. Coffee in rms. Restaurant adj 11 am-10 pm. Ck-out noon. Meeting rms. In-rm modem link. Guest lndry. Some refrigerators. Cr cds: A, C, D, DS, ER, JCB, MC, V.

★★ **DRURY INN.** *2006 N Bishop Ave (65401).* 573/364-4000; toll-free 800/ 436-3310. *www.drury-inn.com.* 86 rms, 2 story. S, D $49.95-$74.95; each addl $10; under 18 free. Crib free. Pet accepted. TV; cable. Complimentary continental bkfst. Pool. Ck-out noon. Meeting rms. Business servs avail. Valet serv. Health club privileges. Cr cds: A, C, D, DS, MC, V.

★★ **ZENO'S MOTEL AND STEAK HOUSE.** *1621 Martin Springs Dr (65401).* 573/364-1301. 51 rms. S $47; D $52-$57; each addl $3; higher rates special events. Crib $3. TV; cable. 2 pools, 1 indoor; whirlpool. Sauna. Restaurant 7 am-10 pm. Bar 4 pm-midnight. Ck-out noon. Meeting rms. Business servs avail. In-rm modem link. Valet serv. Cr cds: A, C, D, DS, MC, V.

Restaurant

★ **JOHNNY'S SMOKE STAK.** *201 US 72 (65401).* 573/364-4838. Hrs: 11 am-8:30 pm; Fri, Sat to 9:30 pm. Closed Jan 1, Thanksgiving, Dec 25. Lunch $5-$5.50, dinner $6-$15. Children's menu. Specializes in hickory-smoked beef, ribs, ham. Salad bar. Cr cds: A, MC, V.

St. Charles

(C-6) *See also St. Louis, Wentzville*

Settled 1769 **Pop** 54,555 **Elev** 536 ft
Area code 636

Information Convention and Visitors Bureau, 230 S Main, 63301; 636/946-7776 or 800/366-2427

Web www.historicstcharles.com

St. Charles, one of the early settlements on the Missouri River, was the first capital of the state (1821-1826). Between 1832-1870 a wave of German immigrants settled here and developed the town but St. Louis, by virtue of its location on the Mississippi, became the state's most important city. St. Charles is the home of Sacred Heart Convent (1818) and Lindenwood University (1827). Frenchtown, a northern ward of old St. Charles, is home to many antique shops.

Katy Trail State Park, St. Charles

What to See and Do

***Goldenrod* Showboat.** Restored 1909 showboat dinner theater. Show only or dinner/show seating combination. (Thurs-Sun eves; also Wed and Thurs matinee) 1000 blk Riverside Dr. Phone 636/946-2020.

Katy Trail State Park. A 185-mi bicycling and hiking trail across Missouri, among the longest of its kind in the US. (Daily) Contact the Missouri Department of Natural Resources. Trailheads in St. Charles and other towns. Phone 660/882-8196.

Miniature World. Miniature representations by renowned artists. "History in miniature" with a focus on WW II (Apr-Sept, Tues-Sat; rest of yr, Wed-Sun). 132-36 N. Main St. Phone 636/916-0550. ¢¢¢

☒ St. Charles Historic District. Nine-blk area along S Main St with restored houses, antique and gift shops, restaurants, the 1836 Newbill-McElhiney House. Also here are

> **First Missouri State Capitol State Historic Site.** Eleven rms of capitol have been restored to original state; nine rms have 1820 period furnishings; also restoration of Peck Brothers General Store and house. Interpretive center. (Daily; closed hols) 200-216 S Main St. Phone 636/946-9282. ¢

> **Lewis and Clark Center.** Museum depicts the 1804-1806 expedition from St. Charles to the Pacific Ocean. Hands-on exhibits, lifesize models of Sacagawea and the men of the expedition; Mandan and Sioux villages, display of Missouri River; gift shop. (Daily; closed hols) 701 Riverside Dr. Phone 636/947-3199. ¢

Special Events

Lewis and Clark Rendezvous. Frontier Park, on Riverside Dr. Reenactment of the explorers' encampment in 1804 prior to embarking on their exploration of the Louisiana Purchase; parade, fife and drum corps. Mid-May.

Festival of the Little Hills. Frontier Park and Main St. Bluegrass and country music; 19th-century crafts, antiques. Late Aug.

Christmas Traditions. Historic District. Month-long celebration with carolers, Santas of the Past, living history characters, parade, fife and drum corps. Day after Thanksgiving-Dec 24.

Motels/Motor Lodges

★ **DAYS INN NOAH'S ARK.** *1500 S 5th St (63303). 636/946-1000; fax 636/723-6670; toll-free 800/332-3448. www.daysinn.com.* 122 rms, 6 story. S $45-$65; D $50-$72; each addl $6; suites $109.95-$175; under 18 free;

Lewis and Clark Center, St. Charles

wkend, hol rates; higher rates special events. Crib free. TV; cable. Pool; whirlpool. Complimentary continental bkfst. Ck-out 11 am. Coin lndry. Meeting rms. Business servs avail. In-rm modem link. Free airport transportation. Exercise equipt; sauna. Game rm. Some refrigerators. Cr cds: A, C, D, DS, MC, V.

🄳 ⌯ 🛉 🔄 🔥 SC

★★ HAMPTON INN. *3720 W Clay St (63301). 636/947-6800; fax 636/947-0020; toll-free 800/426-7867. www.hamptoninn.com.* 122 rms, 4 story. S $65-$70; D $68-$73; under 19 free. Crib free. TV; cable. Indoor pool; whirlpool. Complimentary continental bkfst. Restaurant nearby. Ck-out noon. Meeting rms. Business servs avail. Bellhops. Valet serv. Exercise equipt. Cr cds: A, C, D, DS, MC, V.

🄳 ⌚ ⌯ 🛉 🔄 🔥

★★ HOLIDAY INN SELECT ST. PETER'S. *I-70 and Cave Springs, St. Peters (63376). 636/928-1500; toll-free 800/767-3837. www.holiday-inn.com.* 199 rms, 6 story. S $89; D $99; suites $145; under 18 free. Pet accepted; deposit. TV; cable. Indoor/outdoor pool; whirlpool, poolside serv. Restaurant 6 am-2 pm, 5-11 pm. Bar 11-1 am; entertainment wkends. Ck-out noon. Coin lndry. Meeting rms. Business center. Bellhops. Valet serv. Free airport, bus depot transportation. Exercise equipt; sauna. Game rm. Rec rm. Some bathrm phones; refrigerators, microwaves avail. Luxury level. Cr cds: A, C, D, DS, JCB, MC, V.

🄳 🔄 ⌯ 🛉 ✈ 🔄 🔥 🚶

★ MOTEL 6. *3800 Harry S. Truman Blvd (63301). 636/925-2020; fax 314/946-3480; toll-free 800/466-8356. www.motel6.com.* 110 rms. S $49.95-$55; D, kit. units $55-$65; under 18 free. Crib free. Pet accepted. TV; cable. Pool. Complimentary coffee in lobby. Restaurant opp 6 am-10:30 pm. Ck-out noon. Coin lndry. Some refrigerators. Cr cds: A, C, D, DS, MC, V.

🄳 🔄 ⌯ 🔄 🔥 SC

B&B/Small Inn

★ BOONE'S LICK TRAIL INN. *1000 S Main St (63301). 636/947-7000; fax 636/946-2637; toll-free 800/366-2427.*

www.booneslick.com. 5 rms, 2½ story. S $95; D $135; each addl $15-$40; wkend rates. TV; VCR avail. Complimentary full bkfst. Restaurant adj 11 am-midnight. Ck-out 11 am, ck-in 3:30 pm. Built in 1840; English style. Totally nonsmoking. Cr cds: A, C, D, DS, MC, V.

🄳 🔄 🔥

Restaurant

★★ PAUL MANNO'S CAFE. *75 Forum Ctr (63017). 314/878-1274.* Hrs: 11 am-2 pm, 5-10 pm; Sat from 5 pm; Sun 4:30-8 pm. Closed Mon; hols. Res accepted. Italian menu. Bar. Lunch, dinner $4.50-$15.95. Children's menu. Specialties: linguini del marinaio, capelli d'Angelo alla boscagliola, rigatoni con pollo. Elegant atmosphere. Cr cds: A, C, D, DS, MC, V.

🄳

★★ ST. CHARLES VINTAGE HOUSE. *1219 S Main St (63301). 636/946-7155.* Hrs: 11 am-10 pm; Fri, Sat to midnight; Sun 10 am-8 pm; early-bird dinner Tues-Sat 5-7 pm; Sun brunch to 1 pm. Closed Mon; Dec 25. Res accepted. German, American menu. Bar. Lunch $3.95-$6.50, dinner $7.95-$15.95. Sun brunch $6.95. Children's menu. Specializes in barbecued ribs, fresh seafood, German dishes. Outdoor dining. Former winery (1860). Cr cds: A, C, D, DS, MC, V.

SC

Ste. Genevieve

(E-6) *See also St. Louis*

Founded 1735 **Pop** 4,411 **Elev** 401 ft **Area code** 573 **Zip** 63670

Information Great River Road Interpretive Center, 66 S Main; 573/883-7097 or 800/373-7007

Ste. Genevieve, the first permanent settlement in Missouri, developed on the banks of the Mississippi River early in the 18th century when Frenchmen began mining lead in the region. After a great flood in 1785, the village was moved to higher ground. Once St. Louis's chief rival, Ste. Genevieve preserves its French heritage in its festivals, old houses, and massive redbrick church. Today the town is an important lime-producing center.

What to See and Do

Bolduc House Museum. (ca 1770) Restored French house with walls of upright heavy oak logs; period furnishings, orchard and herb garden. (Apr-Nov, daily) 125 S Main St. Phone 573/883-3105. ¢

Felix Valle Home State Historic Site. (1818) Restored and furnished Federal-style stone house of early fur trader. Guided tours. (Daily; closed hols) 198 Merchant St. Phone 573/883-7102. ¢

Guibourd-Valle House. Late 18th-century restored vertical log house on stone foundation; French heirlooms. Attic with Norman truss and hand-hewn oak beams secured by wooden pegs. Courtyard; rose garden; stone well; costumed guides. (Apr-Oct, daily; Mar and Nov wkends only) 1 N 4th St. Phone 573/883-7544. ¢¢

Ste. Genevieve Museum. Display of salt manufacturing, state's first industry. Scale model of rail car transfer boat Ste. Genevieve, which carried trains across the Mississippi. Native American artifacts; local mementos. (Daily; closed hols) Merchant St and DuBourg Pl. Phone 573/883-3461. ¢

Special Event

Jour de Fête à Ste. Geneviève. 4 mi E via I-55, MO 32. Tours of historic French houses; art show, French market, antiques. Phone 573/883-7097. Second wkend Aug.

B&Bs/Small Inns

★ **INN ST. GEMME BEAUVAIS.** *78 N Main St (63670). 573/883-5744; fax 573/883-3899; toll-free 800/818-5744. www.bbhost.com/innstgemme.* 8 rms, 3 story. No elvtr. No rm phones. S, D $89; each addl $15. TV; cable; VCR avail. Complimentary full bkfst; afternoon refreshments. Ck-out 11 am, ck-in 2 pm. Business servs avail. In-rm modem link. Columned, red-brick Greek-revival inn (1848); antiques. Cr cds: A, DS, MC, V.

★ **MAIN STREET INN BED & BREAKFAST.** *221 N Main St (63670). 573/883-9199; fax 573/883-9911; res 800/918-9199. www.mainstreetinnbb.com.* 8 rms, 3 story. No elvtr. S $65-$75; D $85-$95; each addl $10. Adults only. TV avail; cable; VCR. Complimentary full bkfst. Restaurant nearby. Ck-out noon, ck-in 4 pm. Business servs avail. In-rm modem link. Game rm. Lawn games. Some in-rm whirlpools. Built in 1880 as a hotel; antiques. Totally nonsmoking. Cr cds: A, DS, MC, V.

★★ **SOUTHERN HOTEL BED & BREAKFAST.** *146 S 3rd St (63670). 573/883-3493; fax 573/883-9612; toll-free 800/275-1412. www.southernhotelbb.com.* 8 rms, 3 story. No rm phones. S $70-$103; D $88-$138. Children over 12 yrs only. Complimentary full bkfst; afternoon refreshments. Restaurant nearby. Ck-out 11 am, ck-in 4-6 pm. Gift shop. Game rm. Built 1791. Totally nonsmoking. Cr cds: A, DS, MC, V.

Restaurants

★ **ANVIL SALOON.** *46 S 3rd St (63670). 573/883-7323.* Hrs: 11 am-11 pm. Closed hols. German, American menu. Bar. Lunch, dinner $1.95-$13.50. Specializes in steak, catfish, fried chicken. Own pies. Oldest commercially operated building in city (ca 1850); early Western saloon decor. Cr cds: A, DS, MC, V.

★ **BIG RIVER.** *163 Merchant St (63670). 573/883-5647.* Hrs: 11 am-9 pm; Sun to 7 pm; Mon to 2 pm. Closed Thanksgiving, Dec 25. Res accepted. Southwestern menu. Bar. Lunch, dinner $4.95-$15.95. Children's menu. Specializes in fajitas, barbecue ribs, steaks. Street parking. Outdoor dining. Two-story historic brick building. Totally nonsmoking. Cr cds: MC, V.

★ **OLD BRICK HOUSE.** *90 S 3rd St (63670). 573/883-2724.* Hrs: 8 am-9 pm; Sat to 10 pm; Sun 11 am-7 pm. Closed Thanksgiving, Dec 25. Bar to 1 am. Bkfst $3.75-$5.75, lunch $2.25-$4.95, dinner $5.95-$18.95. Children's menu. Specializes in fried chicken. Salad bar. One of the first brick buildings (1785) west of Mississippi. Cr cds: MC, V.

St. Joseph

(B-2) *See also Cameron, Kansas City, Mound City; also see Atchison, KS*

Settled 1826 **Pop** 71,852 **Elev** 833 ft
Area code 816
Information Convention & Visitors Bureau, 109 S 4th St, 64501; 816/233-6688 or 800/785-0360
Web www.stjomo.com

A historic city with beautiful parks and large industries, St. Joseph retains traces of the frontier settlement of the 1840s in the "original town" near the Missouri River. It was founded and named by Joseph Robidoux III, a French fur trader from St. Louis, who established his post in 1826. St. Joseph, the western terminus of the first railroad to cross the state, became the eastern terminus of the Pony Express, whose riders carried mail to and from Sacramento, California from 1860-1861 using relays of fast ponies. The record trip, which carried copies of President Lincoln's inaugural address, was made in seven days and 17 hours. The telegraph ended the need for the Pony Express. The Civil War disrupted the region, largely Southern in sympathy, but postwar railroad building and cattle trade restored the city.

What to See and Do

Albrecht-Kemper Museum of Art. Exhibits of 18th-, 19th-, and 20th-century American paintings, sculptures, graphic art. Formal gardens. (Tues-Sun; closed hols) 2818 Frederick Blvd. Phone 816/233-7003. ¢¢

First Street Trolley. Reproductions of turn-of-the-century streetcars tour the historically significant sites of St. Joseph. (May-Oct, Mon-Sat) Begin tour at Patee House, 12th and Penn. Phone 800/785-0360. ¢

Glore Psychiatric Museum. Housed in a ward of the original 1874 administration building, the museum displays the evolution of treatment philosophy and techniques over a 400-yr period. (Mon-Fri; also Sat, Sun, and hol afternoons) 3406 Frederick Ave. Phone 816/387-2310. **FREE**

Jesse James Home. One-story frame cottage where the outlaw had been living quietly as "Mr. Howard" until he was killed here Apr 3, 1882, by an associate, Bob Ford. Some original furnishings. (Daily) 12th and Penn sts. Phone 816/232-8206. ¢

Missouri Theater. Renovated 1926 movie palace decorated in pre-Persian motif with bas relief on exterior. (Daily by appt; closed hols) 717 Edmund. Phone 816/271-4628. ¢

Patee House Museum. Built in 1858 as a hotel; in 1860 it served as headquarters of the Pony Express. Contains pioneer exhibits related to transportation and communication; incl restored 1860 Buffalo Saloon; woodburning engine and the original last mail car from the Hannibal and St. Joseph railroad. Also 1917 Japanese tea house; ice-cream parlor. (Apr-Oct, daily; Jan-Mar and Nov, wkends) 12th and Penn sts. Phone 816/232-8206. ¢¢

Pony Express Museum. Museum in old Pikes Peak (Pony Express) Stables, the starting point of the first westward ride. Original stables; displays illustrate the creation, operation, management, and termination of the famed mail service. (Daily; closed hols) 914 Penn St. Phone 816/279-5059. ¢¢

Pony Express Region Tourist Information Centers. Housed in historic railroad cabooses, centers provide brochures and information on St. Joseph, northwest Missouri, and northeast Kansas; free maps. (Apr-Oct, daily) W of I-29 exit 47; also at I-35 and US 36 at Cameron. Phone 816/232-1839.

Robidoux Row Museum. (ca 1850) Built by city's founder, French fur trader Joseph Robidoux, as temporary housing for newly arrived settlers who had purchased land from him. Authentically restored; some original furnishings. Tours. (Tues-Fri, also Sat and Sun afternoons; closed hols) 3rd and Poulin sts. Phone 816/232-5861. ¢

St. Joseph Museum. Native American collections; natural history; local and western history exhibits, incl Civil War, Pony Express, and Jesse James era. (Daily; closed hols) Free on Sun. 11th and Charles sts. Phone 816/232-8471.

St. Joseph Park System. Approximately 26 mi of parkway system stretching over 1,500 acres of land. Of the more than 40 parks and facilities, most are along a 9½-mi drive from Krug Park (W of St. Joseph Ave in the N end of the city) to Hyde Park (4th and Hyde Pk Ave in the S end of the city). The park system provides a variety of recreational facilities incl 18-hole golf, tennis courts, ballfields, and an indoor ice arena. (Daily) Phone 816/271-5500.

Society of Memories Doll Museum. More than 600 antique dolls; miniature rms and houses, old toys, antique clothing. (Tues-Sun; tour by appt) 1115 S 12th St. Phone 816/233-1420. ¢

Special Events

Apple Blossom Parade and Festival. Originally a celebration of area apple growers. Parade with more than 200 entries; food, music, crafts. Phone 816/271-8604. First wkend May.

Historic Homes Tour. Historic mansions open for tours. Styles range from pre-Civil War to Victorian. First wkend June.

Trails West. Arts festival celebrating cultural heritage. Stage performances, historical reenactments, music, food. Phone 800/216-7080. Mid-Aug.

Southside Fall Festival. Crafts, parade, entertainment, rodeo. Phone 816/238-1450. Mid-Sept.

Motels/Motor Lodges

★ **DAYS INN.** *4312 Frederick Blvd (64506). 816/279-1671; fax 816/279-6729; toll-free 800/329-7466. www. daysinn.com.* 100 rms, 2 story. S $44-$64; D $50-$72; each addl $6; under 12 free. Crib free. TV; cable (premium), VCR avail (movies). Pool. Complimentary continental bkfst. Restaurant 6:30-9:30 am, 5:30-9 pm. Bar 5-9 pm. Ck-out 11 am. Meeting rms. Business servs avail. Cr cds: A, C, D, DS, ER, JCB, MC, V.
⌑ ⊠ 🐾 SC

★★ **DRURY INN.** *4213 Frederick Blvd (64506). 816/364-4700; res 800/378-*

7946. 133 rms, 4 story. S $60-$70; D $70-$80; each addl $10; under 18 free. Crib free. Pet accepted. TV; cable (premium). Pool. Complimentary continental bkfst. Coffee in rms. Restaurant adj 6 am-11 pm. Ck-out noon. Meeting rms. Business servs avail. In-rm modem link. Valet serv. Sundries. Exercise equipt. Cr cds: A, C, D, DS, MC, V.
⌐ 🐾 ⌑ 🏋 ⊠ 🔥 🏃

★★ **HOLIDAY INN RIVERFRONT.** *102 S 3rd St (64501). 816/279-8000; res 800/824-7402. www.holiday-inn. com.* 170 rms, 6 story. S, D $76; suites $100-$150; under 18 free; wkend rates. Crib free. Pet accepted. TV; cable. Indoor pool; whirlpool. Restaurant 6:30 am-2 pm, 5:30-10:30 pm. Bar 4 pm-1 am; Sun to 9 pm. Ck-out noon. Meeting rms. Business servs avail. Bellhops. Sundries. Gift shop. Exercise equipt; sauna. Health club privileges. Game rm. Refrigerator, wet bar in suites. Opp river. Cr cds: A, C, D, DS, JCB, MC, V.
⌐ 🐾 ⌑ 🏋 ⊠ 🔥

★ **RAMADA INN.** *4016 Frederick Ave (64506). 816/233-6192; fax 816/233-6001; res 800/748-0036. ramada.com.* 161 rms, 2 story. S $60-$70; D $65-$75; suites $85; under 18 free. Crib free. Pet accepted. TV; cable (premium). Indoor pool; whirlpool. Restaurants 6 am-2 pm, 5-10 pm. Bar 4 pm-midnight. Ck-out noon. Coin lndry. Meeting rms. Business servs avail. Valet serv. Exercise equipt. Rec rm. Picnic tables. Cr cds: A, C, D, DS, MC, V.
⌐ 🐾 ⌑ 🏋 ⊠ 🔥 SC

Hotel

★★★ **SHERATON ST. LOUIS CITY CENTER.** *400 S 14th St, St. Louis (63103). 314/231-5007. www.sheraton. com.* 288 rms, 10 story. S, D $150-$225; each addl $20; under 17 free. Crib avail. Indoor pool. TV; cable (premium), VCR avail. Complimentary coffee, newspaper in rms. Restaurant 6 am-10 pm. Ck-out noon. Meeting rms. Business center. Gift shop. Exercise rm. Some refrigerators, minibars. Cr cds: A, C, D, DS, ER, JCB, MC, V.
⌑ 🏋 🏃 🔥

Restaurants

★ **BARBOSA'S CASTILLO.** *906 Sylvanie St (64501). 816/233-4970.* Hrs: 11 am-9 pm; Fri, Sat to 10 pm. Closed Sun; hols. Mexican menu. Bar. Lunch, dinner $5.50-$9.85. Children's menu. Specializes in enchiladas, tamales, tacos. Dining on 2 levels in restored Victorian mansion (1891). Enclosed rooftop beer garden. Cr cds: A, DS, MC, V.

★★ **36TH STREET FOOD & DRINK COMPANY.** *501 N Belt Hwy (64506). 816/364-1564.* Hrs: 11 am-10 pm; Sat from noon. Closed Sun; hols. Res accepted. Bar 11-1:30 am. Lunch $5.95-$19.25, dinner $5.95-$29.95. Specializes in barbecued ribs, steak, fresh seafood. Country French decor. Cr cds: A, DS, MC, V.

St. Louis (D-6)

Settled 1764 **Pop** 396,685 **Elev** 470 ft
Area code 314
Information Convention & Visitors Commission, 1 Metropolitan Sq, Suite 1100, 63102; 314/421-1023 or 800/325-7962
Web www.st-louis-cvc.com

Suburbs Clayton, St. Charles, Wentzville.

One of the oldest settlements in the Mississippi Valley, St. Louis was founded by Pierre Laclede as a fur trading post and was named for Louis IX of France. Early French settlers, a large German immigration in the mid-1800s, and a happy mix of other national strains contribute to the city's cosmopolitan flavor. A flourishing French community by the time of the Revolutionary War, St. Louis was attacked by a band of British-led Native Americans but was successfully defended by its citizens and a French garrison. In 1804 it was the scene of the transfer of Louisiana to the United States, which opened the way to the westward expansion that overran the peaceful town with immigrants and

adventurers. The first Mississippi steamboat docked at St. Louis in 1817. Missouri's first constitutional convention was held here in 1820. During the Civil War, though divided in sympathy, the city was a base of Union operations. In 1904 the Louisiana Purchase Exposition, known as the St. Louis World's Fair, brought international fame to the city and added to its cultural resources; its first art museum was established in connection with the fair.

For more than 200 years St. Louis has been the dominant city in the state. It is the home of St. Louis University (1818), the University of Missouri-St. Louis (1963), and Washington University (1853), which lies at the border of St. Louis and Clayton. Distinguished by wealth, grace, and culture, St. Louis is also a city of solid and diversified industry. It is one of the world's largest markets for wool, lumber, and pharmaceuticals, and a principal grain and hog center. It is also the center for the only industrial area in the country producing six basic metals: iron, lead, zinc, copper, aluminum, and magnesium. St. Louis is an important producer of beer, chemicals, and transportation equipment. Strategically located near the confluence of the Missouri and Mississippi rivers, the city is one of the country's major railroad terminals and trucking centers. Seven bridges span the Mississippi here.

After the steamboat era, St. Louis grew westward, away from the riverfront, which deteriorated into slums. This original center of the city has now been developed as the Jefferson National Expansion Memorial. Municipal and private redevelopment of downtown and riverfront St. Louis also has been outstanding: America's Center, St. Louis's convention complex, is the hub of the 16-square-block Convention Plaza; Busch Stadium brings St. Louis Cardinals fans into the downtown area; and the rehabilitated Union Station offers visitors a unique shopping experience within a restored turn-of-the-century railroad station.

Additional Visitor Information

The St. Louis Convention & Visitors Commission, 1 Metropolitan Sq,

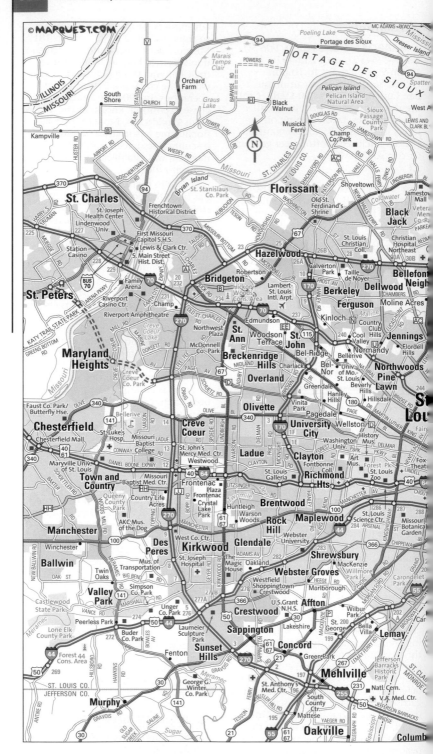

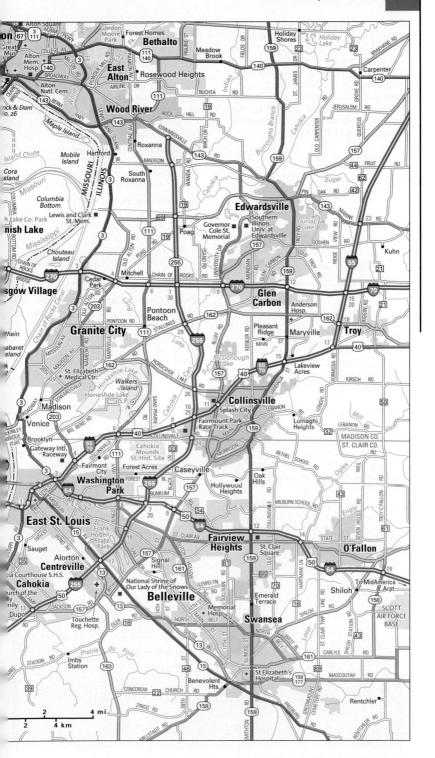

Suite 1100, 63102, has brochures on things to see in St. Louis; phone 314/421-1023 or 800/325-7962. Also obtain brochures at the St. Louis Visitors Center, 7th and Washington. *St. Louis Magazine,* at newsstands, has up-to-date information on cultural events and articles of interest to visitors. For 24-hour tourist information phone 314/421-2100.

Transportation

Airport. St. Louis Lambert Airport Information: 314/426-8000. Lost and found: 314/426-8100. Weather: 314/321-2222. Cash Machines: Main Terminal, Concourse level.

Car Rental Agencies. See IMPORTANT TOLL-FREE NUMBERS.

Public Transportation. Bi-State Transit System, phone 314/231-2345.

Rail Passenger Service. Amtrak 800/872-7245.

Airport Information

St. Louis Lambert Airport Area. For additional accommodations, see ST. LOUIS LAMBERT AIRPORT AREA, which follows ST. LOUIS.

What to See and Do

Aloe Plaza. Across from Union Station. Contains extensive fountain group by Carl Milles symbolizing the meeting of the Mississippi and Missouri rivers. Market St between 18th and 20th sts.

Anheuser-Busch, Inc. Guided brewery tours. (Mon-Sat; closed hols) 12th and Lynch St. Phone 314/577-2626. **FREE**

Butterfly House and Education Center. Three-story crystal palace conservatory with over 2,000 butterflies in free flight. Educational programs, films, miracle of metamorphosis display. (Tues-Sun) 20 mi W via US 40, Olive St exit, in Faust Park. Phone 314/361-3365. ¢¢

Campbell House Museum. Mansion with original 1840-1880 furnishings. (Mar-Dec, Tues-Sun; closed hols) 1508 Locust St. Phone 314/421-0325. ¢¢

Cathedral of St. Louis. (1907) The city's cathedral is a fine example of Romanesque architecture with Byzantine details; the interior mosaic work is among the most extensive in the world. Mosaic museum (fee). Tours (by appt, fee). 4431 Lindell Blvd, at Newstead Ave. Phone 314/533-2824.

Christ Church Cathedral. (1859-1867) The first Episcopal parish west of the Mississippi River, founded 1819. English Gothic sandstone building; altar carved in England from stone taken from a quarry in Caen, France; Tiffany windows on north wall. Occasional concerts. (Mon-Fri, Sun) Tours (Sun). 1210 Locust St. Phone 314/231-3454.

County parks.

    Edgar M. Queeny Park. A 569-acre park. Swimming pool; hiking trail, tennis, ice rink (fee), picnicking, playground. (Daily) 19 mi W via I-64 (US 40) or Clayton Rd, S on Mason Rd. Phone 314/615-7275.

Mississippi Queen paddle wheeler

Laumeier Sculpture Park. Sculpture by contemporary artists on grounds of the Laumeier mansion; art gallery (Wed-Sun). Nature trails, picnic area. (Daily) Geyer and Rott rds. Phone 314/821-1209. **FREE**

Lone Elk Park. Approx 400-acre preserve for bison, elk, deer, and Barbados sheep. Picnicking. (Daily) MO 141 and N Outer Rd, 23 mi SW on I-44, adj to Castlewood State Park. Phone 314/615-7275. **FREE**

DeMenil Mansion and Museum. Antebellum, Greek Revival house with period furnishings; restaurant (lunch) in carriage house. Mansion on old Arsenal Hill in the colorful brewery district. Gift shop. (Tues-Sat) 3352 DeMenil Place. Phone 314/771-5828. ¢¢

The Dog Museum. Museum with exhibits of dog-related art; reference library, videotapes. (Tues-Sat, also Sun afternoons; closed hols) W via I-64 (US 40) to 1721 Mason Rd, in Edgar M. Queeny Park. Phone 314/821-3647. ¢¢

Eugene Field House and Toy Museum. (1845) Birthplace of famous children's poet; mementos, manuscripts, and many original furnishings; antique toys and dolls. (Wed-Sat, also Sun afternoons; closed hols) 634 S Broadway. Phone 314/421-4689. ¢¢

⭐ **Forest Park.** This 1,200-acre park was the site of most of the 1904 Louisiana Purchase Exposition. Many of the city's major attractions are here. (See SPECIAL EVENTS) W via I-64 (US 40), bounded by Skinker and Kingshighway blvds and Oakland Ave. Phone 314/289-5300.

Grant's Farm. This 281-acre wooded tract contains a log cabin (1856) and land once owned by Ulysses S. Grant. Anheuser-Busch Clydesdale barn; carriage house with horse-drawn vehicles, trophy rm; deer park where deer, buffalo, longhorn steer, and other animals roam freely in their natural habitat; bird and elephant show, small animal feeding area. Tours by miniature train. (May-Sept, Tues-Sun; mid-Apr-May, Sept-mid-Oct, Thurs-Sun) 10501 Gravois Rd, SW via I-55. Phone 314/843-1700. **FREE**

Gray Line bus tours. Phone 314/421-4753.

International Bowling Hall of Fame and Museum. Exhibits and displays trace history of bowling from Egyptian child's game to present. Computerized and old-time alleys where visitors may bowl. Gift and snack shop. (Daily; closed hols) 111 Stadium Plaza, across from Busch Stadium. Phone 314/231-6340. ¢¢

Jefferson Barracks Historical Park. Army post established in 1826, used through 1946. St. Louis County now maintains 424 acres of the original tract. Restored buildings incl stable (1851), laborer's house (1851), two powder magazines (1851 and 1857), ordnance rm, and visitor center. Picnicking. Buildings (Tues-Sun; closed hols) S Broadway at Kingston, 10 mi S on I-55, S Broadway exit. Phone 314/544-5714. **FREE**

Jewel Box Floral Conservatory. Site, on 17½ acres, with formal lily pools; floral displays; special hol shows. Free admission Mon and Tues mornings. (Daily) Wells and McKinley drs. ¢

The Magic House, St. Louis Children's Museum. Hands-on exhibits incl electrostatic generator and a three-story circular slide. (Tues-Sun; closed hols) 8 mi W via I-44, Lindbergh Exit at 516 S Kirkwood Rd in Kirkwood. Phone 314/822-8900. ¢¢¢

Missouri Botanical Garden. This 79-acre park incl rose, woodland, and herb gardens; scented garden for the blind; electric tram rides (fee). Restaurant, floral display hall. Sections of the botanical garden are well over a century old. (Daily; closed Dec 25) 4344 Shaw Blvd. Phone 314/577-9400. ¢¢ Incl in admission are

Climatron. Seventy-ft high, prize-winning geodesic dome—first of its kind to be used as a conservatory—houses a two-level, ½-acre tropical rain forest with canopies, rocky outcrops, waterfalls, and mature tree collection; exhibits explain the many facets of a rain forest. Entrance to Climatron through series of sacred lotus and lily pools.

Japanese Garden. Largest traditional Japanese garden in North America, with lake landscaped with many varieties of water iris, waterfalls, bridges, and teahouse. Phone 800/642-8842. Also here is

Tower Grove House. (ca 1859) Restored country residence of garden founder, Henry Shaw; Victorian furnishings. In grove of trees before house is Shaw's Gothic Revival tomb. (Feb-Dec, daily; closed Dec 25) Phone 314/577-5150.

Missouri History Museum-Missouri Historical Society. Exhibits on St. Louis and the American West; artwork, costumes, and decorative arts; toys, firearms; 19th-century fire-fighting equipt; St. Louis history slide show; ragtime rock 'n' roll music exhibit; 1904 World's Fair and Charles A. Lindbergh collections. (Daily; closed hols) Jefferson Memorial Building, Lindell Blvd and DeBaliviere. Phone 314/746-4599. **FREE**

Museum of Transportation. Collection of locomotives, railway cars; city transit conveyances from horse-pulled carts to buses; highway vehicles. (Daily; closed Jan 1, Thanksgiving, Dec 25) 16 mi SW via I-44, N on I-270 to Big Bend and Dougherty Ferry Rd exits, at 3015 Barrett Station Rd in Kirkwood. Phone 314/965-7998. ¢¢

Powell Symphony Hall. (1925) Decorated in ivory and 24-karat gold leaf, the hall, built as a movie and vaudeville house, is now home of the St. Louis Symphony Orchestra (Mid-Sept-mid-May). After-concert tours

avail by appt. 718 N Grand Blvd. Phone 314/534-1700.

Professional sports.

St. Louis Blues (NHL). Savvis Center, 1401 Clark Ave. Phone 314/241-1888.

St. Louis Cardinals (MLB). Busch Stadium, 250 Stadium Plaza. Phone 314/421-3060.

St. Louis Rams (NFL). Trans World Dome, 901 N Broadway. Phone 314/425-8830.

Purina Farms. Domestic animals, educational graphic displays, videos, hands-on activities. Grain bin theater. Petting areas, animal demonstrations, play area with maze, ponds. Snack bar, gift shop. Self-guided tours. (Mid-Mar-Nov, Wed-Sun) Reservations required. 35 mi W via I-44, Gray Summit exit, then 2 blks N on MO 100 and 1 mi W on County MM, in Gray Summit. Phone 314/982-3232. **FREE**

Riverfront area.

⭐ *Delta Queen* and *Mississippi Queen.* Paddlewheelers offer 3-12 night cruises on the Ohio, Cumberland, Mississippi, and Tennessee rivers. Contact Delta Queen Steamboat Co, 30 Robin St Wharf, New

Skyline, St. Louis

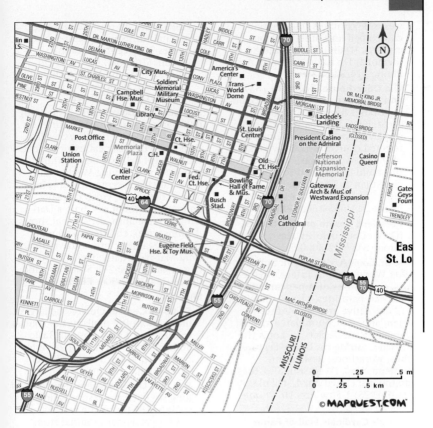

© MAPQUEST.COM

Orleans, LA 70130-1890. Phone 800/543-1949.

Eads Bridge. (1874) Designed by engineer James B. Eads, the Eads was the first bridge to span the wide southern section of the Mississippi and the first bridge in which steel and the cantilever were used extensively; approach ramps are carried on enormous Romanesque stone arches.

Gateway Riverboat Cruises. One-hr narrated cruise of the Mississippi River aboard the *Huck Finn, Tom Sawyer,* and *Becky Thatcher* riverboats, replicas of 19th-century sternwheelers. (Memorial Day-Labor Day, daily) Dock below Gateway Arch. Phone 314/621-4040. ¢¢¢

Jefferson National Expansion Memorial. Eero Saarinen's Gateway Arch is a 630-ft stainless steel arch that symbolizes the starting point of the westward expansion of the US. Visitor center (fee) incl capsule transporter to observation deck

(fee). **Museum of Westward Expansion** offers exhibits on people and events of 19th-century western America, special exhibits and films (fee) on St. Louis, construction of the arch, and the westward movement (Daily; closed Jan 1, Thanksgiving, Dec 25). Videotapes for the hearing impaired; tours for the visually impaired. Observation deck inaccessible to wheelchairs. **Note:** There is often a wait for observation deck capsules, which are small and confining. 11 N 4th St. Phone 314/982-1410. ¢

Laclede's Landing. Early St. Louis commercial district (mid-1800s) incl nine-block area of renovated pre-Civil War and Victorian buildings that house specialty shops, restaurants, and nightclubs. N edge of riverfront, between Eads and King bridges. Phone 314/241-1155.

Old Cathedral. (1831) Basilica of St. Louis, King of France, on the site of the first church built in St. Louis in 1770; museum on the west side contains the original church bell and other religious artifacts. (Daily) 209 Walnut St, at Memorial Dr, under Gateway Arch. Phone 314/231-3250. ¢

Old Courthouse. Begun in 1837 and completed in 1862, this building houses five museum galleries on St. Louis history, incl various displays, dioramas, and films; two restored courtrms. First two trials of the Dred Scott case were held in this building. Guided tour. (Daily; closed Jan 1, Thanksgiving, Dec 25) 11 N 4th St, at Market St. Phone 314/655-1600. **FREE**

President Casino on the *Admiral*. (Daily) Dock below Gateway Arch. Phone 314/622-3000.

The St. Louis Art Museum. Built for 1904 World's Fair as Palace of Fine Arts. Collections of American and European paintings, prints, drawings, and decorative arts. Also African, Asian, and pre-Columbian art; 47-ft statue in front depicts St. Louis the Crusader astride his horse. Lectures, films, workshops. Restaurant, museum shop. (Wed-Sun, also Tues afternoons; closed Jan 1, Thanksgiving, Dec 25) 1 Fine Arts Dr. Phone 314/721-0072.

St. Louis Cardinals Hall of Fame Museum. St. Louis baseball from 1860-present; Stan Musial memorabilia. Gift shop. Also stadium tours (Apr-Dec, daily; rest of yr, limited hrs). Building (daily). Busch Stadium, 100 Stadium Plaza; between gates 5 and 6. Phone 314/421-3263. ¢¢¢

St. Louis Science Center. Features 11 galleries with more than 600 exhibits. Also Omnimax theater, planetarium, Alien Research Project, children's discovery rm (various fees). Outdoor science park. Gift shops. Restaurant. (Daily; closed Jan 1, Thanksgiving, Dec 25) 5050 Oakland Ave. Phone 314/289-4400.

Saint Louis University. (1818) 10,000 students. Oldest university west of the Mississippi River; incl Pius XII Memorial Library with Vatican Microfilm Library—the only depository for copies of Vatican documents in the Western Hemisphere (academic yr, daily; closed hols). 221 N Grand. Phone 314/977-8886. Also here is

Cupples House and Art Gallery. Historic Romanesque building (1889) with 42 rms, 22 fireplaces, original furnishings, period pieces; houses 20th-century graphics collection. (Tues-Sat, hrs vary) On John E. Connelly Mall (formerly W Pine Blvd.), W of Pious XII Library. Phone 314/977-3025. ¢¢

St. Louis Zoological Park. More than 6,000 animals in natural settings on 83 acres; apes and monkeys; walk-through aviary; big cat exhibit, cheetah survival exhibit; herpetarium; aquatic house. Living World education and visitor center features interactive computers, video displays, animatronic robot of Charles Darwin, and live animals. Animal shows (summer; fee); children's zoo with contact area (fee); miniature railroad (mid-Mar-Nov, daily; fee). Zoo (daily; closed Jan 1, Dec 25). S side of park. Phone 314/781-0900. **FREE**

Shopping.

St. Louis Centre. One of the largest urban shopping malls in the country; features 130 shops and Taste of St. Louis food court with 28 restaurants. (Daily) Locust and 6th sts, Downtown.

St. Louis Union Station. This blk-long stone chateauesque railroad station (1894) was the world's busiest passenger terminal from 1905 until the late 1940s. After the last train pulled out—on Oct 31, 1978—the station and train shed were restored and redeveloped as a marketplace with more than 100 specialty shops and restaurants, nightclubs, and hotels, as well as entertainment areas, plazas, and a 1½ acre lake. The station was designed by a local architect to be modeled after a walled medieval city in southern France; its interior features high Romanesque and Sullivanesque design. "Memories," a collection of photographs, letters, memorabilia, and films, brings the station's history to life. Market St, between 18th and 20th sts. Phone 314/421-6655.

West Port Plaza. Alpinelike setting with approx 30 European-style shops and 20 restaurants. (Daily) Approx 15 mi W via I-64 (US 40), N on I-270, E on Page Blvd to W Port Plaza Dr, in Maryland Heights. Phone 314/576-7100.

Six Flags St. Louis. A 200-acre entertainment park with more than 100

rides, shows, and attractions, incl wooden and looping steel roller coasters and whitewater raft rides. (Late May-late Aug, daily; Mar-late May and late Aug-late Oct, wkends) 30 mi SW via I-44, exit 261, in Eureka. Phone 314/938-4800.

Skiing. Hidden Valley Ski Area. Two triple chairlifts, four rope tows; patrol, school, rentals, snowmaking; cafeteria, restaurant, concession, bar. Longest run 1,760 ft; vertical drop 282 ft. Night skiing. (Dec-Mar, daily; closed Dec 24, 25) 28 mi W on I-44, then 3 mi S on MO F to Hidden Valley Dr in Eureka. ¢¢¢¢

Soldiers' Memorial Military Museum. Honoring St. Louis's war dead; memorabilia from pre-Civil War, WWI, WWII, Korea, and Vietnam. (Daily; closed Jan 1, Thanksgiving, Dec 25) 1315 Chestnut St. Phone 314/622-4550. **FREE**

State parks.

  Dr. Edmund A. Babler Memorial. Approx 2,500 acres. Swimming pool; hiking trail, picnicking, playground, improved camping (dump station). Interpretive center, naturalist. Standard fees. (Daily) 25 mi W on MO 100, then N on MO 109. Phone 314/458-3813. **FREE**

Mastodon State Historic Site. Excavation of mastodon remains and Native American artifacts; museum (fee). Fishing; hiking, picnicking. Standard fees. (Daily) 20 mi S off US 55, near US 67 Imperial exit. Phone 314/464-2976. **FREE**

Steinberg Memorial Skating Rink. Roller skating (June-Sept), ice-skating (Nov-Mar); rentals. ¢¢

Ulysses S. Grant National Historic Site. Site consists of five historic structures: two-story residence known as White Haven, stone outbuilding, barn, ice house, and chicken house. The White Haven property was a focal point in Ulysses' and wife Julia's lives for four decades. Grounds feature more than 50 species of trees and are a haven for a variety of wildlife. Visitor center incl exhibits and information on the Grants and White Haven. Guided tours. (Daily; closed Jan 1, Thanksgiving, Dec 25) 7400 Grant Rd. Grant Rd, off Gravois Rd. Phone 314/842-3298.

Special Events

Gypsy Caravan. One of the largest flea markets in the Midwest, with more than 600 vendors; arts and crafts, entertainment, concessions. Memorial Day.

Muny Opera. Forest Park. 12,000-seat outdoor theater. Light opera and musical comedy. Phone 314/361-1900. Mid-June-Aug.

Fair St. Louis. On riverfront. Three-day festival with parade, food, air and water shows, entertainment. July 4 wkend.

Great Forest Park Balloon Race. Forest Park. Food, entertainment, parachute jumps, and other contests. Phone 314/289-5300. Mid-Sept.

Repertory Theatre of St. Louis. 130 Edgar Rd, off I-44 Elm St exit in Webster Groves. Nine-play season incl classics and new works. Phone 314/968-4925. Sept-Apr.

St. Louis Symphony Orchestra. Powell Symphony Hall. Phone 314/534-1700. Sept-May.

Motels/Motor Lodges

★★ **CHESHIRE LODGE.** *6300 Clayton Rd (63117). 314/647-7300; fax 314/647-0442; toll-free 800/325-7378. www.cheshirelodge.com.* 106 rms, 4 story. S, D $80-$120; each addl $10; suites $130-$200; under 12 free; wkend rates. Crib free. TV; cable (premium), VCR avail. Indoor/outdoor pool; poolside serv. Restaurant (see also CHESHIRE INN). Bar 11-1:30 am; entertainment Mon-Sat. Ck-out 2 pm. Meeting rms. Business servs avail. In-rm modem link. Bellhops. Valet serv Mon-Fri. Some refrigerators. Elegant Tudor decor. English garden. Cr cds: A, D, DS, MC, V.
➤ ➤ ➤ SC

★★ **COURTYARD BY MARRIOTT.** *2340 Market St (63103). 314/241-9111; fax 314/241-8113; toll-free 800/321-2211. www.courtyard.com.* 151 units, 4 story, 12 suites. S, D $109-$129; suites $129-$159; under 18 free; wkly rates. Crib free. TV; cable (premium). Indoor pool; whirlpool. Complimentary coffee in rms. Bar. Ck-out noon. Business servs avail. In-rm modem link. Valet serv.

Exercise equipt. Some balconies. Cr cds: A, C, D, DS, ER, JCB, MC, V.

★★ **DRURY INN.** *Convention Plaza and Broadway (21001). 314/231-8100; toll-free 800/325-8300. www.drury-inn.com.* 178 rms, 2 flrs in 6-story building. May-Sept: S $96-$112; D $106-$122; each addl $10; under 18 free; wkend rates; higher rates July 4th; lower rates rest of yr. Crib free. Pet accepted, some restrictions. TV; cable (premium). Indoor pool; whirlpool, poolside serv, lifeguard. Complimentary continental bkfst. Restaurant adj 11 am-2 pm, 4:30-11 pm; wkend hrs vary. Ck-out noon. Meeting rms. Business servs avail. In-rm modem link. No bellhops. Health club privileges. Some refrigerators; microwaves avail. Cr cds: A, C, D, DS, MC, V.

★★ **DRURY INN.** *201 S 20th St (63103). 314/231-3900. www.drury-inn.com.* 176 rms, 7 story. Apr-Oct: S $98-$113; D $108-$123; each addl $10; suites $150; under 18 free; hol rates; lower rates rest of yr. Crib avail. Pet accepted, some restrictions. TV; cable (premium), VCR avail. Indoor pool; whirlpool, lifeguard. Complimentary continental bkfst. Restaurant (see LOMBARDO'S). Bar. Ck-out noon. Coin lndry. Meeting rms. In-rm modem link. No bellhops. Exercise equipt. Some refrigerators. Restored 1907 railroad hotel. Cr cds: A, C, D, DS, MC, V.

★★ **HAMPTON INN - UNION STATION.** *2211 Market St (63103). 314/241-3200; fax 314/241-9351. www.hamptoninn.com.* 239 rms, 11 story, 14 suites. S $79; D $89-$99; suites $110-$135; under 18 free; wkend rates. Crib free. Pet accepted, some restrictions. TV; cable (premium). Indoor pool; whirlpool. Complimentary continental bkfst. Restaurant adj 11-2 am. Bar. Ck-out noon. Coin lndry. Business servs avail. In-rm modem link. No bellhops. Free garage parking. Exercise equipt. Health club privileges. Refrigerators avail. Cr cds: A, MC, V.

★★ **HOLIDAY INN FOREST PARK.** *5915 Wilson Ave (63110). 314/645-0700; toll-free 800/465-4329. www.holiday-inn.com.* 120 rms, 7 story. S $99-$110; D $109-$125; each addl $10; under 18 free; family rates. Crib free. Pet accepted. TV; VCR avail. Complimentary coffee in rms. Restaurant 5:30 am-10 pm. Bar 4 pm-midnight; Sun to 10 pm. Ck-out noon. Meeting rms. Business center. In-rm modem link. Pool. Refrigerators. Balconies. Cr cds: A, C, D, DS, MC, V.

★★ **HOLIDAY INN SELECT ST. LOUIS.** *811 N Ninth St (63101). 314/421-4000; fax 314/421-5974; res 800/289-8338. www.holiday-inn.com.* 295 rms, 4 story, 36 suites. S, D $109-$139; each addl $10; suites $129-$295; under 18 free. Crib avail. Pet accepted, some restrictions. Garage parking $7. TV; cable (premium). Complimentary coffee in rms. Restaurant 6 am-2 pm, 5-11 pm. Bar 11-1 am. Ck-out noon. Convention facilities. Business center. In-rm modem link. Bellhops. Concierge. Sundries. Gift shop. Coin lndry. Exercise equipt; sauna. Indoor pool; whirlpool. Game rm. Luxury level. Cr cds: A, MC, V.

★★ **HOLIDAY INN SOUTHWEST.** *10709 Watson Rd (63127). 314/821-6600; fax 314/821-4673; toll-free 800/682-6338. www.holiday-inn.com.* 212 rms, 4 story. May-Sept: S, D $104-$115; each addl $10; suites $109-$130; under 18 free; lower rates rest of yr. Crib free. TV; cable (premium). 2 pools, 1 indoor. Complimentary coffee in rms. Restaurant 6:30 am-2 pm, 5-10 pm. Bar 11-1 am; entertainment. Ck-out noon. Meeting rms. Business servs avail. In-rm modem link. Bellhops. Valet serv. Exercise equipt. Game rm. Some bathrm phones, refrigerators. Cr cds: A, C, D, DS, ER, JCB, MC, V.

★★ **SUMMERFIELD SUITES.** *1855 Craigshire Rd (63121). 314/878-1555; fax 314/878-9203; toll-free 800/833-4353. www.wyndham.com.* 106 kit. suites, 2 story. 1-bedrm $89; 2-bedrm $109; wkend rates. Crib free. Pet accepted, some restrictions; $75. TV; cable (premium), VCR (movies). Heated pool; whirlpool. Complimentary continental bkfst, coffee in rms.

Grant's Farm, St. Louis

Restaurant nearby. Ck-out noon. Coin lndry. Meeting rms. Business servs avail. In-rm modem link. Valet serv. Sundries. Free airport transportation. Exercise equipt. Health club privileges. Microwaves. Picnic tables, grills. Cr cds: A, C, D, DS, MC, V.

D ☎ ≈ 🏋 🍽 🔥 SC

Hotels

★★ **ADAM'S MARK HOTEL.** *112 N 4th St (63102). 314/241-7400; fax 314/241-6618; toll-free 800/444-2326. www.adamsmark.com.* 910 rms, 18 story. S $174-$214, D $194-$234; each addl $20; suites $185-$1,200; under 18 free; wkend packages. Crib free. Garage parking $4/hr, in/out $12 unlimited; valet $5. TV; cable, VCR avail. 2 heated pools, 1 indoor; whirlpool, poolside serv. Restaurant 6 am-midnight (see also FAUST'S). Rm serv 24 hrs. Bar 11-2 am; entertainment Mon-Sat. Ck-out noon. Convention facilities. Business center. In-rm modem link. Concierge. Shopping arcade. Barber, beauty shop. Exercise equipt; sauna. Massage. Bathrm phones; some refrigerators. Three-story atrium lobby decorated with bronze equestrian sculpture by De Luigi. View of Gateway Arch and riverfront from many rms; near Laclede's Landing and riverfront show-boats. Luxury level. Cr cds: A, C, D, DS, MC, V.

D ≈ 🏋 🍽 🔥 SC 🏋

★★★ **DOUBLETREE HOTEL AND CONFERENCE CENTER.** *16625 Swingley Ridge Rd, Chesterfield (63017). 314/532-5000; fax 314/532-9984; toll-free 800/222-8733. www.doubletree.com.* 223 rms, 12 story. S, D $150; under 18 free; wkend rates. Crib free. TV; cable (premium), VCR avail. 2 pools, 1 indoor; wading pool, whirlpool, poolside serv, lifeguard. Supervised children's activities; ages 1-13. Coffee in rms. Restaurant 6.30-10 pm. Bar 11-1 am. Ck-out noon. Meeting rms. Business center. In-rm modem link. Airport transportation. Lighted tennis. Exercise rm; sauna, steam rm. Rec rm. Refrigerators, microwaves avail. Luxury level. Cr cds: A, C, D, DS, ER, JCB, MC, V.

D 🏌 ≈ 🏋 🍽 🔥 SC 🏋

★★★ **HILTON FRONTENAC.** *1335 S Lindbergh Blvd (63131). 314/993-1100; fax 314/993-8546; toll-free 800/445-8667. www.hilton.com.* 266 rms, 3 story. S, D $99-$235; each addl $10; suites $130-$500; under 18 free; wkend, wkly rates. Crib free. TV; cable (premium), VCR avail. Pool; poolside serv. Restaurant. Bar 11-1 am; entertainment Thurs-Sat. Ck-out noon. Convention facilities. Business center.

In-rm modem link. Bellhops. Valet serv. Sundries. Gift shop. Barber shop. Free airport transportation. Exercise equipt; sauna. Microwaves avail. Luxury level. Cr cds: A, C, D, DS, MC, V.

★★★ **HYATT REGENCY ST. LOUIS.** *1 St. Louis Union Station (63103). 314/231-1234; fax 314/923-3970; toll-free 800/233-1234. www. hyatt.com.* 538 rms, 6 story. S $179-$214; D $204-$244; each addl $25; under 18 free; wkend rates. Crib free. Valet parking $13. TV; cable (premium). Pool; lifeguard. Restaurant 6:30 am-10:30 pm. Bar 11-1:30 am. Ck-out noon. Convention facilities. Business servs avail. In-rm modem link. Shopping arcade. Exercise equipt. Refrigerators avail. Bathrm phones. In renovated Union Station railroad terminal (1894); main lobby and lounge occupy Grand Hall. Luxury level. Cr cds: A, C, D, DS, MC, V.

★★★ **MARRIOTT PAVILION DOWNTOWN ST. LOUIS .** *1 S Broadway (63102). 314/421-1776; fax 314/331-9029; toll-free 800/228-9290. www.marriott.com.* 672 rms, 22-25 story. S $154; D $169; under 18 free; wkend rates. Garage, in/out $12, valet $15. TV; cable (premium). Pool; whirlpool, poolside serv, lifeguard. Coffee in rms. Restaurant 6:30 am-11 pm. Bar 11-1 am. Ck-out noon. Coin lndry. Convention facilities. Business center. In-rm modem link. Concierge. Gift shop. Exercise equipt; sauna. Some bathrm phones, refrigerators. Luxury level. Cr cds: A, C, D, DS, ER, JCB, MC, V.

★★★ **MARRIOTT WEST ST. LOUIS.** *660 Maryville Center Dr (63141). 314/878-2747; fax 314/878-3005. www.marriott.com.* 297 rms, 8 story. S, D $150-$225; each addl $20; under 17 free. Crib avail. Indoor pool. TV; cable (premium), VCR avail. Complimentary coffee, newspaper in rms. Restaurant 6 am-10 pm. Ck-out noon. Meeting rms. Business center. Gift shop. Exercise rm. Some refrigerators, minibars. Cr cds: A, C, D, DS, ER, JCB, MC, V.

★★ **MAYFAIR WYNDHAM GRAND HERITAGE HOTEL.** *806 St. Charles St (63101). 314/421-2500; fax 314/421-6254; res 800/757-8483. www. wyndham.com.* 132 rms, 18 story. S, D $119-$189; each addl $10; under 12 free. Crib free. Pet accepted; $50 deposit. TV; cable (premium). Complimentary coffee in rms. Restaurant 6:30 am-2 pm, 5-10:30 pm. Bar 11:30 am-midnight. Ck-out noon. Meeting rms. Business center. In-rm modem link. Concierge. Exercise equipt. Bathrm phones, refrigerators, minibars. Luxury level. Cr cds: A, C, D, DS, JCB, MC, V.

★★★ **OMNI MAJESTIC HOTEL.** *1019 Pine St (63101). 314/436-2355; fax 314/436-0223; toll-free 800/843-6664. www.omnihotels.com.* 91 units, 9 story. S, D $179-$199; each addl $15; suites $290-$350; wkend rates. Crib free. Valet, in/out parking $12. TV; cable (premium), VCR avail. Coffee in rms. Restaurant 6 am-10 pm. Bar 11-1 am. Ck-out noon. Meeting rms. Business servs avail. In-rm modem link. Concierge. Airport transportation. Exercise equipt. Health club privileges. Bathrm phones. European elegance in 1913 building; marble floors, Oriental rugs. Cr cds: A, MC, V.

★★ **RADISSON HOTEL AND SUITES DOWNTOWN.** *200 N 4th St (36102). 314/621-8200; fax 314/621-8073; toll-free 800/333-3333. www. radisson.com.* 454 rms, 29 story, 282 kits. S $145; D $165; each addl $15; suites $175-$225; under 17 free; wkend rates; higher rates July 4th. Crib free. TV; VCR avail. Pool; lifeguard. Restaurant 6:30 am-10 pm. Bar 11-3 am; Sun 1 pm-midnight. Ck-out noon. Meeting rms. Business servs avail. In-rm modem link. Gift shop. Health club privileges. Game rm. Microwaves avail. Some balconies. Cr cds: A, C, D, DS, ER, MC, V.

★★★ **REGAL RIVERFRONT.** *200 S 4th St (63102). 314/241-9500; fax 314/241-9601; toll-free 800/325-7353. www.regalhotel.com.* 780 rms, 28 story. S $149-$189; D $169-$209; each addl $20; suites $350-$1,000; under 17 free; weekly, wkend rates; higher rates: baseball games, some hols. Crib free. Garage parking $11. Pet accepted; $50 deposit. TV; cable (premium), VCR avail. 2 pools, 1 indoor; wading pool, poolside serv, lifeguard. Restaurant 6:30 am-midnight. Bar. Ck-out noon. Coin lndry. Convention facilities. Business center. In-rm modem link. Gift shop. Exercise equipt. Health club privileges. Game rm. Renovated hotel near river. Luxury level. Cr cds: A, C, D, DS, MC, V.

🅳 💺 ⛳ ≈ 🏋 ⛷ 🔥 🏃

★★★ **RENAISSANCE ST. LOUIS SUITES HOTEL.** *823 Washington Ave (63101). 314/241-9100; fax 314/244-9910. www.renaissancehotels.com.* 300 rms, 24 story. S, D $175-$250; each addl $20; under 17 free. Crib avail. Indoor pool. TV; cable (premium), VCR avail. Complimentary coffee, newspaper in rms. Restaurant 6 am-10 pm. Ck-out noon. Meeting rms. Business center. Gift shop. Exercise rm. Some refrigerators, minibars. Cr cds: A, C, D, DS, ER, JCB, MC, V.

🏋 ≈ 🏃 🔥

★★★ **SHERATON.** *191 Westport Plaza (63146). 314/878-1500; fax 314/878-2837; toll-free 800/822-3535. www.sheraton.com.* 300 rms, 4-6 story. S, D $145-$155; suites $175-$340; under 18 free; wkend rates. TV; cable (premium), VCR avail. Pool; poolside serv, lifeguard. Complimentary coffee in rms. Restaurant 6:30 am-10:30 pm. Bar 11-1 am; pianist Tues-Sat. Ck-out 1 pm. Convention facilities. Business servs avail. In-rm modem link. Concierge. Free covered parking. Free airport transportation. Health club privileges. Some refrigerators. Some balconies. In shopping plaza. Cr cds: A, C, D, DS, JCB, MC, V.

🅳 ≈ 🏃 🔥 **SC**

★★★ **SHERATON CLAYTON PLAZA HOTEL.** *7730 Bonhomme Ave (63105). 314/863-0400. www.sheraton. com.* 257 rms, 15 story. S, D $150-$225; each addl $20; under 17 free. Crib avail. Pet accepted. Indoor pool. TV; cable (premium), VCR avail. Complimentary coffee, newspaper in rms. Restaurant 6 am-10 pm. Ck-out noon. Meeting rms. Business center. Gift shop. Exercise rm. Some refrigerators, minibars. Cr cds: A, C, D, DS, ER, JCB, MC, V.

🐾 🔥 ≈ 🏋 🏃

★★★ **SHERATON PLAZA.** *900 Westport Plaza (63146). 314/434-5010; fax 314/434-0140; toll-free 800/822-*

3535. www.sheraton.com. 209 rms, 12 story. S $145; D $145-$155; each addl $10; suites $179-$477; under 18 free; wkend rates. Crib free. TV; cable (premium), VCR avail (movies). Indoor pool; whirlpool. Sauna. Complimentary coffee in rms. Restaurant 6:30 am-10:30 pm. Bar 11-1 am. Ck-out 1 pm. Meeting rms. Business servs avail. In-rm modem link. Concierge. Free covered parking. Free airport transportation. Tennis privileges. Health club privileges. Some refrigerators. Cr cds: A, D, DS, MC, V.

🅳 💺 ⛳ 🏋 ≈ 🏃 🔥 🏃

★★★ **WESTIN ST. LOUIS.** *811 Spruce St (63102). 314/621-2000. www.westin.com.* 221 rms, 9 story. S, D $150-$225; each addl $20; under 17 free. Crib avail. TV; cable (premium), VCR avail. Complimentary coffee, newspaper in rms. Restaurant 6 am-10 pm. Ck-out noon. Meeting rms. Business center. Gift shop. Exercise rm. Some refrigerators, minibars. Cr cds: A, D, DS, ER, JCB, MC, V.

🏃 🏃 🔥

B&B/Small Inn

★ **LAFAYETTE HOUSE B&B.** *2156 Lafayette Ave (63104). 314/772-4429; fax 314/664-2156; res 800/641-8965.* 6 rms, 3 share bath, 3 story. No elvtr. S, D $60-$150; under 5 free; wkends (2-day min) (May-Oct). TV in some rms; cable (premium) VCR (movies). Complimentary full bkfst. Restaurant nearby. Ck-out 11 am, ck-in 3-6 pm. Built in 1876; Victorian elegance Totally nonsmoking. Cr cds: A, MC, V.

≈ 🔥

All Suite

★★ **EMBASSY SUITES.** *901 N 1st St (63102). 314/241-4200; fax 314/241-6513; toll-free 800/362-2779. www. embassysuitesstl.com.* 297 suites, 8 story. S, D $140-$200; each addl $5; under 18 free; wkend rates. Crib free. TV; cable (premium). Indoor pool; wading pool, whirlpool, lifeguard. Complimentary bkfst served in atrium. Restaurant 11 am-11 pm. Bar to 1 am; wkends to 3 am. Ck-out noon. Coin lndry. Meeting rms. Business servs avail. In-rm modem link. Exercise equipt. Game rm. Refrigerators, wet bars, microwaves avail. Bal-

conies. 8-story atrium courtyard. Cr
cds: A, C, D, DS, MC, V.

[icons]

Extended Stay

**★★ RESIDENCE INN BY MAR-
RIOTT.** *1881 Craigshire Dr, Maryland
Hgts (63146). 314/469-0060; fax 314/
469-3751; toll-free 800/331-3131.
www.marriott.com.* 128 kit. suites, 2
story. Suites $79-$139; wkend plans.
Crib free. Pet accepted, some restrictions; $25. TV; cable (premium).
Pool; whirlpool. Complimentary
continental bkfst. Restaurant nearby.
Ck-out noon. Coin lndry. Meeting
rm. Business servs avail. In-rm
modem link. Airport transportation.
Health club privileges. Refrigerators,
microwaves; many fireplaces. Private
patios, balconies. Picnic tables, grills.
Cr cds: A, D, DS, MC, V.

[icons]

Restaurants

★★ BALABAN'S. *405 N Euclid Ave
(63108). 314/361-8085. www.cafe
balaban.com.* Hrs: 11 am-2:30 pm, 6-
10:30 pm; Fri, Sat 11 am-3 pm, 5:30-
11:30 pm; Sun 10 am-2:30 pm
(brunch), 5-10:30 pm. Closed hols.
Res accepted. Continental menu. Bar.
Lunch $6.95-$12.95, dinner $10.95-
$24.95. Sun brunch $15. Specialties:
beef Wellington, barbecued spiced
salmon, half roast duckling. Own
baking, pasta. Musicians Sun. Valet
parking. Two dining areas—one formal, one more casual—feature artwork, chandeliers. Family-owned. Cr
cds: A, D, DS, MC, V.

[icon]

★ BAR ITALIA. *13 Maryland Pl
(63108). 314/361-7010.* Hrs: 11:30
am-9:30 pm; Fri, Sat to 10 pm; Sat to
8:30 pm. Closed Mon; Thanksgiving,
Dec 25. Res accepted. Italian menu.
Bar. Lunch $4.75-$8.95, dinner
$4.75-$17.95. Children's menu. Specializes in pasta, seafood, chicken.
Own baking. Outdoor dining. European cafe atmosphere. Cr cds: A, D,
DS, MC, V.

[icon]

★★ BEVO MILL. *4749 Gravois Ave
(63116). 314/481-2626. www.bevomill.
com.* Hrs: 11 am-9 pm; Fri, Sat to 10
pm; early-bird dinner Mon-Fri 3-6

pm; Sun brunch 9:30 am-2 pm.
Closed Dec 25. Res accepted. German
menu. Bar. Lunch $5.95-$9.50, dinner $7.95-$17.95. Sun brunch
$10.95. Children's menu. Specialties:
sauerbraten, Wiener schnitzel. Own
baking. Entertainment Thurs, Fri,
Sun eves. Large stone fireplace.
Bavarian exterior; operable windmill.
Cr cds: A, D, MC, V.

[icons]

★★ BIG SKY CAFE. *47 S Old
Orchard, Webster Groves (63119).
314/962-5757. www.bigskycafe.net.*
Hrs: 5:30-10 pm; Fri, Sat to 11 pm;
Sun 4:30-9:30 pm. Closed hols. Res
accepted. Bar. A la carte entrees: dinner $7.50-$15.95. Specialties: rosemary grilled chicken breast, barbecued
salmon, roasted garlic mashed potatoes. Outdoor dining. Eclectic decor.
Cr cds: A, D, DS, MC, V.

[icon]

★ BRISTOL'S SEAFOOD GRILL.
*11801 Olive Blvd, Creve Coeur
(63141). 314/567-0272. www.
houlahans.com.* Hrs: 11:30 am-2:30
pm, 5:30-10 pm; Fri, Sat 5-10:30 pm;
Sun 10 am-2 pm, 5-9 pm. Closed
Memorial Day, July 4, Labor Day,
Dec 25. Res accepted. Bar to 11:30
pm. Lunch $6.95-$13.95, dinner
$9.95-$21.95. Sun brunch $13.95.
Children's menu. Specializes in
mesquite-grilled seafood, steak, fresh
fish. Menu changes daily. Own pastries. Stained-glass windows. Cr cds:
A, D, DS, MC, V.

[icons]

★ BROADWAY OYSTER BAR. *736 S
Broadway (63102). 314/621-8811.
www.broadwayoysterbar.com.* Hrs: 11-
1:30 am; Sun to midnight. Closed
Easter, Dec 25. Cajun/Creole menu.
Bar. Lunch $5.50-$11.50, dinner
$8.75-$13. Blues, jazz nightly. Park-
ing. Outdoor dining. New Orleans
Mardi Gras atmosphere. Cr cds: A, D,
DS, MC, V.

[icon]

★★ BUSCH'S GROVE. *9160 Clayton
Rd, Ladue (63124). 314/993-0011.*
Hrs: 11:30 am-10 pm; Fri, Sat to 11
pm. Closed Mon, Sun; hols. Res
accepted. Bar. Lunch $6.50-$9.95,
dinner $7.99-$23.95. Children's
menu. Specializes in seafood, steak.
Outdoor dining. Built in 1860. Fire-

places. Original art. Family-owned for 106 yrs. Cr cds: A, DS, MC, V.
D ⊒

★★★★ **CAFE DE FRANCE.** *410 Olive St (63102). 314/231-2204. artthis.com/cdef/index.html.* Husband and wife Marcel and Monique Keraval run the kitchen and front-of-house respectively at this formal French restaurant in the heart of downtown. Specialties of duck, seafood, and game, such as quail escolier stuffed with golden raisins, truffles, and pecans with juniper sauce, can be ordered prix fixe or a la carte and have attracted diners for over 20 years. French menu. Specializes in fresh seafood, breast of duck, game. Hrs: 5:30-10:30 pm; Fri, Sat to 11:30 pm. Closed Sun; hols. Res accepted. Bar. Wine cellar. A la carte entrees: dinner $17-$25. Complete meals: 3-course dinner $20.75, 4-course $25.50, 5-course $36. Own baking. Valet parking. European ambience. Jacket. Cr cds: A, C, D, DS, MC, V.
D

★★ **CANDICCI'S.** *12513 Olive St, Creve Couer (63141). 314/878-5858. www.candiccis.com.* Hrs: 11 am-11 pm; Fri, Sat to midnight; Sun noon-9:30 pm. Closed hols. Res accepted. Italian menu. Bar. Lunch $4.95-$8, dinner $8.95-$19.95. Children's menu. Specialties: fettuccini with lobster, pasta a la Lilly, beef spedini. Outdoor dining. Entertainment Thurs-Sat. Casual Italian decor. Cr cds: A, D, DS, MC, V.
D ⊒

★★ **CARDWELL'S.** *94 Plaza Frontenac (63131). 314/997-8885.* Hrs: 11 am-10 pm; Fri, Sat to 11 pm; Sun noon-9 pm. Closed Easter, Thanksgiving, Dec 25. Res accepted. Eclectic menu. Bar. Lunch $7.50-$15.75, dinner $10.95-$21.95. Children's menu. Specialties: spicy Vietnamese chicken stir-fry, Chinese barbecued chicken salad, grilled smoked shrimp. Parking. Euro-bistro style. Cr cds: A, D, MC, V.
D

★ **CHARCOAL HOUSE.** *9855 Manchester Rd (63119). 314/968-4842.* Hrs: 11:30 am-2:30 pm, 5-10:30 pm. Closed Sun; hols. Res accepted Mon-Thurs. Bar. Lunch $5.95-$12; dinner $13.50-$35.95. Children's menu. Specializes in steak, fresh seafood. Cr cds: A, MC, V.
⊒

★ **CHARLIE GITTO'S.** *207 N 6th St (63101). 314/436-2828.* Hrs: 11 am-10:30 pm; Fri, Sat to 11:30 pm. Closed Sun; hols. Italian, American menu. Bar. A la carte entrees: lunch $5-$8, dinner $7.95-$15.15. Children's menu. Specializes in veal, seafood, pasta. Sports bar atmosphere. Cr cds: A, D, DS, MC, V.
D SC ⊒

★★ **CHESHIRE INN.** *6300 Clayton Rd (63117). 314/647-7300.* Hrs: 7-10 am, 11 am-2 pm, 5-10 pm; Wed-Sun to 11 pm; Sat brunch 7-10 am; Sun brunch 9 am-2 pm. Res accepted. Bar 11-3 am. Lunch $5.95-$8.95, dinner $14.95-$25.95. Sat brunch $7.95. Sun brunch $12.95. Children's menu. Specializes in prime rib, steak, fresh seafood. Pianist. Valet parking. Spit roasting in view. Old English architecture, decor. Carriage ride with dinner Fri, Sat (weather permitting; res one wk in advance suggested; fee). Cr cds: A, D, DS, MC, V.
D ⊒

★ **CHINA ROYAL.** *5911 N Lindbergh, Hazelwood (63042). 314/731-1313.* Hrs: 11 am-9:30 pm; Fri, Sat to 10:30 pm; Sun brunch to 3:30 pm. Closed hols. Res accepted. Chinese menu. Bar. Lunch $4.75-$6.95, dinner $6.75-$15.95. Sun brunch $1.95-$3.50. Specialties: sizzling "Three Musketeers," chicken pot Szechuan style, crispy shrimp Hunan style. Own baking. Cr cds: A, D, MC, V.
D ⊒

★ **CHUY ARZOLA'S.** *6405 Clayton Ave (63139). 314/644-4430.* Hrs: 11 am-10 pm; Fri, Sat to 11 pm; Sun 4-9 pm. Closed hols. Mexican menu. Bar. Lunch, dinner $4.50-$9.95. Specializes in fajitas, burritos, Lone Star quesadilla. Cr cds: DS, MC, V.
D ⊒

★ **CICERO'S.** *6691 Delmar Blvd, University City (63130). 314/862-0009.* Hrs: 11-1 am; Sun to midnight. Closed Thanksgiving, Dec 25. Italian menu. Bar. Lunch, dinner $4.95-$14.90. Children's menu. Specializes in pizza, pasta, desserts. Musicians.

Outdoor dining. Over 150 different beers avail; modern decor. Family-owned. Cr cds: A, D, MC, V.

[D] [SC] [⊟]

★ **CRAVINGS.** *8149 Big Bend, Webster Groves (63119).* 314/961-3534. Hrs: 10:30 am-6 pm; Fri, Sat 9 am-11 pm. Closed Mon; Thanksgiving, Dec 25. Res accepted. Wine, beer. Lunch $6.50-$13.50, dinner $12-$22. Specializes in seasonal dishes. Own breads. Some original art. Totally nonsmoking. Cr cds: MC, V.

[D]

★★ **CUNETTO HOUSE OF PASTA.** *5453 Magnolia Ave (63139).* 314/781-1135. Hrs: 11 am-2 pm, 5-10:30 pm; Fri to 11:30 pm; Sat 5-11:30 pm. Closed Sun; hols. Italian menu. Bar 11 am-11:30 pm. Lunch $5.50-$7, dinner $8-$15. Children's menu. Specialties: linguine tutto mare, veal with crabmeat, Sicilian steak. In old Italian neighborhood. Cr cds: A, D, MC, V.

[D] [⊟]

★★ **DIERDORF & HART'S STEAK HOUSE.** *323 Westport Plaza (63146).* 314/878-1801. www.dierdorfhartssteakhouse.com. Hrs: 11 am-10 pm; Fri to 11 pm; Sat 4:30-11 pm; Sun 4:30-10 pm. Closed July 4, Thanksgiving. Res accepted. Bar to 12:30 am; Fri, Sat to 1:30 am. Lunch $5.95-$12.95, dinner $14.75-$37.50. Specializes in broiled steak, broiled seafood. Pianist Wed-Sat. 1940s steakhouse atmosphere. Cr cds: A, C, D, DS, MC, V.

[D]

★★★ **DOMINIC'S RESTAURANT.** *5101 Wilson Ave, St Louis (63110).* 314/231-0911. Hrs: 5-11 pm; Fri, Sat to midnight. Closed Sun; hols. Res accepted. Italian menu. Bar. Wine cellar. Dinner $17.50-$27.50. Specialties: osso buco, shrimp elegante, artichoke stuffed with shrimp. Own pastries, pasta. Valet parking. Family-owned. Jacket. Cr cds: A, C, D, DS, ER, MC, V.

[⊟]

★★★ **FAUST'S.** *4th and Chestnut (63102).* 314/342-4690. www.adamsmark.com. Hrs: 5:30-10 pm; Fri, Sat to 10:30 pm. Res accepted. Bar. Wine list. A la carte entrees: lunch $9-$17, dinner $20-$35. Children's menu. Specialties: rack of lamb, halibut

Chardonnay, chateaubriand. Own baking. Valet parking. 2-tiered dining rm with beamed ceilings; upper tier with view of Gateway Arch. Jacket (dinner). Cr cds: A, D, DS, MC, V.

[D] [⊟]

★★ **FRANK PAPA'S.** *2241 S Brentwood Blvd, Brentwood (63144).* 314/961-3344. Hrs: 11 am-2 pm, 5-10 pm; Sat 5-11 pm. Closed Sun; hols. Res accepted. Italian menu. Bar. Lunch $7.95-$14.95, dinner $14.95-$21.95. Specialties: penne amatriciana, carpaccio, vitello alla Diana. Own baking. Storefront restaurant. Cr cds: A, D, DS, MC, V.

[D] [⊟]

★ **FRAZER'S TRAVELING BROWN BAG.** *1811 Pestalozzi (63118).* 314/773-8646. Hrs: 4-11 pm; Fri, Sat to midnight. Closed Sun; hols. Eclectic menu. Bar. Dinner $5.50-$17.25. Specialty: baked salmon. Keyboard Fri, Sat. Parking. Outdoor dining. Cr cds: MC, V.

[D] [⊟]

★★ **GIAN PEPPE'S.** *2126 Marconi Ave (63110).* 314/772-3303. Hrs: 11 am-2 pm, 5-11 pm; Sat from 5 pm. Closed Sun; hols; also Mon Oct-Jan. Res accepted. Italian menu. Bar. Wine list. Lunch $6.25-$15.99, dinner $12.50-$26.50. Specializes in veal, fresh seafood. Own pastries. Valet parking. Jacket. Cr cds: A, D, MC, V.

[D]

★ **GINO'S.** *4502 Hampton Ave (63109).* 314/351-4187. Hrs: 11 am-2 pm, 5-10 pm; Fri to 11 pm; Sat 5-11 pm; Sun 5-9 pm. Closed Mon; hols. Italian menu. Bar. Lunch $5.99-$10.95, dinner $6.95-$19.95. Children's menu. Specialties: veal Spedine, linguine pescatore, veal chops. Cafe atmosphere. Cr cds: A, MC, V.

[D] [⊟]

★★★ **GIOVANNI'S.** *5201 Shaw Ave (63110).* 314/772-5958. Hrs: 5-11 pm; Fri, Sat to midnight. Closed Sun; hols. Res accepted. Italian menu. Wine cellar. A la carte entrees: dinner $16.95-$29.95. Specialties: tuna San Martino, maltagliati al funchetto, osso buco originale, involtini di pesce spada. Own pastries and homemade pasta. Valet parking. Cr cds: A, DS, MC, V.

⊡ 🏷

★★★ **GIOVANNI'S LITTLE PLACE.** *14560 Manchester Rd, Ballwin (63011).* *636/227-7230.* Hrs: 5-10 pm. Closed Sun; hols. Res accepted. Italian menu. Bar. Wine cellar. Dinner $10.95-$30. Specialties: fusilli ai quattro formaggi, involtini di vitello alla villa Igea, vitello alla Maria. Own pastries. Cr cds: A, D, MC, V.

⊡

★★ **GIUSEPPE'S.** *4141 S Grand Blvd (63118).* *314/832-3779.* Hrs: 11 am-10 pm; Sat 4-10:30 pm; Sun 4-9 pm. Closed Mon; hols; July 1. Res accepted. Italian menu. Bar. Lunch $4.95-$6.95, dinner $6.50-$17.95. Children's menu. Specialties: breaded speidini, breaded veal cutlet, linguini with clam sauce. Mahogany woodwork; ornately framed artwork. Family-owned. Cr cds: A, C, D, MC, V.

⊡ 🏷

★★★ **GP AGOSTINO'S.** *15846 Manchester Rd, Ellisville (63011).* *636/391-5480.* Hrs: 11 am-2:30 pm, 5 pm-midnight. Closed Jan 1, Thanksgiving, Dec 25. Res accepted. Italian menu. Bar. Wine cellar. Lunch $3.95-$9.95, dinner $8.95-$19.95. Sun brunch $11.95 Specialties: veal salto in bocca Romano, osso buco Milanese, salmon con pappardelle. Chef-owned. Jacket (dinner). Cr cds: A, D, DS, MC, V.

⊡

★★ **HACIENDA.** *9748 Manchester Rd, Rockhill (63119).* *314/962-7100.* *www.hacienda-slt.com.* Hrs: 11 am-10 pm; Fri, Sat to midnight; Sun noon-9 pm. Closed hols. Res accepted. Mexican menu. Bar. Lunch, dinner $4.95-$10.95. Specialties: chicken mole, fajitas. Parking. Outdoor dining. Built as residence for steamboat captain (1861). Cr cds: A, DS, MC, V.

⊡ 🏷

★ **HAMMERSTONE'S.** *2028 S 9th (63104).* *314/773-5565.* Hrs: 11-1:30 am; Sun noon-midnight. Closed Easter, Memorial Day, Dec 25. Bar. Lunch, dinner $4.75-$11.95. Children's menu. Specialties: prime rib sandwich, Hammerstone's nachos, prime rib melt. Musicians. Street parking. Outdoor dining. Cr cds: A, MC, V.

🏷

★ **HANNEGAN'S.** *719 N 2nd St (63102).* *314/241-8877.* *www.hannegansrestaurant.com.* Hrs: 11 am-10 pm; Fri, Sat to 11 pm. Closed Thanksgiving, Dec 25. Bar. Lunch $5-$8, dinner $10-$17. Children's menu. Specializes in fresh seafood, steak. Oyster bar in season. Jazz Fri, Sat. Outdoor dining. Replica of US Senate dining rm; political memorabilia. Cr cds: A, D, DS, MC, V.

⊡ 🏷

★★ **HARRY'S.** *2144 Market St (63103).* *314/421-6969.* Hrs: 11 am-3 pm, 5-11 pm; Sun 5-10 pm. Closed hols. Res accepted. Bar. Lunch $5-$16, dinner $8-$25. Specializes in smoked meats, fish. Entertainment Wed, Fri, Sat. Valet parking. Patio dining with view of Union Station and skyline. Cr cds: A, C, D, DS, MC, V.

⊡

★ **HARVEST.** *1059 S Big Bend (63117).* *314/645-3522.* *www.harvest saintlouis.com.* Hrs: 5:30-10 pm; Sun from 5 pm. Closed Mon; July 4, Thanksgiving, Dec 25. Res accepted. Bar. Dinner $16.95-$23.95. Children's menu. Specialties: crab cake, bread pudding. Parking. Menu changes seasonally. Cr cds: A, C, D, DS, MC, V.

⊡

★ **HOUSE OF INDIA.** *8501 Delmar Blvd (63124).* *314/567-6850.* Hrs: 11:30 am-2:30 pm, 5-10 pm. Res accepted. Indian menu. Serv bar. Buffet lunch $5.95. Dinner $6.95-$13.95. Children's menu. Specialty: yogi thali. Indian art. Totally nonsmoking. Cr cds: A, DS, MC, V.

⊡

★★ **J. F. SANFILIPPO'S.** *705 N Broadway (63102).* *314/621-7213.* Hrs: 11 am-2 pm, 4:30-11 pm; Sat from 4:30 pm. Closed Sun (exc football season); hols. Res accepted. Italian menu. Bar. Lunch $4.50-$10.25, dinner $4.75-$18.50. Children's menu. Specializes in pasta, fresh seafood, veal. Free garage parking. Low slatted ceiling of metal and wood. Cr cds: A, C, D, DS, MC, V.

⊡ 🏷

★ **JOHN D. MCGURK'S.** *1200 Russell Blvd (63104).* *314/776-8309. www. mcgurks.com.* Hrs: 11-1:30 am; Sat from 11:30 am; Sun 4 pm-midnight. Closed hols. Res accepted. Irish, American menu. Bar. Lunch $5.95-$10.95, dinner $5.95-$17.95. Children's menu. Specialties: Irish soda bread, corned beef and cabbage, Irish stew. Traditional Irish music. Street parking. Housed in 1861 building. Family-owned. Cr cds: A, C, D, DS, MC, V.
D ⊐

★★★ **JOHN MINEO'S.** *13490 Clayton Rd, Town and Country (63131).* *314/434-5244.* Hrs: 5 pm-midnight. Closed Sun. Res accepted. Italian menu. Bar. Wine list. A la carte entrees: dinner $9.95-$18.95. Specialties: veal alla panna, Dover sole, fresh fish. Chef-owned. Jacket. Cr cds: A, C, D, DS, MC, V.
D

★★ **JOSEPH'S ITALIAN CAFE.** *107 N 6th St (63101).* *314/421-6366.* Hrs: 11 am-2 pm, 5:30-9:30 pm; Sat 5-10 pm. Closed Sun. Res accepted. Italian menu. Bar. Lunch $3.95-$10.95, dinner $8.99-$25.99. Children's menu. Specializes in pasta. Pianist. Outdoor dining. Contemporary decor. Totally nonsmoking. Cr cds: A, C, D, DS, MC, V.
D

★★ **K.C. MASTERPIECE.** *611 N Lindbergh (63141).* *314/991-5811.* Hrs: 11 am-10 pm; Fri, Sat to 11 pm; Sun to 9:30 pm. Closed Jan 1, Dec 25. Barbecue menu. Bar. Lunch $5.59-$17.49, dinner $6.79-$17.99. Children's menu. Specialties: babyback ribs, burnt ends, Doc's dip. Parking. Cr cds: A, DS, MC, V.
D ⊐

★★★ **KEMOLL'S.** *1 Metropolitan Sq (63102).* *314/421-0555. www.kemolls. com.* Hrs: 11 am-2 pm, 5-9 pm; Fri to 10 pm; Sat 5-10 pm; early-bird dinner 5-6:30 pm. Closed Sun; hols. Res accepted. Italian menu. Wine list. Lunch, dinner $15-$32. Specialties: veal Francesco, carciofi fritti. 5 dining rms. Family-owned. Cr cds: A, D, DS, MC, V.
D

★ **KING & I.** *3157 S Grand Blvd (63118).* *314/771-1777. www.kingan direst.com.* Hrs: 11 am-2:30 pm, 5-9:30 pm; Sat, Sun noon-3 pm, 5-10 pm. Closed Mon; also hols. Res accepted. Thai menu. Bar. Lunch $4.50-$6.95, dinner $6.95-$11.95. Specialties: pad Thai, pad spicy, red curry duck. Street parking. Thai decor. Cr cds: A, D, DS, MC, V.
D ⊐

★★★ **KREIS'S.** *535 S Lindbergh, Ladue (63131).* *314/993-0735.* Hrs: 5-10:30 pm; Sat to 11 pm; Sun 4:30-9:30 pm. Closed hols. Res accepted. Bar. Dinner $11.95-$39. Specializes in prime rib, steak, fresh fish. Valet parking. In renovated 1930s brick house with beamed ceilings. Cr cds: A, DS, MC, V.
D ⊐

★★ **LEONARDO'S LITTLE ITALY.** *5901 Southwest Ave (63139).* *314/781-5988.* Hrs: 5-11 pm. Closed Mon, Sun; hols. Res accepted Fri-Sun. Italian menu. Bar. Dinner $15.95-$20.95. Specialties: papardelle alla Genovese, veal Vesuvio, fresh salmon. Own pastries. Located in old Italian neighborhood. Antiques, stained glass, original art. Cr cds: A, D, DS, MC, V.
D

★★★ **LOMBARDO'S.** *201 S 20th St (63103).* *314/621-0666.* Hrs: 11 am-10 pm; Fri to 11:30 pm; Sat 4-11:30 pm. Closed Sun; hols. Res accepted. Italian menu. Bar. Wine list. Lunch $4.75-$8.95, dinner $7.50-$22. Children's menu. Specialties: ravioli, calzoni. Jazz Fri, Sat. Valet parking (dinner). Several dining areas on lower level of historic hotel. Cr cds: A, D, MC, V.
D ⊐

★★ **LORUSSO'S CUCINA.** *3121 Watson Rd (63139).* *314/647-6222. www.lorussos.com.* Hrs: 11:30 am-2 pm, 5-10 pm; Fri, Sat 5-11 pm. Closed Mon, Sun; hols. Italian menu. Bar 11 am-11 pm. Lunch $6.25-$10.95, dinner $8.50-$19.95. Children's menu. Specialties: chicken spedini, mushroom risotto, tenderloin Mudega. Entertainment Fri, Sat. Cr cds: A, D, DS, MC, V.
D ⊐

★★ **LYNCH STREET BISTRO.** *1031 Lynch St (63118).* *314/772-5777. www.lynchstreetbistro.com.* Hrs: 11 am-3 pm, 5-10 pm; Fri, Sat to 11 pm.

Closed Sun; hols. Res accepted. Eclectic menu. Bar. Wine list. Lunch $6-$10. A la carte entrees: dinner $14-$22. Children's menu. Specialties: lobster, barbecue-crusted salmon, grilled pork tenderloin. Live entertainment. Outdoor dining. Original paintings, art and posters. Cr cds: A, D, MC, V.

D

★ **MAGGIE O'BRIEN'S.** *2000 Market St (63103). 314/421-1388.* Hrs: 11-3 am; Sat, Sun from 4 pm. Closed hols. Res accepted. Irish, American menu. Lunch, dinner $5.25-$13.95. Children's menu. Specialties: corned beef and cabbage, chicken O'Brien. Own potato chips. Valet parking. Outdoor dining. Irish atmosphere. Family-owned since 1979. Cr cds: A, D, DS, MC, V.

D

★★★ **MALMAISON AT ST. ALBANS.** *St. Albans Rd, St. Albans (63073). 636/458-0131.* Hrs: 5-10 pm; Sat, Sun 11:30 am-3:30 pm, 5-10 pm. Closed Mon, Tues. Res accepted. French menu. Bar. Wine list. A la carte entrees: dinner $16-$23. Specializes in wild game, duckling. Outdoor dining. French country decor. Jacket. Cr cds: A, MC, V.

D

★★ **MAMA CAMPISI'S.** *2132 Edwards St (63110). 314/771-1797. www.mamacampisi.com.* Hrs: 11 am-10 pm. Closed Mon; hols. Res accepted. Italian menu. Bar. Lunch $5.95-$7.95, dinner $7.25-$16.95. Specialties: petto de polo picante, vitello alla parmigiano, lasagna al forno. Casual dining. Cr cds: A, C, D, DS, MC, V.

SC

★ **MANDARIN HOUSE.** *162 Union Station (63103). 314/621-6888.* Hrs: 10 am-10 pm. Res accepted. Chinese menu. Bar. Lunch, dinner $6.25-$14. Lunch buffet $5.65. Specializes in Szechuan, Peking dishes. Chinese decor. Inside shopping mall at Union Station. Cr cds: A, D, DS, MC, V.

D

★ **MARCIANO'S.** *333 Westport Plaza (63146). 314/878-8180.* Hrs: 11 am-10:30 pm; Fri, Sat to midnight; Sun from 3 pm. Closed Easter, Thanksgiving, Dec 25. Res accepted. Italian menu. Bar. Lunch $6.50-$7.95. A la carte entrees: dinner $6.95-$16.95. Children's menu. Specializes in pasta, seafood, desserts. Outdoor dining. Multilevel dining; Italian posters. Cr cds: A, D, DS, MC, V.

D

★★ **MIKE SHANNON'S.** *100 N 7th St (63101). 314/421-1540. www.bitestl.com/shannons.* Hrs: 11 am-11 pm; Sat, Sun 5-10 pm. Closed Easter, Thanksgiving, Dec 25. Res accepted. Bar. Lunch $5.25-$10.95, dinner $11.95-$35.95. Specializes in prime dry-aged beef, seafood. Sports memorabilia. Cr cds: A, C, D, DS, MC, V.

D

★ **MUSEUM CAFE.** *1 Fine Arts Dr (63110). 314/721-5325. www.slam.org.* Hrs: 11 am-2 pm, 3:30-8:30 pm; Tues 11 am-2 pm, 5-8:30 pm; Sun 10 am-3:30 pm; Sun brunch to 2 pm. Closed Mon; Dec 25. Res accepted. Continental menu. Wine, beer. Lunch $5.50-$8.50, dinner $6.50-$8.95. Children's menu. Specializes in salads, fresh fish. Own soups. Menu items reflect current museum exhibits. Cr cds: DS, MC, V.

D

★ **ONCE UPON A VINE.** *3559 Arsenal St (63118). 314/776-2828. www.bitestl.com/once.* Hrs: 10:30 am-9 pm; Fri, Sat to 10:30 pm. Closed Sun; hols. Res accepted. Bar. Lunch, dinner $5.95-$18.95. Children's menu. Specialties: chicken salad, smoked pork chops, penne with wild mushrooms and chicken. Outdoor dining. Storefront restaurant; casual dining. Totally nonsmoking. Cr cds: A, C, D, DS, MC, V.

D

★★ **PATRICK'S.** *342 Westport Plaza (63146). 314/878-6767.* Hrs: 11 am-11 pm; Fri, Sat to midnight; Sun 9:30 am-2 pm, 4-11 pm. Closed hols. Res accepted. Bar. Lunch $4.95-$8.95, dinner $8.95-$26.95, Sun brunch $9.95. Children's menu. Specialties: fresh seafood, prime rib, pasta. Entertainment. Outdoor dining. Casual decor. Cr cds: A, C, D, MC, V.

D

★★ **PROVINCES.** *1335 S Lindbergh Rd (63131). 314/993-8979. www.*

hilton.com. Hrs: 6:30 am-10 pm; Sun brunch 10 am-2 pm. Res accepted. Eclectic menu. Bar 11-1:30 am; Sun to 11:30 pm. Bkfst $5.25-$9.75, lunch $5.75-$11.25, dinner $13-$20. Sun brunch $19.95. Children's menu. Specialties: seafood fettucine, Chilean sea bass, crusted lamb chops. Cr cds: A, D, DS, MC, V.

D SC

★ **RED SEA.** *6511 Delmar Blvd (63130).* 314/863-0099. Hrs: 11 am-3 pm, 5-10 pm; Fri to 11 pm; Sat 3 pm-1 am; Sun (brunch) 11 am-3:30 pm, 5-11 pm. Closed Dec 25. Res accepted. Ethiopian menu. Bar. Lunch $5.95-$7, dinner $6.95-$15. Specialties: special tips, spicy lemon shrimp, chicken Calypso. Sun brunch $5.95. Jazz. Street parking. Cr cds: A, D, DS, MC, V.

D

★ **RIDDLE PENULTIMATE.** *6307 Delmar Blvd, University City (63130).* 314/725-6985. *www.riddlescafe.com.* Hrs: 11-1 am; Sat from 11:30 am; Sun 5 pm-midnight. Closed Mon; July 4, Thanksgiving, Dec 25. Res accepted. Eclectic menu. Bar. Lunch $4.25-$10, dinner $9-$22. Specializes in pasta, veal, fresh fish. Blues, jazz, bluegrass. Street parking. Outdoor dining. Known for extensive wine list—over 370 varieties. Cr cds: A, C, D, MC, V.

⊒

★ **ROBATA OF JAPAN.** *111 Westport Plaza (63146).* 314/434-1007. Hrs: 11:30 am-1:30 pm, 5:30-9 pm; wkend hrs vary. Closed Thanksgiving. Res accepted. Japanese menu. Bar. Lunch $5-$12, dinner $11-$22. Children's menu. Specializes in steak, seafood, chicken. Japanese decor; teppanyaki cooking. Cr cds: A, D, DS, MC, V.

D

★★ **ST. LOUIS BREWERY & TAP ROOM.** *2100 Locust St (63103).* 314/241-2337. *www.schlafly.com.* Hrs: 11 am-10 pm; Fri, Sat to midnight; Sun noon-9 pm. Closed Jan 1, Easter, Dec 25. Bar. Lunch, dinner $6-$12. Specialties: sticky toffee pudding, beer cheese soup, goat cheese rarebit. English brew pub atmosphere. Cr cds: A, DS, MC, V.

D ⊒

★ **SALEEM'S LEBANESE CUISINE.** *6501 Delmar Blvd (63130).* 314/721-

7947. Hrs: 5-10 pm; Fri, Sat to 11:30 pm. Closed Sun; Thanksgiving, Dec 25. Middle Eastern menu. Serv bar. Dinner $11.95-$15.95. Specializes in vegetarian, chicken, lamb. Middle Eastern decor. Cr cds: DS, MC, V.

D ⊒

★★★ **SCHNEITHORST'S HOFAMBERG INN.** *1600 S Lindbergh Blvd, Ladue (63131).* 314/993-5600. *www.schneithorst.com.* Hrs: 11 am-9 pm; Fri, Sat to 11 pm; Sun 10 am-8 pm; early-bird dinner Mon-Fri 4-6:30 pm (exc hols); Sun brunch to 1:30 pm. Closed Dec 25. Res accepted. German, American menu. Bar. Lunch $5.95-$16.95, dinner $10.95-$23.95. Sun brunch $11.95. Children's menu. Specializes in steak, prime rib, fresh seafood. Outdoor dining. Antique clocks, stein display. Cr cds: A, C, D, DS, MC, V.

D ⊒

★★★ **SEVENTH INN.** *100 Seven Trails, Ballwin (63011).* 636/227-6686. Hrs: 5 pm-1:30 am. Closed Mon, Sun; Easter, Thanksgiving, Dec 25. Res accepted. Continental menu. Bar. Wine list. Prices: $19.95-$29.95. Children's menu. Specializes in fresh seafood, prime aged beef. Entertainment Fri, Sat. Elegant European decor. Cr cds: A, D, DS, MC, V.

D ⊒

★★ **SIDNEY STREET CAFE.** *2000 Sidney St (63104).* 314/771-5777. Hrs: 5-9:30 pm; Fri, Sat to 10:30 pm. Closed Mon and Sun. Res accepted. Continental menu. Bar. Dinner $16-$23. Specializes in grilled seafood, lamb, steak au poivre. In restored building (ca 1885); antiques. Dinner menu recited. Cr cds: A, D, DS, MC, V.

D

★ **SPIRO'S.** *3122 Watson Rd (63134).* 314/645-8383. Hrs: 11 am-2 pm, 5-10 pm; Fri to 11 pm; Sat 5-11 pm; early-bird dinner 5-6:30 pm; Fri to 6 pm. Closed Sun; hols. Res required Fri, Sat (dinner). Continental menu. Serv bar. Lunch $5.50-$10.50, dinner $9-$20.95. Children's menu. Specializes in lamb, steak, fish. Valet parking Sat. Family-owned since 1972. Cr cds: A, DS, MC, V.

D ⊒

★ **SUNFLOWER CAFE.** *5513 Pershing Ave (63112).* 314/367-6800. Hrs:

11 am-2:30 pm, 5-10 pm; Fri, Sat to 11 pm. Closed Sun; hols. Italian, American menu. Bar. Lunch, dinner $4-$15.25. Children's menu. Specializes in pizza, pasta, fresh focaccia. Street parking. Outdoor dining. Totally nonsmoking. Cr cds: A, C, D, DS, MC, V.
D

★ **THAI CAFE.** 6170 Delmar Blvd (63112). 314/862-6868. Hrs: 11:30 am-2:30 pm, 5-10 pm; Fri, Sat to 10:30 pm. Closed Sun; Dec 25. Res accepted. Thai menu. Serv bar. Lunch, dinner $3.90-$10.95. Specialties: Thai satay, pad Thai, red curry. Valet parking. Thai artwork; one rm has only traditional Thai seating (no chairs). Totally nonsmoking. Cr cds: A, DS, MC, V.
D

★★★★ **TONY'S.** 410 Market St (63102). 314/231-7007. Tony Bommarito and his three sons oversee this landmark, special-occasion destination. The hearty, classic-Italian menu presents beef, veal, homemade pastas, and seafood, including the signature lobster albanello in a creamy, mushroom-flecked sauce, all served with energetically warm service. A lucky few may spot a celebrity, but regardless, everyone feels like a VIP in this pristine, classy dining room. Specializes in prime veal and beef, fresh seafood, homemade pasta. Own baking. Hrs: 5-11 pm; Fri, Sat to 11:30 pm. Closed Sun; hols; also 1st wk Jan, 1st wk July. Res accepted. Bar. Wine cellar. Dinner $19.75-$31.75. Valet parking. Family-owned. Jacket. Cr cds: A, C, D, DS, MC, V.
D

★★ **TRATTORIA MARCELLA.** 3600 Watson Rd (63109). 314/352-7706. Hrs: 5-10 pm; Fri, Sat to 11 pm. Closed Mon, Sun; hols. Res accepted. Italian menu. Bar. Dinner $8.95-$15.95. Specialties: frito misto of calamari and spinach, risotto with lobster and wild mushrooms. Own baking, pasta. Outdoor dining. Authentic Italian decor; mirrored walls. Family-owned since 1911. Cr cds: A, D, MC, V.
D

★ **YACOVELLI'S.** 407 Dunn Rd, Florissant (63031). 314/839-1000.

www.yacovellis.com. Hrs: 4-10 pm; early-bird dinner 4-5:30 pm (seasonal). Closed Easter, Thanksgiving, Dec 25. Res accepted. Italian menu. Bar. Dinner $10-$21.95. Children's menu. Specialties: prime rib, steak Diane, filet Yacovelli. Valet parking. Italian decor and atmosphere. Family-owned since 1918. Cr cds: A, D, DS, MC, V.
D 🖼

★★ **YEMANJA BRASIL.** 2900 Missouri Ave (63118). 314/771-7457. Hrs: 11 am-10 pm; Sat 5-11 pm. Closed Mon; also hols. Res accepted. Brazilian menu. Bar. Lunch $4.50-$7.95, dinner $7.95-$16.95. Specialties: ferjoada, shrimp yemanja. Street parking. Outdoor dining. Tropical atmosphere; Brazilian decor. Cr cds: A, DS, MC, V.
D

★ **ZIA'S.** 5256 Wilson Ave (63110). 314/776-0020. www.zias.com. Hrs: 11 am-10 pm; winter hrs vary. Closed Sun; Memorial Day, July 4. Italian menu. Bar. Lunch $5-$8, dinner $8.25-$16.95. Specializes in veal, pasta, chicken. Informal, modern corner restaurant. Outdoor dining. Cr cds: A, D, DS, MC, V.
🖼

★★ **ZINNIA.** 7491 Big Bend Blvd, Webster Groves (63119). 314/962-0572. www.zinniarestaurant.com. Hrs: 11 am-2 pm, 5:30-9:30 pm; Fri to 10:30 pm; Sat 5:30-10:30 pm; Sun 4:30-9 pm. Closed Mon; hols. Res accepted. Bar. Lunch $7.50-$9.50, dinner $13.50-$20.50. Specialties: sauteed veal sweetbreads, trout Zinnia. Own pasta. Outdoor dining. Upscale dining; wall murals, many flower boxes. Cr cds: DS, MC, V.
D

Unrated Dining Spots

AMIGHETTI'S. 5141 Wilson Ave (63110). 314/776-2855. www.amighettis.com. Hrs: 7:30 am-6 pm. Closed Mon, Tues; also hols. Res accepted. Italian menu. Serv bar. Lunch, dinner $2.99-$4.99. Children's menu. Specializes in breads, sandwiches, pastas. Band Sat. Street parking. Outdoor dining. Cr cds: MC, V.

BARN DELI. *180 Dunn Rd, Florissant (63031). 314/838-3670.* Hrs: 11 am-4 pm. Closed Sun; hols. Wine, beer. Lunch $3.50-$4.95. Specializes in deli sandwiches, salads. Own soups, desserts. Outdoor dining. In late 1800s barn. Cr cds: A, DS, MC, V.
D SC ⊸

BLUEBERRY HILL. *6504 Delmar Blvd (63130). 314/727-0880. www.blueberryhill.com.* Hrs: 11-1:30 am; Sun to midnight. Closed Superbowl Sun. Res accepted. Bar to 1:30 am; Sun to midnight. Lunch, dinner $3.25-$7. Specializes in hamburgers, vegetarian platters, soups. Entertainment Wed-Sat eves. Large displays of pop culture memorabilia incl Chuck Berry, The Simpsons, and Elvis. Vintage jukeboxes, toys. Sidewalk has "Walk of Fame" stars for celebrities from St. Louis. Cr cds: A, MC, V.
D ⊸

CROWN CANDY KITCHEN. *1401 St. Louis Ave (63106). 314/621-9650.* Hrs: 10:30 am-10 pm; Sun from noon. Closed hols. Specialty: ice cream. Also sandwiches, chili $2-$4. Homemade candy. Old neighborhood building (1889) with old-fashioned soda fountain (1930s), antique juke box, and Coca-Cola memorabilia. Cr cds: A, DS, MC, V.
D ⊸

O'CONNELL'S PUB. *4652 Shaw Ave (63110). 314/773-6600.* Hrs: 11 am-midnight; Sun noon-10 pm. Closed hols. Bar. Lunch, dinner $3.50-$6.50. Specializes in hamburgers, roast beef sandwiches, soup. Pub atmosphere; antique bar; blackboard menu. Cr cds: A, D, DS, MC, V.
⊸

St. Louis Lambert Airport Area

See also St. Charles, St. Louis

Services and Information

Information. 314/426-8000.

Lost and Found. 314/426-8100.

Weather. 314/321-2222.

Cash Machines. Main Terminal, concourse level.

Airlines. Air Canada, American, America West, Canadian Airlines, Casino Express, Continental, Delta, Frontier Airlines, Lone Star Airlines, Midwest Express, Northwest, Southwest, TWA, United, USAir.

Motels/Motor Lodges

★★ **BEST WESTERN AIRPORT INN.** *10232 Natural Bridge Rd (63134). 314/427-5955; fax 314/427-3079; toll-free 800/872-0070. www.bestwestern.com.* 138 rms, 2 story. May-Sept: S $59-$75; D $59-$80; under 12 free; lower rates rest of yr. Crib free. TV; cable (premium). Pool. Restaurant nearby. Ck-out noon. Coin lndry. Meeting rms. Business servs avail. In-rm modem link. Free airport transportation. Cr cds: A, C, D, DS, JCB, MC, V.
D ⊸ ✈ ⊸ 🖐 SC

★★ **DRURY INN AIRPORT.** *I-70 and Lambert International Airport (63134). 314/423-7700; fax 314/423-7700. www.druryhotels.com.* 172 rms, 6 story. S $79.95-$85.95; D $89.95-$99.95; suites $103-$123; under 18 free; wknd rates. Crib free. Pet accepted, some restrictions. TV; cable (premium), VCR avail. Heated pool. Complimentary continental bkfst. Restaurant adj noon-10 pm. Ck-out noon. Meeting rms. Business servs avail. In-rm modem link. Free airport transportation. Cr cds: A, C, D, DS, ER, JCB, MC, V.
D ⊸ 🖐 ⊸ ✈ ⊸ 🖐

★★ **FAIRFIELD INN.** *9079 Dunn Rd, Hazelwood (63042). 314/731-7700; fax 314/731-1898. www.fairfieldinn.com.* 135 rms, 3 story. May-Sept: S, D $49-$75; under 12 free; wkend rates; higher rates VP Fair. Crib free. TV; cable (premium). Pool. Complimentary continental bkfst. Ck-out noon. Business servs avail. In-rm modem link. Cr cds: A, C, D, DS, MC, V.
D ⊸ ⊸ 🖐

★★ **HAMPTON INN.** *10800 Pear Tree Ln, St. Ann (63074). 314/427-3400; fax 314/423-7765. www.hamptoninn.com.* 155 rms, 4 story. May-Aug: S, D $75.95-$89.95; each addl

$10; under 18 free. Crib free. Pet accepted. TV; cable (premium). Complimentary continental bkfst, coffee in rms. Restaurant adj 6 am-midnight. Ck-out noon. Meeting rms. Business center. In-rm modem link. Free airport transportation. Pool. Refrigerators, microwaves avail. Cr cds: A, C, D, DS, MC, V.

★★ HOLIDAY INN AIRPORT OAKLAND PARK. *4505 Woodson Rd (63134). 314/427-4700; fax 314/427-6086; toll-free 800/426-4700. www. holiday-inn.com.* 156 rms, 5 story, 13 suites. S $109.50; D $119.50; each addl $10; suites $125-$230; under 19 free; wkend rates. Crib free. TV; cable (premium). Pool; whirlpool. Restaurant 6:30-10:30 am, 5-10 pm. Bar 4:30 pm-midnight. Ck-out 1 pm. Coin lndry. Meeting rms. Business servs avail. In-rm modem link. Bellhops. Valet serv. Free airport transportation. Exercise equipt; sauna. Cr cds: A, MC, V.

★★ HOLIDAY INN ST. LOUIS AIRPORT NORTH. *4545 N Lindbergh Blvd (63044). 314/731-2100; fax 314/731-4970. www.holiday-inn.com.* 392 rms, 4 story. May-Dec: S, D $79-$109; under 18 free; family, wkly, wkend, hol rates; lower rates rest of yr. Crib $10. TV; cable (premium). Complimentary coffee in rms. Restaurant 6 am-11 pm. Bar 4 pm-midnight. Ck-out noon. Convention facilities. Business center. In-rm modem link. Bellhops. Valet serv. Concierge. Gift shop. Coin lndry. Free airport transportation. Exercise equipt. Indoor pool; wading pool, whirlpool, poolside serv. Game rm. Many balconies. Luxury level. Cr cds: A, C, D, DS, MC, V.

★★ RAMADA INN ST. LOUIS AIRPORT AND CONFERENCE CENTER. *3551 Pennridge, St. Louis (63044). 314/291-5100; fax 314/291-3546. www.ramada.com.* 245 rms, 4 story. S, D $69-$99; each addl $10; under 18 free. Crib free. Pet accepted. TV; cable (premium), VCR avail. Complimentary coffee in rms. Restaurant 6-10 am. Bar 4 pm-1 am. Ck-out noon. Convention facilities. Business center. In-rm modem link.

Bellhops. Valet serv. Coin lndry. Free airport transportation. Exercise equipt; sauna. Indoor pool; whirlpool. Game rm. Rec rm. Some refrigerators. Luxury level. Cr cds: A, C, D, DS, MC, V.

★ SUPER 8. *12705 St. Charles Rock Rd, Bridgeton (63044). 314/291-8845. www.super8.com.* 99 rms, 3 story. Apr-Sept: S $37-$49; D $49-$55; under 12 free; wkly rates; higher rates: hols, special events; lower rates rest of yr. Crib free. Pet accepted, some restrictions; $25 deposit. TV; cable (premium). Complimentary coffee in lobby. Restaurant nearby. Ck-out 11 am. Business servs avail. Coin lndry. Free airport transportation. Some refrigerators. Cr cds: A, DS, MC, V.

Hotels

★★★ CROWNE PLAZA. *11228 Lone Eagle Dr, Bridgeton (63044). 314/291-6700; fax 314/770-1205. www.crowneplaza.com.* 351 rms, 8 story. S $115-$125; D $125-$135; each addl $10; suites $379; under 18 free; wkend rates. Crib $10. TV. Indoor pool; whirlpool. Restaurant 6:30 am-midnight. Bar from 11 am. Ck-out noon. Convention facilities. Business servs avail. In-rm modem link. Gift shop. Free airport transportation. Exercise equipt. Game rm. Wet bar in suites. Some balconies. Atrium with waterfall. Cr cds: A, C, D, DS, ER, JCB, MC, V.

★★ DOUBLETREE CLUB ST. LOUIS AIRPORT. *9600 Natural Bridge Rd (63134). 314/427-7600; fax 314/427-1614. www.doubletreeclub. com.* 197 rms, 7 story. S $89-$129; D $99-$139; each addl $10; under 18 free; wkend rates. Crib free. TV. Pool, whirlpool. Restaurant 6 am-11 pm. Bar 5:30 pm-midnight. Ck-out noon. Meeting rms. Business servs avail. In-rm modem link. Free airport transportation. Exercise equipt. Cr cds: A, C, D, DS, JCB, MC, V.

★★★ HILTON ST. LOUIS AIRPORT. *10330 Natural Bridge Rd, St. Louis (63134). 314/426-5500; fax 314/426-3429. www.hilton.com.* 220 rms, 9

story. S, D $99-$150; each addl $10; suites $200-$350; under 18 free; wkend package plan. Crib free. TV; cable, VCR avail. Indoor pool; whirlpool, poolside serv. Complimentary coffee in rms. Restaurant 6 am-10 pm; wkends to 11 pm. Bars 11-1:30 am, Sun to midnight. Coin lndry. Ck-out 1 pm. Meeting rms. Business servs avail. In-rm modem link. Gift shop. Free airport transportation. Exercise equipt; sauna. Game rm. Some refrigerators; microwaves avail. Luxury level. Cr cds: A, MC, V.

★★★ **MARRIOTT.** *10700 Pear Tree, St. Louis. 314/423-9700; fax 314/423-0213; toll-free 800/228-9290. www.marriott.com.* 601 rms, 9 story. S, D $99-$134; suites $200-$375. Crib free. Pet accepted. TV; cable (premium), VCR avail. 2 pools, 1 indoor/outdoor; poolside serv, whirlpool. Restaurant 6 am-midnight. Bars 11:30-1 am. Ck-out 1 pm. Coin lndry. Convention facilities. Business center. In-rm modem link. Gift shop. Free airport transportation. 2 lighted tennis courts. Exercise equipt; sauna. Luxury level. Cr cds: A, C, D, DS, ER, JCB, MC, V.

★★★ **RENAISSANCE ST. LOUIS.** *9801 Natural Bridge Rd (63134). 314/429-1100; fax 314/429-3625; toll-free 800/468-3571. www.renaissance hotels.com.* 394 rms, 12 story. S $119-$169; D $139-$185; each addl $15; suites $195-$800; under 18 free; wkend rates. Crib free. TV; cable (premium), VCR avail. 2 pools, 1 indoor; whirlpool, poolside serv. Coffee in rms. Restaurant 6:30 am-11 pm. Rm serv until 1 am. Bar 3 pm-1 am. Ck-out 1 pm. Convention facilities. Business center. In-rm modem link. Gift shop. Concierge. Free airport transportation. Exercise equipt; sauna. Bathrm phones, minibars; microwaves avail. Luxury level. Cr cds: A, DS, MC, V.

All Suite

★★★ **EMBASSY SUITES ST. LOUIS AIRPORT.** *11237 Lone Eagle Dr, Bridgeton (63044). 314/739-8929; fax 314/739-6355. www.embassysuites.com.* 159 suites, 6 story. S $129; D $139; wkend rates; higher rates special events. Crib avail. TV; cable (premium). Indoor pool; whirlpool. Complimentary full bkfst, coffee in rms. Restaurant 11 am-11 pm. Bar 5 pm-midnight. Ck-out noon. Coin lndry. Meeting rms. Business servs avail. In-rm modem link. Gift shop. Free airport transportation. Exercise equipt; sauna. Game rm. Refrigerators, microwaves. Cr cds: A, C, D, DS, JCB, MC, V.

Restaurants

★★ **LOMBARDO'S.** *10488 Natural Bridge Rd (63134). 314/429-5151.* Hrs: 11 am-10 pm; Sat from 5 pm. Closed Sun; hols. Res accepted. Italian menu. Bar. Lunch $4.95-$12.75, dinner $9-$24. Specializes in fresh seafood, steak, pasta. Original art; sculptures. Family-owned since 1934. Cr cds: A, C, D, DS, MC, V.

★★★ **TORNATORE'S.** *12315 Natural Bridge Rd, Bridgeton (63044). 314/739-6644. www.tornatores.com.* Hrs: 11 am-3 pm, 5-10 pm; Sat from 5 pm; early-bird dinner 5-6:30 pm. Closed Sun; hols. Res accepted. Continental Italian menu. Bar. Extensive wine list. Lunch $8.95-$16.95, dinner $16.95-$32.95. Specializes in fresh seafood, Sicilian veal chops, barbecued pork chops. Own desserts. Modern art; etched glass-paneled rm divider. Cr cds: A, D, DS, MC, V.

Sedalia

(D-3) *See also Jefferson City*

Pop 19,800 **Elev** 919 ft **Area code** 660 **Zip** 65301

Information Chamber of Commerce, 113 E 4th St; 660/826-2222 or 800/827-5295

Web www.tourism.sedalia.mo.us

Known as the "queen city of the prairies," Sedalia was a prosperous railhead town in the 1800s with great cattle herds arriving for shipment to eastern markets. During the Civil War the settlement functioned as a military post. A monument at

Lamine and Main streets marks the site of the Maple Leaf Club, one of the city's many saloons that catered to railroad men. The monument is dedicated to Scott Joplin, who composed and performed the "Maple Leaf Rag" here, triggering the ragtime craze at the turn of the 20th century. Whiteman Air Force Base is 21 miles to the west of Sedalia.

What to See and Do

Bothwell Lodge State Historic Site. Approx 180 acres, incl hiking trails, picnicking. Tours of stone lodge (Mon-Sat and Sun afternoons). (See SPECIAL EVENTS) 6 mi N on US 65. Phone 660/827-0510. ¢

Knob Noster State Park. Lakes and streams on more than 3,500 acres. Fishing, boating, canoeing; hiking, picnicking, improved camping (dump stations), lndry facilities. Visitor center, naturalist program. Standard fees. (Daily) 20 mi W on US 50, then S on MO 132. Phone 660/563-2463. **FREE**

Pettis County Courthouse. Historic courthouse contains local artifacts and exhibits. (Mon-Fri; closed hols) 415 S Ohio, downtown. Phone 660/826-4892. **FREE**

Sedalia Ragtime Archives. Incl original sheet music, piano rolls, tapes of interviews with Eubie Blake. (Mon-Fri; closed school hols) State Fair Community College Library, Maple Leaf Rm, 3201 W 16th St. Phone 660/530-5800. **FREE**

Special Events

State Fair Motor Speedway. Racing on ½-mi dirt track featuring three racing classes. Phone 800/499-RACE. Phone 660/826-1600. Fri eves. May-Sept.

Bothwell Lodge Garden Party. Period games, speakers, demonstrations. Phone 660/827-0510. Early June.

Scott Joplin Ragtime Festival. Entertainment by ragtime greats. Phone 660/826-2271. Early June.

Band concerts. Liberty Park band shell. Thurs eves. Mid-June-early Aug.

Missouri State Fair. Fairgrounds, 16th St and Limit Ave. One of the country's leading state fairs; held here since 1901. Stage shows, rodeo, competitive exhibits, livestock, auto races. Phone 660/530-5600. Aug.

Motels/Motor Lodges

★★ **BEST WESTERN STATE FAIR MOTOR INN.** *3120 S Limit Ave (US 65 S and 32nd) (65301).* 660/826-6100; fax 660/827-3850. www.best western.com. 119 rms, 2 story. S $40-$50; D $55-$65; each addl $5; under 18 free. Crib free. Pet accepted. TV; cable (premium). Indoor pool; wading pool, whirlpool, poolside serv. Restaurant 5:45 am-2 pm, 5-9:30 pm. Bar. Ck-out noon. Coin lndry. Meeting rms. Business servs avail. Free airport transportation. Exercise equipt; sauna. Miniature golf. Game rm. Cr cds: A, C, D, DS, MC, V.

⬛ 🐾 ⬛ ⬛ 🕴 ⬛ ⬛

★ **RAMADA INN.** *3501 W Broadway Blvd (65301).* 660/826-8400; fax 660/826-1230; toll-free 800/272-6232. www.ramada.com. 125 rms, 2-3 story. No elvtr. S, D $54-$61; each addl $5; under 18 free. Crib free. TV; cable. Pool. Restaurant 6:30 am-2 pm, 5-10 pm. Bar 4 pm-1:30 am. Ck-out noon. Meeting rms. Business servs avail. Sundries. Cr cds: A, C, D, DS, JCB, MC, V.

⬛ ⬛ ⬛ **SC**

Restaurant

★ **AROUND THE FIRESIDE.** *1975 W Broadway (65301).* 660/826-9743. Hrs: 11 am-10 pm. Closed hols. Res accepted. Bar to 11:30 pm. Lunch $3.95-$7.95, dinner $6-$25. Children's menu. Specializes in steak, seafood. Salad bar. Cr cds: A, C, D, DS, MC, V.

⬛ **SC** ⬛

Sikeston

(F-7) *See also Cape Girardeau*

Founded 1860 **Pop** 17,641 **Elev** 325 ft
Area code 573 **Zip** 63801

Information Sikeston-Miner Convention & Visitors Bureau, 1 Industrial Dr, PO Box 1983; 888/309-6591

Although settlers were in this region before the Louisiana Purchase, John Sikes established the town of Sikeston in 1860 on El Camino Real, the overland route from St. Louis to New Orleans, at the terminus of the Cairo and Fulton Railway (now the Union Pacific).

What to See and Do

Southeast Missouri Agricultural Museum. Collection of antique farm machinery; reconstructed log cabins, 1920s service station. Relocated railroad depot, wooden caboose. (Apr-Oct, daily) 4 mi E via MO 532 in Bertrand. Phone 573/471-3945. ¢¢

Special Events

Bootheel Rodeo. Country music and rodeo events; parade. Four days first full wk Aug.

Cotton Carnival. Parades, contests. Last full wk Sept.

Motels/Motor Lodges

★★ **BEST WESTERN COACH HOUSE INN & SUITES.** *220 S Interstate Dr (63801). 573/471-9700; fax 573/471-4285; toll-free 887/471-9700.* 63 suites, 2 story. S $49-$59; D $58-$69; each addl $8; under 18 free; higher rates rodeo. Crib free. Pet accepted, some restrictions. TV; cable. Complimentary coffee in rms. Restaurant 7-11 am, 5-9 pm. Bar 4-11 pm; entertainment. Ck-out noon. Meeting rms. Business servs avail. In-rm modem link. Free guest lndry. Pool; poolside serv. Game rm. Rec rm. Refrigerators; microwaves avail. Cr cds: A, C, D, DS, MC, V.
🔄 🛏 🏊 🐾

★★ **DRURY INN.** *2602 E Malone Ave (81321). 573/471-4100; toll-free 800/ 325-8300. www.druryinn.com.* 78 rms, 4 story. S $58-$72; D $68-$82; each addl $10; suites $72-$82; under 18 free. Crib free. Pet accepted, some restrictions. TV; cable (premium), VCR avail (movies). Complimentary continental bkfst. Restaurant nearby. Ck-out noon. Meeting rms. Business servs avail. Valet serv. Heated indoor/outdoor pool; whirlpool. Some refrigerators, microwaves. Cr cds: A, C, D, DS, MC, V.
D 🐾 🛏 🏊 🐾 SC

★ **MINER SUPER 8 MOTEL.** *2609 E Malone (63801). 573/471-7944; fax 573/471-7946. www.super8.com.* 63 rms, 2 story. Apr-Sept: S $46; D $55; suites $67; under 12 free; higher rates rodeo; lower rates rest of yr. Crib free. TV; cable. Restaurant adj 10:30 am-10:30 pm. Ck-out 11 am. Cr cds: A, C, D, DS, MC, V.
D 🛏 🐾

★★ **PEAR TREE INN.** *2602 Rear E Malone (63801). 573/471-8660. www.druryinn.com.* 67 rms, 3 story. No elvtr. S $50; D $60; each addl $8; under 19 free. Crib free. Pet accepted, some restrictions. TV; cable (premium). Complimentary continental bkfst. Restaurant adj 6 am-10 pm. Meeting rms. Business servs avail. In-rm modem link. Valet serv. Pool. Microwaves avail. Cr cds: A, D, DS, MC.
D 🐾 ✈ 🛏 🐾

Restaurants

★ **FISHERMAN'S NET.** *915 River Birch Mall (63801). 573/471-8102.* Hrs: 11 am-9 pm. Res accepted. Closed Mon, Sun; hols. Lunch, dinner $3.95-$17.95. Buffet: lunch $4.99, dinner (Fri, Sat) $6.99. Children's menu. Specializes in catfish. Nautical decor. Cr cds: A, D, DS, MC, V.
D SC 🛏

★ **LAMBERT'S.** *2515 E Malone (63801). 573/471-4261.* Hrs: 10:30 am-9 pm. Closed hols. Lunch, dinner $9.99-$14.95. Children's menu. Specialties: throwed rolls and sorghum molasses, chicken and dumplings, chicken-fried steak. Entertainment Thurs-Sun. Country decor. Family-owned.
D

Silver Dollar City

(see Branson/Table Rock Lake Area)

Springfield

(F-3) *See also Branson/Table Rock Lake Area*

Pop 140,494 **Elev** 1,316 ft
Area code 417
Information Convention & Visitors Bureau, 3315 E Battlefield Rd, 65804-4048; 417/881-5300 or 800/678-8767
Web www.springfieldmo.org

In the southwest corner of the state and at the northern edge of the Ozark highlands, Springfield, known as Ozark Mountain Country's Big City, is near some of Missouri's most picturesque scenery and recreational areas. A few settlers came here as early as 1821 but settlement was temporarily discouraged when the government made southwestern Missouri a reservation. Later the tribes were moved west and the town began to develop. Its strategic location made it a military objective in the Civil War. The Confederates took the town in the Battle of Wilson's Creek, August 10, 1861; Union forces recaptured it in 1862. Confederate attempts to regain it were numerous but unsuccessful. "Wild Bill" Hickock, later one of the famous frontier marshals, was a scout and spy for Union forces headquartered in Springfield.

Springfield's growth has been largely due to a healthy economy based on diversified industry; manufacturing and the service industry provide the majority of jobs. Springfield is the home of six major colleges and universities, including Southwest Missouri State University.

What to See and Do

⭐ **Bass Pro Shops Outdoor World Showroom and Fish and Wildlife Museum.** This 300,000-sq-ft sporting goods store features a four-story waterfall, indoor boat and RV showrm, art gallery, and indoor firing range. Restaurant has 30,000-gallon saltwater aquarium. (Daily) 1935 S Campbell Ave. Phone 417/887-7334. ¢¢

Crystal Cave. Once a Native American habitat; contains a variety of colorful formations; temperature 59°F; guided tours. Gift shop, picnic area.

(Daily) 5 mi N of I-44 on MO H, exit 80B. Phone 417/833-9599. ¢¢¢

Dickerson Park Zoo. Animals in naturalistic setting; features elephant herd; animal rides. Playground; concession, picnic area. Gift shop. (Daily; closed Jan 1, Thanksgiving, Dec 25) 3043 N Fort. Phone 417/864-1800. ¢¢

Discovery Center. Interactive hands-on museum; incl "Discovery Town Theatre," where you can be a star on stage, create a newspaper, run a make-believe TV station, or dig for dinosaur bones. (Wed-Sun) 438 St. Louis St. Phone 417/862-9910. ¢¢¢

Exotic Animal Paradise. Approx 3,000 wild animals and rare birds may be seen along nine-mi drive. (Daily; closed Thanksgiving, Dec 25; winter hrs vary according to weather) 12 mi E on I-44 exit 88, Strafford, then E on outer road to entrance. Phone 417/859-2016. ¢¢¢

Fantastic Caverns. Cave tours (45-min) in jeep-drawn tram. (Daily; closed Thanksgiving, Dec 24, and 25) Restaurant (May-Oct). 4 mi NW via I-44, then N 1½ mi at MO 13. 4872 Farm Rd 125. Phone 417/833-2010. ¢¢¢

The History Museum. Permanent and rotating exhibits on Springfield, Greene County, and the Ozarks. (Tues-Sat; limited hrs) 830 Boonville, in historic City Hall. Phone 417/864-1976. ¢¢

⭐ **Laura Ingalls Wilder-Rose Wilder Lane Museum and Home.** House where Laura Ingalls Wilder wrote the Little House books; artifacts and memorabilia of Laura, husband Almanzo, and daughter Rose Wilder Lane; four handwritten manuscripts; many items mentioned in Wilder's books, incl Pa's fiddle. (Mar-Nov, Mon-Sat; also Sun afternoons) 50 mi E on US 60, at MO 5 in Mansfield. Phone 417/924-3626.

Springfield Art Museum. American and European paintings, sculpture, and graphics. (Tues-Sat, also Wed eves and Sun afternoons; closed hols) (See SPECIAL EVENTS) 1111 E Brookside Dr. Phone 417/837-5700. **Donation**

Springfield National Cemetery. One of the few national cemeteries where Union and Confederate soldiers from the same state are buried side-by-side. (Daily) 1702 E Seminole. Phone 417/881-9499.

Wilson's Creek National Battlefield. Scene of Aug 10, 1861, Civil War battle between Confederate and Union forces for control of Missouri. At entrance is visitor center, which has film, battle map light display, and a museum area. Also here are maps of self-guided five-mi road tour featuring waysides, exhibits, and walking trails. Highlights are the Bloody Hill trail, the Ray House, and the headquarters of General Price. Living History program (Memorial Day-Labor Day, Sun and hols). Battlefield (Daily; closed Jan 1, Dec 25). Contact Superintendent, Rte 2, Box 75, Republic 65738. 10 mi SW via I-44, County M and County ZZ, near Republic. Phone 417/732-2662. ¢¢

Special Events

Watercolor USA. Springfield Art Museum. National competitive exhibition of aquamedia painting. Phone 417/837-5700. Early June-early Aug.

Tent Theater. Southwest Missouri State University campus. Dramas, comedies, and musicals in repertory in circuslike tent. Phone 417/836-5979. Late June-early Aug.

Ozark Empire Fair. (regional) Phone 417/833-2660. Late July-early Aug.

Motels/Motor Lodges

★★ **BEST WESTERN DEERFIELD INN.** 3343 E Battlefield St (65804). 417/887-2323; fax 417/887-1242; toll-free 877/822-6560. www.bestwestern.com. 104 rms, 3 story. S $58-$63; D $63-$69; each addl $5; suites $125; under 18 free. TV; cable (premium). Indoor pool. Complimentary continental bkfst. Coffee in rms. Restaurant adj open 24 hrs. Ck-out noon. Meeting rm. Business servs avail. Cr cds: A, C, D, DS, ER, JCB, MC, V.
🄳 ≈ ⊠ 🐾 SC

★★ **BEST WESTERN ROUTE 66 RAIL HAVEN.** 203 S Glenstone Ave (65802). 417/866-1963; toll-free 800/528-1234. www.bestwestern.com. 93 rms. May-Oct: S, D $48-$53; each addl $5; suites $60-$65; under 18 free; lower rates rest of yr. Crib free. Pet accepted, some restrictions. TV; cable (premium), VCR avail (movies).

Pool; whirlpool. Complimentary continental bkfst. Restaurant adj open 24 hrs. Ck-out noon. Business servs avail. In-rm modem link. Valet serv. Refrigerator in suites. Cr cds: A, C, D, DS, MC, V.
🄳 ≈ ⊠ 🐾 SC

★ **CLARION HOTEL.** 3333 S Glenstone Ave (65803). 417/883-6550; fax 417/883-5720; toll-free 800/756-7318. www.clarionhotel.com. 199 rms, 11 with shower only, 2 story. S $69; D $79; each addl $5; suites $150; under 18 free. Crib free. Pet accepted, some restrictions; $10. TV; cable (premium). Pool. Restaurant 6:30 am-11 pm. Rm serv to 2 pm. Bar 11-1 am. Ck-out noon. Meeting rms. Business servs avail. In-rm modem link. Bellhops. Valet serv. Sundries. Free airport transportation. Health club privileges. Some refrigerators. Picnic tables. Cr cds: A, C, D, DS, JCB, MC, V.
🄳 🦃 ≈ ✈ ⊠ 🐾 SC

★ **ECONO LODGE.** 2611 N Glenstone Ave (65803). 417/864-3565; fax 417/865-0567; toll-free 800/553-2666. www.econolodge.com. 122 rms, 2 story. S $40-$47; D $45-$52; each addl $5; under 18 free. Crib free. TV; cable (premium), VCR avail (movies). Pool. Complimentary continental bkfst, coffee in rms. Restaurant nearby. Ck-out 11 am. Valet serv. Cr cds: A, C, D, DS, MC, V.
🄳 ≈ ⊠ 🐾 SC

★ **ECONO LODGE.** 2808 N Kansas Expy (65803). 417/869-5600; fax 417/869-3421; toll-free 800/553-2666. www.econolodge.com. 83 rms, 2-3 story. S $38.95-$43.95; D $45.95; suites $110; under 18 free. Crib free. TV; cable. Complimentary coffee in lobby. Restaurant adj 6 am-9:30 pm. Ck-out 11 am. Business servs avail. Cr cds: A, C, D, DS, ER, MC, V.
🄳 ⊠ 🐾

★★ **HAMPTON INN EAST.** 222 N Ingram Mill Rd (65802). 417/863-1440; fax 417/863-2215; toll-free 800/426-7866. www.hamptoninn.com. 99 rms, 2 story. S $57-$67; D $64-$74; suites $72-$88; under 18 free. Crib free. TV; cable (premium), VCR avail. Pool; whirlpool. Complimentary continental bkfst. Coffee in rms. Restaurant adj 6 am-midnight. Ck-out noon. Meeting rm. Business servs avail. In-rm modem link. Sundries. Exercise equipt. Cr cds: A, MC, V.

D ⚊ 🎿 ⊠ ♨

★★ **HAWTHORN SUITES.** *1550 E Raynell Pl (65804). 417/883-7300; fax 417/520-7900; res 800/527-1133. www.hawthorn.com.* 80 kit. suites, 2 story. S, D $99-$139. Crib $5. Pet accepted, some restrictions; $100 deposit ($75 refundable). TV; cable (premium). Pool; whirlpool. Complimentary continental bkfst. Restaurant nearby. Ck-out noon. Coin lndry. Meeting rms. Business servs avail. Valet serv. Health club privileges. Picnic tables, grills. Gazebo. Cr cds: A, D, DS, MC, V.

D ⬦ ⚊ ⊠ ♨

★★ **HOLIDAY INN NORTH.** *2720 N Glenstone (65803). 417/865-8600; fax 417/862-9415; toll-free 800/465-4329. holiday-inn.com/sgf-northi44.* 188 rms, 6 story, 36 suites. S, D $88.50-$100; suites $200; under 18 free. Crib free. TV; cable (premium), VCR avail. 2 pools, 1 indoor; whirlpool, poolside serv. Restaurant 6 am-2 pm, 5-10:30 pm. Bar 4 pm-1 am. Ck-out noon. Meeting rms. Business servs avail. In-rm modem link. Bellhops. Valet serv. Free airport, bus depot transportation. Exercise equipt; sauna. Some refrigerators. Cr cds: A, MC, V.

D 🎿 ⚊ ⊠ ♨ SC

★ **RAMADA INN.** *2820 N Glenstone Ave (65803). 417/869-3900; fax 417/865-5378; toll-free 800/707-0236. www.ramada.com.* 130 rms, 3 story. May-Oct: S, D $55-$65; each addl $5; under 18 free; higher rates special events; lower rates rest of yr. Crib avail. Pet accepted. TV; cable (premium). Pool. Complimentary continental bkfst, coffee in rms. Restaurant 6:30 am-8 pm. Bar. Ck-out noon. Meeting rms. Business center. In-rm modem link. Valet serv. Free airport transportation. Exercise equipt. Health club privileges. Some refrigerators. Cr cds: A, C, D, DS, MC, V.

D ⬦ ⚊ 🎿 ⊠ ♨ SC 🎿

Hotels

★★ **HOLIDAY INN UNIVERSITY PLAZA.** *333 John Q. Hammons Pkwy (65806). 417/864-7333; fax 417/831-5893; toll-free 800/465-4329. www.*

holiday-inn.com. 271 rms. S, D $79.50-$98.50; each addl $10; suites $111.50; under 19 free. Crib free. Pet accepted, some restrictions. TV; cable (premium), VCR avail. 2 pools, 1 indoor; whirlpool, poolside serv. Restaurant 6 am-10 pm. Bar noon-1 am; entertainment. Ck-out noon. Coin lndry. Convention facilities. Business servs avail. In-rm modem link. Gift shop. Barber, beauty shop. Free airport, bus depot transportation. Lighted tennis. Exercise equipt; sauna. Game rm. Refrigerators. Some private patios. 9-story atrium tower with multitiered waterfall. Cr cds: A, C, D, DS, JCB, MC, V.

D ⬦ 🎿 ⚊ 🎿 ⊠ ♨ SC

★★★ **SHERATON HAWTHORN PARK HOTEL.** *2431 N Glenstone Ave (65803). 417/831-3131; fax 417/831-9786; toll-free 800/223-0092. www.sheraton.com.* 203 rms, 10 story. S $99; D $109; under 18 free. Crib free. TV; cable, (premium). Indoor/outdoor pool; whirlpool. Complimentary coffee in rms. Restaurant 6:30 am-1:30 pm, 5:30-10:30 pm. Bar 1 pm-1 am; Sun to midnight. Ck-out 11 am. Coin lndry. Meeting rms. Business servs avail. In-rm modem link. Concierge. Free airport, bus transportation. Exercise equipt; sauna. Game rm. Luxury level. Cr cds: A, C, D, DS, MC, V.

D ⚊ 🎿 ⊠ ♨ SC

B&Bs/Small Inns

★★ **THE MANSION AT ELFINDALE.** *1701 S Fort (65807). 417/831-5400; fax 417/831-5415; toll-free 800/443-0237. www.cwoc.org/mansion/suites.htm.* 13 suites, 3 story. S, D $75-$125; each addl $10. Children over 11 yrs only. TV in sitting rm, VCR avail (free movies). Complimentary full bkfst. Ck-out 11 am, ck-in 3 pm. Business servs avail. Ornate 35-rm Victorian mansion (1892) built by stone masons brought from Germany; fireplaces, stained-glass windows. Variety of specimen trees on grounds. Totally nonsmoking. Cr cds: A, MC, V.

D ⊠ ♨

★★ **WALNUT STREET INN.** *900 E Walnut St (65806). 417/864-6346; fax 417/864-6184; toll-free 800/593-6346.*

www.walnutstreetinn.com. 12 rms, 3 story. S $69-$119; D $84-$159; each addl $20. TV; cable, VCR avail. Complimentary full bkfst. Restaurants nearby. Ck-out 11 am, ck-in 2 pm. Concierge. Queen Anne-style Victorian inn built 1894. Antiques; sittings. Some in-rm whirlpools, fireplaces. Totally nonsmoking. Cr cds: A, C, D, DS, MC, V.

Restaurants

★ **DIAMOND HEAD.** 2734 S Campbell Ave (US 160) (65807). 417/883-9581. Hrs: 11 am-9:30 pm; Fri, Sat to 10:30 pm. Closed Thanksgiving, Dec 25. Res accepted. Chinese, Polynesian menu. Bar. Lunch $2.95-$4.95, dinner $4.95-$10.95. Buffet: lunch $5.45, dinner $6.45. Children's menu. Specialties: Mongolian barbecue, steak teriyaki. Oriental decor. Cr cds: A, DS, MC, V.

★★ **GEE'S EAST WIND.** 2951 E Sunshine (65804). 417/883-4567. Hrs: 11 am-9:30 pm. Closed Sun; Thanksgiving, Dec 25; also last wk June, 1st wk July. Res accepted. Chinese, American menu. Bar 11 am-9:30 pm. Lunch $5.25-$10, dinner $6.65-$22.75. Children's menu. Specialties: cashew chicken, moo goo gai pan. Chinese screens, wood carvings. Cr cds: A, MC, V.

★ **J. PARRIONO'S PASTA HOUSE.** 1550 E Battlefield (65804). 417/882-1808. Hrs: 10:30 am-11 pm; Fri, Sat to midnight; Sun 4-7 pm. Closed Dec 25. Italian menu. Bar. Lunch $5-$10, dinner $5-$15. Children's menu. Specializes in pasta. Tableside magician Sat eves. Cr cds: A, D, DS, MC, V.

★★★ **LE MIRABELLE.** 2620 S Glenstone Ave (65804). 417/883-2550. Hrs: 5-9 pm; Fri, Sat to 9:30 pm. Closed Sun; hols. Res accepted. French menu. Bar. Wine list. Dinner $12-$20. Specialties: beef Wellington, duck a l'orange, seafood. Own pastries. 3 dining rms, one with fireplace. Cr cds: A, C, D, DS, MC, V.

★★ **SHADY INN.** 524 W Sunshine St (65807). 417/862-0369. Hrs: 11 am-10 pm. Closed Sun; Thanksgiving, Dec 25. Res accepted. Bar 10-1 am. Lunch $3.95-$7.95, dinner $6.95-$38. Children's menu. Specializes in prime rib, steak, seafood. Pianist, entertainment. Old English decor; fireplace. Family-owned. Cr cds: A, D, MC, V.

Unrated Dining Spot

MRS O'MEALLEY'S. 210 E Sunshine (65807). 417/881-7770. Hrs: 11 am-2 pm, 4:30-7:30 pm; Fri, Sat to 8 pm; Sun 11 am-7 pm. Closed Dec 25. Avg ck: lunch $4.50, dinner $5. Specializes in salads, chicken. Own desserts. New Orleans decor. Cr cds: A, MC, V.

Stockton (E-3)

Pop 1,579 **Elev** 965 ft **Area code** 417
Zip 65785

Stockton is the seat of Cedar County. The Stockton Dam, located two miles from the town square, offers many recreational activities.

What to See and Do

Stockton State Park. On shore of 25,000-acre Stockton Lake, impounded by Stockton Dam. Swimming, fishing in stocked lake for bass, crappie, walleye, catfish, and bluegill; boating, canoeing; playground, lodging, restaurant, improved camping, lndry facilities. Standard fees. (Daily) On MO 215. Phone 417/276-4259. **FREE**

Sullivan (D-5)

Pop 5,661 **Elev** 987 ft **Area code** 573
Zip 63080
Information Chamber of Commerce, 2 W Springfield, PO Box 536; 573/468-3314
Web www.ne3.com/vs

What to See and Do

Jesse James Wax Museum. Life-size wax figures of the James gang; $100,000 gun collection; personal belongings of notorious raiders of the Old West; antiques; doll collection. Guided tours. (Mar-mid-Dec, daily; closed Thanksgiving, Dec 25) 5 mi E on I-44 exit 230, on S Service Rd in Stanton. Phone 573/927-5233. ¢¢

Meramec Caverns. Cave used for gunpowder manufacture during Civil War and by Jesse James as a hideout in the 1870s; five levels; lighted; concrete walks; 60°F; guided tours (1 hr, 20 min). Picnicking. Camping; motel, restaurant, gift shop. Canoe rentals; boat rides. (Daily; closed Thanksgiving, Dec 25) 5 mi E on I-44 exit 230, then 3 mi S through La Jolla Park, follow signs. Phone 573/468-3166. ¢¢¢

Meramec State Park. This is one of the largest and most scenic of the state's parks. In its more than 6,700 acres are 30 caves and many springs. Swimming on the Meramec River, fishing, boating (ramp, rentals), canoeing; hiking trails, picnicking, playground, dining lodge, camping (trailer hookups, dump station), cabins, motel, lndry facilities. Nature center, naturalist. Cave tours. Standard fees. (Daily) 4 mi SE on MO 185; off I-44 exit 226. Phone 573/468-6072. **FREE**

Onondaga Cave State Park. Contains historical cave site in 1,300-acre park. Picnicking, camping (fee). Visitor center. Cave tour (Mar-Oct, daily). Park (Daily). 10 mi SW on I-44, then 6 mi SE on County H, past Leasburg. Phone 573/245-6600. ¢¢¢

Motels/Motor Lodges

★ **BUDGET LODGING.** 866 S Outer Rd, St. Clair (63077). 636/629-1000; toll-free 800/958-4354. 66 rms, 2 story. Mid-May-mid-Oct: S $54; D $79; each addl $5; under 16 free; higher rates: wkends, hols; lower rates rest of yr. Crib $5. Pet accepted; $5. TV; cable, VCR avail (movies). Complimentary continental bkfst. Restaurant adj 10 am-11 pm. Ck-out 11 am. Meeting rm. Business servs avail. Coin lndry. Pool. Cr cds: A, C, D, DS, MC, V.
🅳 🔧 🏊 ➰ 🔥

★ **ECONO LODGE PENBERTHY INN.** 307 N Service Rd (63080). 573/468-3136; fax 573/860-3136; toll-free 800/361-4185. www.econolodge.com. 48 rms. S $42; D $55; each addl $5; cottage $150. Crib $5. TV. Pool. Complimentary continental bkfst. Restaurant adj 6 am-10 pm. Ck-out 11 am. Cr cds: A, C, D, DS, MC, V.
🅳 🛁 🏊 ➰ 🔥

★ **FAMILY MOTOR INN.** 209 N Service Rd W (63080). 573/468-4119; fax 573/468-3891. 63 rms. Late May-early Sept: S $39.95; D $47.95; each add $4; suites $45-$55; under 12 free; lower rates rest of yr. Crib $4. Pet accepted; $3. TV; VCR avail (movies $5). Pool; whirlpool. Complimentary coffee. Restaurant nearby. Ck-out 11 am. Business servs avail. Coin lndry. Microwaves avail. Antique shop adj. Cr cds: A, C, D, DS, MC, V.
🅳 🔧 🛁 🏋 🏊 🏋 ➰ 🔥

★ **SUPER 8.** 601 N Service Rd W (63080). 573/468-8076. www.super8.com. 60 rms, 3 story. No elvtr. S $43.88; D $48.88-$58.88; each addl $3; suites $69.88; under 12 free. Crib. Pet accepted; $5. TV; cable. Complimentary coffee. Ck-out 11 am. Coin lndry. Whirlpool in suites. Cr cds: A, D, DS, MC, V.
🅳 🔧 🛁 ➰ 🔥

Table Rock Lake Area

(see Branson/Table Rock Lake Area)

Theodosia

(see Bull Shoals Lake Area, AR)

Motel/Motor Lodge

★ **THEODOSIA MARINA RESORT.** Lake Rd 160-25 (65761). 417/273-4444; fax 417/273-4263. www.tmr bullshoals.com. 20 rms, 7 kit. cottages. Mar-Sept: S $35-$45; D $50-$55; each addl $5; under 6 free; hols 3-day min; lower rates rest of yr. Crib $5. Pet accepted; $2. TV; cable.

Restaurant 7 am-9 pm. Ck-out 2 pm. Meeting rms. Coin lndry. Lighted tennis. Pool. Playground. Refrigerators; some microwaves. Balconies. Picnic tables, grills. On lake. Cr cds: A, DS, MC, V.

Cottage Colony

★ **TURKEY CREEK RANCH.** *HC 3, Box 3180 (65761). 417/273-4362. www.turkeycreekranch.com.* 24 (1-4 bedrm) kit. cottages. Memorial Day-Labor Day (1-wk min): kit. cottages $57-$110; each addl $6; lower rates Sept-May. Crib free. TV. 2 pools, 1 indoor; wading pool, whirlpool. Playground. Ck-out 11 am, ck-in 3 pm. Grocery 9 mi. Coin lndry. Putting green. Tennis. Sailboats, paddleboats, canoes avail; bass boats, pontoons for rent; dock. Lawn games. Rec rm. 700 acres on lake.

Van Buren

(F-5) *See also Poplar Bluff*

Pop 893 **Elev** 475 ft **Area code** 573
Zip 63965

Information Van Buren-Big Spring Area Chamber of Commerce, PO Box 356; 800/692-7582
Web www.semo.net/vanburen

A Ranger District office of the Mark Twain National Forest is located here.

What to See and Do

Clearwater Lake. Formed by dam on Black River. Five different parks surround lake. Swimming, waterskiing, fishing, hunting, boating (ramps, dock, rentals); nature and exercise trails, picnicking, camping (spring-fall, fee; electric hookups, dump stations). Nature trail paved for wheelchair access. Visitor center. (Daily) 12 mi E on US 60, then 6 mi N on MO 34, then NE on County HH, near Piedmont. Phone 573/223-7777. **FREE**

⭐ **Ozark National Scenic Riverways.** More than 80,000 acres with 134 mi of riverfront along the Current and Jacks Fork rivers, both clear, free-flowing streams that are fed by numerous springs. Big Spring, south of town, is one of the largest single-outlet springs in the US with a flow of 276 million gallons daily. Swimming, fishing, floating, boat trips (Memorial Day-Labor Day; some fees); picnicking,

Ozark National Scenic Riverways, near Jacks Fork River

seven campgrounds (daily; fee). Cave tours (Memorial Day-Labor Day, daily; fee). Cultural demonstrations, incl corn milling, at Alley Spring Mill, tours; quilting and wooden jon boat making at Big Spring. There is a visitor center at Alley Spring Mill, 6 mi W of Eminence on MO 106 (Memorial Day-Labor Day, daily). Contact the Superintendent, Ozark National Scenic Riverways, PO Box 490. Off US 60, reached from MO 17, 19, 21, or 106. Phone 573/323-4236.

Waynesville

(E-4) *See also Lebanon, Rolla*

Pop 3,207 **Elev** 805 ft **Area code** 573 **Zip** 65583

Information Waynesville/St. Robert Chamber of Commerce, PO Box 6; 573/336-5121 or 800/447-4617

Special Events

Wild Water Weekend. City park. Man-made boat race, innertube and cooler race. Trout fry. Phone 573/336-5121. First Sat Aug.

Christmas on the Square. Carolers, vendors, crafts, food. Sleigh rides. Phone 573/335-5121. First Thurs Dec.

Motels/Motor Lodges

★ ★ **BEST WESTERN MONTIS INN.** *14086 Hwy Z, St. Robert (65584). 573/336-4299; fax 573/336-2872. www.bestwestern.com.* 45 rms, 2 story, 4 kit. units. May-Oct: S, D $55; each addl $5. Crib $5. Pet accepted, some restrictions. TV; cable, VCR avail (movies). Pool. Complimentary continental bkfst. Restaurant adj 6 am-9 pm. Ck-out noon. Coin lndry. Business servs avail. Some refrigerators, microwaves. Cr cds: A, C, D, DS, ER, JCB, MC, V.

🅳 🐾 ≈ 🔌 🕭 SC

★ **RAMADA INN.** *I 44, exit 16A (65583). 573/336-3121; fax 573/336-4752. www.ramada.com.* 82 rms, 2 story. S $53-$65; D $62-$74; each addl $9; suites $75-$115; under 18 free. Crib free. Pet accepted. TV; cable (premium), VCR avail. 2 pools,

1 indoor; whirlpool. Restaurant 6 am-2 pm, 5-10 pm. Bar 5 pm-1 am, Sun to midnight; entertainment. Ck-out noon. Meeting rms. Business center. In-rm modem link. Gift shop. Exercise rm; sauna. Game rm. Near Ft Leonard Wood. Cr cds: A, C, D, DS, JCB, MC, V.

🅳 🐾 ≈ 🔌 ≈ 🕭 SC 🕴

Wentzville

(C-6) *See also St. Charles, St. Louis*

Pop 5,088 **Elev** 603 ft **Area code** 636 **Zip** 63385

Information Chamber of Commerce, 9 West Allen, PO Box 11; 636/327-6914

Daniel Boone and his family were the first to settle in the area around Wentzville, which was named after Erasmus L. Wentz, principal engineer of the North Missouri Railroad. Between 1850-1880 the area was devoted to growing tobacco; the original Liggett and Myers Tobacco Company factory still stands in Wentzville.

What to See and Do

Cuivre River State Park. One of the state's largest and most natural parks, this 6,251-acre area contains rugged, wooded terrain, native prairie, and an 88-acre lake. Swimming, beach, fishing, boating (ramp); 30 mi of hiking and horseback riding trails, picnicking, camping (hookups, dump station). Standard fees. (Daily) 13 mi N on US 61, then 3 mi E on MO 47 to MO 147. Phone 636/528-7247. **FREE**

Daniel Boone Home. (ca 1803) Built by Boone and his son Nathan, this stone house is where Boone died in 1820; restored and authentically furnished; museum. Guided tours. Picnicking, snack bar. (Mid-Mar-mid-Dec, daily; rest of yr, Sat and Sun; closed Thanksgiving, Dec 25) 5 mi SE via County Z, F, near Defiance. Phone 636/987-2221. ¢¢

Motel/Motor Lodge

★★ **HOLIDAY INN.** *900 Corporate Pkwy (63385). 636/327-7001; fax 314/327-7019. www.holiday-inn.com.* 138 rms, 4 story. S, D $66-$76; suites $115-$125; under 18 free. Crib free. Pet accepted, some restrictions. TV; cable (premium). Pool; poolside serv. Restaurant 6 am-10 pm. Bar 4-11 pm. Ck-out 1 pm. Meeting rms. Business servs avail. In-rm modem link. Bellhops. Valet serv. Sundries. Health club privileges. Some refrigerators. Cr cds: A, C, D, DS, MC, V.
D ➪ ⬤ ⑂ ⌫ ⊠ ▨

Weston

See also Kansas City, St. Joseph

Settled 1837 **Pop** 1,528 **Elev** 800 ft
Area code 816 **Zip** 64098
Information Information Center, 502 Main St, PO Box 53; 816/640-2909
Web www.ci.weston.mo.us

Before the Civil War, Weston was at its peak. Founded on whiskey, hemp, and tobacco, it rivaled St. Louis as a commercial trade center and promised to become a major US city. But disasters—fire, floods, and the Civil War—felled Weston's urban future. Today Weston, the first "district" west of the Mississippi entered into the National Register of Historic Sites, is a quiet town with more than 100 antebellum homes and other buildings.

What to See and Do

Historical Museum. On the site of the International Hotel built by stagecoach king and distillery founder Benjamin Holladay. (Mid-Mar-mid-Dec, Tues-Sun; closed hols) 601 Main St. Phone 816/640-2977. **FREE**

Lewis and Clark State Park. Approx 120 acres on southeast shore of Sugar Lake. Swimming, fishing, boating, canoeing; picnicking, playground, improved camping (dump station). Standard fees. (Daily) 17 mi NW on MO 45 and MO 138. Phone 816/579-5564. **FREE**

Pirtle's Weston Winery. Winery in old brick church (1867); tasting rm furnished with antiques; stained-glass windows. (Daily; closed hols) 502 Spring St. Phone 816/386-5588. **FREE**

Price/Loyles Tour House. Federal-style home occupied by Robert E. Lee's and Daniel Boone's descendants from 1864-1989. Original furnishings; Civil War memorabilia. Tours. (Wed-Sat) 718 Spring St. Phone 816/640-2383. ¢¢

Skiing. Snow Creek Ski Area. Two triple, double chairlift, rope tow; nine intermediate trails. Rentals; ski school, snowmaking. Lodge, restaurant. Vertical drop 300 ft. (Mid-Dec-mid-Mar, daily) 5 mi N on MO 45 at Snow Creek Dr. Phone 816/386-2200. ¢¢¢¢

Weston Brewing Company. Photographs and brewery memorabilia on display. Tours, tasting rm, gift shop. (Wed-Sun) 504 Welt St. Phone 816/640-5245. **FREE**

Special Event

Tobacco Auctions. Three warehouses handle six million pounds of tobacco annually in this "tobacco capital of the west." Thanksgiving-Jan.

B&B/Small Inn

★★ **INN AT WESTON LANDING.** *526 Welt (64098). 816/640-5788.* 4 rms, 2 story. No rm phones. S, D $75-$90. TV in sitting rm; cable. Complimentary full bkfst. Restaurant adj 11:30 am-3 pm, Fri, Sat to 9 pm; Sun to 6 pm. Ck-out 11 am, ck-in 4-6 pm. Downhill ski 5 mi. Built atop the cellars of former brewery (1842). Irish atmosphere; each rm individually decorated. Cr cds: MC, V.
⊠ ⊠ ▨

Restaurant

★★ **AMERICA BOWMAN.** *500 Welt St (64098). 816/640-5235.* Hrs: 11:30 am-3 pm; Fri, Sat to 9 pm; Sun to 6 pm. Closed Mon; hols. Res accepted. Bar. Complete meals: lunch $5.65-$7.95, dinner $9.95-$14.95. Specializes in desserts. Entertainment; Irish balladeer, wkends. Mid-19th-century Irish pub atmosphere. Cr cds: DS, MC, V.
D ⊡

Unrated Dining Spot

PLUM PUDDING. *519 Main St (64098). 816/386-2415. www.weston wares.com.* Hrs: 11:30 am-3 pm. Closed Mon, Sun; Thanksgiving, Dec 25. Lunch $6.50. Specializes in croissant sandwiches with soup or salad. Own desserts. In Victorian building. Gift shop. Cr cds: MC, V.

West Plains (F-5)

Settled 1840 **Pop** 8,913 **Elev** 1,007 ft **Area code** 417 **Zip** 65775

Information Greater West Plains Area Chamber of Commerce, 401 Jefferson Ave; 417/256-4433

Web www.townsqr.com

Motel/Motor Lodge

★ **RAMADA INN.** *1301 Preacher Roe Blvd (65775). 417/256-8191; fax 417/256-8069; toll-free 800/272-6232. www.ramada.com.* 80 rms, 2 story. S $38-$50; D $45-$57; each addl $7; suites $50-$60; under 18 free. Crib free. Pet accepted. TV; cable (premium), VCR avail. Pool. Restaurant 6 am-10 pm. Bar 4 pm-midnight. Ck-out noon. Meeting rms. Business servs avail. Coin lndry. Sundries. Cr cds: A, C, D, DS, JCB, MC, V.

NEBRASKA

In little more than a century, Nebraska—part of what was once called the "great American desert"—has grown from Native American-fighting, buffalo-slaughtering prairie to a farming, ranching, and manufacturing mainstay of America, with an ample variety of recreational and cultural opportunities.

Spaniards visited the region first, but it was on the basis of explorations by Father Marquette and Louis Jolliet in 1673 that French voyageurs, fur traders, and missionaries swept over the land and France claimed it. Nevertheless, it was recognized as Spanish land until 1800, when it became a plaything of European politics and was sold by Napoleon to the United States as part of the Louisiana Purchase in 1803. Famous pathfinders like John C. Frémont, Kit Carson, and the men who trapped for John Jacob Astor thought it a land unfit for cultivation.

Population: 1,578,385
Area: 77,358 square miles
Elevation: 840-5,424 feet
Peak: Near Bushnell (Kimball County)
Entered Union: March 1, 1867 (37th state)
Capital: Lincoln
Motto: Equality before the law
Nickname: Cornhusker State
Flower: Goldenrod
Bird: Western Meadowlark
Tree: Cottonwood
Fair: August 23-September 2, 2002, in Lincoln
Time Zone: Central and Mountain
Website: www.visitnebraska.org

Nebraska was the path for many westward-bound travelers. Native Americans, fur trappers and explorers, pioneers, the Pony Express, the Mormon and Oregon trails, the Overland Freight Company, and the railroads all made their way through the state, following the natural path of the Platte River. In 1854 Nebraska became a United States territory along with Kansas. Febold Feboldson, the Paul Bunyan of the Great Plains, is said to be responsible for the perfectly straight southern boundary line with Kansas. According to the legend, he bred bees with eagles for 15 years until he had an eagle-sized bee. He then hitched the critter to a plow and made a beeline between the two states.

Storm on Nebraska prairie

Within 13 years after being named a territory, statehood was approved by Congress; the town of Lincoln won the fight for the state capital over Omaha and the Homestead Act opened the way for settlement. The Pawnee were often friendly with settlers but were devastated by the smallpox, cholera, and tuberculosis the settlers brought with them. Wars with the Native Americans ended by 1890; by then the land was teeming with farms and ranches, railroads were creating new towns for repairs and supplies, and the twin aids of irrigation and better stock pushed up farm profits.

Farming is big business in southern and eastern Nebraska. With continually improving crop returns, Nebraska has few equals in total output of farm production. It is a leading producer of wild hay, beans, grain sorghum, sugar beets, wheat, soybeans, rye, corn, and alfalfa. Good grazing land can be found in the north central and northwest parts of the state. America's largest formation of stabilized sand dunes is located in the Sandhills, heart of Nebraska's nearly $5-billion cattle industry. Real cowboy country, the ranches of the Sandhills have given starts to many professional rodeo stars.

The fine highway system makes it a pleasure to drive in the state. Several villages and towns settled by Old World immigrants still celebrate their ethnic heritage in folk festivals each year. Native Americans on the Santee, Winnebago, and Omaha reservations also keep their customs at annual powwows. Besides pioneer and Native American history, Nebraska offers a wealth of state parks and recreation areas. The angler has many well-stocked fishing streams and lakes from which to choose. For hunters, game birds, waterfowl, and deer are abundant, and seasons are long.

When to Go/Climate

Nebraska experiences the typically extreme temperatures of the Plains states. Winters are icy cold, summers stifling hot. The state is dry and prone to droughts; tornadoes are a summer reality. Fall and spring are good times to visit.

AVERAGE HIGH/LOW TEMPERATURES (°F)

OMAHA

Jan 30/11	**May** 73/52	**Sept** 75/55
Feb 35/17	**June** 82/67	**Oct** 64/43
Mar 48/28	**July** 87/67	**Nov** 48/30
Apr 62/40	**Aug** 84/64	**Dec** 33/16

SCOTTSBLUFF

Jan 38/12	**May** 71/42	**Sept** 77/46
Feb 44/17	**June** 82/59	**Oct** 66/34
Mar 50/22	**July** 90/52	**Nov** 50/22
Apr 61/32	**Aug** 87/56	**Dec** 40/13

Parks and Recreation Finder

Directions to and information about the parks and recreation areas below are given under their respective town/city sections. Please refer to those sections for details.

NATIONAL PARK AND RECREATION AREAS

Key to abbreviations. I.H.S. = International Historic Site; I.P.M. = International Peace Memorial; N.B. = National Battlefield; N.B.P. = National Battlefield Park; N.B.C. = National Battlefield and Cemetery; N.C.A. = National Conservation Area; N.E.M. = National Expansion Memorial; N.F. = National Forest; N.G. = National Grassland; N.H.P. = National Historical Park; N.H.C. = National Heritage Corridor; N.H.S. = National Historic Site; N.L. = National Lakeshore;

CALENDAR HIGHLIGHTS

MAY

Willa Cather Spring Conference (Hastings). Willa Cather State Historic Site. Features a different Cather novel each year. Discussion groups, banquet, entertainment. Tour of "Cather Country." Phone 402/746-2653.

JUNE

NCAA College Baseball World Series (Omaha). Rosenblatt Stadium. Phone 402/444-4750.

Cottonwood Prairie Festival (Hastings). Brickyard Park. Music, crafts, food. Phone 800/967-2189.

"NEBRASKAland DAYS" Celebration (North Platte). Parades, entertainment, food, and the famous PRCA Rodeo. Phone 308/532-7939.

JULY

Oregon Trail Days (Gering). Parades, chili cook-off, contests, square dancing, barbecue, music festival. Phone Scotts Bluff-Gering United Chamber of Commerce, 308/632-2133.

Central Nebraska Ethnic Festival (Grand Island). Music, dance, ethnic meals, dramatic presentations. Phone 308/385-5455.

July Jamm (Lincoln). Art show, music festival. Phone 402/434-6900.

AUGUST

Nebraska State Fair (Lincoln). State Fair Park. Phone 402/474-5371.

SEPTEMBER

River City Round-Up (Omaha). Fairgrounds. Celebration of agriculture and western heritage includes parade, barbecues, trail rides. Phone 402/554-9610.

DECEMBER

The Light of the World **Christmas Pageant** (Minden). Kearney County Courthouse, Town Square. A town tradition for many years; highlight of outdoor pageant is illumination of courthouse dome by 10,000 lights. Phone the Chamber of Commerce, 308/832-1811.

N.M. = National Monument; N.M.P. = National Military Park; N.Mem. = National Memorial; N.P. = National Park; N.Pres. = National Preserve; N.R.A. = National Recreational Area; N.R.R. = National Recreational River; N.Riv. = National River; N.S. = National Seashore; N.S.R. = National Scenic Riverway; N.S.T. = National Scenic Trail; N.Sc. = National Scientific Reserve; N.V.M. = National Volcanic Monument.

Place Name	Listed Under
Agate Fossil Beds N.M.	SCOTTS BLUFF
Chimney Rock N.H.S.	same
Homestead N.M.	same
Nebraska N.F.	CHADRON, THEDFORD, VALENTINE
Oglala N.G.	CRAWFORD
Scotts Bluff N.M.	same

STATE PARK AND RECREATION AREAS

Key to abbreviations. I.P. = Interstate Park; S.A.P. = State Archaeological Park; S.B. = State Beach; S.C.A. = State Conservation Area; S.C.P. = State Conservation Park; S.Cp. = State Campground; S.F. = State Forest; S.G. = State Garden; S.H.A. = State Historic Area; S.H.P. = State Historic Park; S.H.S. = State Historic Site; S.M.P. = State Marine Park; S.N.A. = State Natural Area; S.P. = State Park;

S.P.C. = State Public Campground; S.R. = State Reserve; S.R.A. = State Recreation Area; S.Res. = State Reservoir; S.Res.P. = State Resort Park; S.R.P. = State Rustic Park.

Place Name	Listed Under
Alexandria Lakes S.R.A.	FAIRBURY
Arbor Lodge S.H.P.	NEBRASKA CITY
Arnold Lake S.R.A.	NORTH PLATTE
Ash Hollow S.H.P.	OGALLALA
Atkinson Lake S.R.A.	O'NEILL
Bluestem Lake S.R.A.	LINCOLN
Branched Oak Lake S.R.A.	LINCOLN
Bridgeport S.R.A.	BRIDGEPORT
Brownville S.R.A.	AUBURN
Buffalo Bill Ranch S.H.P.	NORTH PLATTE
Chadron S.P.	CHADRON
Conestoga Lake S.R.A.	LINCOLN
Crystal Lake S.R.A.	HASTINGS
Eugene T. Mahoney S.P.	LINCOLN
Fort Atkinson S.H.P.	BLAIR
Fort Kearny S.H.P.	KEARNEY
Fort Robinson S.P.	CRAWFORD
Fremont S.R.A.	FREMONT
Gallagher Canyon S.R.A.	COZAD
Indian Cave S.P.	AUBURN
Johnson Lake S.R.A.	LEXINGTON
Lake Maloney S.R.A.	NORTH PLATTE
Lake McConaughy S.R.A.	OGALLALA
Lake Minatare S.R.A.	SCOTTS BLUFF
Lake Ogallala S.R.A.	OGALLALA
Lewis and Clark Lake S.R.A.	CROFTON
Louisville S.R.A.	OMAHA
Medicine Creek Reservoir S.R.A.	McCOOK
Merritt Reservoir S.R.A.	VALENTINE
Mormon Island S.R.A.	GRAND ISLAND
Pawnee Lake S.R.A.	LINCOLN
Pibel Lake S.R.A.	O'NEILL
Platte River S.P.	OMAHA
Ponca S.P.	SOUTH SIOUX CITY
Red Willow Reservoir S.R.A.	McCOOK
Rock Creek Station S.H.P.	FAIRBURY
Schramm Park S.R.A.	OMAHA
Swanson Reservoir S.R.A.	McCOOK
Two Rivers S.R.A.	OMAHA
Verdon Lake S.R.A.	AUBURN
Victoria Springs S.R.A.	BROKEN BOW
Walgreen Lake S.R.A.	CHADRON
Wildcat Hills S.R.A.	SCOTTS BLUFF
Willa Cather S.H.S.	HASTINGS

Water-related activities, hiking, riding, various other sports, picnicking and visitor centers, as well as camping, are available in many of these areas. The state maintains 87 areas, including state parks, recreation areas, and historical parks; park-user permit required ($2.50/day, $14/yr). Seven areas have cabins ($30-$210/night). Camping ($3-$13/site/night, plus $3 for electricity, at some parks), 14-day limit at most sites. Some facilities are open May-September only. Pets on leash only; health certificate required for pets of out-of-state owners. All mechanically powered boats must be registered. Cross-country skiing is a popular winter sport in the larger state parks. For detailed information contact Game and Parks Commission, Division of State Parks, PO Box 30370, Lincoln 68503; 402/471-0641.

FISHING AND HUNTING

Nonresident fishing permit: annual $35; three-day $10.75; aquatic stamp for all fishing permits $5. Nonresident small game hunting permit: $55; deer permit, $150; antelope permit, $112; wild turkey, $56; habitat stamp for game birds and animals and fur-bearing animals, $10.

Nebraska has 11,000 miles of streams and more than 3,300 lakes with trout, northern pike, walleye, sauger, white bass, striped bass, large and small mouth bass, catfish, bluegill, and crappie. Pheasant, quail, prairie chicken, wild turkey, sharp-tailed grouse, cottontail rabbit, squirrel, ducks, geese, antelope, and deer are available here also.

For details, write the Game and Parks Commission, PO Box 30370, Lincoln 68503-0370; 402/471-0641.

Driving Information

Safety belts are mandatory for all persons in the front seat of any 1973 or newer vehicle. Children under five years must be in an approved passenger restraint anywhere in vehicle: ages four-five may use a regulation safety belt; under age four must use an approved safety seat. For further information phone 402/471-2515.

INTERSTATE HIGHWAY SYSTEM

The following alphabetical listing of Nebraska towns in *Mobil Travel Guide* shows that these cities are within ten miles of the indicated Interstate highways. A highway map, however, should be checked for the nearest exit.

Highway Number	Cities/Towns within ten miles
Interstate 80	Cozad, Gothenburg, Grand Island, Kearney, Kimball, Lexington, Lincoln, North Platte, Ogallala, Omaha, Sidney, York.

Additional Visitor Information

The Department of Economic Development, Travel and Tourism Division, PO Box 98913, 700 S 16th, Lincoln 68509, phone 800/228-4307, supplies visitor information about the state; events, parks, hiking, biking, camping, and boating are some of the topics featured. *NEBRASKAland,* published monthly, is available from the Game and Parks Commission, PO Box 30370, Lincoln 68503.

To aid the traveler, visitor centers are located at Melia Hill, off I-80 between Omaha and Lincoln (daily) and at the Nebraska/Omaha Travel Information Center at 10th St and Deer Park Blvd (intersection of I-80 and 13th St) in Omaha (May-October, daily). There are also 25 information centers at rest areas along I-80 (June-August).

HOMESTEADING ALONG THE MISSOURI RIVER

Wooded river bluffs, historic towns, and Homestead National Monument are among the attractions of this drive through southeast Nebraska. Take US 77 from Lincoln south to Beatrice, the first of several charming small towns on this route. A few miles west of town, Homestead National Monument showcases a restored tallgrass prairie and explains the Homestead Act of 1862, which led to widespread settlement in the western United States. From Beatrice, drive east through the farmlands along US 136 to Auburn, a town known for its antique stores. Continue on to Brownville, which features a Missouri River History Museum aboard the dry-docked *Captain Meriwether Lewis,* and riverboat cruises aboard the *Spirit of Brownville.* From Brownville, backtrack to Auburn and head north on US 75 to Nebraska City, the birthplace of Arbor Day. Head west on US 34 north of Nebraska City to return to Lincoln. **(APPROX 180 MI)**

NEBRASKA FROM CRAZY HORSE TO CARHENGE

Vast, lightly populated, and filled with raw beauty, the Sandhills country of western Nebraska takes visitors by surprise. Start in North Platte with a visit to Buffalo Bill Ranch State Historical Park, which preserves the Western icon's home on the range. Head north on US 83 to the Nebraska National Forest; at 90,000 acres, it's the largest hand-planted forest in the country. Continue north to Valentine, set along the Niobrara River, a favorite for canoeing. Drive west on US 20 to Merriman, site of the Sandhills Ranch State Historical Park (still a working ranch despite its name), then on to Chadron to visit the Museum of the Fur Trade. Continue west to Fort Robinson State Park, where Crazy Horse died. The nearby Pine Ridge and Oglala National Grassland are great spots for horseback riding, mountain biking, and hiking. To return to civilization, take NE 2 south from Crawford to Alliance, home to the famous "Carhenge" spoof on England's Stonehenge. From Alliance, head south on US 385 to pick up the Oregon Trail route at Bridgeport, or return to North Platte on NE 2 east and NE 83 south. **(APPROX 550 MI)**

Auburn

(E-8) *See also Nebraska City*

Pop 3,443 **Elev** 994 ft **Area code** 402
Zip 68305
Information Chamber of Commerce, 1211 J St; 402/274-3521
Web www.ci.auburn.ne.us/

What to See and Do

☒ **Brownville.** Restored riverboat town of the 1800s. Over 30 buildings, many of which are open to the public. 9 mi E on US 136. Site incl

Agriculture Museum. (May-Aug, daily) Phone 402/274-3521. **FREE**

Brownville State Recreation Area. Approx 20 acres. Fishing, boat ramps; picnicking, camping. Entry permit required. In Brownville. Phone 402/883-2575. ¢¢

Captain Bailey Museum. (June-Aug, daily; May, Sept-Oct, wkends only) ¢

Carson House. Original 1864-1872 furnishings. (Memorial Day-Labor Day, daily; Apr, May, Sept, and Oct, wkends) ¢

Depot. Museum. (May-Aug, daily) **FREE**

Land Office. Reproduction of the land office where Daniel Freeman filed for the first homestead in the US; houses Tourist Center and Brownville Historical Society Headquarters. **FREE**

Missouri River History Museum. Contains exhibits on river history. (May-mid-Sept, daily) Aboard the *Captain Meriwether Lewis,* former Corps of Engineers dredge, which has been drydocked and restored. Phone 402/825-3341. ¢

Old Dental Office. (May-Aug, daily) **FREE**

Schoolhouse Art Gallery. (May-Sept, Sat and Sun) **FREE**

Spirit of Brownville. Cruises (two hrs) on Missouri River. (July-mid-Aug, Thurs-Sun) Departs from Brownville State Recreation Area. Phone 402/825-6441.

Village Theater. Nebraska's oldest repertory theater; plays produced by Nebraska Wesleyan University in converted church; eight wks beginning last Sat June. Phone 402/825-4121. ¢¢¢

Indian Cave State Park. On approx 3,400 acres, incl oak-covered Missouri River bluffs and the old St. Deroin townsite, which has been partially reconstructed; living history demonstrations. Fishing; hiking trails (20 mi), horseback riding, x-country skiing, sledding, picnicking. Primitive and improved camping (fee, dump station). Also here are ancient petroglyphs in Indian Cave; scenic overlooks of the river. Redbud trees bloom in profusion during spring. 9 mi E on US 136, then 14 mi S on NE 67 then E on NE 64. Phone 402/883-2575. ¢¢

Nemaha Valley Museum. Exhibits trace history of Nemaha County; period rms; farm equipt. (Tues-Sat afternoons) 1423 19th St. Phone 402/274-3203. **FREE**

Verdon Lake State Recreation Area. Approx 30 acres on 33-acre lake. Fishing. Picnicking. Camping. Entry permit required. 17 mi S via US 73, 75, then E on US 73. Phone 402/883-2575. ¢¢

Special Events

Spring Festival with Antique Flea Market. Brownville. Phone 402/825-6001. Memorial Day wkend.

Tour of Homes. Brownville. Phone 402/825-6001. June, Nov-Dec.

Nemaha County Fair. Auburn fairgrounds. Early Aug.

Summer Affair. First Sat Aug.

Fall Festival. First wkend Oct.

Motels/Motor Lodges

★ **AUBURN INN.** *517 J St (68305). 402/274-3143; fax 402/274-4404; toll-free 800/272-3143.* 36 rms. S $32; D $38-$45; each addl $5. Pet accepted, some restrictions. TV; cable (premium). Coffee in rms. Restaurant opp 7 am-10 pm. Ck-out 11 am. Refrigerators, microwaves. Cr cds: A, C, D, DS, MC, V.
🐾 📵 🔥

★ **PALMER HOUSE.** *1918 J St (68305). 402/274-3193; fax 402/274-4165; toll-free 800/272-3143.* 22 rms, 8 suites. S $32; D $38; each addl $3; suites from $49. TV; cable (premium). Complimentary coffee in lobby. Restaurant nearby. Ck-out 11 am. Refrigerators. Cr cds: A, DS, MC, V.
✈ 📵 🔥

Restaurant

★ **WHEELER INN.** *1905 J St (68305). 402/274-4931.* Hrs: 5-10 pm. Closed hols. Res accepted. Bar to 1 am. A la carte entrees: dinner $6-$34.50. Specializes in prime rib, fried chicken, scampi. Salad bar. Casual country atmosphere. Cr cds: A, D, MC, V.

[D] [≡]

Beatrice

(E-7) *See also Fairbury, Lincoln*

Founded 1857 **Pop** 12,354 **Elev** 1,284 ft **Area code** 402 **Zip** 68310
Information Chamber of Commerce, 226 S 6th St; 402/223-2338 or 800/755-7745
Web www.beatrice-ne.com

Beatrice (be-AT-riss), a prosperous farm and industrial community, was named for the daughter of Judge John Kinney, a member of the Nebraska Association that founded this settlement on the Blue River. Hollywood stars Harold Lloyd and Robert Taylor grew up in Beatrice.

What to See and Do

Gage County Historical Museum. Local historical artifacts housed in former Burlington Northern Depot (1906). History and artifacts of all towns of the county displayed. Artifacts of industry, medicine, agriculture, railroads, and rural life. Special exhibits (fee). Tours by appt. (June-Labor Day, Tues-Sun; rest of yr, Tues-Fri, also Sun afternoons; closed hols) 2nd and Court sts. Phone 402/228-1679. **FREE**

Homestead National Monument. (see) 4 mi NW, just off NE 4.

Special Events

Homestead Days. Four-day event with pioneer theme. Demonstrations, parade. Last full wkend June.
Gage County Fair. Fairgrounds, W Scott St. Last wk July.

Motels/Motor Lodges

★★ **BEATRICE INN.** *3500 N 6th St (68501). 402/223-4074.* 63 rms, 2 story. May-Dec: S $35-$42; D $41-$48; each addl $3; under 12 free; lower rates rest of yr. Crib $4. Pet accepted, some restrictions. TV; cable (premium). Heated pool. Restaurant 6 am-9 pm; Sun to 8 pm. Bar 5 pm-1 am. Ck-out 11 am. Coin lndry. Meeting rms. Sundries. Cr cds: A, C, D, DS, MC, V.

[icons] SC

★ **HOLIDAY VILLA MOTEL.** *1820 N 6th St (68310). 402/223-4036; fax 402/228-3875.* 46 rms, 1-2 story, 8 kits. S $26-$29; D $34-$40; each addl $4; kit. units $42; under 10 free. Crib free. Pet accepted, some restrictions. TV; cable. Playground. Complimentary coffee in lobby. Ck-out 11 am. Meeting rms. Cr cds: A, MC, V.

[icons]

★ **VICTORIAN INN 4 LESS.** *1903 N 6th St (68310). 402/228-5955; fax 402/228-2020.* 44 rms, 2 story. S $29.95; D $36.95-$39.95; each addl $3. Pet accepted. TV; cable (premium), VCR avail. Complimentary continental bkfst. Ck-out 11 am. Cr cds: A, C, D, DS, MC, V.

[icons]

Blair

(C-8) *See also Fremont, Omaha*

Founded 1869 **Pop** 6,860 **Elev** 1,075 ft **Area code** 402 **Zip** 68008
Information Chamber of Commerce, 1526 Washington St; 402/533-4455

What to See and Do

Dana College. (1884) 500 students. Liberal arts school founded by Danish pioneers; campus incl Danish immigrant archives, gas lamps from Copenhagen, and Hans Christian Andersen beech trees. Heritage and Lauritz Melchior memorial rms in library incl complete collections of Royal Copenhagen and Bing & Grondahl Christmas plates (After Labor Day-mid-May, daily; early June-early Aug, Mon-Fri; closed hols). ½ mi W,

2848 College Dr. Phone 402/426-7216. On campus is

Tower of the Four Winds. Set on a hill overlooking Blair, the 44-ft tower displays a mosaic interpretation of a vision seen by Black Elk, an Oglala Sioux prophet and medicine man. Phone 402/533-4455.

De Soto National Wildlife Refuge. (See MISSOURI VALLEY, IA) 4 mi E on US 30.

Fort Atkinson State Historical Park. Ongoing reconstruction of military post established in 1820 (16 yrs after Lewis and Clark recommended the site) to protect the fur trade and secure the Louisiana Purchase; museum (Late May-early Sept, daily). Park (Daily). Watch reconstruction of old barracks. 1 mi E of US 75 and Fort Calhoun. Phone 402/468-5611. ¢¢

Special Events

"Gateway to the West" Days. Carnival, parade, street dance. Phone 402/533-4455. Mid-June.

Sights and Sounds of Christmas. Dana College. Danish, German, French, American, and other ethnic Christmas customs, foods, traditions; smorgasbord (res); concert in a setting of hundreds of poinsettias and evergreen trees, dramatic presentations. Phone 402/426-7216 (After Oct 1). Early Dec.

Motel/Motor Lodge

★ **RATH INN.** *1355 US 30 S (68008). 402/426-2340; fax 402/426-8703.* 32 rms, 2 story. S $32; D $41; each addl $5; suites $43. Pet accepted. TV; cable (premium). Heated pool. Restaurant adj 6 am-11 pm. Ck-out 11 am. Refrigerator in suites. Cr cds: A, C, D, DS, MC, V.
🔁 🐾 🏊 ⬇ 🔥

Bridgeport

(C-1) *See also Scottsbluff*

Founded 1900 **Pop** 1,581 **Elev** 3,666 ft **Area code** 308 **Zip** 69336

Information Chamber of Commerce, 428 Main St, PO Box 640; 308/262-1825

What to See and Do

Bridgeport State Recreation Area. Approx 190 acres of sand pit lakes on North Platte River. Swimming, fishing, boating (ramp); hiking, picnicking, camping (dump station). W edge of town on US 26. Per vehicle ¢¢

Carhenge. This roadside spoof on England's Stonehenge is made of more than 30 discarded cars. (Daily) 38 mi N on US 385. Phone 308/762-1520. **FREE**

Oregon Trail Wagon Train. Recreation of an 1840s wagon train, with authentic covered wagons. Chuck wagon cookouts, canoeing, camping and one- and four-day wagon trips. Fees charged for meals, rentals, and activities; res necessary for eve events. (May-Sept) 12 mi W via US 26, NE 92. Phone 308/586-1850.

Broken Bow (C-4)

Founded 1882 **Pop** 3,778 **Elev** 2,475 ft **Area code** 308 **Zip** 68822

What to See and Do

Victoria Springs State Recreation Area. Approx 60 acres; mineral springs. Fishing, nonpower boating (rentals); hiking, picnicking, camping (fee), shelters, rental cabins. Standard fees. 21 mi NW on NE 2, then 7 mi E on Secondary NE 21A. Phone 308/749-2235.

Motels/Motor Lodges

★ **GATEWAY MOTEL.** *628 E Southeast St (68822). 308/872-2478; fax 308/872-2055.* 23 rms. S $25; D $34. Crib $1. Pet accepted, some restrictions. TV; cable (premium). Restaurant nearby. Ck-out 11 am. Sauna. Cr cds: A, DS, MC, V.
🔁 ⬇ 🔥

★ **SUPER 8 MOTEL.** *215 E Southeast St (68822). 308/872-6428; fax 308/872-5031; res 800/800-8000. www.super8.com.* 32 rms, 2 story. Apr-Sept: S $45; D $54. Crib $3. TV; cable (premium). Restaurant adj 6 am-11 pm. Ck-out 11 am. Meeting rm. Coin lndry. Whirlpool. Cr cds: A, C, D, DS, JCB, MC, V.

★ **WAGON WHEEL MOTEL AND CAMPGROUNDS.** *1545 E Southeast St (68822). 308/872-2433; toll-free 800/770-2433.* 15 rms. S $22-$25; D $26-$34; each addl $3. Crib $4. TV; cable (premium). Heated pool. Ck-out 10:30 am. Cr cds: A, D, DS, MC, V.

★ **WILLIAM PENN LODGE.** *853 E Southeast St (68822). 308/872-2412; fax 308/872-6376.* 28 rms. S $24-$30; D $28-$40; each addl $3. Crib $5. Pet accepted. TV; cable (premium). Restaurant opp 6 am-11 pm. Ck-out 10 am. Refrigerators, microwaves. Cr cds: A, MC, V.

Chadron

(B-2) *See also Crawford*

Founded 1885 **Pop** 5,588 **Elev** 3,380 ft
Information Chamber of Commerce, 706 W Third, PO Box 646; 308/432-4401 or 800/603-2937

Starting point of a sensational 1,000-mile horse race to Chicago in 1893, Chadron saw nine men leave in competition for a $1,000 prize. Doc Middleton, former outlaw, was one of the starters, but John Berry beat him to the door of Buffalo Bill's Wild West Show in 13 days and 16 hours. The headquarters and a Ranger District office of the Nebraska National Forest and headquarters of the Oglala National Grasslands are located here.

What to See and Do

Chadron State College. (1911) 3,600 students. Tours. Planetarium, museum open to public by appt. 1000 Main St. Phone 308/432-6000.

Chadron State Park. Approx 950 acres; scenic pine ridge, lagoon, creek. Swimming pool (daily; fee); fishing, paddleboats (rentals); hiking, horseback riding, x-country skiing, picnicking, playground. Camping

(dump station, hookups, standard fees), cabins. Scenic drives. 9 mi S on US 385. Phone 308/432-6167. ¢¢

Museum of the Fur Trade. Displays depict history of the North American fur trade 1500-1900; fine gun collection; Native American exhibits. Restored trading post (1833) and storehouse used by James Bordeaux, a French trader; garden of primitive crops. (June-Sept, daily; rest of yr, by appt) 3½ mi E on US 20. Phone 308/432-3843. ¢

Nebraska National Forest. Fishing, hunting. Picnicking. Camping. S off US 20. Phone 308/432-0300.

Walgreen Lake State Recreation Area. Approx 80 acres on 50-acre lake. According to legend, a Loch Ness-type creature inhabits the Sandhills Lake here. Fishing, boating (nonpower or electric). Picnicking. Camping. Standard hrs, fees. 20 mi SE via US 20, then 2 mi S via NE 87.

Special Events

Fur Trade Days. Phone 308/432-4401. Three days early July.

Ride the Ridge. Twelve-mi trail ride through scenic Pine Ridge. Catered meal and ranch rodeo at end of ride. Phone 308/432-4475. July.

Dawes County Fair. Phone 308/432-4401. Five days early Aug.

Motels/Motor Lodges

★★ **BEST WESTERN WEST HILLS INN.** *1100 W 10th St (69337). 308/432-3305; fax 308/432-5990; res 800/780-7234. www.bestwestern.com.* 67 rms, 2 story. S $60; D $70; each addl $5; suites $85-$125. Crib free. Pet accepted. TV; cable (premium). Indoor pool; whirlpool. Complimentary continental bkfst. Coffee in rms. Restaurant nearby. Ck-out 11 am. Coin lndry. Meeting rms. Exercise equipt. Game rm. Some refrigerators, microwaves, in-rm whirlpools. Cr cds: A, MC, V.

★ **SUPER 8.** *840 W Hwy 20 (69337). 308/432-4471; fax 308/432-3991; res 800/800-8000. www.super8.com.* 45 rms, 2 story. June-Sept: S $45-$53; D $50-$60; lower rates rest of yr. Crib $3. TV; cable (premium). Indoor pool; whirlpool. Restaurant adj 6 am-

9:30 pm. Ck-out 11 am. Coin lndry.
Cr cds: A, D, DS, MC, V.
D 🏊 🐾 🔥 SC

Chimney Rock National Historic Site

See also Bridgeport, Gering, Scottsbluff

(13 mi W of Bridgeport off US 26, NE 92)

A landmark of the Oregon Trail, Chimney Rock rises almost 500 feet above the south bank of the North Platte River. Starting as a cone-shaped mound, it becomes a narrow 150-foot column towering above the landscape. For early travelers, many of whom sketched and described it in their journals, Chimney Rock marked the end of the prairies. It became a National Historic Site in 1956. Visitor center (fee). Phone 308/586-2581.

Columbus (C-7)

Founded 1856 **Pop** 19,480 **Elev** 1,449 ft **Area code** 402 **Zip** 68602

Information Platte County Convention and Visitors Bureau. 764 33rd Ave, Box 515; 402/564-2769

Web www.ci.columbus.ne.us

Named by its founders for Ohio's capital, Columbus has become a center of industry, agriculture, and statewide electrical power.

What to See and Do

Parks. Pawnee Park. Swimming pool. Ball fields, tennis. Picnicking facilities, playground on 130 acres along Loup River. Quincentenary bell tower dedicated to Columbus's voyage to the new world. S on US 30, 81. Phone 402/564-0914. **Lake North and Loup Park.** Swimming, waterskiing, fishing, boating (ramps, docks). Picnicking. Camping. 4 mi N on Monastery Rd. Phone 402/564-3171. **Wilkinson Wildlife Management Area.** 630 acres of permanent

Chimney Rock National Historic Site

wetland area. Hiking; fishing and hunting. SE of Platte Center/NW of Columbus. Phone 402/471-0641. **FREE**

Platte County Historical Society. Exhibits on local history; period schoolrm, barbershop; research library; cultural center. (Apr-mid-Oct, Wed-Sun) 29th Ave and 16th St. Phone 402/564-1856. ¢

Special Events

Horse racing. Agricultural Park. Pari-mutuel betting. May-mid-June.

Platte County Fair. Agricultural Park, E edge of town. Phone 402/563-4901. Mid-July.

Columbus Days. Phone 402/564-2769. Mid Aug.

Motels/Motor Lodges

★ **ECO-LUX INN.** 3803 23rd St (68601). 402/564-9955; fax 402/564-9436; toll-free 877/221-6722. 39 rms, 2 story. S $36-$39; D $43-$45; Crib $4. TV; cable (premium). Restaurant adj 6-2:30 am. Ck-out 11 am. Meeting rm. Coin lndry. Cr cds: A, C, D, DS, MC, V.

★ **JOHNNIE'S MOTEL.** 222 W 16th St, Schuyler (68661). 402/352-5454; fax 402/352-5456. 31 rms. S $27; D $33; each addl $4. Crib $4. TV; cable (premium). Restaurant nearby. Ck-out 11 am. Cr cds: A, DS, MC, V.

★★ **NEW WORLD INN.** 265 33rd Ave (68601). 402/564-1492; fax 402/563-3989; toll-free 800/433-1492. www.newworldinn.com. 154 rms, 2 story. S $46-$54; D $49-$56; each addl $5; suites $100; under 19 free. Crib free. TV; cable. Indoor pool; whirlpool, poolside serv. Restaurant 6 am-2 pm, 5-10 pm. Bar 4 pm-1 am; entertainment Tues, Wed, Fri, Sat. Ck-out noon. Coin lndry. Meeting rms. Business servs avail. Sundries. Free airport transportation. Indoor courtyard. Cr cds: A, C, D, DS, MC, V.

★ **SUPER 8.** 3324 20th St (68601). 402/563-3456; fax 402/563-3456; res 800/800-8000. www.super8.com. 64 rms, 2 story. S $43.98; D $52.98; each addl $3. Crib free. TV; cable

(premium). Complimentary coffee in lobby. Restaurant nearby. Ck-out 11 am. Business servs avail. Cr cds: A, C, D, DS, MC, V.

Cozad

(D-4) See also Gothenburg, Lexington

Pop 3,823 **Elev** 2,490 ft
Area code 308 **Zip** 69130
Information Chamber of Commerce, 211 W 8th St, PO Box 14; 308/784-3930

Cozad is headquarters for a number of industries, as well as a shipping and agricultural center known for the production of alfalfa.

What to See and Do

Gallagher Canyon State Recreation Area. Approx 20 acres of park surround 400 acres of water. Fishing, boating (ramp); hiking, picnicking, camping. Standard hrs, fees. 8 mi S on NE 21. Phone 308/784-3907.

Robert Henri Museum and Historical Walkway. Museum occupies the childhood home of artist Robert Henri, founder of the Ash Can School, and former hotel built by Henri's father. Other historic buildings along walkway are an original Pony Express station, a pioneer school, and an early 20th-century church. (Memorial Day-Sept, Mon-Sat, also by appt) 218 E 8th St. Phone 308/784-4154. ¢

Motel/Motor Lodge

★ **BUDGET HOUSE CIRCLE S.** 440 S Meridian St (69130). 308/784-2290; fax 308/784-3917; res 800/237-5852. 49 rms, 2 story. S $30; D $38; each addl $4. Crib $3. Pet accepted. TV; cable (premium). Heated pool. Restaurant 7 am-9 pm. Ck-out 11 am. Cr cds: A, DS, MC, V.

Restaurant

★ **PLAINSMAN.** 128 E 8th (69130). 308/784-2080. Hrs: 6 am-7 pm; Fri,

Sat to 2 pm; Sun 11 am-1 pm. Closed Mon; hols. Bkfst $2-$5, lunch $3-$5. Specialty: broasted chicken. Salad bar. Street parking. Country motif. 🗗

Crawford

(B-1) *See also Chadron*

Founded 1885 **Pop** 1,115 **Elev** 3,673 ft **Area code** 308 **Zip** 69339

What to See and Do

🌟 **Fort Robinson State Park.** Approx 22,000 acres of pine-covered hills; rocky buttes. Fort established in 1874 in the midst of Native American fighting (the Sioux leader, Crazy Horse, was killed here). Swimming pool (fee), fishing; hiking, horseback riding. X-country skiing. Picnicking, restaurant, lodge (see MOTEL). Camping (dump station), cabins. Post Playhouse; stagecoach and jeep rides (Daily, summer); cookouts. Displays herds of buffalo. Park entry permit required. 3 mi W on US 20. Phone 308/665-2660. Also here are

Fort Robinson Museum. Main museum located in former headquarters building (1905); authentic costumes and weapons of Native Americans and soldiers. Other exhibit buildings incl 1874 guardhouse, 1904 harness repair, 1906 blacksmith and 1900 wheelwright shops, 1887 adobe officer quarters, and 1908 veterinary hospital. Site of Red Cloud Indian Agency (1873-1877). Guided tours (Memorial Day-Labor Day). Museum (Memorial Day-Labor Day, daily; Apr-May and Sept-Oct, Sat and Sun). Maintained by State Historical Society. Phone 308/665-2919. ¢

Trailside Museum. Exhibits of natural history from Fort Robinson area. Museum also offers natural history tours of the area and daily science field trips to Toadstool Park and fossil sites (fee). (Memorial Day-Labor Day, daily; May, Wed-Sun) Operated by University of Nebraska State Museum. Phone 308/665-2929. **Donation**

Nebraska National Forest. 8 mi S on NE 2 (see CHADRON).

Oglala National Grassland. Nearly 95,000 acres of prairie grasses in the badlands of northwestern Nebraska, popular for hunting (in season), hiking, and backpacking. 10 mi N via NE 2, 71. Phone 308/432-4475.

Motel/Motor Lodge

★ **FORT ROBINSON LODGE.** *3200 W Hwy 20 (69339). 308/665-2900; fax 308/665-2906.* 22 rms in inn, 1-2 story; 24 kit. cabins (2-5 bedrm), 7 kit. units (6-9 bedrm). No A/C in cabins. No rm phones. Mid-Apr-late Nov: S, D $30; cabins $60-$90. Closed rest of yr. Crib $5. Indoor pool. Playground. Restaurant 6:30 am-9 pm (Memorial Day-Labor Day). Ck-out 11 am. Sundries. Tennis. Access to facilities of state park. Cr cds: MC, V.
🏊 🏃 🛏 🔥 🐾

Crofton

(B-6) *Also see Vermillion and Yankton, SD*

Pop 820 **Elev** 1,440 ft **Area code** 402 **Zip** 68730

What to See and Do

Lewis and Clark Lake State Recreation Area. Approx 1,300 acres with 7,982-acre lake. Six separate recreation areas on Lewis and Clark Trail. Swimming, fishing, boating (ramps). Picnicking. Tent and trailer camping (dump station). 9 mi N via NE 121. Phone 605/668-2985.

Fairbury

(E-7) *See also Beatrice*

Pop 4,335 **Area code** 402 **Zip** 68352
Information Chamber of Commerce, 515 4th St, PO Box 274; 402/729-3000

What to See and Do

Alexandria Lakes State Recreation Area. Approx 50 acres with 46 acres of water. Swimming, fishing, boating (no motors). Picnicking, concession.

Camping (dump station). Standard hrs, fees. 12 mi W via US 136, then 3½ mi N on NE 53. Phone 402/729-3000.

Rock Creek Station State Historical Park. Located on site of Pony Express station and Oregon Trail ruts. Reconstructed post office and ranch buildings, covered wagon rides, picnic area, and visitor center with interpretive material and slide presentation. Hiking, nature trails. Picnicking, playground. Camping. (Daily) 5½ mi E, 1 mi S on marked country roads. Phone 402/729-5777. ¢¢

Special Event

Germanfest. Parade, crafts, dances. Phone 402/729-3000. Second full wkend Sept.

Motel/Motor Lodge

★ **CAPRI MOTEL.** *1100 14th St (68352). 402/729-3317.* 36 rms. S $30; D $76; each addl $2. Crib $5. TV; cable (premium). Complimentary coffee in lobby. Restaurant nearby. Ck-out 11 am. Cr cds: A, DS, MC, V.

D 🛁 ≋ 🔥

Fremont

(C-7) *See also Omaha*

Founded 1856 **Pop** 23,680 **Elev** 1,198 ft **Area code** 402

Information Fremont Area Chamber and Dodge County Convention and Visitors Bureau, 92 W 5th St, PO Box 182, 68026-0182; 402/721-2641

Web www.visitdodgecountyne.org

This town was named for John C. Frémont, Union general in the Civil War, who ran for president of the United States. In the town's early days the crops were so bad that lots sold for 75 cents; each. Finally, travelers on the Overland Trail brought in enough trade that the town began to prosper and grow. Midland Lutheran College gives a collegiate atmosphere to an otherwise industrial town, chiefly involved in food processing and retail trade.

What to See and Do

Fremont and Elkhorn Valley Railroad. Train rides to Nickerson and Hooper aboard vintage rail cars. Res recommended. (Schedule varies) 1835 N Somers Ave. Phone 402/727-0615. ¢¢¢¢ Also boarding here is

Fremont Dinner Train. Two restored 1940s rail cars make 30-mi round-trips through Elkhorn Valley. Dinner and varied entertainment. (Fri-Sun, also hols) Phone 402/727-8321. ¢¢¢¢

Fremont State Recreation Area. Approx 660 acres with 22 lakes. Swimming, fishing, boating (ramp, rentals). Picnicking, concession. Tent and trailer sites (dump station). (Apr-mid-Oct) Standard fees. 3 mi W on US 30. Phone 402/727-3290. ¢¢

Louis E. May Historical Museum. (1874) A 25-rm house of Fremont's first mayor; oak and mahogany paneling, art glass windows, rooms furnished in late 19th-century style. (Apr-Dec, Wed-Sun afternoons; closed Jan 1, Thanksgiving, Dec 25) 1643 N Nye Ave. Phone 402/721-4515. ¢¢

Special Events

Old Settlers Celebration and Parade. 18 mi W via US 30, in North Bend. Festivities incl parade, carnival, ice cream-social. Late June.

John C. Frémont Days. Balloon race, train rides, historical reenactments, barbecue. Phone 402/727-9428. Mid-July.

Motels/Motor Lodges

★ **BUDGET HOST INN.** *1435 E 23rd St (68025). 402/721-5656; fax 402/721-2514; toll-free 800/283-4678; res 800/228-5150. www.budgethost.com.* 35 rms. S $36-$40; D $46-$50; each addl $5. Crib $3. TV; cable (premium). Coffee in lobby. Restaurant opp 6 am-11 pm. Ck-out 11 am. Cr cds: A, DS, MC, V.

🛁 ✈ ≋ 🔥 SC

★ **COMFORT INN.** *1649 E 23rd St (68025). 402/721-1109. www.comfortinn.com.* 48 rms, 2 story. June-Sept: S $47-$52; D $50-$55; each addl $5; suites $59-$64; under 16 free; higher rates special events. Crib free. Pet accepted, some restrictions. TV;

cable (premium). Indoor pool; whirl-pool. Complimentary continental bkfst. Restaurant adj 6 am-midnight. Ck-out 11 am. Business servs avail. Refrigerator in suites; microwaves avail. Cr cds: A, C, D, DS, MC, V.

★★ **HOLIDAY LODGE.** *1220 E 23rd St (68025). 402/727-1110; fax 402/ 727-4579; toll-free 800/743-7666.* 100 rms, 2 story. S $42-$45; D $49-$63. Crib free. Pet accepted. TV; cable (premium). Indoor pool; whirlpool. Restaurant 6 am-9:30 pm. Bar 3 pm-1 am. Ck-out noon. Meeting rms. Business servs avail. Exercise equipt. Cr cds: A, C, D, DS, MC, V.

★ **SUPER 8.** *1250 E 23rd St (68025). 402/727-4445; fax 402/727-4445; toll-free 800/800-8000. www.super8.com.* 43 rms, 2 story. S $39; D $50; each addl $5; under 12 free. Crib free. TV; cable (premium). Complimentary coffee. Restaurant nearby. Cr cds: ER, JCB, MC, V.

Restaurant

★ **K. C.'S CAFE.** *631 N Park Ave (68025). 402/721-3353.* Hrs: 11 am-2 pm, 5-9:30 pm. Closed Mon, Sun; hols. Res accepted. Bar. Lunch $2.85-$6.50, dinner $5.95-$11.95. Children's menu. Specializes in prime rib, quiche. Many antiques. Cr cds: A, MC, V.

Gering

(C-1) *See also Scotts Bluff National Monument*

Pop 7,946 **Elev** 3,914 ft
Information Scotts Bluff-Gering United Chamber of Commerce, 1517 Broadway, Scotts Bluff 69361; 308/632-2133 or 800/788-9475

What to See and Do

North Platte Valley Museum. Sod house (1889), log house (1890), items and literature of local historical interest. (May-Sept, daily; rest of yr,

by appt) 11th and J sts. Phone 308/436-5411. ¢

Scotts Bluff National Monument. (see) 3 mi W on NE 92.

Special Events

Sugar Valley Rally. Gathering of antique automobiles; precision driving contest. Early June.

Oregon Trail Days. Parades, chili cook-off, contests, square dancing, barbecue, music festival. Four days mid-July.

Gothenburg

(D-4) *See also Cozad, North Platte*

Pop 3,232 **Elev** 2,567 ft
Area code 308 **Zip** 69138
Information Chamber of Commerce, PO Box 263; 308/537-3505 or 800/482-5520
Web www.ci.gothenburg.ne.us

What to See and Do

Pony Express Station. (1854). Pony Express station 1860-1861; later a stop for the Overland Stage; memorabilia, artifacts. (May-Sept, daily) Carriage rides (fee). Ehmen Park. Phone 308/537-3505. **FREE**

Special Events

Pony Express Rodeo. Carnival, barbecue, "mutton busting." July 3-4. Phone 308/537-3505.

Summerfest. Carnival, arts and crafts, contests, parade. Late Aug.

Harvest Festival. Art show, contests, antique farm machinery. Early Oct. Phone 308/537-3505.

Grand Island

(D-6) *See also Hastings*

Founded 1857 **Pop** 39,386 **Elev** 1,870 ft **Area code** 308
Information Grand Island/Hall County Convention and Visitors Bureau, PO Box 1486, 68802; 308/382-4400 or 800/658-3178
Web www.grand-island.com

Named by French trappers for a large island in the Platte River, the town was moved five miles north in 1869 to its present location on the Union Pacific Railroad, which dominated Grand Island's early existence. Traditionally a trade center for a rich irrigated agriculture and livestock region, the city now has diversified industry, including meat and food processing, agricultural and irrigation equipment, and mobile homes.

What to See and Do

Crane Meadows Nature Center. Educational center features exhibits and programs about Platte River habitat. Five miles of public nature trails. (Daily; closed hols) S side of Exit 305 on I-80. Phone 308/382-1820. ¢¢

Fonner Park. Thoroughbred racing. Pari-mutuel betting. (Mid-Feb-late Dec) 700 E Stolley Park Rd, N of I-80. Phone 308/382-4515. ¢

Heritage Zoo. The zoo (7½ acres) features more than 200 native Nebraska and exotic animals; train; special exhibits, events. (Daily) Stolley Park. Phone 308/385-5416. ¢¢

Island Oasis Water Park. Six-acre park has four water slides, wave pool, children's pool, lazy river. Sand volleyball; concessions. (Memorial Day-Labor Day, daily) 321 Fonner Rd, exit 312 off I-80. Phone 308/385-5381. ¢¢

Mormon Island State Recreation Area. Approx 90 acres; 61 water acres on Mormon Trail. Swimming, fishing, boating (nonpower or electric). Picnicking. Tent and trailer sites (standard fees, dump station). 10 mi S via US 34, 281. Phone 308/385-6211.

⚓ Stuhr Museum of the Prairie Pioneer. Museum, on 200 acres situated on island surrounded by man-made lake, was designed by Edward Durell Stone. (Daily; closed Jan 1, Thanksgiving, Dec 25) 4 mi N of I-80 at jct US 281 and US 34. Phone 308/385-5316. ¢¢ Incl are

Antique Auto and Farm Machinery Exhibit. Over 200 items on display, incl many steam tractors. (May-mid-Oct, daily) Phone 308/382-4400.

Gus Fonner Memorial Rotunda. Native American and Old West collections of Gus Fonner. (Daily) Phone 308/382-4400.

Railroad Town. Turn-of-the-century outdoor museum contains 60 original buildings, incl three houses; cottage where Henry Fonda was born; schoolhouse, newspaper office, bank, post office, hotel, country church, depot and railstock; blacksmith, shoe and barber shops. (May-mid-Oct, daily) Phone 308/382-4400.

Special Events

"Wings Over the Platte" Celebration. Each spring, more than 500,000 sandhill cranes, as well as ducks, geese, hawks, and eagles, pause at the Mormon Island Preserve on the Platte River before continuing north to nesting destinations in Canada, Alaska, and Siberia. Guided tours (res necessary) take visitors to carefully concealed blind, where they may observe the birds feeding and resting. For information contact Visitors Bureau, 308/382-4400 or 800/658-3178. Seven wks Mar, Apr.

Central Nebraska Ethnic Festival. Music, dance, ethnic meals, dramatic presentations. Phone 308/385-5455, exit 230. Fourth wkend July.

Harvest of Harmony Festival & Parade. Band and queen competitions. First Sat Oct.

Husker Harvest Days. Cornhusker Army Ammunition Plant, US 30 W. Agricultural exhibits, techniques, and equipt used in irrigation. Phone 308/382-9210. Mid-Sept.

Motels/Motor Lodges

★★ **BEST WESTERN RIVERSIDE INN.** *3333 Ramada Rd (68801). 308/384-5150; fax 308/384-6551; toll-free 800/780-7234. www.bestwestern. com.* 183 rms, 2 story. S $54; D $59; suites $89; under 18 free. Crib free. Pet accepted, some restrictions. TV; cable (premium). Heated pool; whirlpool. Complimentary continental bkfst. Restaurant 6 am-1:30 pm, 5-9 pm. Bar 5 pm-1 am. Ck-out noon. Coin lndry. Meeting rms. Business servs avail. Sundries. Cr cds: A, D, DS, JCB, MC, V.

🅳 🐾 ⌷ ✕ ⬚ 🛠

★ **DAYS INN.** *2620 N Diers Ave (68803). 308/384-8624; fax 308/384-1626; toll-free 888/384-8624. www.*

daysinn.com. 63 rms, 2 story. S $43; D $48-$53; each addl $5; under 12 free. Crib free. TV; cable (premium). Complimentary continental bkfst. Restaurant nearby. Ck-out 11 am. Coin lndry. Business servs avail. Whirlpool. Sauna. Cr cds: A, MC, V.

[D] [≋] [🐾] [SC]

★★ **HOLIDAY INN.** *2503 S Locust St (68801). 308/384-1330; fax 308/382-4615; toll-free 800/548-5542. www. holiday-inn.com.* 206 rms, 2 story. S $69; D $74; suites $95; under 18 free. Crib free. TV; cable (premium). Heated pool; wading pool, whirlpool, poolside serv. Restaurant 6:30 am-1:30 pm, 5:30-9:30 pm. Bar 4 pm-1 am. Ck-out noon. Coin lndry. Meeting rms. Cr cds: A, D, DS, JCB, MC, V.

[D] [≈] [✕] [≋] [🐾] [SC]

★ **OAK GROVE INN.** *3205 S Locust St (68801). 308/384-1333; fax 308/384-3109; toll-free 800/766-1706.* 60 rms, 2 story. Mid-Feb-Sept: S $27; D $33; each addl $3; suites $38; under 18 free; lower rates rest of yr. Crib free. TV; cable. Complimentary coffee in lobby. Restaurant nearby. Ck-out 11 am. Cr cds: A, C, D, DS, MC, V.

[D] [≋] [🐾] [SC]

★ **SUPER 8 MOTEL.** *2603 S Locust St (68801). 308/384-4380; fax 308/384-5015; res 800/800-8000. www.super8. com.* 80 rms, 2 story. S $36; D $41; each addl $2; suites $50-$60; under 12 free. Crib free. Pet accepted, some restrictions. TV; cable. Indoor pool; whirlpool. Complimentary continental bkfst. Restaurant opp 6 am-midnight. Ck-out 11 am. Cr cds: A, C, D, DS, MC, V.

[D] [🐾] [≈] [≋] [🐾] [SC]

Restaurants

★★ **DREISBACH'S.** *1137 S Locust St (68801). 308/382-5450.* Hrs: 11 am-1:30 pm, 5-10 pm; Sat from 4:30 pm; Sun, Mon 11 am-1:30 pm, 4:30-10 pm. Closed hols. Res required. Bar. Lunch $2.95-$6.95, dinner $3.95-$20.95. Lunch buffet: (Sun) $6.95. Children's menu. Specializes in dry-aged beef, chicken, rabbit. Family-owned. Cr cds: A, D, MC, V.

[D] [SC] [⊣]

★ **HUNAN.** *2249 N Webb Rd (68803). 308/384-6964. www.hunan.*

com. Hrs: 11:30 am-9:30 pm; wkends to 10:30 pm. Closed Jan 1, Dec 25. Res accepted. Chinese menu. Bar. Lunch $3.25-$4.75, dinner $4.95-$8.95. Specialties: crispy shrimp, Hunan Flower steak, princess chicken. Cr cds: A, D, MC, V.

[D] [⊣]

Hastings

(E-6) *See also Grand Island*

Founded 1872 **Pop** 22,837 **Elev** 1,931 ft **Area code** 402 **Zip** 68901

Information Convention and Visitors Bureau, PO Box 941, 68902; 402/461-2370 or 800/967-2189

Web www.hastingsnet.com

Hastings came into being almost overnight when two railroad lines crossed. Within eight years of its founding, its population swelled to almost 3,000. After 75 years as a depot and supply center, the town turned out large quantities of ammunition during World War II and the Korean Conflict.

What to See and Do

Crosier Asmat Museum. Collection of art and artifacts from the Asmat people of Irian Jaya, Indonesia. Many fine examples of the woodcarvings for which these people are famous. (Daily; by appt) 223 E 14th St. Phone 402/463-3188. **FREE**

Crystal Lake State Recreation Area. Approx 30 acres surrounding 30-acre lake. Swimming, fishing, boating (nonpower or electric); picnicking. Camping, trailer pads. Standard hrs, fees. 10 mi S on US 281. Phone 402/461-2370.

Hastings Museum. Incl natural science, pioneer history, Native American lore, bird displays; guns, antique cars, horse-drawn vehicles; sod house, country store, coin rm. (Daily; closed Jan 1, Thanksgiving, Dec 24 eve-Dec 25) J. M. McDonald Planetarium, sky shows (daily). IMAX Theatre (fee). 1330 N Burlington Ave. Phone 402/461-2399. ¢¢

Lake Hastings. Waterskiing, fishing, boating; picnicking. (May-Sept, daily) 1 mi N off US 281.

Willa Cather State Historic Site.
Author's letters, first editions, photos; Cather family memorabilia; art gallery; research library; bookstore. (Daily; closed hols) Other buildings incl Cather childhood home, Red Cloud depot, St. Juliana Falconieri Catholic Church, Grace Episcopal Church, and *My Antonia* farmhouse. Tours of properties (5 times daily). (See SPECIAL EVENTS) 38 mi S via US 281 on Webster St, in Red Cloud (branch museum of Nebraska State Historical Society). Phone 402/746-2653. ¢¢

Special Events

Willa Cather Spring Conference.
Willa Cather State Historic Site, Red Cloud. Features different each year. Discussion groups, banquet, entertainment. Tour of "Cather Country." Phone 402/746-2653. First wkend May.

Cottonwood Prairie Festival. Brickyard Park. Music, crafts, foods. Phone 800/967-2189. Mid-June.

Oregon Trail PRCA Rodeo. Labor Day wkend.

Kool-Aid Days. World's largest Kool-Aid stand. Free games and prizes. Downtown Hastings. Phone 800/967-2189. Mid-Aug.

Motels/Motor Lodges

★★ **HOLIDAY INN.** *2205 Osborne Dr E (68901). 402/463-6721; fax 402/463-6874; toll-free 888/905-1200. www.holiday-inn.com.* 100 rms, 2 story. S $50-$60; D $55-$65; each addl $7; suites $75; under 19 free. Crib free. Pet accepted, some restrictions. TV; cable (premium). Indoor pool; whirlpool. Sauna. Restaurant 6:30 am-10 pm. Bar 4 pm-1 am. Ck-out 11 am. Meeting rms. Business servs avail. In-rm modem link. Sundries. Cr cds: A, MC, V.
🄳 🔹 ≈ ⊠ 🅰

★ **SUPER 8.** *2200 N Kansas Ave (68901). 402/463-8888; fax 402/463-8899; res 800/800-8000. www.super8.com.* 50 rms, 2 story. May-Sept: S $55-$60, D $60-$65; lower rates rest of yr. Crib free. Pet accepted. TV; cable (premium). Restaurant adj 6

am-10 pm. Ck-out 11 am. Cr cds: A, D, DS, MC, V.
🄳 🔹 ✕ ⊠ 🅰 🆂🅲

★ **USA INNS.** *2424 E Osborne Dr (68901). 402/463-1422; fax 402/463-2956; toll-free 800/348-0426.* 62 rms, 2 story. S $37; D $46; each addl $2. Crib free. Pet accepted, some restrictions. TV; cable (premium), VCR avail. Complimentary coffee. Ck-out 11 am. Some refrigerators. Cr cds: A, MC, V.
🄳 🔹 ⊠ 🅰 🆂🅲

★ **X-L MOTEL.** *1400 W J St (68901). 402/463-3148.* 41 rms, 2 kit. units. S $35; D $37; each addl $5; kit. units $2 addl. Crib $5. TV; cable. Heated pool; whirlpool. Continental bkfst, coffee in rms. Restaurant nearby. Ck-out 11 am. Guest lndry. Refrigerators, microwaves. Cr cds: A, D, DS, MC, V.
≈ ✕ ⊠ 🅰

Restaurants

★ **BERNARDO'S STEAK HOUSE.**
1109 S Baltimore (68901). 402/463-4666. Hrs: 11 am-1:30 pm, 5-11 pm; Sat 5 pm-midnight; Sun 5-10 pm. Closed hols. Res accepted Mon-Fri, Sun. Bar. Lunch $3.75-$6.25, dinner $6-$14. Children's menu. Specializes in steak, prime rib. Family-owned. Cr cds: A, D, MC, V.
🄳 ⊡

★★ **TAYLOR'S STEAKHOUSE.**
1609 N Kansas (68901). 402/462-8000. Hrs: 11 am-1:30 pm, 4:30-10 pm; Fri, Sat to 10:30 pm; Sun 4:30-9 pm. Closed Jan 1, Dec 25. Res accepted. Bar. Lunch $3.95-$6.95, dinner $5.95-$30. Children's menu. Specializes in prime rib, aged beef, freshwater fish. Fireplace. Cr cds: A, D, DS, MC, V.
🄳 🆂🅲

Homestead National Monument

(4 mi NW of Beatrice, just off NE 4)

This is one of the first sites claimed under terms of the Homestead Act of 1862. A quarter section, 160 acres, went for a nominal fee to citizens who lived and worked on it for five years; eventually, grants equaling the combined states of Texas and Louisiana were made. Set aside in 1939, the site is a memorial to the pioneer spirit that began cultivation of the West.

At the Brownville Land Office Daniel Freeman filed Application No. 1 under the act for this land, built a log cabin and, later, a brick house. A surviving homesteader's cabin similar to Freeman's has been moved to the grounds and furnished as an exhibit. Visitors may take a self-guided tour (2½ miles) of the area. Many other historical items are on display in the Visitor Center museum. Freeman school, ¼ mile west of the Visitor Center, is a one-room brick schoolhouse restored to turn-of-the-century appearance; it commemorates the role of education in frontier society. The homestead story is explained in detail. Camping nearby. (Daily; closed Jan 1, Thanksgiving, Dec 25) Phone 402/223-3514. **FREE**

Kearney

(D-5) *See also Grand Island, Lexington, Minden*

Founded 1873 **Pop** 24,396
Elev 2,153ft **Area code** 308 **Zip** 68848
Information Visitors Bureau, PO Box 607; 308/237-3101 or 800/652-9435
Web www.kearneycoc.org

Kearney (CAR-nee), named for the frontier outpost Fort Kearney. Kearney is one of the largest migratory bird flyways of the world, a temporary home for millions of species.

What to See and Do

Fort Kearny State Historical Park. The first Fort Kearny was erected at Nebraska City in 1846; it was moved here in 1848 to protect the Oregon Trail. In park are restored 1864 stockade, sod blacksmith-carpenter shop, museum and interpretive center (Memorial Day-Labor Day, daily). Swimming, fishing, electric boating;

hiking and bicycling on nature trail (approx 1½ mi) along Platte River. Picnicking. Campground (standard fees, dump station). 4 mi S on NE 10, 3 mi W on link 50A. Phone 308/865-5305. ¢¢

✪ **Harold Warp Pioneer Village.** (See MINDEN) 12 mi S via NE 10.

Kearney Area Children's Museum. A hands-on learning experience for children and adults. (Thurs-Sun afternoons) 2013 Ave A. Phone 308/236-5437. ¢

Museum of Nebraska Art. Collection of paintings, sculptures, drawings, and prints created by Nebraskans or with Nebraska as the subject. (Tues-Sat, also Sun afternoons; closed hols) 24th and Central. Phone 308/865-8559. **FREE**

Trails and Rails Museum. Restored 1898 depot, 1880s freighters' hotel, 1871 country schoolhouse; displays of pioneer trails and rails, exhibits in baggage rm; steam engine, flat car, caboose. (Memorial Day-Labor Day, daily; rest of yr, by appt) 710 W 11th St. Phone 308/234-3041. **FREE**

University of Nebraska at Kearney. (1905) 10,000 students. Offers undergraduate, graduate, and specialist degrees. Two art galleries, planetarium; theater productions, concerts; campus tours. 905 W 25th St. Phone 308/865-8441. Also here is

George W. Frank House. (1889) Three-story mansion with Tiffany window; turn-of-century showplace and center of city's social life. (June-Aug, Tues-Sun) W Hwy 30. Phone 308/865-8284.

Motels/Motor Lodges

★★ **BEST WESTERN INN.** *1010 3rd Ave (68845). 308/237-5185; fax 308/234-1002; res 800/780-7234. www.bestwestern.com.* 69 rms, 2 story. June-Aug: S $66; D $79; each addl $6; under 12 free; lower rates rest of yr. Crib free. Pet accepted. TV; cable (premium), VCR avail (movies). Heated pool; wading pool, whirlpool. Complimentary full bkfst. Restaurant 5-9 pm. Ck-out noon. Meeting rms. Business servs avail. Exercise equipt; sauna. Cr cds: A, D, DS, MC, V.
🐾 🛁 🛌 🛐 🏊

★ **BUDGET MOTEL SOUTH.** *411 S 2nd Ave (68847). 308/237-5991; fax*

303/237-5991. 70 rms, 2 story. June-Labor Day: S, D $34-$56; each addl $4; lower rates rest of yr. Crib free. TV; cable (premium). Indoor pool. Sauna. Complimentary coffee in lobby. Restaurant adj open 24 hrs. Ck-out 11 am. Coin lndry. Meeting rms. Game rm. Cr cds: A, D, DS, MC, V.

★★ **FIRST INN GOLD FORT KEARNEY.** S 2nd Ave and I-80 (68848). 308/234-2541; fax 308/237-4512; toll-free 800/652-7245. 104 rms, 3 story. S $38; D $45; each addl $7; suites $75; under 12 free. Crib free. Pet accepted; $5/day. TV; cable (premium). Heated pool. Restaurant 6 am-10 pm. Bar 4 pm-1 am. Ck-out noon. Coin lndry. Meeting rms. Sundries. Cr cds: A, C, D, DS, MC, V.

★★ **HOLIDAY INN.** 110 S 2nd Ave (68848). 308/237-5971; fax 308/236-7549; res 800/465-4329. www.holiday-inn.com. 155 rms, 2 story. S $69-$79; D $89-$99; suites $110; under 18 free. Crib free. Pet accepted. TV; cable (premium). Indoor pool; whirlpool. Restaurant 6 am-9 pm. Bar 11-1 am; Sun 6-9 pm. Ck-out 11 am. Coin lndry. Meeting rms. Business servs avail. In-rm modem link. Gift shop. Game rm. Cr cds: A, C, D, DS, JCB, MC, V.

★★ **MIDTOWN WESTERN INN.** 1401 2nd Ave (68847). 308/237-3153; fax 308/234-6073; res 800/333-1401. www.midtownwesterninn.com. 34 rms, 2 story. June-Aug: S $38; D $48; each addl $5; under 12 free; lower rates rest of yr. Crib free. TV; cable (premium). Heated pool. Restaurant 6:30 am-9 pm. Bar from 10 am. Ck-out 11 am. Cr cds: A, MC, V.

★ **RAMADA INN.** 301 2nd Ave (68847). 308/237-3141; fax 308/234-4675; res 888/298-2054. www.ramada.com. 210 rms, 2 story. S, D $61-$76; suites $80-$119; under 20 free. Crib free. Pet accepted. TV; cable (premium). Indoor pool; wading pool, whirlpool, poolside serv. Sauna. Restaurant 6 am-10 pm. Bar 11-1 am; entertainment Mon-Sat. Ck-out 11 am. Coin lndry. Meeting rms. Busi-ness servs avail. Sundries. Private patios, balconies. Cr cds: A, MC, V.

★ **WESTERN INN.** 510 3rd Ave (68845). 308/234-1876; fax 308/237-2169; toll-free 800/437-8457. 45 rms. June-Aug: S $45; D $48-$59; each addl $5; under 12 free; lower rates rest of yr. Crib $3. TV; cable (premium). Indoor pool; whirlpool. Sauna. Continental bkfst. Restaurant nearby. Ck-out 11 am. Cr cds: A, D, DS, MC, V.

Restaurants

★★ **ALLEY ROSE.** 2013 Central Ave (68847). 308/234-1261. Hrs: 11 am-10 pm. Closed Memorial Day, Labor Day, Dec 25; also Sun Labor Day-Memorial Day. Res accepted. Bar Fri, Sat to 1 am. Lunch $2.99-$6.29, dinner $3.99-$28.99. Children's menu. Specializes in prime rib, chicken. Salad bar. Piano player wkends. Many antiques, fireplace. Cr cds: A, D, MC, V.

★★ **GRANDPA'S STEAK HOUSE.** 13 Central Ave (68847). 308/237-2882. Hrs: 5-11 pm; Sun 11:30 am-2 pm. Closed hols. Bar. Dinner $6-$17. Buffet: lunch (Sun) $7.25. Children's menu. Specializes in seafood, prime rib, steak. Salad bar. Fireplace. Cr cds: A, D, DS, MC, V.

Kimball

(D-1) *See also Sidney*

Pop 2,574 **Elev** 4,709 ft
Area code 308 **Zip** 69145
Information Chamber of Commerce, 119 E 2nd St; 308/235-3782
Web www.ci.kimball.ne.us

What to See and Do

Recreation. Oliver Reservoir. Swimming, waterskiing, fishing, boating. Camping. 8 mi W on US 30. **Gotte Park.** Swimming pool. Tennis. Picnicking, playground. In park is Titan I missile. E on US 30.

Lexington

(D-4) *See also Cozad, Gothenburg, Kearney*

Founded 1872 **Pop** 6,601 **Elev** 2,390 ft **Area code** 308 **Zip** 68850
Information Lexington Area Chamber of Commerce, 200 W Pacific, PO Box 97; 308/324-5504 or 888/966-0564
Web www.ci.lexington.ne.us

Originally a frontier trading post and settlement along the Oregon Trail, Plum Creek was established in 1872. Completion of the Union Pacific Railroad brought more settlers to this farmland; it was at this time that the name was changed to Lexington. The economy of Lexington has been boosted by the addition of agricultural equipment, machine manufacturing, and beef processing to its already prosperous farming and cattle operations. Lexington is also known as the "Antique Center of Nebraska" with its variety of antique and collectible shops.

What to See and Do

Dawson County Historical Museum. Exhibits incl Dawson County history gallery, furnished rural schoolhouse (1888), 1885 Union Pacific depot, 1903 locomotive, farm equipt, and 1919 experimental biplane. Collection also incl quilts and prehistoric Native American artifacts. Art gallery and archives. (Mon-Sat, also Sun afternoons; closed Jan 1, Thanksgiving, Dec 25) 805 N Taft St. Phone 308/324-5340. ¢

Heartland Museum of Military Vehicles. Collection of restored military vehicles. Incl Bradley fighting Vehicle, Airman retriever, troop carriers. (Daily) I-80 exit 237. Phone 308/324-5504. **Donation**

Johnson Lake State Recreation Area. Approx 80 acres on 2,061-acre lake. Swimming, fishing, boating (ramps). Picnicking. Tent and trailer sites (standard fees, dump station). 7 mi S on US 283. Phone 308/785-2685. ¢¢

Special Events

Johnson Lake Open Regatta. At Johnson Lake. Mid-June.
Dawson County Fair. Mid-Aug.

Antique & Craft Extravaganza. Over 275 antiques, craft and flea market dealers (fee). Labor Day wk.

Motels/Motor Lodges

★ **BUDGET HOST MINUTE MAN MOTEL.** *801 Plum Creek Pkwy (68850). 308/324-5544; fax 308/324-7287; res 800/283-4678. www.budgethost.com.* 36 rms. S $34; D $38; each addl $4. Crib free. TV; cable (premium). Heated pool. Complimentary coffee in lobby. Restaurant adj 6 am-11 pm. Ck-out 11 am. Cr cds: A, C, D, DS, MC, V.
🅳 🐕 ⚲ ✈ 🖎 🐾

★★ **FIRST INTERSTATE INN.** *2503 Plum Creek Pkwy (68850). 308/324-5601; fax 308/324-4284. www.firstinns.com.* 52 rms, 2 story. May-Nov: S $29.95-$31.95; D $33.95-$37.95; each addl $5; kit. units $5 addl; lower rates rest of yr. Crib free. Pet accepted. TV; cable (premium). Heated pool. Complimentary continental bkfst. Ck-out noon. Lndry facilities. Meeting rm. Cr cds: A, C, D, DS, MC, V.
🐕‍🦺 🐕 ⚲ 🖎 🐾

★ **GABLE VIEW INN.** *2701 Plum Creek Pkwy (68850). 308/324-5595; fax 308/324-2267.* 24 rms, 2 story. May-Sept: S $32.95-$37.95; D $42.95-$48.95; lower rates rest of yr. Crib free. TV; cable. Heated pool. Complimentary coffee in lobby. Ck-out 11 am. Cr cds: A, DS, MC, V.
⚲ 🖎 🐾 **SC**

★ **SUPER 8.** *104 E River Rd (68850). 308/324-7434; fax 308/324-4433; res 800/800-8000. www.super8.com.* 47 rms, 2 story. S $34.09; D $40.39; each addl $3; under 6 free. Crib $2. TV; cable (premium). Complimentary coffee in lobby. Restaurant adj open 24 hrs. Cr cds: A, C, D, DS, MC, V.
🅳 🖎 🐾

Lincoln

(D-7) *See also Nebraska City, Omaha*

Settled 1856 **Pop** 191,972 **Elev** 1,176 ft **Area code** 402

Information Convention and Visitors Bureau, 1135 M St, Suite 200, PO Box 83737, 68501; 402/434-5348 or 800/423-8212

Web www.lincoln.org

Second-largest city in Nebraska, Lincoln feuded with Omaha, the territorial seat of government, for the honor of being capital of the new state. When the argument was settled in Lincoln's favor in 1867, books, documents, and office furniture were moved in covered wagons late one night to escape the armed band of Omaha boosters. At that time, only 30 people lived in the new capital but a year later there were 500, and in 1870, 2,500. As a young lawyer in the 1890s, William Jennings Bryan went to Congress from Lincoln; in 1896, 1900, and 1908 he ran unsuccessfully for president. General John J. Pershing taught military science at the University of Nebraska. Business and many cultural activities revolve around state government and the university. Lincoln is also a major grain market, as well as a manufacturing, insurance, finance, printing, and trade center.

The unicameral form of government in Nebraska, which was set up by an amendment to the state constitution in 1934 (mostly by the efforts of Nebraska's famous senator, George W. Norris), is of great interest to students of political science. It works efficiently and avoids delays and deadlocks common to two-house legislatures.

What to See and Do

American Historical Society of Germans from Russia. Located here are the society's headquarters, archives, library, special displays and museum; also chapel, summer kitchen replicas. (Tues-Fri, also Sat mornings; closed hols) 631 D St. Phone 402/474-3363. **FREE**

Bluestem Lake State Recreation Area. Approx 400 acres on 325-acre lake. Swimming, fishing, boating; picnicking, camping (dump station).

13 mi SW via US 77, NE 33. Phone 402/471-5566.

Branched Oak Lake State Recreation Area. Approx 1,150 acres on 1,800-acre lake. Swimming, fishing, boating (ramps), picnicking, concession, camping (dump station). Standard fees. 12 mi NW via US 34, NE 79. Phone 402/783-3400.

City parks.

Antelope Park. Nine-hole junior golf course (fee) at Normal and South sts. Sunken Garden and Rose Garden at 27th and D sts. 23rd and N sts to 33rd and Sheridan sts.

Holmes Park. Approx 550 acres with large lake. Fishing, boating (no motors). Golf course (fee), ball fields. Ice-skating. Picnicking, playground. Hyde Memorial Observatory (Sat eves). Park (daily). 70th and Van Dorn sts. **FREE**

Pioneers Park. Hiking, bike trails, bridle path; golf course (fee). Picnicking, playgrounds. Nature preserve and center, outdoor amphitheater. (Daily) ½ mi S of jct Coddington Ave and W Van Dorn St. Phone 402/441-7895. **FREE**

Wilderness Park. Approx 1,450 acres. Hiking, biking, bridle trails. (Daily) First and Van Dorn to 27th and Saltillo Rd. **FREE**

Conestoga Lake State Recreation Area. Approx 450 acres on 230-acre lake. Fishing, boating (ramps); picnicking, camping (dump station). 6 mi W on US 6, then 3 mi S off NE 55A. Phone 402/471-5566.

Eugene T. Mahoney State Park. More than 570 acres with two lakes. Swimming pool, waterslide (Memorial Day-Labor Day, daily), fishing, paddleboats. Hiking, horseback riding, minature golf, driving range, tennis courts. Picnicking, lodging, restaurant. Camping, cabins. Greenhouse, conservatory. 25 mi NE on I-80, exit 426. Phone 402/944-2523. ¢¢

Folsom Children's Zoo. Exotic animals, contact areas, botanical gardens. (Apr-Labor Day, daily) Train and pony rides (fee). 1222 S 27th St. Phone 402/475-6741. ¢¢

Lincoln Children's Museum. A variety of cultural and scientific exhibits invite exploration and involve the senses. (Tues-Sun; closed hols) 1420 P St. Phone 402/477-0128. ¢¢

Museum of Nebraska History. History of Nebraska summarized in exhibits covering events from prehistoric times through the 1950s. Native American Gallery, period rms. (Daily; closed hols) 15th and P sts. Phone 402/471-4754. **FREE**

National Museum of Roller Skating. Skates, costumes, and photographs documenting the sport and industry from 1700 to the present; also archives dealing with world and national competitions since 1910. The only museum in the world devoted solely to roller skating. (Mon-Fri; closed hols) 4730 South St. Phone 402/483-7551. **FREE**

Nebraska Wesleyan University. (1887) 1,500 students. Liberal arts school founded by the United Methodist Church. On campus is Elder Art Gallery (Late Aug-mid-May, Tues-Sun). Also here is the Old Main Building (1888) and the Nebraska United Methodist Historical Center, containing archives. 50th and St Paul sts. Phone 402/466-2371.

Pawnee Lake State Recreation Area. Approx 1,800 acres on 740-acre lake. Blue rock area. Swimming, fishing, boating (ramps); picnicking, concession, camping (dump station). Standard fees. 6 mi W on US 6, then 3 mi N on NE 55A. Phone 402/471-5566.

State Capitol. Designed by Bertram Goodhue, the most dominant feature of the building is the central tower, which rises 400 ft. Ground was broken in 1922 for this third capitol building at Lincoln; it was completed ten yrs later. Sculpture by Lee Lawrie incl reliefs and friezes depicting the history of law and justice, great philosophers, symbols of the state, and a bronze statue of the Sower (32 ft) atop the tower dome. The great hall, rotunda, and legislative chambers are decorated in tile and marble murals, tapestries, and wood-inlaid panels. One-half hr (June-Aug) and hrly guided tours (Daily; closed hols). 1445 K St. Phone 402/471-0448. Nearby are

Executive Mansion. (1957) Georgian Colonial architecture. Guided tours. (Thurs afternoons; closed hols) 1425 H St. Phone 402/471-3466. **FREE**

Lincoln Monument. (1912) This standing figure of Lincoln was designed by sculptor Daniel

Chester French, who also produced the seated Lincoln statue for Henry Bacon's Lincoln Memorial in Washington, D.C. Architectural setting by Bacon. Phone 402/434-5348.

Statehood Memorial—Thomas P. Kennard House. (1869) Restored residence of Nebraska's first secretary of state. (Tues-Fri; closed hols) 1627 H St. Phone 402/471-4764. ¢

Strategic Air Command Museum. Features permanent collection of 33 aircrafts and six missiles relating to history of SAC and its importance in preservation of world peace. Interactive children's gallery, theater, museum store. (Daily; closed hols) 28210 W Park Hwy, Ashland. Phone 402/944-3100. ¢¢¢

Union College. (1891) 600 students. Tours of campus. 3800 S 48th St, between Bancroft and Prescott sts. Phone 402/488-2331. On campus is

College View Seventh-day Adventist Church. Church noted for its stained-glass windows and Rieger pipe organ. Phone 402/486-2880.

University of Nebraska. (1869) 33,900 students. The university has research-extension divisions throughout the state. 14th and R sts; E campus at 33rd and Holdrege. Phone 402/472-7211. On grounds are

Great Plains Art Collection. Works by Remington, Russell, and other masters are among the nearly 700 pieces of this collection. Also featured are 4,000 volumes of Great Plains and Western Americana. (Tues-Sun; closed hols and between academic semesters) 205 Love Library, 13th and R sts. Phone 402/472-6220. **FREE**

Sheldon Memorial Art Gallery and Sculpture Garden. Designed by Philip Johnson. Fine collection of 20th-century American art; changing exhibitions; film theater. (Tues-Sun; closed hols) 12th and R sts. Phone 402/472-2461.

University of Nebraska State Museum. Displays of fossils (dinosaurs and mounted elephants), rocks and minerals, ancient life, Nebraska plants and animals. Native American exhibits; changing exhibits. (Mon-Sat and Sun afternoons; closed Jan 1,

Thanksgiving, Dec 25) **Encounter Center** (Tues-Sun). **Ralph Mueller Planetarium** (Tues-Sun; fee). 14th and U sts. Phone 402/472-2642. ¢

Special Events

Horse racing. State Fair Park, 1800 State Fair Park Dr. Thoroughbred racing. Phone 402/474-5371. Mid-June-mid-Aug.

Camp Creek Antique Machinery and Threshing Association Festival. 12 mi NE via US 6, in Waverly. Antique tractor pull; parades of antique farm machinery, cars, and horse-drawn equipt; demonstrations of farm tasks and crafts. Phone 402/786-3003. Mid-July.

July Jamm. Art show, music festival. Downtown. Late July.

Nebraska State Fair. State Fair Park, 1800 State Fair Park Dr. Contact the State Fair, PO Box 81223, 68501; 402/474-5371. Aug 23-Sept 2.

Motels/Motor Lodges

★ ★ **BEST WESTERN VILLAGER COURTYARD AND GARDENS.** *5200 O St (68510). 402/464-9111; fax 402/467-0505; res 800/780-7234. www.bestwestern.com.* 190 rms, 2 story. S $64-$69; D $74-$79; each addl $10; suites $150; under 18 free. Crib free. Pet accepted, some restrictions. TV; cable (premium), VCR avail. Pool; whirlpool. Restaurant 6 am-10 pm; Fri, Sat to 11 pm. Bar 3:30 pm-1 am. Ck-out noon. Coin lndry. Meeting rms. Bellhops. Valet serv. Exercise equipt. Cr cds: A, D, DS, MC, V.

★ ★ **CHASE SUITE HOTEL BY WOODFIN.** *200 S 68th Pl (68510). 402/483-4900; fax 402/483-4464; toll-free 888/433-6183. www.woodfinsuite hotels.com.* 120 kit. suites, 2 story. S $79-$101; D $99-$141. Crib free. Pet accepted; $100 ($50 refundable). TV; cable (premium), VCR avail. Heated pool; whirlpool. Complimentary full bkfst, coffee in rms. Ck-out noon. Coin lndry. Meeting rms. Business servs avail. Valet serv. Sundries. Lighted tennis. Exercise equipt. Health club privileges. Microwaves.

Balconies. Picnic tables, grills. Cr cds: A, C, D, DS, JCB, MC, V.

[icons]

★ **COMFORT INN.** *2940 NW 12th St (68521). 402/475-2200; fax 402/475-2200; toll-free 800/228-5150. www. comfortinn.com.* 67 rms, 2 story. May-Oct: S $45-$50; D $48-$55; each addl $5; under 18 free; higher rates university football season; lower rates rest of yr. Crib free. Pet accepted. TV; cable (premium). Complimentary continental bkfst. Restaurant adj open 24 hrs. Ck-out 11 am. Meeting rms. Business servs avail. Whirlpool. Game rm. Microwaves avail. Cr cds: A, C, D, DS, ER, JCB, MC, V.

[icons] SC

★ **DAYS INN.** *2920 NW 12th St (68521). 402/475-3616; fax 402/475-4356; res 800/329-7466. www. daysinn.com.* 84 rms, 2 story. S $44-$56; D $50-$65; each addl $5; under 12 free. Crib free. TV; cable (premium). Complimentary continental bkfst. Restaurant nearby. Ck-out 11 am. Cr cds: A, C, DS, MC, V.

[icons]

★ **FAIRFIELD BY MARRIOTT.** *4221 Industrial Ave (68504). 402/476-6000; fax 402/476-6000; res 800/228-2800. www.fairfieldinn.com.* 63 rms, 3 story. June-Sept: S $49-$59; D $59-$69; under 18 free; lower rates rest of yr. Crib free. TV; cable (premium). Complimentary coffee in lobby. Restaurant opp 11 am-11 pm. Meeting rms. Indoor pool; whirlpool. Cr cds: A, C, D, DS, MC, V.

[icons]

★ **GREAT PLAINS BUDGET HOST INN.** *2732 O St (68510). 402/476-3253; fax 402/476-7540; toll-free 800/ 283-4678. www.budgethost.com.* 42 rms, 2 story, 6 kits. S $34-$38; D $42-$46; each addl $5; kit. units $34-$48; under 12 free; wkly rates. Crib free. TV; cable (premium). Coffee in rms. Restaurant nearby. Ck-out noon. Refrigerators. Cr cds: A, C, D, DS, ER, MC, V.

[icons] SC

★★ **HAMPTON INN.** *1301 W Bond Cir (68521). 402/474-2080; fax 402/474-3401; toll-free 800/426-7866. www.hamptoninn.com.* 111 rms, 3 story. S $65-$79; D $69-$89; suites $85-$150; under 18 free. Crib free.

TV; cable (premium). Heated pool. Complimentary continental bkfst. Restaurant nearby. Ck-out noon. Meeting rms. Business servs avail. In-rm modem link. Refrigerators, microwaves in suites. Private balconies. Cr cds: A, C, D, DS, ER, MC, V.

[icons] SC

★ **HORIZON INN.** *2901 NW 12th St (68501). 402/474-5252; fax 402/474-5259.* 40 rms, 2 story, 5 suites. June-Aug: S $39; D $47; each addl $4; suites $40-$90; under 18 free; lower rates rest of yr. Crib free. TV; cable. Complimentary coffee in lobby. Restaurant adj open 24 hrs. Ck-out noon. Cr cds: A, MC, V.

[icons]

★ **HOWARD JOHNSON.** *5250 Cornhusker Hwy (68504). 402/464-3171; fax 402/464-7439; toll-free 800/446-4656. www.hojo.com.* 104 rms, 2 story. S $51; D $77; each addl $8-$15; under 18 free. TV; cable (premium). Indoor pool. Restaurant 6:30 am-2 pm, 5-10 pm. Bar 5 pm-1 am. Ck-out noon. Coin lndry. Meeting rms. Exercise equipt. Game rm. Cr cds: A, C, D, DS, MC, V.

[icons]

★ **RAMADA LIMITED SOUTH.** *1511 Center Park Rd (68512). 402/ 423-3131; fax 402/423-3155; res 888/298-2054. www.ramada.com.* 80 rms, 28 with shower only, 2 story. S $62; D $76; under 12 free. Crib free. TV; cable (premium). Complimentary continental bkfst, coffee in rms. Restaurant adj 6:30 am-8 pm. Meeting rms. Pool. Cr cds: A, C, D, DS, MC, V.

[icons] SC

Hotels

★★★ **CORNHUSKER.** *333 S 13th St (68508). 402/474-7474; fax 402/474-1847; toll-free 800/793-7474. www. thecornhusker.com.* 290 rms, 10 story. S $135-$150; D $150-$165; each addl $15; suites $175-$450; under 18 free; wkend rates. Crib free. TV; cable (premium), VCR avail. Indoor pool. Restaurants 6:30 am-10 pm. Rm serv 24 hrs. Bar 4 pm-1 am. Ck-out noon. Convention facilities. Business servs avail. Gift shop. Valet parking. Free airport transportation. Exercise equipt. Health club privileges. Cr cds: A, C, D, DS, MC, V.

D ⊠ 🏋 ✕ ➷ 🔥

★★ **HOLIDAY INN DOWNTOWN.** *141 N 9th St (68508). 402/475-4011; fax 402/475-9011; toll-free 800/432-0002. www.holiday-inn.com.* 233 rms, 16 story. S, D $80-$110; each addl $10; suites $135-$240; family, wkend rates. Crib free. TV; cable (premium). Indoor pool; whirlpool, poolside serv. Coffee in rms. Restaurant 6:30 am-10 pm. Bar 11-1 am. Ck-out noon. Meeting rms. In-rm modem link. Gift shop. Free garage parking. Game rm. Cr cds: A, C, D, DS, MC, V.

D 🐾 ⊠ ➷ 🔥

B&B/Small Inn

★ **ROGERS HOUSE BED & BREAKFAST INN.** *2145 B St (68502). 402/476-6961; fax 402/476-6473. www.rogershouseinn.com.* 12 rms, 4 with shower only, 2 story. S $58; D $78. Children over 10 yrs only. Complimentary full bkfst. Ck-out 11 am, ck-in 4 pm. Built in 1914; historical landmark. Totally nonsmoking. Cr cds: A, DS, MC, V.

➷ 🔥

Restaurants

★★ **BILLY'S.** *1301 H St (68508). 402/474-0084.* Hrs: 11 am-2 pm, 5-10 pm, Sat from 5 pm. Closed Sun; hols. Res accepted. Continental menu. Bar. Lunch $5.25-$7.25, dinner $10.95-$17.95. Children's menu. Specializes in fresh fish, beef, veal. In historic house; antiques. Each of 3 dining rms pays tribute to a famous Nebraskan. Cr cds: A, D, DS, MC, V.

D

★ **JABRISCO.** *700 P St (68508). 402/434-5644.* Hrs: 11 am-10:30 pm. Closed hols. Continental menu. Bar. Lunch $2.95-$8.95, dinner $2.95-$11.95. Specialties in pasta, chicken, pizza. Cr cds: A, D, DS, MC, V.

D

McCook (E-4)

Founded 1882 **Pop** 8,112 **Elev** 2,576 ft **Area code** 308 **Zip** 69001

Information Chamber of Commerce, PO Box 337; 308/345-3200 or 800/657-2179

Web www.ci.mccook.ne.us

McCook began as the small settlement of Fairview. The Lincoln Land Company and the Burlington & Missouri Railroad gave the town its name and ensured its growth. It is now a trading center in the middle of a vast reclamation, irrigation, and oil production area.

What to See and Do

George W. Norris House. (Branch museum of Nebraska State Historical Society) Restored house of former senator (1861-1944); original furnishings; museum depicts events in his life. (Wed-Sat; also Tues and Sun afternoons; closed hols) 706 Norris Ave. Phone 308/345-8484. ¢

Medicine Creek Reservoir State Recreation Area. Approx 1,200 acres on 1,768-acre reservoir. Swimming, fishing, boating (ramps, rentals); picnicking, concession. Tent and trailer camping (dump station, standard fees). 23 mi NE via US 6, 34, then 7 mi N on unnumbered road.

Museum of the High Plains. Pioneer and Native American artifacts; World War II prisoner of war paintings; apothecary shop; fossils; flour mill; oil industry exhibit; special exhibits. (Tues-Sun afternoons; closed hols) 423 Norris Ave. Phone 308/345-3661. **FREE**

Red Willow Reservoir State Recreation Area. Approx 1,300 acres on 1,628-acre reservoir. Swimming, fishing, boating (ramps); picnicking, concession. Tent and trailer camping (dump station, standard fees). 11 mi N on US 83. Phone 308/345-6507.

Swanson Reservoir State Recreation Area. Approx 1,100 acres on 4,973-acre reservoir. Swimming, fishing, boating (ramps); picnicking, concession. Tent and trailer camping (dump station, standard fees). 23 mi W on US 34.

Special Events

Sailing Regatta. Phone 308/345-3610. Early July.

Red Willow County Fair and Rodeo. Fairgrounds, M St and 5th St W. Late July.

Heritage Days. Entertainment, parade, arts and crafts fair, carnival. Last wkend Sept.

Motels/Motor Lodges

★★ **BEST WESTERN CHIEF MOTEL.** *612 W B St, McCook (69001). 308/345-3700; fax 308/345-7182; res 800/780-7234. www.bestwestern.com.* 111 rms, 2 story. May-Dec: S $47-$59; D $59-$69; each addl $5; suites $74-$84; higher rates pheasant season, first wk Nov; lower rates rest of yr. Crib $5. Pet accepted. TV; cable (premium). Complimentary continental bkfst. Coffee in rms. Indoor pool; whirlpool, poolside serv. Restaurant 6 am-11 pm. Ck-out 11 am. Exercise equipt. Lndry. Meeting rm. Business servs avail. Cr cds: A, C, D, DS, MC, V.

🄳 🐾 ⛖ 🏋 🏊 🖃 🐾

★ **SUPER 8 MOTEL.** *1103 E B St, McCook (69001). 308/345-1141; fax 308/345-1144; toll-free 800/800-8000. www.super8.com.* 40 rms. S $37.98; D $45.98; each addl $4; under 12 free. Crib $3. Pet accepted. TV; cable (premium). Complimentary coffee in rms. Ck-out 11 am. Cr cds: A, C, D, DS, MC, V.

🄳 🐾 🖃 🐾 SC

Minden

(E-5) *See also Kearney*

Founded 1878 **Pop** 2,749 **Elev** 2,172 ft **Area code** 308 **Zip** 68959

Information Chamber of Commerce, 325 N Colorado Ave, PO Box 375; 308/832-1811

Web www.mindenne.com

What to See and Do

🌟 **Harold Warp Pioneer Village.** Large collection of Americana that follows progress since 1830. Three city blks and over 30 buildings, incl original sod house, schoolhouse, and pony

express station, chronologically represent the country's pioneer heritage. More than 50,000 historic items, incl farm implements, 100 vintage tractors, locomotives, 350 antique autos, and 22 historic flying machines. Restaurant; lodging (see MOTEL). Camping. (Daily) Jct US 6, 34, and NE 10. Phone 308/832-1181.

Special Event

The Light of the World **Christmas Pageant.** Kearney County Courthouse, Town Square. A town tradition for many yrs; highlight of outdoor pageant is illumination of courthouse dome by 10,000 lights. Contact the Chamber of Commerce for details. Sat after Thanksgiving and first two Sun Dec.

Motel/Motor Lodge

★ **PIONEER MOTEL.** *224 E Hwy 6 (68959). 308/832-2750. www.pioneer-village.org.* 90 rms. May-Oct: S $36-$40; D $42-$45; each addl $4; under 5 free; lower rates rest of yr. Crib $2. TV. Restaurant 6 am-9 pm; winter 7 am-8 pm. Ck-out 11 am. Campground. Harold Warp Pioneer Village adj. Cr cds: DS, MC, V.

🄳 🖃 🐾

Nebraska City

(D-8) *See also Auburn, Lincoln*

Founded 1855 **Pop** 6,547 **Elev** 1,029 ft **Area code** 402 **Zip** 68410

Information Chamber of Commerce, 806 First Ave; 402/873-3000 or 800/514-9113

Web www.nebraskacity.com

Nebraska City began as a trading post but grew larger and wilder as the Missouri River and overland traffic brought bullwhackers, muleskinners, and riverboat men with bowie knives and pistols in their belts. Located on the Missouri River, Nebraska City ships grain and agricultural products worldwide.

What to See and Do

Arbor Lodge State Historical Park. More than 60 acres of wooded grounds surround 52-rm, Neo-Colonial mansion of J. Sterling Morton (originator of Arbor Day and secretary of agriculture under Grover Cleveland) and summer residence of son Joy Morton (founder of Morton Salt Co). Picnicking. (See SPECIAL EVENTS) Mansion (Mar-Dec, daily). Park grounds (Daily). 1 mi W on 2nd Ave. Phone 402/873-7222. ¢¢

John Brown's Cave. Original log cabin and cave where slaves were hidden before and after the Civil War. (Apr-Nov, daily) 1900 4th Corso (Hwy 2). Phone 402/873-3115. ¢¢

River Country Nature Center. Mounted animals native to Nebraska, 80-ft panoramic mural of the state; library, gift shop. (Late Apr-Oct, Sun; rest of yr, by appt) 110 N 6th St. Phone 402/873-5491. **FREE**

Sightseeing tour. Old Time Trolleys. Historical tour and narrative. (Daily; closed hols) 806 1st Ave. Phone 402/873-3000. ¢¢

Wildwood Park. Picnicking, playground. W on 4th Corso, then N. Phone 402/873-3000. In park is

Wildwood Historic Home. (1869). A ten-rm house with mid-Victorian furnishings; formal parlor; antique lamps and fixtures. Original brick barn is now art gallery. (Apr-Nov; Tues-Sat, also Sun afternoons) Steinhart Park Rd. Phone 402/873-6340. ¢

Special Events

Arbor Day Celebration. Tree-planting ceremonies in Arbor Lodge State Historical Park; parade, arts festival, fly-in, breakfast. Last wkend Apr.

Applejack Festival. Celebration of the apple harvest. Parade, antique and craft show, classic car show, football game. Third wkend Sept.

Motel/Motor Lodge

★ **APPLE INN.** *502 S 11th St (68410). 402/873-5959; fax 402/873-6640; toll-free 800/659-4446. www. appleinn.net.* 65 rms, 1-2 story. S $35; D $44; each addl $5. TV; cable (premium). Pool. Complimentary continental bkfst. Restaurant nearby. Coin lndry. Ck-out 11 am. Business servs

avail. Some refrigerators. Cr cds: A, MC, V.

B&B/Small Inn

★ **WHISPERING PINES BED AND BREAKFAST.** *21st St and 6th Ave (68410). 402/873-5850; res 800/632-8477.* 5 air-cooled rms, 3 share bath, 2 story. 2 rm phones. S, D $50-$75; under 3 free. TV in some rms. Complimentary full bkfst. Ck-out 10:30 am, ck-in 5 pm. Whirlpool. Picnic tables, grills. Built in 1883; country atmosphere. Family-owned for 100 yrs. Totally nonsmoking. Cr cds: DS, MC, V.

Restaurant

★★ **EMBERS STEAKHOUSE.** *1102 4th Corso (68410). 402/873-6416.* Hrs: 11 am-10 pm; Sun to 8:30 pm. Closed Jan 1, Dec 25. Bar. Lunch $4.95-$14.95, dinner $8.95-$18.95. Children's menu. Specializes in prime rib, chicken, steak. Contemporary decor. Cr cds: A, MC, V.

Norfolk

(C-6) *See also Wayne*

Founded 1866 **Pop** 21,476 **Elev** 1,527 ft **Area code** 402 **Zip** 68701

Information Madison County Convention and Visitors Bureau, PO Box 386, 68702-0386; 402/371-2932 or 888/371-2932

Web www.norfolk.ne.us

German families from Wisconsin were the first to till the rich soil around Norfolk. The town's livestock business and expanding industries have brought prosperity, making Norfolk the chief marketplace of northeastern Nebraska.

What to See and Do

The Cowboy Trail. This 321-mi trail follows former Chicago & North Western railroad line from Norfolk to Chadron, NE. Incl 13,878 ft of handrailed bridges. Trail is suitable for hiking and mountain biking, with horseback riding allowed alongside the trail. Contact local Chamber of Commerce for more information. Phone 402/371-4862.

Neligh Mills. Complete 19th-century flour mill; milling exhibits. Maintained by the Nebraska State Historical Society. (May-Sept, daily; rest of yr, by appt) W off US 275 at Wylie Dr and N St, in Neligh. Phone 402/887-4303. ¢

Skyview Lake. Fishing, boating (no motors), canoeing; picnicking. 1 mi W on Maple Ave. Phone 403/371-2932.

Special Event

LaVitsef Celebration. Fall festival featuring entertainment, parade, softball tournaments. Phone 402/371-4862. Last wkend Sept.

Motels/Motor Lodges

★ **ECO-LUX INN.** *1909 Krenzien Dr (68701). 402/371-7157.* 39 rms, 4 suites, 2 story. S $40-$42; D $46-$51; each addl $4; under 12 free. Crib free. TV; cable (premium). Complimentary continental bkfst. Restaurant adj 24 hrs. Ck-out 11 am. Cr cds: A, MC, V.
SC

★★ **NORFOLK COUNTRY INN.** *1201 S 13th St (68701). 402/371-4430; fax 402/371-6373; toll-free 800/233-0733. www.norfolkcountry inn.com.* 127 rms, 2 story. S $38-$46; D $44-$55; each addl $6; under 16 free. Crib free. TV; cable (premium). Pool; poolside serv. Restaurant 6 am-2 pm, 5-10 pm. Bar 11-1 am. Ck-out noon. Meeting rms. Cr cds: A, C, D, DS, MC, V.
D ♣ 🖈 ➔ ◪ ⦿

★ **RAMADA INN.** *1227 Omaha Ave (68701). 402/371-7000; fax 402/371-7000; res 888/298-2054. www.ramada. com.* 98 rms, 2 story. S $48-$99; D $55-$119; each addl $7; suites $75; under 12 free. Crib free. TV; cable (premium). Indoor pool. Playground. Restaurant 6 am-2 pm, 5-10 pm. Bar 4 pm-1 am. Ck-out 11 am. Meeting rms. Business servs avail. Sundries. Cr cds: A, C, D, DS, ER, JCB, MC, V.
D ➔ ✗ ◪ ⦿

★ **SUPER 8 MOTEL.** *1223 Omaha Ave (68701). 402/379-2220; fax 402/379-3817; toll-free 800/800-8000. www.super8.com.* 66 rms, 2 story. S $42.98; D $51.98; each addl $3. Crib $2. TV; cable (premium). Restaurant adj 6 am-11 pm. Ck-out 11 am. Business servs avail. Cr cds: A, C, D, DS, MC, V.
D ◪ ⦿ SC

Restaurants

★★ **BRASS LANTERN.** *1018 S 9th St (68701). 402/371-2500.* Hrs: 11 am-2 pm, 5-10 pm; Sat 5-11 pm; early-bird dinner Mon-Sat 5-7 pm. Bar. Lunch $3-$5, dinner $5-$20. Children's menu. Specializes in steak, seafood, prime rib. Salad bar. Family-owned. Cr cds: A, D, DS, MC, V.
D ⊟

★ **GRANARY.** *922 S 13th St (68701). 402/371-5334.* Hrs: 11 am-9:30 pm; Thurs-Sat to 10:30 pm. Closed Sun; hols. Bar. Lunch $4.25, dinner $4.25-$6.45. Children's menu. Specialty: fried chicken. Country kitchen antiques. Family-owned. Cr cds: A, D, MC, V.
D ⊟

★★ **PRENGER'S.** *115 E Norfolk Ave (68701). 402/379-1900.* Hrs: 11 am-2 pm; 5-10 pm; Sun 11-1:30 pm. Closed hols. Res accepted. Bar to midnight. Lunch $4.25-$8.95, dinner $4.50-$13.95. Children's menu. Specializes in steak, seafood. Old World atmosphere; dark wood, brass railing. Family-owned. Cr cds: A, D, MC, V.
D SC ⊟

★★★ **THE UPTOWN CAFE.** *326 Norfolk Ave (68701). 402/371-7171. www.theuptowncafe.com.* Hrs: 10 am-2 pm, 5-10 pm; Sat 8 am-2 pm, 5-11 pm. Res accepted. Bar. Wine list. Bkfst $1.50-$4.25, lunch $3-$5, dinner $8-$12. Specialties: seafood, prime rib, beef Wellington. Johnny Carson started his 1st radio show in upstairs ballrm. Cr cds: A, D, DS, MC, V.
D ⊟

North Platte (D-4)

Founded 1866 **Pop** 22,605 **Elev** 2,800 ft **Area code** 308 **Zip** 69103
Information North Platte/Lincoln County Convention and Visitors Bureau, 219 S Dewey, PO Box 1207; 308/532-4729 or 800/955-4528
Web www.northplatte-tourism.com

North Platte, Buffalo Bill Cody's hometown, is the retail railroad and agricultural hub of west central Nebraska. Cattle, hogs, corn, wheat, alfalfa, and hay are the principal crops.

What to See and Do

Buffalo Bill Ranch State Historical Park. Remaining of William F. Cody's ranch are the 18-rm house, barn, and many outbuildings. Interpretive film; display of buffalo. (Apr-late Oct, daily) 1 mi N on Buffalo Bill Ave. Phone 308/535-8035. ¢¢

Cody Park. Heated swimming pool (June-Aug; fee). Tennis, softball, children's circus rides (fee). Picnicking, playgrounds. Camping (fee). Wildlife refuge. Railroad display and museum. (Daily) 3 mi N on US 83. Phone 308/534-7611. **FREE**

Fort McPherson National Cemetery. Soldiers and scouts of Native American and later wars buried here. 14 mi E on I-80 to Maxwell, then 3 mi S on county road.

Lincoln County Historical Museum. Several authentically furnished rooms and exhibits, incl a WWII canteen, depict the life and history of Lincoln County. In back is re-creation of railroad village with restored depot, house, church, schoolhouse, log house, barn. (Memorial Day-Labor Day, daily; rest of yr, by appt) 2403 N Buffalo Bill Ave. Phone 308/534-5640. **Donation**

State recreation areas.

Arnold Lake. Approx 15 acres with 22-acre lake on upper reaches of the Loup River. Fishing, nonpower or electric boating; picnicking, camping. Standard hrs, fees. 37 mi NE via NE 70, 92 near Arnold. Phone 308/532-4729.

Lake Maloney. Approx 1,100 acres on 1,000-acre lake. Swimming, fishing, boating (ramps); picnicking, camping (dump station). Standard hrs, fees. 6 mi S on US 83. Phone 308/532-4729.

Special Event

"NEBRASKAland DAYS" Celebration. Parades, entertainment, food, and the famous PRCA Rodeo. Phone 308/532-7939. Mid-late June.

Motels/Motor Lodges

★★ **BEST WESTERN CHALET LODGE.** *920 N Jeffers St (69101). 308/532-2313; fax 308/532-8823; res 800/780-7234. www.bestwestern.com.* 38 rms, 2 story. June-Aug: S $48-$53; D $53-$58; each addl $3; under 12 free; lower rates rest of yr. Crib $3. Pet accepted. TV; cable (premium). Heated pool. Complimentary continental bkfst, coffee in rms. Restaurant nearby. Ck-out 11 am. Some refrigerators. Cr cds: A, MC, V.
🐾 ⛱ ✈ 🐾

★ **BLUE SPRUCE MOTEL.** *821 S Dewey St (69101). 308/534-2600; toll-free 800/434-2602.* 14 rms. June-mid-Sept: S $24-$31; D $31-$39; each addl $2; lower rates rest of yr. Crib $2. Pet accepted, some restrictions. TV; cable (premium). Complimentary coffee. Restaurant nearby. Ck-out 11 am. Cr cds: A, DS, MC, V.
🐾 🐾 🐾 SC

★★ **COUNTRY INN.** *321 S Dewey St (69101). 308/532-8130; fax 308/534-0588; toll-free 800/532-8130.* 40 rms, 2 story. Mid-May-Aug: S, D $29-$52; lower rates rest of yr. Crib free. Pet accepted, some restrictions. TV; cable (premium). Pool; whirlpool. Restaurant nearby. Cr cds: A, DS, MC, V.
🐾 🏃 🏋 ⛱ ✈ 🐾 🐾

★ **1ST INTERSTATE INN.** *US 83 and I-80 (69103). 308/532-6980; fax 308/532-6981.* 29 rms. Mid-May-mid-Sept: S $34.95; D $40.95; each addl $2; under 12 free; lower rates rest of yr. Crib $3. Pet accepted. TV; cable (premium). Coffee in lobby. Restaurant nearby. Ck-out 11 am. Some refrigerators. Cr cds: A, DS, MC, V.
D 🐾 🏃 🏋 🐾 🐾

★★ **HAMPTON INN.** *200 Platte Oasis Pkwy (69101). 308/534-6000; fax 308/534-3415; toll-free 800/426-7866. www.hamptoninn.com.* 111 rms, 4 story. June-Sept: S $62-$72; D $72-$82; lower rates rest of yr. Crib free. TV; cable (premium), VCR avail. Indoor pool; whirlpool. Complimentary continental bkfst. Restaurants nearby. Ck-out noon. Business servs avail. Cr cds: A, C, D, DS, MC, V.
🄳 ⬚ ⬚ ⬚ 🆂🅲

★ **RAMADA LIMITED.** *3201 S Jeffers St (69101). 308/534-3120; fax 308/534-7745; res 800/298-2054. www.ramada.com.* 80 rms, 2 story. S $49.95-$52.95; D $52.95-$62.95; each addl $4; under 12 free. Crib free. TV; cable (premium). Heated pool. Complimentary coffee in lobby. Restaurant adj 11 am-9:30 pm; wkends to 10:30 pm. Bar 4 pm-1 am. Ck-out 11 am. Coin lndry. Sundries. Gift shop. Cr cds: A, C, D, DS, MC, V.
🄳 ⬚ ⬚ ⬚ ⬚

★ **SANDS MOTOR INN.** *501 Halligan Dr (69101). 308/532-0151; fax 308/532-6299.* 81 rms, 2 story. May-Sept: S $39-$49; D $52; each addl $6; under 12 free; lower rates rest of yr. Crib $5. TV; cable (premium). Heated pool. Restaurant open 24 hrs. Ck-out 11 am. Meeting rm. Cr cds: A, MC, V.
🄳 ⬚ ⬚ ⬚

★ **STANFORD LODGE.** *1400 E 4th St (69101). 308/532-9380; fax 308/532-9634; res 800/743-4934.* 32 rms. June-Aug: S $34.95; D $39.95; each addl $4; lower rates rest of yr. Crib $3. Pet accepted; $3. TV; cable. Complimentary coffee in lobby. Ck-out 11 am. Cr cds: A, DS, MC, V.
⬚ ⬚ ⬚ ⬚

★★ **STOCKMAN INN.** *1402 S Jeffers St (69101). 308/534-3630; fax 308/534-0110; toll-free 800/624-4643.* 140 rms, 2 story. S $45-$50; D $50-$55; each addl $5; higher rates June-Aug. Crib free. Pet accepted, some restrictions. TV; cable (premium). Heated pool. Restaurant 6 am-10 pm. Bar 4:30 pm-1 am. Ck-out noon. Meeting rms. Business servs avail. Cr cds: A, MC, V.
🄳 ⬚ ⬚ ⬚ ⬚

★ **SUPER 8 MOTEL.** *220 Eugene Ave (69101). 308/532-4224; fax 308/534-4317; toll-free 800/800-8000. www.super8.com.* 113 rms, 2 story. S

$34.88; D $39.88-$41.88; each addl $4; under 12 free. Crib $3. TV; cable (premium). Complimentary continental bkfst. Restaurant nearby. Ck-out 11 am. Coin lndry. Exercise equipt. Cr cds: A, D, DS, MC, V.
🄳 ⬚ ⬚ ⬚ 🆂🅲

Restaurant

★ **GOLDEN DRAGON.** *120 W Leota (69101). 308/532-5588.* Hrs: 11 am-2:30 pm, 4:30-9:30 pm; Fri, Sat to 10 pm. Closed hols. Chinese menu. Wine, beer. Lunch $3.60-$5; dinner $6-$15. Cr cds: A, MC, V.
⬚

Ogallala (D-3)

Founded 1868 **Pop** 5,095 **Elev** 3,223 ft **Area code** 308 **Zip** 69153

Information Chamber of Commerce, 204 E A St, PO Box 628; 308/284-4066 or 800/658-4390

Web www.ci.ogallala.com

Developed as a shipping point on the Union Pacific Railroad for the great western cattle herds, Ogallala was the goal of the cattle-driving cowboys who rode day and night with their "eyelids pasted open with tobacco." Many of them are buried in a genuine Boot Hill Cemetery, between 11th and 12th streets, on a 100-foot rise above the South Platte River, where there have been no burials since the 1880s.

What to See and Do

Ash Hollow State Historical Park. Approx 1,000 acres on the Oregon Trail. The hills, cave, and spring of Ash Hollow have sheltered humans from prehistoric times through the pioneer days. Hiking. Picnicking. Interpretive center, restored school. 29 mi NW on US 26. Phone 308/778-5651. ¢¢

Crescent Lake National Wildlife Refuge. A nesting and migratory bird refuge comprising more than 45,000 acres with numerous pothole lakes. Birds found in the refuge incl Canadian geese, great blue herons, American bitterns, prairie chickens, prairie falcons, and long-billed curlews.

Fishing. Nature trail (1½ mi). Refuge office (Mon-Fri). 43 mi NW on US 26 to Oshkosh, then 28 mi N on unnumbered, partially paved road. Phone 308/762-4893. **FREE**

Front Street. Cowboy museum (free), general store, saloon, arcade, restaurant. Shows in Crystal Palace (summer, nightly; fee). (Daily) 519 E First St (E NE 30). Phone 308/284-4066.

Lake McConaughy State Recreation Area. Approx 5,500 acres on Nebraska's largest lake (35,700 acres). Swimming, fishing, boating (ramps, rentals); picnicking, concession, camping (dump station). 9 mi N on NE 61. Phone 308/284-3542. ¢¢

Lake Ogallala State Recreation Area. Approx 300 acres on 320-acre lake. Swimming, fishing, boating (ramps, rentals); picnicking, camping (dump station nearby at Martin Bay). Standard fees. 9 mi N on NE 61, below Kingsley Dam. Phone 308/284-3542. ¢¢

Mansion on the Hill. This 1890s mansion contains period furniture, pioneer household items. (Memorial Day-Labor Day, daily, afternoons) Contact the Chamber of Commerce for further information. 1004 N Spruce St. **FREE**

Special Events

Keith County Fair and Round-Up Rodeo. Phone 308/284-4569. Early Aug.

Governor's Cup Sailboat Regatta. Labor Day wkend.

Motels/Motor Lodges

★★ **BEST WESTERN STAGE-COACH INN.** *201 Stagecoach Tr (69153). 308/284-3656; fax 308/284-6734; res 800/780-7234. www.best western.com.* 100 rms, 2 story. May-Sept: S $57-$67; D $62-$67; each addl $5; under 12 free; lower rates rest of yr. Crib free. Pet accepted. TV; cable, VCR (movies). Indoor/outdoor pool; wading pool, whirlpool. Playground. Restaurant 6 am-9 pm. Bar 5-10 pm. Ck-out 11 am. Coin lndry. Meeting rms. Free airport transportation. Cr cds: A, C, D, DS, MC, V.

D 🔄 ➰ 🏳 🐾 SC

★ **COMFORT INN.** *110 Pony Express Ln (69153). 308/284-4028; fax 308/284-4028; res 800/228-5150. www. comfortinn.com.* 49 rms, 2 story. June-Aug: S $45-$65; D $55-$75; each addl $5; suites $64.95-$84.95; under 18 free; lower rates rest of yr. Crib free. TV; cable (premium). Indoor pool; whirlpool. Complimentary continental bkfst. Restaurant nearby. Ck-out 11 am. Coin lndry. Meeting rms. Cr cds: A, D, DS, MC, V.

D 🐾 ⚡ ➰ 🏳 🐾 SC

★ **RAMADA LIMITED.** *201 Chuck-wagon Rd (69153). 308/284-3623; fax 308/284-4949; res 888/298-2054. www.ramada.com.* 152 rms, 2 story. S, D $75; each addl $7; under 18 free. Pet accepted. TV; cable. Heated pool; wading pool, poolside serv. Continental bkfst. Restaurant 6 am-10 pm. Bar 5 pm-1 am. Ck-out noon. Coin lndry. Meeting rms. Business servs avail. Free airport transportation. Game rm. Cr cds: A, DS, MC, V.

D 🔄 🐾 ➰ 🏳 🐾

Restaurant

★★ **HILL TOP INN.** *197 Kingsley Dr (69153). 308/284-4534.* Hrs: 4:30-9 pm; Sun 11 am-7 pm. Closed Mon; Thanksgiving, Dec 25; also Jan-Mid-Feb. Bar. Dinner $7.95-$17.95. Children's menu. Specializes in steak, seafood. Hilltop view of Kingsley Dam, Lake McConaughy. Family-owned. Cr cds: A, D, MC, V.

D 🏳

Omaha

(D-8) *See also Blair, Lincoln; also Council Bluffs, IA*

Founded 1854 **Pop** 335,795
Elev 1,040 ft **Area code** 402

Information Greater Omaha Convention and Visitors Bureau, 6800 Mercy Rd, Suite 202, 68106-2627; 402/444-4660 or 800/332-1819

Web www.visitomaha.org

The largest city in Nebraska, Omaha is named for the Native American people who lived here until they signed a treaty with the federal gov-

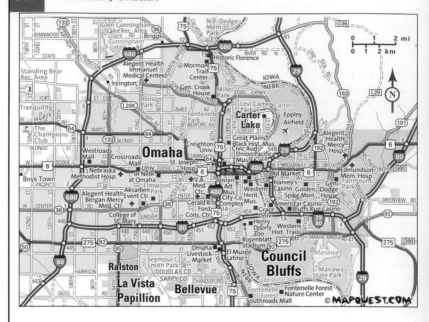

ernment on June 24, 1854. Opportunists across the Missouri River in Council Bluffs, Iowa, who had been waiting for the new territory to open, then rushed to stake out property, triggering a real estate boom. Omaha also saw the trial of Standing Bear, chief of the Ponca Tribe, which established the precedent that Native Americans were human beings and entitled to constitutional rights and protections.

During early boom times, steamboats docked in Omaha daily, bringing gold-seekers and emigrants to be outfitted for the long journey west. Local merchants further prospered when Omaha was named the eastern terminus for the Union Pacific. The first rail was laid in 1865. Public buildings rose on the prairie; schools, plants, and stockyards flourished in the 1870s and 1880s. Fighting tornadoes, grasshopper plagues, floods, and drought, the people built one of the farm belt's great commercial and industrial cities.

Today, Omaha continues to be a major transportation and agribusiness center, but it is also a recognized leader in telecommunications, insurance, and manufacturing as well as the home of five *Fortune* 500 companies. Omaha is also the headquarters of STRATCOM, the Strategic Air Command, one of the vital links in the national defense chain.

Visitors are not in Omaha long before hearing the term "Aksarben." It is, in fact, only Nebraska spelled backward and the name of a civic organization.

Transportation

Car Rental Agencies. See IMPORTANT TOLL-FREE NUMBERS.

Public Transportation. Buses (Metro Area Transit), phone 402/341-0800.

Rail Passenger Service. Amtrak 800/872-7245.

Airport Information

Eppley Airfield. Information, lost and found, 402/422-6817; 402/422-6800; weather, 402/392-1111; cash machines, Terminal Building.

What to See and Do

Aksarben Field and Coliseum. Site of Omaha Lancers (hockey), stock shows, a rodeo, and a variety of fairs, festivals, and family entertainment. 6800 Mercy Rd. Phone 402/561-7000.

Belle **Riverboat..** An old-time riverboat offering sightseeing, dinner and dance cruises on the Missouri River. Res recommended. (Memorial Day-Labor Day, Tues-Sun) Departs Miller's Landing, off Abbott Dr. Phone 402/342-3553.

Boys Town. A community for abandoned, abused, neglected, and handicapped boys and girls. Founded in 1917 by Father Flanagan, Boys Town now has six direct care programs: a residential care facility for 550 boys and girls on the Boys Town campus; a national diagnostic, treatment, and research institute for children with hearing, speech, and learning disorders; an urban high school for troubled youths who may have difficulty in traditional school settings; Boys Town mini-campuses around the nation; a national training program for other child-care facilities; and a family-based program. Boys Town provides services to more than 17,000 youths annually. Tours of Father Flanagan museum and the Hall of History. Visitor center (daily; closed hols). 138th and W Dodge Rd. Phone 402/498-1140. **FREE**

City parks.

Heartland of America Park. Bounded by Missouri River on the E, 8th St on the W, and Douglas St on the N. A 31-acre site features picnic facilities, arbors, and waterfalls. The park's 15-acre lake has a computer-driven fountain that has a colored light show at night. Excursion boat rides on *The General Marion* (Memorial Day-Labor Day, Wed-Sun, afternoons and eves; fee). **Gene Leahy Mall,** bounded by Douglas and Farnam, 10th and 14th sts. **N. P. Dodge Memorial Park,** John Pershing Dr, 7 mi N. Fishing, boating (ramp, marina); tennis, lighted ball fields, picnicking, playground, camping (fee). Inquire about facilities for the disabled. **Elmwood Park,** Dodge and 60th sts. Swimming pool. Golf course. Picnicking. **Memorial Park,** Dodge and 63rd sts, across street from Elmwood Park. WWII memorial, rose garden, walking and jogging paths. Bounded by Missouri River on the E, 8th St on the W, and Douglas St on the N. Phone 402/444-6362.

Durham Western Heritage Museum. Restored Art Deco railroad depot is now a history museum. Exhibits on Omaha history from 1880 to 1954; Byron Reed coin collection. (Tues-Sun; closed hols) In Omaha Union Station, 801 S 10th St. Phone 402/444-5071. ¢¢

Fontenelle Forest Nature Center. Approx 1,250 acres of forest; 17 mi of foot trails through forest marsh, lake, prairie, floodplain environments; indoor animal exhibits; guided walks, lectures, films. (Daily; closed Jan 1, Thanksgiving, Dec 25) 7 mi S via US 75, in Bellevue, 1111 N Bellevue Blvd. Phone 402/731-3140. ¢¢

Fun Plex. Nebraska's largest waterpark incl waterslides, wave-making pool, bumper cars, go-karts. (Memorial Day-Labor Day, daily) 72nd and Q, I-80 72nd St exit. Phone 402/331-8436. ¢¢¢¢

General Crook House. Built in 1878 to serve as the residence of the commander of the Department of the Platte. Originally called Quarters I, Fort Omaha, the house soon came to be known by the name of its first occupant, General George Crook. Italianate architecture; many antiques from the Victorian era; Victorian garden in summer. Guided tours (by appt). (Mon-Fri, also Sun afternoons; closed hols) 30th and Fort sts. Phone 402/455-9990. ¢¢

Gerald Ford Birth Site. Model of original house, White House memorabilia; park, gardens, Betty Ford Memorial Rose Garden. (Daily) 32nd and Woolworth Ave. **FREE**

Great Plains Black History Museum. Housed in a building designed in 1907 by prominent Nebraska architect Thomas R. Kimball, the museum preserves the history of black Americans and their part in the heritage of Omaha and Nebraska since the territorial period of the 1850s. Incl are rare photographs, relics, historical displays; films. (Mon-Fri) 2213 Lake St. Phone 402/345-2212. ¢

Henry Doorly Zoo. More than 18,500 animals, many quite rare, are on display in 110-acre park. Exhibits incl aquarium, indoor rainforest, walk-through aviary, white tigers, and polar bears. Steam train rides (Memorial Day-Labor Day, daily). IMAX 3-D theater (Daily; fee). Restaurant. Picnic areas. (Daily; closed Jan 1, Thanksgiving, Dec 25) 3701 S 10th St, I-80 13th St S exit. Phone 402/733-8401. ¢¢¢

Historic Bellevue. Restored buildings incl old church (1856), the first

Gerald Ford Birth Site, Omaha

church in the Nebraska territory; old depot (1869), contains period artifacts; settlers' log cabin (ca 1830); and Fontenelle Bank (1856). Sarpy County Historical Museum, 2402 SAC Place, has displays concerning the history of the county and changing exhibits (daily; closed Jan 1, Thanksgiving, Dec 25). 9 mi S via US 75. Phone 402/293-3080. Museum ¢

Joslyn Art Museum. (1931) Museum building of Art Deco design with collections of art, ancient through modern, incl European and American paintings, sculpture; art of the Western frontier, Native American art; traveling exhibitions. Guided tours, lectures, workshops, films, gallery talks, concerts. A 30,000-volume art reference library; museum shop. (Tues-Sun; closed hols) 2200 Dodge St. Phone 402/342-3300. ¢¢¢

Louisville State Recreation Area. Approx 192 acres with 50 acres of water area. Swimming, fishing, boating (no motors); picnicking, concession, camping (standard fees, dump station). 25 mi SW via I-80, NE 50. Phone 402/234-6855.

Mormon Trail Center at Winter Quarters. The winter of 1846-1847 took the lives of more than 600 Mormon emigrants who camped near here. A monument commemorates their hardship. Films and pioneer exhibits in visitor center. 3215 State St. Phone 402/453-9372.

Old Market. Art galleries, antique shops, restaurants. Revitalization of old warehouse district; some of Omaha's oldest commercial buildings line the market's brick-paved streets. Center at 11th and Howard sts extending E to 10th St and W to 13th.

Omaha Children's Museum. Self-directed exploration and play for children and families; constantly changing series of hands-on exhibits in science, the arts and humanities, health, and creative play. (Tues-Sun; closed hols) 500 S 20th St. Phone 402/342-6163.

Platte River State Park. 413 acres located on rolling bluffs overlooking the Platte River. Swimming pool, paddleboats; hiking, horseback riding; tennis courts, archery range, recreational fields, x-country skiing, picnicking, concession, restaurant. Camper cabins and housekeeping cabins. Arts and crafts building; observation tower; free use of recreational equipt. 17 mi SW on I-80, then 14 mi S on NE 50 to NE Spur 13 E, then W. Phone 402/234-2217.

Schramm Park State Recreation Area. Approx 330 acres along the north bank of the Platte River. A day-use area offering hiking and nature trails, picnicking, and several other activities. In the park are geological displays, fish hatchery ponds, and the Gretna Fish Hatchery Museum, which uses displays and audiovisual presentations to tell the story of fish and fishery management in Nebraska. Museum (Memorial Day-Labor Day, daily; Apr-late May and after Labor Day-Nov, Mon, Wed-Sun; rest of yr, Wed-Sun; closed hols). Park (Daily). I-80 exit 432, then 6 mi S on NE 31. Phone 402/332-3901. ¢¢ Also located here is

Ak-Sar-Ben Aquarium. Modern facility featuring more than 50 species of fish native to Nebraska, a terrarium, World Herald Auditorium, a natural history classrm, and orientation and display areas. (Seasons same as Gretna Fish Hatchery Museum) Phone 402/332-3901. ¢

Trolley. Trackless *Ollie the Trolley* provides transportation along Douglas and Farnam sts to the Old Market, Gene Leahy Mall, and 16th St Mall. Stops posted along route. (Daily) Phone 402/597-3596. ¢

Two Rivers State Recreation Area. More than 600 acres with water area of 320 acres. Swimming, trout fishing (fee), boating; picnicking, concession; camping (standard fees, dump station), trailer pads (fee), rental cabins (converted Union Pacific Railroad cabooses; late Apr-Oct). 23 mi W off US 275, NE 92. Phone 402/359-5165. ¢¢

University of Nebraska at Omaha. (1908) 16,000 students. 60th and Dodge sts. Phone 402/554-2393. On campus is

Kountze Planetarium. Planetarium shows display galaxies, stars, planets, and other celestial phenomena. Observatory (First Fri, Sat each month). Shows (limited hrs; fee). 68th and Dodge sts, on first floor of Durham Science Center. Phone 402/554-3722. ¢¢

Special Events

NCAA College Baseball World Series. Rosenblatt Stadium, 13th St and Bert Murphy Dr. Phone 402/444-4750. Early June.

Summer Arts Festival. Downtown. Last wkend June.

River City Round-up. Fairgrounds. Celebration of agriculture and western heritage incl parade, barbecues, trail rides. Phone 402/554-9610. Late Sept.

Christmas at Union Station. For details, contact Durham Western Heritage Museum. Dec.

Motels/Motor Lodges

★★ **BAYMONT INN.** *10760 M St (68127). 402/592-5200; fax 402/592-1416; res 877/229-6668. www.baymontinns.com.* 96 rms, 2 story. S $42; D $49; suites $49-$51; under 19 free; wkend, special events rates. Crib free. Pet accepted. TV; cable (premium). Complimentary continental bkfst, coffee in rms. Restaurant nearby. Ck-out noon. Business servs avail. In-rm modem link. Cr cds: A, D, DS, MC, V.

★ **BEST INN.** *9305 S 145th St (68138). 402/895-2555; fax 402/895-1565; res 800/237-8466.* 56 rms, 3 story. No elvtr. S $44; D $52; each addl $5; suites $85; under 16 free. Crib free. Pet accepted; $25. TV; cable (premium). Complimentary continental bkfst. Bar 3 pm-1 am. Ck-out noon. Coin lndry. Whirlpool. Microwaves. Cr cds: A, C, D, DS, MC, V.

★★ **BEST WESTERN CENTRAL - EXECUTIVE CENTER.** *3650 S 72nd St (68124). 402/397-3700; fax 402/397-8362; toll-free 800/528-1234. www.bestwestern.com.* 212 rms, 5 story. June-Aug: S $59-$69; D $69-$89; each addl $6; suites $85-$150; under 18 free; wkend rates; lower rates rest of yr. Crib free. Pet accepted, some restrictions. TV; cable (premium). Indoor pool; whirlpool. Sauna. Restaurant 6:30 am-10 pm. Bar 4 pm-1 am. Ck-out noon. Coin lndry. Meeting rms. Business servs avail. In-rm modem link. Bellhops. Airport transportation. Game rm.

Refrigerator in suites. Cr cds: A, C, D, DS, ER, JCB, MC, V.

[D] [icons] SC

★★ **BEST WESTERN REDICK TOWER.** *1504 Harney St (68102). 402/342-1500; fax 402/342-5554; res 800/780-7234. www.bestwestern.com.* 89 rms, 11 story. Apr-Oct: S, D $115; each addl $15; suites $145-$275; under 18 free; wkend rates. Crib free. Garage $4. TV; cable (premium). Complimentary bkfst. Rm serv 24 hrs. Bar. Ck-out noon. Meeting rms. Business servs avail. In-rm modem link. Free airport, railroad station, bus depot transportation. Exercise equipt; sauna. Whirlpool. Cr cds: A, D, DS, MC, V.

[D] [icons] SC

★★ **DAYS HOTEL CARLISLE.** *10909 M St (68137). 402/331-8220; fax 402/331-8729; res 800/526-6242.* 137 rms, 2-3 story. S $125; D $125; suites $175; under 18 free. Crib free. Pet accepted, some restrictions; $30. TV; cable. Indoor pool; whirlpool. Complimentary full bkfst. Coffee in rms. Restaurant 6:30 am-2 pm, 5-10 pm. Bar 4 pm-midnight. Ck-out noon. Coin lndry. Meeting rms. Business center. In-rm modem link. Bellhops. Free airport transportation. Cr cds: A, C, D, DS, ER, JCB, MC, V.

[D] [icons] SC [icon]

★★ **DAYS INN.** *1811 Hillcrest Dr, Bellevue (68005). 402/292-3800; fax 402/292-6373; res 800/329-7466. www.daysinn.com.* 126 rms, 2 story. S $60; D $66; each addl $6; under 18 free. Crib free. TV; cable. Indoor pool; wading pool, whirlpool, poolside serv. Complimentary full bkfst. Restaurant 6 am-9 pm. Bar noon-1 am. Ck-out noon. Coin lndry. Meeting rms. Business servs avail. Game rm. Some refrigerators. Balconies. Cr cds: A, C, D, DS, JCB, MC, V.

[D] [icons]

★ **ECONO LODGE.** *3511 S 84th St (68124). 402/391-4321; fax 402/397-9260; res 800/553-2666. www.econo lodge.com.* 81 rms, 2 story. S $34.95; D $39.95; each addl $4; suites $59.95-$78.95; under 12 free. TV; cable (premium), VCR avail (movies $2). Restaurant adj open 24 hrs. Ck-out 11 am. Meeting rms. Cr cds: A, DS, MC, V.

[D] [icons]

★★ **FOUR POINTS BY SHERATON OMAHA.** *4888 S 118th St (68137). 402/895-1000; fax 402/896-9247; toll-free 888/625-5144. www.sheraton.com.* 168 rms, 6 story. S, D $69-$79; under 17 free. Crib free. Pet accepted, some restrictions. TV; cable (premium). Indoor pool; wading pool, whirlpool. Sauna. Restaurant 6:30 am-10 pm. Bar 11-1 am. Ck-out noon. Coin lndry. Meeting rm. Business servs avail. Valet serv. Sundries. Free airport transportation. Game rm. Sun deck. Cr cds: A, C, D, DS, MC, V.

[D] [icons]

★★ **HAMPTON INN.** *10728 L St (68127). 402/593-2380; fax 402/593-0859; toll-free 800/426-7866. www. hamptoninn.com.* 133 rms, 4 story. S $56-$62; D $61-$68; under 18 free. Crib free. Pet accepted. TV; cable, VCR avail (movies). Pool. Complimentary continental bkfst. Restaurant nearby. Meeting rms. Business servs avail. In-rm modem link. Cr cds: A, C, D, DS, MC, V.

[D] [icons] SC

★★ **HAMPTON INN.** *9720 W Dodge Rd (68114). 402/391-5300; fax 402/391-8995; res 800/426-7866. www. hamptoninn.com.* 129 rms, 4 story. S $59-$69; D $69-$70; suites $90-$170; under 18 free. Crib free. TV; cable (premium). Complimentary continental bkfst. Ck-out noon. Meeting rms. Business servs avail. In-rm modem link. Sundries. Valet serv. Cr cds: A, C, D, DS, MC, V.

[D] [icons] SC

★★ **HOLIDAY INN.** *3001 Chicago St (68131). 402/345-2222; fax 402/345-2501; res 800/465-4329. www.hi express.com.* 123 rms, 6 story. S, D $81; suites $100-$140; under 18 free. Crib free. TV; cable (premium). Complimentary continental bkfst. Restaurant nearby. Ck-out noon. Coin lndry. Meeting rms. Business servs avail. In-rm modem link. Valet serv. Free airport transportation. Exercise equipt; sauna. Refrigerators. Cr cds: A, C, D, DS, JCB, MC, V.

[D] [icons] SC

★★ **HOWARD JOHNSON PLAZA HOTEL OMAHA INN.** *4706 S 108th St (68137). 402/339-7400; fax 402/339-5155; toll-free 800/446-4656. www.hojo.com.* 102 rms, 7 story. May-Sept: S $59-$67; D $67-$77; under 12

IN AND AROUND THE OLD MARKET AREA

Begin a walking tour of Omaha in the Old Market Area. One of the few downtown areas that preserves Omaha's original Victorian-era architecture, the Old Market Area is a five-block-square shopping, dining, and gallery district that's the heart and soul of the entire city center. Window shop, stop for coffee, pop into art-filled boutiques—the Old Market Area is made for leisurely strolling. Bounded by Farnam and Jones streets and 10th and 13th streets, the Old Market Area was originally the food-processing center for the region: Swanson Food and Anheuser Busch and other stalwarts of the food industry once occupied these buildings. Food is still one of the finest reasons to visit the Old Market Area. Find provisions for a picnic at one of Omaha's best bakeries, Delice European Bakery and Coffee Bar (1206 Howard), and pick up cheese and wine at La Buvette Wine and Grocery (511 South 11th Street). On Wednesdays and Saturdays in summer and fall, shop for fresh local produce at the farmers market, held on 11th Street between Jackson and Howard.

Directly south of the Old Market Area on 10th Street is the Durham Western Heritage Museum (801 South 10th Street), housed in the architecturally stunning Union Station, an Art Deco gem from Omaha's past. The museum tells the story of Omaha and Nebraska's past, complete with vintage cars and railroad equipment—plus a period soda fountain still in operation.

Walk north on 10th Street five blocks to reach Gene Leahy Mall, a ten-acre park with a lake that serves as a reflecting pond for the modern high-rise architecture of Omaha. Trails wind through the park, linking formal flower gardens, a playground for children, a bandstand, and public art displays. To the east, the Leahy Mall connects to Heartland of America Park and Fountain, which is bounded by 8th Street and the Missouri River. The highlight of the park is its lake and fountain, which shoots streams of water 300 hundred feet into the air. The General Marion tour boat navigates the lake to take visitors closer to the fountain. At night, the water display is accompanied by pulsing lights.

Return to the Leahy Mall along Douglas Street, which leads into the modern city center. At 24th Street, turn north one block to the Joslyn Art Museum (2200 Dodge Street), Nebraska's premier center for the visual arts. The museum building is itself a work of art, a fanciful Art Deco structure faced with shimmering pink marble. The permanent collection consists of American and European art from the 19th and 20th centuries. A highlight is the cache of works from Karl Bodmer, a German watercolorist who traveled up the Missouri River in the 1830s, capturing the pristine landscapes, Native Americans, and wildlife before white pioneer settlement.

For a longer walk, continue west on Dodge Street to the Cathedral Neighborhood, which is filled with 19th-century mansions and Victorian homes. The neighborhood is named for St. Cecelia's Cathedral, a massive Spanish Mission-style church at 701 North 40th Street. The Joslyn Castle (3902 Davenport) was built by the family that endowed the city's art museum. A fanciful stone edifice that resembles a Scottish baronial castle, the house stands amid five acres of gardens and forest.

free; wkend rates; lower rates rest of yr. Crib free. TV; cable (premium), VCR avail (movies). Indoor pool; whirlpool. Complimentary continental bkfst. Bar 5 pm-1 am. Ck-out noon. Meeting rms. Business servs avail. In-rm modem link. Exercise equipt. Rec rm. Some refrigerators. Cr cds: A, C, D, DS, MC, V.

★★ **LA QUINTA INN.** *3330 N 104th Ave (68134). 402/493-1900; fax 402/ 496-0750; res 800/687-6667. www. laquinta.com.* 130 rms, 2 story. S $56; D $54-$61; each addl $5; suites $68-$80; under 18 free. Crib free. Pet accepted, some restrictions. TV; cable (premium). Heated pool. Continental bkfst in lobby. Restaurant adj open 24 hrs. Ck-out noon. Coin lndry. Meeting rms. In-rm modem link. Sundries. Cr cds: A, C, D, DS, MC, V.

★ **RAMADA INN CENTRAL.** *7007 Grover St (68106). 402/397-7030; fax 402/397-8449; res 800/228-5299. www.ramada.com.* 215 rms, 9 story. S, D $89-$94; each addl $10; suites $135-$145; under 18 free; wkend rates. Crib free. Pet accepted. TV; cable (premium). Indoor pool; whirlpool. Sauna. Playground. Restaurant 6 am-10 pm; Sat, Sun from 7 am. Bar 5 pm-1 am. Ck-out noon. Meeting rms. Business servs avail. In-rm modem link. Gift shop. Free airport transportation. Cr cds: A, D, DS, MC, V.

★ **SLEEP INN.** *2525 Abbott Dr (68110). 402/342-2525; fax 402/342-9214; toll-free 800/753-3746. www. sleepinn.com.* 93 rms, shower only, 2 story, 12 suites. S $49-$51; D $55-$62; each addl $6; suites $60; under 18 free. Crib free. TV; cable. Complimentary continental bkfst. Ck-out noon. In-rm modem link. Free airport transportation. Cr cds: A, C, D, DS, ER, JCB, MC, V.

★ **SUPER 8 MOTEL.** *10829 M St (68137). 402/339-2250; fax 402/339-6922; res 800/800-8000. www.super8. com.* 118 rms, 3 story. No elvtr. S $40; D $49; each addl $3; under 13 free. Crib $2. TV; cable (premium). Complimentary continental bkfst. Ck-out 11 am. Meeting rm. Sundries. Cr cds: A, MC, V.

★ **SUPER 8 MOTEL.** *303 S Fort Crook Rd, Bellevue (68005). 402/291-1518; fax 402/292-1726; toll-free 800/800-8000. www.super8.com.* 40 rms, 2 story. S $33-$39; D $42-$52; each addl $4. Crib $6. TV; cable (premium). Complimentary continental bkfst. Restaurant adj open 24 hrs. Ck-out 11 am. Business servs avail. In-rm modem link. Cr cds: A, C, D, DS, ER, JCB, MC, V.

Hotels

★★ **DOUBLETREE DOWNTOWN.** *1616 Dodge St (68102). 402/346-7600; fax 402/346-5722; res 800/222-8733. www.doubletreehotels.com.* 413 rms, 19 story. S, D $139; each addl $15; suites $150-$450; under 18 free; wkend rates. Crib free. TV; cable (premium). Indoor pool; whirlpool. Coffee in rms. Restaurant 6 am-midnight. Bar 11-1 am; entertainment Mon-Sat. Ck-out noon. Meeting rms. Business center. In-rm modem link. Gift shop. Barber, beauty shop. Free airport transportation. Exercise equipt; sauna, steam rm. Some refrigerators. Cr cds: A, C, D, DS, ER, JCB, MC, V.

★★★ **MARRIOTT OMAHA.** *10220 Regency Cir (68114). 402/399-9000; fax 402/399-0223; toll-free 800/228-9290. www.marriott.com.* 301 rms, 4-6 story. S, D $69-$169; suites $275; under 18 free. Crib free. Pet accepted, some restrictions. TV; cable, VCR avail. Indoor/outdoor pool; whirlpool, poolside serv, lifeguard. Restaurants 6:30 am-11 pm. Bar 4 pm-1 am. Ck-out noon. Convention facilities. Business servs avail. In-rm modem link. Shopping arcade. Exercise equipt; sauna, steam rm. Private patios, balconies. Luxury level. Cr cds: A, C, D, DS, JCB, MC, V.

★★★ **SHERATON OMAHA.** *1615 Howard St (68102). 402/342-2222. www.sheraton.com.* 145 rms, 6 story. S, D $150-$225; each addl $20; under 17 free. Crib free. TV; cable (premium), VCR avail. Complimentary coffee, newspaper in rms. Restaurant 6 am-10 pm. Ck-out noon. Meeting rms. Business center. Gift shop. Exercise rm. Some refrigerators, minibars. Cr cds: A, C, D, DS, ER, JCB, MC, V.

All Suite

★★ **DOUBLETREE GUEST SUITES.** *7270 Cedar St (68124). 402/397-5141; fax 402/397-1624; res 800/222-8733. www.doubletreehotels.com.* 189 kit. suites, 6 story. S $109; D $119; each addl $10; under 16 free; wkend rates. Crib free. TV; cable (premium), VCR avail (movies). Indoor pool; whirlpool. Complimentary bkfst. Restaurant 7 am-2 pm, 5-10

Western Heritage Museum

pm; Fri, Sat to 11 pm. Coin lndry. Meeting rms. Business servs avail. In-rm modem link. Gift shop. Free airport transportation. Exercise equipt; sauna. Indoor tropical courtyard. Cr cds: A, C, D, DS, ER, JCB, MC, V.

Extended Stay

★★ RESIDENCE INN BY MAR-RIOTT. 6990 Dodge St (68132). 402/553-8898; fax 402/553-8898; toll-free 800/331-3131. www.residenceinn. com. 80 kit. suites. S, D $109-$114. Crib free. Pet accepted, some restrictions; $25. TV; cable (premium), VCR avail (movies). Heated pool; whirlpool. Complimentary continental bkfst. Ck-out noon. Business servs avail. In-rm modem link. Tennis. Health club privileges. Fireplaces. Balconies. Cr cds: A, C, D, DS, JCB, MC, V.

Restaurants

★ BOHEMIAN CAFE.
1406 S 13th St (68108). 402/342-9838. Hrs: 11 am-9 pm; Fri, Sat to 10 pm. Closed Dec 25. Res accepted. Czechoslovakian, American menu. Lunch $4.95, dinner $6.99-$11.95. Specialties: jagerschnitzel, hasenpfeffer, roast pork. European atmosphere; Czechoslovakian prints. Cr cds: D, MC, V.

★★ BUSTY LE DOUX'S.
1014 Howard St (68102). 402/346-5100. Hrs: 11:30 am-10 pm; Fri, Sat to 11 pm. Closed Sun; hols. Cajun menu. Bar. Lunch $3.50-$7.25, dinner $7.25-$15.95. Specializes in bayou boiled crawfish, blackened fish, voodoo stew. Entertainment Fri, Sat eves in summer. Parking. Outdoor dining. Collection of Salvador Dali paintings. Cr cds: A, DS, MC, V.

★★★ CAFE DE PARIS. 1228 S 6th St (68108). 402/344-0227. Hrs: 6-10:30 pm. Closed Sun; hols. Res required. French menu. Bar. Wine cellar. A la carte entrees: dinner $16-$36. Specializes in fresh fish, veal. Own breads. Parking. Intimate atmosphere. Chef-owned. Jacket. Cr cds: A.

★ CHU'S CHOP SUEY & STEAK-HOUSE. 6455 Center St (68106). 402/553-6454. Hrs: 11 am-9 pm; Fri, Sat to 10 pm; Sun, hols from noon. Closed Tues; Jan 1, Thanksgiving, Dec 24, 25. Res accepted. Chinese menu. Bar. Lunch $4.25-$4.95, dinner $5.25-$14.75. Children's menu. Specialties: chicken subgum, sweet and sour pork. Parking. Family-owned. Cr cds: A, D, MC, V.

★★★ FRENCH CAFE. 1017 Howard St (68102). 402/341-3547. www.french

cafe.com. Hrs: 11 am-2 pm, 5:30-10 pm, Fri, Sat to 11 pm; Sun brunch 10:30 am-2 pm. Res accepted. French, American menu. Bar. Wine list. Lunch $6.95-$10.50, dinner $15.95-$27.95. Cr cds: A, D, DS, MC, V.
D ⏐

★ **GARDEN CAFE.** *1212 Harney St (68102). 402/422-1574.* Hrs: 6 am-10 pm. Closed Dec 25. Wine, beer. Bkfst $2.99-$5.99, lunch $3.99-$7.99, dinner $5.99-$14.99. Children's menu. Own desserts. Parking. Café-style dining. Totally nonsmoking. Cr cds: A, D, DS, MC, V.
D SC

★★ **GORAT'S STEAK HOUSE.** *4917 Center St (68106). 402/551-3733.* Hrs: 11 am-2 pm, 5-10:30 pm; Mon 5-10 pm; Fri, Sat to midnight. Closed Sun; hols. Res accepted; required Fri, Sat. Bar. Lunch $3.50-$6.25, dinner $6.25-$29. Children's menu. Specializes in steak, seafood, Italian dishes. Piano bar; entertainment Fri, Sat. Parking. Fireplace. Cr cds: A, MC, V.
D ⏐

★ **GRANDMOTHER'S.** *8989 W Dodge St (68114). 402/391-8889.* Hrs: 11 am-11 pm; Fri, Sat to midnight; Sun 10 am-11 pm. Closed Thanksgiving, Dec 25. Bar. Lunch, dinner $4.25-$11.99. Buffet (Sun): $8.49. Children's menu. Specialties: taco salad, quiche. Parking. Rustic, early-American decor. Cr cds: A, DS, MC, V.
D SC ⏐

★★★ **IMPERIAL PALACE.** *11201 Davenport St (68154). 402/330-3888.* Hrs: 11:30 am-2:30 pm, 5-9:30 pm; Fri to 10:30 pm; Sat 5-10:30 pm; Sun noon-9 pm. Closed hols. Chinese menu. Bar. Wine list. A la carte entrees: lunch $4.35-$5.95, dinner $6.50-$12.95. Specializes in Peking duck, Szechwan dishes, family dinners. Parking. Chinese artwork and decor. Cr cds: A, MC, V.
D ⏐

★★ **INDIAN OVEN.** *1010 Howard St (68102). 402/342-4856.* Hrs: 11:30 am-2 pm, 5:30-10 pm; Fri, Sat to 11 pm; Sun 5:30-10 pm. Closed Mon; Thanksgiving, Dec 25. Res accepted; required Fri, Sat. Northern Indian menu. Bar. A la carte entrees: lunch $5.50-$6.75, dinner $12-$15. Special-

izes in chicken, lamb, fish. Parking. Outdoor dining. East Indian decor. Cr cds: A, D, DS, MC, V.
D

★ **JOHNNY'S CAFE.** *4702 S 27th St (68107). 402/731-4774. www.johnnys cafe.com.* Hrs: 11 am-2 pm, 5-10 pm; Fri, Sat to 10:30 pm. Closed Sun; hols. Res accepted; required hols. Bar. Lunch $5-$8.65, dinner $9-$20. Children's menu. Specializes in steak, prime rib, fresh seafood. Parking. Western decor. Family-owned. Cr cds: A, D, DS, MC, V.
D ⏐

★★★ **LA STRADA 72.** *3125 S 72nd St (68124). 402/397-8389. www. lastrada72.com.* Hrs: 11 am-2 pm, 5:30-10 pm; Fri, Sat 5:30-11 pm. Closed Sun; hols. Res accepted. Italian menu. Bar to midnight. Wine list. Lunch $6-$8, dinner $10-$30. Specializes in veal, pasta, fresh seafood. Own pastries. Parking. Outdoor dining. European bistro decor. Cr cds: A, D, DS, MC, V.
D ⏐

★★★ **SIGNATURE'S.** *1616 Dodge St (68102). 402/346-7600.* Hrs: 11 am-2 pm, 5-10 pm; Fri, Sat 5-11 pm; Sun 9:30 am-2 pm, 5-9 pm; Sun brunch to 2 pm. Res accepted. Bar. Lunch $6.95, dinner $16-$24. Sun brunch $12.95. Specializes in steak, fresh seafood. Own pastries. Parking. Panoramic view of city from 19th floor. Cr cds: A, D, DS, MC, V.
D SC

★ **TRINI'S.** *1020 Howard St (68102). 402/346-8400.* Hrs: 11:30 am-10 pm; Fri, Sat to 11 pm. Closed Sun; hols. Mexican menu. Bar. Lunch $3.95-$6.95, dinner $4.95-$7.95. Specializes in seafood, enchiladas, fajitas. Parking. Cr cds: A, DS, MC, V.
D ⏐

★★★ **V. MERTZ.** *1022 Howard St (68102). 402/345-8980. www.vmertz. com.* Hrs: 11:30 am-2 pm, 6-10 pm; Fri, Sat to 11 pm. Res accepted. Continental menu. Bar. Lunch $6.95-$9.50, dinner $21.95-$29.95. Specializes in fresh fish, steak. Parking. Cr cds: A, D, DS, MC, V.
D

O'Neill (B-5)

Settled 1874 **Pop** 3,852 **Elev** 2,000 ft
Area code 402 **Zip** 68763
Information Chamber of Commerce,
315 E Douglas; 402/336-2355
Web www.hearte.com/chamber

General John J. O'Neill founded this
Irish colony along the Elkhorn River
in the north central portion of the
state. His colorful career included
fighting as a captain of black troops
for the North in the Civil War and
attacking Canada in the armed Fen-
ian invasion of Irish patriots. O'Neill
is known as the Irish capital of
Nebraska and holds an annual St.
Patrick's Day celebration.

What to See and Do

**Atkinson Lake State Recreation
Area.** Approx 53 acres on the
Elkhorn River. Fishing, boating (non-
power or electric); picnicking, camp-
ing. Standard hrs, fees. 18 mi W on
US 20, near Atkinson.

Pibel Lake State Recreation Area.
Approx 40 acres with a 24-acre lake.
Fishing, boating (nonpower or elec-
tric); picnicking, camping. Standard
hrs, fees. 51 mi S on US 281, near
Bartlett.

Motels/Motor Lodges

★ **ELMS BEST VALUE INN.** *414 E
US 20 (68763). 402/336-3800; fax
402/336-1419; toll-free 800/315-2378.
www.bestvalueinn.com.* 21 rms. S $25;
D $30-$38; each addl $3. Crib $2. Pet
accepted. TV; cable (premium). Playground. Restaurant opp 7 am-11 pm.
Ck-out 11 am. Cr cds: A, DS, MC, V.

★ **GOLDEN HOTEL.** *406 E Douglas
St (68763). 402/336-4436; fax 402/
336-3549; toll-free 800/658-3148.
www.historicgoldenhotel.com.* 27 rms, 3
story. S $27; D $32; each addl $5.
Crib free. Pet accepted, some restrictions. TV; cable (premium), VCR
(movies). Complimentary continental
bkfst. Restaurant adj 6 am-10 pm. Ck-
out 11 am. Valet serv. Restored hotel
built 1913. Cr cds: A, DS, MC, V.

Scottsbluff

(C-1) *See also Gering*

Pop 13,711 **Elev** 3,885 ft
Area code 308 **Zip** 69361
Information Scottsbluff-Gering
United Chamber of Commerce, 1517
Broadway; 308/632-2133 or 800/788-
9475
Web www.scottsbluff.net/chamber

Scottsbluff is the trading center for a
large area of western Nebraska and
eastern Wyoming.

What to See and Do

**Agate Fossil Beds National Monu-
ment.** An approx 2,700-acre area;
two self-guided nature trails; visitor
center with exhibits of the fossil
story of mammals that roamed the
area 19-21 million yrs ago; also
exhibits of Plains Native Americans.
Visitor center (daily; closed Dec 25).
Park (all yr). 9 mi NW on US 26 to
Mitchell, then 34 mi N on NE 29.
Phone 308/668-2210. ¢¢

**Lake Minatare State Recreation
Area.** Approx 800 acres on 2,158-
acre lake. Swimming; fishing; boating
(ramps). Hiking. Picnicking, concession. Camping (dump station). (Mid-
Jan-Sept) 10 mi E on US 26, then 10
mi N on Stonegate Rd. Phone
308/783-2911.

**Mexican American Historical
Museum.** Aztec and Mayan artifacts;
ancient cooking tools; photo, clothing, art, dolls display, gift shop. (May-
Sept, daily; winter by appt only;
closed hols) Broadway and 27th St.
Phone 308/635-1044. **Donation**

Rebecca Winters Grave. A pioneer
on the Mormon Trail in 1852, Winters died of cholera and was buried
near Scottsbluff. Her grave, marked
with a wagon wheel, is one of the
most accessible along the old emigrant routes. (Daily) E on S Beltline
Rd. Phone 308/632-2133. **FREE**

Riverside Zoo. More than 97 species
of both native and exotic animals in
a lush park setting. Walk-through
aviary, white tiger, moose woods.
(Daily, weather permitting). 1600 S
Beltline West, W of NE 71. Phone
308/630-6236. ¢¢

Scotts Bluff National Monument.
(see). 3 mi S on NE 71 to Gering,
then 3 mi W on NE 92.

West Nebraska Arts Center. Changing gallery shows in all media
throughout the yr showcasing the
finest artists in the region. (Daily;
Sat, Sun afternoon) 106 E 18th St.
Phone 308/632-2226. **Donation**

**Wildcat Hills State Recreation Area
Reserve and Nature Center.** Approx
650 acres in unusual, rugged terrain
of the high country of western
Nebraska. Buffalo and elk in natural
scenic habitat. Shelter houses. Hiking, picnicking, camping. 13 mi S on
NE 71. Phone 308/436-2383.

Motels/Motor Lodges

★ **CANDLELIGHT INN.** *1822 E 20th
Pl (69361). 308/635-3751; fax 308/
635-1105; toll-free 800/424-2305.* 60
rms, 2 story. S $50-$59; D $55-$64;
each addl $6. Crib $5. TV; cable (premium). Heated pool. Complimentary
continental bkfst. Restaurant adj 6-2
am. Bar 4 pm-midnight. Ck-out 11
am. Airport transportation. Exercise
equipt. Some refrigerators, microwaves. Cr cds: A, C, D, DS, ER, JCB,
MC, V.

[D] [≈] [禾] [✈] [☼] [SC]

★ **COMFORT INN.** *2018 Delta Dr
(69361). 308/632-7510; fax 308/632-
8495; res 800/228-5150. www.
comfortinn.com.* 46 rms, 2 story, 4
suites. S $48; D $58; each addl $5;
suites $75; under 18 free. Crib free.
TV; cable (premium). Indoor pool;
whirlpool. Complimentary continental bkfst. Ck-out 11 am. Coin lndry.
Meeting rms. Refrigerator, microwave
in suites. Cr cds: A, C, D, DS, ER,
JCB, MC, V.

[D] [≈] [禾] [≥] [☼]

Scotts Bluff National Monument

See also Gering, Scottsbluff

(3 mi W of Gering on NE 92)

This 800-foot bluff in western
Nebraska was a landmark to pioneers
who traveled the California/Oregon
Trail by wagon trains. Historians
often speak of this natural promontory in the North Platte Valley, which
was originally named me-a-pa-te,
"hill that is hard to go around," by
the Plains Native Americans. Many
people, including fur traders, Mormons, and gold seekers, came this
way. Westward-bound pioneers, Pony
Express riders, and the first transcontinental telegraph all passed through
Mitchell Pass (within Monument
boundaries) to skirt this pine-studded
bluff. The Oregon Trail Museum at
the monument's visitor center (daily;
closed Dec 25) depicts the story of
westward migration along the trail;
artwork by the famous pioneer artist
and photographer William Henry
Jackson is on permanent display.
Check with the Oregon Trail Museum
for a schedule of special events. A
paved road and hiking trail provide
access to the summit for a view of the
North Platte Valley and other landmarks such as Chimney Rock (see).
The summit road is open to traffic
daily. Visitors also may walk along the
old Oregon Trail, remnants of which
still exist within the park. Covering
five square miles, Scotts Bluff became
a national monument in 1919.
(Daily) For further information contact PO Box 27, Gering 69341-0027;
308/436-4340. Per vehicle ¢¢

Sidney (D-2)

Founded 1867 **Pop** 5,959 **Elev** 4,085
ft **Area code** 308 **Zip** 69162
Information Cheyenne County Visitor's Committee, 740 Illinois St;
800/421-4769

In 1867, Sidney was established as a
division point on the Union Pacific
Railroad. Fort Sidney was established
shortly thereafter, providing military
protection for railroad workers and
immigrants. Many relics of the Fort
Sidney era remain and have been
restored. Sidney, the seat of Cheyenne
County, is also a peaceful farm, trading, and industrial center.

What to See and Do

Cabela's. Corporate headquarters for
one of world's largest outdoor gear

outfitters. The 73,000-sq-ft building displays over 60,000 products; also over 500 wildlife mounts. Other attractions in showrm are an 8,000-gallon aquarium; art gallery; gun library; restaurant; and "Royal Challenge," a larger-than-life bronze sculpture of two battling elk. (Daily) I-80, exit 59. Phone 308/254-5505.

Fort Sidney Post Commander's Home. (1871) One of the original buildings of old Fort Sidney; used in the 19th century to protect railroad workers during the Native American wars; authentically restored. (Memorial Day-Labor Day, daily, afternoons) 1108 6th Ave. Phone 308/254-2150. **FREE** Other restored buildings in the Fort Sidney complex incl

> **Double Set Officer's Quarters Museum.** Built in 1884 as quarters for married officers. (Daily, afternoons) 6th and Jackson. Phone 308/254-2150. **FREE**
>
> **Powder House.** Can be viewed only from the outside. 1033 Fifth Ave.

Special Events

County Fair and NSRA Rodeo. Late July-early Aug.

Oktoberfest. First wkend Oct.

Motels/Motor Lodges

★ **COMFORT INN.** 730 E Jennifer Ln (69162). 308/254-5011; fax 308/254-5122; res 800/228-5150. www.comfort inn.com. 55 rms, 2 story. June-Oct: S $55 D $65; each addl $5; under 18 free; lower rates rest of yr. Crib free. TV; cable (premium). Complimentary continental bkfst. Restaurant nearby. Ck-out 11 am. Coin lndry. Whirlpool. Cr cds: A, MC, V.
[D] [≈] [≥] [⚑]

★ **DAYS INN.** 3042 Silverberg Dr (69162). 308/254-2121; res 800/329-7466. www.daysinn.com. 47 rms, 2 story. June-Sept: S $52-$65; D $60-$70; each addl $5; suites $73-$83; under 12 free; lower rates rest of yr. Crib free. TV; cable (premium). Indoor pool; whirlpool. Complimentary continental bkfst, coffee in rms. Restaurant adj 6:30 am-10 pm. Ck-out 11 am. Coin lndry. Business servs

avail. Valet serv. Sundries. Refrigerator in suites. Cr cds: A, DS, MC, V.
[D] [≈] [≥] [⚑]

South Sioux City

Also see Sioux City, IA

Pop 9,677 **Elev** 1,096 ft
Area code 402 **Zip** 68776
Information Visitors Bureau, 2700 Dakota Ave; 402/494-1307 or 800/793-6327
Web www.sscdc.net

What to See and Do

Ponca State Park. Approx 850 acres. Panoramic views of the Missouri River valley. Swimming pool (fee), fishing, boating (ramps); hiking, horseback riding, x-country skiing. Picnicking. Camping (14-day max, standard fees; dump station, trailer pads), cabins (Mid-Apr-mid-Nov), primitive camping during off-season. 18 mi NW off NE 12, on Missouri River. Phone 402/755-2284.

Special Events

Waterfest Weekend. On the bank of the Missouri River. Outdoor concert, Mighty MO 5k run/walk, waterskiing expo, athletic tournaments. Phone 800/793-6327. Third wkend June.

Horse racing. Atokad Park, 2½ mi SW. Thoroughbred racing; pari-mutuel betting. For information phone 402/494-3611. Early Sept-late Oct.

Motels/Motor Lodges

★ **ECONO LODGE.** 4402 Dakota Ave (68776). 402/494-4114; fax 402/494-4114; toll-free 800/553-2666. www.econolodge.com. 60 rms, 2 story. S $39-$54; D $51-$66; each addl $5; under 12 free. Crib free. TV; cable (premium). Complimentary full bkfst. Restaurant nearby. Ck-out 11 am. Coin lndry. Business servs avail. Cr cds: A, C, D, DS, JCB, MC, V.
[D] [🛏] [≥] [⚑] [SC]

★★★ **MARINA INN CONFERENCE CENTER.** 4th and B sts (68776). 402/

494-4000; fax 402/494-2550; toll-free 800/798-7980. 182 rms, 5 story. S $77-$87; D $87-$97; each addl $10; under 18 free. Crib free. Pet accepted. TV; cable, VCR avail. Indoor pool; whirlpool. Restaurant 6:30 am-10 pm. Bars noon-1 am. Ck-out 11 am. Meeting rms. Free airport transportation. Some private patios. On Missouri River. Cr cds: A, C, D, DS, MC, V.

★ **PARK PLAZA MOTEL.** *1201 1st Ave (68776). 402/494-2021; fax 402/494-5998; toll-free 800/341-8000.* 52 rms. S $35-$45; D $43-$53; each addl $3. Crib $5. TV; cable. Pool. Restaurant 6 am-9 pm. Ck-out 11 am. Cr cds: A, C, D, DS, MC, V.

★ **TRAVELODGE.** *400 Dakota Ave (68776). 402/494-3046; fax 402/494-8299; res 888/515-6375. www. travelodge.com.* 61 rms, 2 story. S $40; D $48-$60; each addl $4. Pet accepted. TV; cable (premium). Complimentary continental bkfst. Restaurant nearby. Ck-out 11 am. Business servs avail. Airport transportation. Cr cds: A, D, DS, MC, V.

Thedford (C-4)

Pop 243 **Elev** 2,848 ft **Area code** 308 **Zip** 69106

What to See and Do

Nebraska National Forest. Site of the Bessey Nursery (1902), oldest Forest Service tree nursery in the US. Swimming pool (fee); hiking, tennis, picnicking. Camping (some fees). 15 mi E on NE 2. Bessey Ranger District office is 2 mi W of Halsey. Phone 308/533-2257.

Valentine

(B-4) *Also see Mission, SD*

Settled 1882 **Pop** 2,826 **Elev** 2,579 ft **Area code** 402 **Zip** 69201

Valentine, the seat of Cherry County, depends on cattle raising for its economy.

What to See and Do

Cherry County Historical Museum. Items and exhibits related to the history of Cherry County; 1882 log cabin; newspapers dating back to 1883; genealogy library. (May-Sept, daily) S Main St and US 20. Phone 402/376-2015. **Donation**

Fishing. Bass, crappie, perch, northern pike in numerous lakes S of town, incl

Big Alkali Lake Wildlife Area. Swimming, boating; hunting, picnicking, camping. 17 mi S on US 83, then 3 mi W on NE 16B.

Valentine National Wildlife Refuge. Eight fishing lakes, waterfowl, upland game bird and deer hunting. Nature study, bird-watching. (Daily, daylight hrs) 17 mi S on US 83, then 13 mi W on NE 16B. Phone 402/376-3789. **FREE**

Fort Niobrara National Wildlife Refuge. Visitor center with exhibits. Nature study, canoeing, wildlife observation, picnicking. Also here are Fort Falls Nature Trail, Fort Niobrara Wilderness Area, a prairie dog town, and herds of buffalo, Texas longhorns, and elk. (Memorial Day-Labor Day, daily; rest of yr, Mon-Fri) 5 mi E on NE 12. Phone 402/376-3789. **FREE**

Samuel R. McKelvie National Forest. Hunting, hiking, picnicking, camping. Part of the Bessey Ranger District of the Nebraska National Forest (see CHADRON and THEDFORD). 30 mi W on US 20, then 19 mi S on NE 97. For information contact PO Box 38, Halsey 69142. Phone 308/533-2257. In the forest on Merritt Reservoir is

Merritt Reservoir State Recreation Area. Approx 6,000 acres with a 2,906-acre reservoir in sandhill area. Swimming, fishing, boating (ramps); picnicking, concession, camping (dump station). Wildlife refuges nearby. Standard hrs, fees. 25 mi SW on NE 97.

Canoeing the Niobrara River, near Valentine

Sawyer's Sandhills Museum. Pioneer and Native American artifacts, antique autos. (Memorial Day-Labor Day, daily; rest of yr, by appt) On US 20, 4 blks W of US 83. Phone 402/376-3293. ¢

Special Events

Cherry County Fair. Cherry County Fairgrounds. Midway, rodeo, agricultural and crafts exhibits; races; concessions. Aug.

Old West Days & Poetry Gathering. Music and fun celebrating Old West heritage. Sept.

Motels/Motor Lodges

★ **DUNES MOTEL.** *3131 E Hwy 20 (69201). 402/376-3131; fax 402/376-5998; toll-free 800/357-3131.* 24 rms. May-mid-Sept: S $30; D $36-$38; each addl $3; lower rates rest of yr. Crib $2. TV; cable. Restaurant nearby. Ck-out 11 am. Cr cds: A, DS, MC, V.

★ **MOTEL RAINE.** *W US 20 (69201). 402/376-2030; toll-free 800/999-3066.* 34 rms. May-Oct: S $42; D $46-$48; each addl $2; lower rates rest of yr. Crib $2. Pet accepted. TV; cable. Coffee in rms. Restaurant nearby. Ck-out 11 am. Free airport transportation. Cr cds: A, MC, V.

★ **TRADE WINDS LODGE.** *US 20 and US 83 (69201). 402/376-1600; fax 402/376-3651; res 800/341-8000.* 32 rms. May-Sept: S $32-$50; D $40-$61; each addl $2; lower rates rest of yr. Crib free. Pet accepted. TV; cable. Heated pool. Complimentary coffee. Ck-out 11 am. Free airport transportation. Cr cds: A, D, DS, MC, V.

Wayne

(B-7) See also Norfolk

Founded 1881 **Pop** 5,142 **Elev** 1,500 ft **Area code** 402 **Zip** 68787

Information Wayne Area Chamber of Commerce, 108 W 3rd St; 402/375-2240

Laid out when the railroad connecting St. Paul to Sioux City was being built, the town was named after General "Mad Anthony" Wayne.

What to See and Do

Wayne State College. (1910) 4,000 students. Liberal arts, business, and teacher education. Tours. 200 E 10th. Phone 402/375-7000. On campus is

Fred G. Dale Planetarium. Features dome-shaped screen, dozens of auxiliary and special effects projectors, and unique sound system. (Oct-Apr; by appt; closed hols) Phone 402/375-7329. **FREE**

Special Events

Chicken Show. Music contests, parade, omelet feed, chicken dinner feed, egg games, craft show, antique show and sale. Second Sat July.

Wayne County Fair. ½ mi W on NE 35. 4-H exhibits, agricultural displays, carnival, nightly entertainment, free barbecue. Aug.

Motel/Motor Lodge

★ **THE K-D INN MOTEL.** *311 E 7th St (68787). 402/375-1770; fax 402/256-3442.* 21 rms, 2 story. S $34; D $42. Crib $2. Pet accepted. TV; cable (premium). Continental bkfst. Restaurant nearby. Ck-out 11 am. Cr cds: A, MC, V.

West Point (C-7)

Founded 1857 **Pop** 3,250 **Elev** 1,335 ft **Area code** 402 **Zip** 68788

Named by early settlers who considered it the western extremity of settlement, West Point was originally a mill town.

What to See and Do

John G. Neihardt Center. Contains memorabilia of Nebraska's late poet laureate; restored one-rm study; Sioux Prayer Garden symbolizes Sioux Hoop of the World. (Daily; closed Jan 1, Thanksgiving, Dec 25) 11 mi N on NE 9, then 8 mi E on NE 51, at Elm and Washington sts in Bancroft. Phone 402/648-3388. **FREE**

York

(D-6) *See also Grand Island, Lincoln*

Founded 1869 **Pop** 7,884 **Elev** 1,609 ft **Area code** 402 **Zip** 68467

What to See and Do

Anna Bemis Palmer Museum. Items and displays relating to the history of the city, York County, and the state of Nebraska. (Daily; closed hols) 211 E 7th St. Phone 402/363-2630. **FREE**

Motels/Motor Lodges

★★ **BEST WESTERN PALMER INN.** *2426 S Lincoln Ave (68467). 402/362-5585; fax 402/362-6053; res 800/780-7234. www.bestwestern.com.* 41 rms. S $36-$40; D $47-$50; each addl $4; under 12 free. Crib $3. TV; cable (premium). Heated pool. Playground. Restaurant nearby. Ck-out 11 am. Coin lndry. Cr cds: A, C, D, DS, MC, V.

★ **DAYS INN.** *3710 S Lincoln Ave (68467). 402/362-6355; fax 402/362-2827; res 800/329-7466. www.daysinn.com.* 39 rms, 2 story. Apr-Sept: S $42-$48; D $55; lower rates rest of yr. Crib free. TV; cable (premium). Indoor pool; whirlpool. Complimentary continental bkfst. Restaurant adj 6 am-11 pm. Ck-out 11 am. Cr cds: A, D, DS, MC, V.

★★ **HOLIDAY INN.** *4619 S Lincoln Ave (68467). 402/362-6661; fax 402/362-3727; toll-free 800/934-5495. www.holiday-inn.com.* 120 rms, 2 story. S $34; D $39; each addl $5; under 18 free. Crib free. TV; cable (premium). Pool. Complimentary bkfst. Restaurant 6 am-11 pm; Fri, Sat to 2 am. Rm serv avail. Bar 4 pm-1 am. Ck-out 11 am. Meeting rms. Cr cds: A, C, D, DS, ER, JCB, MC, V.

★ **WAYFARER II MOTEL.** *905 Road B, Henderson (68371). 402/723-5856; fax 402/723-5856; toll-free 800/543-0577.* 34 rms. June-mid-Sept: S $28;

D $34; each addl $4; lower rates rest of yr. Crib $3. TV. Heated pool. Playground. Restaurant open 24 hrs. Ck-out 11 am. Coin lndry. Cr cds: A, C, D, MC, V.

⊠ ⊠ 🔥 SC

★ **YORKSHIRE MOTEL.** *3402 S Lincoln Ave (68467). 402/362-6633; fax 402/362-5197; toll-free 888/362-6633.* 29 rms, 3 story. S $45; D $54; each addl $4; suites $45-$50. Crib $4. TV; cable (premium). Playground. Coffee in lobby. Restaurant adj 6 am-11 pm. Ck-out 11 am. Cr cds: A, C, D, DS, MC, V.

⊠ 🔥

Restaurant

★★ **CHANCES R.** *124 W 5th (68467). 402/362-7755.* Hrs: 6-1 am; Sun 8 am-midnight; Sun brunch 10 am-2 pm. Closed Dec 24 and Jan 1 eves, Dec 25. Res accepted. Bar. Bkfst $1.75-$5.95, lunch $4.75-$5.75, dinner $6.25-$15.45. Sun brunch $10.45. Children's menu. Specialties: pan-fried chicken, charcoal steak, prime rib. Salad bar. Turn-of-the-century decor; many antiques. Family-owned. Cr cds: A, D, MC, V.

D

NORTH DAKOTA

In Bismarck stands a heroic statuary group, *Pioneer Family,* by Avard Fairbanks; behind it, gleaming white against the sky, towers the famous skyscraper capitol. One symbolizes the North Dakota of wagon trains and General Custer. The other symbolizes the North Dakota that has emerged in recent years—a land where a thousand oil wells have sprouted, dams have harnessed erratic rivers, vast lignite resources have been developed, and industry is absorbing surplus farm labor created by mechanization.

At various times Spain, France, and England claimed what is now North Dakota as part of their empires. French Canadian fur trappers were the first Europeans to explore the land. With the Louisiana Purchase, Lewis and Clark crossed Dakota, establishing Fort Mandan. The earliest permanent European settlement was at Pembina with the establishment of Alexander Henry's trading post in 1801. Settlers from the Earl of Selkirk's colony in Manitoba arrived in 1812. The first military post at Fort Abercrombie served as a gateway into the area for settlers. The Dakota Territory was organized March 2, 1861, but major settlement of what later became North Dakota followed after the entry of the Northern Pacific Railroad in the early 1870s.

Population: 638,800
Area: 69,299 square miles
Elevation: 750-3,506 feet
Peak: White Butte (Slope County)
Entered Union: November 2, 1889 (39th state, same day as South Dakota)
Capital: Bismarck
Motto: Liberty and union, now and forever, one and inseparable
Nickname: Flickertail State, Sioux State, Peace Garden State
Flower: Wild Prairie Rose
Bird: Western Meadowlark
Tree: American Elm
Fair: Late July, 2002 in Minot
Time Zone: Central and Mountain
Website: www.ndtourism.com

This is a fascinating land of prairies, rich river valleys, small cities, huge ranches, and vast stretches of wheat. Bordering Canada for 320 miles to the north, it shares straight-line borders with Montana to the west and South Dakota to the south. The Red River of the North forms its eastern boundary with Minnesota. The Garrison Dam (see) has changed much of the internal geography of the state's western areas, converting the Missouri River, known as "Big Muddy," into a broad waterway with splendid recreation areas bordering the reservoir, Lake Sakajawea. In addition, the Oahe Dam in South Dakota impounds Lake Oahe, which stretches north almost to Bismarck. To the southwest stretch the Badlands in all their natural grandeur, amid the open range about which Theodore Roosevelt wrote so eloquently in his *Ranch Life and the Hunting Trail.*

North Dakota's wealth is still in its soil—agriculture, crude oil, and lignite (a brown variety of very soft coal). It is estimated that one-third of the state is under oil and gas lease, and it ranks high in the nation for the production of oil; the largest deposits of lignite coal in the world are here. The same land through which Custer's men rode with range grass growing up to their stirrups now makes North Dakota the nation's number one cash grain state. North Dakota leads the nation in the production of barley, durum, spring wheat, pinto beans, oats, and flaxseed. Nearly 2,000,000 head of cattle and more than 165,000 sheep are produced on North Dakota grass.

While the rural areas comprise the economic backbone of North Dakota, attractions attributed to a "big city" can be found. In July of 1981 blackjack became a legal form of gambling, causing a number of casinos to open statewide. High-stakes games and slot machines can be found in casinos operated by Native Americans on four reservations. Pari-mutuel horse racing was legalized in 1987. All gambling profits, above expenses, go to nonprofit and charitable organizations.

This is the state in which to trace 19th-century frontier history, to explore the International Peace Garden (see BOTTINEAU), to stand at the center of the continent, to watch Native American dances and outdoor dramas, to fish in the 180-mile-long Lake Sakajawea, or just to watch the ten million migratory waterfowl that soar across the sky each spring and fall.

When to Go/Climate

North Dakota winters are long and merciless, with bitter cold temperatures and insistent winds. Spring is cool and rainy; summers are hot and sunny. Summer hailstorms and thunderstorms are not uncommon in the Badlands.

AVERAGE HIGH/LOW TEMPERATURES (°F)

BISMARCK

Jan 20/-2	**May** 68/42	**Sept** 71/43
Feb 26/5	**June** 77/56	**Oct** 59/33
Mar 39/18	**July** 84/56	**Nov** 39/18
Apr 55/31	**Aug** 83/54	**Dec** 25/3

FARGO

Jan 15/-4	**May** 69/44	**Sept** 69/46
Feb 21/3	**June** 77/59	**Oct** 57/35
Mar 35/17	**July** 83/59	**Nov** 37/19
Apr 54/32	**Aug** 81/57	**Dec** 20/3

Parks and Recreation Finder

Directions to and information about the parks and recreation areas below are given under their respective town/city sections. Please refer to those sections for details.

NATIONAL PARK AND RECREATION AREAS

Key to abbreviations. I.H.S. = International Historic Site; I.P.M. = International Peace Memorial; N.B. = National Battlefield; N.B.P. = National Battlefield Park; N.B.C. = National Battlefield and Cemetery; N.C.A. = National Conservation Area; N.E.M. = National Expansion Memorial; N.F. = National Forest; N.G. = National Grassland; N.H.P. = National Historical Park; N.H.C. = National Heritage Corridor; N.H.S. = National Historic Site; N.L. = National Lakeshore; N.M. = National Monument; N.M.P. = National Military Park; N.Mem. = National Memorial; N.P. = National Park; N.Pres. = National Preserve; N.R.A. = National Recreational Area; N.R.R. = National Recreational River; N.Riv. = National River; N.S. = National Seashore; N.S.R. = National Scenic Riverway; N.S.T. = National Scenic Trail; N.Sc. = National Scientific Reserve; N.V.M. = National Volcanic Monument.

Place Name	Listed Under
Fort Union Trading Post N.H.S.	WILLISTON
Knife River Indian Villages N.H.S.	GARRISON DAM
Theodore Roosevelt N.P.	same

STATE PARK AND RECREATION AREAS

Key to abbreviations. I.P. = Interstate Park; S.A.P. = State Archaeological Park; S.B. = State Beach; S.C.A. = State Conservation Area; S.C.P. = State Conservation Park; S.Cp. = State Campground; S.F. = State Forest; S.G. = State Garden; S.H.A. = State Historic Area; S.H.P. = State Historic Park; S.H.S. = State Historic Site; S.M.P. = State Marine Park; S.N.A. = State Natural Area; S.P. = State Park;

CALENDAR HIGHLIGHTS

JUNE

Buffalo Trails Day (Williston). Parade, chuck wagon breakfast, old-time music, contests, games. Phone 701/859-4361.

Fort Seward Wagon Train (Jamestown). A week-long wagon train experience. Wagons are pulled by draft horses or mules; train stops along the way at historical sites. Participants dress and camp in the manner of the pioneers. Phone 701/252-6844.

Medora Musical (Medora). Outdoor musical extravaganza; Western songs, dance. Phone 800/633-6721.

JULY

Grand Forks County Fair (Grand Forks). County fairgrounds. Phone 701/772-3421.

North Dakota State Fair (Minot). State Fairgrounds. 4-H, livestock, commercial exhibits; horse and tractor pulls, carnival, machinery show, concerts, auto races, demolition derby. Phone 701/852-FAIR.

AUGUST

Pioneer Days (Fargo). Bonanzaville, USA. Celebration of area pioneer heritage. People in period costume, parades, arts and crafts. Phone 701/282-2822.

SEPTEMBER

United Tribes PowWow (Bismarck). One of the largest in the nation, featuring Native American dancing and singing, events, food, games, crafts, and contests. Phone 701/255-3285.

S.P.C. = State Public Campground; S.R. = State Reserve; S.R.A. = State Recreation Area; S.Res. = State Reservoir; S.Res.P. = State Resort Park; S.R.P. = State Rustic Park.

Place Name	Listed Under
Butte View S.P.	BOWMAN
Camp Hancock S.H.S.	BISMARCK
Chateau de Mores S.H.S.	MEDORA
Former Governors' Mansion S.H.S.	BISMARCK
Fort Abercrombie S.H.S.	WAHPETON
Fort Abraham Lincoln S.P.	MANDAN
Fort Buford S.H.S.	WILLISTON
Fort Totten S.H.S.	DEVILS LAKE
Lake Metigoshe S.P.	BOTTINEAU
Lake Sakajawea S.P.	GARRISON DAM
Lewis and Clark S.P.	WILLISTON
Turtle River S.P.	GRAND FORKS
Whitestone Hill Battlefield S.H.S.	JAMESTOWN

Water-related activities, hiking, riding, various other sports, picnicking and visitor centers, as well as camping, are available in many of these areas. Camping facilities ($11-$15/night with electricity; $8-$10/night, no electricity; $3 less with annual permit) at state parks. All motor vehicles entering a state park must obtain a motor vehicle permit: annual $20; daily $3. Pets on leash only. The North Dakota Tourism Department, 604 E Boulevard Ave, Bismarck 58505, offers info on facilities at national, state, and local parks and recreation areas; phone 800/HELLO-ND.

SKI AREAS

Place Name	Listed Under
Bottineau Winter Park Ski Area	BOTTINEAU
Huff Hills Ski Area	MANDAN

FISHING AND HUNTING

Species found in the state are trout, pike, sauger, walleye, bass, salmon, panfish, catfish, and muskie. Fishing season is year-round in many waters. Obtain state's fishing regulations for details. Nonresident license, $25; seven-day nonresident license, $15; three-day nonresident license, $10.

The pothole and slough regions of central North Dakota annually harbor up to four million ducks; waterfowl hunting is tops. Pheasants, sharptails, Hungarian partridge, and deer are also found here. Nonresident small game license $85; with waterfowl $95.

For further information contact the State Game and Fish Department, 100 N Bismarck Expressway, Bismarck 58501-5095; 701/328-6300.

Driving Information

Children ten years and under must be in an approved passenger restraint anywhere in vehicle: children ages three-ten must be properly secured in an approved safety seat or buckled in a safety belt; children under age three must be properly secured in an approved safety seat. For further info phone 701/328-2455.

INTERSTATE HIGHWAY SYSTEM

The following alphabetical listing of North Dakota towns in *Mobil Travel Guide* shows that these cities are within ten miles of the indicated Interstate highways. A highway map, however, should be checked for the nearest exit.

Highway Number	Cities/Towns within ten miles
Interstate 29	Fargo, Grafton, Grand Forks, Wahpeton.
Interstate 94	Bismarck, Dickinson, Fargo, Jamestown, Mandan, Medora, Valley City.

Additional Visitor Information

North Dakota Tourism Department, 604 E Blvd, Bismarck 58505; phone 800/435-5663, has helpful travel information. *North Dakota Horizons,* published quarterly, is avail from the Greater North Dakota Assn, 2000 Shafer St, Bismarck 58501.

Three tourist information centers are open year-round. These centers are: Fargo Information Center, located at I-94, 45th St exit; Grand Forks Travel Center, located on I-29, exit 141; Pembina Travel Center, located in tower building with observation deck, on ND 59, adj to I-29.

Five tourist information centers are open Memorial Day-Labor Day. These centers are: Beach Tourist Information Center, located at North Dakota-Montana border on I-94; Bowman Info Center, located on US 12 W; Lake Agassiz Travel Center. Located on I-29, exit 2; Oriska Info Center. Located at Oriska Rest area, 12 mi E of Valley City on I-94; Williston Info Center, located at US 2 and 6th Ave W.

THE FREE-FLOWING MISSOURI RIVER

There's very little of the free-flowing Missouri River left in North Dakota; only one portion, from Garrison Dam to Bismarck, resembles the broad prairie river as seen by Lewis and Clark. This route explores a section of Missouri River wetlands, allowing modern-day explorers the chance to see the cottonwood forests and wetlands that once stretched along the Missouri, before hydroelectric dams tamed the river.

From Mandan, travel north on Highway 25, which follows the Missouri's western banks. The route passes through farmland and then drops onto a broad, arid basin, with the green, cottonwood-fringed Missouri in the distance. If you don't mind traveling a few miles on gravel roads, turn off Highway 25 east toward the community of Price. Follow the road north along the banks of the river. A number of wildlife refuges string along the river; you may see wild turkeys, deer, or bald eagles. Stop at the Cross Ranch State Park, a wetlands preserve with summer canoe rentals.

At Hensler, turn west on Highway 200A to visit Fort Clark State Historic Site. Fort Clark was built between 1830-1831 by the American Fur Company as a trading post near a Mandan Indian earthlodge village. A second fort, Primeau's Post, was built on the site in the early 1850s and operated in competition with Fort Clark for much of that decade. Artists Karl Bodmer and George Catlin visited the site, as did German Prince Maximilian, John James Audubon, and more than 50 steam boats per year. Many of Bodmer's paintings were of the people and village of Fort Clark. Fort Clark was the scene of small pox and cholera epidemics that decimated the Mandan and Arikara Indian villages located here. The site contains foundations of both fort structures, the remains of the earthlodge village, and a large native burial ground.

Continue west along Highway 200A. At Stanton, follow County Highway 37 north to the Knife River Indian Village National Historic Site. One of the largest Hidatsa villages was located at the confluence of the Missouri and the Knife rivers, where this new interpretive center and earthlodge reconstruction are now found. Displays in the interpretive center are excellent and explain the culture and lifestyle of the Hidatsa. Trails lead out to a reconstructed earthlodge; in summer docents demonstrate traditional Hidatsa crafts and activities. Other trails lead to actual village sites. More than 50 earthlodge remains suggest that Native Americans lived in this location for nearly 8,000 years, ending with five centuries of Hidatsa earthlodge village occupation. The circular depressions at the three village sites are up to 40 feet in diameter and are a silent testimony to the people that lived here.

Continue north to join Highway 200 and follow it across the Garrison Dam, the third-largest earth-filled dam in the United States. The dam backs up the Missouri River 175 miles to the west in 378,000-acre Lake Sakakawea. Continue to Highway 83, then head south, zipping past the coal strip mines at Underwood. At Washburn, leave the freeway and follow signs to the Fort Mandan Historic Site, where volunteers have reconstructed Lewis and Clark's log fort. The Lewis and Clark Expedition spent the winter of 1804-1805 here in a cottonwood blockade above the Missouri River. It was here that they met French-Canadian Toussaint Charbonneau, who would serve as their interpreter, and his young Shoshone wife, Sacajawea. This reconstruction of Fort Mandan is downstream from the original site, which has been eaten away by the river. The triangular fort is quite modest and small, considering that there were 40-odd members of the expedition living here. Also at the park are a visitor center, gift shop, and a picnic area along the river.

Return to Highway 83 and travel south for seven miles, then exit at Highway 1804 and follow this scenic route south along the free-flowing Missouri's eastern banks to Bismarck. (**APPROX 162 MI**)

EXPLORING THE SHEYENNE RIVER VALLEY

The wide, forested valley of the Sheyenne River is a green and shady oasis in the prairies of North Dakota. This peaceful country road is a nice break both from the prairies and from freeway driving. Highway 21 follows the Sheyenne River closely, winding through fields and into basswood, oak, and elm forests, past historic frontier forts and pioneer settlements.

From Valley City, follow Highway 21 south. The route passes the old Ellis-Nelson one room school, built in 1883, and then winds through the Daily Historical Site. When James Daily built the first bridge across the Sheyenne River here in 1878, he established the settlement that became the social and economic center of the entire region. However, when the Northern Pacific Railroad built its own bridge across the river and founded Kathryn just a few miles south in 1900, the old town drifted into ghost town status. Today, Kathryn is a slumbering little village that retains a pleasant turn-of-the-century main street with historic churches and school buildings.

South of Kathryn is the Standing Rock State Historic Site. Called *Inyan Bosendata* by Sioux Indians who consider it sacred, the rock, which is four feet tall and shaped like an inverted cone, stands above a complex of prehistoric burial mounds dating from the Woodland Period, A.D. 1 to 1400. Across the highway is Little Yellowstone Park, which provides picnic and camping facilities.

The town of Fort Ransom, established in 1878, boasts a number of compelling sites in a small area. The town is located at the base of Pyramid Hill, which is a man-made mound nearly 100 feet high and 600 feet on each side. Although the mound was built an estimated 5,000 to 9,000 years ago, recent Scandinavian residents have built a Viking memorial on the hillock. Fort Ransom has a national historic district, which contains the county historical museum, a water-powered mill, and a general store. The Standing Rock Church dates from the 1880s.

At Fort Ransom State Park, explore the hiking trails that lead through the woods, or rent a canoe and paddle along the slow-moving river. Of the original Fort Ransom, which was built as a deterrent to the Sioux during the 1860s, a gun turret remains, and the wooden stockade has been rebuilt. Just across a ravine from the old fort site is Writing Rock, a monolith with peculiar inscriptions and figures carved into it. The site is mentioned in the legends of local Native Americans. East from Fort Ransom toward Lisbon, the route passes through the Sheyenne State Forest, with 508 acres of prairie and woodlands and a network of hiking and mountain biking trails.
(APPROX 55 MI)

Bismarck

(E-4) See also Mandan

Settled 1873 **Pop** 49,256 **Elev** 1,680 ft
Area code 701

Information Bismarck-Mandan Convention and Visitors Bureau, 107 W Main St, PO Box 2274, 58501; 701/222-4308 or 800/767-3555

Web www.bismarck-mandancvb.org

Lewis and Clark camped near here in 1804 and Jim Bridger, Prince Maximilian of Wied, Sitting Bull, General Sully, General Sibley, Theodore Roosevelt, and the Marquis de Mores all figured in Bismarck's history. On the east bank of the Missouri, near the geographic center of the state and within 150 miles of the geographic center of the continent, the city flourished as a steamboat port called "the crossing." As the terminus of the Northern Pacific Railway, it gained new importance and was named for the Chancellor of Germany to attract German capital to invest in building transcontinental railroads. General Custer came to Bismarck to take command of the newly constructed Fort Abraham Lincoln nearby and in 1876 rode out to

his fatal rendezvous with Sitting Bull. In 1883 Bismarck became the capital of the Dakota Territory, and in 1889, the seat of the new state.

What to See and Do

Camp Hancock State Historic Site. This site preserves part of a military camp established in 1872 to provide protection for workers then building the Northern Pacific Railroad. Site incl headquarters building (now wood sheathed), an early Northern Pacific Railroad locomotive, and one of Bismarck's oldest churches, which was moved to the site and restored. (Mid-May-mid-Sept, Wed-Sun) Main and 1st sts. Phone 701/328-2666. **FREE**

Double Ditch Indian Village. State historic site contains the ruins of large Mandan Native American earth lodge village inhabited from 1675-1780; earth lodge and two surrounding fortifications are clearly discernible. (Daily) 9½ mi NW via ND 1804. Phone 701/328-2666. **FREE**

***Lewis & Clark* Riverboat.** Daily cruises to Fort Abraham Lincoln State Park; also dinner, family, pizza, and moonlight cruises. (Memorial Day-Labor Day, daily) North River Rd at Riverboat jct. Phone 701/255-4233.

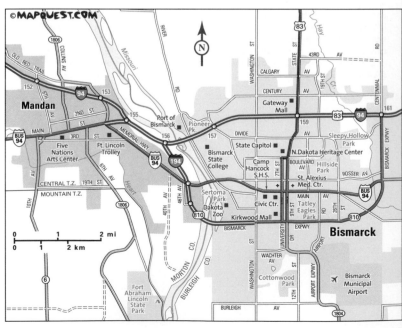

McDowell Recreation Area. Swimming beach, boating (no motors; ramp, dock; canoe, paddle, and sailboat rentals); walking trails, picnicking (shelters by res), playground. Alcoholic beverage permit required. (May-Sept, daily) 6 mi E on ND 10. Phone 701/255-7385.

Riverside-Sertoma Park. Playground; amusement park with miniature golf, children's rides. (Late Apr-Labor Day wkend, daily; some fees). Along Missouri River at W Bowen Ave and Riverside Park Rd. Phone 701/255-1107. ¢¢ Adj is

> **Dakota Zoo.** More than 600 mammals, birds, and reptiles on 80 acres. Miniature train ride (fee); concessions. (Early May-Sept, daily) Phone 701/223-7543. ¢¢

⭐ **State Capitol.** (1933-1934) "Skyscraper of the Prairies," 18 stories high, topped with an observation tower. White limestone shaft houses offices of officials and departments; three-story circular wing serves as forum for legislature. Unique and distinctive interiors with exotic wood paneling, stone, and metals. Tours (daily; closed hols). N 6th St. Phone 701/328-2480. **FREE** Also on grounds are

> **Former Governors' Mansion State Historic Site.** (1884) Restored three-story Victorian mansion occupied 1893-1960. Interpretive exhibits; governors' portraits. (Mid-May-mid-Sept, Wed-Sun afternoons, also by appt) Corner of 4th St and Ave B. Phone 701/328-2666.

> **North Dakota Heritage Center.** Permanent and changing exhibits on history and settlement of northern Great Plains. State archives and research library. Gift shop. (Daily, limited hrs Sun; closed hols) Phone 701/224-2666. **FREE**

> **The Pioneer Family.** Statue by Avard Fairbanks.

> **Statue of Sakajawea.** Memorial to the Native American woman who guided Lewis and Clark. Phone 701/222-4308.

> **Ward Earthlodge Village Historic Site.** Mandan Indians once occupied this bluff above the Missouri River, living in dome-shaped homes built of logs and earth. By the time Lewis and Clark passed

through the region, the village was deserted; however, depressions remain where the houses once stood, and the site is now part of the city park system. Interpretive signs explain how the village was constructed and elements of Mandan cultural life. Spectacular views from the bluff. (Daily, dawn-dusk) Contact Bismarck Parks and Recreation. Near Burnt Boat Dr at Grandview Ln. Phone 701/222-6455. **FREE**

Special Events

Folkfest. Downtown. Mid-Sept.

United Tribes PowWow. One of the largest in the nation, featuring Native American dancing and singing, events, food, games, crafts, and contests. Phone 701/255-3285. Mid-Sept.

Motels/Motor Lodges

★★ **AMERICINN.** 3235 State St (58501). 701/250-1000; fax 701/250-1103; res 800/634-3444. 46 rms, 2 story, 8 suites. Mid-May-mid-Sept: S, D $49.90; each addl $6; suites $55.90-$104.90; under 18 free; lower rates rest of yr. Crib free. TV; cable. Complimentary continental bkfst. Restaurant nearby. Ck-out 11 am. Meeting rms. Business servs avail. In-rm modem link. Coin lndry. Indoor pool; whirlpool. Game rm. Some in-rm whirlpools, refrigerators, microwaves. Cr cds: A, D, DS, MC, V.
🅳 🐾 ⊠ ⊠ 🔥 🕹

★★ **BEST WESTERN DOUBLE-WOOD INN.** 1400 E Interchange Ave (58501). 701/258-7000; fax 701/258-2001; res 800/780-7234. www.bestwestern.com. 143 rms, 2 story. S $61; D $71; each addl $5; suites $89; under 18 free. Crib free. Pet accepted; deposit. TV; cable, VCR avail. Indoor pool; whirlpool, poolside serv. Sauna. Restaurant 6:30 am-2 pm, 5-10 pm. Bar 11-1 am. Ck-out noon. Meeting rms. Bellhops. Valet serv. Sundries. Free airport, bus depot transportation. Some refrigerators. Cr cds: A, C, D, DS, ER, MC, V.
🅳 🐕 🐾 ⊠ ⊠ 🕹

★ **COMFORT INN.** 1030 Interstate Ave (58501). 701/223-1911; fax 701/223-6977; res 800/228-5150. www.comfortinn.com. 148 rms, 3

story. No elvtr. S $38; D
$44-$53; suites $62; under
16 free. Crib $3. TV; cable
(premium). Indoor pool;
whirlpool. Complimentary
continental bkfst. Ck-out
noon. Meeting rms. Free
airport transportation.
Game rm. Cr cds: A, C, D,
DS, MC, V.

Statue of Sakajawea, State Capitol

★★ **COMFORT SUITES.**
929 Gateway Ave (58501).
701/223-4009; fax 701/
223-9119; res 800/517-
4000. www.comfortsuites.
com. 60 rms, 2 story. June-
Aug: S $57; D $60-$75;
under 16 free; lower rates
rest of yr. Crib free. TV;
cable (premium). Compli-
mentary continental
bkfst, coffee in rms.
Restaurant nearby. Ck-out
noon. Meeting rms. Busi-
ness servs avail. In-rm
modem link. Bellhops.
Guest lndry. Free airport
transportation. Exercise
equipt. Indoor pool;
whirlpool, waterslide.
Game rm. Refrigerators,
microwaves. Cr cds: A, D,
DS, MC, V.

★ **DAYS INN.** *1300 E Capitol Ave*
(58501). 701/223-9151; fax 701/223-
9423; res 800/329-7466.
www.daysinn.com. 110 rms, 2 story. S
$39; D $44-$54; each addl $5. Crib
free. TV; cable (premium). Indoor
pool; whirlpool. Sauna. Complimentary continental bkfst. Restaurant
nearby. Ck-out noon. Meeting rms.
Cr cds: A, C, D, DS, JCB, MC, V.

★ **EXPRESSWAY INN.** *200 E Bis-*
marck Expy (58504). 701/222-2900;
fax 701/222-2900; toll-free 800/456-
6388. www.fargoweb.com/expressway.
163 rms, 5 story. S $35-$45; D $50-
$56; each addl $4; suites $67; under
14 free. Crib free. TV; cable (premium), VCR avail. Pool. Playground.
Complimentary continental bkfst.
Restaurant nearby. Ck-out noon. Coin
lndry. Meeting rms. Business servs
avail. Free airport transportation.
Game rm. Cr cds: A, D, DS, MC, V.

★ **EXPRESSWAY SUITES.** *180 E Bis-*
marck Expy (58504). 701/222-3311;
fax 701/222-3311; toll-free 888/774-
5566. www.expresswayinnandsuites.
com. 64 rms, 3 story. June-Oct: S $49-
$65; D $60-$65; each addl $5; under
14 free; wkly rates; higher rates special events; lower rates rest of yr. Crib
free. TV; cable (premium). Complimentary continental bkfst, coffee in
rms. Restaurant adj open 24 hrs. Bar
4 pm-midnight. Ck-out noon. Meeting rms. Business servs avail. Coin
lndry. Free airport transportation.
Exercise equipt. Indoor pool; whirlpool. Game rm. Refrigerators, microwaves. Cr cds: A, D, DS, MC, V.

★★ **FAIRFIELD INN.** *1120 Century*
Ave (58501). 701/223-9077; fax
701/223-9077. www.fairfieldinn.com.
63 rms, 3 story, 16 suites. S $59.95; D
$65.95; each addl $5; suites $69.95-
$75.95; under 18 free; higher rates
mid-May-mid-Sept. Crib free. TV;
cable (premium). Indoor pool; whirlpool. Complimentary continental

bkfst. Ck-out noon. Meeting rms. Sundries. Game rm. Refrigerator in suites. Cr cds: A, C, D, DS, MC, V.

★★ **FAIRFIELD INN.** *135 Ivy Ave (58504). 701/223-9293; fax 701/223-9293. www.fairfieldinn.com.* 63 rms, 3 story. S $60.95; D $65.95; each addl $5; suites $75-$85; under 18 free; higher rates special events. Crib free. Indoor pool; whirlpool. Complimentary continental bkfst. Restaurant adj 6 am-10 pm. Ck-out noon. Game rm. Some refrigerators. Cr cds: A, C, D, DS, MC, V.

★★ **KELLY INN.** *1800 N 12th St (58501). 701/223-8001; fax 701/223-8001.* 101 rms, 2 story. S $45-$49; D $55-$59; each addl $5; suites $65-$95; under 18 free. Crib free. Pet accepted. TV; cable. Indoor pool; whirlpool. Sauna. Restaurant 6:30 am-10 pm; Fri, Sat to 11 pm. Bar 11 am-1:30 pm, 4 pm-1 am. Ck-out noon. Meeting rms. Business servs avail. Valet serv. Free airport transportation. Game rm. Cr cds: A, C, D, DS, ER, MC, V.

★ **RAMADA LTD SUITES.** *3808 E Divide Ave (58501). 701/221-3030; res 800/228-2828. www.ramada.com.* 66 rms, 3 story. Mar-Sept: S $75; D $80; each addl $5; under 18 free; family rates; lower rates rest of yr. Crib $5. Pet accepted. TV; cable (premium), VCR avail. Complimentary continental bkfst. Restaurant opp open 24 hrs. Ck-out 11 am, ck-in 3 pm. Business servs avail. Exercise equipt. Indoor pool; whirlpool. Game rm. Refrigerators, microwaves. Cr cds: A, C, D, DS, ER, JCB, MC, V.

★ **SUPER 8.** *1124 E Capitol Ave (58501). 701/255-1314; res 800/800-8000. www.super8.com.* 61 rms, 3 story. S $36.88; D $43.88-$47.88; each addl $5. Crib free. Pet accepted, some restrictions; $5. TV; cable (premium). Complimentary coffee. Restaurant nearby. Ck-out 11 am. Cr cds: A, C, D, DS, MC, V.

Hotels

★★ **HOLIDAY INN BISMARCK.** *605 E Broadway Ave (58501). 701/255-6000; fax 701/223-0400; toll-free 800/465-4329. www.holiday-inn.com.* 215 rms, 9 story. S, D $85; suites $89-$199; under 19 free; wkend rates. Crib free. Pet accepted. TV; cable, VCR avail. Indoor pool; whirlpool, poolside serv. Restaurant 6 am-10:30 pm. Bar 11:30-1 am. Ck-out noon. Meeting rms. Business servs avail. Beauty shop. Free airport transportation. Exercise equipt; sauna. Game rm. Refrigerator, microwave in suites. Cr cds: A, C, D, DS, ER, JCB, MC, V.

★★ **RADISSON INN.** *800 S 3rd St (58504). 701/258-7700; fax 701/224-8212; res 800/333-3333. www.radisson.com.* 306 rms, 3 story. S $70-$80; D $75-$85; each addl $10; suites $130-$185; under 18 free. Crib free. TV; cable. Indoor pool; wading pool, whirlpool. Restaurant 6 am-10:30 pm; Sat, Sun from 7 am. Bar 11-1 am. Ck-out noon. Meeting rms. Business servs avail. Bellhops. Valet serv. Sundries. Gift shop. Free airport transportation. Exercise equipt; sauna. Game rm. Rec rm. Casino. Some refrigerators. Many private patios, balconies. Shopping mall opp. Cr cds: A, C, D, DS, JCB, MC, V.

Restaurants

★★ **CASPAR'S EAST 40.** *1401 Interchange Ave (58501). 701/258-7222.* Hrs: 11:30 am-9:30 pm. Closed Sun; hols. Res accepted. Continental menu. Bar to 1 am. Lunch $3.95-$9.50, dinner $8.95-$16.50. Children's meals. Specializes in prime rib, steak, seafood. Salad bar. Antique decor; fireplaces. Cr cds: A, D, MC, V.

★★ **PEACOCK ALLEY.** *422 E Main St (58501). 701/255-7917.* Hrs: 11 am-2 pm, 5:30-10 pm; Mon to 9 pm; Sun brunch 9 am-1 pm. Closed hols. Res accepted. Continental menu. Bar to 1 am; closed Sun. Lunch $4.25-$7.25, dinner $9.95-$25.50. Sun brunch $4.95. Children's menu. Specialties: pasta primavera, sliced tenderloin, pan-blackened prime rib. Turn-of-the-century decor; located in

historic former hotel (1915). Cr cds:
A, D, DS, MC, V.

[D] [≞]

Bottineau (A-4)

Founded 1883 **Pop** 2,598 **Elev** 1,635
ft **Area code** 701 **Zip** 58318

Information Greater Bottineau Area
Chamber of Commerce, 103 E 11th
St; 701/228-3849 or 800/735-6932

Web www.tradecorridor.com/
bottineau

What to See and Do

Bottineau Winter Park Ski Area. Two
T-bars, hand tow; patrol, triple chairlift, school, rentals, snowmaking;
snack bar. Longest run 1,200 ft; vertical drop 200 ft. (Mid-Nov-mid-Mar,
Thurs-Sun) 11 mi NW via county
roads in the Turtle Mtns. Phone
701/263-4556. ¢¢¢¢

⭐ International Peace Garden. This
2,339-acre landscaped park symbolizes lasting friendship between
Canada and the US. Formal gardens,
floral clock, arboretum, peace chapel,
bell tower, pavilion, Masonic Auditorium, intrepretive center, Peace
Tower. Picnicking, lodge. Camping
(May-mid-Oct). Grounds (daily,
weather permitting). Astride Canadian border, 18 mi E on ND 5 to
Dunseith, then 13 mi N on US 281,
ND 3. Phone 701/263-4390. ¢¢¢

**J. Clark Salyer National Wildlife
Refuge.** Long, narrow, irregularly
shaped 58,693-acre refuge stretching
from Canadian border to point about
25 mi S of Bottineau. Fishing; hunting, picnicking, bird-watching, photography permitted on some parts of
refuge during specified periods. Self-
guided auto tour (May-Oct); also
canoe trail on Souris River. Details at
headquarters, 2 mi N of Upham
(daily; office closed wkends, hols). 12
mi W on ND 5, then 14 mi S on ND
14. Contact Refuge for road conditions. Phone 701/768-2548. **FREE**

Lake Metigoshe State Park. One of
the largest, most attractive lakes in
the state amid heavily wooded hills
of Turtle Mtns. Wildlife. Swimming
beach, bathhouses, fishing, boating
(ramp); hiking (guides), x-country

skiing, snowmobiling, picnicking,
playground, primitive and improved
camping. Amphitheater programs.
Standard fees. 12 mi N on Lake Rd, 2
mi E of Bottineau Fairgrounds.
Phone 701/263-4651. ¢¢

Turtle Mountain Provincial Park. NE
on county roads in Manitoba,
Canada.

Special Events

International Music Camp. International Peace Garden. Music, dance,
drama, art; Sat concerts with guest
conductors; old-time fiddlers' contest. Seven wks early June-July.

Sports Camp. Sponsored by the
Canadian Legion. Equestrian events,
volleyball, wilderness adventure,
judo, sailing, weights, gymnastics,
basketball, track, soccer, football,
lacrosse. Late July-Aug.

Motels/Motor Lodges

★ NORWAY HOUSE. *1255 ND 5 E
(58318). 701/228-3737; fax 701/228-
3740.* 46 rms. S $29-$33; D $35-$37;
each addl $2. Crib $2. TV; cable.
Restaurant 7 am-2 pm, 5-10 pm. Bar
4 pm-1 am. Ck-out 11 am. Meeting
rm. Free airport transportation.
Downhill/x-country skiing 12 mi. Cr
cds: A, DS, MC, V.

[D] [⚘] [⤢] [⊠] [▦]

Bowman (F-1)

Pop 1,741 **Elev** 2,960 ft
Area code 701 **Zip** 58623

What to See and Do

Bowman-Haley Lake. Rolled earth-fill
dam 74 ft high, 5,730 ft long. Two-
mi-long reservoir, fishing for panfish,
boating (ramp); picnicking, concession. 21 mi SE via US 12 or US 85.
Phone 701/252-7666. **FREE**

Butte View State Park. Picnicking,
camping (electric hookups, dump
station). (Mid-May-mid-Sept, daily)
Standard fees. 1 mi E on US 12.
Phone 701/859-3071.

Carrington (D-6)

Founded 1882 **Pop** 2,267 **Elev** 1,587 ft **Area code** 701 **Zip** 58421

Information Chamber of Commerce, 871 Main St, PO Box 439; 701/652-2524

What to See and Do

Arrowwood Lake Area. James River flows through Arrowwood Lake, Mud Lake, and Jim Lake in a 30-mi interconnecting chain of waterways to Jamestown (see). 14 mi S on US 281, then 6 mi E on gravel road. Along E and W shores is

Arrowwood National Wildlife Refuge. Hunting, picnicking. Self-guided auto tour, wildlife observation. (May-Sept, daily) Headquarters are 6 mi E of Edmunds on gravel road. Phone 701/285-3341. **FREE**

Garrison Diversion Conservancy District. "Nerve center" for the multipurpose 130,000-acre irrigation Garrison Diversion Unit. Project tours with advance notice. (Mon-Fri) 1 mi N on US 281. Phone 701/652-3194.

Special Event

Harvest Festival. Entertainment, dance, crafts. First wkend Sept.

Motels/Motor Lodges

★★ **CHIEFTAIN CONFERENCE CENTER.** *60 4th Ave 50 US 281 (58421). 701/652-3131; fax 701/652-2151.* 51 rms, 2 story. S $40-$46; D $46-$52; each addl $5; suites $45.95-$85.95; under 12 free. Crib avail. TV; cable (premium), VCR avail. Restaurant 6 am-midnight. Rm serv 9 am-10 pm. Bar 11-1 am. Ck-out 11 am. Meeting rms. Business servs avail. In-rm modem link. Casino. Native American artifacts on display. Cr cds: A, C, D, DS, MC, V.
🄳 ✗ ⊠ 🕴

★ **SUPER 8.** *101 4th Ave S (58421). 701/652-3982; fax 701/652-3984; res 800/800-8000. www.super8.com.* 40 rms, 2 story. S $32.95-$36.95; D $41.95-$45.95; each addl $5; suites $45.95-$75.95; under 12 free. Crib

$5. Pet accepted. TV; cable. Complimentary continental bkfst. Restaurant opp 6 am-midnight. Ck-out 11 am. Coin lndry. Business servs avail. In-rm modem link. Sundries. Cr cds: A, C, D, DS, MC, V.
🄳 🐾 ⊠ 🕴

Devils Lake (B-6)

Settled 1882 **Pop** 7,782 **Elev** 1,473 ft **Area code** 701 **Zip** 58301

Information Devils Lake Area Chamber of Commerce, PO Box 879; 701/662-4903 or 800/233-8048

Located near the shore of Devils Lake, the city is in the heart of some of the best fishing in the North. The opening of the federal land office here in 1883 sparked growth of the city.

What to See and Do

Devils Lake. Derives its name from the Indian name Miniwaukan which means "Bad Water." Bolstered by legends of drowned warriors, the name evolved into Devils Lake. Fishing, boating; hunting, golfing, biking, snowmobiling, picnicking, camping (fee). 6 mi S.

Devils Lake Area Welcome Center. Tourist information. (Daily) 1½ mi E on US 2. Phone 701/662-4903. **FREE**

⊠ **Fort Totten State Historic Site.** (1867) Built to protect overland route to Montana; last outpost before 300 mi of wilderness. One of the best preserved military forts west of the Mississippi; 16 original buildings. Pioneer Daughters Museum; interpretive center, commissary display; videotape program of site history. Summer theater (see SPECIAL EVENT). Self-guided tours. (Memorial Day-Labor Day, daily; rest of yr, by appt) 18 mi SW on ND 20. Phone 701/766-4441. ¢¢

Sullys Hill National Game Preserve. More than 1,600 scenic acres of which 700 acres are a big-game enclosure populated by bison, deer, elk, prairie dogs, turkeys; four-mi self-guided auto tour. (May-Oct, daily) Nature trail. Observation towers. 18 mi SW on ND 20, on Devils

Lake, 1 mi E of Fort Totten. Phone 701/766-4272. **FREE**

Special Event

Fort Totten Little Theater. Fort Totten Historic Site. Adaptive use of historic auditorium (1904). Broadway musical productions. (Wed, Thurs, Sat, Sun) Phone 701/662-8888. July.

Motels/Motor Lodges

★ **COMFORT INN.** *215 US 2 E (58301). 701/662-6760; res 888/266-3948. www.comfortinn.com.* 87 rms, 2 story. S $42.95-$49.95; D $49.95-$59.95; each addl $5; under 18 free. Crib free. Pet accepted. TV; cable (premium). Indoor pool; whirlpool. Coffee in rms. Complimentary continental bkfst. Restaurant opp 6 am-11 pm. Ck-out 11 am. Business servs avail. Sundries. Game rm. Refrigerators avail. Cr cds: A, C, D, DS, JCB, MC, V.

🄳 🔌 ⇌ ⊠ 🔥 SC

★ **DAYS INN.** *ND 20 S (58301). 701/662-5381; fax 701/662-3578; toll-free 800/622-1191. www.daysinn.com.* 45 rms, 2 story. S $39-$44; D $49-$54; each addl $5; under 12 free. Crib free. Pet accepted; $3. TV; cable. Complimentary continental bkfst. Restaurant nearby. Ck-out 11 am. Business servs avail. Some refrigerators. Cr cds: A, D, DS, MC, V.

🄳 🔌 🕭 ✈ ⊠ 🔥

★ **SUPER 8 MOTEL.** *1001 US 2 E (58301). 701/662-8656; res 800/800-8000. www.super8.com.* 39 rms, 1-2 story. S $45.88; D $49.88-$59.88. Crib free. TV; cable (premium). Complimentary continental bkfst. Restaurant opp open 24 hrs. Ck out 11 am. Cr cds: A, D, DS, MC, V.

🄳 🕭 ⊠ 🔥

Dickinson

(D-2) *See also Medora*

Settled 1880 **Pop** 16,097 **Elev** 2,420 ft
Area code 701 **Zip** 58601
Information Chamber of Commerce, 314 Third Ave W, PO Box C; 701/225-5115

What to See and Do

Joachim Regional Museum. Art gallery; dinosaur exhibit. (May-Sept, daily) 1266 Museum Dr. Phone 701/225-4409.

Patterson Reservoir. Part of Missouri River Valley reclamation project. Swimming (June-Aug, daily), fishing, boating; volleyball, horseshoes, picnicking, camping (Memorial Day wkend-Labor Day wkend; fee). Park (Apr-Sept, daily). 3 mi W on US 10, then 1 mi S. Phone 701/225-2074.

Special Event

Roughrider Days Celebration. Rodeo, parade, tractor pulls, street dance, demolition derby, races, carnival. July 4th wkend.

Motels/Motor Lodges

★★ **AMERICINN.** *229 15th St W (58601). 701/225-1400; fax 701/225-5230; toll-free 800/634-3444.* 46 rms, 2 story. June-Aug: S $61-$70; D $67-$80; each addl $6; suites $95-$115; under 12 free; higher rates wkends, special events; lower rates rest of yr. Crib avail. Pet accepted. TV; cable (premium). Complimentary continental bkfst, coffee in rms. Restaurant nearby. Ck-out noon, ck-in 3 pm. Meeting rms. Business servs avail. In-rm modem link. Coin lndry. Free airport transportation. Indoor pool; whirlpool. Game rm. Some in-rm whirlpools, refrigerators, microwaves. Cr cds: A, C, D, DS, MC, V.

🄳 🔌 ⇌ ⊠ 🔥

★ **COMFORT INN.** *493 Elk Dr (58601). 701/264-7300; res 800/228-5150.* 117 rms, 2 story. June-mid-Sept: S $45.50; D $59.50; each addl $4; suites $69.50; under 18 free; higher rates special events; lower rates rest of yr. Crib free. Pet accepted. TV; cable. Pool; whirlpool. Complimentary continental bkfst. Ck-out 11 am. Coin lndry. Free airport transportation. Many refrigerators, microwaves. Cr cds: A, C, D, DS, MC, V.

🄳 🔌 🕭 ⇌ ⊠ 🔥

★ **TRAVELODGE.** *532 W 15th St (58602). 701/227-1853; fax 701/225-0090; toll-free 800/422-0949. www.travelodge.com.* 149 rms, 2-3 story. S, D $59; each addl $10; suites $100-$150; under 18 free. Crib free. TV;

cable. Heated pool; whirlpool, poolside serv. Sauna. Restaurant 6 am-10
pm. Bar 11:30-1 am. Ck-out noon.
Coin lndry. Meeting rms. Business
servs avail. Bellhops. Free airport, bus
depot transportation. Rec rm.
Casino. Some private patios, balconies. Cr cds: A, C, D, DS, MC, V.

Fargo (D-8)

Founded 1872 **Pop** 74,111 **Elev** 900 ft
Area code 701
Information Fargo-Moorhead Convention and Visitors Bureau, 2001
44th St SW, 58103; 701/282-3653 or
800/235-7654
Web www.fargomoorhead.org

Fargo, largest city in North Dakota, is
the leading retail and wholesale center of the rich Red River valley and
one of the leading commercial centers in the Northwest. Farm products
and byproducts keep many factories
busy. The city is named for William
G. Fargo of the Wells-Fargo Express
Company. It is also the home town
of baseball great Roger Maris; a display museum filled with his personal
memorabilia is located in West Acres
Mall.

With blackjack legal in North
Dakota, Fargo has taken the lead in
promoting its gaming tables. There
are approximately 30 casinos in the
city, making it a tourist attraction for
the three-state region incl Minnesota
and South Dakota. Charities and
nonprofit organizations run the casinos and collect all profits above
expenses.

What to See and Do

❇ **Bonanzaville, USA.** More than 45
buildings reconstruct the 19th-cen-
tury farm era. Hemp Antique Vehicle
Museum, 1884 locomotive, train
depot, model railroad, pioneer farm
homes, church, school, log cabins,
sod house, home of Kodak film
inventor, general stores, farm
machinery buildings, operating farm-
steads, doll house, Plains Indian

Museum, and more. (See SPECIAL
EVENTS) Village and museums (May-
late Oct, daily; rest of yr, Mon-Fri).
4½ mi W of I-29 on Main Ave or via
I-94, exit 343 (US 10W). 1351 W
Main Ave. Phone 701/282-2822.
Museum only ¢¢; Village and
museum combination (exc during
special events) ¢¢¢

Children's Museum at Yunker Farm.
Hands-on exhibits incl Legoland,
infant-toddler play center, puppet
theater. Also outdoor playground;
picnic shelters. (Summer, daily; rest
of yr, Tues-Sun) 1201 28th Ave N.
Phone 701/232-6102. ¢¢

**Fargo-Moorhead Community The-
atre.** Units for the hearing impaired
available. 333 Fourth St. Phone
701/235-1901.

Fargo Theatre. (1937) Classic and
first-run films; stage productions;
Wurlitzer organ concerts (wkends) in
streamlined *moderne* theater. 314
Broadway. Phone 701/235-4152.

North Dakota State University.
(1890) 9,534 students. Herbarium
and wildlife museum in Stevens Hall;
North Dakota Institute for Regional
Studies at NDSU Library (Mon-Fri;
closed hols). Campus tours. N University Dr and 12th Ave N. Phone
701/231-8643.

Special Events

Red River Valley Fair. Fairgrounds, 5
mi W on I-94, exit 85, in West Fargo.
Pioneer village, livestock exhibits.
Phone 701/239-4129. Late June.

Pioneer Days. Bonanzaville, USA.
Celebration of area pioneer heritage.
People in period costume, parades,
arts and crafts. Phone 701/282-2822.
Third wkend Aug.

Motels/Motor Lodges

★★ **AMERICINN MOTEL.** *1423
35th St SW (58103). 701/234-9946;
fax 701/234-9946; toll-free 800/634-
3444. www.americinn.com.* 43 rms, 2
story. May-Sept: S $47.90-$64.90; D
$53.90-$109.90; each addl $4; under
18 free; lower rates rest of yr. Crib
free. Pet accepted. TV; cable (premium), VCR avail (movies). Indoor
pool; whirlpool. Sauna. Complimentary continental bkfst. Restaurant
nearby. Ck-out 11 am. Business servs

avail. Valet serv. Coin lndry. Some refrigerators. Cr cds: A, C, D, DS, MC, V.

D ⬛ ⬛ ⬛ ⬛ SC

★★ BEST WESTERN DOUBLE-WOOD INN. *3333 S 13th Ave (58103). 701/235-3333; fax 701/280-9482; res 800/780-7234. www.best western.com.* 174 rms, 3 story. S $60-$74; D $70-$84; each addl $5; suites $95-$200; under 18 free; wkend rates. Crib free. TV; cable (premium). Heated pool; whirlpool, poolside serv. Sauna. Coffee in rms. Restaurant 6:30 am-10 pm. Bar 11-1 am. Ck-out noon. Meeting rms. Business servs avail. In-rm modem link. Bellhops. Valet serv. Barber, beauty shop. Free airport, railroad station, bus depot transportation. X-country ski 4 mi. Health club privileges. Casino. Refrigerators. Balconies. Cr cds: A, C, D, DS, MC, V.

D ⬛ ⬛ ⬛ ⬛ ⬛

★★ BEST WESTERN KELLY INN. *3800 Main Ave (58103). 701/282-2143; fax 701/281-0243; res 800/780-7234. www.bestwestern.com.* 133 rms, 2 story, 13 suites. Apr-Sept: S $64; D $74; each addl $5; suites $100-$180; under 18 free; lower rates rest of yr. Crib free. Pet accepted. TV; cable (premium), VCR avail. 2 pools, 1 indoor; whirlpool. Sauna. Restaurant 6:30 am-midnight. Bar 11-1 am. Ck-out 11 am. Coin lndry. Meeting rms. Business servs avail. Valet serv. Sundries. Free airport, railroad station, bus depot transportation. Wet bar in suites. Some patios. Cr cds: A, C, D, DS, ER, MC, V.

D ⬛ ⬛ ✈ ⬛ ⬛

★ COMFORT INN. *3825 9th Ave SW (58103). 701/282-9596; fax 701/282-9596; toll-free 800/228-5150. www. comfortinn.com.* 56 rms, 2 story, 14 suites. S $40-$60; D $44-$70; each addl $5; suites $66-$76; under 18 free. Crib free. Pet accepted. TV; cable. Indoor pool; whirlpool. Complimentary continental bkfst. Restaurant nearby. Ck-out 11 am. Business servs avail. In-rm modem link. Sundries. Game rm. Refrigerator in suites. Cr cds: A, C, D, DS, ER, JCB, MC, V.

D ⬛ ⬛ ⬛ ⬛ SC

★ COMFORT INN. *1407 35th St S (58103). 701/280-9666; fax 701/280-9666; toll-free 800/228-5150. www. comfortinn.com.* 66 rms, 2 story. June-Sept: S $49.95-$59.95; D $59.95; each addl $5; suites $54.95-$64.95; family rates; higher rates special events; lower rates rest of yr. Crib free. Pet accepted. TV; cable. Indoor pool; whirlpool. Complimentary continental bkfst. Restaurant nearby. Ck-out 11 am. Business servs avail. Game rm. Refrigerator in suites. Cr cds: A, C, D, DS, ER, MC, V.

D ⬛ ⬛ ⬛ ⬛ SC

★★ COMFORT SUITES. *1415 35th St S (58103). 701/237-5911; fax 701/237-5911; toll-free 800/517-4000. www.comfortsuites.com.* 66 rms, 2 story. June-Aug: S $58.95-$73.95; D $63.95-$78.95; each addl $5; under 18 free; higher rates special events; lower rates rest of yr. Crib free. Pet accepted; $5. TV; cable. Indoor pool; whirlpool. Complimentary continental bkfst. Restaurant nearby. Ck-out 11 am. Business servs avail. In-rm modem link. Valet serv. Game rm. Refrigerators. Cr cds: A, C, D, DS, ER, JCB, MC, V.

D ⬛ ⬛ ⬛ ⬛ SC

★★ COUNTRY SUITES BY CAL-SON. *3316 13th Ave S (58102). 701/234-0565; fax 701/234-0565; toll-free 800/456-4000.* 99 rms, 3 story, 42 suites. S $65-$71; D $68-$74; suites $75-$139; under 18 free. Crib free. Pet accepted. TV; cable. Indoor pool; whirlpool. Complimentary continental bkfst. Coffee in rms. Restaurant adj 6 am-11 pm. Bar 4:30 pm-1 am. Ck-out noon. Meeting rms. Business servs avail. In-rm modem link. Valet serv. Sundries. Free airport transportation. Exercise equipt. Game rm. Refrigerators, wet bars. Cr cds: A, MC, V.

D ⬛ ⬛ 🍴 ⬛ ⬛ SC

★ ECONO LODGE. *1401 35th St (58103). 701/232-3412; fax 701/232-3412. www.econolodge.com.* 44 rms, 2 story. S $28.96-$33.96; D $38.96-$44.96; each addl $5; under 16 free. Crib free. Pet accepted. TV; cable. Complimentary continental bkfst. Restaurant adj open 24 hrs. Ck-out 11 am. Business servs avail. In-rm modem link. Cr cds: A, MC, V.

D ⬛ ⬛ ⬛ SC

★★ FAIRFIELD INN. *3902 9th Ave SW (58103). 701/281-0494; fax*

701/281-0494; res 800/228-2800. www.fairfieldinn.com. 63 rms, 3 story. Mid-May-mid-Sept: S $47.95-$53.95; D $53.95-$59.95; each addl $6; suites $54.95-$69.95; under 18 free; lower rates rest of yr. Crib free. TV; cable. Indoor pool; whirlpool. Complimentary continental bkfst. Ck-out noon. Business servs avail. In-rm modem link. Sundries. Game rm. Refrigerator in suites. Cr cds: A, C, D, DS, ER, JCB, MC, V.

★★ **HAMPTON INN.** 3431 14th Ave SW (58103). 701/235-5566; fax 701/235-7382; res 800/426-7866. www.hamptoninn.com. 75 rms, 2 story. S $56.95-$63; D $66.95-$73; under 18 free. Crib free. TV; cable (premium), VCR avail (movies). Indoor pool; whirlpool. Complimentary continental bkfst. Restaurant nearby. Ck-out 11 am. Business servs avail. Valet serv. Exercise equipt. Game rm. Some refrigerators. Cr cds: A, D, DS, MC, V.

★★ **HOLIDAY INN.** 3803 13th Ave S (58103). 701/282-2700; fax 701/281-1240; toll-free 877/282-2700. www.holiday-inn.com. 309 rms, 2-7 story. S, D $65-$109; suites $95-$145; under 19 free; wkend rates; package plans. Crib free. Pet accepted. TV; cable (premium). Indoor pool; wading pool, whirlpool, poolside serv. Restaurant 6 am-11 pm; Sat from 7 am; Sun 7 am-10 pm. Bar 11-1 am; Sat from 10 am; Sun 7 am-10 pm; entertainment. Ck-out noon. Convention facilities. Business servs avail. In-rm modem link. Bellhops. Valet serv. Concierge. Sundries. Free airport, railroad station, bus depot transportation. Exercise equipt. Rec rm. Casino. Cr cds: A, DS, MC, V.

★★ **HOLIDAY INN.** 1040 40th St S (58103). 701/282-2000; fax 701/282-4721; res 800/465-4329. www.holiday-inn.com. 77 rms, 4 story. S, D $45-$59; under 18 free. Crib free. Pet accepted. TV; cable. Indoor pool; whirlpool. Complimentary continental bkfst. Restaurant adj 6 am-11 pm. Ck-out noon. Business servs avail.

Sundries. Valet serv. Coin lndry. Game rm. Cr cds: A, C, D, DS.

★★ **KELLY INN 13TH AVENUE.** 4207 13th Ave SW (58103). 701/277-8821; fax 701/277-0208; res 800/635-3559. 59 rms, 2 story. S $65; D $69; each addl $5; suites $80-$100; under 18 free. Crib free. Pet accepted. TV; cable (premium). Indoor pool; whirlpool. Sauna. Complimentary continental bkfst. Restaurant adj 6 am-11 pm. Ck-out 11 am. Business servs avail. Valet serv. Coin lndry. Game rm. Some refrigerators, microwaves. Cr cds: A, D, DS, MC, V.

★ **RED ROOF INN.** 901 SW 38th St (58103). 701/282-9100; fax 701/277-1581; res 800/843-7663. www.redroof.com. 99 rms, 2 story. S $31.90-$37.90; D $45.90-$57.90; each addl $6; under 18 free. Crib free. TV; cable, VCR avail (movies). Complimentary continental bkfst. Restaurant nearby. Ck-out 11 am. Business servs avail. Sundries. Cr cds: A, C, D, DS, MC, V.

★ **SLEEP INN.** 1921 44th St SW (58103). 701/281-8240; fax 701/281-2041; res 800/905-7533. www.sleepinn.com. 61 rms, shower only, 2 story. Mid-May-Sept: S, D $49-$79; each addl $4; under 18 free; lower rates rest of yr. Crib $6. Pet accepted. TV; cable (premium). Complimentary continental bkfst. Restaurant opp open 24 hrs. Ck-out 11 am. Business servs avail. Valet serv. Exercise equipt. Cr cds: A, C, D, DS, MC.

★ **SUPER 8 HOTEL & SUITES.** 3518 Interstate Blvd (58103). 701/232-9202; fax 701/232-4543; res 800/800-8000. www.super8.com. 109 units, 2 story, 25 suites. S $32-$41; D $41-$51; suites $45-$99; each addl $2-$5. Crib $2. Pet accepted. TV; cable (premium). Indoor pool; whirlpool. Complimentary continental bkfst. Restaurant nearby. Ck-out 11 am. Coin lndry. Business servs avail. Some in-rm whirlpools. Cr cds: A, D, DS, MC, V.

Hotel

★ ★ **RADISSON.** *201 5th St N (58102). 701/232-7363; fax 701/298-9134; toll-free 800/333-3333. www. radisson.com.* 151 rms, 18 story. S, D $85; suites $130-$185; under 18 free; wkend rates; package plans. Crib free. Pet accepted. TV; cable. Coffee in rms. Restaurant 6:30 am-10:30 pm. Bar 11-1 am; Sat from 4:30 pm. Ck-out noon. Meeting rms. Business servs avail. In-rm modem link. Free airport transportation. Exercise equipt; sauna. Game rm. Rec rm. Minibars. Cr cds: A, C, D, DS, ER, JCB, MC, V.

D ⌦ ♨ 🕇 ✈ ⊇ 🐾 SC

Restaurants

★ ★ **THE GRAINERY.** *3902 13th Ave SW (58103). 701/282-6262.* Hrs: 11 am-10 pm; Fri, Sat to 11 pm; Sun 11 am-4 pm. Closed Easter, Thanksgiving, Dec 25. Res accepted. Bar to 1 am; Sun noon-6 pm. Lunch $4.25-$7.95, dinner $5.75-$18.95. Children's menu. Specialties: beer cheese soup, prime rib, broiled shrimp. Salad bar. Theodore Roosevelt memorabilia. Cr cds: A, D, DS, MC, V.

D ⊇

★ ★ **MEXICAN VILLAGE.** *814 Main Ave (58103). 701/293-0120.* Hrs: 11 am-11 pm; Fri, Sat to midnight; Sun to 10 pm. Closed Easter, Thanksgiving, Dec 25. Res accepted. Mexican menu. Serv bar. Lunch $4-$5, dinner $5-$8. Specializes in burritos, fajitas. Cr cds: A, D, DS, MC, V.

D ⊇

Garrison Dam

(58 mi N of Bismarck on US 83, then 11 mi W on ND 200)

Area Code 701

Garrison Project represents one of the key projects of the Missouri River Basin constructed by the US Army Corps of Engineers. The project cost nearly $300 million. Flood control, power generation, irrigation, navigation, recreation, and fish and wildlife are the project purposes. Garrison Dam is one of the largest rolled earthfill dams in the world. It cuts more than two miles across the Missouri River and rises 210 feet above the river channel with ND 200 carried on its crest. Behind the dam, Lake Sakajawea stretches approximately 180 miles. Beaches, fishing, and boating (ramps) are available on the 1,300-mile shoreline. There are also picnic areas and camping facilities (early May-mid-October; fee) and resorts. Displays in powerhouse lobby. (Memorial Day-Labor Day, daily; rest of year, Monday-Friday) Guided tours (Memorial Day-Labor Day, daily; rest of year, by appointment). Phone 701/654-7441.

What to See and Do

Audubon National Wildlife Refuge. Wildlife observation and eight-mi auto trail. (Daily; closed hols) 16 mi SE of Garrison via ND 37 to US 83. Phone 701/442-5474. **FREE**

Garrison Dam National Fish Hatchery. Produces northern pike, paddlefish, walleye, rainbow trout, and chinook salmon for waters in nothern Great Plains; visitor center and aquarium. (Memorial Day-Labor Day, daily) Phone 701/654-7451. **FREE**

Knife River Indian Villages National Historic Site. Three visible Hidatsa earth lodge village sites. Ranger-guided tours to reconstructed earth and self-guided trails, canoe and x-country ski trails. Visitor center; museum exhibits, demonstrations, orientation film. (Daily; closed Jan 1, Thanksgiving, Dec 25) 19 mi S of Garrison Dam via ND 200, ¼ mi N of Stanton via County 37. Phone 701/745-3309.

Lake Sakajawea State Park. Swimming (beach); fishing for pike, salmon, walleye, sauger, trout, and catfish; boating (ramp, rentals, marina); ice fishing; hiking; x-country skiing; snowmobiling; picnicking; playground; concession; tent and trailer facilities. Summer interpretive programs, sailing regattas. Standard fees. On the south shore of 180-mi-long lake. Phone 701/487-3315. Per vehicle ¢¢

Earthlodge, Knife River Indian Villages National Historic Site

Grafton

(B-7) *See also Grand Forks*

Pop 4,840 **Elev** 825 ft **Area code** 701
Zip 58237
Information Chamber of Commerce,
PO Box 632; 701/352-0781

The seat of Walsh County and a
transportation and farming junction,
Grafton bears the name of the New
Hampshire county where the pioneer
settlers of this area began their westward trek.

What to See and Do

Heritage Village. Incl furnished farmhouse; country church; depot with
caboose; taxidermy shop and working carousel. (May-Sept, Sun; also by
appt) Just west of Downtown on ND
17. Phone 701/352-3280. **Donation**

Homme Dam Recreation Area. In
wooded valley of Park River, well
stocked for fishing. Boating (docks,
ramps); winter sports, picnicking,
camping (fee). (Apr-Nov, daily) 19 mi
W on ND 17. ¢

Motel/Motor Lodge

★ **SUPER 8.** *948 W 12th St (58237).*
701/352-0888; fax 701/352-0422; res
800/800-8000. www.super8.com. 32

rms, 2 story. S $38.88; D $43.88-
$48.88. Crib free. TV; cable (pre-
mium). Complimentary continental
bkfst. Restaurant nearby. Ck-out 11
am. Business servs avail. Cr cds: A,
DS, MC, V.

🄳 🐾 🕭 🖾 🔥

Grand Forks (C-8)

Settled 1871 **Pop** 49,425 **Elev** 834 ft
Area code 701
Information Convention and Visitors
Bureau, 4251 Gateway Dr, 58203;
701/746-0444 or 800/866-4566
Web www.grandforkscvb.org

Grand Forks stands at the point
where the Red River of the North
and Red Lake River form a fork.
Socially, culturally, and commercially
the town is closely allied with its
cousin city across the river, East
Grand Forks, Minnesota. First a
French fur trading post, Grand Forks
later developed as a frontier river
town. The arrival of the railroad and
cultivation of nearby farmland
brought about another change in its
personality. The University of North
Dakota plays a dominant role in the
city's culture and economy. Grand
Forks AFB is 14 miles west on US 2.

What to See and Do

Grand Forks County Historical Society. Society maintains **Campbell House,** historic pioneer cabin of agricultural innovator Tom Campbell. Original log cabin portion dates from 1879. Also on grounds are log post office (1870), one-rm schoolhouse, and Myra Carriage Museum. **Myra Museum** houses collection of late 19th- and early 20th-century artifacts from surrounding area. (May-Oct, daily) 2405 Belmont Rd. Phone 701/775-2216. ¢¢

Turtle River State Park. This 784-acre park is named for Bell's Terrapins (mud turtles). Swimming pool; hiking, x-country skiing, chalet warming house, snowmobiling, ice-skating, other winter recreation (mid-Dec-mid-Mar; fees), picnicking, playground, camping, trailer facilities. Standard fees. 22 mi W on US 2. Phone 701/594-4445.

University of North Dakota. (1883) 12,430 students. *Eternal Flame of Knowledge,* an immense steel-girded sphere, commemorates Old Main and past presidents. J. Lloyd Stone Alumni Center, historic turn-of-the-century mansion; Center for Aerospace Sciences Atmospherium; North Dakota Museum of Art; Chester Fritz Library houses artwork. Tours. W end of University Ave. Phone 701/777-3304.

Waterworld. Water slides, tube slide, body slide, baby slide. Miniature golf. Picnic area. (June-Aug, daily) 3651 S Washington St. Phone 701/746-2795. ¢¢

Special Events

State Hockey Tournament. Engelstad Arena, University of North Dakota. Late Feb.

Native American Annual Time Out and Wacipi. University of North Dakota Indian Association. Late Mar, early Apr.

Summerthing. University Park. Arts festivals. June and July.

Grand Forks County Fair. County fairgrounds. July.

Potato Bowl Week. Queen pageant, parade, football game, other events. Mid-Sept.

Motels/Motor Lodges

★★ **BEST WESTERN TOWN HOUSE.** *710 1st Ave N (58203). 701/746-5411; fax 701/746-1407; res 800/780-7234. www.bestwestern.com.* 103 units, 2 story. S $54-$65; D $65-$75; each addl $5; suites $90-$125; under 18 free. Crib free. TV; cable (premium). Indoor pool; whirlpool. Sauna. Restaurant 6:30 am-2 pm, 5-10 pm; Sun 7 am-1:30 pm, 6-8 pm. Bar 4:30 pm-1 am. Ck-out noon. Meeting rms. Business servs avail. Valet serv. Airport, railroad station, bus depot transportation. Indoor miniature golf. Game rm. Cr cds: A, MC, V.
🅓 ⊷ 🏊 🐾 SC

★★ **C'MON INN.** *3051 32nd Ave S (58201). 701/775-3320; fax 701/780-8141; toll-free 800/255-2323. www.cmoninn.com.* 80 rms, 2 story. S $40.70-$48.70; D $46.70-$67.90; each addl $6; suites $83.90-$91.90; under 13 free. Crib free. TV; cable (premium), VCR (movies). Indoor pool; wading pool, whirlpools. Complimentary continental bkfst. Restaurant opp 6 am-11 pm. Ck-out noon. Meeting rms. Business servs avail. Sundries. Valet serv. X-country ski 2 mi. Exercise equipt. Game rm. Some refrigerators. Cr cds: A, MC, V.
🅓 🏋 🏊 🕱 🐾 SC

★ **COMFORT INN.** *3251 30th Ave S (58201). 701/775-7503; fax 701/775-7503; toll-free 800/228-5150. www.comfortinn.com.* 67 rms, 2 story. June-Aug: S $43.95-$54.95; D $43.95-$65.95; each addl $6; suites $55.95-$65.95; under 19 free; lower rates rest of yr. Crib free. Pet accepted. TV; cable. Indoor pool; whirlpool. Complimentary continental bkfst. Restaurant nearby. Ck-out 11 am. Business servs avail. Game rm. Refrigerator in suites. Cr cds: A, C, D, DS, ER, JCB, MC, V.
🅓 🐾 ⊷ 🏊 🐾 SC

★★ **COUNTRY INN & SUITES.** *3350 S 32nd Ave (58201). 701/775-5000; fax 701/775-9073; res 800/456-4000.* 89 rms, 3 story, 45 suites. S $40.95-$56.95; D $46.95-$62.95; each addl $6; under 18 free. Crib free. TV; VCR (movies free). Indoor pool; whirlpool. Sauna. Complimentary continental bkfst. Ck-out 11 am. Coin lndry. Business servs avail. Valet

serv. Refrigerators, minibars. Cr cds:
A, C, D, DS, MC, V.

D 🏊 ⛳ 🐾

★ **DAYS INN.** *3101 34th St S
(58201). 701/775-0060; res 800/329-
7466. www.daysinn.com.* 52 rms, 2
story. June-Aug: S, D $50.95-$68.95;
each addl $6; suites $55.95-$73.95;
under 16 free; lower rates rest of yr.
Crib free. TV; cable. Indoor pool;
whirlpool. Complimentary continental bkfst. Ck-out 11 am. Business servs
avail. Game rm. Refrigerator in suites.
Cr cds: A, C, D, DS, JCB, MC, V.

D 🏊 ⛳ 🐾

★ **ECONO LODGE.** *900 N 43rd St
(58203). 701/746-6666; fax 701/746-
6666; res 800/553-2666. www.econo
lodge.com.* 44 rms, 2 story, 6 suites.
Apr-Oct: S $44-$49; D $49-$54; each
addl $5; under 18 free; lower rates
rest of yr. Crib free. TV; cable (premium). Complimentary continental
bkfst. Restaurant nearby. Ck-out 11
am. Business servs avail. In-rm
modem link. Refrigerator, wet bar in
suites. Cr cds: A, C, D, DS, MC, V.

D ⛳ 🐾 SC

★ **FABULOUS WESTWARD HO
MOTEL.** *3400 Gateway Dr (58203).
701/775-5341; fax 701/775-3703; toll-
free 800/437-9562.* 108 rms, 1-2 story.
S $41; D $49-$55; each addl $5;
suites $80; under 12 free. Crib free.
Pet accepted. TV; cable, VCR avail
(movies). Heated pool. Sauna.
Restaurant 6:30 am-10 pm; Sun 8
am-10 pm. Bars 11-1 am; entertainment Wed-Sat eves. Ck-out noon.
Meeting rms. Business servs avail. In-
rm modem link. Bathrm phones. Picnic tables. Old West motif; model
Western village. Casino. Cr cds: A, C,
D, DS, ER, MC, V.

🐾 🏊 ⛳ 🐾 SC

★★ **FAIRFIELD INN.** *3051 S 34th St
(58201). 701/775-7910; res 800/228-
2800 www.fairfieldinn.com.* 62 rms, 3
story. S $45.95-$53.95; D $51.95-
$59.95; each addl $6; under 18 free.
Crib free. TV; cable. Indoor pool;
whirlpool. Complimentary continental bkfst. Ck-out noon. Business servs
avail. In-rm modem link. Sundries.
Valet serv. Game rm. Cr cds: A, C, D,
DS, MC, V.

D 🏊 ⛳ 🐾

★★ **HOLIDAY INN.** *1210 N 43rd St
(58203). 701/772-7131; fax 701/780-
9112; res 888/249-1464. www.holiday-
inn.com.* 150 rms, 2 story. S, D $74;
under 19 free. Crib free. TV; cable
(premium). Indoor pool; wading pool,
whirlpool. Restaurant 6:30 am-2 pm,
5-10 pm. Bar 2 pm-1 am. Ck-out
noon. Coin lndry. Meeting rms. Business servs avail. In-rm modem link.
Bellhops. Valet serv. Sundries. Free airport, railroad station, bus depot transportation. Putting green. Exercise
equipt; sauna. Game rm. Casino. Cr
cds: A, C, D, DS, JCB, MC, V.

D 🏊 🏋 🛫 ⛳ 🐾

★ **RAMADA INN.** *1205 N 43rd St
(58203). 701/775-3951; fax 701/775-
9774; toll-free 800/228-2828. www.
ramada.com.* 100 rms, 2 story. S $60-
$68; D $70-$78; each addl $7; under
18 free. Crib free. TV; cable (premium), VCR avail. Indoor pool; wading pool, whirlpool, poolside serv.
Sauna. Restaurant 6:30 am-9 pm. Bar
3 pm-1 am. Ck-out noon. Coin
lndry. Meeting rms. Business servs
avail. In-rm modem link. Bellhops.
Valet serv. Free airport, railroad station, bus depot transportation. Rec
rm. Casino. Cr cds: A, C, D, DS, ER,
JCB, MC, V.

D 🏊 🛫 ⛳ 🐾

★★ **ROAD KING INN.** *3300 S 30th
Ave (58201). 701/746-1391; fax 701/
746-8586; toll-free 800/707-1391.
www.roadkinginn.com.* 85 rms, 2 story.
S $39-$53; D $47-$63; each addl $6;
suites $84-$92; under 12 free. Crib
free. TV; cable (premium). Indoor
pool; wading pool, whirlpool. Complimentary continental bkfst. Restaurant nearby. Ck-out noon. Coin
lndry. Meeting rm. Business servs
avail. In-rm modem link. Valet serv.
Health club privileges. Game rm.
Whirlpool in suites. Cr cds: A, DS,
MC, V.

D 🏊 ⛳ 🐾

★ **ROAD KING INN.** *1015 N 43rd St
(58203). 701/775-0691; fax 701/775-
9964; toll-free 800/950-0691. www.
roadkinginn.com.* 98 rms, 2 story. S
$27.95-$42.95; D $36.95-$42.95;
each addl $5; under 12 free. Crib
free. TV; cable. Complimentary continental bkfst; afternoon refreshments. Restaurant nearby. Ck-out
noon. Coin lndry. Business servs

avail. Valet serv. Health club privileges. Cr cds: A, C, D, DS, MC, V.
⊠ 🐾 SC

★ **SELECT INN OF GRAND FORKS.** *1000 N 42nd St (58203). 701/775-0555; fax 701/775-9967; res 800/641-1000. www.selectinn.com.* 120 rms. S $27.95-$35.95; D $36.95-$45.95; each addl $4; under 13 free. Crib free. Pet accepted. TV; cable (premium), VCR avail (movies). Complimentary continental bkfst. Restaurant nearby. Ck-out noon. Coin lndry. Business servs avail. Valet serv. Cr cds: A, MC, V.
◀ ✕ 🐾

★ **SUPER 8 MOTEL.** *1122 N 43rd St (58203). 701/775-8138; res 800/800-8000. www.super8.com.* 33 rms, 2 story. S $38.88-$48.88; D $43.88-$63.88; each addl $6; under 12 free. Crib free. TV; cable. Restaurant nearby. Ck-out 11 am. Business servs avail. Cr cds: A, MC, V.
✕ 🐾

Restaurant

★★ **G F GOODRIBS.** *4223 N 12th Ave (58203). 701/746-7115.* Hrs: 11 am-10 pm; Fri, Sat to 11 pm; Sun 10:30 am-9 pm; Sun brunch to 2 pm. Closed Dec 24, 25. Res accepted. Bar to 1 am; Sun from noon. Lunch $4-$6, dinner $9-$15. Sun brunch $6.39. Children's menu. Specializes in ribs, steak, seafood. Cr cds: A, DS, MC, V.
D SC ⊸

Jamestown

(D-6) *See also Carrington, Valley City*

Settled 1872 **Pop** 15,571 **Elev** 1,410 ft
Area code 701 **Zip** 58401
Information Jamestown Promotion and Tourism Center, 212 Third Ave NE; 701/252-4835 or 800/222-4766

Settlers and businessmen in the wake of soldiers and railroad workers established Jamestown as a transportation center guarded by Fort Seward. When farmers discovered they could pay for their rich land with two years' crops, the area developed as a prosperous diversified agricultural sector. The James River, known as the longest unnavigable river in the world, flows through the town. On the northeastern edge of town is Jamestown College (1883).

What to See and Do

Fort Seward Historic Site and Interpretive Center. Built on the original site of Fort Seward, the center preserves the early military history of the region with a collection of historical documents and artifacts. There is also a picnic area on the grounds. (Apr-Oct, daily) US 281 and 8th St NW. Phone 701/252-8421. **FREE**

Frontier Village. Large statue of bison; restored school, church, log cabin, railroad depot, old shops, art exhibits, trading post, jail. Entertainment. (May-Sept, daily) Also **National Buffalo Museum** (All yr; fee). Home of "White Cloud," an albino buffalo. On I-94, SE edge of town. Phone 701/252-6307. **FREE**

Whitestone Hill Battlefield State Historic Site. Most probably triggered by the 1862 Sioux uprising in Minnesota, the Sept 1863 Battle of Whitestone Hill marked the beginning of a war between the US Cavalry and the Plains Sioux that lasted for more than 20 yrs. Granite monument of bugler, graves of soldiers; small museum. Picnicking, playgrounds. (Mid-May-mid-Sept, Thurs-Mon) 37 mi S on US 281, then 15 mi W on ND 13 to Kulm, then 15 mi S on ND 56, then E on unimproved road. **FREE**

Special Events

Fort Seward Wagon Train. A wk-long wagon train experience. Wagons are pulled by draft horses or mules; train stops along the way at historical sites. Participants dress and camp in the manner of the pioneers. For info phone 701/252-6844. One wk late June.

Stutsman County Fair. Late June or early July.

Motels/Motor Lodges

★ **COMFORT INN.** *811 SW 20th St (58401). 701/252-7125; res 800/228-5150. www.comfortinn.com.* 52 rms, 2 story, 8 suites. S $49.95; D $55.95; each addl $5; suites $61.95; under 18 free; wkly rates; higher rates: county fair, stockcar stampede. Crib free. Pet accepted. TV; cable. Indoor pool; whirlpool. Complimentary continental bkfst. Restaurant adj 6 am-10 pm. Ck-out 11 am. Business servs avail. Game rm. Refrigerator in suites. Cr cds: A, D, DS, MC, V.

★★ **DAKOTA INN.** *US 281 S (58402). 701/252-3611; fax 701/252-5711; toll-free 800/726-7924.* 120 rms, 2 story. S $40-$50; D $45-$60; each addl $5; under 16 free. Crib $5. Pet accepted. TV; cable. Indoor pool; whirlpool. Restaurant 7 am-10 pm. Bar 3 pm-1 am; entertainment Fri, Sat. Ck-out 11 am. Meeting rms. Business servs avail. Bellhops. Valet serv. Free airport, bus depot transportation. Game rm. Lawn games. Cr cds: A, DS, MC, V.

★★ **GLADSTONE SELECT HOTEL.** *111 2nd St NE (58401). 701/252-0700; fax 701/252-0700; toll-free 800/641-1000. www.selectinn.com.* 117 rms, 2 story. S, D $50-$65; each addl $5; under 18 free. Crib $3. Pet accepted. TV; cable. Indoor pool; whirlpool. Restaurant 6:30 am-10 pm. Bar. Ck-out 11 am. Meeting rms. Business servs avail. Free airport, bus depot transportation. Casino. Cr cds: A, C, D, DS, MC, V.

★ **SUPER 8 MOTEL.** *US 281 S and I-94 (58402). 701/252-4715; fax 701/251-1647; res 800/800-8000. www.super8.com.* 62 rms, 2 story. S $38-$47; D $47-$54. Crib $2. TV; cable. Complimentary coffee in lobby. Ck-out 11 am. Business servs avail. Cr cds: A, D, DS, MC, V.

Kenmare

(B-3) *See also Minot*

Settled 1897 **Pop** 1,214 **Elev** 1,850 ft
Area code 701 **Zip** 58746
Information Chamber of Commerce, 320 Central Ave, PO Box 517; 701/385-4857

In the center of a rich farming area that produces durum wheat and sunflowers, Kenmare also enjoys the beauties of nature from its hillside location overlooking Middle Des Lacs Lake. At one time, grain was shipped down the lake by steamboat from the Canadian border area for shipment by rail to US markets.

What to See and Do

Des Lacs National Wildlife Refuge. Rings Upper, Middle, and Lower Des Lacs Lakes, a 30-mi finger of water pointing down from Canadian border. A six-mi stretch of the Upper Lake has a picnic site (Memorial Day-Labor Day, daily). The Taskers Coulee Recreational Area (3 mi SW of town) offers picnicking, bird-watching (Memorial Day-Labor Day, daily). Refuge headquarters is ½ mi W of town (Mon-Fri; closed hols). Phone 701/385-4046. **FREE**

Lake Darling. (See Upper Souris National Wildlife Refuge in MINOT.) 6 mi N on US 52, then 18 mi E on ND 5, then S.

Mandan

(E-4) *See also Bismarck*

Settled 1881 **Pop** 15,177 **Elev** 1,651 ft
Area code 701 **Zip** 58554
Information Bismarck-Mandan Convention and Visitor Bureau, PO Box 2274, Bismarck 58502; 701/222-4308 or 800/767-3555
Web www.bismarck-mandancvb.org

The Mandan originally farmed this area, and today the agricultural tradition persists in the dairy and dry farms that surround the city. Lignite, a soft coal, is mined in this region. Mandan has been an important railroad city since the tracks crossed the Missouri River the year the city was founded.

What to See and Do

Cross Ranch Nature Preserve. The Nature Conservancy. This 6,000-acre nature preserve has mixed grass prairies, Missouri River floodplain forest, upland woody draws. Bison herd. Hiking and self-guided nature trails. (Daily) 30 mi N via ND H1806 (gravel). Phone 701/794-8741. **FREE**

Five Nations Art Depot. Home to Native American arts and crafts; works avail to purchase. (Daily) Main St. **FREE**

★ Fort Abraham Lincoln State Park. Historic site marks fort which Custer commanded prior to his "last stand." Reconstructed fort buildings (tours Memorial Day-Labor Day) and Mandan earth lodge village. Fishing, hiking, x-country skiing, snowmobiling, picnicking, playground, concession, camping. Visitor center, amphitheater, museum, summer interpretive program. 7 mi S on ND 1806. Phone 701/663-9571. ¢¢

Railroad Museum. Houses exhibits from early 1900s. Handmade models, photographs, and uniforms; miniature train carries passengers on Sun. (Memorial Day-Labor Day, afternoons) N of Mandan on Old Red Trail. **FREE**

Skiing. Huff Hills Ski Area. Two double chairlifts. Rentals (snowboard and ski). Chalet. Longest run 3,600 ft; vertical drop 425 ft. (Mid-Nov-Mar, Thurs-Sun) 15 mi S on ND 1806. ¢¢¢¢

Special Events

Stock Car Racing. Dacotah Speedway. ⅜-mi dirt, high-banked, oval track. Fri. Phone 701/663-6843. Mid-May-first wkend Sept.

Buggies 'n Blues. 205 2nd Ave NW. Live entertainment, over 300 classic roadsters on display. Phone 701/663-1136. Early June.

Jaycees Rodeo Days. Rodeo, parade, midway, arts and crafts. Early July.

Motel/Motor Lodge

★★ BEST WESTERN SEVEN SEAS INN. 2611 Old Red Tr (58554). 701/663-7401; fax 701/663-0025; res 800/780-7234. www.bestwestern.com. 103 rms, 3 story. S $59; D $69; each addl $5; suites $99-$150; under 18 free. Crib free. TV; cable. Indoor pool; whirlpool. Coffee in rms. Restaurant 6:30 am-10:30 pm. Bar 11-1 am; entertainment. Ck-out noon. Ck-in 3 pm. Meeting rms. Business servs avail. Valet serv. Sundries. Free airport transportation.

Refrigerators, microwaves avail. Cr cds: A, C, D, DS, MC, V.

D 🐾 🕏 🐟 🏕 🔥

Unrated Dining Spot

MERIWETHERS. 1700 River Rd (58554). 701/224-0455. Hrs: 11 am-10 pm. Closed Thanksgiving, Dec 25. Bar. Lunch, dinner $4.95-$14.95. Children's menu. Specializes in steak, seafood, barbecue. Entertainment (summer). Outdoor dining. On Missouri River. Cr cds: A, D, DS, MC, V.

D SC 🔌

Medora

(D-5) See also Dickinson

Founded 1883 **Pop** 101 **Elev** 2,271 ft
Area code 701 **Zip** 58645

This village is a living museum of two of the most colorful characters found on the raw badlands frontier: young, bespectacled Theodore Roosevelt, and the hot-blooded, visionary Marquis de Mores. The Marquis, a wealthy Frenchman, established the town and named it for his wife, daughter of a New York banker. He built a packing plant and icehouses, then planned to slaughter cattle on the range and ship them to metropolitan markets in refrigerated railroad cars. The plan fizzled, but not before the mustachioed Frenchman left his stamp on the community. Roosevelt came here in 1883 and won respect as part owner of the Maltese Cross and Elkhorn ranches and as organizer and first president of the Little Missouri Stockmen's Association.

What to See and Do

★ Chateau de Mores State Historic Site. The site commemorates the life of Antoine de Vallombrosa, the Marquis de Mores. The Marquis busied himself with many undertakings such as a stagecoach line, an experiment with refrigerated railroad cars, and a beef packing plant. Remaining are the ruins of a packing plant; a 26-rm, two-story frame mansion filled with French furnishings; also library, servants' quarters, relic rm

THE LITTLE MISSOURI BADLANDS

Medora sits at the base of the dramatic Little Missouri Badlands, a deeply eroded gorge that exposes hundreds of millions of years of sedimentary deposits in colorful horizontal striations. Medora itself is a fascinating historical town: Teddy Roosevelt lived near here in the 1880s, as did the flamboyant Marquis de Mores, a French nobleman who journeyed to Dakota Territory to live out his cowboy fantasies. Before setting out to explore bluffs that rise behind the town, be sure to visit the Chateau de Mores, the luxurious frontier home built by the marquis. When it was built in 1883, this 26-room mansion was the finest and most modern private home for hundreds of miles.

The Maah Daah Hey Trail is 100 miles long and connects the northern and southern sections of the Theodore Roosevelt National Park, passing through the Little Missouri National Grassland. The following hike covers 4 1/2 miles at the trail's southern extreme and explores the scenic badlands above Medora, passing through the fascinating and ruggedly beautiful badlands ecosystem, home to prairie wildlife including pronghorn antelope, coyotes, white-tail deer, prairie dogs, and rattlesnakes. This section of the Maah Daah Hey Trail makes a wonderful 1/2-day hike for fit hikers.

Begin the hike at Sully Creek State Park, two miles south of Medora (the Maah Daah Hey Trail is also popular with mountain bikers, so be aware that you'll share the trail). The trail crosses the Little Missouri River, which is ankle-deep and easily waded in summer, and follows the river valley through stands of cottonwood, willow, and silver sage. The trail then begins to climb up the face of a badland mesa, eventually reaching a plateau. From a rocky escarpment, enjoy a magnificent overlook onto Medora nestled in the Little Missouri River breaks. Continue north on the trail through prairie grassland to a side path, the Canyon Trail, which drops steeply down a rugged canyon wall to a prairie dog town. Follow the trail north, through a self-closing gate, to where the Canyon Trail rejoins the Maah Daah Hey. From here, hikers have a choice of returning to Medora along a gravel road or continuing north through more badlands landscape to the South Unit of the Theodore Roosevelt National Park headquarters.

displaying the Marquis' saddles, guns, boots, coats, and other possessions. An interpretive center is on the grounds. The site is not heated. Picnicking avail. Self-guided tours (mid-May-mid-Sept, daily; rest of yr, by appt; closed Jan 1, Thanksgiving, Dec 25). 1 mi W, off US 10, I-94. Phone 701/623-4355. ¢¢

Historic buildings. Rough Riders Hotel (1884) provided the name of T. R.'s regiment in the Spanish-American War; remodeled. **St. Mary's Catholic Church** (1884), built by the Marquis. **Joe Ferris Store** (1885), owned by Roosevelt partner; remodeled (1965). On or near US 10, I-94.

Theodore Roosevelt National Park-South Unit. (see) Phone 701/623-4466.

Special Event

Medora Musical. Outdoor musical extravaganza; western songs, dance. Phone 800/633-6721. June.

Motel/Motor Lodge

★★ **AMERICINN MOTEL & SUITES.** *75 E River Rd S (58645). 701/623-4800; fax 701/623-4890; res 800/634-3444. www.americinn.com.* 56 rms, 2 story. June-Aug: S, D $89.90; each addl $6; suites $140-$160; under 12 free; higher rates special events; lower rates rest of yr. Crib $6. Pet accepted. TV; cable (premium). Complimentary continental bkfst, coffee in rms. Restaurant nearby. Ck-out 11 am. Meeting rms. Business servs avail. In-rm modem link. Coin lndry. Indoor pool; whirlpool. Game rm. Some in-rm whirlpools, refrigerators, microwaves. Cr cds: A, C, D, DS, MC, V.

[icons]

Minot (B-3)

Settled 1886 **Pop** 34,544 **Elev** 1,580 ft
Area code 701 **Zip** 58701
Information Convention and Visitors Bureau, 1020 S Broadway, PO Box 2066, 58702; 701/857-8206 or 800/264-2626
Web www.minotchamber.org

Minot's advance from tepee and tarpaper to a supersonic-age city has been so vigorous that it lays claim to being the "Magic City." Where buffalo bones were once stacked by "plainscombers" stands a city rich from agriculture, lignite coal reserves, oil pools, industries, and railroad yards on both sides of the Mouse River. Minot is the commercial center of a radius that sweeps into Canada. Minot State University is located here.

What to See and Do

Minot AFB. Air Combat Command base for B-52 bombers, UH-1 helicopters, and Minuteman III missiles under 91st Space Wing. 13 mi N on US 83. For tour information contact Base Public Affairs. Phone 701/723-6212. **FREE**

Oak Park. Heated swimming pool, wading pool, bathhouse, lifeguards (fee; schedule same as Roosevelt Park); exercise trail; picnicking, playground, fireplaces. Park (daily). 4th Ave NW between 10th and 16th sts NW. **FREE**

Roosevelt Park and Zoo. Incl 90 acres of formal lawns and sunken gardens. On the grounds are a swimming pool, water slide, and bathhouse, lifeguards on duty (late May-early Sept, daily; fee). Also in the park are picnic facilities, playgrounds, tennis courts, mini train (fee), carousel (fee), a bandshell, and a 28-acre zoo (May-Sept, daily; fee). Park (daily). 1219 Burdick Expy E. Phone 701/857-4166.

Scandinavian Heritage Center. A 220-yr-old house from Sigdal, Norway; Danish windmill; flag display; statues of famous people. (Daily; Memorial Day-Labor Day, wkends) Broadway and 11th Ave. Phone 701/852-9161. **Donation**

Upper Souris National Wildlife Refuge. Lake Darling, a 20-mi lake within the refuge, is home to more than 290 species of birds. Ice fishing and open-water fishing for walleye, northern pike, smallmouth bass, and perch in designated areas, boat and bank fishing in summer, canoe areas; picnic facilities, three-mi auto tour route, hiking trails. Refuge headquarters are 7 mi N of Foxholm. 18 mi NW on US 52 to Foxholm, then continue 7 mi N, or travel 15 mi N on US 83, then 12 mi W on County 6. For more information contact Upper Souris National Wildlife Refuge, Rural Rte 1, Box 163, Foxholm 58738. Phone 701/468-5467. **FREE**

Ward County Historical Society Museum and Pioneer Village. First county courthouse, early schoolhouse, depot, blacksmith shop, pioneer cabin, church, and ten-rm house, barbershop, dental parlor; museum with antiques. (May-Sept, limited hrs; also by appt) State Fairgrounds. Phone 701/839-0785. **FREE**

Special Events

North Dakota State Fair. State Fairgrounds. 4-H, livestock, commercial exhibits; horse and tractor pulls, carnival, machinery show, concerts, auto races, demolition derby. Phone 701/852-FAIR. Last wk July.

Norsk Hostfest. All Seasons Arena. Norwegian folk festival. Phone 701/852-2368. Mid-Oct.

Motels/Motor Lodges

★★ **BEST WESTERN-KELLY INN.** *1510 26th Ave SW (58701). 701/852-4300; fax 701/838-1234; toll-free 800/780-7234. www.bestwestern.com.* 100 rms, 2 story. S $55; D $61; each addl $6; suites $69-$85; under 18 free; higher rates special events. Crib avail. Pet accepted. TV; cable (premium), VCR (movies). Indoor pool; whirlpool. Complimentary continental bkfst. Bar 5 pm-1 am. Ck-out 11 am. Meeting rm. Business servs avail. Game rm. Cr cds: A, C, D, DS, MC, V.

[icons]

★ **COMFORT INN.** *1515 22nd Ave SW (58701). 701/852-2201; fax*

701/852-2201; res 800/228-5150. www.comfortinn.com. 141 rms, 3 story. S, D $58; each addl $5; under 18 free. Crib free. Pet accepted. TV; cable. Indoor pool; whirlpool. Complimentary continental bkfst. Restaurant adj 6-1 am. Ck-out 11 am. Meeting rms. Business servs avail. Valet serv. Sundries. Game rm. Cr cds: A, C, D, DS, JCB, MC, V.
D 🐾 ≈ ≧ 🔥

★ **DAYS INN.** 2100 4th St SW (58701). 701/852-3646; fax 701/852-0501; res 800/544-8313. www.daysinn.com. 82 rms, 3 story. S $42-$49; D $48-$59; suites $48-$65; each addl $3; under 18 free. Crib free. TV; cable, VCR avail. Indoor pool; whirlpool. Sauna. Complimentary continental bkfst. Ck-out noon. Business servs avail. Cr cds: A, C, D, DS, MC, V.
D 🛆 ≈ ≧ 🔥

★★ **FAIRFIELD INN.** 900 24th Ave SW (58701). 701/838-2424; fax 701/838-2424; res 800/228-2800. www.fairfieldinn.com. 62 rms, 3 story. May-Aug: S $45; D $51; each addl $6; suites $60.95; under 18 free; higher rates Norsk Hostfest; lower rates rest of yr. Crib free. TV; cable (premium). Indoor pool; whirlpool. Complimentary continental bkfst. Restaurant nearby. Ck-out noon. Meeting rms. Business servs avail. Sundries. Game rm. Cr cds: A, C, D, DS, MC, V.
D ≈ ≧ 🔥

★★ **HOLIDAY INN.** 2200 Burdick Expy E (58702). 701/852-2504; fax 701/852-2630; toll-free 800/468-9968. www.holiday-inn.com/minotnd. 173 rms. S $53-$94; D $63-$94; each addl $5; suites $125-$150; under 18 free; higher rates special events. Crib free. TV; cable. Heated pool; whirlpool, poolside serv. Sauna. Complimentary coffee in rms. Restaurant 6-1 am. Bar 5 pm-midnight. Ck-out noon. Meeting rms. Business servs avail. Gift shop. Barber, beauty shop. Airport, railroad station, bus depot transportation. Golf privileges. Game rm. Balconies. Cr cds: A, C, D, DS, JCB, MC, V.
D 🍴 ≈ ≧ 🔥 SC

Restaurant

★★ **FIELD & STREAM.** US 83 N (58703). 701/852-3663. Hrs: 5-9:30

pm. Closed Sun; hols. Res accepted. Dinner $8.95-$25.95. Children's menu. Specializes in prime rib, steak, seafood. Cr cds: A, C, D, DS, MC, V.
D ≧

Rugby

(B-5) See also Minot

Founded 1886 **Pop** 2,909 **Elev** 1,545 ft **Area code** 701 **Zip** 58368

The geographical center of North America has been located by the US Geological Survey as one-half mile south of Rugby. The location is marked by a monument.

What to See and Do

Geographical Museum and Pioneer Village. A rather unusual museum featuring 27 buildings from Pierce County and the surrounding area. Each building is furnished with materials from the period when it was in use. Gun collections, displays of farm implements, dolls, and glass items. (May-Sept, daily) US 2 E. Phone 701/776-6414. ¢¢

Theodore Roosevelt National Park

See also Medora

The 70,447 scenic acres of spectacular badlands that compose this park are the state's foremost tourist attraction. This national park is a monument to Theodore Roosevelt, who, in addition to all of his other vigorous pursuits, was the nation's champion of conservation of natural resources. Roosevelt, who came to the badlands in September 1883 to hunt buffalo and other big game, became interested in the open-range cattle industry and purchased interest in the Maltese Cross Ranch near Medora (see). He returned the next year and established another ranch, the Elkhorn, about 35 miles north of

North Dakota Badlands

Medora. The demands of his political career and losses in cattle production eventually forced him to abandon his ranching ventures.

The park preserves the landscape as Roosevelt knew it. General Sully, during his campaign against the Sioux in 1864, described it as "hell with the fires out...grand, dismal, and majestic." From a thick series of flat-lying sedimentary rocks, wind and water have carved curiously sculptured formations, tablelands, buttes, canyons, and rugged hills. Exposed in eroded hillsides are thick, dark layers of lignite coal that sometimes are fired by lightning and burn slowly for many years, often baking adjacent clay layers into a red, bricklike substance called scoria, or clinker.

Many forms of wildlife inhabit the area. Elk and bison have been reintroduced here and may be seen by visitors. There are several large prairie dog towns; mule and white-tail deer are abundant; wild horses can be seen in the South Unit; and the area is rich in bird life incl hawks, falcons, eagles, and other more common species.

The park is divided into three units: the South Unit is accessible from I-94 at Medora, where there is a visitor center (daily) and Roosevelt's Maltese Cross cabin; the Elkhorn

Ranch Site on the Little Missouri River can be reached only by rough dirt roads, and visitors should first obtain current information from rangers at the Medora Visitor Center, phone 701/623-4466, before attempting the trip; the North Unit is accessible from US 85, near Watford City, and this unit also has a visitor center. An additional visitor center is located at Painted Canyon Scenic Overlook on I-94 (Apr-Oct, daily). There are self-guided trails, picnic areas, camping (standard fees, daily), and evening campfire programs in both the North and South Units (June-mid-September). The park is open all year (fee). Visitor centers are closed January 1, Thanksgiving, December 25. Golden Eagle and Golden Age passports are accepted (see MAKING THE MOST OF YOUR TRIP).

Valley City

(D-7) *See also Jamestown*

Settled 1872 **Pop** 7,163 **Elev** 1,222 ft
Area code 701 **Zip** 58072
Information Valley City Area Chamber of Commerce, 205 NE 2nd St, PO Box 724; 701/845-1891

The railroad and the first settlers arrived here simultaneously to establish a community then known as Worthington. Later, as the seat of Barnes County, the town in the deeply forested Sheyenne River valley changed to its present name. The grain fields and dairy farms of the surrounding area provide the basis of its economy.

What to See and Do

Baldhill Dam and Lake Ashtabula. Impounds Sheyenne River and Baldhill Creek in water supply project, creating 27-mi-long Lake Ashtabula; eight recreational areas. Swimming, waterskiing, fishing, boating (ramps); picnicking (shelters), concessions, camping (hookups; fee). Fish hatchery. (May-Oct) 11 mi NW on county road. Phone 701/845-2970.

Clausen Springs Park. A 400-acre park with a 50-acre lake. Fishing, canoes, boating (electric motors only); nature trails, bicycling, picnicking, playground, camping, tent and trailer sites (electric hookups, fee). (May-Oct, daily) 4 mi W on I-94, then 16 mi S on ND 1, then 1 mi E, ½ mi S following signs.

Little Yellowstone Park. Picnicking, camping (electric hookups, fee) in sheltered portion of rugged Sheyenne River valley; fireplaces, shelters, rustic bridges. (May-Oct, daily) 4 mi W on I-94, then 19 mi S on ND 1, then 6 mi E off ND 46.

Valley City State University. (1890) 1,100 students. Teacher education, business, industrial technology, liberal arts. Planetarium on campus; phone 701/845-7452. Campus tours. South side of town. Phone 701/845-7101.

Special Event

Dakota Soap Box Derby. Two-day downhill gravity race. Mid-June.

Motel/Motor Lodge

★ **SUPER 8 MOTEL.** 822 11th St SW (58072). 701/845-1140; fax 701/845-1145; toll-free 800/800-8000. www.super8.com. 30 rms, 2 story. S $31.95; D $37.95; each addl $3. Crib free. TV; cable, VCR avail (movies). Complimentary coffee in lobby. Restaurant

nearby. Ck-out 11 am. Business servs avail. Cr cds: A, C, D, DS, MC, V.
◹ ⚑ SC

Wahpeton

(E-8) *See also Fargo*

Settled 1871 **Pop** 8,751 **Elev** 963 ft
Area code 701 **Zip** 58075
Information Visitors Center, 120 N 4th St; 701/642-8559 or 800/892-6673
Web www.wahpchamber.com/visitors

Where the waters of the Bois de Sioux and Otter Tail rivers integrate to become the Red River of the North, Wahpeton, derived from an Indian word meaning "dwellers among the leaves," is situated at the start of the Red River. Wahpeton is the marketplace for a large segment of the southeast corner of the state.

What to See and Do

Chahinkapa Park. Chahinkapa Zoo incl petting zoo; many North American animals, several exotic displays, nature center. Restored 1926 **Prairie Rose Carousel** (Memorial Day-Labor Day; fee). Swimming, water slide (fee), trails, basketball, tennis, 18-hole golf, softball, picnicking, camping (fee). 1st St and 7th Ave N, on banks of Red River of the North. Phone 701/642-2811. ¢¢

✪ **Fort Abercrombie State Historic Site.** First federal military post in state, rebuilt on authentic lines; blockhouses, guardhouse, stockade. Built on the west bank of the Red River, the fort regulated fur trade, kept peace between Chippewa and Sioux, served as gateway through which wagon trains, stagecoaches, and Army units moved west. Established in 1858, abandoned in 1859, reoccupied in 1860 and moved to present site, repelled a six-wk siege in 1862, and abandoned in 1877. Museum interprets history of the fort; displays of relics and early settlers' possessions (mid-May-mid-Sept, daily; fee). Picnicking. 20 mi N, ½ mi E off US 81, in Abercrombie. Phone 701/224-2666. **FREE**

Kidder Recreation Area. Fishing, boating (docks, ramp); picnicking. 4th St and 19th Ave N. Phone 701/642-2811. **FREE**

Richland County Historical Museum. Pioneer artifacts trace county's history; display of Rosemeade pottery. (Apr-Nov, limited hrs) 2nd St and 7th Ave N. Phone 701/642-3075. **FREE**

Special Events

Winter Wonderland. Second wkend Feb.

Carousel Days. Second wkend June.

Motel/Motor Lodge

★ **SUPER 8.** *995 N 21st Ave (58075). 701/642-8731; fax 701/642-8733; res 800/800-8000. www.super8.com.* 58 rms, 2 story. S $40.88; D $44.88-$47.88; each addl $3; under 18 free. Crib free. TV; cable. Indoor pool; whirlpool. Complimentary continental bkfst. Restaurant 6 am-10 pm; Sun 7 am-2 pm. Bar 3 pm-1 am. Ckout 11 am. Meeting rms. Business servs avail. In-rm modem link. X-country ski 1½ mi. Casino. Cr cds: A, D, DS, MC, V.

Williston (B-1)

Settled 1870 **Pop** 13,131 **Elev** 1,880 ft
Area code 701 **Zip** 58801
Information Convention and Visitors Bureau, 10 Main St; 800/615-9041

The city, which was first called "Little Muddy," has grown from its origin as a small supply center for ranchers. As the area populated, the production of grains became an important business. The refining of high-grade petroleum has also had a major effect on the local economy since it was discovered in the early 1950s. Today Williston is a trading center for some 90,000 people.

What to See and Do

Buffalo Trails Museum. Seven-building complex with dioramas of Native American and pioneer life; fossils; interior of homesteader's shack; regional historical exhibits. (June-Aug, daily; Sept-Oct, Sun only; other days and May by appt) 6 mi N on US 2, 85, then 13 mi E on County

Fort Union Trading Post National Historic Site

Rd 6 in Epping. Phone 701/859-4361. ¢

Fort Buford State Historic Site. Established near the confluence of the Missouri and Yellowstone rivers in 1866, Fort Buford served primarily as the distribution point for government annuities to peaceful natives in the vicinity. During the war with the Sioux (1870s and 1880s), the post became a major supply depot for military field operations. The fort is perhaps best remembered as the site of the surrender of Sitting Bull in 1881. Original features still existing on the site incl a stone powder magazine, the post cemetery, and a large officers' quarters, which now houses a museum. Picnicking. (Mid-May-mid-Sept, daily; rest of yr, by appt) 7 mi W on US 2, then 17 mi SW on ND 1804. Phone 701/572-9034. ¢

Fort Union Trading Post National Historic Site. American Fur Company built this fort in 1829 at the confluence of the Yellowstone and Missouri rivers. During the next three decades it was one of the most important trading depots on the western frontier. In 1867, the government bought the fort, dismantled it, and used the materials to build Fort Buford two mi away. Much of the fort has been reconstructed. A National Park Service visitor center is located in the Bourgeois House. Guided tours and interpretive programs (summer). Site (daily). For details contact Superintendent, Fort Union Trading Post NHS, Buford Rte. 7 mi W on US 2, then SW on ND 1804W. Phone 701/572-9083. **FREE**

Lewis and Clark State Park. Situated on an upper bay of Lake Sakajawea and surrounded by beautiful scenery. Swimming, fishing; hiking, x-country skiing and snowmobiling, picnicking, playground, camping. Amphitheater; summer interpretive program. Standard fees. 19 mi SE off ND 1804. Phone 701/859-3071.

Lewis and Clark Trail Museum. Diorama of Fort Mandan; rms furnished as pioneer home, country store, blacksmith, shoe and saddle shops, post office; farm machinery. (Memorial Day-Labor Day, daily) 19 mi S on US 85 in Alexander. Phone 701/828-3595. ¢

Spring Lake Park. Landscaped park area, lagoons. Picnicking. (Daily) 3 mi N on US 2, 85. **FREE**

Special Events

Fort Union Trading Post Rendezvous. Phone 701/572-9083. Mid-June.

Buffalo Trails Day. Parade, chuck wagon breakfast, old-time music, contests, games. July.

Fort Buford 6th Infantry State Historical Encampment. Reenactment of Indian Wars frontier army exercises. Phone 701/572-9034. July.

OKLAHOMA

Populated by Native Americans, the area that was to become the state of Oklahoma was practically unknown to Americans at the time of the Louisiana Purchase of 1803. Believing these unsettled lands to be of little value, the government set them aside as "Indian Territory" in 1830, assigning a portion to each of the Five Civilized Tribes. Between 1830-46, 20,000 Creeks of Georgia and Alabama, 5,000 Choctaws of Mississippi and Louisiana, 4,000 Chickasaws of Mississippi, and 3,000 Seminoles of Florida were forced to move to Oklahoma. In 1838 some 16,000 Cherokees were marched west from their lands in North Carolina, Tennessee, and Georgia by troops under the command of General Winfield Scott. Many hid out in the hills and swamps of their homeland, where their descendants still remain. About one-fourth of those forced west over this "Trail of Tears" died en route of hunger, disease, cold, and exhaustion. But those who reached the Indian Territory were soon running their own affairs with skill and determination. By 1890, 67 different tribal groups resided in Oklahoma. Today Oklahoma has the largest Native American population in the United States.

Population: 3,145,585
Area: 69,919 square miles
Elevation: 287-4,973 feet
Peak: Black Mesa (Cimarron County)
Entered Union: November 16, 1907 (46th state)
Capital: Oklahoma City
Motto: Labor conquers all things
Nickname: Sooner State
Flower: Mistletoe
Bird: Scissor-tailed Flycatcher
Tree: Redbud
Fair: September 13-29, 2002, in Oklahoma City
Time Zone: Central
Website: www.state.ok.us

As the nation moved west settlers squatted in the Indian Territory, wanting the land for their own. On April 22, 1889, portions of the land were opened for

Turner Falls Park, Arbuckle Mountains, near Davis

settlement. In the next few years all unassigned Oklahoma land was opened by a series of six "runs." People who jumped the gun were called "Sooners," hence Oklahoma's nickname, the "Sooner State." Close to 17 million acres of land in the state were settled in this way; the last "lottery," a form of run, took place on August 16, 1901. Previously unsettled tracts became cities within eight hours.

Oklahoma produces many millions of barrels of oil a year and great quantities of natural gas. It is a leader in coal production and also produces gypsum limestone, tripoli, granite, and other minerals. The state's three largest industries are agriculture, tourism, and petroleum. The McClellan-Kerr Arkansas River Navigation System has given Oklahoma a direct water route to the Mississippi River and to the Gulf of Mexico. The ports of Muskogee on the Arkansas River and Catoosa on the Verdigris River connect Oklahoma to the inland waterway system and to major US markets.

Oklahoma is developing its recreational resources at a rapid rate. Every year millions of tourists and vacationers visit the growing number of lakes, built mostly for electric power, and the state park system, one of the best in the country.

When to Go/Climate

Oklahoma is a state of extremes. Located in the heart of Tornado Alley, temperatures can change dramatically in minutes. An unusual amount of sunny days and entire months of mild temperatures help compensate for the often sweltering summer heat.

AVERAGE HIGH/LOW TEMPERATURES (°F)

OKLAHOMA CITY

Jan 47/25	**May** 79/58	**Sept** 84/62
Feb 52/30	**June** 87/66	**Oct** 74/50
Mar 62/39	**July** 93/71	**Nov** 60/39
Apr 72/49	**Aug** 93/70	**Dec** 50/29

TULSA

Jan 45/25	**May** 80/59	**Sept** 84/63
Feb 51/30	**June** 88/68	**Oct** 74/51
Mar 62/39	**July** 94/73	**Nov** 60/40
Apr 73/50	**Aug** 93/71	**Dec** 49/29

Parks and Recreation Finder

Directions to and information about the parks and recreation areas below are given under their respective town/city sections. Please refer to those sections for details.

NATIONAL PARK AND RECREATION AREAS

Key to abbreviations. I.H.S. = International Historic Site; I.P.M. = International Peace Memorial; N.B. = National Battlefield; N.B.P. = National Battlefield Park; N.B.C. = National Battlefield and Cemetery; N.C.A. = National Conservation Area; N.E.M. = National Expansion Memorial; N.F. = National Forest; N.G. = National Grassland; N.H.P. = National Historical Park; N.H.C. = National Heritage Corridor; N.H.S. = National Historic Site; N.L. = National Lakeshore; N.M. = National Monument; N.M.P. = National Military Park; N.Mem. = National Memorial; N.P. = National Park; N.Pres. = National Preserve; N.R.A. = National Recreational Area; N.R.R. = National Recreational River; N.Riv. = National River; N.S. = National Seashore; N.S.R. = National Scenic

CALENDAR HIGHLIGHTS

JANUARY

International Finals Rodeo (Oklahoma City). Myriad Convention Center. International Pro Rodeo Association's top 15 cowboys and cowgirls compete in seven events to determine world championships. Phone 405/235-6540 or 405/948-6800.

APRIL

Medieval Fair (Norman). University of Oklahoma, Brandt Park. Living history fair depicting life in the Middle Ages; strolling minstrels, jugglers, jesters; knights in armor joust; storytellers. Phone 405/366-8095.

Festival of the Arts (Oklahoma City). International foods, entertainment, children's learning and play area; craft market; artists from many states display their work. Contact Convention & Visitors Bureau, 405/297-8912 or 800/225-5652.

MAY

Tri-State Music Festival (Enid). Phone 580/237-4964.

Antique Car Swap Meet (Chickasha). Phone 405/224-6552.

AUGUST

American Indian Exposition (Anadarko). Parade, dance contests, horse races, arts and crafts. Phone 405/247-6651.

SEPTEMBER

Cherokee National Holiday (Tahlequah). Celebration of the signing of the first Cherokee Constitution in September 1839. Championship Cornstalk bow and arrow shoot, powwow, rodeo, tournaments, and other events. Contact Cherokee Nation 918/456-0671 extension 2544 or 800/850-0348.

Chili Cookoff & Bluegrass Festival (Tulsa). The best in bluegrass and country music and the International Chili Society Mid-America Regional Chili Cookoff. Phone 918/583-2617.

State Fair of Oklahoma (Oklahoma City). Livestock, crafts, art exhibits; ice show, circus, rodeo; truck pull contests; auto races; concerts; international show, flower and garden show; Native American ceremonial dances; carriage collection; monorail, space tower, carnival, parades. Arena and grandstand attractions. Phone 405/948-6700.

NOVEMBER

World Championship Quarter Horse Show (Oklahoma City). More than 1,800 horses compete on the state fairgrounds. Contact Convention & Visitors Bureau, 405/297-8912 or 800/225-5652.

Riverway; N.S.T. = National Scenic Trail; N.Sc. = National Scientific Reserve; N.V.M. = National Volcanic Monument.

Place Name	Listed Under
Chickasaw N.R.A.	SULPHUR

STATE PARK AND RECREATION AREAS

Key to abbreviations. I.P. = Interstate Park; S.A.P. = State Archaeological Park; S.B. = State Beach; S.C.A. = State Conservation Area; S.C.P. = State Conservation Park; S.Cp. = State Campground; S.F. = State Forest; S.G. = State Garden; S.H.A. = State Historic Area; S.H.P. = State Historic Park; S.H.S. = State Historic Site; S.M.P. = State Marine Park; S.N.A. = State Natural Area; S.P. = State Park;

S.P.C. = State Public Campground; S.R. = State Reserve; S.R.A. = State Recreation Area; S.Res. = State Reservoir; S.Res.P. = State Resort Park; S.R.P. = State Rustic Park.

Place Name	Listed Under
Alabaster Caverns S.P.	ALVA
Arrowhead S.P.	EUFAULA
Beavers Bend Resort S.P.	BROKEN BOW
Black Mesa S.P.	BOISE CITY
Boggy Depot S.P.	ATOKA
Boiling Springs S.P.	WOODWARD
Fort Cobb S.P.	ANADARKO
Foss S.P.	CLINTON
Fountainhead S.P.	EUFAULA
Great Salt Plains S.P.	ALVA
Greenleaf Lake S.P.	MUSKOGEE
Hochatown S.P.	BROKEN BOW
Lake Keystone S.P.	TULSA
Lake Murray S.P.	same
Lake Texoma S.P.	LAKE TEXOMA
Lake Thunderbird S.P.	NORMAN
Lake Wister S.P.	POTEAU
Little Sahara S.P.	ALVA
Okmulgee S.P.	OKMULGEE
Osage Hills S.P.	PAWHUSKA
Quartz Mountain S.P.	same
Raymond Gary S.P.	HUGO
Red Rock Canyon S.P.	WEATHERFORD
Robber's Cave S.P.	MCALESTER
Roman Nose S.P.	same
Sallisaw S.P. at Brushy Lake	SALLISAW
Sequoyah S.P.	same
Spiro Mound Archaeological S.P.	POTEAU
Tenkiller S.P.	TENKILLER FERRY LAKE
Walnut Creek S.P.	TULSA

Water-related activities, hiking, riding, various other sports, picnicking and visitor centers, as well as camping, are available in many of these areas. Many of the state parks have lodges and cabins as well as campsites and trailer parks. Camping fee ($12-$25) required for assigned campgrounds and trailer hookups; tent camping ($7); camping fee ($11-$17) in unassigned areas. For state park reservations, phone the park directly. Pets on leash only. For further information contact the Division of State Parks, 15 N Robinson, PO Box 52002, Oklahoma City 73152-2002; 405/521-3411, 800/652-6552 or 800/654-8240 (reservations).

For further information write Oklahoma Tourism & Recreation Department, Literature Distribution Center, PO Box 60789, Oklahoma City 73146.

FISHING AND HUNTING

Nonresident fishing license: 5-day, $10; 14-day, $20; annual, $28.50; nonresident hunting license: small game, 5-day, $35 (except pheasant, turkey, or deer), annual, $85; deer, $201. Trout fishing license: $7.75.

Many species of fish are found statewide: largemouth bass, white bass, catfish, crappie, and bluegill. Rainbow trout can be found throughout the year in the Illinois River, Mountain Fork River, Lake Pawhuska, and Broken Bow Lake; during the winter at Lake Watonga, Blue River, Lake Carl Etling, and below

Altus-Lugert dam; striped bass in Lake Keystone, Lake Texoma, and the
Arkansas River Navigation System; and smallmouth bass in several eastern
streams as well as in Broken Bow, Murray, and Texoma lakes.

For information about fishing and hunting regulations and changes in fees,
contact Oklahoma Department of Wildlife Conservation, 1801 N Lincoln Blvd,
Oklahoma City 73105; 405/521-3851. For boating regulations contact Lake
Patrol Division, Department of Public Safety, 3600 N Martin Luther King Ave,
Oklahoma City 73136; 405/425-2143.

Driving Information

Safety belts are mandatory for all persons in front seat of vehicle. Children
under six years must be in an approved passenger restraint anywhere in vehicle: ages four and five may use a regulation safety belt; age three and under
may use a regulation safety belt in back seat, however, in front seat children
must use an approved safety seat. For further information phone 405/523-1570.

INTERSTATE HIGHWAY SYSTEM

The following alphabetical listing of Oklahoma towns in *Mobil Travel Guide*
shows that these cities are within ten miles of the indicated Interstate highways. A highway map should, however, be checked for the nearest exit.

Highway Number	Cities/Towns within ten miles
Interstate 35	Ardmore, Guthrie, Marietta, Norman, Oklahoma City, Pauls Valley, Perry.
Interstate 40	Clinton, Elk City, El Reno, Henryetta, Oklahoma City, Sallisaw, Shawnee, Weatherford.
Interstate 44	Chickasaw, Lawton, Miami, Oklahoma City, Tulsa.

Additional Visitor Information

Free information on the state may be obtained from the Oklahoma Tourism &
Recreation Department, Literature Distribution Center, PO Box 52002, Okla-
homa City 73152-2002; 405/521-3831 or 800/652-6552. Also available from the
Tourism Department, *Oklahoma Today* magazine, published bimonthly. The
Department of Wildlife Conservation produces a monthly publication, *Outdoor
Oklahoma*.

There are ten traveler information centers in Oklahoma; visitors who stop
will find information and brochures most helpful in planning stops at points of
interest. Their locations are as follows: from the N, 10 mi S of OK-KS border on
I-35; from the E, 14 mi W of OK-AR border on I-40; from the S, 2 mi N of OK-
TX border on US 69/75, or 4 mi N of OK-TX border on I-35; from the SW, on I-
44 at the Walters exit; from the W, 9 mi E of OK-TX border on I-40. (Daily,
summer, 7 am-7 pm; winter, 8:30 am-5 pm) Also: from the NE, on Will Rogers
Tpke E of Miami, Catoosa-intersection of Will Rogers Tpke & US 66; at intersection of I-35 and NE 50th in Oklahoma City; and at the State Capitol Building,
NE 23rd & Lincoln Blvd; all centers are closed December 25.

OKLAHOMA'S NATIVE AMERICAN HERITAGE

Drive west from Oklahoma City on Highway 270 to Highway 81 south, a designated scenic route. Cross the Canadian River and head west on OK 37/152 and south on Highway 281 to Anadarko, a center of Native American heritage, with an American Indian Hall of Fame, Southern Plains Indian Museum, art galleries, tribal museums, and overnight stays in tepees. Continue south on Highway 281 to Medicine Park, a funky old resort town with cobblestone buildings and access to Mount Scott, a remarkable viewpoint for the region, which includes the Wichita Mountains Wildlife Refuge. Immediately south is Lawton/Fort Sill, with a sensational history museum showcasing Geronimo, buffalo soldiers, and tribes, as well as historic cemeteries and granite cliff scenery. Head east on OK 7 to Duncan to see the marvelous Chisholm Trail Statue and Museum, then go north on Highway 81 back to Oklahoma City. **(Approx 160 mi)**

EXPLORING OKLAHOMA'S STATE PARKS

Begin your tour of southeastern and eastern Oklahoma at the small town of Broken Bow, located at the edge of the Ouachita National Forest. This is a good place to stock up on picnic supplies for lunch or dinner at one of the gorgeous state parks that lie ahead on this two-day driving route. About six miles east of town on Highway 70, history buffs will enjoy exploring the 1880s home of Choctaw Chief Jefferson Gardner. If you would prefer to investigate nature's offerings, head seven miles north of town along US 259 to Beavers Bend State Park, one of the most gorgeous places in this part of the country. Lake Broken Bow, at 14,200 acres, offers park visitors 180 miles of pretty, wooded shoreline, as well as bass fishing, paddleboating, canoeing, and swimming. The park is also adjacent to Mountain Fork River, popular for its trout fishing and canoe trips. On land, you'll get a kick out of horseback riding, miniature golf, and golf on Cedar Creek Golf Course. Stay overnight here, or continue on for an overnight at Lake Wister.

Continue north on scenic US 259 through the tree-covered Kiamichi Mountains and you'll enter the Ouachita National Forest. If you turn west on OK 1, you'll be on the spectacular Talimena Scenic Drive, which makes a 54-mile reach between Talihina, Oklahoma, and Mena, Arkansas. Take plenty of film to capture the vistas from various look-out spots on the sides of the road; look to the north to see the beautiful Winding Stair Mountains. Once you're in Talihina, go four miles southwest on US 271 to Talimena State Park, a wonderful place for picnicking. Back on US 259, continue north and pick up US 59 north to Lake Wister State Park, a pretty, wooded spread of 33,428 acres that showcases 4,000-acre Lake Wister and a 2,000-acre waterfowl refuge. You could spend time here hiking, mountain biking (if you bring your own wheels), horseback riding, fishing, and swimming. This is a good overnight spot, and some of the park's 15 cabins have fireplaces. Less than three miles northeast of US 59 and US 270, Heavener Runestone State Park is the place to go to see gigantic stone tablets carved with runic alphabet characters. Nobody seems to understand the meaning, but the markings are attributed to Vikings around 1012.

Stay north on US 59 about 50 miles to Sallisaw, on the eastern edge of Oklahoma's Green Country. Eleven miles northeast of town via OK 101, you'll find the Sequoyah's Home Site, with exhibits about the leader who created the Cherokee alphabet. Drive west from Sallisaw via US 64 about ten miles, then follow Oklahoma

Highway 82 north to wonderful Tenkiller State Park, hugging the southern end of magnificent Lake Tenkiller. There's great scuba diving here, as well as cabins for taking a break from the world. Follow Highway 82 along the lake's eastern edge, and you'll find scenic park areas called Snake Creek Cove, Sixshooter Camp, Cookson Bend, and Standing Rock Landing. Lodges and resorts surround the lake, too. Follow scenic Highway 82 north about ten miles from the lake's northern end and you'll finish your driving tour at Tallequah, capital city of the Cherokee Nation. Destinations here include the Cherokee Heritage Center, with a good museum, outdoor theater, and authentic Indian village; the Murrell Home, a restored antebellum home that belonged to a prominent early citizen; and the restored 1889 Cherokee National Female Seminary, at Northeastern State University. **(APPROX 90 MI)**

Ada

(D-6) *See also Pauls Valley, Sulphur*

Founded 1890 **Pop** 15,820 **Elev** 1,010 ft **Area code** 580 **Zip** 74820
Information Chamber of Commerce, 300 W Main, PO Box 248, 74821; 580/332-2506
Web www.chickasaw.com/~adachamb

Ada is one of the principal cities of southeastern Oklahoma. Important manufactured products here are automotive parts, farm implements, furniture, feed, denim clothing, and biomedical supplies. South of the city are fine silica sand and limestone quarries that provide the raw material for cement. Cattle operations are still important, and oil is produced throughout the county.

What to See and Do

East Central University. (1909) 4,000 students. At the entrance to the campus is the fossilized stump of a rare giant Callixylon tree of the Devonian Age. Main St and Francis Ave. Phone 580/332-8000.

Wintersmith Park. Park covering approx 140 acres has arboretum, restored one-rm schoolhouse (1907), small zoo, carousel, ½-mi miniature train ride, concerts. Swimming pool, stocked fishing lake; miniature golf, picnic area. Fee for some activities. (Daily) 18th St at Scenic Dr. Phone 580/436-6300. **FREE**

Special Event

Western Heritage Week. Five days of celebration. First full wk Aug.

Motel/Motor Lodge

★★ **BEST WESTERN RAINTREE MOTOR INN.** *1100 N Mississippi Ave (74820). 580/332-6262; fax 580/436-4929; toll-free 888/563-9411. www.bestwestern.com.* 40 rms, 2 story. S $54; D $64; each addl $4; under 12 free. Crib $4. TV; cable (premium). Indoor pool. Complimentary full bkfst Tues-Fri. Restaurant 6 am-10 pm; closed Mon; Sun to 2:30 pm. Ck-out 11 am. Business servs avail.

In-rm modem link. Bathrm phones. Cr cds: A, C, D, DS, MC, V.
D 🐾 ➿ ✈ 🔧 🐾

Altus (D-4)

Founded 1891 **Pop** 21,910 **Elev** 1,398 ft **Area code** 580
Information Chamber of Commerce, Main and Broadway, PO Box 518, 73522; 580/482-0210
Web www.intplsrv.net/c-of-c/

In the spring of 1891, a flood on Bitter Creek forced a group of settlers to flee to higher ground, taking with them what possessions they could. Gathered together to escape destruction, they founded a town and called it Altus because one of them said the word meant "high ground."

On the border between the high plains and the southland, Altus lies between winter wheat on the north and cotton on the south. The Lugert-Altus irrigation district, using water from Lake Altus on the North Fork of the Red River, feeds 70,000 acres of prosperous farmland growing cotton, wheat, alfalfa seed, and cattle. Nearby Altus Air Force Base is the home of the 97th Air Mobility Wing.

What to See and Do

Museum of the Western Prairie. Changing exhibits depict all aspects of pioneer living in southwestern Oklahoma. Also, building featuring displays of early farm implements, coaches, wagons; original reconstructed half-dugout house. Reference library. (Tues-Sun; closed hols) 1100 N Hightower St. Phone 580/482-1044. **Donation**

Special Events

Great Plains Stampede Rodeo. PRCA-sanctioned rodeo; special events. Late Aug.

Jackson County Fair. Livestock, carnival, games, food. Phone 740/384-6587. Late Aug.

Motels/Motor Lodges

★★ **BEST WESTERN ALTUS.** *2804 N Main St (73521). 580/482-9300; fax 580/482-2245; res 800/528-1234. www.bestwestern.com.* 100 rms, 2 story. S, D $50-$54.50; each addl $6; under 12 free. Crib free. Pet accepted. TV; cable (premium). Indoor/outdoor pool. Complimentary continental bkfst. Ck-out noon. Coin lndry. Meeting rms. Business center. In-rm modem link. Sauna. Some bathrm phones, refrigerators, microwaves. Cr cds: A, MC, V.

D ⬛ ⬛ ⬛ ⬛ SC ⬛

★ **DAYS INN.** *3202 N Main St (73521). 580/477-2300; fax 405/477-2379; toll-free 800/329-7466. www.daysinn.com.* 36 rms, 2 story. S $37; D $42; each addl $5; under 18 free. Crib free. Pet accepted. TV; cable (premium). Complimentary continental bkfst. Ck-out 11 am. Business servs avail. Cr cds: A, C, D, DS, ER, MC, V.

⬛ ⬛ ⬛ SC

★ **RAMADA INN.** *2515 E Broadway St (73521). 580/477-3000; fax 580/477-0078; toll-free 800/272-6232. www.ramada.com.* 120 units, 12 suites, 2 story. S $47-$53; D $53-$59; each addl $8; suites $86-$102. Crib free. Pet accepted. TV; cable (premium). Indoor pool. Coffee in rms. Restaurant 6:30 am-2 pm, 5-10 pm. Bar 5 pm-2 am. Ck-out noon. Meeting rms. Business servs avail. Valet serv. Refrigerators. Balconies. Cr cds: A, C, D, DS, MC, V.

D ⬛ ⬛ ⬛ ⬛ SC

Alva (B-4)

Pop 5,495 **Elev** 1,350 ft
Area code 580 **Zip** 73717
Information Chamber of Commerce, 410 College; 580/327-1647

What to See and Do

Cherokee Strip Museum. Historical display of Cherokee Strip; Lincoln pictures; collection of flags, soldiers' uniforms; antiques, dolls, toys, furniture; general store, kitchen; miniature trains; authentic covered wagon; adj annex houses small farm machinery. Old schoolhouse. (Summer hrs vary; rest of yr, Sat, Sun afternoons; closed hols) 901 14th St. Phone 580/327-2030. **FREE**

State parks.

Alabaster Caverns. On approx 200 acres, Alabaster is said to be largest known natural gypsum cavern in world; tours (daily); Cedar Canyon. Swimming, bathhouse; picnicking, playground, camping area, trailer sites. (Daily) 25 mi W on US 64, then 7 mi S via OK 50, 50A. Phone 580/621-3381. ¢¢

Great Salt Plains. Approx 840 acres with 9,300-acre lake. Swimming, waterskiing, fishing, boating (ramps); nature trails, picnic area, playground, camping areas, trailer hookups (fee), cabins. (Daily) 16 mi E on US 64, then 11 mi E on OK 11, then S on OK 38. Phone 580/626-4731.

Little Sahara. Approx 1,600 acres. Sand dunes. Picnicking, playground. Trailer hookups (fee). (Daily) 28 mi S and W on US 281. Phone 580/824-1471.

Motels/Motor Lodges

★ **RANGER INN.** *420 E Oklahoma Blvd (73717). 580/327-1981; fax 580/327-1981.* 41 rms. S $34-$36; D $38; under 16 free. Pet accepted, some restrictions. TV; cable (premium). Complimentary coffee. Ck-out 11 am. Microwaves avail. Cr cds: A, C, D, DS, MC, V.

D ⬛ ⬛ ⬛

★ **WESTERN MOTEL.** *608 E Oklahoma Blvd (73717). 580/327-1363.* 21 rms. S $28-$30; D $34; each addl $3; under 12 free. Crib $4. TV; cable (premium). Pool. Complimentary coffee in rms. Ck-out 11 am. Business servs avail. In-rm modem link. Free airport transportation. Refrigerators avail. Picnic tables. Cr cds: A, C, D, DS, MC, V.

⬛ ⬛ ⬛ SC

Anadarko

(D-5) *See also Chickasha*

Founded 1901 **Pop** 6,586 **Elev** 1,183 ft **Area code** 405 **Zip** 73005

Information Chamber of Commerce, 516 W Kentucky, PO Box 366; 405/247-6651

Web www.tanet.net/city

Anadarko first came into being in 1859 as the Wichita Indian Agency after eastern tribes were relocated here. The Bureau of Indian Affairs area office is located here.

What to See and Do

Anadarko Philomathic Museum. Railroad memorabilia displayed in old ticket office; Native American doll collection; paintings, costumes, and artifacts; military equipt and uniforms; excellent photographic collection; early physician's office; country store. (Tues-Sun; closed hols) 311 E Main St, in Rock Island Depot. Phone 405/247-3240. **FREE**

Fort Cobb State Park. A 2,850-acre park; 4,100-acre lake. Swimming, waterskiing, fishing, boating (ramps, marina); hunting, 18-hole golf, picnic facilities, camping, trailer hookups (fee). (Daily) 8 mi W on US 62, then 12 mi NW off OK 9. Phone 405/643-2249. **FREE**

Indian City—USA. Authentic reconstruction of seven Plains tribes' villages (Pawnee, Wichita, Caddo, Kiowa, Navajo, Pueblo, and Apache) with Native American guides (45-min tours) and actual dance ceremonies (summer, daily; winter, wkends). Petting zoo. Arts and crafts shop. Swimming. Concession. Camping. (Daily; closed Jan 1, Thanksgiving, Dec 25) (See SPECIAL EVENTS) 2½ mi SE on OK 8. Phone 405/247-5661. ¢¢¢

National Hall of Fame for Famous American Indians. Outdoor museum with sculptured bronze busts of famous Native Americans (daily). Visitor center (daily; closed Thanksgiving, Dec 25). E on US 62E. Phone 405/247-5555. **FREE**

Southern Plains Indian Museum and Crafts Center. Exhibits of historic and contemporary Native American arts from the southern plains region. (June-Sept, daily; rest of yr, Tues-Sun; closed Jan 1, Thanksgiving, Dec 25) E on US 62 E. Phone 405/247-6221. ¢¢

Special Events

Kiowa Veterans Black Leggins Ceremonial. Indian City. Mid-May and mid-Oct.

American Indian Exposition. Caddo County Fairground. Parade, dances, horse races; arts and crafts. Mid-Aug.

Wichita-Caddo-Delaware Ceremonial. Wichita Park. Late Aug.

Caddo County Free Fair. Early Sept.

Holiday Celebration. Randlett Park. Hand-built lighted Christmas displays. Phone 405/247-6651. Late Nov-Dec.

Ardmore

(E-6) *See also Marietta, Sulphur*

Founded 1887 **Pop** 23,079 **Elev** 881 ft **Area code** 580 **Zip** 73401

Information Chamber of Commerce, 410 W Main, PO Box 1585; 580/223-7765

Web www.ardmore.org

This is an oil and cattle town and a good center for recreation. The Arbuckle Mountains are a few miles north of town.

What to See and Do

Charles B. Goddard Center. Contemporary Western graphics, painting, and sculpture. National touring exhibits. Community theater, dance, concerts. (Mon-Fri, also wkend afternoons; closed hols) First Ave and D St SW. Phone 580/226-0909.

Eliza Cruce Hall Doll Museum. Collection of more than 300 antique dolls, some dating to 1728; display incl porcelain, bisque, leather, wood, wax dolls. (Mon-Sat; closed hols) 320 E St NW, in public library. Phone 580/223-8290. **FREE**

Greater Southwest Historical Museum. "Living" exhibits; oil and agricultural machinery; military memorabilia; re-creation of a pioneer community. (Tues-Sat, Sun afternoon) 35 Sunset Dr. Phone 580/226-3857. **Donation**

Lake Murray State Park. (see) 7 mi SE, off I-35 exit 24 or 29.

Special Events

Ardmoredillo Chili Cookoff. Main St. Early Apr.

Charity Club Rodeo. Hardy Murphy Coliseum. PRCA sanctioned. Early Apr.

Barry Burk Jr. Calf Roping. Hardy Murphy Coliseum. Memorial Day wkend.

Carter County Free Fair. Hardy Murphy Coliseum. Various festivities. Early Sept.

Motels/Motor Lodges

★ **DORCHESTER INN.** *2614 W Broadway St (73401). 580/226-1761; fax 580/223-3131.* 47 rms, 2 story. S $29.95; D $39; under 12 free. Crib free. Pet accepted, some restrictions. TV; cable (premium). Complimentary continental bkfst. Restaurant adj open 24 hrs. Ck-out 11 am. Refrigerators avail. Cr cds: A, C, D, DS, MC, V.
🄳 🐾 ⛆ 🛏 🐾

★ **GUEST INN.** *2519 W Hwy 142 (73401). 580/223-1234; fax 580/223-1234; toll-free 800/460-4064.* 126 rms, 2 story. S $36; D $40; suites $65; each addl $4; under 12 free; wkly rates. Crib free. Pet accepted, some restrictions. TV; cable (premium), VCR avail (movies). Pool. Coffee in rms. Restaurant adj 6 am-9 pm. Ck-out 1 pm. Coin lndry. Business servs avail. Valet serv. Cr cds: A, C, D, DS, MC, V.
🄳 🐾 ⛆ 🛏 🐾 SC

★★ **HOLIDAY INN.** *2705 W Holiday Dr (73401). 580/223-7130; toll-free 800/465-4329. www.holiday-inn.com.* 171 rms, 2 story. S, D $52-$64; suites $95-$150. Crib free. Pet accepted. TV; cable. Pool; wading pool. Playground. Restaurant open 24 hrs. Bar 4 pm-midnight, closed Sun. Ck-out noon. Coin lndry. Valet serv. Business servs avail. In-rm modem link. Meeting rms. Sundries. Free airport transportation. Cr cds: A, C, D, DS, JCB, MC, V.
🄳 🐾 ⛆ 🛏 🐾 SC

Restaurant

★ **BILL & BARB'S.** *1225 N Washington (73401). 580/223-1976.* Hrs: 6 am-9 pm; Sun to 3 pm. Closed Mon; July 4, Thanksgiving, Dec 25-Jan 1.

Bkfst $2.05-$6.85, lunch, dinner $4.75-$12.25. Specialties: fresh vegetables, corn bread. Salad bar. Family-owned. Cr cds: A, D, DS, MC, V.
🄳 🖃

Atoka (D-7)

Founded 1867 **Pop** 3,298 **Elev** 583 ft **Area code** 580 **Zip** 74525

Information Chamber of Commerce, PO Box 778; 580/889-2410

What to See and Do

Boggy Depot State Park. Approx 420 acres. Picnicking, playgrounds. Camping areas, trailer hookups (fee). Historical area. (Daily) 11 mi W on OK 7, then 4 mi S on Park Ln. Phone 580/889-5625. **FREE**

Confederate Memorial Museum and Cemetery. Site reserved as an outpost throughout the Civil War. Museum features artifacts and memorabilia. Cemetery contains remains of Confederate soldiers. (Mon-Sat; closed hols) ½ mi N on OK 69. Phone 580/889-7912. **FREE**

Motel/Motor Lodge

★★ **BEST WESTERN INN.** *2101 S Mississippi Ave (74525). 580/889-7381; fax 580/889-6695; res 800/528-1234. www.bestwestern.com.* 54 rms, 2 story. S $54-$59; D $59-$64; each addl $5; under 17 free. TV; cable. Pool. Ck-out noon. Meeting rms. Business servs avail. Cr cds: A, C, D, DS, MC, V.
⛆ 🛏 🐾 SC

Bartlesville

(B-7) *See also Pawhuska*

Founded 1875 **Pop** 34,256 **Elev** 715 ft **Area code** 918

Information Bartlesville Area Chamber of Commerce, 201 SW Keeler, PO Box 2366, 74005; 918/336-8708

Web www.bartlesville.com

The Bartlesville area is proud of its Western and Native American heritage, which involves three tribes—the Cherokee, Delaware, and Osage. Oklahoma's first electricity was produced here in 1876 when Jacob Bartles, an early settler, hitched a dynamo to the Caney River. Oil, first tapped in the area in 1897, is the economic base of the city, which is the headquarters of the Phillips Petroleum Company.

Bartlesville has become internationally known for its distinguished, modern architecture, a building trend initiated by the H. C. Price family. The town boasts a number of both public and private buildings by Frank Lloyd Wright and Bruce Goff.

What to See and Do

Dewey Hotel Museum. Victorian structure built by Jacob Bartles. Period furnishings. (Apr-Oct, Tues-Sat and Sun afternoons; closed hols) 801 N Delaware. Phone 918/534-0215. ¢

Frank Phillips Mansion. Built in 1909 by the founder of the Phillips Petroleum Company. This Greek Revival house has been restored to 1930s period; interior incl imported woods, marble, Oriental rugs, and original furnishings. (Wed-Sun; closed hols). 1107 S Cherokee Ave. Phone 918/336-2491. **Donation**

Nellie Johnstone Oil Well. Replica of the original rig, first commercial oil well in state. An 83-acre park with a low water dam on the Caney River. Fishing; picnicking, playgrounds, children's rides (late May-Labor Day, daily; closed July 4). Park (daily). In Johnstone Park, 300 blk of N Cherokee. **FREE**

Price Tower. Designed by Frank Lloyd Wright, this 221-ft office building was built by pipeline construction pioneer H. C. Price as headquarters for his company. The building design is based on a diamond module of 30- to 60-degree triangles. Although Wright designed many skyscrapers, Price Tower was his only tall building to be completed. Guided tours (45 min). (Thurs or by appt) On Sixth and Dewey sts. Phone 918/333-8558.

Tom Mix Museum. Exhibits and memorabilia of silent movie star Tom Mix, the first "King of the Cowboys"; displays of his cowboy gear; stills from his films. (Tues-Sun; closed

hols) 721 N Delaware, Dewey. Phone 918/534-1555. **Donation**

⬛ **Woolaroc.** Complex covering 3,600 acres with wildlife preserve for herds of American bison, longhorn cattle, Scottish Highland cattle, elk, deer, and other native wildlife. These are wild animals and may be dangerous; it is mandatory to stay in car. At museum are paintings by Russell, Remington, and other great Western artists; exhibits on development of America; artifacts of several Native American tribes, pioneers, and cowboys; also one of finest collections of Colt firearms in country. The Woolaroc Lodge (1925), once a private dwelling, has paintings, bark-covered furnishings, and blankets. The National Y-Indian Guide Center has multimedia shows, authentic Native American crafts, art displays, and a nature trail (1½ mi). Picnic area. (Late May-early Sept, daily; rest of yr, Tues-Sun; closed Thanksgiving, Dec 25). 12 mi SW on OK 123. Phone 918/336-0307. ¢¢

Motels/Motor Lodges

★★ **BEST WESTERN.** *222 SE Washington Blvd (74006). 918/335-7755; fax 918/335-7763; res 800/780-7234. www.bestwestern.com.* 111 rms, 2 story, 5 suites. S $42-$49; D $45-$53; under 12 free. Crib free. TV; cable (premium). Pool. Complimentary continental bkfst, coffee in rms. Restaurant 6 am-9 pm. Ck-out noon. Coin lndry. Meeting rms. Business servs avail. Some refrigerators, in-rm whirlpools; microwaves avail. Cr cds: A, C, D, DS, ER, JCB, MC, V.

⬛ 🏊 ⬛ 🔥 **SC**

★★ **HOLIDAY INN.** *1410 SE Washington Blvd (74006). 918/333-8320; fax 918/333-8979; toll-free 877/371-5920. www.holiday-inn.com.* 104 rms, 3 story. S $60-$65; D $66-$71; each addl $6; suites $75; under 18 free. Crib free. Pet accepted; $15 deposit. TV; cable (premium). Indoor pool. Complimentary coffee in rms. Restaurant 6-11 am, 5-9 pm; Sun to 2 pm. Bar. Ck-out noon. Coin lndry. Meeting rm. Business servs avail. In-rm modem link. Valet serv. Exercise equipt; sauna. Cr cds: A, C, D, DS, MC, V.

⬛ 🐾 ⬛ 🏃 ⬛ 🔥 **SC**

★ **TRAVELERS MOTEL.** *3105 E Frank Phillips Blvd (74006). 918/333-1900.* 24 rms. S $31-$34; D $35-$38. Pet accepted. TV; cable (premium). Complimentary coffee in lobby. Restaurant nearby. Ck-out 11 am. Cr cds: A, C, DS, MC, V.

◨ ⊠ ⟠

Hotel

★★★ **HOTEL PHILLIPS.** *821 Johnstone (74003). 918/336-5600; fax 918/336-0350; toll-free 800/331-0706.* 145 rms, 7 story, 25 suites. S, D $70-$105; each addl $10; suites $80-$150; under 16 free. Crib free. TV; cable (premium). Restaurant 6:30 am-10 pm; Sun to 2 pm. Bar 11 am-midnight. Ck-out noon. Meeting rms. Business servs avail. In-rm modem link. Concierge. Gift shop. Exercise equipt. Health club privileges. Rms individually decorated. Rooftop terrace. Luxury level. Cr cds: A, MC, V.

◨ ⅟ ⊠ ⟠ SC

Restaurants

★ **MURPHY'S ORIGINAL STEAK HOUSE.** *1625 W Frank Phillips Blvd (74003). 918/336-4789.* Hrs: 11 am-11:30 pm. Closed Mon; Thanksgiving, Dec 25. Lunch, dinner $4-$16.95. Specializes in steak, hamburgers. Open kitchen. Family-owned. Cr cds: MC, V.

⊟

★★ **STERLING'S GRILLE.** *2905 E Frank Phillips Blvd (74006). 918/335-0707.* Hrs: 11 am-9 pm; Fri, Sat to 10 pm; Sun 10 am-8 pm; early-bird dinner 4-6 pm. Closed hols. Res accepted. Bar. Lunch $5.95-$7.95, dinner $8.95-$17.95. Sun brunch $3.95-$6.95. Children's menu. Specializes in steak, seafood, pasta. Pianist Mon, Fri, Sat. Outdoor dining. 3 separate rms with different motifs. Cr cds: A, DS, MC, V.

◨ ⊟

Boise City (B-1)

Pop 1,509 **Elev** 4,165 ft
Area code 580 **Zip** 73933

Information Chamber of Commerce, 6 NE Square, in red caboose, PO Box 1027; 580/544-3344

Web www.ccccok.org

What to See and Do

Black Mesa State Park. Lake Carl Etling (260 acres) offers fishing facilities, boating (ramps); picnic area, playground. Camping, trailer hookups (fee). (Daily) 19 mi NW on OK 325, then 9 mi W on unnumbered roads. Phone 580/426-2222. **FREE**

Special Event

Santa Fe Trail Daze Celebration. Guided tour of Santa Fe Trail crossing, autograph rock, dinosaur tracks, and excavation site. Phone 580/544-3344. First wkend June.

Broken Bow

(E-8) *See also Idabel*

Pop 3,961 **Elev** 467 ft **Area code** 580 **Zip** 74728

Information Chamber of Commerce, 113 W Martin Luther King; 580/584-3393 or 800/52-TREES

What to See and Do

Beavers Bend Resort State Park. This 3,522-acre mountainous area is crossed by the Mountain Fork River and incl the Broken Bow Reservoir. Swimming, bathhouse, fishing, boating (no motors); nature trail, picnic areas, playground, grocery, restaurant, camping, trailer hookups (fee), cabins. Nature center. (Daily) 6 mi N on US 259, then 3 mi E on OK 259A. Phone 580/494-6300. **FREE**

Hochatown State Park. Covers 1,713 acres on 14,220-acre Broken Bow Lake. Swimming, waterskiing, fishing, bait and tackle shop, boating (ramps; marina, rentals, gas dock, boathouses); hiking trails, 18-hole golf course, picnicking, playground, snack bar, trailer hookups (fee), dump station, rest rms. (Daily) 10 mi N on US 259. Phone 580/494-6452. **FREE**

CLAREMORE/OKLAHOMA 445

Special Event

Kiamichi Owa Chito Festival. Beavers Bend Resort State Park. Contests, entertainment, food. Phone 580/494-6509. Third wkend June.

Motel/Motor Lodge

★ **CHARLES WESLEY MOTOR LODGE.** *302 N Park Dr (74728). 580/584-3303; fax 580/584-3433. www.charleswesleymotorlodge.com.* 50 rms, 1-2 story, 6 kits. S $35; D $44; each addl $4. Crib $4. TV; cable. Pool. Restaurant 6 am-10 pm; Sun to 8 pm. Ck-out 11 am. Cr cds: A, MC, V. 🏊✈️🐾

Chickasha

(D-5) *See also Anadarko*

Founded 1892 **Pop** 14,988 **Elev** 1,095 ft **Area code** 405
Information Chamber of Commerce, 221 W Chickasha Ave, PO Box 1717, 73023; 405/224-0787
Web www.chickasha-ok.com

Established to serve as a passenger and freight division point for the Rock Island and Pacific Railroad in 1892, this town site was on land originally given to the Choctaw in 1820. It became part of the Chickasaw Nation in 1834. In 1907, when the Oklahoma and Indian territories were joined to form the 46th state, Chickasha became the county seat of Grady County. Today agriculture, livestock, dairy production, manufacturing, and energy-related industries play an important part in the economy of the city and surrounding area.

What to See and Do

Recreation areas. Lake Burtschi. Fishing. Picnic areas. Camping. 11 mi SW on OK 92. **Lake Chickasha**, swimmimg, waterskiing, fishing; hunting, picnic areas, camping. 15 mi NW off US 62.

Special Events

Grady County Fair. Phone 405/224-2031. Last wk Aug.

Antique Car Swap Meet. Mid-Oct and mid-May.

Festival of Light. Lighted displays; 16-story Christmas tree; crystal bridge; shopping. Phone 405/224-0787. Thanksgiving-Dec 31.

Motels/Motor Lodges

★★ **BEST WESTERN INN.** *2101 S 4th St, PO Box 1439 (73023). 405/224-4890; fax 405/224-3411; toll-free 877/489-0647. www.bestwestern.com.* 154 rms, 2 story. S $50-$55; D $60-$65; each addl $5; under 18 free. Crib free. Pet accepted. TV; cable. Heated pool; whirlpool, sauna. Restaurant 6 am-9 pm. Ck-out noon. Meeting rms. Business servs avail. Valet serv. Refrigerator in suites. Cr cds: A, C, D, DS, JCB, MC, V.

★ **DAYS INN.** *2701 S 4th St (73018). 405/222-5800; toll-free 800/329-7466. www.daysinn.com.* 106 rms, 2 story. S $39; D $44; each addl $5; under 18 free. Crib free. Pet accepted. TV; cable (premium). Pool. Restaurant 6 am-9 pm. Ck-out 11 am. Meeting rms. Business servs avail. In-rm modem link. Valet serv. Some refrigerators, microwaves. Cr cds: A, C, D, DS, JCB, MC, V.

Claremore

(B-7) *See also Pryor, Tulsa*

Pop 13,280 **Elev** 602 ft **Area code** 918 **Zip** 74017
Information Claremore Area Chamber of Commerce, 419 W Will Rogers Blvd; 918/341-2818

Claremore is most famous as the birthplace of Will Rogers. He was actually born about halfway between this city and Oologah but used to talk more of Claremore because, he said, "nobody but an Indian could pronounce Oologah." Rogers County, of which Claremore is the seat, was named not for Will Rogers but for his father, Clem.

www.exxonmobiltravel.com

Will Rogers Memorial, Claremore

What to See and Do

J. M. Davis Arms & Historical Museum. Houses 20,000 firearms, steins, arrowheads, saddles, posters, other historical and Native American artifacts, collection of "John Rogers Group" statuaries. (Mon-Sat, also Sun afternoons; closed Thanksgiving, Dec 25). 333 N Lynn Riggs Blvd (OK 66). Phone 918/341-5707. **Donation**

Lynn Riggs Memorial. Houses author's personal belongings, sculpture of Riggs, original manuscripts, and the original "surrey with the fringe on top" from *Oklahoma!* (Mon-Fri; closed hols) Rogers County Historical Society, 4th and Weenonah. Phone 918/342-1127. **FREE**

Will Rogers Birthplace and Dog Iron Ranch. Home where "Oklahoma's favorite son" was born Nov 4, 1879. (Daily) 12 mi NW on OK 88, then 2 mi N. **Donation**

⭐ **Will Rogers Memorial.** Mementos; murals; saddle collection; dioramas; theater, films, tapes, research library. Jo Davidson's statue of Rogers stands in the foyer. The memorial is on 20 acres once owned by the humorist. Garden with Rogers's tomb. (Daily). 1720 W Will Rogers Blvd (OK 88).

Special Events

Will Rogers PRCA Rodeo. Early June.
Rogers County Free Fair. Mid-Sept.

Will Rogers Birthday Celebration. Early Nov.

Motel/Motor Lodge

★★ **BEST WESTERN WILL ROGERS INN.** *940 S Lynn Riggs Blvd (74017). 918/341-4410; fax 918/341-6045; toll-free 800/644-9455. www. bestwestern.com.* 52 rms. S $44; D $54; each addl $4. Crib $5. Pet accepted. TV; cable (premium). Pool. Coffee in rms. Restaurant adj 6 am-9:30 pm; closed Sun. Bar noon-1:30 am, closed Sun, hols. Ck-out noon. Coin lndry. Meeting rm. Business servs avail. Many refrigerators; microwaves avail. Cr cds: A, C, D, DS, ER, JCB, MC, V.
🄳 🐾 ➴ 🖎 🔥 SC

Restaurant

★★ **HAMMETT HOUSE.** *1616 W Will Rogers Blvd (74017). 918/341-7333. www.hammetthouse.com.* Hrs: 11 am-9 pm. Closed Mon; Thanksgiving, Dec 25. Bar. Lunch $4-$6, dinner $4-17. Children's menu. Specialties: pamper-fried chicken, lamb and turkey fries. Own baking. Family-owned. Cr cds: A, C, D, DS, MC, V.
🄳 🍽

Unrated Dining Spot

PINK HOUSE. *210 W 4th St (74017). 918/342-2544.* Hrs: 11 am-3 pm.

Closed wk of July 4, Thanksgiving wkend, wk of Dec 25. Lunch $3-$7. Children's menu. Specializes in soups, desserts. House (1902) with Victorian decor; antiques. Cr cds: A, DS, MC, V.

D

Clinton

(C-4) *See also Elk City, Weatherford*

Founded 1903 **Pop** 9,298 **Elev** 1,592 ft **Area code** 580 **Zip** 73601
Information Chamber of Commerce, 600 Avant; 580/323-2222

This is a cattle, farming, manufacturing, and shipping center founded when Congress approved the purchase of acreage owned by Native Americans at the junction of two railroads. Oil and gas drilling and production take place here.

What to See and Do

Foss State Park. An 8,800-acre lake created by dam on Washita River. Waterskiing, fishing, enclosed dock, boating (ramps, docks, marina); picnic facilities, playgrounds, camping, trailer hookups (fee). (Daily) 14 mi W on I-40, exit 53, then 7 mi N on OK 44. Phone 580/592-4433. **FREE**

Special Events

Art in the Park Festival. McLain-Rogers Park. Features art from Oklahoma and surrounding states. Second Sat May.

Route 66 Festival. McLain-Rogers Park. Car show, motorcycle rally, foot races. Wkend after Labor Day.

Duncan

(D-5) *See also Lawton, Waurika*

Founded 1893 **Pop** 21,732 **Elev** 1,126 ft **Area code** 580 **Zip** 73533
Information Chamber of Commerce, 911 Walnut, PO Box 699; 580/255-3644

Once a cattle town on the old Chisholm Trail, Duncan has become an oil services and agricultural center. It was here that Erle P. Halliburton developed his oil well cementing business, which now operates all over the world.

What to See and Do

Chisholm Trail Museum. Interactive displays demonstrating the history of the Chisholm Trail. Historical movies; gift shop. (Summer, daily; winter, wkends) 1000 N 29th St. Phone 580/252-5580. **FREE** Also here is
   On the Chisholm Trail. Large bronze statue depicts life-size cowboys, horses, cattle, and chuckwagon. (Daily) **FREE**

Stephens County Historical Museum. Houses pioneer and Native American artifacts, antique toys, gem and lapidary display; Plains Indian exhibit. Also log cabin, old schoolhouse, pioneer kitchen (1892), blacksmith shop, dentist's office, law office. (Thurs, Sat, and Sun; closed hols) On E side of US 81 and Beech Ave, in Fuqua Park. Phone 580/252-0717. **FREE**

Motel/Motor Lodge

★ ★ **HOLIDAY INN.** *1015 N US 81 (73533).* 580/252-1500; fax 580/255-1851; res 800/465-4329. www.holiday-inn.com. 138 rms, 2 story. S $51-$61; D $57-$68; under 18 free. Crib free. Pet accepted, some restrictions. TV; cable (premium). Indoor pool; wading pool. Restaurant 6 am-10 pm; Sat to 11 pm; Sun to 9 pm. Bar 5 pm-2 am. Ck-out noon. Meeting rms. Business servs avail. In-rm modem link. Sauna. Valet serv. Picnic tables. Cr cds: A, C, D, DS, JCB, MC, V.

D ➲ ⬧ ⬧ ⬧ ⬧ ⬧

Durant

(E-7) *See also Lake Texoma*

Settled 1832 **Pop** 12,823 **Elev** 647 ft **Area code** 580 **Zip** 74701
Information Chamber of Commerce, 215 N 4th St; 580/924-0848
Web www.durantokla.com

Long a farm and livestock-producing town in Oklahoma's Red River Valley, Durant has become a recreation center since the completion of Lake Texoma. Oil and industry have also stimulated the city's economy. Durant, home of Southeastern Oklahoma State University (1909), has many mansions, magnolia trees, and gardens.

What to See and Do

Fort Washita. Originally built in 1842 to protect the Five Civilized Tribes from the Plains Indians; used during the Civil War as Confederate supply depot; remains of 48 buildings are visible. Picnicking. Special events (fee). (Daily; closed hols) 16 mi NW via OK 78, 199, on N shore of Lake Texoma. Phone 580/924-6502. **FREE**

Three Valley Museum. Museum housed in the Choctaw Nation Headquarters building; contains turn-of-the-century artifacts, antique dolls, art, and beadwork. (Tues-Sat, also by appt; closed Thanksgiving, Dec 25) 16th and Locust. Phone 580/920-1907. **FREE**

Special Events

Magnolia Festival. Downtown. Crafts, rides, art show, entertainment. Last wkend May.

The Oklahoma Shakespearean Festival. On the campus of Southeastern Oklahoma State University. Musical; children's show, teen cabaret; dinner theatre. Phone 580/924-0121, ext 2442. Late June-July.

Motels/Motor Lodges

★★ **BEST WESTERN MARKITA INN.** *2401 W Main St (74701). 580/924-7676; fax 580/924-3060; toll-free 800/528-1234. www.bestwestern. com.* 60 rms, 2 story. S $40; D $60; each addl $5; suites $75-$125; under 12 free. Crib $5. TV; cable (premium). Pool. Restaurant open 24 hrs. Rm serv 7-11 am. Ck-out noon. Meeting rm. Business servs avail. In-rm modem link. Refrigerators. Picnic tables. Cr cds: A, C, D, DS, MC, V.
[D] [≈] [⊠] [⦾] [SC]

★★ **COMFORT INN AND SUITES.** *2112 W Main St (74701). 580/924-8881; fax 580/924-0955; toll-free 800/228-5150. www.comfortinn.com.*
62 rms, 2 story, 16 suites. Apr-Oct: S $64-$74; D $69-$79; each addl $5; suites $84-$89; under 16 free; lower rates rest of yr. Crib $5. Pet accepted: $10. TV; cable (premium). Complimentary continental bkfst. Restaurant nearby. Ck-out noon. Meeting rms. Business servs avail. In-rm modem link. Sundries. Coin lndry. Pool. Bathrm phones; refrigerator, microwave in suite. Cr cds: A, C, D, DS, JCB, MC, V.
[D] [⦿] [≈] [⊠] [⦾] [SC]

★★ **HOLIDAY INN.** *2121 W Main St (74701). 580/924-5432; fax 580/924-9721; res 800/465-4329. www.holiday-inn.com.* 81 rms, 2 story. May-mid-Sept: S, D $54-$59; each addl $5; under 18 free. Crib free. TV; cable (premium). Pool. Restaurant 6 am-10 pm, wkends to midnight. Ck-out noon. Meeting rm. Business servs avail. Cr cds: A, C, D, DS, JCB, MC, V.
[D] [≈] [⊠] [⦾] [SC]

Elk City

(C-4) *See also Clinton*

Pop 10,428 **Elev** 1,928 ft
Area code 580 **Zip** 73644
Information Chamber of Commerce, 1016 Airport Blvd, PO Box 972; 580/225-0207 or 800/280-0207
Web www.elkcitychamber.com

This was once a stopping point for cattlemen driving herds from Texas to railheads in Kansas. It was known as the "Great Western" or "Dodge City Cattle Trail." Elk City, centrally located on historic Route 66, lies near the center of the Anadarko Basin, where extensive natural gas exploration takes place.

What to See and Do

Old Town Museum. Turn-of-the-century house has Victorian furnishings, Native American artifacts, Beutler Brothers Rodeo memorabilia; Memorial Chapel; early one-rm school; wagon yard; gristmill; depot and caboose. (Tues-Sun; closed hols) Pioneer Rd and US 66. Phone 580/225-2207. ¢¢

Special Events

Beachfest. Lake Elk City. Watersports, concerts. Early Aug.

Rodeo of Champions. Rodeo grounds, A Ave at W edge of town. PRCA sanctioned. Labor Day wkend.

Fall Festival of the Arts. Exhibits, children's show, performing arts, and music. Third wkend Sept.

Motels/Motor Lodges

★ **DAYS INN.** *1100 OK 34 and I-40 (73644). 580/225-9210; fax 580/225-1278; toll-free 800/329-7466. www. daysinn.com.* 100 rms, 63 kits. S $35-$45; D $40-$50. Crib free. Pet accepted. TV; cable. Pool. Complimentary continental bkfst. Restaurant opp open 24 hrs. Ck-out noon. Business servs avail. Gift shop. Some refrigerators. Cr cds: A, MC, V.

★★ **HOLIDAY INN.** *101 Meadow Ridge (73644). 580/225-6637; res 800/465-4329. www.holiday-inn.com.* 151 rms, 2 story. S, D $59-$75; each addl $6; suites $85-$105; under 19 free. Crib free. Pet accepted. TV; cable (premium), VCR avail (movies). Indoor pool; whirlpool. Complimentary coffee in rms. Restaurant 6 am-2 pm, 5-10 pm. Bar 5 pm-midnight; Fri, Sat to 2 am. Ck-out noon. Meeting rms. Business servs avail. In-rm modem link. Valet serv. Exercise equipt; sauna. Lawn games. Miniature golf. Wet bar in suites. Cr cds: A, C, D, DS, MC, V.

Restaurants

★ **COUNTRY DOVE.** *610 W 3rd (73644). 580/225-7028.* Hrs: 11 am-2 pm. Closed Sun; hols. Res accepted. Lunch $3.50-$5.95. Specialties: chicken avocado sandwich, French silk pie. Gift shop. Cr cds: DS, MC, V.

★ **LUPE'S.** *905 N Main St (73644). 580/225-7109.* Hrs: 11 am-2 pm, 4-11 pm; Sat from 4 pm. Closed Sun; hols. Mexican, American menu. Bar. Lunch $4.35-$6.55, dinner $4.25-$15.35. Children's menu. Specialties: rib-eye steak, fajitas. Mexican decor. Cr cds: A, DS, MC, V.

El Reno

Founded 1889 **Pop** 15,414 **Elev** 1,365 ft **Area code** 405 **Zip** 73036
Information Chamber of Commerce, 206 N Bickford, PO Box 67; 405/262-1188

Established in 1889, El Reno was named for Civil War General Jesse L. Reno, who was killed during the Battle of Antietam in 1862. The city lies in the heart of the Canadian River valley. Farming, livestock, and cotton are its principal agricultural pursuits.

What to See and Do

Canadian County Historical Museum. Former Rock Island Depot (1907) houses Native American and pioneer artifacts; Agriculture Exhibit Barn; railroad exhibit and caboose; historical hotel, log cabin, jail, and rural schoolhouse on grounds. (Wed-Sun; closed hols) 300 S Grand St. Phone 405/262-5121. **FREE**

Motel/Motor Lodge

★★ **BEST WESTERN - HENSLEY'S.** *2701 S Country Club Rd (73036). 405/262-6490; fax 405/262-7642; toll-free 800/263-3844. www.bestwestern. com.* 60 rms, 2 story. Mar-Oct: S $44-$54; D $47-$57; each addl $4; under 12 free; lower rates rest of yr. Crib $2. Pet accepted, some restrictions. TV; cable (premium). Heated pool. Complimentary continental bkfst. Restaurant adj. Ck-out 11 am. Meeting rms. Business servs avail. Cr cds: A, MC, V.

Enid (B-5)

Founded 1893 **Pop** 45,309 **Elev** 1,246 ft **Area code** 580
Information Chamber of Commerce, 210 Kenwood Blvd, PO Box 907, 73702; 580/237-2494 or 800/299-2494
Web www.chamber.enid.com

Like many Oklahoma cities, Enid was born of a land rush. When the Cherokee Outlet (more popularly known as the Cherokee Strip) was opened to settlement on September 16, 1893, a tent city sprang up. It is now a prosperous community, a center for farm marketing and oil processing. Just south of town is Vance Air Force Base, a training base for jet aircraft pilots.

What to See and Do

Homesteader's Sod House. (1894) A two-rm sod house built by Marshall McCully in 1894; said to be the only original example of this type of structure still standing in Oklahoma. Period furnishings; farm machinery. (Tues-Fri, also Sat and Sun afternoons; closed hols) 30 mi W on US 60, then 5½ mi N of Cleo Springs on OK 8. Phone 580/463-2441. **FREE**

Museum of the Cherokee Strip. Artifacts covering Oklahoma history of the Plains Indians, the Land Run of 1893, and events from 1900-present. (Tues-Fri, also Sat and Sun afternoons; closed hols) 507 S 4th St. Phone 580/237-1907. **FREE**

Special Events

Tri-State Music Festival. One wk late Apr or early May.

Cherokee Strip Celebration. City-wide festival commemorates opening of the Cherokee Strip to settlers. Incl entertainment, parade, rodeo, arts and crafts, food. Four days mid-Sept.

Grand National Quail Hunt. Late Nov.

Motels/Motor Lodges

★★ **BEST WESTERN.** *2818 S Van Buren St (73703). 580/242-7110; fax 580/242-6202; res 800/378-6308. www.bestwestern.com.* 100 rms, 2 story. S $50-$52; D $55-$57; each addl $5. Crib free. Pet accepted. TV; cable (premium). Indoor pool. Restaurant 6 am-2 pm, 5-10 pm. Bar 5 pm-2 am, closed Sun. Ck-out noon. Meeting rms. Business servs avail. In-rm modem link. Valet serv. Health club privileges. Game rm. Refrigerators, microwaves avail. Cr cds: A, C, D, DS, JCB, MC, V.
D 🐕 ⛱ 🏊 🔥 SC

★★ **HOLIDAY INN.** *2901 S Van Buren St (73703). 580/237-6000; fax 580/234-3270; res 800/465-4329. www.holiday-inn.com.* 100 rms, 2 story. S $46-$50; D $52-$56; each addl $6. Crib free. Pet accepted. TV; cable (premium). Pool. Restaurant 6 am-9 pm; Sun to 2 pm. Bar 4 pm-2 am, closed Sun. Ck-out noon. Meeting rms. Business servs avail. Sundries. Cr cds: A, D, DS, JCB, MC, V.
D 🐕 ⛱ 🏊 🔥

★ **RAMADA INN.** *3005 W Owen K. Garriott Rd (73703). 580/234-0440; fax 580/233-1402; res 888/298-2054. www.ramada.com.* 125 rms, 2 story. S $42; D $48; each addl $6; under 18 free. Crib free. Pet accepted. TV; cable (premium). Pool; whirlpool. Restaurant 6 am-2 pm, 5-9 pm. Ck-out noon. Coin lndry. Meeting rms. Exercise equipt; sauna. Health club privileges. Game rm. Microwaves avail. Cr cds: A, C, D, DS, ER, JCB, MC, V.
D 🐕 🏋 ⛱ 🏊 🔥 🏃

Restaurant

★★ **SAGE ROOM.** *1927 S Van Buren St (US 81) (73703). 580/233-1212.* Hrs: 5-9:30 pm; Fri, Sat to 10 pm. Closed Sun; hols. Serv bar. Dinner $6.95-$59.95. Children's menu. Specializes in beef, seafood, chicken. Pianist Tues-Sun. Antique clock collection. Cr cds: DS, MC, V.
D SC 🔒

Eufaula

(C-7) *See also McAlester*

Settled 1836 **Pop** 2,652 **Elev** 617 ft
Area code 918 **Zip** 74432

Information Greater Eufaula Area Chamber of Commerce, 64 Memorial Dr, PO Box 738; 918/689-2791

Eufaula was first a Native American settlement and later a trading post. The town is still the home of the Eufaula Boarding School for Indian Girls (1849), which was renamed the Eufaula Dormitory after becoming coeducational. Eufaula is also the home of the state's oldest continuously published newspaper, *The*

Indian Journal, and the Eufaula Dam, which impounds the Canadian River to form one of the largest man-made lakes in the world.

What to See and Do

Arrowhead State Park. Approx 2,450 acres located on south shore of 102,500-acre Lake Eufaula. Beach, bathhouse, waterskiing, fishing, boating (ramps, marina); golf, nature walk, hiking, picnicking, playground, restaurant, lodges, full resort facilities, camping, trailer hookups (fee), cabins. Airstrip. (Daily) 11 mi S on US 69, then E. Phone 918/339-2204. **FREE**

Eufaula Dam. Camping at Dam site East (early Apr-Oct; fee). Swimming beach; nature trail. 18 mi NE via OK 9, 71. Phone 918/484-5135.

Fountainhead State Park. Approx 3,400 acres on shore of Lake Eufaula. Beach, bathhouse, waterskiing, fishing, boating (ramps, marina); golf, tennis, nature walk, hiking and bridle paths, picnicking, playground, restaurant, lodges, full resort facilities (see RESORT), camping, trailer hookups (fee). Airstrip. Gift shop. (Daily) 6 mi N on US 69, then 2 mi NW on OK 150. Phone 918/689-5311. **FREE**

Special Event

McIntosh County Fair. Three days late Aug.

Motel/Motor Lodge

★★ **BEST WESTERN INN.** HC 60, Box 1835, Checotah (74426). 918/473-2376; fax 918/473-5774; toll-free 800/528-1234. 48 rms. S $42; D $47-$57; each addl $5. Crib $3. TV; cable (premium). Pool. Continental bkfst. Ck-out noon. Coin lndry. Business servs avail. Cr cds: A, C, D, DS, MC, V.

Resort

★ **FOUNTAINHEAD RESORT.** Rural Rte 60, Box 1355, Checotah (74426). 918/689-9173; fax 918/689-9493; toll-free 800/345-6343. www.fountainhead. com. 188 units, 5 story. Apr-Oct: S, D $75-$95; each addl $10; suites $200-$300; under 16 free; lower rates rest

of yr. Crib free. TV. 2 pools, 1 indoor; wading pool. Playground. Dining rm (see COLOURS). Box lunches, picnics. Bar 5 pm-1 am; Sat to 2 am. Ck-out 11 am, ck-in 3 pm. Coin lndry. Grocery, package store 7 mi. Meeting rms. Gift shop. Sports dir. Lighted tennis. 18-hole golf, greens fee $9-$11, putting green, driving range. Swimming beach. Hiking. Lawn games. Soc dir. Rec rm. Game rm. Sauna. Fishing/hunting guides. Some refrigerators. Fountainhead State Park facilities avail to guests. Cr cds: A, C, D, DS, MC, V.

Restaurant

★★ **COLOURS.** HC 60, Checotah (74426). 918/689-9173. www.fountain headresort.com. Hrs: 7 am-1 pm, 5-8 pm; Fri, Sat to 9 pm. Res accepted. Bar. Bkfst $2.95-$4.95, lunch $4.95-$6.95, dinner $8.95-$21.95. Children's menu. Salad bar. Overlooks Lake Eufaula. Cr cds: A, DS, MC, V.

Grand Lake

See also Miami, Pryor, Vinita

Also called "Grand Lake O' the Cherokees," this 66-mile, 59,200-acre lake above Pensacola Dam is primarily a source of electric power. It also offers swimming, water sports, fishing, boating, and camping along 1,300 miles of shoreline, and is a popular resort area that has drawn millions of visitors. There are more than 100 resorts and fishing camps. Twenty-nine enclosed fishing docks are here; some are heated for year-round use. Grove is a major center of activity, but Ketchum, Langley, and Disney are also important. The lake is convenient to Miami, Pryor, and Vinita (see all).

What to See and Do

Boat cruises. *Cherokee Queen I & II.* Narrated cruise (90-min) on Grand Lake O' the Cherokees; entertainment, refreshments. Honey Creek Bridge on US 59, south end of Grove. Phone 918/786-4272.

Har-Ber Village. Reconstructed old-time village with 90 buildings and shops typical of a pioneer town; also a variety of memorabilia collections. Picnicking. (Mar-Nov, daily) 4404 W 20th St, Grove. Phone 918/786-6446. **FREE**

Lendonwood Gardens. Houses one of the largest collections of chamaecy-parais in the US, plus rhododendrons, day lilies, and azaleas. Gardens incl Display Garden, English Terrace Garden, and Japanese Garden. (Daily) 1308 W 13th St (Har-Ber Rd) in Grove. Phone 918/786-2938. ¢¢

Special Events

Picture in Scripture Amphitheater. 6 mi S via OK 85 and OK 82, 3 mi E via OK 28, in Disney. Biblical drama of Jonah and the Whale. Phone 918/435-8207. June-Aug.

Pelican Festival. Grand Lake O' the Cherokees, in Grove. Viewing of white pelicans on their southward migration; tours and cruises to view pelicans; events; parade. Phone 918/786-2289. Last wkend Sept.

Resort

★★★ **SHANGRI-LA RESORT.** *57401 E Hwy 125 S, Afton (74331). 918/257-4204; fax 918/257-5916; toll-free 800/331-4060. shangrilagrandlake. com.* 380 units, 101 suites. Memorial Day-Labor Day: S, D $89-$134; each addl (after 2nd person) $15; suites $139-$387; under 18 free; tennis, golf packages; lower rates rest of yr. Crib free. TV; cable (premium). 2 pools, 1 indoor; whirlpool, lifeguard (wkends). Playground. Supervised children's activities (Memorial Day-Labor Day); ages 5-12. Dining rms 6:30 am-10 pm; Thurs-Sat to 11 pm. Box lunches, snack bar. Bar 1 pm-1 am. Ck-out noon, ck-in 4 pm. Convention facilities. Business servs avail. Valet serv. Gift shop. Beauty shop. Sports dir. Lighted and indoor tennis. 36-hole golf, pro, putting green, driving range. Private beach; marina, boats, waterskiing, swimming. Bicycles. Lawn games. Soc dir. Game rm. Bowling. Exercise equipt; sauna. Fireplace in houses. Some balconies. Picnic tables. 660-acre resort on shores of Grand Lake o' the Cherokees. Cr cds: A, C, D, DS, ER, JCB, MC, V.

Guthrie

(C-6) *See also Oklahoma City*

Founded 1889 **Pop** 10,518 **Elev** 946 ft **Area code** 405 **Zip** 73044

Information Chamber of Commerce, 212 W Oklahoma, PO Box 995; 405/282-1947

Guthrie was founded in just a few hours during the great land rush. Prior to the "run" only a small frame railroad station and a partially completed land registration office stood on the site. A few hours later perhaps 20,000 inhabited the tent city on the prairie.

Oklahoma's territorial and first state capital, Guthrie now has the most complete collection of restored Victorian architecture in the United States, with 1,400 acres of the city listed on the National Historic Register. Included are 160 buildings in the central business district and the center of town and numerous Victorian mansions. The town is being restored to the 1907-1910 era, including the expansive Guthrie Railroad Hotel and the former opera house, the Pollard Theatre. Some who have called Guthrie home at one time or another are Tom Mix, Lon Chaney, Will Rogers, Carry Nation, and O. Henry.

What to See and Do

Oklahoma Territorial Museum. Exhibits and displays of life in territorial Oklahoma during the turn of the century. Adj is the Carnegie Library (1902-1903), site of inaugurations of the last territorial and the first state governor. (Tues-Sun; closed hols) 406 E Oklahoma Ave. Phone 405/282-1889. **FREE**

Scottish Rite Masonic Temple. A multimillion-dollar Classical Revival building, said to be the largest structure used for Masonic purposes. Building contains the original state capitol; 13 artistic rms; 200 stained-glass windows. Surrounding it is a ten-acre park. Visitors welcome; children must be accompanied by adult. (Mon-Fri; closed hols) 900 E Oklahoma Ave. Phone 405/282-1281. ¢

State Capital Publishing Museum. Located in the four-story State Capital Publishing Company Building

(1902). Houses a collection of original furnishings, vintage letterpress equipt; exhibits featuring the history of the first newspaper in Oklahoma Territory and period printing technology. (Tues-Sun; closed hols) 301 W Harrison. Phone 405/282-4123. **FREE**

Special Events

Eighty-niner Celebration. PRCA rodeo, "chuck wagon feed," parade, carnival, races. Mid- or late Apr.

Oklahoma International Bluegrass Festival. Performances by top bluegrass bands and musicians. Children's activities, music workshops, concessions; celebrity golf tournament. Phone 405/282-4446. Four days early Oct.

Road Show. Street display of antique automobiles. Mid-Sept.

Territorial Christmas. Seven mi of lights outline architecture in Historic District; streets are filled with persons clad in turn-of-the-century style clothes, horse-drawn vehicles; window displays echo 1890-1920 era. Fri after Thanksgiving-late Dec.

Motel/Motor Lodge

★★ **BEST WESTERN INN.** *2323 Territorial Tr (73044). 405/282-8831; toll-free 800/528-1234. www.best western.com.* 84 units, 2 story. S $51-$65; D $61-$69; each addl $6; under 12 free. Crib free. Pet accepted, some restrictions. TV; cable. Pool. Restaurant 6 am-2 pm, 5-9 pm. Bar 5 pm-2 am. Ck-out 11 am. Meeting rms. Cr cds: A, C, D, DS, MC, V.

D ⬛ ⬛ ⬛ ⬛ SC

B&B/Small Inn

★★ **HARRISON HOUSE BED & BREAKFAST INN.** *124 W Harrison (73044). 405/282-1000; toll-free 800/ 375-1001. www.machtolff.com.* 30 rms, 3 story. S $70-$75; D $70-$95; each addl $15; under 12 free. TV in parlor; VCR avail. Complimentary continental bkfst. Ck-out 11 am, ck-in after 3 pm. Business servs avail. Pollard Theatre adj. Cr cds: A, C, D, DS, MC, V.

D ⬛ ⬛ SC

Restaurant

★ **STABLES CAFE.** *223 N Division (73044). 405/282-0893.* Hrs: 11 am-9 pm; Fri, Sat to 10 pm. Closed July 4, Thanksgiving, Dec 25. Lunch, dinner $3.65-$14. Children's menu. Specializes in barbecue, steak, hamburgers. Salad bar. Western atmosphere; pictures, memorabilia. Cr cds: A, DS, MC, V.

D SC ⬛

Guymon (B-2)

Founded 1890 **Pop** 7,803 **Elev** 3,121 ft **Area code** 580 **Zip** 73942

Information Chamber of Commerce, Rte 3, Box 120; 580/338-3376

Web www.guymoncofc.com

Located approximately at the center of Oklahoma's panhandle, Guymon owes its growth to oil, natural gas, irrigation, manufacturing, commercial feed lots, and swine production.

What to See and Do

Oklahoma Panhandle State University. (1909) 1,200 students. Agricultural research station; golf course (fee). Campus tours. 10 mi SW on US 54, in Goodwell. Phone 580/349-2611, ext 275. On campus is

    No Man's Land Museum. (1932) Exhibit divisions relating to panhandle region incl archives, anthropology, biology, geology, pioneer history, and art gallery; changing exhibits; notable archaeological collection and alabaster carvings. (Tues-Sat; closed hols) 207 W Sewell St. Phone 580/349-2670. **FREE**

Sunset Lake. Fishing, paddle boats; picnicking, playground, miniature train rides. Fee for activities. Adj game preserve has buffalo, llamas, aoudad sheep, longhorn cattle, and elk. (Daily) W end of 5th St in Thompson Park. Phone 580/338-2178. **FREE**

Special Events

Pioneer Days. Chuck wagon bkfst, parade, PRCA rodeo, dancing, entertainment. First wkend May.

Panhandle Exposition. Texas County Fairgrounds, 5th and Sunset. Livestock, field, and garden crop displays; grandstand attractions; midway. Phone 580/338-5446. Mid-Sept.

Motels/Motor Lodges

★★ **AMBASSADOR INN.** *US 64 N at 21st St (73942). 580/338-5555; fax 580/338-1784; res 800/338-3301.* 70 rms, 2 story. S $45-$55; D $48-$58; each addl $4; under 12 free. Crib free. Pet accepted, some restrictions. TV; cable (premium). Pool. Restaurant 6 am-9 pm. Bar. Ck-out 11 am. Meeting rms. Business servs avail. Valet serv. Cr cds: A, MC, V.

★ **ECONO LODGE.** *923 US 54 E (73942). 580/338-5431; fax 580/338-0554; res 800/638-4854. www.econo lodge.com.* 40 rms. S $39-$43; D $48-$53; each addl $4; under 12 free. Crib $4. TV; cable (premium). Complimentary coffee in lobby. Restaurant adj 11 am-9 pm. Ck-out 11 am. Business servs avail. Cr cds: A, C, D, DS, MC, V.

Henryetta

(C-7) See also Okmulgee

Founded 1900 **Pop** 5,872 **Elev** 691 ft **Area code** 918 **Zip** 74437
Information Chamber of Commerce, 115 S 4th St; 918/652-3331
Web www.ocevnet.org/henryetta

Motels/Motor Lodges

★ **HENRYETTA INN AND DOME.** *810 E Trudgeon St (74437). 918/652-2581; res 800/515-3663.* 85 rms, 2 story. S $56.99-$64.99; D $68.99-$76.99; each addl $8; under 19 free. Crib free. Pet accepted. TV; cable. Indoor pool. Complimentary coffee in lobby. Restaurant 6 am-10 pm. Bar 5 pm-2 am; closed Sun. Ck-out noon. Coin lndry. Meeting rms. Business servs avail. Sundries. Exercise equipt;

sauna. Rec rm. Cr cds: A, C, D, DS, JCB, MC, V.

★ **LE BARON MOTEL.** *1001 E Main St (74437). 918/652-2531.* 24 rms, 2 story. S $29.95; D $36.85-$39.95. Crib free. Pet accepted. TV; cable (premium). Restaurant nearby. Ck-out noon. Sundries. Some in-rm whirlpools. Cr cds: A, C, D, DS, ER, JCB, MC, V.

Hugo (E-7)

Pop 5,978 **Elev** 541 ft **Area code** 580 **Zip** 74743
Information Chamber of Commerce, 200 S Broadway; 580/326-7511
Web www.net.com/hugook

What to See and Do

Hugo Lake. Nine recreation areas. Swimming, beaches (fee), boat ramps (fee); picnicking, tent and trailer sites (fee). Electrical, water hookups in some areas. (Daily) 8 mi E on US 70. Phone 580/326-3345. **FREE**

Raymond Gary State Park. Approx 46 acres with 295-acre lake. Swimming beach, fishing, boating; picnicking, playgrounds, camping (showers, dump station). Standard fees. (Daily) 16 mi E on US 70; 2 mi S of Fort Towson on OK 209. Phone 580/873-2307. **FREE**

Special Event

Grant's Bluegrass & Old-Time Music Festival. Salt Creek Park. Bluegrass performances. Phone 580/326-5598. Early Aug.

Motel/Motor Lodge

★ **VILLAGE INN MOTEL.** *610 W Jackson St (74743). 580/326-3333; fax 580/326-2670.* 50 rms. S $37; D $43; each addl $5. TV; cable. Pool. Restaurant 6 am-9 pm. Ck-out 11 am. Business servs avail. Cr cds: A, D, DS, MC, V.

Idabel

(E-8) *See also Broken Bow*

Pop 6,957 **Elev** 489 ft **Area code** 580
Zip 74745
Information Chamber of Commerce,
13 N Central; 580/286-3305
Web www.oio.net/usrs/idabel/iah.htm

The western portion of the Ouachita
National Forest (see HOT SPRINGS
and HOT SPRINGS NATIONAL PARK,
ARKANSAS) is located to the east of
Idabel. Although predominantly
evergreen, the deciduous growth—a
mixture of oak, gum, maple,
sycamore, dogwood, and persim-
mon—makes the forest notable for
its magnificent fall color. For information contact Supervisor, PO Box
1270, Federal Building, Hot Springs
National Park, AR 71902; 501/321-
5202. A Ranger District office of the
forest is also located in Idabel; phone
580/286-6564.

What to See and Do

Museum of the Red River. Interpretive exhibits of historic and prehistoric Native Americans; local
archeology; changing exhibits. (Tues-
Sat; closed hols) S of city on US
70/259 Bypass. Phone 580/286-3616.
Donation

Special Events

Dogwood Days Festival. Early Apr.
**Kiamichi Owa Chito Festival of the
Forest.** Third wkend June.

Motel/Motor Lodge

★★ **HOLIDAY INN.** *Hwy 70 W
(74745).* 580/286-6501; fax 580/286-
7482; res 800/465-4329. www.holiday-
inn.com. 99 rms, 2 story. S $62; D
$70; each addl $8; under 19 free.
Crib free. TV; cable (premium), VCR
avail. Pool. Restaurant 6-10:30 am, 6-
9 pm. Private club 5 pm-1 am, closed
Sun. Ck-out noon. Meeting rm. Business servs avail. In-rm modem link.
Cr cds: A, C, D, DS, JCB, MC, V.
🄳 ⏛ ⍟ 🐾 SC

Lake Murray State Park

See also Ardmore

*(7 mi SE of Ardmore, off I-35 exit 24 or
29)*

This 12,496-acre state park, which
includes a 5,728-acre man-made lake,
can be reached from either Marietta
or Ardmore. The museum in Tucker
Tower (Feb-Nov, Wed-Sun; fee) has
historical and mineral exhibits,
including a large, rare meteorite. The
park is hilly and wooded with beach,
bathhouse, swimming pool, waterskiing, two fishing piers, heated fishing
dock, boating (rentals, ramps,
marina); horseback riding, 18-hole
golf, tennis, two hiking trails, picnic
facilities, playground, miniature golf,
grocery, lodge (see RESORT), club,
camping areas, trailer hookups (fee).
Airstrip. (Daily) Phone 580/223-4044.
FREE

Resort

★ **LAKE MURRAY LODGE AND
COUNTRY INN.** *3310 S Lake Murray
Dr (73401).* 580/223-6600; fax 580/
223-6154. 51 rms in lodge, 80 cottages. Mid-May-mid-Sept: S, D $63-
$78; each addl $10; suites $150;
lower rates rest of yr; kit. cottages
(no equipt) $53-$98; cottages for 6-
12, $110-$275; 1-2 bedrm cottages
$78-$98; under 18 free in lodge rms;
golf plans. Crib free. Pet accepted,
cabins only. TV in lodge rms, lobby;
VCR avail (movies). Pool; lifeguard.
Playgrounds. Free supervised children's activities; ages 6-18. Dining
rm 7 am-2 pm, 5-10 pm. Bar 5 pm-
midnight. Ck-out noon, ck-in 3 pm.
Meeting rms. Business servs avail.
Airport transportation. Gift shop.
Grocery. Tennis. 18-hole golf privileges. Miniature golf. Paddleboats.
Sport facilities of Lake Murray State
Park. Lawn games. Soc dir. Rec rm.
Movies. Chapel; services Sun. Some
refrigerators, fireplaces. 2,500-ft
lighted, paved airstrip. On Lake Mur-
ray. State operated. Cr cds: A, C, D,
DS, MC, V.
🄳 🐾 ⍟ 🏕 🎿 ⏛ 🐾 SC

Restaurant

★★ **FIRESIDE DINING.** *Lake Murray Village (73401)*. *580/226-4070*. Hrs: 5-10 pm. Closed Mon, Sun; hols. Continental menu. Dinner $13.95-$21.95. Children's menu. Specializes in prime cut aged beef, fresh seafood. Western decor; pioneer artifacts, fireplace, gardens. Cr cds: A, DS, MC, V.
D ➔

Lake Texoma

See also Durant, Marietta

14 mi W on US 70.
Area code 580
Information Project Office, Lake Twxoma, Rte 3, Box 493, Denison TX 75020; 903/465-4990

This lake is so named because it is impounded behind Denison Dam on the Red River, the boundary between Oklahoma and Texas. With shores in both states, this is one of the finest and most popular of the lakes in either.

Approximately two-thirds pf the lake's 89,000 acres are in Oklahoma. The total shoreline is 580 miles. About 105,000 acres surrounding the lake are federally owned, but the state of Oklahoma has leased 1,600 acres between Madill and Durant for Lake Texoma State Park. The remainder of the lake is under control of the US Army Corps of Engineers, which built the dam. Project office (Monday-Friday; closed holidays).

Fishing boats and outboard motors may be rented at several locations on the lake. Guides are available. Duck and goose hunting is good. Swimming beaches have been developed at many points on the lake. Picnicking, camping, and trailer hookups (fee), cabins and supplies at many points, some privately operated and some state owned. Also here are beach, swimming pool, bathhouse, waterskiing, fishing dock, boat dock, storage, and marina; horseback riding, 18-hole golf course, driving range, putting range, tennis courts, shuffleboard; three playgrounds, restaurant, grocery, lodging (see RESORT), cabins, and a 2,500-foot airstrip at Lake Texoma State Park.

At the northern end of the lake, on the courthouse grounds in Tishomingo, is the Chickasaw Council House, the log cabin used as the first seat of government of the Chickasaw Nation in the Indian Territory. Enclosed in a larger building, it has displays on Native American history (Tuesday-Sunday; closed holidays; free).

Fees may be charged at federal recreation sites.

Lake Texoma

Resort

★★ **LAKE TEXOMA RESORT.** *US 70 E, Kingston (73439).* 580/564-2311; *fax 580/564-9322.* 100 rms in main lodge; 20 rms in annex (dorm-type baths, phone in lobby); 67 cottages with kits. (no equipt). Mid-Apr-mid-Sept: S, D $50-$64; suites $87-$150; kit. cottages for 1-8, $57-$94; MAP, golf, fishing, honeymoon plans; lower rates rest of yr. Crib free. TV in main lodge, cottages; VCR avail (movies $3). Pool; wading pool, lifeguard in summer. Playground. Free supervised children's activities. Dining rm 6:30 am-9:30 pm. Rm serv in lodge. Box lunches, snacks in summer. Ck-out noon, ck-in varies. Coin lndry. Meeting rms. Business servs avail. Bellhops. Gift shop. Lighted tennis. 18-hole golf, greens fee $11-$13, pro. Miniature golf. Volleyball, horseshoe pit. Go-carts; bumper boats. Full-service marina. Exercise equipt; sauna. Sports dir; all facilities of state park. Fishing guides. Rec rm. Indoor, outdoor games. Refrigerator, wet bar in suites. Fireplace in cottages. Airstrip in park. State-owned, operated. Cr cds: A, C, D, DS, MC, V.

🄳 ⬤ ⛵ 🏋 🎣 ≋ 🚶 🔻 🎿

Restaurant

★ **SANFORD'S.** *US 70 E, Kingston (73439).* 580/564-3764. Hrs: 4:30-9 pm; Fri, Sat to 10 pm. Closed Mon, Sun; Thanksgiving, Dec 25. Dinner $7.45-$15.95. Specializes in catfish, steak. Salad bar. Cr cds: A, C, D, DS, ER, MC, V.

🄳 ⊟

Lawton

(D-5) *See also Duncan*

Founded 1901 **Pop** 80,561 **Elev** 1,109 ft **Area code** 580

Information Chamber of Commerce, 607 C Ave, PO Box 1376, 73502; 580/355-3541

Web www.lcci.org

Last of the many Oklahoma cities that sprang up overnight, Lawton had its land rush on August 6, 1901.

It is now the state's third-largest city and serves as a prominent shopping, recreational, medical, and educational center for the area. Much of the city's prosperity is due to Fort Sill, established in 1869, and the world's largest Goodyear Tire plant. The Wichita Mountains provide a dramatic backdrop to the city.

What to See and Do

Fort Sill Military Reservation. A 94,268-acre army installation, US Army Field Artillery Center and School. Geronimo, war leader of the Apaches, spent his final yrs here and is buried in the post's Apache cemetery. There are many historic sites here. (Daily) 4 mi N on US 277. Phone 580/442-2521. **FREE** Also here are

Fort Sill National Historic Landmark. Forty-three buildings built of native stone during the 1870s, many of which are still being used for their original purpose. Incl

Sherman House. Commandant's home. In 1871 General William Tecumseh Sherman was almost killed by the Kiowa on the front porch. Not open to the public.

Old Post Headquarters. From which Generals Grierson and Mackenzie conducted Native American campaigns.

Old Post Chapel. One of the oldest houses of worship still in use in state.

Old Guardhouse. Commissary Storehouse, Quartermaster warehouse, School of Fire, Quartermaster Corral, Visitor Center, and Cannon Walk. Depicts history of field artillery and missiles. Cavalry, Native American relics. Film presentation of Fort Sill history, 25 min (daily). Self-guided tour map. (Daily; closed hols) Phone 580/442-2521. **FREE**

Mattie Beal Home. Fourteen-rm Greek Revival mansion built in 1908. Tours second Sun of each month. 1006 SW 5th St. Phone 580/353-6884. ¢

Museum of the Great Plains. Displays on Native Americans, fur trade, exploration, cattle industry, and settlement of the area; period rms depict Main St of frontier town; outdoor exhibits of a 300-ton Baldwin steam locomotive, depot, and wooden threshers; fortified trading post with a 100-sq-ft log stockade, two-story blockhouses and furnished trader's cabin representing such a post in the 1830s-1840s. Trading post (Wed-Sun) has living history programs. (Tues-Sun; closed Jan 1, Thanksgiving, Dec 25) In Elmer Thomas Park, 601 Ferris Blvd. Phone 580/581-3460. ¢¢

Percussive Arts Society Museum. Displays of percussion instruments from around the world. Visitors can try several different instruments. Tours by appt. (Daily) 7th and Ferris. Phone 580/353-1455. ¢

Wichita Mountains Wildlife Refuge. This 59,060-acre refuge has 12 man-made lakes. Nonmotorized boating permitted on four lakes, trolling motors on three lakes; picnicking, camping only at Doris Campground; limited backcountry camping by res only (camping fee). Quanah Parker Visitor Center (Mar-Nov, Fri-Sun); self-guided trails. Longhorn cattle, herds of buffalo, elk, deer, and other wildlife can be viewed from several wildlife/scenic viewing areas. (Daily) (See SPECIAL EVENTS) Headquarters are 13 mi W on US 62 to Cache, then 12 mi N on OK 115. Phone 580/429-3222. **FREE**

Special Events

Arts For All. Shelper Park. Features visual arts and entertainment of local artists; food; street dance. Easter Eve.

Easter Sunday Pageant. Holy City of the Wichitas, in Wichita Mtns National Wildlife Refuge. Phone 580/429-3361. Begins Sat eve before Easter.

Lawton Birthday and Rodeo Celebration. Street dancing, rodeo, races, parade. Three days early Aug.

International Festival. Celebrates various cultures of area; arts and crafts, entertainment, food. Sept.

Motels/Motor Lodges

★ **DAYS INN.** *3110 Cache Rd (73505). 580/353-3104; fax 580/353-0992; toll-free 800/329-7466. www. daysinn.com.* 96 rms, 2 story. S, D $40-$54; each addl $5; under 18 free. Crib free. Pet accepted. TV; cable (premium). Indoor/outdoor pool; whirlpool. Complimentary continental bkfst. Ck-out noon. Business servs avail. Free airport, bus depot trans-

portation. Some bathrm phones, refrigerators. Cr cds: A, C, D, DS, MC, V.

D ◨ ☒ ☒ ☒ SC

★ **HOWARD JOHNSON HOTEL & CONVENTION CENTER.** *1125 E Gore Blvd (73501). 580/353-0200; fax 580/353-6801; res 800/359-0020. www.hojo.com.* 145 rms, 2 story. S, D $49-$63; suites $110-$140; each addl $5; under 16 free. Crib free. Pet accepted; $25. TV; cable (premium), VCR avail. 3 pools, 1 indoor; wading pool, poolside serv. Complimentary coffee in lobby. Restaurant 6 am-2 pm, 4-9 pm. Bar 4 pm-2 am. Ck-out noon. Meeting rms. Business center. In-rm modem link. Free airport transportation. Lighted tennis. Exercise equipt; sauna. Some refrigerators. Private patios, balconies. Picnic tables. Cr cds: A, D, DS, MC, V.

D ◨ ☒ ☒ ☒ ☒ ☒ ☒ ☒ ☒

★ **RAMADA INN.** *601 N 2nd St (73507). 580/355-7155; fax 580/353-6162; toll-free 800/749-7155. www. ramada.com.* 98 rms, 2 story. S $46-$48; D $50-$54; each addl $6; under 18 free. Crib free. TV; cable (premium), VCR avail (movies). Pool. Complimentary coffee in rms. Restaurant 6 am-2 pm, 5-9 pm; Sun to 2 pm. Bar. Ck-out noon. Meeting rms. Business servs avail. Cr cds: A, C, D, DS, JCB, MC, V.

D ☒ ☒ ☒ ☒ SC

Restaurants

★★ **FISHERMEN'S COVE.** *6 Wildwood Rd (73501). 580/529-2672.* Hrs: 4-10 pm; Sun 11 am-9 pm. Closed Mon, Tues; Thanksgiving, Dec 25. Res accepted. Dinner $5.95-$23.95. Children's menu. Specializes in seafood, hickory-smoked meat, Cajun dishes. Nautical decor. Family-owned. Cr cds: A, D, DS, MC, V.

D SC ☒

★★★ **MARTIN'S.** *2107 N Cache Rd (73505). 580/353-5286.* Hrs: 5:30-10 pm. Closed Mon, Sun; hols. Res accepted. Bar. Wine list. Dinner $12.95-$19.95. Children's menu. Specialties: veal Oscar, duck a l'orange, prime rib. Own baking. Piano. Family-owned. Cr cds: A, D, DS, MC, V.

☒

★★ **SALAS.** *111 W Lee Blvd (OK 7) (73501). 580/357-1600.* Hrs: 11 am-10 pm. Closed Mon, Tues; Jan 1, Thanksgiving, Dec 25. Res accepted. Mexican, American menu. Lunch, dinner $4.75-$8.50. Mexican cantina atmoshpere. View of kitchen. Family-owned. Cr cds: A, DS, MC, V.
D ⊒

Marietta

(E-6) *See also Ardmore, Lake Texoma*

Pop 2,306 **Elev** 841 ft **Area code** 580 **Zip** 73448
Information Love County Chamber of Commerce, 112 W Main, Box 422; 580/276-3102
Web www.bright.net/chickasaw/marietta

What to See and Do

Lake Murray State Park. (see) 11 mi NE, off I-35 or OK 77.

Special Event

Love County Frontier Days Celebration. Courthouse lawn. Parade, musical entertainment, games, races. First wkend June.

Restaurant

★ **MCGEHEE CATFISH.** *Rural Rte 2 (73448). 580/276-2751.* Hrs: 5-9 pm; Sat, Sun from 1 pm. Closed Wed; Thanksgiving, Dec 24-26. Dinner $9.49-$11.49. Children's menu. Specialties: catfish, hot cherry tarts. Limited menu. Old West decor; fireplace, antiques. Overlooks Red River. Cr cds: DS, MC, V.
D

McAlester

(D-7) *See also Eufaula*

Founded 1870 **Pop** 16,370 **Elev** 723 ft **Area code** 918 **Zip** 74501
Information McAlester Area Chamber of Commerce & Agriculture, 17 E Carl Albert Pkwy, PO Box 759, 74502; 918/423-2550
Web www.icok.net/~macok

James J. McAlester came to the Indian Territory in 1870 armed with a geologist's notebook describing some coal deposits and a fine sense of commercial strategy. He set up a tent store where the heavily traveled Texas Road crossed the California Trail. Later, McAlester married a Native American woman, which made him a member of the Choctaw Nation with full rights. When the railroad came through, he started mining coal. After a dispute with the Choctaw Nation over royalties McAlester came to terms with the Choctaw, and in 1911 became lieutenant governor of the state.

Cattle raising, peanut farming, women's sportswear and lingerie, aircraft, electronics, and boat and oil field equipment give diversity to the town's economy.

What to See and Do

Lake McAlester. Fishing, boating. Stocked by the city. Supplies avail on road to lake. (Daily) NW of town. Phone 918/423-2550. **FREE**

McAlester Scottish Rite Temple. Unusual copper dome containing multicolored lenses makes this a landmark when lighted. One of its most illustrious members was Will Rogers, taking degrees in 1908. Tours (Mon-Fri by appt; closed hols). Adams Ave and 2nd St. Phone 918/423-6360. **FREE**

Robber's Cave State Park. Approx 8,200 acres incl lakes, alpine forests, "outlaw cave." Swimming, bathhouse, fishing, boating; hiking and horseback riding trails, picnicking, playground, restaurant, grocery, camping, trailer hookups (fee), cabins. Amphitheater. (Daily) 35 mi E to Wilburton on US 270, then 5 mi N on OK 2. Phone 918/465-2565. **FREE**

Special Event

Sanders Family Bluegrass Festival. 5 mi W via US 270. Bluegrass performances, entertainment. Phone 918/423-4891. Early-mid-June.

Motels/Motor Lodges

★★ **BEST WESTERN INN.** *1215 George Nigh Expy (74502). 918/426-0115; fax 918/426-3634; res 800/528-1234. www.bestwestern.com.* 61 rms, 2 story. S $38-$41; D $48-$52; each addl $4; suite $75; under 18 free. Crib free. Pet accepted. TV; cable (premium). Pool. Complimentary continental bkfst. Restaurant 6 am-10 pm. Ck-out noon. Business servs avail. Some refrigerators. Cr cds: A, MC, V.

★ **DAYS INN CONFERENCE HOTEL.** *1217 S George Nigh Expy (74502). 918/426-5050; fax 918/426-5055; res 800/329-7466. www.daysinn.com.* 100 rms, 2 story. S $49; D $54; each addl $5; under 18 free. Crib free. Pet accepted. TV; cable (premium). Indoor pool; whirlpool. Coffee in rms. Restaurant 6-10 am, 5-10 pm. Bar 6 pm-midnight, closed Sun. Ck-out noon. Meeting rm. Business servs avail. Coin lndry. Some refrigerators. Near Municipal Airport. Cr cds: A, C, D, DS, JCB, MC, V.

★ **RAMADA INN.** *1500 S George Nigh Expy (74501). 918/423-7766; fax 918/426-0068; res 800/228-2828. www.ramada.com.* 161 rms, 2 story. S, D $52-$57; each addl $5; suites $99-$199; under 19 free. Crib free. Pet accepted. TV; cable. Heated pool; whirlpool. Restaurant 6 am-10 pm. Bar 4 pm-2 am, closed Sun. Ck-out noon. Coin lndry. Meeting rms. Business servs avail. Bellhops. Valet serv. Sundries. Miniature golf. Sauna. Game rm. Cr cds: A, C, D, DS, JCB, MC, V.

Restaurants

★ **GIACOMO'S.** *501 S George Nigh Expy (74501). 918/423-2662.* Hrs: 11:30 am-9:30 pm. Closed Mon, Sun; hols; also wk after Memorial Day and Labor Day. Italian, American menu. Beer. Complete meals: lunch, dinner $8.50-$15.50. Children's menu. Specializes in steak, lamb fries, shrimp scampi. Family-owned. Cr cds: DS, MC, V.

★★ **ISLE OF CAPRI.** *150 SW 7th, Krebs (74554). 918/423-3062.* Hrs: 5-10:30 pm. Closed Sun; hols; also wks of July 4 and Thanksgiving. Res accepted. Italian, American menu. Bar. Complete meals: dinner $8-$15. Children's menu. Specializes in steak, shrimp, chicken, lamb fries, Italian sausage. Family-owned. Cr cds: A, DS, MC, V.

★★ **PETE'S PLACE.** *120 SW 8th St, Krebs (74554). 918/423-2042.* Hrs: 4-9 pm; Fri, Sat to 10 pm; Sun noon-9 pm. Closed hols. Res accepted. Italian menu. Serv bar. Complete meals: dinner $8.50-$15.95. Children's menu. Specializes in lamb fries, steak. Microbrewery. Family-owned. Cr cds: A, DS, MC, V.

★★ **TROLLEY'S.** *21 E Monroe St (74501). 918/423-2446. www.trolleysrestaurant.com.* Hrs: 5-10 pm. Closed Mon, Sun; Thanksgiving, Dec 25. Res accepted. Serv bar. Dinner $7.50-$25.95. Children's menu. Specializes in seafood, steak, Cajun dishes. Located in restored house (1886) with former streetcar (1908) addition; decor from early movie theaters. Cr cds: A, D, DS, MC, V.

Miami

(A-8) *See also Vinita*

Founded 1891 **Pop** 13,142 **Elev** 798 ft **Area code** 918 **Zip** 74354

Information Chamber of Commerce, 111 N Main, PO Box 760; 918/542-4481; or Traveler Information Center, E on Will Rogers Turnpike; 918/542-9303

Situated on the headwaters of Grand Lake, Miami boasts many recreational facilities. Agriculture is diversified and a number of outstanding foundation breeding herds are raised in the area. In recent years many industries have been attracted to Miami by the low-cost electricity generated by the Grand River Dam Authority.

What to See and Do

Coleman Theatre Beautiful. Built as a vaudeville theatre and movie palace in 1929, theatre features Spanish Mission Revival exterior and Louis XV interior with gold-leaf trim and carved mahogany staircases. Original pipe organ, the "Mighty Wurlitzer," is restored and reinstalled. Tours (Tues-Sat, also by appt). 103 N Main St. Phone 918/540-2425. **FREE**

Riverview Park. Swimming, fishing, boating; picnicking, camping. On Neosho River, end of S Main St.

Motel/Motor Lodge

★★ **BEST WESTERN INN OF MIAMI.** *2225 E Steve Owens Blvd (74354). 918/542-6681; fax 918/542-3777; toll-free 877/884-5422. www. bestwestern.com.* 80 rms. S $49-$59; D $59-$69; each addl $4; under 12 free. Crib $3. Pet accepted. TV; cable (premium). Pool. Restaurant 6 am-10 pm. Bar 5 pm-midnight. Ck-out noon. Airport transportation. Valet serv. Refrigerators. Cr cds: A, MC, V.
🔥 ⇔ 🗙 🐾 SC

Muskogee (C-7)

Founded 1872 **Pop** 37,708 **Elev** 602 ft
Area code 918
Information Convention & Tourism, 425 Boston, PO Box 2361, 74402; 918/684-6464 or 888/687-6137

Located near the confluence of the Verdigris, Grand, and Arkansas rivers, Muskogee was a logical site for a trading center, especially since it was in Cherokee and Creek country. Southward on the old Texas Road, over which families moved to Texas, and northward, over which cattle were driven to market, the town's location was commercially ideal. The railroad superseded the rivers in transportation importance, however, almost before the town was settled.

Today Muskogee is a diversified agricultural and industrial center where glass, paper products and paper containers, rare metals, structural steel and iron, optical machinery, and many other products are manufactured. It is an attractive town dotted with 32 small parks and is the gateway to the eastern lakes area. The port of Muskogee is part of the McClellan-Kerr Arkansas River Navigation System, handling barges that go through the inland waterway system from Pittsburgh and Minneapolis to Houston and New Orleans.

The area's surroundings made it a logical location for the US Union Agency for the Five Civilized Tribes (Cherokee, Chickasaw, Choctaw, Creek, and Seminole). The agency is in the Old Union Building, Honor Heights Dr.

What to See and Do

Five Civilized Tribes Museum. (1875) Art and artifacts of the Cherokees, Chickasaws, Choctaws, Creeks, and Seminoles; displays relating to their history and culture. (Mar-Dec, daily; rest of yr Tues-Sat; closed Jan 1, Thanksgiving, Dec 25). Agency Hill in Honor Heights Park. Phone 918/683-1701. ¢

Fort Gibson Historic Site. Established as state's first military post in 1824, park incl 12 reconstructed or restored buildings on 55-acre site; period rms depict army life in the 1830s and 1870s. Fort Gibson National Cemetery 1½ mi E. (Daily) 7 mi E on US 62 to Fort Gibson, then 1 mi N on OK 80. Phone 918/478-4088. ¢¢

Greenleaf Lake State Park. On a 930-acre lake stocked with crappie, channel catfish, and black bass. Beach, swimming pool, bathhouse, enclosed fishing dock, boating (boat and equipt rentals, marina, boathouse); hiking, picnicking, playground, camping trailer hookups (fee), cabins. (Daily) 20 mi SE on OK 10. Phone 918/487-5196. **FREE**

Honor Heights Park. A 112-acre park with azalea (mid-Apr), rose (May-Oct), and chrysanthemum gardens (Sept-Nov); nature walks, lakes, waterfall. Picnicking. (Daily) 641 Park Dr. Phone 918/684-6302. **FREE**

Tenkiller State Park. (see TENKILLER FERRY LAKE) 30 mi SE on US 64, N on OK 10, 10A.

USS *Batfish.* WWII submarine. Also military museum; Teddy Roosevelt

Historical Monument. (Mid-Mar-mid-Oct, daily). 3500 Batfish Rd. Phone 918/682-6294.

Special Events

Azalea Festival. Parade, art shows, garden tours, entertainment. Mid-Apr.

River Rhumba. Riverboat rides, kiddie carnival, hot-air balloon rides, music, fireworks, food. Phone 918/684-6305. Mid-Sept.

Motels/Motor Lodges

★ **DAYS INN.** 900 S 32nd St (74401). 918/683-3911; fax 918/683-5744; toll-free 800/329-7466. www.daysinn.com. 43 rms, 2 story. S $38; D $45; each addl $5; under 12 free. Crib free. TV; cable (premium), VCR avail. Pool. Complimentary coffee in rms. Restaurant nearby. Ck-out 11 am. Meeting rms. Business servs avail. Some refrigerators. Microwaves avail. Cr cds: A, C, D, DS, MC, V.
⬚ ⬚ ⬚ ⬚ SC

★ **MUSKOGEE INN.** 2360 E Shawnee Rd (74403). 918/683-6551; fax 918/682-2877; res 800/783-0103. 122 rms, 2 story. S $46; D $51; each addl $5; under 12 free. Crib $5. TV; cable (premium). Pool. Restaurant 6 am-noon. Bar 4 pm-midnight, closed Sun. Ck-out noon. Meeting rms. Cr cds: A, DS, MC, V.
⬚ ⬚ ⬚ ⬚ ⬚

★ **RAMADA INN.** 800 S 32nd St (74401). 918/682-4341; fax 918/682-7400; res 800/272-6232. www.ramada.com. 135 rms, 2 story. S $52; D $58; each addl $5; suites $95-$125; under 18 free. Crib free. Pet accepted; some restrictions. TV; cable (premium), VCR avail. Indoor pool; whirlpool, sauna. Restaurant 6 am-2 pm, 5-10 pm; Sun to 2 pm. Bar 5 pm-2 am; closed Sun; entertainment. Ck-out noon. Meeting rms. Business servs avail. Exercise equipt. Game rm. Microwaves avail. Cr cds: A, MC, V.
⬚ ⬚ ⬚ ⬚ ⬚ ⬚ SC

★ **TRAVELODGE.** 534 S 32nd St (74401). 918/683-2951; fax 918/683-5848; toll-free 800/578-7878. www.travelodge.com. 109 rms, 2 story. S $42; D $51; each addl $5; suites $70; under 12 free. Crib free. Pet accepted, some restrictions. TV; cable (premium). Pool; poolside serv. Bar 5 pm-2 am, closed Sun. Ck-out 11 am. Meeting rms. Business servs avail. Inrm modem link. Valet serv. Cr cds: A, C, D, DS, MC, V.
⬚ ⬚ ⬚ ⬚ SC

Restaurant

★ **OKIES.** 219 S 32nd St (US 69) (74401). 918/683-1056. Hrs: 11 am-10 pm. Closed Sun; Jan 1, Thanksgiving, Dec 25. Res accepted. Bar. Lunch, dinner $4.75-$24.95. Children's menu. Specializes in chicken breast, prime rib. Own ice cream. Antiques. Cr cds: A, D, DS, MC, V.
⬚ ⬚

Norman (D-6)

Founded 1889 **Pop** 80,071 **Elev** 1,104 ft **Area code** 405

Information Convention & Visitors Bureau, 224 W Gray, Suite 104, 73069; 405/366-8095 or 800/767-7260

Web www.ncvb.org

Norman was founded on April 22, 1889 in the famous land rush known as the "Oklahoma land run." The run opened what was once the Indian Territory to modern-day settlement. A year later the University of Oklahoma was founded. The city now offers numerous restaurants, museums, shopping areas, parks, and lodgings as well as convention, conference, and symposium sites. The city of Norman has a well-balanced economy with education, oil, industry, tourism, high technology, research and development, and agriculture.

What to See and Do

Hunting preserves. Lexington. Lake **Thunderbird**, Little River Arm and Hog Creek Arm, NE of town. 9 mi S, off US 77.

Lake Thunderbird State Park. A 4,010-acre park on 6,070-acre Thunderbird Lake. Swimming, bathhouse, fishing, boating (ramp, rentals, marina); hiking, riding, archery, miniature golf (fee), picnicking, playground, grocery, camping, trailer hookups (fee). (Daily) 12 mi E on Hwy 9. Phone 405/360-3572. **FREE**

Sooner Theatre. (1929) Seasonal concerts, ballet, and theater productions. 101 E Main at Norman's Performing Arts Center. Phone 405/321-9600. ¢¢¢

University of Oklahoma. (1890) 25,000 students. An approx 3,100-acre campus with more than 225 buildings. Its University of Oklahoma Press is a distinguished publishing house. On campus are the Fred Jones Jr. Museum of Art (Tues-Sun; phone 405/325-3272); Oklahoma Museum of Natural History (phone 405/325-4712); Rupel Jones Theater (phone 405/325-4101); University Research Park. (Museums closed hols) Contact OU Visitor Center, Jacobson Hall, 550 Parrington Oval, 73019. Phone 405/325-1188.

Special Events

Chocolate Festival. 1700 Asp Ave, in Commons Restaurant. Artwork with chocolate theme; culinary delights. Sat before Feb 14.

Medieval Fair. Brandt Park duck pond at University of Oklahoma. Living history fair depicting life in the Middle Ages; strolling minstrels, jugglers, jesters; knights in armor joust; storytellers. Phone 405/288-2536. Second wkend Apr.

89er Celebration. Parade, contests, wagon train river crossing. Third wk Apr.

Little River Zoo. Educational zoo with over 400 species of wild and domesticated animals. Petting zoo. (Daily; closed hols) 120th Ave SE Phone 405/366-7229. ¢¢

Motels/Motor Lodges

★ **DAYS INN.** *609 N Interstate Dr (73069). 405/360-4380; fax 405/321-5767; toll-free 800/329-7466. www. daysinn.com.* 72 rms, 2 story. S $40; D $45-$50; each addl $5; suites $55; under 12 free. Pet accepted, some restrictions. TV; cable (premium). Pool. Ck-out 11 am. Business servs avail. Some refrigerators. Cr cds: A, C, D, DS, MC, V.
🄳 🔧 🌊 🔀 🐾 SC

★ **GUEST INN NORMAN.** *2543 W Main St (73069). 405/360-1234; toll-free 800/460-4619.* 110 units, 2 story. S $42-$47; D $52-$55; suites $62-$95;

wkly plans. Crib $2. Pet accepted; $10. TV; cable (premium), VCR avail. Pool. Complimentary coffee in lobby. Restaurant open 24 hrs. Ck-out noon. Coin lndry. Meeting rms. Business servs avail. Valet serv. Game rm. Refrigerators, microwaves avail. Picnic tables, grills. Cr cds: A, C, D, DS, MC, V.
🄳 🔧 🌊 🔀 🐾 SC

★ **RAMADA INN.** *1200 24th Ave SW (73072). 405/321-0110; fax 405/360-5629; res 800/500-9869. www.ramada. com.* 146 rms, 2 story. S, D $60; each addl $6; suites $95-$165; under 15 free; higher rates: football wkends, special events. Crib free. TV; cable (premium). Pool. Coffee in rms. Restaurant 6 am-2 pm, 5-9 pm. Bar 2 pm-2 am. Ck-out noon. Coin lndry. Meeting rms. Business servs avail. In-rm modem link. Valet serv. Exercise equipt. Game rm. Cr cds: A, C, D, DS, MC, V.
🄳 🌊 🍴 🔀 🐾 SC

★ **TRAVELODGE.** *225 N Interstate Dr (73069). 405/329-7194; res 800/ 578-7878. www.travelodge.com.* 40 rms, 2 story. S $39.95; D $49.95; higher rates special events; each addl $5. Pet accepted. TV; cable (premium). Pool. Complimentary continental bkfst. Coffee in rms. Restaurant nearby. Ck-out 11 am. Cr cds: A, D, DS, MC, V.
🄳 🔧 🌊 🔀 🐾 SC

B&Bs/Small Inns

★★ **HOLMBERG HOUSE BED AND BREAKFAST.** *766 Debarr Ave (73069). 405/321-6221; toll-free 877/621-6221. www.holmberghouse.com.* 4 rms, 2 story. Rm phones avail. S, D $75-$85. TV; cable. Complimentary full bkfst. Ck-out noon, ck-in 3 pm. Built in 1914 by first dean of the University of Oklahoma's College of Fine Arts. Totally nonsmoking. Cr cds: A, DS, MC, V.
🔀 🐾 SC

★★★ **MONTFORD INN BED & BREAKFAST.** *322 W Tonhawa St (73069). 405/321-2200; fax 405/321-8347; toll-free 800/321-8969. www. montfordinn.com.* 13 rms. S $90; D $130; each addl $20; suites $100-$195. Crib free. TV; cable, VCR (movies). Complimentary full bkfst; afternoon refreshments. Restaurant nearby. Ck-out noon, ck-in 3 pm. Luggage handling. Concierge serv. Business servs avail. In-rm modem link. Health club privileges. Picnic tables. Replica of 1900s house; antiques. Totally nonsmoking. Cr cds: A, D, DS, MC, V.

🄓 ▨ ▨

Extended Stay

★★ **RESIDENCE INN BY MAR-RIOTT.** *2681 Jefferson St (73072). 405/366-0900; fax 405/360-6552; toll-free 800/331-3131. www.whghotels. com.* 126 kit. suites, 2 story. Kit. suites $79-$89; family, wkly, monthly rates. Crib free. Pet accepted; $75. TV; cable (premium). Pool; whirlpool. Complimentary continental bkfst, coffee in rms. Ck-out noon. Coin lndry. Meeting rms. Business servs avail. In-rm modem link. Lighted tennis. Health club privileges. Microwaves. Cr cds: A, C, D, DS, ER, JCB, MC, V.

🄓 ▨ ▨ ▨ ▨ ▨ SC

Restaurants

★★ **CAFE PLAID.** *333 W Boyd St (73069). 405/364-6469. www.cafe plaid.com.* Hrs: 8 am-9 pm; Mon to 4 pm; Fri, Sat to 10 pm; Sun brunch 9 am-3 pm. Closed Jan 1, Thanksgiving, Dec 25. Res accepted. Bar. Bkfst $1.49-$5.25, lunch $1.50-$6.50, dinner $2.95-$12.95. Sun brunch $2.49-$6.95. Children's menu. Specialty: rosemary chicken. Own salads. Music Fri, Sat. Parking. Outdoor dining. Totally nonsmoking. Cr cds: A, MC, V.

🄓

★★★ **LEGEND'S.** *1313 W Lindsey St (73069). 405/329-8888.* Hrs: 11 am-11 pm; Sun 10 am-10 pm; Sun brunch to 4:30 pm. Closed hols. Continental menu. Bar. Lunch $5.45-$8.95, dinner $5.45-$19.95. Sun brunch $5.95-$8.95. Specializes in fresh seafood, steak, pasta. Salad bar. Own desserts. Garden dining. Eclectic decor; artwork. Cr cds: A, D, DS, MC, V.

🄓

★ **VISTA SPORTS GRILL.** *111 N Peters (73069). 405/447-0909.* Hrs: 11-2 am. Closed hols. Bar. Lunch $2.95-$6.50, dinner $4.75-$9.95. Children's menu. Specializes in sand-wiches, salads, burgers. Sports memorabilia. Cr cds: A, DS, MC, V.

🄓 ▨

Oklahoma City

(C-6)

Founded 1889 **Pop** 444,719
Elev 1,207 ft **Area code** 405
Information Convention & Visitors Bureau, 189 W Sheridan, 73102; 405/297-8912 or 800/225-5652
Web www.okccvb.org

What is now the site of Oklahoma's capital was barren prairie on the morning of April 22, 1889. Unassigned land was opened to settlement that day, and by nightfall the population numbered 10,000. No city was ever settled faster than during this famous run.

The city sits atop one of the nation's largest oil fields, with wells even on the lawn of the Capitol. First discovered in 1928, the field was rapidly developed throughout the city. It still produces large quantities of high-gravity oil. Oil well equipment manufacture became one of the city's major industries.

Oklahoma City's stockyards and meat packing plants are the largest in the state. The city is also a grain milling and cotton processing center. Iron and steel, furniture, tire manufacturing, electrical equipment, electronics, and aircraft and automobile assembly are other industries. Tinker Air Force Base is southeast of the city.

Additional Visitor Information

The following organizations can provide travelers with assistance and additional information: Oklahoma City Convention and Visitors Bureau, 189 W Sheridan, 73102, phone 405/297-8912 or 800/225-5652; Oklahoma City Chamber of Commerce, 123 Park Ave, 73102, phone 405/297-8900; Oklahoma Tourism and Recreation Dept, 15 N Robinson, 73102, phone 405/521-2406. *Oklahoma Today,* the state's official magazine, has up-to-date information and articles of interest to the tourist.

Transportation

Car Rental Agencies. See IMPOR-
TANT TOLL-FREE NUMBERS.

Public Transportation. Buses (Central
Oklahoma Transportation and Parking Authority), phone 405/235-7433.

Airport Information

Will Rogers World Airport. Information 405/680-3200; lost and found
405/680-3233; weather 405/478-
3377; cash machines, located at
upper level Main Terminal.

What to See and Do

Civic Center Music Hall. Home of
the Oklahoma City Philharmonic,
Canterbury Choral Society, and Ballet Oklahoma. A variety of entertainment is provided, incl Broadway
shows and popular concerts. 6420 SE
15th. Phone 405/297-2584.

45th Infantry Division Museum.
Exhibits state military history from
its beginnings in the early Oklahoma
Territory through WWII, Korea to
the present National Guard; Desert
Storm exhibit; uniforms, vehicles,

Oklahoma City National Memorial

aircraft, artillery, and an extensive military firearms collection with pieces dating from the American Revolution; memorabilia and original cartoons by Bill Mauldin. (Tues-Sun; closed Jan 1 and Dec 25) 2145 NE 36th St. Phone 405/424-5313.

Frontier City. A 40-acre Western theme park; incl more than 75 rides, shows, and attractions; entertainment; shops, restaurants. (Memorial Day-late Aug, daily; Easter-Memorial Day and late Aug-Oct, wkends only) 11501 NE Expy. Phone 405/478-2412. ¢¢¢¢

Garden Exhibition Building and Horticulture Gardens. Azalea trails; butterfly garden; rose, peony, and iris gardens; arboretum; conservatory has one of the country's largest cactus and succulent collections (daily). Exhibition Building (Mon-Fri; closed hols; open Sat, Sun during flower shows). 3400 NW 36th St. Phone 405/943-0827. **FREE**

Harn Homestead and 1889er Museum. Historic homestead claimed in Land Run of 1889; 1904 farmhouse furnished with prestatehood objects dating from period of the run. Three-story stone and cedar barn; one-rm schoolhouse; working farm. Ten acres of picnic area, shade

trees. (Tues-Sat; closed hols) 313 NE 16th St. Phone 405/235-4058. ¢¢

Metro Concourse. A downtown "city beneath the city," the underground tunnel system connects nearly all the downtown buildings in a 20-sq-blk area. It is one of the most extensive all-enclosed pedestrian systems in the country. Offices, shops, and restaurants line the concourse system. (Mon-Fri)

Myriad Botanical Gardens. A 17-acre botanical garden in the heart of the city's redeveloping central business district. Features lake, amphitheater, botanical gardens, and seven-story Crystal Bridge Tropical Conservatory. Reno and Robinson sts. Phone 405/297-3995. ¢¢

⭐ **National Cowboy Hall of Fame & Western Heritage Center.** Major art collections depict America's Western heritage; Rodeo Hall of Fame; sculpture, incl *End of the Trail*, *Buffalo Bill*, and *Coming Through the Rye*; portrait gallery of Western film stars; landscaped gardens. (Daily; closed Jan 1, Thanksgiving, Dec 25) 1700 NE 63rd St, off I-44 near I-35, between Martin Luther King, Jr., and Kelley aves. Phone 405/478-2250. ¢¢¢

National Softball Hall of Fame and Museum. Displays of equipt and memorabilia trace the history of the sport; Hall of Fame; stadium complex. (Mar-Oct, Mon-Sat; rest of yr, Mon-Fri) 2801 NE 50th St, just W of I-35. Phone 405/424-5266. ¢

Oklahoma City Art Museum. Permanent collection of 13th- to 20th-century European and American paintings, prints, drawings, photographs, sculpture, and decorative arts. Changing exhibitions of regional, national, and international artists. (Tues-Sun; closed hols) 3113 Pershing Blvd, Oklahoma State Fairgrounds. Phone 405/946-4477. ¢¢

Oklahoma City National Memorial. Series of monuments in honor of the men, women, and children killed by a bomb at the Murrah Federal Building on Apr 19, 1995. "Gates of Time" memorial represents the moment of the blast, forever frozen in time. "Field of Empty Chairs" pays tribute to the 168 lives lost in the bombing. "Survivor Tree," an American elm tree that withstood the blast. Also reflecting pool, orchard, and children's area. (Daily) NW 5th St at N Robinson Ave. Phone 405/235-3313. **FREE**

Oklahoma City Zoo. Covers 110 acres with more than 2,000 animals representing 500 species; expansive hoofstock collection; naturalistic island life exhibit; walk-through aviaries; herpetarium; pachyderm building; big cat exhibit; primate and gorilla exhibit; children's zoo with discovery area; Safari Tram, Sky Safari. (Daily; closed Jan 1, Dec 25) Exit 50th St off I-35, 1 mi W to zoo entrance. Phone 405/424-3344. ¢¢ On zoo grounds is

Aquaticus. A unique marine-life science facility contains comprehensive collection of aquatic life; dolphin/sea lion shows; shark tank; adaptations and habitat exhibits; underwater viewing. (Daily; closed Jan 1, Dec 25) Phone 405/424-3344. ¢

Oklahoma Firefighters Museum. Antique fire equipt dating back to 1736; also first fire station (1869) in Oklahoma reassembled here. (Daily; closed hols) 2716 NE 50th St. Phone 405/424-3440. ¢¢

Oklahoma Heritage Center. Restored Hefner family mansion (1917) maintained as a museum; antique furnish-

ings; collection of bells, art; Oklahoma Hall of Fame galleries (third floor) feature work by Oklahoma artists; memorial chapel and gardens. (Daily; closed hols) 201 NW 14th St. Phone 405/235-4458. ¢¢

Oklahoma National Stockyards. One of world's largest cattle markets; auction of cattle, hogs, and sheep; Livestock Exchange Building. (Mon, Tues; closed hols) 2501 Exchange Ave. Phone 405/235-8675. **FREE**

✪ **Omniplex.** Houses several museums and attractions within ten-acre facility. (Daily; closed Dec 25). 2100 NE 52nd St. Phone 405/602-6664. ¢¢¢ Incl

International Photography Hall of Fame and Museum. Permanent and traveling exhibits; one of world's largest photographic murals. (Daily; closed Thanksgiving, Dec 25) Phone 405/424-4055.

Kirkpatrick Science and Air Space Museum. Incl hands-on science museum, Air Space Museum, Kirkpatrick Galleries, gardens/greenhouse; Kirkpatrick Planetarium (shows change quarterly). (Daily; closed Thanksgiving, Dec 25) Phone 405/602-6664.

Red Earth Indian Center. Exhibits and educational programs encourage appreciation of Native American cultures. (Daily; closed Thanksgiving, Dec 25) Phone 405/427-5228.

Remington Park. Thoroughbred racing with four-level grandstand and more than 300 video monitors. Restaurants. (Aug-Dec; Thurs-Mon) One Remington Place, at jct I-35 and I-44. Phone 405/424-1000. ¢¢

State Capitol. Greco-Roman, neoclassical building designed by S. A. Layton and Wemyss Smith. Oil well beneath Capitol building reaches 1¼ mi underground. After pumping oil from 1941-1986, it is now preserved as a monument. Legislature meets annually for 78 days beginning on the first Mon in Feb. Tours (daily; closed Dec 25). NE 23rd St and Lincoln Blvd. Phone 405/521-3356. **FREE** Opp is

State Museum of History. Exhibits on the history of Oklahoma; extensive collection of Native American artifacts. (Mon-Sat; closed hols) Phone 405/521-2491. **FREE**

White Water Bay. Outdoor water park with body surfing, water chutes, slides, rapids, and swimming pool; special playland for tots. (June-Aug, daily; May and Sept, wkends) 3908 W Reno, via I-40, Meridian exit. Phone 405/943-9687. ¢¢¢¢¢

Special Events

International Finals Rodeo. Myriad Convention Center. International Pro Rodeo Association's top 15 cowboys and cowgirls compete in seven events to determine world championships. Phone 405/235-6540 or 405/236-5000. Mid-Jan.

Festival of the Arts. International foods, entertainment, children's learning and play area; craft market; artists from many states display their work. Six days late Apr.

Red Earth. Native American heritage and culture featuring dancers and artists from most North American tribes. Dance competition, arts festival. Phone 405/427-5228. Second wkend June.

Aerospace America. Will Rogers World Airport. Air show incl precision performers, aerobatics, parachute jumpers, warbird displays. Phone 405/685-9546. Mid-June.

Lyric Theatre. 2501 N Blackwelder Ave, in Kirkpatrick Fine Arts Auditorium of Oklahoma City University. Professional musical theater. Phone 405/521-5227. Mid-June-mid-Aug.

Oklahoma City Philharmonic Orchestra. Civic Center Music Hall. Phone 405/297-2584. Sept-Apr.

State Fair of Oklahoma. Fair Park, NW 10th St and N May Ave. Livestock, crafts, art exhibits; ice show, circus, rodeo; truck pull contests; auto races; concerts; international show, flower and garden show; Native American ceremonial dances; carriage collection; monorail, space tower, carnival, parades. Arena and grandstand attractions. Phone 405/948-6700. Sept.

Ballet Oklahoma. 2501 N Blackwelder Ave. Phone 405/843-9898 or 405/848-TOES. Oct-Apr.

World Championship Quarter Horse Show. State fairgrounds. More than 1,800 horses compete. Phone 405/946-4477. Early-mid-Nov.

Motels/Motor Lodges

★★ **BEST WESTERN SADDLE-BACK INN.** *4300 SW 3rd St (73108). 405/947-7000; fax 405/948-7636; res 800/228-3903. www.bestwestern.com.* 220 rms, 2-3 story. S, D $65-$72; each addl $7; suites $79-$86; under 17 free; wkend rates. Crib free. Pet accepted. TV; cable (premium), VCR avail. Heated pool; whirlpool, poolside serv. Coffee in rms. Restaurant 6 am-2 pm, 5-10 pm; Sun 7 am-2 pm. Bar 4 pm-midnight. Ck-out noon. Coin lndry. Meeting rms. Business servs avail. In-rm modem link. Bellhops. Valet serv. Gift shop. Sundries. Free airport transportation. Exercise equipt; sauna. Southwestern decor. Cr cds: A, MC, V.

D ⬟ ⬟ 🏋 ⬟ ⬟ SC

★★ **BEST WESTERN SANTA FE INN.** *6101 N Santa Fe Ave (73118). 405/848-1919; fax 405/840-1581; res 800/369-7223. www.bestwestern.com.* 96 rms, 3 story. S $59-$65; D $66-$72; each addl $10; suites $85-$125; under 12 free. Crib free. TV; cable (premium). Pool; whirlpool. Complimentary full bkfst, coffee in rms. Restaurant 6 am-1:30 pm, 5-9 pm. Bar 5 pm-midnight. Ck-out 11 am. Meeting rms. Business servs avail. In-rm modem link. Valet serv. Health club privileges. Some refrigerators. Cr cds: A, C, D, DS, MC, V.

D 🛏 ⬟ ⬟ ⬟ ⬟ SC

★★ **BILTMORE HOTEL.** *401 S Meridian Ave (73108). 405/947-7681; fax 405/947-4253; res 800/522-6620.* 509 rms, 2 story. S $64; D $59; each addl $10; suites $89-$195; family, wkend rates. Crib free. Pet accepted, some restrictions. TV; cable (premium), VCR avail. 4 pools, 1 indoor; whirlpool, poolside serv. Restaurants 6 am-11 pm. Bars 11:30-2 am; entertainment. Ck-out noon. Meeting rms. Business servs avail. In-rm modem link. Bellhops. Sundries. Gift shop. Barber shop. Free airport transportation. Tennis. Exercise equipt; sauna. Rec rm. Bathrm phone, wet bar in townhouse suites; whirlpool in some suites. Cr cds: A, C, D, DS, ER, JCB, MC, V.

D ⬟ ⬟ 🏋 🏊 ⬟ ⬟

★★ **COURTYARD BY MARRIOTT.** *4301 Highline Blvd (73108). 405/946-6500; fax 405/946-7638; toll-free 800/*

THE OKLAHOMA CITY EXPERIENCE

Single-day events have shaped both the past and present of this settlement in the American heartland. Oklahoma City was born on April 22, 1889, when the area known as the Unassigned Lands in Oklahoma Territory was opened for settlement; a cannon was fired at noon that day, signaling a rush of thousands of settlers who raced into the two million acres of land to make their claims on the plains.

Just over a century later, the city's spirited energy was put to a horrific challenge with the April 19, 1995, bombing of the Alfred P. Murrah Federal Building. Today, the strength, unity, and hope generated between the city and its nation can be experienced at the new Oklahoma City National Memorial. You'll want to allow ample time to explore and appreciate this breathtaking site.

Begin at the Gates of Time, twin monuments that frame the moment of destruction: 9:02 am. The east gate represents 9:01 a.m. and the west gate 9:03 a.m. The Field of Empty Chairs consists of 168 bronze-and-stone chairs arranged in nine rows, representing the lives lost and the floor each victim was on at the time of the blast. The smaller ones memorialize the 19 children killed. The glass seats of the chairs are etched with the names of the victims and are lit up at night. Also at the site are an American elm called the Survivors Tree; fruit and flower trees in the Rescuers Orchard; the peaceful Reflection Pool; and the Children's Area, with a wall of hand-painted tiles sent to Oklahoma City in 1995 by children across the nation.

After this sobering start, you'll walk four blocks south of Robinson to a cheerful place called the International Gymnastics Hall of Fame. Located in the First National Center, the Hall of Fame honors such Oklahoma and Olympic gymnastic greats as Shannon Miller, Bart Connor, and Nadia Comenici. Hundreds of photos, medals, uniforms, videos, and memorabilia are on display here.

Walk just another block south of Robinson to its intersection with Reno to find the beautiful Myriad Botanical Gardens, a 17-acre sanctuary in the center of downtown with lovely hills surrounding a sunken lake. At the center is the seven-story Crystal Bridge Tropical Conservatory, featuring an intriguing collection of palm trees, flowers, and exotic plants from across the globe. Along the Adventure Walk, you'll wind beneath a 35-foot-high waterfall, and you can gaze at the tropics from a skywalk. Check out the Crystal Bridge Gift Shop, featuring an outstanding collection of botanical and garden-related items.

Backtrack on Robinson just two blocks to Sheridan, turning right (east) on Sheridan. Continue walking two blocks and you'll reach Bricktown, a hot new entertainment and dining district. The old warehouse district just east of the Santa Fe railroad tracks saw its birth just before World War I, but the latest boom came in the last 15 years. Roam around the old brick streets, poke around in the shops, then take a load off at one of the restaurants, such as Crabtown, the Varsity Sports Grill, Windy City Pizza, or Bricktown Brewery (Oklahoma's first brew pub and microbrewery). Be sure to get tickets for a game at the new Bricktown Ballpark, home of the popular AAA baseball club called the Oklahoma RedHawks. Feet worn out from walking? In Bricktown, you can hop on the new rubber-wheeled trolleys, the Oklahoma Spirit, to tour downtown, or catch a ride on the Water Taxi, a narrated tour boat that cruises the Bricktown Canal.

321-2211. www.courtyard.com. 149 rms, 3 story. S $89; D $99; suites $109-$119; under 12 free; wkend rates. TV; cable (premium), VCR avail (movies). Heated pool; whirlpool. Complimentary coffee in rms. Restaurant 6:30- 10:30 am; wkends 7-11 am. Bar 4:30-10:30 pm. Ck-out noon. Coin lndry. Meeting rms. Business servs avail. In-rm modem link. Valet serv. Sundries. Free airport transportation. Exercise equipt. Refrigerator in suites. Balconies. Cr cds: A, C, D, DS, MC, V.

[icons]

★ **DAYS INN.** *12013 N I-35 Service Rd (73131). 405/478-2554; fax 405/478-5033; res 888/605-9055. www. daysinn.com.* 47 rms, 2 story, 22 suites. Apr-Oct: S, D $55-$85; each addl $5; suites $95-$125; under 12 free. Crib free. Pet accepted, some restrictions. TV; cable (premium). Complimentary continental bkfst, coffee in rms. Restaurant nearby. Ck-out 11 am. Business servs avail. In-rm modem link. Sundries. Indoor pool. Refrigerators, microwaves. Cr cds: A, D, DS, MC, V.

[icons]

★ **DAYS INN NORTHWEST.** *2801 NW 39th Expy (73112). 405/946-0741; fax 405/942-0181; res 800/992-3297. www.hotels-oklahomacity.com.* 117 rms, 2 story. S $39; D $45; each addl $6; suites $150; under 16 free; wkend rates. Crib free. Pet accepted. TV; cable (premium). Coffee in rms. Pool. Restaurant 6:30 am-1 pm, 5-9 pm. Bar 2 pm-2 am. Ck-out 11 am. Coin lndry. Meeting rms. Business servs avail. Valet serv. Sundries. Free airport transportation. Some bathrm phones, refrigerators. Cr cds: A, C, D, DS, ER, JCB, MC, V.

[icons]

★ **GOVERNORS SUITES INN.** *2308 S Meridian Ave (73108). 405/682-5299; fax 405/682-3047; res 888/819-7575. www.governorssuites-okc.com.* 50 units, 3 story. S, D $65-$95. TV; cable (premium). Pool; whirlpool. Complimentary full bkfst, coffee in rms. Restaurant nearby. Ck-out 11 am. Meeting rm. Business servs avail. Free airport transportation. Exercise equipt, sauna. Microwaves. Cr cds: A, C, D, DS, MC, V.

[icons]

★ **HOWARD JOHNSON EXPRESS.** *400 S Meridian Ave (73108). 405/943-9841; fax 405/942-1869; res 800/458-8186. www.the.hojo.com.* 96 rms, 2 story. S, D $42-$45; under 17 free. Crib free. Pet accepted, some restrictions. TV; cable (premium). Pool. Complimentary continental bkfst, coffee in rms. Restaurant adj 10:30 am-11 pm. Ck-out noon. Coin lndry. Business servs avail. Health club privi-

leges. Many refrigerators; microwaves avail. Cr cds: A, C, D, DS, MC, V.

[icons]

★ **HOWARD JOHNSON EXPRESS INN.** *4017 NW 39th Expy (73112). 405/947-0038; fax 405/946-7450. www.hojo.com.* 112 rms, 2 story, 15 kit. units. S, D $51-$62; each addl $6; kit. units $59-$71; under 18 free. Crib free. Pet accepted, some restrictions. TV; cable (premium), VCR avail (movies). Pool. Complimentary continental bkfst. Coffee in rms. Restaurant adj open 24 hrs. Ck-out noon. Coin lndry. Meeting rms. Business servs avail. In-rm modem link. Valet serv. Health club privileges. Some refrigerators; microwaves avail. Cr cds: A, C, D, DS, ER, JCB, MC, V.

[icons]

★★ **LA QUINTA INN.** *800 S Meridian Ave (73108). 405/942-0040; fax 405/942-0638; toll-free 800/531-5900. www.laquinta.com.* 168 rms, 2 story. S $69-$89; D $79-$99; each addl $10; under 18 free. Pet accepted, some restrictions. TV; cable (premium), VCR avail. Pool; wading pool, poolside serv. Complimentary continental bkfst. Restaurant 6:30 am-midnight. Bar from 10 am. Ck-out noon. Meeting rms. Business servs avail. In-rm modem link. Free airport, bus depot transportation. Exercise equipt. Refrigerators, microwaves avail. Cr cds: A, C, D, DS, MC, V.

[icons]

★★ **LA QUINTA INN.** *8315 S I-35 Service Rd (73149). 405/631-8661; fax 405/631-1892; toll-free 800/687-6667. www.laquinta.com.* 122 rms, 2 story. S, D $62-$72; each addl $7; under 18 free. Crib free. TV; cable (premium). Pool. Complimentary continental bkfst. Coffee in rms. Restaurant opp open 24 hrs. Ck-out noon. Business servs avail. Valet serv. Health club privileges. Refrigerators, microwaves avail. Cr cds: A, C, D, DS, MC, V.

[icons]

★ **LEXINGTON HOTEL SUITES.** *1200 S Meridian Ave (73108). 405/943-7800; fax 405/943-8346; toll-free 800/927-8483. www.lexres.com.* 145 kit. suites, 3 story. S $69-$79; D $76-$86; under 16 free; wkend rates; higher rates special events. Crib free. TV; cable (premium), VCR avail. Complimentary continental bkfst, coffee in rms. Restaurant opp open 24 hrs. Ck-out noon. Meeting rms. Business servs avail. In-rm modem link. Valet serv. Coin lndry. Free airport transportation. Health club privileges. Heated pool. Refrigerators; many microwaves. Cr cds: A, D, DS, MC, V.

[D] [≈] [✕] [≈] [🔥] [SC]

★ **QUALITY INN NORTH.** *12001 NE Expy (73131). 405/478-0400; fax 405/478-2774; res 800/228-5151. www.qualityinn.com.* 213 rms, 2 story. S $55-$67; D $60-$72; each addl $5; suites $125; under 18 free. Crib avail. Pet accepted. TV; cable (premium). Complimentary continental bkfst, coffee in rms. Restaurant 5-9 pm. Ck-out noon. Meeting rms. Business servs avail. Valet serv. Sundries. Coin lndry. 2 pools, 1 indoor; whirlpool. Playground. Game rm. Cr cds: A, C, D, DS, MC, V.

[D] [🏌] [🛁] [🏃] [≈] [≈] [🔥]

★ **RAMADA INN.** *1401 NE 63rd St (73111). 405/478-5221. www.ramada. com.* 52 rms, 2-3 story. No elvtr. S $51-$56; D $56-$61; each addl $7; under 12 free; wkend rates. Crib free. Pet accepted; $25 deposit; $7/day. TV; cable (premium). Complimentary continental bkfst. Restaurant adj 10 am-9 pm. Ck-out noon. Meeting rms. Business servs avail. In-rm modem link. Valet serv. Sundries. Coin lndry. Free airport transportation. Some refrigerators, microwaves. Cr cds: A, D, DS, MC, V.

[D] [🏌] [≈] [≈] [🔥]

★ **RAMADA INN & CONFERENCE CENTER.** *4345 N Lincoln Blvd (73105). 405/528-2741; fax 405/525-8185; res 800/741-2741. www.ramada. com.* 306 rms, 7 story. S $69-$89; D $79-$99; each addl $10; suites $125-$200; under 18 free; family rates; package plans; lower rates rest of yr. Crib free. Pet accepted, some restrictions. TV; cable (premium), VCR avail. Complimentary coffee in rms. Restaurant 6:30 am-11 pm; Sun to 9 pm. Bar 11 am-11 pm; entertainment Fri, Sat. Ck-out noon. Convention facilities. Business center. In-rm modem link. Bellhops. Valet serv. Concierge. Sundries. Gift shop. Airport transportation. Lighted tennis. Health club privileges. Pool; poolside serv. Game rm. Some bathrm

phones; refrigerators avail. Luxury level. Cr cds: A, C, D, DS, ER, MC, V.

[D] [🏌] [🏃] [≈] [≈] [🔥] [🏃]

★★ **RAMADA PLAZA HOTEL.** *930 E 2nd St, Edmond (73034). 405/341-3577; fax 405/341-9279; toll-free 800/272-6232. www.ramada.com.* 145 rms, 8 story. S $69; D $79; each addl $10; suites $89-$150; under 18 free; wkend rates. Crib free. TV; cable (premium). Pool; whirlpool. Complimentary full bkfst, coffee in rms. Restaurant 6 am-2 pm, 5-10 pm. Bar 5 pm-midnight; Fri, Sat to 1:30 am, Sun 4-10 pm; entertainment Fri, Sat. Ck-out 11 am. Meeting rms. Business servs avail. In-rm modem link. Exercise equipt. Microwaves avail. Cr cds: A, C, D, DS, ER, JCB, MC, V.

[D] [≈] [🏃] [≈] [🔥] [SC]

★ **SUPER 8 FAIRGROUNDS.** *2821 NW 39th (73112). 405/946-9170; fax 405/942-0181; res 800/800-8000. www.super8.com.* 71 rms, 2 story. S, D $39.88-$43.88; each addl $4; under 16 free. Crib free. Pet accepted, some restrictions; $25. TV; cable (premium). Complimentary coffee in rms. Restaurant adj 6 am-10 pm. Ck-out 11 am. Business servs avail. In-rm modem link. Coin lndry. Free airport transportation. Cr cds: A, MC, V.

[D] [🏌] [≈] [🔥] [SC]

★ **TRAVELERS INN.** *504 S Meridian (75108). 405/942-8294; fax 405/947-3529; res 800/633-8300.* 130 rms, 2 story. S $34.99; D $41.99; each addl $4; suites $47.99-$54.99; under 18 free. Crib free. TV; cable (premium). Heated pool. Complimentary continental bkfst. Restaurant adj 11 am-11 pm. Ck-out 11 am. Coin lndry. Business servs avail. In-rm modem link. Valet serv. Near airport. Cr cds: A, MC, V.

[D] [≈] [≈] [🔥] [SC]

Hotels

★★★ **HILTON INN.** *2945 NW Expy (73112). 405/848-4811; fax 405/842-4328; toll-free 800/445-8667. www.hilton.com.* 218 rms, 9 story. S $95-$149; D $99-$159; each addl $10; suites $175-$299; under 18 free; wkend rates. Crib free. TV; cable (premium). Heated pool; whirlpool, poolside serv. Complimentary coffee in rms. Restaurant 6 am-2 pm, 5-11

Red Earth Native American Festival

pm. Bar 4 pm-midnight; Fri, Sat to 1 am; Sun to 10 pm. Ck-out noon. Meeting rms. Business servs avail. In-rm modem link. Free airport transportation. Exercise equipt. Health club privileges. Refrigerator avail. Cr cds: A, C, D, DS, ER, MC, V.

★★ **HOLIDAY INN.** *6200 N Robinson Ave (73118). 405/843-5558; fax 405/840-3410; res 800/522-9458. www.holiday-inn.com.* 202 rms, 3 story, 27 suites. S, D $49-$99; each addl $10; suites $95-$150; under 12 free. Crib free. Pet accepted, some restrictions. TV; cable (premium). Indoor pool; poolside serv. Complimentary full bkfst, coffee in rms. Restaurant 6:30 am-2 pm, 5-10 pm. Bar 4 pm-midnight. Ck-out noon. Coin lndry. Meeting rms. Business servs avail. Gift shop. Health club privileges. Refrigerator, minibar in suites. Cr cds: A, C, D, DS, JCB, MC, V.

★★★ **MARRIOTT OKLAHOMA CITY.** *3233 NW Expy (73112). 405/842-6633; fax 405/842-3152; res 800/228-9290. www.marriott.com.* 354 rms, 15 story. S, D $119; suites $175-$350; studio rms $99; under 18 free; wkend rates. Crib free. Pet accepted, some restrictions. TV; cable (premium). Indoor/outdoor pool. Coffee in rms. Restaurant (see JW'S STEAKHOUSE). Bar. Ck-out noon. Coin

lndry. Convention facilities. Business center. In-rm modem link. Concierge. Gift shop. Exercise equipt. Health club privileges. Some balconies. Luxury level. Cr cds: A, C, D, DS, JCB, MC, V.

★★★ **RENAISSANCE DOWNTOWN.** *10 N Broadway (73102). 405/228-8000; fax 405/228-8080. www.renaissancehotels.com.* 311 rms, 15 story. S, D $150-$225; each addl $20; under 17 free. Crib avail. TV; cable (premium), VCR avail. Complimentary coffee, newspaper in rms. Restaurant 6 am-10 pm. Ck-out noon. Meeting rms. Business center. Gift shop. Exercise rm. Some refrigerators, minibars. Cr cds: A, C, D, DS, ER, JCB, MC, V.

★★★ **WATERFORD MARRIOTT.** *6300 Waterford Blvd (73118). 405/848-4782; fax 405/848-7810; toll-free 800/992-2009. www.marriott.com.* 197 rms, 9 story. S, D $114-$149; each addl $10; suites $165-$750; under 18 free; package plans. Crib free. TV; cable (premium), VCR avail. Heated pool; whirlpool, poolside serv. Restaurant (see THE WATERFORD). Bar 11-1 am; entertainment. Ck-out noon. Business center. In-rm modem link. Concierge. Barber. Exercise rm; sauna. Massage. Bathrm phones; some refrigerators. Some balconies. Luxury level. Cr cds: A, D, DS, MC, V.

★★★ **WESTIN OKLAHOMA CITY.** *1 N Broadway Ave (73102). 405/ 235-2780; fax 405/232-8752; toll-free 800/937-8461. www.westin.com.* 395 rms, 15 story. S $119-$169; D $129-$179; each addl $10; suites $250-$850; wkend rates. Crib free. Pet accepted. Garage $4. TV; cable (premium), VCR avail. Pool. Restaurant (see ARIA GRILL). Rm serv 24 hrs. Bar 4 pm-2 am. Ck-out noon. Convention facilities. Business center. In-rm modem link. Valet parking. Exercise equipt. Health club privilege. Cr cds: A, MC, V.

All Suite

★★ **EMBASSY SUITES HOTEL.** *1815 S Meridian Ave (73108). 405/682-6000; fax 405/682-9835; res 800/362-2779. www.embassysuites. com.* 236 suites, 6 story. S, D $129; each addl $10; under 12 free; wkend rates. Crib free. Pet accepted; some restrictions. TV; cable (premium). Indoor pool; whirlpool. Complimentary bkfst, coffee in rms. Restaurant 6 am-10 pm. Bar 4 pm-2 am. Ck-out noon. Meeting rms. Business center. In-rm modem link. Gift shop. Airport transportation. Exercise equipt, sauna. Refrigerators, microwaves, wet bars. Some balconies. Atrium. Cr cds: A, C, D, DS, JCB, MC, V.

Extended Stay

★★ **RESIDENCE INN BY MARRIOTT.** *4361 W Reno Ave (73107). 405/942-4500; fax 405/942-7777; toll-free 800/331-3131. www.residenceinn. com.* 135 kit. suites, 1-2 story. 1-bedrm suites $89-$105; 2-bedrm suites $99-$139. Crib free. Pet accepted, some restrictions. TV; cable (premium). Heated pool; whirlpool. Complimentary continental bkfst, coffee in rms. Ck-out noon. Coin lndry. Meeting rms. Business center. In-rm modem link. Valet serv. Airport transportation. Health club privileges. Refrigerators, microwaves, fireplaces. Private patios, balconies.

Picnic tables, grills. Cr cds: A, C, D, DS, JCB, MC, V.

Restaurants

★★ **APPLEWOODS.** *2747 Memorial Rd (73134). 405/752-4484.* Hrs: 11 am-10 pm; Fri, Sat 4-11 pm; Sun 11 am-3 pm, 4:30-10 pm. Closed Thanksgiving, Dec 25. Bar. Lunch $3.95-$7.95, dinner $9.95-$19.95. Buffet: lunch (Sun) $6.95. Children's menu. Specializes in pot roast, pork chops, hot apple dumplings. Cr cds: A, D, DS, MC, V.

★★ **ARIA GRILL.** *1 N Broadway (73102). 405/815-6063.* Hrs: 6 am-11 pm. Res accepted. Continental menu. Bar 4 pm-2 am. Bkfst $2.75-$10.25, lunch, dinner $4.75-$19.95. Buffet: bkfst $10.95. Children's menu. Specialty: prime rib. Valet parking. Cr cds: A, D, DS, MC, V.

★★★ **BELLINI'S.** *6305 Waterford Blvd #1 (73118). 405/848-1065. www. bellinis.net.* Hrs: 11 am-10 pm; Fri, Sat to 11:30 pm; Sun to 9 pm; Sun brunch to 2:30 pm. Closed hols. Italian, American menu. Bar. Lunch $4.80-$12.95, dinner $7.95-$21.95. Sun brunch $4.95-$8.95. Specializes in Angus beef, pasta, pizza. Patio dining; view of park and fountain. Open brick pizza oven. Cr cds: A, D, DS, MC, V.

★★ **BRICKTOWN BREWERY.** *1 N Oklahoma Ave (73104). 405/232-2739. www.bricktownbrewery.com.* Hrs: 11 am-midnight; Sun, Mon to 10 pm; Fri, Sat to 2 am. Closed Thanksgiving, Dec 24, 25. Res accepted. Bar. Lunch, dinner $4.95-$12.95. Children's menu. Specializes in hearty American cuisine, handcrafted beers. Entertainment Fri, Sat. Renovated building in warehouse district. Cr cds: A, D, DS, MC, V.

★★ **CAFE 501.** *501 S Boulevard St, Edmond (73034). 405/359-1501.* Hrs: 7 am-9 pm; Fri, Sat to 10 pm; Sun brunch 9 am-2 pm. Closed Jan 1, Thanksgiving, Dec 25. Eclectic menu. Wine, beer. Bkfst $2-$6.50, lunch

$3.29-$7.49, dinner $3.29-$12.99. Sun brunch $2-$7.29. Children's menu. Specializes in wrapps, whole grain pizza. Totally nonsmoking. Cr cds: A, D, DS, MC, V.
D

★★ **CATTLEMAN'S STEAK-HOUSE.** *1309 S Agnew St (73108). 405/236-0416.* Hrs: 6 am-10 pm; Fri, Sat to midnight. Closed Thanksgiving, Dec 25. Serv bar. Bkfst $1.40-$6, lunch $2.25-$17.95, dinner $5.95-$17.95. Buffet: Sat, Sun bkfst $5.50. Specializes in steak, lamb fries. In historic Stockyards City district, opened in 1910. Cr cds: A, D, DS, MC, V.
D

★★★ **COACH HOUSE.** *6437 Avondale Dr (73116). 405/842-1000.* Hrs: 11:30 am-2 pm, 6-10 pm; Sat from 6 pm. Closed Sun; hols. Res accepted. French, American menu. Serv bar. Lunch $9-$14, dinner $19-$34. Specialties: rack of lamb, Dover sole, Grand Marnier souffle. Formal dining. Cr cds: A, D, DS, MC, V.
D

★ **COUNTY LINE.** *1226 NE 63rd St (73111). 405/478-4955. www.airribs. com.* Hrs: 11 am-9 pm; Fri, Sat to 10 pm. Closed hols. Bar. Lunch $4.95-$10.95, dinner $6.95-$16.95. Children's menu. Specializes in barbecue, prime rib. Nostalgic decor and atmosphere. Cr cds: A, D, DS, MC, V.
D

★★ **DEEP FORK GRILL.** *5418 N Western (73118). 405/848-7678.* Hrs: 11 am-2:30 pm, 5:30-10 pm. Closed hols. Res accepted. Bar. Lunch $6-$15, dinner $7-$26. Specialties: cedar planked salmon, penne pasta with roasted tomato and smoked cheese, wood-grilled veal chop. Parking. Cr cds: A, D, DS, MC, V.
D

★★ **EDDY'S OF OKLAHOMA CITY.** *4227 N Meridian Ave (73112). 405/787-2944. www.eddys-steakhouse.com.* Hrs: 4:30-10:30 pm; Fri, Sat to 11 pm; early-bird dinner Tues-Fri 4:30-6 pm. Closed Mon, Sun; Thanksgiving, Dec 25. Complete meals: dinner $9.95-$18.95. Children's menu. Specializes in Lebanese hors d'oeuvres, steak, seafood. Own pastries. Display of crystal, collectables. Family-owned. Cr cds: A, C, D, DS, MC, V.
D

★ **GOPURAM TASTE OF INDIA.** *4559 NW 23rd St (73127). 405/948-7373. www.members.aol.com/gopuram.* Hrs: 11 am-2 pm, 5:30-10 pm; Sat, Sun brunch 11:30 am-2:30 pm. Res accepted. East Indian menu. Bar. Buffet: lunch $6.25. A la carte entrees: dinner $9.95-$14.95. Sat, Sun brunch $8.95. Children's menu. Specializes in tandoori dishes, vegetarian dishes. Parking. East Indian decor. Cr cds: A, D, DS, MC, V.
D

★★★ **JW'S STEAKHOUSE.** *3233 NW Expressway St (73112). 405/842-6633.* Hrs: 6-10 pm; Fri, Sat to 11 pm. Closed Sun; Jan 1, Thanksgiving, Dec 25. Res accepted. A la carte entrees: dinner $13.95-$27.95. Children's menu. Specializes in seafood, steaks. Valet parking. Cr cds: A, DS, MC, V.
D

★★★ **KELLER IN THE KASTLE GERMAN RESTAURANT.** *820 N MacArthur (73127). 405/942-6133.* Hrs: 5:30-10 pm. Closed Mon, Sun; hols. Res accepted. German menu. Bar. Dinner $7.95-$26.95. Specialties: spiesbraten, wurstplatte, jaeger schnitzel. Parking. Outdoor dining. Building designed after castle in Normandy (France). Cr cds: A, DS, MC, V.
D

★★ **KONA RANCH STEAKHOUSE.** *2037 S Meridian (73108). 405/681-1000.* Hrs: 11 am-10 pm; Fri, Sat to 11 pm. Closed Thanksgiving, Dec. 25. Hawaiian menu. Bar. Lunch $5.75-$9.95, dinner $7.65-$17. Children's menu. Specialties: coconut shrimp, smoked prime rib. Unique Hawaiian/cowboy decor. Cr cds: A, D, DS, MC, V.
D

★ **LA BAGUETTE BISTRO.** *7408 N May Ave (73116). 405/840-3047. www.labaguette.com.* Hrs: 8 am-10 pm; Mon to 5 pm; Sun brunch 9:30 am-2:30 pm. Closed hols. Res accepted. French menu. Bar. Bkfst $2.75-$6.95, lunch $5-$10.50, dinner $6.95-$20.95. Sun brunch $4.95-$8.95. Specializes in French cuisine. Bistro atmosphere. Cr cds: A, D, DS, MC, V.
D

★★ **LAS PALOMAS.** *2329 N Meridian (73107). 405/949-9988.* Hrs: 11 am-9:30 pm; Fri, Sat to 10 pm. Closed Thanksgiving, Dec 25. Mexican menu. Beer. Lunch $5.15-$6.95, dinner $7.50-$10.95. Children's menu. Specialties: asado de puerco, fajitas estilo mi pueblo, entomatadas. Parking. Totally nonsmoking. Cr cds: A, DS, MC, V.
[D]

★★ **SLEEPY HOLLOW.** *1101 NE 50th St (73111). 405/424-1614.* Hrs: 11 am-4 pm, 5-9:30 pm; Sat from 5 pm. Closed hols. Res accepted. Bar. Lunch $4-$8. Complete meals: dinner $9.95-$19.95. Specializes in pan-fried chicken, steak. Own biscuits. Valet parking. Country decor. Cr cds: A, D, DS, MC, V.
[D] [≡]

★★ **SUSHI NEKO.** *4318 N Western Ave (73118). 405/528-8862. www. sushineko.com.* Hrs: 11:30 am-2 pm, 5-11 pm. Closed Sun; hols. Res accepted. Japanese menu. Bar. Lunch $7-$10, dinner $10-$20. Children's menu. Specializes in sushi, teriyaki, curry. Parking. Japanese decor; sushi bar. Cr cds: A, D, DS, MC, V.
[D] [≡]

★★★ **THE WATERFORD.** *6300 Waterford Blvd (73118). 405/848-4782. www.marriott.com/waterford.* Hrs: 6-10:30 pm; Fri, Sat to 11 pm. Closed Sun. Res accepted. Continental menu. Bar. Wine list. A la carte entrees: dinner $6.75-$25.95. Specializes in black Angus beef. Own baking, sauces. Valet parking. English country decor. Cr cds: A, D, DS, MC, V.
[D] [≡]

Unrated Dining Spot

CLASSEN GRILL. *5124 N Classen Blvd (73118). 405/842-0428.* Hrs: 7 am-10 pm; Sat from 8 am; Sun 8 am-2 pm. Closed Mon; hols. Bar from 10 am. Bkfst $2.50-$5.95, lunch $4-$6, dinner $5-$9. Children's menu. Specializes in chicken-fried steak, fresh seafood. Local artwork. Cr cds: A, D, DS, MC, V.
[D]

Okmulgee

(C-7) *See also Henryetta*

Founded ca 1900 **Pop** 13,441
Elev 670 ft **Area code** 918 **Zip** 74447
Information Chamber of Commerce, 112 N Morton, PO Box 609; 918/756-6172 or 800/355-5552.

The capital of the Creek Nation was established in 1868 and operates at the Creek Indian Complex. The Creeks gave the town its name, which means "bubbling water." Within Okmulgee County nearly five million pounds of wild pecans are harvested annually. The city is the home of Oklahoma State University/Okmulgee, one of the country's largest residential-vocational training schools and a branch of Oklahoma State University.

What to See and Do

Creek Council House Museum. Museum houses display of Creek tribal history. (Tues-Sun; closed hols) Council House, 6th St between Grand and Morton aves. Phone 918/756-2324. **FREE**

Okmulgee State Park. Covers 575 acres; 678-acre lake. Fishing, boating (ramps); picnicking, playground, camping, trailer hookups (fee). (Daily) 5 mi W on OK 56. Phone 918/756-5971. **FREE**

Special Events

Creek Nation Rodeo and Festival. Third wkend June.

Pecan Festival. Carnival, entertainment, arts and crafts, eight-km run. Phone 918/756-6172. Third wkend June.

Motel/Motor Lodge

★★ **BEST WESTERN OKMULGEE.** *3499 N Wood Dr (74447). 918/756-9200; fax 918/752-0022; res 800/552-9201. www.bestwestern.com.* 50 units, 2 story, 5 suites. S $50-$60; D $50-$65; suites $77-$90; under 12 free. Crib avail. Pet accepted. TV; cable (premium). Pool. Coffee in rms. Restaurant 7 am-9 pm; closed Sun. Bar 4 pm-2 am; entertainment. Ck-out 11 am. Meeting rms. Business

servs avail. In-rm modem link. Refrigerators, microwaves. Cr cds: A, MC, V.
D 🐕 🛏 🖳 🖢

Pauls Valley (D-6)

Settled 1847 **Pop** 6,150 **Elev** 876 ft
Area code 405 **Zip** 73075
Information Chamber of Commerce, 112 E Paul St, Box 638; 405/238-6491

What to See and Do

Murray-Lindsay Mansion. (1880) A three-story Classic Revival mansion built by Frank Murray, an Irish immigrant who married a woman of Choctaw descent. Starting small, Murray eventually controlled over 20,000 acres of land within the Chickasaw Nation. The mansion, a showplace within the Nation, contains original period furnishings. (Tues-Sun afternoons; closed hols) 21 mi W on OK 19, 2 mi S on OK 76, in Erin Springs. Phone 405/756-2121. **FREE**

Pauls Valley City Lake. Fishing, boating (ramps, dock); hiking, picnicking, camping. Fee for some activities. (Daily) 2 mi E on OK 19, then 1 mi N. Phone 405/238-5134.

Washita Valley Museum. Artifact collection of the Washita River Culture People (A.D. 600-800) with paintings by a local artist; collection of antique medical and surgical instruments; Pioneer clothing, photos, and other memorabilia from the early 1900s. (Wed-Sun; closed Thanksgiving, Dec 25) 1100 N Ash St. Phone 405/238-3048. **FREE**

Special Events

International Rodeo Association Competition. Last wkend June.

Garvin County Free Fair. Fairgrounds. Early Sept.

Motel/Motor Lodge

★ **DAYS INN.** *3203 W Grant Ave (73075). 405/238-7548; fax 405/238-1262; toll-free 800/329-7466. www.daysinn.com.* 54 rms, 2 story. May-Sept: S $41; D $52; each addl $5; under 12 free. Crib free. Pet accepted, some restrictions. TV; cable. Complimentary continental bkfst. Restaurant nearby. Ck-out noon. Cr cds: A, C, D, DS, MC, V.
D 🐕 🖳 🖢 SC

Pawhuska

(B-7) *See also Bartlesville*

Pop 3,825 **Elev** 818 ft **Area code** 918
Zip 74056
Information Chamber of Commerce, 222 W Main St; 918/287-1208
Web www.chamber.pawhuska.ok.us

This is the county seat of Oklahoma's largest county and is the Osage capital (county boundaries are same as those of the Osage Nation). This is a good fishing and hunting area with approximately 5,000 private lakes and five major lakes nearby.

The first Boy Scout troop in America was organized here in May 1909 by the Reverend John Mitchell.

What to See and Do

Drummond Home. (1905) Restored three-story Victorian house of merchant/cattleman Fred Drummond. Native sandstone, central square tower, second-floor balcony, and false dormers; original furnishings. (Fri, Sat, and Sun afternoons; closed hols) 21 mi S on OK 99, in Hominy. Phone 918/885-2374. **FREE**

Osage County Historical Society Museum. Old Santa Fe depot; chuck wagon display; saddles, Western, Native American, pioneer, and oil exhibits. Monument to the first Boy Scout troop in America (1909); correspondence and pictures about the beginning of the Boy Scouts. (Mon-Fri, also Sat and Sun afternoons; closed Thanksgiving, Dec 25) 700 N Lynn Ave. Phone 918/287-9924. **FREE**

Osage Hills State Park. A 1,005-acre park with 18-acre lake. Swimming pool, fishing; picnic facilities, playgrounds, camping areas, trailer hookups (fee). (Daily) 11 mi NE on US 60. Phone 918/336-4141. **FREE**

Osage Tribal Museum. Treaties; costumes, beadwork; arts and crafts center. (Tues-Sat; closed hols) 814

Grandview Ave. Phone 918/287-4622. **FREE**

Tallgrass Prairie Preserve. On 37,000 acres. Buffalo herd. 17 mi N on county road. Phone 918/287-1208. **FREE**

Special Events

Ben Johnson Memorial Steer-Roping Contest. Father's Day wkend.

International Roundup Clubs Cavalcade. State's largest amateur rodeo. Third wkend July.

Osage County Fair. Late Sept.

Pawnee

(B-6) *See also Perry*

Pop 2,197 **Elev** 900 ft **Area code** 918 **Zip** 74058
Information Chamber of Commerce, 608 Harrison St; 918/762-2108

What to See and Do

Pawnee Bill Ranch Site. House of Pawnee Bill, completed in 1910; 14 rms with original furnishings; Wild West show mementos. Buffalo, longhorn cattle pasture. (Daily, hrs vary; closed hols) On US 64. Phone 918/762-2513. **FREE**

Special Events

Steam Show and Threshing Bee. Fairgrounds. Steam engine races; exhibits. First full wkend May.

Indian Powwow. Tribal dances, contests. First wkend July.

Pawnee Bill Memorial Rodeo. Cattle drive, wagon trains, cowboy poet gathering. Third wk Aug.

Perry

(B-6) *See also Pawnee, Stillwater*

Pop 4,978 **Elev** 1,002 ft
Area code 580 **Zip** 73077
Information Chamber of Commerce, PO Box 426; 580/336-4684

What to See and Do

Cherokee Strip Museum. Schoolhouse (1895), implement building, pioneer artifacts, and documents depict era of the 1893 land run; picnic area. (Tues-Fri; closed hols) 2617 W Fir. Phone 405/336-2405. **FREE**

Special Event

Cherokee Strip Celebration. Commemorates opening of Cherokee Strip to settlers. Parade, entertainment, rodeo, contests, Noble County Fair. Mid-Sept.

Motel/Motor Lodge

★★ **BEST WESTERN CHEROKEE STRIP MOTEL.** *2903 US 77 and I-35 (73077). 580/336-2218; fax 580/336-9753; toll-free 800/528-1234. www.bestwestern.com.* 90 rms. S $45-$51; D $51-$57; each addl $5. Crib free. Pet accepted, some restrictions. TV; cable (premium), VCR avail. Indoor pool. Restaurant 6 am-10 pm. Bar 5-11 pm; closed Sun. Ck-out noon. Cr cds: A, C, D, DS, MC, V.
🄳 🐾 ☒ ☒ 🔥 SC

Ponca City (B-6)

Founded 1893 **Pop** 26,359 **Elev** 1,019 ft **Area code** 580
Information Ponca City Tourism, PO Box 1450, 74602; 580/763-8067 or 800/475-4400
Web www.poncacitynews.com/tourism

Ponca City was founded in a single day in the traditional Oklahoma land rush manner. Although in the Cherokee Strip, the town was named for the Ponca tribe. Ponca City is a modern industrial town surrounded by cattle and wheat country.

What to See and Do

Cultural Center & Museums. Indian Museum, 101 Ranch Room, Bryant Baker studio, and D.A.R. Memorial Museum. (Daily; closed Jan 1, Thanksgiving, Dec 25) 1000 E Grand Ave, in Marland-Paris Historic House. Phone 580/767-0427. ¢

Kaw Lake. On the Arkansas River; shoreline covers 168 mi. Water sports, fishing, boating; hunting. Recreation and camping areas (fee) located 1 mi off US 60. (Daily) 8 mi E on Lake Rd. Phone 580/762-5611. **FREE**

Lake Ponca. Waterskiing (license required), fishing, boating; camp and trailer park (fee). 4 mi NE.

Marland Mansion Estate. A 55-rm mansion built in 1928 by E.W. Marland, oil baron, governor, and philanthropist. Modeled after the Davanzati Palace in Florence, Italy; features elaborate artwork and hand-painted ceilings. Tours. (Daily; closed Jan 1, Thanksgiving, Dec 25) 901 Monument Rd. Phone 580/767-0420. ¢¢

Motels/Motor Lodges

★ **DAYS INN.** *1415 E Bradley Ave (74604). 580/767-1406; fax 580/762-9589; res 800/329-7466. www.daysinn. com.* 59 rms, 3 story. No elvtr. S $34; D $36; each addl $5; under 12 free. Crib free. Pet accepted, some restrictions. TV; cable (premium). Complimentary continental bkfst. Restaurant nearby. Ck-out noon. Microwaves avail. Cr cds: A, D, DS, MC, V.

🅳 ⬛ 🕿 ✕ ➖ ⬛

★★ **HOLIDAY INN.** *2215 N 14 St (74601). 580/762-8311; fax 580/765-0014; toll-free 800/465-4329. www. holiday-inn.com/poncacityok.* 139 rms, 2 story. S $65-$69; D $69-$76; each addl $8; under 19 free. Crib free. TV; cable (premium). Pool. Coffee in rms. Restaurant 6 am-10 pm; Sat, Sun from 7 am. Bar 5 pm-midnight. Ck-out noon. In-rm modem link. Valet serv. Cr cds: A, C, D, DS, JCB, MC, V.

🅳 ➖ ➖ ⬛ SC

B&B/Small Inn

★ **ROSE STONE INN.** *120 S 3rd St (74601). 580/765-5699; res 800/763-9922.* 25 rms, 2 story, 3 suites. S, D $49; each addl $5; suites $79; under 16 free; wkend, hol rates. Crib free. Pet accepted, some restrictions. TV; cable (premium), VCR avail (movies). Complimentary full bkfst; afternoon refreshments. Restaurant nearby. Ck-out 11 am, ck-in 3 pm. Business servs avail. In-rm modem link. Luggage handling. Concierge serv. Guest lndry. Exercise equipt. Health club

privileges. Some refrigerators; microwaves in suites. Former home of one of the first S & L west of the Mississippi. Totally nonsmoking. Cr cds: A, C, D, DS, ER, MC, V.

🅳 ⬛ ➖ 🕿 ✕ ➖ ⬛ SC

Poteau (D-8)

Founded 1898 **Pop** 7,210 **Elev** 480 ft
Area code 918 **Zip** 74953
Information Chamber of Commerce, 201 S Broadway St; 918/647-9178

Rich in ancient history and pioneer heritage, Poteau is located in an area of timber and high hills. Just off US 271, a 4½-mile paved road winds to the peak of Cavanal Hill for a spectacular view of the entire Poteau River valley. Poteau lies approximately 15 miles north of Ouachita National Forest (see HOT SPRINGS, AR).

What to See and Do

Heavener Runestone. Scandinavian cryptograph in eight runes that scholars believe were inscribed by Vikings in A.D. 1012. Other runes from the Scandinavian alphabet of the third-tenth centuries have been found engraved on several stones in the area. NE of Heavener off US 59.

Kerr Museum. Home of former Senator Robert S. Kerr contains material detailing the history and development of eastern Oklahoma; incl natural history, pioneer, Choctaw, and special exhibits. (Tues-Sun afternoons; also by appt; closed Jan 1, Thanksgiving, Dec 25) 6 mi SW. Phone 918/647-8221. ¢

Lake Wister State Park. On 4,000-acre lake, facilities incl swimming pool, waterskiing, fishing, boating (ramps); hiking trails, picnic facilities, playground, miniature golf, grocery, camping, trailer hookups (fee), cabins. (Daily) 9 mi SW on US 271, then 2 mi SE on US 270. Phone 918/655-7756. **FREE**

Spiro Mound Archeological State Park. A 138-acre site with 12 earthen mounds dated from A.D. 600-A.D. 1450. Reconstructed Native American house; excavated items on display in Interpretive Center (summer, Tues-Sun; winter, Wed-Sun). Hiking trails, picnicking. 17 mi N on US 59, 6 mi E on OK 9, then 4 mi N on Spiro Mounds Rd. Phone 918/962-2062. **FREE**

Special Event

Poteau Frontier Days Rodeo. Memorial Day wkend.

Pryor

(B-8) *See also Claremore, Grand Lake, Miami, Vinita*

Pop 8,327 **Elev** 626 ft **Area code** 918 **Zip** 74361

Information Chamber of Commerce, PO Box 367, 74362; 918/825-0157

Pryor was named in honor of Nathaniel Pryor, a scout with Lewis and Clark who built a trading post near the town to do business with the Osage. For years a farming community, Pryor now has a 9,000-acre industrial park with plants producing cement, fertilizers and chemicals, castings, and wallboard.

What to See and Do

Coo-Y-Yah Country Museum. Artifacts from Mayes County representing several cultures incl clothing, artwork, Native American and pioneer items; also temporary exhibits. The museum is housed in an old railroad depot. (Apr-Dec, Wed-Fri and Sun afternoons; rest of yr, by appt) 8th St at US 69 S. Phone 918/825-2222. **FREE**

Lake Hudson. Robert S. Kerr Dam impounds waters of Grand River. Swimming, waterskiing, fishing, boating; camping. 10 mi E on OK 20. **FREE**

Motel/Motor Lodge

★ **PRYOR HOUSE MOTOR INN.** *123 S Mill St (74361).* 918/825-6677. 35 rms, 2 story. S $35; D $40; each addl $5; suites $40-$42; under 12 free. Pet accepted. TV; cable (premium). Pool. Complimentary continental bkfst. Restaurant open 24 hrs. Ck-out 11 am. Cr cds: A, D, DS, MC, V.

D 🐾 🛄 🛏️ 🖼️ 🎣

Quartz Mountain State Park

18 mi N of Altus via US 283, OK 44, 44A.

This 4,284-acre scenic preserve is on Lake Altus-Lugert, a 6,260-acre lake with excellent fishing for bass, catfish, and crappie. The wild rock-strewn park has 29 varieties of trees and 140 species of wildflowers.

Recreational facilities include beach, swimming pool, bathhouse, waterskiing, fishing, boating (ramps); hiking, golf, tennis, picnic facilities; playground, cafe, grocery, lodge, camping, trailer hookups (fee), cabins. Amphitheater. For camping reservations and additional information, phone 800/654-8240 or contact Oklahoma Tourism and Recreation Department, 15 N Robinson, Oklahoma City 73105; 405/521-2406.

Roman Nose State Park

(7 mi N of Watonga via OK 8, 8A)

Named after Chief Henry Roman Nose of the Cheyenne, this is a 750-acre area with a 55-acre man-made lake stocked with bass, crappie, bluegill, rainbow trout, and catfish. Its many recreational facilities include swimming pool, bathhouse, fishing, boating, paddleboats on Lake Boecher; golf, tennis, picnicking (grills), playgrounds, concession, lodge (see RESORT). Campsites, trailer hookups (fee). Contact Park Manager, Rte 1, Box 2-2, Watonga 73772; 580/623-7281.

Resort

★★ **ROMAN NOSE RESORT.** *Rte 1, Watonga (73772).* 580/623-7281; fax 580/623-2538; toll-free 800/654-8240. 57 units, 1-3 story; 47 lodge rms, 10 cottages with kits. Mid-May-mid-Sept: S, D $65-$68; each addl $10;

kit. cottages $70-$78; under 18 free; lower rates rest of yr. TV; VCR avail (movies). Pool. Supervised children's activities (Memorial Day-Labor Day); ages 3-15. Playground. Restaurant 7 am-9 pm; summer to 10 pm. Box lunches. Ck-out noon, ck-in 3 pm. Meeting rm. Business servs avail. Lighted tennis. 9-hole golf, pro, greens fee $8-$10, putting green. Recreation program. Paddle boats, canoes. Soc dir. State-owned, operated; all facilities of state park avail. On bluff overlooking Lake Boecher. Cr cds: A, C, D, DS, MC, V.

D 🛗 🍴 🏋 🎿 ⛵ 🛶 🐾 SC

Sallisaw (C-8)

Pop 7,122 **Elev** 533 ft **Area code** 918 **Zip** 74955

Information Chamber of Commerce, 111 N Elm, PO Box 251; 918/775-2558

What to See and Do

Blue Ribbon Downs. Thoroughbred, quarter horse, appaloosa, and paint horse racing. Pari-mutuel betting. (Schedule varies) Phone 918/775-7771. ¢

Robert S. Kerr Lake. Approx 42,000 acres with 250 mi of shoreline, Kerr Lake was formed with the creation of the inland waterway along the Arkansas River. Swimming, fishing, boating (ramps); hunting (in season), picnicking, camping (fee). (Daily) 8 mi S on OK 59. Phone 918/775-4474. **FREE**

Sallisaw State Park at Brushy Lake. Fishing, boating (ramp); picnicking, camping (fee). (Daily) 8 mi N on Marble City Rd, then 1 mi W on county road. Phone 918/775-6507. **FREE**

🔲 **Sequoyah's Home.** (ca 1830) Historic one-rm log cabin built by Sequoyah, famous Cherokee who created an 86-character alphabet for the Cherokee language. Historic landmark incl visitor center, mini-museum, artifacts; picnicking. (Tues-Sun; closed hols) 11 mi NE on OK 101. Phone 918/775-2413. **FREE**

Special Event

Grapes of Wrath Festival. Costume contest, parade. Antique and specialty car show. Chili cook-off, entertainment, children's activities. Phone 918/775-2558. Second wkend Oct.

Motels/Motor Lodges

★★ **BEST WESTERN.** *706 S Kerr Blvd (74955). 918/775-6294; fax 918/775-5151; toll-free 800/528-1234.* 81 rms, 2 story. June-Aug: S $39; D $45; each addl $5; suites $60-$75; under 12 free; lower rates rest of yr. Crib $5. Pet accepted; $5. TV; cable (premium). 2 pools, 1 indoor; whirlpool. Restaurant adj 6 am-10 pm. Ck-out 11 am. Lndry facilities. Meeting rms. Gift shop. Exercise equipt. Some refrigerators. Cr cds: A, C, D, DS, MC, V.

D 🍴 ⛵ 🏋 🐾 SC

★ **DAYS INN.** *1700 W Cherokee St (74955). 918/775-4406; fax 918/775-4440; res 800/329-7466. www.days inn.com.* 33 rms, 2 story. S, D $34-$46; each addl $5; under 12 free. Crib $5. Pet accepted, some restrictions. TV; cable (premium). Complimentary continenal bkfst. Restaurant adj 6 am-8:30 pm. Ck-out 11 am. Some refrigerators, microwaves. Cr cds: A, C, D, DS, MC, V.

D 🍴 🛗 🐾

★ **GOLDEN SPUR MOTEL.** *US 59 and I-40 (74955). 918/775-4443.* 28 rms, 2 story. S $30; D $32-$34; each addl $5; under 12 free. Crib $3. Pet accepted, some restrictions. TV; cable (premium). Pool. Complimentary coffee in lobby. Ck-out 11 am. Cr cds: A, C, D, DS, MC, V.

🍴 ⛵ 🐾 SC

★ **MCKNIGHT SALLISAW INN.** *1611 W Ruth St (74955). 918/775-9126; fax 918/775-9126.* 39 units, 2 story. S $26-$33; D $33-$50; wkly rates. Crib free. TV; cable (premium), VCR (movies). Pool. Restaurant nearby. Ck-out 11 am. Coin lndry. Cr cds: A, C, D, DS, MC, V.

D 🛗 🍴 ⛵ 🐾

Sequoyah State Park

See also Tahlequah

(8 mi E of Wagoner on OK 51)

These approximately 2,800 acres in Oklahoma's Cookson Hills, once a bandits' hideout, offer many attractions to vacationers. The park is on Fort Gibson Reservoir, created by the dam of the same name. This 19,100-acre reservoir shifts its level less than most hydroelectric power lakes in Oklahoma and is stocked with bass, catfish, and crappie. Fees may be charged at federal recreation sites at the reservoir.

The park has many features: beach, swimming pool, bathhouse, water sports, fishing, boating (ramps, docks, marina, rentals); hiking trail, mountain bike trail, horseback riding, 18-hole golf, tennis, picnic facilities, playgrounds, games, grocery, lodge (see RESORT), camping area, trailer hookups (fee), cabins. Contact Park Manager, Rte 1, Box 198-3, Hulbert 74441; phone 918/772-2046 or 918/772-2545.

Motel/Motor Lodge

★ **INDIAN LODGE.** *Rural Rte 2, Box 393, Wagoner (74467). 918/485-3184.* 25 rms, 9 kits. Apr-Oct: D $40-$55; each addl $7.50; kit. units $55-$60; suites $90-$155. Closed rest of yr. Crib $5. TV; cable. Pool. Playground. Restaurant nearby. Ck-out noon. Lawn games. Picnic tables, grill. Shaded grounds, near Fort Gibson Reservoir. Cr cds: A, MC, V.

Resort

★★ **WESTERN HILLS GUEST RANCH.** *19808 Park No. 10, Wagoner (74441). 918/772-2545; fax 918/772-2030; toll-free 800/368-1486. www.otrd.state.ok.us.* 98 rms in lodge; 44 cottages (1-2 bedrm), 18 kits. (no equipt). Mid-Apr-mid-Sept: lodge: S, D $70-$75; each addl $10; studio rms from $60; cabana $110; suites $100-$175; under 18 free; golf plans; lower rates rest of yr. Crib free. TV; VCR

avail (movies). Pool; wading pool, lifeguard in summer. Supervised children's activities (Memorial Day-Labor Day). Playground. Dining rm 7 am-9 pm. Box lunches, snack bar. Rm serv, lodge only. Bar 6 pm-1 am. Ck-out noon, ck-in 3 pm. Meeting rms. Business servs avail. Grocery 3 mi. Gift shop. Sundries. Lighted tennis. Golf, greens fee $12, pro. Boats, paddleboats. Bicycles, lawn games, hayrides. Soc dir. Rec rm. Poolside, lakeside rms. State owned, operated; all facilities of park avail. On Fort Gibson Reservoir. Cr cds: A, D, DS, MC, V.

Shawnee (C-6)

Founded 1895 **Pop** 26,017 **Elev** 1,055 ft **Area code** 405 **Zip** 74801
Information Chamber of Commerce, 131 N Bell, PO Box 1613; 405/273-6092

The history of Shawnee is that of Oklahoma in miniature. In the center of the state; it stands on what was originally Sac and Fox land, which was also claimed at various times by Spain, France, and England; and it was opened by a land rush on September 22, 1891. Oil was struck in 1926. Now it has diversified industries in addition to the processing of fruits, vegetables, poultry, and dairy products.

Shawnee is the home of Oklahoma Baptist University (1910). Jim Thorpe, the great Native American athlete, and Dr. Brewster Higley, the physician who wrote "Home on the Range," lived here. Astronaut Gordon Cooper was born and raised in Shawnee.

What to See and Do

Mabee-Gerrer Museum of Art. Art gallery features works by 19th- and 20th-century European and American artists as well as works from the Middle Ages and the Renaissance. Museum features artifacts of Egyptian, Babylonian, Grecian, Roman, Persian, Chinese, African, and Polynesian civilizations as well as North, Central, and South American native civilizations. (Tues-Sun; closed hols) St. Gregory's College, 1900 W MacArthur Dr. Phone 405/878-5300. **Donation**

Seminole Nation Museum. Traces the tribe's history from its removal from Florida over the "Trail of Tears" to establishing the capital. Displays incl collection of Native American peace medals; replicas of a Chické (Florida Seminole house), dioramas of the stickball game, the Whipping tree, the Old Wewoka Trading Post; artifacts from pioneer through oil boom days of 1920s. Art gallery with Native American paintings and sculpture. (Tues-Sun; closed hols) 524 S Wewoka Ave, 30 mi SE via US 177, OK 9, US 270, in Wewoka. Phone 405/257-5580. **FREE**

Shawnee Twin Lakes. Fishing, boating, swimming; hunting. Fee for activities. 8 mi W.

Special Events

Potawatomie Powwow. Late June.

Pott County Fair. Late Aug.

Heritage Fest. Late Sept.

Motels/Motor Lodges

★★ **BEST WESTERN CINDERELLA MOTOR INN.** *623 Kickapoo Spur St (74801). 405/273-7010; res 800/528-1234. www.bestwestern.com.* 92 rms, 2 story. S $49-$69; D $52-$72; each addl $5; under 18 free. Crib free. Pet accepted. TV; cable (premium). Indoor pool; whirlpool, poolside serv. Restaurant 6 am-10 pm. Bar 4 pm-midnight; closed Sun. Ck-out noon. Coin lndry. Meeting rms. Business servs avail. Sundries. Health club privileges. Cr cds: A, C, D, DS, JCB, MC, V.
D ⮌ ⇌ ▨ ▨ SC

★ **FLEETWOOD MOTEL.** *1301 N Harrison St (74801). 405/273-7561.* 17 rms. S $24-$26; D $32-$35. TV; cable. Restaurant nearby. Ck-out 11 am. Cr cds: A, DS, MC, V.
▨

★ **RAMADA INN.** *4900 N Harrison Blvd (74801). 405/275-4404; fax 405/275-4998; toll-free 800/228-2828. www.ramada.com.* 106 rms, 2 story. S $55; D $65; each addl $5; suites $125; under 18 free. Crib free. Pet accepted; $20 deposit. TV; cable (pre-

mium). Pool; poolside serv. Complimentary coffee in rms. Restaurant 6 am-10 pm. Bar 4 pm-midnight; Fri, Sat to 2 am; entertainment Fri, Sat. Coin lndry. Meeting rms. Business servs avail. In-rm modem link. Sundries. Game rm. Some refrigerators. Minibars. Cr cds: A, C, D, DS, JCB, MC, V.
D ⮌ ⇌ ▨ ▨ SC

Stillwater

(B-6) *See also Perry*

Founded 1889 **Pop** 36,676 **Elev** 900 ft **Area code** 405

Information Visitors and Special Events Bureau, 409 S Main, PO Box 1687, 74076; 405/372-5573

Stillwater was born overnight in the great land run of 1889. The settlement was less than a year old when on Christmas Day 1890, the territorial legislature established Oklahoma State University (formerly Oklahoma A & M). At the time the settlement had a mayor but no real town government. Yet less than four months later, the new settlers voted to incorporate as a city and to issue $10,000 in bonds to help build the college.

What to See and Do

Lake Carl Blackwell. A 19,364-acre recreation area operated by Oklahoma State University. Swimming, waterskiing, fishing, boating, sailing; hunting, picnic areas, campgrounds, cabins. Fees for various activities. 9 mi W on OK 51. Phone 405/372-5157. ¢

National Wrestling Hall of Fame. Houses Museum of Wrestling History and Honors Court. (Mon-Fri; also Sat during university sports events; closed hols) 405 W Hall of Fame Ave. Phone 405/377-5243. **FREE**

Oklahoma State University. (1890) 18,567 students. On a campus of 840 acres with an additional 4,774 acres of experimental university farms statewide. On campus is the Noble Research Center for Agriculture and Renewable Natural Resources, education/research complex with emphasis on the biological sciences. Buildings vary in style from "Old Central," the oldest collegiate building in the state, built in 1894 of pink brick, to attractive modified Georgian buildings of redbrick with slate roofs. Of special interest are Museum of Higher Education in Oklahoma (Tues-Sat; phone 405/624-3220); Bartlett Center for Studio Arts (Mon-Fri; phone 405/744-6016); and Gardiner Art Gallery (daily; phone 405/744-6016). Relief maps for the visually impaired. Washington St and University Ave, jct US 177 and OK 51. Phone 405/744-9341.

Payne County Free Fair. Payne County Expo Center. Livestock shows, commercial booths, carnival, children's barnyard, antique farm equipt, tractor pull. Phone 405/377-1275.

Sheerar Museum. Historical building houses local history museum, incl a 4,000-specimen button collection; also changing exhibits. (Tues-Sun; closed hols) 702 S Duncan St. Phone 405/377-0359. **FREE**

Special Event

Run for the Arts. Fine arts and jazz festival. Fiddle, banjo, and guitar contests; antique auto show. Apr.

Motels/Motor Lodges

★★ **BEST WESTERN OF STILLWATER.** 600 E McElroy Rd (74075). 405/377-7010; fax 405/743-1686; toll-free 800/353-6894. www.bestwestern. com. 122 rms, 4 story. S $46-$65; D $51-$70; each addl $5; suites $95-$120; under 12 free. Crib free. Pet accepted, some restrictions. TV; cable (premium). Indoor pool. Restaurant 6 am-11 am, 4-9 pm; Sun to noon. Bar 4 pm-2 am; closed Sun. Ck-out noon. Coin lndry. Meeting rms. Business center. In-rm modem link. Valet serv. Health club privileges. Game rm. Some refrigerators. Balconies. Cr cds: A, MC, V.

D ⊶ ≍ ⊠ ⋒ SC ⍾

★★ **HOLIDAY INN.** 2515 W 6th Ave (74074). 405/372-0800; fax 405/377-8212; res 800/465-4329. www.holiday-inn.com. 141 rms, 2 story. S $55-$65; D $62-$75; each addl $7; suites from $69; town house $128; under 19 free. Crib free. Pet accepted. TV; cable (premium). Indoor pool; whirlpool. Restaurant 6 am-8 pm. Bar from 4

pm. Ck-out noon. Coin lndry. Meeting rms. Game rm. Cr cds: A, C, D, DS, MC, V.

D ⊶ ⍾ ≍ ⊠ ⋒

Restaurant

★★ **STILLWATER BAY.** $623^1/2$ S Husband St (74074). 405/743-2780. www.stillwaterbay.com. Hrs: 11 am-10 pm; Fri, Sat to 11 pm; Sun to 9 pm; Sun brunch to 2 pm. Closed hols. Bar. Lunch $2.95-$8.95, dinner $4.95-$19.95. Sun brunch $2.95-$8.95. Children's menu. Specializes in fresh seafood, prime rib, chicken. Cr cds: A, DS, MC, V.

D ⊒

Sulphur

(D-6) *See also Ada, Ardmore*

Pop 4,824 **Elev** 976 ft **Area code** 580 **Zip** 73086

Information Chamber of Commerce, 717 W Broadway; 580/622-2824

Web www.brightok.net/chickasaw/sulphur

What to See and Do

Arbuckle Wilderness. A six-mi scenic drive through animal park; exotic, free-roaming animals; aviaries, zoo, hayrides, camel rides; petting park, catfish feeding; paddle and bumper boats; go-carts; playground; snack bar; gifts. (Daily, weather permitting; closed Dec 25) Approx 9 mi W via OK 7, 3 mi S of Davis near jct I-35, US 77; exit 51. Phone 580/369-3383. ¢¢¢

Chickasaw National Recreation Area. Travertine District (912 acres), near Sulphur, has mineral and freshwater springs, which contain sulphur, iron, bromide, and other minerals. There are streams for wading and swimming and 20 mi of hiking trails. Travertine Nature Center (daily; closed hols) has exhibits of natural history of area. Guided tours (summer and wkends; rest of yr, by appt). Veterans Lake has a fishing dock with access for the disabled. Lake of the Arbuckles offers fishing for catfish, largemouth bass, sunfish, crappie, and walleyed pike. There is also swimming, waterskiing, boating (launching at three designated ramps only; fee); picnicking, camping (fee), first-come, first-served basis; (Daily) Contact Superintendent, PO Box 201. S off OK 7. Phone 580/622-3165. **FREE**

Motel/Motor Lodge

★ **CHICKASAW LODGE.** *W First and Muskogee (73086).* *580/622-2156; fax 580/622-3094.* 69 rms, 1-2 story. S $34; D $39; each addl $5. Crib $7. TV; cable. Pool; wading pool. Restaurant 6 am-7 pm. Ck-out 11 am. Meeting rms. Cr cds: A, C, D, MC, V.
🄳 🕭 ⇌ 🔀 🐾

Restaurant

★ **BRICKS.** *2112 W Broadway (OK 7) (73086). 580/622-3125.* Hrs: 11 am-9 pm. Closed Jan 1, Thanksgiving, Dec 25. Lunch, dinner $3.75-$10.95. Children's menu. Specializes in barbecue, catfish. Cr cds: A, D, DS, MC, V.
🄳 🖳

Tahlequah (C-8)

Founded 1845 **Pop** 10,398 **Elev** 800 ft
Area code 918 **Zip** 74464
Information Tahlequah Area Chamber of Commerce, 123 E Delaware St; 918/456-3742 or 800/456-4860
Web www.tahlequah.com/chamber

Tribal branches of the Cherokee met here in 1839 to sign a new constitution forming the Cherokee Nation. They had been driven by the US Army from North Carolina, Alabama, Tennessee, and Georgia over the "Trail of Tears." Many died during the long forced march; a new life then began for the survivors, whose influence has since permeated the history and life of Tahlequah.

Sequoyah had created a written alphabet. The Cherokee were the only tribe with a constitution and a body of law written in their own language. These talented people published the first newspaper in Indian Territory (Oklahoma) and in 1885 established the first commercial telephone line in Oklahoma. The Southwestern Bell Telephone Company, to

which it was later sold, established a monument to this remarkable enterprise on the Old Courthouse Square.

The scene of these historic events is now rapidly growing as a vacation area with lakes and a river offering fishing and water sports of all types.

What to See and Do

🆉 **Cherokee Heritage Center.** National Museum of Cherokee artifacts; also reconstructed 1890 rural village (weather permitting). Guided tours of 1650 ancient village (May-late Aug, Mon-Sat). *Trail of Tears* drama (see SPECIAL EVENTS) is presented in Tsa-La-Gi outdoor amphitheater. Museum (Mon-Sat; closed Jan 1, Thanksgiving, Dec 25). Combination ticket avail. 3½ mi S on US 62, then 1 mi E on Willis Rd. Phone 918/456-6007. ¢¢

Float trips on the Illinois River. Contact the Chamber of Commerce.

Murrell Home. Pre-Civil War mansion; many original furnishings. (Wed-Sun; closed Jan 1, Thanksgiving, Dec 25) 3 mi S on OK 82, then 1 mi E on Murrell Rd. Phone 918/456-2751. **FREE** Also park and

  Murrell Home Nature Trail. Three-quarter-mi trail with special features for those in wheelchairs. Railroad ties line edges as guides; bird sanctuary, flower beds. **FREE**

Northeastern State University. (1909) 9,500 students. Founded on site of National Cherokee Female Seminary (1889), now Seminary Hall; John Vaughan Library; arboretum; theater productions. Tours of campus and Tahlequah historic places. On OK 82. Phone 918/458-2088.

Special Events

Trail of Tears. Tsa-La-Gi Amphitheater. Professional cast presents musical drama depicting history of Cherokee Tribe. Mon-Sat eves. Phone 918/456-6007. Late May-early June.

Illinois River Balloon Fest. Balloon race, balloon glow, arts and crafts, carnival, skydiving exhibition, food. Mid-Aug.

Cherokee National Holiday. Celebration of Constitutional Convention. Championship cornstalk bow and arrow shoot, powwow. Labor Day wkend.

Cherokee County Fair. Mid-Sept.

Motel/Motor Lodge

★ **TAHLEQUAH MOTOR LODGE.**
*2501 S Muskogee Ave (74464). 918/
456-2350; res 800/480-8705.* 53 rms,
2 story. S $35-$55; D $40-$55; under
12 free. TV; cable (premium). Indoor/
outdoor pool; whirlpool, sauna.
Complimentary full bkfst. Restaurant
24 hrs; Sun to 2 pm. Ck-out noon.
Coin lndry. Meeting rm. Refrigerators, microwaves. Cr cds: A, D, DS,
ER, MC, V.

Restaurant

★★ **JASPER'S.** *2600 S Muskogee
(74464). 918/456-0100.* Hrs: 11 am-
10 pm. Closed Sun; Thanksgiving,
Dec 25. Bar. Lunch $3.99-$5.99, dinner $7.99-$22.99. Children's menu.
Specializes in steak, seafood. Entertainment. Cr cds: A, DS, MC, V.

Tenkiller Ferry Lake

See also Muskogee, Tahlequah

(40 mi SE of Muskogee, off US 64)

This is one of Oklahoma's most beautiful lakes. Its shores consist of recreation areas, cliffs, rock bluffs, and
wooded slopes. The Tenkiller Ferry
Dam on the Illinois River is 197 feet
high and backs up the stream for 34
miles, creating more than 130 miles
of shoreline. There are 12,900 acres
of water surface.

Tenkiller State Park is on OK 100,
nine miles north of Gore. There are
four recreation areas on its 1,180
acres, with nature center; pool, bathhouse, waterskiing, fishing, boating
(rentals, ramps, marina); picnic facilities, playground, restaurant, gift
shop, camping areas, trailer hookups
(fee), plus cabins.

Like other Oklahoma lakes,
Tenkiller is lined with marinas, lodges,
and boat docks. The lower Illinois
River is famous for its striped bass

fishing. It is stocked with 96,000 trout
annually. Black bass and channel catfish are also plentiful, but the fish
causing the most excitement among
anglers are white bass and crappie.

There are 12 federal recreational
areas that provide camping for the
public. Six of these have electrical
hookups, showers, and other facilities. Contact Superintendent; phone
918/489-5643.

Resort

★★★ **FIN & FEATHER RESORT.**
*Rural Rte 1, Box 194, Gore (74435).
918/487-5148; fax 918/487-5025.
www.finandfeatherresort.com.* 83 units
(1-8 bedrm), 35 kits. Easter-Sept
(wkends, 2-day min; kit. units, 3-day
min): 1-bedrm $61-$68; 2-bedrm kit.
units $103-$155; 3-5-bedrm $310; 8-
bedrm $620. Closed rest of yr. Crib
$5. Pet accepted, some restrictions.
TV; cable, VCR avail (movies). Pool;
wading pool, whirlpool. Playground.
Dining rms 8 am-2 pm, 6-8 pm. Box
lunch, snacks. Ck-out noon, ck-in 2
pm. Grocery. Coin lndry. Convention facilities. Business servs avail.
Gift shop. Tennis. Private pond. Basketball. Volleyball. Roller-skating.
Lawn games. Rec rm. Game rm; mini
golf. Refrigerators. Picnic tables,
grills. Cr cds: A, DS, MC, V.

Tulsa (B-7)

Founded 1879 **Pop** 367,302 **Elev** 750
ft **Area code** 918

Information Metro Tulsa Chamber of
Commerce, 616 S Boston Ave, Suite
100, 74119-1298; 918/585-1201or
800/558-3311

Web www.tulsachamber.com

Not an oil derrick is visible to the
casual tourist, yet Tulsa is an important energy city. Oil and gas fields
surround it and offices of energy
companies are prevalent: more than
600 energy and energy-oriented firms
employ 30,000 people. It is the second-largest city in Oklahoma; its
atmosphere is cosmopolitan.

The first well came in across the river in 1901. Tulsa invited oilmen to "come and make your homes in a beautiful little city that is high and dry, peaceful and orderly, where there are good churches, stores, schools, and banks, and where our ordinances prevent the desolation of our homes and property by oil wells."

Oil discoveries came in 1905 and 1912 but Tulsa maintained its aloof attitude. Although most of the town owned oil, worked in oil, or supplied the oil fields, culture remained important. Concerts, theater, museums, and activities at three universities, including the University of Tulsa (1894) and Oral Roberts University (1963), give the city a sophisticated quality.

Tulsa has a well-balanced economy. Aviation and aerospace is the city's second-largest industry; it includes Rockwell International and the American Airlines maintenance base, engineering center, reservations center, and revenue and finance division.

With the completion of the Arkansas River Navigation System, Tulsa gained a water route to the Great Lakes and the Gulf of Mexico. The Port of Catoosa, three miles from the city and located on the Verdigris River, is at the headwaters of the waterway and is now America's westernmost inland water port.

Transportation

Car Rental Agencies. See IMPORTANT TOLL-FREE NUMBERS.

Public Transportation. Buses (Tulsa Transit), phone 918/585-1195.

Airport Information

Tulsa International Airport. Information 918/838-5000; lost and found 918/838-5090; weather 918/743-3311; cash machines, Main Terminal, upper level.

What to See and Do

Allen Ranch. A working horse ranch offering horseback riding, hayrides, children's barnyard and animal park, camping and chuckwagon dinners with entertainment. (Mon-Sat; closed Thanksgiving, Dec 25) Res requested. 19600 S Memorial Dr. Phone 918/366-3010. ¢¢¢¢

Arkansas River Historical Society Museum. Located in the Port Authority Building; pictorial displays and operating models trace the history of the 1,450-mi Arkansas River and McClellan-Kerr Navigation System. (Mon-Fri; closed hols) Tulsa Port of Catoosa, 5350 Cimarron Rd, 17 mi E on I-44 in Catoosa. Phone 918/266-2291. **FREE**

Bell's Amusement Park. Rides incl large wooden roller coaster, log ride, skyride; two miniature golf courses. (June-Aug, eves, also Sat and Sun afternoons; Apr-May, Fri-Sun; Sept, Sat and Sun) Free parking. 21st and S New Haven sts. Phone 918/744-1991. ¢¢¢¢

Big Splash Water Park. Park with two speed slides (75 ft), three flume rides, wave pool, tube ride; children's pool. (May-Labor Day) 21st St and Yale. Phone 918/749-7385. ¢¢¢

Boston Avenue United Methodist Church. (1929) Designed by Adah Robinson, the church facade was executed in Art Deco, the first large-scale use of the style in sacred architecture, and features a main 225-ft tower and many lesser towers decorated with bas-relief pioneer figures. The sanctuary is ornamented with Italian mosaic reredos. (Sun-Fri; closed hols) 1301 S Boston Ave, at 13th St. Phone 918/583-5181.

Creek Council Oak Tree. Landscaped plot housing the "Council Oak," which stands as a memorial to the Lochapokas Creek tribe. In 1834 this tribe brought law and order to a near wilderness. 18th and Cheyenne.

Frankoma Pottery. Guided 20-min tour (Mon-Fri). Shop (Sun afternoons). 2400 Frankoma Rd, 4 mi SW off I-44, in Sapulpa. Phone 918/224-5511. **FREE**

⭐ **Gilcrease Museum.** Founded by Thomas Gilcrease, oil man of Creek descent. Collection of art concerning westward movement, North American development, and the Native American. Works by Frederic Remington, Thomas Moran, Charles Russell, George Catlin, and others, incl colonial artists such as Thomas Sully; Native American artifacts from 12,000 yrs ago-present. Library houses some 90,000 items, incl the earliest known letter sent to Europe from the New World. Beautiful grounds with historic theme gardens. (Daily; closed

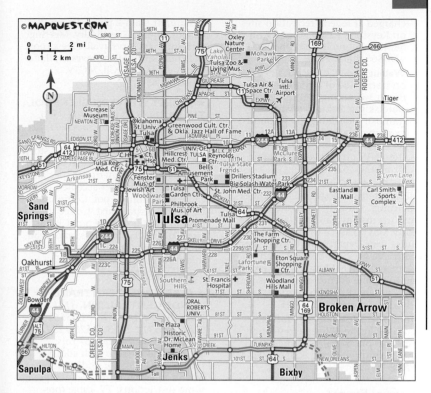

Dec 25). 1400 Gilcrease Museum Rd. Phone 918/596-2700. **Donation**

Mohawk Park. Fishing; golf course (fee), picnicking, restaurant. Nature center by appt. Park entrance fee. E 36th St N. Phone 918/669-6272. Within the park is

> **The Tulsa Zoo.** More than 200 varieties of animals set within 68 acres of landscaped grounds. Zoo features Native American artifacts, geological specimens, dinosaur replica, live plants and animals; train ride (fee). (Daily; closed Dec 25). 5701 E 36th St. Phone 918/669-6200. **¢¢**

Oxley Nature Center. An 800-acre wildlife sanctuary with numerous nature trails. Visitor center has exhibits and displays. Guided tours by appt. (Daily; closed hols) 5701 E 36th St N. Phone 918/669-6644. **FREE**

Philbrook Museum of Art. Exhibits incl Italian Renaissance, 19th-century English, American, and Native American paintings; Native American baskets and pottery; Chinese jades and decorative material; Southeast Asian tradeware; African sculpture. Housed in Italian Renaissance-revival villa on 23 acres; formal and sculpture gardens. Many national touring exhibitions. A 75,000-sq-ft addition houses an auditorium, museum school, and restaurant. (Tues-Sun; closed hols). 2727 S Rockford Rd. Phone 918/749-7941. **¢¢**

Sherwin Miller Museum of Jewish Art. Southwest's largest collection of Judaica contains objects representative of Jewish history, art, ceremonial events, and daily life from around the world. (Mon-Thurs, also Sun afternoons; closed Jewish hols) 1223 E 17th Place, in the B'nai Emunah Synagogue. **FREE**

State parks.

> **Lake Keystone.** Covers 715 acres on south shore of 26,300-acre Keystone Lake. Swimming, waterskiing, fishing, boating (marina, boathouse); hiking trails, picnicking, playground, grocery, snack bar (seasonal), camping, 14-day limit (fee), trailer hookups, cabins. Standard fees. (Daily) (Fees may be

charged at federal recreation sites on Keystone Lake.) 20 mi W on US 64, then S on OK 151. Phone 918/865-4991. **FREE**

Walnut Creek. Covers 1,429 acres on north side of Keystone Lake. Beach swimming, bathhouse, waterskiing, fishing, boating (ramps); picnicking, playground, camping, trailer hookups. Standard fees. (Daily) 19 mi W on US 64, then NW on 209 W Ave. Phone 918/242-3362. **FREE**

Tulsa Garden Center. Library, arboretum; extensive dogwood and azalea plantings. Directly north are rose and iris display gardens (late Apr-early May). East of the Center is the Tulsa Park Department Conservatory, with five seasonal displays each yr. Garden Center (Mon-Fri; also wkends during some events; closed hols and Dec 25-Jan 1). 2345 S Peoria Ave. Phone 918/746-5125. **FREE**

Tulsa Historical Society Museum. Located in the Gilcrease residence. Features photographs, rare books, and furniture. Phone 918/712-9484. **FREE**

Special Events

Gilcrease Rendezvous. Patterned after fur traders' engagements of days gone by. May.

Tulsa Powwow. Expo Square. Early June.

Discoveryland! Outdoor Theater. 10 mi W via W 41st St. Presents Rodgers and Hammerstein's *Oklahoma!* in a 2,000-seat outdoor theater complex with western theme. Authentic Native American dancing, Western musical revue, and barbecue dinner prior to performance. Mon-Sat. Phone 918/742-5255. Mid-June-late Aug.

Chili Cookoff & Bluegrass Festival. Early Sept.

Tulsa State Fair. Expo Square. Phone 918/744-1113. Late Sept-early Oct.

Motels/Motor Lodges

★★ **BEST WESTERN AIRPORT.** *222 N Garnett Rd (74116). 918/438-0780; fax 918/438-9296; res 888/438-0780. www.bestwestern.com.* 118 rms, 2 story. S, D $60-$90; each addl $5; suites $100; under 18 free. Crib free. TV; cable (premium). Pool. Complimentary continental bkfst. Coffee in rms.

Restaurant 6 am-2 pm, 5-10 pm. Bar. Ck-out 11 am. Guest lndry. Meeting rms. Business servs avail. Free airport transportation. Microwaves avail. Cr cds: A, C, D, DS, JCB, MC, V.
D ⛵ ✕ ⬜ 🔥 SC

★★ **BEST WESTERN GLENPOOL TULSA.** *14831 S Casper (US 75 S), Glenpool (74033). 918/322-5201; fax 918/322-9604; res 800/678-5201. www.bestwestern.com.* 64 rms, 2 story. S $45-$50; D $50-$60; each addl $5; under 12 free; higher rates special events. Crib free. Pet accepted. TV; cable (premium). Pool. Complimentary continental bkfst. Coffee in rms. Restaurant adj 6 am-9 pm. Ck-out 11 am. Coin lndry. Business servs avail. In-rm modem link. Refrigerators, microwaves. Cr cds: A, MC, V.
D 🐾 ⛵ ⬜ 🔥 SC

★★ **BEST WESTERN TRADE WINDS CENTRAL INN.** *3141 E Skelly Dr (74105). 918/749-5561; fax 918/749-6312; res 800/528-1234. www.bestwestern.com.* 167 rms, 2 story. S $64; D $69; each addl $4; studio rms $70-$86; under 18 free; wkend rates. Crib free. Pet accepted, some restrictions. TV; cable (premium), VCR avail (movies). Heated pool; poolside serv. Complimentary continental bkfst. Coffee in rms. Restaurant 6 am-10 pm. Bar 11-2 am; closed Sun; entertainment. Ck-out noon. Coin lndry. Meeting rms. Business servs avail. In-rm modem link. Valet serv. Sundries. Airport transportation. Exercise equipt. Wet bar, whirlpool in suites. Some balconies. Cr cds: A, C, D, DS, ER, JCB, MC, V.
D 🐾 ⛵ 🏋 ✕ ⬜ 🐾

★★ **COMFORT SUITES.** *8338 E 61st S (74133). 918/254-0088; fax 918/254-6820. www.comfortsuites.com.* 49 suites, 3 story. S $69; D $74; each addl $8; under 18 free; wkend rates. Crib free. TV; cable (premium), VCR avail. Pool. Complimentary full bkfst, coffee in rms. Ck-out 11 am. Meeting rm. Business servs avail. In-rm modem link. Sundries. Health club privileges. Refrigerators, microwaves. Cr cds: A, C, D, DS, ER, JCB, MC, V.
D ⛵ ⬜ 🔥 SC

★★ **GUESTHOUSE SUITES PLUS.** *8181 E 41st St (74145). 918/664-7241; fax 918/622-0314. www.guest*

house.net. 135 kit. units, 2 story. S, D $80-$115; under 12 free. Crib free. Pet accepted, some restrictions. TV; cable (premium), VCR avail. Pool; whirlpool. Complimentary continental bkfst, coffee in rms. Ck-out noon. Coin lndry. Meeting rm. Business servs avail. In-rm modem line. Sundries. Valet serv. Free airport transportation. Health club privileges. Microwaves. Balconies. Picnic tables. Cr cds: A, C, D, DS, MC, V.

[D] [icons]

★★ **HAMPTON INN.** *3209 S 79th E Ave (74145). 918/663-1000; fax 918/ 663-0587; res 800/426-7866. www. hamptoninn.com.* 148 rms, 4 story. S $66; D $79; suites $89-$99; under 18 free; wkend rates. Crib free. TV; cable (premium). Heated pool. Complimentary continental bkfst. Restaurant adj open 24 hrs. Ck-out noon. Meeting rms. Business servs avail. In-rm modem link. Health club privileges. Refrigerator in suites; microwaves avail. Cr cds: A, C, D, DS, JCB, MC, V.

[D] [icons]

★★ **HAWTHORN SUITES.** *3509 S 79th E Ave (74145). 918/663-3900; fax 918/664-0548; res 800/527-1133. www.hawthorn.com.* 131 units, 3 story. S, D $69-$99; 1-bedrm kit. suites $89-$129; 2-bedrm kit. suites $139-$189; wkend rates. Crib free. Pet accepted. TV; cable (premium). Heated pool; whirlpool. Complimentary full bkfst; eve refreshments Mon-Thurs. Coin lndry. Meeting rms. Business servs avail. Free airport transportation. Bellhops. Valet serv. Sport court. Microwaves, fireplaces. Private patios, balconies. Cr cds: A, D, DS, MC, V.

[D] [icons] SC

★★ **HERITAGE INN.** *6030 E Skelly Dr (74135). 918/665-2630; fax 918/ 665-2630; res 800/447-0660.* 130 rms, 4 story. S $47; D $51; each addl $5; suites $99; under 10 free. Crib free. TV; cable (premium), VCR avail. Pool. Complimentary continental bkfst. Ck-out noon. Meeting rms. Business servs avail. Some in-rm whirlpools in suites; microwaves avail. Cr cds: A, MC, V.

[D] [icons] SC

★★ **HOLIDAY INN EAST AIRPORT.** *1010 N Garnett Rd (74116). 918/437-*7660; fax 918/438-7538; res 800/465-4329. www.holiday-inn.com.* 158 rms, 2 story. S, D $99; each addl $10; under 19 free. Pet accepted. TV; cable (premium). Indoor pool. Playground. Restaurant 6 am-2 pm, 5-10 pm; Sat, Sun from 7 am. Bar 4 pm-2 am. Ck-out noon. Meeting rms. Business servs avail. In-rm modem link. Bellhops. Valet serv. Free airport transportation. Health club privileges. Game rm. Microwaves avail. Cr cds: A, C, D, DS, MC, V.

[D] [icons]

★★ **LA QUINTA INN.** *35 N Sheridan Rd (74115). 918/836-3931; fax 918/ 836-5428; toll-free 800/687-6667. www.laquinta.com.* 101 rms, 2 story. S, D $63; each addl $7; units for 6, $73; suites $89-$110; under 18 free. Crib free. Pet accepted, some restrictions. TV; cable (premium). Pool. Complimentary continental bkfst. Coffee in rms. Restaurant adj open 24 hrs. Ck-out noon. Business servs avail. In-rm modem link. Valet serv. Free airport transportation. Cr cds: A, C, D, DS, JCB, MC, V.

[D] [icons] SC

★★ **LEXINGTON SUITES.** *8525 E 41st St (74145). 918/627-0030; fax 918/627-0587. www.lexres.com.* 162 kit. suites, 3 story. S $65; D $85; each addl $7; under 16 free; wkly, monthly rates. Crib free. TV; cable (premium). Heated pool. Complimentary continental bkfst, coffee in rms. Ck-out noon. Coin lndry. Meeting rms. Business servs avail. In-rm modem link. Valet serv. Free airport transportation. Microwaves avail. Cr cds: A, D, DS, MC, V.

[icons]

★ **TRAVELODGE SOUTH.** *4717 S Yale Ave (74135). 918/622-6776; fax 918/622-1809; res 800/578-7878. www.travelodge.com.* 106 rms, 3 story. S $44-$49; D $46-$58; suites $65-$110; under 18 free. TV; cable. Pool. Complimentary continental bkfst. Restaurant adj. Ck-out 11 am. In-rm modem link. Cr cds: A, D, DS, MC, V.

[D] [icons]

Hotels

★★ **ADAM'S MARK HOTEL.** *100 E 2nd St (74103). 918/582-9000; fax 918/560-2232; toll-free 800/444-2326.*

Creek Council Oak Tree, Tulsa

www.adamsmark.com/tulsa. 462 rms, 15 story. S $135-$180; D $147-$195; suites $275-$975; under 17 free; wkend rates; package plans. Crib free. TV; cable, VCR avail. Heated pool. Restaurants 6:30 am-10 pm; Fri, Sat to 11 pm; Sun to 10 pm. Rm serv 24 hrs. Bar 11-1 am. Ck-out noon. Meeting rms. Business center. In-rm modem link. Gift shop. Free airport transportation. Exercise equipt. Refrigerator, minibar in suites. Balconies. Luxury level. Cr cds: A, D, DS, MC, V.

★★★ DOUBLETREE HOTEL AT WARREN PLACE. *6110 S Yale Ave (74136). 918/495-1000; fax 918/495-1944; res 800/222-8733. www.double treehotels.com.* 370 rms, 10 story. S, D $99-$119; each addl $15; suites $200-$500; under 18 free; wkend rates. Crib free. Pet accepted; some restrictions. Valet parking $7.50. TV; cable (premium), VCR avail. Indoor pool; whirlpool. Coffee in rms. Restaurants 6:30 am-11 pm (see also WARREN DUCK CLUB). Bar 3 pm-1 am. Ck-out noon. Convention facilities. Business center. In-rm modem link. Concierge. Gift shop. Free covered parking. Free airport transportation. Exercise equipt, sauna, steam rm. Health club privileges. Refrigerator,

wet bar in suites. Some balconies. Elaborate landscaping. Common rms decorated with Chippendale, Hepplewhite furniture. Luxury level. Cr cds: A, C, D, DS, ER, JCB, MC, V.

★★ DOUBLETREE HOTEL DOWNTOWN. *616 W 7th St (74127). 918/587-8000; fax 918/587-3001; res 800/222-8733. www.double treehotels.com.* 417 rms, 18 story. S, D $79-$150; each addl $15; suites $400-$700; under 18 free; wkend rates. Crib free. Pet accepted; $50 deposit ($25 refundable). Valet parking $8, garage $4. TV; cable (premium), VCR avail. Indoor pool; whirlpool, poolside serv. Coffee in rms. Restaurant 6:30 am-10:30 pm. Bar; entertainment. Ck-out noon. Convention facilities. Business center. In-rm modem link. Gift shop. Free airport transportation. Exercise equipt. Microwaves avail. Cr cds: A, C, D, DS, ER, JCB, MC, V.

★★★ HILTON TULSA SOUTHERN HILLS. *7902 S Lewis St (74136). 918/492-5000; fax 918/492-7256. www.hilton.com.* 350 rms, 11 story. S, D $150-$225; each addl $20; under 17 free. Crib avail. Pool. TV; cable (premium), VCR avail. Complimentary coffee, newspaper in rms. Restaurant 6 am-10 pm. Ck-out noon. Meeting rms. Business center. Gift shop. Exercise rm. Some refrigerators, minibars. Cr cds: A, C, D, DS, MC, V.

★★★ **MARRIOTT SOUTHERN HILLS TULSA.** *1902 E 71st St (74136). 918/493-7000; fax 918/523-0950; res 800/228-9290. www.marriott.com.* 382 rms, 11 story. S $139; D $149; each addl $10; suites $250-$500; under 18 free; wkend rates. Crib free. TV; cable (premium), VCR avail. Indoor pool; poolside serv. Restaurant 6:30 am-10 pm. Bar 4 pm-2 am. Ck-out noon. Convention facilities. Business center. In-rm modem link. Concierge. Gift shop. Free valet parking. Airport transportation. Exercise equipt; sauna. Some bathrm phones. Fountain in lobby. Cr cds: A, MC, V.

★★ **RADISSON INN TULSA AIRPORT.** *2201 N 77th E Ave (74115). 918/835-9911; fax 918/838-2452; res 800/333-3333. radisson.com/tulsaok.* 172 rms, 2 story. S, D $99-$119; each addl $10; suites from $135; under 17 free; wkend rates. Crib free. TV; cable (premium). Pool. Restaurants 6 am-10:30 pm; Sat, Sun 6:30 am-10 pm. Bar 11 am-midnight. Ck-out 1 pm. Meeting rms. Business servs avail. Bellhops. Free airport transportation. Exercise equipt; sauna. Grill. Cr cds: A, C, D, DS, ER, JCB, MC, V.

★★★ **SHERATON HOTEL.** *10918 E 41st St (74146). 918/627-5000; fax 918/627-4003; toll-free 800/325-3535. www.sheraton.com/tulsa.* 325 rms, 11 story. S, D $69-$129; suites $250-$500; under 18 free; wkend plans. Crib free. Pet accepted, some restrictions. TV; cable (premium), VCR avail (movies). Indoor/outdoor pool; whirlpool, poolside serv. Restaurant 6 am-10 pm. Bar. Ck-out 11 am. Coin lndry. Convention facilities. Business center. In-rm modem link. Concierge. Gift shop. Free parking. Free airport transportation. Exercise equipt; sauna. Health club privileges. Luxury level. Cr cds: A, D, DS, MC, V.

B&B/Small Inn

★★★★ **INN AT JARRETT FARM.** *38009 US 75 N, Ramona (74061). 918/371-1200; fax 918/371-1300; res 887/371-1200. www.jarrettfarm.com.* Perched on a hilltop 20 miles north of Tulsa, this 115-acre countryside bed and breakfast offers plenty of relaxation space and beautifully serene views. One 1,100-square-foot master suite is located in the ranch-style main house while the other ten suites are in charming yellow cottages dotting the property. Fine American/Continental cuisine is served at the inn's dining room. 5 rms. No rm phones. S, D $205; each addl $25. TV; VCR (movies avail). Pool; whirlpool. Spa. Complimentary full bkfst, coffee in rms. Ck-out noon, ck-in 4 pm. Business servs avail. Minibars. Totally nonsmoking. Cr cds: A, DS, MC, V.

All Suite

★★ **EMBASSY SUITES.** *3332 S 79th E Ave (74145). 918/622-4000; fax 918/665-2347; res 800/362-2779. www.embassysuites.com.* 240 kit. suites, 9 story. S, D $129-$250; each addl $10; suites $165-$195; under 18 free; wkend rates. Crib free. TV; cable (premium). Indoor pool; whirlpool. Complimentary full bkfst. Coffee in rms. Restaurant 11 am-2 pm, 5-10 pm; Fri, Sat to 11 pm. Bar 11 am-midnight. Ck-out noon. Coin lndry. Meeting rms. Business servs avail. In-rm modem link. Gift shop. Free airport transportation. Exercise equipt; sauna. Refrigerators, microwaves, wet bars. Balconies. Skylight over atrium. Cr cds: A, C, D, DS, ER, JCB, MC, V.

Restaurants

★★★ **ATLANTIC SEA GRILL.** *8321-A E 61St (74133). 918/252-7966.* Hrs: 11:30 am-2:30 pm, 5:30-10 pm; Fri to 11 pm; Sat 5:30-11 pm; Sun from 5:30 pm. Closed hols. Res accepted. Continental menu. Bar. Wine list. Lunch $4.95-$9.95, dinner $8.95-$21.95. Specializes in fresh seafood, steak, veal. Own pastries. Outdoor dining in

park setting. 350-gallon saltwater aquarium. Cr cds: A, D, MC, V.
D SC

★★★ **BODEAN SEAFOOD.** 3323 E 51st (74135). 918/743-3861. Hrs: 11 am-2:30 pm, 5-10:30 pm; Sat from 5 pm; Sun 5-9 pm. Closed hols. Res accepted. Bar 11 am-10:30 pm. Lunch $5.95-$15.95, dinner $11.95-$25.95. All seafood fresh daily. Valet parking wkends. Cr cds: A, D, DS, MC, V.
D SC

★★ **CAMMERELLI'S.** 1536 E 15th (74120). 918/582-8900. Hrs: 11 am-2 pm, 5-10:30 pm; Fri, Sat 5-11:30 pm; Sun from 5 pm. Closed Thanksgiving, Dec 25. Res accepted. Italian menu. Bar to 2 am. Lunch $6.95-$10.95, dinner $9.95-$18.95. Specializes in pasta, chicken, veal. Entertainment Tues-Thurs. Parking. Cr cds: A, D, DS, MC, V.
D SC

★ **FINNS CHOWDER HOUSE.** 1748 Utica Sq (74114). 918/712-0592. Hrs: 11 am-10 pm; Fri, Sat to 11 pm. Closed Sun; hols. Serv bar. Lunch $5.50-$13.99, dinner $7.99-$14.99. Specializes in seafood, steak, chicken. Outdoor dining. Wall murals. Cr cds: A, DS, MC, V.
D SC

★★★ **FOUNTAINS.** 6540 S Lewis Ave (74136). 918/749-9916. www.fountainsrestaurant.com. Hrs: 11:30 am-2 pm, 5:30-10 pm; Fri to 11 pm; Sat 5:30-11 pm; Sun to 9 pm; early-bird dinner 5:30-6:30 pm; Sun brunch 11 am-2 pm. Res accepted. Bar. Wine list. Lunch $4.95-$8.95, dinner $9.95-$16.95. Buffet: lunch $6.95. Sun brunch $9.95. Children's menu. Specialties: Beef Oscar, roast duck. Dessert bar. Entertainment Thurs-Sun; pianist Sun. Multilevel dining overlooks pool and fountains. Cr cds: A, D, DS, MC, V.
D SC

★★ **GRADY'S AMERICAN GRILL.** 7007 S Memorial Dr (74133). 918/254-7733. Hrs: 11 am-10 pm; Fri, Sat to 11 pm. Closed Thanksgiving, Dec 25. Bar. Lunch, dinner $5.25-$15.45. Specializes in prime rib, steak, fresh seafood. Open kitchen. Rustic decor. Cr cds: A, D, DS, MC, V.
D SC

★ **JAMIL'S.** 2833 E 51st (74170). 918/742-9097. Hrs: 4 pm-midnight. Res accepted. Dinner $8.50-$27.50. Children's menu. Specializes in Lebanese-style dishes, steak, smoked chicken. Family-owned. Cr cds: A, D, DS, MC, V.
D SC

★★★ **POLO GRILL.** 2038 Utica Sq (74114). 918/744-4280. www.thepologrill.com. Hrs: 11 am-10 pm; Fri, Sat to 11 pm. Closed Sun; hols. Res accepted. Bar. Wine list. A la carte entrees: lunch $5.95-$14.95, dinner $7.95-$23.95. Specializes in fresh seafood. Pianist eves. Outdoor dining. English hunting decor, collectibles. Cr cds: A, D, MC, V.
D

★ **RICARDOS.** 5629 E 41st (74135). 918/622-2668. www.ricardostulsa.com. Hrs: 11 am-2 pm, 5-9:30 pm; Fri to 10 pm; Sat 11 am-10 pm. Closed Sun; July 4, Thanksgiving, Dec 25. Mexican menu. Serv bar. Lunch $3.50-$7.50, dinner $4-$8.95. Children's menu. Specialties: chili relleños, chili con queso. Cr cds: A, D, DS, MC, V.
D SC

★ **ROMANO'S MACARONI GRILL.** 8112 E 66th (74133). 918/254-7800. Hrs: 11 am-10 pm; Fri, Sat to 11 pm. Closed Thanksgiving, Dec 25. Italian menu. Bar. Lunch $4.95-$8.95, dinner $6.95-$16. Children's menu. Specializes in Northern Italian cuisine. Entertainment; opera singers. Italian villa decor. Stone walls, archways. Fireplaces. Cr cds: A, D, DS, MC, V.
D SC

★★ **ROSIE'S RIB JOINT.** 8125 E 49th (74145). 918/663-2610. www.rosiesribjoint.com. Hrs: 11 am-2 pm, 5-10 pm; Sat from 5 pm; Sun 11 am-9 pm. Closed hols. Res accepted. Bar. Lunch $5.95-$11.95, dinner $7.50-$18.95. Specializes in smoked ribs, prime rib, seafood. Salad bar. Cr cds: A, DS, MC, V.
D SC

★★ **TIAMO.** 8151 E 21st (74129). 918/665-1939. Hrs: 11 am-2 pm, 5-9 pm; Fri, Sat to 10 pm. Sun 11 am-9 pm. Closed hols. Res accepted. Italian menu. Bar. Lunch $4.95-$8.95, dinner $6.95-$15.95. Specialties: scampi coriana, vitello ramano, fil-leto alla tiamo. Parking. Cr cds: A, DS, MC, V.

🄳 ➡

★★ TIAMO. *6024A S Sheridan (74145). 918/499-1919.* Hrs: 11 am-2 pm, 5-9 pm; Fri to 10 pm; Sat 5-10 pm; Sun 11 am-9 pm. Closed hols. Italian menu. Bar. Lunch $4.95-$6.95, dinner $6.95-$14.95. Specialties: rigatoni alla Sicilliano, chicken della casa, vitello ramano. Parking. Classic Italian decor. Cr cds: A, DS, MC, V.

🄳 ➡

★★★ WARREN DUCK CLUB. *6110 S Yale (74136). 918/495-1000. www.doubletreehotels.com.* Hrs: 11:30 am-2 pm, 6-10 pm; Fri, Sat 6-11 pm. Closed Sun; hols. Res accepted. Continental menu. Bar. Lunch $8.95-$13.95, dinner $17.95-$55. Children's menu. Specialties: blackened tenderloin, rotisserie duck, seafood. Pianist Fri, Sat. Valet parking. Cr cds: MC, V.

🄳 ➡

Unrated Dining Spots

BAXTER INTERURBAN. *717 S Houston (74127). 918/585-3134.* Hrs: 11 am-10:30 pm; Fri, Sat to midnight; Sun 5-10:30 pm. Closed hols. Bar to midnight. Lunch, dinner $4.95-$12.95. Children's menu. Specializes in gourmet hamburgers, salads, Mexican dishes. Trolley theme. Cr cds: A, D, DS, MC, V.

🄳 ➡

CASA BONITA. *2120 S Sheridan Rd (74129). 918/836-6464.* Hrs: 11 am-9:30 pm; Fri, Sat to 10 pm. Closed Thanksgiving, Dec 24, 25. Mexican, American menu. Lunch $4.99-$8.79, dinner $5.99-$8.79. Children's menu. Specializes in all-you-can-eat Mexican dinner. Strolling Mexican musicians; entertainment, puppet shows. Mexican village decor; waterfalls, caves. Gift shop. Game rm. Cr cds: A, C, D, DS, MC, V.

🄳 🆂🅲 ➡

METRO DINER. *3001 E 11th (74104). 918/592-2616.* Hrs: 7 am-10 pm; Fri, Sat to 11 pm. Closed Easter, Thanksgiving, Dec 25. Bar. Bkfst $2.95-$6.50, lunch, dinner $3.99-$10. Children's menu. Specializes in chicken-fried steak, homemade pies.

1950s diner atmosphere. Cr cds: A, DS, MC, V.

🄳 ➡

Vinita

(B-8) *See also Grand Lake, Miami, Pryor*

Pop 5,804 **Elev** 700 ft **Area code** 918 **Zip** 74301
Information Vinita Area Chamber of Commerce, 125 S Scraper, PO Box 882; 918/256-7133

Among the oldest towns in the state, Vinita was established in 1871 within the Cherokee Nation. Many stately homes attest to the town's cultural significance during the late 1800s. Vinita is also home to one of the world's largest McDonald's restaurants.

What to See and Do

Eastern Trails Museum. Historic displays, articles belonging to Vinnie Ream, Native American artifacts. (Mon-Sat afternoons; closed hols) 215 W Illinois. Phone 918/256-2115. **FREE**

Special Event

Will Rogers Memorial Rodeo and Parade. Late Aug.

Waurika

(E-5) *See also Duncan*

Pop 2,088 **Elev** 881 ft **Area code** 580 **Zip** 73573

Waurika is the site of Monument Rocks, a high point of the Chisholm Trail in southern Oklahoma. Early drovers made two piles of sandstone boulders, each about 12 feet high, on a flat-topped mesa, enabling the viewer to see 10-15 miles in either direction.

What to See and Do

Chisholm Trail Historical Museum. Chisholm Trail Gallery depicts his-

tory and artifacts from 1867-1889;
Pioneer Gallery shows development
of local history; slide presentation.
(Tues-Sun; closed hols) 1 mi E via US
70. Phone 580/228-2166. **FREE**

Waurika Lake. Dam on Beaver Creek,
a tributary of the Red River. Swimming, waterskiing, fishing, boating;
hunting, picnicking, camping (fee;
many sites have electrical hookups).
Information center (Mon-Fri). (Daily)
6 mi NW via OK 5. Phone 580/963-
2111. **FREE**

Weatherford

(C-4) *See also Clinton*

Settled 1898 **Pop** 10,124 **Elev** 1,647 ft
Area code 580 **Zip** 73096
Information Chamber of Commerce,
522 W Rainey, PO Box 729; 580/772-
7744 or 800/725-7744
Web www.weatherford.net

Weatherford is a progressive, growing
city with a diversified economy and
is the home of Southwestern Oklahoma State University (1901) as well
as Gemini and Apollo astronaut
Thomas P. Stafford.

What to See and Do

Crowder Lake. Swimming, fishing,
boating. 9 mi S on OK 54, then ¾
mi E.

Red Rock Canyon State Park. Covers
310 acres. Swimming pool, bathhouse; hiking, picnicking, playground, camping, trailer hookups
(fee). (Daily) 20 mi E on I-40, then
4½ mi S on US 281, near Hinton.
Phone 580/542-6344. **FREE**

Thomas P. Stafford Museum. Houses
memorabilia of former astronaut.
(Daily) Stafford Field. Phone
580/772-6143. **FREE**

Special Event

Southwest Festival of the Arts.
Crafts, performing arts, concerts. Second Sat Sept.

Motel/Motor Lodge

★★ **BEST WESTERN MARK
MOTOR HOTEL.** *525 E Main St
(73096).* 580/772-3325; *fax 580/772-*
8950; *res 800/598-3089. www.best
western.com.* 63 rms, 1-2 story. S $45-
$49; D $49-$59; each addl $3. Crib
$4. Pet accepted. TV; cable (pre-
mium), VCR avail. Pool. Complimentary coffee in rms. Restaurant opp 6
am-10 pm. Ck-out noon. Meeting
rms. Business servs avail. In-rm
modem link. Refrigerators. Cr cds: A,
C, D, DS, MC, V.
🅓 🐾 ⌨ 🛏 🔥

Restaurant

★★ **T-BONE STEAK HOUSE.** *1805
E Main St (73096).* 580/772-6329.
www.tbonesteakhouse.com. Hrs: 5-10
pm; Sun to 9 pm; Sun brunch 11 am-
2 pm. Bar. Dinner $6.99-$17.99. Sun
brunch $6.99. Children's menu. Spe-
cialties: hickory-smoked prime rib,
mushrooms tempura, mud pie. Fireplace. Cr cds: A, C, D, DS, MC, V.
🅓 ⊒

Woodward (B-4)

Pop 12,340 **Elev** 1,905 ft
Area code 580
Information Chamber of Commerce,
1006 Oklahoma Ave, PO Box 1026,
73802; 580/256-7411 or 800/364-5352

What to See and Do

Boiling Springs State Park. Covers 820
acres with seven-acre lake. Swimming
pool, bathhouse, fishing; hiking, picnicking, playground, concession,
camping, trailer hookups (fee), cabins.
(Daily) 1 mi N on OK 34, then 5 mi E
on OK 34C. Phone 580/256-7664.
FREE

Fort Supply Lake. Swimming, fishing; hunting, camping (hookups;
fees). (Daily) 15 mi NW via US 270; 1
mi S of Fort Supply. Phone 580/766-
2701. **FREE**

Glass Mountains. Name derived from
the mountains' surface, which is
made up of sparkling selenite crystals.
Roadside rest area. E on OK 15, just E
of jct US 281, OK 15, W of Orienta.

Historic Fort Supply. Established as a
temporary cavalry supply camp in
the late 1800s, the fort endured as a
trail stop between Kansas, Texas, and
Oklahoma. Restored original build-

ings incl the Powder Monkey's House and Teamsters Cabin (ca 1870), the Commanding Officer's Quarters (1878), and the Officer's Quarters (ca mid-1880s). The Guard House (1892) is now a museum. Tours. (Mon-Fri, closed hols) 15 mi NW via US 270. Phone 580/766-3767. **FREE**

Plains Indians & Pioneers Museum.
Changing and permanent displays depict Native American culture and early life on the plains. Pioneer, cowboy, and Native American artifacts and clothing; collection of personal belongings of Temple Houston, son of Sam Houston; exhibits from early-day banks; original building from historic Fort Supply; agriculture building; art center with changing exhibits. (Tues-Sun; closed hols) 2009 Williams Ave (US 270). Phone 580/256-6136. **FREE**

Motels/Motor Lodges

★★ **NORTHWEST INN.** *US 270 S and 1st St (73802). 580/256-7600; fax 580/254-2274; toll-free 800/727-7606.* 124 rms, 2 story. S $69; D $76; each addl $7; under 18 free. Crib free. Pet accepted. TV; cable (premium). Indoor pool. Restaurant 6 am-11 am, 5-10 pm. Bar 5 pm-2 am; closed Sun; entertainment. Ck-out noon. Coin lndry. Meeting rms. Business servs avail. Game rm. Some refrigerators. Cr cds: A, C, D, DS, MC.

★ **SUPER 8 MOTEL.** *4120 Williams Ave (73801). 580/254-2964; res 800/ 800-8000. www.super8.com.* 60 rms, 2 story. S $35-$55; D $40-$65; under 12 free; wkly rates. Crib avail. Pet accepted; $7. TV; cable (premium). Pool. Complimentary continental bkfst. Restaurant nearby. Ck-out 11 am. Business servs avail. Cr cds: A, C, D, DS, MC, V.

SOUTH DAKOTA

This land was once dominated by the proud and mighty Sioux. They, along with mountain men who trapped for the American Fur Company, the Missouri Fur Company, and the Hudson's Bay Company, slowly gave way to the settlers. Today most Sioux descendants live on nine reservations in South Dakota. Many South Dakota museums and shops display and sell Native American art and artifacts.

Many settlers who came for the free land offered under the Homestead Act of 1862 built sod houses on the prairies; others, who came for gold discovered in 1874, set up gold rush camps in the Black Hills. Three groups of immigrants—Germans, Scandinavians, and Czechs—retain their traditional customs and cookery in their home life. Several colonies of Hutterites prosper in the eastern part of the state.

In South Dakota human achievements are strikingly contrasted with nature's design. Near the town of Wall are the Badlands, a colorful and spectacular result of eons of erosion. In the Black Hills the largest sculpture in the world, the Crazy Horse Memorial, is being created. The combination of natural wonders with Native American and frontier legend is a made-to-order attraction for tourists.

Population: 696,004
Area: 75,953 square miles
Elevation: 962-7,242 feet
Peak: Harney Peak (Pennington County, in Black Hills)
Entered Union: November 2, 1889 (40th state, same day as North Dakota)
Capital: Pierre
Motto: Under God, the people rule
Nickname: Mount Rushmore State; Coyote State
Flower: Pasque
Bird: Chinese Ring-Necked Pheasant
Tree: Black Hills Spruce
Fair: July 29-August 4, 2002, in Huron
Time Zone: Central and Mountain
Website: www.state.sd.us

Badlands National Park

The wide-open spaces of eastern and central South Dakota are famous for pheasant and offer some of the finest hunting in the nation. The Missouri River, with its four great lakes, is a paradise for those who love water recreation. Walleye fishing in the area is superlative. Fishing for northern pike is also superb, especially in Lake Oahe, where they often reach trophy size.

Throughout the state hundreds of markers inform visitors of history or natural phenomena. Many sites of natural, historical, and cultural significance are also preserved in a number of the state parks and recreation areas.

When to Go/Climate

Unpredictable, sometimes erratic, weather conditions are common in South Dakota. Summers are hot and humid, although less so than in other midwestern states. September brings cool temperatures, while winter can get downright frigid, and it has been known to snow as late as May.

AVERAGE HIGH/LOW TEMPERATURES (°F)

RAPID CITY

Jan 34/11	May 68/42	Sept 74/46
Feb 38/15	June 78/52	Oct 63/35
Mar 46/22	July 86/58	Nov 47/23
Apr 58/32	Aug 85/56	Dec 36/13

SIOUX FALLS

Jan 24/3	May 71/46	Sept 73/49
Feb 30/10	June 81/56	Oct 61/36
Mar 42/23	July 86/62	Nov 43/23
Apr 59/35	Aug 83/59	Dec 28/9

Parks and Recreation Finder

Directions to and information about the parks and recreation areas below are given under their respective town/city sections. Please refer to those sections for details.

NATIONAL PARK AND RECREATION AREAS

Key to abbreviations. I.H.S. = International Historic Site; I.P.M. = International Peace Memorial; N.B. = National Battlefield; N.B.P. = National Battlefield Park; N.B.C. = National Battlefield and Cemetery; N.C.A. = National Conservation Area; N.E.M. = National Expansion Memorial; N.F. = National Forest; N.G. = National Grassland; N.H.P. = National Historical Park; N.H.C. = National Heritage Corridor; N.H.S. = National Historic Site; N.L. = National Lakeshore; N.M. = National Monument; N.M.P. = National Military Park; N.Mem. = National Memorial; N.P. = National Park; N.Pres. = National Preserve; N.R.A. = National Recreational Area; N.R.R. = National Recreational River; N.Riv. = National River; N.S. = National Seashore; N.S.R. = National Scenic Riverway; N.S.T. = National Scenic Trail; N.Sc. = National Scientific Reserve; N.V.M. = National Volcanic Monument.

Place Name	Listed Under
Badlands N.P.	same
Black Hills N.F.	BLACK HILLS
Jewel Cave N.M.	same
Mount Rushmore N.Mem.	same
Wind Cave N.P.	same

STATE PARK AND RECREATION AREAS

Key to abbreviations. I.P. = Interstate Park; S.A.P. = State Archaeological Park; S.B. = State Beach; S.C.A. = State Conservation Area; S.C.P. = State Conservation

CALENDAR HIGHLIGHTS

JUNE

10K Volksmarch (Crazy Horse Memorial). Only time mountain top is open to the public. Phone 605/673-4681.

L. Frank Baum Oz Festival (Aberdeen). At Wylie Park. Oz characters, storytelling, book memorabilia, educational lectures. Art and food vendors, band concerts. Phone 800/645-3851.

JULY

Summer Festival (Brookings). Pioneer Park. Largest arts and crafts festival in the state. Entertainment, food. Phone 605/692-6125.

Corvette Classic (Spearfish). Main St. Sports car enthusiasts gather each summer for their convention. Highlight is Main St Show and Shine, when hundreds of Corvettes line Main St. Phone 605/336-7140.

AUGUST

South Dakota State Fair (Huron). Largest farm machinery exhibit in midwest. Carnival, entertainment, horse shows, car races, rodeos, livestock. Phone 605/353-7340.

Central States Fair (Rapid City). Central States Fairground. Rodeo, carnival, horse and tractor pulls, auto races, demo derby. Phone 605/355-3861.

SEPTEMBER

Corn Palace Festival (Mitchell). Music and entertainment. Phone Chamber of Commerce, 605/996-5667 or 605/996-6223 or 800/257-CORN.

Park; S.Cp. = State Campground; S.F. = State Forest; S.G. = State Garden; S.H.A. = State Historic Area; S.H.P. = State Historic Park; S.H.S. = State Historic Site; S.M.P. = State Marine Park; S.N.A. = State Natural Area; S.P. = State Park; S.P.C. = State Public Campground; S.R. = State Reserve; S.R.A. = State Recreation Area; S.Res. = State Reservoir; S.Res.P. = State Resort Park; S.R.P. = State Rustic Park.

Place Name	Listed Under
Angostura Reservoir S.R.A.	HOT SPRINGS
Bear Butte S.P.	STURGIS
Custer S.P.	same
Farm Island S.R.A.	PIERRE
Fisher Grove S.P.	REDFIELD
Fort Sisseton S.P.	SISSETON
Hartford Beach S.P.	MILBANK
Lake Herman S.P.	MADISON
Mina S.R.A.	ABERDEEN
Oakwood Lakes S.P.	BROOKINGS
Platte Creek S.R.A.	PLATTE
Richmond Lake S.R.A.	ABERDEEN
Roy Lake S.P.	SISSETON
Snake Creek S.R.A.	PLATTE
Union County S.P.	BERESFORD

Water-related activities, hiking, riding, various other sports, picnicking and visitor centers, as well as camping, are available in many of these areas. Entrance fee (daily). Annual $20/carload permit is good at all state parks and recreation areas or $2/person daily (Custer, $3 May-Oct); under age 12 free. There is a camping fee at most areas ($6-$13/site/night; electricity $3). Cabins (where available) $32/night. All areas open daily. Pets on leash only. For further information write Division of Parks and Recreation, Department of Game, Fish, and Parks, 523 E Capitol Ave, Pierre 57501-3182 or phone 605/773-3391. Phone 800/710-2267 for reservations at parks.

SKI AREAS

Place Name	Listed Under
Deer Mountain Ski Area	LEAD
Terry Peak Ski Area	LEAD

FISHING AND HUNTING

Nonresident: annual fishing license $59; family $59 (allows one limit); visitor's three-day $30; one-day $12; no license required for nonresidents under 16, but fish taken will be counted as part of string limit of a licensed accompanying adult. Nonresident: big game $155-$205; small game $100 (good for two 5-day periods). Nonresident waterfowl license $105 (good for ten consecutive days except in southeast counties); nonresident turkey license $75; nonresident predator license $35.

All nonresident big game firearm licenses are issued through a computer lottery.

Regulations, seasons, and limits for both fish and game vary in different waters and areas of South Dakota. For detailed information write to Department of Game, Fish, and Parks, 523 E Capitol Ave, Pierre 57501 or phone 605/773-3485.

Driving Information

Children under five yrs must be in an approved child passenger restraint system anywhere in vehicle: ages two-five may use a regulation safety belt; age one and under must use an approved safety seat. For further information phone 605/773-4493.

INTERSTATE HIGHWAY SYSTEM

The following alphabetical listing of South Dakota towns in *Mobil Travel Guide* shows that these cities are within ten miles of the indicated Interstate highways. A highway map, however, should be checked for the nearest exit.

Highway Number	Cities/Towns within ten miles
Interstate 29	Beresford, Brookings, Sioux Falls, Sisseton, Vermillion, Watertown.
Interstate 90	Badlands National Park, Belle Fourche, Chamberlain, Deadwood, Mitchell, Murdo, Rapid City, Sioux Falls, Spearfish, Sturgis, Wall.
Interstate 229	Sioux Falls.

Additional Visitor Information

A state highway map and the annual *South Dakota Vacation Guide* are free from the South Dakota Department of Tourism, 711 E Wells Ave, Pierre 57501-3369 or phone 800/S-DAKOTA. A periodical also worth looking at is *South Dakota Conservation Digest,* bimonthly, from South Dakota Department of Game, Fish, and Parks, 445 E Capitol Ave, Pierre 57501.

There are information centers (mid-May-September, daily) at rest areas along I-90 near Chamberlain, Tilford, Salem, Spearfish, Valley Springs, Vivian, and Wasta; and along I-29 near New Effington, Vermillion, and Wilmot.

BLACK HILLS AND BUFFALO: THE PETER NORBECK SCENIC BYWAY

This route passes through the rugged high country of the Black Hills, an isolated, pine-covered mountain range that rises from the northern prairies. Although the Black Hills look gently domed from a distance, in fact they are highly eroded, with many steep canyons, rocky peaks, and precipitous winding roads.

From Keystone, follow Highway 16A south into the Black Hills, ascending one of the most scenic—and challenging—roads in the Black Hills. Called the Iron Mountain Road, this road passes over three "Pigtail Bridges," trestles that spiral up a mountain slope too steep for traditional switchbacks. The road was also designed so that drivers emerge from the tunnels with Mount Rushmore perfectly framed in the distance. The Norbeck Memorial Overlook, at 6,445 feet, is named for Black Hills conservationist Peter Norbeck and is the highest point reached by paved road in the Black Hills. From here you can take in views that include Mount Rushmore, the granite cliffs and forests of the Black Elk Wilderness, and hundreds of miles of distant prairie.

Continuing south, the route passes into Custer State Park, the star of the South Dakota state park system. Custer State Park is home to the world's largest free-roaming buffalo herd, and hikers are apt to glimpse deer, elk, beaver, coyote, and raptors.

At Hermosa junction, continue on Highway 16A west into the park. Stop by the Peter Norbeck Visitors Center for information on hiking and other recreation, and visit the State Game Lodge and Resort, a venerable hotel built in 1920 that served as the Summer White House for President Calvin Coolidge.

Continue west on Highway 16A. Legion Lake, near the junction with Highway 87, has a campground, swimming beach, picnic area, and rustic lodge. Turn north on Highway 87 to join the Needles Highway, which passes through a maze of spired granite formations that rise above the Black Hills' heavy forest mantle. To carve a road through this precipitous landscape, engineers had to blast tunnels and corkscrew roadbeds down sheer cliffs. Rock climbing is a popular sport along the spires of the Needles formations; watch for brightly clad climbers clambering up the sheer rock faces. Less ambitious visitors can hike one of the many trails in this part of the Black Hills.

Continue north on Highway 87, passing Sylvan Lake, a cliff-lined lake popular for canoeing and swimming. Boat rentals and lodgings are available from the Sylvan Lake Lodge, whose buildings were inspired by Frank Lloyd Wright. From Sylvan Lake, continue north, climbing steeply through more tunnels and up more pigtail switchbacks to the junction with Highway 244 and roll east across the forested uplands. To the south is Mount Harney, which boasts an elevation of 7,242 feet, making it the continent's highest point east of the Rocky Mountains.
Whether you first see the crowds and tour buses or the carved busts of past presidents, you'll soon know you're near Mount Rushmore National Monument. Designed by Gutzon Borglum in the 1930s, the 60-feet-high carvings on Mount Rushmore are both more and less than you imagine them to be. Stop at the new visitor center and museum and explore the Presidential Trail, a walking trail and boardwalk that provide spectacular close-up views of the mountain sculpture. From Mount Rushmore, continue east, dropping down the steep switchbacks to Keystone. **(Approx 70 mi)**

Aberdeen

(B-6) *See also Redfield, Webster*

Settled 1880 **Pop** 24,927 **Elev** 1,304 ft **Area code** 605 **Zip** 57401
Information Convention & Visitors Bureau, 514¹/₂ S Main St, PO Box 1179, 57402-1179; 605/225-2414 or 800/645-3851

The roots of Aberdeen's commerce are the three railroads that converge here and make it a wholesale and distribution center, giving it the fitting nickname "Hub City." Alexander Mitchell, a railroader of the 19th century, named the town for his Scottish birthplace. German-Russian immigrants arrived in 1884. Hamlin Garland, author of *Son of the Middle Border*, and L. Frank Baum, author of *The Wizard of Oz*, lived here.

What to See and Do

Dacotah Prairie Museum. Pioneer and Native American artifacts; area history and art. **Hatterscheidt Wildlife Gallery** features specimens from around the world. (Tues-Sun; closed hols) 21 S Main St. Phone 605/626-7117. **FREE**

Mina State Recreation Area. On 300 acres. Swimming, bathhouses, fishing, boating (ramps, dock); hiking, picnicking (shelters), playground. Camping (electrical hookups). Interpretive programs. Standard fees. 11 mi W off US 12. Phone 800/710-2267.

Richmond Lake State Recreation Area. On 346 acres. Swimming, bathhouses, fishing, boating (ramps, dock); hiking, picnicking (shelters), playground. Camping (electrical hookups). Interpretive program. Standard fees. 10 mi NW via US 12, County 6, and County 13. Phone 800/710-2267.

Wylie Park. Man-made lake, swimming beach, waterslide, picnic areas, concession; zoo with buffalo, deer, elk. **Storybook Land**, a theme park inspired by children's stories and **Land of Oz** theme park. Camping (standard fees). (Late Apr-mid-Oct, daily) 1 mi N on US 281. Phone 605/626-3512. **FREE**

Special Events

Snow Queen Festival. Two wkends in Jan.

Pari-mutuel horse racing. Brown County Fairgrounds. Quarterhorse and thoroughbred racing. Three wkends May.

L. Frank Baum Oz Festival. June.

Motels/Motor Lodges

★★ **BEST WESTERN RAMKOTA HOTEL.** *1400 NW 8th Ave (57401). 605/229-4040; fax 605/229-0480; toll-free 800/528-1234. www.bestwestern. com.* 154 rms, 2 story. S $61; D $69; each addl $6; suites $85-$175; under 18 free. Crib free. Pet accepted. TV; cable. Indoor pool; wading pool, whirlpool, sauna. Restaurant 6:30 am-10 pm. Bar 11-2 am. Ck-out noon. Meeting rms. Business servs avail. Free airport, railroad station, bus depot transportation. X-country ski 2 mi. Health club privileges. Cr cds: A, C, D, DS, ER, JCB, MC, V.
🅳 ⭓ ⮚ ➰ ✕ ⊠ 🔥 🏊

★ **BREEZE INN MOTEL.** *1216 6th Ave SW (57401). 605/225-4222; toll-free 800/288-4248.* 20 rms, 3 kits. S $24; D $34.95-$36.95; each addl $2. Crib $2. Pet accepted. TV; cable. Restaurant adj. Ck-out 11 am. X-country ski 1 mi. Cr cds: C, D, DS, MC, V.
⭓ ⮚ ⊠ 🔥 🏊

★ **RAMADA INN.** *2727 SE 6th Ave (57401). 605/225-3600; fax 605/225-6704; toll-free 800/272-6232. www. ramada.com.* 153 rms, 2 story. S $48-$61; D $55-$69; each addl $8; under 18 free. Crib free. Pet accepted, some restrictions. TV; cable. Indoor pool. Playground. Restaurant 6 am-10 pm. Bar 4 pm-2 am. Ck-out 11 am. Meeting rms. Business servs avail. Valet serv. Sundries. Free airport, bus depot transportation. X-country ski 1 mi. Rec rm. Cr cds: A, C, D, DS, JCB, MC, V.
🅳 ⭓ ⮚ ⟲ ➰ ✕ ⊠ 🔥 🆂🅲

★ **SUPER 8.** *2405 SE 6th Ave (57401). 605/229-5005; res 800/800-8000. www.super8.com.* 108 rms, 2-3 story. No elvtr. S $37.98; D $44.98; each addl $5. Crib free. TV; cable. Indoor pool; sauna. Restaurant nearby. Ck-out 11 am. Coin lndry. Business servs avail. In-rm modem link. Airport transportation. X-country ski 1 mi. Cr cds: A, C, D, DS, MC, V.

★★ **WHITE HOUSE INN.** *500 SW 6th Ave (57402). 605/225-5000; fax 605/225-6730; toll-free 800/225-6000.* 96 rms, 3 story. S $32; D $36-$38; each addl $3; suites $40-$55; under 12 free. Crib free. Pet accepted. TV; cable. Complimentary continental bkfst. Restaurant nearby. Ck-out 11 am. Business servs avail. Airport, railroad station, bus depot transportation. X-country ski 1½ mi. Cr cds: A, DS, MC, V.

Restaurants

★★ **THE FLAME.** *2 S Main St (57401). 605/225-2082.* Hrs: 11 am-11 pm; Fri, Sat to midnight. Closed Sun; hols. Res accepted. Bar. Lunch $4.75-$8.95, dinner $7.75-$15.95. Children's plates. Specializes in steak, ribs, seafood. Family-owned. Cr cds: A, DS, MC, V.

★ **HONG KONG.** *1721 SE 6th Ave (57401). 605/229-2639.* Hrs: 11 am-9 pm; Fri, Sat to 10 pm. Closed hols. Res accepted. Chinese menu. Wine, beer. Lunch $4-$6, dinner $6-$8. Asian decor. Cr cds: MC, V.

Badlands National Park

(75 mi E of Rapid City via I-90, SD 240)

This fantastic, painted landscape of steep canyons, spires, and razor-edged ridges was made a national monument by President Franklin D. Roosevelt in 1939 and became a national park in 1978. Its stark and simple demonstration of geologic processes has an unusual beauty. Soft clays and sandstones deposited as sediments 26 to 37 million years ago by streams from the Black Hills created vast plains that were inhabited by the saber-toothed cat, the rhinoceroslike brontothere, and ancestors

of the present-day camel and horse. Their fossilized bones make the area an enormous prehistoric graveyard. Herds of bison, gone for many years, roam the area again. Pronghorn antelope, mule deer, prairie dogs, and Rocky Mountain bighorn sheep can also be seen.

More than 600 feet of volcanic ash and other sediments were laid down. About 500,000 years ago streams began carving the present structures, leaving gullies and multicolored canyons.

The Ben Reifel Visitor Center with exhibits and an audiovisual program is open all year at Cedar Pass (daily; closed January 1, Thanksgiving, December 25). The "Touch Room" is open to children of all ages. Evening programs and activities conducted by ranger-naturalists are offered during the summer. Camping at Cedar Pass (fee) and Sage Creek (free). The White River Visitor Center, 60 miles SW of the Ben Reifel Visitor Center, features colorful displays on the history and culture of the Oglala Sioux. Vehicle fee; Golden Eagle, Golden Age, and Golden Access Passports accepted (see MAKING THE MOST OF YOUR TRIP). For further information contact PO Box 6, Interior 57750; 605/433-5361.

Belle Fourche

(C-1) *See also Deadwood, Lead, Spearfish, Sturgis*

Founded 1890 **Pop** 4,335 **Elev** 3,023 ft **Area code** 605 **Zip** 57717

Information Chamber of Commerce, 415 5th Ave; 605/892-2676

Web www.bellefourche.org/regional/

Belle Fourche, rich in Western heritage, is a destination for those in search of the West. Cowboys and sheepherders once fought a range war here. Belle Fourche, seat of Butte County, still ships the largest volume of livestock of any town in western South Dakota, Wyoming, or Montana and is the wool-shipping capital of the nation. Industry includes bentonite (industrial clay) mills and mines. However, around July 4 there is little work done, for the Black Hills Roundup, one of the West's outstanding rodeos, keeps the town at fever pitch. The geographical center of the United States, with Alaska included, is marked at a point 20 miles north of Belle Fourche on US 85.

What to See and Do

Belle Fourche Reservoir and Orman Dam. Recreation on 52-mi shoreline. Swimming, waterskiing, windsurfing. Walleye and northern pike fishing. NE of town off US 212.

Johnny Spaulding Cabin. Two-story cabin, built in 1876 and restored. Tourist info. (June-Aug, Mon-Sat) 801 State St opp Post Office. **FREE**

Tri-State Museum. Regional and historical exhibits; fossils; dolls. (Mid-May-mid-Sept, daily; closed Labor Day) 831 State St. Phone 605/892-3705. **FREE**

Special Events

All Car Rally. Mid-June.

Black Hills Roundup. Rodeo. Phone 605/892-2676 for ticket prices and res. Early July.

Butte County Fair. 17 mi E on US 212, in Nisland. Mid-Aug.

Buffalo Western Show. 1111 National St. Lariat trick roping, bullwhip show, stunts with miniature horses. Phone 605/892-2676 or 888/345-5859. Mid-late June and late July-mid-August. ¢¢¢

Beresford

(E-8) *See also Sioux Falls, Vermillion*

Pop 1,849 **Elev** 1,498 ft
Area code 605 **Zip** 57004

What to See and Do

Union County State Park. Approx 500 acres. Hiking, bridle trails, picnicking, camping. Standard fees. 11 mi S off I-29. Phone 605/987-2263. ¢

Motel/Motor Lodge

★ **CROSSROADS.** *1409 W Cedar St (57004). 605/763-2020; fax 605/763-*

2504. 32 rms. S $28; D $38; each addl $4-$6. Crib $5. Pet accepted; $5. TV. Restaurant adj 6 am-10 pm. Ck-out 11 am. Cr cds: A, C, D, DS, MC, V.

Black Hills

See also Crazy Horse Memorial, Custer, Custer State Park, Deadwood, Hill City, Hot Springs, Jewel Cave National Monument, Keystone, Lead, Mount Rushmore National Memorial, Rapid City, Spearfish, Sturgis, Wind Cave National Park

Magnificent forests, mountain scenery, ghost towns, Mount Rushmore National Memorial (see), Harney Peak (highest mountain east of the Rockies), Crazy Horse Memorial (see), swimming, horseback riding, rodeos, hiking, skiing, and the Black Hills Passion Play make up only a partial list of attractions. Memories of Calamity Jane, Wild Bill Hickock, and Preacher Smith (all buried in Deadwood) haunt the old Western towns. There are parks, lakes, and picturesque mountain streams. Bison, deer, elk, coyotes, mountain goats, bighorn sheep, and smaller animals make this area home.

Black Hills National Forest includes 1,247,000 acres—nearly half of the Black Hills. The forest offers 28 campgrounds, 20 picnic grounds and one winter sports area (see LEAD). Daily fees are charged at most campgrounds. Headquarters are in Custer (see). For information and a map ($4) of the National Forest write Forest Supervisor, RR 2, Box 200, Custer 57730. Two major snowmobile trail systems, one in the Bearlodge Mountains and the other in the northern Black Hills, offer 330 miles of some of the best snowmobiling in the nation. There are also 250 miles of hiking, bridle, and mountain biking trails.

There is a story that whimsically explains the formation of the Black Hills. Paul Bunyan, the legendary logger, had a stove so large that boys with hams strapped to their feet skated on the top to grease it for the famous camp flapjacks. One day when the stove was red hot, "Babe,"

Paul's favorite blue ox, swallowed it whole and took off in all directions. He died of a combination of indigestion and exhaustion. Paul, weeping so copiously his tears eroded out the Badlands, built the Black Hills as a cairn over his old friend.

Geologists, however, state that the Black Hills were formed by a great geologic uplift that pushed a mighty dome of ancient granite up under the sandstone and limestone layers. Water washed away these softer rocks, exposing the granite. This uplift was slow. It may still be going on. The Black Hills offer rich rewards in gold and silver from the famous Homestake and other mines. Pactola Visitor Center, on US 385 at Pactola Reservoir, west of Rapid City, has information and interpretive exhibits on Black Hills history, geology, and ecology (Memorial Day-Labor Day).

Brookings

(C-8) *See also Madison, Watertown*

Founded 1879 **Pop** 16,270 **Elev** 1,623 ft **Area code** 605 **Zip** 57006

Information Chamber of Commerce/Convention & Visitor Bureau, 2308 6th St, PO Box 431; 605/692-6125 or 800/699-6125

Web www.brookings.com/chamber/

Research done at South Dakota State University has helped make Brookings the agricultural capital of the state; it has developed diversified farming and the manufacturing of devices for seed cleaning, counting, and planting.

What to See and Do

Laura Ingalls Wilder Home. Laura Ingalls Wilder and her family lived in these houses from 1887 to 1928, and they figure into her book *Little Town on the Prairie*. Tours are offered of the two houses, and interested visitors can follow a self-guided tour of 16 other De Smet sites mentioned by Ingalls in her books. (Memorial Day-mid-Sept, daily) 105 Olivet St SE, De Smet. Phone 605/854-3383. ¢¢

McCrory Gardens. Twenty acres of formal gardens and 45 acres of arboretum. (Daily) 2308 6th St E. **FREE**

Oakwood Lakes State Park. On 255 acres. Swimming, fishing, boating, canoeing; hiking, picnicking, playground, camping (electrical hookups, dump station). Visitor center (Daily). Interpretive program. Standard fees. 8 mi N on I-29, then 9 mi W on county road. Phone 605/627-5441.

South Dakota Art Museum. Features Harvey Dunn paintings of pioneers, Oscar Howe paintings; Native American arts; South Dakota collection; changing exhibits. (Daily; closed Jan 1, Thanksgiving, Dec 25) Medary Ave at Harvey Dunn St. Phone 605/688-5423. **Donation**

South Dakota State University. (1881) 8,090 students. McCrory Gardens and South Dakota Arboretum, 65 acres of horticultural gardens incl 15 acres of theme gardens. Walking tours. Guided tours on request. NE part of town. Phone 605/688-4541. Also on campus is

   Agricultural Heritage Museum. Displays on historical development of South Dakota agriculture. Changing exhibits. (Daily; closed hols) Medary Ave and 11th St. Phone 605/688-6226. **FREE**

Special Event

Summer Festival. Pioneer Park. Largest arts and crafts festival in the state. Entertainment, food. Second full wkend July.

Motels/Motor Lodges

★★★ **BROOKINGS INN.** *2500 E 6th St (57006). 605/692-9471; fax 605/692-5807; toll-free 877/831-1562. www.brookingsinn.net.* 125 rms, 2 story. S $49-$61; D $54-$61; each addl $4; under 18 free. Crib free. Pet accepted. TV; cable. Indoor pool; whirlpool. Restaurant 6:30 am-10 pm. Bar 4 pm-2 am, closed Sun; entertainment. Ck-out noon. Coin lndry. Meeting rms. Business center. In-rm modem link. Bellhops. Valet serv. Sundries. Free airport transportation. X-country ski 1½ mi. Rec rm. Exercise equipt; sauna. Some balconies. Cr cds: A, D, DS, MC, V.
D ⬛ 🖹 ➰ 🏋 🔀 🐾 🏃

★★ **QUALITY INN AND SUITES.** *2515 E 6th St (57006). 605/692-9421; toll-free 800/228-5151. www.quality inn.com.* 102 rms, 2 story. S $43-$49;

Laura Ingalls Wilder Home, Brookings

D $48-$56; each addl $2; suites $90; under 18 free. Crib free. Pet accepted. TV; cable. Indoor pool; wading pool, whirlpool. Restaurant 6 am-9 pm. Bar 4 pm-2 am; entertainment Mon-Sat. Ck-out 11 am. Meeting rms. Business servs avail. In-rm modem link. Bellhops. Valet serv. Sundries. Free airport, bus depot transportation. X-country ski 1 mi. Health club privileges. Private patios, balconies. Picnic tables. Cr cds: A, C, D, DS, ER, MC, V.

⬛⬛⬛⬛⬛ SC

Restaurant

★★ **THE RAM & O'HARE'S.** *327 Main Ave (57006). 605/692-2485.* Hrs: 11:30 am-10:30 pm. Closed Sun; hols. Res accepted. Bar 4:30 pm-2 am. Lunch $4.95-$9.25, dinner $5.25-$12.95. Specializes in prime rib, pasta, hamburgers. 3 dining levels in restored 1920 bank. Cr cds: A, D, DS, MC, V.

⬛

Chamberlain

(D-5) *See also Platte, Winner*

Pop 2,347 **Elev** 1,465 ft
Area code 605 **Zip** 57325

This town on the Missouri River is situated in the middle of the state, between corn farms and western cattle ranches.

What to See and Do

Akta Lakota Museum. Features large collection of Sioux artifacts and handcrafts, as well as several dioramas that depict daily life on the prairie. Also features large collection of Native American paintings and sculpture. Gift shop carries an extensive selection of books of Native American history and culture, as well as locally made jewelry and art. (Mon-Fri; free admission Memorial Day-Labor Day) Call for pricing. On campus of St. Joseph's Indian School (I-90, exit 263). Phone 605/734-3455.

American Creek Recreational Area. On Lake Francis Case; swimming (May-Oct, fee), sand beaches, waterskiing, fishing, boat docks; picnicking, camping (May-Oct; fee). Park (Daily; ranger, May-Oct). N end of Main St, SD 50. Phone 605/734-6772.

Big Bend Dam-Lake Sharpe. One of a series of six dams on the Missouri River built by the US Army Corps of Engineers as units in the "Pick-Sloan Plan" for power production, flood control, and recreation. Guided tours of powerhouse (June-Aug, daily; rest of yr, by appt). Visitor center at dam site (mid-May-mid-Sept, daily). Many recreation areas along reservoir have swimming, fishing, boating (docks, ramps, fee); winter sports, picnicking, camping (May-mid-Sept, fee). 21 mi NW via SD 50. Phone 605/245-2255. **FREE**

Motels/Motor Lodges

★★ **BEST WESTERN LEE'S MOTOR INN.** *220 W King Ave (57325). 605/734-5575; toll-free 800/ 528-1234. www.bestwestern.com.* 60 rms, 2 story. June-Aug: S $50; D $65-$75; family units $80-$90; family plan; lower rates rest of yr. Crib $5. TV; cable. Indoor pool. Ck-out 11 am. Cr cds: A, C, D, DS, MC, V.
≈ ⊠ 🐾 SC

★★ **OASIS INN.** *1100 E Hwy 16, Oacoma (57365). 605/734-6061; fax 605/734-4161. kellyinns.com.* 69 rms, 2 story. June-mid-Oct: S $40-$77; D $46-$81; each addl $5; under 12 free; lower rates rest of yr. Crib free. Pet accepted. TV; cable (premium). Restaurant adj 6 am-10:30 pm. Bar 5 pm-midnight. Ck-out 11 am. Coin lndry. Sundries. Airport, bus depot transportation. Miniature golf. Whirlpool. Sauna. Picnic tables, grills. Pond. On river. Cr cds: A, C, D, DS, ER, MC, V.
🔺 ⊠ 🐾 SC

★ **RIVERVIEW INN.** *128 N Front St (57325). 605/734-6057; fax 605/734-6058.* 29 rms, 2 story. May-Oct: S, D $50-$75; each addl $5. Closed rest of yr. Crib $5. TV; cable. Indoor pool; whirlpool. Sauna. Complimentary coffee in lobby. Restaurant nearby. Ck-out 10:30 am. Coin lndry. Meeting rms. Cr cds: A, DS, MC, V.
D 🛆 ≈ ⊠ 🐾

★ **SUPER 8 MOTEL.** *I-90; Lakeview Heights Rd (57325). 605/734-6548; res 800/800-8000. www.super8.com.* 56 rms, 2 story. Mid-May-mid-Sept: S $48.88; D $52.88-$62.88; each addl $3; lower rates rest of yr. Crib $2. TV; cable. Restaurant nearby. Ck-out 11 am. Cr cds: A, C, D, DS, MC, V.
D ⊠ 🐾 SC

Restaurant

★ **AL'S OASIS.** *I-90 exit 260 (57325). 605/734-6054.* Hrs: 6 am-10:30 pm; winter 7 am-9 pm. Closed Jan 1, Thanksgiving, Dec 25. Bar from 4 pm. Bkfst $2.75-$5.75, lunch $2.95-$7.25, dinner $6.95-$15.25. Children's menu. Specializes in buffalo burgers, steak, prime rib. Salad bar. Western artifacts display. Family-owned. Cr cds: A, DS, MC, V.
D

Crazy Horse Memorial

See also Custer

(5 mi N of Custer off US 16, 385)

This large sculpture, still being carved from the granite of Thunderhead Mountain, was the life work of Korczak Ziolkowski (1908-1982), who briefly assisted Gutzon Borglum on Mount Rushmore. With funds gained solely from admission fees and contributions, Ziolkowski worked alone on the memorial, refusing federal and state funding. The work is being continued by the sculptor's wife, Ruth, and several of their children.

The sculpture will depict Crazy Horse—the stalwart Sioux chief who helped defeat Custer and the United States Seventh Cavalry—astride a magnificent horse. It is meant to honor not only Crazy Horse and the unconquerable human spirit, but also all Native American tribes. It is merely a part of what is planned by Ziolkowski's family and the Crazy Horse Memorial Foundation. Near the mountain Ziolkowski visualized a great Native American center with a museum, medical training center, and university.

Crazy Horse's emerging head and face are nearly nine stories tall. When completed in the round, the mountain carving will be 563 feet high and 641 feet long—the largest sculpture in the world. To date 8.4 million tons of granite have been blasted off the mountain. Audiovisual programs and displays show how the mountain is being carved.

The Indian Museum of North America is on the grounds and houses some 20,000 artifacts in three wings. A Native American educational and cultural center opened in 1997. The visitor complex also includes the sculptor's log studio/home and workshop filled with sculpture, fine arts, and antiques. A restaurant is open daily (in season). Memorial open daylight-dark; closed December 25. Phone 605/673-4681 or 605/673-2828 (museum). ¢¢¢-¢¢¢¢

Special Events

10K Volksmarch. Only time mountain top is open to public. First full wkend June.

Night blasting. Late June and early Sept.

Custer

(D-1) *See also Hill City, Hot Springs, Keystone, Rapid City*

Settled 1876 **Pop** 1,741 **Elev** 5,318 ft **Area code** 605 **Zip** 57730

Information Custer County Chamber of Commerce, 615 Washington St; 605/673-2244 or 800/992-9818

Web www.custersd.com

This is where a prospector with Lieutenant Colonel Custer's expedition of 1874 discovered gold, prompting the gold rush of 1875-1876. Main Street was laid out in the 1880s, wide enough for wagons pulled by teams of oxen to make U-turns. Custer is the seat of Custer County, headquarters of the Black Hills National Forest (see BLACK HILLS) and center of an area of great mineral wealth. Gold, quartz, beryl, mica, and gypsum are some of the minerals that are mined in commercial quantities. Lumbering, tourism, and ranching are also important to the economy. Custer is a popular area for winter sports activities.

What to See and Do

Custer County Courthouse Museum. (1881) Features historical and cultural memorabilia of Custer County. (June-Aug, daily) 411 Mt Rushmore Rd. Phone 605/673-2443. Also here is

  1875 Log Cabin. Oldest cabin in the Black Hills. Preserved as a pioneer museum. (Days same as Courthouse Museum) Way Park. **FREE**

Flintstones Bedrock City. Adventures with the modern stone-age family: Fred, Wilma, Barney, Betty, Pebbles, Bamm Bamm, and Dino. Village tour; train ride; concessions. Campground. (Mid-May-mid-Sept, daily) US 16, 385. Phone 605/673-4079. ¢¢¢

Golden Circle Tours. Mini-bus tours of the area. (May-Sept, daily) Write L&J, Box 454 or phone 605/673-4349. ¢¢¢¢

Mountain Music Show. Country music show with comedy; family entertainment. (Late May-Labor Day, daily) 3 mi N on US 16, 385, in Flintstone Theater. Phone 605/673-2405. ¢¢¢

National Museum of Woodcarving. Features woodcarvings by an original Disney animator and other professional woodcarvers; Wooden Nickel Theater, museum gallery, carving area, and snack bar. (May-Oct, daily) 2 mi W on US 16. Phone 605/673-4404.

Special Events

Gold Discovery Days. Pageant of Paha Sapa, festival, carnival, parade, balloon rally. Late July.

Buffalo Wallow Chili Cook-off. Musical entertainment, art fair, chili contests. Early Oct.

Motels/Motor Lodges

★★ **BAVARIAN INN.** *US 16 and 385 N (57730).* 605/673-2802; fax 605/673-4777; toll-free 800/657-4312. www.custer-sd.com/bavarian. 64 rms, 2 story. Mid-June-late Aug: S $69; D $96; each addl $5; suites $120-$150; lower rates rest of yr. Crib free. Pet accepted. TV; cable (premium). 2 pools, 1 indoor; whirlpool, sauna. Playground. Coffee in rms. Restaurant 7-11 am, 4-10 pm. Bar 4 pm-1 am. Ck-out noon. Meeting rms. Gift shop. Lighted tennis. Game rm. Lawn games. Patios, balconies. Cr cds: A, MC, V.

★ **SUPER 8.** *415 W Mt Rushmore Rd (US 16) (57730).* 605/673-2200; fax 605/673-2201; res 800/800-8000. www.super8.com. 40 rms. Early June-Labor Day: S $75.88; D $85.88; suites $91.88; lower rates rest of yr. Crib free. TV; cable. Complimentary coffee in lobby. Restaurant nearby. Ck-out 11 am. Coin lndry. Cr cds: A, DS, MC, V.

D ☒ ♨

B&B/Small Inn

★★ **CUSTER MANSION BED & BREAKFAST.** *35 Centennial Dr (57730). 605/673-3333; fax 605/673-3033; toll-free 877/519-4948. www. custermansionbb.com.* 5 rms, 2 story. No A/C. No rm phones. Mid-May-mid-Sept: S $63-$95; D $68-$98; each addl $10; family rates; lower rates rest of yr. TV in sitting rm. Complimentary full bkfst. Restaurant nearby. Ck-out 10:30 am, ck-in 3 pm. Balconies. Picnic tables. Built 1891; antiques. Totally nonsmoking. Cr cds: MC, V.

♿ ⚕ ☒ ♨

Restaurant

★ **SKYWAY.** *511 Mt Rushmore Rd (US 16) (57730). 605/673-4477.* Hrs: 6:30 am-10 pm. Closed Jan 1, Thanksgiving, Dec 25. Res accepted. Mexican, American menu. Bar. Bkfst $2.69-$6.29, lunch $3.75-$6.59, dinner $5.25-$15.95. Children's menu. Specialties: teriyaki chicken, chicken fried steak, Tex-Mex dishes. Salad bar. Contemporary dining. Cr cds: A, D, DS, MC, V.

D ⊟

Custer State Park

See also Custer, Hill City, Hot Springs, Keystone

(5 mi E of Custer on US 16A.)
Area Code 605 **Information** Information Director, HC 83, PO Box 70, Custer 57730; 605/255-4515
Web www.state.sd.us/sdparks

This is one of the largest state parks in the United States—73,000 acres. A mountain recreation area and game refuge, the park has one of the largest publicly owned herds of bison in the country (more than 1,400), as well as Rocky Mountain bighorn sheep, mountain goats, burros, deer, elk, and other wildlife. Four man-

made lakes and three streams provide excellent fishing and swimming. Near the park is the site of the original gold strike of 1874 and a replica of the Gordon stockade, built by the first gold rush party in 1874.

Peter Norbeck Visitor Center (May-Oct, daily) has information about the park and naturalist programs, which are offered daily (May-Sept). Paddleboats; horseback riding, hiking, bicycle rentals, Jeep rides, camping, hayrides, chuckwagon cookouts. Standard fees. A park entrance license is required. Per vehicle ¢¢¢ or per person ¢¢

The Black Hills Playhouse, in the heart of the park, is the scene of productions for 11 wks (mid-June-late Aug, schedule varies); phone 605/255-4141.

Motels/Motor Lodges

★★ **STATE GAME LODGE.** *US 16A; Custer State Park (57730). 605/255-4541; fax 605/255-4706; toll-free 800/658-3530. www.custerresorts. com.* 68 rms, 3 story, 21 cabins, 8 kits. No A/C in cabins, lodge, motel units. Some rm phones. Mid-May-mid-Oct: S, D $89; 2-bedrm house $185-$265; 4-bedrm house $315; kit. cabins for 2-8, $89-$115. Closed rest of yr. Pet accepted; some restrictions. TV; cable. Restaurant 7 am-9 pm. Snack bar, box lunches. Bar noon-10 pm. Ck-out 10 am. Meeting rms. Gift shop. Grocery ¼ mi, package store. Jeep rides into buffalo area. Hiking trails. Fireplace in lobby. Picnic tables. Served as "summer White House" for Presidents Coolidge and Eisenhower. Cr cds: A, MC, V.

🔄 ♿ ⚕ ♨

★★ **SYLVAN LAKE RESORT.** *Rural Rte 2, Box 240 (57730). 605/574-2561; fax 605/574-4943; toll-free 800/658-3530.* 35 rms in 3-story lodge, 31 cabins, 19 kits. No A/C. Mid-May-Oct: S, D $90-$125; kit. cabins $75-$200; cabins $85-$125; lower rates rest of yr. Crib $5. Restaurant 7 am-9 pm. Bar 11:30 am-midnight. Ck-out 10 am. Meeting rms. Gift shop. Grocery. Paddleboats. Hiking. Some fireplaces. Some private balconies. Picnic tables. Lake swimming. Cr cds: A, D, MC, V.

D ☒ ♨

Cottage Colonies

★★ **BLUE BELL LODGE & RESORT.** *SD 87 S; Custer State Park (57730). 605/255-4531; fax 605/255-4407; toll-free 800/658-3530. www. custerresorts.com.* 29 cabins, 13 kits. No A/C. Mid-May-early Oct: S, D $120; each addl $5; kit. units $80-$160; lower rates rest of yr. Crib $5. TV; cable. Restaurant 7 am-9 pm. Bar. Ck-out 10 am, ck-in after 2 pm. Coin lndry. Meeting rms. Grocery, package store opp. Campground; hiking trails. Hayrides. Chuckwagon cookouts. Overnight pack trips. Lawn games. Refrigerators; many fireplaces. Picnic tables, grills. Cr cds: A, DS, MC, V.

★ **LEGION LAKE LODGE.** *HC 83 Box 67; Custer State Park (57730). 605/255-4521; fax 605/255-4581; toll-free 800/658-3530. www.custerresorts. com.* 25 cabins, 12 kits. May-Sept: S, D $69; kits. $110; each addl $5. Closed rest of yr. Crib $5. Pet accepted; $5. Playground. Restaurant 7 am-9 pm. Ck-out noon. Grocery. Swimming beach; boating. Hiking. Bicycle rentals. On lake. Cr cds: A, DS, MC, V.

Deadwood

(C-1) *See also Belle Fourche, Lead, Rapid City, Spearfish, Sturgis*

Pop 1,830 **Elev** 4,537 ft
Area code 605 **Zip** 57732
Information Deadwood Area Chamber of Commerce and Visitors Bureau, 735 Main St; 605/578-1876 or 800/999-1876
Web www.deadwood.org

This town is best known for gold and such Wild West characters as Calamity Jane, Preacher Smith, and Wild Bill Hickock. The main street runs through Deadwood Gulch; the rest of the town crawls up the steep canyon sides. A bust of Hickock by Korczak Ziolkowski—creator of the Crazy Horse Memorial—stands on Sherman Street. At the height of the 1876 gold rush, 25,000 people swarmed over the hillsides to dig gold. When gold was first struck at Deadwood, nearly the entire population of Custer rushed to Deadwood; predictably, at the height of a newer strike, nearly the entire population of Deadwood rushed to the town of Lead. Recently legalized gambling has given Deadwood another boom.

The Nemo Ranger District office of the Black Hills National Forest (see BLACK HILLS) is located in Deadwood.

What to See and Do

Adams Museum. Exhibits of local interest. (May-Sept, daily; rest of yr, Mon-Sat) Sherman and Deadwood sts. Phone 605/578-1714. **FREE**

Broken Boot Gold Mine. See how gold was mined in the historic gold camp days; underground guided tour. (Mid-May-Sept, daily) S edge of town on US 14A. Phone 605/578-9997. ¢¢

Casino gambling. On historic Main St. Most facilities have dining and lodging avail. **First Gold Hotel**, 270 Main St, phone 605-578-9777 or 800/274-1876; **Four Aces**, 531 Main St, phone 800/825-ACES; **Gold Dust**, 688 Main St, phone 605/578-2100 or 800/456-0533; **Historic Franklin Hotel**, 700 Main St, phone 605/578-2241 or 800/688-1876; **Midnight Star**, 677 Main St, phone 800/999-6482; **Miss Kitty's**, 649 Main St, phone 605/578-1811; **Silverado**, 709 Main St, phone 800/584-7005; **Wild West Winners Club**, 622 Main St, phone 605/578-1100 or 800/500-7711.

Mount Moriah Cemetery. "Boot Hill" of Deadwood. Graves of Wild Bill Hickock, Calamity Jane, Preacher Smith, Seth Bullock, and others.

Old Style Saloon #10. Collection of Western artifacts, pictures, guns; this is the saloon in which Wild Bill Hickock was shot. Entertainment, gambling, refreshments. (Daily; closed Dec 25) 657 Main St. Phone 605/578-3346. **FREE**

Sightseeing tours.

Boot Hill Tours. One-hr narrated open-air bus tours through historic Deadwood and Mt Moriah Cemetery ("Boot Hill"). Visit graves of Wild Bill Hickock and Calamity Jane. Res required for groups. (June-

Main Street, Deadwood

early Oct, daily) Departs from cafe at center of Main St. Phone 605/578-3758. ¢¢¢

Original Deadwood Tour. One-hr narrated open-air bus tours through historic Deadwood and "Boot Hill." Res recommended. (May-late Sept, daily) Departs from Midnight Star, 677 Main St. Phone 605/578-2091. ¢¢¢

Special Events

Ghosts of Deadwood Gulch Wax Museum. Old Town Hall, Lee and Sherman sts. Audiovisual tour of more than 70 life-size wax figures depicting 19 historic episodes in the settling of the Dakota Territory. Daily. Phone 605/578-3583. Mid-May-Sept.

Trial of Jack McCall. Old Town Hall, Lee and Sherman sts. Reenactment of McCall's capture and trial for killing Wild Bill Hickock. Mon-Sat. Phone 605/578-3583. June-Aug.

Days of '76. Rodeo at Amusement Park, 1 mi N. Historic parade down Main St; reenactment of early days. Last wkend July.

Kool Deadwood Nites. Free concert, show, adult prom. Third wk Aug.

Deadwood Jam. Free concert and entertainment. Second wk Sept.

Motels/Motor Lodges

★★ **BULLOCK HOTEL & CASINO.** *633 Main St (57732). 605/578-1745; fax 605/578-1382; toll-free 800/336-1876. www.bullockhotel.com.* 28 rms, 3 story. Late May-mid-Sept: S, D $65-$85; each addl $10; suites $155; under 12 free; lower rates rest of yr. Crib $10. TV; cable. Complimentary coffee. Restaurant 7 am-2 pm, 5-10 pm. Bar to 2 am; entertainment. Ck-out 11 am. Meeting rms. Bellhops. Minibar in suites. Restored Victorian hotel (1895). Cr cds: A, DS, MC, V.
D ⚞ 🕭

★ **DEADWOOD GULCH RESORT.** *US 85 S (57732). 605/578-1294; fax 605/578-2505; toll-free 800/695-1876. www.deadwoodgulch.com.* 97 rms, 2 story. Late May-mid-Sept: S, D $90-$99; under 18 free; lower rates rest of yr. Crib free. TV; cable. Pool; whirl-pool. Restaurant 6 am-10 pm. Bar 7-2 am. Ck-out 11 am. Meeting rms. Sundries. Gift shop. Game rm. Cr cds: A, MC, V.
D ⚞ 🏊 ⚞ 🕭 SC

★ **MINERAL PALACE HOTEL.** *601 Historic Main St (57732). 605/578-*

2036; fax 605/578-2037; toll-free 800/847-2522. www.mineralpalace. com. 63 rms, 3 story. June-Aug: S, D $69-$99; each addl $5; suites $125-$195; under 18 free; ski plan; higher rates Christmas wk; lower rates rest of yr. Crib free. TV; cable, VCR avail (movies $3.50). Coffee in rms. Restaurant 6 am-10 pm. Bar 7-2 am. Ck-out 11 am. Meeting rms. Business servs avail. Bellhops. Gift shop. Game rm. Refrigerator, minibar in suites. Cr cds: A, C, D, DS, MC, V.

Restaurant

★ ★ ★ JAKE'S ATOP THE MID-NIGHT STAR. 677 Main St (57732). 605/578-3656. www.themidnightstar. com. Hrs: 5-10 pm; Fri, Sat to midnight. Closed Dec 24, 25. Res accepted. Bar. Dinner $17-$25. Specialties: herb-crusted rack of lamb, Cajun seafood tortellini, filet mignon. Pianist. Elegant dining in atrium setting; skylight. Cr cds: A, D, DS, MC, V.

Hill City

(D-1) See also Custer, Deadwood, Keystone, Rapid City

Settled 1876 **Pop** 650 **Elev** 4,979 ft
Area code 605 **Zip** 57745
Information Chamber of Commerce, PO Box 253; 605/574-2368 or 800/888-1798

Hill City is a beautiful mountain town in the heart of the Black Hills. The Black Hills Institute of Geological Research and a Ranger District office of the Black Hills National Forest (see BLACK HILLS) are located here.

What to See and Do

■ 1880 Train. Steam train runs on gold-rush era track; vintage railroad equipt. Two-hr round trip between Hill City and Keystone through national forest, mountain meadow-

lands. Vintage car restaurant, gift shop. (Mid-May-mid-Oct, daily) Hill City Depot. Phone 605/574-2222. ¢¢¢¢

Recreation areas. In Black Hills National Forest. **Sheridan Lake.** 4 mi NE on US 16, then 2 mi NE on US 385. Swimming beaches. **Pactola Lake.** 4 mi NE on US 16, then 12½ mi NE off US 385. Both areas offer fishing, boating (ramps, rental); picnicking, camping supplies, grocery. Tent and trailer sites (fee). Visitor center (Memorial Day-Sept, daily). **Deerfield Lake.** 16 mi NW on Forest Highway. Fishing, waveless boating only (ramps); picnicking, camping (fee). Contact Forest Supervisor, Rural Rte 2, Box 200, Custer 57730.

Wade's Gold Mill. Authentic mill showing four methods of recovering gold. Panning for gold (fee). (May-Sept, daily) Deerfield Rd, ¾ mi NW. Phone 605/574-2680.

Special Events

Bank Robbery and Shoot-Out. Main St. Tues-Thurs eves. Memorial Day-Labor Day.

Fife and Drum Corps Concerts. Main St. Free performances every Mon eve. Memorial Day-Labor Day.

Heart of the Hills Celebration. Parade, barbecue, timber and logging show. Second wkend July.

Motels/Motor Lodges

★ ★ BEST WESTERN GOLDEN SPIKE. 106 Main St (57745). 605/574-2577; fax 605/574-4719; res 800/528-1234. www.bestwestern.com. 61 rms, 2 story. Mid-June-Aug: S $86; D $99; each addl $5; lower rates Apr-mid-June and Sept-Nov. Closed rest of yr. Crib $5. TV; cable. Heated pool; whirlpool. Coffee in rms. Restaurant 7 am-9 pm. Ck-out 11 am. Coin lndry. Meeting rms. Gift shop. Exercise equipt. Bicycle rentals. Cr cds: A, MC, V.

★ COMFORT INN. 678 Main St (57745). 605/574-2100; fax 605/574-4936. www.comfortinn.com. 42 rms, 2 story. June-Sept: S $78; D $78-$87; suites $133; under 18 free; higher rates special events; lower rates rest of yr. Crib free. TV; cable (premium).

Complimentary continental bkfst. Restaurant nearby. Ck-out noon. Business servs avail. Coin lndry. Indoor pool; whirlpool. Cr cds: A, DS, MC, V.

D ⟐ ⟐ ⟐ SC

Restaurant

★★ **ALPINE INN.** *225 Main St (57745). 605/574-2749.* Hrs: 11 am-2:30 pm, 5-10 pm. Closed Sun; Thanksgiving; also Dec 24-mid-Jan. No A/C. Wine, beer. Lunch $4.25-$5.95, dinner $5.95-$7.95. Specialty: filet mignon. Outdoor dining (lunch). Old World German decor. Totally nonsmoking.

Hot Springs

(E-1) *See also Custer, Keystone*

Settled 1879 **Pop** 4,325 **Elev** 3,464 ft **Area code** 605 **Zip** 57747
Information Chamber of Commerce, 801 S 6th St; 605/745-4140 or 800/325-6991 outside SD.
Web www.hotsprings-sd.com

Hot Springs, seat of Fall River County, is on the southeast edge of Black Hills National Forest. Many local buildings are of pink, red, and buff sandstone. A Ranger District office of the Nebraska National Forest (see CHADRON, NE) is located here.

What to See and Do

Angostura Reservoir State Recreation Area. On 1,480 acres. Swimming, fishing, boating, canoeing; hiking, picnicking, concession, lodging. Camping nearby. Interpretive program. Standard fees. 10 mi SE off US 18. Phone 605/745-6996.

Black Hills Wild Horse Sanctuary. Guided two-hr tours. Camping and chuckwagon dinners avail. (Memorial Day-Labor Day) Phone 605/745-5955. ¢¢¢¢

Evans Plunge. Large indoor, natural warm-water pool. Also health club with sauna, steam bath, spas, and exercise equipt; indoor water slides. Outdoor pool with water slide open during summer months. (Daily; closed Dec 25) 1145 N River St, N

edge of town on US 385. Phone 605/745-5165. ¢¢

Fall River County Museum. Artifacts and memorabilia documenting history of Black Hills. In former school (1893). (June-early Sept, Mon-Sat) 300 N Chicago St. Phone 605/745-5147. **FREE**

⊠ **Historic District.** Thirty-nine Richardsonian-Romanesque buildings, constructed of locally quarried sandstone. Architectural tours avail at the Chamber of Commerce. Near town center. **FREE**

⊠ **Mammoth Site of Hot Springs.** Excavation of a remarkable concentration of mammoth skeletons; to date the remains of 51 mammoths, a camel, and giant short-faced bear have been unearthed. (Daily) Southern city limits on US 18 truck bypass. Phone 605/745-6017. ¢¢

Huron

(C-6) *See also Brookings, Mitchell*

Founded 1879 **Pop** 12,448 **Elev** 1,275 ft **Area code** 605 **Zip** 57350
Information Huron Convention and Visitors Bureau, 15 4th St SW; 605/352-0000 or 800/HURONSD

Huron, seat of Beadle County, is also administrative center for a number of federal and state agencies. It is a trade and farm products processing center for a 10,500-square-mile area. Twelve city parks feature swimming, picnicking, golf, tennis, and ballfields. The area offers excellent northern and walleye fishing, and good pheasant hunting brings enthusiasts here when the season opens in mid-October.

What to See and Do

Centennial Center. Gothic stone structure (1887) houses state centennial memorabilia, Native American artifacts, railroad items, and memoirs of Hubert and Muriel Humphrey. (Mon-Fri, afternoons; also by appt) 48 Fourth St SE. Phone 605/352-1442. **Donation**

Dakotaland Museum. Pioneer exhibits, log cabin. (Memorial Day-Labor Day, Mon-Fri) 8 blks W on US

14 at State Fairgrounds. Phone 605/352-4626. ¢

Gladys Pyle Historic Home. (1894) This Queen Anne-style house was the residence of the first elected female US senator. Stained glass, carved woodwork, original furnishings. (Daily, afternoons only) 376 Idaho Ave SE. Phone 605/352-2528. ¢

Hubert H. Humphrey Drugstore. Mid-1930s atmosphere; owned by the former senator and vice-president until his death; still owned by Humphrey family. (Mon-Sat) 233 Dakota S. Phone 605/352-4064. **FREE**

Laura Ingalls Wilder Memorial. Laura Ingalls Wilder wrote a series of children's books based on her childhood experiences in De Smet. Here are restored surveyors' house, the family home from 1879-1880; original family home (1887); replica of period schoolhouse; memorabilia; many other sites and buildings mentioned in her books. Guided tours (Late May-mid-Sept, daily). 105 Olivet St SE, in De Smet. Phone 605/854-3383. ¢¢

Special Events

State Fair Speedway. US 14 W. South Dakota's largest racing program. Phone 605/352-1896 or 605/352-1431. Late Apr-early Sept.

Laura Ingalls Wilder Pageant. In De Smet. Fri-Sun, last wkend June and first two wkends July.

South Dakota State Fair. State Fairgrounds, W on US 14, at 3rd St SW and Nevada Ave SW. Phone 605/353-7340. July 29-Aug 4.

Meadowood Fair. Memorial Park. Art, craft exhibits, demonstrations; children's activities, entertainment, concessions. First wkend Aug.

Parade of Lights. Day after Thanksgiving.

Motels/Motor Lodges

★ ★ ★ **CROSSROADS HOTEL & CONVENTION CENTER.** *100 4th St SW (57350). 605/352-3204; toll-free 800/876-5858.* 100 rms, 3 story. S $51-$61; D $56-$69; each addl $5; suites $130; family rates. Crib free. Pet accepted. TV; cable. Indoor pool; whirlpool, poolside serv. Sauna. Restaurant 6:30 am-10 pm. Bar 4 pm-

2 am. Ck-out 11 am. Meeting rms. Business servs avail. In-rm modem link. Valet serv. Airport, railroad station, bus depot transportation. Health club privileges. Some refrigerators. Cr cds: A, MC, V.

D ♦ ➤ ⊠ ⚑ SC

★ ★ **DAKOTA PLAINS INN.** *924 NE 4th St (57350). 605/352-1400; toll-free 800/648-3735.* 77 rms, 2 story. S $35-$65; D $40-$65; each addl $5; under 12 free. Crib free. Pet accepted. TV; cable. Pool. Restaurant adj 6-10 pm. Bar 11:30-2 am. Ck-out 11 am. Meeting rm. Business servs avail. In-rm modem link. X-country ski 1½ mi. Cr cds: A, D, DS, MC, V.

♦ ➤ ⊠ ⚑

★ **SUPER 8.** *2189 S Dakota Ave (SD 37 S) (57350). 605/352-0740; res 800/800-8000. www.super8.com.* 68 rms, 2 story. S $38.88-$65.88; D $40.88-$65.88; each addl $4. Crib free. TV; cable. Indoor pool. Restaurant adj open 24 hrs. Ck-out 11 am. Business servs avail. X-country ski ½ mi. Cr cds: A, D, DS, MC, V.

D ➤ ⊠ ⚑

Jewel Cave National Monument

See also Custer, Hill City

(13 ml W of Custer on US 16.)

On a high rolling plateau in the Black Hills is Jewel Cave, with an entrance on the east side of Hell Canyon. More than 100 miles of passageways make this cave system the second longest in the United States. Formations of jewellike calcite crystals produce unusual effects. The surrounding terrain is covered by ponderosa pine. Many varieties of wildflowers bloom from early spring through summer on the 1,274-acre monument.

There is a guided 1¼-hr scenic tour of the monument (May-September) and a 1½-hr historic tour (Memorial Day-Labor Day; age six years or older only). There is also a four- to five-hr spelunking tour (June-August);

advance reservations required; minimum age 16. Note: All tours recommended only for those in good physical condition. For spelunking, wear hiking clothes and sturdy, lace-up boots. Visitor center. (Daily) Contact Rural Rte 1, PO Box 60 AA, Custer 57730; 605/673-2288. Tours: Scenic or historic ¢¢; Spelunking ¢¢¢¢

Keystone

(D-1) *See also Custer, Hill City, Rapid City*

Pop 232 **Elev** 4,323 ft **Area code** 605 **Zip** 57751
Information Chamber of Commerce, PO Box 653; 605/666-4896 or 800/456-3345

Keystone is the entrance to Mount Rushmore and Custer State Park. A former mining town supplying miners for the Peerless, Hugo, and the Holy Terror Gold Mine, it was also home to Carrie Ingalls and the men who carved Mount Rushmore.

What to See and Do

Big Thunder Gold Mine. Authentic 1880s gold mine. Visitors may dig gold ore or pan it by the stream. Guided tours; historic film. (May-Oct, daily) 5 blks E of stop light. Phone 605/666-4847. ¢¢¢

✪ **Borglum Historical Center.** Exhibits on Gutzon Borglum and the carving of Mt Rushmore. Newsreels of carving in progress. Original models and tools, collection of his paintings, unpublished photos of the memorial, sculptures, historical documents. Full-size replica of Lincoln's eye. (Apr-Oct, daily) US 16A, in town. Phone 605/666-4449. ¢¢

Cosmos of the Black Hills. Curious gravitational and optical effects. Guided tours every 12 min. (Apr-Oct, daily) 4 mi NE, ½ mi off US 16. Phone 605/343-9802. ¢¢

✪ **Mount Rushmore National Memorial.** (see) 3 mi SW off US 16A.

Parade of Presidents Wax Museum. Nearly 100 life-size wax figures depict historic scenes from nation's past. (May-Sept, daily) S on US 16A, at E entrance to Mt Rushmore. Phone 605/666-4455. ¢¢¢

Rushmore Aerial Tramway. This 15-min ride allows a view of the Black Hills and Mt Rushmore across the valley. (May-mid-Sept, daily) S on US 16A. Phone 605/666-4478. ¢¢

Rushmore Cave. Guided tours (May-Oct, daily). 5 mi E via SD 40, turn at Keystone traffic light. Phone 605/255-4467. ¢¢

Rushmore Helicopter Sightseeing Tours. Helicopter rides over Mt Rushmore and nearby points of interest. (Late May-late Sept, daily) S on US 16A. Phone 605/666-4461. ¢¢¢¢

Motels/Motor Lodges

★★ **BEST WESTERN FOUR PRESIDENTS MOTEL.** *250 Winter St (57751). 605/666-4472; fax 605/666-4574; toll-free 800/528-1234. www.bestwestern.com.* 33 rms, 3 story. No elvtr. Mid-June-Sept: S $82; D $92; lower rates Apr-mid-June and Oct-Nov. Closed rest of yr. Crib $5. Pet accepted, some restrictions. TV. Complimentary coffee in rms. Restaurant adj 7 am-10 pm. Ck-out 10 am. Cr cds: A, C, D, DS, MC, V.
🔄 🖥️ 🐾 SC

★ **FIRST LADY INN.** *702 US 16A (57751). 605/666-4990; fax 605/666-4676; toll-free 800/252-2119.* 41 rms, 3 story. No elvtr. Late May-early Sept: S $84; D $89; each addl $5; suites $119; lower rates rest of yr. Crib $5. Pet accepted; $7. TV; cable. Complimentary coffee in rms. Ck-out 10 am. Whirlpool. Cr cds: A, DS, MC, V.
D 🔄 🐾 ⛷️ 🖥️ 🐾

★ **KELLY INN.** *320 Old Cemetery Rd (57751). 605/666-4483; fax 605/666-4883; res 800/635-3559. www.kellyinns.com.* 44 rms, 2 story. Mid-May-mid-Sept: S $70; D $70-$80; each addl $5; under 6 free; lower rates rest of yr. Crib free. Pet accepted. TV; cable. Complimentary continental bkfst. Restaurant nearby. Ck-out 11 am. Meeting rm. Whirlpool, sauna. Cr cds: A, MC, V.
D 🔄 🖥️ 🐾

Lead

(C-1) *See also Belle Fourche, Deadwood, Rapid City, Spearfish, Sturgis*

Founded 1876 **Pop** 3,632 **Elev** 5,400 ft **Area code** 605 **Zip** 57754

Information Deadwood Area Chamber of Commerce and Visitors Bureau, 735 Historic Main St, Deadwood 57732; 605/578-1876 or 800/999-1876

Web www.deadwood.org

The chain of gold mines that began in Custer and spread through the Black Hills to Deadwood ended in Lead. The discovery of gold here in 1876 eventually led to the development of the Homestake Mine, one of the largest gold producers in this hemisphere. Lead is located on mountaintops with the Homestake Mine burrowing under the town.

What to See and Do

⭐ **Black Hills Mining Museum.** Exhibits trace development of mining in the Black Hills since 1876; incl guided tour of underground mine; gold panning; historic displays. (May-mid-Oct, daily) 323 W Main St. Phone 605/584-1605. ¢¢

Homestake Gold Mine Surface Tours. (since 1876) A one-hr tour of surface workings in an 8,000 ft mine; explanation of gold production. (May-Sept, daily; closed hols) 160 W Main St. Phone 605/584-3110. ¢¢

Ski Areas.

Deer Mountain. Triple chairlift, two Pomalifts; patrol, school, rentals; cafeteria, bar. X-country trails. Night skiing. Halfpipe for snowboards. Vertical drop 850 ft. (Nov-Mar, Wed-Sun; closed Dec 25) 3 mi S on US 85. Contact PO Box 622, Deadwood 57732. Phone 605/584-3230 or 888/410-3337.

Terry Peak. Two quads, two triple, two double chairlifts, Mitey-Mite; patrol, school, rentals; snowmaking; two chalets; snack bar, cafeteria, bar. Longest run 1¼ mi; vertical drop 1,052 ft. (Thanksgiv-

ing-Easter, daily) 3 mi SW on US 85, then N, in Black Hills National Forest. Phone 605/584-2165. ¢¢¢¢

Motels/Motor Lodges

⭐⭐ **GOLDEN HILLS INN.** *900 Miners Ave (57754). 605/584-1800; fax 605/584-3933; res 888/465-3080.* 100 rms, 5 story. S $89; D $99-$104; each addl $10; suites $185; under 18 free. Crib free. TV; cable (premium). Indoor pool; wading pool, whirlpool, lifeguard. Restaurant 6 am-1:30 pm, 5-10 pm. Bar 3 pm-2 am. Ck-out 11 am. Meeting rms. Business servs avail. Downhill/x-country ski 3 mi. Exercise rm; sauna. Refrigerator, wet bar; whirlpool in some suites. Cr cds: A, C, D, DS, JCB, MC, V.
🄳 ⚡ ✈ ☕ 🛂 ✕ ⛷ 🔥

⭐ **WHITE HOUSE INN.** *395 Glendale Dr (57754). 605/584-2000; toll-free 800/654-5323.* 71 rms, 4 story. June-Sept: S $60; D $70-$75; each addl $5; suites $90-$110; under 16 free; lower rates rest of yr. Crib free. TV; cable (premium). Complimentary continental bkfst. Restaurant nearby. Ck-out 11 am. Meeting rms. Whirlpool. Cr cds: A, D, DS, MC, V.
🄳 ⛷ 🔥

Madison

(D-8) *See also Brookings, Sioux Falls*

Founded 1875 **Pop** 6,257 **Elev** 1,670 ft **Area code** 605 **Zip** 57042

Information Greater Madison Chamber of Commerce, 315 S Egan St, PO Box 467; 605/256-2454

Web www.madison.sd.us

Madison, seat of Lake County, is the marketing, processing, and trade center for meat, grain, and dairy products and has some diversified industry. Madison is wellknown for its pheasant hunting as well as walleye fishing at many area lakes.

What to See and Do

Dakota State University. (1881) 1,400 students. Karl E. Mundt Library contains archives of the South Dakota senator. The Dakota Prairie

Playhouse offers varied entertainment; located off campus at 1205 N Washington Ave. Corner of Egan Ave and 8th St NE. Phone 605/256-5111. On campus is

Smith-Zimmermann State Museum. History of eastern South Dakota from 1860-1940. (Tues-Fri, daily) Phone 605/256-5308. **FREE**

Lake Herman State Park. 226 acres. Swimming, fishing, boating, canoeing; hiking, picnicking, playground. Interpretive program, children's activities. Camping (electrical hookups, dump station). Standard fees. 2 mi W off SD 34. Phone 605/256-5003.

Prairie Village. Replica of pioneer town; 40 restored buildings, antique tractors, autos; steam merry-go-round (1893) and three steam trains. (May-Sept, daily) Limited camping. 2 mi W on SD 34. Phone 605/256-3644. ¢¢

Special Events

Art in the Park. DSU campus. Late June.

Steam Threshing Jamboree. Prairie Village. Antique farm machinery; plowing; parades, arts and crafts display; steam merry-go-round, train rides. Last wkend Aug.

Fall Festival. Mid-Sept.

Motels/Motor Lodges

★ **LAKE PARK MOTEL.** *1515 NW 2nd St (57042). 605/256-3524; fax 605/256-4199.* 40 rms. S $35; D $40; each addl $5. Crib $7. Pet accepted, some restrictions. TV; cable (premium). Heated pool. Restaurant adj. Ck-out 11 am. X-country ski 1 mi. Some refrigerators. Cr cds: A, C, D, DS, MC, V.
[D][symbols]SC

★ **SUPER 8 OF MADISON.** *Jct of US 81 and SD 34 (57042). 605/256-6931. www.super8.com.* 34 rms, 2 story. S $39-$41; D $43-$47; each addl $3-$4; under 12 free. Crib free. Pet accepted. TV; cable. Restaurant adj 6 am-10 pm. Ck-out 11 am. Cr cds: A, C, D, DS, MC, V.
[D][symbols]

Milbank

(B-8) *See also Watertown*

Pop 3,879 **Elev** 1,150 ft
Area code 605 **Zip** 57252
Information Milbank Area Chamber of Commerce, 401 S Main; 605/432-6656 or 800/675-6656
Web www.visitmilbank

Milbank, the county seat of Grant County, is set in the Whetstone Valley, where granite production and the dairy industry figure prominently. Milbank is the birthplace of American Legion baseball, proposed here on July 17, 1925.

What to See and Do

Hartford Beach State Park. On 331 acres. Swimming, bathhouse, fishing, boating, canoeing; hiking, picnicking, playground, camping (fee; hookups, dump station). Standard fees. 15 mi N on SD 15. Phone 605/432-6374.

Old Windmill. (1882) Picturesque English-style gristmill (not operating), open to public. Operates as tourist information center May-Aug. E on US 12 near Milbank Insurance Co.

Special Event

Train Festival. Ride the rails on the Whetstone Valley Express. Second wkend Aug.

Motels/Motor Lodges

★★ **IMA MANOR MOTEL.** *US 12 E (57252). 605/432-4527; fax 605/432-4529; res 800/341-8000.* 30 rms, 1-2 story. S $34-$40; D $44-$52; each addl $4; under 16 free; higher rates Oct hunting season. Crib free. Pet accepted. TV. Indoor pool; whirlpool. Saunas. Restaurant 6 am-11 pm. Ck-out 11 am. Cr cds: A, C, D, DS, MC, V.
[symbols]SC

★ **LANTERN MOTEL.** *1010 S Dakota St (57252). 605/432-4591; fax 605/432-4806; toll-free 800/627-6075.* 30 rms. S $29-$32; D $33-$38; each addl $5; under 12 free. Crib $5. TV; cable (premium). Complimentary continental bkfst. Restaurant 5:30-10 pm.

Ck-out 11 am. X-country ski 1 mi. Sauna. Cr cds: A, D, DS, MC, V.

★ **SUPER 8.** *US 12 E (57252). 605/432-9288; res 800/800-8000. www.super8.com.* 39 rms, 2 story. S $38; D $50; each addl $3; under 12 free. Crib free. TV; cable (premium). Restaurant nearby. Ck-out 11 am. Meeting rm. Business servs avail. In-rm modem link. Cr cds: A, C, D, DS, MC, V.

Restaurant

★ **MILLSTONE FAMILY RESTAU-RANT.** *US 12 E and Hwy 77 (57252). 605/432-6866.* Hrs: 6 am-11 pm; Sun from 7 am. Closed Thanksgiving, Dec 25. Res accepted. Bkfst $2.50-$5, lunch $3.75-$5, dinner $4-$8. Sun brunch $5.95. Children's menu. Specializes in hamburgers. Salad bar. Cr cds: DS, MC, V.

Mission

(E-4) *See also Murdo, Winner*

Pop 730 **Elev** 2,581 ft **Area code** 605 **Zip** 57555

Information Rosebud Sioux Tribal Office, PO Box 430, Rosebud 57570; 605/747-2381

This is a trading center for the Rosebud Sioux Reservation.

What to See and Do

Buechel Memorial Lakota Museum. Lakota Sioux artifacts. (Late May-Sept, daily) 5 mi W on US 18, then 16 mi SW on Bureau of Indian Affairs Rd, in St. Francis. Phone 605/747-2745. FREE

Ghost Hawk Park. Swimming, fishing; picnicking, playground, camping (fee). (Mid-May-Sept, daily) 3 mi NW of Rosebud on Bureau of Indian Affairs Rd; on Little White River.

Rosebud. Powwows can be seen Sat, Sun nights during summer. Inquire for swimming, fishing, golf in area. HQ for Rosebud Reservation. 5 mi W

on US 18, then 8 mi SW on Bureau of Indian Affairs Rd. Phone 605/747-2381.

Special Event

Rosebud Sioux Tribal Fair and Pow-wow. In Rosebud. Dances, traditional buffalo dinner; arts and crafts exhibits. Late Aug.

Mitchell (D-7)

Founded 1879 **Pop** 13,798 **Elev** 1,293 ft **Area code** 605 **Zip** 57301

Information Chamber of Commerce, 601 N Main St, PO Box 1026; 605/996-5567 or 800/257-2676

Web www.cornpalace.org

This is a tree-shaded town in the James River valley, where agriculture is celebrated with a colorful, nine-day festival each September. The economy is based on agriculture, light industry, and tourism. Pheasant shooting attracts hunters from around the country.

What to See and Do

The Corn Palace. A huge building (seats 3,500), turreted, towered, dome-capped, flamboyantly Byzantine. Annually decorated, incl scenic murals, entirely in colored corn and grasses. Erected in 1892, the structure has been rebuilt twice. (May-Sept, daily; rest of yr, Mon-Fri; closed hols) 604 N Main St. Phone 800/257-2676. **FREE**

Enchanted World Doll Museum. More than 4,000 antique and modern dolls displayed in scenes from fairy tales and story books; dollhouses; accessories. (Apr-Nov, daily) 615 N Main. Phone 605/996-9896. ¢¢

Lake Mitchell. Swimming, fishing, boating (rentals); playground, grocery, camping (electrical and sewer hookups, fee). (Mid-Apr-late Oct) Main St and Lakeshore Dr, 1½ mi N on SD 37. Phone 605/995-4057.

Middle Border Museum of American Indian & Pioneer Life. Seven-building complex features Case Art Gallery; 1886 restored house, 1885 territorial school, 1900 railroad depot; pioneer life exhibits, horse-drawn vehicles, antique autos; American Indian Gallery; 1909 country church. (May-Sept, daily; rest of yr, by appt) 1311 S Duff St. Phone 605/996-2122. ¢¢

★ **Oscar Howe Art Center.** Former Carnegie Library Building (1902) housing permanent gallery with original paintings by Sioux artist Oscar Howe. Changing exhibits; summer exhibits focus on Native American art and culture. (Memorial Day-Labor Day, Mon-Sat; rest of yr, Tues-Sat, also by appt; closed hols) 119 W Third. Phone 605/996-4111.

Prehistoric Indian Village National Historic Landmark Archaeological Site. Ongoing study of 1,000-yr-old Native American village. Boehnen Memorial Museum; excavation and exhibits; guided tours; visitor center. (May-Oct, daily; rest of yr, by appt) 2 mi N via SD 37, exit 23rd Ave to Indian Village Rd, then N. Phone 605/996-5473. ¢¢

Soukup and Thomas International Balloon and Airship Museum. Exhibits detailing history of ballooning from 1700s to present; *Hindenburg* china, antiques. Video presentations. (Memorial Day-mid-Sept, daily; rest of yr, Mon,Tues, and Thurs-Sun, afternoons) 700 N Main St. Phone 605/996-2311.

Special Events

Corn Palace Stampede. Rodeo. Third wkend July.

Dakotafest. Third Tues-Thurs Aug.

Corn Palace Festival. Second or third wk Sept.

Motels/Motor Lodges

★ **ANTHONY MOTEL.** *1518 W Havens St (57301). 605/996-7518; fax 605/996-7251; toll-free 800/477-2235.* 34 rms. June-Sept: S $30-$45; D $42-$50; each addl $4; lower rates rest of yr. Crib free. TV; cable. Heated pool. Restaurant adj 6 am-midnight. Ck-out 11 am. Coin lndry. Meeting rm. Business servs avail. Free airport, bus depot transportation. Cr cds: A, MC, V.

★ **COACHLIGHT.** *1000 W Havens St (57301). 605/996-5686; fax 605/996-2798.* 20 rms. June-Oct: S $36; D $42; each addl $4; lower rates rest of yr. Crib free. Pet accepted. TV; cable. Restaurant nearby. Ck-out 11 am. Airport, bus depot transportation. X-country ski 1½ mi. Cr cds: A, DS, MC, V.

★ **COMFORT INN.** *1117 S Burr St (57301). 605/996-1333; fax 605/996-6022; res 800/228-5150. www.comfort*

Corn Palace, Mitchell

inn.com. 60 rms, 2 story. May-Oct: S $53-$58; D $68-$78; each addl $5; under 19 free; lower rates rest of yr. Crib $3. TV; cable. Indoor pool; whirlpool, sauna. Complimentary continental bkfst. Restaurant adj 6 am-11 pm. Ck-out 11 am. Coin lndry. Meeting rm. Cr cds: A, C, D, DS, ER, JCB, MC, V.

🄳 🖼 🔌 🔥

★ **DAYS INN.** *1506 S Burr St (57301). 605/996-6208; fax 605/996-5220; res 800/329-7466. www.daysinn.com.* 65 rms, 2 story. S $38-$50; D $50-$70; each addl $5; under 12 free. Crib free. TV; cable (premium). Indoor pool; whirlpool. Complimentary continental bkfst. Restaurant opp 6 am-11 pm. Ck-out 11 am. Meeting rm. Coin lndry. Cr cds: A, D, DS, MC, V.

🄳 🖼 🔌 🔥

★ **ECONO LODGE INN.** *1313 S Ohlman (57301). 605/996-6647; fax 605/996-7339; toll-free 800/283-4678. www.econolodge.com.* 44 rms, 2 story. S $38.95; D $46.95; each addl $6; under 12 free. TV; cable (premium). Restaurant nearby. Ck-out 11 am. Cr cds: A, C, D, DS, MC, V.

🔌 🔥 SC

★★ **HOLIDAY INN.** *1525 W Havens St (57301). 605/996-6501; fax 609/996-3228; toll-free 800/888-4702. www.holiday-inn.com.* 153 rms, 2 story. June-Oct: S $84-$94; D $89-$99; each addl $5; under 19 free; lower rates rest of yr. Crib free. Pet accepted. TV; cable. Indoor pool; wading pool, whirlpool, sauna, poolside serv. Restaurant 6 am-10 pm. Bar 11-2 am. Ck-out noon. Coin lndry. Meeting rms. Business servs avail. In-rm modem link. Bellhops. Free airport, bus depot transportation. Rec rm. Private patios, balconies. Cr cds: A, D, DS, MC, V.

🄳 🐾 🖼 🔌 🔥

★ **MOTEL 6.** *1309 S Ohlman St (57301). 605/996-0530; fax 605/995-2019. www.motel6.com.* 122 rms. Mid-June-mid-Sept: S $29.95; D $35.95; under 17 free; lower rates rest of yr. Crib free. Pet accepted. TV. Heated pool. Restaurant nearby. Ck-out noon. X-country ski 2 mi. Cr cds: A, C, D, DS, MC, V.

🐾 ⏩ 🖼 🔌 🔥

★ **SIESTA MOTEL.** *1210 W Havens (57301). 605/996-5544; fax 605/996-4946; toll-free 800/424-0537. www.siestamotel.com.* 23 rms. Memorial Day-Labor Day: S $38; D $38-$48; each addl $4; lower rates rest of yr. Crib free. Pet accepted. TV; cable. Pool. Restaurant nearby. Ck-out 10 am. Cr cds: A, MC, V.

🐾 🖼 🔌 🔥 SC

★ **SUPER 8 MOTEL.** *I-90 and US 37 (57301). 605/996-9678; fax 605/996-5339; toll-free 800/800-8000. www.super8.com.* 107 rms, 3 story. S $38.88; D $43.88-$48.88; each addl $2. Crib $3. TV; cable. Indoor/outdoor pool; whirlpool. Restaurant adj open 24 hrs. Ck-out 11 am. Business servs avail. In-rm modem link. X-country ski 1 mi. Some in-rm whirlpools. Cr cds: A, C, D, DS, MC, V.

🄳 ⏩ 🖼 🔌 🔥 SC

★★ **THUNDERBIRD LODGE.** *1601 S Burr St (57301). 605/996-6645; fax 605/995-5883.* 48 rms, 2 story. June-Nov: S $38; D $52; each addl $5; suites $68; lower rates rest of yr. Crib $5. TV; cable (premium). Restaurant adj open 24 hrs. Ck-out 11 am. Coin lndry. Meeting rm. Airport transportation. Whirlpool, sauna. Cr cds: A, DS, MC, V.

🄳 🔌 🔥

Restaurant

★★ **CHEF LOUIE'S.** *601 E Havens (57301). 605/996-7565.* Hrs: 11 am-11 pm; Sun Jun-Aug 10 am-8 pm. Closed hols. Bar to 2 am. Lunch $4.25-$5.95, dinner $6.95-$19.95. Specializes in steak, seafood. Cr cds: A, C, D, DS, MC, V.

🄳 ⏪

Mobridge (B-4)

Founded 1906 **Pop** 3,768 **Elev** 1,676 ft **Area code** 605 **Zip** 57601

Information Chamber of Commerce, 212 Main; 605/845-2387 or 888/614-3474

Web www.mobridge.org

The Milwaukee Railroad built a bridge across the Missouri River in

1906 at what was once the site of an Arikara and Sioux village. A telegraph operator used the contraction "Mobridge" to indicate his location. The name has remained the same. Today Mobridge is centered in farm and ranch country and is still home for a large Native American population. Located on the Oahe Reservoir, Mobridge is noted for its ample fishing and recreational activities.

What to See and Do

Klein Museum. Changing art exhibits; local pioneer artifacts and antiques; Sioux and Arikara artifacts; farm machinery collection; restored schoolhouse. (June-Aug, daily; Apr, May, Sept, Oct, Mon and Wed-Sun; closed Easter, Labor Day) 2 mi W on US 12. Phone 605/845-7243. ¢

Recreation Areas. Indian Creek. 2 mi E on US 12, then 1 mi S. **Indian Memorial.** 2 mi W off US 12. Both on Oahe Reservoir (see PIERRE). Swimming, bathhouse, boating (ramps, marinas), fishing; picnicking, playgrounds. Tent and trailer sites (Memorial Day-Labor Day; hookups, dump station; fee). Phone 605/845-2252.

Scherr Howe Arena. Colorful murals by Oscar Howe, a Dakota Sioux and art professor at University of South Dakota, depict history and ceremonies of Native Americans. (Mon-Sat; closed hols) Main St. Phone 605/845-3700. **FREE**

Sitting Bull Monument. Korczak Ziolkowski sculpted the bust for this monument. The burial ground on the hill affords beautiful view of Missouri River and surrounding country. 3 mi W on US 12, then 4 mi S on County 1806.

Motels/Motor Lodges

★ **SUPER 8 MOTEL.** *1301 Grand Crossing US 12 W (57601). 605/845-7215; fax 605/845-5270; toll-free 800/800-8000. www.super8.com.* 31 rms, 2 story. S $34.52; D $39.83. Crib free. TV; cable. Restaurant nearby. Ck-out 11 am. Cr cds: A, C, D, DS, MC, V.
🖼️ 🐾 **SC**

★★ **WRANGLER MOTOR INN.** *820 W Grand Crossing (57601). 605/845-3641; fax 605/845-3641; toll-free 888/315-BEST.* 61 rms, 1-2 story. S

$52; D $62; each addl $5; under 12 free. Crib $5. TV; cable. Indoor pool; whirlpool. Restaurant 6 am-10 pm. Bar. Ck-out 11 am. Meeting rms. Business servs avail. Exercise equipt; sauna. Game rm. Rec rm. Overlooks Lake Oahe. Cr cds: A, DS, MC, V.
🅓 🐾 🖼️ ♨ 🏊 🖼️ 🔥

Mount Rushmore National Memorial

See also Custer, Hill City, Keystone, Rapid City

(25 mi SW of Rapid City off US 16A and SD 244)

The faces of four great American presidents—Washington, Jefferson, Lincoln, and Theodore Roosevelt—stand out on a 5,675-foot mountain in the Black Hills of South Dakota, as grand and enduring as the contributions of the men they represent. Senator Peter Norbeck was instrumental in the realization of the monument. The original plan called for the presidents to be sculpted to the waist. It was a controversial project when sculptor Gutzon Borglum began his work on the carving in 1927. With crews often numbering 30 workers, he continued through 14 years of crisis and heartbreak and had almost finished by March, 1941, when he died. Lincoln Borglum, his son, brought the project to a close in October of that year. Today the memorial is host to almost three million visitors a year. To reach it, follow the signs south from I-90 on US 16. Then take US 16A through Keystone to SD 244 and the Memorial entrance. The orientation center, administrative and information headquarters, gift shop, and a snack bar (daily) are on the grounds; also Buffalo Room Cafeteria (see KEYSTONE). Evening program followed by sculpture lighting and other interpretive programs (mid-May-mid-September, daily). Sculptor's studio museum (summer). Phone 605/574-2523. Per vehicle ¢¢¢

Mount Rushmore National Memorial

Murdo (D-4)

Founded 1906 **Pop** 679 **Elev** 2,326 ft
Area code 605 **Zip** 57559

The old Fort Pierre-Custer stage route and one of the main routes of the old Texas Cattle Trail passed through the site where Murdo is now located. The town is named for pioneer cattleman Murdo McKenzie. Seat of Jones County, Murdo is still dominated by the cattle business. It is on the dividing line between Mountain and Central time.

Motel/Motor Lodge

★ ★ **BEST WESTERN GRAHAM'S.** *301 W 5th St, PO Box 78 (57559). 605/669-2441; fax 605/669-3139. www.bestwestern.com/grahams.* 45 rms. June-mid-Sept: S $46-$55; D $52-$78; lower rates rest of yr. Crib $2. TV; cable (premium). Heated pool. Playground. Restaurant nearby. Ck-out

11 am. Business servs avail. Cr cds: A, MC, V.
🅳 ☄ ⊠ 🔥 SC

Restaurant

★ **STAR.** *I-90 Business (57559). 605/669-2411.* Hrs: 7 am-10 pm. Closed Oct-early May. Bkfst $1.95-$5.50, lunch $3-$5.50, dinner $4.95-$16.75. Children's menu. Salad bar. Own pies. Family-owned. Cr cds: DS, MC, V.
⊠

Pierre (C-4)

Settled 1880 **Pop** 12,906 **Elev** 1,484 ft
Area code 605 **Zip** 57501

Information Chamber of Commerce, 800 W Dakota, PO Box 548; 605/224-7361 or 800/962-2034

Web www.pierre.org

Pierre (PEER) is the capital of South Dakota, an honor for which it campaigned hard and won, in part, because of its central location—the geographic center of the state. The town's prosperity was built by cattle ranchers from the west, farmers from the east, local businesspeople, and government officials.

What to See and Do

Cultural Heritage Center. Pioneer life, Native American, mining, and historic exhibits; the Verendrye Plate, a lead plate buried in 1743 at Fort Pierre by French explorers, the first known Europeans in South Dakota. (Daily; closed Jan 1, Thanksgiving, Dec 25) 900 Governors Dr. Phone 605/773-3458. ¢¢

Farm Island State Recreation Area. On 1,184 acres. Swimming, bathhouse, fishing, boating, canoeing; hiking, picnicking, playground. Interpretive program. Camping (electrical hookups, dump station). Visitor center (May-Sept, daily). Standard fees. 4 mi E off SD 34. Phone 605/224-5605.

Fighting Stallions Memorial. Replica of a carving by Korczak Ziolkowski honors Governor George S. Mickelson and seven others who died in an airplane crash in 1993.

Oahe Dam and Reservoir. This large earthfill dam (9,300 ft long, 245 ft high) is part of the Missouri River Basin project. Lobby with exhibits (Late May-early Sept, daily; rest of yr Mon-Fri; free). Recreation areas along reservoir offer waterskiing, fishing, boating; nature trails, picnicking. Primitive and improved camping (mid-May-mid-Sept; fee). 6 mi N on SD 1804, 1806. Phone 605/224-5862.

South Dakota Discovery Center and Aquarium. Hands-on science and technology exhibits; aquarium features native fish. (Daily, afternoons) 805 W Sioux Ave. Phone 605/224-8295. ¢¢

State Capitol. Built of Bedford limestone, local boulder granite, and marble. Guided tours (Mon-Fri). Capitol Ave E. Phone 605/773-3765. **FREE** Adj is

Flaming Fountain. The artesian well that feeds this fountain has a natural sulphur content so high that the waters can be lit. The fountain serves as a memorial to war veterans. On the northwest shore of Capitol Lake.

State National Guard Museum. Historical guard memorabilia. (Mon, Wed, Fri afternoons) 303 E Dakota. Phone 605/224-9991.

Motels/Motor Lodges

★ **CAPITOL INN & SUITES.** *815 E Wells Ave (57501). 605/224-6387; fax 605/224-8083; toll-free 800/658-3055.* 83 rms, 2 story. S $26.95; D $35.95-$41.95; each addl $3; suites $58-$76. Crib free. Pet accepted. TV; cable. Pool. Restaurant nearby. Ck-out 11 am. Business servs avail. Some refrigerators. Balconies. Cr cds: A, DS, MC, V.
🄳 🐾 🖼 🆚 🔥

★ **DAYS INN.** *520 W Sioux Blvd (57501). 605/224-0411. www.daysinn. com.* 79 rms, 2 story. S $45-$55; D $55-$65; each addl $5. Crib free. TV; cable. Complimentary continental bkfst. Restaurant nearby. Ck-out 11 am. Business servs avail. X-country ski 1 mi. Cr cds: A, C, D, DS, MC, V.
🄳 📺 🆚 🔥 🆂🅲

★★ **KINGS INN HOTEL AND CONVENTION CENTER.** *220 S Pierre St (57501). 605/224-5951; fax 605/224-5301; toll-free 800/232-1112.* 104 rms, 2 story. S $44; D $49-$52; each addl $5; under 12 free. Crib free. Pet accepted. TV; cable. Restaurant 6 am-11 pm. Bar 11-2 am. Ck-out noon. Business servs avail. Sundries. X-country ski 1 mi. Whirlpool, sauna. Some refrigerators. Cr cds: A, D, DS, MC, V.
🐾 📺 ✈️ 🆚 🔥

★★ **RAMKOTA HOTEL.** *920 W Sioux Ave (57501). 605/224-6877; fax 605/224-1042. www.ramkotahotel.com.* 151 rms, 2 story. S $69; D $79; each addl $6; suites $150; under 17 free. Crib avail. Pet accepted. TV; cable. Indoor pool; wading pool, whirlpool. Restaurant 6 am-10 pm. Bar. Ck-out noon. Coin lndry. Meeting rms. Business servs avail. Bellhops. Valet serv. Free airport, railroad station, bus depot transportation. Exercise equipt; sauna. Game rm. Some refrigerators. Balconies. At Missouri River. Cr cds: A, C, D, DS, ER, MC, V.
🄳 🐾 🛝 🖼 🏃 ✈️ 🆚 🔥

★ **SUPER 8.** *320 W Sioux Ave (57501). 605/224-1617; fax 605/224-1617; res 800/800-8000. www.super8. com.* 78 rms, 3 story. S $39.98; D $45.98. Crib free. Pet accepted. TV; cable (premium), VCR avail. Restaurant adj open 24 hrs. Ck-out 11 am. Cr cds: A, C, D, DS, MC, V.

⬛ 🔌 🏃 ✕ 🔲 🔥

Restaurant

★ **KOZY KORNER.** *217 E Dakota (57501).* 605/224-9547. Hrs: 5 am-10 pm; winter from 6 am. Closed Dec 25. Res accepted. Bkfst $2.50-$5.75, lunch $3.35-$5.25, dinner $3.95-$8.95. Specializes in steak, seafood, soup. Salad bar. Own pies. Artwork displayed.

⬛ 🔲

Pine Ridge

(E-2) *See also Badlands National Park, Hot Springs; also see Chadron, NE*

Pop 2,596 **Elev** 3,232 ft
Area code 605 **Zip** 57770

This is the administrative center for the Oglala Sioux nation at the Pine Ridge Indian Reservation.

What to See and Do

Red Cloud Indian School Heritage Art Museum. Features works by various Native American tribes. (June-Aug, daily; rest of yr, Mon-Fri) Holy Rosary Mission, 4 mi W on US 18. Phone 605/867-5491. **FREE**

■ **Wounded Knee Historical Site.** Grounds where, on Dec 29, 1890, almost 150 Minniconjou Sioux, incl women and children, were shot by the US Army. A monument marks their mass grave. 8 mi E on US 18, then 7 mi N on unnumbered paved road to Wounded Knee.

Special Event

Oglala Nation Fair and Rodeo. Powwow and dance contest with participants from 30 tribes; displays; activities. Phone 605/867-5821. Early Aug.

Platte (E-6)

Settled 1882 **Pop** 1,311 **Elev** 1,612 ft
Area code 605 **Zip** 57369

Settled by immigrants from the Netherlands, Platte has a strategic location at the end of a railroad line.

What to See and Do

Fort Randall Dam-Lake Francis Case. Part of the Missouri River Basin project, Fort Randall Dam is 10,700 ft long and 165 ft high. Powerhouse guided tours (Memorial Day-Labor Day, daily). Many recreation areas along reservoir have swimming, fishing, boating; picnicking, camping (May-Oct; fee, electricity addl). The project also incl the former site of Fort Randall just below the dam. 7 mi E on SD 44, then 24 mi S on SD 50, then 6 mi S on US 18, 281, in Pickstown. Contact Lake Manager, PO Box 199, Pickstown 57367; Phone 605/487-7847.

Platte Creek State Recreation Area. On 190 acres. Fishing, boating (ramp), canoeing; picnicking, camping (electrical hookups, dump station). Standard fees. 8 mi W on SD 44, then 6 mi S on SD 1804. Phone 605/337-2587.

Snake Creek State Recreation Area. On 735 acres. Swimming, bathhouse; fishing; boating (ramp), canoeing. Picnicking, concession. Camping (electrical hookups, dump station). Standard fees. 14 mi W off SD 44. Phone 605/337-2587.

Motels/Motor Lodges

★ **DAKOTA COUNTRY INN.** *821 E 7th St (SD 44 E) (57369). 605/337-2607; fax 605/337-9933; toll-free 800/336-2607.* 30 rms. S $39-$42; D $48-$52; each addl $3; higher rates pheasant season. Crib $2. TV; cable (premium). Complimentary continental bkfst, coffee in lobby. Restaurant nearby. Ck-out 11 am. Business servs avail. In-rm modem link. Cr cds: A, DS, MC, V.

⬛ 🔲 🔲 🔲 🔲

★ **KINGS INN OF PLATTE.** *221 E 7th St (57369). 605/337-3385; toll-free 800/337-7756.* 34 rms. S $24-$28; D

$31.95-$35.95. Crib $3. Pet accepted. TV; cable. Playground. Complimentary continental bkfst. Restaurant nearby. Ck-out 10 am. Cr cds: A, DS, MC, V.

Rapid City

(D-2) *See also Hill City, Keystone, Sturgis*

Founded 1876 **Pop** 54,523 **Elev** 3,247 ft **Area code** 605

Information Convention and Visitors Bureau, 444 Mount Rushmore Rd N, PO Box 747, 57709; 605/343-1744 or 800/487-3223

Web www.rapidcitycvb.com

In the last few decades tourism has replaced gold mining as one of the chief industries of Rapid City. Founded only two years after gold was discovered in the Black Hills, Rapid City is a boomtown that came to stay. It is the seat of Pennington County, second-largest city in South Dakota, and home of Ellsworth Air Force Base. There is a substantial industrial life based on mining, lumbering, and agriculture. The Pactola Ranger District office of the Black Hills National Forest (see BLACK HILLS) is located in Rapid City.

What to See and Do

Bear Country USA. Drive-through wildlife park with bears, mountain lions, wolves, elk, deer, buffalo, antelope, bighorn sheep, Rocky Mountain goats, and moose. (Late May-mid-Oct, daily) 8 mi S via US 16. Phone 605/343-2290. ¢¢¢¢

Black Hills Caverns. Series of chambers connected by a fissure 160 ft high at some points; many types of formations, incl amethyst and boxwork. Three different tours. (May 1-Oct 15, daily) 4 mi W on SD 44. Phone 605/343-0542. ¢¢

Black Hills Petrified Forest. Incl interpretive film on the Black Hills geology and petrifaction process; five-blk walk through area of logs ranging from 5 ft-100 ft in length and up to 3 ft in diameter and stumps 3 ft-5 ft in height. Guided tours. Rock, fossil, and mineral museum; gift and rock/lapidary shops. (Memorial Day-Labor Day, daily; weather permitting) Campground nearby. 11 mi NW on I-90, exit 46, then 1 mi E on Elk Creek Rd. Phone 605/787-4560. ¢¢

Black Hills Reptile Gardens. Incl reptile exhibit, alligator show, birds-of-prey show, snake lecture, jungle orchid trail. Children may ride giant tortoises and miniature horses. (Apr-Oct, daily) 6 mi S on US 16. Phone 605/342-5873. ¢¢

Chapel in the Hills. Replica of 12th-century Borgund Stavkirke. Vespers during summer months. SW off Jackson Blvd. Phone 605/342-8281.

Chuckwagon Suppers and Western Shows.

Circle B. Also covered wagon ride, shoot-outs. Supper (Early June-Labor Day, daily; res required). 15 mi W via SD 44, then 1 mi N on US 385. Phone 605/348-7358. ¢¢¢¢

Flying T Chuckwagon. Supper and show (Late May-mid-Sept, daily). Res suggested. 6 mi S via US 16; adj to Reptile Gardens. Phone 605/342-1905. ¢¢¢¢

Crystal Cave Park. Park with nature trail leading to replica of Native American village, petrified garden, rock and mineral display, and cave; picnic grounds. (Mid-May-Sept, daily) 3 mi W via SD 44. Phone 605/342-8008. ¢¢

Dahl Fine Arts Center. Visual arts center with three galleries. Mural Gallery with 200-ft cyclorama depicting 200 yrs of US history; narration. Two regional artists' galleries. (Daily; closed hols) 713 7th St. Phone 605/394-4101. **FREE**

Dinosaur Park. Life-size steel and cement models of dinosaurs once numerous in the area. (Daily) W on Quincy St to Skyline Dr. Phone 605/343-8687. **FREE**

Gray Line Sightseeing Tours. Trips to Black Hills and Badlands. Phone 605/342-4461.

🌟 **The Journey.** This important historical center utilizes state-of-the-art technology to reveal the geography, people, and historical events that shaped the history of the Black Hills. Fully interactive exhibits take visitors back in time to discover the land as

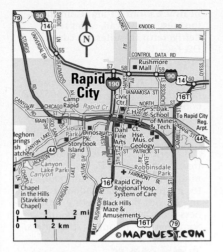

it was 2½ billion yrs ago and trace its development to today. Home to five substantial collections of artifacts, memorabilia, and specimens from the area. Gallery features traveling exhibits and is workplace for artists and craftspeople. Museum store. (Daily) Third and New York sts. Phone 605/394-6923.

✪ **Mount Rushmore National Memorial.** (see) 25 mi SW off US 16A.

Sitting Bull Crystal Cave. Believed to be only dogtooth spar cave in North America; fossils of sea life embedded in walls. (Mid-May-mid-Oct, daily) 9 mi S on US 16. Phone 605/342-2777. ¢¢¢

South Dakota School of Mines and Technology. (1885) 2,358 students. Computer and scanning electron microscope laboratories. St Joseph St. On campus is

Museum of Geology. Exceptional display of minerals, fossils, gold samples, and other geological material; first tyrannosaurus rex skull found in SD. (Mon-Sat, Sun afternoons; closed hols) O'Harra Memorial Building. Phone 605/394-2467. **FREE**

Stagecoach West. Lecture tours to Mt Rushmore, Custer State Park, Crazy Horse Memorial, Black Hills. (June-Sept, daily) Contact PO Box 264, 57709. Phone 605/343-3113. ¢¢¢¢

Storybook Island. Fairyland park illustrating children's stories and rhymes; outdoor settings with music and animation. (Memorial Day-Labor Day, daily, weather permitting) Sheridan Lake Rd, 2 mi SW. Phone 605/342-6357. **FREE**

Thunderhead Underground Falls. One of the oldest (1878) gold mining tunnels in Black Hills area; stalactites and gold-bearing granite formations. Falls are 600 ft inside mine. (May-Oct, daily) 10 mi W via SD 44. Phone 605/343-0081. ¢¢

Special Events

Black Hills Powwow and Art Expo. Early July.

Central States Fair. Rodeo, carnival, horse and tractor pulls, auto races, demolition derby. Mid-Aug.

Motels/Motor Lodges

★★ **AMERICINN MOTEL AND SUITES.** *1632 Rapp St (57701). 605/343-8424; fax 605/343-2220; res 800/634-3444. www.americinn.com.* 64 rms, 3 story, 12 suites. Mid-May-Aug: S $99; D $109; each addl $10; under 13 free; higher rates special events; lower rates rest of yr. TV; cable (premium). Complimentary continental bkfst. Restaurant opp open 24 hrs. Ck-out 11 am. Meeting rms. Business servs avail. In-rm modem link. Bellhops. Coin lndry. Indoor pool; whirlpool. Some in-rm whirlpools; refrigerator, microwave in suites. Cr cds: A, D, DS, MC, V.
D ⊵ ⊠ ⚒ SC

★★ **BEST WESTERN RAMKOTA.** *2111 N Lacrosse St (57701). 605/343-8550; fax 605/343-9107; res 800/528-1234. www.bestwestern.com.* 272 rms, 2 story. June-Aug: S $89; D $99; each addl $10; suites $150; under 18 free; lower rates rest of yr. Crib free. TV; cable. Indoor/outdoor pool; whirlpool, poolside serv. Playground. Restaurant 6 am-11 pm. Bar 11-2 am, Sun 1 pm-midnight; entertainment Mon-Sat. Ck-out noon. Coin lndry. Meeting rms. Business servs avail. Sundries. Airport, bus depot transportation. Exercise equipt; sauna, steam rm. Some refrigerators. Private patios, balconies. Cr cds: A, D, DS, MC, V.
D ⊵ 🛉 ⊠ ⚒ 🖷

★★ **BEST WESTERN TOWN & COUNTRY.** *2505 Mt Rushmore Rd (57701). 605/343-5383; fax 605/343-*

9670; toll-free 800/666-5383. www. bestwestern.com. 100 rms, 1-2 story. June-mid-Aug: S $85; D $85-$95; each addl $5; under 12 free; lower rates rest of yr. Crib $5. TV; cable. 2 pools, 1 indoor. Playground. Coffee in rms. Restaurant 7 am-9 pm. Ck-out 11 am. Free airport transportation. Some refrigerators, microwaves. Cr cds: A, MC, V.

⊠ ≋ 🏂 **SC**

★ **COMFORT INN.** *1550 N Lacrosse St (57701). 605/348-2221; fax 605/348-3110. www.comfortinn.com.* 72 rms, 2 story. June-Aug: S, D $69-$159; each addl $10; under 18 free; higher rates Rally Week; lower rates rest of yr. Crib $8. TV; cable. Indoor pool; whirlpool. Restaurant adj 7 am-10 pm. Ck-out 11 am. Game rm. Cr cds: A, D, DS, MC, V.

D ≋ 🏂 🔥

★ **DAYS INN.** *1570 Rapp St (57701). 605/348-8410; fax 605/348-3392; res 800/329-7466. www.daysinn.com.* 77 rms, 2 story, 16 suites. Mid-June-Aug: S $45-$99; D $69-$119; each addl $10; suites $109-$169; under 18 free; higher rates Sturgis Bike Rally; lower rates rest of yr. Crib free. TV; cable (premium), VCR avail (movies). Indoor pool; whirlpool. Complimentary continental bkfst. Restaurant adj 6 am-10 pm. Ck-out 11 am. Coin lndry. Meeting rms. Business servs avail. In-rm modem link. Bellhops. Valet serv. Sundries. Exercise equipt. Game rm. Refrigerator, microwave in suites. Cr cds: A, D, DS, MC, V.

D ≋ 🕴 🏂 🔥 **SC**

★ **FAIR VALUE INN.** *1607 N Lacrosse St (57701). 605/342-8118; toll-free 800/954-8118.* 25 rms, 2 story. June-Aug: S, D $65; each addl $3; higher rates motorcycle rally; lower rates rest of yr. Crib $3. TV; cable (premium). Restaurant adj open 24 hrs. Ck-out 11 am. Cr cds: A, C, D, DS, MC, V.

D 🏂 🔥 **SC**

★★ **HOLIDAY INN.** *750 Cathedral Dr (57701). 605/341-9300; fax 605/341-9333; res 800/465-4329. www.holiday-inn.com.* 63 rms, 3 story. June-mid-Sept: S, D $104; under 18 free; lower rates rest of yr. Crib free. TV; cable (premium). Indoor pool; whirlpool. Complimentary continental bkfst. Coffee in rms. Restaurant

nearby. Ck-out 11 am. Coin lndry. Business servs avail. Valet serv. Refrigerator in suites. Cr cds: A, C, D, DS, MC, V.

D ≋ 🏂 🔥

★ **RAMADA INN.** *1721 Lacrosse St (57701). 605/342-1300; fax 605/342-0663; res 800/272-6232. www.ramada.com.* 139 rms, 4 story. June-Aug: S $114; D $129; each addl $10; suites $150; under 18 free; higher rates special events; lower rates rest of yr. Crib free. Pet accepted. TV; cable (premium). Indoor pool; whirlpool. Coffee in rm. Restaurant adj. Bar 7-12:30 am. Ck-out noon. Meeting rms. Business servs avail. Bellhops. Game rm. Some bathrm phones, refrigerators. Cr cds: A, MC, V.

D 🐾 ≋ 🏂 🔥 **SC**

★ **SUPER 8.** *2124 N Lacrosse St (57701). 605/348-8070; fax 605/348-0833. www.super8.com.* 119 rms, 3 story. No elvtr. June-Aug: S $77; D $87; lower rates rest of yr. Crib free. Pet accepted. TV; cable (premium), VCR avail (movies). Complimentary coffee in lobby. Restaurant adj open 24 hrs. Ck-out 11 am. Sundries. Game rm. Cr cds: A, C, D, DS, MC, V.

D 🐾 🏂 🔥

★ **TRAVELODGE.** *620 Howard St (57701). 605/343-5434; fax 605/343-7085; toll-free 800/456-0061. www.travelodge.com.* 98 rms, 2 story. July-mid-Aug: S $69; D $69-$89; each addl $8; under 18 free; lower rates rest of yr. Crib $3. TV; cable, VCR avail (movies $6). Pool. Complimentary continental bkfst, coffee in rms. Restaurant adj 11 am-10 pm. Ck-out 11 am. Cr cds: A, D, DS, MC, V.

D ≋ 🏂 🔥

Hotels

★★ **ALEX JOHNSON.** *523 6th St (57701). 605/342-1210; toll-free 800/888-2539. www.alexjohnson.com.* 143 rms, 6 story, 25 suites. June-Sept: S $98; D $102-$110; each addl $10; suites $115-$250; under 18 free; wkly, wkend, hol rates; lower rates rest of yr. Crib free. TV; cable. Restaurant 5:30 am-10 pm. Bar noon-2 am; entertainment Fri, Sat. Ck-out 11 am. Meeting rms. Concierge. Gift shop. Airport transportation. Refrigerators in suites. Renovated historic hotel (1928) pairing European and Native

American decor. Cr cds: A, D, DS, MC, V.

⬜ 🔲 🔲

★★ **HOLIDAY INN.** *505 N 5th St (57701). 605/348-4000; fax 605/348-9777. www.holiday-inn.com.* 205 rms, 8 story, 48 suites. S, D $108-$115; suites $125-$250; under 18 free. Crib free. TV; cable (premium). Indoor pool; whirlpool, poolside serv. Restaurant 6 am-10 pm. Bar 11-midnight. Ck-out noon. Convention facilities. Gift shop. Free airport, railroad station, bus depot transportation. Exercise equipt; sauna. Refrigerator, wet bar in some suites. Next to Rushmore Plaza Civic Center. Cr cds: A, D, DS, MC, V.

⬜ 🔲 🔲 🔲 🔲

★★ **RADISSON HOTEL-MOUNT RUSHMORE.** *445 Mt Rushmore Rd (57701). 605/348-8300; fax 605/348-3833; toll-free 800/333-3333. www.radissonrapidcity.com.* 176 rms, 9 story. Mid-May-Sept: S, D $89-$114; each addl $10; suites $125; under 18 free; family rates; higher rates special events; lower rates rest of yr. Crib free. TV; cable (premium). Complimentary coffee in rms. Restaurant 6 am-10 pm. Bar 3 pm-2 am; entertainment Fri-Sun. Ck-out noon. Meeting rms. Business center. Concierge. Gift shop. Beauty shop. Free airport transportation. Exercise equipt. Indoor pool; whirlpool. Game rm. Some refrigerators, microwaves. Cr cds: A, C, D, DS, ER, JCB, MC, V.

⬜ 🔲 🔲 🔲 🔲 🔲 🔲 🔲 🔲

B&B/Small Inn

★★ **ABEND HAUS COTTAGES & AUDRIE'S BED & BREAKFAST.** *23029 Thunderhead Falls Rd (57702). 605/342-7788. www.audriesbb.com.* 10 rms, all with shower only, 1-2 story, 4 cottages, 6 suites. No rm phones. S $95-$175; D $145-295; each addl $15; suites $95. Adults only. TV; cable, VCR (movies). Complimentary continental bkfst, coffee in rms. Restaurant nearby. Ck-out 11 am, ck-in 4-9 pm. Luggage handling. Gift shop. Refrigerators, microwaves; some fireplaces. European antiques. Totally nonsmoking.

🔲 🔲 🔲

Restaurants

★ **FIREHOUSE BREWING CO.** *610 Main St (57701). 605/348-1915. www.firehousebrewing.com.* Hrs: 11-2 am; Sun 4-10 pm. Closed Easter, Thanksgiving, Dec 25. Res accepted. Bar. Lunch $3.95-$7.50, dinner $6.95-$13.95. Children's menu. Specialties: Cajun gumbo, beef brisket, buffalo steaks. Outdoor dining. In 1915 firehouse; microbrewery. Cr cds: A, D, DS, MC, V.

⬜ 🔲

★★ **GREAT WALL.** *315 E North St (57701). 605/348-1060.* Hrs: 11 am-10 pm; Fri, Sat to 10:30 pm. Closed Thanksgiving, Dec 24, 25. Res accepted. Chinese menu. Wine, beer. Lunch $4.50-$6.95, dinner $5.75-$9.95. Children's menu. Specialties: Hunan-style orange chicken, Mandarin-style sesame beef. Chinese decor. Cr cds: A, D, DS, MC, V.

🔲

★★ **IMPERIAL.** *702 E North St (57701). 605/394-8888.* Hrs: 11 am-10 pm. Res accepted. Chinese menu. Bar. Lunch $4.50-$6.95, dinner $6.50-$9.50. Children's menu. Specialties: pineapple chicken, tangerine beef, General Tao's Hunan-style chicken. Parking. Contemporary Chinese decor. Cr cds: A, D, DS, MC, V.

⬜ 🔲

Unrated Dining Spot

FLYING T. CHUCKWAGON SUPPER & SHOW. *8971 S SD 16 (57702). 605/342-1905. www.flyingt.com.* Hrs: one sitting at 7:30 pm. Closed mid-Sept-late May. Res accepted. Beer. Complete meals: dinner and show $12; age 4-10, $5. Western dinner of barbecue beef, baked potato, beans. Cr cds: MC, V.

⬜

Redfield

(C-6) *See also Aberdeen*

Pop 2,770 **Elev** 1,303 ft
Area code 605 **Zip** 57469
Information Chamber of Commerce, 626 N Main St; 605/472-0965

Web www.nsu-cc.northern.edu/red-field

What to See and Do

Fisher Grove State Park. On 277 acres. Fishing, boating, canoeing; hiking, golf, picnicking, playground. Interpretive program. Camping (electrical hookups, dump station). Standard fees. 7 mi E on US 212. Phone 605/472-1212.

Spink County Historical Memorial Museum. Early-day furniture, household items, tools, machinery; collections of mounted birds, butterflies, other insects. (June-Aug, daily) SE corner of Courthouse Sq. Phone 605/472-0758. ¢

Motels/Motor Lodges

★ **SUPER 8.** 824 W 4th St (57469). 605/472-0720; fax 605/472-0855; res 800/800-8000. www.super8.com. 27 rms, 2 story. S $31.88; D $36.88; each addl $3; under 12 free. Crib avail. TV; cable. Restaurant nearby. Ck-out 11 am. Cr cds: A, C, D, DS, JCB, MC, V.
🄳 ⚡ 🐾 ⛽

★ **WILSON MOTOR INN.** 1109 E 7th Ave (57469). 605/472-0550; toll-free 800/690-0551. 24 rms. S $24-$30; D $30-$40; each addl $4; higher rates special events. Crib $2.50. TV; cable. Ck-out 11 am. Cr cds: DS, MC, V.
⛽ 🐾

Sioux Falls (D-8)

Founded 1856 **Pop** 100,814
Elev 1,442 ft **Area code** 605
Information Chamber of Commerce and Convention and Visitors Bureau, 200 N Phillips Ave, Suite 102; 57101; 605/336-1620 or 800/333-2072
Web www.siouxfalls.org

At the falls of the Sioux River, this city has been developing at a constant pace since it was reestablished in 1865, having been abandoned in 1862 after threats of a Lakota attack. Its prosperity is based on diversified industry and farming. Cattle are shipped from a three-state area, slaughtered and packed here, then shipped east. Manufactured goods from the east are distributed throughout much of South Dakota from Sioux Falls.

Jean Nicolet saw the falls here in 1839 and described them impressively. The Dakota Land Company of Minnesota (1856) and the Western Town Company (1857) of Dubuque set out to develop the area and apparently worked together successfully. In September, 1858, the thirty-odd residents elected members to a Territorial Legislature, casting (it is said) votes for all their relatives as well as for themselves. On July 2, 1859, the first Sioux Falls newspaper, the *Democrat*, appeared.

Sioux Falls is the center for EROS (Earth Resources Observation Systems), an international center for space and aircraft photography of the Earth.

What to See and Do

Augustana College. (1860) 2,100 students. Gilbert Science Center with Foucault pendulum, miniature dioramas of state wildlife. Center for Western Studies has museum and archival center on Western heritage. Art exhibits. Replica of Michelangelo's statue of Moses is on campus. Tours. 29th St and Summit Ave. Phone 605/336-5516.

EROS (Earth Resources Observation Systems). Data Center of Department of the Interior aids in research and development of land and natural resource management. Houses millions of frames of satellite and aircraft photography of Earth. Visitor center containing audiovisual displays (Mon-Fri; closed federal hols); other buildings not open to public. NE off I-90 on County Rd 121. Phone 605/594-6511. **FREE**

Sherman Park. Formal flower garden, ballfields, picnicking. Kiwanis Ave from 12th to 22nd sts. Also here are

Delbridge Museum of Natural History. Displays of five climatic eco-zones; more than 150 mounted animals; hands-on exhibits. (Daily) Phone 605/367-7003.

Great Plains Zoo. More than 300 reptiles, birds, and mammals from around the world; penguin exhibit; children's zoo. (Daily) 805 S Kiwanis Ave. Phone 605/367-7003. ¢¢

■ **Siouxland Heritage Museums.** Unified museum system comprised of two sites:

Old Courthouse Museum. Restored Richardsonian-Romanesque quartzite stone courthouse (1890) contains exhibits of Siouxland history, special exhibits on local culture. (Daily; closed hols) 200 W 6th St. Phone 605/367-4210. **FREE**

Pettigrew Home and Museum. Restored Queen Anne historic house (1889) furnished to show life of state's first senator; galleries of Native American items and cultural history of the Siouxland. (Daily; closed hols) 8th St and Duluth Ave. Phone 605/367-7097. **FREE**

University of Sioux Falls. (1883) 900 students. Has Lorene B. Burns Indian Collection and Lucy Borneman Chinese Collection (Academic yr, daily; summer, Mon-Fri; closed school vacations). The historic Yankton Trail crossed this area; marker indicates the site. 22nd St and Prairie Ave. Phone 605/331-5000.

USS South Dakota Battleship Memorial. Memorial has the same dimensions as the battleship and is bordered by the ship's lifeline stanchions. Museum houses WWII mementos. (Memorial Day-Labor Day, daily) W 12th St and Kiwanis Ave. Phone 605/367-7060.

Motels/Motor Lodges

★★ **AMERICINN.** 3508 S Gateway Blvd (57106). 605/361-3538; toll-free 800/634-3444. www.americinn.com. 65 rms, 2 story. June-Aug: S $54-$57; D $58-$67; suites $78-$111; under 12 free; lower rates rest of yr. Crib free. TV; cable (premium). Indoor pool; whirlpool. Complimentary continental bkfst. Restaurant adj open 24 hrs. Ck-out 11 am. Meeting rms. Business servs avail. X-country ski 10 mi. Cr cds: A, MC, V.
🏊 🖾 🖾 🔥 SC

★★ **BAYMONT INN.** 3200 S Meadow Ave (57106). 605/362-0835; fax 605/362-0836; res 800/301-0200. www.baymontinns.com. 82 rms, 3 story. Late-May-Sept: S $46.99-$59.99; D $56.99-$69.99; suites $70.99-$84.99; under 18 free; lower rates rest of yr.

Crib free. Pet accepted. TV; cable (premium). Indoor pool; whirlpool. Complimentary coffee in rms. Restaurant adj open 24 hrs. Ck-out 11 am. Meeting rms. X-country ski 2 mi. Some refrigerators. Cr cds: A, D, DS, MC, V.
D 🖘 🖾 🖾 🖾 🔥

★★ **BEST WESTERN RAMKOTA HOTEL.** 2400 N Louise Ave (57107). 605/336-0650; fax 605/336-1687; toll-free 800/528-1234. www.ramkota.com. 226 rms, 2 story. S, D $69-$109; each addl $8; suites $140-$229; under 18 free. Crib free. Pet accepted. TV; cable (premium), VCR avail. 2 pools, 1 indoor; whirlpool, sauna. Playground. Restaurant 6 am-10 pm. Bar 11-2 am. Ck-out 11 am. Coin lndry. Convention facilities. Business servs avail. Bellhops. Valet serv. Sundries. Free airport, bus depot transportation. X-country ski 2 mi. Game rm. Rec rm. Cr cds: A, D, DS, MC, V.
D 🖘 🖾 🖾 🗶 🖾 🔥

★ **BUDGET HOST INN.** 2620 E 10th St (57103). 605/336-1550; fax 605/338-4752; res 888/336-1550. 35 rms. June-Sept: S $39-$46; D $49-$55; each addl $6; under 12 free; lower rates rest of yr. Crib free. Pet accepted, some restricitons. TV; cable. Restaurant adj open 24 hrs. Ck-out 11 am. Meeting rm. Cr cds: A, D, DS, MC, V.
🖘 🖾 🖾 🔥

★ **COMFORT INN SOUTH.** 3216 S Carolyn Ave (57106). 605/361-2822; toll-free 800/638-7949. www.comfortinn.com. 67 rms, 2 story. Mid-May-mid-Sept: S $45.95-$65.95; D $50.95-$75.95; each addl $5; under 18 free; lower rates rest of yr. Crib free. Pet accepted. TV; cable (premium). Indoor pool; whirlpool. Complimentary continental bkfst. Restaurant adj open 24 hrs. Ck-out 11 am. Meeting rms. Game rm. Some refrigerators. Cr cds: A, C, D, DS, ER, JCB, MC, V.
D 🖘 🖾 🖾 🔥 SC

★★ **COMFORT SUITES.** 3208 Carolyn Ave (57106). 605/362-9711; res 800/228-5150. www.comfortinn.com. 61 rms, 3 story. Mid-May-mid-Sept: S $59.95-$79.95; D $63.95-$89.95; each addl $5; under 18 free; lower rates rest of yr. Crib free. Pet accepted. TV; cable (premium). Indoor pool; whirlpool. Complimen-

A CITY OF PARKS

Sioux Falls has a handsome Victorian town center accented with progressive cultural institutions; with over 60 parks, it's a walker's dream. No wonder the community repeatedly leads many surveys of most livable small cities in the nation. Begin a walking tour at the Falls Park Visitor Information Center, near the corner of Phillips and 6th Avenue. From the center's observation tower, take in views of the town and its namesake waterfalls.

Falls Park contains a number of attractions, including terraced rock formations over which the Big Sioux River tumbles in a series of waterfalls. Trails lead to the falls and to picnic areas scattered around the park; at night, light programs play across the falls. At the north end of the park is the Horse Barn Arts Center, an artists cooperative housed in an old stone barn. The second-floor gallery features exhibits of local artists and crafters.

Continue south on Phillips Avenue, past the Sioux Falls Brewing Company (431 North Phillips Avenue), which is housed in a classic stone-and-brick storefront, to 6th Street. West on 6th lies the modern downtown core of Sioux Falls, plus the city's Historic District. The Old Courthouse Museum, at 6th Street and Main Avenue, is a grand structure built of local quartzite that now serves as a historical museum, activity center for kids, and gift shop featuring local crafts. In summer, live music plays in the neighboring plaza.

Continue south on Main to 8th Street, and turn west to Duluth Avenue. The Pettigrew Home and Museum, 8th Street and Duluth Avenue, is the Queen Anne Victorian home of South Dakota's first US Senator. This beautifully restored home contains period furniture and artifacts from the frontier era of Sioux Falls. Follow 8th Street, past more Victorian homes, to Grange Avenue. Turn north and continue to 6th Street and Terrace Park. The Shoto-Teien Japanese Gardens, with formal gardens, pagodas, and exotic Asian plants, flank Covell Lake in the park. If it's a warm day and you've got kids in tow, the swimming pools and water slides of Terrace Park Aquatic Center are a perfect spot to cool down.

From Terrace Park, walk south on Grange Avenue to 12th Street, and turn west. The 205-acre Sherman Park, at 12th and Kiwanis Avenue, contains the Great Plains Zoo and Delbridge Museum of Natural History, plus a memorial for the USS *South Dakota*, the most decorated battleship in World War II. The park also features a number of unexcavated Native American burial mounds.

From Sherman Park, head back east toward downtown along 12th Avenue. At Main Avenue is Sioux Falls's largest entertainment, cultural, and educational facility, the Washington Pavilion of Arts and Science. Formerly the city's original high school, the complex is a model of architectural repurposing. The pavilion contains the Visual Arts Center, with a permanent collection of regional artists, plus changing exhibitions and art shows. Also in the pavilion are the Wells Fargo Cinedome Theater, Kirby Science Discovery Center, Husby Performing Arts Center, restaurants, and gift shops.

Continue east along 11th Street, passing a full-size casting of Michelangelo's *David* just before crossing the Big Sioux River. From here, drop down onto the Sioux River Greenway, and follow the hiking and biking trail north to Falls Park.

tary continental bkfst. Restaurant adj open 24 hrs. Ck-out 11 am. Business servs avail. X-country ski 1 mi. Cr cds: A, D, DS, MC, V.

⬛ 🐾 🏊 ⚿ 🎿 🖼

★ **DAYS INN AIRPORT.** *5001 N Cliff Ave (57104). 605/331-5959; res 800/ 329-7466. www.daysinn.com.* 87 rms, 2 story. S $42-$89; D $49-$119; each addl $5. TV; cable. Complimentary continental bkfst. Ck-out noon. Business servs avail. Airport transportation. X-country ski 3 mi. Cr cds: A, C, D, DS, JCB, MC, V.

[D] [X] [>] [~] [m] [SC]

★ **DAYS INN EMPIRE.** *3401 Gateway Blvd (57106). 605/361-9240; fax 605/361-5419; 800/329-7466. www. daysinn.com.* 76 rms, 2 story. S $38-$45; D $48-$55; each addl $5. Crib free. TV; cable. Complimentary continental bkfst. Restaurant adj open 24 hrs. Ck-out noon. Business servs avail. X-country ski 1 mi. Cr cds: A, MC, V.

[D] [>] [~] [m] [SC]

★ **EXEL INN.** *1300 W Russell St (57104). 605/331-5800; fax 605/331-4074. www.exelinn.com.* 105 rms, 2 story. S $32.99-$38.99; D $43.99-$49.55; each addl $5; under 18 free. Crib free. Pet accepted. TV; cable. Complimentary continental bkfst. Restaurant nearby. Ck-out noon. Coin lndry. X-country ski 1½ mi. Cr cds: A, D, DS, MC, V.

[D] [>] [>] [X] [~] [m]

★ ★ **HOLIDAY INN.** *100 W 8th St (57104). 605/339-2000; fax 605/339-3724. www.holiday-inn.com/fsd-cityctr.* 299 rms, 10 story. S $79-$119; D $79-$129; each addl $10; suites $183; under 18 free. Crib free. TV; cable (premium), VCR avail. Indoor pool; whirlpool, poolside serv. Restaurants 6 am-10 pm. Bar noon-2 am. Ck-out noon. Meeting rms. Business servs avail. In-rm modem link. Bellhops. Valet serv. Sundries. Gift shop. Free airport, bus depot transportation. Exercise equipt; sauna. Rec rm. Balconies. Cr cds: A, C, D, DS, ER, JCB, MC, V.

[D] [~] [X] [X] [~] [m] [SC]

★ ★ **KELLY INN.** *3101 W Russell St (57107). 605/338-6242; fax 605/338-5453; res 800/635-3559.* 43 rms, 2 story. June-Aug: S $57-$64; D $62-69; each addl $5; under 12 free; lower rates rest of yr. Crib free. Pet accepted. TV; cable. Complimentary continental bkfst. Restaurant adj 6 am-11 pm. Ck-out 11 am. Coin lndry. Meeting rm. Airport transportation. Whirlpool, sauna. Cr cds: A, C, D, DS, ER, JCB, MC, V.

[D] [>] [X] [~] [m] [SC]

★ **MOTEL 6.** *3009 W Russell St (57107). 605/336-7800; fax 605/330-9273; res 800/466-8356. www.motel6. com.* 87 rms, 2 story. May-Sept: S $29.99; D $35.99; each addl $6; under 17 free; lower rates rest of yr. Crib free. Pet accepted, some restrictions. TV; cable. Heated pool. Restaurant adj 6 am-11 pm. Ck-out noon. Business servs avail. Cr cds: A, D, DS, MC, V.

[D] [>] [~] [~] [m]

★ ★ **OAKS HOTEL.** *3300 W Russell St (57107). 605/336-9000; toll-free 800/326-4656.* 200 rms, 2 story. S $59-$68; D $59-$74; each addl $6; suites $85; under 18 free. Crib free. TV; cable. Indoor/outdoor pool; whirlpool, sauna. Playground. Restaurant 6 am-10 pm. Bar 1 pm-2 am, Sun to midnight; entertainment. Ck-out noon. Coin lndry. Meeting rms. Business servs avail. Bellhops. Valet serv. Sundries. Free airport, bus depot transportation. X-country ski 1 mi. Game rm. Private patios, balconies. Cr cds: A, D, DS, MC, V.

[D] [>] [>] [~] [X] [X] [~] [m]

★ **RAMADA INN AIRPORT.** *1301 W Russell St (57104). 605/336-1020; fax 605/336-3030. www.ramada.com.* 200 rms, 2 story. S $57-$74; D $69-$84; each addl $8; under 18 free; Crib free. Pet accepted. TV; cable. Indoor pool; whirlpool, sauna. Restaurant 6 am-10 pm. Bar 4 pm-2 am; Sun to 10 pm; entertainment. Ck-out noon. Coin lndry. Meeting rms. Business servs avail. In-rm modem link. Bellhops. Valet serv. Sundries. Free airport, bus depot transportation. Putting green. Game rm. Cr cds: A, C, D, DS, MC, V.

[D] [>] [~] [X] [~] [m]

★ **SELECT INN.** *3500 Gateway Blvd (57106). 605/361-1864; fax 605/361-9287; toll-free 800/641-1000. www. selectinn.com.* 100 rms, 2 story. S $29.90-$39.90; D $35.90-$39.90; each addl $3; under 12 free. Crib $3. Pet accepted. TV; cable, VCR avail (movies). Complimentary continental bkfst. Ck-out 11 am. Cr cds: A, MC, V.

[D] [>] [~] [m] [SC]

★ **SUPER 8 MOTEL.** *1508 W Russell St (57104). 605/339-9330; fax 605/ 339-9330; res 800/800-8000. www.*

super8.com. 95 rms, 3 story. No elvtr. S $27.29-$38.88; D $29.59-$47.88; each addl $5; under 12 free. Crib free. Pet accepted. TV; cable (premium). Restaurant adj open 24 hrs. Ck-out 11 am. Business servs avail. In-rm modem link. X-country ski 1 mi. Cr cds: A, MC, V.
⬛⬛⬛⬛⬛

Hotels

★★ **RADISSON HOTEL.** *4300 W Empire Pl (57106). 605/361-6684; fax 605/362-0916; toll-free 800/333-3333. www.radisson.com.* 106 rms, 3 story. S, D $89-$99; suites $150-$425; under 18 free. Crib free. TV; cable. Indoor pool; whirlpool. Coffee in rms. Restaurant 6:30 am-noon. Rm serv 6:30 am-11 pm. Ck-out noon. Meeting rms. Business servs avail. In-rm modem link. Bellhops. Valet serv. Sundries. Free airport, railroad station, bus depot transportation. Health club privileges. Refrigerator in suites. Cr cds: A, C, D, DS, ER, MC, V.
⬛⬛⬛⬛ SC

★★★ **SHERATON.** *1211 N West Ave (57104). 605/331-0100. www. sheraton.com.* 184 rms, 5 story. S, D $150-$225; each addl $20; under 17 free. Crib avail. Pet accepted. Indoor pool. TV; cable (premium), VCR avail. Complimentary coffee, newspaper in rms. Restaurant 6 am-10 pm. Ck-out noon. Meeting rms. Business center. Gift shop. Exercise rm. Some refrigerators, minibars. Cr cds: A, C, D, DS, ER, JCB, MC, V.
⬛⬛⬛⬛⬛⬛

Restaurants

★★★ **C.J. CALLAWAY'S.** *500 E 69th St (57109). 605/334-8888. www. cjcallaways.com.* Menu changes seasonally. Hrs: 9 am-10 pm; Fri, Sat to 11 pm. Closed hols. Res accepted. Wine, beer. Lunch $5.95-$8.50; dinner $16.95-$25.99. Cr cds: A, D, DS, MC, V.
⬛⬛

★★ **MINERVA'S.** *301 S Phillips (57104). 605/334-0386.* Hrs: 11 am-2:30 pm, 5:30-10 pm; Fri, Sat 5-11 pm. Closed Sun; hols. Res accepted. Continental menu. Bar 11 am-midnight. Lunch $4.95-$8.95, dinner $8.95-$28.95. Children's menu. Spe-

cializes in pasta, fresh seafood, aged steaks. Salad bar. Cr cds: A, D, DS, MC, V.
⬛⬛

Sisseton

(A-8) *See also Webster*

Pop 2,181 **Elev** 1,204 ft
Area code 605 **Zip** 57262

What to See and Do

Fort Sisseton State Park. Established in 1864 to protect settlers, the fort housed 400 soldiers and contained more than 45 wooden, stone, and brick buildings. The post was abandoned in 1889; during the 1930s it was used as a federal transient camp by the Works Progress Administration, which restored 14 of the fort's brick and stone buildings. Hiking trail, picnicking, camping. Visitor center with historical exhibits (Memorial Day-Labor Day, daily). Standard fees. 20 mi W on SD 10, then S on SD 25. Phone 605/448-5701.

Roy Lake State Park. On 509 acres. Swimming beach, bathhouse, fishing; boating, canoeing; hiking, picnicking, playground, concession. Camping (electrical hookups, dump station), cabins. Res accepted after Jan 1 annually. Standard fees. 18 mi W on SD 10, then 3 mi SW near Lake City. Phone 605/448-5701. ¢

Tekakwitha Fine Arts Center. Eight galleries featuring more than 200 works by Sisseton/Wahpeton Dakota Sioux. Gift shop. (Memorial Day-Labor Day, daily; rest of yr, Tues-Fri, also wkend afternoons; closed hols) 401 S 8th Ave. Phone 605/698-7058. **Donation**

Special Event

Fort Sisseton Historical Festival. Fort Sisseton State Park. Incl muzzleloading rendezvous, cavalry and infantry drills, square dancing, melodrama, frontier crafts, and Dutch oven cookoff. First wkend June.

Motel/Motor Lodge

★ **HOLIDAY MOTEL.** *SD 10 E and 127 (57262). 605/698-7644; fax 605/*

742-0487; toll-free 888/460-9548. 19 rms. S $22-$28; D $30-$34; each addl $3. Crib free. Pet accepted. TV; cable. Complimentary coffee. Restaurant nearby. Ck-out 11 am. Cr cds: A, C, D, DS, MC, V.

Restaurant

★ **AMERICAN HEARTH.** *6 Hickory St E (57262).* *605/698-3077.* Hrs: 6 am-11 pm. Closed Dec 25. Res accepted. Bkfst $4-$6, lunch $4-$7, dinner $5-$9. Children's menu. Specializes in steak. Parking.

Spearfish

(C-1) *See also Belle Fourche, Deadwood, Lead, Rapid City, Sturgis*

Pop 6,966 **Elev** 3,643 ft
Area code 605 **Zip** 57783
Information Chamber of Commerce, 106 W Kansas, PO Box 550; 605/642-2626 or 800/626-8013
Web www.spearfish.sd.us

The fertile valley in which Spearfish lies is at the mouth of Spearfish Canyon, famous for its scenery and fishing. A Ranger District office of the Black Hills National Forest (see BLACK HILLS) is located in Spearfish.

What to See and Do

Black Hills State University. (1883) 2,800 students. Located in the northern Black Hills overlooking the community. Library has Lyndle Dunn wildlife art, Babylonian tablets, and Rachetts porcelain miniature dolls of First Ladies. Donald E. Young Sports and Fitness Center open to public (fees). Walking tours. 1200 University Ave. Phone 605/642-6343.

City Campgrounds. Incl 150 campsites, 57 with hookups (addl fee). Fishing. (Mid-May-Oct, daily) I-90 exit 12, left at second light, on S canyon St. Phone 605/642-1340. ¢¢¢

DC Booth Historic Fish Hatchery. (1899) One of the first in the West;

facilities incl ponds, visitor center, historic displays, restored Booth home. Visitor fish feeding. Historic buildings tour. 423 Hatchery Circle. Phone 605/642-7730. **FREE**

High Plains Heritage Center and Museum. Western art, sculpture. Special events. (Daily; closed hols) 825 Heritage Dr. Phone 605/642-9378. ¢¢

Star Aviation Air Tours. Airplane tours of the Gold Country, Devils Tower, Mt Rushmore, and the Badlands. Min two persons per ride. Phone 605/642-4112. ¢¢¢¢

Special Events

Black Hills Passion Play. Amphitheater, 400 St. Joe St. Dramatization of last days of Jesus Christ, presented on 350-ft outdoor stage. Tues, Thurs, and Sun. Phone 605/642-2646. June-Aug.

Matthews Opera House. 614 Main. For program schedule phone 605/642-7973. June-Aug.

Corvette Classic. Main St. Sports car enthusiasts gather each summer for their convention. Highlight is Main St show and shine, when hundreds of corvettes line Main St. Phone 605/361-1243. July 17-20.

Motels/Motor Lodges

★ **ALL AMERICAN INN.** *2275 E Colorado Blvd (57783).* *605/642-2350; fax 605/642-9312; toll-free 800/606-2350.* 40 rms, 2 story. June-Aug: S, D $79; each addl $6; under 12 free; higher rates special events; lower rates rest of yr. Crib $5. TV; cable (premium). Indoor pool; whirlpool. Complimentary continental bkfst. Ck-out 11 am. Cr cds: A, MC, V.

★ **COMFORT INN.** *2725 1st Ave (57783).* *605/642-2337; fax 605/642-0866; res 800/228-5150.* www.comfort inn.com. 40 rms, 2 story. June-Aug: S $76-$86; D $81-$96; each addl $5; under 18 free; ski plan; higher rates special events; lower rates rest of yr. Pet accepted, some restrictions. TV; cable. Indoor pool; whirlpool. Complimentary continental bkfst. Restaurant nearby. Ck-out 11 am. Coin lndry. Meeting rm. Cr cds: A, C, D, DS, MC, V.

★ **DAYS INN.** *240 Ryan Rd (57783). 605/642-7101; fax 605/642-7120; toll-free 800/329-7466.* 50 rms, 2 story. June-Sept: S $65; D $70; each addl $5; suites $80; under 12 free; higher rates motorcycle rally, Corvette rally; lower rates rest of yr. Crib free. TV; cable (premium). Complimentary continental bkfst. Restaurant nearby. Ck-out 11 am. Coin lndry. Cr cds: A, DS, MC, V.

🆔 📶 📱 🐾

★★ **FAIRFIELD INN.** *2720 E 1st Ave (57783). 605/642-3500; 800/450-4442. www.fairfieldinn.com.* 57 rms, 3 story. May-Sept: S $65.95-$78.95; D $78.95; each addl $5; suites $90-$150; under 18 free; lower rates rest of yr. Crib free. TV; cable (premium). Indoor pool; whirlpool. Complimentary continental bkfst. Ck-out noon. Meeting rm. Downhill/x-country ski 16 mi. Refrigerator, microwave in suites. Picnic tables. Cr cds: A, D, DS, MC, V.

🆔 📶 📱 🎿 📱 🐾

★★ **HOLIDAY INN & CONVENTION CENTER.** *305 N 27th St (57783). 605/642-4683; fax 605/642-0203; toll-free 800/999-3541. www. holiday-inn.com.* 145 rms, 2 story, 24 suites. June-Aug: S, D $75; suites $120; under 18 free; ski plans; higher rates special events; lower rates rest of yr. Crib $10. Pet accepted. TV; cable (premium). Complimentary coffee in rms. Restaurant 6 am-2 pm, 5-10 pm. Bar 4 pm-1 am. Ck-out noon. Meeting rms. Business servs avail. Sundries. Gift shop. Coin lndry. Downhill ski 15 mi. Exercise equipt. Indoor pool; whirlpools. Game rm. Refrigerator, microwave in suites. Some balconies. Cr cds: A, MC, V.

🆔 📶 📱 🎿 📱 🐾 SC

★★ **KELLY INN.** *540 E Jackson (57783). 605/642-7795; fax 605/642-7751; res 800/635-3559.* 50 rms, 2 story. June-Aug: S $70; D $75; each addl $5; under 12 free; lower rates rest of yr. Crib free. Pet accepted. TV; cable (premium). Complimentary continental bkfst. Restaurant adj open 24 hrs. Ck-out 11 am. Coin lndry. Whirlpool, sauna. Some in-rm whirlpools. Cr cds: A, D, DS, MC, V.

🆔 📶 📱 📱 🐾

★★ **SPEARFISH CANYON.** *US 14A (57783). 605/584-3435; fax 605/584-*

3990; toll-free 800/439-8544. 54 rms, 2 story. Mid-May-mid-Oct: S, D $89; each addl $6; suites $129-$195; under 12 free; wkend rates; higher rates Sturgis Black Hills Bike Rally; lower rates rest of yr. Crib $10. TV; cable. Whirlpool. Complimentary coffee in lobby. Restaurant opp 7 am-9 pm. Bar 8-2 am. Ck-out 11 am. Coin lndry. Meeting rms. Business servs avail. Bellhops. Gift shop. Downhill ski 6 mi; x-country ski 8 mi. Massage. Bicycle rentals. Minibars; refrigerator in suites. Some balconies. Cr cds: DS, MC, V.

🆔 📶 📱 🐾

Sturgis

(C-1) *See also Belle Fourche, Deadwood, Lead, Rapid City, Spearfish*

Founded 1878 **Pop** 5,330 **Elev** 3,440 ft **Area code** 605 **Zip** 57785

Information Chamber of Commerce, 606 Anna St, PO Box 504; 605/347-2556

Originally a "bullwhackers" (wagon drivers) stop on the way to Fort Meade, this was once known as "Scooptown" because soldiers who came in were "scooped" (cleaned out) by such characters as Poker Alice, a famed cigar-smoking scoop-expert. Now Sturgis is a bustling Black Hills trade center.

What to See and Do

Bear Butte State Park. On 1,941 acres. Hiking trail to Bear Butte summit; ending point for 111-mi Centennial Trail through the Black Hills (see WIND CAVE NATIONAL PARK). Picnicking, playground, camping. Visitor center has displays on Native American culture and history (May-Sept, daily). Park (Daily). Standard fees. 6 mi NE off SD 79. Phone 605/347-5240.

Fort Meade Museum. On site of original Fort Meade (1878-1944), to which surviving members of the Seventh Cavalry came after the Custer Massacre. Old cavalry quarters, post cemetery; museum has displays of artifacts, documents. Video presentation. (May-Sept, daily) 1 mi E on SD 34, 79. Phone 605/347-9822.

Motorcycle Museum and Hall of Fame. Vintage motorcycles; gift shop. (Daily) 2438 Junction Ave. Phone 605/347-4875. ¢¢

Wonderland Cave. Scenic tours of underground caverns 60 million yrs old; two-level living cave with largest variety of crystal formations in the Northwest. Picnicking, snack bar; gift shop; hiking trails. (May-Oct, daily) S via I-90, exit 32, then 15 mi S on Vanocker Canyon Rd or S of Deadwood on SD 385. Phone 605/578-1728. ¢¢¢

Motels/Motor Lodges

★ **DAYS INN.** *HC 55, Box 348 (57785). 605/347-3027; fax 605/720-0313; res 800/329-7466. www.days inn.com.* 53 rms, 2 story. June-Aug: S $76; D $81; each addl $5; suite $90; under 13 free; higher rates motorcycle rally; lower rates rest of yr. Crib free. TV; cable (premium). Complimentary continental bkfst. Restaurant opp 6 am-11 pm. Ck-out 11 am. Coin lndry. Meeting rms. Business servs avail. Whirlpool. Cr cds: A, DS, MC, V.

⬛ 🏕 🖼

★ **SUPER 8 MOTEL.** *HC 55, Box 306 (57785). 605/347-4447; fax 605/347-2334; res 800/800-8000. www.super8. com.* 59 rms, 3 story. June-Sept: S $63.88; D $73.88; each addl $3; lower rates rest of yr. Crib $5. Pet accepted. TV; cable (premium). Complimentary coffee in lobby. Restaurant adj open 24 hrs. Ck-out 11 am. Coin lndry. Exercise equipt; sauna. Whirlpool. Some balconies. Cr cds: A, MC, V.

⬛ 🔙 🏋 🖼 🔥 SC

Vermillion

(F-8) *See also Beresford, Yankton; also see Sioux City, IA*

Settled 1859 **Pop** 10,034 **Elev** 1,221 ft **Area code** 605 **Zip** 57069

Information Chamber of Commerce, 906 E Cherry St; 605/624-5571 or 800/809-2071

Web www.mainstreetweb.com

Vermillion, the seat of Clay County, was settled originally below the bluffs of the Missouri River until the flood of 1881 changed the river's course, forcing residents to higher ground. Located in a portion of the state that was claimed twice by France and once by Spain before being sold to the United States, Vermillion has prospered and now prides itself as being a combination of rich farmland, good industrial climate, and home to the University of South Dakota.

What to See and Do

Clay County Recreation Area. On 121 acres. Fishing, boating, canoeing (landing); picnicking. 4 mi W, 1½ mi S off SD 50, on banks of Missouri River. Phone 605/987-2263.

University of South Dakota. (1862) 7,300 students. On campus is the DakotaDome, a physical education, recreation, and athletic facility with an air-supported roof. Art galleries and theaters are located in the Warren M. Lee Center for the Fine Arts and Coyote Student Center. Tours. Dakota St, on SD 50 Bypass. Phone 605/677-5326. Also on campus is

Shrine to Music Museum. More than 6,000 antique musical instruments from all over the world and from all periods. (Daily; closed Jan 1, Thanksgiving, Dec 25) Clark and Yale sts. Phone 605/677-5306. **FREE**

W. H. Over State Museum. State museum of natural and state history. Exhibits incl life size diorama of a Teton Dakota village; the Stanley J. Morrow collection of historical photographs; pioneer artifacts. Changing gallery. Gift shop. (Daily; closed hols) 1110 Ratingen St. Phone 605/677-5228. **FREE**

Motels/Motor Lodges

★ **COMFORT INN.** *701 W Cherry St (57069). 605/624-8333; toll-free 800/228-5150. www.comfortinn.com.* 46 rms, 2 story. S $43.95-$63.95; D $59.95-$79.95; each addl $5; under 18 free; higher rates some special events. Crib free. Pet accepted. TV; cable (premium). Indoor pool; whirlpool. Complimentary continental bkfst. Ck-out 10 am. Meeting rms.

Business servs avail. Exercise equipt; sauna. Outdoor patio. Cr cds: A, C, D, DS, ER, JCB, MC, V.

D 🐾 ⤳ 🕅 🖳 🖐 SC

★ **WESTSIDE INN.** *1313 W Cherry St (57069). 605/624-2601; fax 605/624-2449.* 19 rms. S $35; D $38; each addl $3; under 10 free; higher rates special events. Crib $2. TV; cable. Pool. Complimentary continental bkfst, coffee in rms. Restaurant nearby. Ck-out 11 am. Business servs avail. Aiport, bus depot transportation. X-country ski 1 mi. Cr cds: A, C, D, DS, MC, V.

🏊 ⤳ 🖐 SC

Restaurant

★ **SILVER DOLLAR.** *1216 E Cherry (SD 50) (57069). 605/624-4830.* Hrs: 11 am-midnight. Closed Thanksgiving, Dec 25. Res accepted. Bar. Lunch $2.95-$5.95, dinner $3.95-$13.95. Specializes in chicken breast, prime rib. Cr cds: A, DS, MC, V.

D SC ⤙

Wall

(D-3) *See also Rapid City*

Founded 1907 **Pop** 834 **Elev** 2,818 ft **Area code** 605 **Zip** 57790

Established as a station on the Chicago and North Western Railroad in 1907, Wall is a gateway to Badlands National Park (see). The town is a trading center for a large area of farmers and ranchers, and it is noted for its pure water, which is brought up from wells 3,200 feet deep. A Ranger District office of the Nebraska National Forest (see CHADRON, NE) is located here.

What to See and Do

🌟 **Wall Drug Store.** World-famous for roadside advertising, store features animated cowboy orchestra and chuckwagon quartet; 80-ft dinosaur; art gallery; 23 Western shops; travelers' chapel; cafe. (Daily; closed hols) On US 14, I-90, SD 240. Phone 605/279-2175. **FREE**

Motels/Motor Lodges

★★ **BEST WESTERN PLAINS.** *712 Glenn St (57790). 605/279-2145; fax 605/279-2977; res 800/528-1234. www.bestwestern.com.* 74 rms, 1-2 story, 8 suites. Aug: S, D $94; each addl $7; lower rates rest of yr. Crib $5. Pet accepted. TV; cable (premium). Heated pool. Complimentary coffee in rms. Restaurant nearby. Ck-out 11 am. Gift shop. Rec rm. Cr cds: A, C, D, DS, MC, V.

🐾 ⤳ 🖳 🖐

★ **DAYS INN WALL.** *Tenth and Norris (57790). 605/279-2000; fax 605/279-2004; res 800/325-2525.* 32 rms, 2 story. June-Aug: S $80; D $90; each addl $5; under 12 free; higher rates motorcycle rally; lower rates rest of yr. Crib free. TV; cable. Complimentary coffee in lobby. Restaurant adj 5 am-10 pm. Ck-out 11 am. Whirlpool. Sauna. Pool privileges. Cr cds: A, MC, V.

D 🖳 🖐 SC

★ **SUPER 8 MOTEL.** *711 Glenn St (57790). 605/279-2688; fax 605/279-2396; toll-free 800/800-8000. www.super8.com.* 29 rms. June-Aug: S $65.88; D $69.88-$73.88; each addl $2; lower rates rest of yr. Crib free. TV; cable (premium). Complimentary coffee in lobby. Restaurant nearby. Ck-out 11 am. Cr cds: A, C, D, DS, MC, V.

D 🖳 🖐

Restaurant

★ **WALL DRUG.** *510 Main St (57790). 605/279-2175. www.walldrug.com.* Hrs: 6 am-10 pm; winter to 6 pm. Closed hols. Res accepted. Wine, beer. Bkfst $2.75-$7.39, lunch, dinner $2.98-$9.98. Specializes in buffalo burgers, hot beef sandwiches. Salad bar. Original Western artwork; memorabilia. Cr cds: A, DS, MC, V.

D ⤙

Watertown

(B-8) *See also Brookings*

Founded 1879 **Pop** 17,592 **Elev** 1,739 ft **Area code** 605 **Zip** 57201

Information Convention and Visitors Bureau, 1200 33 St SE, Suite 209, PO Box 1113; 605/886-5814 or 800/658-4505
Web www.watertownsd.com

Originally called Waterville, the settlement owed its boom to the railroads. Two large lakes, Kampeska and Pelican, are on the edges of town.

What to See and Do

Bramble Park Zoo. Municipal zoo (21 acres) features more than 400 birds and mammals of 100 different species. Live animal demonstrations; picnic area, playground; discovery center features displays and hands-on programs; band concerts in summer. (Daily, weather permitting) 901 Sixth Ave NW (SD 20). Phone 605/882-6269. ¢¢

Kampeska Heritage Museum. Exhibits depict pioneer history, local history through WWII and Native American artifacts. (Tues-Sat, afternoons) 27 1st Ave SE. Phone 605/886-7335. **FREE**

Lake Kampeska. Parks along shore offer swimming, bathhouses, water-skiing, fishing, boating (launch); picnicking, camping, trailer sites. Standard fees. There is also a 25-mi scenic drive around the lake. NW on SD 20. Phone 605/882-6260.

Mellette House. (1883) Built by Arthur C. Mellette, last territorial and first state governor of South Dakota. Original Victorian furnishings, heirlooms, family portraits. (May-Sept, Tues-Sun; afternoons) 421 5th Ave NW. Phone 605/886-4730. **FREE**

Redlin Art Center. Houses over 100 of Terry Redlin's original oil paintings. Center also incl the only planetarium in the state, an amphitheater, gift shop, and Glacial Lakes and Prairie Tourism Association. (Daily; seasonal schedule) Jct US 212 and I-29. Phone 605/882-3877. ¢

Motels/Motor Lodges

★★ **BEST WESTERN RAMKOTA INN.** *1901 SW 9th Ave (57201). 605/886-8011; fax 605/886-3667; toll-free 800/528-1234. www.bestwestern. com.* 101 rms, 2 story. S $53; D $61; each addl $5; suites $130; under 18 free. Crib free. Pet accepted. TV; cable. Indoor pool; whirlpool. Coffee in rms. Restaurant 7 am-10 pm. Bar 4 pm-1 am. Ck-out noon. Meeting rms. Business servs avail. In-rm modem link. Sauna. Valet serv. Sundries. Free airport, bus depot transportation. Cr cds: A, C, D, DS, MC, V.

★ **SUPER 8 MOTEL WATERTON.** *503 14th Ave SE (57201). 605/882-1900; fax 605/882-1900; res 800/800-8000. www.super8.com.* 58 rms, 3 story. No elvtr. S $38.88; D $47.88; each addl $6. Crib $1. TV; cable. Indoor pool; whirlpool. Sauna. Restaurant nearby. Ck-out 11 am. X-country ski 1 mi. Cr cds: A, MC, V.

★ **TRAVELERS INN.** *920 SE 14th St (57201). 605/882-2243; fax 605/882-0968; toll-free 800/568-7074.* 50 rms, 2 story. S $30-$37; D $44-$49; each addl $5; under 12 free. Crib free. Pet accepted. TV; cable. Complimentary continental bkfst. Restaurant nearby. Ck-out 11 am. Cr cds: A, D, DS, MC, V.

★ **TRAVEL HOST.** *1714 SW 9th Ave (57201). 605/886-6120; fax 605/886-5352; toll-free 800/658-5512.* 29 units, 2 story. S $36; D $46; each addl $5; under 12 free. Crib free. Pet accepted, some restrictions. TV; cable. Complimentary continental bkfst. Restaurant adj 7 am-10 pm. Ck-out 11 am. Cr cds: A, DS, MC, V.

Webster

(B-7) *See also Aberdeen, Sisseton*

Founded 1881 **Pop** 2,017 **Elev** 1,847 ft **Area code** 605 **Zip** 57274
Information Chamber of Commerce, 513 Main, PO Box 123; 605/345-4668

What to See and Do

Museum of Wildlife, Science and Industry. Antique automobiles, tractors; international animal display. (Daily) Exit 207 off I-29, W US 12. Phone 605/345-4751. **Donation**

Waubay National Wildlife Refuge.
This 4,694-acre wildlife refuge has
nature and bird-watching trails; six-
mi x-country ski trails; 100-ft tall
observation tower; outdoor classrm
activities and wildlife exhibits. (Mon-
Fri) 19 mi NE via US 12, then 7 mi N
on County Rd 1, in Waubay. Phone
605/947-4521.

Special Events

**Glacial Lakes Stampede and Rodeo
Days.** July.

Day County Fair. Grandstand shows,
animals on display, special programs.
Fair is over 110 yrs old. Aug.

Motels/Motor Lodges

★ **HOLIDAY MOTEL.** *US 12 W
(57274). 605/345-3323.* 20 rms. S
$24-$26; D $32; suites $44-$50. Crib
free. TV. Restaurant adj 5-11 pm. Ck-
out 10 am. Cr cds: DS, MC, V.
⊠ 🐾

★ **SUPER 8 MOTEL.** *US 12 W
(57274). 605/345-4701; toll-free
800/800-8000. www.super8.com.* 27
rms, 2 story. S $36.88; D $41.88; each
addl $5; under 12 free. Crib free. TV;
cable. Complimentary coffee in
lobby. Restaurant nearby. Ck-out 11
am. Cr cds: A, C, D, DS, MC, V.
⊠ 🐾 SC

Wind Cave National Park

*See also Custer, Hill City, Hot Springs,
Keystone*

(11 mi N of Hot Springs on US 385)

Wind Cave, one of many caves in
the ring of limestone surrounding
the Black Hills, is a maze of subter-
ranean passages known to extend
more than 79 miles. It is named for
the strong currents of wind that
blow in or out of its entrance according to atmospheric pressure. When
the pressure is decreasing, the wind
blows outward; when it increases,
the wind blows in. It was the rushing
sound of air coming out of the
entrance that led to its discovery in
1881. The cave and surrounding area

became a national park in 1903;
today it comprises 44 square miles.

Wind Cave is a constant 53°F. Various one- to two-hr guided tours
(daily; no tours Thanksgiving,
December 25) and four-hr tours
(June-mid-August, daily). Tours are
moderately strenuous. A sweater or
jacket is advised; shoes must have
low heels and nonslip soles.

On the surface are prairie grasslands, forests, and a wildlife preserve—the home of bison, pronghorn
elk, deer, prairie dogs, and other animals. The Centennial Trail, a 111-
mile, multiuse trail, takes visitors
from one end of the Black Hills to the
other. The trail begins here and ends
at Bear Butte State Park (see STUR-
GIS). In addition, there is hiking,
bicycling, picnicking, and camping at
Elk Mountain near headquarters. Visitor center (Daily; closed Thanksgiving, December 25). Hrs may vary
throughout yr. Park (Daily). Phone
605/745-4600. Tours ¢¢-¢¢¢¢

Winner (E-5)

Settled 1909 **Pop** 3,354 **Elev** 1,972 ft
Area code 605 **Zip** 57580
Information Chamber of Commerce,
Tripp County Courthouse, PO Box
268; 605/842-1533 or 800/658-3079
Web www.state.sd.us/state/execu-
tive/tourism/adds/winner.htm

Winner is a sports-oriented town; a
pheasant hunting autumn follows a
baseball summer. It is the seat of
Tripp County and one of the largest
producers of cattle and wheat in the
state.

Special Events

Regional High School Rodeo. Early
June.

Shrine Circus. July.

Mid-Dakota Fair. Early Aug.

Motels/Motor Lodges

★ **BEST VALUE BUFFALO TRAIL
MOTEL.** *1030 W 2nd St (57580).
605/842-2212; fax 605/842-3199; toll-
free 800/341-8000. www.bestvalue
inn.com.* 31 rms. S $45-$110; D $48-
$110; each addl $5; higher rates hunt-

ing season. Crib $5. Pet accepted. TV; cable. Pool. Complimentary continental bkfst. Restaurant nearby. Ck-out 11 am. Free airport transportation. 9-hole golf privileges, putting green, driving range. Rec rm. Picnic tables. Cr cds: A, C, D, DS, MC, V.

★ **WARRIOR INN.** *845 SD 44 E (57580). 605/842-3121; fax 605/842-0600; toll-free 800/658-4705.* 39 rms. S $36; D $46; each addl $4; family rates. Crib $5. TV; cable. Indoor pool. Restaurant nearby. Bar 5 pm-1 am. Ck-out 11 am. Sundries. Free airport transportation. Cr cds: A, C, D, DS, MC, V.

Yankton

(E-7) *See also Beresford, Vermillion*

Settled 1859 **Pop** 12,703 **Elev** 1,205 ft
Area code 605 **Zip** 57078
Information Chamber of Commerce, 218 W 4th St, PO Box 588-D; 605/665-3636 or 800/888-1460
Web www.yanktonsd.com

First capital of Dakota Territory (1861-1883), Yankton has restored homes and mansions dating to territorial days.

What to See and Do

Dakota Territorial Capitol. Replica of first capitol of Dakota Territory. Original building (1862) was auctioned for scrap after the territorial capital was moved to Bismarck in 1883. Riverside Park. **FREE**

Dakota Territorial Museum. Museum in complex incl restored Dakota Territorial Legislative Council Building; railroad depot, caboose; rural schoolhouse; blacksmith shop; 1870 parlor, 1900 bedrm, grandma's kitchen; saloon; military display. (Memorial Day-Labor Day, Tues-Sun; rest of yr Tues-Fri, daily) 610 Summit Ave, in Westside Park. Phone 605/665-3898. **FREE**

Lewis and Clark Lake/Gavins Point Dam. This reservoir of Missouri River has 15 developed recreation areas for camping (fee), swimming beaches, boat and fishing access. Primitive areas for hunting, scenic drives, hiking. Other attractions incl tour of powerhouse, visitor center, fish hatchery and aquarium, campground programs. 5 mi W on SD 52. Phone 402/667-7873. **FREE**

Special Events

Riverboat Days. Entertainment, crafts, food, rodeo. Phone 605/665-1657. Third wkend Aug.

Great Plains Oldtime Fiddlers Contest. Mid-Sept.

Dacotah Territorial Reunion. Late Sept.

Motels/Motor Lodges

★★ **BEST WESTERN INN.** *1607 E SD 50 (57078). 605/665-2906; fax 605/665-4318; res 800/528-1234. www.bestwestern.com.* 123 rms, 2 story. S $55-$89; D $65-$89; each addl $5; under 14 free. Crib free. Pet accepted. TV; cable. Indoor pool; wading pool, whirlpool. Restaurant adj 7 am-10 pm. Ck-out 11 am. Meeting rms. Business servs avail. Bellhops. Exercise equipt. Game rm. Some refrigerators. Near lake. Cr cds: A, D, DS, MC, V.

★ **BROADWAY INN MOTEL.** *1210 Broadway Ave (57078). 605/665-7805; fax 605/668-9519; res 800/336-3087.* 37 rms. S $34.95-$49.95; D $43.95-$57.95; each addl $3. Crib $4. Pet accepted. TV; cable (premium), VCR avail. Pool. Restaurant nearby. Ck-out 11 am. Bar 11-2 am. X-country ski 1 mi. Cr cds: A, MC, V.

★ **COMFORT INN.** *2118 Broadway St (57078). 605/665-8053; fax 605/665-8165; res 800/517-4000.* 45 rms, 2 story. S $39.95; D $47.95-$65.95; each addl $4; under 19 free. Crib $5. Pet accepted, some restrictions. TV; cable. Whirlpool. Complimentary continental bkfst. Restaurant nearby. Ck-out 11 am. Business servs avail. In-rm modem link. Cr cds: A, D, DS, MC, V.

★ **DAYS INN.** *2410 Broadway (57078). 605/665-8717; res 605/665-8717. www.daysinn.com.* 45 rms, 2

story. S $40-$47; D $48-$52; each
addl $4; under 13 free. Crib free. TV;
cable. Whirlpool. Complimentary
continental bkfst. Restaurant adj. Ck-
out 11 am. Business servs avail. In-
rm modem link. Cr cds: A, MC, V.

✈ 🐾

★ **SUPER 8 MOTEL.** *1705 SD 50 E
(57078). 605/665-6510; toll-free
800/800-8000. www.super8.com.* 58
rms, 3 story. No elvtr. S $31.88; D
$36.88-$42.88; each addl $2. Crib $3.
TV; cable. Restaurant adj open 24
hrs. Bar 3 pm-2 am. Ck-out 11 am.
X-country ski 1 mi. Cr cds: A, C, D,
DS, MC, V.

🛥 📠 🐾 **SC**

ATTRACTION LIST

Attraction names are listed in alphabetical order followed by a symbol identifying their classification and then city. The symbols for classification are: [S] for Special Events and [W] for What to See and Do.

Abilene Smoky Valley Excursion Train [W] *Abilene, KS*

Adams Museum [W] *Deadwood, SD*

Adventureland Park [W] *Des Moines, IA*

Adventures of Tom Sawyer Diorama Museum [W] *Hannibal, MO*

Aerial Lift Bridge [W] *Duluth, MN*

Aerospace America [S] *Oklahoma City, OK*

Afton Alps [W] *Hastings, MN*

Agassiz National Wildlife Refuge [W] *Thief River Falls, MN*

Agate Fossil Beds National Monument [W] *Scottsbluff, NE*

Agricultural Heritage Museum [W] *Brookings, SD*

Agriculture Museum [W] *Auburn, NE*

Ak-Sar-Ben Aquarium [W] *Omaha, NE*

AKsarben Field and Coliseum [W] *Omaha, NE*

Akta Lakota Museum [W] *Chamberlain, SD*

Alabaster Caverns [W] *Alva, OK*

Albrecht-Kemper Museum of Art [W] *St. Joseph, MO*

Al Brumley's Memory Valley Show [W] *Branson/Table Rock Lake Area, MO*

Alexander Faribault House [W] *Faribault, MN*

Alexander Ramsey House [W] *St. Paul, MN*

Alexandria Lakes State Recreation Area [W] *Fairbury, NE*

Alexis Bailly Vineyard [W] *Hastings, MN*

All Car Rally [S] *Belle Fourche, SD*

Allen County Fair [S] *Iola, KS*

Allen County Historical Museum Gallery [W] *Iola, KS*

Allen-Lambe House Museum and Study Center [W] *Wichita, KS*

Allen Ranch [W] *Tulsa, OK*

All-Iowa Fair [S] *Cedar Rapids, IA*

Aloe Plaza [W] *St. Louis, MO*

Alpine Slide [W] *Lutsen, MN*

Amana [W] *Amana Colonies, IA*

Ambrose A. Call State Park [W] *Algona, IA*

Amelia Earhart Birthplace [W] *Atchison, KS*

Amelia Earhart Festival [S] *Atchison, KS*

America Fest [S] *St. Cloud, MN*

American Creek Recreational Area [W] *Chamberlain, SD*

American Historical Society of Germans from Russia [W] *Lincoln, NE*

American Indian Exposition [S] *Anadarko, OK*

American Royal Barbecue [S] *Kansas City, MO*

American Royal Livestock, Horse Show and Rodeo [S] *Kansas City, MO*

American Swedish Institute [W] *Minneapolis, MN*

Anadarko Philomathic Museum [W] *Anadarko, OK*

Andy Williams Moon River Theatre [W] *Branson/Table Rock Lake Area, MO*

Angostura Reservoir State Recreation Area [W] *Hot Springs, SD*

Anheuser-Busch, Inc [W] *St. Louis, MO*

Anna Bemis Palmer Museum [W] *York, NE*

Anoka County Suburban Fair [S]
   Anoka, MN
Antelope Park [W] *Lincoln, NE*
Antique Airplane Fly-In [S] *Atchi-son, KS*
Antique & Craft Extravaganza [S]
   Lexington, NE
Antique Auto and Farm Machin-ery Exhibit [W] *Grand Island, NE*
Antique Car Swap Meet [S] *Chickasha, OK*
Antique Show/Sale [S] *Arrow Rock, MO*
Antonin Dvorak Memorial [W]
   Decorah, IA
Apple Blossom Parade and Festival
   [S] *St. Joseph, MO*
Applejack Festival [S] *Nebraska City, NE*
Apple Trees Historical Museum, The [W] *Burlington, IA*
Aquaticus [W] *Oklahoma City, OK*
Arabia Steamboat Museum [W]
   Kansas City, MO
Arbor Day Celebration [S]
   Nebraska City, NE
Arbor Lodge State Historical Park
   [W] *Nebraska City, NE*
Arbuckle Wilderness [W] *Sulphur, OK*
Ardmoredillo Chili Cookoff [S]
   Ardmore, OK
Arkalalah Celebration [S] *Arkansas City, KS*
Arkansas River Historical Society
   Museum [W] *Tulsa, OK*
Arnold Lake [W] *North Platte, NE*
Arnolds Park Amusement Park
   [W] *Okoboji, IA*
Arrowhead State Park [W] *Eufaula, OK*
Arrow Rock Lyceum Theater [S]
   Arrow Rock, MO
Arrow Rock State Historic Site [W]
   Arrow Rock, MO
Arrowwood Lake Area [W] *Carrington, ND*
Arrowwood National Wildlife
   Refuge [W] *Carrington, ND*
Art-a-Fest [S] *Charles City, IA*
Art and Antique Center [W]
   Kansas City, MO
Art in the Park [S] *Madison, SD*

Art in the Park Festival [S] *Clinton, OK*
Artist Alley and Fall Festival [S]
   Chanute, KS
Art On The Square [S] *Oskaloosa, IA*
Arts For All [S] *Lawton, OK*
Ash Hollow State Historical Park
   [W] *Ogallala, NE*
Atchison County Fair [S] *Atchison, KS*
Atchison County Historical Society Museum [W] *Atchison, KS*
Atchison Trolley [W] *Atchison, KS*
Atkinson Lake State Recreation
   Area [W] *O'Neill, NE*
Augustana College [W] *Sioux Falls, SD*
Austin Fine Arts Center [W]
   Austin, MN
Autumn Historic Folklife Festival
   [S] *Hannibal, MO*
Azalea Festival [S] *Muskogee, OK*
Backbone [W] *Strawberry Point, IA*
Baker University [W] *Lawrence, KS*
Bald Eagle Appreciation Days [S]
   Keokuk, IA
Baldhill Dam and Lake Ashtabula
   [W] *Valley City, ND*
Baldknobbers Jamboree [W] *Branson/Table Rock Lake Area, MO*
Ballet Oklahoma [S] *Oklahoma City, OK*
Balloon Days [S] *Storm Lake, IA*
Band concerts [S] *Cedar Falls, IA*
Band concerts [S] *Sedalia, MO*
Bank Robbery and Shoot-Out [S]
   Hill City, SD
Barry Burk Jr. Calf Roping [S] *Ardmore, OK*
Barton County Fair [S] *Great Bend, KS*
Barton County Historical Society
   Museum and Village [W]
   Great Bend, KS
Basilica of St. Mary [W] *Minneapolis, MN*
Bass Pro Shops Outdoor World
   Showroom and Fish and
   Wildlife Museum [W] *Springfield, MO*
Battle of Carthage Civil War
   Museum [W] *Carthage, MO*

Battle of Lexington State Historic Site [W] *Lexington, MO*

Bayfront Blues Festival [S] *Duluth, MN*

Beachfest [S] *Elk City, OK*

Beach—Ottumwa, The [W] *Ottumwa, IA*

Bear Butte State Park [W] *Sturgis, SD*

Bear Country USA [W] *Rapid City, SD*

Beavers Bend Resort State Park [W] *Broken Bow, OK*

Becker County Fair [S] *Detroit Lakes, MN*

Becker County Historical Society Museum [W] *Detroit Lakes, MN*

Becky Thatcher House [W] *Hannibal, MO*

Beed's Lake State Park [W] *Hampton, IA*

Beef Empire Days [S] *Garden City, KS*

Belle Fourche Reservoir and Orman Dam [W] *Belle Fourche, SD*

Belle of Sioux City [W] *Sioux City, IA*

Belle Riverboat [W] *Omaha, NE*

Bellevue State Park [W] *Dubuque, IA*

Bell Museum of Natural History [W] *Minneapolis, MN*

Bell's Amusement Park [W] *Tulsa, OK*

Beltrami County Fair [S] *Bemidji, MN*

Bemidji State University [W] *Bemidji, MN*

Bemidji Tourist Information Center [W] *Bemidji, MN*

Benjamin Ranch [W] *Kansas City, MO*

Ben Johnson Memorial Steer-Roping Contest [S] *Pawhuska, OK*

Bennett Spring Hillbilly Days [S] *Lebanon, MO*

Bennett Spring State Park [W] *Lebanon, MO*

Bentonsport-National Historic District [W] *Fairfield, IA*

Bethel College Fall Festival [S] *Newton, KS*

Bicentennial Center [W] *Salina, KS*

Big Alkali Lake Wildlife Area [W] *Valentine, NE*

Big Bend Dam-Lake Sharpe [W] *Chamberlain, SD*

Big Island Rendezvous and Festival [S] *Albert Lea, MN*

Big Lake State Park [W] *Mound City, MO*

Big Shot Family Action Park [W] *Osage Beach, MO*

Big Sing USA [S] *St. Cloud, MN*

Big Splash Water Park [W] *Tulsa, OK*

Big Surf Water Park [W] *Osage Beach, MO*

Big Thunder Gold Mine [W] *Keystone, SD*

Big Well [W] *Greensburg, KS*

Bike Tour [S] *Mora, MN*

Biking [W] *Red Wing, MN*

Bily Clocks [W] *Decorah, IA*

Bingham-Waggoner Estate [W] *Independence, MO*

Birger Sandzen Memorial Art Gallery [W] *Lindsborg, KS*

Bix Beiderbecke Memorial Jazz Festival [S] *Davenport, IA*

Black Hawk Park [W] *Cedar Falls, IA*

Black Hawk State Park [W] *Carroll, IA*

Black Hills Caverns [W] *Rapid City, SD*

Black Hills Mining Museum [W] *Lead, SD*

Black Hills Passion Play [S] *Spearfish, SD*

Black Hills Petrified Forest [W] *Rapid City, SD*

Black Hills Powwow and Art Expo [S] *Rapid City, SD*

Black Hills Reptile Gardens [W] *Rapid City, SD*

Black Hills Roundup [S] *Belle Fourche, SD*

Black Hills State University [W] *Spearfish, SD*

Black Hills Wild Horse Sanctuary [W] *Hot Springs, SD*

Black Mesa State Park [W] *Boise City, OK*

Blackwood Family Music Show [W] *Branson/Table Rock Lake Area, MO*

Blackwood Quartet [W] *Branson/Table Rock Lake Area, MO*

Blanden Memorial Art Museum [W] *Fort Dodge, IA*

Blank Park Zoo [W] *Des Moines, IA*

Blueberry/Art Festival [S] *Ely, MN*

Bluegrass Festival [S] *Colby, KS*

Blue Mounds State Park [W] *Luverne, MN*

Blue Ribbon Downs [W] *Sallisaw, OK*

Bluestem Lake State Recreation Area [W] *Lincoln, NE*

Board of Trade [W] *Kansas City, MO*

Boat cruises. *Cherokee Queen I & II.* [W] *Grand Lake, OK*

Boat Excursions [W] *Taylors Falls, MN*

Boatyard [W] *Dubuque, IA*

Boggy Depot State Park [W] *Atoka, OK*

Boiling Springs State Park [W] *Woodward, OK*

Boise Cascade Paper Mill [W] *International Falls, MN*

Boji Bay [W] *Okoboji, IA*

Bolduc House Museum [W] *Ste. Genevieve, MO*

Bollinger Mill State Historic Site [W] *Cape Girardeau, MO*

Bonanzaville, USA [W] *Fargo, ND*

Bonne Terre Mine Tours [W] *Bonne Terre, MO*

Boone and Scenic Valley Railroad [W] *Boone, IA*

Boone County Fair [S] *Columbia, MO*

Boone County Heritage Festival [S] *Columbia, MO*

Bootheel Rodeo [S] *Sikeston, MO*

Boot Hill Museum [W] *Dodge City, KS*

Boot Hill Tours [W] *Deadwood, SD*

Borglum Historical Center [W] *Keystone, SD*

Boston Avenue United Methodist Church [W] *Tulsa, OK*

Botanica, The Wichita Gardens [W] *Wichita, KS*

Botany Greenhouses and Herbarium [W] *Columbia, MO*

Bothwell Lodge Garden Party [S] *Sedalia, MO*

Bothwell Lodge State Historic Site [W] *Sedalia, MO*

Bottineau Winter Park Ski Area [W] *Bottineau, ND*

Bourbon County Fair [S] *Fort Scott, KS*

Bowlus Fine Arts Center [W] *Iola, KS*

Bowman-Haley Lake [W] *Bowman, ND*

Boyhood Home of Major General Frederick Funston [W] *Iola, KS*

Boys Town [W] *Omaha, NE*

Brainerd International Raceway [S] *Brainerd, MN*

Bramble Park Zoo [W] *Watertown, SD*

Branched Oak Lake State Recreation Area [W] *Lincoln, NE*

Branson Scenic Railway [W] *Branson/Table Rock Lake Area, MO*

Branson's Magical Mansion [W] *Branson/Table Rock Lake Area, MO*

Breakthrough [W] *Fulton, MO*

Brenton National Bank— Poweshiek County [W] *Grinnell, IA*

Bridal Cave [W] *Camdenton, MO*

Bridgeport State Recreation Area [W] *Bridgeport, NE*

Brit Spaugh Park and Zoo [W] *Great Bend, KS*

Broken Boot Gold Mine [W] *Deadwood, SD*

Bronko Nagurski Museum [W] *International Falls, MN*

Brown County AG Museum [W] *Hiawatha, KS*

Brown County Fair [S] *New Ulm, MN*

Brown County Historical Museum [W] *New Ulm, MN*

Brown Grand Theatre, The [W] *Concordia, KS*

Brown Mansion [W] *Coffeyville, KS*

Brownville [W] *Auburn, NE*

Brownville State Recreation Area [W] *Auburn, NE*

Brucemore [W] *Cedar Rapids, IA*

Brush Creek Canyon [W] *Strawberry Point, IA*

Buck Hill [W] *Minneapolis, MN*

Buddy Holly Tribute [S] *Mason City, IA*

Buechel Memorial Lakota Museum [W] *Mission, SD*

Buena Vista County Historical Museum [W] *Storm Lake, IA*

Buffalo Bill Cody Homestead [W] *Bettendorf, IA*

Buffalo Bill Ranch State Historical Park [W] *North Platte, NE*

Buffalo Trails Day [S] *Williston, ND*

Buffalo Trails Museum [W] *Williston, ND*

Buffalo Wallow Chili Cook-off [S] *Custer, SD*

Buffalo Western Show [S] *Belle Fourche, SD*

Buggies 'n Blues [S] *Mandan, ND*

Bunnell House [W] *Winona, MN*

Burlington Steamboat Days & the American Music Festival [S] *Burlington, IA*

Bushwhacker Days [S] *Nevada, MO*

Bushwhacker Museum [W] *Nevada, MO*

Buster Keaton Festival [S] *Iola, KS*

Bus tour [W] *Hibbing, MN*

Butte County Fair [S] *Belle Fourche, SD*

Butterfly House and Education Center [W] *St. Louis, MO*

Butte View State Park [W] *Bowman, ND*

Cabela's [W] *Sidney, NE*

Caddo County Free Fair [S] *Anadarko, OK*

Camden State Park [W] *Marshall, MN*

Campanile [W] *Ames, IA*

Campbell House Museum [W] *St. Louis, MO*

Camp Creek Antique Machinery and Threshing Association Festival [S] *Lincoln, NE*

Camp Hancock State Historic Site [W] *Bismarck, ND*

Canadian County Historical Museum [W] *El Reno, OK*

Cannon Valley Trail [W] *Red Wing, MN*

Canoe Country Outfitters [W] *Ely, MN*

Canoeing [W] *Grand Rapids, MN*

Canoe Race [S] *Mora, MN*

Canoe trips [W] *Ely, MN*

Canoe trips [W] *Grand Marais, MN*

Cape River Heritage Museum [W] *Cape Girardeau, MO*

Cape Rock Park [W] *Cape Girardeau, MO*

Capitol City Trolley [W] *St. Paul, MN*

Captain Bailey Museum [W] *Auburn, NE*

Carhenge [W] *Bridgeport, NE*

Carleton College [W] *Northfield, MN*

Carousel Days [S] *Wahpeton, ND*

Carpenter St. Croix Valley Nature Center [W] *Hastings, MN*

Carry A. Nation Home Memorial [W] *Medicine Lodge, KS*

Carson House [W] *Auburn, NE*

Carter County Free Fair [S] *Ardmore, OK*

Carver-Hawkeye Arena [W] *Iowa City, IA*

Casino gambling [W] *Deadwood, SD*

Casino Pier [W] *Lake of the Ozarks, MO*

Cathedral of St Louis [W] *St. Louis, MO*

Cathedral of St. Paul [W] *St. Paul, MN*

Cathedral Square [W] *Dubuque, IA*

Cedar Bluff State Park [W] *WaKeeney, KS*

Cedar Falls Historical Society Victorian Home Museum [W] *Cedar Falls, IA*

Cedar Rapids Museum of Art [W] *Cedar Rapids, IA*

Celebration of the Arts [S] *Cedar Rapids, IA*

Centennial Center [W] *Huron, SD*

Central College [W] *Pella, IA*

Central Kansas Flywheels Historical Museum [W] *Salina, KS*

Central Kansas Free Fair and PRCA Wild Bill Hickock Rodeo [S] *Abilene, KS*

Central Missouri Regional Fair [S] *Rolla, MO*

Central Nebraska Ethnic Festival [S] *Grand Island, NE*

Central Park [W] *Crookston, MN*

Central School [W] *Grand Rapids, MN*

Central States Fair [S] *Rapid City, SD*

Century II Convention Center [W] *Wichita, KS*

Chadron State College [W] *Chadron, NE*

Chadron State Park [W] *Chadron, NE*

Chahinkapa Park [W] *Wahpeton, ND*

Chalet Campsite [W] *Glenwood, MN*

Chalk beds [W] *WaKeeney, KS*

Chanute Art Gallery [W] *Chanute, KS*

Chapel in the Hills [W] *Rapid City, SD*

Chaplin Nature Center [W] *Arkansas City, KS*

Charity Club Rodeo [S] *Ardmore, OK*

Charles A. Lindbergh House and History Center [W] *Little Falls, MN*

Charles A. Lindbergh State Park [W] *Little Falls, MN*

Charles A. Weyerhaeuser Memorial Museum [W] *Little Falls, MN*

Charles B. Goddard Center [W] *Ardmore, OK*

Charles H. MacNider Museum [W] *Mason City, IA*

Charley Pride Theatre [W] *Branson/Table Rock Lake Area, MO*

Chateau de Mores State Historic Site [W] *Medora, ND*

Cheney State Park [W] *Wichita, KS*

Cherokee County Fair [S] *Cherokee, IA*

Cherokee County Fair [S] *Tahlequah, OK*

Cherokee Heritage Center [W] *Tahlequah, OK*

Cherokee National Holiday [S] *Tahlequah, OK*

Cherokee Rodeo [S] *Cherokee, IA*

Cherokee Strip Celebration [S] *Enid, OK*

Cherokee Strip Celebration [S] *Perry, OK*

Cherokee Strip Land Rush Museum [W] *Arkansas City, KS*

Cherokee Strip Museum [W] *Alva, OK*

Cherokee Strip Museum [W] *Perry, OK*

Cherry County Fair [S] *Valentine, NE*

Cherry County Historical Museum [W] *Valentine, NE*

Cheyenne Bottoms [W] *Great Bend, KS*

Chickasaw National Recreation Area [W] *Sulphur, OK*

Chicken Show [S] *Wayne, NE*

Children's Museum at Yunker Farm [W] *Fargo, ND*

Children's Museum of Kansas City, The [W] *Kansas City, KS*

Chili Cookoff & Bluegrass Festival [S] *Tulsa, OK*

Chippewa National Forest [W] *Deer River, MN*

Chippewa National Forest [W] *Grand Rapids, MN*

Chisholm Trail Festival [S] *Abilene, KS*

Chisholm Trail Festival [S] *Newton, KS*

Chisholm Trail Historical Museum [W] *Waurika, OK*

Chisholm Trail Museum [W] *Duncan, OK*

Chocolate Festival [S] *Norman, OK*

Christ Church Cathedral [W] *St. Louis, MO*

Christian Petersen Sculptures [W] *Ames, IA*

Christmas at Union Station [S] *Omaha, NE*

Christmas on the Square [S] *Waynesville, MO*

Christmas Traditions [S] *St. Charles, MO*

Chuckwagon Suppers and Western Shows [W] *Rapid City, SD*

Circle B [W] *Rapid City, SD*

City Campgrounds [W] *Spearfish, SD*

City Hall and Court House [W] *St. Paul, MN*

City Lake [W] *Winfield, KS*

City Market [W] *Kansas City, MO*

City Park [W] *Manhattan, KS*

City parks [W] *Atchison, KS*

City parks [W] *Lincoln, NE*

City parks [W] *Omaha, NE*

City Parks. Wescott [W] *Cherokee, IA*

City recreation areas. Riverside Park. [W] *St. Cloud, MN*

Citywide Garage Sales [S] *Blue Earth, MN*

Civic Center [W] *Des Moines, IA*

Civic Center Music Hall [W] *Oklahoma City, OK*

Civil War Museum of Jackson County [W] *Blue Springs, MO*

Civil War Reenactment [S] *Clinton, IA*

Civil War Reenactment [S] *Keokuk, IA*

Clarke College [W] *Dubuque, IA*

Clausen Springs Park [W] *Valley City, ND*

Clay County Fair [S] *Spencer, IA*

Clay County Recreation Area [W] *Vermillion, SD*

Clear Lake [W] *Clear Lake, IA*

Clearwater Lake [W] *Van Buren, MO*

Clemens Gardens & Munsinger Gardens [W] *St. Cloud, MN*

Clifton Square Shopping Village [W] *Wichita, KS*

Climatron [W] *St. Louis, MO*

Clinton State Park [W] *Lawrence, KS*

Cloud County Fair [S] *Concordia, KS*

Cody Park [W] *North Platte, NE*

Cole County Fair [S] *Jefferson City, MO*

Cole County Historical Society Museum [W] *Jefferson City, MO*

Coleman Theatre Beautiful [W] *Miami, OK*

College Hill Arts Festival [S] *Cedar Falls, IA*

College of St. Benedict [W] *St. Cloud, MN*

College of the Ozarks [W] *Branson/Table Rock Lake Area, MO*

College View Seventh-day Adventist Church [W] *Lincoln, NE*

Colonial Hall Museum [W] *Anoka, MN*

Columbus Days [S] *Columbus, NE*

Combat Air Museum [W] *Topeka, KS*

Como Park [W] *St. Paul, MN*

Comstock Historic House [W] *Moorhead, MN*

Conestoga Lake State Recreation Area [W] *Lincoln, NE*

Confederate Memorial Museum and Cemetary [W] *Atoka, OK*

Cook County Fair [S] *Grand Marais, MN*

Coo-Y-Yah Country Museum [W] *Pryor, OK*

Coralville Lake [W] *Iowa City, IA*

Corbin Education Center [W] *Wichita, KS*

Corn Palace, The [W] *Mitchell, SD*

Corn Palace Festival [S] *Mitchell, SD*

Corn Palace Stampede [S] *Mitchell, SD*

Coronado Museum [W] *Liberal, KS*

Corvette Classic [S] *Spearfish, SD*

Cosmos of the Black Hills [W] *Keystone, SD*

Costello's Old Mill Gallery [W] *Maquoketa, IA*

Coterie—Kansas City's Family Theatre [W] *Kansas City, MO*

Cotton Carnival [S] *Sikeston, MO*

Cottonwood Prairie Festival [S] *Hastings, NE*

Council Grove Federal Lake [W] *Council Grove, KS*

Council Oak Shrine [W] *Council Grove, KS*

Country Club Plaza [W] *Kansas City, MO*

Country Relics Little Village and Homestead [W] *Webster City, IA*

County Fair [S] *Jackson, MN*

County Fair and NSRA Rodeo [S] *Sidney, NE*

County parks [W] *St. Louis, MO*

Court of Common Pleas Building [W] *Cape Girardeau, MO*

Covered Bridge Festival [S] *Winterset, IA*

Covered bridges [W] *Winterset, IA*

Cowboy Trail, The [W] *Norfolk, NE*

Cowley County Historical Museum [W] *Winfield, KS*

Craft Alliance Gallery [W] *Clayton, MO*

Crane Meadows Nature Center [W] *Grand Island, NE*

Crapo and Dankwardt Parks [W] *Burlington, IA*

Crawford County Historical Museum [W] *Pittsburg, KS*

Crawford State Park [W] *Pittsburg, KS*

Creek Council House Museum [W] *Okmulgee, OK*

Creek Council Oak Tree [W] *Tulsa, OK*

Creek Nation Rodeo and Festival [S] *Okmulgee, OK*

Crescent Lake National Wildlife Refuge [W] *Ogallala, NE*

Creston Hot Air Balloon Days [S] *Creston, IA*

Croatian Fest [S] *Centerville, IA*

Crosier Asmat Museum [W] *Hastings, NE*

Cross Ranch Nature Preserve. The Nature Conservancy [W] *Mandan, ND*

Crossroads of Yesteryear Museum [W] *Belleville, KS*

Crowder Lake [W] *Weatherford, OK*

Crown Center [W] *Kansas City, MO*

Crow Wing County Fair [S] *Brainerd, MN*

Crow Wing County Historical Society Museum [W] *Brainerd, MN*

Crystal Cave [W] *Springfield, MO*

Crystal Cave Park [W] *Rapid City, SD*

Crystal Lake Cave [W] *Dubuque, IA*

Crystal Lake State Recreation Area [W] *Hastings, NE*

Cuivre River State Park [W] *Wentzville, MO*

Cultural Center & Museums [W] *Ponca City, OK*

Cultural Heritage Center [W] *Pierre, SD*

Cupples House and Art Gallery [W] *St. Louis, MO*

Custer County Courthouse Museum [W] *Custer, SD*

Custer House [W] *Junction City, KS*

Custer's Elm Shrine [W] *Council Grove, KS*

Cut Foot Sioux Lakes [W] *Deer River, MN*

Czech Village [W] *Cedar Rapids, IA*

Dacotah Prairie Museum [W] *Aberdeen, SD*

Dacotah Territorial Reunion [S] *Yankton, SD*

Dahl Fine Arts Center [W] *Rapid City, SD*

Dakotafest [S] *Mitchell, SD*

Dakotaland Museum [W] *Huron, SD*

Dakota Soap Box Derby [S] *Valley City, ND*

Dakota State University [W] *Madison, SD*

Dakota Territorial Capitol [W] *Yankton, SD*

Dakota Territorial Museum [W] *Yankton, SD*

Dakota Zoo [W] *Bismarck, ND*

Dalton Defenders Day [S] *Coffeyville, KS*

Dalton Defenders Museum [W] *Coffeyville, KS*

Dana College [W] *Blair, NE*

Daniel Boone Home [W] *Wentzville, MO*

Danish Windmill [W] *Atlantic, IA*

Dan Nagle Walnut Grove Pioneer Village [W] *Davenport, IA*

Davenport Museum of Art [W] *Davenport, IA*

Davis Memorial [W] *Hiawatha, KS*

Dawes County Fair [S] *Chadron, NE*

Dawson County Fair [S] *Lexington, NE*

Dawson County Historical Museum [W] *Lexington, NE*

Day County Fair [S] *Webster, SD*

Days of '76 [S] *Deadwood, SD*

DC Booth Historic Fish Hatchery [W] *Spearfish, SD*

Deadwood Jam [S] *Deadwood, SD*

Decatur County Fair [S] *Oberlin, KS*

Decatur County Museum [W] *Oberlin, KS*

Deer Mountain [W] *Lead, SD*

Defeat of Jesse James Days [S] *Northfield, MN*

Deines Cultural Center [W] *Russell, KS*

Delbridge Museum of Natural History [W] *Sioux Falls, SD*

Delta Queen and *Mississippi Queen.* [W] *St. Louis, MO*

DeMenil Mansion and Museum [W] *St. Louis, MO*

Department of Natural Resources, Area Fisheries Headquarters [W] *Glenwood, MN*

Depot [W] *Auburn, NE*

Depot Museum [W] *Two Harbors, MN*

Depot Museum Complex [W] *Webster City, IA*

Depot Square [W] *Duluth, MN*

Depot, St Louis County Heritage and Arts Center, The [W] *Duluth, MN*

Des Lacs National Wildlife Refuge [W] *Kenmare, ND*

Des Moines Art Center [W] *Des Moines, IA*

Des Moines Botanical Center [W] *Des Moines, IA*

Des Moines Metro Opera Summer Festival [S] *Indianola, IA*

De Soto National Wildlife Refuge [W] *Blair, NE*

DeSoto National Wildlife Refuge [W] *Missouri Valley, IA*

Detroit Lakes City Park [W] *Detroit Lakes, MN*

Detroit Mountain Ski Area [W] *Detroit Lakes, MN*

Deutsche Schule Arts and Crafts [W] *Hermann, MO*

Deutschheim State Historic Site [W] *Hermann, MO*

Devils Lake [W] *Devils Lake, ND*

Devils Lake Area Welcome Center [W] *Devils Lake, ND*

Dewey Hotel Museum [W] *Bartlesville, OK*

Diamond Jo Casino. [W] *Dubuque, IA*

Dickerson Park Zoo [W] *Springfield, MO*

Dickinson County Historical Museum [W] *Abilene, KS*

Dietrich Cabin Museum [W] *Ottawa, KS*

Dillon Nature Center [W] *Hutchinson, KS*

Dinosaur Park [W] *Rapid City, SD*

Discovery Center [W] *Springfield, MO*

Discoveryland! Outdoor Theater [S] *Tulsa, OK*

Dodge City Days [S] *Dodge City, KS*

Dodge City Trolley [W] *Dodge City, KS*

Dog Museum, The [W] *St. Louis, MO*

Dogwood Days Festival [S] *Idabel, OK*

Dogwood Festival [S] *Camdenton, MO*

Dolliver Memorial [W] *Fort Dodge, IA*

Donna Reed Festival for the Performing Arts [S] *Denison, IA*

Doors to the Past [S] *Des Moines, IA*

Dorothea B. Hoover Historical Museum [W] *Joplin, MO*

Dorothy Molter Museum [W] *Ely, MN*

Double Ditch Indian Village [W] *Bismarck, ND*

Double Set Officer's Quarters Museum [W] *Sidney, NE*

Douglas County Free Fair [S] *Lawrence, KS*

Drake Relays [S] *Des Moines, IA*

Drake University [W] *Des Moines, IA*

Dr. Edmund A. Babler Memorial [W] *St. Louis, MO*

Driving tour [W] *Osawatomie, KS*

Drummond Home [W] *Pawhuska, OK*

Dubuque Arboretum and Botanical Gardens [W] *Dubuque, IA*

Dubuque Catfish Festival [S] *Dubuque, IA*

Dubuque County Courthouse [W] *Dubuque, IA*

Dubuque County Fair [S] *Dubuque, IA*

Dubuque Heritage Center [W] *Dubuque, IA*

Dubuque Museum of Art/Old County Jail [W] *Dubuque, IA*

Duluth Children's Museum [W] *Duluth, MN*

Duluth Lakewalk [W] *Duluth, MN*

Duluth-Superior Excursions [W] *Duluth, MN*

Durham Western Heritage Museum [W] *Omaha, NE*

Dutton Family Theatre [W] *Branson/Table Rock Lake Area, MO*

Eads Bridge [W] *St. Louis, MO*

Eagle Point Park [W] *Clinton, IA*

Eagle Point Park [W] *Dubuque, IA*

East Amana [W] *Amana Colonies, IA*

East Central University [W] *Ada, OK*

Eastern Trails Museum [W] *Vinita, OK*

Easter Sunday Pageant [S] *Lawton, OK*

East Leach Park Campground [W] *Spencer, IA*

Ed Clark Museum of Missouri Geology [W] *Rolla, MO*

Edgar M. Queeny Park [W] *St. Louis, MO*

Edison Electric Dynamo [W] *Columbia, MO*

Edwards Mill [W] *Branson/Table Rock Lake Area, MO*

Edwin A. Ulrich Museum of Art [W] *Wichita, KS*

Effigy Mounds National Monument [W] *Marquette, IA*

1859 Marshall's Home and Jail Museum [W] *Independence, MO*

1880 Train [W] *Hill City, SD*

1875 Log Cabin [W] *Custer, SD*

Eighty-niner Celebration [S] *Guthrie, OK*

89er Celebration [S] *Norman, OK*

Eisenhower Center [W] *Abilene, KS*

Eisenhower State Park [W] *Emporia, KS*

Elbow Lake [W] *Cook, MN*

El Dorado State Park [W] *El Dorado, KS*

Eliza Cruce Hall Doll Museum [W] *Ardmore, OK*

Ellis County Fair [S] *Hays, KS*

Ellis County Historical Society and Museum [W] *Hays, KS*

Ellis Library [W] *Columbia, MO*

Eloise Butler Wildflower Garden and Bird Sanctuary [W] *Minneapolis, MN*

Elvis and the Superstars Show [W] *Branson/Table Rock Lake Area, MO*

Emporia Gazette Building [W] *Emporia, KS*

Emporia Zoo [W] *Emporia, KS*

Enchanted World Doll Museum [W] *Mitchell, SD*

Enger Tower [W] *Duluth, MN*

Entertainment shows [W] *Branson/Table Rock Lake Area, MO*

EROS (Earth Resources Observation Systems) [W] *Sioux Falls, SD*

Ethnic Enrichment Festival [S] *Kansas City, MO*

Eufaula Dam [W] *Eufaula, OK*

Eugene Field House and Toy Museum [W] *St. Louis, MO*

Eugene Saint Julien Cox House [W] *St. Peter, MN*

Eugene T. Mahoney State Park [W] *Lincoln, NE*

Evah C. Cray Historical Home Museum [W] *Atchison, KS*

Evans Plunge [W] *Hot Springs, SD*

Excelsior Springs Historical Museum [W] *Excelsior Springs, MO*

Executive Mansion [W] *Lincoln, NE*

Exotic Animal Paradise [W] *Springfield, MO*

Fairgrounds and Pecan Grove [W] *Winfield, KS*

Fairmont Opera House [W] *Fairmont, MN*

Fair St Louis [S] *St. Louis, MO*

Fall Fest [S] *Concordia, KS*

Fall Festival [S] *Auburn, NE*

Fall Festival [S] *Madison, SD*

Fall Festival of the Arts [S] *Elk City, OK*

Fall Festival of the Arts [S] *Red Wing, MN*

Fall River County Museum [W] *Hot Springs, SD*

Fall River State Park [W] *Eureka, KS*

Family Museum of Arts & Science [W] *Bettendorf, IA*

Fantastic Caverns [W] *Springfield, MO*

Fargo-Moorhead Community Theatre [W] *Fargo, ND*

Fargo Theatre [W] *Fargo, ND*

Faribault County Fair [S] *Blue Earth, MN*

Faribault County Historical Society [W] *Blue Earth, MN*

Faribault Woolen Mill Company [W] *Faribault, MN*

Farm City Days [S] *Iola, KS*

Farm House [W] *Ames, IA*

Farm Island State Recreation Area [W] *Pierre, SD*

Fasching [S] *New Ulm, MN*

Father Hennepin Stone [W] *Anoka, MN*

Fejevary Park [W] *Davenport, IA*

Felix Valle Home State Historic Site [W] *Ste. Genevieve, MO*

Fenelon Place Elevator [W] *Dubuque, IA*

Ferry Service to Isle Royale National Park [W] *Grand Portage, MN*

Festival of America [S] *Branson/Table Rock Lake Area, MO*

Festival of Birds [S] *Detroit Lakes, MN*

Festival of Light [S] *Chickasha, OK*

Festival of the Arts [S] *Oklahoma City, OK*

Festival of the Little Hills [S] *St. Charles, MO*

Festival Weekend [S] *Jefferson City, MO*

Fick Fossil and History Museum [W] *Oakley, KS*

Field of Dreams Movie Site [W] *Dubuque, IA*

Fife and Drum Corps Concerts [S] *Hill City, SD*

Fighting Stallions Memorial [W] *Pierre, SD*

Finney County Fair [S] *Garden City, KS*

Finney Game Refuge [W] *Garden City, KS*

Finnup Park and Lee Richardson Zoo [W] *Garden City, KS*

1st Infantry Division Museum [W] *Junction City, KS*

First Missouri State Capitol State Historic Site [W] *St. Charles, MO*

First Street Trolley [W] *St. Joseph, MO*

First Territorial Capitol [W] *Junction City, KS*

Fisher Community Center Art Gallery [W] *Marshalltown, IA*

Fisher Grove State Park [W] *Redfield, SD*

Fisherman's Picnic [S] *Grand Marais, MN*

Fish House Parade [S] *Aitkin, MN*

Fishing [W] *Mora, MN*

Fishing [W] *Osawatomie, KS*

Fishing [W] *Valentine, NE*

Fishing, picnicking, boating. Neosho County State Fishing Lake [W] *Parsons, KS*

Fishing. Rainy Lake [W] *International Falls, MN*

Fishing. Whitman Dam and Locks #5 [W] *Winona, MN*

Fitger's Brewery Complex [W] *Duluth, MN*

Five Civilized Tribes Museum [W] *Muskogee, OK*

Five Flags Theater [W] *Dubuque, IA*

Five Nations Art Depot [W] *Mandan, ND*

Five-State Free Fair [S] *Liberal, KS*

Flagfest Summer Festival [S] *Spencer, IA*

Flaming Fountain [W] *Pierre, SD*

Flandrau [W] *New Ulm, MN*

Flatlander Fall Classic [S] *Goodland, KS*

Fleming Park [W] *Blue Springs, MO*

Flint Hills National Wildlife Refuge [W] *Emporia, KS*

Flintstones Bedrock City [W] *Custer, SD*

Float trips on the Illinois River [W] *Tahlequah, OK*

Floyd County Historical Society Museum [W] *Charles City, IA*

Flying T Chuckwagon [W] *Rapid City, SD*

Folkfest [S] *Bismarck, ND*

Folsom Children's Zoo [W] *Lincoln, NE*

Fonner Park [W] *Grand Island, NE*

Fontenelle Forest Nature Center [W] *Omaha, NE*

Forest History Center [W] *Grand Rapids, MN*

Forest Park [W] *Clayton, MO*

Forest Park [W] *St. Louis, MO*

Forestville/Mystery Cave State Park [W] *Spring Valley, MN*

Former Governors' Mansion State Historic Site [W] *Bismarck, ND*

Fort Abercrombie State Historic Site [W] *Wahpeton, ND*

Fort Abraham Lincoln State Park [W] *Mandan, ND*

Fort Atkinson State Historical Park [W] *Blair, NE*

Fort Atkinson State Preserve [W] *Decorah, IA*

Fort Belmont [W] *Jackson, MN*

Fort Buford 6th Infantry State Historical Encampment [S] *Williston, ND*

Fort Buford State Historic Site [W] *Williston, ND*

Fort Cobb State Park [W] *Anadarko, OK*

Fort Defiance State Park [W] *Estherville, IA*

Fort Dodge Historical Museum, Fort Museum and Frontier Village [W] *Fort Dodge, IA*

Fort Gibson Historic Site [W] *Muskogee, OK*

Fort Kearny State Historical Park [W] *Kearney, NE*

Fort Larned National Historic Site [W] *Larned, KS*

Fort Leavenworth [W] *Leavenworth, KS*

Fort Markley and Indian Village [W] *Seneca, KS*

Fort McPherson National Cemetery [W] *North Platte, NE*

Fort Meade Museum [W] *Sturgis, SD*

Fort Mille Lacs Village [W] *Onamia, MN*

Fort Niobrara National Wildlife Refuge [W] *Valentine, NE*

Fort Osage [W] *Independence, MO*

Fort Randall Dam-Lake Francis Case [W] *Platte, SD*

Fort Ridgely [W] *New Ulm, MN*

Fort Riley [W] *Junction City, KS*

Fort Robinson Museum [W] *Crawford, NE*

Fort Robinson State Park [W] *Crawford, NE*

Fort Scott National Cemetery [W] *Fort Scott, KS*

Fort Scott National Historic Site [W] *Fort Scott, KS*

Fort Seward Historic Site and Interpretive Center [W] *Jamestown, ND*

Fort Seward Wagon Train [S] *Jamestown, ND*

Fort Sidney Post Commander's Home [W] *Sidney, NE*

Fort Sill Military Reservation [W] *Lawton, OK*

Fort Sill National Historic Landmark [W] *Lawton, OK*

Fort Sisseton Historical Festival [S] *Sisseton, SD*

Fort Sisseton State Park [W] *Sisseton, SD*

Fort Snelling State Park [W] *Minneapolis, MN*

Fort Snelling State Park [W] *St. Paul, MN*

Fort Supply Lake [W] *Woodward, OK*

Fort Totten Little Theater [S] *Devils Lake, ND*

Fort Totten State Historic Site [W] *Devils Lake, ND*

Fort Union Trading Post National Historic Site [W] *Williston, ND*

Fort Union Trading Post Rendezvous [S] *Williston, ND*

45th Infantry Division Museum [W] *Oklahoma City, OK*

Fort Washita [W] *Durant, OK*

Fossil Station Museum [W] *Russell, KS*

Foss State Park [W] *Clinton, OK*

Fountainhead State Park [W] *Eufaula, OK*

Fountain Lake [W] *Albert Lea, MN*

Francesca's House [W] *Des Moines, IA*

Frank A. Gotch Park [W] *Humboldt, IA*

Franklin County Fair [S] *Ottawa, KS*

Frankoma Pottery [W] *Tulsa, OK*

Frank Phillips Mansion [W] *Bartlesville, OK*

Frederick R. Weisman Art Museum [W] *Minneapolis, MN*

Fred G. Dale Planetarium [W] *Wayne, NE*

Fred Maytag Park [W] *Newton, IA*

Freeborn County Fair [S] *Albert Lea, MN*

Freeborn County Historical Museum, Library, and Village [W] *Albert Lea, MN*

Freedom Festival [S] *Cedar Rapids, IA*

Fremont and Elkhorn Valley Railroad [W] *Fremont, NE*

Fremont Dinner Train [W] *Fremont, NE*

Fremont State Recreation Area [W] *Fremont, NE*

Frontier City [W] *Oklahoma City, OK*

Frontier Village [W] *Jamestown, ND*

Front Street [W] *Ogallala, NE*

Ft Homes Tour and Frontier Army Encampment [S] *Leavenworth, KS*

Full Harvest Moon Festival [S] *Ely, MN*

Fun Plex [W] *Omaha, NE*

Fur Trade Days [S] *Chadron, NE*

Gage County Fair [S] *Beatrice, NE*

Gage County Historical Museum [W] *Beatrice, NE*

Gage Park [W] *Topeka, KS*

Gallagher Canyon State Recreation Area [W] *Cozad, NE*

Gallery of Also-Rans [W] *Norton, KS*

Gallery of Art [W] *Cedar Falls, IA*

Garden Exhibition Building and Horticulture Gardens [W] *Oklahoma City, OK*

Garden Tour [S] *Abilene, KS*

Gardner Cabin [W] *Okoboji, IA*

Garrison Diversion Conservancy District [W] *Carrington, ND*

Garvin County Free Fair [S] *Pauls Valley, OK*

Garvin Heights [W] *Winona, MN*

Gateway Riverboat Cruises [W] *St. Louis, MO*

"Gateway to the West" Days [S] *Blair, NE*

Gathering, The [S] *WaKeeney, KS*

Geary County Historical Museum [W] *Junction City, KS*

General Crook House [W] *Omaha, NE*

General John J. Pershing Boyhood Home State Historic Site [W] *Chillicothe, MO*

General Zebulon Pike Lock and Dam [W] *Dubuque, IA*

Geode State Park [W] *Burlington, IA*

Geographical Museum and Pioneer Village [W] *Rugby, ND*

George Caleb Bingham House [W] *Arrow Rock, MO*

George Washington Carver National Memorial [W] *Carthage, MO*

George W. Frank House [W] *Kearney, NE*

George W. Norris House [W] *McCook, NE*

George Wyth House [W] *Cedar Falls, IA*

George Wyth Memorial State Park [W] *Cedar Falls, IA*

Gerald Ford Birth Site [W] *Omaha, NE*

Germanfest [S] *Fairbury, NE*

Ghost Hawk Park [W] *Mission, SD*

Ghosts of Deadwood Gulch Wax Museum [S] *Deadwood, SD*

Gibbs Farm Museum [W] *St. Paul, MN*

Gilcrease Museum [W] *Tulsa, OK*

Gilcrease Rendezvous [S] *Tulsa, OK*

Glacial Lakes Stampede and Rodeo Days [S] *Webster, SD*

Gladys Pyle Historic Home [W] *Huron, SD*

Glass Mountains [W] *Woodward, OK*

Glen Elder State Park [W] *Beloit, KS*

Glenn House [W] *Cape Girardeau, MO*

Glenn Miller Festival [S] *Clarinda, IA*

Glensheen [W] *Duluth, MN*

Glick-Sower Historical Homestead [W] *Marshalltown, IA*

Glockenspiel, The [W] *New Ulm, MN*

Glore Psychiatric Museum [W] *St. Joseph, MO*

Gold Discovery Days [S] *Custer, SD*

Golden Circle Tours [W] *Custer, SD*

Goldenrod Showboat [W] *St. Charles, MO*

Golden Spike [W] *Council Bluffs, IA*

Gondola Skyride [W] *Lutsen, MN*

Goodhue County Historical Museum [W] *Red Wing, MN*

Goodnow House Museum [W] *Manhattan, KS*

Good Ol' Days Celebration [S] *Fort Scott, KS*

Gooseberry Falls State Park [W] *Two Harbors, MN*

Government Buildings [W] *Kansas City, MO*

Governor's Cup Sailboat Regatta [S] *Ogallala, NE*

Governor's Mansion [W] *Jefferson City, MO*

Governor's Mansion (Cedar Crest) [W] *Topeka, KS*

Grady County Fair [S] *Chickasha, OK*

Graham Cave State Park [W] *Hermann, MO*

Grand Army of the Republic Hall [W] *Litchfield, MN*

Grand Forks County Fair [S] *Grand Forks, ND*

Grand Forks County Historical Society [W] *Grand Forks, ND*

Grand Mound History Center [W] *International Falls, MN*

Grand National Quail Hunt [S] *Enid, OK*

Grand Opera House [W] *Dubuque, IA*

Grandpa Bill's Farm [W] *Burlington, IA*

Grand Palace, The [W] *Branson/Table Rock Lake Area, MO*

Grand Portage [W] *Grand Portage, MN*

Grand Portage National Monument [W] *Grand Marais, MN*

Grand Portage National Monument [W] *Grand Portage, MN*

Grant's Bluegrass & Old-Time Music Festival [S] *Hugo, OK*

Grant's Farm [W] *St. Louis, MO*

Grant Wood Murals [W] *Ames, IA*

Grapes of Wrath Festival [S] *Sallisaw, OK*

Gray Line bus tours [W] *Minneapolis, MN*

Gray Line bus tours [W] *St. Louis, MO*

Gray Line bus tours [W] *St. Paul, MN*

Gray Line Sightseeing Tours [W] *Rapid City, SD*

Great American History Theatre [W] *St. Paul, MN*

Great American Music Festival [W] *Branson/Table Rock Lake Area, MO*

Greater Southwest Historical Museum [W] *Ardmore, OK*

Great Forest Park Balloon Race [S] *St. Louis, MO*

Great Plains Art Collection [W] *Lincoln, NE*

Great Plains Black History Museum [W] *Omaha, NE*

Great Plains Oldtime Fiddlers Contest [S] *Yankton, SD*

Great Plains Stampede Rodeo [S] *Altus, OK*

Great Plains Zoo [W] *Sioux Falls, SD*

Great Raccoon River Fun Float [S] *Carroll, IA*

Great Salt Plains [W] *Alva, OK*

Great Stone Hill Grape Stomp [S] *Hermann, MO*

Greenleaf Lake State Park [W] *Muskogee, OK*

Greenstone outcropping [W] *Ely, MN*

Green Valley State Park [W] *Creston, IA*

Greenwood County Historical Society and Museum [W] *Eureka, KS*

Greyhound Hall of Fame [W] *Abilene, KS*

Grinnell College [W] *Grinnell, IA*

Grinnell Historical Museum [W] *Grinnell, IA*

Grinter House [W] *Kansas City, KS*

Grotto of the Redemption [W] *West Bend, IA*

Grout Museum of History and Science [W] *Waterloo, IA*

Guibourd-Valle House [W] *Ste. Genevieve, MO*

Gull Point [W] *Okoboji, IA*

Gull Point State Park [W] *Spencer, IA*

Gunflint Trail [W] *Grand Marais, MN*

Gunn Park [W] *Fort Scott, KS*

Gus Fonner Memorial Rotunda [W] *Grand Island, NE*

Gustavus Adolphus College [W] *St. Peter, MN*

Guthrie Theater [W] *Minneapolis, MN*

Gypsum Hills [W] *Medicine Lodge, KS*

Gypsy Caravan [S] *St. Louis, MO*

Ha Ha Tonka State Park [W] *Camdenton, MO*

Half Marathon [S] *Mora, MN*

Hallmark Visitors Center [W] *Kansas City, MO*

Hall of Waters [W] *Excelsior Springs, MO*

Halloween Parade [S] *Hiawatha, KS*

Hannibal Trolley [W] *Hannibal, MO*

Har-Ber Village [W] *Grand Lake, OK*

Harkin Store [W] *New Ulm, MN*

Harn Homestead and 1889er Museum [W] *Oklahoma City, OK*

Harold Warp Pioneer Village [W] *Kearney, NE*

Harold Warp Pioneer Village [W] *Minden, NE*

Harrison County Historical Village/Welcome Center [W] *Missouri Valley, IA*

Harry S Truman Birthplace State Historic Site [W] *Lamar, MO*

Harry S. Truman Courtroom and Office Museum [W] *Independence, MO*

Harry S Truman Library and Museum [W] *Independence, MO*

Harry S. Truman National Historic Site (Truman House) [W] *Independence, MO*

Harry S. Truman State Park [W] *Clinton, MO*

Hartford Beach State Park [W] *Milbank, SD*

Hartford House [W] *Manhattan, KS*

Harvest Festival [S] *Carrington, ND*

Harvest Festival [S] *Gothenburg, NE*

Harvest of Harmony Festival & Parade [S] *Grand Island, NE*

Haskell Indian Nations University [W] *Lawrence, KS*

Hastings Museum [W] *Hastings, NE*

Haunted Home Tours [S] *Atchison, KS*

Haunted House on Hill Street [W] *Hannibal, MO*

Hawkeye Log Cabin [W] *Burlington, IA*

Hawthorne Ranch Trail Rides [W] *Eureka, KS*

Hayes Lake State Park [W] *Roseau, MN*

Hays House [W] *Council Grove, KS*

Heartland Museum of Military Vehicles [W] *Lexington, NE*

Heartland of America Park [W] *Omaha, NE*

Heartland Park Topeka [W] *Topeka, KS*

Heart of the Hills Celebration [S] *Hill City, SD*

Heavener Runestone [W] *Poteau, OK*

Hennepin History Museum [W] *Minneapolis, MN*

Henry County Historical Society Museum and Cultural Arts Center [W] *Clinton, MO*

Henry Doorly Zoo [W] *Omaha, NE*

Herbert Hoover National Historic Site [W] *Iowa City, IA*

Herbert Hoover Presidential Library-Museum [W] *Iowa City, IA*

Heritage Days [S] *McCook, NE*

Heritagefest [S] *New Ulm, MN*

Heritage Fest [S] *Shawnee, OK*

Heritage Halls Museum [W] *Owatonna, MN*

Heritage Hill National Historic District [W] *Burlington, IA*

Heritage-Hjemkomst Interpretive Center [W] *Moorhead, MN*

Heritage Trail [W] *Dubuque, IA*

Heritage Village [W] *Des Moines, IA*

Heritage Village [W] *Grafton, ND*

Heritage Zoo [W] *Grand Island, NE*

Hermannhof Winery [W] *Hermann, MO*

Hermann's Monument [W] *New Ulm, MN*

Hibbing World Classic Rodeo [S] *Hibbing, MN*

Hidden Valley Ski Area [W] *St. Louis, MO*

Higgins Museum [W] *Okoboji, IA*

High Amana [W] *Amana Colonies, IA*

High Plains Heritage Center and Museum [W] *Spearfish, SD*

High Plains Museum [W] *Goodland, KS*

Hiking [W] *Red Wing, MN*

Hinckley Fire Museum [W] *Hinckley, MN*

Historical Museum [W] *Weston, MO*

Historic Bellevue [W] *Omaha, NE*

Historic buildings [W] *Medora, ND*

Historic buildings [W] *Spring Valley, MN*

Historic Claybrook Plantation [W] *Excelsior Springs, MO*

Historic District [W] *Hot Springs, SD*

Historic Fort Hays [W] *Hays, KS*

Historic Fort Hays Days [S] *Hays, KS*

Historic Fort Snelling [W] *St. Paul, MN*

Historic Fort Supply [W] *Woodward, OK*

Historic Fox Theatre [W] *Hutchinson, KS*

Historic Front Street [W] *Dodge City, KS*

Historic General Dodge House [W] *Council Bluffs, IA*

Historic Hermann Museum [W] *Hermann, MO*

Historic Homes Tour [S] *Atchison, KS*

Historic Homes Tour [S] *St. Joseph, MO*

Historic Pottawattamie County Jail [W] *Council Bluffs, IA*

Historic Trolley Tour [W] *Fort Scott, KS*

Historic Walking Tour [W] *Hastings, MN*

Historic Ward-Meade Historical Park [W] *Topeka, KS*

History Museum, The [W] *Springfield, MO*

Hochatown State Park [W] *Broken Bow, OK*

Holiday Animated Lighting Extravaganza [S] *Carroll, IA*

Holiday Celebration [S] *Anadarko, OK*

Hollenberg Pony Express Station [W] *Marysville, KS*

Holmes Park [W] *Lincoln, NE*

Home of Stone & Ford County Museum [W] *Dodge City, KS*

Home on the Range Cabin [W] *Smith Center, KS*

Homestake Gold Mine Surface Tours [W] *Lead, SD*

Homestead [W] *Amana Colonies, IA*

Homestead Days [S] *Beatrice, NE*

Homesteader's Sod House [W] *Enid, OK*

Homestead National Monument [W] *Beatrice, NE*

Homme Dam Recreation Area [W] *Grafton, ND*

Honey Creek State Park [W] *Centerville, IA*

Honor Heights Park [W] *Muskogee, OK*

Horse racing [S] *Columbus, NE*

Horse racing [S] *Lincoln, NE*

Horse racing [S] *South Sioux City, NE*

Houby Days [S] *Cedar Rapids, IA*

Hoyt Sherman Place [W] *Des Moines, IA*

Hubbard County Historical Museum/North Country Museum of Arts [W] *Park Rapids, MN*

Hubbard House [W] *Mankato, MN*

Hubert H. Humphrey Drugstore [W] *Huron, SD*

Hubert H. Humphrey Metrodome [W] *Minneapolis, MN*

Huff Hills Ski Area [W] *Mandan, ND*

Huff 'n Puff Balloon Rally [S] *Topeka, KS*

Hugo Lake [W] *Hugo, OK*

Hull-Rust Mahoning Mine [W] *Hibbing, MN*

Humboldt County Historical Museum [W] *Humboldt, IA*

Hunting preserves. Lexington. [W] *Norman, OK*

Huron Indian Cemetery [W] *Kansas City, KS*

Husker Harvest Days [S] *Grand Island, NE*

Hyland Hills [W] *Minneapolis, MN*

Ice Cream Days [S] *Le Mars, IA*

Icefest [S] *Brainerd, MN*

Icehouse Museum [W] *Cedar Falls, IA*

IDS Tower [W] *Minneapolis, MN*

Illinois River Balloon Fest [S] *Tahlequah, OK*

Independence Museum [W] *Independence, KS*

Independence Park [W] *Atchison, KS*

Independence Science & Technology Center [W] *Independence, KS*

Indian Arts Show [S] *Lawrence, KS*

Indian Cave State Park [W] *Auburn, NE*

Indian Center Museum [W] *Wichita, KS*

Indian City—USA [W] *Anadarko, OK*

Indian Creek Nature Center [W] *Cedar Rapids, IA*

Indian Powwow [S] *Pawnee, OK*

Indian Powwow [S] *Wichita, KS*

International Bowling Hall of Fame and Museum [W] *St. Louis, MO*

International Falls City Beach [W] *International Falls, MN*

International Festival [S] *Lawton, OK*

International Finals Rodeo [S] *Oklahoma City, OK*

International Folk Festival [S] *Duluth, MN*

International Forest of Friendship [W] *Atchison, KS*

International Music Camp [S] *Bottineau, ND*

International Pancake Race [S] *Liberal, KS*

International Peace Garden [W] *Bottineau, ND*

International Photography Hall of Fame and Museum [W] *Oklahoma City, OK*

International Rodeo Association Competition [S] *Pauls Valley, OK*

International Rolle Bolle Tournament [S] *Marshall, MN*

International Roundup Clubs Cavalcade [S] *Pawhuska, OK*

International Wolf Center [W] *Ely, MN*

Interstate [W] *Taylors Falls, MN*

Inter-State Fair and Rodeo [S] *Coffeyville, KS*

Intertribal Pow Wow [S] *Coffeyville, KS*

Iowa Arboretum [W] *Ames, IA*

Iowa Arts Festival [S] *Iowa City, IA*

Iowa Children's Museum [W] *Iowa City, IA*

Iowa Hall [W] *Iowa City, IA*

Iowa Historical Building [W] *Des Moines, IA*

Iowa Star Clipper Dinner Train [W] *Waverly, IA*

Iowa State Center [W] *Ames, IA*

Iowa State Fair [S] *Des Moines, IA*

Iowa State University [W] *Ames, IA*

Iowa Welcome Center [W] *Dubuque, IA*

Iowa Wesleyan College [W] *Mount Pleasant, IA*

Ironworld USA [W] *Hibbing, MN*

Island Oasis Water Park [W] *Grand Island, NE*

Itasca County Fair [S] *Grand Rapids, MN*

Jackson County Fair [S] *Altus, OK*

Jackson County Historical Museum [W] *Maquoketa, IA*

Jackson Park [W] *Atchison, KS*

Jacob's Cave [W] *Lake of the Ozarks, MO*

James J. Hill House [W] *St. Paul, MN*

Japanese Garden [W] *St. Louis, MO*

Jasper County Courthouse [W] *Carthage, MO*

Jasper County Historical Museum [W] *Newton, IA*

Jaycees Rodeo Days [S] *Mandan, ND*

Jay Cooke State Park [W] *Duluth, MN*

Jazz Festival [S] *Wichita, KS*

Jazz Fest on the River [S] *Burlington, IA*

J.C. Hormel Nature Center [W] *Austin, MN*

J. Clark Salyer National Wildlife Refuge [W] *Bottineau, ND*

Jefferson Barracks Historical Park [W] *St. Louis, MO*

Jefferson County Park [W] *Fairfield, IA*

Jefferson Landing State Historic Site [W] *Jefferson City, MO*

Jefferson National Expansion Memorial [W] *St. Louis, MO*

Jesse James Bank Museum [W] *Kansas City, MO*

Jesse James' Farm [W] *Excelsior Springs, MO*

Jesse James Home [W] *St. Joseph, MO*

Jesse James Wax Museum [W] *Sullivan, MO*

Jewel Box Floral Conservatory [W] *St. Louis, MO*

Jim Stafford Theatre [W] *Branson/Table Rock Lake Area, MO*

J.M. Davis Arms & Historical Museum [W] *Claremore, OK*

Joachim Regional Museum [W] *Dickinson, ND*

Joe Sheldon Park [W] *Humboldt, IA*

John Beargrease Sled Dog Marathon [S] *Duluth, MN*

John Brown Jamboree [S] *Osawatomie, KS*

John Brown Memorial Park [W] *Osawatomie, KS*

John Brown's Cave [W] *Nebraska City, NE*

John C. Frémont Days [S] *Fremont, NE*

John Deere Ottumwa Works [W] *Ottumwa, IA*

John Deere Waterloo Works [W] *Waterloo, IA*

John F. Kennedy Memorial Park [W] *Fort Dodge, IA*

John G. Neihardt Center [W] *West Point, NE*

John L. Lewis Museum of Mining and Labor [W] *Chariton, IA*

John M. Clemens Law Office [W] *Hannibal, MO*

Johnny Spaulding Cabin [W] *Belle Fourche, SD*

Johnson Lake Open Regatta [S] *Lexington, NE*

Johnson Lake State Recreation Area [W] *Lexington, NE*

Johnson's Shut-Ins State Park [W] *Pilot Knob, MO*

John Wayne Birthplace [W] *Winterset, IA*

John Wornall House Museum [W] *Kansas City, MO*

Jonathan Emerson Monument [W] *Anoka, MN*

Joslyn Art Museum [W] *Omaha, NE*

Jour de FÍte à Ste Geneviè:ve [S] *Ste. Genevieve, MO*

Journey, The [W] *Rapid City, SD*

Judy Garland Birthplace and Children's Museum [W] *Grand Rapids, MN*

Judy Garland Festival [S] *Grand Rapids, MN*

Julien Dubuque Monument [W]
Dubuque, IA

Julius C. Wilkie Steamboat Center
[W] *Winona, MN*

July Jamm [S] *Lincoln, NE*

Kabetogama Lake [W] *Lake
Kabetogama, MN*

Kaleidoscope [W] *Kansas City, MO*

Kalona Fall Festival [S] *Iowa City,
IA*

Kalona Historical Village [W] *Iowa
City, IA*

Kalsow Prairie [W] *Fort Dodge, IA*

Kampeska Heritage Museum [W]
Watertown, SD

Kanabec History Center [W] *Mora,
MN*

Kandiyohi County Historical Society Museum [W] *Willmar,
MN*

Kanopolis State Park [W] *Lindsborg, KS*

Kansas City Art Institute [W]
Kansas City, MO

Kansas City Blades (IHL) [W]
Kansas City, MO

Kansas City Blues and Jazz Festival
[S] *Kansas City, MO*

Kansas City Chiefs (NFL) [W]
Kansas City, MO

Kansas City Museum [W] *Kansas
City, MO*

Kansas City Pro Rodeo [S] *Kansas
City, MO*

Kansas City Royals (MLB) [W]
Kansas City, MO

Kansas City Symphony [S] *Kansas
City, MO*

Kansas City Trolley [W] *Kansas
City, MO*

Kansas City Wizards (MLS) [W]
Kansas City, MO

Kansas City Zoological Gardens
[W] *Kansas City, MO*

Kansas Cosmosphere and Space
Center [W] *Hutchinson, KS*

Kansas Learning Center for Health
[W] *Newton, KS*

Kansas Museum of History [W]
Topeka, KS

Kansas Oil Museum and Butler
County Historical Museum
[W] *El Dorado, KS*

Kansas State Fair [S] *Hutchinson,
KS*

Kansas State Fish Hatchery/Nature
Center [W] *Pratt, KS*

Kansas State Historical Society [W]
Topeka, KS

Kansas State University [W] *Manhattan, KS*

Karpeles Manuscript Library
Museum [W] *Duluth, MN*

Katy Trail State Park [W] *St.
Charles, MO*

Kauffman Museum [W] *Newton,
KS*

Kaw Lake [W] *Ponca City, OK*

Kaw Mission State Historic Site
[W] *Council Grove, KS*

Kearney Area Children's Museum
[W] *Kearney, NE*

Kearney Park [W] *Emmetsburg, IA*

Keith County Fair and Round-Up
Rodeo [S] *Ogallala, NE*

Kemper Museum of Contemporary Art and Design [W]
Kansas City, MO

Keokuk Dam [W] *Keokuk, IA*

Keokuk River Museum [W]
Keokuk, IA

Kerr Museum [W] *Poteau, OK*

Kiamichi Owa Chito Festival [S]
Broken Bow, OK

Kiamichi Owa Chito Festival of
the Forest [S] *Idabel, OK*

Kidder Recreation Area [W] *Wahpeton, ND*

Kilen Woods State Park [W] *Jackson, MN*

Kingdom Days [S] *Fulton, MO*

Kingdom Expo and Car Museum
[W] *Fulton, MO*

Kinney Pioneer Museum [W]
Mason City, IA

Kiowa Veterans Black Leggins Ceremonial [S] *Anadarko, OK*

Kirkpatrick Science and Air Space
Museum [W] *Oklahoma City,
OK*

Kirwin National Wildlife Refuge
[W] *Phillipsburg, KS*

Klein Museum [W] *Mobridge, SD*

Klokkenspel at Franklin Place [W]
Pella, IA

Knob Noster State Park [W]
Sedalia, MO

Koester House Museum [W]
   Marysville, KS
Koochiching County Historical
   Museum [W] International
   Falls, MN
Kool-Aid Days [S] Hastings, NE
Kool Deadwood Nites [S] Dead-
   wood, SD
Kountze Planetarium [W] Omaha,
   NE
KristKindl Markt [S] Hermann, MO
Kumberland Gap Pioneer Settle-
   ment [W] Clinton, MO
Lacey-Keosauqua State Park [W]
   Fairfield, IA
Laclede County Fair [S] Lebanon,
   MO
Laclede County Museum [W]
   Lebanon, MO
Laclede's Landing [W] St. Louis,
   MO
Lac qui Parle State Park [W] Gran-
   ite Falls, MN
Lady Luck Casino [W] Bettendorf,
   IA
Lafayette County Courthouse [W]
   Lexington, MO
Lake Afton Public Observatory
   [W] Wichita, KS
Lake Ahquabi State Park [W] Indi-
   anola, IA
Lake Bemidji State Park [W]
   Bemidji, MN
Lake Carl Blackwell [W] Stillwater,
   OK
Lake Carlos State Park [W] Alexan-
   dria, MN
Lake cruises [W] Lake of the
   Ozarks, MO
Lake Darling [W] Kenmare, ND
Lake Darling State Park [W] Wash-
   ington, IA
Lake Hastings [W] Hastings, NE
Lake Herman State Park [W] Madi-
   son, SD
Lake Hudson [W] Pryor, OK
Lake Kampeska [W] Watertown, SD
Lake Keomah State Park [W]
   Oskaloosa, IA
Lake Keystone [W] Tulsa, OK
Lake Macbride State Park [W] Iowa
   City, IA
Lake Maloney [W] North Platte, NE

Lake Manawa State Park [W]
   Council Bluffs, IA
Lake McAlester [W] McAlester, OK
Lake McConaughy State Recre-
   ation Area [W] Ogallala, NE
Lake Metigoshe State Park [W]
   Bottineau, ND
Lake Minatare State Recreation
   Area [W] Scottsbluff, NE
Lake Mitchell [W] Mitchell, SD
Lake Murray State Park [W] Ard-
   more, OK
Lake Murray State Park [W] Ard-
   more, OK
Lake Murray State Park [W] Mari-
   etta, OK
Lake Murray State Park [W] Mari-
   etta, OK
Lake of the Ozarks State Park [W]
   Lake of the Ozarks, MO
Lake of the Woods [W] Baudette,
   MN
Lake of the Woods County
   Museum [W] Baudette, MN
Lake of Three Fires State Park [W]
   Clarinda, IA
Lake Ogallala State Recreation
   Area [W] Ogallala, NE
Lake Ponca [W] Ponca City, OK
Lake Queen Cruises [W]
   Branson/Table Rock Lake
   Area, MO
Lakes [W] Cook, MN
Lake Scott State Park [W] Scott
   City, KS
Lake Shawnee [W] Topeka, KS
Lake Shetek State Park [W] Tracy,
   MN
Lake Superior Maritime Visitors
   Center [W] Duluth, MN
Lake Superior Railroad Museum
   [W] Duluth, MN
Lake Superior Zoological Gardens
   [W] Duluth, MN
Lake Thunderbird State Park [W]
   Norman, OK
Lake Vermilion [W] Cook, MN
Lake Vermilion [W] Tower, MN
Lake Wapello State Park [W]
   Ottumwa, IA
Lake Wappapello State Park [W]
   Poplar Bluff, MO
Lake Wister State Park [W] Poteau,
   OK

Lamar Free Fair [S] *Lamar, MO*

Landmark Center [W] *St. Paul, MN*

Land Office [W] *Auburn, NE*

Land of Memories [W] *Mankato, MN*

Lansing Daze [S] *Leavenworth, KS*

Last Chance Curling Bonspiel [S] *Hibbing, MN*

Last Run Car Show [S] *Arkansas City, KS*

Laumeier Sculpture Park [W] *St. Louis, MO*

Laura Ingalls Wilder Home [W] *Brookings, SD*

Laura Ingalls Wilder Memorial [W] *Huron, SD*

Laura Ingalls Wilder Museum and Tourist Center [W] *Tracy, MN*

Laura Ingalls Wilder Pageant [S] *Huron, SD*

Laura Ingalls Wilder Pageant [S] *Tracy, MN*

Laura Ingalls Wilder-Rose Wilder Lane Museum and Home [W] *Springfield, MO*

LaVitsef Celebration [S] *Norfolk, NE*

Lawrence Arts Center [W] *Lawrence, KS*

Lawrence Welk Show [W] *Branson/Table Rock Lake Area, MO*

Lawton Birthday and Rodeo Celebration [S] *Lawton, OK*

Leavenworth River Fest [S] *Leavenworth, KS*

Leavenworth's Victorian Carroll Museum [W] *Leavenworth, KS*

Lebold-Vahsholtz Mansion [W] *Abilene, KS*

Ledges State Park [W] *Boone, IA*

Leech Lake [W] *Walker, MN*

Lee County Courthouse [W] *Fort Madison, IA*

Lee Mace's Ozark Opry [S] *Osage Beach, MO*

Leif Erikson Park [W] *Duluth, MN*

Lendonwood Gardens [W] *Grand Lake, OK*

Lewis and Clark Center [W] *St. Charles, MO*

Lewis and Clark Lake/Gavins Point Dam [W] *Yankton, SD*

Lewis and Clark Lake State Recreation Area [W] *Crofton, NE*

Lewis and Clark Monument [W] *Council Bluffs, IA*

Lewis and Clark Rendezvous [S] *St. Charles, MO*

Lewis & Clark *Riverboat [W] *Bismarck, ND*

Lewis and Clark State Park [W] *Onawa, IA*

Lewis and Clark State Park [W] *Weston, MO*

Lewis and Clark State Park [W] *Williston, ND*

Lewis and Clark Trail Museum [W] *Williston, ND*

Lexington Historical Museum [W] *Lexington, MO*

L. Frank Baum Oz Festival [S] *Aberdeen, SD*

Liberal Air Museum [W] *Liberal, KS*

Lighted Christmas Parade [S] *Oskaloosa, IA*

Lighthouse Point and Harbor Museum [W] *Two Harbors, MN*

The Light of the World Christmas Pageant [S] *Minden, NE*

Lillian Russell Theatre [W] *Clinton, IA*

Lime Creek Nature Center [W] *Mason City, IA*

Lincoln Children's Museum [W] *Lincoln, NE*

Lincoln County Historical Museum [W] *North Platte, NE*

Lincoln Monument [W] *Council Bluffs, IA*

Lincoln Monument [W] *Lincoln, NE*

Lincoln Park [W] *Pittsburg, KS*

Little Dixie Lake Conservation Area [W] *Fulton, MO*

"Little House on the Prairie" [W] *Independence, KS*

Little Red School, The [W] *Cedar Falls, IA*

Little River Zoo [S] *Norman, OK*

Little Sahara [W] *Alva, OK*

Little Yellowstone Park [W] *Valley City, ND*

Living Heritage Tree Museum [W] *Storm Lake, IA*

Living History Farms [W] *Des Moines, IA*

Loess Hills Scenic Byway [W] *Missouri Valley, IA*

Log Cabin Festival [S] *Harrisonville, MO*

Log Hotel [W] *Stockton, KS*

Log House Museum [W] *Lexington, MO*

Lone Elk Park [W] *St. Louis, MO*

Long Branch Saloon [S] *Dodge City, KS*

Long Branch State Park [W] *Macon, MO*

Loras College [W] *Dubuque, IA*

Louis E. May Historical Museum [W] *Fremont, NE*

Louisville State Recreation Area [W] *Omaha, NE*

Love County Frontier Days Celebration [S] *Marietta, OK*

Lovewell State Park [W] *Mankato, KS*

Lower Sioux Agency and History Center [W] *Redwood Falls, MN*

Lucas County Historical Museum [W] *Chariton, IA*

Lucia Fest [S] *Lindsborg, KS*

Lumberjack Days [S] *Stillwater, MN*

Luther Northwestern Theological Seminary [W] *St. Paul, MN*

Lutsen Mountains Ski Area [W] *Lutsen, MN*

Lyndale Park [W] *Minneapolis, MN*

Lynn Riggs Memorial [W] *Claremore, OK*

Lyon County Free Fair [S] *Emporia, KS*

Lyon County Historical Museum [W] *Emporia, KS*

Lyric Opera [S] *Kansas City, MO*

Lyric Theatre [S] *Oklahoma City, OK*

Mabee-Gerrer Museum of Art [W] *Shawnee, OK*

Madison County Fair [S] *Winterset, IA*

Madison County Museum and Complex [W] *Winterset, IA*

Madonna of the Trail Monument, The [W] *Council Grove, KS*

Magic House, St Louis Children's Museum, The [W] *St. Louis, MO*

Magnolia Festival [S] *Durant, OK*

Maifest [S] *Hermann, MO*

Main Street Opry [S] *Osage Beach, MO*

Mall of America [W] *Bloomington, MN*

Mamie Doud Eisenhower Birthplace [W] *Boone, IA*

Mammoth Site of Hot Springs [W] *Hot Springs, SD*

Mansion on the Hill [W] *Ogallala, NE*

Maple Leaf Festival [S] *Carthage, MO*

Maquoketa Caves State Park [W] *Maquoketa, IA*

Maramec Spring Park and Remains of Old Ironworks [W] *Rolla, MO*

Margaret M. MacNider/East Park [W] *Mason City, IA*

Mark Twain Birthplace and State Park [W] *Monroe City, MO*

Mark Twain Cave [W] *Hannibal, MO*

Mark Twain Museum and Boyhood Home [W] *Hannibal, MO*

Mark Twain National Forest [W] *Bonne Terre, MO*

Mark Twain National Forest [W] *Cassville, MO*

Mark Twain National Forests [W] *Poplar Bluff, MO*

Mark Twain National Forests [W] *Rolla, MO*

Mark Twain Outdoor Theater [S] *Hannibal, MO*

Mark Twain Overlook [W] *Muscatine, IA*

Mark Twain Riverboat Excursions [W] *Hannibal, MO*

Marland Mansion Estate [W] *Ponca City, OK*

Marshall W. Alworth Planetarium [W] *Duluth, MN*

Martin and Osa Johnson Safari Museum [W] *Chanute, KS*

Martin H. Bush Outdoor Sculpture Collection [W] *Wichita, KS*

Masonic Library [W] *Cedar Rapids, IA*

Mastodon State Historic Site [W] *St. Louis, MO*

Mathias Ham House Historic Site [W] *Dubuque, IA*

Matthews Opera House [S] *Spearfish, SD*

Mattie Beal Home [W] *Lawton, OK*

Maxwell Wildlife Refuge [W] *McPherson, KS*

Mayo Clinic [W] *Rochester, MN*

Mayowood [W] *Rochester, MN*

McAlester Scottish Rite Temple [W] *McAlester, OK*

McCarthy Beach State Park [W] *Hibbing, MN*

McCrory Gardens [W] *Brookings, SD*

McDowell Recreation Area [W] *Bismarck, ND*

McIntosh County Fair [S] *Eufaula, OK*

McIntosh Woods [W] *Clear Lake, IA*

McPherson County Old Mill Museum and Park [W] *Lindsborg, KS*

McPherson Museum [W] *McPherson, KS*

Meade County Historical Society [W] *Meade, KS*

Meade State Park [W] *Meade, KS*

Meadowood Fair [S] *Huron, SD*

Medical Museum [W] *Iowa City, IA*

Medicine Creek Reservoir State Recreation Area [W] *McCook, NE*

Medicine Lodge Stockade [W] *Medicine Lodge, KS*

Medieval Fair [S] *Norman, OK*

Medora Musical [S] *Medora, ND*

Meeker County Historical Society Museum [W] *Litchfield, MN*

Mellette House [W] *Watertown, SD*

Mel Tillis Theater [W] *Branson/Table Rock Lake Area, MO*

Memoryville, USA [W] *Rolla, MO*

Meramec Caverns [W] *Sullivan, MO*

Meramec State Park [W] *Sullivan, MO*

Meredith Wilson Boyhood Home [W] *Mason City, IA*

Meredith Wilson Footbridge [W] *Mason City, IA*

Merritt Reservoir State Recreation Area [W] *Valentine, NE*

Messiah Festival [S] *Lindsborg, KS*

Methodist Church [W] *Spring Valley, MN*

Metro Concourse [W] *Oklahoma City, OK*

MetroConnections [W] *Minneapolis, MN*

Mexican-American Fiesta [S] *Emporia, KS*

Mexican American Historical Museum [W] *Scottsbluff, NE*

Mexican Fiesta [S] *Chanute, KS*

Mexican Fiesta [S] *Garden City, KS*

Mid-Dakota Fair [S] *Winner, SD*

Middle Amana [W] *Amana Colonies, IA*

Middle Border Museum of American Indian & Pioneer Life [W] *Mitchell, SD*

Midsummer's Day Festival [S] *Lindsborg, KS*

Midwest Old Threshers Heritage Museum [W] *Mount Pleasant, IA*

Midwest Old Threshers Reunion [S] *Mount Pleasant, IA*

Mighty Summer Farm Toy Show [S] *Dubuque, IA*

Milford Lake [W] *Junction City, KS*

Milford State Park [W] *Junction City, KS*

Mille Lacs Kathio State Park [W] *Onamia, MN*

Mille Lacs Lake [W] *Aitkin, MN*

Mille Lacs Lake [W] *Onamia, MN*

Mina State Recreation Area [W] *Aberdeen, SD*

Minerals Museum [W] *Rolla, MO*

Mines of Spain Recreation Area [W] *Dubuque, IA*

Mine View in the Sky [W] *Virginia, MN*

Miniature World [W] *St. Charles, MO*

Mini-Sapa Days [S] *Oberlin, KS*

Mini-Wakan State Park [W] *Spirit Lake, IA*

Minneapolis Aquatennial [S] *Minneapolis, MN*

Minneapolis City Hall [W] *Minneapolis, MN*

Minneapolis College of Art and Design [W] *Minneapolis, MN*

Minneapolis Grain Exchange [W] *Minneapolis, MN*

Minneapolis Institute of Arts [W] *Minneapolis, MN*

Minneapolis Planetarium [W] *Minneapolis, MN*

Minneapolis Sculpture Garden [W] *Minneapolis, MN*

Minnehaha Park [W] *Minneapolis, MN*

Minneopa State Park [W] *Mankato, MN*

Minneopa-Williams Outdoor Learning Center [W] *Mankato, MN*

Minnesota Baseball Hall of Fame [W] *St. Cloud, MN*

Minnesota Children's Museum [W] *St. Paul, MN*

Minnesota Ethnic Days [S] *Hibbing, MN*

Minnesota History Center [W] *St. Paul, MN*

Minnesota Inventors Congress [S] *Redwood Falls, MN*

Minnesota Lynx (WNBA) [W] *Minneapolis, MN*

Minnesota Military Museum [W] *Little Falls, MN*

Minnesota Museum of American Art—Landmark Center [W] *St. Paul, MN*

Minnesota Museum of Mining [W] *Hibbing, MN*

Minnesota Orchestra [S] *Minneapolis, MN*

Minnesota State Fair [S] *St. Paul, MN*

Minnesota State Public School Orphanage Museum [W] *Owatonna, MN*

Minnesota Timberwolves (NBA) [W] *Minneapolis, MN*

Minnesota Transportation Museum [W] *Minneapolis, MN*

Minnesota Twins (MLB) [W] *Minneapolis, MN*

Minnesota Valley National Wildlife Refuge [W] *Bloomington, MN*

Minnesota Vikings (NFL) [W] *Minneapolis, MN*

Minnesota Wild (NHL) [W] *St. Paul, MN*

Minnesota Zoo [W] *Bloomington, MN*

Minot AFB [W] *Minot, ND*

Mississippi Belle II [W] *Clinton, IA*

Mississippi Belle II [W] *Council Bluffs, IA*

Mississippi Melodie Showboat [S] *Grand Rapids, MN*

Mississippi Music Fest [S] *St. Cloud, MN*

Mississippi River Art Fair [S] *Hannibal, MO*

Mississippi River Museum [W] *Dubuque, IA*

Miss Kansas Pageant [S] *Pratt, KS*

Missouri Botanical Garden [W] *St. Louis, MO*

Missouri History Museum-Missouri Historical Society [W] *St. Louis, MO*

Missouri Repertory Theatre [S] *Kansas City, MO*

Missouri River History Museum [W] *Auburn, NE*

Missouri Southern State College [W] *Joplin, MO*

Missouri State Fair [S] *Sedalia, MO*

Missouri State Museum [W] *Jefferson City, MO*

Missouri Theater [W] *St. Joseph, MO*

Missouri Town 1855 [W] *Blue Springs, MO*

Missouri Valley Antique and Craft Mall [W] *Missouri Valley, IA*

Mohawk Park [W] *Tulsa, OK*

Molly Brown Birthplace and Museum [W] *Hannibal, MO*

Molly Brown Dinner Theater [S] *Hannibal, MO*

Montauk [W] *West Union, IA*

Montauk State Park [W] *Rolla, MO*

Monument to Slain Settlers [W] *Jackson, MN*

Mormon Island State Recreation Area [W] *Grand Island, NE*

Mormon Trail Center at Winter Quarters [W] *Omaha, NE*

Mormon Trail Memorial [W] *Council Bluffs, IA*

Morningside College [W] *Sioux City, IA*

Mosquito Park [W] *Burlington, IA*

Motorcycle Museum and Hall of Fame [W] *Sturgis, SD*

Mounds Park [W] *St. Paul, MN*

Mountain Music Show [W] *Custer, SD*

Mount Frontenac [W] *Red Wing, MN*

Mount Kato Ski Area [W] *Mankato, MN*

Mount Moriah Cemetery [W] *Deadwood, SD*

Mount Rushmore National Memorial [W] *Keystone, SD*

Mount Rushmore National Memorial [W] *Rapid City, SD*

Mower County Fair [S] *Austin, MN*

Mower County Historical Center [W] *Austin, MN*

Muny Opera [S] *St. Louis, MO*

Murray-Lindsay Mansion [W] *Pauls Valley, OK*

Murrell Home [W] *Tahlequah, OK*

Murrell Home Nature Trail [W] *Tahlequah, OK*

Muscatine Art Center [W] *Muscatine, IA*

Museum Annex [W] *Hannibal, MO*

Muscum Complex [W] *Joplin, MO*

Museum of Amana History [W] *Amana Colonies, IA*

Museum of Anthropology [W] *Columbia, MO*

Museum of Art [W] *Iowa City, IA*

Museum of Art and Archaeology [W] *Columbia, MO*

Museum of Geology [W] *Rapid City, SD*

Museum of Independent Telephony [W] *Abilene, KS*

Museum of Natural History [W] *Iowa City, IA*

Museum of Nebraska Art [W] *Kearney, NE*

Museum of Nebraska History [W] *Lincoln, NE*

Museum of the Cherokee Strip [W] *Enid, OK*

Museum of the Fur Trade [W] *Chadron, NE*

Museum of the Great Plains [W] *Lawton, OK*

Museum of the High Plains [W] *McCook, NE*

Museum of the Red River [W] *Idabel, OK*

Museum of the Western Prairie [W] *Altus, OK*

Museum of Transportation [W] *St. Louis, MO*

Museum of Wildlife, Science and Industry [W] *Webster, SD*

Museum Room [W] *Iola, KS*

Music on the March [S] *Dubuque, IA*

Mutton Hollow Craft and Entertainment Village [W] *Branson/Table Rock Lake Area, MO*

Myre-Big Island State Park [W] *Albert Lea, MN*

Myriad Botanical Gardens [W] *Oklahoma City, OK*

Mystery Cave [W] *Spring Valley, MN*

My Waterloo Days Festival [S] *Waterloo, IA*

National Agricultural Center and Hall of Fame [W] *Kansas City, KS*

National Balloon Classic [S] *Indianola, IA*

National Balloon Museum [W] *Indianola, IA*

National Barrow Show [S] *Austin, MN*

National Baseball Congress World Series [S] *Wichita, KS*

National Cemetery [W] *Keokuk, IA*

National Cowboy Hall of Fame & Western Heritage Center [W] *Oklahoma City, OK*

National Czech and Slovak Museum & Library [W] *Cedar Rapids, IA*

National Farm Toy Museum [W] *Dubuque, IA*

National Festival of Craftsmen [S] *Branson/Table Rock Lake Area, MO*

National Frontier Trails Center [W] *Independence, MO*

National Greyhound Meet [S] *Abilene, KS*

National Hall of Fame for Famous American Indians [W] *Anadarko, OK*

National Junior College Basketball Tournament [S] *Hutchinson, KS*

National Museum of Roller Skating [W] *Lincoln, NE*

National Museum of Woodcarving [W] *Custer, SD*

National Rivers Hall Of Fame [W] *Dubuque, IA*

National Skillet-Throwing Contest [S] *Winterset, IA*

National Softball Hall of Fame and Museum [W] *Oklahoma City, OK*

National Teachers Hall of Fame [W] *Emporia, KS*

National Wrestling Hall of Fame [W] *Stillwater, OK*

Native American Annual Time Out and Wacipi [S] *Grand Forks, ND*

Native American Pictographs [W] *Ely, MN*

NCAA College Baseball World Series [S] *Omaha, NE*

"NEBRASKAland DAYS" Celebration [S] *North Platte, NE*

Nebraska National Forest [W] *Chadron, NE*

Nebraska National Forest [W] *Crawford, NE*

Nebraska National Forest [W] *Thedford, NE*

Nebraska State Fair [S] *Lincoln, NE*

Nebraska Wesleyan University [W] *Lincoln, NE*

"Neewollah" [S] *Independence, KS*

Neligh Mills [W] *Norfolk, NE*

Nellie Johnstone Oil Well [W] *Bartlesville, OK*

Nelson-Atkins Museum of Art [W] *Kansas City, MO*

Nelson Pioneer Farm & Craft Museum [W] *Oskaloosa, IA*

Nemaha County Fair [S] *Auburn, NE*

Nemaha County Historical Museum [W] *Seneca, KS*

Nemaha Valley Museum [W] *Auburn, NE*

Nerstrand Woods State Park [W] *Northfield, MN*

New Beginning Festival [S] *Coffeyville, KS*

Newton Fiesta [S] *Newton, KS*

Nicollet Mall [W] *Minneapolis, MN*

Nifong Park [W] *Columbia, MO*

Night blasting [S] *Crazy Horse Memorial, SD*

Nine Eagles State Park [W] *Osceola, IA*

Nodaway Valley Historical Museum [W] *Clarinda, IA*

No Man's Land Museum [W] *Guymon, OK*

Nordic Fest [S] *Decorah, IA*

Norsk Hostfest [S] *Minot, ND*

North Central Kansas Free Fair [S] *Belleville, KS*

North Central Kansas Rodeo [S] *Concordia, KS*

North Dakota Heritage Center [W] *Bismarck, ND*

North Dakota State Fair [S] *Minot, ND*

North Dakota State University [W] *Fargo, ND*

Northeastern State University [W] *Tahlequah, OK*

Northern Minnesota Car Show and Swap Meet [S] *Grand Rapids, MN*

Northfield Arts Guild [W] *Northfield, MN*

North Iowa Band Festival [S] *Mason City, IA*

North Iowa Fair [S] *Mason City, IA*

North Platte Valley Museum [W] *Gering, NE*

North Shore Drive [W] *Grand Marais, MN*

North Shore Scenic Railroad [W] *Duluth, MN*

North Star Stampede [S] *Grand Rapids, MN*

Northwest Angle/Islands [W] *Baudette, MN*

North West Company Fur Post [W] *Hinckley, MN*

Northwest Kansas District Free Fair [S] *Goodland, KS*

Northwest Research Extension Center [W] *Colby, KS*

Northwest Water Carnival [S] *Detroit Lakes, MN*

Norwest Bank Owatonna, NA Building [W] *Owatonna, MN*

Norwest Center Skyway [W] *St. Paul, MN*

Oahe Dam and Reservoir [W] *Pierre, SD*

Oakland Mills Park [W] *Mount Pleasant, IA*

Oak Park [W] *Minot, ND*

Oakwood Cemetery [W] *Parsons, KS*

Oakwood Lakes State Park [W] *Brookings, SD*

Oceans of Fun [W] *Kansas City, MO*

Octoberfest [S] *Hermann, MO*

Octoberfest [S] *Ottumwa, IA*

Octoberfest of Bands [S] *Maquoketa, IA*

Oglala National Grassland [W] *Crawford, NE*

Oglala Nation Fair and Rodeo [S] *Pine Ridge, SD*

Oil Patch Museum [W] *Russell, KS*

O.J. Watson Park [W] *Wichita, KS*

Oklahoma City Art Museum [W] *Oklahoma City, OK*

Oklahoma City National Memorial [W] *Oklahoma City, OK*

Oklahoma City Philharmonic Orchestra [S] *Oklahoma City, OK*

Oklahoma City Zoo [W] *Oklahoma City, OK*

Oklahoma Firefighters Museum [W] *Oklahoma City, OK*

Oklahoma Heritage Center [W] *Oklahoma City, OK*

Oklahoma International Bluegrass Festival [S] *Guthrie, OK*

Oklahoma National Stockyards [W] *Oklahoma City, OK*

Oklahoma Panhandle State University [W] *Guymon, OK*

Oklahoma Shakespearean Festival, The [S] *Durant, OK*

Oklahoma State University [W] *Stillwater, OK*

Oklahoma Territorial Museum [W] *Guthrie, OK*

Okmulgee State Park [W] *Okmulgee, OK*

Okoboji Queen II [W] *Okoboji, IA*

Okoboji Summer Theater [S] *Okoboji, IA*

Oktoberfest [S] *Atchison, KS*

Oktoberfest [S] *Hays, KS*

Oktoberfest [S] *Sidney, NE*

Old Calaboose [W] *Council Grove, KS*

Old Capitol [W] *Iowa City, IA*

Old Cathedral [W] *St. Louis, MO*

Old Courthouse [W] *St. Louis, MO*

Old Courthouse Museum [W] *Sioux Falls, SD*

Old Cowtown Museum [W] *Wichita, KS*

Old Creamery Theatre Company [W] *Amana Colonies, IA*

Old Dental Office [W] *Auburn, NE*

Old Depot Museum [W] *Ottawa, KS*

Old Dutch Mill [W] *Smith Center, KS*

Old Fort Bissell [W] *Phillipsburg, KS*

Old Fort Madison [W] *Fort Madison, IA*

Old Guardhouse. [W] *Lawton, OK*

Old Jail Museum [W] *Iola, KS*

Old Market [W] *Omaha, NE*

Old Post Chapel. [W] *Lawton, OK*

Old Post Headquarters. [W] *Lawton, OK*

Old Sedgwick County Fair [S] *Wichita, KS*

Old Settlers Celebration and Parade [S] *Fremont, NE*

Old Settlers Park [W] *Fairfield, IA*

Old Shawnee Town [W] *Overland Park, KS*

Old Shot Tower [W] *Dubuque, IA*

Old St. Vincent's Church [W] *Cape Girardeau, MO*

Old Style Saloon #10 [W] *Deadwood, SD*

Old Tavern [W] *Arrow Rock, MO*

Old Town Museum [W] *Elk City, OK*

Old West Days & Poetry Gathering [S] *Valentine, NE*

Old West Lawrence Historic District [W] *Lawrence, KS*

Old Windmill [W] *Milbank, SD*

Ole Oppe Fest [S] *Alexandria, MN*

Oliver H. Kelley Farm [W] *Elk River, MN*

Olmsted County History Center and Museum [W] *Rochester, MN*

Olof Swensson Farm Museum [W] *Granite Falls, MN*

Omaha Children's Museum [W] *Omaha, NE*

Omniplex [W] *Oklahoma City, OK*

Omnisphere and Science Center [W] *Wichita, KS*

Oneota State Park [W] *Spencer, IA*

Onondaga Cave State Park [W] *Sullivan, MO*

On the Chisholm Trail [W] *Duncan, OK*

Optical Science Center and Museum [W] *Hannibal, MO*

Oregon Trail Days [S] *Gering, NE*

Oregon Trail PRCA Rodeo [S] *Hastings, NE*

Oregon Trail Wagon Train [W] *Bridgeport, NE*

Original Deadwood Tour [W] *Deadwood, SD*

Osage County Fair [S] *Pawhuska, OK*

Osage County Historical Society Museum [W] *Pawhuska, OK*

Osage Hills State Park [W] *Pawhuska, OK*

Osage Tribal Museum [W] *Pawhuska, OK*

Oscar Howe Art Center [W] *Mitchell, SD*

Osmond Family Theater [W] *Branson/Table Rock Lake Area, MO*

Ottawa Indian Burial Grounds [W] *Ottawa, KS*

Otter Tail County Historical Society Museum [W] *Fergus Falls, MN*

Ottumwa Park [W] *Ottumwa, IA*

Ottumwa Pro Balloon Races [S] *Ottumwa, IA*

Outdoor Theater [W] *Branson/Table Rock Lake Area, MO*

Overland Park Arboretum and Botanical Gardens [W] *Overland Park, KS*

Owatonna Arts Center [W] *Owatonna, MN*

Ox Cart Days [S] *Crookston, MN*

Oxley Nature Center [W] *Tulsa, OK*

Ozark Empire Fair [S] *Springfield, MO*

Ozark National Scenic Riverways [W] *Van Buren, MO*

Ozark Wonder Cave [W] *Cassville, MO*

Oztoberfest [S] *Liberal, KS*

Paddlewheeler *Tom Sawyer* Excursion Boat [W] *Lake of the Ozarks, MO*

Paddlewheel Towboat Logsdon [W] *Dubuque, IA*

Page County Fair [S] *Clarinda, IA*

Palisades-Kepler State Park [W] *Cedar Rapids, IA*

Pancake Day [S] *Centerville, IA*

Panhandle Exposition [S] *Guymon, OK*

Parade of Lights [S] *Huron, SD*

Parade of Presidents Wax Museum [W] *Keystone, SD*

Paramount Theatre [W] *Cedar Rapids, IA*

Pari-mutuel horse racing [S] *Aberdeen, SD*

Parker Carousel [W] *Leavenworth, KS*

Park Point Recreation Center [W] *Duluth, MN*

Parks [W] *Davenport, IA*

Parks [W] *St. Paul, MN*

Parks [W] *Topeka, KS*

Parks. Pawnee Park [W] *Columbus, NE*

Parsons Historical Museum [W] *Parsons, KS*

Patee House Museum [W] *St. Joseph, MO*

Patterson Reservoir [W] *Dickinson, ND*

Paul Bunyan Amusement Center [W] *Brainerd, MN*

Paul Bunyan and "Babe" [W] *Bemidji, MN*

Paul Bunyan Playhouse [S] *Bemidji, MN*

Paul Bunyan State Trail [W] *Brainerd, MN*

Paul Bunyan Water Carnival [S] *Bemidji, MN*

Pauls Valley City Lake [W] *Pauls Valley, OK*

Paulucci Space Theatre [W] *Hibbing, MN*

Pawnee Bill Memorial Rodeo [S] *Pawnee, OK*

Pawnee Bill Ranch Site [W] *Pawnee, OK*

Pawnee Indian Village Museum [W] *Belleville, KS*

Pawnee Indian Village Rendezvous [S] *Belleville, KS*

Pawnee Lake State Recreaction Area [W] *Lincoln, NE*

Payne County Free Fair [W] *Stillwater, OK*

Pearl Button Museum [W] *Muscatine, IA*

Pearson-Skubitz Big Hill Lake [W] *Parsons, KS*

Pecan Festival [S] *Okmulgee, OK*

Pelican Festival [S] *Grand Lake, OK*

Pelican Lake [W] *Cook, MN*

Pella Historical Village Museum [W] *Pella, IA*

Percussive Arts Society Museum [W] *Lawton, OK*

Perry State Park [W] *Topeka, KS*

Pershing State Park [W] *Chillicothe, MO*

Peter Pan Park [W] *Emporia, KS*

Pettigrew Home and Museum [W] *Sioux Falls, SD*

Pettis County Courthouse [W] *Sedalia, MO*

Phelps House [W] *Burlington, IA*

Philbrook Museum of Art [W] *Tulsa, OK*

Phillips County Fair [S] *Phillipsburg, KS*

Pibel Lake State Recreation Area [W] *O'Neill, NE*

Picture in Scripture Amphitheater [S] *Grand Lake, OK*

Pikes Peak State Park [W] *Marquette, IA*

Pikes Point [W] *Okoboji, IA*

Pilaster House and Grant's Drugstore [W] *Hannibal, MO*

Pilot Knob State Park [W] *Garner, IA*

Pioneer Days [S] *Fargo, ND*

Pioneer Days [S] *Guymon, OK*

The Pioneer Family [W] *Bismarck, ND*

Pioneer Farm and Village [W] *Roseau, MN*

Pioneer Harvest Fiesta [S] *Fort Scott, KS*

Pioneer Museum [W] *Fairmont, MN*

Pioneers Park [W] *Lincoln, NE*

Pioneer Spring Cabin [W] *Independence, MO*

Pipestone County Museum [W] *Pipestone, MN*

Pirtle's Weston Winery [W] *Weston, MO*

Plains Indians & Pioneers Museum [W] *Woodward, OK*

Platte County Fair [S] *Columbus, NE*

Platte County Historical Society [W] *Columbus, NE*

Platte Creek State Recreation Area [W] *Platte, SD*

Platte River State Park [W] *Omaha, NE*

Plum Grove [W] *Iowa City, IA*

Plummer House of the Arts [W] *Rochester, MN*

Plymouth County Fair [S] *Le Mars, IA*

Plymouth County Historical Museum [W] *Le Mars, IA*

Pokegama Dam [W] *Grand Rapids, MN*

Polar Fest [S] *Detroit Lakes, MN*

Polk County Heritage Gallery [W] *Des Moines, IA*

Polk County Historical Museum [W] *Crookston, MN*

Polynesian Princess [W] *Branson/Table Rock Lake Area, MO*

Pomme de Terre City Park [W] *Morris, MN*

Pomme de Terre State Park [W] *Camdenton, MO*

Pomona Reservoir [W] *Ottawa, KS*

Pomona State Park [W] *Ottawa, KS*

Ponca State Park [W] *South Sioux City, NE*

Pony Express Barn Museum [W] *Marysville, KS*

Pony Express Museum [W] *St. Joseph, MO*

Pony Express Region Tourist Information Centers [W] *St. Joseph, MO*

Pony Express Rodeo [S] *Gothenburg, NE*

Pony Express Station [W] *Gothenburg, NE*

Pope County Fair [S] *Glenwood, MN*

Pope County Historical Museum [W] *Glenwood, MN*

Post Memorial Art Reference Library [W] *Joplin, MO*

Post Office Oak [W] *Council Grove, KS*

Potato Bowl Week [S] *Grand Forks, ND*

Potawatomie Powwow [S] *Shawnee, OK*

Poteau Frontier Days Rodeo [S] *Poteau, OK*

Potlatch Paper Mill [W] *Brainerd, MN*

Pott County Fair [S] *Shawnee, OK*

Potwin Place [W] *Topeka, KS*

Powder House [W] *Sidney, NE*

Powder Ridge Ski Area [W] *St. Cloud, MN*

Powell Symphony Hall [W] *St. Louis, MO*

Powers Museum [W] *Carthage, MO*

Prairie Day Celebration [S] *McPherson, KS*

Prairie Dog State Park [W] *Norton, KS*

Prairie Heritage Day [S] *Colby, KS*

Prairie Island Park [W] *Winona, MN*

Prairie Meadows Racetrack & Casino [W] *Des Moines, IA*

Prairie Museum of Art & History [W] *Colby, KS*

Prairie Passage [W] *Emporia, KS*

Prairie Pioneer Days [S] *Morris, MN*

Prairie Rose State Park [W] *Avoca, IA*

Prairie State Park [W] *Lamar, MO*

Prairie Village [W] *Madison, SD*

Pratt County Fair [S] *Pratt, KS*

Pratt County Historical Society Museum [W] *Pratt, KS*

Precious Moments Chapel [W] *Carthage, MO*

Prehistoric Indian Village National Historic Landmark Archaeological Site [W] *Mitchell, SD*

President Casino [W] *Davenport, IA*

President Casino on the *Admiral* [W] *St. Louis, MO*

Presleys' Jubilee [W] *Branson/Table Rock Lake Area, MO*

Price/Loyles Tour House [W] *Weston, MO*

Price Tower [W] *Bartlesville, OK*

Primeval Pine Grove Municipal Park [W] *Little Falls, MN*

Professional sports [W] *Kansas City, MO*

Professional sports [W] *Minneapolis, MN*

Professional sports [W] *St. Louis, MO*

Pufferbilly Days [S] *Boone, IA*

Purina Farms [W] *St. Louis, MO*

Putnam Museum of History & Natural Science [W] *Davenport, IA*

Quadna Mountain Resort Ski Area [W] *Grand Rapids, MN*

Quarter horse racing [S] *Eureka, KS*

Quivira National Wildlife Refuge [W] *Great Bend, KS*

Railroad Museum [W] *Mandan, ND*

Railroad Town [W] *Grand Island, NE*

RailsWest Railroad Museum [W] *Council Bluffs, IA*

Rainy River [W] *Baudette, MN*

Ralph Foster Museum [W] *Branson/Table Rock Lake Area, MO*

Ramsey Mill [W] *Hastings, MN*

Ramsey Park [W] *Redwood Falls, MN*

Rand Park [W] *Keokuk, IA*

Rapid River Logging Camp [W] *Park Rapids, MN*

Rathbun Lake [W] *Centerville, IA*

Raymond Gary State Park [W] *Hugo, OK*

Rebecca Winters Grave [W] *Scottsbluff, NE*

Recreation [W] *Winfield, KS*

Recreational Areas [W] *Brainerd, MN*

Recreation areas [W] *Hill City, SD*

Recreation areas. Elk City State Park [W] *Independence, KS*

Recreation Areas. Indian Creek [W] *Mobridge, SD*

Recreation areas. Lake Burtschi. [W] *Chickasha, OK*

Recreation areas. Pebble Lake City Park [W] *Fergus Falls, MN*

Recreation. Oliver Reservoir [W] *Kimball, NE*

Red Cloud Indian School Heritage Art Museum [W] *Pine Ridge, SD*

Red Earth [S] *Oklahoma City, OK*

Red Earth Indian Center [W] *Oklahoma City, OK*

Red Haw State Park [W] *Chariton, IA*

Red Lake Wildlife Management Area and Norris Camp [W] *Baudette, MN*

Redlin Art Center [W] *Watertown, SD*

Red River Valley Fair [S] *Fargo, ND*

Red Rock Canyon State Park [W] *Weatherford, OK*

Red Rock Lake [W] *Pella, IA*

Redstone Inn [W] *Dubuque, IA*

Red Willow County Fair and Rodeo [S] *McCook, NE*

Red Willow Reservoir State Recreation Area [W] *McCook, NE*

Red Wing Stoneware [W] *Red Wing, MN*

Regional High School Rodeo [S] *Winner, SD*

Regional Science Center-Planetarium [W] *Moorhead, MN*

Reiman Gardens [W] *Ames, IA*

Remington Park [W] *Oklahoma City, OK*

Renaissance Faire of the Midlands [S] *Council Bluffs, IA*

Renaissance Festival [S] *Bloomington, MN*

Renaissance Festival [S] *Kansas City, KS*

Reno County Museum [W] *Hutchinson, KS*

Rensselaer Russell House Museum [W] *Waterloo, IA*

REO Auto Museum [W] *Lindsborg, KS*

Repertory Theatre of St Louis [S] *St. Louis, MO*

Research Center and Archives [W] *Emporia, KS*

Research Reactor Facility [W] *Columbia, MO*

Rice County Historical Society Museum [W] *Faribault, MN*

Rice Lake National Wildlife Refuge [W] *Aitkin, MN*

Rice Lake State Park [W] *Garner, IA*

Richland County Historical Museum [W] *Wahpeton, ND*

Richmond Lake State Recreation Area [W] *Aberdeen, SD*

Ride the Ducks [W] *Branson/Table Rock Lake Area, MO*

Ride the Ridge [S] *Chadron, NE*

Riley County Historical Museum [W] *Manhattan, KS*

Ripley's Believe It Or Not! Museum [W] *Branson/Table Rock Lake Area, MO*

River Bend Nature Center [W] *Faribault, MN*

Riverboat Days [S] *Clinton, IA*

Riverboat Days [S] *Yankton, SD*

Riverboat Heritage Days [S] *Aitkin, MN*

River-Cade Festival [S] *Sioux City, IA*

River City Days [S] *Red Wing, MN*

River City Round-up [S] *Omaha, NE*

River City Trolley [W] *Minneapolis, MN*

River Country Nature Center [W] *Nebraska City, NE*

Riverfest [S] *Cape Girardeau, MO*

Riverfront area [W] *St. Louis, MO*

River of Dreams [W] *Dubuque, IA*

River Rhumba [S] *Muskogee, OK*

Riverside Park [W] *Independence, KS*

Riverside-Sertoma Park [W] *Bismarck, ND*

Riverside Zoo [W] *Scottsbluff, NE*

Rivertown Art Fair [S] *Stillwater, MN*

Rivertown Days [S] *Hastings, MN*

River Valley Art Festival [S] *Arkansas City, KS*

Riverview Park [W] *Clinton, IA*

Riverview Park [W] *Fort Madison, IA*

Riverview Park [W] *Hannibal, MO*

Riverview Park [W] *Marshalltown, IA*

Riverview Park [W] *Miami, OK*

Road Show [S] *Guthrie, OK*

Roaring River State Park [W] *Cassville, MO*

Robber's Cave State Park [W] *McAlester, OK*

Robert Henri Museum and Historical Walkway [W] *Cozad, NE*

Robert S. Kerr Lake [W] *Sallisaw, OK*

Robidoux Row Museum [W] *St. Joseph, MO*

Rochester Carillon, The [W] *Rochester, MN*

Rockcliffe Mansion [W] *Hannibal, MO*

Rock Creek State Park [W] *Grinnell, IA*

Rock Creek Station State Historical Park [W] *Fairbury, NE*

Rodeo [S] *Phillipsburg, KS*

Rodeo of Champions [S] *Elk City, OK*

Rodeo Park [W] *Fort Madison, IA*

Rogers County Free Fair [S] *Claremore, OK*

Rooks County Museum [W] *Stockton, KS*

Roosevelt Park and Zoo [W] *Minot, ND*

Roseau City Park [W] *Roseau, MN*

Roseau County Historical Museum and Interpretive Center [W] *Roseau, MN*

Roseau River Wildlife Management Area [W] *Roseau, MN*

Rosebud [W] *Mission, SD*

Rosebud Sioux Tribal Fair and Powwow [S] *Mission, SD*

Rose Display Garden [W] *Cape Girardeau, MO*

Roughrider Days Celebration [S] *Dickinson, ND*

Route 66 Festival [S] *Clinton, OK*

Roy Clark Celebrity Theatre [W] *Branson/Table Rock Lake Area, MO*

Roy Lake State Park [W] *Sisseton, SD*

Rt 66 Summerfest [S] *Rolla, MO*

Runestone Museum [W] *Alexandria, MN*

Run for the Arts [S] *Stillwater, OK*

Runge Conservation Nature Center [W] *Jefferson City, MO*

Rushmore Aerial Tramway [W] *Keystone, SD*

Rushmore Cave [W] *Keystone, SD*

Rushmore Helicopter Sightseeing Tours [W] *Keystone, SD*

Rustic Hills Carriage Tours [W] *Dubuque, IA*

Ruth Anne Dodge Memorial [W] *Council Bluffs, IA*

Sailing Regatta [S] *McCook, NE*

St. Anthony Falls [W] *Minneapolis, MN*

St. Benedict's Convent [W] *St. Cloud, MN*

St. Charles Historic District [W] *St. Charles, MO*

St. Cloud State University [W] *St. Cloud, MN*

St. Croix and Lower St. Croix National Scenic Riverway [W] *Taylors Falls, MN*

St. Croix Scenic Highway [W] *Stillwater, MN*

St. Croix State Park [W] *Hinckley, MN*

St. Francois State Park [W] *Bonne Terre, MO*

Ste. Genevieve Museum [W] *Ste. Genevieve, MO*

St. James Winery [W] *Rolla, MO*

St. John's University and Abbey, Preparatory School [W] *St. Cloud, MN*

St. Joseph Museum [W] *St. Joseph, MO*

St. Joseph Park System [W] *St. Joseph, MO*

St. Louis Art Fair [S] *Clayton, MO*

St. Louis Art Museum, The [W] *St. Louis, MO*

St. Louis Blues (NHL) [W] *St. Louis, MO*

St. Louis Cardinals Hall of Fame Museum [W] *St. Louis, MO*

St. Louis Cardinals (MLB) [W] *St. Louis, MO*

St. Louis Centre [W] *St. Louis, MO*

St. Louis County Fair [S] *Hibbing, MN*

St. Louis County Historical Society [W] *Duluth, MN*

St. Louis Iron Mountain and Southern Railway [W] *Cape Girardeau, MO*

St. Louis Rams (NFL) [W] *St. Louis, MO*

St. Louis Science Center [W] *St. Louis, MO*

Saint Louis Symphony Orchestra [S] *St. Louis, MO*

St. Louis Union Station [W] *St. Louis, MO*

Saint Louis University [W] *St. Louis, MO*

St. Louis Zoological Park [W] *St. Louis, MO*

St. Mary's Chapel [W] *Junction City, KS*

St. Olaf College [W] *Northfield, MN*

St. Patrick's Day Celebration [S] *Emmetsburg, IA*

St. Patrick's Parade [S] *Kansas City, MO*

St. Pat's Celebration [S] *Rolla, MO*

Salina Art Center [W] *Salina, KS*

Salisbury House [W] *Des Moines, IA*

Sallisaw State Park at Brushy Lake [W] *Sallisaw, OK*

Sam A. Baker State Park [W] *Pilot Knob, MO*

Sammy Lane Pirate Cruise [W] *Branson/Table Rock Lake Area, MO*

Samuel F. Miller House and Museum [W] *Keokuk, IA*

Samuel R. McKelvie National Forest [W] *Valentine, NE*

Sanders Family Bluegrass Festival [S] *McAlester, OK*

Sanford Museum and Planetarium [W] *Cherokee, IA*

Santa-Cali-Gon [S] *Independence, MO*

Santa Fe Railway Bridge [W] *Fort Madison, IA*

Santa Fe Trail Center [W] *Larned, KS*

Santa Fe Trail Daze Celebration [S] *Boise City, OK*

Santa's Castle [S] *Storm Lake, IA*

Sante Fe Depot Historic Museum and Complex [W] *Fort Madison, IA*

Saturday in the Park [S] *Sioux City, IA*

Saulsbury Bridge Recreation Area [W] *Muscatine, IA*

Savanna Portage State Park [W] *Aitkin, MN*

Sawyer's Sandhills Museum [W] *Valentine, NE*

Scandinavian Heritage Center [W] *Minot, ND*

Scandinavian Hjemkomst Festival [S] *Moorhead, MN*

Scenic North Shore Drive [W] *Duluth, MN*

Scenic State Park [W] *Grand Rapids, MN*

Schell Garden and Deer Park [W] *New Ulm, MN*

Schell Osage Wildlife Area [W] *Nevada, MO*

Scherr Howe Arena [W] *Mobridge, SD*

Scholte House [W] *Pella, IA*

Schoolhouse Art Gallery [W] *Auburn, NE*

Schramm Park State Recreation Area [W] *Omaha, NE*

Science Center of Iowa [W] *Des Moines, IA*

Science Museum of Minnesota [W] *St. Paul, MN*

Science Station [W] *Cedar Rapids, IA*

Scott County Park [W] *Davenport, IA*

Scottish Festival and Highland Games [S] *McPherson, KS*

Scottish Rite Masonic Temple [W] *Guthrie, OK*

Scott Joplin Ragtime Festival [S] *Sedalia, MO*

Scotts Bluff National Monument [W] *Gering, NE*

Scotts Bluff National Monument [W] *Gering, NE*

Scotts Bluff National Monument [W] *Scottsbluff, NE*

Scotts Bluff National Monument [W] *Scottsbluff, NE*

Scout Fishing Derby [S] *Glenwood, MN*

Sedalia Ragtime Archives [W] *Sedalia, MO*

Sedgwick County Zoo and Botanical Garden [W] *Wichita, KS*

Seed Savers Heritage Farm [W] *Decorah, IA*

Seelye Mansion and Museum [W] *Abilene, KS*

Seminole Nation Museum [W] *Shawnee, OK*

Semo District Fair [S] *Cape Girardeau, MO*

Sequoyah's Home [W] *Sallisaw, OK*

Sergeant Floyd Monument [W] *Sioux City, IA*

Sergeant Floyd Welcome Center and Museum [W] *Sioux City, IA*

76 Music Hall [W] *Branson/Table Rock Lake Area, MO*

Shades of the Past 50's Revival Weekend [S] *Marshall, MN*

Shady Creek Recreation Area [W] *Muscatine, IA*

Sharon Bluffs Park [W] *Centerville, IA*

Shawnee Indian Mission State History Site [W] *Overland Park, KS*

Shawnee Twin Lakes [W] *Shawnee, OK*

Sheerar Museum [W] *Stillwater, OK*

Sheldon Memorial Art Gallery and Sculpture Garden [W] *Lincoln, NE*

Sheldon Theatre [W] *Red Wing, MN*

Shelter Gardens [W] *Columbia, MO*

Shepherd of the Hills [W] *Branson/Table Rock Lake Area, MO*

Shepherd of the Hills Trout Hatchery [W] *Branson/Table Rock Lake Area, MO*

Sherburne National Wildlife Refuge [W] *Elk River, MN*

Sherman House. [W] *Lawton, OK*

Sherman Park [W] *Sioux Falls, SD*

Sherwin Miller Museum of Jewish Art [W] *Tulsa, OK*

Shimek State Forest [W] *Fort Madison, IA*

Shoji Tabuchi Theatre [W] *Branson/Table Rock Lake Area, MO*

Shopping [W] *St. Louis, MO*

Showboat [S] *Minneapolis, MN*

Showboat *Branson Belle* [W] *Branson/Table Rock Lake Area, MO*

Show-Me State Games [S] *Columbia, MO*

Shrine Circus [S] *Winner, SD*

Shrine to Music Museum [W] *Vermillion, SD*

Sibley Historic Site [W] *St. Paul, MN*

Sibley Park [W] *Mankato, MN*

Sibley State Park [W] *Willmar, MN*

Sidewheeler William M. Black [W] *Dubuque, IA*

Sight of Music, The [S] *Burlington, IA*

Sights and Sounds of Christmas [S] *Blair, NE*

Sightseeing [W] *Branson/Table Rock Lake Area, MO*

Sightseeing [W] *Kansas City, MO*

Sightseeing cruises [W] *St. Paul, MN*

Sightseeing tour. Old Time Trolleys [W] *Nebraska City, NE*

Sightseeing tours [W] *Deadwood, SD*

Simpson College [W] *Indianola, IA*

Sinclair Lewis Boyhood Home [W] *Sauk Centre, MN*

Sinclair Lewis Days [S] *Sauk Centre, MN*

Sinclair Lewis Interpretive Center [W] *Sauk Centre, MN*

Sioux City Art Center [W] *Sioux City, IA*

Sioux City Public Museum [W] *Sioux City, IA*

Siouxland Heritage Museums [W] *Sioux Falls, SD*

Site of Fond du Lac [W] *Duluth, MN*

Site of Old Fort Dodge [W] *Fort Dodge, IA*

Sitting Bull Crystal Cave [W] *Rapid City, SD*

Sitting Bull Monument [W] *Mobridge, SD*

Six Flags St Louis [W] *St. Louis, MO*

Skiing [W] *Lead, SD*

Skiing [W] *Minneapolis, MN*

Skiing [W] *Red Wing, MN*

Skyline Parkway Drive [W] *Duluth, MN*

Skyview Lake [W] *Norfolk, NE*

Smith Lake Park [W] *Algona, IA*

Smith-Zimmermann State Museum [W] *Madison, SD*

Smokey the Bear Statue [W] *International Falls, MN*

Smoky Hill Museum [W] *Salina, KS*

Smoky Hill River Festival [S] *Salina, KS*

Smoky Hills Artisan Community [W] *Park Rapids, MN*

Snake Alley [W] *Burlington, IA*

Snake Alley Criterium Bicycle Races [S] *Burlington, IA*

Snake Creek State Recreation Area [W] *Platte, SD*

Snow Creek Ski Area [W] *Weston, MO*

Snow Queen Festival [S] *Aberdeen, SD*

Society of Memories Doll Museum [W] *St. Joseph, MO*

Soden's Grove Park [W] *Emporia, KS*

Soldiers' Memorial Military Museum [W] *St. Louis, MO*

Soldiers' Memorial Park/East End Recreation Area [W] *Red Wing, MN*

Sommerfest [S] *Minneapolis, MN*

Song of Hiawatha Pageant [S] *Pipestone, MN*

Sons of the Pioneers [W] *Branson/Table Rock Lake Area, MO*

Sooner Theatre [W] *Norman, OK*

Soudan Underground Mine State Park [W] *Tower, MN*

Soukup and Thomas International Balloon and Airship Museum [W] *Mitchell, SD*

South Amana [W] *Amana Colonies, IA*

South Dakota Art Museum [W] *Brookings, SD*

South Dakota Discovery Center and Aquarium [W] *Pierre, SD*

South Dakota School of Mines and Technology [W] *Rapid City, SD*

South Dakota State Fair [S] *Huron, SD*

South Dakota State University [W] *Brookings, SD*

Southeast Missouri Agricultural Museum [W] *Sikeston, MO*

Southern Iowa Fair [S] *Oskaloosa, IA*

Southern Plains Indian Museum and Crafts Center [W] *Anadarko, OK*

South River Festival [S] *Winterset, IA*

Southside Fall Festival [S] *St. Joseph, MO*

Southwest Festival of the Arts [S] *Weatherford, OK*

Southwest Iowa Band Jamboree [S] *Clarinda, IA*

Southwest State University [W] *Marshall, MN*

SpamTown USA Festival/Spam Jam [S] *Austin, MN*

Spink County Historical Memorial Museum [W] *Redfield, SD*

Spirit Lake [W] *Spirit Lake, IA*

Spirit Mountain Ski Area [W] *Duluth, MN*

Spirit of Brownville [W] *Auburn, NE*

Spirit of Dubuque [W] *Dubuque, IA*

Spiro Mound Archeological State Park [W] *Poteau, OK*

Split Rock Creek State Park [W] *Pipestone, MN*

Split Rock Lighthouse State Park [W] *Two Harbors, MN*

Spook Cave and Campground [W] *Marquette, IA*

Sports Camp [S] *Bottineau, ND*

Spring Festival with Antique Flea Market [S] *Auburn, NE*

Springfield Art Museum [W] *Springfield, MO*

Springfield National Cemetery [W] *Springfield, MO*

Spring Lake Park [W] *Williston, ND*

Squaw Creek National Wildlife Refuge [W] *Mound City, MO*

S/S *William A. Irvin* [W] *Duluth, MN*

Stagecoach West [W] *Rapid City, SD*

Star Aviation Air Tours [W] *Spearfish, SD*

Starlight Theater [S] *Kansas City, MO*

Star-Spangled Spectacular [S] *Storm Lake, IA*

State Capital Publishing Museum [W] *Guthrie, OK*

State Capitol [W] *Bismarck, ND*

State Capitol [W] *Des Moines, IA*

State Capitol [W] *Jefferson City, MO*

State Capitol [W] *Lincoln, NE*

State Capitol [W] *Oklahoma City, OK*

State Capitol [W] *Pierre, SD*

State Capitol [W] *St. Paul, MN*

State Capitol [W] *Topeka, KS*

State Fair Motor Speedway [S] *Sedalia, MO*

State Fair of Oklahoma [S] *Oklahoma City, OK*

State Fair Speedway [S] *Huron, SD*

State Hockey Tournament [S] *Grand Forks, ND*

Statehood Memorial—Thomas P. Kennard House [W] *Lincoln, NE*

State Museum of History [W] *Oklahoma City, OK*

State National Guard Museum [W] *Pierre, SD*

State parks [W] *Alva, OK*

State parks [W] *Clear Lake, IA*

State parks [W] *Fort Dodge, IA*

State parks [W] *New Ulm, MN*

State parks [W] *Okoboji, IA*

State parks [W] *St. Louis, MO*

State parks [W] *Strawberry Point, IA*

State parks [W] *Taylors Falls, MN*

State parks [W] *Tulsa, OK*

State recreation areas [W] *North Platte, NE*

Station 15 [W] *Norton, KS*

Statue of Sakajawea [W] *Bismarck, ND*

Steam Engine and Antique Farm Engine Show [S] *Salina, KS*

Steam locomotive and coach [W] *Tower, MN*

Steam Show and Threshing Bee [S] *Pawnee, OK*

Steam Threshing Jamboree [S] *Madison, SD*

Stearns County Heritage Center [W] *St. Cloud, MN*

Steinberg Memorial Skating Rink [W] *St. Louis, MO*

Stephens College [W] *Columbia, MO*

Stephens County Historical Museum [W] *Duncan, OK*

Stephens State Forest [W] *Chariton, IA*

Sternberg Museum of Natural History [W] *Hays, KS*

Stock Car Racing [S] *Mandan, ND*

Stockman House [W] *Mason City, IA*

Stockton State Park [W] *Stockton, MO*

Stone Hill Winery [W] *Branson/Table Rock Lake Area, MO*

Stone Hill Winery [W] *Hermann, MO*

Stone State Park [W] *Sioux City, IA*

Storm Lake [W] *Storm Lake, IA*

Storybook Hill Children's Zoo [W] *Dubuque, IA*

Storybook Island [W] *Rapid City, SD*

Story Lady Doll and Toy Museum [W] *Albert Lea, MN*

Strategic Air Command Museum [W] *Lincoln, NE*

Stuhr Museum of the Prairie Pioneer [W] *Grand Island, NE*

Sturgis Falls Days Celebration [S] *Cedar Falls, IA*

Stutsman County Fair [S] *Jamestown, ND*

Sugar Creek State Forest [W] *Kirksville, MO*

Sugar Valley Rally [S] *Gering, NE*

Sullys Hill National Game Preserve [W] *Devils Lake, ND*

Summer Affair [S] *Auburn, NE*

Summer Arts Festival [S] *Omaha, NE*

Summerfest [S] *Gothenburg, NE*

Summer Festival [S] *Brookings, SD*

Summerthing [S] *Grand Forks, ND*

Sundown Mountain Ski Area [W] *Dubuque, IA*

Sunflower Festival [S] *Goodland, KS*

Sunset Lake [W] *Guymon, OK*

Sunset Zoo [W] *Manhattan, KS*

Superior-Quetico Wilderness [W] *Ely, MN*

Surf Ballroom [W] *Clear Lake, IA*

Swan Lake National Wildlife Refuge [W] *Chillicothe, MO*

Swan Lake Park [W] *Carroll, IA*

Swanson Reservoir State Recreation Area [W] *McCook, NE*

Sweet Corn Days [S] *Estherville, IA*

Symphony of Lights [S] *Clinton, IA*

Table Rock Dam and Lake [W] *Branson/Table Rock Lake Area, MO*

Table Rock Helicopters [W] *Branson/Table Rock Lake Area, MO*

Table Rock State Park [W] *Branson/Table Rock Lake Area, MO*

Tallgrass Prairie Preserve [W] *Pawhuska, OK*

Tall Timber Days and US Chainsaw Carving Championships [S] *Grand Rapids, MN*

Tamarac National Wildlife Refuge [W] *Detroit Lakes, MN*

Tekakwitha Fine Arts Center [W] *Sisseton, SD*

Tenkiller State Park [W] *Muskogee, OK*

10K Volksmarch [S] *Crazy Horse Memorial, SD*

Tent Theater [S] *Springfield, MO*

Terrace Hill [W] *Des Moines, IA*

Terrace Mill Heritage Festival [S] *Glenwood, MN*

Terrence Mill Fiddlers' Contest [S] *Glenwood, MN*

Territorial Christmas [S] *Guthrie, OK*

Terry Peak [W] *Lead, SD*

Theodore Roosevelt National Park-South Unit [W] *Medora, ND*

Thomas County Free Fair [S] *Colby, KS*

Thomas Hart Benton Exhibit [W] *Joplin, MO*

Thomas Hart Benton Home and Studio State Historic Site [W] *Kansas City, MO*

Thomas P. Stafford Museum [W] *Weatherford, OK*

Thousand Hills State Park [W] *Kirksville, MO*

Three Valley Museum [W] *Durant, OK*

Thunderhead Underground Falls [W] *Rapid City, SD*

Tobacco Auctions [S] *Weston, MO*

Tom and Huck Statue [W] *Hannibal, MO*

Tom and Woods' Moose Lake Wilderness Canoe Trips [W] *Ely, MN*

Tom Mix Museum [W] *Bartlesville, OK*

Tom Sawyer Days [S] *Hannibal, MO*

Topeka Zoo [W] *Topeka, KS*

Toronto State Park [W] *Yates Center, KS*

Tour of Homes [S] *Auburn, NE*

Tours [W] *Minneapolis, MN*

Tours. Main Street Trolley [W] *Clear Lake, IA*

Tourtelotte Park [W] *Mankato, MN*

Tower Grove House [W] *St. Louis, MO*

Tower of the Four Winds [W] *Blair, NE*

Town and Country Day Celebration [S] *Jackson, MN*

Town Square Park [W] *St. Paul, MN*

Toy and Miniature Museum of Kansas City [W] *Kansas City, MO*

Trail of Tears. [S] *Tahlequah, OK*

Trail of Tears State Park [W] *Cape Girardeau, MO*

Trails and Rails Museum [W] *Kearney, NE*

Trailside Museum [W] *Crawford, NE*

Trails West [S] *St. Joseph, MO*

Train Festival [S] *Milbank, SD*

Trainland, USA [W] *Newton, IA*

Treasure Island Casino and Bingo [W] *Hastings, MN*

Treaty Site History Center [W] *St. Peter, MN*

Tree Frog Music Festival [S] *Faribault, MN*

Trego County Free Fair [S] *WaKeeney, KS*

Trial of Jack McCall. [S] *Deadwood, SD*

Trinity Heights [W] *Sioux City, IA*

Tri-Rivers Fair and Rodeo [S] *Salina, KS*

Tri-State Mineral Museum [W] *Joplin, MO*

Tri-State Museum [W] *Belle Fourche, SD*

Tri-State Music Festival [S] *Enid, OK*

Tri-State Rodeo [S] *Fort Madison, IA*

Trolley [W] *Omaha, NE*

Trolleys of Dubuque, Inc [W] *Dubuque, IA*

Truman Celebration [S] *Independence, MO*

Truman Days [S] *Lamar, MO*

Truman Farm Home [W] *Independence, MO*

Truman State University [W] *Kirksville, MO*

Tulip Time Festival [S] *Pella, IA*

Tulsa Garden Center [W] *Tulsa, OK*

Tulsa Historical Society Museum [W] *Tulsa, OK*

Tulsa Powwow [S] *Tulsa, OK*

Tulsa State Fair [S] *Tulsa, OK*

Tulsa Zoo, The [W] *Tulsa, OK*

Tumbleweed Festival [S] *Garden City, KS*

Turtle Mountain Provincial Park [W] *Bottineau, ND*

Turtle River State Park [W] *Grand Forks, ND*

Tuttle Creek State Park [W] *Manhattan, KS*

Twainland Express [W] *Hannibal, MO*

Tweed Museum of Art [W] *Duluth, MN*

Twin Lakes [W] *Fort Dodge, IA*

Twin Rivers Festival [S] *Emporia, KS*

Two Rivers State Recreation Area [W] *Omaha, NE*

Ulysses S. Grant National Historic Site [W] *St. Louis, MO*

UMR Nuclear Reactor [W] *Rolla, MO*

UM-Rolla Stonehenge [W] *Rolla, MO*

Union Cemetery [W] *Kansas City, MO*

Union College [W] *Lincoln, NE*

Union County State Park [W] *Beresford, SD*

United States Cellular Balloon Classic [S] *Columbia, MO*

United Tribes PowWow [S] *Bismarck, ND*

University of Dubuque [W] *Dubuque, IA*

University of Iowa [W] *Iowa City, IA*

University of Kansas [W] *Lawrence, KS*

University of Minnesota, Duluth [W] *Duluth, MN*

University of Minnesota, Twin Cities [W] *Minneapolis, MN*

University of Minnesota, Morris [W] *Morris, MN*

University of Minnesota, Twin Cities Campus [W] *St. Paul, MN*

University of Missouri-Columbia [W] *Columbia, MO*

University of Missouri-Kansas City [W] *Kansas City, MO*

University of Missouri-Rolla [W] *Rolla, MO*

University of Nebraska at Kearney [W] *Kearney, NE*

University of Nebraska State Museum [W] *Lincoln, NE*

University of Nebraska [W] *Lincoln, NE*

University of Nebraska at Omaha [W] *Omaha, NE*

University of North Dakota [W] *Grand Forks, ND*

University of Northern Iowa [W] *Cedar Falls, IA*

University of Oklahoma [W] *Norman, OK*

University of Sioux Falls [W] *Sioux Falls, SD*

University of South Dakota [W] *Vermillion, SD*

University Theatre [S] *Minneapolis, MN*

Upper Iowa River [W] *Decorah, IA*

Upper Midwest Woodcarvers and Quilters Expo [S] *Blue Earth, MN*

Upper Mississippi River National Wildlife and Fish Refuge [W] *Winona, MN*

Upper Sioux Agency State Park [W] *Granite Falls, MN*

Upper Souris National Wildlife Refuge [W] *Minot, ND*

US Cavalry Museum [W] *Junction City, KS*

US Cellular Center [W] *Cedar Rapids, IA*

US Hockey Hall of Fame [W] *Eveleth, MN*

USS *Batfish.* [W] *Muskogee, OK*

USS *South Dakota* Battleship Memorial [W] *Sioux Falls, SD*

Vaile Mansion [W] *Independence, MO*

Valentine National Wildlife Refuge [W] *Valentine, NE*

Valley City State University [W] *Valley City, ND*

Valleyfair [W] *Bloomington, MN*

Van Horn's Antique Truck Museum [W] *Mason City, IA*

Van Meter State Park [W] *Arrow Rock, MO*

Vasaloppet Cross-Country Ski Race [S] *Mora, MN*

Veishea Spring Festival [S] *Ames, IA*

Verdon Lake State Recreation Area [W] *Auburn, NE*

Vermilion Interpretive Center [W] *Ely, MN*

Vesterheim, the Norwegian-American Museum [W] *Decorah, IA*

Victorian Fair [S] *Winona, MN*

Victoria Springs State Recreation Area [W] *Broken Bow, NE*

Viking Lake State Park [W] *Red Oak, IA*

Vikingland Band Festival [S] *Alexandria, MN*

Vikingland Drum Corps Classic [S] *Alexandria, MN*

Viking Mooring Stones [W] *Moorhead, MN*

Village of Yesteryear [W] *Owatonna, MN*

Village Theater [W] *Auburn, NE*

Volga River State Recreation Area [W] *West Union, IA*

Voyageurs National Park [W] *International Falls, MN*

Voyageurs National Park [W] *Lake Kabetogama, MN*

Voyageur Winter Festival [S] *Ely, MN*

Wade's Gold Mill [W] *Hill City, SD*

Wah-Shun-Gah Days [S] *Council Grove, KS*

Walgreen Lake State Recreation Area [W] *Chadron, NE*

Walker Art Center [W] *Minneapolis, MN*

Walking tour [W] *Arrow Rock, MO*

Wallace State Park [W] *Cameron, MO*

Wall Drug Store [W] *Wall, SD*

Walnut Creek [W] *Tulsa, OK*

Waltzing Waters [W] *Branson/Table Rock Lake Area, MO*

Wapsipinicon State Park [W] *Cedar Rapids, IA*

Ward County Historical Society Museum and Pioneer Village [W] *Minot, ND*

Ward Earthlodge Village Historic Site [W] *Bismarck, ND*

Warkentin House [W] *Newton, KS*

War Memorial Monuments [W] *Carroll, IA*

Warnock Lake Recreation Area [W] *Atchison, KS*

Wartburg College [W] *Waverly, IA*

Washburn Sunflower Music Festival [S] *Topeka, KS*

Washburn University of Topeka [W] *Topeka, KS*

Washburn-Zittleman House [W] *Spring Valley, MN*

Washington County Historical Museum [W] *Stillwater, MN*

Washington State Park [W] *Bonne Terre, MO*

Washington University Gallery of Art [W] *Clayton, MO*

Washington University [W] *Clayton, MO*

Washita Valley Museum [W] *Pauls Valley, OK*

Waterama [S] *Glenwood, MN*

Watercolor USA [S] *Springfield, MO*

Waterfest Weekend [S] *South Sioux City, NE*

Waterloo Community Playhouse [W] *Waterloo, IA*

Waterloo Museum of Art [W] *Waterloo, IA*

Water Park [W] *Taylors Falls, MN*

Watertower Festival [S] *Pipestone, MN*

Waterworld [W] *Grand Forks, ND*

Watkins Community Museum [W] *Lawrence, KS*

Watkins Woolen Mill State Historic Site [W] *Excelsior Springs, MO*

Waubay National Wildlife Refuge [W] *Webster, SD*

Waurika Lake [W] *Waurika, OK*

Wayne County Fair [S] *Wayne, NE*

Wayne County Historical Museum [W] *Chariton, IA*

Wayne State College [W] *Wayne, NE*

Webster State Park [W] *Stockton, KS*

WE Country Music Fest [S] *Detroit Lakes, MN*

Welch Village [W] *Red Wing, MN*

West Amana [W] *Amana Colonies, IA*

Western Fest Stampede Rodeo [S] *Granite Falls, MN*

Western Heritage Week [S] *Ada, OK*

Western Historic Trails Center [W] *Council Bluffs, IA*

Westminster College [W] *Fulton, MO*

West Nebraska Arts Center [W] *Scottsbluff, NE*

Weston Brewing Company [W] *Weston, MO*

Westport [W] *Kansas City, MO*

West Port Plaza [W] *St. Louis, MO*

W.H.C. Folsom House [W] *Taylors Falls, MN*

Wheels, Wings & Water Festival [S] *St. Cloud, MN*

White Earth Powwow [S] *Detroit Lakes, MN*

White House [W] *Hermann, MO*

Whitestone Hill Battlefield State Historic Site [W] *Jamestown, ND*

White Water [W] *Branson/Table Rock Lake Area, MO*

White Water Bay [W] *Oklahoma City, OK*

Whitewater State Park [W] *Rochester, MN*

White Water University [W] *Des Moines, IA*

W.H. Over State Museum [W] *Vermillion, SD*

Wichita Art Museum [W] *Wichita, KS*

Wichita-Caddo-Delaware Ceremonial [S] *Anadarko, OK*

Wichita Center for the Arts [W] *Wichita, KS*

Wichita Mountains Wildlife Refuge [W] *Lawton, OK*

Wichita River Festival [S] *Wichita, KS*

Wichita-Sedgwick County Historical Museum [W] *Wichita, KS*

Wildcat Den State Park [W] *Muscatine, IA*

Wildcat Hills State Recreation Area Reserve and Nature Center [W] *Scottsbluff, NE*

Wilder Memorial Museum [W] *Strawberry Point, IA*

Wilderness Park [W] *Lincoln, NE*

Wild Mountain Ski Area [W] *Taylors Falls, MN*

Wild River [W] *Taylors Falls, MN*

Wild Water Weekend [S] *Waynesville, MO*

Wild West Festival [S] *Hays, KS*

Wildwood Historic Home [W] *Nebraska City, NE*

Wildwood Park [W] *Nebraska City, NE*

Willa Cather Spring Conference [S] *Hastings, NE*

Willa Cather State Historic Site [W] *Hastings, NE*

William O'Brien State Park [W] *Stillwater, MN*

Will Rogers Birthday Celebration [S] *Claremore, OK*

Will Rogers Birthplace and Dog Iron Ranch [W] *Claremore, OK*

Will Rogers Memorial [W] *Claremore, OK*

Will Rogers Memorial Rodeo and Parade [S] *Vinita, OK*

Will Rogers PRCA Rodeo [S] *Claremore, OK*

Will Rogers Theatre [W] *Branson/Table Rock Lake Area, MO*

Wilson Dam and Reservoir [W] *Russell, KS*

Wilson Island State Recreation Area [W] *Missouri Valley, IA*

Wilson's Creek National Battlefield [W] *Springfield, MO*

Wilson State Park [W] *Russell, KS*

Wineries [W] *Hermann, MO*

"Wings Over the Platte" Celebration [S] *Grand Island, NE*

Winona County Historical Society Museum [W] *Winona, MN*

Winona Steamboat Days [S] *Winona, MN*

Winston Churchill Memorial and Library [W] *Fulton, MO*

Winter Carnival [S] *St. Paul, MN*

Winter Frolic [S] *Hibbing, MN*

Wintersmith Park [W] *Ada, OK*

Winter Sports Festival [S] *Estherville, IA*

Winter Wonderland [S] *Wahpeton, ND*

Wonderland Cave [W] *Sturgis, SD*

Woodbury County Courthouse [W] *Sioux City, IA*

Woodlands, The [W] *Kansas City, KS*

Woodland School and Krosch Log House, The [W] *Blue Earth, MN*

Woodward Riverboat Museum [W] *Dubuque, IA*

Woolaroc [W] *Bartlesville, OK*

World Championship Quarter Horse Show [S] *Oklahoma City, OK*

World Headquarters Complex, Reorganized Church of Jesus

Christ of Latter Day Saints [W] *Independence, MO*

World's Largest Floating Loon [W] *Virginia, MN*

Worlds of Fun [W] *Kansas City, MO*

Wounded Knee Historical Site [W] *Pine Ridge, SD*

W.W. Mayo House [W] *Le Sueur, MN*

Wyandotte County Historical Society and Museum [W] *Kansas City, KS*

Wylie Park [W] *Aberdeen, SD*

Yellow Medicine County Museum [W] *Granite Falls, MN*

Yellow Smoke Park [W] *Denison, IA*

Yule Feast Weekend [S] *Ottawa, KS*

Zippel Bay State Park [W] *Baudette, MN*

LODGING LIST

Establishment names are listed in alphabetical order followed by a symbol identifying their classification and then city and state. The symbols for classification are: [AS] for All Suites, [BB] for B&Bs/Small Inns, [CAS] for Casinos, [CC] for Cottage Colonies, [CON] for Villas/Condos, [CONF] for Conference Centers, [EX] for Extended Stays, [HOT] for Hotels, [MOT] for Motels/Motor Lodges, [RAN] for Guest Ranches, and [RST] for Resorts.

ABBEY HOTEL [BB] *Bettendorf, IA*

ABEND HAUS COTTAGES & AUDRIE'S BED & BREAKFAST [BB] *Rapid City, SD*

ADAM'S MARK [HOT] *Kansas City, MO*

ADAM'S MARK HOTEL [HOT] *St. Louis, MO*

ADAM'S MARK HOTEL [HOT] *Tulsa, OK*

ADVENTURELAND INN [MOT] *Des Moines, IA*

AFTON HOUSE INN [BB] *Stillwater, MN*

ALEX JOHNSON [HOT] *Rapid City, SD*

ALL AMERICAN INN [MOT] *Spearfish, SD*

ALLYNDALE MOTEL [MOT] *Duluth, MN*

AMBASSADOR INN [MOT] *Guymon, OK*

AMBER INN [MOT] *Le Mars, IA*

AMERICINN [MOT] *Bemidji, MN*

AMERICINN [MOT] *Bismarck, ND*

AMERICINN [MOT] *Cloquet, MN*

AMERICINN [MOT] *Dickinson, ND*

AMERICINN [MOT] *Elk River, MN*

AMERICINN [MOT] *Minneapolis, MN*

AMERICINN [MOT] *Sioux Falls, SD*

AMERICINN [MOT] *Walker, MN*

AMERICINN MOTEL [MOT] *Alexandria, MN*

AMERICINN MOTEL [MOT] *Fargo, ND*

AMERICINN MOTEL [MOT] *Hastings, MN*

AMERICINN MOTEL & SUITES [MOT] *Medora, ND*

AMERICINN MOTEL AND SUITES [MOT] *Rapid City, SD*

AMERICINN MOTEL AND SUITES [MOT] *Willmar, MN*

AMERICINN OF BAXTER [MOT] *Brainerd, MN*

AMERICINN OF GRAND RAPIDS [MOT] *Grand Rapids, MN*

AMERICINN STEWARTVILLE [MOT] *Rochester, MN*

AMERISTAR CASINO [HOT] *Council Bluffs, IA*

AMERISUITES [MOT] *Overland Park, KS*

ANDERSON'S PINE EDGE INN [MOT] *Little Falls, MN*

ANTHONY MOTEL [MOT] *Mitchell, SD*

APPLE INN [MOT] *Nebraska City, NE*

APPLE TREE INN [MOT] *Coffeyville, KS*

APPLETREE INN [MOT] *Independence, KS*

APPLE TREE INN [MOT] *Indianola, IA*

AQUA CITY MOTEL [MOT] *Minneapolis, MN*

ARCHER HOUSE HOTEL [BB] *Northfield, MN*

ARROW MOTEL [MOT] *Pipestone, MN*

ARROWWOOD A RADISSON RESORT [RST] *Alexandria, MN*

ASPEN LODGE [MOT] *Grand Marais, MN*

AUBURN INN [MOT] *Auburn, NE*

AUGUSTA LINDENHOF BED & BREAKFAST [BB] *Hermann, MO*

BASS POINT RESORT [CC] *Lake of the Ozarks, MO*

BAVARIAN INN [MOT] *Custer, SD*

BAYMONT INN [MOT] *Bloomington, MN*

BAYMONT INN [MOT] *Omaha, NE*

BAYMONT INN [MOT] *Sioux Falls, SD*

BAYMONT INN & SUITES [MOT] *Ames, IA*

BAYMONT INN & SUITES [MOT] *Kansas City, MO*

BAYMONT INN AND SUITES [MOT] *Minneapolis, MN*

BEARSKIN LODGE [RST] *Grand Marais, MN*

BEATRICE INN [MOT] *Beatrice, NE*

BEL-AIRE MOTOR INN [MOT] *Albert Lea, MN*

BERNING MOTOR INN [MOT] *Creston, IA*

BEST INN [MOT] *Alexandria, MN*

BEST INN [MOT] *Des Moines, IA*

BEST INN [MOT] *Omaha, NE*

BEST INN-EMPORIA [MOT] *Emporia, KS*

BEST VALUE BUFFALO TRAIL MOTEL [MOT] *Winner, SD*

BEST VALUE INN CAMELOT MOTOR INN [MOT] *Winfield, KS*

BEST VALUE SUBURBAN MOTEL [MOT] *Emmetsburg, IA*

BEST WESTERN [MOT] *Ames, IA*

BEST WESTERN [MOT] *Bartlesville, OK*

BEST WESTERN [MOT] *Bemidji, MN*

BEST WESTERN [MOT] *Chillicothe, MO*

BEST WESTERN [MOT] *Emporia, KS*

BEST WESTERN [MOT] *Enid, OK*

BEST WESTERN [MOT] *Goodland, KS*

BEST WESTERN [MOT] *Grand Marais, MN*

BEST WESTERN [MOT] *Mankato, MN*

BEST WESTERN [MOT] *Marshall, MN*

BEST WESTERN [MOT] *Pratt, KS*

BEST WESTERN [MOT] *Red Wing, MN*

BEST WESTERN [MOT] *Sallisaw, OK*

BEST WESTERN [MOT] *St. Paul, MN*

BEST WESTERN [MOT] *Stillwater, MN*

BEST WESTERN ABILENE'S PRIDE [MOT] *Abilene, KS*

BEST WESTERN AIRPORT [MOT] *Tulsa, OK*

BEST WESTERN AIRPORT INN [MOT] *St. Louis, MO*

BEST WESTERN ALTUS [MOT] *Altus, OK*

BEST WESTERN AMERICANNA INN AND CONFERENCE CENTER [MOT] *St. Cloud, MN*

BEST WESTERN ANGUS INN [MOT] *Great Bend, KS*

BEST WESTERN BEL VILLA [MOT] *Belleville, KS*

BEST WESTERN CENTRAL - EXECUTIVE CENTER [MOT] *Omaha, NE*

BEST WESTERN CHALET LODGE [MOT] *North Platte, NE*

BEST WESTERN CHEROKEE STRIP MOTEL [MOT] *Perry, OK*

BEST WESTERN CHIEF MOTEL [MOT] *McCook, NE*

BEST WESTERN CINDERELLA MOTOR INN [MOT] *Shawnee, OK*

BEST WESTERN CITY CENTRE [MOT] *Sioux City, IA*

BEST WESTERN CLIFF DWELLER [MOT] *Lutsen, MN*

BEST WESTERN COACH HOUSE INN & SUITES [MOT] *Sikeston, MO*

BEST WESTERN COACHLIGHT [MOT] *Rolla, MO*

BEST WESTERN COOPERS MILL [MOT] *Cedar Rapids, IA*

BEST WESTERN COUNTRY INN [MOT] *Kansas City, MO*

BEST WESTERN COUNTRY MANOR INN [MOT] *Jackson, MN*

BEST WESTERN COURTYARD AND GARDENS VILLAGER [MOT] *Lincoln, NE*

BEST WESTERN CROWN HOTEL [MOT] *Colby, KS*

BEST WESTERN DEERFIELD INN [MOT] *Springfield, MO*

BEST WESTERN DOGWOOD HILLS RESORT INN [MOT] *Osage Beach, MO*

BEST WESTERN DOUBLEWOOD INN [MOT] *Bismarck, ND*

BEST WESTERN DOUBLEWOOD INN [MOT] *Fargo, ND*

BEST WESTERN DOWNTOWN [MOT] *Minneapolis, MN*

BEST WESTERN DROVER'S INN AND CONFERENCE CENTER [MOT] *St. Paul, MN*

BEST WESTERN EDGEWATER [MOT] *Duluth, MN*

BEST WESTERN FAIRFIELD INN [MOT] *Fairfield, IA*

BEST WESTERN FIFTH AVENUE [MOT] *Rochester, MN*

BEST WESTERN FOUR PRESIDENTS MOTEL [MOT] *Keystone, SD*

BEST WESTERN FRONTIER MOTOR INN [MOT] *Clinton, IA*

BEST WESTERN GLENPOOL TULSA [MOT] *Tulsa, OK*

BEST WESTERN GOLDEN PLAINS [MOT] *Oakley, KS*

BEST WESTERN GOLDEN SPIKE [MOT] *Hill City, SD*

BEST WESTERN GRAHAM'S [MOT] *Murdo, SD*

BEST WESTERN - HENSLEY'S [MOT] *El Reno, OK*

BEST WESTERN HILLS RESORT [MOT] *Lead, SD*

BEST WESTERN HOLIDAY LODGE [MOT] *Clear Lake, IA*

BEST WESTERN HOLIDAY MANOR [MOT] *McPherson, KS*

BEST WESTERN HOLLAND HOUSE [MOT] *Detroit Lakes, MN*

BEST WESTERN HOTEL CLEMENS [MOT] *Hannibal, MO*

BEST WESTERN INN [MOT] *Atoka, OK*

BEST WESTERN INN [MOT] *Chickasha, OK*

BEST WESTERN INN [MOT] *Des Moines, IA*

BEST WESTERN INN [MOT] *Dubuque, IA*

BEST WESTERN INN [MOT] *Eufaula, OK*

BEST WESTERN INN [MOT] *Fort Scott, KS*

BEST WESTERN INN [MOT] *Guthrie, OK*

BEST WESTERN INN [MOT] *Harrisonville, MO*

BEST WESTERN INN [MOT] *Iola, KS*

BEST WESTERN INN [MOT] *Jefferson City, MO*

BEST WESTERN INN [MOT] *Kearney, NE*

BEST WESTERN INN [MOT] *Lawrence, KS*

BEST WESTERN INN [MOT] *Macon, MO*

BEST WESTERN INN [MOT] *McAlester, OK*

BEST WESTERN INN [MOT] *Rochester, MN*

BEST WESTERN INN [MOT] *Thief River Falls, MN*

BEST WESTERN INN [MOT] *Yankton, SD*

BEST WESTERN INN OF MIAMI [MOT] *Miami, OK*

BEST WESTERN J-HAWK [MOT] *Greensburg, KS*

BEST WESTERN KELLY INN [MOT] *Fargo, ND*

BEST WESTERN KELLY INN [MOT] *Minneapolis, MN*

BEST WESTERN KELLY INN [MOT] *Minneapolis, MN*

BEST WESTERN-KELLY INN [MOT] *Minot, ND*

BEST WESTERN KELLY INN [MOT] *St. Cloud, MN*

BEST WESTERN KELLY INN [MOT] *St. Paul, MN*

BEST WESTERN LA GRANDE HACIENDA [MOT] *Cherokee, IA*

BEST WESTERN LEE'S MOTOR INN [MOT] *Chamberlain, SD*

BEST WESTERN LONGBRANCH [MOT] *Cedar Rapids, IA*

BEST WESTERN MARKITA INN [MOT] *Durant, OK*

BEST WESTERN MARK MOTOR HOTEL [MOT] *Weatherford, OK*

BEST WESTERN MEADOW ACRES [MOT] *Topeka, KS*

BEST WESTERN MID-AMERICA INN [MOT] *Salina, KS*

BEST WESTERN MIDWAY HOTEL [MOT] *Dubuque, IA*

BEST WESTERN MONTIS INN [MOT] *Waynesville, MO*

BEST WESTERN MOUNTAIN OAK LODGE [MOT] *Branson/Table Rock Lake Area, MO*

BEST WESTERN NEWTON INN [MOT] *Newton, IA*

BEST WESTERN NORSEMAN INN [MOT] *Webster City, IA*

BEST WESTERN OF STILLWATER [MOT] *Stillwater, OK*

BEST WESTERN OKMULGEE [MOT] *Okmulgee, OK*

BEST WESTERN PALMER INN [MOT] *York, NE*

BEST WESTERN PLAINS [MOT] *Wall, SD*

BEST WESTERN PRAIRIE INN [MOT] *Independence, KS*

BEST WESTERN PRAIRIE INN [MOT] *Morris, MN*

BEST WESTERN PZAZZ MOTOR INN [MOT] *Burlington, IA*

BEST WESTERN QUIET HOUSE SUITES [MOT] *Amana Colonies, IA*

BEST WESTERN RAINTREE MOTOR INN [MOT] *Ada, OK*

BEST WESTERN RAMKOTA [MOT] *Rapid City, SD*

BEST WESTERN RAMKOTA HOTEL [MOT] *Aberdeen, SD*

BEST WESTERN RAMKOTA HOTEL [MOT] *Sioux Falls, SD*

BEST WESTERN RAMKOTA INN [MOT] *Watertown, SD*

BEST WESTERN RED COACH INN [MOT] *El Dorado, KS*

BEST WESTERN RED COACH INN [MOT] *Newton, KS*

BEST WESTERN RED COACH INN [MOT] *Wichita, KS*

BEST WESTERN REDICK TOWER [MOT] *Omaha, NE*

BEST WESTERN REGENCY INN [MOT] *Marshalltown, IA*

BEST WESTERN RIVERPORT INN [MOT] *Winona, MN*

BEST WESTERN RIVERSIDE INN [MOT] *Grand Island, NE*

BEST WESTERN ROUTE 66 RAIL HAVEN [MOT] *Springfield, MO*

BEST WESTERN SADDLEBACK INN [MOT] *Oklahoma City, OK*

BEST WESTERN SANTA FE INN [MOT] *Oklahoma City, OK*

BEST WESTERN SEVEN SEAS INN [MOT] *Mandan, ND*

BEST WESTERN SILVER SPUR LODGE [MOT] *Dodge City, KS*

BEST WESTERN SOLDIERS' FIELD [MOT] *Rochester, MN*

BEST WESTERN STAGECOACH INN [MOT] *Ogallala, NE*

BEST WESTERN STARLITE VILLAGE MOTELS [MOT] *Fort Dodge, IA*

BEST WESTERN STARLITE VILLAGE [MOT] *Waterloo, IA*

BEST WESTERN STATE FAIR MOTOR INN [MOT] *Sedalia, MO*

BEST WESTERN STEEPLEGATE INN [MOT] *Davenport, IA*

BEST WESTERN SURF MOTEL [MOT] *Marysville, KS*

BEST WESTERN THUNDERBIRD HOTEL [MOT] *Bloomington, MN*

BEST WESTERN TOWN & COUNTRY [MOT] *Rapid City, SD*

BEST WESTERN TOWN HOUSE [MOT] *Grand Forks, ND*

BEST WESTERN TOWNSEND [MOT] *Larned, KS*

BEST WESTERN TRADE WINDS CENTRAL INN [MOT] *Tulsa, OK*

BEST WESTERN VAGABOND [MOT] *Hays, KS*

BEST WESTERN WEST HILLS INN [MOT] *Chadron, NE*

BEST WESTERN WHEAT LANDS HOTEL AND CONFERENCE CENTER [MOT] *Garden City, KS*

BEST WESTERN WILL ROGERS INN [MOT] *Claremore, OK*

BEST WESTERN WYOTA INN [MOT] *Lebanon, MO*

BIG CEDAR LODGE [MOT] *Branson/Table Rock Lake Area, MO*

BIG ROCK RESORT [CC] *Walker, MN*

BILTMORE HOTEL [MOT] *Oklahoma City, OK*

BISMARCK INN [MOT] *Lawrence, KS*

BLONDELL [MOT] *Rochester, MN*

BLUE BELL LODGE & RESORT [CC] *Custer, SD*

BLUEFIN BAY ON LAKE SUPERIOR [MOT] *Lutsen, MN*

BLUE HAVEN MOTEL [MOT] *Osceola, IA*

BLUE SPRUCE MOTEL [MOT] *North Platte, NE*

BLUE STEM LODGE [MOT] *Eureka, KS*

BLUE TOP INN [MOT] *Lamar, MO*

BOONE'S LICK TRAIL INN [BB] *St. Charles, MO*

BOYD LODGE [CC] *Crosslake, MN*

BRANSON HOTEL BED & BREAKFAST [BB] *Branson/Table Rock Lake Area, MO*

BRANSON HOUSE BED & BREAKFAST [BB] *Branson/Table Rock Lake Area, MO*

BRANSON INN [MOT] *Branson/Table Rock Lake Area, MO*

BREEZE INN MOTEL [MOT] *Aberdeen, SD*

BREEZY POINT RESORT TIME SHARES [RST] *Brainerd, MN*

BRIARWOOD RESORT [CC] *Branson/Table Rock Lake Area, MO*

BROADWAY INN MOTEL [MOT] *Humboldt, IA*

BROADWAY INN MOTEL [MOT] *Yankton, SD*

BROOKINGS INN [MOT] *Brookings, SD*

BROOKS, THE [MOT] *Norton, KS*

BROOKSIDE RESORT [CC] *Park Rapids, MN*

BUDGET HOLIDAY [MOT] *New Ulm, MN*

BUDGET HOST [MOT] *Albert Lea, MN*

BUDGET HOST [MOT] *Jackson, MN*

BUDGET HOST [MOT] *Mount Vernon, MO*

BUDGET HOST ELY [MOT] *Ely, MN*

BUDGET HOST INN [MOT] *Fremont, NE*

BUDGET HOST INN [MOT] *Grand Rapids, MN*

BUDGET HOST INN [MOT] *Owatonna, MN*

BUDGET HOST INN [MOT] *Sioux Falls, SD*

BUDGET HOST MINUTE MAN MOTEL [MOT] *Lexington, NE*

BUDGET HOST VILLAGE INN [MOT] *Kirksville, MO*

BUDGET HOST VILLA INN [MOT] *Hays, KS*

BUDGET HOUSE CIRCLE S [MOT] *Cozad, NE*

BUDGET INN [MOT] *Clear Lake, IA*

BUDGET INN [MOT] *Fairmont, MN*

BUDGET INN [MOT] *Storm Lake, IA*

BUDGET LODGING [MOT] *Sullivan, MO*

BUDGET MOTEL SOUTH [MOT] *Kearney, NE*

BULLOCK HOTEL & CASINO [MOT] *Deadwood, SD*

BURR OAK [MOT] *Algona, IA*

CAMBRIDGE SUITES [MOT] *Wichita, KS*

CAMPUS INN [MOT] *Columbia, MO*

CANDLELIGHT INN [MOT] *Scottsbluff, NE*

CANTERBURY INN [MOT] *Parsons, KS*

CAPITAL CENTER INN [MOT] *Topeka, KS*

CAPITOL INN & SUITES [MOT] *Pierre, SD*

CAPITOL PLAZA HOTEL [HOT] *Jefferson City, MO*

CAPRI MOTEL [MOT] *Avoca, IA*

CAPRI MOTEL [MOT] *Fairbury, NE*

CAPRI MOTEL [MOT] *O'Neill, NE*

CARIBOU HIGHLANDS LODGE [RST] *Lutsen, MN*

CARROLLTON INN [MOT] *Carroll, IA*

CASCADE LODGE [RST] *Lutsen, MN*

CEDAR RAPIDS INN AND CONFERENCE CENTER [MOT] *Cedar Rapids, IA*

CELEBRITY INN MOTEL [MOT] *Clarinda, IA*

CHANHASSEN INN [MOT] *Minneapolis, MN*

CHARLES WESLEY MOTOR LODGE [MOT] *Broken Bow, OK*

CHASE HOTEL [EX] *Kansas City, MO*

CHASE SUITE HOTEL [EX] *Des Moines, IA*

CHASE SUITE HOTEL [AS] *Overland Park, KS*

CHASE SUITE HOTEL BY WOODFIN [MOT] *Lincoln, NE*

CHATEAU ON THE LAKE [RST] *Branson/Table Rock Lake Area, MO*

CHESHIRE LODGE [MOT] *St. Louis, MO*

CHESTNUT CHARM BED & BREAKFAST [BB] *Atlantic, IA*

CHICKASAW LODGE [MOT] *Sulphur, OK*

CHIEF MOTEL [MOT] *Pocahontas, IA*

CHIEFTAIN CONFERENCE CENTER [MOT] *Carrington, ND*

CLARION HOTEL [AS] *Bloomington, MN*

CLARION HOTEL [MOT] *Davenport, IA*

CLARION HOTEL [MOT] *Springfield, MO*

CLARION HOTEL [MOT] *Wichita, KS*

CLARION HOTEL AND CONFERENCE CENTER [MOT] *Iowa City, IA*

CLEARWATER CANOE OUTFITTERS AND LODGE [RST] *Grand Marais, MN*

CLUBHOUSE INN [MOT] *Overland Park, KS*

CLUBHOUSE INN [MOT] *Topeka, KS*

C'MON INN [MOT] *Grand Forks, ND*

C'MON INN [MOT] *Thief River Falls, MN*

COACHLIGHT [MOT] *Mitchell, SD*

COLLEGE CITY MOTEL [MOT] *Northfield, MN*

COLLINS PLAZA [HOT] *Cedar Rapids, IA*

COLONIAL INN [MOT] *New Ulm, MN*

COMFORT INN [MOT] *Ames, IA*

COMFORT INN [MOT] *Atchison, KS*

COMFORT INN [MOT] *Bemidji, MN*

COMFORT INN [MOT] *Bismarck, ND*

COMFORT INN [MOT] *Bloomington, MN*

COMFORT INN [MOT] *Burlington, IA*

COMFORT INN [MOT] *Cedar Rapids, IA*

COMFORT INN [MOT] *Davenport, IA*

COMFORT INN [MOT] *Devils Lake, ND*

COMFORT INN [MOT] *Dickinson, ND*

COMFORT INN [MOT] *Dubuque, IA*

COMFORT INN [MOT] *Duluth, MN*

COMFORT INN [MOT] *Fargo, ND*

COMFORT INN [MOT] *Fargo, ND*

COMFORT INN [MOT] *Fergus Falls, MN*

COMFORT INN [MOT] *Fort Dodge, IA*

COMFORT INN [MOT] *Fremont, NE*

COMFORT INN [MOT] *Grand Forks, ND*

COMFORT INN [MOT] *Hill City, SD*

COMFORT INN [MOT] *Hutchinson, KS*

COMFORT INN [MOT] *Independence, MO*

COMFORT INN [MOT] *Jamestown, ND*

COMFORT INN [MOT] *Lincoln, NE*

COMFORT INN [MOT] *Marshall, MN*

COMFORT INN [MOT] *Marshalltown, IA*

COMFORT INN [MOT] *Mason City, IA*

COMFORT INN [MOT] *Minneapolis, MN*

COMFORT INN [MOT] *Minot, ND*

COMFORT INN [MOT] *Mitchell, SD*

COMFORT INN [MOT] *Ogallala, NE*

COMFORT INN [MOT] *Rapid City, SD*

COMFORT INN [MOT] *Salina, KS*

COMFORT INN [MOT] *Scottsbluff, NE*

COMFORT INN [MOT] *Sioux City, IA*

COMFORT INN [MOT] *Spearfish, SD*

COMFORT INN [MOT] *St. Cloud, MN*

COMFORT INN [MOT] *Vermillion, SD*

COMFORT INN [MOT] *Yankton, SD*

COMFORT INN & CONFERENCE CENTER [MOT] *Rochester, MN*

COMFORT INN AND SUITES [MOT] *Durant, OK*

COMFORT INN OF SIDNEY [MOT] *Sidney, NE*

COMFORT INN SOUTH [MOT] *Cedar Rapids, IA*

COMFORT INN SOUTH [MOT] *Des Moines, IA*

COMFORT INN SOUTH [MOT] *Sioux Falls, SD*

COMFORT SUITES [MOT] *Bismarck, ND*

COMFORT SUITES [MOT] *Duluth, MN*

COMFORT SUITES [MOT] *Fargo, ND*

COMFORT SUITES [MOT] *Sioux Falls, SD*

COMFORT SUITES [MOT] *Tulsa, OK*

COMFORT SUITES LIVING [MOT] *Des Moines, IA*

COMFORT SUITES WICHITA AIRPORT [MOT] *Wichita, KS*

COPA [MOT] *Medicine Lodge, KS*

CORNHUSKER [HOT] *Lincoln, NE*

COTTAGE HOUSE HOTEL & MOTEL, THE [MOT] *Council Grove, KS*

COUNTRY CLUB MOTEL [MOT] *Okoboji, IA*

COUNTRY INN [MOT] *Deerwood, MN*

COUNTRY INN [MOT] *Grand Rapids, MN*

COUNTRY INN [MOT] *North Platte, NE*

COUNTRY INN [MOT] *Shenandoah, IA*

COUNTRY INN [MOT] *St. Paul, MN*

COUNTRY INN & SUITES [MOT] *Grand Forks, ND*

COUNTRY INN & SUITES - BLOOMINGTON [MOT] *Bloomington, MN*

COUNTRY INN & SUITES - BAXTER [MOT] *Brainerd, MN*

COUNTRY INN AND SUITES BY CARLSON [MOT] *Stillwater, MN*

COUNTRY INN BY CARLSON [MOT] *Two Harbors, MN*

COUNTRY INN BY CARLSON, NORTHFIELD [MOT] *Northfield, MN*

COUNTRY SUITES BY CALSON [MOT] *Fargo, ND*

COURTYARD BY MARRIOTT [MOT] *Bettendorf, IA*

COURTYARD BY MARRIOTT [MOT] *Oklahoma City, OK*

COURTYARD BY MARRIOTT [MOT] *Overland Park, KS*

COURTYARD BY MARRIOTT [MOT] *St. Louis, MO*

COVER PARK MANOR BED AND BREAKFAST [BB] *Stillwater, MN*

CRAGUN'S PINE BEACH LODGE AND CONFERENCE CENTER [RST] *Brainerd, MN*

CREST-VUE MOTEL [MOT] *Mankato, KS*

CROSSROADS [MOT] *Beresford, SD*

CROSSROADS HOTEL & CONVENTION CENTER [MOT] *Huron, SD*

CROSSROADS MOTEL [MOT] *Iola, KS*

CROWNE PLAZA [HOT] *St. Louis Lambert Airport Area, MO*

CROWNE PLAZA FIVE SEASONS [HOT] *Cedar Rapids, IA*

CROWNE PLAZA MINNEAPOLIS/ST. PAUL AIRPORT (MALL OF AMERICA AREA) [HOT] *St. Paul, MN*

CROWNE PLAZA NORTHSTAR HOTEL [HOT] *Minneapolis, MN*

CUSTER MANSION BED & BREAKFAST [BB] *Custer, SD*

DAKOTA COUNTRY INN [MOT] *Platte, SD*

DAKOTA INN [MOT] *Jamestown, ND*

DAKOTA PLAINS INN [MOT] *Huron, SD*

DANIELE HOTEL [HOT] *Clayton, MO*

DAS GAST HAUS NADLER [BB] *Clayton, MO*

DAYS HOTEL CARLISLE [MOT] *Omaha, NE*

DAYS INN [MOT] *Albert Lea, MN*

DAYS INN [MOT] *Alexandria, MN*

DAYS INN [MOT] *Altus, OK*

DAYS INN [MOT] *Bismarck, ND*

DAYS INN [MOT] *Bloomington, MN*

DAYS INN [MOT] *Brainerd, MN*

DAYS INN [MOT] *Brainerd, MN*

DAYS INN [MOT] *Branson/Table Rock Lake Area, MO*

DAYS INN [MOT] *Carthage, MO*

DAYS INN [MOT] *Cedar Rapids, IA*

DAYS INN [MOT] *Chickasha, OK*

DAYS INN [MOT] *Davenport, IA*

DAYS INN [MOT] *Davenport, IA*

DAYS INN [MOT] *Devils Lake, ND*

DAYS INN [MOT] *Dubuque, IA*

DAYS INN [MOT] *Duluth, MN*

DAYS INN [MOT] *Elk City, OK*

DAYS INN [MOT] *Emporia, KS*

DAYS INN [MOT] *Fergus Falls, MN*

DAYS INN [MOT] *Grand Forks, ND*

DAYS INN [MOT] *Grand Island, NE*

DAYS INN [MOT] *Hays, KS*

DAYS INN [MOT] *Hibbing, MN*

DAYS INN [MOT] *International Falls, MN*

DAYS INN [MOT] *Junction City, KS*

DAYS INN [MOT] *Kansas City, MO*

DAYS INN [MOT] *Lawrence, KS*

DAYS INN [MOT] *Lawton, OK*

DAYS INN [MOT] *Lebanon, MO*

DAYS INN [MOT] *Lincoln, NE*

DAYS INN [MOT] *Manhattan, KS*

DAYS INN [MOT] *Mankato, MN*

DAYS INN [MOT] *Mason City, IA*

DAYS INN [MOT] *Minneapolis, MN*

DAYS INN [MOT] *Minot, ND*

DAYS INN [MOT] *Mitchell, SD*

DAYS INN [MOT] *Muskogee, OK*

DAYS INN [MOT] *Newton, IA*

DAYS INN [MOT] *Norman, OK*

DAYS INN [MOT] *Oklahoma City, OK*

DAYS INN [MOT] *Omaha, NE*

DAYS INN [MOT] *Pauls Valley, OK*
DAYS INN [MOT] *Pierre, SD*
DAYS INN [MOT] *Ponca City, OK*
DAYS INN [MOT] *Rapid City, SD*
DAYS INN [MOT] *Red Wing, MN*
DAYS INN [MOT] *Rochester, MN*
DAYS INN [MOT] *Rochester, MN*
DAYS INN [MOT] *Sallisaw, OK*
DAYS INN [MOT] *Sidney, NE*
DAYS INN [MOT] *Spearfish, SD*
DAYS INN [MOT] *St. Cloud, MN*
DAYS INN [MOT] *St. Joseph, MO*
DAYS INN [MOT] *St. Paul, MN*
DAYS INN [MOT] *Sturgis, SD*
DAYS INN [MOT] *Topeka, KS*
DAYS INN [MOT] *West Plains, MO*
DAYS INN [MOT] *Wichita, KS*
DAYS INN [MOT] *Winona, MN*
DAYS INN [MOT] *Yankton, SD*
DAYS INN [MOT] *York, NE*
DAYS INN AIRPORT [MOT] *Sioux Falls, SD*
DAYS INN CONFERENCE HOTEL [MOT] *McAlester, OK*
DAYS INN EAST [MOT] *Wichita, KS*
DAYS INN EMPIRE [MOT] *Sioux Falls, SD*
DAYS INN MOTEL [MOT] *Grinnell, IA*
DAYS INN MOUNDS VIEW [MOT] *Minneapolis, MN*
DAYS INN NOAH'S ARK [MOT] *St. Charles, MO*
DAYS INN NORTHWEST [MOT] *Oklahoma City, OK*
DAYS INN OF HINCKLEY [MOT] *Hinckley, MN*
DAYS INN WALL [MOT] *Wall, SD*
DAYS INN WILLMAR [MOT] *Willmar, MN*
DEADWOOD GULCH RESORT [MOT] *Deadwood, SD*
DIAMOND MOTEL [MOT] *Abilene, KS*
DIE HEIMAT COUNTRY INN [BB] *Amana Colonies, IA*
DOANLEIGH INN [BB] *Kansas City, MO*
DODGE HOUSE HOTEL AND CONVENTION CENTER [MOT] *Dodge City, KS*
DOGWOOD INN [MOT] *Branson/Table Rock Lake Area, MO*

DORCHESTER INN [MOT] *Ardmore, OK*
DOUBLETREE [HOT] *Overland Park, KS*
DOUBLETREE CLUB ST. LOUIS AIRPORT [HOT] *St. Louis, MO*
DOUBLETREE DOWNTOWN [HOT] *Omaha, NE*
DOUBLETREE GUEST SUITES [HOT] *Minneapolis, MN*
DOUBLETREE GUEST SUITES [AS] *Omaha, NE*
DOUBLETREE HOTEL [HOT] *Kansas City, MO*
DOUBLETREE HOTEL AND CONFERENCE CENTER [HOT] *St. Louis, MO*
DOUBLETREE HOTEL AT WARREN PLACE [HOT] *Tulsa, OK*
DOUBLETREE HOTEL DOWNTOWN [HOT] *Tulsa, OK*
DOUBLETREE MINNEAPOLIS AIRPORT AT THE MALL [HOT] *Bloomington, MN*
DOUBLETREE PARK PLACE [HOT] *Minneapolis, MN*
DOUGLAS LODGE [RST] *Itasca State Park, MN*
DRIFTWOOD RESORT AND GOLF COURSE [RST] *Pine River, MN*
DRURY INN [MOT] *Joplin, MO*
DRURY INN [MOT] *Overland Park, KS*
DRURY INN [MOT] *Poplar Bluff, MO*
DRURY INN [MOT] *Rolla, MO*
DRURY INN [MOT] *Sikeston, MO*
DRURY INN [MOT] *St. Joseph, MO*
DRURY INN [MOT] *St. Louis, MO*
DRURY INN [MOT] *St. Louis, MO*
DRURY INN AIRPORT [MOT] *St. Louis, MO*
DRURY LODGE [MOT] *Cape Girardeau, MO*
DRURY SUITES [MOT] *Cape Girardeau, MO*
DUNES MOTEL [MOT] *Valentine, NE*
DUSK TO DAWN BED & BREAKFAST [BB] *Amana Colonies, IA*
EAST BAY HOTEL AND DINING ROOM [MOT] *Grand Marais, MN*
ECO-LUX INN [MOT] *Columbus, NE*
ECO-LUX INN [MOT] *Norfolk, NE*
ECONO LODGE [MOT] *Atlantic, IA*

ECONO LODGE [MOT] *Bettendorf, IA*

ECONO LODGE [MOT] *Carthage, MO*

ECONO LODGE [MOT] *Cedar Rapids, IA*

ECONO LODGE [MOT] *Concordia, KS*

ECONO LODGE [MOT] *Council Bluffs, IA*

ECONO LODGE [MOT] *Fargo, ND*

ECONO LODGE [MOT] *Grand Forks, ND*

ECONO LODGE [MOT] *Guymon, OK*

ECONO LODGE [MOT] *Hinckley, MN*

ECONO LODGE [MOT] *Mankato, MN*

ECONO LODGE [MOT] *Minneapolis, MN*

ECONO LODGE [MOT] *Muscatine, IA*

ECONO LODGE [MOT] *Omaha, NE*

ECONO LODGE [MOT] *Rochester, MN*

ECONO LODGE [MOT] *South Sioux City, NE*

ECONO LODGE [MOT] *Springfield, MO*

ECONO LODGE [MOT] *Springfield, MO*

ECONO LODGE INN [MOT] *Cameron, MO*

ECONO LODGE INN [MOT] *Mitchell, SD*

ECONO LODGE PENBERTHY INN [MOT] *Sullivan, MO*

ECONOMY INN [MOT] *Fairfield, IA*

ELDRIDGE HOTEL [HOT] *Lawrence, KS*

ELMS BEST VALUE INN [MOT] *O'Neill, NE*

EMBASSY SUITES [AS] *Bloomington, MN*

EMBASSY SUITES [AS] *Des Moines, IA*

EMBASSY SUITES [AS] *Kansas City, MO*

EMBASSY SUITES [AS] *Overland Park, KS*

EMBASSY SUITES [HOT] *St. Paul, MN*

EMBASSY SUITES [AS] *Tulsa, OK*

EMBASSY SUITES BLOOMINGTON [AS] *Bloomington, MN*

EMBASSY SUITES DOWNTOWN MPLS [AS] *Minneapolis, MN*

EMBASSY SUITES HOTEL [AS] *Oklahoma City, OK*

EMBASSY SUITES ST. LOUIS DOWNTOWN ON HISTORIC LACLEDE'S LANDING [AS] *St. Louis, MO*

EMBASSY SUITES ST. LOUIS AIRPORT [AS] *St. Louis Lambert Airport Area, MO*

ESTHER'S AUSBLICK BED & BREAKFAST [BB] *Hermann, MO*

EVELETH INN [MOT] *Eveleth, MN*

EVERGREEN LODGE FAMILY RESORT AND GOLF [CC] *Park Rapids, MN*

EXECUTIVE INN [MOT] *Owatonna, MN*

EXECUTIVE INN [MOT] *Rochester, MN*

EXECUTIVE INN [MOT] *Webster City, IA*

EXECUTIVE SUITES AND INN [MOT] *Rochester, MN*

EXEL INN [MOT] *Bloomington, MN*

EXEL INN [MOT] *Cedar Rapids, IA*

EXEL INN [MOT] *Davenport, IA*

EXEL INN [MOT] *Sioux Falls, SD*

EXEL INN OF ST. PAUL [MOT] *St. Paul, MN*

EXPRESSWAY INN [MOT] *Bismarck, ND*

EXPRESSWAY SUITES [MOT] *Bismarck, ND*

FABULOUS WESTWARD HO MOTEL [MOT] *Grand Forks, ND*

FAIRFIELD BY MARRIOTT [MOT] *Lincoln, NE*

FAIRFIELD INN [MOT] *Bismarck, ND*

FAIRFIELD INN [MOT] *Bismarck, ND*

FAIRFIELD INN [MOT] *Bloomington, MN*

FAIRFIELD INN [MOT] *Cedar Rapids, IA*

FAIRFIELD INN [MOT] *Council Bluffs, IA*

FAIRFIELD INN [MOT] *Davenport, IA*

FAIRFIELD INN [MOT] *Des Moines, IA*

FAIRFIELD INN [MOT] *Fargo, ND*

FAIRFIELD INN [MOT] *Grand Forks, ND*

FAIRFIELD INN [MOT] *Minot, ND*

FAIRFIELD INN [MOT] *Ottumwa, IA*

FAIRFIELD INN [MOT] *Overland Park, KS*

FAIRFIELD INN [MOT] *Spearfish, SD*

FAIRFIELD INN [MOT] *St. Cloud, MN*

FAIRFIELD INN [MOT] *St. Louis Lambert Airport Area, MO*

FAIRFIELD INN [MOT] *Waterloo, IA*

FAIR HILLS [RST] *Detroit Lakes, MN*

FAIRMONT KANSAS CITY AT THE PLAZA [HOT] *Kansas City, MO*

FAIR VALUE INN [MOT] *Rapid City, SD*

FAMILY BUDGET INN [MOT] *Bethany, MO*

FAMILY INNS OF AMERICA [MOT] *Wichita, KS*

FAMILY MOTOR INN [MOT] *Sullivan, MO*

5TH STREET MANSION BED AND BREAKFAST [BB] *Hannibal, MO*

FIKSDAL HOTEL AND SUITES [MOT] *Rochester, MN*

FILLENWARTH BEACH [MOT] *Okoboji, IA*

FIN & FEATHER RESORT [RST] *Tenkiller Ferry Lake, OK*

FINN AND FEATHER RESORT [CC] *Bemidji, MN*

FIRST INN GOLD FORT KEARNEY [MOT] *Kearney, NE*

FIRST INTERSTATE INN [MOT] *Lexington, NE*

1ST INTERSTATE INN [MOT] *North Platte, NE*

1ST INTERSTATE INN [MOT] *Oakley, KS*

FIRST LADY INN [MOT] *Keystone, SD*

FITGERS INN [HOT] *Duluth, MN*

FLEETWOOD MOTEL [MOT] *Shawnee, OK*

FORT ROBINSON LODGE [MOT] *Crawford, NE*

FOUNTAINHEAD RESORT [RST] *Eufaula, OK*

FOUR POINTS BY SHERATON [MOT] *Cedar Rapids, IA*

FOUR POINTS BY SHERATON [MOT] *Des Moines, IA*

FOUR POINTS BY SHERATON [MOT] *Des Moines, IA*

FOUR POINTS BY SHERATON MINNEAPOLIS [MOT] *Minneapolis, MN*

FOUR POINTS BY SHERATON OMAHA [MOT] *Omaha, NE*

FOUR SEASONS RESORT [MOT] *Okoboji, IA*

FOXBOROUGH INN [MOT] *Branson/Table Rock Lake Area, MO*

FULTON'S LANDING GUEST HOUSE [BB] *Davenport, IA*

GABLE VIEW INN [MOT] *Lexington, NE*

GALAXIE INN & SUITES [MOT] *Faribault, MN*

GARDEN CITY PLAZA INN [MOT] *Garden City, KS*

GARTH WOODSIDE MANSION B&B [BB] *Hannibal, MO*

GASLIGHT INN [MOT] *Rochester, MN*

GATEWAY INN [MOT] *Liberal, KS*

GATEWAY MOTEL [MOT] *Broken Bow, NE*

GAZEBO INN [MOT] *Branson/Table Rock Lake Area, MO*

GLADSTONE SELECT HOTEL [MOT] *Jamestown, ND*

GOLDEN HOTEL [MOT] *O'Neill, NE*

GOLDEN LANTERN INN [BB] *Red Wing, MN*

GOLDEN SPUR MOTEL [MOT] *Sallisaw, OK*

GOLDEN WHEAT BUDGET INN [MOT] *Junction City, KS*

GOLD KEY [MOT] *Hampton, IA*

GOLD PINE INN [MOT] *Hinckley, MN*

GOVERNORS SUITES INN [MOT] *Oklahoma City, OK*

GRAND AVE BED AND BREAKFAST [BB] *Carthage, MO*

GRAND HINCKLEY INN [MOT] *Hinckley, MN*

GRAND HOTEL MINNEAPOLIS, THE [HOT] *Minneapolis, MN*

GRAND NORTHERN INN [MOT] *Hinckley, MN*

GRAND RIVER INN [MOT] *Chillicothe, MO*

GRAND VIEW LODGE [RST] *Brainerd, MN*

GREAT BEND HOLIDAY INN [MOT] *Great Bend, KS*

GREAT PLAINS BUDGET HOST INN [MOT] *Lincoln, NE*

GUEST HOUSE MOTOR INN [MOT] *Amana Colonies, IA*

GUESTHOUSE SUITES PLUS [MOT] *Tulsa, OK*

GUEST INN [MOT] *Ardmore, OK*

GUEST INN NORMAN [MOT]
Norman, OK

HALCYON HOUSE BED &
BREAKFAST [BB] *Lawrence, KS*

HALLMARK INN [MOT] *Arkansas
City, KS*

HALLMARK INN [MOT] *Joplin, MO*

HALLMARK INN [MOT] *Ottawa, KS*

HALLMARK INN LEAVENWORTH
[MOT] *Leavenworth, KS*

HAMPTON INN [MOT] *Bloomington,
MN*

HAMPTON INN [MOT] *Bloomington,
MN*

HAMPTON INN [MOT] *Cape
Girardeau, MO*

HAMPTON INN [MOT] *Cedar Rapids,
IA*

HAMPTON INN [MOT] *Davenport, IA*

HAMPTON INN [MOT] *Des Moines,
IA*

HAMPTON INN [MOT] *Fargo, ND*

HAMPTON INN [MOT] *Hays, KS*

HAMPTON INN [MOT] *Iowa City, IA*

HAMPTON INN [MOT] *Lincoln, NE*

HAMPTON INN [MOT] *Minneapolis,
MN*

HAMPTON INN [MOT] *North Platte,
NE*

HAMPTON INN [MOT] *Omaha, NE*

HAMPTON INN [MOT] *Omaha, NE*

HAMPTON INN [MOT] *Overland
Park, KS*

HAMPTON INN [MOT] *Rochester,
MN*

HAMPTON INN [MOT] *St. Charles,
MO*

HAMPTON INN [MOT] *St. Louis
Lambert Airport Area, MO*

HAMPTON INN [MOT] *St. Paul, MN*

HAMPTON INN [MOT] *Tulsa, OK*

HAMPTON INN BRANSON WEST
[MOT] *Branson/Table Rock Lake
Area, MO*

HAMPTON INN EAST [MOT]
Springfield, MO

HAMPTON INN - UNION STATION
[MOT] *St. Louis, MO*

HANNIBAL INN AND CONFERENCE
CENTER [MOT] *Hannibal, MO*

HARRISON HOUSE BED &
BREAKFAST INN [BB] *Guthrie,
OK*

HARTWOOD INN [MOT] *Charles
City, IA*

HASTINGS INN [MOT] *Hastings, MN*

HAWTHORN SUITES [MOT]
Bloomington, MN

HAWTHORN SUITES [MOT]
Springfield, MO

HAWTHORN SUITES [MOT] *Tulsa,
OK*

HEARTLAND INN [MOT] *Ames, IA*

HEARTLAND INN [MOT] *Bettendorf,
IA*

HEARTLAND INN [MOT] *Cedar
Rapids, IA*

HEARTLAND INN [MOT] *Clear Lake,
IA*

HEARTLAND INN [MOT] *Council
Bluffs, IA*

HEARTLAND INN [MOT] *Davenport,
IA*

HEARTLAND INN [MOT] *Decorah, IA*

HEARTLAND INN [MOT] *Des
Moines, IA*

HEARTLAND INN [MOT] *Dubuque,
IA*

HEARTLAND INN [MOT] *Dubuque,
IA*

HEARTLAND INN [MOT] *Iowa City,
IA*

HEARTLAND INN [MOT] *Mount
Pleasant, IA*

HEARTLAND INN [MOT] *Ottumwa,
IA*

HEARTLAND INN [MOT] *Waterloo,
IA*

HEARTLAND INN [MOT] *Waterloo,
IA*

HENRYETTA INN AND DOME
[MOT] *Henryetta, OK*

HENRY VIII HOTEL [MOT] *St. Louis
Lambert Airport Area, MO*

HERITAGE HOUSE [BB] *Topeka, KS*

HERITAGE INN [MOT] *Tulsa, OK*

HERMANN [MOT] *Hermann, MO*

HIAWATHA INN [MOT] *Hiawatha,
KS*

HILLCREST MOTEL [MOT] *Norton,
KS*

HILLCREST MOTEL [MOT] *Sauk
Centre, MN*

HILTON [HOT] *Minneapolis, MN*

HILTON AIRPORT [HOT] *Wichita,
KS*

HILTON FRONTENAC [HOT] *St.
Louis, MO*

HILTON INN [HOT] *Oklahoma City,
OK*

HILTON KANSAS CITY AIRPORT
[HOT] *Kansas City, MO*

HILTON MINNEAPOLIS NORTH [HOT] *Minneapolis, MN*

HILTON MINNEAPOLIS/ST. PAUL AIRPORT [HOT] *Bloomington, MN*

HILTON SIOUX CITY [HOT] *Sioux City, IA*

HILTON ST LOUIS AIRPORT [HOT] *St. Louis Lambert Airport Area, MO*

HILTON TULSA SOUTHERN HILLS [HOT] *Tulsa, OK*

HISTORIC CALUMET INN [HOT] *Pipestone, MN*

HISTORIC SUITES OF AMERICA [HOT] *Kansas City, MO*

HI-VIEW MOTEL [MOT] *Glenwood, MN*

HOLIDAY INN [MOT] *Alexandria, MN*

HOLIDAY INN [MOT] *Ardmore, OK*

HOLIDAY INN [MOT] *Austin, MN*

HOLIDAY INN [MOT] *Bartlesville, OK*

HOLIDAY INN [MOT] *Bettendorf, IA*

HOLIDAY INN [MOT] *Bloomington, MN*

HOLIDAY INN [MOT] *Bloomington, MN*

HOLIDAY INN [MOT] *Brainerd, MN*

HOLIDAY INN [MOT] *Columbia, MO*

HOLIDAY INN [MOT] *Davenport, IA*

HOLIDAY INN [MOT] *Detroit Lakes, MN*

HOLIDAY INN [MOT] *Dubuque, IA*

HOLIDAY INN [MOT] *Duncan, OK*

HOLIDAY INN [MOT] *Durant, OK*

HOLIDAY INN [MOT] *Elk City, OK*

HOLIDAY INN [MOT] *Enid, OK*

HOLIDAY INN [MOT] *Fairmont, MN*

HOLIDAY INN [MOT] *Fargo, ND*

HOLIDAY INN [MOT] *Fargo, ND*

HOLIDAY INN [MOT] *Fort Dodge, IA*

HOLIDAY INN [MOT] *Grand Forks, ND*

HOLIDAY INN [MOT] *Grand Island, NE*

HOLIDAY INN [MOT] *Hastings, NE*

HOLIDAY INN [MOT] *Hays, KS*

HOLIDAY INN [MOT] *Idabel, OK*

HOLIDAY INN [MOT] *International Falls, MN*

HOLIDAY INN [MOT] *Kansas City, MO*

HOLIDAY INN [HOT] *Kansas City, MO*

HOLIDAY INN [MOT] *Kearney, NE*

HOLIDAY INN [MOT] *Lawrence, KS*

HOLIDAY INN [MOT] *Manhattan, KS*

HOLIDAY INN [MOT] *Mankato, MN*

HOLIDAY INN [HOT] *Minneapolis, MN*

HOLIDAY INN [MOT] *Minot, ND*

HOLIDAY INN [MOT] *Mitchell, SD*

HOLIDAY INN [MOT] *Muscatine, IA*

HOLIDAY INN [MOT] *New Ulm, MN*

HOLIDAY INN [HOT] *Oklahoma City, OK*

HOLIDAY INN [MOT] *Omaha, NE*

HOLIDAY INN [MOT] *Ponca City, OK*

HOLIDAY INN [MOT] *Rapid City, SD*

HOLIDAY INN [HOT] *Rapid City, SD*

HOLIDAY INN [MOT] *Salina, KS*

HOLIDAY INN [MOT] *Sioux Falls, SD*

HOLIDAY INN [MOT] *St. Paul, MN*

HOLIDAY INN [MOT] *St. Paul, MN*

HOLIDAY INN [MOT] *Stillwater, OK*

HOLIDAY INN [MOT] *Waterloo, IA*

HOLIDAY INN [MOT] *Wentzville, MO*

HOLIDAY INN [MOT] *Wichita, KS*

HOLIDAY INN [MOT] *Willmar, MN*

HOLIDAY INN [MOT] *York, NE*

HOLIDAY INN AIRPORT [MOT] *Kansas City, MO*

HOLIDAY INN AIRPORT & CONFERENCE CENTER [MOT] *Des Moines, IA*

HOLIDAY INN AIRPORT OAKLAND PARK [MOT] *St. Louis, MO*

HOLIDAY INN AMANA COLONIES [MOT] *Amana Colonies, IA*

HOLIDAY INN & CONVENTION CENTER [MOT] *Joplin, MO*

HOLIDAY INN & CONVENTION CENTER [MOT] *Spearfish, SD*

HOLIDAY INN BISMARCK [HOT] *Bismarck, ND*

HOLIDAY INN CITY CENTRE [HOT] *Rochester, MN*

HOLIDAY INN DOWNTOWN [HOT] *Des Moines, IA*

HOLIDAY INN DOWNTOWN [HOT] *Lincoln, NE*

HOLIDAY INN EAST [MOT] *Columbia, MO*

HOLIDAY INN EAST AIRPORT [MOT] *Tulsa, OK*

HOLIDAY INN EXPRESS [MOT] *Branson/Table Rock Lake Area, MO*

HOLIDAY INN EXPRESS [MOT] *Branson/Table Rock Lake Area, MO*

HOLIDAY INN EXPRESS [MOT] *Burlington, IA*

HOLIDAY INN EXPRESS [MOT] *Keokuk, IA*

HOLIDAY INN EXPRESS [MOT] *Overland Park, KS*

HOLIDAY INN EXPRESS [MOT] *Pittsburg, KS*

HOLIDAY INN EXPRESS [MOT] *Sioux City, IA*

HOLIDAY INN EXPRESS AIRPORT [MOT] *Kansas City, MO*

HOLIDAY INN EXPRESS AT DRAKE [MOT] *Des Moines, IA*

HOLIDAY INN FOREST PARK [MOT] *St. Louis, MO*

HOLIDAY INN GATEWAY CENTER [MOT] *Ames, IA*

HOLIDAY INN HOTEL & SUITES - DOWNTOWN WATERFRONT [HOT] *Duluth, MN*

HOLIDAY INN HOTEL & SUITES [HOT] *Overland Park, KS*

HOLIDAY INN KANSAS CITY/ LENEXA [MOT] *Overland Park, KS*

HOLIDAY INN NORTH [MOT] *Springfield, MO*

HOLIDAY INN RIVERFRONT [MOT] *St. Joseph, MO*

HOLIDAY INN SELECT [MOT] *Bloomington, MN*

HOLIDAY INN SELECT [MOT] *Wichita, KS*

HOLIDAY INN SELECT ST LOUIS [MOT] *St. Louis, MO*

HOLIDAY INN SELECT ST. PETER'S [MOT] *St. Charles, MO*

HOLIDAY INN SOUTH [MOT] *Rochester, MN*

HOLIDAY INN SOUTHWEST [MOT] *St. Louis, MO*

HOLIDAY INN SPORTS COMPLEX [MOT] *Kansas City, MO*

HOLIDAY INN ST. CLOUD [MOT] *St. Cloud, MN*

HOLIDAY INN ST. LOUIS AIRPORT NORTH [MOT] *St. Louis, MO*

HOLIDAY INN ST PAUL NORTH [MOT] *St. Paul, MN*

HOLIDAY INN SUNSPREE RESORT [MOT] *Lake Ozark, MO*

HOLIDAY INN UNIVERSITY PLAZA [MOT] *Cedar Falls, IA*

HOLIDAY INN UNIVERSITY PLAZA AND CONFERENCE C [HOT] *Springfield, MO*

HOLIDAY INN WEST PARK [MOT] *Cape Girardeau, MO*

HOLIDAY LODGE [MOT] *Fremont, NE*

HOLIDAY MOTEL [MOT] *Sisseton, SD*

HOLIDAY MOTEL [MOT] *Webster, SD*

HOLIDAY SHORES [MOT] *Marquette, IA*

HOLIDAY VILLA MOTEL [MOT] *Beatrice, NE*

HOLMBERG HOUSE BED AND BREAKFAST [BB] *Norman, OK*

HORIZON INN [MOT] *Lincoln, NE*

HOTEL, THE [MOT] *Spencer, IA*

HOTEL DEVILLE [MOT] *Jefferson City, MO*

HOTEL FORT DES MOINES [HOT] *Des Moines, IA*

HOTEL PATTEE [HOT] *Boone, IA*

HOTEL PHILLIPS [HOT] *Bartlesville, OK*

HOTEL PHILLIPS [HOT] *Kansas City, MO*

HOTEL SAVOY [HOT] *Kansas City, MO*

HOWARD JOHNSON [MOT] *Goodland, KS*

HOWARD JOHNSON [MOT] *Lincoln, NE*

HOWARD JOHNSON EXPRESS [MOT] *Oklahoma City, OK*

HOWARD JOHNSON EXPRESS INN [MOT] *Oklahoma City, OK*

HOWARD JOHNSON HOTEL & CONVENTION CENTER [MOT] *Lawton, OK*

HOWARD JOHNSON PLAZA HOTEL OMAHA INN [MOT] *Omaha, NE*

HYATT REGENCY [HOT] *Minneapolis, MN*

HYATT REGENCY CROWN CENTER [HOT] *Kansas City, MO*

HYATT REGENCY CROWN CENTER [HOT] *Kansas City, MO*

HYATT REGENCY ST LOUIS [HOT] *St. Louis, MO*

HYATT REGENCY WICHITA [HOT]
Wichita, KS
HYATT WHITNEY [HOT]
Minneapolis, MN
IMA CORNER INN [MOT] *Humboldt,
IA*
IMA FRIENDLY HOST INN [MOT]
Lakeville, MN
IMA MANOR MOTEL [MOT]
Milbank, SD
INDIAN LODGE [MOT] *Sequoyah
State Park, OK*
INN AT GRAND GLAIZE [MOT]
Osage Beach, MO
INN AT JARRETT FARM [BB] *Tulsa,
OK*
INN AT THE PARK [BB] *Wichita, KS*
INN AT UNIVERSITY [MOT] *Des
Moines, IA*
INN AT WESTON LANDING [BB]
Weston, MO
INN ON CRESCENT LAKE, THE [BB]
Excelsior Springs, MO
INN ON THE FARM [BB]
Minneapolis, MN
INN PRATT TABOR [BB] *Red Wing,
MN*
INN RESORT COMPLEX [MOT]
Okoboji, IA
INN ST. GEMME BEAUVAIS [BB] *Ste.
Genevieve, MO*
IRON HORSE INN [MOT] *Sheldon, IA*
IRON HORSE MOTEL [MOT] *Spencer,
IA*
ISLAND VIEW LODGE [CC]
International Falls, MN
ISLE OF CAPRI MARQUETTE [MOT]
Marquette, IA
IZATY'S GOLF AND YACHT CLUB
[RST] *Onamia, MN*
JAMES A. MULVEY INN [BB]
Stillwater, MN
JOHNNIE'S MOTEL [MOT]
Columbus, NE
JULIEN INN [MOT] *Dubuque, IA*
JUMER'S CASTLE LODGE [HOT]
Bettendorf, IA
KAHLER HOTEL [HOT] *Rochester,
MN*
KALFRAN LODGE [RST] *Osage Beach,
MO*
K-D INN MOTEL, THE [MOT]
Wayne, NE
KELLY INN [MOT] *Bismarck, ND*
KELLY INN [MOT] *Keystone, SD*

KELLY INN [MOT] *Sioux Falls, SD*
KELLY INN [MOT] *Spearfish, SD*
KELLY INN 13TH AVENUE [MOT]
Fargo, ND
KEY MOTEL [MOT] *Maquoketa, IA*
KINGS INN HOTEL AND
CONVENTION CENTER
[MOT] *Pierre, SD*
KINGS INN OF PLATTE [MOT]
Platte, SD
KINGSLEY INN [BB] *Fort Madison, IA*
KIRKWOOD CIVIC CENTER HOTEL
[HOT] *Des Moines, IA*
KNOLLS, THE [RST] *Osage Beach, MO*
LA CORSETTE MAISON INN [BB]
Newton, IA
LAFAYETTE HOUSE B&B [BB] *St.
Louis, MO*
LAKE CHATEAU RESORT INN
[MOT] *Osage Beach, MO*
LAKE MURRAY LODGE AND
COUNTRY INN [RST] *Ardmore,
OK*
LAKE PARK MOTEL [MOT] *Madison,
SD*
LAKE RIPLEY RESORT [MOT]
Litchfield, MN
LAKESHORE MOTOR INN [MOT]
Virginia, MN
LAKE TEXOMA RESORT [RST] *Lake
Texoma, OK*
LANGDON'S UPTOWN MOTEL
[MOT] *Rochester, MN*
LANTERN MOTEL [MOT] *Milbank,
SD*
LA QUINTA INN [MOT] *Oklahoma
City, OK*
LA QUINTA INN [MOT] *Oklahoma
City, OK*
LA QUINTA INN [MOT] *Omaha, NE*
LA QUINTA INN [MOT] *Overland
Park, KS*
LA QUINTA INN [MOT] *Tulsa, OK*
LA QUINTA INN [MOT] *Wichita, KS*
LE BARON MOTEL [MOT] *Henryetta,
OK*
LEGION LAKE LODGE [CC] *Custer,
SD*
LEMARS SUPER 8 MOTEL [MOT] *Le
Mars, IA*
LEWIS AND CLARK INN [MOT]
Hermann, MO
LEXINGTON HOTEL SUITES [MOT]
Oklahoma City, OK

LEXINGTON INN PROPERTIES INC [MOT] *Lexington, MO*

LEXINGTON SUITES [MOT] *Tulsa, OK*

LIBERAL INN [MOT] *Liberal, KS*

LIBERTY INN [MOT] *Topeka, KS*

LILAC MOTEL [MOT] *West Union, IA*

LODGE OF FOUR SEASONS [RST] *Lake Ozark, MO*

LODGE OF THE OZARKS ENTERTAINMENT COMPLEX [MOT] *Branson/Table Rock Lake Area, MO*

LOWELL INN [BB] *Stillwater, MN*

LUDLOW ISLAND LODGE [CC] *Cook, MN*

LUMBER BARON'S HOTEL [HOT] *Stillwater, MN*

LUXURY INN [MOT] *Elk City, OK*

MADDEN'S ON GULL LAKE [RST] *Brainerd, MN*

MADISON INN [MOT] *Fort Madison, IA*

MAGNOLIA INN [MOT] *Branson/Table Rock Lake Area, MO*

MAIN STREET INN BED & BREAKFAST [BB] *Ste. Genevieve, MO*

MANSION AT ELFINDALE, THE [BB] *Springfield, MO*

MARINA INN CONFERENCE CENTER [MOT] *South Sioux City, NE*

MARK V MOTEL [MOT] *Phillipsburg, KS*

MARQUETTE HOTEL, THE [HOT] *Minneapolis, MN*

MARRIOTT [HOT] *St. Louis Lambert Airport Area, MO*

MARRIOTT AT MAYO CLINIC ROCHESTER [HOT] *Rochester, MN*

MARRIOTT CITY CENTER MINNEAPOLIS [HOT] *Minneapolis, MN*

MARRIOTT COUNTRY CLUB PLAZA KANSAS CITY [HOT] *Kansas City, MO*

MARRIOTT DES MOINES [HOT] *Des Moines, IA*

MARRIOTT DOWNTOWN KANSAS CITY [HOT] *Kansas City, MO*

MARRIOTT KANSAS CITY AIRPORT [HOT] *Kansas City, MO*

MARRIOTT MINNEAPOLIS AIRPORT [HOT] *Bloomington, MN*

MARRIOTT OKLAHOMA CITY [HOT] *Oklahoma City, OK*

MARRIOTT OMAHA [HOT] *Omaha, NE*

MARRIOTT OVERLAND PARK [HOT] *Overland Park, KS*

MARRIOTT PAVILION DOWNTOWN ST. LOUIS [HOT] *St. Louis, MO*

MARRIOTT SOUTHERN HILLS TULSA [HOT] *Tulsa, OK*

MARRIOTT SOUTHWEST MINNEAPOLIS [HOT] *Minneapolis, MN*

MARRIOTT WEST DES MOINES [HOT] *Des Moines, IA*

MARRIOTT WEST ST. LOUIS [HOT] *St. Louis, MO*

MARRIOTT WICHITA [HOT] *Wichita, KS*

MAYFAIR WYNDHAM GRAND HERITAGE HOTEL [HOT] *St. Louis, MO*

MC KNIGHT SALLISAW INN [MOT] *Sallisaw, OK*

MELODY LANE INN [MOT] *Branson/Table Rock Lake Area, MO*

METRO INN [MOT] *Minneapolis, MN*

MIDTOWN WESTERN INN [MOT] *Kearney, NE*

MILLENNIUM HOTEL MINNEAPOLIS [HOT] *Minneapolis, MN*

MINERAL PALACE HOTEL [MOT] *Deadwood, SD*

MINER SUPER 8 MOTEL [MOT] *Sikeston, MO*

MODERN AIRE MOTEL [MOT] *Smith Center, KS*

MONROE CITY INN [MOT] *Monroe City, MO*

MONTFORD INN BED & BREAKFAST [BB] *Norman, OK*

MOOSEHORN LODGE BED & BREAKFAST [RST] *Grand Marais, MN*

MORRIS MOTEL [MOT] *Morris, MN*

MOTEL 6 [MOT] *Des Moines, IA*

MOTEL 6 [MOT] *Lakeville, MN*

MOTEL 6 [MOT] *Mitchell, SD*

MOTEL 6 [MOT] *Sioux Falls, SD*

MOTEL 6 [MOT] *St. Charles, MO*

MOTEL 6 [MOT] *St. Cloud, MN*

MOTEL MORA [MOT] *Mora, MN*

MOTEL RAINE [MOT] *Valentine, NE*

MOUNTAIN INN [MOT] *Lutsen, MN*

MUSKOGEE INN [MOT] *Muskogee, OK*

NANIBOUJOU LODGE [MOT] *Grand Marais, MN*

NELSON'S RESORT [CC] *Crane Lake, MN*

NEW WORLD INN [MOT] *Columbus, NE*

NICOLLET ISLAND INN [BB] *Minneapolis, MN*

NORFOLK COUNTRY INN [MOT] *Norfolk, NE*

NORTH COUNTRY INN [MOT] *Cook, MN*

NORTHERNAIRE HOUSEBOATS OF RAINY LAKE [CC] *International Falls, MN*

NORTHERN INN [MOT] *Bemidji, MN*

NORTHLAND INN [MOT] *Crookston, MN*

NORTHLAND INN AND EXECUTIVE CONFERENCE CENTER [HOT] *Minneapolis, MN*

NORTHWEST INN [MOT] *Woodward, OK*

NORWAY HOUSE [MOT] *Bottineau, ND*

NORWESTER LODGE [RST] *Grand Marais, MN*

OAK GROVE INN [MOT] *Grand Island, NE*

OAKS HOTEL [MOT] *Sioux Falls, SD*

OASIS INN [MOT] *Chamberlain, SD*

OLSON BAY RESORT [CC] *Ely, MN*

OMNI MAJESTIC HOTEL [HOT] *St Louis, MO*

OSAGE VILLAGE MOTEL [MOT] *Osage Beach, MO*

OSKALOOSA SUPER 8 [MOT] *Oskaloosa, IA*

PALACE INN [MOT] *Branson/Table Rock Lake Area, MO*

PALMER HOUSE [MOT] *Auburn, NE*

PALMER HOUSE MOTEL [MOT] *Sioux City, IA*

PARK INN SUITES INTERNATIONAL [HOT] *Bloomington, MN*

PARK PLACE HOTEL [HOT] *Kansas City, MO*

PARK PLAZA MOTEL [MOT] *South Sioux City, NE*

PARSONIAN HOTEL [HOT] *Parsons, KS*

PAUL BUNYAN INN [MOT] *Brainerd, MN*

PEAR TREE INN [MOT] *Cape Girardeau, MO*

PEAR TREE INN [MOT] *Sikeston, MO*

PETERS' SUNSET BEACH RESORT [RST] *Glenwood, MN*

PINEY RIDGE LODGE [RST] *Pine River, MN*

PIONEER MOTEL [MOT] *Minden, NE*

PLAZA HOTEL WESTPORT [MOT] *Kansas City, MO*

PLAZA ONE MOTEL [MOT] *Spencer, IA*

POINT BREEZE RESORT [MOT] *Osage Beach, MO*

POINTE ROYALE [RST] *Branson/Table Rock Lake Area, MO*

PRESIDENT CASINO'S BLACKHAWK HOTEL [HOT] *Davenport, IA*

PRESIDENTIAL MOTOR INN [MOT] *Iowa City, IA*

PRYOR HOUSE MOTOR INN [MOT] *Pryor, OK*

QUALITY INN [MOT] *Council Bluffs, IA*

QUALITY INN [MOT] *Hutchinson, KS*

QUALITY INN [MOT] *St. Cloud, MN*

QUALITY INN AND SUITES [MOT] *Brookings, SD*

QUALITY INN & SUITES [MOT] *Des Moines, IA*

QUALITY INN & SUITES [MOT] *Minneapolis, MN*

QUALITY INN AND SUITES [MOT] *Rochester, MN*

QUALITY INN NORTH [MOT] *Oklahoma City, OK*

QUALITY INN OF WINONA [MOT] *Winona, MN*

QUARTERAGE HOTEL [MOT] *Kansas City, MO*

QUEEN MARIE VICTORIAN BED & BREAKFAST [BB] *Emmetsburg, IA*

RADISSON [HOT] *Fargo, ND*

RADISSON [HOT] *Minneapolis, MN*

RADISSON HOTEL [HOT] *Sioux Falls, SD*

RADISSON HOTEL AND SUITES DOWNTOWN [HOT] *St. Louis, MO*

RADISSON HOTEL BRANSON [HOT] *Branson/Table Rock Lake Area, MO*

RADISSON HOTEL CLAYTON [HOT] *Clayton, MO*

RADISSON HOTEL DULUTH-HARBORVIEW [HOT] *Duluth, MN*

RADISSON HOTEL METRODOME [HOT] *Minneapolis, MN*

RADISSON HOTEL-MT. RUSHMORE [HOT] *Rapid City, SD*

RADISSON HOTEL SOUTH & PLAZA TOWER [HOT] *Bloomington, MN*

RADISSON INN [HOT] *Bismarck, ND*

RADISSON INN TULSA AIRPORT [HOT] *Tulsa, OK*

RADISSON PLAZA [HOT] *Minneapolis, MN*

RADISSON PLAZA [HOT] *Rochester, MN*

RADISSON RIVERFRONT HOTEL [HOT] *St. Paul, MN*

RAINBOW [MOT] *Monroe City, MO*

RAINBOW INN, THE [MOT] *Grand Rapids, MN*

RAMADA CONFERENCE CENTER [MOT] *Hutchinson, KS*

RAMADA INN [MOT] *Aberdeen, SD*

RAMADA INN [MOT] *Altus, OK*

RAMADA INN [MOT] *Ames, IA*

RAMADA INN [MOT] *Branson/Table Rock Lake Area, MO*

RAMADA INN [MOT] *Clinton, IA*

RAMADA INN [MOT] *Colby, KS*

RAMADA INN [MOT] *Enid, OK*

RAMADA INN [MOT] *Grand Forks, ND*

RAMADA INN [MOT] *Iowa City, IA*

RAMADA INN [MOT] *Jefferson City, MO*

RAMADA INN [MOT] *Joplin, MO*

RAMADA INN [MOT] *Kearney, NE*

RAMADA INN [MOT] *Lawton, OK*

RAMADA INN [MOT] *Leavenworth, KS*

RAMADA INN [MOT] *McAlester, OK*

RAMADA INN [MOT] *Minneapolis, MN*

RAMADA INN [MOT] *Muskogee, OK*

RAMADA INN [MOT] *Norfolk, NE*

RAMADA INN [MOT] *Norman, OK*

RAMADA INN [MOT] *Oklahoma City, OK*

RAMADA INN [MOT] *Owatonna, MN*

RAMADA INN [MOT] *Poplar Bluff, MO*

RAMADA INN [MOT] *Rapid City, SD*

RAMADA INN [MOT] *Salina, KS*

RAMADA INN [MOT] *Sedalia, MO*

RAMADA INN [MOT] *Shawnee, OK*

RAMADA INN [MOT] *Springfield, MO*

RAMADA INN [MOT] *St. Joseph, MO*

RAMADA INN [MOT] *Waynesville, MO*

RAMADA INN [MOT] *West Plains, MO*

RAMADA INN [MOT] *Wichita, KS*

RAMADA INN AIRPORT [MOT] *Sioux Falls, SD*

RAMADA INN AND CONFERENCE CENTER [MOT] *Emporia, KS*

RAMADA INN & CONFERENCE CENTER [MOT] *Oklahoma City, OK*

RAMADA INN AT MERLE HAY [MOT] *Des Moines, IA*

RAMADA INN CENTRAL [MOT] *Omaha, NE*

RAMADA INN DOWNTOWN [MOT] *Topeka, KS*

RAMADA INN MINNEAPOLIS AIRPORT [MOT] *Bloomington, MN*

RAMADA INN ST. LOUIS AIRPORT AND CONFERENCE CENTER [MOT] *St. Louis Lambert Airport Area, MO*

RAMADA INN WEST DES MOINES [MOT] *Des Moines, IA*

RAMADA LIMITED [MOT] *Bloomington, MN*

RAMADA LIMITED [MOT] *North Platte, NE*

RAMADA LIMITED [MOT] *Ogallala, NE*

RAMADA LIMITED [MOT] *Rochester, MN*

RAMADA LIMITED SOUTH [MOT] *Lincoln, NE*

RAMADA LTD [MOT] *Amana Colonies, IA*

RAMADA LTD SUITES [MOT] *Bismarck, ND*

RAMADA PLAZA [MOT] *Manhattan, KS*

RAMADA PLAZA [MOT] *Minneapolis, MN*

RAMADA PLAZA HOTEL [MOT] *Oklahoma City, OK*

RAMBLER MOTEL [MOT] *Nevada, MO*

RAMKOTA HOTEL [MOT] *Pierre, SD*

RAMSEY'S [MOT] *Nevada, MO*
RANGER INN [MOT] *Alva, OK*
RAPHAEL [HOT] *Kansas City, MO*
RATH INN [MOT] *Blair, NE*
RED CARPET INN [MOT] *Elk River, MN*
RED CARPET INN [MOT] *Junction City, KS*
RED CARPET INN [MOT] *Oskaloosa, IA*
RED CARPET INN [MOT] *Rochester, MN*
RED COACH INN [MOT] *McPherson, KS*
RED COACH INN [MOT] *Red Oak, IA*
RED ROOF INN [MOT] *Cedar Rapids, IA*
RED ROOF INN [MOT] *Fargo, ND*
RED ROOF INN [MOT] *Independence, MO*
RED ROOF INN ST.PAUL [MOT] *St. Paul, MN*
REDSTONE INN, THE [BB] *Dubuque, IA*
REGAL RIVERFRONT [HOT] *St. Louis, MO*
REGENCY COURT INN [MOT] *Arkansas City, KS*
RENAISSANCE DOWNTOWN [HOT] *Oklahoma City, OK*
RENAISSANCE ST. LOUIS [HOT] *St. Louis, MO*
RENAISSANCE ST. LOUIS SUITES HOTEL [HOT] *St. Louis, MO*
RESIDENCE INN BY MARRIOTT [EX] *Bloomington, MN*
RESIDENCE INN BY MARRIOTT [EX] *Norman, OK*
RESIDENCE INN BY MARRIOTT [EX] *Oklahoma City, OK*
RESIDENCE INN BY MARRIOTT [EX] *Omaha, NE*
RESIDENCE INN BY MARRIOTT [EX] *St. Louis, MO*
RESIDENCE INN BY MARRIOTT [EX] *Wichita, KS*
RIPPLE RIVER MOTEL & RV PARK [MOT] *Aitkin, MN*
RITZ-CARLTON, ST. LOUIS, THE [HOT] *Clayton, MO*
RIVERFRONT INN [MOT] *Mankato, MN*
RIVERVIEW INN [MOT] *Chamberlain, SD*

ROAD KING INN [MOT] *Grand Forks, ND*
ROAD KING INN [MOT] *Grand Forks, ND*
ROCHESTER INN [MOT] *Rochester, MN*
ROCKWOOD LODGE & OUTFITTERS [RST] *Grand Marais, MN*
RODEWAY INN [MOT] *Oskaloosa, IA*
RODEWAY INN [MOT] *Red Wing, MN*
ROGERS HOUSE BED & BREAKFAST INN [BB] *Lincoln, NE*
ROMAN NOSE RESORT [RST] *Roman Nose State Park, OK*
ROSE STONE INN [BB] *Ponca City, OK*
RUTTGER'S BAY LAKE LODGE [RST] *Deerwood, MN*
RUTTGER'S BIRCHMONT LODGE [RST] *Bemidji, MN*
ST. JAMES [HOT] *Red Wing, MN*
SAINT PAUL HOTEL, THE [HOT] *St. Paul, MN*
SALINA RED COACH INN [MOT] *Salina, KS*
SANDS MOTOR INN [MOT] *North Platte, NE*
SAVANNAH SUITES [MOT] *Omaha, NE*
SAVERY HOTEL AND SPA [HOT] *Des Moines, IA*
SAWMILL INN [MOT] *Grand Rapids, MN*
SCENIC VALLEY MOTEL [MOT] *Granite Falls, MN*
SCHUMACHER'S HOTEL [BB] *Lakeville, MN*
SCHWEGMANN HOUSE BED & BREAKFAST [BB] *Hermann, MO*
SCOTMAN INN WEST [MOT] *Wichita, KS*
SCOTWOOD [MOT] *Litchfield, MN*
SCOTWOOD MOTEL [MOT] *Glenwood, MN*
SELECT INN [MOT] *Bloomington, MN*
SELECT INN [MOT] *Faribault, MN*
SELECT INN [MOT] *Sioux Falls, SD*
SELECT INN OF GRAND FORKS [MOT] *Grand Forks, ND*
SENATE LUXURY SUITES [MOT] *Topeka, KS*
SENECA MOTEL [MOT] *Seneca, KS*

SETTLE INN [MOT] *Branson/Table Rock Lake Area, MO*

SEVEN GABLES [BB] *Clayton, MO*

SHADOWBROOK MOTEL [MOT] *Branson/Table Rock Lake Area, MO*

SHAMROCK INN [MOT] *Kirksville, MO*

SHANGRI-LA RESORT [RST] *Grand Lake, OK*

SHERATON [HOT] *Sioux Falls, SD*

SHERATON [HOT] *St. Louis, MO*

SHERATON CLAYTON PLAZA HOTEL [HOT] *St. Louis, MO*

SHERATON HAWTHORN PARK HOTEL [HOT] *Springfield, MO*

SHERATON HOTEL [HOT] *Tulsa, OK*

SHERATON INN [HOT] *St. Paul, MN*

SHERATON IOWA CITY HOTEL [HOT] *Iowa City, IA*

SHERATON OMAHA [HOT] *Omaha, NE*

SHERATON PLAZA [HOT] *St. Louis, MO*

SHERATON ST. LOUIS CITY CENTER [HOT] *St. Joseph, MO*

SHERATON SUITES COUNTRY CLUB PLAZA [HOT] *Kansas City, MO*

SHORELINE [MOT] *Grand Marais, MN*

SIESTA MOTEL [MOT] *Mitchell, SD*

SIGNATURE INN [MOT] *Bettendorf, IA*

SKI VIEW [MOT] *Virginia, MN*

SLEEP INN [MOT] *Fargo, ND*

SLEEP INN [MOT] *Omaha, NE*

SLOVENE MOTEL [MOT] *Eveleth, MN*

SOFITEL [HOT] *Bloomington, MN*

SOUTHERN HOTEL BED & BREAKFAST [BB] *Ste. Genevieve, MO*

SOUTHERN OAKS INN [MOT] *Branson/Table Rock Lake Area, MO*

SOUTHMORELAND ON THE PLAZA [BB] *Kansas City, MO*

SPEARFISH CANYON [MOT] *Spearfish, SD*

SPORTSMAN'S LODGE [CC] *Baudette, MN*

SQUIERS MANOR BED & BREAKFAST [BB] *Maquoketa, IA*

STANFORD LODGE [MOT] *North Platte, NE*

STAR LITE MOTEL [MOT] *Seneca, KS*

STATE GAME LODGE [MOT] *Custer, SD*

STERLING MOTEL [MOT] *Winona, MN*

STOCKMAN INN [MOT] *North Platte, NE*

STRATFORD HOUSE INNS [MOT] *Wichita, KS*

SUMMERFIELD SUITES [MOT] *St. Louis, MO*

SUMMERSET INN RESORT [MOT] *Osage Beach, MO*

SUNSET LODGE [CC] *Park Rapids, MN*

SUNTERRA RESORT AT FALL CREEK [MOT] *Branson/Table Rock Lake Area, MO*

SUPER 8 [MOT] *Aberdeen, SD*

SUPER 8 [MOT] *Alexandria, MN*

SUPER 8 [MOT] *Bismarck, ND*

SUPER 8 [MOT] *Bloomington, MN*

SUPER 8 [MOT] *Carrington, ND*

SUPER 8 [MOT] *Chadron, NE*

SUPER 8 [MOT] *Columbus, NE*

SUPER 8 [MOT] *Creston, IA*

SUPER 8 [MOT] *Custer, SD*

SUPER 8 [MOT] *Denison, IA*

SUPER 8 [MOT] *Dodge City, KS*

SUPER 8 [MOT] *Duluth, MN*

SUPER 8 [MOT] *Fremont, NE*

SUPER 8 [MOT] *Grafton, ND*

SUPER 8 [MOT] *Grand Marais, MN*

SUPER 8 [MOT] *Hastings, NE*

SUPER 8 [MOT] *Hibbing, MN*

SUPER 8 [MOT] *Hinckley, MN*

SUPER 8 [MOT] *Huron, SD*

SUPER 8 [MOT] *Kansas City, MO*

SUPER 8 [MOT] *Keokuk, IA*

SUPER 8 [MOT] *Lexington, NE*

SUPER 8 [MOT] *Manhattan, KS*

SUPER 8 [MOT] *Marshall, MN*

SUPER 8 [MOT] *Milbank, SD*

SUPER 8 [MOT] *Minneapolis, MN*

SUPER 8 [MOT] *Newton, IA*

SUPER 8 [MOT] *Onawa, IA*

SUPER 8 [MOT] *Pierre, SD*

SUPER 8 [MOT] *Pipestone, MN*

SUPER 8 [MOT] *Rapid City, SD*

SUPER 8 [MOT] *Red Wing, MN*

SUPER 8 [MOT] *Redfield, SD*

SUPER 8 [MOT] *Rochester, MN*

SUPER 8 [MOT] *Rochester, MN*
SUPER 8 [MOT] *Sauk Centre, MN*
SUPER 8 [MOT] *St. Louis Lambert Airport Area, MO*
SUPER 8 [MOT] *Sullivan, MO*
SUPER 8 [MOT] *Wahpeton, ND*
SUPER 8 [MOT] *Waterloo, IA*
SUPER 8 FAIRGROUNDS [MOT] *Oklahoma City, OK*
SUPER 8 HOTEL & SUITES [MOT] *Fargo, ND*
SUPER 8 MOTEL [MOT] *Abilene, KS*
SUPER 8 MOTEL [MOT] *Albert Lea, MN*
SUPER 8 MOTEL [MOT] *Amana Colonies, IA*
SUPER 8 MOTEL [MOT] *Atlantic, IA*
SUPER 8 MOTEL [MOT] *Atlantic, IA*
SUPER 8 MOTEL [MOT] *Bemidji, MN*
SUPER 8 MOTEL [MOT] *Blue Earth, MN*
SUPER 8 MOTEL [MOT] *Brainerd, MN*
SUPER 8 MOTEL [MOT] *Broken Bow, NE*
SUPER 8 MOTEL [MOT] *Burlington, IA*
SUPER 8 MOTEL [MOT] *Centerville, IA*
SUPER 8 MOTEL [MOT] *Chamberlain, SD*
SUPER 8 MOTEL [MOT] *Cherokee, IA*
SUPER 8 MOTEL [MOT] *Clear Lake, IA*
SUPER 8 MOTEL [MOT] *Clinton, IA*
SUPER 8 MOTEL [MOT] *Columbia, MO*
SUPER 8 MOTEL [MOT] *Davenport, IA*
SUPER 8 MOTEL [MOT] *Decorah, IA*
SUPER 8 MOTEL [MOT] *Detroit Lakes, MN*
SUPER 8 MOTEL [MOT] *Devils Lake, ND*
SUPER 8 MOTEL [MOT] *Dubuque, IA*
SUPER 8 MOTEL [MOT] *Ely, MN*
SUPER 8 MOTEL [MOT] *Fairmont, MN*
SUPER 8 MOTEL [MOT] *Fergus Falls, MN*
SUPER 8 MOTEL [MOT] *Grand Forks, ND*
SUPER 8 MOTEL [MOT] *Grand Island, NE*

SUPER 8 MOTEL [MOT] *Grand Rapids, MN*
SUPER 8 MOTEL [MOT] *Grinnell, IA*
SUPER 8 MOTEL [MOT] *Hannibal, MO*
SUPER 8 MOTEL [MOT] *Hastings, MN*
SUPER 8 MOTEL [MOT] *International Falls, MN*
SUPER 8 MOTEL [MOT] *Jamestown, ND*
SUPER 8 MOTEL [MOT] *Junction City, KS*
SUPER 8 MOTEL [MOT] *Kirksville, MO*
SUPER 8 MOTEL [MOT] *Little Falls, MN*
SUPER 8 MOTEL [MOT] *Luverne, MN*
SUPER 8 MOTEL [MOT] *Mankato, MN*
SUPER 8 MOTEL [MOT] *Marshalltown, IA*
SUPER 8 MOTEL [MOT] *McCook, NE*
SUPER 8 MOTEL [MOT] *Mitchell, SD*
SUPER 8 MOTEL [MOT] *Mobridge, SD*
SUPER 8 MOTEL [MOT] *Moorhead, MN*
SUPER 8 MOTEL [MOT] *Mount Pleasant, IA*
SUPER 8 MOTEL [MOT] *Nevada, MO*
SUPER 8 MOTEL [MOT] *Norfolk, NE*
SUPER 8 MOTEL [MOT] *North Platte, NE*
SUPER 8 MOTEL [MOT] *Northfield, MN*
SUPER 8 MOTEL [MOT] *Omaha, NE*
SUPER 8 MOTEL [MOT] *Omaha, NE*
SUPER 8 MOTEL [MOT] *Ottumwa, IA*
SUPER 8 MOTEL [MOT] *Owatonna, MN*
SUPER 8 MOTEL [MOT] *Park Rapids, MN*
SUPER 8 MOTEL [MOT] *Poplar Bluff, MO*
SUPER 8 MOTEL [MOT] *Sioux City, IA*
SUPER 8 MOTEL [MOT] *Sioux Falls, SD*
SUPER 8 MOTEL [MOT] *Spencer, IA*
SUPER 8 MOTEL [MOT] *St. Cloud, MN*
SUPER 8 MOTEL [MOT] *St. Paul, MN*
SUPER 8 MOTEL [MOT] *Stillwater, MN*

SUPER 8 MOTEL [MOT] *Sturgis, SD*

SUPER 8 MOTEL [MOT] *Thief River Falls, MN*

SUPER 8 MOTEL [MOT] *Valley City, ND*

SUPER 8 MOTEL [MOT] *Wall, SD*

SUPER 8 MOTEL [MOT] *Webster, SD*

SUPER 8 MOTEL [MOT] *Willmar, MN*

SUPER 8 MOTEL [MOT] *Winona, MN*

SUPER 8 MOTEL [MOT] *Woodward, OK*

SUPER 8 MOTEL [MOT] *Yankton, SD*

SUPER 8 MOTEL - EVELETH [MOT] *Eveleth, MN*

SUPER 8 MOTEL WATERTON [MOT] *Watertown, SD*

SUPER 8 OF IOWA CITY [MOT] *Iowa City, IA*

SUPER 8 OF MADISON [MOT] *Madison, SD*

SUPERIOR SHORES RESORT [RST] *Two Harbors, MN*

SWEDISH COUNTRY INN [BB] *Lindsborg, KS*

SYLVAN LAKE RESORT [MOT] *Custer, SD*

TAHLEQUAH MOTOR LODGE [MOT] *Tahlequah, OK*

TANEYCOMO MOTOR LODGE [MOT] *Rockaway Beach, MO*

TAN-TAR-A RESORT GOLF CLUB AND SPA [RST] *Osage Beach, MO*

THEODOSIA MARINA RESORT [MOT] *Theodosia, MO*

THISTLE HILL BED & BREAKFAST [BB] *WaKeeney, KS*

THORWOOD BED AND BREAKFAST INN [BB] *Hastings, MN*

THUNDERBIRD HOTEL [MOT] *Joplin, MO*

THUNDERBIRD INN [MOT] *Marysville, KS*

THUNDERBIRD LODGE [MOT] *Mitchell, SD*

TIMBER BAY LODGE AND HOUSEBOATS [CC] *Ely, MN*

TIMMERMAN'S HOTEL & RESORT [MOT] *Dubuque, IA*

TOWNHOUSE [MOT] *O'Neill, NE*

TOWNSMAN MOTEL [MOT] *Parsons, KS*

TRADE WINDS LODGE [MOT] *Valentine, NE*

TRAVELER'S INN [BB] *Kirksville, MO*

TRAVELERS INN [MOT] *Oklahoma City, OK*

TRAVELERS INN [MOT] *Watertown, SD*

TRAVELER'S LODGE [MOT] *Marshall, MN*

TRAVELERS MOTEL [MOT] *Bartlesville, OK*

TRAVEL HOST [MOT] *Watertown, SD*

TRAVEL INN [MOT] *Clinton, IA*

TRAVEL INN [MOT] *Waterloo, IA*

TRAVEL INN BUDGET HOST [MOT] *WaKeeney, KS*

TRAVELODGE [MOT] *Columbia, MO*

TRAVELODGE [MOT] *Des Moines, IA*

TRAVELODGE [MOT] *Dickinson, ND*

TRAVELODGE [MOT] *Muskogee, OK*

TRAVELODGE [MOT] *Norman, OK*

TRAVELODGE [MOT] *Rapid City, SD*

TRAVELODGE [MOT] *South Sioux City, NE*

TRAVELODGE [MOT] *St. Cloud, MN*

TRAVELODGE FORGET-ME-NOT INN [MOT] *Branson/Table Rock Lake Area, MO*

TRAVELODGE SOUTH [MOT] *Tulsa, OK*

TURKEY CREEK RANCH [CC] *Theodosia, MO*

TURTLE MOUNTAIN LODGE [MOT] *Bottineau, ND*

UNIVERSITY INN [MOT] *Ames, IA*

USA INNS [MOT] *Hastings, NE*

U S CENTER MOTEL [MOT] *Smith Center, KS*

VACATIONAIRE SUPPER CLUB [RST] *Park Rapids, MN*

VAGABOND INN [MOT] *Salina, KS*

VICTORIAN INN 4 LESS [MOT] *Beatrice, NE*

VIKING JR MOTEL [MOT] *Granite Falls, MN*

VIKING MOTEL [MOT] *Lindsborg, KS*

VILLAGE EAST [MOT] *Okoboji, IA*

VILLAGE INN MOTEL [MOT] *Hugo, OK*

VILLAGER INN [MOT] *Mount Vernon, MO*

VILLAGER LODGE [MOT] *Cedar Falls, IA*

VILLAGE VIEW MOTEL [MOT] *Winterset, IA*

WAGON WHEEL MOTEL AND CAMPGROUNDS [MOT] *Broken Bow, NE*

WALLEYE INN MOTEL [MOT]
  Baudette, MN
WALNUT STREET INN [BB]
  Springfield, MO
WARRIOR INN [MOT] Winner, SD
WATERFORD MARRIOTT [HOT]
  Oklahoma City, OK
WAYFARER II MOTEL [MOT] York,
  NE
WELCOME INN [MOT] Nevada, MO
WESTERN HILLS GUEST RANCH
  [RST] Sequoyah State Park, OK
WESTERN INN [MOT] Kearney, NE
WESTERN INN MOTOR LODGE
  [MOT] Council Bluffs, IA
WESTERN MOTEL [MOT] Alva, OK
WESTGATE MOTEL [MOT] Ely, MN
WESTIN CROWN CENTER [HOT]
  Kansas City, MO
WESTIN OKLAHOMA CITY [HOT]
  Oklahoma City, OK
WESTIN ST. LOUIS [HOT] St. Louis,
  MO
WESTMINSTER INN [MOT]
  Lawrence, KS
WESTSIDE INN [MOT] Vermillion, SD
WESTWOOD [MOT] Joplin, MO
WHISPERING PINES BED AND
  BREAKFAST [BB] Nebraska
  City, NE
WHITE HAVEN MOTOR LODGE
  [MOT] Overland Park, KS
WHITE HOUSE INN [MOT]
  Aberdeen, SD
WHITE HOUSE INN [MOT] Lead, SD
WICHITA INN EAST [MOT] Wichita,
  KS
WICHITA SUITES HOTEL [MOT]
  Wichita, KS
WILDERNESS LODGE [RST] Pilot
  Knob, MO
WILDWOOD LODGE [HOT] Des
  Moines, IA
WILLIAM PENN LODGE [MOT]
  Broken Bow, NE
WILSON MOTOR INN [MOT]
  Redfield, SD
WINDHOMME HILL [BB] Hermann,
  MO
WOODSTOCK INN BED &
  BREAKFAST [BB] Independence,
  MO
WRANGLER MOTOR INN [MOT]
  Mobridge, SD

WYNDHAM GARDEN HOTEL
  [MOT] Bloomington, MN
WYNDHAM GARDEN HOTEL [HOT]
  Kansas City, MO
WYNDHAM GARDEN HOTEL
  [MOT] Overland Park, KS
WYNDHAM GARDEN HOTEL
  [MOT] Wichita, KS
X-L MOTEL [MOT] Hastings, NE
YORKSHIRE MOTEL [MOT] York, NE
ZENO'S MOTEL AND STEAK HOUSE
  [MOT] Rolla, MO

RESTAURANT LIST

Establishment names are listed in alphabetical order followed by a symbol identifying their classification and then city and state. The symbols for classification are: [RES] for Restaurants and [URD] for Unrated Dining Spots.

AFTON HOUSE [RES] *Stillwater, MN*

A LITTLE BIT OF ITALY [RES] *Spearfish, SD*

ALLEY ROSE [RES] *Kearney, NE*

ALPINE INN [RES] *Hill City, SD*

AL'S OASIS [RES] *Chamberlain, SD*

AMANA BARN RESTAURANT, THE [RES] *Amana Colonies, IA*

AMERICA BOWMAN [RES] *Weston, MO*

AMERICAN [RES] *Kansas City, MO*

AMERICAN HEARTH [RES] *Sisseton, SD*

AMIGHETTI'S [URD] *St. Louis, MO*

ANDRE'S CONFISERIE SUISSE [URD] *Kansas City, MO*

ANGRY TROUT CAFE [RES] *Grand Marais, MN*

ANNIE GUNN'S [RES] *Clayton, MO*

ANVIL SALOON [RES] *Ste. Genevieve, MO*

APPLEWOODS [RES] *Oklahoma City, OK*

ARIA GRILL [RES] *Oklahoma City, OK*

AROUND THE FIRESIDE [RES] *Sedalia, MO*

ARTHUR BRYANT'S BARBEQUE [RES] *Kansas City, MO*

ASIA GRILLE [RES] *Bloomington, MN*

A TASTE OF THAILAND [RES] *Des Moines, IA*

ATLANTIC SEA GRILL [RES] *Tulsa, OK*

AUGUST MOON [RES] *Minneapolis, MN*

AVIARY [RES] *Rochester, MN*

BACKSTAGE AT BRAVO [RES] *Minneapolis, MN*

BALABAN'S [RES] *St. Louis, MO*

BAMBOO GARDEN [RES] *Carthage, MO*

BARBOSA'S CASTILLO [RES] *St. Joseph, MO*

BAR HARBOR SUPPER CLUB [RES] *Brainerd, MN*

BAR ITALIA [RES] *St. Louis, MO*

BARN DELI [URD] *St. Louis, MO*

BAXTER INTERURBAN [URD] *Tulsa, OK*

BAYPORT AMERICAN COOKERY [RES] *Stillwater, MN*

BELLINI'S [RES] *Oklahoma City, OK*

BELLISIO'S [RES] *Duluth, MN*

BENEDETTO'S [RES] *Clayton, MO*

BENTLEY'S [RES] *Lake Ozark, MO*

BERLINER BEAR [RES] *Kansas City, MO*

BERNARDO'S STEAK HOUSE [RES] *Hastings, NE*

BEVO MILL [RES] *St. Louis, MO*

BG'S OLDE TYME DELI & SALOON [RES] *Cape Girardeau, MO*

BIG RIVER [RES] *Ste. Genevieve, MO*

BIG SKY CAFE [RES] *St. Louis, MO*

BILL & BARB'S [RES] *Ardmore, OK*

BILLY'S [RES] *Lincoln, NE*

BIRCH TERRACE [RES] *Grand Marais, MN*

BLACK FOREST INN [RES] *Minneapolis, MN*

BLUEBERRY HILL [URD] *St. Louis, MO*

BODEAN SEAFOOD [RES] *Tulsa, OK*

BOHEMIAN CAFE [RES] *Omaha, NE*

BOONE TAVERN [RES] *Columbia, MO*

BRASS DOOR [RES] *Osage Beach, MO*

BRASS LANTERN [RES] *Norfolk, NE*

BRICK HAUS [RES] *Amana Colonies, IA*

BRICKS [RES] *Sulphur, OK*

BRICKTOWN BREWERY [RES] *Oklahoma City, OK*

BRISTOL'S SEAFOOD GRILL [RES] *St. Louis, MO*

BRIX [RES] *Des Moines, IA*

BROADSTREET CAFE AND BAR [RES] *Rochester, MN*

BROADWAY OYSTER BAR [RES] *St. Louis, MO*

BROILER STEAKHOUSE [RES] *Ames, IA*

BROOKS [RES] *Charles City, IA*

BROOKVILLE HOTEL DINING ROOM [RES] *Abilene, KS*

BROUSSARD'S CAJUN CUISINE [RES] *Cape Girardeau, MO*

BRUNSWICK HOTEL [RES] *Lindsborg, KS*

BUCA DI BEPPO [RES] *Minneapolis, MN*

BUCA DI BEPPO [RES] *St. Paul, MN*

BUGATTI'S LITTLE ITALY [RES] *Kansas City, MO*

BUSCH'S GROVE [RES] *St. Louis, MO*

BUSTY LE DOUX'S [RES] *Omaha, NE*

CAFE 501 [RES] *Oklahoma City, OK*

CAFE ALLEGRO [RES] *Kansas City, MO*

CAFE BARCELONA [RES] *Kansas City, MO*

CAFE BRENDA [RES] *Minneapolis, MN*

CAFE DE FRANCE [RES] *St. Louis, MO*

CAFE DE PARIS [RES] *Omaha, NE*

CAFE ITALIA [RES] *Overland Park, KS*

CAFE MIRA [RES] *Clayton, MO*

CAFE NAPOLI [RES] *Clayton, MO*

CAFE PERIWINKLE [RES] *Blue Springs, MO*

CAFE PLAID [RES] *Norman, OK*

CAFE PROVENCAL [RES] *Clayton, MO*

CAFE UN DEUX TROIS [RES] *Minneapolis, MN*

CALIFORNOS [RES] *Kansas City, MO*

CAMMERELLI'S [RES] *Tulsa, OK*

CAMPIELLO [RES] *Minneapolis, MN*

CANDICCI'S [RES] *St. Louis, MO*

CANDLESTICK INN [RES] *Branson/Table Rock Lake Area, MO*

CANYON CAFE [RES] *Kansas City, MO*

CARAVAN SERAI [RES] *St. Paul, MN*

CARAVELLE [RES] *Minneapolis, MN*

CARDWELL'S [RES] *Clayton, MO*

CARDWELL'S [RES] *St. Louis, MO*

CARLOS O'KELLY'S [RES] *Topeka, KS*

CASA BONITA [URD] *Tulsa, OK*

CASCONE'S [RES] *Kansas City, MO*

CASPAR'S EAST 40 [RES] *Bismarck, ND*

CASSSIDY'S [RES] *Hinckley, MN*

CATTLEMAN'S STEAKHOUSE [RES] *Oklahoma City, OK*

CECIL'S [URD] *St. Paul, MN*

CHANCES R [RES] *York, NE*

CHAPELL'S [RES] *Kansas City, MO*

CHARCOAL HOUSE [RES] *St. Louis, MO*

CHARDONNAY [RES] *Rochester, MN*

CHARLIE GITTO'S [RES] *St. Louis, MO*

CHAR-TONY'S [RES] *Hermann, MO*

CHEF LOUIE'S [RES] *Mitchell, SD*

CHESHIRE INN [RES] *St. Louis, MO*

CHEZ BANANAS [RES] *Minneapolis, MN*

CHINA PALACE [RES] *Des Moines, IA*

CHINA ROYAL [RES] *St. Louis, MO*

CHINA WOK [RES] *Des Moines, IA*

CHRISTIE'S [RES] *Davenport, IA*

CHRISTOPHER'S [RES] *Des Moines, IA*

CHRISTOS [RES] *Minneapolis, MN*

CHU'S CHOP SUEY & STEAKHOUSE [RES] *Omaha, NE*

CHUY ARZOLA'S [RES] *St. Louis, MO*

CIAO BELLA [RES] *Bloomington, MN*

CIATTI'S [RES] *St. Paul, MN*

CICERO'S [RES] *St. Louis, MO*

C.J. CALLAWAY'S [RES] *Sioux Falls, SD*

CLASSEN GRILL [URD] *Oklahoma City, OK*

CLASSIC CUP [RES] *Kansas City, MO*

CLASSIC CUP SIDEWALK CAFE [RES] *Kansas City, MO*

COACH HOUSE [RES] *Oklahoma City, OK*

COLONIAL STEAK HOUSE [RES] *Oakley, KS*

COLONY VILLAGE [RES] *Amana Colonies, IA*

COLOURS [RES] *Eufaula, OK*

COUNTRY DOVE [RES] *Elk City, OK*

COUNTY LINE [RES] *Oklahoma City, OK*

COYOTE GRILL [RES] *Overland Park, KS*

CRAVINGS [RES] *St. Louis, MO*

CRAZY FISH FRESH GRILL [RES] *Clayton, MO*

CRONK'S [RES] *Denison, IA*

CROWN CANDY KITCHEN [URD] *St. Louis, MO*

CUNETTO HOUSE OF PASTA [RES] *St. Louis, MO*

DA AFGHAN [URD] *Bloomington, MN*

DAKOTA BAR AND GRILL [RES] *St. Paul, MN*

D'AMICO CUCINA [RES] *Minneapolis, MN*

DANIELE [RES] *Clayton, MO*

DAVID FONG'S [RES] *Bloomington, MN*

D. B. SEARLE'S [RES] *St. Cloud, MN*

DEEP FORK GRILL [RES] *Oklahoma City, OK*

DELI, THE [URD] *St. Joseph, MO*

DIAMOND HEAD [RES] *Springfield, MO*

DICK CLARK'S AMERICAN BANDSTAND GRILL [URD] *Overland Park, KS*

DIERDORF & HART'S STEAK HOUSE [RES] *St. Louis, MO*

DIMITRIS [RES] *Branson/Table Rock Lake Area, MO*

DIXIE'S [RES] *St. Paul, MN*

D.J.'S [RES] *New Ulm, MN*

DOMENICO'S CARRY-OUT PIZZA [RES] *Osage Beach, MO*

DOMINIC'S RESTAURANT [RES] *St. Louis, MO*

DON CHILITO'S [RES] *Overland Park, KS*

DREISBACH'S [RES] *Grand Island, NE*

EBT [RES] *Kansas City, MO*

EDDY'S OF OKLAHOMA CITY [RES] *Oklahoma City, OK*

EL CARIBE [RES] *Overland Park, KS*

EL SAMBRE [RES] *Nevada, MO*

ELWELL'S CHEF'S INN [RES] *Ames, IA*

EMBERS STEAKHOUSE [RES] *Nebraska City, NE*

EMILY'S LEBANESE DELI [URD] *Minneapolis, MN*

ESTEBAN'S [RES] *Stillwater, MN*

FAUST'S [RES] *St. Louis, MO*

FEDORA CAFE [RES] *Kansas City, MO*

FIELD & STREAM [RES] *Minot, ND*

FIFI'S [RES] *Lawrence, KS*

FIGLIO [RES] *Kansas City, MO*

FIGLIO [RES] *Minneapolis, MN*

FINNS CHOWDER HOUSE [RES] *Tulsa, OK*

FIORELLA'S JACK STACK BAR-B-Q [RES] *Kansas City, MO*

FIORELLA'S SMOKE STACK BAR-B-Q [RES] *Kansas City, MO*

FIO'S LA FOURCHETTE [RES] *Clayton, MO*

FIREHOUSE BREWING CO [RES] *Rapid City, SD*

FIRESIDE [RES] *Detroit Lakes, MN*

FIRESIDE DINING [RES] *Lake Murray State Park, OK*

FISHERMAN'S BAY [RES] *Ottumwa, IA*

FISHERMAN'S NET [RES] *Sikeston, MO*

FISHERMEN'S COVE [RES] *Lawton, OK*

510 RESTAURANT [RES] *Minneapolis, MN*

FLAME, THE [RES] *Aberdeen, SD*

FLAT BRANCH PUB & BREWING [RES] *Columbia, MO*

FLYING T. CHUCKWAGON SUPPER & SHOW [URD] *Rapid City, SD*

FOREPAUGH'S [RES] *St. Paul, MN*

FOUNTAINS [RES] *Tulsa, OK*

FRANK PAPA'S [RES] *St. Louis, MO*

FRAZER'S TRAVELING BROWN BAG [RES] *St. Louis, MO*

FRENCH CAFE [RES] *Omaha, NE*

FRENCH HEN [RES] *Tulsa, OK*

FRIENDSHIP HOUSE [RES] *Branson/Table Rock Lake Area, MO*

GALLIVAN'S [RES] *St. Paul, MN*

GARDEN CAFE [RES] *Omaha, NE*

GARDENS - SALONICA [RES] *Minneapolis, MN*

GAROZZO'S [RES] *Kansas City, MO*

GAROZZO'S DUE [RES] *Independence, MO*

GASLIGHT ROOM [RES] *Macon, MO*

GASTHAUS BAVARIAN HUNTER [RES] *Stillwater, MN*

GATES BAR-B-QUE [URD] *Overland Park, KS*

GEE'S EAST WIND [RES] *Springfield, MO*

G F GOODRIBS [RES] *Grand Forks, ND*

GIACOMO'S [RES] *McAlester, OK*

GIAN PEPPE'S [RES] *St. Louis, MO*

GINO'S [RES] *St. Louis, MO*

GIORGIO [RES] *Minneapolis, MN*

GIOVANNI'S [RES] *St. Louis, MO*

GIOVANNI'S LITTLE PLACE [RES] *St. Louis, MO*

GIUSEPPE'S [RES] *St. Louis, MO*
GOLDEN DRAGON [RES] *North Platte, NE*
GOLDEN OX [RES] *Kansas City, MO*
GOODFELLOW'S [RES] *Minneapolis, MN*
GOPURAM TASTE OF INDIA [RES] *Oklahoma City, OK*
GORAT'S STEAK HOUSE [RES] *Omaha, NE*
GP AGOSTINO'S [RES] *St. Louis, MO*
GRADY'S AMERICAN GRILL [RES] *Tulsa, OK*
GRAINERY, THE [RES] *Fargo, ND*
GRAMMA'S KITCHEN [RES] *Davenport, IA*
GRANARY [RES] *Norfolk, NE*
GRANDMA'S CANAL PARK [RES] *Duluth, MN*
GRANDMOTHER'S [RES] *Omaha, NE*
GRANDPA'S STEAK HOUSE [RES] *Kearney, NE*
GRAND STREET CAFE [RES] *Kansas City, MO*
GRAPE [RES] *Wichita, KS*
GREAT WALL [RES] *Rapid City, SD*
GREENBRIER [RES] *Des Moines, IA*
GREEN CIRCLE INN [RES] *Centerville, IA*
GREEN GABLES [RES] *Sioux City, IA*
GREEN MILL INN [URD] *St. Paul, MN*
GRILL, THE [RES] *St. Louis, MO*
GUTIERREZ [RES] *Hays, KS*
GUTIERREZ [RES] *Salina, KS*
HACIENDA [RES] *St. Louis, MO*
HAMMERSTONE'S [RES] *St. Louis, MO*
HAMMETT HOUSE [RES] *Claremore, OK*
HANNEGAN'S [RES] *St. Louis, MO*
HAPPY FISHERMAN [RES] *Osage Beach, MO*
HARDWARE CAFE [RES] *Kansas City, MO*
HARRY'S [RES] *St. Louis, MO*
HARRY'S BAR & TABLES [RES] *Kansas City, MO*
HARRY'S UPTOWN SUPPER CLUB [RES] *Manhattan, KS*
HARVEST [RES] *St. Louis, MO*
HARVEST INN [RES] *Stillwater, MN*
HAYS HOUSE 1857 [RES] *Council Grove, KS*

HEARTLAND [RES] *Hiawatha, KS*
HENRY WELLINGTON [RES] *Rochester, MN*
HEREFORD HOUSE [RES] *Kansas City, MO*
HEREFORD HOUSE [RES] *Overland Park, KS*
HERITAGE HOUSE [RES] *Topeka, KS*
HICKORY PARK [RES] *Ames, IA*
HILLSIDE INN [RES] *Rockaway Beach, MO*
HILL TOP INN [RES] *Ogallala, NE*
HOMESTEAD KITCHEN [RES] *Amana Colonies, IA*
HONG KONG [RES] *Aberdeen, SD*
HOUSE OF HUNAN [RES] *Des Moines, IA*
HOUSE OF INDIA [RES] *St. Louis, MO*
HOUSTON'S [RES] *Overland Park, KS*
HUBBELL HOUSE [RES] *Rochester, MN*
HUNAN [RES] *Grand Island, NE*
HUNAN PALACE [RES] *Sioux City, IA*
ICHIBAN JAPANESE STEAK HOUSE [RES] *Minneapolis, MN*
ILIKI CAFE [RES] *Kansas City, MO*
IL TRULLO [RES] *Overland Park, KS*
IMPERIAL [RES] *Rapid City, SD*
IMPERIAL PALACE [RES] *Omaha, NE*
INDIAN OVEN [RES] *Omaha, NE*
INDIA PALACE [RES] *Overland Park, KS*
IOWA MACHINE SHED [RES] *Davenport, IA*
IOWA RIVER POWER COMPANY [RES] *Iowa City, IA*
ISLE OF CAPRI [RES] *McAlester, OK*
ITALIAN GARDENS [RES] *Kansas City, MO*
IT'S GREEK TO ME [RES] *Minneapolis, MN*
IVEN'S ON THE BAY [RES] *Brainerd, MN*
JABRISCO [RES] *Lincoln, NE*
JACK STACK BARBECUE [RES] *Overland Park, KS*
JAKE'S ATOP THE MIDNIGHT STAR [RES] *Deadwood, SD*
JAMIL'S [RES] *Tulsa, OK*
JAPENGO [RES] *Kansas City, MO*
JASPER'S [RES] *Tahlequah, OK*
JAX CAFE [RES] *Minneapolis, MN*

J B HOOK'S GREAT OCEAN FISH [RES] *Lake Ozark, MO*

J. BRUNER'S [RES] *Clarinda, IA*

J.D. HOYT'S [RES] *Minneapolis, MN*

JERUSALEM'S [RES] *Minneapolis, MN*

JESS & JIM'S STEAK HOUSE [RES] *Kansas City, MO*

JESSE'S EMBERS [RES] *Des Moines, IA*

J.F. SANFILIPPO'S [RES] *St. Louis, MO*

J GILBERT'S WOOD FIRED STEAKS [RES] *Overland Park, KS*

JJ'S [RES] *Kansas City, MO*

JOHN BARLEYCORN [RES] *Rochester, MN*

JOHN D. MCGURK'S [RES] *St. Louis, MO*

JOHN MINEO'S [RES] *St. Louis, MO*

JOHNNY CASCONE'S [RES] *Overland Park, KS*

JOHNNY'S CAFE [RES] *Omaha, NE*

JOHNNY'S SMOKE STAK [RES] *Rolla, MO*

JOSEPH'S ITALIAN CAFE [RES] *St. Louis, MO*

J. PARRIONO'S PASTA HOUSE [RES] *Springfield, MO*

J.T. MALONEY'S [RES] *Nevada, MO*

JUMER'S [RES] *Bettendorf, IA*

JUN'S JAPANESE RESTAURANT [RES] *Overland Park, KS*

JW'S STEAKHOUSE [RES] *Oklahoma City, OK*

K.C. MASTERPIECE [RES] *Kansas City, MO*

K.C. MASTERPIECE [RES] *Overland Park, KS*

K.C. MASTERPIECE [RES] *St. Louis, MO*

K. C.'S CAFE [RES] *Fremont, NE*

KELCY'S FINE FOODS [RES] *Grinnell, IA*

KELLER IN THE KASTLE GERMAN RESTAURANT [RES] *Oklahoma City, OK*

KEMOLL'S [RES] *St. Louis, MO*

KIKUGAWA [RES] *Minneapolis, MN*

KINCAID'S [RES] *Bloomington, MN*

KING AND I, THE [RES] *Minneapolis, MN*

KING & I [RES] *St. Louis, MO*

KING'S PIT BAR-B-Q [RES] *Liberal, KS*

KIRBY HOUSE [RES] *Abilene, KS*

KITCHEN PASS [RES] *Joplin, MO*

KOBE STEAK HOUSE OF JAPAN [RES] *Topeka, KS*

KONA RANCH STEAKHOUSE [RES] *Oklahoma City, OK*

KOZLAKS ROYAL OAK [RES] *St. Paul, MN*

KOZY KORNER [RES] *Pierre, SD*

KREIS'S [RES] *St. Louis, MO*

LA BAGUETTE BISTRO [RES] *Oklahoma City, OK*

LA CORSETTE MAISON INN [RES] *Newton, IA*

LA FOUGASSE [URD] *Bloomington, MN*

LAKE ELMO INN [RES] *St. Paul, MN*

LAKESIDE [RES] *Detroit Lakes, MN*

LAMAR'S DONUTS [RES] *Kansas City, MO*

LAMBERT'S [RES] *Sikeston, MO*

LANGE'S CAFE [RES] *Pipestone, MN*

LAS PALOMAS [RES] *Oklahoma City, OK*

LA STRADA 72 [RES] *Omaha, NE*

LAVENDER INN [RES] *Faribault, MN*

L B STEAKHOUSE [RES] *Iowa City, IA*

L.C.'S BAR-B-Q [RES] *Kansas City, MO*

LEEANN CHIN [RES] *Bloomington, MN*

LEEANN CHIN [RES] *St. Paul, MN*

LE FOU FROG [RES] *Kansas City, MO*

LEGEND'S [RES] *Norman, OK*

LE MIRABELLE [RES] *Springfield, MO*

LEONARDO'S LITTLE ITALY [RES] *St. Louis, MO*

LEONA YARBROUGH'S [RES] *Overland Park, KS*

LEXINGTON [RES] *St. Paul, MN*

LIBERTY'S [RES] *Red Wing, MN*

LIDIA'S [RES] *Kansas City, MO*

LINDEY'S PRIME STEAKHOUSE [RES] *St. Paul, MN*

LINGUINI AND BOB [RES] *Minneapolis, MN*

LOGUE'S [RES] *Hannibal, MO*

LOMBARDO'S [RES] *St. Louis, MO*

LOMBARDO'S [RES] *St. Louis, MO*

LONG BRANCH [RES] *Macon, MO*

LORD FLETCHER'S OF THE LAKE [RES] *Minneapolis, MN*

LORING CAFE [RES] *Minneapolis, MN*

LORUSSO'S CUCINA [RES] *St. Louis, MO*

LOWELL INN [RES] *Stillwater, MN*

LUCIA'S [RES] *Minneapolis, MN*
LUCULLANS [RES] *Ames, IA*
LUPE'S [RES] *Elk City, OK*
LYNCH STREET BISTRO [RES] *St. Louis, MO*
MABEL MURPHY'S EATING LTD [RES] *Fergus Falls, MN*
MACALUSO'S [RES] *Kansas City, MO*
MACHINE SHED, THE [RES] *Des Moines, IA*
MACNAMERA'S [RES] *Cameron, MO*
MADISON'S CAFE [RES] *Jefferson City, MO*
MAGGIE O'BRIEN'S [RES] *St. Louis, MO*
MAJESTIC STEAKHOUSE [RES] *Kansas City, MO*
MALMAISON AT ST. ALBANS [RES] *St. Louis, MO*
MAMA CAMPISI'S [RES] *St. Louis, MO*
MANCINI'S CHAR HOUSE [RES] *St. Paul, MN*
MANDARIN HOUSE [RES] *St. Louis, MO*
MANNY'S [RES] *Minneapolis, MN*
MARCIANO'S [RES] *St. Louis, MO*
MARINA GROG & GALLEY [RES] *Blue Springs, MO*
MARIO'S [RES] *Dubuque, IA*
MARKET BAR-B-QUE [URD] *Minneapolis, MN*
MARSH [RES] *Minneapolis, MN*
MARTIN'S [RES] *Lawton, OK*
MAXIE'S [RES] *Des Moines, IA*
MCFARLAND'S [RES] *Topeka, KS*
MCGEHEE CATFISH [RES] *Marietta, OK*
MEADOWS [RES] *Minneapolis, MN*
MERIWETHERS [URD] *Mandan, ND*
METRO DINER [URD] *Tulsa, OK*
METROPOLIS AMERICAN GRILL [RES] *Kansas City, MO*
MEXICAN VILLAGE [RES] *Fargo, ND*
MICHAEL'S FINE DINING [RES] *Rochester, MN*
MIKE SHANNON'S [RES] *St. Louis, MO*
MILANO [RES] *Kansas City, MO*
MILLSTONE FAMILY RESTAURANT [RES] *Milbank, SD*
MINERVA'S [RES] *Sioux Falls, SD*
MINNEWASKA HOUSE SUPPER CLUB [RES] *Glenwood, MN*

MISSISSIPPI BELLE [RES] *Hastings, MN*
MORTON'S OF CHICAGO [RES] *Minneapolis, MN*
MR G'S CHICAGO STYLE PIZZA [RES] *Branson/Table Rock Lake Area, MO*
MRS O'MEALLEY'S [URD] *Springfield, MO*
MUD PIE [URD] *Minneapolis, MN*
MUFFULETTA IN THE PARK [RES] *St. Paul, MN*
MURPHY'S ORIGINAL STEAK HOUSE [RES] *Bartlesville, OK*
MUSEUM CAFE [RES] *St. Louis, MO*
MUSTARDS [URD] *Des Moines, IA*
NACHO MAMMAS [RES] *Des Moines, IA*
NEW FRENCH CAFE [RES] *Minneapolis, MN*
NIKKO [RES] *Overland Park, KS*
NO WAKE CAFE [URD] *St. Paul, MN*
NYE'S POLONAISE [RES] *Minneapolis, MN*
OCEANAIRE SEAFOOD INN [RES] *Minneapolis, MN*
O'CONNELL'S PUB [URD] *St. Louis, MO*
O'DOWD'S LITTLE DUBLIN [RES] *Kansas City, MO*
OHANA STEAKHOUSE [RES] *Des Moines, IA*
OKIES [RES] *Muskogee, OK*
OLD BRICK HOUSE [RES] *Ste. Genevieve, MO*
OLDE BROOM FACTORY [RES] *Cedar Falls, IA*
OLIVE TREE [RES] *Wichita, KS*
ONCE UPON A VINE [RES] *St. Louis, MO*
ORIGAMI [RES] *Minneapolis, MN*
OX YOKE INN [RES] *Amana Colonies, IA*
PALOMINO [RES] *Minneapolis, MN*
PAPAGALLO [RES] *Kansas City, MO*
PARADISE GRILL [RES] *Kansas City, MO*
PASTA HOUSE COMPANY [RES] *St. Louis, MO*
PATRICK'S [RES] *St. Louis, MO*
PAUL MANNO'S CAFE [RES] *St. Louis, MO*
PAULO & BILL [RES] *Kansas City, KS*
PEACOCK ALLEY [RES] *Bismarck, ND*

PETE'S PLACE [RES] *McAlester, OK*

PHOENIX PIANO BAR & GRILL [RES] *Kansas City, MO*

PICKLED PARROT [RES] *Minneapolis, MN*

PICKWICK [RES] *Duluth, MN*

PING'S SZECHUAN BAR AND GRILL [RES] *Minneapolis, MN*

PINK HOUSE [URD] *Claremore, OK*

PLAINSMAN [RES] *Cozad, NE*

PLANET HOLLYWOOD [URD] *Bloomington, MN*

PLAZA III THE STEAKHOUSE [RES] *Kansas City, MO*

PLUM PUDDING [URD] *Weston, MO*

POLO GRILL [RES] *Tulsa, OK*

PORTABELLA [RES] *Clayton, MO*

POTTED STEER [RES] *Osage Beach, MO*

PRACNA ON MAIN [RES] *Minneapolis, MN*

PRENGER'S [RES] *Norfolk, NE*

PROVINCES [RES] *St. Louis, MO*

RAINFOREST CAFE [URD] *Bloomington, MN*

RAM & O'HARE'S, THE [RES] *Brookings, SD*

RANCH FAMILY RESTAURANT, THE [RES] *Fairmont, MN*

RAOUL'S VELVET ROOM [RES] *Overland Park, KS*

RAPHAEL DINING ROOM [RES] *Kansas City, MO*

RED SEA [RES] *St. Louis, MO*

REMY'S [RES] *Clayton, MO*

RHEINLAND [RES] *Independence, MO*

RICARDOS [RES] *Tulsa, OK*

RIDDLE PENULTIMATE [RES] *St. Louis, MO*

RISTORANTE LUCI [RES] *St. Paul, MN*

ROBATA OF JAPAN [RES] *St. Louis, MO*

ROMANO'S MACARONI GRILL [RES] *Tulsa, OK*

RONNEBURG [RES] *Amana Colonies, IA*

ROSIE'S RIB JOINT [RES] *Tulsa, OK*

ROTISSERIE [RES] *Overland Park, KS*

RUTH'S CHRIS STEAK HOUSE [RES] *Kansas City, MO*

RUTH'S CHRIS STEAK HOUSE [RES] *Minneapolis, MN*

SAGE ROOM [RES] *Enid, OK*

ST. CHARLES VINTAGE HOUSE [RES] *St. Charles, MO*

ST. LOUIS BREWERY & TAP ROOM [RES] *St. Louis, MO*

ST. PAUL GRILL, THE [RES] *St. Paul, MN*

SAKURA [RES] *St. Paul, MN*

SALAS [RES] *Lawton, OK*

SALEEM'S LEBANESE CUISINE [RES] *St. Louis, MO*

SANDY POINT [RES] *Rochester, MN*

SANFORD'S [RES] *Lake Texoma, OK*

SANTORINI [RES] *Minneapolis, MN*

SAVOY GRILL [RES] *Kansas City, MO*

SAWATDEE [RES] *Minneapolis, MN*

SAWATDEE [RES] *St. Paul, MN*

SCHNEITHORST'S HOFAMBERG INN [RES] *St. Louis, MO*

SCHUMACHER'S [RES] *Lakeville, MN*

SEASONS [RES] *Anoka, MN*

SEVENTH INN [RES] *St. Louis, MO*

SHADY INN [RES] *Springfield, MO*

SHIRAZ [RES] *Kansas City, MO*

SHUANG CHENG [RES] *Minneapolis, MN*

SIDNEY'S PIZZA CAFE [RES] *Minneapolis, MN*

SIDNEY STREET CAFE [RES] *St. Louis, MO*

SIGNATURE'S [RES] *Omaha, NE*

SILVER DOLLAR [RES] *Vermillion, SD*

SISTER SARAH'S [RES] *Algona, IA*

SKYVIEW [RES] *Leavenworth, KS*

SKYWAY [RES] *Custer, SD*

SLEEPY HOLLOW [RES] *Oklahoma City, OK*

SMUGGLER'S INN [RES] *Kansas City, MO*

SOPHIA [RES] *Minneapolis, MN*

SPAGHETTI WORKS [RES] *Des Moines, IA*

SPEARS [RES] *Newton, KS*

SPIRO'S [RES] *St. Louis, MO*

SPOT FIREHOUSE [RES] *International Falls, MN*

STABLES CAFE [RES] *Guthrie, OK*

STAR [RES] *Murdo, SD*

STEAK UND SCHITZEL HAUS [RES] *Sedalia, MO*

STEPHENSON'S APPLE FARM [RES] *Kansas City, MO*

STERLING'S GRILLE [RES] *Bartlesville, OK*

STEWART'S [RES] *Lake Ozark, MO*

STILLWATER BAY [RES] *Stillwater, OK*

STOLEN GRILL [RES] *Kansas City, MO*

STONEGATE STATION [RES] *Lebanon, MO*

STONE HEARTH INN [RES] *Decorah, IA*

STROUD'S [RES] *Kansas City, MO*

STUBBS EDDY RESTAURANT/PUB [RES] *Bettendorf, IA*

SUNFLOWER CAFE [RES] *St. Louis, MO*

SUSHI GIN [RES] *Overland Park, KS*

SUSHI NEKO [RES] *Oklahoma City, OK*

SWEDISH CROWN [RES] *Lindsborg, KS*

TABLE OF CONTENTS [RES] *Minneapolis, MN*

TABLE OF CONTENTS [RES] *St. Paul, MN*

TATSU'S [RES] *Overland Park, KS*

TAYLOR'S STEAKHOUSE [RES] *Hastings, NE*

T-BONE STEAK HOUSE [RES] *Weatherford, OK*

TEJAS [RES] *Bloomington, MN*

THAI CAFE [RES] *St. Louis, MO*

1313 NICOLLET [RES] *Minneapolis, MN*

36TH STREET FOOD & DRINK COMPANY [RES] *St. Joseph, MO*

THUNDER BAY GRILLE [RES] *Davenport, IA*

TIAMO [RES] *Tulsa, OK*

TIAMO [RES] *Tulsa, OK*

TIME OUT FAMILY RESTAURANT [RES] *Atchison, KS*

TIPPINS [RES] *Independence, MO*

TOBIE'S [RES] *Hinckley, MN*

TOBY'S ON THE LAKE [RES] *St. Paul, MN*

TOLEDO'S [RES] *Lake Ozark, MO*

TONY'S [RES] *Carroll, IA*

TONY'S [RES] *St. Louis, MO*

TOP OF THE HARBOR [RES] *Duluth, MN*

TORNATORE'S [RES] *St. Louis Lambert Airport Area, MO*

TRATTORIA MARCELLA [RES] *St. Louis, MO*

TRINI'S [RES] *Omaha, NE*

TROLLEY'S [RES] *McAlester, OK*

TULIPS [RES] *St. Paul, MN*

UCHIE'S FINE FOODS [RES] *Clinton, MO*

UNCLE JOE'S BAR-B-Q [RES] *Branson/Table Rock Lake Area, MO*

UPTOWN CAFE, THE [RES] *Norfolk, NE*

VEIGEL'S KAISERHOF [RES] *New Ulm, MN*

VEIT'S DIAMOND [RES] *Jefferson City, MO*

VELVET DOG, THE [RES] *Kansas City, MO*

VENETIAN INN [RES] *St. Paul, MN*

VINEYARD, THE [RES] *Anoka, MN*

VINTAGE [RES] *Hermann, MO*

VISTA GRANDE [RES] *Osage Beach, MO*

VISTA SPORTS GRILL [RES] *Norman, OK*

VITTORIO'S [RES] *Stillwater, MN*

V. MERTZ [RES] *Omaha, NE*

V'S ITALIANO [RES] *Independence, MO*

W. A. FROST AND COMPANY [RES] *St. Paul, MN*

WALL DRUG [RES] *Wall, SD*

WARREN DUCK CLUB [RES] *Tulsa, OK*

WATERFORD, THE [RES] *Oklahoma City, OK*

WATERFRONT SEAFOOD MARKET [RES] *Des Moines, IA*

WHEELER INN [RES] *Auburn, NE*

WHITNEY GRILLE [RES] *Minneapolis, MN*

WILDER'S [RES] *Joplin, MO*

WOKS, THE [RES] *Overland Park, KS*

YACOVELLI'S [RES] *St. Louis, MO*

YAHOOZ [RES] *Overland Park, KS*

YEMANJA BRASIL [RES] *St. Louis, MO*

YEN CHING [RES] *Dubuque, IA*

YIAYIAS EUROBISTRO [RES] *Overland Park, KS*

ZIA'S [RES] *St. Louis, MO*

ZINNIA [RES] *St. Louis, MO*

ZUBER'S [RES] *Amana Colonies, IA*

CITY INDEX

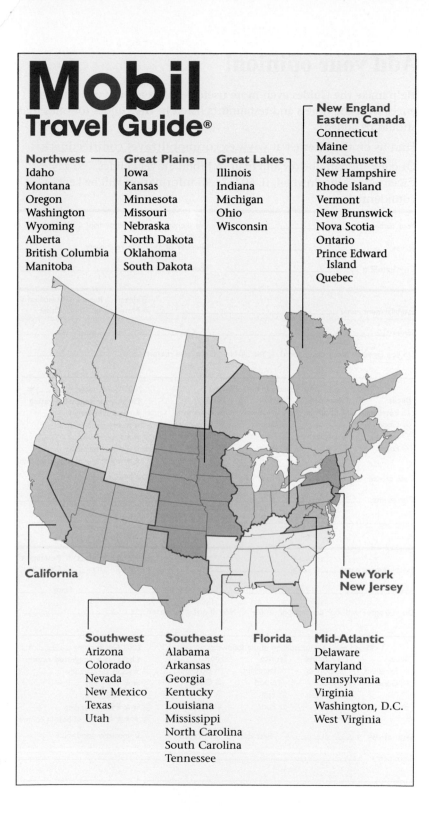

Mobil
Travel Guide®

New England
Eastern Canada
Connecticut
Maine
Massachusetts
New Hampshire
Rhode Island
Vermont
New Brunswick
Nova Scotia
Ontario
Prince Edward
  Island
Quebec

Northwest
Idaho
Montana
Oregon
Washington
Wyoming
Alberta
British Columbia
Manitoba

Great Plains
Iowa
Kansas
Minnesota
Missouri
Nebraska
North Dakota
Oklahoma
South Dakota

Great Lakes
Illinois
Indiana
Michigan
Ohio
Wisconsin

California

New York
New Jersey

Southwest
Arizona
Colorado
Nevada
New Mexico
Texas
Utah

Southeast
Alabama
Arkansas
Georgia
Kentucky
Louisiana
Mississippi
North Carolina
South Carolina
Tennessee

Florida

Mid-Atlantic
Delaware
Maryland
Pennsylvania
Virginia
Washington, D.C.
West Virginia

Add your opinion!

Help make the Guides even more useful. Tell us about your experiences with the hotels and restaurants listed in the Guides (or ones that should be added).

Find us on the Internet at **www.exxonmobiltravel.com/feedback**

Or copy the form below and mail to Mobil Travel Guides, 7373 N Cicero Ave, Lincolnwood, IL 60712. All information will be kept confidential.

Your name _____   Were children with you on trip? ☐ Yes ☐ No

Street _____   Number of people in your party _____

City/State/Zip _____   Your occupation _____

Establishment name_____
☐ Hotel ☐ Resort ☐ Restaurant
☐ Motel ☐ Inn ☐ Other

Street_____ City_____ State _____

Do you agree with our description? ☐ Yes ☐ No   If not, give reason_____

Please give us your opinion of the following:

Decor	Cleanliness	Service	Food
☐ Excellent	☐ Spotless	☐ Excellent	☐ Excellent
☐ Good	☐ Clean	☐ Good	☐ Good
☐ Fair	☐ Unclean	☐ Fair	☐ Fair
☐ Poor	☐ Dirty	☐ Poor	☐ Poor

2002 Guide rating _____ ★

Check your suggested rating
☐ ★good, satisfactory
☐ ★★very good
☐ ★★★excellent
☐ ★★★★outstanding
☐ ★★★★★ one of best in country
☐ ✓unusually good value

Date of visit _____   First visit? ☐ Yes ☐ No

Comments _____

Establishment name_____
☐ Hotel ☐ Resort ☐ Restaurant
☐ Motel ☐ Inn ☐ Other

Street_____ City_____ State _____

Do you agree with our description? ☐ Yes ☐ No   If not, give reason_____

Please give us your opinion of the following:

Decor	Cleanliness	Service	Food
☐ Excellent	☐ Spotless	☐ Excellent	☐ Excellent
☐ Good	☐ Clean	☐ Good	☐ Good
☐ Fair	☐ Unclean	☐ Fair	☐ Fair
☐ Poor	☐ Dirty	☐ Poor	☐ Poor

2002 Guide rating _____ ★

Check your suggested rating
☐ ★good, satisfactory
☐ ★★very good
☐ ★★★excellent
☐ ★★★★outstanding
☐ ★★★★★ one of best in country
☐ ✓unusually good value

Date of visit _____   First visit? ☐ Yes ☐ No

Comments _____

Notes

Notes